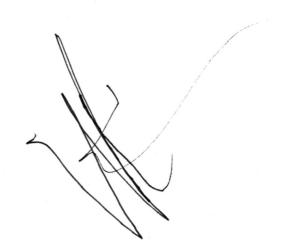

# CORRECTIONS

## A COMPREHENSIVE VIEW

# CORRECTIONS
## A COMPREHENSIVE VIEW

**Ira J. Silverman**

*Professor, Department of Criminology*
*University of South Florida*


**Manuel Vega**

*Associate Professor Emeritus, Department of Criminology*
*University of South Florida at Sarasota*

**West Publishing Company**
Minneapolis/Saint Paul   New York   Los Angeles   San Francisco

## ▪ PRODUCTION CREDITS

Composition: Carlisle Communications, Ltd.
Copyeditor: Lorretta Palagi
Art: Nancy Wirsig McClure, Hand to Mouse Arts
Photo Research: Eva Tucholka, New York
Index: Schroeder Indexing Services
Cover photo: © Matthew Naythons, Epicenter Communications

## ▪ WEST'S COMMITMENT
### TO THE ENVIRONMENT

In 1906, West Publishing Company began recycling materials left over from the production of books. This began a tradition of efficient and responsible use of resources. Today, 100% of our legal bound volumes are printed on acid-free, recycled paper consisting of 50% new paper pulp and 50% paper that has undergone a de-inking process. We also use vegetable-based inks to print all of our books. West recycles nearly 27,700,000 pounds of scrap paper annually—the equivalent of 229,300 trees. Since the 1960s, West has devised ways to capture and recycle waste inks, solvents, oils, and vapors created in the printing process. We also recycle plastics of all kinds, wood, glass, corrugated cardboard, and batteries, and have eliminated the use of polystyrene book packaging. We at West are proud of the longevity and the scope of our commitment to the environment.

West pocket parts and advance sheets are printed on recyclable paper and can be collected and recycled with newspapers. Staples do not have to be removed. Bound volumes can be recycled after removing the cover.

Production, Prepress, Printing and Binding by West Publishing Company.

 TEXT IS PRINTED ON 10% POST CONSUMER RECYCLED PAPER      Printed with **Printwise** Environmentally Advanced Water Washable Ink

British Library Cataloguing-in-Publication Data. A catalogue record for this book is available from the British Library.

COPYRIGHT ©1996     By WEST PUBLISHING COMPANY
610 Opperman Drive
P.O. Box 64526
St. Paul, MN  55164-0526

All rights reserved
Printed in the United States of America
03 02 01 00 99 98 97 96          8 7 6 5 4 3 2 1 0
Library of Congress Cataloging-in-Publication Data
Silverman, Ira J.
    Corrections : a comprehensive view / Ira J. Silverman, Manuel
Vega.
       p.    cm.
    Includes bibliographical references and index.
    ISBN 0-314-04575-9 (hard : alk. paper)
    1. Corrections—History.  2. Criminal justice, Administration of—
—History,  3. Imprisonment—Philosophy.  4. Punishment—Philosophy.
5. Prisoners—Social conditions.  6. Prisons—Overcrowding.
I. Vega, Manual, 1929-  .  II. Title.
HV8705.S55  1996                    96-2164
365'.9—dc20                          CIP

# PREFACE

During the last third of the twentieth century, a parade of events and changes in the United States has had a major impact on correctional systems. These changes have resulted in substantial increases in violent crime (particularly gun-related offenses by youth), the movement of crime out of the inner city and into the suburbs, and the randomness of victimization (e.g., car jackings, the Oklahoma City bombing, and home invasions). These events have led to a growing public hatred and intolerance for criminals, creating a demand for immediate solutions to the crime problem (e.g., mandatory sentencing, three strikes laws, harsh treatment for those convicted). This backlash has caused massive increases in prison populations (with a need for many new prisons) and the creation of programs such as boot camps and the revival of chain gangs. Two other trends affecting corrections are the increasing number of women and older individuals in the prisons. All of these changes are likely to require increases in funding and specialized programming well into the next century.

Because corrections is under intense scrutiny we feel it is very important for students to know and understand the many aspects of this field. Thus, these are the primary goals of this book:

**1.** To provide students with an accurate, detailed, and up-to-date account of the development of correctional practices.
**2.** To show how historical events and social issues have helped to shape today's correctional systems.
**3.** To describe objectively and in detail contemporary corrections in the United States in terms of its present structure, clients, management and personnel, and programs.
**4.** To provide a historic perspective of prisoners rights and the current constitutional guarantees to which inmates are entitled.

Numerous references and sources have been used to provide a well-rounded and broad presentation of the information that constitutes this intrinsically interesting topic.

## ORGANIZATION OF THE TEXT

Part One introduces the student to the correctional system, its relationship to the other segments of the criminal justice system, and the role of sentencing. The first chapter deals with the place of corrections in the criminal justice system, and Chapter 2 considers the various justifications, aspects, and strategies surrounding sentencing.

Part Two provides a four-chapter picture of the historical development of corrections from ancient times through the development of U.S. prisons during the nineteenth century, the approaches taken in the deep south, and the Big House prisons of the first half of the twentieth century.

Part Three contains four chapters detailing the emergence of modern prisons and the factors that influenced them. This includes the development of rehabilitative institutions, the massive social changes that occurred during the 1960s and their impact on race relations, the environment of contemporary prisons, and the development of prison gangs.

Part Four describes and discusses correctional clientele and is divided into two chapters. The first of these chapters deals with the male inmate and the various special categories of inmates that are found in prison. The next chapter profiles the female inmate population, and discusses the special problems of incarcerated women and their adaptations to prison life.

The fifth part, containing five chapters, deals with a variety of issues related to prison administration and management. The first of these chapters discusses correctional administrators and managers and the organizational contexts in which they work. The next chapter deals with line correctional officers and their roles, work environment, training, relations with inmates, and other important issues. The next two chapters are concerned with correctional law and inmate rights and the ways in which these factors impact the operation of prisons. The final chapter in this section addresses classification issues, including the assessment of inmates regarding custody, security and treatment needs.

Part Six, which includes four chapters, focuses on the basic programs and services that must be maintained by correctional institutions to provide for inmate needs. First to be discussed are educational and work programs and their importance in dealing with inmate deficits in these areas. The next chapter deals with medical and mental health services and treatment. Chapter 20 considers the importance of prison food services and the problems and issues associated with this activity and also the role of religion and the part played by chaplains in the prison environment. This section concludes with a chapter that focuses on family ties, visitation, and recreational programs, all of which play a central role in the normalization of the very restrictive prison environment.

The seventh part concerns itself with correctional programs and facilities found in the community. Chapter 22 deals with jails and detention facilities and the role they play in the criminal justice and correctional processes. Chapter 23 describes and discusses probation and parole programs, which represent the largest and most important segment of community corrections. Chapter 24 closes this section and treats the various intermediate sanctions that fall between standard probation and incarceration.

We close the book with an epilogue in which we examine contemporary trends in light of the directions we feel should be taken with respect to correctional policy.

## SPECIAL FEATURES OF THIS TEXT

This book presents a **comprehensive treatment of correctional history**, issues, and practices. The authors feel this treatment is necessary if the reader is to understand the contemporary state of corrections, especially the growing emphasis on punishment. The views of those who lived or worked in corrections during earlier times can make the past come alive for students and will help them analyze the issues and problems in the field today and to think critically about solutions. Much of this research is supported by the extensive use of primary references. The inclusion of various chapters

not usually found in other texts (e.g., Southern prisons, gangs) can enhance students' understanding of differences existing in the various state systems. The following is a list of the special chapters and/or sections that emphasize aspects of corrections not usually found in other corrections texts:

**1.** Chapter 3 examines the historical evolution of the punishments used to deal with rule/law violators.
**2.** Chapter 5 traces correctional practices developed in the various Southern states.
**3.** Chapter 6 examines the Big House prisons that existed in Northern states during the first half of the twentieth century.
**4.** Chapter 7 deals with the rehabilitative type of prison that existed during the 30-year period following World War II.
**5.** Chapter 8 details the sociopolitical developments of the 1960s and their impact on American corrections.
**6.** Chapter 10 examines the development of prison gangs and their impact on the environment of the contemporary prison.
**7.** Chapters 15 and 16 review a large number of cases and issues dealing with legal issues germane to corrections.
**8.** Part 6 covers in some detail the programs and services necessary in modern correctional facilities.

**"Close-ups"** are special boxed features, many of which were prepared exclusively for this text, that highlight actual events, unique and controversial programs and issues, personal experiences by inmates and their family members, personal experiences by correctional staff and others associated with the criminal justice process, and important court cases. Most of the Close-ups conclude with questions challenging students to think about the issues presented.

**The bibliography and case lists** include both primary and secondary sources as well as an extensive compilation of books, monographs, and articles on historical and contemporary aspects of corrections. Also included is a list of court cases dealing with inmate constitutional rights and other major correctional legal issues.

The **glossary** at the end of the book provides students with definitions of the important terms found throughout the text. This serves as an excellent reference source and can also be used to review important concepts discussed in the text.

## LEARNING TOOLS

The text contains the following features, which are designed to help the student learn, organize, and understand the material:

1. *Terms to remember* appear at the beginning of each chapter and serve to alert students to be on the lookout for important material.
2. *Learning objectives* are provided for each chapter.
3. *Topical readings and subheadings* provide students with a clear idea of the content that follows.
4. Each chapter concludes with a *comprehensive topical outline* that summarizes the chapter.
5. *Questions for review* and some *objective questions* are presented at the end of each chapter.

## ANCILLARIES

A complete instructor's manual is available. It includes chapter summaries, definitions of terms to know, complete chapter outlines, and overhead transparency masters. Also included will be an extensive test bank and the thoroughly revised Westtest 3.1.

## ACKNOWLEDGMENTS

The preparation of this text was immeasurably enhanced by the help of a number of academic colleagues and of professionals in the field of corrections. They contributed information and material for our use and/or read and critiqued chapters or parts of them. We particularly wish to thank Harvey Landress, Jo Gustafson, and Karen Roth. Jo, a corrections information specialist at the National Institute of Corrections, was a continual source of information whose help went above and beyond the call of duty. Harvey, a friend and colleague, contributed many hours reading, writing, and revising parts of the manuscript, particularly the material on drugs and infectious diseases, and provided valuable insights and information.

Karen, a member of the USF library staff, was extremely helpful in obtaining reference materials. Terry Danner of St. Leo College also assisted us by reading the manuscript and developing some pedagogical aspects of the book, as did Christine Sellers of our Department. We wish to thank and acknowledge the expertise of the authors who contributed chapters to the book: Gerasimos (Gerry) Gianakis, Chapter 13—Correctional Administration; Larry R. Ard and Ken Kerle, Chapter 22—Jails and Detention; and Linda Smith, Chapter 24—Intermediate Sanctions: Getting Tough in the Community. Also special thanks are due William Blount, friend, colleague, and chair of our department for all his support and encouragement throughout this project. Others who provided assistance and support include Cecil Geek, Kathleen Heide, Eldra Solomon, and Leonard Territo. Others at USF who were very helpful include Norm Voissem and members of the USF library staff: Susan Silver, Larry Heilos, and Marilyn Burke.

Typing and other related clerical services were provided by many people. We would like to especially thank Marianne Bell of USF's Information Processing Center, who typed numerous drafts of our chapters and assisted us in numerous related tasks that were necessary to complete this project. We are also grateful to Vicki Andrews who provided word processing assistance and without whose help we would not have been able to complete the second draft of this manuscript in so timely a fashion. Additionally, we wish to acknowledge Hertha Simon for the time and effort she devoted to typing parts of this manuscript. Secretarial support was also provided by Shirley Latt, Laura Pierce, and Heather Cote. For the work they have done, they have our undying gratitude. We also wish to acknowledge several students—Lisa Landis, Kathryn McPherson, Casey Mickler, and Steve Mislyan—who helped by reading a number of chapters and giving us the "consumer's" perspective.

This text has not only benefited from scholarly literature, as noted by our extensive bibliography, but also from materials and comments supplied by those working in corrections or related fields. The following individuals made special contributions to this text by providing expertise, materials, and comments, and by writing special close-ups that improved the accuracy and/or real-world picture this text has endeavored to furnish:

Howard Abadinsky, professor, Criminal Justice Program, Saint Xavier College, Chicago, Illinois

David Agresti, former director of programs, Pride of Florida

Jaye Anno, chairman, National Commission on Correctional Health Care

Kay Wood Bailey, president, International Corrections Art Network

Ann Bartolo, unit manager, FCI-Morgantown, Federal Bureau of Prisons

Glenda Beale, managing director and editor of research, American Correctional Association

Fred Berlin, director, National Institute for the Study, Prevention and Treatment of Sexual Trauma, and associate professor, School of Medicine, Johns Hopkins University

John Boston, project director, Criminal Appeals Bureau, Prisoners Rights Project, Legal Aid Society, New York City

Peter Breen, director, Centerforce, San Quentin, California

Robert A. Buchanan, president, Correctional Services Group Inc., Kansas City, Missouri

Sammy Buentello, gang specialist and member, State Classification Committee, Institutional Division, Texas Department of Criminal Justice

Russell Clemens, American Federation of State, County and Municipal Employees

Darryl Cheatwood, director and professor of criminal justice and sociology, University of Texas–San Antonio.

Kristina R. Crisafulli, project manager, Bureau of Justice Statistics Clearinghouse, Rockville, Maryland

Terry Danner, associate professor, Division of Social Science, St. Leo College

Michael E. Deutsch, attorney at law, active in the defense of Attica prisoners for more than 20 years

Joel DeVolentine, program administrator, Florida Correctional Mental Institution

Richard Dieter, executive director, Death Penalty Information Center

Jack E Dison, associate professor, Department of Criminology, Arkansas State University

Joan Dolby, staff associate, National Prison Project, Washington, D.C.

Robert Fong, associate professor, Department of Criminal Justice, California State University–Long Beach

Patricia Foote, Director, Corporate Communications, PRIDE of Florida

Mike Gilbert, former correctional officer, currently assistant professor, Department of Social and Policy Sciences, University of Texas–San Antonio

Imam Abdul Hafiz, chaplain, Federal Correctional Institution, Terminal Island, California

Casey F. Hairston, vice president, Parents Inc., and professor and associate dean, Indiana University School of Social Work, Indianapolis

Gwen Ingley, legislative liaison, American Correctional Association

Mike Israel, member, Lifers Board of Directors, Rathway Prison, New Jersey, and criminal justice director, Kean College, Union, New Jersey

Cheryl Johnson, director of instructional services, Windham School District, Texas Department of Criminal justice

Janice LaRosa, Unlimited Gravel Club sponsor, and psychological specialist, Tomoka Correctional Institution, Daytona Beach, Florida

Renee M. Legrand, executive director, Louisiana Junior Chamber of Commerce

Kraig Libstag, psychologist, Vermont Treatment Program for Sexual Offenders

Jess Maghan, executive director, Forum for Comparative Corrections, Office of International Criminal Justice, Chicago, Illinois

Mark Mauer, assistant director, The Sentencing Project, Washington, D.C.

Gail McCall, associate professor, Department of Recreation, University of Florida

Howard McClish, Lieutenant, Recreational Specialist, Minnesota Correctional Facility, Oak Park Heights

Dana Murray, graphics manager, American Correctional Association

Lane Murray, retired superintendent, Windham School District, Texas Department of Criminal Justice

James W. Mustin, director, Family and Corrections Network

David Nunnellee, public information officer, Texas Department of Criminal Justice

Joseph Papy, regional administrator, Probation and Parole Service, Department of Corrections, Florida

Barbara Parrer, executive director, Institutional Programs (in Arts, Crafts, Humanities), Oklahoma City, Oklahoma

William Pithers, director, Vermont Treatment Program for Sexual Offenders

Tom Pospichal, division manager, UNICOR, Federal Bureau of Prisons

Chrisine E. Reynolds, director of business planning, Pride of Florida

Charles Riggs, chaplaincy administrator, Federal Bureau of Prisons

Martin Salisbury, director of education, Patuxent Institute, Maryland

Nancy Schafer, Acting Director, Justice Center, University of Alaska, Anchorage

Pat Scholes, correctional information specialist, National Institute of Corrections

Robert R. Schulze, assistant chaplaincy administrator, Federal Bureau of Prisons

Richard Shaw, chaplain, Albany, Rensselaer and Schenectady County jails, and instructor, Department of Criminal Justice, Sienna College

Emmett Solomon, administrator of chaplaincy programs, Texas Department of Criminal Justice

Judy Ford Stokes, president, Judy Ford Stokes & Associates, Food Management Consultants, Atlanta, Georgia

Steve Steurer, executive director, Correctional Educational Association

Keehna J. Sture, former coordinator, Family Services, New York State Department of Corrections, currently counselor, Rochester Correctional Facility.

William Banks Taylor, professor, Department of Criminal Justice, University of Southern Mississippi

Alice Tracy, assistant director, Correctional Educational Association

Cris Tracy, superintendent, Windham School District, Texas Department of Criminal Justice

Glen Walters, Psychology Services, Federal Correctional Institution–Schuylkill

Kathi Westcott, Coalition Against Stop, National Prison Project

Frank Wood, commissioner, Minnesota Department of Correction

We are also grateful to the staff at West Publishing for their invaluable assistance and support. We wish to especially thank Joan Gill, our editor, for her unflagging support, without which this project would not have been completed. Becky Stovall, developmental editor, also provided invaluable help in coordinating and dealing with the review process. Matt Thurber, our production editor, also deserves our gratitude for the superb job he did in guiding us through the intricacies of publishing a first edition and for making helpful suggestions that improved the final product. Lorretta Palagi, our copyeditor, expertly edited the manuscript, improving its readability and correcting errors in it. This expertly-produced text was the result of the efforts of all of these people.

This book went through a number of meticulous reviews for both content and style. The comments and suggestions of the following reviewers has enhanced the focus and presentation of the material.

Gordon Armstrong
*Fayetteville State University*
Michael B. Blankenship
*University of Memphis*
David Callonick
*Northern Michigan University*
Ben Carmichael
*California State University-Hayward*

Darryl Cheatwood
*University of Baltimore*
John K. Cochran
*University of Oklahoma*
Joe Divver
*Seminole Community College*
Peter J. Grimes
*Nassau Community College*
Joe Jimenez
*Pima Community College-West Campus*
Polly Johnson
*Austin Community College*
Karol Lucken
*University of Central Florida*
Robert Mendelsohn
*South Dakota State College*
Terry Miller
*Clinton Community College*
Cora Moseley
*Tarrant County Community College*
Richard McCorkle
*University of Nevada-Las Vegas*
William E. Osterhoff
*Auburn University at Montgomery*
Jerald Phillips
*Linn-Benton Community College*
Chester L. Quarles
*University of Mississippi*
Kathryn Sullivan
*Hudson Valley Community College*
Thomas Todd
*Carl Sandburg College*
Ellen Van Valkenburgh
*Jamestown Community College*

Finally, the authors would like thank the most important people in their lives who supported them throughout this project. Dr. Silverman would like to express his thanks to his wife Happy. It is impossible to put into words the feeling of gratitude he has for all of the sacrifices she made and for the extraordinary forbearance, love, and tireless support that she provided during the more than 10 years that this book was in preparation. Further, when deadlines were nearing and time was tight she also read and critically edited portions of the manuscript. Were it not for her continuing love, nurturing, and support he could never have completed this project. Dr. Vega would like to thank his wife Allene for the unflagging love, support, and encouragement she provided during this project. Without this, it would not have been possible to complete this book.

# CONTENTS IN BRIEF

# CONTENTS

PART TWO:
HISTORICAL PERSPECTIVE 45

Chapter 3: The Evolution of Punishment 46

## PART SIX:
## INSTITUTIONAL PROGRAMS AND SERVICES 383

### Chapter 18: Basic Prison Programs: Educational and Work 384

# CORRECTIONS

## A COMPREHENSIVE VIEW

# PART ONE

## CORRECTIONS AND CRIMINAL JUSTICE

# CHAPTER 1

# THE CORRECTIONAL PROCESS

■ **LEARNING OBJECTIVES**

*After completing this chapter, you should be able to:*

**1.** Define the terms *corrections* and *penology* and discuss the place of corrections within the criminal justice system.

**2.** Comment on the hidden nature of corrections and on its role in the solution of the crime problem.

**3.** Describe the organization of corrections within the United States.

**4.** Specify the relationship between the police and corrections and describe the correctional functions performed by the police.

**5.** Discuss the impact of prosecutorial discretion on corrections and describe the correctional functions performed by prosecutors.

**6.** Describe the relationship between sentencing and corrections.

**7.** Discuss the courts' role in correcting unconstitutional conditions within prisons.

**8.** Identify, describe, and compare the rehabilitation, justice, and utilitarian models of corrections.

**9.** Discuss the importance of history and social issues in the evolution of corrections.

■ **KEY TERMS AND CONCEPTS**

Cleveland Prosecution Mediation Program
Correctional sieve
Corrections
Judges' review of prison conditions
Justice model
Local corrections
*Nolle prosequi*
Penology
Police role in corrections
Prison crowding
Probation without adjudication
Prosecutors' impact on corrections
Rehabilitative model
Utilitarian model

## CORRECTIONS FACES MANY PROBLEMS

About forty people have gathered in a church Sunday school classroom. Some seem upset and are talking, sometimes heatedly, with one another. Their minister has asked them to discuss the problem of crime and escalating violence which has plagued their neighborhood for a long time. A woman is describing the injuries suffered by her eleven-year-old daughter who was on her way to school when robbed of her lunch money by a young neighborhood tough. She calls for the punishment of the perpetrator. Responding to the woman's anguish and anger, the minister states that those responsible, and indeed all like them, should be imprisoned for life because this would teach all criminals a lesson and prevent them from further injuring others. The audience rises as one and shouts out its approval.

This scenario points to some problems faced by the criminal justice system in general and the corrections subsystem in particular when confronting the issue of how to deal with those who victimize us. Should we expect convicted offenders (and others who might engage in crime) to be swayed by what we do to them? If the answer is yes, in what way(s) should we deal with them? These questions have no easy answers. As we will see, humanity has been wrestling with them for centuries and has yet to devise a satisfactory answer.

Official responses to the punishment of convicted offenders in the United States are collectively referred to as corrections. Currently and historically the system of institutions, programs, and services that comprise corrections in this country has been under fire for not adequately protecting the community. Much current public dissatisfaction with corrections seems to focus on the "lenient treatment" received by convicted criminals (e.g., they do not serve long enough terms, not enough of them are incarcerated, most prisons are too soft on them).

In general, the system is felt by the public not to sufficiently punish the criminal. Many people feel that if enough money were spent on incarcerating all criminals in harsh prisons for the full term of their sentences that the crime problem would be solved. Do you think this would be an appropriate solution? If so, why?

This text attempts to answer this and other questions regarding convicted offenders. We examine the historical events and developments regarding correctional/penal responses to criminal behavior and the social changes that have affected them. In this way, current approaches regarding criminal behavior can be better understood. Perhaps one of the insights we may gain is that corrections can provide only one of many parts of the solution to the high levels of crime currently being experienced in the United States.

### Corrections Is Responsible for the Accused and the Convicted

Technically the term corrections has been limited to only actions taken by agencies to deal with convicted offenders. It is more common today, however, for it to encompass a broader definition. Corrections can be defined as all agencies, programs, and organizations on the local, state, and federal levels that deal with both those accused of crimes—e.g., pretrial detainees—and those convicted of them. In expanding this definition, we recognize that there are limitations placed on what can be done to those accused of crimes versus those convicted.

The efforts directed at those who are convicted involve a variety of methods and approaches that include punishment, treating offenders' problems (e.g., drug addiction), and improving academic and job skills. These efforts may enable them to return to society and lead productive lives and also protect society from criminal acts. Punishment in the form of retribution frequently continues to be viewed as the most basic response of corrections toward convicted offenders because, both historically and contemporarily, people believe that those who victimize others should suffer in some way. Today, for the most part, with the exception of capital punishment, this belief translates into some restriction or deprivation of liberty either by subjecting offenders to some form of probation, parole, or imprisonment. Along with these sanctions offenders may also be subject to methods and approaches designed to deter, incapacitate, or provide opportunities to deal with problems and or improve their chances of becoming productive members of society. With the exception of retribution, some of these methods and approaches are used, with some limitations, on pretrial detainees and those placed in pretrial diversion programs.

Corrections replaced the older term penology, which was derived from a Latin word that means punishment. Penology, which is the generic term for the organized body of concepts, theories, and approaches centered on the prison and the institutional experience, signifies "the study of punishment." The term corrections, which replaced this narrower concept, better describes the broad range of facilities, programs, and services that deal with convicted offenders. The term corrections, with its implication of placing less emphasis on punishment, has created a dilemma regarding its appropriate role in dealing with criminals. That is, should criminals merely be punished or should we attempt to rehabilitate them? Discerning readers are likely to ask themselves "Can't you rehabilitate through punishment?" Although the answer to that question is a qualified "yes," the beneficial results of punishment as applied to criminals have not been amply demonstrated because punishment alone will not rehabilitate. That is, punishment alone will not remediate educational and other deficits affecting inmates.

Our historical review of corrections will show that most correctional systems in the United States have always had an underlying punitive orientation toward criminals. Nevertheless, one of the original intentions of imprisonment was reformation, a goal that has been pursued in a variety of ways, often with limited success. Beginning with the penitentiary, these two objectives of punishment and reform have generally been combined and have become a source of friction, a situation that has made it difficult to fully realize either of them. The difficulty of applying a strict punitive sanction to the vast majority of convicted offenders is that they are not in prisons but under some form of community supervision, which makes it impossible to maintain a rigid punitive regimen. In contrast, most prisons are not structured or organized such that reformation or rehabilitation is easily achieved.

## Much of Corrections Is Hidden from Public View

An important characteristic of the formal corrections process compared with other components of the criminal justice system, both in and out of the community, is its low visibility. Prisons are the least visible of the components because most of them, particularly the older "fortress"-type institutions, are located in isolated, thinly populated rural areas. Visits to them by community leaders, politicians, or by judges who routinely sentence offenders to confinement in these places have, until recently, been a rarity. The remoteness and difficulty of access often also imposes real hardships on the families of inmates who want to remain in close touch.

Within the community, correctional services become visible only in a few instances. One in particular is when an attempt is made to locate a probation office (or some similar service center or facility for offenders) in a specific area of the community. Although they recognize the need for these facilities, citizens often take the position of "not in my back yard" (NIMBY). The furor is even greater when an area is proposed as a site for a prison or jail (Rogers and Haimes, 1987; McShane, Williams, and Wagoner, 1992).

**CORRECTIONAL FACILITIES RECEIVE ATTENTION ONLY WHEN PROBLEMS ARISE** Frequently the public only becomes aware of correctional institutions when adverse publicity occurs, for example, a riot, an escape, a guard or inmate slaying, some dramatic event such as the execution of an infamous criminal, or the commission of a heinous crime by an ex-convict, particularly if, for example, he or she was released prior to the expiration of his or her sentence as a consequence of overcrowded prisons. Our "Close-Up: The Pitfalls of Early Release" illustrates the latter case. These news stories tend to validate the public view of offenders as individuals who are inherently bad, brutal, or beyond change. This serves to move public opinion in the direction of having the corrections system provide less treatment and more punishment.

Unconstitutional conditions (such as poor medical care) and reduced services and programs, often due to overcrowding and budgetary constraints, have also kept prisons in the public eye. There is less concern, however, regarding the loss or reduction of programs and services because of the feeling, by large segments of the population, that inmates are not entitled to these services.

## Racial Conflicts and Crowding Also Add to Corrections' Problems

Racial conflicts represent another source of attention for correctional institutions. In these facilities, in which the population is disproportionately composed of minorities, the animosities between different ethnic groups is magnified by the nature of institutional life. Self-preservation instincts in this tense atmosphere are manifested by the formation

## Close Up  **The Pitfalls of Early Release**

Two men arrested in September 1993 in Tampa, Florida, in the beating death of a Turkish student had been recently released from prison as part of a plan to free 7500 offenders to ease overcrowding, according to corrections officials. The two suspects have extensive criminal records.

"When you have that kind of record, and you're still out in the community and you go and beat someone to death,. . . you know the system has problems," said Tampa police Maj. Ken Taylor.

One of the suspects was released in January after serving 6 months of a five-year sentence for a variety of offenses, which included aggravated battery. The other suspect had been released in June after serving 13 months of a 40-month sentence involving a hit-and-run conviction.

Police said the two suspects were angered after the victim cut them off in traffic, so they followed him home and beat him to death.

Source: "Slaying suspects on early release," *The Bradenton Herald*, Sep. 23, 1993, p. B6.

---

of prison gangs and cliques and of "veneers of toughness by inmates" (Silberman, 1995). Bottled-up anger and frustration can be seen in gang rapes and assaults, intensified racial conflicts between inmates, and hostile inmate-guard relations.

This situation has been further aggravated by prison crowding because when institutions are filled beyond capacity, an inmate cannot escape the inherent dangers of prison life by taking refuge in a safe, single cell. A prison too crowded to restrain its most dangerous and aggressive inmates is likely to generate high levels of anxiety and violence, which further aggravate the conditions mentioned. This crowding has occurred in spite of the fact that the number of prison beds doubled during the 1980s.

### Public Fears Influence Policy

Regardless of the specific factors that raise public fears about crime, the bottom line is that these fears are influencing criminal justice policy. Thus, polls taken in 1992, 1993, and 1994 indicate that crime, violence, and drugs have become the primary concern of Americans, substantially outweighing concerns about health care and jobs. Of those responding to one poll, about two-thirds said they worried more about crime now than they did five years ago (although reported crime had gone down) (Faucheaux, 1994). The fears and concerns about crime have affected public attitudes regarding the performance of the various segments of the criminal justice system. A 1992 survey asking respondents to rate the various segments of the system showed that although almost two-thirds rated police as excellent or good, less than one-third rated corrections in those categories (Maguire, Pastore, and Flanagan, 1993). Another survey reported by Maguire *et al.* indicated that about two-thirds of those respondents reported they wanted stricter law enforcement and more severe penalties in order to combat crime. Support for these tougher policies is being strongly manifested in both black and white communities although whites more strongly support capital punishment. Support by blacks has grown in spite of the fact that they often feel that the system discriminates against them.

These concerns are being affected politically in several ways. First, an increasing number of anticrime propositions have shown up on the ballots of a number of states and have been successful (while noncrime issues tended to be rejected). Second, most politicians have jumped on the crime bandwagon and are promising a variety of anticrime steps including more police, "three strikes and you're out" (some even say "one strike") laws, building more and more prisons, and speedier executions. This rhetoric is particularly strident when it comes to dealing with violence, especially when committed by juveniles. Little concern is being manifested by the public regarding the funding of programs that emphasize treatment and/or prevention. Another aspect of the political implications is that those who are winning elections at this time are usually those espousing the toughest stance in dealing with criminals (Faucheaux, 1994).

## Many of Today's Problems in Corrections Have a Long History

Although the problems currently facing corrections are of great concern, this situation is not unique. It is difficult to find a time when corrections has not experienced a significant number of problems (for reasons that are implicit in the dilemmas faced by a democratic and pluralistic society like ours) in dealing with crime, criminals, and criminal behavior. Some of these factors are explored in the following chapters, which examine the historical background and systematic developments that have helped to shape corrections. However, to place contemporary corrections in the proper perspective, we begin our discussion by examining its place in the criminal justice system. First, we focus on the complex and often conflicting relationships

between corrections and other components of the criminal justice system. Second, we examine the correctional functions performed by these other components either in addition to, or as part of, their regular duties and responsibilities. We believe these considerations bear significantly on the success or failure of corrections.

## THE CRIMINAL JUSTICE PROCESS IS COMPLICATED

The activities of the criminal justice system form a continuum, which includes a series of steps and potential exit points (see Figure 1.1). Felonies, misdemeanors, petty offenses, and juvenile cases each tend to receive different dispositions within the

FIGURE 1.1   Flow of Cases in the Criminal Justice System

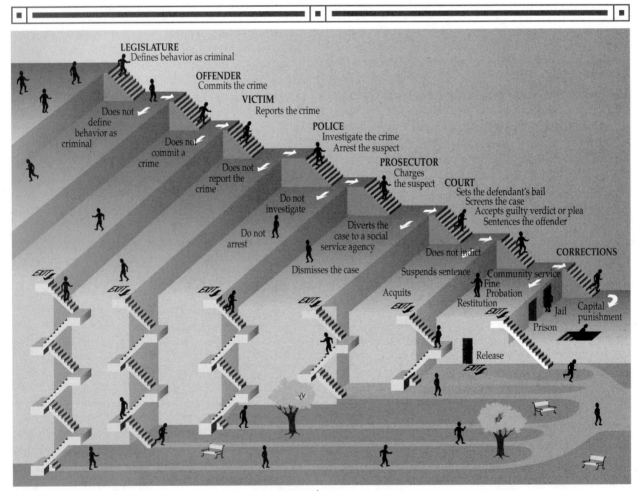

*SOURCE:* Adapted from *The challenge of crime in a free society.* President's Commission on Law Enforcement and Administration of Justice, 1967.

criminal justice system and thus follow separate paths in the process. Apprehended offenders may be screened out of the system at different points along the way. This screening process suggests a correctional sieve (see Figure 1.2), through which most cases "leak" out before they are retained in some correctional program (such as probation or prison).

## Organization of Corrections in the United States

It is important to describe corrections briefly prior to examining interrelationships between it and the other components of the criminal justice system, particularly because there is no single system of corrections in this country. Instead, there are numerous systems: a federal system, fifty state systems, and several thousand local systems. One key distinction is the difference between jails and prisons. Jails are almost always local (although several federal facilities do exist) for detaining pretrial arrestees and convicted misdemeanants. Prisons are state or federal facilities holding sentenced felons.

The federal system, administered by the Bureau of Prisons, consists of sixty-eight prisons, four jails, and a probation service and deals with offenders accused or convicted of breaking federal laws. The prisons are divided into six levels of security rang-

ing from minimum security camps to the super maximum security prisons at Marion, Illinois, and Florence, Colorado.

Each state correctional system is organized according to the wishes of its governor and legislature. State prisons house offenders convicted of felony offenses and who are usually incarcerated for sentences of more than one year or are awaiting execution. Normally state prisons are divided into three or four levels of security. The organizational pattern of state corrections, which varies widely, will be discussed in a later chapter. Both state and federal correctional systems also include probation, other community correctional services such as halfway houses, and may include some form of parole or supervision after release from prison.

Local corrections deals with convicted misdemeanant offenders and pretrial detainees. The major local correctional facilities for convicted misdemeanants are jails, but some jurisdictions also place these offenders on probation, work release, or in boot camps. At this level, terms are normally short—averaging approximately sixty days—so that the turnover in clientele is extremely large. Most local correctional programs are at the county level, but larger cities across the country (e.g., New York City) may also have their own programs. Additionally, jails in six states are run on a

FIGURE 1.2   **The Correctional Sieve**

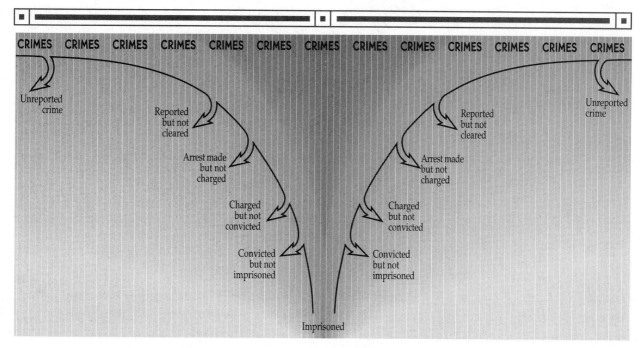

statewide basis. Local programs are more fully discussed in Chapter 22.

## CRIMINAL JUSTICE HAS FOUR MAJOR COMPONENTS

The criminal justice system is composed of four major subsystems: police, prosecution, courts, and corrections, each with different responsibilities. What is often forgotten is that none of these subsystems is mutually exclusive of one another. Thus, what is done in one has some effect on all the others. Prosecutors receive their clientele from the police; courts from the prosecutors; the corrections sector receives its clients from the courts; and the cycle is often repeated when released offenders commit another offense and again become police "clientele." Increased efforts by the police, such as drug sweeps, produce an immediate impact on the other subsystems by overloading what are already heavy work schedules. Finally, if corrections is forced to release potential recidivists because of overcrowding resulting from the increased activity of other subsystems, then they may, in turn, produce an increase in the workload of the police and courts.

Unlike justice systems in other parts of the world, the American process is not composed of a single system. Instead, it includes many separate, relatively independent systems and subsystems of institutions and procedures. In all of the thousands of towns, cities, counties, the fifty states—and even in the federal government—there are criminal justice "systems" of sorts. All apprehend, prosecute, convict, and punish or attempt to rehabilitate lawbreakers, yet no two are exactly alike and few are linked in any systematic way.

## EACH CRIMINAL JUSTICE SUB-SYSTEM HAS SOME CORRECTIONAL ROLE

In addition to what is viewed as their regular functions, the police, prosecution, and courts also perform some correctional functions.

### The Police Play Various Roles in Corrections

The growth in the number of social agencies dealing with the offender has led to an increased police role in corrections. One of these roles is apparent in the interactions between the police and community-based corrections. The neutral ground where the probation or parole officer and the police first meet is usually the court, and this first encounter is likely to be in connection with the presentation of the presentence investigation report by the probation officer (PO). In this circumstance, the PO may make a sentencing recommendation with which the police officer disagrees because he has seen the harm done by the offender first hand. This disagreement could adversely affect the relationship between the police officer and the PO.

Relations between police and probation or parole personnel in the urban setting also tend to be adversely affected by the size of the respective departments and high turnover rates among personnel. POs in many urban areas are not highly visible and may be strictly limited in their mobility as a consequence of an excess of paperwork or administrative responsibilities. However, the increasing use of community control and other intensive supervision programs, which require more face-to-face contacts between POs and offenders in the community, have likely led to greater interaction between POs and law enforcement. Also, in a number of states POs are assuming a larger law enforcement/surveillance role in the management of their supervisees, which would tend to increase their contact with police officers.

**POLICE AGENCIES USUALLY OPERATE JAILS AND DETENTION FACILITIES** Because of their uniforms, weapons, hardware, and traditional roles (i.e., law enforcement, crime control), it may be difficult to conceive of the police as the point at which corrections begins. The most visible corrections function performed by local law enforcement agencies is the operation of short-term detention and postadjudication facilities (i.e., jails). The primary functions of jails are to detain offenders awaiting trial; to hold convicted felons awaiting transfer to state institutions; and to punish convicted misdemeanants. Although programs are usually limited, many county correction agencies provide education, drug treatment, and work release. Participation in these programs may have some correctional benefits. Moreover, a pretrial jail experience may make some individuals conscious of the potential costs of continued criminal activity, which may have some deterrent value.

A school resource officer lectures an elementary school class on crime prevention. This represents an early-stage correctional function.

**POLICE OPERATE SOME CORRECTIONAL PROGRAMS** Some police departments operate programs directed toward the prevention, control, and treatment of delinquency. Police departments with special juvenile units may place youths on informal probation. Informal probation typically involves an agreement between the police, the adolescent, and his/her parents to meet certain conditions that may require the youth to attend school and also restrict after-school activities. In the last decade, many police departments have assigned school resource officers to junior and senior high schools for purposes of preventing and diverting youth from contact with the juvenile justice system. In this capacity, they counsel youth and their parents and provide lectures on law enforcement and related topics. These activities have led many of these officers, who are often better educated (many have BA degrees), to a better understanding of the limited influence that corrections has in deciding which offenders are released into the community (Florida Department of Law Enforcement, 1990).

**POLICE PERFORM A "GATEKEEPER" FUNCTION** A less visible police corrections function involves their discretionary arrest authority. This "gatekeeper function" allows police to determine how

far some individuals are processed into the criminal justice system. Police are sometimes in a position to make a decision as to whether formal action should be taken against an offender.

In those instances in which an offender is not taken into custody, there are several options—all of which may involve some correctional function: (1) Police can warn offenders and release them; (2) in dealing with juveniles, police can take the youngster home and confer with the family; or (3) they can refer the adult or juvenile to a diversion program such as pretrial intervention or community mental health (Finn and Sullivan, 1988). With some first offenders, the only correctional action necessary may be a reprimand, warning, or referral. Much police activity revolves around dealing with either juveniles or public drunks. Finn (1989) studied the decriminalization of public drunkenness. He concluded that thirty-four jurisdictions had decriminalized it since 1971 and that there had been a downward trend in arrests in these jurisdictions since the law had been changed, with police now taking many of these individuals to detoxification centers.

**POLICE PROVIDE INFORMATION ON OFFENDERS TO CORRECTIONAL PERSONNEL** Police also serve as a valuable source of information for various correctional agencies. Probation or parole officers interview police to obtain a more complete picture of the offender, which can be used in preparing a presentence investigation report (PSI). In some jurisdictions, police are consulted as to whether certain offenders should be eligible for work or study release programs or be allowed home furloughs.

### Prosecutors Play Several Roles in Corrections

Prosecutors impact corrections in various ways. The discretion exercised by the office of the prosecutor has indirect but extremely important consequences for corrections. Decisions by prosecutors affect the size and nature of the prison population because they can decide whether to initiate prosecution against people arrested by the police and the specific charges that will be brought against them.

**PROSECUTORIAL DISCRETION CAN LIMIT THE NUMBER AND TYPES OF OFFENDERS ENTERING THE SYSTEM**   The prosecutor must make a determination as to whether to charge the suspect with having committed a crime and whether a case merits prosecution. Recently some prosecutors have developed administrative procedures to assist them in making these decisions. One example is the Prosecutors Information Systems, in which computers are used to generate ratings that help attorneys decide which cases to prosecute and serve as a means of supervising their discretion (Miller, Dawson, Dix, and Parnas, 1976). Second, prosecutors can screen out defendants who have been charged by requesting that the judge or magistrate *nolle prosequi* (i.e., a formal decision by the prosecutor not to prosecute further) a case at the preliminary hearing (Boyce and Perkins, 1989). From a prosecutor's standpoint, screening out questionable cases as early as possible conserves scarce resources. The prosecutor's right to decide not to prosecute despite sufficient evidence to do so is one of the broadest, most powerful examples of discretionary authority available to anyone in the criminal justice system (Newman, 1975). This discretion is allowed on the grounds that near autonomy is a fundamental prerequisite for safeguarding the integrity of the decision-making process in which the prosecutor engages.

A prosecutor arguing a case in court. By making sentencing recommendations, prosecutors can significantly affect corrections.

Prosecutors can also remove cases from the system by requesting that the offender be declared incompetent to stand trial. In the past, this meant an indefinite commitment to a mental hospital until the person was found competent. However, in 1972 the Supreme Court struck this down in *Jackson v. Indiana*. The court ruled that if there was no substantial possibility that individuals declared incompetent could either be restored to competency in a reasonable period of time or effectively treated, the state must either (1) institutionalize these offenders using civil commitment proceedings or (2) release them. Most states now require that this determination be made within a six-month period (Low, Jeffries, and Bonnie, 1986; Boyce and Perkins, 1989).

*A Number of Factors Influence the Decision Not to Prosecute*   Prosecutors may decide not to take official action in a given case for a variety of reasons. They may not have the staff and budget to prosecute all criminal violations, which requires them to develop priorities. The lowest priority is usually assigned to minor offenses and to nonviolent property crimes (e.g., fraud, embezzlement, forgery, and so on) in which the offender is not a serious or persistent violator and/or has made restitution or other amends that satisfy the victim.

Prosecutors may also not take action in cases where the offense is minor and the filing of a criminal charge would result in severe embarrassment or possible injury to the accused or his/her family. For example, if a well-known sports celebrity was arrested for indecent exposure, the prosecutor might drop charges if the defendant agrees to seek professional help. Charges may be dropped in cases in which available alternatives to a criminal proceeding will achieve the same purposes. Thus, the prosecutor may choose to invoke a civil sanction, such as the revocation of a license. For mentally disturbed or mentally retarded individuals, institutionalization in an appropriate treatment facility through civil commitment may be pursued. For those on probation or parole for a prior offense, revocation rather than initiation of new charges may be sought.

*Charges May Be Reduced or the Process May Be Suspended*  Reduction or dismissal of charges can occur because the victim either precipitated the offense by his/her own conduct or is unwilling to cooperate fully in prosecution. Criminal charges may also be reduced or dismissed for individuals who have agreed to "turn state's evidence" (i.e., testify for the prosecution) or act as informers for the prosecutor or police. A plea bargain can also result in the dismissal or reduction of some charges. Offenders who "cop a plea" rather than stand trial often receive a reduced sentence, which lessens the time they will spend under correctional supervision compared to the time spent if convicted by means of a trial.

**PROSECUTORS SERVE AS CORRECTIONAL AGENTS**  The Cleveland Prosecution Mediation Program, which has been copied in other states, provides citizens an out-of-court means for settling disputes that might involve misdemeanor offenses. This program deals with interpersonal disputes involving friends, family members, neighbors, or others, which may lead to violence. Approximately 8400 cases are scheduled for mediation each year.

Cases come to the attention of program personnel when one party initiates a complaint. In lieu of a court proceeding, mediation is initiated. Specially trained second- and third-year law students function as referees between the disputants. Each party

is given an opportunity to tell his/her version of the case without interruption. The mediator then helps the two parties fashion possible solutions to the problem. Once a solution is agreed on, the mediator makes a record of this accord and gets a commitment from the participants to its provisions. In two weeks the mediator is required to contact the parties to determine if they are adhering to the agreement. Warrants may be issued in instances of noncompliance.

This program has benefitted both the criminal justice system and participants (Weis, 1985). The system benefits by not expending funds on relatively minor cases while individuals get a speedier resolution to problems that might have escalated to more serious levels. Also the time for case disposition has been reduced from an average of three and one-half months for court hearings to fifteen days for the mediation program. Additionally, most parties involved in the program were satisfied with its outcome and were still adhering to their commitments after a year.

The Office of the State Attorney in Jacksonville, Florida, operates eight separate and distinct pretrial/diversion programs with correctional implications. These programs include a pretrial intervention program, a literacy enhancement program, a dispute settlement program, a youth mediator program, a youth work program, and a restitution program (Weinstein, 1989; Garrett, 1993).

The literacy enhancement program represents a unique correctional activity. It is aimed at providing young adult offenders who have not completed school with the opportunity to obtain a General Equivalency Diploma (GED). To be selected for the program offenders must meet criminal history and residency requirements. Volunteer community mentors are recruited to guide and motivate these youth during this educational process. The local community college handles classroom instruction and testing. Job placement is also provided for unemployed offenders.

## The Courts Play Several Roles in Corrections

Courts determine guilt or innocence, which, along with sentencing, impact corrections. Additionally, the courts review prison conditions with respect to constitutionality, mandating changes when necessary. They also operate some correctional programs.

**SENTENCING IS A KEY COURT CORRECTIONAL FUNCTION**   The most obvious relationship between the courts and corrections revolves around sentencing. For adults, the correctional process begins formally when a court finds them guilty of having violated a criminal law. The sentencing process is the most crucial phase of the court procedure because of the wide range of sanctions that might be imposed. Although historically discretion has played a varying role in sentencing, recently this discretion has been limited by statutory changes in many states that have included the increased use of determinate sentences, sentencing guidelines, and mandatory sentencing. (For an expanded discussion of sentencing, see Chapter 2.) On a purely mechanical level, sentencing determines (1) whether an individual will be referred or committed to a particular agency, institution, or facility; and (2) the conditions under which the agency or facility will receive the offender. As the Task Force on the Courts (1973) stated in its report to the National Advisory Commission on Criminal Justice Standards and Goals:

> Sentencing also affects the correctional process on a more subtle level. The extent to which a defendant regards his sentence as fair may influence his willingness to participate in correctional programs. Moreover, certain sentencing practices give correctional officials authority to detain an offender until his chances of successful integration into the community are at a maximum; other sentencing practices may require earlier release or detention beyond that point. Sentencing is related to community security insofar as it affects the ability of correctional agencies to change the behavior of convicted offenders. It may also help curtail crimes by persons other than the offender being sentenced. This may occur through deterrence—the creation of conscious fear of swift and certain punishment—or through more complex means, such as reinforcing social norms by the imposition of severe penalties (p. 109).

There is no monolithic community view regarding how we should deal with specific offenses or individual offenders. The level of public support for different approaches to controlling and correcting crime varies over time, and at any given point one or another of these approaches will have majority support. Although the most vocal members of the community have frequently viewed punishment as the major objective of sentencing, other

segments of the community have considered rehabilitation or reformation or reintegration to be the most important objective. The question facing judges (and the legislators making laws impinging on sentencing) has been one of which view they should consider when imposing sentences. The creation of sentencing guidelines and mandatory sentencing paradigms increasingly appears to be taking this decision out of judges' hands.

*Many Factors Affect the Sentencing Process*   Many factors affect the type of disposition an offender receives but among the most important are the following:

   **1.** The statutory sanctions mandated for the offense.
   **2.** The judges' perceptions of the community's view of the purpose of corrections. These perceptions are affected by the community's social structure and conditions such as increasing crime, or the recent occurrence of particularly brutal or heinous offenses.
   **3.** Judges' personalities and their own views of the offense, the place where it occurred, the way in which it was perpetrated, and the offender.
   **4.** The presentence investigation report almost always influences the judge's perception of the offender. This adds another dimension to the sentencing process because, to some extent, the probation officer's view of the offender and his/her crime will affect the report. This may involve either the inclusion or exclusion of, or emphasis on, certain information and/or recommendations.
   **5.** The attitude of the victim, which in recent years has been more often taken into consideration in sentencing.
   **6.** The viewpoint of the police, which is either presented to the prosecutor who in turn presents it to the judge or expressed directly by the police in open court.
   **7.** The persuasiveness of counsel at the sentencing hearing.
   **8.** The political climate in the community in which the judge presides.
   **9.** The limitations imposed by the lack of appropriate correctional facilities.
   **10.** The plea bargaining process, which in most instances influences the sentence that the defendant will receive. In these cases, the sentence is usually negotiated before a guilty plea is made. Judges can reject a plea bargain but it is not done

in too many cases, because it would clog an already overburdened system.

The thrust of sentencing reform has revolved around changes in procedures and decision-making intended to result in dispositions that are more fair, rational, humane, open to inspection, subject to accountability, and—however measured—more effective. However, the explosion of drug-related crime has resulted in intense pressure on judges simply to impose longer sentences.

There is an especially thin line between sentencing and corrections. The sentencing function is interwoven with and invokes all of the substantive issues confronting and comprising corrections. Indeed, it is scarcely possible to conceptualize sentencing adequately without concurrently considering the correctional framework within which it will be carried out and its consequences for the individual and for society. These issues are more fully discussed in Chapter 2.

**JUDGES SERVE AS MONITORS OF CONDITIONS IN THE CORRECTIONAL SYSTEM**  Another facet of judicial involvement in corrections is the role it has taken in reviewing prison conditions. Until the mid-1960s most state and federal courts refused to consider prisoner complaints concerning prison conditions, a position referred to as the "hands-off" doctrine (Singer and Statsky, 1974; Krantz and Branham, 1991).

Several reasons have been offered for the change in the courts' willingness to intervene in prison operations (Singer and Statsky, 1974). By visiting many prisons, a number of judges recognized the need for intervention in prison management. They also became frustrated by the lack of action taken by the legislative and executive branches to correct the deficiencies that were noted.

During the 1960s, judges began to recognize that if they did not act nothing would happen. On the federal level precedents existed to support court intervention to ensure that basic constitutional rights were accorded to a variety of groups. Historically, this was done regardless of the popularity of the decisions and was exemplified by cases involving changes in criminal procedure, civil rights, and women's rights. Given that federal judges are appointed for life they could render decisions without fear of political repercussions.

We will discuss the specific changes relating to corrections made by the courts in Chapters 15 and 16. Suffice it to say that from this point the courts took the position that people entering our jails and prisons were not deprived of all their constitutional rights once the institutional door closed.

**THE COURTS ALSO OPERATE CORRECTIONAL PROGRAMS**  As in the case of police and prosecution, judges perform correctional functions in the exercise of their authority. For example, Florida employs the concept of probation without adjudication, which allows judges to withhold adjudication in the interests of reducing the penetration of offenders into the criminal justice system. This approach is similar in concept to the use of deferred prosecution in the federal courts, where it has been applied since 1946 to youthful offenders.

Citizen dispute settlement centers or neighborhood justice centers such as the Cleveland Prosecution Mediation Program described earlier are also administered by courts in several jurisdictions. Since 1970 approximately 100 of these court-sponsored programs have been opened across the United States (Roehl and Ray, July 1986).

A study of court processing by the Vera Institute of Justice found that in 56% of all felony arrests for crimes against the person, the victim had a previous relationship with the accused. This report concluded the following:

> Because our society has not found adequate alternatives to arrest and adjudication for coping with interpersonal anger publicly expressed, we pay a price. The price includes large court case loads, long delays in processing and, ultimately, high dismissal rates. These impose high financial costs on taxpayers and high personal costs on defendants and their families. The public pays in another way, too. The congestion and drain on resources caused by an excessive number of such cases in the courts weakens the ability of the criminal justice system to deal quickly and decisively with the "real" felons, who may be getting lost in the shuffle. The risk that they will be returned to the street increases, as does the danger to law-abiding citizens on whom they prey (Vera Institute of Justice, 1977, p. xv).

Complainants in most cases involving people with some prior relationship are usually not interested in having the defendant prosecuted once

**A mediation session in a Citizen Dispute Center.**

they have cooled off. Thus, initial court time spent on these cases is wasted and makes an alternative process more practical and economical. In a society drowning in litigation, neighborhood dispute settlement programs are a valuable alternative to the courts.

Finally, in some states the courts' involvement in the correctional process is very direct often including, on a county level, direct responsibility for probation services for both juvenile and adult offenders. In these jurisdictions, the county's chief judge has administrative oversight for the probation department but usually delegates its management to a chief probation officer.

## DIFFERENT VIEWS REGARDING THE OBJECTIVES OF CORRECTIONS

The preceding discussion has emphasized the point that the total correctional process cannot be understood without considering the relationships between corrections and the other components of the criminal justice system. We have stressed that these criminal justice subsystems affect corrections in several ways. First, they control the intake pro-

cess of offenders into the system and, thus, determine the level, quality, and extent of services that corrections can offer. A present example is the jail and prison crowding caused by the draconian drug policies of the late 1980s and early 1990s. These policies resulted in a glut of arrests and subsequent convictions of large numbers of drug offenders and have strained correctional budgets.

Second, these components perform a variety of correctional functions, sometimes independent of and sometimes in concert with the formal correctional system. These activities occur during all phases of the process, from offenders' initial contact with the police to their being found guilty, after which they become clients of the correctional system. A third effect is the control that is exerted over the correctional system by court mandates and legislative actions. These actions have the effect of controlling policy as well as day-to-day operating procedures.

The correctional subsystem has been plagued by a variety of problems throughout its history, many of which can be traced to overcrowding. Indeed, the present array of problems dogging the correctional subsystem is attributable to a variety of social changes. These changes have resulted in high levels of drug use and related crime and, more recently, in increasing violent crime. Reactions to these problems by the criminal justice system have resulted in severe prison crowding, leading to community placement for many offenders and early releases for many inmates. This has contributed to a hardening of public attitudes regarding the mission and goals of the correctional process and has led to calls for increased severity of punishment. The move toward greater punishment has weakened the "correctional/reform" aspects of corrections, sparking controversy among corrections professionals and criminologists regarding the purposes of sanctions. Wilson (1975), Fogel (1979), Cullen and Gilbert (1982), Bartollas (1985), and Palmer (1992) have reviewed or commented on the various models that currently underlie this controversy: the rehabilitation model, the justice model, and the Utilitarian model.

### The Rehabilitative Model Focuses on Treating the Offender

The objective of the rehabilitative model is to change the offenders' attitudes and behavior and improve their academic and vocational skills so as to reduce the likelihood of their reinvolvement in crime. The rehabilitative model has been approached somewhat differently by means of three submodels (Bartollas, 1985). The medical submodel treats criminals as if they are sick and in need of a cure for the disease of criminality. The adjustment submodel focuses on helping offenders develop socially acceptable attitudes and behavior patterns so as to become more responsible and law abiding. The reintegration submodel believes that offender problems must be solved in the community where they began. It views the role of corrections as securing for offenders contacts, experiences, and opportunities that will provide a stimulus for pursuing a lawful lifestyle (Task Force on Corrections, 1973). All three submodels are driven by some form of treatment. The rehabilitative model has been strongly criticized largely because of its previous emphasis on curing offenders and society's less tolerant attitude of them. However, its more recent focus on providing offenders opportunities for change and self-improvement has resulted in its receiving somewhat more support. Palmer (1992) indicates that the rehabilitation model is beginning to receive more emphasis in the 1990s after being deemphasized in the mid-1970s. Palmer's optimism may have to be tempered in view of the political climate of the mid-1990s.

### The Justice Model Stresses That Offenders Should Be Punished But in a Just and Humane Way

The justice model, developed by David Fogel (1979), takes a "just deserts" or retributive approach. While emphasizing a "justice-as-fairness perspective," this model appears to fit the present public mood toward more punishment and the use of determinate sentencing and away from rehabilitation. It proposes the following:

1. Justice is a more viable goal than rehabilitation.
2. Through free will, perpetrators are liable for the consequences of their law-breaking behavior.
3. Lawbreakers deserve punishment and punishment is not intended to provide social benefits.
4. The state possesses great power and is thus to be distrusted. Discretion in the justice system should be discouraged.
5. The rehabilitative concept of justice has no currency.
6. All individuals who are acted on by the justice process (victims, jurors, witnesses, offenders) should be protected from the overuse of power by the justice system.
7. Offenders should be treated with respect and dignity and as being responsible. Programs should be available for voluntary participation, inmates should have some degree of self-government, and grievance processes should be available.
8. Large unmanageable fortress-like prisons should be abandoned in favor of small facilities.

### The Utilitarian Model Emphasizes Punishment as a Crime Deterrent

The utilitarian model advocates the use of punishment as a way to affect, control, or change future criminal behavior. From this perspective the correctional system should function to punish lawbreakers so as to deter further criminal behavior or to incapacitate the offender. This model also advocates determinate sentences, punishment instead of treatment for serious juvenile offenders, expanded use of the death penalty, and a get-tough policy with drug offenders.

## Effectiveness of Models Should Determine Which of Them Are Implemented

The efficacy of these three models has been argued by a variety of experts. If corrections is to be more effective in its impact on the problem of crime, its philosophies as well as its myriad activities will have to be more well defined, evaluated, and integrated. The bottom line regarding the results of the correctional process—the condition of the offenders being released back into the community—is that a continuous evaluation process must be used to determine what works with which offenders. If we are going to be concerned about the safety of our communities, the effect of the correctional process on offenders will have to be monitored closely, because in the final analysis most inmates who enter the system will be released back into the community. This means that at the very least the corrections process must not make inmates any more dangerous or criminally inclined than when they entered the system. Given our crowded and underfunded correctional systems, even this minimal goal, which offers little solace to those in the community, may not presently be achieved. However, more than this is required if corrections is going to have any impact on the crime problem. To make a difference, corrections must provide offenders with opportunities for self-improvement. It is only in this way that they will have the skills to become productive and responsible members of society. Even if one discounts the humanitarian and social welfare benefits that accrue from this approach, it is hard to ignore the economic benefits. As you will see, the cost of incarcerating and continuing to build prisons to house growing numbers of inmates is greater than the cost of providing academic and vocational training that can prepare them for jobs on release. Under these conditions, then, the understanding and rational implementation of effective correctional programming becomes mandatory.

## THE TEXT VIEWS CONTEMPORARY CORRECTIONS FROM A HISTORICAL PERSPECTIVE

An inescapable fact is that criminals are human beings who, like law-abiding citizens, are part of society. Thus, the treatment to which they are and have been subjected when convicted is better understood when examined in relation to the societal conditions in which it has occurred. The reader will see that many of the events, social issues, and philosophies that have been important throughout the history of humanity (e.g., the industrial revolution, religious movements, the civil rights movement) have affected the manner in which criminals have been treated. One easily discernible pattern is that as we have become more civilized our treatment of criminals has become more humane.

This text spends considerable time examining the various historical events and trends that have produced different reactions to criminal behavior over time. We believe that in order to understand the historical antecedents of contemporary corrections, it is necessary to focus on the eras in which these reactions occurred and the social conditions that produced them. This serves as a foundation for understanding current responses for dealing with criminals and the conditions that characterize our corrections system. Thus during any given time period the sanctions imposed on apprehended offenders and the conditions they experience are the result of an evolutionary process. This process is a blend of historical events and trends and specific current social conditions. The historical overview we present covers many of the things that human societies have done in their attempts to deal with criminal behavior as well as the reasons for these practices. This covers a vast period of time and requires a relatively lengthy account, especially as these events pertain to the United States.

This then is the backdrop against which contemporary corrections exists. The rest of the text is organized around the specific aspects of the corrections system. We begin by examining the dynamics of sentencing, which is the gateway into the corrections systems. Following the historical overview just mentioned, there is a section on correctional clientele, which examines the characteristics of male offenders, special category offenders (e.g., elderly and long term offenders), and female offenders. Institutional administration and management is our next focus, with discussions centering on the structure, management, and control of prisons; the history of prisoner rights and the constitutional guarantees currently accorded inmates; the key role of custodial personnel; and custody and classification.

Next, vital institutional programs and services including education, vocational training and work; medical and psychological services; food; religion; visiting; and recreation are discussed. Also examined are related problems and issues such as mental health, drug treatment, and contagious diseases including HIV/AIDS, tuberculosis, and hepatitis, which are more prevalent in the prison population due to drug use and the lifestyle of many offenders.

Programs set in the community are then examined including jails that house substantial numbers of pretrial detainees and convicted misdemeanants; probation and parole/supervised community release, which represent front-end and back-end correctional programs accounting for three-quarters of those under correctional supervision; and finally intermediate sanctions, which have expanded to accommodate the increasing number of convicted offenders for whom there is no room in prison but who need more intensive supervision than can be provided by traditional probation. Finally, we end the book with an epilogue that deals with our perceptions regarding the future of corrections.

## CHAPTER RECAP

**Corrections Faces Many Problems**
Corrections Is Responsible for the Accused and Convicted
Much of Corrections Is Hidden from Public View
  Correctional Facilities and Programs Usually Receive Attention Only When Problems Arise
Racial Conflicts and Crowding Also Add to Corrections' Problems
Is Corrections Responsible for Solving Crime?
  Many of Today's Problems in Corrections Have a Long History
**The Criminal Justice Process Is Complicated**
The Organization of Corrections in the United States Is Fragmented
**Criminal Justice Has Four Major Components**
**Each Criminal Justice System Component Has Some Correctional Role**
The Police Play Various Roles in Corrections
  Police Agencies Usually Operate Jails and Detention Facilities
  Police Operate Some Correctional Programs
  Police Perform a "Gatekeeper" Function
  Police Provide Information on Offenders to Correctional Personnel
Prosecutors Play Several Roles in Corrections
  Prosecutorial Discretion Can Limit the Number and Types of Offenders Entering the System
    A Number of Factors Influence the Decision Not to Prosecute
    Charges May Be Reduced or the Process May Be Suspended
  Prosecutors Serve as Correctional Agents
The Courts Play Several Roles in Corrections
  Sentencing Is a Key Court Correctional Function
    Many Factors Affect the Sentencing Process

  Judges Serve as Monitors of Conditions in the Correctional System
  The Courts Also Operate Correctional Programs
**Different Views Regarding the Objectives of Corrections**
The Rehabilitative Model Focuses on Treating the Offender
The Justice Model Stresses That Offenders Should Be Punished But in a Just and Humane Way
The Utilitarian Model Emphasizes Punishment as a Crime Deterrent
Effectiveness of Models Should Determine Which of Them Are Implemented
**The Text Views Contemporary Corrections from an Historical Perspective**

## REVIEW QUESTIONS

**1.** What are some of the consequences of the hidden nature of corrections?
**2.** In what ways do the activities of the police, prosecutors, and the courts impact corrections?
**3.** What correctional services do the police, prosecutors, and courts provide?
**4.** Describe and compare the rehabilitation, justice, and utilitarian models with respect to corrections.
**5.** Describe the various services and programs for inmates and the importance that they have in maintaining order within the prisons.

## TEST YOUR KNOWLEDGE

**1.** Attitude surveys conducted during the 1990s show that about _____ percent of the American public feels that the criminal justice systems should deal more strictly with criminals.

a. 47
b. 67
c. 84
d. 98

2. Correctional functions are performed by
    a. the police.
    b. the courts.
    c. prosecutors.
    d. all of the above.
    e. none of the above.

3. Choose the true statement.
    a. The courts still view inmates as slaves of the state.
    b. The courts continue to refuse to deal with prison conditions because judges feel that they lack the expertise to determine their appropriateness.

c. People beginning sentences in our jails and prisons are not deprived of all their constitutional rights.
    d. None of the above.

4. The chief proponent of the justice model is David Fogel.
    a. true
    b. false

5. If correctional programs could be perfected crime could be eliminated.
    a. true
    b. false

# CHAPTER 2

# SENTENCING: THE IMPOSITION OF CORRECTIONAL SANCTIONS

## ■ LEARNING OBJECTIVES

*After completing this chapter, you should be able to:*

**1.** Specify and discuss the role of sentencing in the correctional process.

**2.** Define, describe, and discuss retribution, deterrence, incapacitation, and rehabilitation as rationales for the sanctions applied to criminals.

**3.** List and describe the various monetary sanctions that may be applied to convicted criminals.

**4.** Specify and discuss the various community sanctions (e.g., probation) that may be applied to convicted criminals.

**5.** Describe the sanction of incarceration and specify the factors that affect the nature of this sentence.

**6.** Discuss the sanction of capital punishment and contrast the various arguments in favor of and against it.

**7.** Compare and contrast indeterminate and determinate sentences and the sentencing justifications of each.

**8.** Define and describe mandatory and presumptive sentences and the problems they appear to be engendering for corrections.

**9.** Describe and discuss sentencing guidelines as a manner of reforming the sentencing process.

## ■ KEY TERMS AND CONCEPTS

Brutalization effect
Capital punishment
Chronic offenders
Day fines
Determinate discretionary sentences
Determinate sentences
Deterrence
Good time
Incapacitation
Indeterminate sentences
Life without parole
Mandatory sentences
Probation
Proportionality
Reformation
Rehabilitation
Reintegration
Restitution
Retribution
Sentence
Sentencing guidelines

Offenders take their first step into a correctional system either when they plead guilty or are convicted of crime at a trial. A judge then imposes a sentence on them, which is one of the most important decisions made in the criminal justice system. The sentence is a primary concern to all major parties associated with any criminal event: offenders and their families; victims and their families; prosecutors; defense counsel; and the correctional personnel who will carry it out. A sentence represents the punishment specified for a given crime by the legislature of a given political jurisdiction, is imposed by one of its courts, and is carried out by its correctional system.

## JUSTIFICATIONS FOR PUNISHMENT OF OFFENDERS ■

Each society develops justifications for the punishments imposed on criminals and these justifications have varied over time. However, some suffering has almost always been a part of the sanctions imposed on offenders. Ever since this country's birth, many reformative and rehabilitative roles have been sought for our penal systems, even when these roles clashed with the objective of social defense and the maintenance of public order. The punishment of criminal behavior has been the paramount purpose, however, and is justified on three grounds:

1. *Retribution:* "You're going to get what's coming to you."
2. *Deterrence:* "We're going to punish you so that you will not do it again." Or the variation, "We're going to punish you so that you will serve as an example to others and they will not do it."
3. *Incapacitation:* "We're going to punish you in such a way that you will not be able to victimize us."

These justifications overlap considerably because all involve some element of offender suffering. A fourth justification for the use of imprisonment has been to rehabilitate the offender: "We're going to put you in prison for your own good (to fix what is wrong with you)."

### Retribution: The Infliction of Deserved Punishment and Its Painful Consequences on the Criminal

The punitive response to criminal behavior is rooted in tradition. Retribution, defined as "deserved punishment for evil done," is a relatively primitive human reaction. In early societies vengeance was the means by which victims repaid offenders for the injury inflicted on them or their property. This function was later taken over by official societal institutions. Some of the philosophical justifications used to support it follow:

1. It serves to fulfill a religious mission through retaliation. Since there are biblical sanctions for the punishment of transgressors, the society is doing God's work in carrying out His punishment.
2. It removes the tension in society caused by the criminal act, creating harmony through retaliation.
3. It washes the guilt of the criminal away through suffering and expresses society's disapproval of the behavior.
4. It makes victims whole again by making the offender suffer as they did.
5. It assures that the most beneficial social consequences occur through the application of a punishment that best fits the particular crime/criminal.

### Deterrence: Pain or Other Consequences Will Inhibit Criminal Behavior

The concept of deterrence as a means of controlling crime dates back over 200 years to the work of Cesare Beccaria and Jeremy Bentham. Referred to as *classical theory,* this position assumes that humans have free will, are rational, and make behavioral decisions based on the consequences of an action before engaging in it. If the consequences are positive they will engage in the behavior. If not they will avoid it.

This view is now reflected in choice theory or rational choice theory (Abell, 1991; Cornish and Clarke, 1986), which pays attention to the rational decision-making elements governing criminal events. Of course, it recognizes that the degree of reasoning involved will vary from offender to offender and from crime to crime. In viewing crime in this way, some criminologists have focused on the factors burglars consider when deciding which homes to target (Are the residents home? Are they open to public view? Is there easy availability to escape routes?) (Cromwell Marks, Olson, and Avary, 1991; MacDonald and Gifford, 1989). Other factors reported to motivate their involvement in crime included obtaining money, impressing friends, and the excitement of the acts (Marshall and Horney, 1991). Finally, attention has focused on factors influencing offenders to desist from crime. These have been found to include shock (e.g., seeing a friend shot or killed during their last crime) or the cumulative effects of factors such as recognition of the inevitability of capture, a reduced ability to do time, fear of incarceration, and general anxiety over a life of crime (Cusson and Pinsonneault, 1986).

The imposition of punishment for purposes of deterrence is based on the belief that these sanctions will prevent future crime because of the painful consequences suffered by convicted offenders. This can be achieved in two ways. First, specific deterrence can be achieved by making the offender suffer in some way. If the pain associated with the punishment outweighs the gains resulting from the crime, this will presumably prevent the offender from committing subsequent crimes.

Punishment is also considered to have general deterrent value because of the belief that an offender's suffering shows others what will happen to them if they engage in similar acts and hence discourages them from doing it. There is also the hope that the punishment of any given crime will deter all types of offenses.

**THE DETERRENT VALUE OF PUNISHMENT IS INCONCLUSIVE** The deterrent effects of punishment have been studied in several different ways. One approach examines general deterrence by measuring the relationship between the probabilities of being punished (i.e., getting arrested, convicted, and imprisoned or otherwise punished) and the rate of crime. If deterrence works, then, for example, as the probability of punishment rises, arrests should go down. However, there is no consistent evidence showing this to be true. Although some studies (e.g., Gibbs, 1968; Tittle and

Rowe, 1974) have shown that certainty of punishment resulted in reduced crime rates, others (e.g., Bursik, Grasmick and Chamlin, 1990; Chiricos and Waldo, 1970; Zedlewski, 1987) have shown an inconsistent or absent relationship.

Another approach is to show that the threat of punishment reduces illegal behavior. The best known of these studies examined the effects of toughened anti–drunk-driving laws and found that when these laws were toughened they had a short-term effect but in the long run their effect was negligible (Ross, McCleary, and LaFree, 1990).

A third approach uses what is referred to as perceptual research. Here subjects are asked to determine how certain they are that they might get caught and punished if they break a specific law. They are then asked whether they actually would commit that crime. If deterrence works, those who feel they would get caught and punished should most likely refrain from committing the crime. The research tends to show that the more certain the perceived punishment, the less likely individuals are to say they do or will engage in the sanctioned crimes (see, e.g., Grasmick and Bursik, 1990; Klepper and Nagin, 1989).

Finally, deterrence is examined based on its effect on those who are punished. The results of this line of research are inconsistent. Some studies indicate that a majority of inmates have a history of previous arrests, convictions, and even incarcerations (e.g., Greenfeld, 1985). They also show that just under two-thirds of convicted felons are rearrested within three years of release from prison, and those with the most extensive records are most likely to recidivate (Beck and Shipley, 1989). However, other studies show that punishment may have a suppressive effect on some forms of criminal behavior. Severely punished delinquents, arrested spouse abusers, arrested drunk drivers, and arrested novice offenders were less likely to commit future offenses when compared with offenders who were treated more leniently (Murray and Cox, 1979; Sherman and Berk, 1984; Shapiro and Votey, 1984; Smith and Gartin, 1989).

**SPEED, SEVERITY, AND CERTAINTY OF PUNISHMENT AFFECT DETERRENCE** Although there is no consensus on the deterrent effects of punishment there is agreement that three factors may significantly affect its success or failure: its severity and the speed and certainty with which it is imposed. There is evidence that certainty is the more influential of these variables, but this conclusion is not consistently supported. All three factors are not usually present together in the typical criminal justice scenario, thus it is very difficult to determine precisely their relative efficacy. The crime clearance rate [only 21% for all UCR index offenses (Federal Bureau of Investigation, 1994)], the relatively slow rate at which the courts operate, and the perceived leniency of the system [in the early 1990s it was expected that prison inmates would only serve about one-third of their sentences (Langan and Dawson, 1993; Langan and Solari, 1993)] interact to reduce the deterrence effects of criminal justice system actions.

### Incapacitation: The Prevention of Future Crime

Incapacitation refers to punishment that is directed at preventing offenders from committing additional crimes. Historically, efforts at permanent prevention have involved capital punishment and dismemberment. Today, in most parts of the world, these punishments have been replaced by imprisonment. Incapacitation is still used to justify imprisonment in that as long as offenders are in confinement they are not free to commit further crimes. This is true, of course, only if offenders do not commit offenses while they are in prison (e.g., assault a correctional officer).

Although relatively infrequently imposed, our most severe punishments—capital punishment and life imprisonment without parole—continue to be supported because they appear to represent a way of totally incapacitating our most serious offenders. This is generally regarded, by both supporters and critics of the punitive approach, as the most plausible utilitarian argument for punishment.

Incapacitation has been suggested as an answer to the problem of chronic offenders (i.e., those arrested for five or more offenses) who, although small in number, account for a disproportionate share of serious crime (Petersilia, Greenwood, and Lavin, 1978; Wolfgang, Figlio, and Sellin, 1972). Wolfgang's research on two cohorts of juveniles from Philadelphia—one born in 1945 and the other in 1958—found that chronics, who represented 6 to 7% of the males in these cohorts, committed more than half of the delinquent and at least two-thirds of the index offenses (Tracy, Wolfgang, and Figlio, 1985). Research by Miller, Dinitz and Conrad (1982), on adults with at least one arrest for a violent offense, found that the more arrests these offenders had, the greater the likelihood they would eventually be arrested for a violent crime. They also concluded that the more arrests offenders have had, the more likely they are to either lose control or assert themselves over others irrespective of the consequences.

### THREE TYPES OF INCAPACITATION STRATEGIES HAVE BEEN PROPOSED

Incapacitation strategies have taken three approaches. The first is collective incapacitation, which would mandate that all individuals convicted of a certain offense (e.g., robbery) receive the same sentence (e.g., five years). Although research has shown this strategy would have only a modest impact (10 to 20%) on crime reduction, it might double, triple, or increase even more dramatically the size of the prison population, depending on which categories of offenders were chosen for incapacitation (Cohen, 1983).

Selective incapacitation would base sentences on predictions that certain offenders will commit serious offenses at higher rates than others convicted of the same types of crimes. These predictions would be used to structure the sentences of individuals convicted of a particular type of crime. This approach suffers from the fact that we can correctly identify no more than 45% of those who will engage in future offenses. Thus, if existing scales to identify high-rate offenders for purposes of incapacitation were used, 55 people out of every 100 of these individuals imprisoned would not commit an offense if they were allowed to remain free (Cohen, 1983). Obviously this level of accuracy is unacceptable and would result in many miscarriages of justice.

Criminal career incapacitation avoids many of the problems associated with selective incapacitation (Cohen, 1983). It involves identification of classes of criminals who on the average have active high rates of crime. Cohen's (1983) research in Washington, D.C., led to two important conclusions. First, individuals convicted of robbery and burglary are prime candidates for incapacitation, because on the average they commit these offenses at relatively high rates and have relatively short careers. Second, prison sentences for these offenders can shorten their expected careers and thus reduce robbery and burglary rates. She found that a two-year prison sentence imposed on convicted robbers would reduce robberies by 8% and only increase the total prison population by 7%.

**AN ALTERNATIVE TO INCAPACITATION IS MORE SEVERE SENTENCES FOR VIOLENT OFFENDERS**
Miller, Dinitz, and Conrad (1982) offer solutions, based on their research on violent offenders, which would achieve the same objectives as incapacitation but not have the ethical and legal problems associated with it. They found that most violent offenders will recidivate and that they are likely to commit new violent offenses. They argue that the perpetration of a violent crime by a recidivist is a sufficiently serious occurrence to warrant substantially more severe punishment than is now imposed as well as a greater degree of certainty that they will in fact be punished. They also argue for changes in the sentencing of violent criminals that require incarceration of offenders causing injury to their victims for a mandatory period of time.

### A Continuing Purpose of Incarceration Has Been to Reform or Rehabilitate the Offender

The concept of reformation can be traced back to the early European antecedents of the prison system. In the United States the development of the penitentiary was based on the idea that imprisonment would reform an inmate by instilling a new sense of morality and purpose. This original notion was later modified in response to a growing belief, espoused in the philosophy of Positivism, that criminal behavior was caused by conditions within the offender as well as those in their environment. Labeled as rehabilitation, it was felt that providing inmates with a variety of services and programs (e.g., education, job training, psychological assistance) during their incarceration would ameliorate these conditions and reduce the probability of future criminality. Although rehabilitation was deemphasized as a justification for imprisonment during the 1970s, programs with an emphasis on providing offenders opportunities to deal with their problems and improve their academic and work skills are still carried out in contemporary prisons (see, e.g., Chapters 18 and 19). However, the survival of these programs is continually threatened by pressure from those who believe inmates are not deserving of these "benefits."

**REINTEGRATION IS MAINTAINING OR INTEGRATING OFFENDERS INTO THE COMMUNITY**
Although imprisonment has been touted as serving one or more of the aforementioned functions, its critics point to the debilitating and sometimes destructive effects that it may have on inmates. These effects are described in the chapters that follow. Thus, reintegration, an approach that emphasizes community-based residential and nonresidential alternatives to incarceration, has been viewed by these critics as a solution to these problems. Supporters argue that only hard-core offenders require imprisonment and that nondangerous offenders can be effectively and more economically supervised in the community. This allows these offenders to maintain ties with family and friends and benefit from community programs and services not available in prisons. These programs also help to relieve prison overcrowding and are less costly to operate.

## TYPES OF DISPOSITIONS

Judges have a variety of dispositions which they may impose on convicted offenders. Suspending the sentence is one option that is typically available in most jurisdictions. This procedure can be accomplished in two ways: deferral of the pronouncement of a sentence or suspension of its implementation. Postponement of sentencing allows the judge to create potential substitutes for the sentence (e.g., offender must successfully complete a specific program). The implied threat of a suspended sentence is that it will be implemented if the offender continues to engage in criminal behavior (Kittrie and Zenoff, 1981).

### Monetary Sanctions: Getting Hit in the Wallet

Fines are monetary sanctions that are usually assessed in the case of minor offenses. They may be the only sanction imposed or be combined with other sentencing alternatives, such as probation, restitution, or confinement. The statutes specifying criminal fines tend to be inconsistent and chaotic and give judges little guidance as to the appropriate monetary amounts to be assessed.

We do not know if fines are effective tools in controlling criminal behavior. Critics of fines argue that they cannot incapacitate and may have detrimental effects on defendants who are poor. Many offenders are confined in local jails for nonpayment of criminal fines, because this is the standard sanction. The Supreme Court in *Tate v. Short* (1971), a case involving an indigent jailed for failing to pay $425 in traffic fines, ruled that imprisoning people unable to pay a fine unconstitutionally discriminated against the poor. However, courts can constitutionally incarcerate offenders for nonpayment when jail time is a sentence option.

**DAY FINES ARE IMPOSED ON THE BASIS OF THE GRAVITY OF THE OFFENSE AND OFFENDER INCOME** The day fine is an innovation proposed to reduce the economic inequities resulting from fines (Hillsman and Greene, 1988). This Scandinavian practice has been adopted in other European countries and was tested in Staten Island, New York, and Milwaukee, Wisconsin, in the United States (McDonald, 1992; Greene, 1992; and Worzella, 1992). Day fines allow judges to impose monetary sanctions that are commensurate with the seriousness of the offense while tying the amount to the offender's income and assets. Thus, a day fine equalizes the monetary burden on offenders from different socioeconomic levels.

To establish a day fine the courts go through a two-step process (McDonald, 1992). First, they determine the monetary units assigned to the offense (the more serious the crime, the higher the number of units). The next step is to calculate the dollar value of each monetary unit based on the economic circumstances of the offender. For example:

> [Joseph Burke] plead guilty to attempted unauthorized use of an auto (a class B misdemeanor). . . . Mr. Burke is 21 years old . . . single and lives with his mother, to whom he contributes support. He works at a restaurant and reports take-home pay of $180 per week. He was sentenced to pay a ten-unit day fine and his unit value was set at $11.78. His fine totaled $117.80 [which he was allowed to pay in five payments over three months].
>
> [Mr. Smith pled guilty to disorderly conduct. He is a 20-year-old Transit Authority employees, with no dependents and income of $800 every 2 weeks]. He was sentenced to a pay five unit day fine. Each unit was fixed at $32 for a total of $160—which he paid in full at sentencing (Greene, 1992, p. 36).

An obvious problem with this system is the difficulty and expense of establishing the true economic circumstances of each offender.

McDonald (1992) concluded that the day fine programs in Milwaukee and Staten Island increased the proportion of fines collected within those jurisdictions. An evaluation of the Staten Island program concluded that judges have become comfortable with this approach to levying fines (Winterfield and Hillsman, 1991).

Other economic sanctions imposed on convicted offenders include court costs, surcharges on fines, and asset forfeiture. The economic burden of these sanctions on offenders sometime causes judges to reduce or eliminate them from sentences (Hillsman, Mahoney, Cole, and Auchter, 1987).

**RESTITUTION REQUIRES THAT THE OFFENDER MAKE AMENDS TO THE VICTIM OR THE COMMUNITY** Restitution as a sentence or part of a sentence requires the offender to repay the victim (or the community) money or services so that the losses or damages caused by the criminal act can be restored or repaired. Restitution is usually imposed as a condition of another sanction, such as probation or incarceration. It suffers from the same problems as fines. That is, lower income offenders, who comprise the vast majority of the offenders processed through our courts, are least likely to pay. Some jurisdictions may have restitution centers with programs that require offenders to work to help them meet these obligations. Also, most prisons that pay inmates for their work require that a portion of their income go toward restitution (see Chapter 18).

### Community Programs Can Be Residential or Non-residential

In between fines or unsupervised suspended sentences and incarceration, judges usually have the option to allow convicted offenders to remain in the community under some form of correctional supervision and control.

**PROBATION IS SERVING A SENTENCE UNDER SUPERVISION IN THE COMMUNITY** The most common sentence in the American judicial system is probation. This involves placing the offender under community supervision by a probation agency and usually requires compliance with legally imposed conditions. A new series of options known as intensive probation supervision, house arrest or community control has been designed for offenders who require more intensive supervision than can be provided under ordinary probation. These may involve confinement to one's residence except to go to work, attend school, or engage in some other mandated activity and/or more intensive surveillance by probation officers. Programs for higher risk offenders may require them to wear an electronic bracelet that helps monitor their whereabouts during the times they are supposed to be at home, thus increasing the intensity of supervision (Petersilia, 1988).

**RESIDENTIAL COMMUNITY PROGRAMS PROVIDE THE MOST INTENSE SUPERVISION SHORT OF PRISON**   Halfway houses and other residential programs provide more intense supervision than probation and can furnish specific treatment programs for adjudicated individuals. These facilities have been used both as an intermediate step between the community and prison or between the prison and the community.

## Incarceration is Confinement of an Offender in a Prison or Jail

Incarceration, or a sentence to jail or prison, is imposed when the community must be protected from further victimization by the offender. To the American public it represents the most commonly deserved sanction for criminal behavior and is used more often and with longer terms in the United States than anywhere else in the Western world. In 1990 46% of convicted felons were sentenced to state prison terms. Offenders who were sentenced to state prisons in the late 1980s and early 1990s were sentenced to an average of 75 months and expected to serve about one-third of that term (Langan and Dawson, 1993; Langan and Solari, 1993). Crash prison building programs during the 1990s increased the proportion of sentence served to more than 70%. Figure 2.1 shows the average length of felony sentences imposed by state courts in the United States for various crimes

**FIGURE 2.1   State Felony Sentences and Estimated Time to be Served**

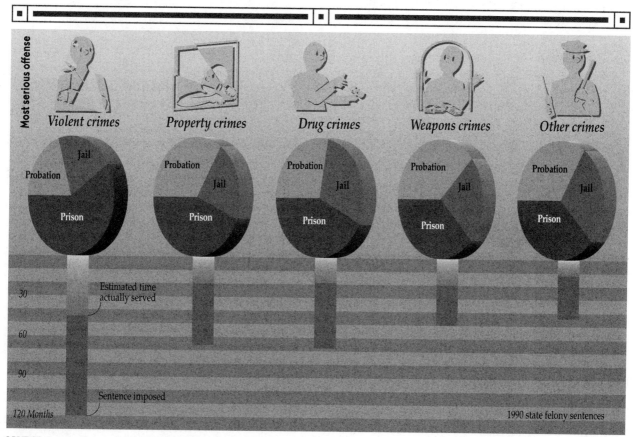

SOURCE: Langan, P. A., and Salari, R. (1993). *National Judicial Reporting Program, 1990.* Washington, D.C.: Bureau of Justice Statistics, p. 4.

and the proportions of offenders sentenced to prison, probation, and jail.

Although the cost of imprisonment can be a limiting factor in its use, some feel that imprisonment can save money (Reynolds, 1992). Several studies indicate that the average criminal commits 187 crimes per year, costing an average of $430,000 per year in lost property, police investigations, etc. Thus, keeping that inmate in prison at a cost of $25,000 per year represents a substantial savings. This leads Zedlewski (1987) to conclude, even when considering prison construction costs, that:

> given the large number of crimes averted by imprisonment ... incapacitating prison-eligible offenders now crowded out of today's [prisons], construction would likely cost communities less than they now pay in social damages and prevention (p. 6).

This may well have some merit if sentencing policies were based on the research of Miller, Dinitz, and Conrad (1982) and Cohen (1983), which emphasized mandatory sentencing for violent offenders who inflicted injury on their victims and for those committing robbery and burglary.

Interviews with 589 incarcerated property offenders provided insight into their perceptions of the deterrent impact of various sanctions, programs, and other criminal justice system actions (Dinitz and Huff, 1988). These offenders indicated that criminal justice system actions increasing the chances of imprisonment or the sentence length were perceived to have the most deterrent effect (see Figure 2.2).

## Capital Punishment Is the Ultimate Sanction

Capital punishment—the death penalty—is our most extreme sanction and in the United States is currently generally reserved for only the most heinous first-degree murderers. Although rarely imposed (about 250 death sentences are given out annually), its highly controversial nature and non-reversible consequences require that arguments for and against its use be discussed.

The death penalty in the United States has been a controversial issue since before the beginning of the Republic. Its early major opponents were the Quakers who based their opposition on humanitarian and practical factors (e.g., it lessens the horror

FIGURE 2.2 Inmate Perception of the Importance of Various Criminal Justice System Actions Aimed at Preventing Property Crimes

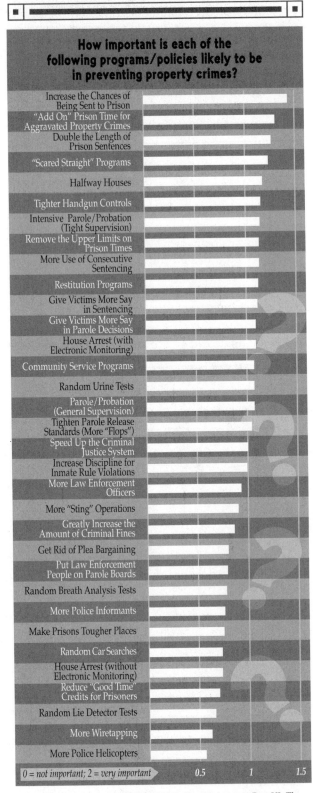

SOURCE: Dinitz, S., and Huff, R. (1988). *The Figgie report Part VI. The business of crime: The criminal perspective.* Richmond, VA: Figgie International, Inc., p. 39. Reprinted with permission of the publisher.

of taking a human life and tends to multiply murders).

Between 1608 and 1959 there were about 14,379 legal executions (Schneider and Smykla, 1991). Fewer than 1% of those executed during this period were women (Streib, 1992). There were 3879 executions between 1930 and 1967, of which 32 were women (Agresti, undated). From 1968 to 1972 death sentences were imposed but not implemented because the U.S. Supreme Court was considering their constitutionality. In 1972 the Court struck down existing capital punishment statutes on the grounds that they were in violation of the Eighth and Fourteenth Amendments (*Furman v. Georgia,* 1972). Led by the success of Georgia's revised capital punishment statute (*Gregg v. Georgia,* 1976), many states modeled their statutes to conform to constitutional standards. Most of the statutes approved permitted the death penalty after consideration of mitigating and aggravating circumstances. Executions began again in 1977 and by early 1995, 266 offenders, including one woman, had been put to death (Stephan, Brien, and Greenfeld, 1994; Death Penalty Information Center, 1995).

As of October 1994 there were 2948 inmates, including 41 women, on death rows in 34 of the 37 jurisdictions that had death penalty statutes (Death Penalty Information Center, 1995). In 1995 New York became the 38th state to have a death penalty statute. Inmates on death row as of December 1993 had all been convicted of murder and had been there an average of about six years. Almost two-thirds had prior felony convictions (with 1 in 10 having committed a prior murder) and about 40% had a criminal justice status (e.g., had escaped from prison, were on parole) at the time they committed the murder. More than half of these offenders were white (57.7%) and their median age was 36, the youngest was 18 and the oldest was 78 years of age (Stephan, Brien, and Greenfeld, 1994).

Figure 2.3 shows the race proportions of the 266 defendants executed between 1977 and 1995, victims killed by those on death row, and inmates on death row as of late 1994. More than 80% of the executions occurred in southern states. The methods of execution used included lethal injection (28 states), electrocution (12 states), lethal gas (7 states), hanging (4 states), and firing squad (2 states) with

**FIGURE 2.3  Race Data Regarding the Death Penalty**

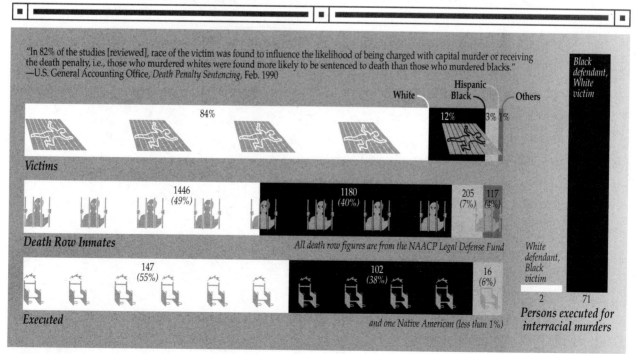

SOURCE: Death Penalty Information Center (February 1995) *Facts about the Death Penalty.* Washington, D.C.: Author. Reproduced with permission of the publisher.

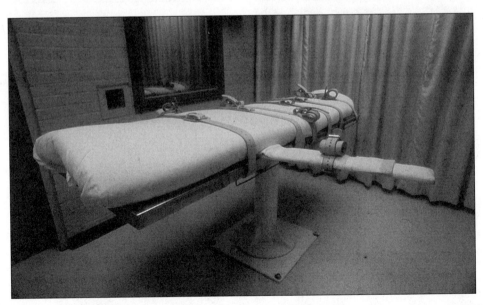

These are forms of capital punishment. Each was introduced to make the process more humane. Today the lethal injection is the most commonly used method, which involves the introduction of a lethal chemical into the bloodstream.

several states authorizing two or more of these methods (Death Penalty Information Center, 1995).

Approximately three-quarters of the U.S. population favors the execution of murderers. Support is usually higher among males, whites, Republicans, those with higher levels of education and income, and those who live in the Midwest, South, or West. The Death Penalty Information Center (1995) reports that support drops to almost 40% when a sentence of life without parole is an alternative.

**THE DEATH PENALTY HAS SUPPORTERS AND DETRACTORS**   There is a broad range of opinions on capital punishment. At one extreme are individuals who feel that criminals, especially violent ones, are not deserving of public support in what they perceive as "country club" prisons and should be summarily executed. At the other extreme are those who feel that life is sacred and the government has no right to execute offenders, regardless of the crimes committed. In between these extremes is the large majority of individuals whose views are affected by such factors as the nature of the crime and the degree to which the system provides assurances that the offender will not be released. Those favoring capital punishment are referred to as retentionists; those against it are called abolitionists.

Retentionists justify the death penalty with the same arguments used to support other penal sanctions. They believe it is either deserved (retribution), that it will keep the individual who is executed from victimizing others again (incapacitation), that it will serve as an example (general deterrence), or that it serves the purpose of revenge ("an eye for an eye"). Among the strongest proponents of the death penalty is Ernest van den Haag (1975), who contends that the punishment for misbehavior must fit the crime. He feels that the death penalty is particularly appropriate for heinous murders because it protects society more than other possible sanctions.

Retribution has been associated with two views: revenge, in which the offender is paid back for his wrongful behavior, and "just deserts," which demands that the offender be punished so as to make recompense to society for the harm done (Fickenauer, 1988). However, Bohm (1992) found that there were generally two views of revenge underlying attitudes on the death penalty: one based on an emotional, "get even" feeling and the other based on a "taking a life deserves execution" feeling.

Proportionality is another argument used to justify the death penalty. Its proponents argue that sanctions for criminal behavior should be proportional to the seriousness of the crime. By imposing capital punishment the scales of justice are balanced. For many, execution represents total or ultimate incapacitation in that this criminal will never "do it again." Concern about recidivism is real and is supported by research. A study of 52,000 inmates serving sentences for murder found that 810 had been convicted for a homicide once before (Markman and Cassell, 1988). Additionally, as noted earlier, 10% of the inmates on death row had previously committed homicides (Stephan and Brien, 1994).

Proponents of the death penalty have also pointed to the recent high level of public support for capital punishment as a sanction for murderers. Indeed, this factor was considered by the Supreme Court in *Gregg v. Georgia* (1976) when it affirmed newly formulated capital punishment statutes. It noted that the appropriateness of this sanction lies in the fact that it represents "an expression of the community's belief that [these offenses] are themselves so grievous an affront to humanity that the only adequate response may be the penalty of death" (p. 859).

Advocates of the death penalty strongly believe that executions serve a deterrent function. Not only is the person who is executed unable to commit another murder, but through general deterrence others contemplating killing someone may also be dissuaded. The deterrent effects of executions have been studied in several ways. One approach compares murder rates in states with capital punishment to those without it. Another strategy compares the murder rates in a given jurisdiction before and after executions. A third approach examines rates for murder and other crimes in a specific state before and after the abolition or institution of capital punishment. Only a few of these studies find evidence that capital punishment is a deterrent (e.g., Layson, 1986). Zimring and Hawkins (1973) indicate that punishment is likely to be an effective deterrent for individuals who are generally law abiding, but not for those who are predisposed to commit crimes.

The issue of morality is a complicated one that can be construed to support both retentionist and

**This graphically shows public support for the death penalty.**

abolitionist arguments. Supporters point to the mention of death as a penalty in the Bible. According to Friedrichs (1989), capital punishment may also serve a moral purpose by holding those who commit a serious violent crime responsible for it in a special way. Through execution, the scales of justice may come closer to being balanced in the eyes of society as well as those most affected by the crime. Further, the death of the criminal makes a statement that the victim is no less important than the criminal.

Although challenges to the constitutionality of capital punishment persist, it continues to be supported by the federal courts. The Eighth Amendment's prohibition against cruel and unusual punishment does not include death because it was a common penalty when the Constitution was written. Advocates thus point to its legality to help justify it.

In comparing the cost of capital punishment to life without parole (LWOP), retentionists maintain that executing an individual costs considerably less. Thus, a 25-year-old offender sentenced to LWOP might be expected to live 45 years in prison. At a cost of $25,000 per year it would cost $1,125,000, not counting the costs associated with his or her arrest and court processing, to punish that individual.

Arguments against the death penalty generally counter those offered by retentionists. Although public support for the death penalty is strong, the vast majority of articles on the subject appearing in the professional criminology and legal literature are against it. The following represents a summary of the common arguments used by abolitionists.

Executions by the state are morally repugnant to some groups, in that they feel that life is sacred and not to be taken by man. They also note that the

Some offenders sentenced to death are not guilty. Like Andrew Golden and Sylvester Adams, Randall Dale Adams spent over twelve years in a Texas prison, most of it on death row before winning release. He had been convicted of murdering a police officer, a crime someone else later confessed to.

biblical admonition—Thou shalt not kill—applies to the state as well as to the individual.

Many abolitionists believe the death penalty should not be applied because of its finality. Once carried out there is no way to reverse its effects if a mistake was made and an innocent person was executed. There is no doubt that mistakes are made and there are a number of examples of them. Bedau and Radelet (1987) maintain that of the thousands of persons sentenced to death in the United States, 350 were erroneously convicted. Of these, 23 were executed and 21 others narrowly won reprieves. They assert that since 1976, 24 of the over 2000 defendants sentenced to death were erroneously convicted; 23 were eventually released but 1 was executed. Some common reasons for erroneous conviction include perjury by prosecution witnesses and mistaken eyewitness testimony (Radelet, Bedau, and Putnam, 1992).

Sometimes mistakes are resolved. In the late 1960s James Richardson was tried, convicted, and sentenced to death for killing six of his children. Before his death warrant could be signed his sentence was commuted to life and he spent 21 years in prison. He was released in 1989 after it was determined that during his trial crucial evidence had been withheld by the prosecution (Radelet, Bedau, and Putnam, 1992; Malcolm, 1989).

Other issues involve the competence of the attorneys defending the accused. Failure to fully present available evidence has resulted in death sentences for individuals who have either been potentially innocent, not guilty by reason of insanity, or guilty of a lesser crime. Our Close-Up "Indigents Don't Usually Get the 'Dream Team' in Capital Cases" examines this problem.

Abolitionists argue that the death penalty does not deter but may, instead, have a brutalizing effect, i.e., it may cause an increase in the number of murders because it reinforces violence (Bowers and Pierce, 1980). They cite research on deterrent effects of capital punishment that show it to be inconclusive (e.g., Archer, Gartner, and Beittel, 1983; McFarland, 1983; Bedau, 1982). Studies by Bailey (1990) and Peterson and Bailey (1991) found no support for either deterrence or brutalization.

A major issue surrounding the death penalty involves its biased application in that it appears to be employed in a racially discriminatory manner. Historically, more than 50% of those executed in the United States have been black. Further, while the proportion of blacks presently on death row (40%) is somewhat lower than in the past, it is still disproportionate to their number in the general population (12%). Although blatant racism in the use of the death penalty was the norm until the middle of the twentieth century, especially for rape, since 1976, the issue of its discriminatory imposition has shifted to the race of the victim. Statistics show that 86% of white victims are killed by other whites, while blacks account for most of the rest. With very few exceptions, blacks on death row are there for killing a white even though the large majority of black murderers kill blacks. Twenty-three of 28 studies conducted between 1976 and 1990 showed that murderers who killed whites were more likely to be sentenced to death than those who killed blacks (General Accounting Office, 1990a). Further, many of these studies showed that black defendants were more likely than whites to get the death penalty. These data suggest that black victims' lives may be less valued than those of whites and that there is still discrimination for those receiving the death penalty. However,

Oppenents of capital punishment often demonstrate outside prisons where individuals are executed. Many times these demonstrations take the form of candlelight vigils and/or prayer sessions.

despite a pattern of racial bias in death penalty sentencing, the Supreme Court ruled that only evidence of racial bias particular to the case was relevant to these proceedings (*McClesky v. Kemp*, 1987).

Because a very small number of those charged with murder actually receive the death penalty its use is seen as arbitrary by critics. Although about 7000 offenders are convicted of murder annually, 2.2% receive the death penalty and 31% are sentenced to life in prison (Langan and Dawson, 1993). The findings in a three-state survey appear to support the notion that it is arbitrary. The survey found that 80% of those surveyed agreed strongly with the statement "the death penalty is too arbi-

trary because some people are executed and others go to prison" (Bowers, 1993, p. 166).

Several factors help reduce the number of offenders given a death sentence. State statutes designate only certain types of murders as capital crimes. These include first-degree murder, felony murder, murder of a corrections or peace officer or firefighter performing official duties, murder for hire, and murder by an inmate serving a life sentence (Foster, Siegel, and Jacobs, 1992). These types of murder represent a relatively small proportion of the murders committed each year. Additionally, many death penalty-eligible cases receive a prison sentence because of prosecutors' discretion in the charging and plea bargaining phases of the

## Close Up  Indigents Don't Usually Get The "Dream Team" In Capital Cases

Given the publicity surrounding the trial and acquittal of O.J. Simpson in 1995 on 1st degree murder charges, the importance of his lawyers, referred to as the "dream team", was focused on. However, many capital trials involve poor individuals who cannot afford to pay a lawyer and are thus defended by poorly compensated appointed attorneys whose efforts on behalf of their clients are sometimes commensurate with their level of compensation. Compensation for appointed attorneys varies according to state policy and may involve very low hourly or flat rates that provide no resources to conduct necessary investigations. For example, in Alabama appointed attorneys working on capital cases received up to $1,000. Even if they only spent 500 hours on the case—the average amount spent is 2,000 hours—they would earn $2.00 per hour. Obviously they could earn more flipping hamburgers and probably earn more respect and incur fewer headaches.

Thus, far from the legal "dream team" assembled in the O.J. Simpson case, capital defendants are given attorneys who fail to investigate, who fall asleep during trials or come into court drunk, attorneys barely out of law school, or attorneys who say nothing when their client's life is on the line. Some States allow elected judges to pick attorneys not on the basis of experience or merit but because they will cause the least trouble in trying the case. [A number of] former death row inmates such as Andrew Golden . . . received poor representation at trials and could have been executed (Dieter, 1995, p.iii).

Golden, who had no previous criminal record (not even a traffic ticket) was sent to death row in 1991 after being convicted of murdering his wife. It was a weak case and even the police investigators and the medical examiner felt she had committed suicide. His lawyer did nothing to prepare for the trial, assuming the case would be thrown out. When it was not, he did not present the jury with the very reasonable scenario that his wife had committed suicide because she was depressed over her father's recent death. With the help of a competent lawyer Golden had his conviction overturned after spending three years on death row.

Others have not been as lucky as Golden.

Sylvester Adams was executed in South Carolina on August 17 1995. Adams was a poor, black man suffering from mental retardation and mental illness. But his court-appointed lawyer failed to mention those critical facts at trial. Later, at least one of the jurors came forward and said that she would not have voted for death if she had known Adams was retarded. Her vote for life would have spared Adams. The subsequent intervention of David Bruck (who represented Susan Smith at [her] trial) and the South Carolina Resource Center came too late. (Dieter, 1995, p.6).

The very fact that the execution of an individual who is erroneously convicted and sentenced is irreversible makes a good defense mandatory. Irrespective of your view on the death penalty, a system that permits an individual to be put to death under a cloud of doubt creates a serious doubt as to the quality and fairness of its justice.

How do you feel about the fact that individuals who are tried for a capital crime may not receive the strongest defense possible? About the length of time taken by the appeals process for death row inmates? What might be some solutions regarding the error problem? What argument(s) do you think make(s) the strongest case for or against the death penalty?

Source for this material is Dieter, R.C. (1995). With Justice for few: The growing crisis in death penalty representation. Washington, D.C.: Death Penalty Information Center.

judicial process. Data from six states and two large urban counties show that the average proportion of guilty pleas accepted in death-eligible cases was 61%. In three of these jurisdictions, prosecutors also waived the penalty phase (required for imposition of capital punishment) in about two-thirds of the cases (Baldus, Woodworth, and Pulaski, 1990).

Finally, several studies showed that although offense seriousness had the greatest influence on prosecutorial discretion, the victim's race was next in importance. Other factors influencing this process were the offender's race and whether the victim was a stranger (Baldus, et al, 1990; Paternoster, 1991; Keil and Vito, 1991).

Amnesty International (AI) (1989a) has carried on a continuing fight to abolish executions. AI argues that the fundamental human rights protected by the United Nations' Universal Declaration of Human Rights, which includes the right to life, limit what a state may do to a human being. AI asserts that "No matter what reason a government gives for executing prisoners and what method of execution is used, the death penalty cannot be separated from the issue of human rights" (p. 1). In 1991, 43% of the countries in the world either did not have or had abolished the death penalty (AI, 1992). Further, of the Western/industrialized countries, the United States is the only one that retains it. This fact is used by abolitionists to question why we alone of the more socially advanced countries of the world continue to execute people. The implication is that those countries retaining the death penalty are less civilized and more barbaric.

Abolitionists counter arguments regarding the high expense of life imprisonment with economic arguments of their own. They point to the extremely high cost of capital trials and the cost of appeals, which can run into the millions of dollars. Research done at Duke University found that it costs North Carolina taxpayers $163,000 more, on average, to try, convict, and execute a murderer when compared with the cost of a life prison term (Cook and Slawson, 1993). Wright (1991) asserts that life without parole in a "hellish" prison may not only cost less but may be a more severe punishment than a painless death by lethal injection.

### Life without Parole Represents an Alternative to Execution

A life without parole (LWOP) sentence is a relatively new innovation available in thirty states. It can serve as an alternative to either capital punishment or to a regular life sentence (with parole possible) by ensuring that those thusly sentenced will remain in prison for the rest of their lives. It can also be used to incapacitate career criminals. Although it is presumed that LWOP will keep offenders in prison for the rest of their lives, there are loopholes that might result in the release of these inmates. LWOP statutes are usually written to exclude common methods of release such as parole and expiration of sentence due to the accumulation of good time credits. However, sometimes placement in a work release program or

being allowed home furloughs can permit access to the community. With the exception of Washington, no state forbids all of these forms of release (Cheatwood, 1988).[a]

These statutes also rarely address whether governors, through executive clemency, can pardon LWOP inmates. Executive clemency may be the only way governors can deal with two unpleasant realities. The first is the high cost of caring for older inmates suffering from age-related illnesses. Second, it provides a safety valve for dealing with overcrowding., If only relatively few offenders are sentenced to LWOP and they are released quietly after twenty years or more, a public outcry is unlikely (Cheatwood, 1988).

Would the same passive attitude prevail if LWOP was generally used as a substitute for capital punishment or would citizen watchdog groups organize to block releases? Would there be mercy for older offenders deemed nondangerous, infirm, and/or suffering from terminal illness? What would happen if one or more of these offenders escaped, or had their sentences commuted to time served, or were released on furloughs or placed in a work release program and then committed a heinous crime? The answers to these questions pose substantial dilemmas for correctional decision makers.

## SENTENCING STRATEGIES

■

Two major sentencing strategies, indeterminate and determinate sentences, have been commonly used.

### Indeterminate Sentences Have Been Tied to Rehabilitation

In practice, indeterminate sentences are normally tied to rehabilitation and consist of a range of time that is defined in terms of a minimum period to be served before release can be considered, and a maximum period after which the inmate has to be released. A period of parole supervision is generally required following release, which is supposed to consolidate treatment gains made while in prison and assist inmates in adjusting to the community.

Each penal code specifies the minimum/maximum time frames to be imposed for each offense and sets limits on judges' discretion in setting the gap between the two. Most states limit the minimum sentence to no more than one-half of the maximum (e.g., 5 to 10 years). Some permit wider judicial discretion, allowing sentences ranging from bare minimums, such as six months, to an unrealistic maximum, such as 200 years. Although these absurdly long sentences create the appearance of toughness, parole commissions can make releases independent of the courts, which effectively negates these harsh sentences. The discretion at both ends of this process creates severe discrepancies in the sentences given to, and time served by, individuals with similar offenses, which in turn has led to much criticism and inmate dissatisfaction. Also, the uncertainties over the length of time to be served generates stress, which could lead to psychological problems and increased hostility toward the corrections system (Mason, 1990).

### A Determinate Sentence Represents a Fixed Term

A determinate sentence imposes a specified period during which the offender is subject to the control of the state. In practice, determinate sentences are usually associated with good time, which is a statutory provision for the reduction of time served through the accumulation of automatic and/or earned credits. Automatic good time is credits specified by law or regulation and awarded based on such factors as length of sentence. For example, inmates in Colorado can take up to 15 days off their sentences per month served. Earned credits are usually given for participation in programs (e.g., work or education) and for exceptional conduct (e.g., heroic deeds). Inmates may lose any or all of their good time as the result of rule violations. The net result of good time provisions considerably reduces the time served by most inmates incarcerated under determinate sentences. The proportion of determinate sentences served by inmates was also substantially reduced by courts that reacted to overcrowding by capping the number of inmates who could be held in a prison or system. Recently some states have legislatively raised population caps and/or built more and more prisons to increase the proportion of sentence served.

Determinate sentencing, in one form or another, has been adopted by almost all of the states and by

the federal system since 1975 as a result of the greater emphasis on retribution (U.S. Department of Justice, 1988; Gottlieb, 1993). This type of sentence can take one of three forms: determinate discretionary sentencing, determinate presumptive sentencing, and mandatory sentencing.

Under determinate discretionary sentencing the legislature typically provides a range (e.g., six to thirty years) for each crime and the judge then has the discretion to decide within that range the exact term an offender will serve (Krantz and Branham, 1991). This eliminates discretionary parole and means that correctional or parole authorities no longer have the power to release an inmate.

As of 1988 twelve states had instituted some form of determinate presumptive sentencing, under which exact sentence lengths, set by law, are specified for each offense or class of offense (U.S. Department of Justice, 1988). Judges must impose these sentences unless there are aggravating or mitigating circumstances, in which case they may lengthen or shorten them within narrow boundaries and with written justification. Rather than being tailored to fit the offender, this type of sentence is constructed to fit the offense. Presumptive sentencing statutes in Illinois, for example, specify three terms (e.g., three, four, or six years) for each class of crime, the middle of which must be imposed under unexceptional circumstances. If there are mitigating or aggravating circumstances, then the lower or higher terms can be imposed (Krantz and Branham, 1991).

### Mandatory Sentences Are Blamed for Prison Crowding

Forty-eight states (all except Utah and Vermont) have required judges to impose mandatory sentences of incarceration, often of a specified length, for certain crimes or for certain categories of offenders. They generally do not permit judges any discretion in sentencing offenders convicted of these offenses and there is no option for probation or suspension of the sentence. Minimum mandatory sentences require a specific term to be served by inmates before they can accumulate good time credits. They are aimed at incarcerating certain types of offenders (e.g., violent or habitual criminals).

Mandatory sentences have been enacted even though there is evidence that they do not work.

Legislators, responding to increasing public anxiety about crime, have passed these laws to demonstrate that they were "tough on crime." According to Tonry (1992), being on the right side of this issue has been more important than making sound and sensible public policy choices. This knee-jerk reaction has had several consequences.

The most obvious consequence has been massive increases in prison populations and concurrently escalating corrections costs. Some idea of the problem can be gleaned from the following statement:

> In the 1980's Pennsylvania's prison population grew 171% and its jail population rose 126% due to the introduction of mandatory sentences and sentencing guidelines (Steffensmeier, 1992).

Has the substantial increase in the number people in prison had an effect in reducing crime? Research shows that the enactment of these penalties had "either no demonstrable effect or a marginal effect or a short term effect that rapidly wasted away" (Tonry, 1992, p. 244). For example, during the heyday of these penalties (1985 to 1991) incarceration rates increased by 32% and the rate of violent crime rose by 38% (Steffensmeier, 1992).

Secondly, evaluations of these penalties indicate that there are judges and prosecutors who have devised ways to avoid their use. Some prosecutors refuse to file charges bearing mandatory penalties, and some judges, as occurred in a Michigan case, acquit factually guilty defendants.

Mandatory minimum statutes are bitterly and almost unanimously detested by federal judges across the political spectrum. For example, these laws prescribe identical mandatory minimum sentences for every convicted participant in a drug transaction, from the leaders down to the lowest participant, based solely on the type of drug and the weight of any "mixture or substance containing a detectable amount" of the drug. The bottom line is that the average length of stay in prison for drug offenders has more than tripled, from 23.1 months to 71.8 months since Congress adopted the first broad mandatory minimum statute in 1986 (Taylor, 1993).

Finally, cases involving mandatory penalties have increased public expenses due to longer trial and case processing times. Offenders looking at long prison sentences without the possibility of parole have little to lose and everything to gain by going to trial. The U.S. sentencing commission found that trial rates rose 2.5 times for crimes imposing mandatory penalties compared to other offenses (i.e., 30% versus 12%) (Tonry, 1992). Our "Close-Up: Three Strikes and You're Out" discusses the newest form of mandatory sentences.

Tonry (1992) suggests four ways of correcting the problems posed by mandatory sentences. First, they should be converted to presumptive sentences. Thus, judges would be provided with the preferred sentence for a given offense but would have discretion to impose another sentence if they saw fit. Second, all mandatory sentence laws should contain sunset clauses, which provide for automatic repeal after a fixed period of time. This would limit the amount of harm they could do. A third strategy would narrow their scope so that only the most serious crimes receive mandatory sentences. Finally, correctional authorities can be given the authority to release inmates serving mandatory sentences after they have completed some reasonable portion of their sentences.

## Some Judges Impose Creative Sentences

Some judges impose sentences that might be described as creative or offbeat (indeed, some people might describe them as off the wall). There is some question as to whether some of these sentences are unconstitutional. Judges using this kind of discretion usually deal with misdemeanants. Our "Close-Up: Judges Who Create Sentences" illustrates the ingenuity of some judges.

## Sentencing Reform Focuses on Proportionality, Equity, and Social Debt

Sentencing laws generally reflect concerns with proportionality, equity, and social debt. Proportionality requires that the severity of the punishment be commensurate with the seriousness of the crime. Equity involves the belief that like treatment should be accorded to similar criminals who have committed similar crimes. Social debt implies that the severity of the punishment should take into account the criminal's prior record.

Current sentencing reform laws were occasioned by rapidly rising crime rates and public dissatisfaction with the wide discretion exercised by judges in imposing sentences (Shane-Dubow, Brown, and Olsen, 1985). This discretion resulted in sentencing disparities whereby individuals with similar crimi-

# Close Up  **Three Strikes and You're Out**

The high level of public concern with crime in the 1990s led many states to consider tougher sentencing policies. One popular approach has been statutes sentencing repeat felons to life without parole. These have been referred to as "three strikes and you're out" because they dictate that offenders be put away for life after being convicted of their third felony. Although this sanction is seen as best fitting for dangerous offenders who have committed violent crimes, there is evidence it may be flawed and misuse scarce correctional resources.

Proponents of three-strikes laws tout their incapacitating effect because they feel that violent criminals will be taken off the streets for good. However, their statutory language allows them to be applied to relatively minor offenders. For example, in Washington, where the nation's first three-strikes law was enacted in 1993, a 35-year-old small time offender, Larry Fisher, was sentenced to life. His first strike involved pushing his grandfather down and taking $390 from him; his second involved robbery of a pizza parlor in which he concealed his finger so it looked like a gun and made off with $100. For his final strike he again used his finger and held up a sandwich shop for $150. While conviction for his third offense would have resulted in a 22-month sentence, under the three-strikes law he faces life in prison. The most ludicrous example involves Jerry Williams, who grabbed a slice of pizza from group of children. This offense was his third strike. Under California law, because he had a prior record of two felonies, including robbery and attempted robbery, he was sentenced to 25 years to life. Others sentenced under this law, like Cecil Davis, charged with kidnapping, rape, and attempted murder, are just the type of offenders this law was designed for. The problem is that unless these laws are very specific or allow some discretion in applying them they will ensnare people like Larry Fisher and Jerry Williams.

There are other reasons for questioning the wisdom of these laws. First, existing state and federal laws already provide for severe penalties for dangerous or violent offenders. About two-thirds of the states have habitual offender statutes, which permit enhanced penalties for repeat offenders. Second, repeat offenders are most likely to avoid enhanced penalties through plea bargaining. If plea bargaining is reduced in these cases (or if the offender is faced with a life sentence) it creates the probability of more trials, placing a severe strain on the courts. Crime statistics indicate that young males commit a disproportionate amount of violent crime and that the rate of offenses drops precipitously with age. This points to another flaw in these laws, that is, that they will incarcerate a group of offenders who are well past their most criminally active years. Thus, putting these individuals in prison will have a minimal impact on crime. It also will ultimately increase the number of older inmates whose medical problems will strain corrections budgets. Additionally, police may be faced with offenders who, facing life in prison, may be more prone to violently resist arrest.

The three-strikes laws will add to the cost of running the criminal justice system in two ways. First, more trials will occur, increasing court costs, since those facing life in prison will have nothing to lose by demanding a trial. The California State Judicial Council estimates that the state's new laws will increase trials by about 17,000 annually at a cost of about $27 million. In fact, by March 1995, a year after this law was passed, California reported that whereas 94% of felony cases were handled by plea bargains in the past, now only 14% of second-strike cases and 6% of the third-strike cases are being disposed of in this way. In Los Angeles, this resulted in a 50% increase in the number of pretrial detainees, forcing the sheriff to release some sentenced offenders early. Second, the California Department of Corrections estimates that the three-strikes law, will add 275,000 new inmates by the year 2028 at an annual cost of $5.7 billion. These added inmates would require new prison construction costing $21 billion. California judges have expressed some opposition to the three-strikes law. One Northern California judge refused to apply it in a case involving a three-time loser whose crimes he felt did not merit such stringent punishment.

As a form of mandatory sentencing the three-strikes laws will likely discriminate against minorities as do other forms of mandatory sentences. Studies at the federal and state levels show black and Hispanic offenders are more likely than whites to be given mandatory sentences or to receive enhanced sentences under habitual offender laws. These outcomes occur even though the offenses and criminal histories of the whites and minority groups are similar (Mauer, 1994; Egan, 1994; California Judge Refuses, 1994; Royko, 1995; Butterfield, 1995).

The three-strikes laws give the appearance of toughness on crime. What do you think? How would you resolve some of the problems indicated above?

## Close Up  Judges Who Create Sentences

Judge Joe B. Brown, [a controversial Memphis, Tennessee, jurist, once sentenced a convicted] drug offender to stand in front of a gorilla cage for an hour. [Brown said,] "I wanted him to get the idea that that could be him locked up and confined, and see how bad that was.". . . "It got to him.". . . [Brown says] the goal of his approach to sentencing...is not to hand out easier punishments but to devise ones that have special meaning to lawbreakers. "You have to make the punishment fit the offender, more so than the offense...His unusual sentences for first-time nonviolent offenders are accompanied by probation and community work, like washing police cars or clearing weed-filled lots. As a condition of probation, Judge Brown also...[imposes] demands that offenders complete a job training course or...[complete] school...Perhaps the most disputed of Judge Brown's sentences has been allowing burglary victims to visit the burglar's home and take something of equal value while the burglar watches. The victims, accompanied by a sheriff's deputy or bailiff, make these visits without warning so that the burglars cannot hide their most valuable possessions...[This aspect of] [t]he sentence troubles Mr. [Scott] Wallace of the Criminal Justice Policy Foundation. "I don't think it's a good idea, to involve the victim in a face-to-face intimidating confrontation," he said...Paul Levine, director of public affairs with the National Association of Criminal Defense Lawyers ...also questioned the constitutionality of the practice...[Others have] applauded his approach. "It's my firm belief that these sentences are not done just for

the purpose of being different, but for the purpose of turning individual lives around," said Leslie Balin, a defense lawyer in Memphis...[According to Judge Brown] "What we are trying to do here is use the coercive power of the court to do a bit of social engineering. That's really what I'm trying to do. (Finger, 1993)[b]"

Judge Howard Boardman, of Visalia, California has also dispensed creative and controversial sentences. In his most controversial sentence he gave a woman convicted of severely abusing her children a choice: four years in prison or probation with the condition that she use Norplant, the long term subcutaneous contraceptive. The woman originally accepted the probation sentence with the Norplant condition but later reversed herself and sued the judge for violating her "reproductive rights." The suit was dismissed about a year later when her probation was revoked and she was sent to prison (she tested positive for cocaine). As a result of the Norplant sentence, an individual who violently opposed its use, and the sentence, entered Judge Boardman's court and tried to shoot him. The judge was not injured in that incident (Southwick, 1992; Castro, 1992)

Do you think that judges should be allowed the type of discretion to hand down sentences like those imposed by Judges Brown and Broadman? Do you think that these sentences can accomplish any of the goals of sentencing that we discussed earlier? Which ones, if any?

nal backgrounds who committed the same crime might receive widely divergent penalties.

These inequities raised questions regarding the operation of the criminal justice system and created problems that interfered with its functioning. First, constitutional issues could be raised regarding the equality of justice since these types of disparities are basically unfair. Secondly, where it was possible, this resulted in defense attorneys engaging in "judge shopping" so their clients might get a lighter/fairer sentence. In turn, this made it more difficult for court administrators to schedule and equitably divide workloads.

Finally, because inmates tend to compare sentences, those who were more severely punished

and hence felt discriminated against tended to react in ways that made their management more difficult. Violation of proportionality raises issues similar to those involved with equity.

A number of solutions have been developed to cope with the problems of disparity and proportionality, including sentencing guidelines of various types and sentence review processes that include appellate review and sentencing councils.

**SENTENCING GUIDELINES ARE DESIGNED TO CREATE UNIFORMITY**  Guidelines have generally been developed to accompany determinate sentences although they could also be used in conjunction with indeterminate sentences. Normally, sentencing guidelines set forth explicit policies and procedures for making decisions regarding individual sentences. The criteria for making these decisions are usually based on the nature and seriousness of the offense and the offender's criminal history. For example, whereas an individual with no previous record might receive a sentence of probation for a specific offense, with a record of one prior felony, he might instead receive prison time.

In some states the guidelines are advisory, providing benchmarks for the judge but not requiring that specific sentences be imposed. In other states they mandate that the judge impose the prescribed sentence and its presumptive length when the offender is convicted for a particular offense. When used in the latter sense, guidelines tend to reduce disparities.

A 1994 survey showed nineteen states were using sentencing guidelines, with several other states considering their implementation (Lillis, 1994a). Of those using guidelines, twelve considered them to be an improvement over their past sentencing practices, while two, Florida and New York, saw them as too rigid and in need of modification. This survey found the effects of the guidelines were mixed. About one-third of the states reported an increase in the number of violent offenders imprisoned, one-quarter reported putting more nonviolent offenders on probation, and in the rest there were either no noticeable effects or the programs were too new to be evaluated.

Figure 2.4 presents a sentencing grid with two axes, adapted from Minnesota's sentencing guide-

FIGURE 2.4  **Minnesota Sentencing Guidelines Grid Showing Sentence Length Changes Made in 1989**

| Severity levels of conviction offense | | Criminal history score 0 | 1 | 2 | 3 | 4 | 5 | 6 or more | Presumptive length of sentence (months) |
|---|---|---|---|---|---|---|---|---|---|
| Sale of a simulated controlled substance | I | 12 | 12 | 12 | 13 | 15 | 17 | 19 / 18–20 | |
| Theft-related crimes ($2,500 or less) Check forgery ($200–$2,500) | II | 12 | 12 | 13 | 15 | 17 | 19 | 21 / 21–22 | |
| Theft crimes ($2,500 or less) | III | 12 | 13 | 15 | 17 | 19 / 18–20 | 21 / 21–23 | 25 / 24–26 | |
| Nonresidential burglary Theft crimes (over $2,500) | IV | 12 | 15 | 18 | 21 | 25 / 24–26 | 32 / 30–34 | 41 / 37–45 | |
| Residential burglary Simple robbery | V | 18 | 23 | 27 | 30 / 29–31 | 38 / 36–40 | 46 / 43–49 | 54 / 50–58 | |
| Criminal sexual conduct, 2nd degree | VI | 21 | 26 | 30 | 34 / 33–35 | 44 / 42–46 | 54 / 50–58 | 65 / 60–70 | |
| Aggravated robbery | VII | 24 / 23–25 / 48 / 44–52 | 32 / 30–34 / 58 / 54–62 | 41 / 38–44 / 68 / 64–72 | 49 / 45–55 / 78 / 74–82 | 65 / 60–70 / 88 / 84–92 | 81 / 75–87 / 98 / 94–102 | 97 / 90–104 / 108 / 104–112 | |
| Criminal sexual conduct, 1st degree Assault, 1st degree | VIII | 43 / 41–45 / 86 / 81–91 | 54 / 50–58 / 98 / 93–103 | 65 / 60–70 / 110 / 105–115 | 76 / 71–81 / 122 / 117–127 | 95 / 89–104 / 134 / 129–139 | 113 / 106–120 / 146 / 141–151 | 132 / 124–140 / 158 / 153–163 | |
| Murder, 3rd degree Murder, 2nd degree (felony murder) | IX | 105 / 102–108 / 150 / 144–156 | 119 / 116–122 / 165 / 159–171 | 127 / 124–130 / 180 / 174–186 | 149 / 143–155 / 195 / 189–201 | 176 / 168–184 / 210 / 204–216 | 205 / 195–215 / 225 / 219–231 | 230 / 218–242 / 240 / 234–246 | |
| Murder, 2nd degree (with intent) | X | 216 / 212–220 / 306 / 299–313 | 236 / 231–241 / 326 / 319–333 | 256 / 250–262 / 346 / 339–353 | 276 / 269–283 / 366 / 359–373 | 296 / 288–304 / 386 / 379–393 | 316 / 307–325 / 406 / 399–413 | 336 / 326–346 / 426 / 419–433 | |

SOURCE: Frase, R. S. (1993, Feb.). Prison population growing under Minnesota guidelines. *Overcrowded Times*, 4(1), p. 12.[c]

# *Close Up*  ACA President Speaks Out on Sentencing

In his keynote address to the American Corrections Association convention in January 1993, ACA president Perry M. Johnson acknowledged that considerable time, energy, and money had been devoted to the issue of overcrowding. Instead of continuing to concentrate on building more prisons to solve the problem he urged the association to challenge the policies that caused the crowding. He argued that because correctional professionals see the effects of court-imposed sanctions they can contribute valuable insights to the sentencing debate. What follows is a distillation of his remarks.

At least four criteria need to be met by appropriate and adequate criminal sanctions which are not dealt with by existing sentencing strategies:

**1.** A sound sentencing policy has to be just and fair, impartial, and proportionate to the harm done by the crime.
**2.** Sentencing policy has to be based on a rational strategy to reduce crime.
**3.** Sentencing policy must maintain respect for the law, not diminish it.
**4.** It should enhance, where possible, the condition of the victim by restoring them to wholeness.

With respect to the first criterion, studies have consistently found that different people receive very different punishments for similar crimes. The same punishment is given to people who have committed crimes that differ widely in their seriousness. For example a study by the Michigan Supreme court of 7000 sentencing decisions found little correlation between the factors that judges claimed to use in making their decisions and their actual sentences. The factors with a significant relationship to sentences were age, race, and gender. Other studies have found that when the race of the victim is white the level of punishment meted out by judges is greater than when the victims are of other races. This fact places greater value on the interests and safety of whites and constitutes a gross injustice. Also there are many examples of disparities in state sentencing policy including such discrepancies as bad check writers receiving longer sentences than child abusers in Michigan.

The second criterion calls for a rational relationship between sentencing and crime reduction. Most states in this country have committed themselves to "get tough on crime" policies during the 1980s and 1990s. The question is: Has this approach had a demonstrable effect on the level of crime? The answer appears to be uncertain. Certainly, the number of people in prison and under other forms of correctional supervision has grown dramatically so that the sentencing policies of this era demonstrate this toughness. However, is there less crime? The answer is relatively straightforward: "No." In fact, the rate of crime has remained quite high and most recent indications are that rates of serious violent crimes are rising. In Michigan, for example, during the period in which the state's sentencing policy was toughened and the number of offenders being sent to prison more than doubled, violent crime rates reached historic highs. In spite of that and other evidence that the get-tough policies

lines. The horizontal axis contains criminal history scores, based on offender characteristics, which predict recidivism; the vertical axis contains the list of offenses, based on increasing seriousness. The offender's criminal history score is obtained by summing points assigned to each of a variety of factors including juvenile and adult convictions, previous incarcerations, supervisory status at the time of the offense (Was the offender on probation or parole? Had he or she escaped?), employment status, and educational achievement. Once the offender's score has been determined, the judge can locate the recommended sentence by finding the cell that denotes the intersection of the criminal history score with the appropriate offense. The cell contains the sentence to be given (along with its permissible range) in months. Thus, an individual who has a criminal history score of 3 and has been convicted of a Level VII offense should be sentenced to 78 months. However, judges have some leeway and can impose sentences of from 74 to 82 months depending on circumstances.

By using sentencing guidelines in combination with an independent commission that could modify sentence lengths, Minnesota was able to control its prison population growth for several years (Frase, 1993).

# Close Up

have not worked very well, supporters still claim that these policies should be even tougher.

If tried, tougher sentencing policies would not likely work. Johnson estimates that if we incarcerated every last felon we can convict this year without letting any already in prison out—give nothing but hard time—it would only have a small effect on crime, but it would double the prison population in one year (at the cost of billions of dollars) and only reduce serious crime by less than 15%. While releasing truly dangerous criminals is not advocated, our tough policies have probably only widened the net.

The practices followed in community corrections are used to demonstrate the problems of sentencing related to respect for the law. These sanctions many times amount to no more than benign neglect. Offenders receive freedom without responsibility and are not held accountable for many violations of the conditions that allow them to remain in the community. Part of the problem is that caseloads for community corrections workers are likely to be considerable and the "overcrowding" which results is invisible. If we believe that more intensive community supervision is helping, we are deluding ourselves because only about 5% of the caseload receives that level of supervision. Given that most individuals on probation are not adequately supervised and many offenders receiving prison sentences only serve a small proportion of those sentences, respect for the law is diminished.

Finally, the degree to which sentences help the victims of the criminal act to return to their previctimization state is low. Although restitution is cited as a benefit for victims, it is ordered in less than one-third of the cases and collected in only half of those. Thus, the victim continues to be the neglected actor in the criminal justice drama.

Johnson concludes that the public should be informed about the costs and effects of sentencing policy and then polled to determine what criminal sanctions ought to be legislated. He believes that an informed public would be less likely to support the policy of high rates of incarceration. Further, any guidelines structured to govern sentences should set time standards for both incarceration and community sanctions. In both types of sanctions convicted offenders should be held accountable to fulfill the punitive conditions attached to their sentences. While programs, like school, trade training, or drug treatment are essential in both environments, they should not form the basis for the sanctions. Without widening the net, community sanctions should be emphasized with prisons used for the truly dangerous and for recalcitrants. As Johnson says, "Developing a system that says to every convicted criminal 'you will be punished in a just and reasonable manner without bias' and then proves it is hardly soft on crime. And if we combine that with real opportunity for positive change—for self-improvement—the public will be well served."

(SOURCE: Adapted from Johnson, P.M. (1993). Corrections should take the lead in changing sentencing practices. *Corrections Today* 55, (2), pp. 54–55, 130–131.[d]

**SENTENCING REVIEW PROCEDURES ARE DESIGNED TO REDUCE DISPARITIES** Other arrangements employed to reduce sentencing inconsistency have involved reviews of sentences to be imposed. More than half of the states permit appellate review of the merits of sentences in some circumstances (Kittrie and Zenoff, 1981). These reviews have the dual purpose of reducing disparities and creating sets of generally agreed-on criteria for sentencing policies. Another approach to review has been sentencing councils. Under this arrangement, sentencing judges meet with several colleagues to find out what sentences they would impose in the case being judged.

It should be obvious that the complex maze of sentencing presents some serious problems for corrections. Our "Close-Up: ACA President Speaks Out on Sentencing" presents some suggestions from the field of corrections to resolve some of these problems.

## Conclusion

It is clear that the sentence, which starts convicted offenders into the correctional process, has immense implications for them. At the very least, it will set the tone for their immediate futures and perhaps for much longer. For better or worse, usually the latter, if they are incarcerated they will be thrown into an environment that will totally dominate their lives. In the chapters that follow, we will try to convey a picture of how these penal and other sanctions, and the processes that accompany them, have evolved into their present form.

### Acknowledgments

[a] D. Cheatwood. The life-without-parole sanction: Its current status and a research agenda. *Crime and Delinquency*, 343, 43–59. National Council on Crime and Delinquency. ©1988 by Sage Publications. Reprinted by permission of Sage Publications.
[b] Copyright ©1993 by the New York Times Company. Reprinted by permission.
[c] Reprinted with permission from *Overcrowded Times*, Vol. 4, No. 1, 1993.
[d] Reprinted with permission of the American Correctional Association, Lanham, MD.

### Chapter Recap

**Justifications for Punishment of Offenders**
Retribution: The Infliction of Deserved Punishment and Its Painful Consequences on the Criminal
Deterrence: Pain or Other Consequences Will Inhibit Criminal Behavior
　The Deterrent Value of Punishment Is Inconclusive
　Speed, Severity, and Certainty of Punishment Affect Deterrence
Incapacitation: The Prevention of Future Crime
　Three Types of Incapacitation Strategies Have Been Proposed
　An Alternative to Incapacitation Is More Severe Sentences for Violent Offenders
A Continuing Purpose of Incarceration Has Been to Reform or Rehabilitate the Offender
　Reintegration Is Maintaining or Integrating Offenders into the Community

**Types of Dispositions**
Monetary Sanctions: Getting Hit in the Wallet
　Day Fines Are Imposed on the Basis of the Gravity of the Offense and Offender Income
　Restitution Requires That the Offender Make Amends to the Victim or the Community
Community-Based Alternatives
　Probation Is Serving A Sentence Under Supervision in the Community
　Residential Community Programs Provide the Most Intense Supervision Short of Prison

Incarceration Is Confinement of an Offender in a Prison or Jail
Capital Punishment Is the Ultimate Sanction
　The Death Penalty Has Supporters and Detractors
Life without Parole Represents an Alternative to Execution

**Sentencing Strategies**
Indeterminate Sentences Have Been Tied to Rehabilitation
A Determinate Sentence Represents A Fixed Term
Mandatory Sentences Are Blamed for Prison Crowding
Some Judges Impose Creative Sentences
Sentencing Reform Focuses on Proportionality, Equity, and Social Debt
Sentencing Guidelines Are Designed to Create Uniformity
Sentencing Review Procedures Are Designed to Reduce Disparities
**Conclusion**

### Review Questions

**1.** Contrast and discuss retribution, deterrence and incapacitation as rationales for the use of the various forms of punishment employed by corrections.
**2.** Compare probation with intermediate sanctions and with incarceration, especially with respect to its impact on retribution and reintegration.
**3.** Summarize the various arguments both for and against capital punishment.
**4.** Describe and discuss the indeterminate sentence. What impact can the discretion afforded by this type of sentence have on treatment programs within corrections? What disadvantages does it have? How do determinate sentences differ from indeterminate ones?
**5.** What factors need to be considered in structuring an appropriate sentence for a given offender?

### Test Your Knowledge

**1.** As a justification for the imposition of a penal sanction, retribution specifies that
　**a.** the pain of punishment will discourage further criminal behavior.

**b.** while being punished, the criminal will not be able to further victimize society.

✓ **c.** the criminal is getting what he/she deserves.

✗ **d.** society is getting revenge for the harm it has suffered.

2. Restitution can be thought of as

   **a.** deserved punishment.

   **b.** a form of nonmonetary punishment.

   ✗ **c.** payment for harm done to the victim.

   ✓ **d.** a sentence that requires the offender to perform community service.

3. The death penalty

   **a.** is legal in all but three states in the United States.

   ✗ **b.** is supported by about 75% of the U.S. public.

   **c.** is imposed for first-degree murder and sadistic rape in the jurisdictions in which it is legal.

   ✓ **d.** all of the above.

4. Indeterminate sentences

   ✓ **a.** require that a specific number of years be served.

   **b.** are typically associated with some form of parole.

   **c.** were developed to implement the modern form of retribution.

   ✗ **d.** none of the above.

# PART TWO

# HISTORICAL PERSPECTIVE

# CHAPTER 3

# THE EVOLUTION OF PUNISHMENT

PUNISHMENT OF THE KNOUT.

## PUNISHMENT OF EARLY CRIMINAL BEHAVIOR

Before discussing the evolution of punishment, it is important to note that methods employed historically to punish offenders do not change abruptly (Spierenburg, 1991). Instead, they evolve gradually and unevenly, especially when comparing different countries. For long periods, capital punishment, dismemberment, and banishment were used to some degree followed by transportation and long-term imprisonment. Although many forms of punishment were eventually abandoned in most countries, some are still used in several parts of the world today.

### Early Societies Had Two Classes of Crimes

Early groups had no written laws, but most had norms or customs that regulated behavior. In ancient times the power of control rested with the father as head of the basic social unit, the family. This authority was so absolute that it included the power of life and death. Clans and tribes had two classes of wrongful acts: **public wrongs** and **private wrongs.** The whole social group was obligated to take repressive action to control public wrongs, whereas individuals and blood relatives dealt with private wrongs (Wines, 1895).

**PUBLIC WRONGS WERE EQUATED WITH SIN** In preliterate societies there were six basic categories of public wrongs or crimes: sacrilege and other offenses against religion, treason, witchcraft, incest and other sex offenses, poisoning, and violations of the hunting rules (Oppenheimer, 1913/1975). Religious offenses were the most heinous because they were believed to expose not only offenders but the entire group to untold disasters due to the wrath of the gods (Oppenheimer, 1913/1975). An offender might be hacked or stoned to death, or suffer some equally gruesome punishment. Today, some religious offenses continue to be punished by extreme fundamentalist nations. In 1989, the Ayatollah Khomeini of Iran called for Muslims to execute Salman Rushdie, offering a reward of $2.6 million, because of statements in his book, *The Satanic Verses*, that were alleged to insult the prophet Muhammad. To survive, Rushdie was forced into hiding and continues to be protected by the British government (Darnton, 1993; Ibrahim, 1989; Smith, 1989).

Incest was believed to offend the spirits and to bring disaster on the land (Oppenheimer, 1913/1975). Witchcraft or sorcery was thought to involve the use of magical powers for individual revenge or advancement or to bring disaster to the group. Poisoning was seen as witchcraft because the action of drugs on the body was thought to involve the manipulation of supernatural powers. Thus, individuals who poisoned others were punished by the group. Good magicians were given high status because they used drugs in a positive way.

Treason usually involved rendering assistance to an enemy at war with the tribe (e.g., joining the opponent or betrayal by revelation of military secrets) and sometimes included refusal to fight against an enemy. These violators were customarily executed. Even today, these actions are subject to severe punishment. Finally, those breaching the hunting and fishing rules were punished by the group because of its need to protect sources of food. For example, in some societies, those guilty of frightening off the herd before the hunt could begin were subsequently executed (Oppenheimer, 1913/1975).

**PRIVATE WRONGS INITIALLY REQUIRED INDIVIDUAL RETALIATION BUT LATER SOME RESPONSIBILITY SHIFTED TO THE GROUP** In primitive groups, private revenge was the only means victims had to deal with most cases of physical injury, property damage, or theft. Striking back was also a way to prevent future attacks on self and property. Of course, the original aggressor defended against a victim's retaliation by reattacking, thereby setting the stage for perpetual conflict (Schafer, 1976).

As tribal societies became more advanced, the responsibility for punishing crimes against individuals from different clans or tribes was assumed by the entire group. Only minor crimes remained the responsibility of the individual. It was during this time that the **"blood feud"** developed. This meant that acts against one individual were viewed as acts against that person's entire kinship group and required the victim's family, tribe, or community to take action. Thus, a criminal offense was an act perpetrated by one tribe against all of the members of another tribe or clan. Revenge was directed at restoring the balance of power between groups and was really a response to the perpetrator's group rather than to the injury suffered by the victim (Schafer, 1969).

Blood feud retaliation was customarily carried out following *lex talionis,* i.e., the principle of an eye-for-an eye. This meant that if a man knocked out the tooth of someone of his own rank, they were permitted to knock out his tooth. Several ancient codes, such as the Babylonian Code of Hammurabi (about 2500 B.C.), the Ten Commandments, and the Indian Manama Dharma Astra, carefully regulated the extent of the revenge (Schafer, 1976). In Europe, between the Roman period and the start of the Middle Ages (the fifth to eleventh centuries), society consisted of such feuding families and tribes.

**COMPENSATION PROVIDED A BRIDGE BETWEEN PRIVATE VENGEANCE AND THE STATE** Many difficulties were associated with blood feuds. The most serious was that no satisfactory way existed for their resolution. One injury could start a perpetual vendetta that made life perilous for both feuding clans. This became a greater problem as tribes settled in an area and developed stable communities.

One widely used solution to the blood feud, though not universal, was the system of **compensation** or *wergild.* Typically, tribes creating cities and towns adopted a compensation system. Among German tribes, compensation became an acceptable alternative to retaliation because the criminal was humiliated to some extent by the act of paying compensation, which in turn appeased the victim's desire for revenge. Even homicide could be atoned for by paying a certain fine in cattle and sheep (Schafer, 1977). Unlike the system of revenge, which was based on maintaining the security of the tribe, compensation was related to the effect of the wrongful act on the victim. The amount of reparations received depended on such factors as the age, rank, sex, or influence of the victim. "A free man was worth more than a slave, a grown-up more than a child, a man more than a woman, and a person of rank more than a freeman" (Barnes, 1930/1972, p. 49).

This system ultimately led to the concept of **outlawry** (Schafer, 1977). Those who would not or could not pay the necessary reparations were declared outlaws and ostracized by the group. Outlaws who did not escape could be killed or might be sold into slavery (Ives, 1914/1970). Only those criminals who paid their blood fines could remain in the community. By 871 A.D., in Saxony, victim retaliation was only permitted after the offender refused to pay the compensation requested by the victim (Schafer, 1977).

The practice of granting sanctuary or protection to those accused of crimes, dating back to the time of Moses, was also an outgrowth of blood feud retaliation (Wines, 1895). Most countries had a city or a special building, such as a temple or church to which the accused could flee and stay for a certain period until the alleged "wrong" could be resolved through mediation and concession. Until the thirteenth century, in England, a criminal could claim refuge in a church for forty days, after which he had to surrender or admit guilt and forfeit his property. After this he was afforded safe passage out of the realm (Ives, 1914/1970). By 1530 offenders could not leave the country but had to spend the rest of their days in a "privileged place"—usually a colony that grew up around a monastery. By 1663, with the dissolution of monasteries, this practice was finally abolished in England (Ives, 1914/1970).

When compensation replaced private revenge, disputes over the amount of payment were resolved at periodically held tribal assemblies (Oppenheimer, 1913/1975). Although they had only peacekeeping functions, these assemblies were an example of early judicial proceedings. The growth of a central authority (e.g., a king) in the fifth and sixth centuries led to the first Anglo-Saxon laws in 601–604 to control violence. Known as "the dooms," these laws provided evidence of the early custom of the "king's peace." Under this law, the king extended his protection to those in his presence and in the local area in which he currently was staying. Those breaching the king's peace were fined in addition to paying the victim compensation. Noblemen imposed a similar type of peace in their jurisdictions and exacted fines from those violating it (Oppenheimer, 1913/1975).

By the mid-fourteenth century kings had gained absolute power and gradually extended their peace to more areas, and when they became strong enough, proclaimed the entire country under their control (Johnson, 1988). With the development of a strong central authority, the definition of crime and its resolution was altered. Private wrongs became offenses against the king's peace, and breaches of public order and the compensation system changed. Initially, kings took only a portion of the compensation a victim received as payment for helping to settle disputes, but greed gradually led them to take increasing amounts of the victim's share until it all went to the state.

### Crimes Become Acts of Revolt against the King

Viewed as acts against both the divine and temporal powers of the king, crime now represented an act of revolt against a king's omnipotence (Oppenheimer, 1913/1975). Offenders were harshly punished for two main reasons. First, when a ruler initially attained control, he severely punished offenders to deter those who might challenge his position. Second, severe punishment also served as a deterrence to the rest of society (Barnes, 1930/1972). Criminals were subjected to corporal or capital punishment and sometimes both (i.e., torture preceded execution).

## HISTORICALLY, OFFENDERS WERE PUNISHED IN VARIOUS WAYS

From early times the most common forms of punishment were exile, corporal punishment, capital punishment, and less often public ridicule and magical spells. In some cases, punishment may have been twofold (e.g., mutilation sometimes accompanied placement in the pillories).

### Magic and Curses Were Used as Punishments

Primitives employed some punishments that involved curses, magic, incantations, and formulas based on notions that the spoken word had a certain potency. Cursing an individual or using special magical words or phrases were believed to cause the result the user intended. Medicine men and shamans devised various procedures that they believed caused a desired result. For example, it was believed that by constructing a doll with things taken from the victim's person (such as hair and nail parings), one could eliminate the individual in question by following certain procedures (Gillin, 1935). In the United States today a form of this approach is used in practicing the contemporary Afro-Caribbean religion of Santeria (Wetli and Martinez, 1981, 1983).

### Some Punishments Were Designed to Humiliate the Offender

**Public humiliation and shame** have been used as punishments from primitive times to the present. In ancient Greece, for example, army deserters

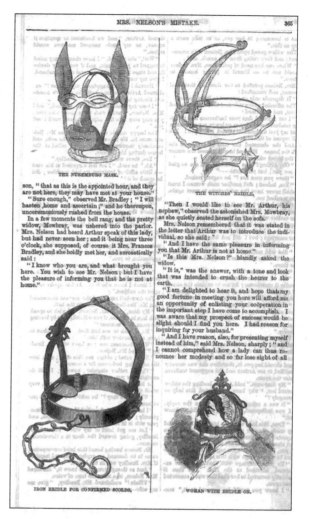

Branks and bridles were means of punishing and disciplining outspoken women. These sexist devices were used until the late 1800s.

were publicly displayed in women's clothes. In England during the Middle Ages, it was used to deal with fraud by merchants. A baker selling short-weighted loaves of bread might be punished by being paraded through the streets with a loaf of bread tied around his neck. Drunkards were sometimes walked through the streets clothed only in a barrel (Ives, 1914/1970).

**GAGS WERE USED TO BOTH SHAME AND CONSTRAIN VERBAL ABUSE** Scolds, persons who openly, habitually, and abusively found fault, unjustly criticized, or lied about others, were punished by being made to wear various gags consisting of metal brands or bridles. A **bridle** was an iron

**Prisoners were often placed in the public pillories.**

cage that fit over the head and had a front plate that was sharpened or covered with spikes designed to fit into the mouth of the offender. This made any movement of the tongue very painful. This was more often employed against women than men due to sexist views of the volatility of women's words. In England it was used until the late 1800s by husbands as a means of keeping their wives subservient and stopping their nagging (Andrews, 1899). When it was used on prostitutes ribbons were added to indicate their crimes (Wilson, 1931). In Colonial America, it was employed on both sexes to control swearing, drunkenness, and so on (Newman, 1978).

**THE STOCKS AND PILLORIES SERVED TO CONFINE AND DISPLAY OFFENDERS** Before the erection of the houses of correction in England, stocks were used as outside jails to punish the idle. Under Henry VIII, vagabonds and the unemployed were ordered to sit in the **stocks** for three days and nights and were given only bread and water. From the Reformation until the nineteenth century they were used for offenses such as swearing, Sabbath breaking, wife abuse, and petty forms of theft. They were also used in Colonial America to deal with similar crimes. For example, a Boston carpenter hired to construct a set of stocks for the city in 1639 was confined in them for charging too much to build them (Wilson, 1931). During the seventeenth and eighteenth centuries they were most frequently used to punish drunks (Newman, 1978).

The use of **pillories** dates to the pre-Christian era of the Greeks and Gauls. In England they were commonly employed during the Tudor period but their peak use occurred in the seventeenth century (Newman, 1978). Like stocks, pillories occupied a prominent place in English towns and villages, and served to show offenders the community's disapproval while advertising their guilt.

Pillories were used for a variety of offenses ranging from blasphemy to treason, to pickpocketing and drunkenness (Earle, 1896/1969). Although this was not a harsh punishment in and of itself, the treatment offenders received while confined was sometimes extremely brutal. Some offenders were secured to them by having their ears nailed to the frame and released by having their ears cut off.

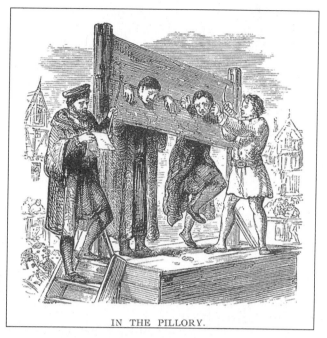

IN THE PILLORY.

**The humiliation of being placed in the pillory was sometimes compounded by the pain of having one's ears nailed to the frame. Rocks and other items might be thrown at the offenders by the crowd.**

With their faces protruding through the pillory, offenders stood defenseless against the cruel jeers and missiles the crowd might throw (including stones), which sometimes caused serious injury and even death (Ives, 1914/1970; Earle, 1896/1969). Their use was abolished in the 1830s in both England and France (Earle, 1896/1969).

In Colonial America the use of the pillory followed the same pattern as in England and continued until 1803. Its earlier decline here may have been because of our disdain for English forms of punishment, but the major reason for the decline of the pillory was likely due to the growth in the size of communities. As the population of towns grew and the nature of social relationships became more impersonal, the stigmatizing power of this punishment declined. With the declining use of the pillory and stocks, branding became the means, at least temporarily, for offenders to be identified and stigmatized.

**BRANDING MARKED A PERSON AS AN OFFENDER**  While certainly painful, **branding** was employed primarily for making offenders, slaves, and prisoners of war recognizable. Reference to this practice can be found in the Code of Hammurabi as well as in ancient Greece (Wines, 1895; Oppenheimer, 1913/1975). By the fourth century, England had begun to use branding, often with other more brutal punishments. Offenders were typically branded on their thumb with a letter denoting their offense (e.g., "M" for murderer; "T" for thief). The mark was used by judges to determine if a person had a prior conviction. In England this practice was abolished in 1779 (Parry, 1934/1975). In the United States it was commonly used during the colonial period, reaching a peak by the late 1700s. After they were branded, offenders were often banished to some offshore location.

Hawthorne's 1850 book, *The Scarlet Letter*, immortalized the requirement in many American colonies that offenders wear letters sewed on their outer garments specifying their crimes. In New

York and Massachusetts this was a common punishment for blasphemers and drunks (Earle, 1896/1969). Finally, a practice in both England and its American colonies was to require offenders to hang a paper around their necks or pinned to their chest describing their offenses.

In the late 1980s a county judge in Sarasota, Florida, ordered those she found guilty of drunk driving to put bumper stickers on their cars identifying them as drunk drivers. It seems that old ideas keep coming back.

## Corporal Punishments Inflicted Pain on the Offender

Until the end of the eighteenth century, corporal punishment represented the most universally employed method of punishing offenders (Barnes and Teeters, 1943). It was typically imposed in public, which represented a means of setting an example for others who violated the law (deterrence), and it inflicted pain on the offender, which served a means of retribution.

**WHIPPING HAS A LONG AND EXTENSIVE HISTORY** Whipping, also known as **flogging** or **scourging,** is one of the oldest most widely employed means of corporal punishment. In fact, its extensive use as a punishment has no equal. It has been employed to punish crimes, as discipline in a correctional setting, on slaves, within religious orders, and for enforcing domestic, family, military, and academic discipline (Newman, 1978).

It earliest recorded use as a coercive punishment dates back to the fifth chapter of Exodus, which indicates that the Israelites were whipped by their Egyptian masters if they failed to produce their quota of bricks (Cooper, 1870). The Romans carried the use of whipping farther than any other nation. Judges surrounded themselves with a variety of whips, scourges, and leather straps to terrify offenders and bring them to a sense of duty. Accounts of Roman life were full of references to masters and mistresses whipping their slaves (sometimes to death) (Cooper, 1870).

Whipping was common in England before the sixteenth century. However, it was not until 1530 that the Whipping Act was passed to deter and punish those who were not productive members of society. This law ordered vagrants (men, women, or children) to be tied to the tail end of a cart, stripped naked, and beaten as they were pulled through the town or village until their bodies were bloody (Parry, 1934/1975; Newman, 1978). Many offenders subjected to this type of brutality died (Scott, 1938). Under Queen Elizabeth in 1597, the cart was replaced by the whipping post and offenders were only stripped to the waist.

Whipping had its greatest use during a 300-year period that began in 1600 (Newman, 1978). Its demise in England began in the early 1800s with abolition of flogging for women. Whipping of men became less frequent and was carried out inside prisons. It was not until 1948 that it was abolished as a punishment for crimes. Thus as late as the 1930s, adolescents and adults were whipped for offenses such as burglary and arson (Scott, 1938).

Whipping was also quite common on the European continent. In Holland, the whipping of women was made into a public spectacle. In a perverse way, the public found this so entertaining they willingly paid an admission charge to witness it (Cooper, 1870).

The despotic and semibarbaric practices in Russia led it to be labeled "the Land of the Whip and the Rod" (Cooper, 1870, p. 242). It was quite common for servants, serfs, workers, and even women of rank to be brought to police stations to be whipped. Russia also invented what Cooper called the "most formidable punisher ever devised," the **Russian knout.** This instrument is a wooden-handled whip typically consisting of several rawhide thongs twisted together and terminating in a single strand that projects about 18 inches beyond the body of the knot. Sometimes the hide was plaited with wire, dipped in liquid, and then frozen before use or the thongs had hooks or rings attached to the ends (Scott, 1938). To spare an offender a painful death, his family sometimes bribed the executioner to wield the knout like an axe and inflict the fatal blow on the first stroke (deLangy, 1854).

In the American colonies flogging and other forms of corporal punishment were more frequently employed than in England because early colonial criminal codes meted out more corporal punishment than capital punishment. Offenders were flogged for such offenses as lying, swearing, perjury, selling rum to Indians, sleeping rather than attending church on the Sabbath, drunkenness, and stealing (Newman, 1978). Whipping was also used to preserve the virtue of young unmarried women. The colonists had no more sympathy for women than they did for men (Earle, 1896/1969).

After the Revolution, imprisonment began to be substituted for both corporal and capital punishment. Pennsylvania abolished whipping in 1786 and four years later the federal government prohibited it and the use of the pillory for federal offenses. Although several states continued to flog offenders well into nineteenth century, by the twentieth century only two states—Maryland and Delaware—retained this form of punishment (Sutherland, 1924). The last known flogging in Maryland took place in 1949; in Delaware the last one occurred in 1952 but the law was not repealed until 1972 (Rubin, 1973; Burns, 1975).

The use of whipping in Delaware well into the second half of the twentieth century provided Caldwell (1947) with an opportunity to examine the major arguments advanced to support flogging. These included:

*The offender must suffer pain:* Proponents argue that for violent offenses, whipping provides some physical suffering but is not barbaric. Opponents counter that it puts a premium on violence, aligns the criminal against society, and brutalizes and blunts the sensibilities of all involved (i.e., offenders, officials, and spectators). Also, imprisonment serves the function of making the offender suffer, at least psychologically, without violence. This satisfies both society's and the victim's desire for retribution.

*Whipping is cheaper:* In Delaware, this argument was invalid because, except for wife beating, all other offenses included a prison sentence. Also, offenders' sentences were not shortened when whipping was imposed because usually the most hardened and serious offenders were the ones flogged.

*Whipping reforms an offender:* Caldwell states that it is astonishing anyone could believe "that so simple a thing as a lash when applied to so complex an organism as a human being, who is striving for adjustment in such an amazingly intricate interplay of geographical, biological, and social forces [can truly reform criminals and in turn have] significance for the welfare an en-

tire society" (p. 86). Also, if the lash truly reformed offenders, why did Delaware imprison most of them?

*"Spare the rod, spoil the child" argument:* Defenders claim "my parents whipped me as a child and I'm a better person today because of it." This confuses spanking children in a loving family context with the impersonal whipping of criminals by the justice system. Discipline may be effective on children because it is part of a continuing positive relationship valued by the child and is likely to be imposed within hours of the offensive behavior.

*Whipping prevents further criminal activities:* Studies conducted in Great Britain, Canada, and Delaware revealed that whipping has not reformed offenders (Caldwell, 1965). In Delaware, Caldwell found that of the 320 offenders whipped between 1920 and 1939, by 1942 61.9% had been convicted of a subsequent offense after their first whipping, and 65.1% of those whipped twice were convicted of a another offense. By comparison, of the 516 offenders not whipped who could have been, during 1928, 1932, 1936, and 1940, only 52.3% were convicted of some offense before 1945. Advocates counter this by arguing that it was ineffective because it was administered by people who did not "lay on the lashes" with sufficient force to make an impression on the offender. This argument falls apart since recidivism data on offenders whipped by Warden Wilson, who was known to lay the lashes on "hard," showed that of 106 offenders he whipped between 1935 and 1942, by 1945 two-thirds had subsequently recidivated (45% of them for a major crime).

Support for whipping continues to exist in Delaware today. In 1989, although it was not passed, a bill was introduced in the Senate that would have brought whipping back as a punishment for dealing in hard drugs (*Public Whipping,* 1989). Moreover, Amnesty International (AI) (1989b, 1990, 1991) reports that whipping is still legal in at least 13 countries including some in the Caribbean, Middle and Far East, and Africa. In Singapore caning is a mandatory penalty for 30 crimes. In the Sudan many people, including women, are publicly flogged after summary trials (Amnesty International, 1991).

In 1994, an 18-year-old American youth living in Singapore confessed to vandalizing several vehicles. He was sentenced to four months in prison and was given four lashes with a ½-inch-thick rattan cane (Shenon, 1994). Regardless of the publicity describing the brutality of this punishment, a *U.S.A. Today* poll found that 53% favored whipping and other harsh punishments as deterrents to crime (Stone, 1994). What are your views?

**THE DUCKING STOOL WAS GENERALLY USED FOR SCOLDS AND GOSSIPS**   The **ducking stool** was used as a punishment as early as the eleventh century. Those sentenced to be "ducked" were placed on a chair and suspended over a body of water and plunged into it. Earle (1896/1969) notes that as an "engine of punishment" (consistent with the sexist views of the time that women's words were a powerful weapon) it was customarily reserved for females who continually nagged and used abusive language.

In England, it was also used for brawlers, slanderers, prostitutes, quarrelsome married couples (tied back-to-back and ducked), wife beaters, male scolds, and sellers of bad beer or bread. Occasionally, offenders were dipped too often and died. The last ducking in England occurred in 1820 for wife-beating (Wilson, 1931).

In America, its use was widespread in the colonies outside of New England (Earle, 1896/1969). During the 1800s it was used infrequently, and by the end of the century it was no longer employed (Andrews, 1899).

## Capital Punishment Rids the Community of the Offender

From earliest times to the present, execution has represented the most extreme reaction to criminal behavior in almost all societies. In many cultures, death was the most frequent way to punish offenders for many centuries (Laurence, 1960). Its heavy

The ducking stool was used to punish a variety of minor "crimes."

use continued even as communities developed because it seemed to provide the only sure means of ridding the community of troublesome and offensive characters, while at the same time satisfying the desire for vengeance. Additionally, it displayed the power of the rulers and what would happen to those who challenged their authority. As far back as the time of Moses, the state's right over the individual in capital cases was recognized (Laurence, 1960).

### CAPITAL PUNISHMENT HAS A LONG HISTORY
The earliest recorded use of execution is in Ancient China where beheading was the prescribed method. In early Egypt and Assyria offenders were also beheaded and some were ordered to kill themselves, usually by taking poison. The oldest recorded death sentence can be found in the Amherst papyri, which included an account of the trial of a state criminal in Egypt in 1500 B.C. The condemned offender was found guilty of using "magic" and sentenced to death. In England capital punishment arose about 450 B.C. At that time condemned offenders were thrown into a quagmire to die (Laurence, 1960).

From the time of the Norman Conquest in the eleventh century through the seventeenth century, the death penalty was frequently combined with estate forfeiture, thereby resulting in the impoverishment of the offender's family. All felonies and high and petty treasons were capital crimes. In fact, from 1688 to 1820 the number of capital offenses in England soared from 50 to more than 200. Many of these were enacted to protect property (Mackay, 1985). Early on, there were two ways to escape the death/forfeiture penalty. One was by refusing to go to trial and instead be pressed to death by giant stones. This saved the family's property from forfeiture. The second was to have the case transferred to an ecclesiastical court (benefit of clergy),[1] which did not have the power to impose the death penalty except in cases of heresy (Greek, 1992). Over time, the second option was curtailed as more crimes were designated "felonies without benefit of clergy."

During this era, the large number of capital crimes led England's criminal code to be called the "Bloody Code." However, the death sentence was not meted out to all individuals convicted of capital crimes. Mackay (1985) asserts that it would have been socially and politically unacceptable to impose the death sentence in all possible cases. In

fact, if it had been used indiscriminately its credibility would have been questioned and public acceptance of the law could have been threatened (Ekirch, 1987). Therefore, the courts actually circumvented the severity of these laws by using a great deal of discretion regarding the death sentence and transportation (discussed later in this chapter) to apportion sentences so as to achieve the proper mixture of example, deterrence, and retribution. Thus, even during a period when execution was more acceptable and as many as 200 offenses were capital crimes, public opinion did not permit full imposition of this penalty (Mackay, 1985).

### THE METHODS OF EXECUTION WERE LIMITED ONLY BY THE IMAGINATION
Historically, methods of execution have been limited only by human imagination and ingenuity and have included flaying alive, boiling in oil, crushing beneath the wheels of vehicles or feet of elephants, throwing to wild beasts, compulsory combat in the arena, burying alive, blowing from the mouth of a cannon, impaling, piercing with javelins, starving to death, poisoning, strangulation, suffocation, drowning, shooting, and, more recently, electrocution, the gas chamber, and lethal injection. The severity of the execution was often based on factors such as the social class of the offender or the degree to which the crime offended the ruling powers.

Methods or devices for making beheading more humane included those by which the blade fell of its own weight and would cut through the neck cleanly. The most notable of these was the guillotine which had its greatest use during the French revolution (1793–1794) when more than 1255 persons were executed (Laurence, 1960).

Before the modern era, an offender's death would often be preceded by excruciating torture. Thus, during the reign of Elizabeth I, in the sixteenth century, the penalty for treason was death preceded by drawing and quartering. Traitors were dragged to the gallows tied to the tail of a horse, hanged by the neck until nearly dead, then cut down and while still alive had their bellies slit open and entrails cut out and burned by the executioner. They were decapitated and their bodies were cut into four quarters and then displayed in public (Laurence, 1960).

The most widely used form of execution has been hanging, which has been used since ancient times to the present.

**Historically executions, such as this hanging, were done in public. Today some people feel they should be televised.**

With the "progress" of humankind, there has been a demand for more humane methods of execution. The invention of the electric chair was one such innovation. Electrocution was developed simultaneously in the United States and Germany in the late 1800s. In the United States, it was adopted in New York in 1888. Today, as noted in Chapter 2, the death penalty has been abolished in 43% of the world's countries and in the rest its use is limited to murderers or wartime offenders (Amnesty International, 1992).

### Mutilation and Dismemberment Were Employed for Retribution, Deterrence, and Incapacitation

Mutilation and dismemberment have been justified on a number of grounds throughout history. They were employed early in connection with the *lex talionis*. If someone injured or cut off the hand of another, that person was to suffer the same fate. This was considered retribution and an equitable way of resolving the conflict. Later, it was used for purposes of both deterrence and incapacitation.

Dismemberment and mutilation as punishment for crimes date from the Egyptians who removed the tongues of those who betrayed state secrets, cut off the hands of forgers and counterfeiters, and castrated rapists. These punishments were employed to fit the crime and to try to prevent its reoccurrence (Wines, 1895). The Code of Hammurabi, which had as its prime objectives the restoration of equity, frequently stipulated that the offender be mutilated. The level of punishment depended on the status of the offender relative to the victim (Adams, Barlow, Kleinfeld, Smith, and Wootten, 1968).

In England, beginning in the 9th century, the codes promulgated by Alfred, Athesltan, and Canute revoked a 4th century ban on mutilation instituted by Constantine of Rome. Punishments became more severe and mutilation was practiced in every form (Pike, 1873-1876). King Canute's use of mutilation was designed to provide a humane substitute for capital punishment. During this era it was common to see men with their tongues cut out or missing limbs. They served as examples of what would befall others committing even petty crimes (Pike, 1873–76). When the Normans gained control of England from the Danes in 1066 they also used mutilation. They believed that it was a more effective punishment than executions because those who were maimed served as warnings to potential criminals (Wines, 1895).

Mutilation began declining by the middle of the thirteenth century (Bellamy, 1973), and during the fourteenth and fifteenth centuries it was uncommon. At the time of the Tudors (1485–1603), the practice of mutilation experienced a renaissance, and the cutting off of ears and hands again became common. Although mutilation has not been used as a punishment in most countries, Amnesty International reports that it continues to be employed in several Muslim countries including Iran, Iraq, Saudi Arabia, Yemen, and in the Sudan (Amnesty International, 1990, 1991, 1992).

## BANISHMENT WAS A MEANS OF EXILING OR ENSLAVING UNDESIRABLES

■

Banishment is an alternative to the death penalty because it has the same result: It rids the community of the offender (Wines, 1895). Among the oldest forms of punishment, **banishment** has historically included both temporary and permanent exclusion from the community, and enslavement or exile of offenders to a penal colony (Oppenheimer, 1913/1975). In primitive societies, those violating a group's major taboos could be outlawed and lose their place in the group. This expulsion could result in injury, loss of possessions, and even death (Johnson, 1988). In ancient Greece permanent banishment was used for serious crimes in lieu of the

death penalty. An exile of ten years was imposed for lesser crimes (Wines, 1895).

## Outlawry: Robin Hood, Fact or Fiction?

The practice of outlawry goes back to about the fourth century in England. Outlaws were men and women who either fled from justice (failed to appear in court to face the charges against them) or had been banished to the wilderness, which became their "penal colony" (Ives, 1914/1970). Their property was forfeited to the king, they could be killed by anyone, and their children were also viewed as outlaws. They could only return to the community by securing a royal pardon (Bellamy, 1973).

During medieval times, outlaws banded together for camaraderie and, unlike the Robin Hood legend, to accomplish criminal objectives. Since most citizens were armed during this period, outlaws had to band together to overcome resistance. Many criminals indicted by local juries failed to appear in court and were subject to pursuit by sheriffs, bounty hunters, and those with grudges against them. When these methods failed to secure justice, medieval kings resorted to "the use of the purse" (i.e., they allowed outlaws to purchase a pardon by either a monetary payment or performance of some service).

By the 1400s being declared an outlaw became less of a hardship. Instead of taking to the woods and becoming professional robbers, some hid out with friends until a pardon could be secured, while others moved a distance away and continued their trades. The penalty of outlawry was not abolished in England until 1938. In the United States, North Carolina had an outlaw statute until 1970. In that year, three escaped prisoners from a county jail were declared outlaws by a court, which made them vulnerable to be killed by any citizen if they resisted apprehension. They were eventually captured peacefully and returned to custody (Walker, 1973).

## Enslavement of Criminals Amounted to Banishment

Slaves in ancient civilizations were acquired in a variety of ways: as prisoners of war, as defaulters on debts, and as criminals. In the Greek city-state of Athens, serious offenders could be banished and enslaved if they violated certain conditions (e.g., if they failed to pay a required tax). In the Roman Empire, most lower class offenders were sentenced for life at hard labor in the Imperial mines, which, in effect, made them slaves. The more fortunate worked on public projects such as building and repairing roads or in state factories (Sellin, 1976). During the Middle Ages penal servitude was revived to relieve labor shortages, to reduce the more brutal punishments used to control crime, and to go beyond merely punishing offenders.

## Maritime Nations Subjected Offenders to Penal Slavery at the Oars

**Galleys** were oar-driven ships used in commerce and warfare for hundreds of years until the seventeenth century by Mediterranean nations. Galley slaves sat four to six per seat in the waist of the boat on benches, manning large oars requiring much strength and skill (Sellin, 1976; Ives, 1914/ 1970).

> Above and between the groups of oarsmen were raised plank-paths, along which walked boatswains or warders, with heavy whips with which they could reach the bare backs of the rowers (Ives, 1914/1970, pp. 102– 103).

In Europe during the Middle Ages, the galley was a major repository for convicts and other undesirables. The value of galleys declined with the discovery of the Americas because they were unsuitable for long ocean voyages. Many nations continued to use them for regional forays because they were cheap to build and operate. Even the land-locked states of Europe (e.g., Switzerland) used galley servitude to deal with criminals by sending them to the French, Venetian, Spanish, and Genoese galleys (Sellin, 1976; Bamford, 1973).

## Some Convicts Were Housed in Facilities Called Bagnes

**Bagnes** were secure stockades established at seaports to house slaves and others. By the 1600s, bagnes began to be used to hold crippled galley convicts while they were in port (Bamford, 1973)[a]. Some bagnes were transformed into "workhouses" so these convicts could contribute to their self-support. However, physical problems did not allow many of these men to work effectively. Since the

government had contracted with businesses to provide workers in these facilities, galley oarsmen who were in port began to be pressed into service and these bagnes became workhouse prisons. The facilities operated on a lease arrangement with businessmen with the state providing the factory building, inmate housing, food, and clothing. The contractor's only expense was a small wage paid to the convicts and they received all profits from the goods produced. Convict labor solved the industrialist's two major problems. Absenteeism was eliminated since convicts were housed where they worked, and discipline was improved because convicts could be punished in ways that free men could not.

Although convicts in the bagnes worked daily from dawn to dusk, it was a great improvement over galleys and jails. The work was typically sedentary and compensation enabled workers to supplement their daily ration. Once assigned to a bagne, an oarsman was unlikely to return to galley service. By the time bagnes developed, galley use was decreasing and all but disappeared by 1800 in France, Italy, and Spain. In these countries, bagnes served as a transition from the galleys to prisons.

**THE FRENCH BAGNES WERE FORERUNNERS OF INDUSTRIAL-TYPE PRISONS**   In France by the mid-1700s, most convicts were sent to one of four bagnes. Although most confinement during this era was bad, the bagnes cared for their inmates because they needed them to work.

At two of the French facilities in the late 1700s, Toulon (2500) and Rochefort (1000+), inmates were housed on decommissioned galleys or hulks. However, at Brest, a large three-story prison building that held 1880 inmates was constructed. This is significant since, by comparison, the largest American prisons, Auburn and Sing-Sing, had each held fewer than 700 inmates as late as 1850. Although some textbooks, notably Barnes and Teeters (1943), have viewed the prison as an American invention, this is a gross oversimplification of its historical origins. The characteristics of the bagnes, particularly the one at Brest, were similar to American industrial prisons. They employed inmates for state profit as well as to reform them. The major differences were that inmates in bagnes were housed in dormitories, not cells, and there was no rule of silence (Bamford, 1973).

Transportation replaced bagnes in France by the mid 1800s as the method for punishing most offenders. Since Italy had no colonies to which to transport its offenders, bagnes were used there until 1889 when they were replaced by cellular prisons (Sellin, 1976).

## TRANSPORTATION WAS AN INTERMEDIATE PUNISHMENT

As early as the fifteenth century, Spain and Portugal shipped convicts to colonies and distant military settlements. However, they abandoned this practice because they needed these men on the galleys (Rusche and Kirchheimer, 1939/1957). England became the first country during the early modern period, which dates from the sixteenth century onward, to systematically ship offenders to its colonies.

### The English System of Transportation

England pioneered the establishment of workhouses, but rather than adapt this system to incarcerate felons, it chose to transport them to its new American colonies. Magistrates were given authority to exile rogues and vagabonds and by 1615 less serious offenders who were sentenced to death were eligible. Thus, transportation served as an intermediate punishment between execution and lesser sanctions such as whipping or pillorying.

**INCREASED CRIME PRODUCED BY SOCIAL AND ECONOMIC CONDITIONS CAUSED A PUBLIC OUTCRY FOR SOLUTIONS**  The widespread use of this sanction began with the Transportation Act of 1718. It was passed to deal with an alarming increase in crime caused by the disorganizing effects of the transition from medieval to modern times. The reduced need for farm workers, along with insufficient industrial development and a doubling of the population during a 100-year period, produced high unemployment. These displaced workers were responsible for increased crime (Ekirch, 1987).[b]

Parliament, pressured to do something about crime, chose transportation rather than expanding their workhouses or using more capital punishment. Although there were well over 200 capital offenses on the books, public support for and the willingness of magistrates to impose capital punishment had declined precipitously (Hughes, 1987).

Imprisonment did not gain favor because of its high costs and the fear that it might be used by a tyrant to subjugate the nation.

Transportation was the perfect solution because it had none of the drawbacks of other alternatives. Undesirables were not supposed to be able to return and prey on English society, the costs were minimal, and it provided a source of labor for the new developing colonies (Ekirch, 1987). By removing offenders from their old companions and surroundings it was thought their energies would be absorbed in useful physical work, old habits broken, and useful trades and new lives acquired (Van der Zee, 1985). From 1718 to 1769, 69.5% of the almost 17,000 felons convicted at the Old Bailey in London were sentenced to transportation, 15.5% were executed, and the remainder were given lesser punishments. Capital felons subject to transportation served fourteen-year terms; other felons served seven years. Most convicts were male, unskilled, from the lower classes, and had likely been driven to crime by economic necessity. Nevertheless, it is estimated that one-fifth to one-third of this population was female (Ekirch, 1987; Blumenthal, 1962).

**THE INDENTURE SYSTEM: WHITE SERVITUDE IN COLONIAL AMERICA**  Before proceeding, we need to clarify the system of white servitude prevailing in the colonies prior to the Revolution because transported convicts were part of this population. The system of indentured servitude provided colonists with needed labor at about one-quarter the cost of a free man. They also tended to be more obedient and dependable workers since the penalties for sassing a boss or running away were severe. Thus, for the period of servitude the indentured servant was a slave (Van der Zee, 1985). This practice involved two types of individuals. First, there were those who came voluntarily. They basically exchanged their labor for the cost of being transported to the Americas. The second major group came involuntarily and included criminals and others (e.g., those who were shanghaied) (Ives, 1914/1970; Smith, 1947/1965). Regardless of how they came, all were considered "slaves" for the term of their indenture. In total, these people represented half (30,000 to 50,000) of all the colonists coming to this country from the early 1600s to the 1700s (Van der Zee, 1985; Blumenthal, 1962).

Convicts awaiting shipment to the colonies were detained in gaols (jails) up to six months or more

**Chained neck to neck and hand to hand, these prisoners were led through the streets to Blackfriars Stairs, where they were taken aboard a barge and carried down the river to the vessel which was to transport them to America.**

under notoriously unhealthy conditions (Ekirch, 1987). Those surviving the gaol were weakened for the arduous trip to the ships and the voyage to the colonies.

Once on the ships, the government cared little about what happened to the convicts. Private contractors transported them to the colonies in exchange for selling their labor for the duration of their sentence. Their voyage differed little from that experienced by African slaves. They were chained below deck in damp, cramped quarters with little fresh air or light with disease posing an ever-present problem. Mortality rates ranged from 10% to 15% in the early years but with improved conditions the death rate dropped to 5%. All colonies received convicts, however, the majority went to Virginia and Maryland. Some also went to other British Colonies in the West Indies.

The sale of convicts and other servants was likened to cattle auctions. Convicts were purchased for all types of agricultural, retail, and industrial work. Women were less valuable because they could not perform heavy labor and might get pregnant and not work for at least six months.

However, since the colonies had a shortage of females, these women "contributed much to make life a bit more tolerable by becoming the wives, mistresses, or even merely existing as amiable parts of the Colonies" (Smith, 1947/1965, p. 274).

Like slaves, the life of indentured servants was harsh. They were the private property of their masters and could be bought and sold, treated harshly, whipped, or placed in iron collars and chains when unruly. Sizable numbers attempted to escape and most were successful. Apprehended escapees were punished by having their servitude extended (Ekirch, 1987). If women became pregnant, either by liaisons with servants or by submitting to their masters' sexual demands, their servitude was increased by up to a year to compensate their masters for lost time due to childbearing.

The practice of indentured servitude made colonization less difficult. However, this does not justify the practice nor the cruelty of many masters, or the kidnapping of innocent victims to bring as servants to the colonies. For the British, the transportation of convicts provided a cheap and easy means of dealing with their criminal population.

Despite colonists' fears of the dangers posed by these criminals, life in America provided many fewer opportunities for property crime. This probably meant that these felons rarely ran afoul of the law (Smith, 1947/1965).

**THE REVOLUTION CAUSED A CRISIS IN ENGLAND'S PUNISHMENT SYSTEM** The outbreak of the American Revolution had a devastating effect on English corrections. It meant that fewer convicts could be shipped to the American colonies, and other methods of dealing with the convict population were not in place (Ekirch, 1987). Although more than 200 offenses still carried the death penalty, its implementation was still not tolerated in large numbers (Ekirch, 1987). However, judges still viewed gallows as an effective deterrent for serious offenders and as robberies and burglaries mounted so did the execution of the most recalcitrant of these offenders (Beattie, 1987).

**CONFINEMENT AT HARD LABOR WAS SUBSTITUTED FOR TRANSPORTATION: FLOATING PRISONS EMERGED AS A TEMPORARY EXPEDIENT** The Hulks Act of 1776 specified that convicts were to be put to work at hard labor on the Thames River raising sand, gravel, and soil and cleaning the water and banks. These convicts were housed aboard two **"hulks"** (broken-down and abandoned war vessels and transport ships) that were transformed into nautical prisons. These hulks were overcrowded, poorly ventilated, unsanitary, and could not handle the number of individuals being sentenced. This forced judges to sentence potential transportees to terms in the gaols and workhouses, which also quickly became overcrowded since they were not designed for long-term imprisonment. In 1779, Parliament passed an act authorizing the construction of two penitentiaries, but the cost of construction made them unaffordable. Instead, the government put more hulks into service despite a death rate aboard these ships of more than one-third of the 5792 inmates confined between 1776–1795 (Branch-Johnson, 1957).

Peak use of the hulks occurred between 1823 and 1844 when ten hulks held close to 5000 convicts in England. Conditions aboard these hulks (e.g., poor sanitation, a starvation diet, harsh discipline) led convicts to use the phrase "hell upon earth" to describe them (Branch-Johnson, 1957). Their demise, like other punishments, was gradual and primarily due to the discovery of Australia.

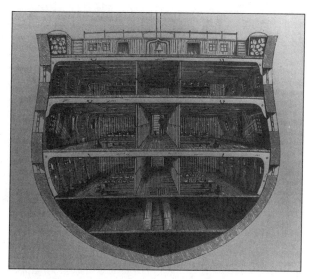

This sectional view of the hulk "Defence" shows how a warship was transformed into a floating prison.

**ENGLAND SEARCHES FOR ALTERNATIVES TO THE PRISON HULKS** During the late 1700s while hulks were being stuffed with convicts, transportation of convicts to a remote location was still being sought with cost as the key factor in site selection. Various West African locations were suggested as was Australia, which was later chosen. However, as our "Close-Up: Lemain: The Historical Antecedent of *'Escape from New York'* " suggests, other ideas were considered first.

**TRANSPORTATION TO AUSTRALIA: THE SEARCH FOR A NEW DUMPING GROUND** After rejecting various African locations, Australia, which had been newly discovered, was chosen because it had a healthy climate, conditions suitable to agricultural development, and was too far for felons to return easily (Mackay, 1985). While convicts were shipped to America to assist in developing existing colonies, in Australia the majority of colonists were to be convicts. Beyond getting rid of the convicts, little thought was given to how this would be accomplished. As with other knee-jerk reactions, it was doomed to disaster for several reasons. The plan called for the creation of a subsistence economy based on communal farming developed and worked by inmates under government supervision. However, there were two problems: No supervisors were supplied, which meant using convict overseers; and no thought was given to selecting convicts—about 4400 arrived between

## Close Up    Lemain: The Historical Antecedent of *"Escape from New York"*

The 1981 movie *Escape from New York* was set in 1997. The movie centers around the hijacking and crash of Air Force One—with the president on board—into the middle of Manhattan Island, which had been converted into a top-security penal colony. A 400% increase in crime prompted its establishment as a permanent prison for recalcitrant offenders unable to live in society. Those entering were given a choice of death or placement on the island for life. There were no guards; the only system of control was that developed by the inmates. Escape was prevented by a 50-foot-high wall surrounding the island and all bridges and waterways were mined. A federal police force patrolled the island's perimeter and anyone attempting to escape that failed to heed the warning to return was shot.

While the above is a fictional account, in 1785 a plan was advanced to place convicts on the island of Lemain—known today as MacCarthy Island—which was 400 miles up the Gambia river in what was then the British West African colony of Gambia. The plan was to transport 150 convicts with enough provisions for six months and some goods to be used for trading. To prevent escape, a private armed ship was to be stationed down river to provide security. The island was fertile and crops could be produced within four months of occupancy. The premise was that if the convicts were left to their own devices, and prevented from escaping they would quickly become planters of cotton, tobacco, indigo, and yams. While realizing in the first year many convicts would die due to the change of climate, it was believed that as the colony became more stable and more convicts arrived, the food supply would improve and eventually 4000 transportees could be accommodated. As the settlement developed the convicts would form their own government, grow prosperous, and therefore become honest and ultimately would return home reformed and upstanding citizens. Thus, in the same way that their old lifestyle in England had corrupted these offenders, exposure to this pristine environment would have a purifying effect. The economics of this solution favored its initiation, however, it was never implemented due to the potentially high death rate resulting from the region's unhealthy climate and the fear that landing criminals among the African natives would trigger a massacre—who died would depend on if the convicts were armed (Ekirch, 1987; Mackay, 1985). One wonders if this idea would have been initiated if Australia had been unavailable as a depository for convicts.

The idea of isolating convicts on a deserted island continues to be raised. Reflect for a moment on the pros and cons of this arrangement as a permanent placement for recalcitrant offenders, those to be executed, or serial sex offenders.

1788 to 1791—who had the farming and construction skills to survive in and develop this new land.

While the first shipment of convicts was transported under government control, private contractors were subsequently used and paid per convict transported. This made the 3½- to 8-month trip disastrous since contractors were initially permitted to carry as many convicts as possible and were provided no incentive to keep the convicts healthy. Thus, a large number of convicts died. To improve convict conditions, some ships had government-appointed doctors to supervise convict health and a payment plan was initiated under which three-quarters of the fee was paid on embarkation and the rest when convicts landed in decent health. This dropped the death rate to about 1% (Hughes, 1987).

*The Establishment of a Colony in Australia Was a Monumental Task* In 1788, after an 8½-month, 15,000-mile journey, the bedraggled first fleet arrived in Australia. Trouble began immediately because most convicts were unskilled and not able to do the tasks needed to develop a colony and the military refused to supervise them (Hughes, 1987; Hirst, 1983). By the end of six months, a structure for convict labor and status evolved. Convicts were employed on government projects (e.g., road building, farming) under convict overseers. Also, some convicts were assigned to free settlers, who had undertaken the development of private farms.

Under the Australian system, convicts served a fixed term and then became free. Those serving the majority of their sentences on the hulks before shipment to Australia were eligible for release after a year. If they wanted to farm they were granted 30 or more acres of land and convicts to help them. By 1791, the colony had a new major social grouping, "the settlers," which was largely comprised of ex-convicts. In time, no distinction was made between those settlers who had been convicts and those who had always been free (Hirst, 1983).[c]

The key to development of the colony was the convict assignment system. It was economical because it shifted responsibility for feeding, clothing, and housing of convicts to private citizens. It also induced prosperous free settlers to consider immigrating because of the lure of free convict labor.

The large farms in Australia were structured similarly to plantations in the pre–Civil War South except convicts were not slaves. Many convicts working for small farmers and tradesmen were sometimes considered partners and/or treated like family, particularly by ex-convict settlers. Some were rewarded with a share of the crop or were given a plot of land to work for their own benefit. However, the conditions under which these convicts served their sentence varied enormously, often depending on their master's disposition. Hirst (1983) asserts that convicts' treatment depended on their disposition as well. Ten to 20% of the convicts were incorrigible and were controlled by flogging or by placement on chain gangs or in penal colonies.

*A New Society Developed from a Colony of Convicts* About 24,000 women were transported to Australia between 1788 and 1852 (Hirst, 1983). Although the government did not formally announce that women were sent for breeding and sexual conveniences, this was implicit in the policies guiding early requests for female convicts. Thus, the colony's first governor requested more women convicts because he wanted them to marry and raise native-born families who would provide the base for an agricultural society of small farms. In the early years women were assigned as mistresses, which was akin to a "mail-order bride" system. Pressure from the evangelical lobby ended this practice, however.

Despite the unfavorable portrait of convict women, many were able to raise children who were a credit to the community. The population of native-born children grew rapidly and schools were established to facilitate their development. The first generation of native children were the most law-abiding, morally conservative people in the country. The

legacy of the convict system was not criminality but its opposite—repulsion from it. Between 1833 and 1838 only 4% of convicts under sentence were native born (Hughes, 1987). Thus, a new society developed from what was largely a convict population. Ex-convicts held positions of trust in government and the private sector. They were lawyers, teachers, magistrates, constables, superintendents, and owners of large enterprises and farms (Hirst, 1987).

Class distinctions existed among wealthy and free families as well as those having ex-convict/emancipist origins. However, there was general agreement not to use the term "convict" because of the permanent degradation implicit in this label. Convicts were called "government men" and assigned as servants, and ex-convicts were referred to as emancipists or free men (Hirst, 1983).

*Tickets of Leave and Pardons Were Issued as Rewards for Good Service* The most enticing reward for convicts was to be released from their sentences, which, in Australia, occurred in three ways. The first was an absolute pardon—rarely given—from the governor, which restored all rights including return to England. The second was a conditional pardon, which gave the convict citizenship in the colony but no right to return to England. The third was a **ticket of leave,** which did not end their sentences but freed convicts from their obligation to work for the government or a master. They could work as free agents, for wages, as long as they remained in the colony until their sentences ended and they committed no crimes.

In time, the "ticket" was considered a reward and issued for various types of good behavior until about 1820 when a more structured system was initiated. The worst thing a master could do to convicts was to stop them from getting their tickets. This was sometimes done by unscrupulous masters to retain a skilled convict worker. Freed ex-convicts were granted a small farm and during the early years about one-third took this opportunity (Hirst, 1983).

*Several Punishments Were Used on Those Who Failed to Conform to the Dictates of Colonial Life* Many convicts lacked the self-restraint to resist the temptations of working in an open confinement setting. The lash and penal colonies served as sanctions to motivate those not eager to work (Hirst, 1983).

The first penal colony was Norfolk Island where both convicts and soldiers committing offenses in Sydney were sent. Newcastle, established in 1801, was the first mainland penal colony in Australia. Here refractory convicts worked in gangs cutting timber, mining coal under extremely inhumane conditions, and producing lime to be used for mortar (Hughes, 1987). Short of execution, assignment to these colonies was the most dreaded punishment for crimes committed in Australia.

In 1824 Norfolk Island was reopened as a last resort penal colony for the absolute worst convicts because its location 400 miles from New Zealand made it escape-proof. Commandants were granted absolute control over the lives of the convicts. These convicts, unlike mainland offenders, forfeited all claims to protections of law and were not entitled to sentence reduction. All offenders served a minimum of 10 years. In the next chapter, we will see how Alexander Maconochie transformed this prison into a model institution in 1840.

*Transportation Was Abandoned in Stages*   The abandonment of transportation began in the 1830s prompted by growing propaganda in England that it was not being punitive enough and had little deterrent effect. In 1847 England began placing offenders in prison and then on public work gangs. They were then exiled to Western Australia, which had acute labor needs. Pressure from other colonies forced Britain to discontinue this practice entirely in 1868. More than 160,000 convicts and exiles were shipped to Australia during the 80-year period during which transportation was in effect.

Although transportation to Australia had its virtues and defects, for years it was a secondary or intermediate punishment. That is, it offered the only alternative to execution in a country that refused to expend funds to construct long-term prisons (Shaw, 1966). For Australia, the end of transportation also meant the sublimation of its convict heritage. It was not until after World War II that Australians "could speak levelly and without shame about the convict origins of their country" (Hirst, 1983, p. 217). While much of the treatment of convicts was cruel and often barbaric, what happened in Australia was truly remarkable. An almost exclusively convict population took an undeveloped land and created a functioning society.

## The French Transportation System Was More Harsh Than the English System

The French initiated their transportation system during the 1700s when they sent some convicts, including women, to the Louisiana territory. This phase was short lived and transportation was not renewed until 1852 when 2000 bagne prisoners were sent to penal colonies in Guiana, on the northeast coast of South America (Rickards, 1968). At these colonies, conditions were incredibly brutal and were only exceeded by those found in the Siberian penal colonies in Russia. These French colonies were in an area of high temperature and tropical rains, thus inmates were plagued by yellow fever, marsh fevers, fatal anemia, and dysentery. These conditions, combined with the work in the jungles from dawn to dark, produced a mortality rate averaging 25% to 32% (Wines, 1895). The penal colonies in Guiana to which most prisoners were sent were on the mainland. There were also island colonies—including Devil's Island—which were reserved for desperate cases, political prisoners, and escapees. The French maintained these inhumane colonies until World War II when they were abolished by the Free French Government (Barnes and Teeters, 1951).[d]

## The Russian Transportation System Was Considered the Most Brutal

The Russians established their major penal colonies in Siberia. They had the most brutal and degrading system of transportation and were the only major nation to continue this practice into the 1990s. Russian law mentions transportation for ridding the country of offenders as early as 1648 (Wines, 1895). Under the Czars, two major types of convict exiles were sent to Siberia. First were those sentenced for life who were considered "dead" and had forfeited all civil, political, and property rights. Their wives and families could accompany them or the wives could remain at home and remarry. The second group, the quasi-colonists, retained all civil rights. Although serving long prison terms, they could either return to European Russia or remain in Siberia on completion of their sentences.

Exile to Siberia began with the long arduous two- to three-year journey. Convicts were herded from European Russia to one filthy and overcrowded waystation or forwarding prison to another until they reached Siberia. Many perished before reaching their final destination. When they finally arrived, those convicts sentenced to forced labor worked in the gold and silver mines from dawn to dusk (Barnes and Teeters, 1951). Others worked in factories and workshops, but lack of work kept many in overcrowded, verminous, unsanitary prisons, which were more repulsive than the hard labor in the mines and qualified as the worst feature of penal servitude (Sellin, 1976).

Penal servitude was continued after the Russian Revolution by the new Soviet government. However, whereas the Czars had exiled primarily conventional criminals, the Soviets sent mainly political offenders. Under the Soviets, most conventional criminals (e.g., robbers) were placed in rehabilitative institutions, which provided inmates with cultural education and vocational training aimed at making them good citizens who could fit into the Communist State. Prior to World War II Western correctional experts visiting these correctional facilities were greatly impressed by them, especially the Bolshevo, because of their programming for young offenders (Sellin, 1976).

During the Stalin era between 3½ and 7 million people, nearly all male, entered the Siberian camps. This large workforce was a major factor in the government's ability to meet its successive five-year plans designed to make the Soviet Union into a major industrial power. Inmate labor was used to build highways and barracks, cut timber, produce oil and cement, mine gold, chromium, coal, and other ores, and operate the fisheries on the Arctic coast. Because of the inhumane conditions the death rate was very high (e.g., up to two dead for every yard dug underground).

Beginning in the late 1940s, and hastened by the death of Stalin in 1953, these penal camps were transformed and absorbed into the corrective labor colony system. However, into the late 1980s a chain of prisons, labor camps, insane asylums, and villages, called *gulags,* operated in Siberia to confine and exile those opposing the government. A. M. Rosenthal, an American reporter, toured one of these gulags, Perm 35. He talked with four prisoners, who spoke of illegal arrests and bad treatment including torture by cold. A later meeting with released prisoners from Perm 35 confirmed these practices (Rosenthal, 1989). In February 1992, the

Russian leader Boris Yeltsin announced that Perm 35 had finally been closed (Burke, 1992).

## People Continue to Advocate the Use of Transportation

Today there is little use of transportation as a means of dealing with offenders. However, some people still occasionally suggest the resurrection of this practice despite its checkered history of brutality, inhumane conditions, and slavery. In the United States, Alaska and other island outposts have been mentioned as potential penal colonies. When space travel becomes more common it is likely that someone will suggest establishing a penal colony on another planet or on the moon (a similar idea appears in some "Star Trek" episodes). Adherents of transportation argue that it allows offenders a chance to start their lives again and an opportunity to live with their families, and to support themselves and their dependents (Caldwell, 1965). Opponents of this practice assert that it is hard to find a suitable location for penal colonies and citizens living in these areas do not want penal colonies close to them. Other objections include that it is impossible to establish a normal community that is made up of criminals, children should not be raised in this environment, and their isolation encourages the use of brutal and sadistic practices (Caldwell, 1965). Thus, unless someone can develop a plan offsetting the extremely negative aspects of using penal colonies, this practice should remain a sordid facet of correctional history. However, as our Close-Up on banishment shows, history repeats itself.

## FORERUNNERS OF LONG-TERM IMPRISONMENT

Prisons as facilities where large numbers of convicted offenders are punished by being deprived of their liberty are a relatively recent development. Prisons and dungeons existed for thousands of years but were not major means of punishing offenders. Before the 1800s, jails and prisons served as detention facilities and only rarely for long-term imprisonment (Barnes, 1930/1972; Spierenburg, 1991).

---

## *Close Up* Indian Youths Banished as Punishment for Their Crimes

Two 17-year-old Alaskan Indian boys, visiting Seattle, pleaded guilty to robbing and beating a pizza delivery man with a baseball bat (Akre, 1994). These first-time offenders were allowed by a Washington State judge to face a tribal court rather than go to prison. The tribal court banished the boys to separate isolated Alaskan islands for one year to eighteen months. Each boy "would be given forks for digging up clams, axes and saws for cutting fire wood, and some food to carry them though the first 5 days. [Also] a sleeping bag and shelter, which would be equipped with a wood stove for cooking and heat" (p. 70).[5] The boys will be checked on regularly but in emergencies will have no means of contacting the outside world. Do you believe this is an appropriate punishment for first-time offenders?

---

In examining the evolution of punishment, it is important to recognize that there was no abrupt transition from corporal and capital punishment to imprisonment, as some authors have implied. Change was gradual and uneven and in the Western world this transition spanned the period from the sixteenth to the middle of the nineteenth century.

### The Roots of Imprisonment Can Be Traced to Monasteries and Asylums

Monasteries and asylums were the earliest facilities resembling prisons (Spierenburg, 1991).[e] The regimented discipline employed at monasteries and convents led them to be viewed as models for prisons. Also, parents placed children, who were often unfit for life outside, in these facilities. Medieval hospitals may also have been used for incarceration (Spierenburg, 1991). These hospitals typically functioned as a refuge for the sick, aged, homeless, and others. Dating back to the twelfth century, those with detention areas usually housed the insane. By the fifteenth century, separate institutions that resembled prisons began to be built for the insane. These "asylums" were the first facilities to confine people for relatively long periods of time. However, their charitable nature and their clientele (people not considered responsible for their actions) kept them from earning the distinction of being the first prisons. That "honor" instead went to workhouses that were developed a century later.

### Workhouses and Houses of Correction Were Early Forms of Imprisonment

**Workhouses** or houses of correction are generally considered the true forerunners of the modern prison. Their development and growth can be traced to a variety of long-term social and cultural changes that include efforts to alter the behavior of offenders through punishment and/or reform (Spierenburg, 1991). Workhouses were first established to reform those who were immoral or living in sin. This involved efforts to regulate and control bad habits—drinking, gambling, and immoral sexual behavior—through the criminalizing of offenses against morality. There was also a change in attitude toward the poor. The able-bodied poor were now seen as undeserving, which led to restrictions on begging and punishment of beggars. At first they were chased away but after workhouses developed they were confined in them and subjected to forced labor (Spierenburg, 1991). The Protestant reformation also helped accelerate the emergence of workhouses because the tenets of the Protestant ethic required that "everyone should work." This norm came to be accepted in Catholic countries as well. This fit in well with the workhouse regimen of forcing the able-bodied poor to work.

These combined developments occurred between the twelfth and fifteenth centuries and were accompanied by increased stability, peace, and the gradual development of centralized governments and justice systems. The high level of stability reinforced the focus on the poor and other marginals because they became a threat to this new social order. Banishment from one area to another became impossible because magistrates were now concerned about how these people would affect neighboring towns. Although workhouses were developed to control and reform the undeserving poor, early on they were also used to incarcerate some convicted criminals. Given the apparent refusal of criminals to work, depriving them of their liberty and reforming them through forced labor was deemed appropriate.

**BRIDEWELLS WERE THE FIRST INSTITUTIONS TO ATTEMPT REFORM**  The first workhouse in England was the **Bridewell,** an old palace donated to the city of London by Edward VI. It was renovated and opened about 1556 to deal with the increasing number of vagabonds (including beggars, prostitutes, con artists, and other petty offenders[2]) who were public nuisances and considered responsible for murders, thefts and other serious crimes. Work was the chief mode of reformation and the profits from this went toward making the facility self-sufficient. Initially, inmates were paid for their work and charged for their meals. By 1563, an apprenticeship program was initiated for delinquent children and was also open to children of poor freemen. Other English counties eventually built workhouses, often also called Bridewells.

In line with the thinking of the times, "correction" of inmates was also achieved by physical punishment. Thus, at the London Bridewell both males and females were flogged twice a week until each had received what was deemed punishment proportionate to their crimes. Flogging, restriction of diet, and placement in stocks were used to punish rule violators and those not meeting work quotas (Ives, 1914/1970; Sellin, 1976; Van der Slice, 1936).

As with many such experiments, the Bridewells achieved varying levels of success in reforming inmates. While established by national legislation, which specified that offenders be housed there and subjected to a program of reform, there was no central government oversight to make sure they met these requirements (Ives, 1914/1970). Local authorities were left to manage and fund them. As a result their quality and effectiveness varied tremendously. By the late 1600s these institutions had deteriorated and became overcrowded places of detention indistinguishable from gaols. Men, women, children, the old, the young, and serious

and minor offenders were housed together indiscriminately. Inmates made their own rules and predators preyed on the weak and innocent. Ruthless cruelty was compounded by unhygienic conditions that produced serious epidemics of gaol fever—mostly typhus—or malignant forms of dysentery. Also, food was not provided, forcing inmates to depend on the charity of family or friends to avoid starvation (Grunhut, 1948/1972; Ives, 1914/1970).

**EUROPEAN COUNTRIES ESTABLISHED WORKHOUSES[3] WITH MANY MODELED AFTER ONE IN AMSTERDAM**  On the continent the **Amsterdam Workhouse** for men opened in 1596 and the Spin House for women was established a year later. They served as models for others developed throughout Holland and other northern European areas during the 17th and 18th centuries.[4] Space precludes the discussion of all European workhouses, however, we will briefly examine the Amsterdam facilities.

The male unit confined three categories of inmates: unemployed vagrants, condemned delinquents (usually petty offenders), and individuals committed at the request of their families. When this facility opened, weaving was the primary type of work. By 1700 it was replaced by rasping, which involved reducing a hardwood log to dust, which was then boiled to extract the pigment used in dying cloth. This led these facilities to be known as "Rasphouses." Workers had quotas to produce each day. Those not meeting them were punished while overproduction was rewarded with special prison coins, which could be used to buy items in the prison store. This represented the first use of prison script and of a token economy. A policy of sentence reductions was also initiated, primarily to reward inmates who snitched (accused and testified against others involved in crimes). Good behavior could also earn an inmate early release.

The Spin House for women was initially more like a charitable asylum than a prison. However, over time it became a penal facility to punish professional beggars, prostitutes, and other petty criminals. Most women initially labored at spinning, but by the eighteenth century most worked at sewing linen.

Our Close-up on the world of early workhouses examines these facilities to determine which of their features survived over time.

## *Close Up* The World of Early Workhouses Had Many Facets

The management of workhouses approximated a household or family model. The offenders sent to these facilities were viewed as having broken away from the disciplinary restraints of family control. Thus, to reform them required a more structured environment.

To accommodate these views, management involved four levels. At the top were the town's magistrates who established the facilities and appointed a board of administrators (the second level) who managed finances and served as an internal court to judge and punish inmate rule violators. The operational administrator occupied the third level. It is here that we can use the family analogy. Known as the indoor father, he and his wife were considered the heads of this household and were viewed as surrogate parents to the inmates. The indoor father had from one to three assistants who were responsible for providing discipline, maintenance, food, other necessities, and supervision of inmates at work. On the fourth level were minor personnel, typically servants and assistants. There were no guards.

Inmates were rarely separated on arrival, suggesting they were not viewed as predisposed to aggressive behavior. While those who conceived of these facilities felt they had the best interest of the inmates in mind, the number of attempted and completed escapes suggests that inmates did not feel the same way. For example, at the Delft facility, 28% of the inmates absconded and remained at large. The frequency of escapes led Spierenburg (1991) to conclude that no day passed without some inmates thinking about it.

Subcultures typically develop whenever individuals interact in groups for any length of time. While data are scant, there were some aspects of prison subculture reported including the use of argot (special words and phrases), the use of graffiti, and tattooing. Additionally, professional criminals were accorded high status. This was possible because their extended terms enabled them to become well acquainted with all aspects of the institutions. Also, as professional criminals, they were viewed as leaders and were respected by other offenders. Their frequent escapes may have also added to their status.

---

At the beginning of the 1600s, workhouses were used primarily for beggars and vagabonds. By the mid-1600s they were used for criminals and the public viewed them as places for the punishment of convicts. Thus, according to Spierenburg, the birth of the prison can be traced to the middle of the seventeenth century, specifically to two institutions: one in Amsterdam and another in Hamburg, Germany. While small in size, rarely holding more than 100 inmates, they were of symbolic importance because they were the first facilities to imprison offenders exclusively to punish them. Their existence also showed public acceptance for this method of dealing with offenders. However, it was not until prisons developed in the United States that this penal philosophy became widespread. Before discussing prison development in the United States, we will examine two other examples in Europe that clearly anticipated modern prisons: the Hospice of San Michele in Rome, and the Maison de Force in Ghent, Belgium. The aim of these facilities was reformation, which was partly achieved by a work program. Both also had some type of classification system and cells for the separation of inmates.

**THE HOSPICE OF SAN MICHELE WAS AN EARLY JUVENILE REFORMATORY** The **Hospice of San Michele** was a composite social welfare institution that developed over several hundred years. Beginning in 1582, and continuing well into the 1700s, this institution added facilities to serve the poor, orphans of both sexes, the aged poor, delinquent boys (1703), and female offenders (1735) (Sellin, 1930). The unit for juveniles, initiated by Pope Clement XI, has historical importance because many of its ideas anticipated features that became an integral part of early adult and juvenile systems in the United States.

The program for juvenile males housed youths under age 20 convicted of crimes, and youths sent by their parents who were beyond their control or inclined toward vice. Funding for the program for convicted youth came from money made by the sale of inmate-produced goods to the church and government. Parents of incorrigible youth paid to have their children placed at this facility. For these youth, this was a cross between a military school and a juvenile institution.

The vocational training program, another unique feature, was directed by skilled artisans so that these youth could learn a trade and be better able to earn a decent living on release. Religious and moral instruction were also an integral part of this program. This emphasis was a central component of the Pennsylvania system to be discussed in the next chapter. The spartan regimen included only enough food for sustenance and this may have been used to make these youth regret the error of their ways.

The cellular design of the facility is considered to represent its most lasting contribution. A logical outgrowth of the sleeping arrangements at monasteries, convents, and Jesuit colleges, it was unique as a method of housing offenders. It influenced the design of the Maison de Force (to be discussed next) and became, in a modified form, one primary architectural model for prison cellblocks (e.g., Auburn) in the United States. Moreover, its deep impression on the noted reformer John Howard, when he visited the facility, led him to alert others by including two etchings in his book showing the exterior and a floor plan of the institution. This facility resembled a cellblock. Along each wall were three tiers with 10 cells per floor. The space running through the middle of the two rows of cells was used as a workshop. The facility for women opened in 1735 used the same design (Sellin, 1930).

On entering, incorrigible boys had their heads shaved and their street clothes were exchanged for institutional garb. They were then whipped.[6] Each was given a paternal lecture urging him to receive his punishments with a penitent spirit and change his life. He was promised release to his parents as soon as he showed he was reformed. Criminal youths were kept either until they were reformed or, failing that, until they reached the age when they could be sent to the galleys.

Those convicted of crimes worked together in silence, chained to the workbench in the central hall, at spinning and knitting tasks. Sometimes they were forced to listen to the monks reading the Bible. At night they were separately confined in small brick cells. These were the essential features of the Auburn system, which, as noted in the next chapter, became the dominant model for prisons in the United States 50 years later (Sellin, 1930; Wines, 1895).

Those in the incorrigible/disobedient group were individually confined in cells day and night without labor. These youth had visits from clergy, who lectured them and attempted to teach them Christian doctrine. This resembled an early version of the Pennsylvania system, which was experimented with at New York's Auburn Prison. Finally, whipping was used to punish youths who disobeyed the rules.

It is interesting to note that St. Michele recognized that delinquent and incorrigible youth required distinct programs. It took until the 1960s for our juvenile justice system to realize this fact.

**THE MAISON DE FORCE HAD MANY INNOVATIVE FEATURES**  The **Maison de Force,** established in 1773 by Vilain in Ghent, Belgium, was also clearly ahead of its time. It had a rudimentary classification system by which felons were separated from misdemeanants and vagrants and provided a separate section for women and one for children. Although opposed to life imprisonment, Vilain believed that offenders should be sentenced to a minimum of one year so that they could learn a trade. He also felt that offenders should be able to have their sentences reduced as a reward for good conduct. This was an early form of "good time" (Wines, 1895).

Work was the primary method of reform at this institution. It offered inmates opportunities to engage in productive occupations (e.g., weaving, shoemaking, tailoring). As incentives, inmates were allowed to keep a percentage of their earnings and could work overtime. A portion of this money was saved, to be given to the inmate on release. In this way, he would not be forced to return to a life of crime. Inmates worked together during the day, but at night they were housed separately. This facility also had a resident chaplain and a physician. Discipline in the institution was maintained by guards who used a system of graduated punishments. These punishments ranged from warnings to whippings to solitary confinement and finally to the extension of the inmate's sentence (one week was added for each day spent in the dungeon). This enlightened perspective earned Vilain the title of "father of modern penitentiary science" (Wines, 1895).

By 1783 what was once a remarkable establishment had lost much of its reformative value. A petition from private industry complaining that the prison's manufacturing operations injured their business persuaded the emperor to terminate this operation and sell the equipment. Inmates were no longer fully employed nor could they learn trades to enable them to become productive citizens on release (Howard, 1791). About 150 years later the United States succumbed to the same pressures during the Big House era, and closed most prison industries with similar consequences. At the Maison there was also a reduction in the quality and quantity of food served inmates and in maintenance of the housing units. The emperor, like others that followed him, did this under the mistaken belief that disagreeable conditions discourage inmates from future criminal acts. In truth, this usually further alienates inmates from conventional society.

---

## ENDNOTES

1. See glossary.
2. It is important to note that Bridewells were only used for misdemeanants since at this time more serious offenders were subject to corporal and capital punishment.
3. Except where otherwise noted, the discussion of the workhouse on the continent is drawn from the work of Spierenburg (1991).
4. The use of galley servitude in Southern Europe for marginals precluded the development of these facilities in these countries with the exceptions of the appearance in 1622 of a workhouse in Lyon, France, and one in Madrid, Spain. This, along with the use of transportation and the employment of offenders in public works, resulted in a delay in the adoption of imprisonment as a means of dealing with both marginal and other offenders until the later part of eighteenth and in some cases well into nineteenth century (Spierenburg, 1991).
5. This experiment came to an end in September of 1995 when problems with the tribal court and reports of inadequate supervision prompted the sentencing judge to recall the boys from the two islands to which they had been banished. One of the boys was sentenced to 55 months in prison and the other to 31 months and both received credit for 12 months on the islands. They were also required pay restitution of $35,000 to the pizza driver they injured (Banished tribal teens, 1995). Even if this experiment had been managed appropriately, the use of this form of punishment as we move toward the end of the 20th century is highly questionable.
6. It is unclear whether convicted youths were also subjected to whipping as part of the orientation process.

## ACKNOWLEDGEMENTS

[a] P.W. Bamford, *Fighting Ships and Prisons: The Mediterranean Galleys of France in the Age of Louis XIV* (University of Minnesota Press, 1973), pp. excerpts used with the permission of the publisher.
[b] *Bound for America: The transportation of British convicts to the colonies 1718–1775.* Oxford University Press Inc. ©1987. Reprinted by permission of Oxford University Press.
[c] J.B. Hirst, *Convict society and its enemies.* Sydney, Australia: George Allen and Unwin. ©1983 Reprinted with the permission of the publisher.
[d] Barnes/Teeters, *New Horizons in Criminology, 2/e,* ©1951, Reprinted by permission of Prentice-Hall, Inc., Upper Saddle River, NJ 07458.
[e] Pieter Spierenburg, *The Prison Experience,* ©1991 by Pieter Spierenburg. Reprinted by permission of Rutgers University Press.

## CHAPTER RECAP

### Punishment of Early Criminal Behavior
Early Societies Had Two Classes of Crimes
    Public Wrongs Were Equated with Sin
    Private Wrongs Initially Required Individual Retaliation But Later Some Responsibility Shifted to the Group
    Compensation Provided a Bridge Between Private Vengeance and the State
Crimes Become Acts of Revolt Against the King

### Historically Offenders Were Punished in Various Ways
Magic and Curses Were Used as Punishments
Some Punishments were Designed to Humiliate the Offender
    Gags Were Used to Both Shame and Constrain Verbal Abuse
    The Stocks and Pillories Served to Confine and Display Offenders
    Branding Marked a Person as an Offender
Corporal Punishments Inflicted Pain on the Offender
    Whipping Has a Long and Extensive History
    The Ducking Stool Was Generally Used for Scolds and Gossips

Capital Punishment Rids the Community of the Of-
fender
Capital Punishment Has a Long History
The Methods of Execution Were Limited Only by the
Imagination
Mutilation and Dismemberment Were Employed for
Retribution, Deterrence, and Incapacitation
**Banishment Was a Means of Exiling or Enslaving
Undesirables**
Outlawry: Robin Hood, Fact or Fiction?
Enslavement of Criminals Amounted to Banishment
Maritime Nations Subjected Offenders to Penal Slavery
at the Oars
Some Convicts Were Housed in Facilities Called Bagnes
The French Bagnes Were Forerunners of Industrial-
Type Prisons
**Transportation Was an Intermediate Punishment**
The English System of Transportation
Increased Crime Produced by Social and Economic
Conditions Caused a Public Outcry for Solutions
The Indenture System: White Servitude in Colonial
America
The Revolution Caused a Crisis in England's Punish-
ment System
Confinement at Hard Labor Was Substituted for
Transportation: Floating Prisons Emerged as a
Temporary Expedient
England Searches for Alternatives to the Prison
Hulks
Transportation to Australia: The Search for a New
Dumping Ground
The Establishment of a Colony in Australia Was
a Monumental Task
A New Society Developed from a Colony of
Convicts
Tickets of Leave and Pardons Were Issued as
Rewards for Good Service
Several Punishments Were Used on Those Who
Failed to Conform to the Dictates of Colonial Life
Transportation Was Abandoned in Stages
The French Transportation System Was More Harsh
Than the English System
The Russian Transportation System Was Considered
the Most Brutal
People Continue to Advance the Use of Transportation
**Forerunners of Long-Term Imprisonment**
The Roots of Imprisonment Can Be Traced to Monaster-
ies and Asylums
Workhouses and Houses of Correction Were Early
Forms of Imprisonment
Bridewells Were the First Institutions to Attempt Re-
form
European Countries Established Workhouses with
Many Modeled After The One in Amsterdam
The Hospice of San Michele Was an Early Juvenile
Reformatory
The Maison de Force Had Many Innovative Features

## REVIEW QUESTIONS

**1.** What were the differences between public and private wrongs and how were these handled in early societies?
**2.** What role did compensation play in the reduction of
blood feuds?
**3.** What were the major purposes of the stocks and pillories in the punishment of offenders?
**4.** Discuss the use of whipping as a punishment for
criminal behavior. What justifications have been used
to support its use in the United States?
**5.** Discuss the use of capital punishment from a historical perspective.
**6.** Discuss galley servitude and the subsequent development of the bagnes.
**7.** Compare and contrast use of transportation to
American colonies with transportation to Australia.
**8.** Identify and describe the early forerunners of long-
term imprisonment.

## TEST YOUR KNOWLEDGE

**1.** Early preliterate societies brutally punished taboo
violators primarily to
  **a.** placate supernatural powers.
  **b.** rehabilitate offenders.
  **c.** deter future deviance.
  **d.** make an example of nonconformists.
**2.** An early practice wherein an offender or his clan
offered an economic settlement to the victim in order to
avoid revenge was known as
  **a.** retribution.
  **b.** compensation.
  **c.** lex talionis.
  **d.** endogamy.
**3.** Bridles were used primarily as punishments for
  **a.** drunkards
  **b.** vagabonds
  **c.** scolds
  **d.** prostitutes
**4.** The early British practice of sending convicts to the
American colonies came to an end as a result of
  **a.** the War of 1812.
  **b.** increasing African slave trade.
  **c.** the increasing use of capital punishment in England.
  **d.** the American Revolution.
**5.** Which of the following institutions had juvenile programs?
  **a.** Maison de Force
  **b.** Bagnes
  **c.** Hospice of St. Michele
  **d.** All of them

# CHAPTER 4

Marching in Lock-Step.

# THE DEVELOPMENT OF PRISONS IN THE UNITED STATES

The last chapter traced the development and employment of different forms of punishment through the eighteenth century. Although imprisonment was used for some offenders, its development as a primary means of punishment did not occur until after the American Revolution. This chapter traces the evolution of imprisonment in the United States to the end of the nineteenth century. To set the stage for this discussion, we briefly examine the forms of punishment employed in colonial America.

## Methods of Punishment during the Colonial Period

Corporal and capital punishment were commonly employed for most offenses. During the 1700s, criminal codes specified a variety of punishments including fines and whippings, banishment, and hanging. Branding was also used (e.g., having a letter burned on a visible part of the body) to identify strangers and community members who had committed crimes. This, along with forms of public ridicule (e.g., stocks, pillory) served as an important social control mechanism in tight-knit communities where people were concerned about their reputations with their neighbors (Rothman, 1971).[a]

Incarceration was an uncommon practice and was never used as the sole form of punishment. Jails held people awaiting trial, those who were sentenced but not punished, and debtors. A few workhouses also existed, but were used primarily as a deterrent to idle strangers, beggars, and pilferers, who, if apprehended, could also be whipped and put to hard labor.

## The Search for New Methods of Social Control after the Revolution

Following the American Revolution, which ended in 1783, the social, economic, and intellectual forces that created this nation led to a reassessment of British methods of social control (Rothman, 1971). Understanding and devising methods to control abnormal behavior would be the first step toward creating a new social system that would bind citizens together and provide a new social organization. New ideas of penal reform, espoused by Cesare Becarria, founder of the classical school of criminology, were adopted. He asserted that the causes of crime and other forms of deviant behavior could be traced to the nature of the antiquated colonial criminal codes. Beccaria's (1764/1963) views on laws and punishment influenced the framing of post-Colonial laws. He felt that to prevent crimes:

> laws must be clear . . .; punishment should be based on the extent of harm that the act causes society . . . [and] used only . . . on the supposition that it prevents crime. . . . Punishment for each crime should be inevitable, prompt and public [and it] . . . should be severe enough to override any pleasure that accrues from the criminal acts (p. 94).

Americans believed a more rational system of crime control, under which punishment was certain but humane, would deter all but a very few from a life of crime. Many reformers embraced the idea of using prisons to control crime not because they believed prisons could reform offenders but because they were more humane than hanging and whipping (Rothman, 1971). However, some who were instrumental in developing the Pennsylvania system *did* believe in the reformative value of prison. In either case, prison allowed for matching the seriousness of the crime to an appropriate level of punishment, that is, the more serious the offense the longer the sentence.

### Penitentiaries Were Developed as Places to Reform Criminals

By the 1820s, attention shifted to viewing crime as having been caused by the life circumstances of the criminal and the penitentiary as the place to counteract these conditions. To determine what factors caused crime, investigators conducted interviews with numerous convicted offenders. They concluded that deviant behavior was caused by an inadequate family life combined with the effects of corruption in the community. A typical sketch of an inmate included reference to an inadequate family situation, for example, a father with a bad drinking habit.

Because convicts were thought to be victims of faulty upbringing and community corruptions, it was felt they could be reeducated and rehabilitated in a well-ordered institutional setting organized around the principles of separation, obedience, and labor. Thus, a prison free of corrupting community influences that provided appropriate training could resocialize offenders. Moreover, in the same way that the "criminal environment led him into crime, the institutional environment would lead him out of it" (Rothman, 1971, p. 83).

## THE PENNSYLVANIA AND AUBURN SYSTEMS

The Pennsylvania and Auburn systems each developed an institutional environment and program directed at reforming offenders. This was to serve as the foundation for our new system of social control.

### The Pennsylvania Reformers Experimented with Several Different Systems

Penal reform in the United States began in Philadelphia after the Revolution. In 1783, a number of prominent citizens, including Benjamin Franklin and Benjamin Rush, organized a movement to reform the harsh criminal code of 1718, which authorized whipping and other punishments common to the English system. During the next decade, this group was successful in abolishing the death penalty for all crimes except first-degree murder and using imprisonment or fines for other offenses previously subject to corporal punishment (Barnes, 1930/1972).

In 1787, penal reformers formed the Philadelphia Society for Alleviating the Miseries of Public Prisons. This group was instrumental in persuading the legislature to designate the **Walnut Street Jail** as a temporary state prison and change its orientation to a new approach that would reform inmates.

**THE WALNUT STREET JAIL WAS THE BIRTHPLACE OF THE U.S. PRISON SYSTEM** In planning this facility, which is viewed as our first prison, reformers faced the same problems that we still grapple with today (Should prisoners be housed separately or in association? Should it be for purposes of punishment? etc.) (Lewis, 1922/1996). The Quakers were concerned with developing a program that reformed offenders while providing humane treat-

**The Walnut Street Jail in Philadelphia, which was remodeled in 1790, was considered to be the first U.S. Penitentiary.**

ment. To accomplish these objectives, the Walnut Street Jail was remodeled in 1790 to provide for the confinement of two classes of offenders.

More serious offenders, previously subject to corporal or capital punishment, were confined in a newly built penitentiary house containing sixteen solitary cells—each 6 feet wide, 8 feet long, and 10 feet high—called punishment cells. They were subject to isolation, harsh conditions, and initially were not allowed to work in order to show the public that this system did punish serious offenders (Grunhut, 1948/1972). In isolation they would reflect on the error of their ways, which would, in turn, change their habits and behavior. After a period of time, inmates could earn the privilege of working while still confined to these cells. After completing a portion of their sentence, they could be released into the general population of the prison.

Less hardened and dangerous offenders were congregately housed in eight large rooms, 20 by 18 feet in size (Lewis, 1922/1996). They were permitted to work at occupations basic to the economy of the period. Males labored at carpentry, weaving, shoemaking, and tailoring. Females, in separate facilities, were employed at spinning cotton, carding wool, washing, and mending clothes.

This prisoner labor system presented authorities with the need to deal with a problem that continues to be an issue today: What incentives encourage inmates to work efficiently and productively? The same two incentives that are typically used today were used then: early release and wages. Inmates were either paid prevailing wages or at a somewhat lower rate. There were deductions for daily maintenance, tools, court costs, and any fines. Most prisoners were released well clothed and with money in their pockets. The major incentive was not the money but the hope of a pardon, which might be awarded for their good work. Discipline of inmates was humane. Thus, prisoners were not shackled nor was corporal punishment used. Wages were a great incentive to behave. As additional punishment, disobedient offenders could be put in solitary cells and still be charged daily maintenance expenses. In contrast, the more industrious inmates were given better clothing and permitted to buy extra food. Although a strict rule of silence prevailed in the shops and at meals, inmates in congregate living rooms could talk at night (Lewis, 1922/1996).

An independent, government-appointed board of twelve citizen inspectors was responsible for determining the prison's policies and supervising its administration. A warden with executive authority was responsible to the board. A board subcommittee frequently visited the prison to assure it was operating according to its policies and daily visits were made by one or more inspectors (Lewis (1922/1996).

During its first decade of operation, the program at the Walnut Street Jail appeared to be successful. Street crime dropped to a point that people felt secure on the streets as well as in their homes and businesses. After seven years of operation, only 4 of the 200 persons pardoned by the governor were recommitted. Also, in the four years preceding this new system there were 104 escapes; there were none in a similar period thereafter. The programs initiated at the Walnut Street Jail formed the basis for the development of early prisons in this country.

*Overcrowding Was the Major Factor in Program Failure*
Although the Walnut Street Jail had great promise, by 1800 a number of factors caused its programs to begin to fail. Discipline in the institution became lax, and pardons, which had been given only as rewards for good behavior and work, were issued to placate convicts and achieve order. This made a mockery of the system because offenders were often released after serving a very short period of time. This is similar to what was happening during the late 1980s and early 1990s, when overcrowding led to many early releases. Indeed, the primary factor causing Walnut Street to fail was its inability to handle the increasing inmate population. The increase in the number of inmates resulted from a

growing state population and the fact that this was the only state institution. Also, the increased substitution of solitary confinement for capital punishment resulted in more commitments and longer terms of confinement.

It is fascinating to see how history repeats itself. Today, part of the reason for prison overcrowding is the failure to recognize the effects of changes in sentencing criteria on the prison population. The irony is that states currently experiencing major overcrowding problems are facing the same criticisms of their early release policies as did the Walnut Street Jail.

Overcrowding made it impossible for humanely oriented prison officers to provide the personal attention that was the primary factor in the institution's success and to maintain silence and good order during the day. By 1820, conditions had deteriorated to the point that solitary confinement and keeping classes of offenders separate were not possible. What happened was the very thing the reformers had tried to prevent: The facility became a school for crime with prisoners exchanging experiences and learning from one another.

Recognizing that reform was impossible under overcrowded conditions, in the acts of 1818 and 1821 the Pennsylvania legislature authorized the construction of two penitentiaries, the Western Penitentiary at Pittsburgh and the Eastern Penitentiary at Cherry Hill. They were to operate under the principle of solitary confinement. A new law in 1829, prompted by pressure from the Philadelphia Society for Alleviating the Miseries of Public Prisons, changed the operating principle to solitary confinement at hard labor (Barnes, 1930/1972). Poor planning and construction made it impossible for the Western Penitentiary to realize either its initial objective of solitary confinement or the later work requirement. It was demolished in 1833 and replaced with a facility similar in design to the one at Cherry Hill, to be discussed next, which could meet these objectives.

**EASTERN PENITENTIARY HAD A PROGRAM OF SOLITARY CONFINEMENT, WORK, AND PENITENCE**   Opened in 1829, **Eastern Penitentiary at Cherry Hill** was the first facility to put into effect the **Pennsylvania System** or "separate system." It was designed so inmates would not have to be removed from their cells except when sick. Inmates ate, slept, read their Bibles, received moral instruction, and worked in their cells. Their only contact was with the warden, guards, the chaplain, and members of some Philadelphia organizations interested in inmate care and welfare. Inmates were not permitted to receive or send letters to family or anyone on the outside (Barnes and Teeters, 1951; Lewis, 1922/1996).

The Cherry Hill facility had seven wings, resembling the spokes of a wheel and extending from a hublike center. Each cell block had a passage running down the center, with cells on either side, connecting the wing to the hub of the building. The hub contained an observatory tower and an alarm bell. The 252 cells were quite spacious, about 12 feet long by 7.5 feet wide and 16 feet high. First floor cells had individual walled exercise yards, which inmates were permitted to use for one hour each day. On the second floor, inmates were allowed an extra cell for exercise purposes.

The institutional program was based on solitary confinement, work, and penitence and was justified on the grounds that:

**1.** communication in any [form] contributed to the contamination of the less hardened by the vicious . . . .

**2.** Solitary confinement without the opportunity of communication with fellow prisoners would stop all such contamination.

**3.** Living in silence day and night, [the inmate] would inevitably reflect upon his sins and resolve never more to return.

**4.** Labor in the cell would enable him to contribute to his support and at the same time would relieve the dreadful monotony of solitary confinement . . . (Gillin, 1935, p. 282).

In this country, this system did not receive wide acceptance. However, many European countries adopted it as a model for their own penal systems. Our Close-Up on "Two Views on the Success of the Pennsylvania Model" provides an example of European perspectives.

### The System Devised at Auburn Became the Model for U.S. Prisons

Although Auburn prison in New York eventually became the model for prisons throughout the United States, when it was first built in 1816, its construction and administration followed traditional patterns of the period. The first part of the

The Eastern Penitentiary at Cherry Hill was opened in 1829. At this facility, the model known as The Pennsylvania or Separate System was fully put into effect.

## Close Up  Two Views on the Success of the Pennsylvania Model

William Crawford was appointed by the London Society for the Improvement of Prisons to study U.S. penal institutions and specifically to evaluate the competing Auburn and Pennsylvania models. After visiting 14 state penitentiaries and several jails, Crawford provided what Barnes (1927/1968) called a glowing [evaluation] of the Pennsylvania system, which eventually led to the construction of "The Model Prison" in London, later known as Pentonville. This became the model for prisons in the British Isles and its colonies, for example, India, Canada, and Australia, and also the prototype for institutions in France, Prussia, Austria, Holland, Denmark, and Belgium (Johnston, 1969). Crawford indicated that:

> I have uniformly found that the deterring influence is extremely great, and such as I believe belongs to no other system of gaol management; for although in large bodies, associated together, silence may by strict discipline be in a great measure maintained, prisoners thus debarred from speaking have inevitably recourse to other modes of communication. . . . The Eastern Penitentiary imparts no such relief . . .the separation from the world is certain and complete. . . . I was indeed particularly struck by the mild and subdued spirit which seemed to pervade the temper of the convicts, and which is essentially promoted by reflection, solitude, and the absence of corporal punishment. The only offenses in the Eastern Penitentiary which the prisoner can commit are idleness and wilful damage to the materials on which he is at work. On such occasions he is punished by the loss of employment, the diminution of his food, or close confinement in a darkened cell. The necessity for correction is extremely rare. There is not a whip nor are there any fire-arms within the walls of the prison (Crawford, 1835/1969, pp. 11–12).
>
> I conclude this account of the Philadelphia penitentiary by stating that . . . I could not perceive, either in their appearance or conversation, any indication that the solitude to which they had been subjected for this long period had injured their health or impaired the understanding. Although generally serious, they were not de-

pressed, and several talked with a cheerfulness which I did not expect to find in men such situated. . . . They universally concurred in the conviction that solitude was of all punishments the most fearful, and declared that if ever they were liberated they should never be found again within those walls. (Crawford, 1835/1969, Appendix X, p. 10).

It is interesting that despite the fact that Crawford spent time examining prison records and interviewing inmates and staff he apparently did not discover the fact that not all inmates were kept in solitary confinement nor were inmates subjected to the mild forms of discipline he reported. Either these practices were hidden from him during his visit or he neglected to report them because he wanted to present as favorable a picture of the system as possible so that it would be adopted in England.

While Crawford had nothing but praise for the Pennsylvania solitary confinement system, a fellow Englishmen and noted author, Charles Dickens, found the system appalling.

> I am well convinced that those who devised this system of Prison Discipline . . . did not know what it is that they are doing . . . very few men are capable of estimating the immense amount of torture and agony which this dreadful punishment, prolonged for years, inflicts upon the sufferers . . . I hesitated once, debating with myself whether, if I had the power of saying 'Yes' or 'No,' I would allow it to be tried in certain cases where the terms of imprison ment were short; but now I solemnly declare that [I could not with good conscience allow] one human creature, for any length of time, no matter what, lay suffering this unknown punishment in his silent cell . . . (as cited by Gillin, 1935, p. 285).

After reading these accounts take a moment and reflect on both of these positions. How would you feel about being placed in this system? Do you think as Crawford did that you would be rehabilitated? Or like Dickens, do you feel that the system imposed cruel and unusual punishment?

prison contained 28 rooms, each intended to house eight to twelve prisoners with 61 additional cells, designed for one convict (or two if necessary). Initially, Auburn followed a system of congregate

work and confinement (Lewis, 1922/1996). However, disorders at this prison—and at Newgate, another New York prison—prompted authorities to search for better methods of prison management.

Sing Sing Prison in New York was built in 1825 as an Auburn-type prison with tiers of cells back to back inside a hollow building. This "Big House" prison was thus the first to have real cell blocks, which are a unique aspect of American prisons.

**AUBURN EXPERIMENTED WITH THREE ALTERNATIVES** A commission devised a plan employing a threefold system of classification assigning inmates to one of three programs. The first group, the least serious criminals, were to work in silence in the prison shops during the day and be confined in separate cells at night. A second group, the more serious and hardened criminals, were to be confined in solitary cells, until there was evidence of repentance. They were then to be kept in solitary at night and permitted to work there during the day. The third group, vicious and hardened criminals, were to be confined in their cells without labor. This plan embodied the predominant views of the period, which held that prisoners could be reformed through penitence and that the appropriate function of imprisonment was punishment (Lewis, 1922/1996).

Unlike the cells at Eastern Penitentiary, which occupied the outside wall of the prison, these newly built solitary confinement cells—for reasons of economy—were built back to back five tiers high in a hollow building. They were very small (7 feet long, 4 feet wide, and 7 feet high) and their doors opened onto galleries or walkways 8 to 10 feet from the outer wall of the building. These cells were dark, dreary, and without much fresh air because the only light and air that entered them came from the small, heavily barred windows in the building wall some 9 feet away (Lewis, 1922/1996). Despite its many faults, this pattern of **inside cell blocks** was adopted by most of the states that built prisons during the next century. The high cost of prison construction has assured that many of the older prisons built according to this plan are still being used today.

Auburn was not designed for total solitary confinement. However, on Christmas Day in 1821, as mandated by the New York State legislature, 80 of the "worst inmates" being held at Auburn were placed in total solitary confinement. Except for a Bible to read, they had no work, no contact with visitors, nor any other methods for passing the lonely hours. The legislature failed to anticipate the disastrous consequences of solitude (e.g., attempted suicides, mental breakdowns, and deaths) without anything to do. After 18 months, the increasing number of convict deaths led the governor to visit the prison. Shocked by what he observed, he terminated the program and pardoned most of the survivors (McKelvey, 1977; Lewis, 1922/1996). (This crude experiment cannot be viewed as a test of the disciplinary and reformative potential of the Pennsylvania system at the Eastern Penitentiary, because Auburn lacked the larger, more roomy cells and failed to provide inmates with productive labor.)

**THE AUBURN PLAN OF CONGREGATE WORK, SILENCE, AND SEPARATE-CELL CONFINEMENT WAS ADOPTED AS AN ACCEPTABLE CONFINEMENT METHOD** With no existing acceptable prison regimens at this point, at Auburn, under the guidance of Warden Elam Lynds, a new system was evolving that involved a compromise between solitary confinement and the congregate confinement of earlier facilities. This new **Auburn system,** was in full operation by 1823 and combined the separate confinement of each inmate at night with work in groups in the prison shops and yards during the day. Silence was rigidly enforced both day and night. Proponents felt that this system met the objectives of imprisonment and also provided an economical system of management and strict discipline, allowing for the safe and efficient functioning of the prison. Silence prevented inmates from corrupting each other or plotting escapes and riots, and work enabled them to pay for the cost of their imprisonment. The emphasis on isolation restricted communication in the prison and separated inmates from the outside world. No communication was permitted through visits[1] or by letter with relatives or friends except under extraordinary circumstances, which meant inmates were almost totally shut off from any world news.

Inmates received no inducements to comply with the system's rigid requirements. Obedience was obtained by a prompt and severe system of punishment involving the use of "stripes," as flogging was called. Disobedient inmates were taken from the work area and flogged with a rawhide whip in a way that would not endanger their health or ability to work. This was seen to have two advantages: (1) It was dreaded by the convicts yet produced the least personal suffering for them, and (2) it required little time to administer, meaning convicts could return to work immediately and thereby avoid substantially reducing shop production. Although flogging appears to be brutal to us today, and we do not condone it, it is important to remember that corporal punishment was widely used at home and in other spheres of society (Lewis, 1922/1996). The brutality of this situation was mitigated by the fact that well-behaved prisoners suffered little corporal punishment. Nevertheless, for the Auburn system to work effectively, a dictatorial regime was required. Without force and the iron hand of authority, the system would have collapsed because inmates would have had

no incentives to obey the rules (Lewis, 1922/1996). Thus, the key features of the Auburn system were silence, hard congregate labor, and corporal punishment for rule violators.

### The Auburn–Pennsylvania Controversy Involved a Debate over Which System Was Superior

By the 1830s, the two American penitentiary systems had achieved worldwide recognition, and attention began to focus on which would provide the best model for future prisons.

The Pennsylvania camp insisted that the separate design eliminated contamination and, once isolated, convicts immediately began the reformation process. This system did not require well-trained guards since contact with inmates was minimal; it facilitated security because plotting and accomplishing escapes were difficult under these conditions; and there was little need for the whip because men in isolation had few chances to violate rules. In short, it was touted as being secure, quiet, humane, efficient, and reformative. Pennsylvania supporters also criticized the Auburn system on the basis that it was nearly impossible to enforce silence when inmates worked, ate, and exercised together. Also, they felt that inmate contact with one another for long periods without talking was unnecessarily painful. The frequent and severe punishments of inmates who broke rules failed to solve the problem and showed that the system was defective.

Auburn advocates criticized the defects of the Pennsylvania system, saying that prolonged isolation was cruel, dangerous, and unnatural, as proven by its trial at Auburn, which bred insanity and suicide. This showed the separate system was no more effective than the congregate system. The most persuasive arguments for the Auburn system were that (1) Auburn-type institutions were less costly to construct because cells could be smaller since inmates only slept in them, and (2) it brought greater returns from convict labor because of greater efficiency and the resulting variety and quantity of products produced when convicts worked together. In fact, in 1828 Auburn's warden announced he no longer needed state funds to run the prison (Lewis, 1922/1996).

Thus, Auburn proponents argued that if both systems had their defects, there was no way to justify the greater costs of the Pennsylvania system (Rothman, 1971; Wines, 1895). Although the Auburn system eventually prevailed in the United States, before looking at its use, we briefly examine the adaptations of the Pennsylvania model.

**THE PENNSYLVANIA MODEL WAS ONLY USED BY A FEW U.S. JURISDICTIONS** Only two states, New Jersey and Rhode Island, built prisons following the Cherry Hill design and adopted the solitary system.[2] However, Rhode Island abandoned it after six years and New Jersey did so after 25 years (Barnes, 1927/1968). Abroad, the Pennsylvania system was adopted by many European countries including England, Sweden, Denmark, Norway, Holland, France, and Belgium. However, its application varied: Some countries used it only for hardened offenders, and in others all offenders were subjected to periods of solitary confinement (Barnes and Teeters, 1951).

As we note in our Close-Up on "The Real Versus Ideal Pennsylvania System," some key goals of this system could not be realized even during the early "honeymoon" years. Even its basic tenet of completely separating inmates was not possible from the start (Teeters, 1970). By the 1860s it was common for inmates to share a cell and by 1867 it became the official policy. This system was abandoned for practical reasons and because of overcrowding, as had occurred at the Walnut Street Jail. When there are more convicts than there are cells, doubling up is inevitable (Wines, 1895). In 1872, it was renamed "the individual treatment system" and by 1913 the program had changed to the point that it no longer resembled the original system and

was abolished. Cherry Hill then became just another Auburn-type prison, existing as a maximum security facility until 1970.

**THE AUBURN MODEL PREVAILED FOR ECONOMIC REASONS** The Auburn system became the model for prisons in the United States, primarily because its economic advantages were more attractive to taxpayers than any arguments in favor of the Pennsylvania system.

Auburn's doctrines of separation, obedience, labor, and silence were consistent with the values of the time regarding reformation. Both prison officials and reformers believed criminals had never learned to respect others, to set limits, or to obey authority. To change this, the prison had to require absolute adherence to a rigid system of rules. Any refusal to conform had to be "broken." Maintaining a daily routine of hard and constant work was consistent with accepted views on the causes and results of involvement in crime. Those not willing to work were seen as prone to commit crime. Idleness also gave inmates opportunities to teach each other the values and techniques of crime. Thus, the tougher the regimen, the greater the possibilities of successful reformation.

**AUBURN-TYPE PRISONS WERE BUILT IN MANY JURISDICTIONS** The dominance of the Auburn model can be seen (Table 4.1) from the 29 prisons built throughout the country between 1825 and 1869 that followed this design (Morse, 1940; McKelvey, 1977).

TABLE 4.1 **Auburn-Type Prisons Built between 1825 and 1869**

| | | | |
|---|---|---|---|
| New York (Sing Sing) | 1825 | Maine (Thomaston) | 1845 |
| Connecticut (Wethersfield) | 1827 | New York (Clinton) | 1845 |
| Maryland (Baltimore) | 1829 | Texas (Huntsville) | 1851 |
| Vermont (Windsor) | 1831 | Minnesota (Stillwater) | 1849 |
| Tennessee (Nashville) | 1831 | California (San Quentin) | 1852 |
| New Hampshire (Concord) | 1832 | Wisconsin (Waupun) | 1852 |
| Illinois (Alton) | 1833 | Illinois (Joliet) | 1858 |
| Ohio (Columbus) | 1834 | Indiana (Michigan City) | 1860 |
| Louisiana (Baton Rouge) | 1835 | Idaho (Boise) | 1863 |
| Missouri (Jefferson City) | 1836 | Kansas (Lansing) | 1864 |
| Michigan (Jackson) | 1838 | Nevada (Carson City) | 1864 |
| Iowa (Ft. Madison) | 1840 | South Carolina (Columbia) | 1865 |
| Alabama (Wetumpka) | 1841 | West Virginia (Moundsville) | 1866 |
| Indiana (Jeffersonville) | 1842 | Nebraska (Lincoln) | 1869 |
| Mississippi (Jackson) | 1842 | | |

**MANY STATES BUILT AUBURN-TYPE PRISONS BUT FAILED TO ADHERE TO ITS RIGID STANDARDS** Although many states embraced the Auburn model, their institutions failed to follow its rigid standards. The degree to which the model was followed depended largely on the varying skills and concerns of those running the institutions. For example, Ohio built an Auburn-type institution with separate cells for inmates, but even though its operational policy forbade communication between convicts, its administration was not strong enough to maintain the silent system. During the 1840s, convicts could roam freely through the prison, determine much of their own routine, and talk with each other at will. To gain inmate cooperation, guards bribed them with food and clothing. This is typical of what happens under any lax and poor administration—and when inmates are organized. Generally, the farther west the state in which the model was followed, the more loosely enforced were its rigid rules of discipline (Rothman, 1971).

**THE AUBURN APPROACH FOLLOWED A QUASI-MILITARY MODEL** To achieve Auburn-type goals, prisons during this era adopted a **quasimilitary model.** Convicts were marched from place to place in "close-order single file," each looking over the next man's shoulder with their faces pointed to the right to prevent conversation, and their feet moving in unison. This type of formation, known as the **lockstep,** became a hallmark of American prisons well into the 1930s.

The daily schedule was also organized in a military fashion:

> . . . At the sound of a horn or bell, keepers opened the cells, prisoners stepped onto the deck, and then in the lockstep marched into the yard. In formation they emptied their night pails, moved on and washed them, took a few more steps, and placed them on a rack to dry. Still in line, they marched to the shops. There they worked at their tasks in rows on long benches until the bell rang for breakfast. They grouped again in single file, passed into the kitchen, picked up their rations (regulations admonished them not to break step) and continued on to their cells, or in some institutions, to a common messroom where they ate their meal. (Regulations again instructed them to sit erect with backs straight.) At the bell they stood, reentered formation, and marched back to the shops. They repeated this routine at noon, and again at six o'clock; then they returned to their

cells for the night and at nine o'clock lights went out, as at a barracks (Rothman, 1971, p. 106).

They also wore uniforms of simple, coarse, striped fabric and had their hair cut short to increase uniformity (Rothman, 1971). The stated purpose of this highly regimented and discipline-oriented organizational structure was to socialize society's most dangerous misfits in such a way as to make them more able to resist corruption, respect authority, and lead ordered lives. Finally, it is important to note that many elements of this system (including the lockstep, silent system, regimented routines, and fortress prisons) evolved over time, and remained part of our penal system well into the twentieth century.

## ANTECEDENTS OF THE REFORMATORY MOVEMENT

By the end of the Civil War, the inadequacies of both the Pennsylvania and Auburn systems were abundantly clear. The rigid discipline of the solitary system in Pennsylvania and of the Auburn congregate system had degenerated to more or less corrupt, lax, and brutal routines (Rothman, 1980).[6] The institutions of this era were overcrowded and understaffed, which made the systems of silence unenforceable (Wines and Dwight, 1867). In addition, many states had recognized the economic advantage of leasing inmate labor to private contractors who supplied machinery, raw materials, and supervisory personnel for producing saleable goods. While benefitting the state, this diminished the authority of prison staff over inmates because (at least during work hours) contractors had control of the inmates. By the 1860s, prison industries were so profitable they became the major focus of institutional operations (Wines and Dwight, 1867). Discipline was used to maintain production and its use for reformative purposes became secondary.

Taken together, these circumstances created turmoil in the prisons and wardens resorted to a variety of bizarre punishments to regain control. One of these punishment devices was a pulley mechanism

> "[B]y means [of which an inmate] . . . bound about both wrists [by a cord was] brought together, and drawn upon an overhead system of pulleys," . . . was

## Close Up   The Real Versus Ideal Pennsylvania System

This Close-Up focuses on the first seven years of Eastern Penitentiary's operation. Typically, if a program is going to adhere to its operational plan it will do so in its early years.

### The Disciplinary System Was Not as Benign as System Planners Intended

Developers of the Pennsylvania system were convinced that they could use solitude as a means of bending the will of the offender without "assalling his flesh." This was how the system was supposed to work and it was the way official reports portrayed it. Under this system punishment involved restricting privileges including work and moral and religious instruction books.

By 1835, the facility had its first 300 inmates. Upon arrival these offenders spent their "first few days in contemplation, after which being cowed and docile, [they] were grateful for being allowed to work and read the bible" (Thibaut, 1982, p. 194).[c] At the outset this plan was flawed because half of the inmates were illiterate. Thus, depriving them of books was a meaningless punishment. Also, work was viewed as a privilege, and it was used as a disciplinary action. This sent mixed messages to inmates as to the purpose of work.

Because those who established and ran this program were convinced it was the most enlightened system of incarceration, they were not inclined to admit the program was not a total success. Public pronouncements tended to obscure the fact that from the beginning some inmates had behaved as they did in other prisons. Thus in the 1836 annual report the warden commented:

> The prisoners seldom show anything like violence in their conduct, and small privation of food is gener-

ally sufficient to correct any small indiscretion of misbehavior (warden's annual report as cited by Thibaut, 1982, p. 194).

The warden's journal indicated that about one-fifth of the first 300 inmates committed disciplinary infractions or displayed mental disturbance. However, this represents a minimum since the warden was often away from the prison and/or frequently occupied and no official records of infractions or punishments were required. The punishments imposed on inmates were supposed to be of a nonviolent nature, but the staff soon learned these methods were ineffective with more rebellious prisoners. The warden, who had full discretion in disciplinary matters, was forced to fall back on more harsh forms of punishment. What developed was a system of graded punishments, starting with those publicly acknowledged, and moving to more severe methods but not as corporally damaging as whipping (Thibaut, 1982).

Lewis (1922/1996) describes this graded system of punishments:

> The first and mildest punishment was a deprivation of the use of the exercise yard by the convict for a given period. The second stage of punishment included a serious reduction in rations. For severer cases, the dark cell was employed, this being an ordinary cell from which light was totally excluded. Often even the single blanket was denied the prisoner. The next degree of punishment . . . was the absolute deprivation of food, for a period of not over three days. A further stage [involved] . . . the infliction of "ducking," in which process the convict was suspended from the yard wall by the wrists, and drenched with buckets of cold water, the degree of severity . . . depended on [the temperature (pp. 221-222)].

lifted "entirely from the ground, with his whole weight suspended upon the small cord." The duration of this punishment ranged from two minutes or less to an hour. . . . Sing-Sing had its own particular mechanism, a "tying up" device that suspended prisoners by their thumbs instead of their wrists . . . "Men have been kept raised so long as to cause bleeding from the mouth, before the doctor would order the prisoner taken down" (New York State Prison Commission, 1876, as cited by Rothman, 1980, pp. 18–19).

Also during this era inmates were flogged, with the number of strokes based on the gravity of their infraction. Solitary confinement to the "dungeon" on a bread and water diet was also employed. The most horrendous punishment was Kansas's "water crib," a coffin-like box in which an inmate was placed face down with hands cuffed behind his back and then a water hose was turned on which allowed water to slowly fill the crib. As the water

# Close Up

Other punishments included the following:

> The "mad or tranquilizing chair" . . . was a large box-chair made of planks . . . [in which] the convict was strapped . . . and his hands were handcuffed. For the feet there was no resting place. It was not possible to move body or limbs, and the consequent pain was intense. Arms and legs swelled frightfully.
>
> The "straight-jacket," . . . was a sack or bagging cloth of three thicknesses, with pocketholes in the front for the admission of the hands. In the back there were rows of eyelets, whereby the jacket might be laced up. . . . Convicts in the Eastern Penitentiary had been so tightly laced into the jacket that their necks and faces were black with congealed blood. The torture could be made excruciating. One convict was reported to have lost the use of his hand. Men of the stoutest nerve would shriek as if on the rack (p.222).

By contemporary standards many of these punishments appear barbaric, but we again remind the reader that punishments were generally severe in this era. In comparison with other prisons, the punishments at Cherry Hill were generally less severe. Our point in discussing them is to show that (1) public pronouncements regarding the success of a program may gloss over deficiencies in order to demonstrate its success; (2) no matter how well intentioned program planners and administrators are there will always be some prisoners who will not conform to program rules and who may be controlled by methods that are outside approved policies.

## The Work Requirement Was Inconsistent with Solitary Confinement

Divergences between the intentions of the Philadelphia Society and the actual conditions at the penitentiary were most . . . evident in prison management and administration during the first five years of operation. The determination of the Society to occupy every prisoner with some form of work, while at the same time maintaining isolation, presented the prison staff with serious organizational difficulties.

Dyeing, blacksmithing, carriage-making, cooking, and washing were difficult, if not impossible, to accomplish in the cells. [Warden] Wood apparently modif[ied] the system [during this time] to suit the needs of prison administration. In fact, men were working all about the premises, some of them in the doubtless convivial company of men brought in to work on prison construction. . . .

Wood's administration, through 1833, was relaxed to the extent that the separate system was certainly in jeopardy. For instance, a communal room, probably equipped with partitions, was used by those inmates who worked as weavers. . . . The Board of Inspectors acknowledged the deterioration of the system in December of 1833, when they ordered that "all the prisoners be confined to the cells in accordance with their sentences and the Warden be directed to employ suitable persons to perform the duties performed by them[11]. . . . Judging from the published reports of the Board of Inspectors, the rules stated that prisoners were not permitted even a glimpse of other inmates. Clearly, Warden Wood accepted a much less stringent application of the principle (Thibaut, 1982, pp. 210–212).

In summary, it is clear that in several important respects the designs of the reformers of the Philadelphia Society for Alleviating the Miseries of Public Prisons had succumbed, during the first years of [operation of] the Eastern State Penitentiary, to compelling forces that reshaped the separate system in practice (Thibaut, 1982, p. 221).

rose the inmate, slowly drowning, fought to keep his head above the rising water. Whereas it took days to bring a man around in solitary, this torture was said to get his cooperation immediately (Rothman, 1980).

Reformers were appalled by these forms of torture and punishment. However, one group of reformers felt that if the prison were abolished it might be replaced by a greater use of capital punishment, corporal punishment, and even banishment. Thus, prisons were the lesser of the possible evils and rather than abolish them, the solution was to look for a better operational model. A second group of reformers simply continued to believe that prisons could rehabilitate criminals and there was a need for a new type of prison. In searching for programs that could be used to develop a new prison system reformers were heavily influenced by the work of Captain Alexander Maconochie and Sir Walter Crofton.

### Alexander Maconochie's Mark System

While serving as a young naval officer in 1810, **Alexander Maconochie** was captured by the French and became a prisoner of war until Napoleon's abdication in 1814. This made him sensitive to the brutalities of prisons and the convict transportation system. He later investigated the process of transportation as the lieutenant governor of Van Damien's Island, a prison colony off the coast of Australia. This led him to develop a revolutionary plan for penal reform (Barry, 1972).

**THE MAJOR OBJECTIVE OF PRISON SHOULD BE REFORM** In developing his system, Maconochie recognized that it was necessary to identify its objectives. He believed pain and suffering were an essential part of any penal system because they served to constrain others from violating the law and reinforced in the offender's mind the wrongfulness of his behavior. However, he felt that its major objective should be to reform offenders. Thus, the primary emphasis was on preventing future misdeeds rather than just punishing past misbehavior. This required a prison program with two components: (1) punishment for past behavior and (2) training to prepare offenders to return to society as useful, honest, and trustworthy members of the community. Reformation had to be the primary goal if offenders were to be returned to society. For this system to work, persuasion, not coercion, had to be the main method of controlling and reforming offenders. He also felt that a system of reformation could not operate effectively without trained personnel. This required the formation of an organizational structure—the Prison Service—providing a distinct status for prison administrators, similar to that of employees of Britain's Foreign Service.[3] In this way, service as a prison administrator would be a career choice with promotion depending on their success in reforming offenders.

**THE MARK SYSTEM ENABLED INMATES TO WORK THEIR WAY OUT OF PRISON** Maconochie believed that for change to take place, an offender's sentence should be "task oriented," that is, based on good conduct and performance of a specified quantity of labor rather than on a period of time.

This came to be known as the **mark system** because sentences were to consist of a specified number of marks or points based on the seriousness of the offense. Rather than a 10-year term for burglary, an offender's sentence might be 10,000 marks. These marks represented a debt, and the offender had to earn enough marks to pay off the debt before he could be released. Maconochie's system consisted of stages that provided convicts with tangible goals and rewards to strive for (Taylor, 1978).

**Penal Stage.** Upon entering prison the inmate would be exposed to a short but severe penal stage designed to punish him for his past offenses. This included placement in solitary confinement, a diet of bread and water, and moral instruction to instill in him a feeling of remorse for his past actions.

**Associational Stage.** Felons then entered a second stage in which they were given more freedom and allowed to associate with other inmates. They were informed that they would remain in prison until they earned enough marks to meet those assigned to them by the court. However, they could choose to do nothing and remain in prison indefinitely on a diet of bread and water.

Marks could be earned by working, participation in educational programs, and good behavior. Maconochie viewed marks as wages and therefore permitted convicts to use them in a variety of ways, including improving their lifestyles (e.g., exchanging them for better clothing and food); depositing them in a prison bank to be redeemed for cash upon discharge; or refusing all luxuries and applying all earned marks toward obtaining an earlier release.

Finally, punishment for offenses committed in prison was imposed by adding marks to an offender's sentence, extending his confinement. Under this system, an inmate knew his status at all times because all transactions were recorded on a daily basis. Maconochie felt this placed the fate of offenders in their own hands. This was the first system employing a form of indeterminate sentence (see Chapter 2).[4]

**Social Stage.** Inmates entered the final stage when they had enough marks to reduce those given by the court to a given percentage. This was labeled the "social stage" because inmates with common interests and accounts were permitted to organize themselves into groups of six. An inmate's daily earnings were determined by dividing the total marks earned by the group of six. Fines inflicted on a group member and luxuries bought by a member were deducted from the group's total. Thus, each inmate was responsible for the conduct of all members of the group. This system was designed to teach inmates a sense of social responsibility, which Maconochie felt was necessary in order to live in a free society.

**Ticket of Leave.** Finally, when convicts had earned a sufficient number of marks to offset those debited to them at sentencing they were entitled to a conditional pardon known as a **ticket of leave.** However, Maconochie felt that once offenders had been reformed by successfully progressing through these stages they should be able to feel totally free. This meant police should not be able to constantly pick them up for questioning nor have summary jurisdiction—the power to arrest and imprison them. He felt the only basis for imprisoning these releasees should be conviction for a new crime (Barry, 1958). Thus, Maconochie did not appear to view a ticket of leave as requiring releasees to be subject to any conditions or supervision. This contradicts those crediting him with contributing to the development of parole (see, e.g., Burns, 1975) since parole has always involved supervision.

**THE MARK SYSTEM WAS FIRST APPLIED AT NORFOLK ISLAND PRISON** Maconochie first applied his system in 1840 when he was appointed administrator of Norfolk Island, a penal colony off the coast of Australia. This was one of Britain's worst colonies because it held "the twice-condemned"—criminals sent from England to penal colonies in Australia who subsequently committed offenses while there. Although not able to implement his program fully, he did establish a system that included an initial penal stage (and two other stages) in which progress was based on the acquisition of marks (Barry, 1958). Also, Maconochie was not able to release offenders earning enough marks to offset those debited against them. However, he did issue them an "island ticket of leave" allowing them to live outside the main barracks and use their leisure to work for themselves.

Despite these limitations, Maconochie was able in four short years to transform Britain's most dreaded penal colony into a modern, open institution. He eliminated or drastically reduced its most brutalizing features (e.g., he dismantled the gallows, and almost totally eliminated whipping and confinement in irons). He built two churches and

obtained books for Jewish convicts. He also established schools, encouraged reading, and gave out prizes. Last, in an effort to provide a more humane atmosphere, he allowed convicts to eat with forks and knives, where they previously had to eat with their fingers.

Maconochie recognized the importance of being open and available to talk to inmates and of treating them with dignity. He managed by walking around, which more than 100 years later came to be viewed as a key element in effective prison management (see Chapter 13).

> I encouraged all to address me with freedom. I would not even listen to a man unless he stood up and spoke to me like one. . . . I encouraged all, if they wanted to come to myself with their request, instead of seeking to make friends among those more immediately about me. To facilitate this I walked and rode about the island quite alone, and rather invited, than discouraged, conversation with any (Maconochie, 1859, as cited by Barry, 1958, p. 116).

**PUNITIVE PUBLIC VIEWS RESULTED IN MACONOCHIE'S RECALL** Maconochie's claim that he found Norfolk Island a turbulent, brutal hell, and left it a peaceful, well ordered community appears to be an accurate assessment. However, English society still associated imprisonment with punishment and misery, and thus many of his superiors were hostile to his views. When word reached London that he had allowed inmates the luxury of celebrating the Queen's birthday with games and dinner, he was removed (Barry, 1958).

Maconochie's recall was also prompted by the fact that under his regime the cost of maintaining a convict increased by 21%. This was seized on by his critics, because he claimed his program would be less expensive than more traditional methods. What he meant was that, in the long run, if offenders were reformed this system would save the government money. This is a problem that has continually plagued corrections: Institutions with good programs will invariably cost more to operate than those without them—in the short run. However, if these programs reduce recidivism rates, their long-term savings outweigh increased short-term costs. Maconochie's superiors apparently ignored this since there is evidence that his program was successful. Less than 3% of 1450 inmates who had been discharged from the penal colony were convicted of new crimes. Also, of the 920 doubly convicted and "allegedly irreclaimable," only 20 were reconvicted (Barry, 1958). This is quite remarkable since there was serious unemployment in the areas to which these inmates were released. Any warden today would be pleased with a success figure of this kind, given the 79.9% recidivism rates of prison inmates during the early 1990s (Snell and Morton, 1994).

**THE SYSTEM WAS ALSO IMPLEMENTED AT BIR-MINGHAM BOROUGH PRISON** In 1849, Maconochie was appointed governor of the new Birmingham Borough Prison. Again, due to legal restraints, he was unable to fully put his system into operation. He only lasted two years in this position and was dismissed because his methods were thought to be too lenient (Barry, 1972). In both instances, Maconochie failed to implement his system fully because of the legally entrenched sentencing system of the time, the inability to recruit a staff that subscribed to his principles, and the outward hostility of public officials.

### Sir Walter Crofton's Irish System Also Influenced the Reformatory

Undoubtedly, the penal philosophy of Alexander Maconochie would have died if Sir **Walter Crofton** had not been appointed chairman of the board of directors of the Irish convict prisons. In 1854 when he assumed this position, he faced a number of problems, including massive overcrowding, poorly designed buildings, and an inadequately prepared staff (Dooley, 1978).[d] The most pressing problem, overcrowding, he solved by developing a new system that was forward-looking rather than retrospective. Like Maconochie's, Crofton's system punished convicts for their past crimes and also prepared them for release. This was accomplished by giving them the opportunity to earn increased responsibility and privileges while progressing through a four-stage system that came to be known as the **Irish system** or intermediate system.

**THE IRISH SYSTEM INVOLVED INCREASING PRIVILEGES AND PHASED RELEASE Solitary Confinement Stage.** When offenders entered the Irish system, they were incarcerated in a conventional prison (for approximately nine months) and subject to a regimen of silence and solitary confinement, except during school, exercise, chapel, and

when they worked. Although Crofton was criticized for allowing offenders to do some work during this stage, he felt that idleness spiced with a taste of labor made offenders realize that work was a privilege (Dooley, 1978).

**Associational Stage.** After successfully completing their period of solitary confinement, convicts entered this second stage and were transferred to public works prisons where they were allowed to earn marks. They were typically required to progress through three conduct classes, which required the accumulation of 108 marks and took about twelve months. As they progressed up the class structure, they were rewarded with better clothes and more privileges.

**Intermediate Stage.** After accumulating 108 marks, convicts entered this third stage, which was Crofton's unique contribution. About three-quarters of all convicts entered this stage. Crofton felt inmates had to prove to society that they were reformed by showing they had developed sufficient powers of self-control to resist temptation under circumstances of relative freedom. Also, training under conditions of partial freedom prepared offenders for full freedom on release (Wines, 1895). Thus, during this intermediate stage inmates were minimally supervised.

This stage represented an early antecedent of current prerelease centers. There were two common objections to inmates' involvement in this type of work: (1) the requirement that prisons had to be built where the work was performed and (2) the high cost of supervising the inmates. Crofton resolved these problems by constructing two portable huts that could be dismantled and moved to another location when a project was completed. Also, at least one work site provided instruction on subjects that prepared inmates for release (Dooley, 1978).

**Conditional Release Stage.** Inmates successfully completing the intermediate stage were granted a conditional pardon (ticket of leave) for the remainder of their sentence. During this period, they were under supervision, and those disobeying regulations could be charged with a misdemeanor, summarily tried, and, if convicted, have their tickets of leave revoked (Dooley, 1978). This was the first extensive use of parole as the term is applied today (Barnes and Teeters, 1951).

**THE IRISH SYSTEM REDUCED RECIDIVISM** A variety of measures was used to gauge the success of this system. Among the most reliable was the decline in the prison population from 3933 in 1854 when Crofton took office to 1314 by 1862. Equally impressive was the number of convicts who were successfully discharged from conditional release as compared with those returned to prison. Between 1856 and 1861, 1227 tickets of leave were issued, of which only 5.6% were revoked (Dooley, 1978).

## THE REFORMATORY SYSTEM

In the United States, the Irish system provided a rallying point for penal reformers. Inspired by this system, they organized to translate these new principles of reform into practice. From this emerged the reformatory movement.

### At the National Congress on Penitentiary and Reformatory Discipline, Prominent Reformers Proposed a New System

In 1870, these reformers held a conference in Cincinnati—the National Congress on Penitentiary and Reformatory Discipline—at which the **National Prison Association** (NPA) was organized[5] (Wines, 1895). At this conference, the leading reform ideas of the era were discussed and were incorporated into a Declaration of Principles that was adopted by the conference. This declaration advocated "A philosophy of reformation as opposed to the adoption of punishment, progressive classification of prisoners based on the mark system, the indeterminate sentence, and the cultivation of the inmate's self-respect" (Barnes and Teeters, 1951, p. 524). Its basic tenets follow:

1. Reformation, not vindictive suffering, should be the purpose of penal treatment of prisoners.
2. Classification should be made on the basis of a mark system, patterned after the Irish system.
3. Rewards should be provided for good conduct.
4. The prisoner should be made to realize that his destiny is in his own hands.
5. The chief obstacles to prison reform are the political appointment of prison officials, and the instability of management.
6. Prison officials should be trained for their jobs.

7. Indeterminate sentences should be substituted for fixed sentences, and the gross disparities and inequities in prison sentences should be removed. Also, the futility of repeated short sentences was emphasized.
8. Religion and education were cited as the most important agencies of reformation.
9. Prison discipline should be such as to gain the will of the prisoner and conserve his self-respect.
10. The aim of the prison should be to make industrious freemen rather than orderly and obedient prisoners.
11. Industrial training should be fully provided for.
12. The system of contract labor in prisons should be abolished.
13. Prisons should be small, and there should be separate institutions for different types of offenders.
14. The law should strike against the so-called "higher-ups" in crime, as well as against the lesser operatives.
15. There should be indemnification for prisoners who are later discovered to be innocent.
16. There should be revision of the laws relating to the treatment of insane criminals.
17. There should be a more judicious exercise of the pardoning power.
18. There should be established a system for the collection of uniform penal statistics.
19. A more adequate architecture should be developed, providing sufficiently for air and sunlight, as well as for prison hospitals, school rooms, etc.
20. Within each state, prison-management should be centralized.
21. The social training of prisoners should be facilitated through proper association, and the abolition of the silence rules.
22. Society at large should be made to realize its responsibility for crime conditions (Wood and Waits, 1941, pp. 532–533).

As McKelvey (1977) suggests, it is truly remarkable that these principles were adopted by this convention in light of the brutalizing conditions of prisons during this era. Although the humane and progressive methods advocated at the Cincinnati meeting were aimed at all offenders, they were only employed on young, first offenders in so-called reformatories (Barnes and Teeters, 1951).

## Elmira Was the First Reformatory

The first reformatory, **Elmira Reformatory in New York,** opened in 1877 and was headed by **Zebulon T. Brockway** for the next 20 years. Brockway made one of the most ambitious attempts to put the declaration of principles into effect at Elmira.

Judges were to send first time felons, ages 16 to 30, who were capable of being reformed, to this institution (Rothman, 1980). These offenders were given modified indeterminate sentences, under which they were incarcerated either until they were reformed or had served their maximum term.

**INMATES COULD PROGRESS THROUGH A "GRADE" SYSTEM, WHICH RESULTED IN EARLY RELEASE** Upon entering the institution, inmates were placed in grade 2. If they behaved acceptably and successfully completed their work and school assignments they received 3 marks per month in each of these three areas (for a total of 9 marks per month). They needed 54 marks (which could be earned in as few as six months) to be promoted to grade 1. Six more months of good behavior in grade one, which yielded an additional 54 marks, entitled the inmate to be paroled. Uncooperative inmates were punished by being demoted to grade 3. Promotion from grade 3 to grade 2 required three months of satisfactory behavior.

**ELMIRA HAD A NUMBER OF INNOVATIVE PROGRAMS** Brockway initiated a number of programs at Elmira. He established a school program that enabled inmates to progress from learning basic arithmetic, reading, and writing skills to classes in psychology, ethics, etc. He also developed an industrial arts program that transformed Elmira into a truly industrial "reformatory" (Pisciotta, 1983). By the late 1880s, inmates could choose from more than twenty trades and within ten years after that, thirty-six were available (e.g., shoemaker, fresco painter, blacksmith, carpenter, tailor). This was also one of the first prisons to use organized sports (e.g., track, basketball) as a contributor to the reformation of inmates.

**ELMIRA HAD THE FIRST PAROLE SYSTEM IN THE UNITED STATES** Finally, Brockway is credited with developing the first parole system in the United States. Inmates successfully completing the grade system could request a hearing before the Parole Board—called the Board of Managers—who would determine their suitability for release after consulting with the superintendent. To be eligible for release, the inmate had to have a job he could start when released. While under supervision, parolees had to submit monthly reports, cosigned by their employers, stating that they were maintaining good work habits. There were no paid parole officers so Brockway had to rely on volunteers to supervise parolees during the six-month parole period. Inmates violating the conditions of their parole were returned to Elmira and placed in the second or third grade at Brockway's discretion and given another chance at reform (Pisciotta, 1983).

**WARDEN BROCKWAY USED REGRESSIVE METHODS OF DISCIPLINE** Despite his progressive ideas for reform, Brockway's methods of discipline were more severe than those advocated in the Declaration of Principles. An investigation of the records of disciplinary abuses at Elmira in 1893 and 1894 shows that disobedient prisoners were beaten with a heavy leather strap by Brockway (Pisciotta, 1983). One of Brockway's so-called "patients," as he liked to refer to errant inmates, provides a graphic account of one of these beatings prompted by his failure to complete a task:

I knew I was in for a beating as I knew the terrible treatment received by others, I had a terror of what was coming. I refused to leave my cell. They stuck into the cell an iron rod with a two foot hook on the end, heated red hot and poked me with it. I tried to defend myself with the bed, but my clothing took fire and the iron burned my breast. My breast is deeply seared to-day [sic] from burn. They also had a shortened hot poker, which burned my hands. I have those scars, too. I [was] finally secured, was handcuffed and taken to the bathroom. I asked Brockway if I had not been punished enough. He laughed at me, and said "Oh yes, we just fixed you up a little though," with that the hook was fastened to my shackles and I was hoisted off the floor. I got a dozen blows with the paddle right across the kidneys. The pain was so agonizing that I fainted. They revived me, and when I begged for mercy, Brockway struck me on the head with the strap, knocked me insensible. The next thing I knew I was lying on the cot in the dungeon, shackled to an iron bar. . . . I stayed in the dungeon that night and the next day shackled and received only bread and water. The next day I was again hoisted and beaten, returned to the dungeon and after one day's rest, beaten again. Then I was put in the cell in Murderer's Row, where I remained for 21 days on bread and water. (New York State Board of Charities, 1894, p. 8–9, as cited by Pisciotta, 1983, p. 621).

In the 1880s, Elmira instituted military training as a means of training inmates and keeping them busy when inmate labor laws abolished prison industries. In the early 1980s, this type of programing became an integral part of Boot Camp programs, which like Elmira, were designed for youthful offenders (see Chapter 24).

This account and others indicated that Brockway did not limit his discipline to paddling his "patients" but employed other methods, including solitary confinement, administering a quick slap or punch in the face, placing inmates on a restrictive diet of bread and water, and whipping them with a rubber hose. Persistent troublemakers were put in "rest cure cells" and some remained there for more than 100 days on diets of bread and water. Apparently Brockway considered these types of discipline appropriate since he never denied administering them and, in fact, argued they were for the inmates' own good (Pisciotta, 1983).

### Reformatory Goals Were Never Achieved

Between 1877 and 1913 reformatories were established in seventeen states. However, even the so-called model reformatory at Elmira, was not able to fully meet the objectives outlined in the Declaration of Principles. Thus, it is not surprising that

these other institutions failed as well. In fact, by 1910 the reformatory movement had reached its peak and was on the decline (Morse, 1940).

A number of factors doomed these reformatories to become nothing more than junior prisons (Barnes and Teeters, 1951; Johnson, 1968). First, both the design of the physical plant and the administrative policy of these facilities placed primary emphasis on security. Most reformatories were designed as maximum security facilities and were predominately staffed with old guard prison employees who viewed prisons as places to lock up and punish convicts. Second, the vocational and educational programs were limited because these institutions were concerned about making money in the shops and/or had inadequate equipment and staff. Third, the populations of these institutions were supposed to be limited to young, first-time offenders (16 to 30) who were thought to be capable of reformation. However, judges failed to restrict their sentencing to this type of offender.

Fourth, the grading system was complicated and led to most inmates being put in grade 1, leaving only a few in grade 2, with grade 3 being used for those being punished for misbehavior while in prison. Finally, states failed to employ indeterminate sentencing universally when committing offenders to these facilities, and to provide an adequately trained and professional parole system to supervise them on release.

Although reformatories failed in practice, they crystallized progressive correctional thought. During the first half of the twentieth century, there continued to be sporadic attempts to introduce bits and pieces of the Declaration of Principles into juvenile programs and even into adult institutions. In "Big House" prisons that dominated adult corrections for the next half century, as discussed in Chapter 6, there were attempts to introduce more elaborate classification systems and small rehabilitation departments. It was not until after World War II, however, that the necessary support became available to create a new type of prison—the "rehabilitation institution" (see Chapter 7)—in which these ideas could be tested more fully.

## ENDNOTES

**1.** At Auburn, like some other prisons, citizens were permitted to observe the inmates without having any contact with them. For a fee of 25 cents, prison visitors could walk along a passageway that ran along the walls of the shops and could observe inmates at work by looking through small holes in the walls. There were different views on this practice. Some wanted to abolish it because it gave the public the idea that prison life was not so hard and severe. Also some penal reformers felt the practice of allowing citizens to view and, in some cases, jeer at inmates provided a sideshow-type atmosphere. This put inmates on display in the same way as the freaks in a circus, which adversely affected efforts to reform them. Proponents argued that if the public was excluded from visiting prisons, people would think it was because the inmates were being subjected to cruel and inhumane punishment (Lewis, 1922/1996).

**2.** A number of other states experimented with solitary confinement for short periods of time during the first third of the nineteenth century, but only New Jersey and Rhode Island systemically tested the Pennsylvania model. These other states included Maryland, Virginia, Massachusetts, and Maine.

**3.** England today does have a professional prison service with two distinct career tracks, one involving those seeking to be governors and the other for prisoner officers (correctional officers). In visiting English institutions, one of the authors was impressed with both groups.

**4.** Chapter 7 also examines indeterminate sentencing with a specific focus on its use as a part of a rehabilitation program.

**5.** In 1941 the NPA was renamed the American Prison Association and in 1954 it became the American Correctional Association.

## ACKNOWLEDGMENTS

[a] *From The Discovery Of The Asylum* by David J. Rothman. Copyright ©1971 by David J. Rothman. By permission Little, Brown and Company.
[b] From *Conscience And Convenience: The Asylum and Its Alternatives In Progressive America* by David J. Rothman. Copyright ©1980 by David J. Rothman. By permission Little, Brown and Company.
[c] Reprinted by permission of The Historical Society of Pennsylvania. 1300 Locust Street: Philadelphia, PA 19107.
[d] ©Copyright New England School of Law 1981. All rights reserved. Reprinted by permission.
[e] Pisciotta, A.W. Scientific reform: The New Penology. *Crime and Delinquency.* 29(4) pp. 613–630. Sage Publications, Inc. ©1983. Reprinted by permission of Sage Publications, Inc.

## CHAPTER RECAP

**Methods of Punishment During the Colonial Period**
**The Search for New Methods of Social Control After the Revolution**
Penitentiaries Were Developed as Places to Reform Criminals
**The Pennsylvania and Auburn Systems**
The Pennsylvania Reformers Experimented with Several Different Systems
  The Walnut Street Jail Was the Birthplace of the U.S. Prison System
  Overcrowding Was the Major Factor in Program Failure
  Eastern Penitentiary Had a Program of Solitary Confinement, Work, and Penitence
The System Devised at Auburn Became the Model for U.S. Prisons
  Auburn Experimented with Three Alternatives

The Auburn Plan of Congregate Work, Silence, and Separate-Cell Confinement Was Adopted as an Acceptable Confinement Method

The Auburn–Pennsylvania Controversy Involved a Debate Over Which System Was Superior

The Pennsylvania Model Was Only Used by a Few U.S. Jurisdictions

The Auburn Model Prevailed for Economic Reasons

Auburn-Type Prisons Were Built in Many Jurisdictions

Many States Built Auburn-Type Prisons But Failed to Adhere to Its Rigid Standards

The Auburn Approach Followed a Quasimilitary Model

**Antecedents of the Reformatory Movement**

Alexander Maconochie's Mark System

The Major Objective of Prison Should be Reform

The Mark System Enabled Inmates to Work Their Way Out of Prison

The Mark System Was First Applied at Norfolk Island Prison

Punitive Public Views Resulted in Maconochie's Recall

The System Was Also Implemented at Birmingham Borough Prison

Sir Walter Crofton's Irish System

The Irish System Involved Increasing Privileges and Phased Release

The Irish System Reduced Recidivism

**The Reformatory System**

At the National Congress on Penitentiary and Reformatory Discipline, Prominent Reformers Proposed a New System

Elmira Was the First Reformatory

Inmates Could Progress Through a "Grade" System, Which Resulted in Early Release

Elmira Had a Number of Innovative Programs

Elmira Had the First Parole System in the United States

Warden Brockway Used Regressive Methods of Discipline

Reformatory Goals Were Never Achieved

## REVIEW QUESTIONS

**1.** Discuss the contributions of the Quakers to the development of prisons.

**2.** What was the importance of the Walnut Street Jail? Describe its program.

**3.** Compare the Pennsylvania and Auburn models.

**4.** Why was the Auburn model adopted by most states in the United States?

**5.** Describe the quasimilitary model and why it was used.

**6.** What caused the failure of the Auburn and Pennsylvania models?

**7.** Detail the roles of Maconochie and Crofton in the development of the reformatory.

**8.** Describe the unique features of the Elmira Reformatory.

**9.** Why did the reformatory movement fail?

## TEST YOUR KNOWLEDGE

**1.** Which of the following was a characteristic of the Walnut Street Jail?
  **a.** pay for work
  **b.** leg irons and chains
  **c.** guards that carried weapons
  **d.** frequent corporal punishment

**2.** Various alternatives were tried before what has come to be known as the Auburn system was finally developed. Which of the following methods was experimented with at Auburn but did not become part of the system?
  **a.** silence
  **b.** 24-hour-a-day solitary confinement
  **c.** congregate labor
  **d.** severe corporal punishment

**3.** Which of the following modern correctional practices was foreshadowed by Maconochie's mark system?
  **a.** disciplinary hearings
  **b.** inmate vocational training
  **c.** indeterminate sentencing
  **d.** prison boot camps

**4.** Which of the following is *not* a key element of the 1870 National Prison Conference's declaration of principles?
  **a.** solitary confinement
  **b.** indeterminate sentencing
  **c.** the mark system
  **d.** classification

# CHAPTER 5

# SOUTHERN PENAL SYSTEMS

Popular views of southern prison systems have been influenced by movies such as *Cool Hand Luke* and *Brubaker*. It is important to examine the southern system separately because different social and economic factors in this region produced methods of handling prisoners distinct from those in other parts of the country. The reader should remember that until the 1950s, southern states were segregated by law and could generally be characterized as strongly racist. The authors are cognizant of the sensitive nature of this issue and its presence in our society. In considering the events and conditions in this historical review, we do not wish to imply that the contemporary South is any more racist than the rest of the country.

Prior to the Civil War, in the South black slaves were the property of their owners, who had unlimited disciplinary power (including death) over them. Normally, however, owners used punishments similar to those inflicted on free men, most often including whipping, the stocks, pillories, mutilation, branding, and jail.

## THE PRE–CIVIL WAR SOUTH

Because slaves were usually punished by their owners, they were not usually found in prisons before the Civil War. Thus, most inmates were white.

### Black Codes Were Designed to Control Slaves

Slave owners had traditionally dominated southern legislatures and protected their slave interests. Recognizing that both slaves and free men needed to be punished for their crimes, they felt separate laws were required to keep their slaves docile and to prevent them from running away. These laws, collectively called **"Black Codes,"** inflicted more severe punishments on slaves than on whites for many offenses. For example, in Virginia slaves could be executed for a dozen or more felonies ranging from rape to buying or receiving stolen property, whereas whites received prison sentences for these offenses. Also, some acts for blacks were not construed as crimes when committed by whites. In Louisiana, slaves could be executed for striking their owners for the third time. Imprisonment was not seen as appropriate for slaves because it deprived their owners of their labor.

### Some Southern States Adopted Auburn-Type Prisons

Prior to the Revolutionary War, in all of the colonies free citizens were punished by corporal, capital, or monetary punishments. However, by the end of the 1700s all states had reformed their penal codes, reducing capital offenses for whites and substituting long-term imprisonment. As Chapter 4 noted, prior to the Civil War most southern states, with the exception of Florida and the Carolinas, opened Auburn-style prisons (Ayers, 1984).[a] These prisons were built only because a small but powerful group of politicians and editors supported this more humane alternative.

**CHARACTERISTICS OF THE PRISON POPULATION** The population of pre–Civil War prisons was composed almost solely of white males and a few free blacks. Prisons in most southern states either had no blacks or they constituted between 1 and 8% of the prison population. The two exceptions were Virginia, where free blacks comprised one-third of the prison population, and Maryland, where they represented more than one-half. Generally, the racial groups were segregated, but wardens in southern prisons, from the 1820s until the late 1850s still complained about having to house whites and blacks in the same facilities. This "problem" was solved in 1858 when blacks began being leased to private contractors for work outside prisons on canals, roads, and bridges (Ayers, 1984).

Women also represented a very small proportion of the prison population during this era. They typically suffered more than their male counterparts because the prisons had no special units for them. Women were generally housed in small, dirty, and unventilated buildings within the prison. Many were also sexually abused, often resulting in pregnancy. However, because so few were imprisoned, their plight was generally ignored. Their best chance was to gain early release through a pardon, which governors, sensitive to their plight, often granted (Ayers, 1984).

### States Resorted to the Lease System for Economic Reasons

Prisons in the South were initially established to reform offenders through compulsory labor. To pay operating costs, like prisons in the North, they established industrial shops that produced goods for sale on the open market. However, these industries failed to produce enough revenue to pay for prison operations. To remedy this, some states experimented with the **lease system.** In some cases a private company was contracted to control and operate prison shops, with the warden retaining overall control of inmates (Ayers, 1984). In other cases, the entire prison operation was handed over to an individual or company who paid the state a fee or a portion of the profits from the convict labor. Because lessees wanted to maximize their profits, they fed and clothed inmates as cheaply as possible; used guards willing to work for substandard wages or used inmates in this capacity; and worked inmates from dawn to dusk. Punishments for inmates who disobeyed orders or violated strict rules included solitary confinement on bread and water and whipping consisting of from 10 to 100 lashes (Sellin, 1976).

## THE POST–CIVIL WAR PERIOD

After the Civil War, the economy and infrastructure of the southern states[1] were in shambles and heavy taxes were required to rebuild them. At the same time they still had to deal with those convicted of crimes. Several factors led most of these states to choose a lease system to deal with inmates (Ayers, 1984).

### The Lease System Solved Various Problems

After the war, large numbers of free blacks began to be arrested as criminals and soon constituted 90% of those incarcerated. Because of deep racist beliefs, the crime problem became confused with "the negro problem." For these racists, this was "proof" of the inherent criminality of blacks and of their "inferiority." A more accurate characterization of southern blacks was that most were disorganized, uneducated, and poverty stricken—a legacy of their former slave status. In one rare instance a courageous Louisiana legislator, Aurel Arnaud, speaking before the General Assembly, offered a remarkably frank explanation of the criminal motives of blacks:

> Can you not see that [the fact that black tenant farmers or laborers rarely had incomes exceeding $40 per year] is not sufficient to support [them]? And

every day you divest him from a chance of earning something is a robbery of his daily bread? Should any one . . . be surprised to hear that negroes steal? I am surprised that they do not steal more (cited in Hair, 1962, as quoted by Carleton, 1971, pp. 44–45).

Efforts like Aranud's fell on deaf ears, however, because most white southerners were convinced of the innate inferiority of blacks and were unwilling to pay for their incarceration. However, once initiated even black legislators supported the lease system.

A second reason was the combination of bad economic times and the run-down condition of many state prisons. They had deteriorated during the war and some had been destroyed by northern troops. Initially most states repaired and rebuilt their prisons because they had become an integral part of their criminal justice systems (Ayers, 1984). However, widespread poverty during the postwar years led to increased crime, swelling the number of offenders entering the prisons. Because states could not afford to build enough new prisons to house this escalating population, many turned to leasing as a temporary solution. This avoided large outlays of state funds while more satisfactory alternatives were sought.

A third factor was the change from an agricultural slave economy to the beginnings of industrial development, which created a demand for labor. This was in short supply in many parts of the region, especially in dangerous jobs such as mining, building railroads, and turpentine production. For example, railroads needed rebuilding after the war but it soon became evident that using free laborers presented management problems because they often got drunk and then fought among themselves. Convicts, however, provided a reliable workforce because they could not get whiskey nor were they allowed to brawl. Also, they were chained together and guarded by men ordered to shoot anyone attempting to escape or to whip those not keeping up the work pace. Mississippi's experience in using inmates to build a railroad through the Canay Swamps illustrates these conditions.

> [Inmates] were placed in the swamp in water ranging to their knees, and in almost nude state they spaded caney and rooty ground, their bare feet chained together by chains that fretted the flesh. They were compelled to attend to the calls of nature in line as they stood day in and day out, their thirst compelling

them to drink the water in which they were compelled to deposit their excrement" (Foreman and Tatum, 1938, p. 260, cited by Sellin, 1976, p. 148).

There was a bright side and a dark side to the lease system. It gave impetus to industrial development in the South, which would not have been possible for many years. However, it did so at a terrible cost to those inmates who were involved in it (Ayers, 1984).

A fourth reason the lease system became popular was that during this period law-abiding citizens had no concern for the welfare of criminals despite the documented horrendous and inhumane conditions under which leased convicts worked. This was undoubtedly due to the fact that most lessees were free blacks and this returned them to a condition of servitude, which most racist southerners felt was appropriate.

Fifth, the lease system was justified on the grounds that it reformed its charges. Claims were made that it taught work and discipline. Indeed, the system gained a reputation, even among foreign visitors, of turning out good workers (Ayers, 1984).

A sixth reason was that there were major economic incentives for maintaining the lease system. It was ideally suited for industrialists whose only concern was making money (Ayers, 1984). In the beginning their labor costs were fixed and very low and they reaped high profits. States soon upped their lease rates when they realized convicts could command much higher prices. Despite higher rates, contractors still made a profit. Further, the lease system provided a constant pool of labor that could be used at any type of job.

A final factor making this system attractive to contractors was that convicts could be forced to work under conditions that free laborers would not tolerate. In many camps guards would wake up convicts at 4:30 A.M. and work them until nightfall with only a forty-minute dinner break. With the exception of Sundays and holidays, they worked every day regardless of the weather.

### The Convict Lease System Turned Offenders into Penal Slaves

This system of penal servitude made both black and white convicts the temporary or lifelong "slaves" of employers or corporations to whom they were assigned. Under the terms of most leases, convicts were turned over to contractors who were responsible for feeding, clothing, disciplining, and sometimes housing them. Contractors also paid annual fees, providing added revenue, which sometimes constituted sizable portions of a state's budget. In Alabama and Tennessee this amounted to about 10% of these states' incomes (Ayers, 1984).

Living conditions in the work camps were scarcely above subsistence level (McKelvey, 1977). Housing usually consisted of wooden huts, which held more than 100 inmates who slept on crude bunks strung along the walls. To prevent escapes, these huts were completely closed up at night and were thus foul smelling. Sanitary conditions were extremely crude and rampant disease was common. Our Close-Up on "The American Siberia: Life Under the Lease System in Florida," from a book by this title, provides a glimpse of these conditions.

Discipline in the work camps was quite severe. Although whipping was the usual punishment, some guards devised ingenious forms of torture or reinstituted others dating from the middle ages. Florida reached back to the Spanish Inquisition and resurrected the "ordeal by water," in which the prisoners were strapped down on their backs and had a funnel forced in their mouth, into which a steady stream of water is poured. The effect was to expand the stomach, producing great agony and a sense of impending death because of the pressure on the heart. Also used was the medieval practice of "hanging by the thumbs," which could cause great agony and even death. Many convicts were also subjected to as many as ten hours or more in the **sweat box:**

[which was] a coffin like cell with just enough space to accommodate a man standing erect. Generally made of wood or tin it was completely closed except for a hole two inches in diameter at nose level. When placed under the blistering southern sun, the temperature inside becomes unbearable. In a few hours, a man's body swells and occasionally bleeds (Moos, 1942, p. 18).

Conditions such as these drove many men to attempt to escape. To prevent this, convicts wore striped uniforms, were usually shackled, and sometimes had heavy iron balls attached to the chains. Dogs and armed guards provided added security measures. To ensure the vigilance of the contractors, some states fined them for every

## Close Up    The American Siberia: Life under the Florida Lease System

The line of the proposed railroad was through a virgin wilderness; there seems to have been no attention whatever paid to proper equipment, and the story of that terrible journey stands unparalleled in criminal annals. Dozens of those who went into the tropical marshes and palmetto jungles of Lake Eustace went to certain death. There was no provision made for either shelter or supplies. Rude huts were built of whatever material came to hand, and in the periods of heavy rain it was no unusual thing for the convicts to awake in the morning half submerged in mud and slime. The commissary department dwindled into nothing . . . there was no food at all. . . . [T]he convicts were driven to live as the wild beasts, except that they were only allowed the briefest intervals from labor to scour the woods for food. They dug up roots and cut the tops from "cabbage" palmetto trees. Noble Hawkins, a ten year Nassau convict, lived for fourteen days on nothing but palmetto tops and a little salt, and his case was but one of many. . . It was not long before the camp was ravaged by every disease induced by starvation and exposure. The pestilential swamps were full of fever, and skin maladies; scurvy and pneumonia ran riot. Dysentery was most common, and reduced the men to a point of emaciation difficult to describe or to credit. Every stopping-place was a shambles, and the line of survey is punctuated by grave-yards (Powell, 1891/1970, pp. 10–13).

**Inmates could be punished by being placed in sweat boxes for up to an entire day. Some Southern prison systems used this form of punishment well into the 20th century.**

escapee. In some cases, guards' jobs were made dependent on their vigilance, resulting in scores of fugitives being shot every year. The escape attempts, harsh discipline, and barbaric and unsanitary conditions produced very high convict mortality rates. In the late 1800s the death rate in twenty-eight northern institutions was 14.9 per 1000, whereas in southern prisons it averaged 41.3 per 1000 (McKelvey, 1977), which for the South was probably a low estimate (Powell, 1891/1970; Ayers, 1984).

Thus, in the South after the Civil War, blacks convicted of crimes were subjected to a new form of slavery that was even worse than that experienced under the plantation system (Sellin, 1976). This **penal slavery** not only enabled the state to transfer its responsibility for convicts to a private authority that would house, clothe, feed, and "punish" them, it was also paid for it. This era represents one of the low points in American corrections.

The lease system was also employed in several western states and territories—Washington territory, Montana, Wyoming, Nebraska, and Oregon—which did not have funds to build and maintain prison facilities (McKelvey, 1977). It was not until 1936 that the system was finally abolished in every state (Barnes and Teeters, 1951). We will see in Chapter 13 that overcrowding and the high cost of prison construction and operation in the 1980s has

Striped uniforms and shackles were used to prevent escape on the chain gangs. This practice is currently being revived in several states.

prompted states and local jurisdictions to reconsider the involvement of private contractors in managing prisons and prisoners.

### Chain Gangs Were Used by Some Jurisdictions to Manage Prisoners

One might think when states terminated the lease system and assumed control of convicts that the lease system's worst features would disappear.

Unfortunately, the only change was that inmates were now under the control of the states or counties who placed them on "chain gangs," "prison farms," or "plantations."

The term **chain gang** has been used to refer to all southern prison camps that employed inmates at hard labor. We will employ it only to refer to the use by counties and states of chained convicts to build railroads and levees and to construct and maintain county roads and state highways.[2] Many

A Southern chain gang cleaning up a road right-of-way.

jurisdictions viewed this as an excellent way to improve roads required by the advent of the automobile and to avoid building expensive prisons. To maximize output and minimize escapes, armed guards and shackles were used. Whipping and other harsh practices were used to discipline those who were unruly or unwilling to work.

Convict housing at these camps took one of two forms (Tannenbaum, 1924). Some convicts were housed in movable prisons called cages because of their resemblance to those used to confine circus animals. These wooden or steel structures were easily moved, allowing this labor supply to be housed wherever needed. Our Close-Up on "Life on the Chain Gang: Even Circus Animals Lived Better" provides a perspective on conditions prevailing in some camps. Tents, which provided a little better housing, were also used in some camps (Tannenbaum, 1924).

Convicts on the chain gang worked ten- to twelve-hour days depending on the season, and were under the control of a camp captain who was hired because of his knowledge of road building or promoted through the ranks. The guards overseeing these inmates were poorly paid, usually illiterate, and could only control the inmates by resorting to brute force (Sellin, 1976).

Moveable cages used to house inmates while they worked on the chain gangs.

Flogging, which was legal in most southern states until just before World War II, was the most common form of punishment. When it was abolished some states devised other equally excruciating punishments, including solitary confinement with a diet of bread and water. Despite the efforts

## *Close Up* **Life on the Chain Gang: Even Circus Animals Lived Better**

Frank Tannenbaum (1924) provides a rare glimpse of life at a camp that employed cages to house its convicts.

. . . As soon as a man comes to a chain gang camp he is shackled. That shackle generally stays put as long as he is there—and that may be a life-time. The chain is riveted to both ankles. . . A dozen men and more will be chained to each other when they are asleep in their beds. There will be a long chain running from one end of the cage to the other. Through this chain all men will be locked by slipping one end of the long chain through the loose end of the cross chain which each prisoner has, in addition to the one riveted around his ankles. This limits the movements of the men to the length of their cross chain. Thus, they sleep. Thus, they lie in their beds on Sundays. Frequently, they are compelled to lie that way when it rains and that may be for two weeks together. The typical cages [they sleep in] are small. They stand on wheels. They range from seven by seven by sixteen to nine by nine by twenty. The typical cage has some 18 beds. There are nine beds on each side of the cage. Three beds lengthwise, three in height one above the other . . . They have chains on their ankles and are often, even in the daytime, locked to each other. That means that the men have no freedom of movement. They lie on their beds, their faces almost touching the bed above them. The cage frequently has tin roofing. On hot days—Sundays, Saturday afternoons, holidays—the sun streams down on the cage and makes an oven of the place, and the human beings in it roast. These cages are not cleaned. Under this crowding it would be impossible to keep them sanitary . . . [These] steel road cage[s were] similar to those used for circus animals, except they did not have the privacy which would be given to a respectable lion, tiger, or bear (pp. 84–86).

At a chain gang work camp, portable wagons were used to house inmates.

of reformers in some states, few if any, changes were made in these conditions until the mid-1950s.

## PRISON FARMS AND PLANTATION PRISONS

When some southern states abolished leasing, they developed large prison farms and plantations for those convicts who were not employed on the roads. These institutions operated primarily to maximize profits and reduce or eliminate the costs of imprisoning convicted offenders. Thus, the treatment inmates received was not much better than that received by inmates on the chain gangs. The development of agricultural work in southern prisons was based on the fact that this was a major industry in the South and the belief that this work was better suited for the black majority of the inmate population.

### In Mississippi, the Parchman Penal Farm Became the Main Prison

The work of William Taylor (1984, 1993[b]) provides an excellent history of the Mississippi penal system. Drawing on his work we briefly examine the development of this system as an example of the prison farm concept.

**FARM ORGANIZATION FOLLOWED A PLANTA-TION MODEL**   Following an antebellum plantation model (drawn from the way pre–Civil War plantations were organized,) each farm was divided into essentially autonomous field camps for purposes of crop rotation, accountability, self-sufficiency, simplified management, and the dispersal of laborers. By 1917 thirteen camps were operating, producing cotton and their own food (Taylor, 1984, 1993).

Labor on these farms, which was "under the gun," began at sunrise, six days a week. Convicts were marched to the fields under the supervision of an unarmed sergeant—who ran the camp—and his unarmed assistants and several armed **trusty-guards.** Any inmates who ventured beyond a defined line could be shot at by trusty-shooters. Convicts labored until sunset and were marched back to their housing units. There they were super-

vised by trusty-guards who served as night watch-men.

The trusty system on this and other southern prison farms was an outgrowth of a slave structure existing on pre–Civil War plantations. On the prison farm trusty-servants had the most desirable jobs and were envied by all other convicts. These special inmates worked as domestic help in the superintendent's mansion and in the homes of camp employees and in service-related camp activities. They held jobs as cooks, janitors, drivers, orderlies in the hospital, etc.

On the next rung were the convict artisans who functioned as support service personnel. Most of these inmates were white and performed skilled jobs such as carpentry, masonry, and other repairs. Next in status were the trusty-shooters, who as the only armed men on the farms, functioned as the camp security force. These men, usually murderers, were appointed by camp sergeants only after years of trouble-free service as field hands. They were the camp police who had two jobs: to prevent escapes and be night watchmen.

Using convicts to perform most guard, service, and support functions kept the prison's payroll quite low. This system's cost effectiveness and efficiency caused it to continue until a federal court finally intervened in 1972 (*Gates v. Collier,* 1972).

To maintain good behavior and foster hard work, camp sergeants bestowed a number of privileges on convicts. They were allowed the freedom of the camp on Sundays, holidays, and week nights. Organized sports were permitted; baseball was popular and teams were formed at the black camps that competed regularly. Trusty status was also a powerful reward for good behavior (Taylor, 1993).

Another major incentive for black inmates was the **conjugal visiting program.** Its origins are not clear and it was not sanctioned by the legislature nor motivated by any concerns for maintaining marital relationships. As early as 1918 this system enabled black convicts to enjoy the favors of commercial prostitutes. Authorities viewed sexual favors as valuable in the management of black convicts (Taylor, 1993).

During the 1930s this privilege continued to be restricted to black convicts. Also, by this time black inmates were allowed to take their wives or girlfriends to their sleeping quarters where privacy was secured by hanging up blankets (Hopper, 1969). Beginning in 1940 some camps constructed a makeshift building to be used for conjugal visiting. Painted red, they became known as "red houses." Although this system may have served camp sergeants as a very effective motivational tool, there is little doubt that it had negative effects on white prisoners who were not given the same privilege initially.[3]

By the early 1950s most male camps, black and white, had "red houses," and prostitutes were no longer permitted in the camps. Nevertheless, there was still no official support or recognition for the program (Hopper, 1969). It was not until 1957, when a reform-oriented superintendent officially established what he described as his "family day program," that it received formal recognition.

Although the Mississippi conjugal visiting system is the oldest in the United States, the reasons it was established were far from humanistically based. However, by the time it received official recognition more humanitarian motives were the predominant basis of the system. Chapter 21 discusses further the issues regarding conjugal visits.

Several forms of early release were part of the reward system to promote good behavior and hard work. A good time program enabled these inmates to reduce the length of their sentence by a specified number of days each month (Taylor, 1993). More appealing to the inmates were the three forms of executive clemency. Pardons were granted along with early release for meritorious conduct (usually given to a trusty-shooter who prevented escapes by shooting the escapees); participation in medical experiments; and general clemency on major holidays (e.g., Christmas) or when a governor left office. About 13% of the convicts were released yearly in this manner.

Convicts refusing to obey the rules were whipped and/or transferred to a tougher camp because these punishments were consistent with the demands of the farm system. In the North, solitary confinement on a restricted diet was the most common punishment. However, in the South, isolation was viewed as a way for convicts to escape labor and food deprivation was considered to weaken convict laborers and create costly health problems. It is interesting that, as at Auburn, the use of the strap was justified as the most expedient means of achieving inmate compliance. No more

than fifteen lashes per day were permitted. All forms of corporal punishment were finally banned by a federal court in 1972 (*Gates v. Collier*, 1972).

## THE PRISON FARM COMPLEX EVOLVED OVER TIME AND WAS FOUNDED ON THE TWIN GOALS OF PROFIT AND REFORMATION

The father of the **Parchman Farm prison plantation** was Governor James K. Vardaman, an individual who might be best described as a "benevolent racist" (Taylor, 1993). In 1906 he was responsible for legislation defining Parchman as Mississippi's primary prison facility. He took a personal interest in developing what was barren land into a prison farm complex. He was also the philosophical architect of this approach to imprisonment. He recognized that the limited opportunities available to ex-convicts upon release contributed to recidivism. His solution was to make the prison into a school to teach inmates the skills needed to survive on the outside. However, his white supremacist views overshadowed his reformative philosophy, because he believed that blacks should not be permitted to do any work above that of common laborers. Therefore, they did not need to learn how to read and write and only required vocational training relating to agricultural work. He believed that if inmates were paid for their labor and provided with incentives they would learn a work ethic.

Vardaman also felt that these institutions should be self-sufficient and profit-making. In fact, between 1906 and 1933, while other systems were operating at a loss, Mississippi prisons made a profit of more than $4 million over and above their operating costs. The self-sufficiency of the farm operations created opportunities for inmates to learn trades and provided housing, food, and medical care that were up to the standards of the period (Taylor, 1993). By 1933, however, with the Great Depression in full swing, the system experienced declining revenues. The legislature was unwilling to fund the prison adequately and this resulted in a deterioration of the physical plant and living conditions for inmates.

*Changes Led to New Goals: Punishment and Profit Then Back to Reform and Profit* In the 1930s the legislature eliminated reform as a goal, making punishment at no cost to the state the prison's major focus. To increase revenues, superintendents diversified prison operations at Parchman by establishing new canning and shoe factories and a modern slaughterhouse. This all helped to pump huge revenues into the state treasury and to provide work for those displaced from farms because of mechanization.

In the 1940s the dual goals of reform and profit again surfaced with the appointment of a reform-oriented superintendent. This period saw improvements in health care, living conditions, and in the quality and quantity of food inmates received. In 1944, with the superintendent's support, a rehabilitation component was introduced by a popular minister who was appointed as chief chaplain. His reform efforts included a modest basic elementary education program, a religious program, Christmas furloughs, and increased visitation. Reform efforts continued in the 1950s with expanded educational offerings, including high school classes and new classification procedures under which tests determined work assignments and educational placements.

The introduction of synthetic fibers resulted in a depressed cotton market and contributed to a big decline in prison revenues in the early 1950s. Increasing numbers of pardons and releases of inmates were used to save money. The resulting loss of these better inmates—including many trusty-shooters who really controlled the camps—worsened the systems' security problems. Reformers used this to justify creating a probation system and constructing a maximum security unit (Taylor, 1993).

*The Writing Was on the Wall: The Racist and Inhumane Conditions Had to Change*   Despite some improvements in working conditions and medical care, by 1956 Mississippi was being targeted by the Civil Rights movement for its racist policies. A new superintendent was brought in who initiated several changes that included television sets for inmates (justified as a reintegrative tool since they could serve a prerelease orientation function), an increased emphasis on religion to build moral character, a formalized conjugal visiting, a program helping inmates to get jobs on release, and new status and support for the inmate newspaper. The real change occurred when the prison's "money-making" philosophy was abolished. In its place "the rehabilitation of prisoners, the protection of society, and the welfare of prisoners" was to be emphasized (Taylor, 1993, p. 156). Also solitary confinement replaced the strap as the main disciplinary tool.

In the early 1960s an attempt was made to restore Parchman's "good old days" when the farm was making money. This was to be accomplished by better management of farm operations. Reform continued to be a goal as manifested in the establishment of a new literacy program. However, the prison's continuing budget deficit forced cuts in expenses, which resulted in reductions in medical services, food services, and staff. A senator visiting the prison found inmates lacking shoes, boots, and winter underwear. These conditions, and the changing character of the inmate population, contributed to increased escapes.

This system was established to handle a largely black, illiterate, unskilled, and rural population. However, in the mid-1960s the offenders admitted were 40% white and almost 90% literate. Thus the prison began to experience problems because white inmates were more unmanageable and often had urban backgrounds, which made them less willing to do farm work. Further, the Civil Rights movement inspired blacks to resist their "oppressive" treatment. While the probation and parole systems removed the most easily managed inmates, attempts continued in the effort to make the farming operation a financial success.

The increasing mechanization of the agricultural system in the mid-1960s may have improved the institution's financial status without other major changes, however, it only added to problems of inmate idleness. Forgotten was the primary reason for the labor-intensive program (i.e., to occupy inmates and tire them out, which reduced their likelihood of engaging in mischief). Although vocational programs and other innovations were added to fill the void, they only involved a small proportion of inmates who tended to be the most well-behaved anyway.

Security then became a critical problem. The prison began to get an increasing number of hard core offenders who were initially placed at the farm units. Inadequate funding, low pay for prison workers, and the farm's isolated location resulted in a short-staffed civilian work force, which was corrupt, inept, or both. Trusty-shooters continued to be the primary security force, but parole had deprived the prison of the best of the trusties. Despite this, the legislature still refused to fund a civilian guard system. By the late 1960s inmates complained about being mistreated, overworked, fed terribly, and forced to endure merciless whippings and other tortures by guards and trusties.

**THE COURTS STEP IN TO PROPEL THE SYSTEM INTO THE TWENTIETH CENTURY**  Although Arkansas was deemed to be the worst system in the country, the Mississippi system was not far behind. After the finding in 1970 that the totality of conditions in Arkansas prisons violated Eighth Amendment protections against cruel and usual punishment, the Mississippi legislature acted to protect itself. Some modest changes were made including hiring a qualified superintendent and eliminating the trusty-shooters. However, it failed to fund newly established staff positions to: replace the inmate guards; ban the lash; and solve the question of racial inequities.

This led to an inmate lawsuit filed in 1971 seeking relief from alleged unconstitutional conditions and practices at Parchman. In reviewing this complaint, Judge Keady determined that it qualified as a class action suit. During the pretrial discovery phase the state admitted "in effect ... that constitutional provisions [had] been violated" (as cited by Taylor, 1993, p. 201). The judge found confinement at the prison deprived inmates of the constitutional rights guaranteed by the First, Eighth, Thirteenth, and Fourteenth Amendments (*Gates v. Collier*, 1972). He ordered immediate changes including the elimination of segregation of inmates by race, mail censorship, and confinement of inmates under improper conditions in solitary confinement. The prison was also required to adopt a meaningful classification system, provide inmates better protection and medical care, phase out the trusty-shooters, and improve physical facilities. In areas requiring more time, much money, or extensive construction, the judge ordered the state to devise a plan that included improving inmate housing, water, treatment, medical services, and fire-fighting facilities.

While Mississippi complied with Judge Keady's orders, the changes occurring in its prisons have both a bright and a dark side. The unconstitutional conditions that existed and the problems addressed by the inmate suit have largely been corrected. However, Taylor (1993), asserts that the Mississippi penal system remains an "ongoing problem" plagued by a number of problems including a lack of political support, poor morale, increasing inmate-on-inmate violence, racially based gangs, inmate idleness, and reduced participation in programs. These problems have been exacerbated by large increases in the inmate population.

## Arkansas Was Considered the Worst of the Southern Systems

Although many prison farms, such as Angola in Louisiana, have vied for the honor of the "worst" prison farm, the Arkansas system appears to win the prize. The horrendous conditions at the two prison farms comprising this system were brought to public attention by an official investigation released to the press in January 1967, when newly elected Governor Winthrop Rockefeller was about to take office. In his inaugural address, Rockefeller described this prison system as the "worst in the nation." He appointed a reform Warden, **Tom Murton,** to bring these institutions, still operating using eighteenth-century methods, up to mid-twentieth-century standards (Murton and Hyams, 1969).

Before examining the system it is necessary to provide a brief perspective on Arkansas penology. The system Murton took over had not changed in about forty years, leading him to call it the "Tucker Time Tunnel" because entering it was like getting in a time machine and going back 100 years (Dison, 1991). It consisted of the Cummins Farm (16,000 acres) and the Tucker Farm (4500 acres) each producing rice, cotton, vegetables, and livestock. The combined inmate population was close to 2000, with only thirty-four civilian employees at the two facilities.

**CONDITIONS WHEN MURTON ASSUMED CONTROL WERE HORRENDOUS**  In this system an inmate's status was all important because it determined his living conditions, treatment, and privileges. The 300 inmates at Tucker were housed in three barracks 50 feet wide by a 100 feet long. Each housed 100 inmates and the facilities within them varied according to the inmates' status.

Trusties were at the top of the inmate hierarchy. Since there were only three civilian employees, trusties were responsible for operating most facets of the prison, including serving as guards and operating prison services (e.g., food, medical, farm). They had their own dormitory, the most freedom, the best food, and were in the best position to extort money and goods from inmates.

The middle status group, half-trusties or **do-pops,** so named because they had duties that included popping doors open for superiors, cleaning buildings, waiting tables, and caring for the animals. They had their own dormitory, ate almost as well the trusties, and were one step from trusty status.

The lowest level in the system was occupied by **rank men** or farm laborers. In the barracks they were subject to being kicked and walked on by trusties. They could be forced to sweep all night and at daybreak be marched to the fields where the trusty guard could beat them all day. They had no socks, underwear, t-shirts, or outerwear to protect them against the cold. Rank men worked hardest but got the worst food; most were 40 to 60 pounds under their normal weight. They did not have even the basic necessities of life and their living conditions were abysmal (e.g., they slept on rotting mattresses with sheets that were washed perhaps every three weeks. Thus when offered a trusty job they took it, even though it involved beating other inmates, because their quality of life improved. This organizational structure perpetuated a system by which the oppressed became the oppressors (Murton and Hyams, 1969).

While all prisons have sub-rosa economies and power structures, inmate control of these farms led to a system of extreme corruption, brutality, and deprivation. Trusties frequently deprived newly arriving inmates of their money or property by threats or with promises of better treatment. They took the food, money, and clothing rank men received from their families on visiting days. For most the only source of money was the "blood sucking program" (i.e., selling their blood at $3 per donation).[4] Also for sale was the "right to continue living." Inmates without outside resources were forced to bargain with their bodies. The open barracks system, combined with lack of civilian staff, enabled more powerful inmates to victimize young and/or weaker ones. Since Arkansas had no minimum age for prison confinement there were many fourteen-year-olds in the system who, according to Murton, were ripe for "punking" (being made into passive homosexual partners for other inmates).

While most rank men ate poorly, those with money could buy extra food from the inmate serving it, who likely had his own "commissary."

Guards sold "good beds" for $1 to $3 (Murton and Hyams, 1969) and even medical care had its price. Rank men wanting to go to the infirmary when the doctor was there or to receive their prescribed medication had to be on good terms with the trusties or be able to pay them (Murton and Hyams, 1969; *Holt v. Sarver,* 1970).

To survive, inmates developed all sorts of rackets. Laundry workers charged a $2 fee to clean clothes. Kitchen workers bought food from the commissary and used institutional equipment to prepare food for sale in the barracks. Gambling flourished. Trusties profited most because they controlled everything in the prison including jobs, discipline, housing, food, and access to services and administration. The trusties' freedom to leave the farm to go to town meant they could bring back free-world items, such as weapons, liquor, and drugs, to sell to other inmates at a considerable profit.

The most incredible aspects of this system were the inmate shacks. A trusty with power and money could scrounge himself some lumber and build a shack. Appropriate payoffs to facility technicians would get him water, electricity, and gas. He then bought a television, a gas range and refrigerator, and became a squatter. When he left he could sell his job, house, and personal property to his successor. They were even allowed to bring women to these "homes." Some trusties did so well they did not want to leave the prison (*Holt v. Sarver,* 1970).

Half of the inmates were employed in housekeeping and maintenance jobs. An inmate armed guard force of fifty, half of whom were convicted murders, manned the institution's perimeter. This group had life and death control over inmates and civilian staff. The maintenance and security requirements of the facility left only fifty-five to sixty inmates to work the fields.

While the prison superintendent was responsible for seeing that there were no inmate escapes, his major function was to operate the farm at a profit. This required planting and harvesting fifty-six different crops. To achieve this, he made a deal with the **yard man**—the chief trusty—who really ran the prison:

He told them, "Get the crops in and keep the men quiet, I will give you extra privileges. I don't care how you manage. Use a lead pipe, anything. Just do it. And keep anything you make on the side" (Murton and Hyams, 1969, pp. 42–43).

## Close Up   Corporal Punishment Arkansas Style

### Whipping—Oh, Captain

LL-34 said that in April 1966 he was whipped for not picking enough "pickles," and Mr. Bruton ordered his head peeled [shaved] and he was given ten more lashes on the bare buttocks. He refused to cry out "Oh, Captain!" and was locked up for another hour, then given twenty more lashes by Mr. Bruton (Murton and Hyams, 1969, p. 11)

### The Infamous "Tucker Telephone"

The telephone designed by prison superintendent Jim Bruton consisted of an electric generator taken from a crank-type telephone and wired in sequence with two dry-cell batteries. An undressed inmate was strapped to the treatment table at Tucker Hospital while electrodes were attached to his big toe and to his penis. The crank was then turned, sending an electrical charge into his body. [This was known as being "rung up" in contrast to receiving a "long distance call" which involved the infliction of several charges]. . . . Sometimes the "telephone" operator's skill was defective, and the sustained current not only caused the inmate to lose consciousness but resulted in irreparable damage to his testicles. Some men were literally driven out of their minds (Murton and Hyams, 1969, p. 7). [The Tucker telephone was not only used to punish inmates but also for getting them to provide information.]

---

The control of men who were cold, hungry, tired, and hopeless required a brutal system of punishment, which included whipping and torture. This was only one of two states—the other being Mississippi—where whipping was authorized and practiced into the 1960s. Many inmates also reported being tortured by having their fingers, toes, noses, ears, or genitals pinched with pliers or having needles inserted under their fingernails. The most dreaded and vicious torture was the **Tucker Telephone.** Our Close-Up on "Corporal Punishment Arkansas Style" provides examples of these types of punishment.

As late as 1966, the Arkansas parole system was an extension of the system of penal slavery. As a parolee, an inmate became an indentured slave; that is, to be paroled an inmate had to be sponsored for a job. Sponsorship was usually accorded to people who had contacts with the parole board. Thus, parolees could be worked like slaves because if they complained or tried to get another job, the employer could call their parole officer, who would send them back to prison.

**MURTON TRIED TO BRING THE SYSTEM NEARER TO CONTEMPORARY STANDARDS** Murton decided to change this system by first assuming control of Tucker Farm, the smaller of the two farms. He planned to learn more about the system, reform this farm, and develop a commando crew later to take over the Cummins Farm (Murton and Hyams, 1969). In this section we briefly discuss some of the changes he made at Tucker.

Taking charge of an institution that was almost entirely run by inmates was extremely difficult because it was impossible to eliminate past practices and abuses without their cooperation. The incongruity of these circumstances is reflected in Murton's first formal comments to the trusties:

> Normally when I take over an institution I come in and say "This is how it's going to be and this is the way we're going to run things. But this is ridiculous in a situation like this because you have the guns and the keys and you're running things so there's no way I can take over" (Murton and Hyams, p. 30).

He also told this group he intended set up an education program, which he did with the help of the local school district. A vocational training program was also instituted with the help of the local gas company. For fifteen years this company tried to establish such a program (it would have provided both equipment and instructors) because it needed 400 repairmen each year and viewed inmates as ideal trainees. After implementation, inmate enthusiasm was so high that the instructor offered a second class. Murton reduced gambling by requiring that inmates turn in their free-world money as well as their prison money. He also reduced inmate access to certain raw materials, which decreased the production of alcohol.

Murton also promised rank men that they would be fed, clothed, and, most importantly, would be coming back at night and not be buried in the fields. He pledged that inmates would be promoted on merit and not by purchasing their jobs.

To keep his promise to promote on merit, he established an elected camp council, which functioned as a classification committee that made decisions regarding custody as well as changes in status, for example, appointment of trusties. Three inmates and the superintendent formed the disciplinary committee. It heard all complaints against inmates, decided guilt or innocence, rendered a judgment, and determined punishment. Murton reserved the right to veto any action and gave inmates the option of having their cases heard only by him.

The strap and the other barbaric punishments were eliminated. These were replaced with solitary confinement of one to two days, under which inmates received the same food provided to other inmates except without condiments. Murton felt that this, along with a loss of newly gained privileges (e.g., visitation, movies), was sufficient to gain inmates' cooperation.

Farm operations and food service were reorganized. Meat was served three times a day and farm produce appeared on the tables. Inmates were given footlockers with padlocks for their belongings. A recreation program was established that included the construction of a baseball field and a farm band. A new doctor was hired who was concerned about inmate welfare.

Within ten months Murton felt he had accomplished enough at Tucker to assume control of Cummins and began making changes similar to those at Tucker. He hired a replacement for himself and increased the civilian staff to include supervisors for special services, probation and parole, education, farm operations, and security.

The most controversial information Murton brought to light involved the high number of inmates who had disappeared—were listed as escapees—and/or died under questionable circumstances. Based on an investigation, he concluded some, if not most, of these inmates had been murdered by prison officials or other inmates. In the controversy following these revelations, Mur-

ton was fired in 1968, ostensibly for being "incapable of and insensitive to the requirements of operating in harmony with his associates in a government structure" (Murton and Hyams, 1969, p. 191).

**THE TOTALITY OF CONDITIONS AT THE PRISONS WERE FOUND CONSTITUTIONALLY UNACCEPTABLE** When Murton left Arkansas, conditions basically reverted to the way they were before his arrival. Fortunately for the inmates, the courts adopted a "hands on approach to prisons" and finally forced the system to change for good. In *Jackson v. Bishop* (1968), the Eighth Circuit Court of Appeals stated that whipping for disciplinary purposes was a violation of Eighth Amendment protections against cruel and unusual punishment. A second series of cases—*Holt v. Sarver,* 1969, and *Holt v. Sarver,* 1970—dealt with broader aspects of the system. Here the court set a precedent by using the concept of "totality of conditions." Thus, taken individually, conditions cited may not have represented constitutional violations, but taken in "their totality" (i.e., together) they did constitute cruel and unusual punishment and violated the eighth amendment. The court found inadequate medical and dental facilities and inmate access to them and unsanitary kitchen facilities. The court went to on say that:

> For the ordinary convict a sentence to the Arkansas Penitentiary today amounts to a banishment from civilized society to a dark and evil world completely alien to the free world, a world that is administered by criminals under rules and customs completely foreign to free world culture. . . . A convict . . . has no assurance whatever that he will not be killed, injured or sexually assaulted . . . confinement involves living under degrading and disgusting conditions. . . However constitutionally tolerable the Arkansas system may have been in former years, it simply will not do today as the Twentieth Century goes into its eighth decade (*Holt v. Sarver,* 1970, p. 381).

The judge ruled that if the state wanted to continue the confining of inmates at these prison farms it had to eliminate the trusty and field guard system, ensure inmate safety, change the barracks system, and eliminate the isolation cells. Although it recognized that a transitional period was necessary to make these changes, the court deemed the conditions so intolerable that it required they be made in

---

## Close Up  **The Arkansas Prison System in the 1990s**

The legal dispute regarding the constitutionality of the Arkansas prison system lasted for thirteen years. By 1982 Arkansas had convinced the court that its prisons met "minimal constitutional standards." Only a very few people associated with Arkansas corrections (e.g., a few inmates with long sentences) saw the case through from its initiation until it was settled.

Many changes came about during the thirteen years the federal courts were involved in Arkansas corrections. Some of the more important ones were replacing inmate trusty supervisors with trained staff; establishing inmate rights through formalized disciplinary and grievance processes; creating sanitary and humane living and working conditions; improved medical care; and construction of millions of dollars worth of new facilities. The number of staff increased from 35 to more than 1000 during this period and budgets increased accordingly.

It is fair to say that the Arkansas system left behind its nineteenth-century approach and became a relatively conventional system in the 1980s. However, problems remain and Arkansas faces the same major issues that most other systems face. In the late 1970s Arkansas toughened sentencing and parole laws. This greatly increased the demand for prison bed space. Between the early 1970s and 1991 the Arkansas prison population almost quadrupled from about 2000 to 7700 inmates. While budgets increased (e.g., $6 million in 1977 to $45 million in 1987), the system is still unable to keep up with the volume of inmates. It is not unusual to have hundreds of convicted inmates in county jails waiting for space in prison. A number of facilities have been built in addition to the facilities known as Cummins and Tucker and a "bootcamp" operation has been established for first offenders. It is reported that Jim Guy Tucker, the Arkansas governor who replaced Bill Clinton, places a high priority on further reforms of the Arkansas system, including expansion of community-based corrections and intermediate sentencing options. Correctional reform in Arkansas thus continues to unfold.

*Source:* Prepared especially for *Corrections: A Comprehensive View* by Jack E Dison, Associate Professor, Department of Criminology Arkansas State University

---

months rather than years and warned Arkansas officials.

Our Close-Up on "The Arkansas Prison System in the 1990s" provides a brief look at how this system has changed since the 1970s.

## THE TEXAS SYSTEM WAS THE LAST MAJOR SYSTEM TO CHANGE

No discussion of southern penal systems would be complete without including the Texas prison system, which was and still is the largest in the region. In 1849 the first Texas penitentiary was opened in Huntsville. It contained 225 cells and was constructed on the Auburn model. Its inmates were expected to produce sufficient quantities of goods to make it self-supporting. The history of how Texas dealt with inmates can be divided into several periods including the lessee period (1871–1883); the contract-lease period (1884–1909); the agricultural expansion period or the era of the plantation farm (1910–1947); the period of reform and stability (1948–1971); and the period of court intervention (1972–1990).

### The Lessee Period: Inmates Were Assigned to Contractors

In the decades following the Civil War, and after failing to operate a profitable prison manufacturing program, Texas officials decided to lease the entire prison operation to private businesses. Thus, convicts were housed, fed, worked, and cared for by contractors whose only concern was making a profit. Although the state saved money, the brutality and neglect to which the inmates were subjected was extreme and ranged from poor clothing and food, to beatings and murder (Copeland, 1980; Crouch and Marquart, 1989). The Texas Penal Code of that time prohibited indiscriminate whipping and other forms of corporal punishment, yet these punishments were routinely used for rule violations.

These poor conditions resulted in an increasing number of inmate deaths and escapes (Martin and Ekland-Olson, 1987).

### The Contract-Lease Period: The State Controlled Inmates and Their Labor Was Contracted to Businesses

In 1883 the state resumed control of Huntsville prison and its inmates. The contractual arrangement with private farmers, railroad, and mining businesses was continued but prison officials supervised, disciplined, and housed the inmates working for these contractors. In 1885, in order to make its prisons more self-sufficient, the state purchased its first prison farm. This established an agricultural component, which in the next era became its major aspect. The contract-lease system failed to improve inmate conditions substantially, leading to continued criticism, yet it persisted for more than twenty-five years (Crouch and Marquart, 1989).[c]

### The Plantation Farm Period: The State Assumed Total Control of Inmates

Around 1880 the prison system began to buy thousands of acres of farmland around Huntsville and Houston. With the demise of the contract-lease system, the prisons went into the agricultural business in a big way. Although not successful economically, these farms provided work for a large proportion of the inmates, who continued to be harshly treated. Legislative investigations repeatedly showed a pattern of abuse of inmates as bad or worse than in preceding periods (Crouch and Marquart, 1989). By 1947 conditions were so bad the Texas prisons were labeled as among the nation's worst.

The prison farms were so spread out and remotely located that no fencing was put up around them. Remoteness also made their wardens essentially autonomous with each viewing his farm as his own private kingdom. Each warden had his own special rules and procedures for controlling inmates and was rarely reprimanded regardless of his actions (Copeland, 1980). Living conditions at these farms were poor and overcrowded. Sheets, blankets, clothing items, soap, toilets, bathing, and laundry facilities were all in short supply. A news account reported that in one camp for young offenders:

> the stench is awful for they get soap enough for only one fourth of the men in the tanks to get a soap and water bath every three weeks and at this farm there is no provision for the prisoners to wash their clothing. . . In rainy weather, the prisoners are unable to wash their own clothing, even in plain water (*Houston Chronicle*, December 14, 1947, as cited by Copeland, 1980, p. 64).

Not only was the there not enough to eat but in some cases the food was spoiled and unfit for human consumption. These terrible conditions led to frequent inmate work strikes.

Living conditions in the tanks (barracks) were aggravated by the fact that guards infrequently entered them, preferring to patrol outside to prevent escapes. This led to the appointment of **building tenders** (BTs), inmates who were given the authority to maintain order within the tanks. From the outset they were described as a plague on the system. BTs performed functions similar to trusty-guards in Mississippi and Arkansas, except that they did not carry firearms (Copeland, 1980). Typically they were long-term inmates who were chosen by the guards for their superior intelligence or physical prowess.

BTs controlled all the gambling, had access to contraband such as narcotics, and controlled such things as putting an inmate on the sick list, which meant he could rest for the day (Copeland, 1980). They maintained order through violence and could carry weapons such as knives and clubs. Thus, tank society was dominated by the strong and vicious with the weak being constantly victimized physically and/or sexually. Also, a substantial number of inmates died from the harsh working conditions, poor sanitation and medical care, and at the hands of civilian prison guards.

On the farms everyone worked. The majority of inmates were assigned to the "field force" or **hoe line.** Work squads, carrying their tools, marched from their living areas to work sites up to 5 miles away. Inmates worked under the close supervision of armed guards mounted on horseback. There were also dog packs and other armed officers on the work perimeter to prevent escapes.

The basic workday went from sunrise to sundown irrespective of the weather. Inmate workers were driven mercilessly by the guards, who used rubber hoses, chains, bullwhips, and even their horses to bully inmates to work. Inmates who lagged or worked too slowly were punished in the field and/or when they returned to the camp. Even inmates falling out because of heat exhaustion or for other physical reasons were likely to be punished.

The terrible conditions under which inmates lived and worked produced some expected and unexpected reactions. Many attempted to escape, however most escapees were recaptured and many were killed even while surrendering. An unconventional way of escaping used by some inmates was self-mutilation, which included amputations (of a foot, hand, or of several fingers), cuts into which lye or some infection-causing materials were placed, fracturing of arms or legs, and severing of the Achilles tendon. Amputating three fingers from one hand was the "million dollar" injury because this made wielding a hoe or other similar tool impossible (Copeland, 1980; Crouch and Marquart, 1989). Seriously injured inmates were transferred to the main prison hospital in Huntsville, where conditions were much better; but those who could be cured were sent back to the farm. Between 1932 and 1948 there were 411 self-mutilations (Koeninger, 1951).

The state had about as little concern for guards as for the inmates they watched. Guards worked from twelve to fourteen hours a day. Vacations were nearly unheard of and even sickness was no excuse for missing work. The guards paid for their own uniforms and weapons. They lived in a room in the same building as the inmates, separated from them only by a common wall, which often had gaping holes in it. The food they ate was almost as bad as that of the inmates. They had little formal education—many were illiterate—and the system provided no formal training. Thus, many inmates found it easy to manipulate their guards. Even with these low standards the system was hard pressed to keep its units fully staffed. To maintain control, prison managers were given greater authority to use inmates to supervise their fellow convicts.

Like the previous period in Texas prison history, the plantation farm era finally succumbed to external criticism. With the election of a reform governor in 1947 efforts began to make major changes in the system.

### The Period of Reform and Stability: TDC Goes from the Worst to the "Best" System

This period saw many system changes and improvements. The election of Governor Jester, who had run on a platform of prison reform, set the stage for this period. He hired O. B. Ellis, who had successfully operated the prison farm program in Tennessee, to manage Texas prisons (Crouch and Marquart, 1989).

Under Ellis, and his successor George Beto, the Texas system went from "worst to first" in less than twenty years. By the 1960s it gained the reputation of being the nation's best system. The reforms effected during that period created an "orderly, steady and philosophically consistent" system (Krajick, 1978). The hallmark of the system was the degree of control exerted over the inmates.

In addition to tightened security and control, there were improvements in inmate conditions. Incorrigible inmates were removed from the farms and placed in isolation; self-mutilators were no longer "rewarded" by being removed from the farms. An attempt was also made to eliminate excessive force against inmates by firing some guards and even a warden. Although extremely flagrant abuses were eliminated, many old punishments continued to be used, including handcuffing inmates to cell bars. Thus, Ellis was unable to change the use of physical punishment to control inmates. Neither he nor Beto eliminated the building tender system but rather modified it to exert more control over inmates. A subject of continuing criticism, the BT system remained even under Beto's successor, W. J. Estelle. It was not abolished until the 1980s, and then it was by court order.

**WHILE WORK CONTINUED TO BE STRESSED, IMPROVEMENTS WERE MADE IN PROGRAMMING** Typically all able-bodied inmates worked during this era. Inmates spent their first six months on the hoe line. If job performance and personal behavior were satisfactory, inmates were then eligible for a "promotion" to some other type of agricultural work, prison industries, construction, or prison maintenance. About 50% of the inmates did agricultural work. Others were employed at jobs in modern dairies, raising livestock and chickens and in running farm machinery. Texas boasted that its inmates were not idle since any not employed in other pursuits worked the line.

Some work programs offered inmates a chance to learn a skill that might lead to employment upon release. Our Close-Up on "Texas Inmates Learn Marketable Skills" looks at two of the more distinctive programs operating during this era. About

## Close Up Texas Inmates Learn Marketable Skills

Visitors to the Ellis unit bus repair facility and the Wayne and Coffield records conversion facilities cannot help but be impressed with these programs, as one of the authors was, because of the extent to which they parallel those on the outside.

The bus repair plant renovates and repairs buses for schools throughout the state at a cost of approximately half their replacement value. The inmates can take a school bus that has been in an accident or has deteriorated to a point where it is no longer functional and completely renovate it, including painting the interior and exterior, frame repair, engine replacement, seat replacement, etc., so that it looks and performs as well as a new one. They also repair and construct bodies for fire engines. This plant is operated by 150 inmates who are supervised by eight employees.

Equally impressive are two records conversion facilities, which employ more than 1300 inmates who work three shifts a day. These facilities place such records as vehicle registrations, traffic tickets, and other records on microfilm, magnetic computer tape, or punch cards. They also provide services such as file maintenance, mail inserting, and zip coding, including preparing and mailing vehicle registration renewal forms. This facility also prepares, maintains, and reproduces textbooks in braille for the blind, which are provided upon request for various school districts. According to the supervisors of these programs, inmates that work in these programs have little difficulty obtaining jobs upon release.

10% of the inmate workforce built and maintained all prison buildings. Using inmate labor, Texas could build facilities at about two-thirds of their free-world cost; consequently, Texas has more new prisons than most other states. The remainder of the Texas Department of Corrections (TDC) inmates (approximately 30%) who were not on the programs described in the Close-Up were assigned to institutional maintenance jobs (e.g., porters, kitchen workers).

Toward the end of this period the Texas system was reputed to be the safest, most orderly, and most economically run in the nation. This was largely attributed to its full employment system, which, while based on the goal of self-sufficiency, also served as a mechanism of control and may have been a vehicle for rehabilitation. However, as we shall see, order and control in this system were achieved through brutal means.

Education was another important facet of TDC programming during this era. Fully accredited programs ranging from remedial education to secondary school academic and vocational classes were offered through the Windham School District, a nongeographical school district established by the state legislature in 1969 specifically for conducting educational programs at TDC. New inmates with less than a fifth-grade equivalency were required to

attend school; others could attend one day a week (Gettinger, 1978). A junior college program offered academic and vocational training leading to an associate of arts degree and courses leading to a bachelor's degree were available.

**CONTROL AND STABILITY WERE ACHIEVED THROUGH AN AUTHORITARIAN SYSTEM** Control and stability were still achieved through a rigid authoritarian system:

Everything is predictable. You know what to expect. You don't have to worry about getting stabbed or raped by other inmates, or what's going to happen from one day to the next, because it's the administration that's totally in control. After a short time here, you realize that if you go to your cell, go to mess, wash up, go to work quietly, all will go well. It's almost more like the service than the penitentiary, except for the bars (as cited by Krajick, 1978, p. 21)

This statement from a TDC inmate, who had served time in two other states, suggests why this system impressed many correctional professionals. While acclaimed for its high level of control, safety, stability, and cleanliness, the question raised by critics was "at what price?" The "cost" was a regimented and brutal system, which had elements of a totalitarian society (Crouch and Marquart,

1989). All facets of an inmate's life were tightly controlled including his dress, movements, speech, correspondence, and visits. Contraband was controlled by requiring all inmates to strip each day prior to returning to their cells, and by barring contact visits. Regimented formations were maintained in all activities inside the prisons.

A second facet of this authoritarian system was the correctional officer (CO) subculture, which was shaped by four characteristics: a strong work ethic; strong personal loyalties to their superiors and the department of corrections; paternalism in dealing with inmates and subordinate officers; and tough self-reliance in handling inmates. Inmates occupied a subordinate status and were viewed as lazy, immature, and inferior, which justified their treatment like children by COs. They developed a reputation for being able to achieve compliance, when necessary, by the use of physical force. Physical punishment was used frequently enough to lend weight to more common verbal reprimands. Thus, while the majority of inmates were not brutalized, all lived under this threat. Ranking officers established a network of snitches who kept them informed about inmate actions and plans (Crouch and Marquart, 1989).

**INMATE-GUARDS PLAYED AN IMPORTANT ROLE IN THE CONTROL SYSTEM** The backbone of the Texas prison system that kept inmates under tight control (in this era as in the past) was the hierarchical trusty-guard system, which featured building tenders, turnkeys, and bookkeepers. At the top were head building tenders, who were in charge of a particular cell block and accountable for all inmate behavior in it. They were the most powerful inmates in the prisoner society. Next were rank-file building tenders, who assisted the head BT in controlling the cell block; turnkeys, who opened and closed riot gates; and bookkeepers, who kept prison records. On the third rung were runners, strikers, or hit men who kept the cell block clean, dispensed supplies, and provided BTs with physical backup when necessary (Marquart and Crouch, 1984; Crouch and Marquart, 1989).

Inmates who became BTs were given status and power as well as tangible rewards. They had freedom of movement within the prison, their own showers, access to food as often as they wanted, freedom to carry weapons, immunity from punishment, and access to gifts and bribes from inmates

for helping them with their problems. Crouch and Marquart (1989) subdivided BT functions into three major roles. BTs functioned as assistant guards by helping guards in such control functions as counts and getting inmates to meals and work assignments. They also protected guards by breaking up fights in the living areas so that officers did not have to get involved and risk personal injury. Second, as mediators, BTs functioned to adjudicate and arbitrate inmate disputes. They tried to settle petty squabbles (e.g., poor hygiene or snoring) as well as more serious inmate disputes including physical or sexual assaults, thefts, and failure to make good on debts. BTs kept the peace by fear, coercion, and moving inmates unable to get along with one another to another cell or unit. Third, they had an intelligence and contraband control function in that they gathered information on inmates and reported it to prison staff. Not all rule violations (e.g., who was playing a radio too loud) were reported since this would adversely reflect on their management of the cell block. As the staff depended on the BTs, they in turn depended on their own network of stool pigeons. As one head BT put it: "The tanks were run through an information system . . . this was how trouble is kept down" (Crouch and Marquart, 1989, p. 95). Force was frequently used and often involved the weapons that BTs were allowed to possess. One BT summed up the way they used coercion as follows:

> If inmates were wrong, it was an eye for an eye and they'd get the shit whipped out of them. . . You can't control people who consider themselves gangsters by word of mouth. You let them know every day who's running the tank—whatever it took to convince them. You don't say, "Would you please do this?" because they'd f**k your ass. You need a certain amount of force and a certain amount of fear and certain amount of respect (as cited by Aric Press, 1986, p. 49).

In short, BTs controlled the tanks through fear, intimidation, and physical force. From the standpoint of prison officials, the inmate elite, and many average inmates, this made prison life more stable and predictable. However, for inmates disliked by BTs or considered problems, life in the tanks was tense and often not safe.

Officials controlled BTs by a policy of divide and conquer. While united when confronting other inmates, BTs regularly snitched on each other for revenge or to help "the man." When they became too abusive, got involved in drugs, or got into the protection rackets, they were fired if the staff found out about it.

**CONTROL OF THE BTs WAS LOST DURING A MAJOR POPULATION INCREASE** Prison officials were able to maintain control of BTs until the early 1970s. In the next decade, the prison population almost doubled but the guard force remained about the same. Thus, officials were increasingly dependent on BTs to control inmates but were less able to exercise control over them. As a result BTs wielded even more discretionary power and they used it routinely to punish inmates physically. Under these circumstances, staff lost control of the prisons.

### The Era of *Ruiz v. Estelle* Converted Texas into a Modern System

By the mid-1970s the once solid support that TDC had enjoyed from the press and more importantly from the legislature started cracking. The death knell for TDC was *Ruiz v. Estelle* (1980). David Ruiz was a habitual repeat offender serving a 25-year sentence for armed robbery when he began to file writs and write letters complaining about conditions in the Texas prisons. One of his petitions reached federal judge William W. Justice, a well-known judicial activist, who decided to combine it with six similar civil actions that were filed by other Texas inmates. Ruiz was named as the plaintiff in this action and Wayne Estelle, director of the Texas Department of Corrections, and several of his wardens were named as defendants.

The *Ruiz* case, the most far reaching in correctional legal history, lasted for nine months and involved 349 witnesses and 1600 exhibits. After listening to this mountain of testimony, the presiding judge, William Justice, issued the most sweeping and detailed order in the history of prison litigation. He found that the conditions in almost every part of this prison system violated minimum constitutional standards. His opinion covered overcrowding, security and supervision, health care, discipline, access to the courts, fire safety and sanitation, work safety and hygiene, unit size, structure, and location. Part of his order mandated the elimination of the "unlawfully maintained building tender" system (p. 1298). To make sure that the changes either ordered or mutually agreed to in a consent degree were implemented, he appointed Vincent M. Nathan to act as Special Master in the case.[5]

The state initially resisted the orders to change, but then began to comply in late 1983. Restrictions were imposed on guards using physical force to control inmates. The BT system was abolished, which created a power vacuum because it dissolved the inmate power structure that had defined and governed the nature of inmate relations for many years. A surge of inmate violence and aggression resulted. One veteran guard explained it in this way:

> The inmates know they're not going to get their asses whipped by nobody. They know there's no BTs to whip their ass. So they do what they want to do. You know, "F**k TDC." There is nobody to stop them from killing somebody. They're trying to stake their claim now that the BTs are gone (as cited by Crouch and Marquart, 1989, p. 198).

Other changes in the control system also had negative effects. The addition of new guards and imposition of greater restrictions on the use of force without creating effective alternative methods of control meant inmates could act out with impunity. Crowding and administrative turnover helped to produce further social disorganization.

In an environment without any controls, "survival of the fittest" became the norm. Inmates became preoccupied with self-protection. Some succumbed to the advances of stronger more aggressive inmates; others got weapons and protected themselves. By the mid-1980s TDC prisons, particularly the hard-core units, had become very dangerous places.

From 1979 to 1985 TDC staff increased from about 2500 to 9000, which meant most COs were inexperienced. When added to the massive changes going on at TDC, this created a disaster. There were not enough experienced personnel to socialize new COs. Unaware of the dangers and manipulative and exploitative nature of many inmates, many COs became overly friendly with them. Thus, in the early 1980s, many COs were receiving money or loans from inmates for performing favors (e.g., giving them a copy of their file) or bringing in contraband (e.g., drugs and weapons) (Crouch and Marquart, 1989).

The crisis in self-protection—created by the removal of the BTs and greater restrictions on guards—was further aggravated by racial tensions. Many inmates ended up joining together into gangs. Chapter 10 provides a detailed discussion of gang development and activities. In the present context these gangs offered their members protection and also provided other things, including access to use and traffic in contraband, such as drugs. As is the case when most gangs first develop and vie for control of illicit markets, the gangs in TDC during this era accounted for a disproportionate amount of violence. Between 1984 and 1985 there were 52 murders and 80,000 reported instances of violence in the system (Aric Press, 1986).

Stability was achieved by a new bureaucratic order and legal control mechanisms. To regain stability, Texas had to come to grips with the requirements of the *Ruiz* decision. TDC's governing board finally did this in the mid-1980s. This ushered in a new legalistic order, which was put into effect when Raymond Procunier[6] assumed control of the system after the resignation of Jim Estelle. Coming from outside TDC, he had no commitment to its traditions. His mandate was to transform the system as rapidly as possible into a constitutionally acceptable operation. To accomplish this, he centralized decision making and expanded rules. He formalized accountability procedures in order to standardize operations and to maximize compliance with rules by all staff. This placed major constraints on official staff discretion in rewarding and punishing inmates. The use of force (except in well-defined situations) was banned. Control was to be achieved by legal devices (including the write-up or report of rule violations, which could affect an inmate's good time and eventual release), administrative segregation, and, when necessary, lockdown.

To deal with the violence and allay concerns that the administration was losing control, in late 1985 a program of indefinite lockdowns for all gang-affiliated or assaultive inmates was instituted. Initially 1700 inmates were locked down. This number rose to more than 3000 and hovered between this figure and 2500 until the late 1980s. The lockdown policy was successful and both guards and inmates reported that this was the major reason the prisons became safer. Homicides dropped from twenty-seven in 1985 to three in 1986. As a result, in 1987 Texas opened a super maximum security unit, similar to the federal facility at Marion (see Chapter 17), to control its high-risk inmates.

The new legalistic approach to controlling inmates gradually filtered down to the unit level and by the late 1980s a new control structure developed. By this time unfamiliar rules, paperwork, and procedures had become routine. COs found that by using discretion in enforcing rules, most inmate behavior could be controlled by threat, frustration, and harassment. As these changes took hold and the system approached compliance with the *Ruiz* requirements, a new bureaucratic order emerged. Court oversight declined and TDC's central office gained greater autonomy in managing the prison, particularly in control issues. In turn, the central office relaxed bureaucratic control on prison operations believing that new compliance policies were sufficiently institutionalized and that greater prison unit autonomy would not jeopardize inmate rights (Crouch and Marquart, 1989).

## WORK CAMPS AND PRISON FARMS CAN BE VALUABLE COMPONENTS OF A CORRECTIONS SYSTEM

This discussion of southern prisons may appear to suggest that work camps or prison farms should not be part of a modern corrections system. However, it is not the model that is objectionable, but the abuses that have characterized it. In fact, there appears to be real value in the employment of inmates in agricultural activities and other outdoor programs, for example, forestry camps and road gangs. These programs give inmates opportunities to work in the fresh air, engage in productive labor, and get some exercise. Further, it tires them out and minimizes problems generated by idleness in the prisons. The placement of inmates serving long sentences, but posing minimum security risks, in small work camps reduces incarceration costs and gives them freedom of movement not available in larger facilities. Agricultural programs also provide food for the prison system and for sale to other state agencies, which helps to reduce imprisonment costs. Finally, given the high cost of constructing and operating traditional prisons, these facilities deserve a place, at least in major state correctional systems.

There are some disadvantages in small work camps. They lack special programs and services because they cannot be cost-effectively maintained in these settings. Additionally, the work opportunities at these camps may not result in many future job skills.

Today, prisons in the South face the same problems as those in the North: They must deal with an escalating prison population.

## ENDNOTES

**1.** The southern states include Mississippi, Louisiana, Alabama, Georgia, Florida, South Carolina, North Carolina, Arkansas, Tennessee, Texas, Kentucky, and Virginia.

**2.** Camps of this kind were established in Arkansas, Alabama, Florida, Louisiana, Mississippi, and Texas.

**3.** Hopper (1969, 1989) offers a somewhat different interpretation of the development of this system. He contends that the small rural nature of these camps and the plantation mindset of those who ran them helped to maintain a view of workers, whether they were slaves or inmates, as not willing to work productively through punishment alone. Moreover, the small rural nature of these camps allowed for a more informal visiting system without the attendant security problems and supervision that would be necessary at large prison complexes. Also the small size of these camps enabled sergeants to get to know the inmates and their families more personally. This, he feels, fostered a greater concern for the physical and emotional needs of their charges. Thus, for Hopper this more liberal visiting program, along with the home furlough program, seemed to be designed to help inmates maintain contacts with their families.

**4.** While the inmates were actually paid $5 per pint of blood, $1 went to the Officers' Welfare Fund and another $1 went to the Inmate Welfare Fund—from which inmates derived little benefit. Thus all the inmate got was $3. The real beneficiary of this system was the doctor who had the contract to sell the blood to Cutter Laboratories. He made between $130,000 and $150,000 per year from these donations.

**5.** It was not until March 31, 1990, that he finally completed his role as master in this case. At that point the burden for overseeing compliance shifted to system's assistant director for compliance, Charles Smith, and his staff members. He had to oversee compliance in ten areas for an additional two years.

**6.** Raymond Procunier was a prison administrator with experience in New Mexico, California, Utah, and Virginia. He resigned after a year and was succeeded by his deputy—Lane McCotter, an army colonel with experience running the stockade at Fort Leavenworth—who had been hired at the same time as Procunier.

## ACKNOWLEDGMENTS

[a] Excerpted from *Vengeance and Justice: Crime and Punishment in the 19th-Century America South* by Edward L. Ayers. Copyright ©1984 by Oxford University Press, Inc. Reprinted by permission.

[b] Material from *Brokered Justice: Race, Politics, and Mississippi Prisons, 1798–1992,* William Banks Taylor, is used by permission. ©1993 by the Ohio State University Press. All rights reserved.

[c] From *An Appeal to Justice: Litigated Reform Of Texas Prisons* by Ben M. Crouch and James W. Marquart, Copyright ©1989. By permission of the author and the University of Texas Press.

## CHAPTER RECAP

**The Pre–Civil War South**
Black Codes Were Designed to Control Slaves
Some Southern States Adopted Auburn-Type Prisons
    Characteristics of the Prison Population
States Resorted to the Lease System for Economic Reasons
**The Post–Civil War Period**
The Lease System Solved Various Problems
The Convict Lease System Turned Offenders into Penal Slaves
Chain Gangs Were Used by Some Jurisdictions to Manage Prisoners
**Prison Farms and Plantation Prisons**
In Mississippi, the Parchman Penal Farm Became the Main Prison
    Farm Organization Followed a Plantation Model
    The Prison Farm Complex Evolved Over Time and Was Founded on the Twin Goals of Profit and Reformation
        Changes Led to New Goals: Punishment and Profit Then Back to Reform and Profit
        The Writing Was on the Wall: The Racist and Inhumane Conditions Had to Stop
    The Courts Step In to Propel the System into the Twentieth Century
Arkansas Was Considered the Worst of the Southern Systems
    Conditions When Murton Assumed Control Were Horrendous
    Murton Tried to Bring the System Nearer to Contemporary Standards
    The Totality of Conditions at the Prisons Were Found Unconstitutionally Acceptable
**The Texas System Was the Last Major System to Change**
The Lessee Period: Inmates Were Assigned to Contractors
The Contract-Lease Period: The State Controlled Inmates and Their Labor Was Contracted to Businesses
The Plantation Farm Period: The State Assumed Total Control of Inmates
The Period of Reform and Stability: TDC Goes from the Worst to the "Best" System

While Work Continued to be Stressed, Improvements Were Made in Programming

Control and Stability Were Achieved through an Authoritarian System

Inmate-Guards Played an Important Role in the Control System

Control of the BTs Was Lost During a Major Population Increase

The Era of *Ruiz v. Estelle* Converted Texas into a Modern System

**Work Camps and Prison Farms Can be Valuable Components of a Corrections System**

## REVIEW QUESTIONS

1. Specify the pre–Civil War conditions that affected the development of corrections in the South. Define and describe the Black Codes.

2. Discuss the operation of the lease system.

3. What was the nature of inmate living conditions on southern chain gangs?

4. Outline the organization and functions of the Parchman Farm prison plantation.

5. Explain why Arkansas prisons were considered the worst of the southern prison farm systems. Describe the process by which Tom Murton changed the prison farm at Tucker.

6. Discuss the precedent-setting *Holt v. Sarver* decisions.

7. Outline the development of the Texas prison system and the phases through which it progressed.

8. Define the role of the building tenders during the different phases of the development of the Texas system.

9. What were the effects of the *Ruiz* decision on the Texas prison system?

10. Suggest some reasons why work camps or prison farms could still be beneficial to corrections.

## TEST YOUR KNOWLEDGE

1. The early practice of handing prisons over to an individual or company who took responsibility for its operation and usually paid the state a fee or a portion of the profits that were derived from the labor of the convicts was known as the
   a. chain gang.
   b. lease system.
   c. lease camp.
   d. plantation prison.

2. The main goal that the lease system, chain gangs, and prison plantations had in common was to
   a. hold prisoners awaiting trial.
   b. rehabilitate offenders.
   c. develop inmate job skills.
   d. maximize profits from convict labor.

3. Conditions in the Arkansas prison system were finally challenged by the courts because they were
   a. unconstitutional.
   b. inefficient.
   c. immoral.
   d. not cost-effective.

4. Which of the following terms was used for the lowest classification of inmates in the Arkansas prison system?
   a. do-pops
   b. yard men
   c. rank men
   d. trusties

5. Which of the following statements regarding the building tenders in the Texas prison is true?
   a. They were paid.
   b. They were armed with shotguns.
   c. They performed maintenance duties such as repairing the plumbing.
   d. All of the above.
   e. None of the above.

# CHAPTER 6

# THE BIG HOUSE

The Leavenworth Prison, built in 1895, is a typical Big House fortress prison. Note the exterior architecture, yard, gun towers, and cell houses.

To understand contemporary prisons, it is necessary to examine the changes that occurred in prisons and their populations during the twentieth century. The era of the Big House lasted from about 1900 to 1950. During this period prison populations grew from about 50,000 to 163,000 inmates (Barnes and Teeters, 1943; Bureau of Justice Statistics, 1982). Any attempt to portray correctional institutions during a given period is hampered by the fact that each state administers its own facilities. As a result, there are wide variations in policies, practices, and facilities. Thus, anything but a broad overview of prisons during a given era is impossible. During this era federal prisons began to be built, with the first three opening between 1902 and 1907.

## BIG HOUSE PRISONS WERE HARSH AND IDLE PLACES

Big House prisons were usually surrounded by thick concrete walls with towers at each corner. They resembled military fortresses. They had an average population of 2500 men housed in large cell blocks containing as many as six tiers of one- or two-man cells. New units were gradually added over a long period of time. Cells in the newer units were usually more spacious and clean, better ventilated and heated, and contained toilets and small sinks. Many of these prisons also allowed inmates

to decorate their quarters with paintings, rugs, and furniture, which helped make these extremely cramped spaces more accommodating. Despite these human touches, the Big House was a harsh and oppressive world of concrete and steel in which inmates were subject to chilling cold in the winter, oppressive heat and stench during the summer, and constant unnerving levels of noise.

Other distinctive features included a mess hall, workshops and industrial facilities, an administration building, and the "yard." Typically enclosed by cell blocks and the prison's exterior wall, the yard often presented the only opportunity for inmates to enjoy some freedom and fresh air. Recreational facilities in the yard may have included a baseball diamond, tables and benches, basketball courts, and handball courts—often created by using the walls of the cell blocks. The better known of these institutions included Stateville in Illinois, Sing Sing in New York, the Ohio Penitentiary in Columbus, and Canyon City in Colorado.

### The Big House Era Saw the Demise of the Industrial Prison

The Big House era saw the collapse of prison industry and the emergence of prison idleness. The heyday of full employment for prison inmates spanned a period of about seventy years, lasting into the early twentieth century. Virtually every prison had workshops. Some had prison factories,

The "yard" at the "Walls" unit in Texas. The yard was the traditional recreation area in the Big House.

which produced items sold on the open market in competition with those made by free enterprises. However, the economic hardships of the 1930s enabled business and labor to persuade states and the federal government to pass legislation restricting the sale of convict-made products on the open market. Most jurisdictions shifted to a **state use system,** which restricted the sale of prison-made goods to state and local governments.[1]

The reduction in prison industries resulted in 50% or more of the prison population being unemployed. As more men than necessary were assigned to the shrinking pool of jobs, the work day was reduced to six or fewer hours, creating more idle time. Without the mass production of the automobile in the late 1920s, which created a de-

mand for license plates, there would have been even more idleness. In some prisons this was the only functioning industry (Barnes and Teeters, 1951). The only other jobs involved institutional maintenance (e.g., kitchen work, cleaning cell blocks, institutional repairs), and a small number of clerical jobs. Very few of these jobs taxed the inmate's energy or time (Barnes and Teeters, 1951). Thus, during the last twenty to thirty years of their existence, Big Houses contended with idleness and its attendant problems (e.g., riots and inmate schemes). As a result, by the mid 1930s, relatively harsh punishment and strict custody functions were being used to control inmates (Morse, 1940). Idleness has continued to be a problem through the present time.

The "Tag Factory" represented one of the few industries in 20th century Big Houses. It taught few usable free world skills because Tags were only made in prisons.

## THE SOCIAL WORLD OF INMATES

Whenever people interact with one another over an extended period of time, they develop a social structure with divisions and strata, informal rules and meanings, and a variety of enterprises (Irwin, 1980). The specific social patterns that develop in a prison result from the interactions between the prison's environmental characteristics and those characterizing the inmates. Inmates bring to prison the values and attitudes developed in their free-world lives and from their prior experiences in other facilities (Irwin and Cressey, 1962). Other inmate characteristics that shape the prison world include (1) population characteristics such as age, race/ethnic origin, rural versus urban background, and educational level; (2) the extent to which inmates identify with outside subcultures; and (3) the adaptations they make to the dehumanizing conditions and deprivations of prison life. The prevailing attitudes and values in society at large also have an influence. These factors interact to produce an inmate world that includes several subcultures, various adaptations to prison life, and a status system.

### The Big House Population Contained Those Who Were Unsuccessful in Both Their Legal and Illegal Pursuits

Clemmer (1940/1958)[a] examined a Big House prison during the 1930s and found its population consisted largely of individuals from the poorer and less well educated segments of the population. They lacked job skills, had irregular work histories, and about one-half had previously been in a prison or reform school. The thief (robber or burglar) was the predominant type of offender. These were not "big score offenders"; instead they were usually amateur, occasional offenders who averaged under $100 per crime. Consistent with prevailing outside practices and prejudices, blacks and other minorities were usually segregated by being housed separately or with cell mates of the same race, were relegated to menial jobs, and by rule or tradition occupied separate sections in the mess hall. Thus, Big Houses were dominated by white lower class individuals, many with reform school experiences. They were not equipped to succeed in either conventional or criminal pursuits.

### The Inmate Subculture Was Influenced by Internal and External Factors

The inmate subculture helps inmates cope with the special circumstances of prison life by providing ways of thinking, feeling, and acting for all aspects of prison life. Much research and debate has centered on the factors influencing the development of this subculture (Thomas and Petersen, 1977). One position, the **deprivation model,** argues that inmate culture is a collective response to the deprivations imposed by prison life, for example, lack of heterosexual relations (Sykes, 1958). In contrast, the **importation model** asserts that it is shaped by a socialization process involving the adoption of a criminal value system to which the inmate is exposed prior to confinement (Irwin and Cressey, 1962). An inmate growing up in an urban lower class community, who has been in a juvenile gang and later involved with adult criminals, comes to prison with values and behaviors similar to those that characterize the inmate subculture.

Rather than arguing which model is valid, it makes better sense to look at the inmate subculture as a dynamic system affected by a variety of factors both within and outside the prison (Thomas and Petersen, 1977). These factors include the historical development of the prison, outside social and political developments, criminal values, and conditions within the prison. When we discuss the prisoner movement in Chapter 8, it will be clear how external conditions, such as the Civil Rights movement, affected the inmate subculture. In the Big Houses two factors produced the inmate subculture: the convict code and the conditions of confinement.

#### THIEF VALUES INFLUENCED THE CONVICT CODE
The dominant value system in the Big House was the **convict code,** which was heavily influenced by the thieves code. Thieves who were involved in for-profit crimes such as larceny, burglary, or robbery were the predominant criminal group in these prisons. Their loyalty to each other, strong commitment to thief values, and communication network enabled them to occupy a superior role in the inmate world (Irwin and Cressey, 1962; Irwin, 1980). Although not all inmates abided by its precepts, many gave lip service to its values and evaluated each other based on its core value—rightness or solidness. A right or solid guy was someone who could be trusted and, most importantly, relied on not to rat on another offender.

Imprisonment was a recurring problem with which thieves had to deal. Their subculture provided ways of doing time that attempted to reduce the discomfort of and time spent in prison. When they came to prison they brought a code emphasizing trustworthiness, which translated into "Do your own time" and "Don't rat on another prisoner." It also expected thieves to (1) maintain dignity and respect, (2) help other thieves, (3) leave most other inmates alone, and (4) manifest no weaknesses. These norms formed the convict code. While admonishing inmates to avoid fights, this code expected inmates to settle conflicts among themselves and not ask for help from prison officials. If assaulted you settled the matter on your own, even if it meant killing someone. Weaker inmates were not to seek help from guards even if they were beaten, raped, or deprived of their property. If you were in a fight started by another inmate and the guards broke it up, you went to solitary rather than turning in the instigator. The code also prohibited inmates from openly cooperating or interacting with the administration or guards. This generated feelings of hostility between inmates and guards. It also created a system of mutual aid for a small number of prisoners, produced patterns of exploitation among others, and helped create a hierarchy among the prisoners (Sykes and Messinger, 1960).

The convict subculture was also influenced by the deprivations and limitations on freedom associated with prison life. At its core were values that stressed utilitarian and manipulative behavior. Those most adept at functioning in this manner were best able to acquire available wealth and positions of influence (Irwin and Cressey, 1962).

### As Total Institutions, Prisons Limit Freedom and Inflict Deprivations

Goffman (1961) used the term **total institution** as a way of describing the prison environment. Like custodial hospitals, boarding schools, and military training bases, prisons are places in which large groups of people live and work together around the clock within a circumscribed space and under a tightly scheduled sequence of activities. As in other restrictive environments, prisons subject inmates to deprivations and limit their freedom. Sykes (1958) has called these deprivations the "pains of imprisonment." These features of institutional life apply to all prisons, from early penitentiaries to prisons today. For this reason, we discuss this material in the present tense while using examples from various eras in prison history. Its inclusion here is appropriate because the study of inmate culture largely originated in this era. These general aspects of inmate culture will not be dealt with in detail in subsequent chapters dealing with contemporary prisons.

**LIFE ACTIVITIES IN PRISONS ARE NOT SEPARATED**   People are accustomed to living, working, and playing with separate groups of people and to using different schemes for organizing their life activities. Prison life does not permit a separation of these facets of life because all activities are carried out within a very circumscribed area.

**INMATES ARE DEPRIVED OF THEIR AUTONOMY** Inmates have no control over scheduling of activities. This is done by administration, which usually imposes a highly regimented schedule. Inmates are generally conveyed in groups from one place to another and have prescribed times for meals, showers, recreation, etc. Routinization discourages individuality, even in thought. They are also subject to an extensive system of formal rules. For example, during the Big House era the Iowa State Penitentiary had 105 rules governing inmate behavior (Wickersham Commission, 1931). The following excerpt shows the frustration felt by inmates under this highly structured regimen, which deprives them of opportunities to exercise initiative:

> AU R N: No feeling of being able to say anything about your life. It is like everything is shoveled to you. You know, you are in this hole, and everything that you need—your room, your board, your house—is shoved through a hole at you. That takes all the responsibility away from a person, and then X amount of years later you are out in the streets again, and then you will be responsible, which you never

had to be, and it is like being in the other world. . . . And you come in here, and you are given your sheets, and you are given your room to sleep in, and they try to make you as comfortable as they can within security, you know, which is another trick. And then you go out in the street, like I said before, and then you have got a whole different ball game (Toch, 1977a, pp. 121–122).[b]

**INMATES ARE DEPRIVED OF PRIVACY**   Inmates carry out their activities in the immediate company of large numbers of other inmates. For most people, privacy is a basic condition of normal life. However, prisons offer few opportunities for privacy. Inmates must shower and use the toilet in the open, and in the contemporary prison this may be done under the watchful eyes of guards of the opposite sex. They are also subject to random cell searches, pat-down body searches, strip searches, and sometimes body cavity examinations. To gain privacy, some inmates violate prison rules in order to be put in solitary confinement. The following excerpt suggests the stress that lack of privacy causes some inmates:

> COX R 27: Sometimes there is twenty or thirty people in the showers, and they're always making remarks to you, and you don't feel free. I'm used to on the streets, where you don't have any paranoia. Taking a shower is a beautiful thing. Here it's a paranoia thing, where they have your back against the wall. And if you turn around and wash your legs and you're bent over, besides getting remarks you might really get hurt. . . . And you take your shower in thirty seconds, and you feel really stupid, and you just pull your pants down, and there is all these guys waiting for you to pull your pants down. It's a sick thing. Even though the physical pressure is there for a short time, the mental pressure is there permanently. . . (Toch, 1977a, p. 149).

**INMATES ARE DEPRIVED OF SECURITY**   The most disturbing feature of prison life is that danger permeates the institutional environment. The levels of violence or danger during different eras have been influenced by various factors: the number of violence-prone inmates entering the system and the ability of more seasoned inmates to control them; the ethnic/racial makeup of the prison population. In every era there have been enough "thugs" or outlaws to threaten many inmates' sense of security. "While . . . every prisoner does not live in constant fear of being robbed or beaten, the constant companionship of thieves, rapists, murderers, and aggressive homosexuals is far from reassuring. . . . [Further,] inmate[s] have always been acutely aware that sooner or later [they] will be "tested"—that someone will "push" [them to] see how far they can go and [they] must be prepared to fight for the safety of [their] person and possessions" (Sykes, 1958, p. 77).

> COX R 6: they told me that you can't run away from it. You have to knock them down, face up to them. The first person that you knock out, you get locked up for three or four days, and then you come out and come back down, and you're going to get a lot more respect . . . (Toch, 1977a, p. 158).

Protecting oneself has a Catch-22 flavor about it. If inmates cannot overcome aggressors, they are in constant danger of being attacked because they are considered unable to stand up for themselves. If they succeed in defeating a bully, they may become a target for inmates looking to enhance their prestige. Thus, prisons may protect the public from prisoners, but they often fail to protect inmates from each other. Chronic understaffing continues to contribute to this problem. With a population of offenders that is increasingly violence prone, this problem is likely to get worse in the future.

**PRISONS RESTRICT CONTACT WITH THE OUTSIDE WORLD** Historically, inmates were totally isolated from the outside world by being prohibited from receiving visits or mail from family and friends or from having newspapers or books other than the Bible. By the 1850s most prisons allowed well-behaved inmates to have visitors who were approved by the prison administration. However, in some prisons, then as now, security concerns restricted visits, the number of visits, and visitors per month. Big Houses usually prohibited contact visits with outsiders, and also restricted the correspondence and reading material that inmates could receive. This contributed to their isolation since many inmates found it difficult to find many people who would be approved for visits or correspondence (Sykes, 1958). Because approved visitors stopped visiting and writing after a period of time, many long-term inmates lost contact with friends and family.

This isolation can be painful because of the loss of emotional ties with close family and friends. Despite more liberal visiting and correspondence policies today, contact with family and friends is still difficult for many inmates.[2] Some inmates view this as a moral rejection by society at large. To deal with this pain and rejection, many identify with the prison subculture, which provides a new reference group, social relationships, and rationalizations that help neutralize feelings of isolation and rejection (Korn and McCorkle, 1954).

**INMATES ARE DEPRIVED OF MANY GOODS AND SERVICES** Many problems arise when comparing the standard of living of inmates with people on the outside (Sykes, 1958). How does one compare life in a cell, in which inmates share a chair with cell mates and may use a scrap of old blanket as a rug, with living even in a sparsely furnished home or apartment? How does one equate often ill-fitting prison clothing with having even a minimal wardrobe on the outside? Even though some inmates live better in prison because they have "three hots (meals) and a cot," clothing, and basic medical care, most, if given a choice, would prefer "going it on their own" on the outside.

Upon admission, inmates are deprived of most personal property. Over and above the basics, they are neither provided with nor permitted to buy many amenities taken for granted on the outside. Items like deodorant, snacks, and cigarettes may be purchased from the commissary by those with access to money. Contraband items, such as alcohol, are only available through the inmate sub-rosa economic system (see Chapter 9). While provided with food, its quality and variety may not be to the inmate's liking. In describing food in the Big House, Nelson (1933) indicates that while "it was plentiful, [it was] badly cooked, sloppily served, and, on the whole, fearfully dry and uninteresting" (p. 222). While prison services and the items available in the commissary have dramatically improved, most inmates still live under impoverished conditions compared with life outside.

**INMATES ARE DEPRIVED OF THE OPPORTUNITY FOR MEANINGFUL WORK** While our prisons were built on the idea that work would reform offenders, by the middle of the Big House era few opportunities for meaningful prison work existed. This meant idleness for many, and for others it involved "make work" tasks using more inmates than a job required. This made prison life monotonous, as the following excerpt suggests:

**Dealing with time was a problem because of the lack of programs and meaningful work.**

One o'clock. Back to work again. The same stuffy shops . . . [and] tiresome work. It is absolute industrial masturbation! [W]orking men . . . to keep them busy, with no pride in the finished product, no care about inculcating habits of craftsmanship, no thought except to make us do something we don't like to do. The guards on their elevated benches become lazy-minded, unpremeditated sadists, and take a senseless delight in giving each man the job he most . . . hates to do . . . Work, . . . day in and day out; hateful, stupefying work, to which we bring nothing but resentment and from which we take nothing but hatred (Nelson, 1933, pp. 14–15).

This type of work often fails to prepare inmates for anything but a return to crime on release and deprives them of a means of making the days pass more rapidly. Chapter 18 examines this topic more fully.

**INMATES ARE DEPRIVED OF HETEROSEXUAL RELATIONSHIPS**  Prison deprives individuals of normal heterosexual outlets and also denies them the civilizing influence of the presence of the opposite sex. Language in prison is coarse, profane, obscene, brutal; manners are almost nonexistent; personal hygiene tends to be poor; and emotions tend to be experienced and expressed in the extreme.

**INMATES ARE RELEGATED TO A SUBSERVIENT STATUS**  The prison world is split by a wall that separates correctional workers, who occupy a superordinate status, from inmates, who occupy a subordinate status (Goffman, 1961). In this world inmates can never achieve equal status with staff. Social distance is typically great and often formally mandated. Staff members usually call inmates by a first name, last name, or nickname, whereas inmates are required to address staff as "Mister," "Officer," or some other title, along with their surnames. Rules forbid fraternization between staff and inmates. Staff are expected to deal with inmates in an impersonal and authoritarian manner. Social distance is also reinforced by the mass handling of prisoners, which allows staff few opportunities to treat prisoners on a personal basis.

The degree to which staff members maintain social distance differs by institution and depends on correctional officer characteristics such as compassion, empathy, and capacity for effective communication. It can also be influenced by differences in institutional architecture. Nevertheless, some correctional officers manage to develop interpersonal relationships with some prisoners.

## Prisonization Is the Socialization of Inmates

Clemmer (1940/1958) used the term **prisonization** to describe the socialization process by which inmates take on (to a greater or lesser degree) the folkways, mores, customs, and general culture of the penitentiary. He described the process as follows:

> Every man who enters the penitentiary undergoes prisonization to some extent. The first . . . step concerns his status. He becomes at once an anonymous figure in a subordinate group. A number replaces a name. He wears the clothes of the other members of the subordinate group. He is questioned and admonished. He soon learns . . . the warden is all-powerful . . [and] the ranks, titles, and authority of various officials. And whether he uses the prison slang and argot or not, he comes to know its meanings. Even though a new man may hold himself aloof from other inmates and remain a solitary figure, he finds himself within a few months referring to or thinking of keepers as "screws," the physician as the "croaker" and using the local nicknames to designate persons. . . . He learns to eat in haste and in obtaining food he imitates the tricks of those near him (p. 299).

Certain universal factors in the prison environment tended to influence most inmates. These included:

> acceptance of an inferior role, accumulation of facts concerning the organization of the prison, the development of somewhat new habits of eating, dressing, working, the adoption of local language, the recognition that nothing is owed to the environment for the supplying of needs, and the eventual desire for a good job (Clemmer, 1940/1958, p. 300).

Other factors affect only some of the inmates. Thus, not all inmates learn new ways to gamble, participate in homosexual relations, or learn to distrust and hate guards, their parole board, or other inmates. Clemmer believed the personality of long-term inmates was so affected by the assimilation of the universal factors that it was next to impossible for them to adjust satisfactorily to the community when released. Occasionally, inmates imprisoned for many years, when offered release, refuse release because they fear an inability to adjust to society and have no family to assist in this process.

Various factors affect the extent of an inmate's assimilation into the prison culture (Clemmer, 1940/1958; Thomas and Petersen, 1977; Johnson and Toch, 1982). These include personal characteristics such as age, race, marital status, socioeconomic status, educational attainment, and extent of criminal involvement. Clemmer found that inmates incarcerated for short periods, such as a year or so, were neither assimilated into the prison culture nor had they become prisonized. Most people can endure deprivations for short periods of time because they can see an end to their torment. For those facing long sentences, prison becomes home. To make it in this environment, inmates must adapt to its more unpleasant features.

The frequency and quality of inmates' relationships with individuals or groups on the outside affects their successful reintegration into the community on release (see Chapter 21). Added to this is the extent to which individuals feel that conviction and confinement has stigmatized them. Adaptation to and participation in the prison world and its subculture is more likely if inmates have little or no contact with the larger society, have their primary group relationships broken by prolonged absence, or feel they are unlikely to be reunited with their family and return to some meaningful position in the community on release (Thomas and Petersen, 1977). Involvement in the inmate culture is also affected by an inmate's past criminal history. Habitual, professional, and gang-involved offenders who expect on release to return to criminal activities will find the prison subculture consistent with their criminal values. Other factors affecting assimilation to the prison culture include an unstable personality, a chance cell or work assignment with inmates involved in this subculture, and readiness to engage in gambling and homosexual relations.

Finally, identification with the prison subculture varies based on an inmate's point in his or her sentence. Those at the beginning of their terms may be more influenced by outside values, experiences, and associations. By the time a few months or a year have passed, prison subcultural values, experiences, and friendships may become more important. As inmates near release, depending on whether they intend "to go straight," considerations such as where to live, getting a job and reuniting with family may result in their adopting more conventional values and behavior.

## Adjustments to Changes in Status Begin at Admission

Entering prison, especially for first timers, can be a terrifying experience that can result in a state of shock. As inmates are separated from the outside world, they undergo **role dispossession,** that is, they lose the opportunity to play certain roles (Goffman, 1961). They lose their roles as workers and lovers. Married men often lose their status as heads of households because they are not at home when day-to-day decisions are made and no longer support their families. Women, while still mothers, can no longer care for their children and may lose them if no relative is willing to care for them. Inmates also lose the right to will money to an heir, write checks, contest a divorce, vote, and freely marry.

What are the first impressions and experiences of inmates entering prison or jail? Procedures call for getting fingerprinted and photographed, handing over cash and personal effects, bathing, getting thoroughly searched, receiving prison clothing, a medical examination, and having prison regulations explained. This begins the **mortification process,** which deprives individuals of key aspects important for maintaining their self-concept (Goffman, 1961). This includes their ability to perform certain roles and participate in certain activities, loss of self-determination, and deprivation of personal items, which gives many individuals their sense of self. While these things (e.g., clothes) may not be the only variables in a person's self-image, they help to maintain a positive image. Haircuts are required by many prisons, and this represents a further personal defacement. Finally, the ill-fitting prison clothing supplied to inmates further deprives many of their ability to present themselves in the most favorable light.

On arrival inmates are given an identification number. Their first moments of socialization within the prison may involve an obedience test and even a will-breaking contest. This, and the feelings of humiliation felt by inmates, are well illustrated in our Close-Up on "The Admission Process."

New inmates may also be subjected to verbal or gestural profanity, that is, called obscene names, cursed, or pointed out. For the first time they have to beg for little things like a cigarette or the use of a telephone, and will begin the deference routine of shuffling and looking down in the presence of a guard and addressing him as "Sir." New prisoners must adhere to a type of life alien to them. For males the lack of heterosexual activity may produce fear of becoming unmasculine. They are exposed to contamination—common use of bathrooms, clothes, towels, blankets, even underwear. The prisoner then goes through a process of social exclusion and status reduction. Their uniforms are symbols of their reduced status. They have no choice of housing, neighbors, or food. They become afraid of official power on one side and the inmate kangaroo court on the other. Things taken for granted on the outside now become privileges that staff can withdraw at their discretion. It is not surprising that inmates become resentful and hostile toward the society that landed them in this mess.

**ABILITY TO ADAPT TO PRISON VARIES** Every **fish** (newcomer) faces the same question: "How am I going to do my time?" Preprison orientations are important in understanding how individuals cope with the prison experience. Some offenders know what to expect in prison, either because they have served time before or have picked up knowledge about prison life from the streets. Others, often those imprisoned for a serious crime but lacking a criminal background, are ill prepared to do time. Preparation spells the difference in whether the inmate suffers disorganization and withdrawal or manages to cope with a minimum of damage to the self (Irwin, 1980). Although prisons have changed since the Big House era, the characteristics we have examined in this section are still more or less applicable.

## The Inmate Status System in the Big House Had Four Levels

Returning to our focus on the Big House era, we examine the inmate status system characterizing

# *Close Up*    **The Admission Process**

This Close-Up profiles two accounts of the admission process. First, Barbara Deming (1966), a pacifist arrested for demonstrating against nuclear testing, gives us a rare glimpse of how this process affects the newly admitted inmate. Then we take an excerpt from the Malcolm Braly (1967) novel, *On The Yard,* which draws on his seventeen years of experience as an inmate beginning in 1943 (Braly, 1976). He captures the essence of the obedience testing process that often is part of the inmate's initiation to the prison.

Barbara Demining describes her experience as follows:

> . . . At the House of Detention, a . . . guard empties the bags [and] keeps every . . . article. We . . . packed a . . . comb, toothbrush, deodorant, a change of underclothes. She takes them all—even . . . some pieces of Kleenex. And if I have to blow my nose? "Find something else to blow it on," she tells me cheerfully. She explains then: I might be smuggling in dope this way. I am led into a large shower room and told to strip . . . and I struggle hard now for self-possession. Her stance reminds me a little of that of an animal trainer. Now she asks me to hold my arms wide for a moment, turn my back and squat. I ask the reason. She, too, is searching for dope—or for concealed weapons. One of my companions has been led in by another woman and has stripped and is sitting on the toilet there. Her face is anguished. She explains her predicament to the guard: she is menstruating, but her extra sanitary napkins have been taken from her. "Just don't think about it," the woman tells her. I don't know how to help her; catch her eye and look away. I am given a very short hospital gown and led now into a small medical-examination room. . . . I climb up on the table. I assume that the examination performed is to check for venereal disease. The woman in the white smock grins at me and then her assistant, who grins back. No, this too is a search for concealed dope or dangerous weapons. . . . They wouldn't be able to admit it to themselves, but their search, of course [is not for drugs but for] something else, and is efficient: their search is for our pride . . . (pp. 3–4).

Braly shows what happens to a newly admitted inmate who fails to comply with a guard's request during the admission process.

. . . When they had all been photographed, the sergeant ordered them to strip down and throw their coveralls into a canvas laundry basket, and their shoes, socks and underwear into a cardboard box next to it. "You take nothing—nothing—inside the walls. . . .

[Stick] . . . stepped in front of the sergeant. . . . He lifted his arms when he was told to, but he hesitated before opening his mouth, and then only parted his lips. "Much wider," the sergeant said. "Show some tonsil." Stick thrust his head forward and jerked his mouth open inches from the sergeant's face, who swayed back and looked at Stick thoughtfully. "All right, lift your nuts." Stick thrust his pelvis forward and exposed his scrotum. The sergeant's eyes flickered . . . "All right, son," he said softly, "let's have a look at your a\*\*." Stick stood rigid. "Don't you hear well?" Still Stick didn't move. "Don't be modest. I see a lot of a\*\*holes. They all look the same." "F\*\*k you," Stick said. The sergeant nodded with the appearance of satisfaction, and pressed a button set in the base of his phone. "This is a place," he told Stick, "where you can buy a great deal of trouble very cheaply. . . ." In less than a minute the door flew open and three guards entered on the double. The goon squad [included guards called] Farmer . . ., the Indian . . ., a small Negro—the Spook. . . .

The sergeant nodded at Stick, who hadn't moved, and told the Spook he had refused to bend over. . . . The Farmer and the Indian closed on Stick like fingers of the same hand as they armlocked him from either side. They raised him straining to his tiptoes. The Spook looked up at him. "You see, you've aroused our curiosity." The Indian and the Farmer bent Stick as easily as they would break a shotgun. The Spook pried open his clamped rump. Stick jerked wildly and made a hissing noise. "My, my," the Spook murmured, "not a feather on him. Some jocker's due to score." He looked up at the sergeant. "You think he might have something keister stashed? We can X-ray." "No," the sergeant said. "He's just some kind of nut." The Spook studied Stick knowingly. "Yes, he's some kind of nut. Yes, put him in a holding cell. I'll think up some charge before I go off duty."

(SOURCES: Deming, B., *Prison Notes.* Boston: Beacon Press, 1966, pp. 3–4. Reissued as *Prisons That Could Not Hold.* Athens, GA: University of Georgia Press, 1995. Braly, M., *On The Yard.* Boston: Little Brown, 1967ᶜ, pp. 33–35. Reproduced with permission.)

these institutions. Much like status systems in a free society, it was based on prestige, privilege, and power.

**THE UPPER CLASS WAS THE ELITE**  At the top of the hierarchy were the **right guys** who achieved this title because they could always be depended on "to do right according to the inmate code" (Korn and McCorkle, 1959). Their high prestige as thieves, their tendency to cooperate with each other, and their demeanor of toughness and coolness further enhanced their position. This elite group included the more sophisticated, intelligent, and urbanized inmates. They usually did not ingratiate themselves with prison officials to obtain special favors. They tended to set themselves apart from other inmates, usually restricting their relationships to one another (Clemmer, 1940/1958).

**MERCHANTS, POLITICIANS, AND GAMBLERS WERE MAJOR FIGURES IN THE UPPER MIDDLE CLASS**  On the next level were merchants, politicians, and gamblers whose high status derived from the goods and services they provided the inmate economy. **Merchants** achieved their status because they obtained or manufactured scarce luxury items, both legal and illegal (e.g., cigarettes, alcohol, weapons, coffee, and pornographic literature), to be sold or traded in the inmate economy. **Politicians** generally occupied positions in the administrative offices or worked for key officials, which gave them access to files and other sources of information. They knew about key decisions before other inmates (e.g., about parole decisions) and had advance warning when things were going to happen (e.g., shakedowns and even lockdowns). Through special relationships with key officials (e.g., serving as a captain's clerk) they could influence job and cell assignments and obtain special privileges. Finally, the key role of gambling in prison resulted in some **gamblers** gaining status among their fellow inmates. Thus, gaming skills or luck enabled them to acquire substantial winnings, putting them in a position of power relative to the inmate economy. Gambling, like drinking, represented one of the few escapes from the monotony of prison life. Clemmer (1940/1958) asserts that "whether the player wins or loses, [it] is a means of keeping the personality keyed up; it serves as a hypodermic with an emotional kick" (p. 240). In-

mates made wagers on all types of sporting events and gambled at cards and dice.

*Characters and Prison Toughs Were Also in the Upper Middle Class*  **Characters,** who were good at providing humorous diversions by virtue of their storytelling abilities, dress, or general behavior, were also included in this class. This accorded them a special status with considerable popularity and respect but without much direct power. Lower in status were the **prison toughs** who manifested a constant hostility toward prison officials, conventional society, and most other prisoners. Cliques of these toughs occasionally hurt or killed inmates, usually those without prestige or power. They had to be respected because of their willingness to use violence (Korn and McCorkle, 1959; Clemmer, 1940/1958; Irwin, 1980). This group will be of much greater importance in subsequent eras of prison development.

**MOST INMATES WERE IN THE MIDDLE CLASS**  Individuals in the **inmate middle class,** which encompassed the majority of inmates, failed to distinguish themselves as either criminals or characters (Clemmer, 1940/1958). This group included lower and working class individuals with little or no criminal skill and, as a result, they had no respect. **Square Johns,** also in this group, were accidental offenders who were not considered criminals by the inmate population and were oriented to conventional society. Their crimes included homicides committed in the heat of an argument or embezzlement.

**THE LOWER CLASSES INCLUDED A VARIETY OF INMATES**  The lowest stratum was occupied by several groups including **Hoosiers,** who were dull, backward, and provincial individuals with little knowledge of crime and came from rural areas; **prison queens,** who were openly homosexual and manifested their "feminine" characteristics in dress and manner; **punks,** who were young inmates coerced by threats or forced to provide sexual favors; **rats,** who were inmates known to inform on others to the staff; and **"rapos"** or **abnormal sex offenders,** who were sentenced for incest and child molesting and considered repulsive by most inmates. There were also **dingbats,** who were crazy but harmless inmates and were typically ignored and excluded from informal inmate activities. There were also the "crazies" who, due to their unpredictable behavior, were considered extremely dangerous and to be treated with caution.

## Three Common Adaptations to Prison Life

Inmate adaptations to being in prison were based on whether they had a prison or free-world orientation, their commitment to criminal values, and their preprison activities.

### "DOING TIME" INVOLVED AVOIDING TROUBLE AND GETTING OUT FAST

The most frequent adaptation to prison life was **doing time** (Irwin, 1980). It was adopted by the thief and most other inmates whose concern was getting out of prison as fast as possible with a minimum amount of pain. These offenders avoided situations that might place them in danger of extending and/or intensifying their punishment. They also avoided "hard time" by spending their free time involved in hobbies, sports, or reading; acquiring luxuries without causing themselves major problems; and developing a group of close friends they could depend on for help, protection, and to share their leisure hours and resources.

### JAILING INVOLVED BECOMING IMMERSED IN THE PRISON WORLD

**Jailing** was generally adopted by state-raised youth, inmates who had spent major portions of their lives in juvenile institutions, jails, or prisons in their early teens or before (Irwin, 1980). These prisoners almost completely oriented themselves to the prison, which became the world around which their lives revolved. Many were more familiar with the institutional world than the outside social world, as the following conversation between Claude Brown, who grew up in Harlem, and a boyhood friend who had served many sentences illustrates:

When I go to jail now, Sonny, I live, man. I'm right at home. That's the good part of it, Sonny, a cat like me is just cut out to be in jail. It never hurt me 'cause I never had what the good folks called a home and all that kind of s**t to begin with. So I went to jail, the first time I went away, I went to Warwick [training school], I made my own home. It was all right. S**t, I learned how to live. Now I go back to the joint, anywhere I go, I know some people. If I go to any of the jails in New York, or if I go to a slam in Jersey, even, I still run into a lot of cats I know. It's almost like a family (Brown, 1965, p. 425).

To these inmates, prison was not particularly depriving in nature. For some, it was even better than life on the outside because in prison they were able to manipulate the system and some even occupied high status positions. Prison became "home," and some even caused problems before release to have their sentences extended, whereas others committed crimes after release to be recommitted. These inmates sought jobs to enhance their power, influence, and status in the inmate hierarchy (e.g., secretary, to the captain or warden). Jobs also provided income; for example, working in the laundry enabled inmates to give special attention to the clothing of paying customers.

### GLEANERS FOCUSED ON SELF-IMPROVEMENT

**Gleaning** was adopted by a small number of inmates who wanted to use available prison resources to improve their minds and post-prison employment potential (Irwin, 1980). They spent their time reading, attending the prison's education programs, and learning trades either through the few vocational training programs or from prison job assignments.

I got tired of losing. I had been losing all my life. I decided that I wanted to win for a while. So I got on a different kick. I knew that I had to learn something so I went to school, got my high school diploma. I cut myself off from my old YA buddies and started hanging around with some intelligent guys who minded their own business. We read a lot, a couple of us paint. We play a little bridge and talk, a lot of time about what we are going to do when we get out. [Interview, Soledad Prison, June 1966 (Irwin, 1970, p. 77)].

They tried to improve their social skills, physical appearance, and do anything else that would better equip them for life on the outside.

## Coping with Prison Deprivation Often Required Improvisation

The scarcity of many goods, services, etc., in prisons led many inmates to improvise substitutes for them in order to make prison life more bearable.

**FOOD, DRINK, AND WEAPONS MADE PRISON LIFE EASIER** Inmates developed creative ways to deal with the deprivation and scarcities of life in prison. Brewing of **prison alcohol**, nicknamed pruno or raisin jack, provides a good illustration of improvisation. This brew was made by accumulating sugar, grains, fruit or potatoes, and yeast, and allowing them to ferment for several days to a few weeks. While foul tasting and highly impure, it was intoxicating, providing inmates the outlet for which they were looking. Although prison rules forbade inmates from cooking in their cells, some managed to get food into the cell block and to fashion devices by which it could be cooked (Clemmer, 1940/1958). Some prisoners also made weapons, usually **"shivs"** (i.e., knives made from materials available in the prison, including kitchen utensils, metal from the shops, and even from seemingly harmless items such as tooth brushes).

**INMATES DEVELOPED ADAPTATIONS TO THEIR SINGLE-SEX WORLD** Homosexual patterns represented a form of prison improvisation in the Big House. Nelson (1933), an ex-long term inmate, provides a perspective on the deprivations of heterosexual contact:

> For all the possible forms of starvation, surely none is more demoralizing than sexual starvation . . . to be starved for month after weary month, year after endless year . . . this is the secret quintessence of human misery. Is it any wonder . . . that the prisoner should seek relief in any available form?. . . . [I]t makes little difference to the average prisoner that the only available means of sexual satisfaction are abnormal . . . [Inmates have] a hunger not only for sexual intercourse, but . . . for the voice, . . . touch, . . . laugh, . . . tears of a woman; and women themselves (p. 143).

By depriving men of an opportunity for normal sexual and affectionate relations, prisons generate conditions that promote homosexual behavior. This also highlights the fact that Big House prisons were an almost totally womanless environment. Few women worked there and, except for visits from wives or girlfriends, inmates had little female contact.

Involvement in homosexual behavior was affected by a variety of factors, including length of sentence, marital status, frequency of pre-prison sexual activity, age, and prior sexual orientation—homosexual versus heterosexual. Inmates satisfied their sexual desires in a variety of ways. Masturbation, frequently accompanied by heterosexual fantasies, was the most common form of release.

On a more active level, homosexual encounters involved two distinctive role patterns. Those known as **jockers, wolves,** or **daddies** performed the traditional masculine role in oral or anal intercourse. They were generally respected because their behavior followed the traditional male pattern, except that the object of their gratification was a male rather than a woman. Other inmates felt that, if desperate enough for sexual satisfaction, they too would assume this role (Nelson, 1933; Sykes, 1958).

Those who played the more traditional "female" role were often younger, weaker, more naive, and more effeminate appearing. They had been "turned out," that is, either seduced or tricked by an experienced wolf who plied them with gifts, kindness, and provided protection from other inmates; and/or they were forced to seek protection from other inmates and became the "girlfriend" of a tough wolf. This group also included those trapped into this role because they had performed as punks—played the female role—in the past in other institutions. There were also homosexual prostitutes who serviced other inmates in exchange for luxuries like tobacco and candy. Inmates who began their careers as wolves might, after a period of continued homosexual activity, play the female role. Finally, for some, involvement in homosexual activities led to a change in their sexual orientation, which meant they would likely continue their homosexuality after being released.

**SOME INMATES MANAGED TO HAVE HETEROSEXUAL RELATIONS** Opportunities for normal sexual relations were restricted because few women worked in these prisons and visits were tightly controlled. A few inmates still found ways to have sexual liaisons with women (usually in badly managed prisons or large city jails where guards got jobs through political influence) (Fishman, 1934). At these facilities, for a price, inmates were allowed to have sexual relationships with wives or mistresses. Wilson (1948) describes how inmates at Leavenworth got the idea of smuggling women into the prison during the 1930s. A wife took a chance to be with her husband by hiding in a truck being loaded for the prison. When inside, an inmate saw her, and while other inmates distracted the guard, he hid her in a storeroom until her husband could be found. Some inmates got the idea that they could bring a prostitute into the prison, who would service many inmates in the same way. After much planning the plot was hatched. Before this escapade ended, four girls had been smuggled into the prison on a once-a-week basis. This might have continued except for the death of one of the girls who was accidentally killed when the truck she was hidden in crashed inside the prison.

## Prison Stupor Was a Form of Psychological Escape

**Prison stupor,** also referred to as prison psychosis, is a mental escape from the deprivations of prison life. The Big House was not a stimulating environment since most inmates spent much of their time in small, poorly ventilated cells. Their only opportunity for sunshine, fresh air, and interactions with persons of their choosing was the short time spent in the prison yard. Meals were depressing events at which inmates ate badly cooked food of inferior quality under unpleasant conditions. Inmates had only a short time to eat—sometimes only 20 minutes—and no talking was permitted. Visits were too limited to give them the kind of mental and emotional stimulation to keep their minds and emotions active, and enable them to remain well balanced (Nelson, 1933). Lack of normal sexual outlets, combined with long periods of dead time spent in cells, generated erotic and other fantasies among inmates. They also had little or no responsibility for meeting their own needs, that is, for planning a day's work or budgeting for necessities like food. The result was often a loss of physical or mental alertness and initiative resulting in prison stupor.

**INMATES SUFFERING FROM PRISON STUPOR WERE OUT OF TOUCH WITH REALITY** Nelson (1933) describes prison stupor as a largely self-induced kind of unconscious habit of autohypnosis or self-dramatization.

> From the host of unsatisfied desires and needs of the imprisoned man (desire for sensual pleasure and comfort, desire to forget the daily round of dullness and misery, the horrible surroundings, the uncongenial associations, the painful realities of unsatisfying life) comes a deep if usually unconscious urge to get away from it all, to escape from the intolerable environment. The prisoner begins mentally (and often physically, as well) to shut his eyes whenever he gets a chance; he begins to project himself into the remembrances of some former life, or into some imagined future world in which his desires will be satisfied and life may be pleasant. He seeks happiness if only in the spurious world of his imaginings. This gives him a certain mild and temporary relief. Slipping farther and farther into this habit of daydreaming and self-dramatization, he is in the end so far gone that he spends nearly all of his waking hours in the world of fantasy. Its final result is occasionally madness, and at least, a pretty strong entrenched neurosis. The danger is that the dream world may become so satisfying and vital to the prisoner that he will eventually slip over the edge, lose control, and spend all of his time in it (pp. 229–230).

Inmates in the advanced stages of stupor usually walked around with an expression of total indifference on their faces, and their eyes were glazed over with absentmindedness. All prisoners in these institutions suffered in varying degrees from stupor. Lapses into stupor depended on an inmate's personal attitudes toward life and were affected by such factors as age, length of time in prison, and the time remaining on his sentence. Inmates with no hope or ambition and/or who were serving life or extended sentences were prime candidates for prison stupor. Some even tried suicide as a means of ending their misery. A few prisoners maintained their mental alertness by planning escapes or actually attempting them, risking the possibility of being killed in the process. Apparently, to some, death was preferable to a meaningless life in prison (Nelson, 1933; Barnes and Teeters, 1951).

## BIG HOUSE PRISON GUARDS

Big House prison guards were referred to as hacks, screws, or bulls. They "did time" in the same way as the inmates. The following description captures the essence of a Big House guard's life:

> The life of the guard, except for his privilege of leaving at night after his twelve hour shift, is in many cases more unpleasant than that of the convict.... The guards are politically appointed, untrained for their work by even an institutional school of instruction, with no assurance of tenure or pension, underpaid, many physically unfit for the crises (escapes,

**A Big House Dining Room. Inmates ate meals quickly, under strict supervision, and in relatively uncomfortable conditions. Inmates often sat on stools without backs. The lack of space between inmates sometimes forced them to keep their elbows on the table while eating.**

mutiny, pursuit, and supervision), [and] inexperienced in prison conditions . . . (Jacobs, 1977[d], p. 21).

Guards functioned in a hostile environment due to the inmate code's admonition not to cooperate or interact openly with them or the administration. This made their jobs difficult since their only contact was with inmates for most of their working hours. They were responsible for supervising inmate activities and for preventing problems (e.g., fights and escapes). Inmate hostility toward guards and their deprived circumstances contributed to making the guard's job difficult. Inmates broke prison rules, got into fights, attempted escapes, and occasionally caused riots and many were a thorn in the lives of their keepers.

The guards also had to cope with the incredibly large number of arbitrary and inclusive prison rules they had to enforce (Wickersham Commission, 1931). Some of these rules included such trivial things as forbidding loud talking in the cells, not getting in or out of bed promptly, and not wearing an outside shirt. The guards were scarcely more free than the prisoners since they also worked under rules sometimes as oppressive and imprecise as those for the inmates (Wickersham Commission, 1931; Rothman, 1980). They were often prohibited from doing anything except watching over inmates and were not supposed to talk to them except to give them orders (Rothman, 1980). Stateville guards probably were under the most stringent controls. They could be disciplined for such things as not saluting a captain or reading a newspaper and their barracks could be searched by their superiors for contraband items (e.g., radios) or to expose any gambling (Jacobs, 1977).

The multiplicity of rules that guards had to enforce, and those under which they operated, placed them in a Catch-22 position. Almost anything an inmate did could be a violation. Guards could enforce the rules rigidly, however, this had practical drawbacks. They required inmate cooperation to operate and maintain the prison and were evaluated in terms of their ability to control inmates. Thus, a noisy, troublesome, dirty cellblock reflected adversely on a guard's ability to handle inmates.

## Close Up   The Hole

In many jails solitary is called the hole. In Nevada, it was a hole. A rough cave under the prison. . . . The actual detention unit was a line of four iron cages. We were stripped, thrown suits of long underwear and locked in. We were supplied with a gunboat of water, a s**t bucket sprinkled with lime, and a single blanket. There was no bed, no mattress, and when the guards left us there they turned out the light, and, except for a brief visit once a day to feed us and change our honey buckets, we were left in darkness. At first our food was a loaf of bread each day and a can of fresh water. . . . The convict orderly who serviced us had . . . been told to keep his mouth shut . . . sometimes he winked at me. Once he dropped a sack of Bull Durham, cigarette papers, and a small bundle of matches. . . . The hole was always warm, and we grew used to living on bread and sleeping on the iron floor, and if the guard wouldn't talk to us we spoke whole books to each other. Time went swiftly. Soon we were sleeping over twelve hours a day and telling each other the stories of our lives.

At first we assumed we'd be here in the dark for thirty days. A standard sentence. But the thirtieth day passed and we immediately assumed we had lost count. . . . At the next feeding period, they added a can of hot soup to our ration and we knew we were going on. If we weren't doing thirty, we were doing sixty or ninety. . . . As the days in the hole wore by, the guard who brought our food began to loosen a little. Sometimes he asked us how we felt. Mick tried to talk to him, but I never did. Once Mick asked him how the weather was and he said it was boiling outside and we were lucky to be in the coolest place in the joint (Braly, 1976, pp. 115–119).

### Guards Used Several Methods of Discipline to Control Inmates

Some guards used brutal techniques, such as beatings, to control inmates. This was the least effective and most exaggerated of the control strategies because guards were greatly outnumbered by inmates. While guards could call for backup from other guards this was not well received by administration since most prisons were understaffed.

Officially, inmate violators could be placed in solitary and, until the 1930s, could be whipped in many prisons (Rothman, 1980). Institutions usually had two kinds of isolation. **Administrative segregation,** which consisted of placement in regularly equipped and ventilated cells in which inmates received three meals a day and could be confined for many months. The other type was **solitary confinement** cells, often called the hole, which was used as punishment. These were frequently bare, unlighted, and unventilated cells with only buckets for bodily needs. Inmates placed here were sometimes stripped and not given blankets, which meant they slept naked on a stone floor. In summer, the lack of ventilation was as great a punishment as was the lack of heat in the winter. Fed only bread and water, some inmates lost up to 15 pounds in a short period of time. By the late 1930s there were improvements in the treatment of inmates in solitary. On the federal level, with the exception of Alcatraz, solitary cells had some light and ventilation, and inmates were given a blanket and a board to sleep on (Bates, 1936; Wilson, 1948). Although confinement was supposed to be limited to short periods of time, that is, a week or two, wardens often circumvented this rule by confining inmates for the maximum period, releasing them for a day, and then confining them again. This cycle could be repeated for months (Rothman, 1980). Our Close-Up on "The Hole" graphically describes Nevada State Prison's solitary confinement unit.

For less serious violations inmates lost privileges, such as attending movies or ball games. For major violations, like fighting or attempted escapes, confinement could be lengthened by loss of good time or additional sentences. However, punishments tend to lose their effectiveness when used too frequently or against too many inmates. Thus, guards were fortunate that most inmates were inclined to do their time as quickly and peacefully as possible.

### Guards Developed Several Informal Methods of Controlling Inmates

Guards in these institutions had few control devices to sustain their authority. Also, since they were evaluated on their ability to control inmates they were under pressure to operate a smooth running cell block in a noncoercive manner. This meant using the few persuasions or rewards that were available (Sykes, 1956). Guards in charge of prison services and shops were also supposed to make sure that their areas produced what was expected. To do this guards had to make deals with inmates to meet certain objectives:

> Well, they caught up with me finally. (What happened?) The Security Officer found some "jack" in the mess hall, so they put four of us on refrigeration (i.e., solitary confinement). (How was it possible for you to make the stuff?) Well, you got to make arrangements with the mess sergeant. He gets the ingredients, and then we're in business. (What was his percentage?) Well, it's sort of hard to explain. It's one of those "you do this for me and I'll do this for you" sort of things. (What do you mean?) Well, look at it this way. The sergeant has to feed 1,500 men. It don't look good if he goofs. He wants the job done right. Now we're the ones who do the work, the cooking and all of that. So the sergeant, he says, "Okay, you can make a little drink. But see to it that you get that food on the lines, or the deal's off." (And what did you do with the "jack"?) Sold it, most of it. There's plenty of guys that would kick over big for a little drink (Cloward, 1969, p. 96).

To obtain inmate cooperation, guards could offer a few things like ignoring minor offenses or not being in places where they would likely discover rule infractions. Some agreements were explicit in that specific inmates agreed not break certain rules in exchange for some special treatment. **Corrupt favoritism** was another informal control mechanism whereby guards granted special privileges to certain key inmates in exchange for their assistance in the maintenance of order. This arrangement involved no explicit agreement but evolved gradually. An inmate would take certain liberties; if the guard failed to take action, he would continue the practice. This included getting things for himself, friends, or clients like more food or cell changes, and even suppressing disciplinary actions. These inmates kept their own violations within acceptable limits and supported the prison value system, which indirectly supported conformity. They also coerced or used violence to control inmates who threatened the prison routine and their privileged arrangements (Korn and McCorkle, 1959). Also, by not strictly enforcing the rules, guards could build a fund of

goodwill, which was a valuable asset during riots when the tables were turned (Sykes, 1956).

Finally, the guards' authority was eroded by their tendency to transfer many responsibilities to trusted inmates (Sykes, 1956). Some guards allowed trusted inmates to assume responsibility for minor chores such as preparing reports, locking and unlocking doors, and making cell checks at periodic counts. Inmates in these key posts had positions analogous to that of an administrative assistant, which gave them power and influence in their area of the prison. However, when a guard was transferred to another position he could find this arrangement was already in operation. The attendant risks of changing the status quo for him or others already trapped in this arrangement were more than many guards were willing to take. Inmates were not above sending a "snitch" or "kite"—an anonymous note—to a guard's superior detailing his past derelictions of duty. This form of blackmail was often enough to sustain the existing balance of power.

## CONDITIONS THAT PRECIPITATED DISTURBANCES AND RIOTS

While the Big Houses were rocked by disturbances from time to time they were relatively peaceful places. There were two reasons for this: The control strategies employed by the guards and administration were generally effective, and inmates tended to want to do their time peacefully and quickly and knew that participation in disturbances could result in longer sentences. While things were generally peaceful, this did not mean that inmates were content and satisfied. The deprivations, tensions, and pressures of prison life added to the pent-up feelings that could not be expressed. The riots and disturbances that occurred were unpredictable and spontaneous, often erupting over minor incidents that disturbed the fragile peace and set off an explosion of suppressed feelings. Bad food was a frequent precipitating cause of riots in these institutions (Bates, 1936). While tainted meat or weevils in the oatmeal might not have caused these men to become enraged on the outside, in prison, where food represented one of the few pleasures, this was sometimes enough to set off a riot.

Many riots occurred after prison administrators made changes in prison routines that resulted in

## Close Up   Prison Riots during the Big House Era

The greatest loss of life reported from a prison uprising was the Ohio Penitentiary fire on Monday, April 21, 1930. The fire began at 6:00 in the evening and was set by inmates apparently intending to create confusion and then escaping. Two thousand prisoners were loose in the yard and were threatening violence which did not materialize. Guards would not open the cells in and near burning buildings. Guard Watkins held the keys, insisting that he did it on orders of [the] Deputy . . . who later denied any such orders. By the time other officers wrested the keys from Watkins and opened the cells, 317 inmates were reported to have died. It is surprising that the property damage resulted in but $11,000 (Fox, 1956, p. 22).

In Colorado, on Friday, October 3, 1929, 150 inmates . . . obtained four guns and barricaded themselves in cell-house No. 3 holding seven guards hostage. Prison officers attacked the cell-house and the inmates felled three officers in the first rush, killing them immediately. They demanded that the prison gates be swung open and that they be allowed to escape. If

their demands were not met, they threatened to kill a hostage each hour on the hour as long as their demands were ignored. The administration demanded unconditional surrender. The body of [the] guard . . . hangman was the first to be thrown from the cell-house. . . . Armed guards had been able to isolate the riot to the cell-house. National guardsmen were called, bringing in one airplane and several three-inch field pieces. [The] Warden . . . was shot seriously, but recovered. The Catholic chaplain . . . set the charge of dynamite at the cell-house and exploded it, after which the cell-house was sprayed with machine gun fire. The prisoners retreated to the undamaged part of the cell-house and continued their fight. The militia advanced, but the prisoners drove them back. Governor Adams endorsed the manner in which the riot was being handled. As their ammunition ran out, inmate leader Danny Daniels shot his lieutenants and then shot himself. The toll was seven guards killed, five inmates killed, $500,000 in property damage, a new record, and an escape prevented (Fox, 1956, pp. 26–27).

the loss of privileges, upset the precarious balance between prison leaders and inmates, or increased punishment and deprivation. Overcrowding also contributed to prison tensions since it resulted in hastily prepared food and reduced privileges, yard time, privacy, and individual attention to inmates (Bates, 1936). While riots were not regular occurrences and happened at a time when inmates had few rights, their seriousness should not be overlooked, as our Close-Up on "Prison Riots During the Big House Era" shows.

## CONFLICTS FACED BY PRISON ADMINISTRATORS REGARDING THE TREATMENT OF INMATES

Big House administrators and their staffs were responsible for maintaining order (e.g., preventing escapes and controlling internal disruption and violence) as well as providing prisoners with the necessities of life—usually on a meager budget. In most Big Houses there was a constant conflict between advocates of humane treatment and those who were punitively oriented.

## Pressures toward Harsh Treatment Came from External and Internal Sources

The Wickersham Commission (1931) noted that the major function of prison was believed to be the suppression and control of dangerous offenders. Efforts at humane treatment and rehabilitation required experimentation and administrative flexibility that were thought to pose custodial problems (Barnes and Teeters, 1951). If inmates were given more freedom and allowed to participate in rehabilitation programs, there was a risk of disturbances and escapes, which the press was quick to report. However, a warden's efforts to introduce humane practices and reform programs for offenders rarely received any positive mention and often left him open to accusations of coddling convicts or running a country club. Thus, prison officials who wanted to keep their jobs, which were often political appointments, took the safe way out and refused to experiment with enlightened practices.

Several other factors contributed to the strong tendency to employ forceful and harsh control measures. Many inmates were considered violent and presented escape risks. Additionally, most wardens were not experienced correctional administrators, and their guard staff was usually of low caliber. This frequently led them to use the most expeditious methods of control (Wickersham Commission, 1931). The geographic isolation of prisons, the autonomy of prison administrators, and the authoritarian paramilitary organizational structure of prisons also contributed to the use of these methods.

## Pressures toward Humane Practices Came from Reformers

Persistent pressures for more humane practices and programs to reform offenders also existed. Often referred to as the "new penology," this movement traced its roots to the principles enunciated in 1870 at the National Congress on Penitentiary and Reformatory Discipline (Barnes and Teeters, 1951). Most states, except for most of those in the South, went through periods when a governor supporting reform appointed a progressive warden. In the more humane prisons, inmates spent more time outside their cells, had better food, and ate it under more normal conditions (i.e., at small tables). In addition, visiting was less restricted and discipline was less cruel.

The new penology model also influenced prison design. Old fortress-type prisons that caged inmates like animals were viewed as inconsistent with efforts to reform offenders. New prisons like the federal facility at Lewisburg were designed to be consistent with this new philosophy. The plans for Lewisburg called for security without depressing restraint, the circulation of light and air within the facility, a library, hospital facilities, and a mess hall. Also various types of housing facilities, which permitted varied degrees of restraint, were built for a population of 1300 inmates. These included 88 steel cells, 450 securely guarded rooms with outside windows, and dormitories of varying sizes for the remaining population.

## Prison Specialization and Classification Paved the Way for the Development of Treatment Programs

The start of efforts to classify inmates was another progressive development that paved the way for treatment programs. As early as 1916, some states created a centralized authority for the operation of an integrated prison system. Some states also initiated institutional specialization, including the estab-

lishment of prisons for the criminally insane, reformatories for those aged sixteen to twenty-five, and separate institutions for women. Some correctional systems also began grouping inmates according to factors such as the need for supervision and the risk of escape, that is, custody and security considerations. These resulted in systems separating younger offenders from more hardened, older ones and gave more freedom to those who could be trusted (Bates, 1936). This often meant the construction of medium and minimum security facilities.

The growing influence of the social sciences, particularly in areas such as psychiatry and psychology, added a new dimension to the classification process in the early part of the twentieth century. Concerned with understanding human behavior, they attempted to unravel the individual causes of criminal behavior. These concerns made themselves felt in the classification process when specialists such as psychologists and social workers joined prison classification teams (Hippchen, 1978).

Beginning in the 1920s, state prisons established a period of isolation and classification for newly admitted inmates before their placement in the general population. In the late 1940s, some states established centralized receiving and diagnostic centers to perform these functions. During this classification period inmates were evaluated for purposes of developing a treatment plan that included decisions regarding placement in a facility (if one existed) best suited to their needs, appropriate work or education, and (if needed and available) treatment. By 1940 a national survey found that forty-five of the eighty-eight institutions polled followed this procedure (Morse, 1940). However, the hitch was that no prison or system of prisons could provide the treatment necessary to correct all of the problems that were diagnosed (Barnes and Teeters, 1943). Thus, while education programs were offered in about one-half the state institutions, only a quarter had programs based on professional standards of education. Vocational training, involving more than just on-the-job instruction, was available in only about one-fifth of the prisons (Morse, 1940). In essence, what occurred during this era was an attempt to separate inmates according to age, sex, and as to whether they were "hopeful," "dangerous," or "hopeless" (mentally ill or psychologically defective).

Another problem affecting reform was that system needs and/or custodial concerns often took precedence over those of the inmate. If a low-risk inmate wanted to learn printing, and the print shop was at a maximum security facility, he would likely be sent to a minimum security farm where inmates were needed to work the farm to produce food for the system. If he was a high-risk inmate and the print shop was at a minimum security facility or outside the prison walls he would be denied access. This points to a conflict that began in a few systems during this era (e.g., Federal Bureau of Prisons and California), and continued into the next period when many more adopted a treatment orientation (see Chapter 7). While custody and treatment were to be given a voice in programming decisions, custody concerns weighed more heavily and usually prevailed over treatment considerations even in prisons that were supposed to prepare inmates for release (Barnes and Teeters, 1951).

## THIS ERA SAW CHANGES IN THE TREATMENT OF INMATES

In looking at the changes that took place in the treatment of offenders from 1900 to 1950, it is fair to conclude that the Big House era was characterized by a gradual and uneven movement toward less

brutality and punishment combined with more humane routines. At the beginning of this era the silent system was in effect. Inmates could routinely be whipped for violations of prison rules and often spent more than two-thirds of their sentences in their cells. As this era progressed, treatment personnel entered prisons, and their reformation and treatment emphasis brought them into conflict with the punishment-oriented views of custodial staff. So began the struggle between these groups which became more pervasive in the next era as more systems established treatment departments.

Finally, not all institutions during the first half of this century could be described as "Big Houses." First, it should be clear from the discussion in the preceding chapter that southern prisons were different from Big House–type prisons in several ways. Also, each state had a small population of female inmates who were either housed in small separate institutions, often known as reformatories, or, in some instances, in special sections of male prisons (Barnes and Teeters, 1951). These institutions differed from Big House–type facilities by virtue of their size and population. The offenses and social patterns characteristic of women in these institutions were also different than those of their male counterparts (see Chapter 12).

## ENDNOTES

1. Chapter 18 provides a more detailed discussion of the history and development of prison industry programs.
2. See Chapter 21 for a discussion of the issue of approved visiting lists and other rules relating to visiting.

## ACKNOWLEDGMENTS

[a] D. Clemmer. *The prison community.* Holt, Rinehart & Winston, Inc. ©1958 by Donald Clemmer. Reprinted with the permission of Holt, Rinehart and Winston, Inc.
[b] H. Toch. (1977) *Living in prison: The ecology of survival.* New York: The Free Press, Div. of MacMillan Publishing Co. Reproduced by permission of the American Psychological Association.
[c] ©1967. Malcolm Braly. Reprinted by permission of Knox Burger Associates.
[d] J. Jacobs. *Stateville: The penitentiary in mass society.* University of Chicago Press. ©1977 by the University of Chicago. All rights reserved. Reprinted by permission of the University of Chicago Press.

## CHAPTER RECAP

**Big House Prisons Were Harsh and Idle Places**
The Big House Era Saw the Demise of the Industrial Prison
**The Social World of Inmates**
The Big House Population Contained Those Who Were Unsuccessful in Both Their Legal and Illegal Pursuits
The Inmate Subculture Was Influenced by Internal and External Factors
   Thief Values Influenced the Convict Code
As Total Institutions, Prisons Limit Freedom and Inflict Deprivations
   Life Activities in Prisons Are Not Separated
   Inmates Are Deprived of Their Autonomy
   Inmates Are Deprived of Privacy
   Inmates Are Deprived of Security
   Prisons Restrict Contact with the Outside World
   Inmates Are Deprived of Many Goods and Services
   Inmates Are Deprived of the Opportunity for Meaningful Work
   Inmates Are Deprived of Heterosexual Relationships
   Inmates Are Relegated to a Subservient Status

Prisonization Is the Socialization of Inmates

Adjustments to Changes in Status Begin at Admission
  Ability to Adapt to Prison Varies

The Inmate Status System in the Big House Had Four
  Levels
  The Upper Class Was the Elite
  Merchants, Politicians, and Gamblers Were Major
    Figures in the Upper Middle Class
    Characters and Prison Toughs Were Also in The
      Upper Middle Class
  Most Inmates Were in the Middle Class
  The Lower Classes Included a Variety of Inmates

Three Common Adaptations to Prison Life
  "Doing Time" Involved Avoiding Trouble and Get-
    ting Out Fast
  Jailing Involved Becoming Immersed in the Prison
    World
  Gleaners Focused on Self-Improvement

Coping with Prison Deprivation Often Required Impro-
  visation
  Food, Drink, and Weapons Made Prison Life Easier
  Inmates Developed Adaptations to Their Single-Sex
    World
  Some Inmates Managed to Have Heterosexual Rela-
    tions

Prison Stupor Was a Form of Psychological Escape
  Inmates Suffering from Prison Stupor Were Out of
    Touch with Reality

**Big House Prison Guards**

Guards Used Several Methods of Discipline to Control
  Inmates

Guards Developed Several Informal Methods of Controlling Inmates

**Conditions That Precipitated Disturbances and Riots**

**Conflicts Faced by Prison Administrators Regarding
  the Treatment of Inmates**

Pressures Toward Harsh Treatment Came from External
  and Internal Sources

Pressures Toward Humane Practices Came from Reformers

Prison Specialization and Classification Paved the Way
  for the Development of Treatment Programs

**This Era Saw Changes in the Treatment of Inmates**

## REVIEW QUESTIONS

**1.** Describe the Big House prison. What major change affected the daily routine of these prisons?

**2.** What were the major factors that affected the nature and character of the inmate social world in the Big House? Describe the inmate code as it existed in these prisons.

**3.** What are "total institutions" and how do they affect inmates?

**4.** Outline the inmate status system and the various roles and positions within it and describe the three common adaptations to prison.

**5.** What are some of the solutions that inmates improvise to cope with the deprivations of prison?

**6.** Describe prison stupor and explain what causes it.

**7.** Describe the role of guards in the Big House and indicate the difficulties they faced in carrying out their delegated responsibilities and the methods developed to handle these problems.

**8.** What is corrupt favoritism?

## TEST YOUR KNOWLEDGE

**1.** The end result of organized labor's opposition to prison industries was that
  **a.** it became illegal to use inmate labor for anything.
  **b.** it became illegal to use inmate labor to manufacture any product.
  **c.** prison products could only be sold to governmental agencies.
  **d.** prison products could compete with those of private industries.

**2.** Which of the following factors is an important influence on the prison social environment?
  **a.** outside subcultures
  **b.** adaptation to deprivation
  **c.** prevailing social conditions
  **d.** all of the above

**3.** Which of the following is a subtle but important attitude change that results as part of the prisonization process?
  **a.** the recognition that nothing is owed to the environment for the supplying of needs
  **b.** a slowly developing respect for the prison administration
  **c.** disregard for the moral wrongness of crime
  **d.** an increasing emphasis on the need for self-rehabilitation

**4.** The elite group of inmates who were more sophisticated, tended to cooperate with each other, and whose demeanor was characterized by toughness and coolness were known as
  **a.** accomplished characters.
  **b.** right guys.
  **c.** hoosiers.
  **d.** dingbats.
  **e.** hard rocks or tush hogs

**5.** The mode of adaptation to prison life in which an inmate used available prison resources to better themselves for life on the outside was known as
  **a.** just doing time.
  **b.** jailing.
  **c.** gleaning.
  **d.** role dispossession.

# PART THREE

# MODERN PRISONS

# CHAPTER 7

# THE RISE AND FALL OF THE REHABILITATIVE INSTITUTION

■ **LEARNING OBJECTIVES**

*After completion of this chapter, you should be able to:*
1. Define and describe the rehabilitative institution.
2. Describe the social changes that preceded and gave rise to the rehabilitative institution.
3. Outline the fundamentals of a sound correctional program.
4. Describe indeterminate sentencing and its role in the rehabilitative institution.
5. Describe the role of classification in the rehabilitative institution and describe its shortcomings.
6. Explain the role of treatment in a correctional setting.
7. Discuss some problems associated with the use of group counseling in a correctional setting.
8. Outline the basic features of prison life at the Soledad Correctional Institution.
9. Enumerate the reasons why the transformation of prisons into "correctional facilities" was doomed to failure.

■ **KEY TERMS AND CONCEPTS**

Adjustment centers
Classification
Correctionalist
Group counseling
Medical model
Prison intelligentsia
Rehabilitation
Rehabilitative institution
State-raised youth
Tips and cliques

The term **rehabilitative institution** refers to the use of the prison as a treatment facility where the major focus is to treat and "cure" the offender.

The blueprint for the treatment-oriented correctional institution was developed at the 1870 meeting of the National Congress on Penitentiary and Reformatory Discipline. The Progressive Movement of the late nineteenth and early twentieth centuries helped to initiate movement toward reformation of inmates. Parole and indeterminate sentences were also initiated and expanded. It was not until after World War II, however, that these types of institutions replaced Big Houses in many states. These newly constructed institutions had a different appearance, organization, type of prisoner, and inmate social world. Most importantly they differed in their impact on offenders. By the 1950s the rehabilitative philosophy dominated corrections, at least in the sense that penologists of the era regarded it as embracing the goals toward which corrections should work (Irwin, 1980). The rehabilitation era spanned the period from 1950 to the early 1970s.

## SOCIAL CHANGES SHAPED THE REHABILITATIVE INSTITUTION

The change from an institutional system warehousing and punishing offenders to one oriented toward rehabilitating them occurred during an era when our society was undergoing many social changes. Some related directly to the emergence of correctional rehabilitation, whereas other changes affected the nature of the inmate population. The post–World War II period in the United States was characterized by prosperity, increasing urbanization, and mobility (Irwin, 1980).

Changes during this period also made it difficult for those in the lower socioeconomic classes to move up the social ladder as easily as many immigrant groups had done in the past. Previously, hard work had been the key to success and upward mobility. Now this mobility became based increasingly on education and the possession of occupational skills. The Horatio Alger myth of the poor boy who worked hard and eventually became a wealthy and influential citizen was not likely to occur. Most immigrants and migrants arriving in the cities could not succeed because they lacked

the necessary educational and occupational background to compete effectively for better jobs. Unlike their predecessors, who worked hard and eventually moved out of the ghettos, these later arrivals were frequently unable to improve their economic situation sufficiently to make such a move.

### Slum Conditions Restricted Social Mobility

The inability of many ghetto residents to improve their economic positions led to the development of hard-core slums that produced enduring lower class subcultures. These areas included second- and third-generation lower class whites who lived in the slums, and descendants of immigrants who had remained in the slum (perhaps because of physical, mental, or other adverse circumstances). Also living in these areas were a disproportionate number of blacks who were relative newcomers to the urban scene. Their lower socioeconomic position was due to educational/occupational skill deficiencies and to racial prejudice and discrimination. Puerto Ricans also lived in slum areas, some remaining in them only temporarily before returning to Puerto Rico while others became permanent residents. Puerto Ricans experienced problems similar to blacks and were also hampered by a language barrier. Mexicans residing in these areas experienced problems paralleling those of the Puerto Ricans, and many had the additional difficulties associated with their illegal entry into this country. Whites from chronically depressed areas of Appalachia had also moved into these neighborhoods. Their problems, which were like those of many blacks who migrated from the South, centered on adjusting from a rural to an urban environment. Their lower socioeconomic position also resulted from deficiencies in education and marketable job skills.

In summary, many people in the groups populating the urban slums of this era, unlike their predecessors, were unable to find the means to move out within a generation. The factors that contributed to keeping them there included (1) poor English language skills that made the educational process more difficult, (2) relatively low quality schools in the slums, (3) a value system of several groups that did not emphasize education, and (4) prejudice and discrimination.

**LIMITED SOCIAL MOBILITY IN URBAN SLUMS HAD AN IMPACT ON THE PRISON SYSTEM**   The result of this lack of mobility was that these areas were home to a succession of poorly educated and occupationally unprepared individuals. This facilitated the development of subcultures that were heavily involved in delinquency and crime, which had several consequences for the prison system. First, the criminal justice system tends to deal most strictly with conventional or street crime, which tends to be overwhelmingly perpetrated by members of the lower class. Therefore, the prison population of this era was largely composed of the urban groups just discussed. The upward mobility difficulties these groups experienced assured a greater consistency in the ethnic mix of the prison population for a longer period than in the past. Second, the street norms of many youth groups in these subcultures contained antisocial dimensions that shaped the inmate world. Third, the difficulties many individuals in these groups experienced when trying to improve their circumstances generated frustration and hostility. This was particularly true of blacks because they were the group most blatantly discriminated against. This also made them susceptible to potentially explosive violence and ripe for participation in the prisoner revolution to be discussed in the next chapter.

### The Manner of Dealing with Problems Began to Change

This era also saw changes in approaches to social problems such as family disorganization, race relations, juvenile delinquency, and urban crime—all of which affected the criminal justice system (Irwin, 1980). Experiences with the 1930s Depression and World War II changed perceptions as to how to deal with these problems from an isolationist to individualistic orientation. We accepted the idea of government intervention and also required it to deal with conditions needing to be rectified. Government agencies at all levels began employing a variety of professionals including psychologists, psychiatrists, physicians, urban planners, social workers, and sociologists.

**CORRECTIONALISTS SOUGHT TO CHANGE PRISONS TO REHABILITATION FACILITIES**   In corrections the new penal specialists were referred to by Irwin (1980) as **correctionalists.** This group included

college-educated administrators and employees of prisons, probation and parole officers, and a few academic penologists. Their objective was to reduce the rapidly growing crime problem by persuading state governments and concerned segments of the general population that the crime problem could be reduced by "curing" offenders of their criminality. Accomplishing this required an understanding of the causes of criminal behavior. Social scientists sought to find these causes on all levels—psychological, biological, and sociological. Their basic assumption was that they could identify the factors causing criminal behavior. They believed these factors, if corrected, would reduce or extinguish this behavior. Thus, the primary function of prisons was to be **rehabilitation,** which was a new form of reformation based on scientific methods (Irwin, 1980).

## Prison Focus Changed from Punishment to Rehabilitation

The rehabilitation of offenders was far from a new idea. Until 1950, however, this objective was not seriously entertained for several reasons.

### Several Factors Gave Rise to the Shift to Rehabilitation

Society was not prepared to entertain the idea of correcting rather than punishing offenders until after World War II. Involvement in this war gave many Americans opportunities to experience new cultural patterns. This made them more receptive to fresh ideas and methods of handling problems. Coupled with our experience in government intervention, dealing with the problems of the Depression made society more willing to experiment with new programs. This climate provided the impetus for many state governments to allocate funds for the construction of new prisons and for hiring new treatment personnel to staff them. The GI Bill for World War II veterans provided funds to former soldiers for college. This created a pool of college-educated professionals who could be employed in these programs.

Also, in the early 1950s prisons around the country were disrupted by a series of riots. During 1952 and 1953 at least twenty-five prisons had to quell revolts among inmates, resulting in a large number of injuries and the loss of millions of dollars due to property damage (Fox, 1956). Responding to this situation, the American Prison Association established a committee, chaired by Richard McGee, to study the nature and causes of inmate violence. McGee concluded that the underlying cause of inmate violence was a failure by the public and inmates to understand the rehabilitative functions and purposes of prisons. Consequently, prison administrators received inadequate support and were dependent on poorly paid and untrained staffs (McKelvey, 1977). Before this era, limited funds made it impossible for prisons to employ professional, educational, and other treatment personnel. Also, restraints on prison industry had produced much inmate idleness. McGee maintained that to reduce the number of riots we needed sufficient support to eliminate the major grounds for convict grievances. In 1954, the American Prison Association further supported the rehabilitation ideal by changing its name to the American Correctional Association and its primary publication, *The Prison World*, to *The American Journal of Corrections*. It also issued a revised and expanded manual of correctional standards (McKelvey, 1977).

### Some Changes Were Substantive But Others Were Only Cosmetic

Some states, like Wisconsin and Minnesota, responded by reorganizing institutional staff structures and introducing new programs into old prisons. Other states, like New York and California, constructed facilities to more adequately test this orientation. Others merely gave lip service to the correctional ideal by relabeling key aspects of the prison environment. Prisons became known as correctional institutions, guards as correctional officers, prisoners as inmates, and solitary confinement as the adjustment center. Thus, Warden Joe Ragen, who ran a strict, punitive prison, simply renamed his system of total control at Stateville in Illinois as "rehabilitation." Although he increased the size of the academic and vocational schools, inmate students spent only a few hours a day in class and the vocational training program primarily consisted of using previously trained inmates to repair staff autos and appliances. Ragen justified his regimen of total control because coercing inmates to conform to prison rules would result in their being resocialized (Jacobs, 1977). That this type of program could be even construed as rehabilitation shows the ambiguity of this concept and why this approach ultimately failed. However, to more fully understand its failure, it is necessary to examine the major features of this approach.

## THREE COMPONENTS CHARACTERIZED THE REHABILITATIVE INSTITUTION

The *Manual of Correctional Standards* of the American Correctional Association [Committee for the Revision of the 1954 Manual (CRTM), 1959] states what correctionalists viewed as the fundamentals of a sound correctional program. It called for an institutional philosophy based on employing individualized treatment to its fullest practical extent, even in maximum security facilities. Thus the basic aim of an institution was to provide rehabilitation. To achieve this, inmates had to be given indeterminate sentences and be involved in institutional programming, classification, and treatment.

### Indeterminate Sentencing Made Release Contingent upon Rehabilitation

Ideally, under strict indeterminate sentencing, judges assign custody of the offender to the department of corrections, and their release is dependent on their readiness to function in a conventional, law-abiding manner in society. Thus, during this period offenders would be released when they had shown they could conform to the model being used to measure their ability to return to society (Barnes and Teeters, 1959). Indeterminate sentencing was critical to this approach because it was impossible to determine in advance the proper length of imprisonment necessary to rehabilitate a given offender. This reflects the rehabilitative approach's reliance on the assumptions of the **medical model** (i.e., that problems would be dealt with as illnesses by diagnosing and treating them) (Rothman, 1980). Thus, in the same way that it is impossible to predict how long it takes to cure someone hospitalized for a physical illness, no prediction can be made on the time it would take for inmates to respond to treatment programs in a correctional institution.

Despite their offenses, the indeterminate sentence was supposed to lead to parole for inmates amenable to treatment and to protect society from those unwilling to change their criminal lifestyles. This facilitated the operation of rehabilitation programs, which was society's best guarantee of safety, while not "coddling the real criminal" (Rothman, 1980).

**INDETERMINATE SENTENCES GAVE RISE TO SEVERAL PROBLEMS**   The indeterminate sentence suffered from many problems in its underlying assumptions and its implementation. It assumed we had the knowledge to develop programs to "reform" many offenders. This presumed we (1) were skillful enough to determine the crucial factors behind the criminality of specific inmates; (2) had or could develop programs that could bring about appropriate changes in the offender's behavior and/or personality (i.e., cure them); and (3) had the tools and diagnostic instruments to determine when an offender was ready for release. In fact, we had none of these skills (Irwin, 1980). All we had was the faith that with adequate resources and qualified professionals, we could acquire the knowledge necessary for developing a sound correctional program.

Also, several problems arose when trying to implement the indeterminate sentence. First, it provided correctional administrators and parole board members with considerable discretionary authority. For prison administrators it was a powerful management tool. Wardens could influence parole decisions by noting on reports that an inmate was dangerous and/or listing his many disciplinary infractions. This gave them a disciplinary mechanism that was more potent than the lash. Thus, they could openly punish recalcitrant inmates while rewarding those who "behaved" (Rothman, 1980). This also gave parole authorities the opportunity to avoid unfavorable criticism by keeping "notorious" and heinous offenders in prison, while giving preferential treatment to high-status offenders. This discretion generated a great deal of hostility among inmates.

From a treatment standpoint, however, conformity to prison rules is not always the best indicator of an inmate's ability to adapt to conventional society. An inmate who rigidly abides by prison rules may be incapable of handling the openness of conventional society. In a true treatment setting, a certain amount of rule violation is expected because it may represent experimentation on the client's part with different patterns of behaviors.

Second, indeterminate sentencing was criticized because it resulted in longer terms of confinement and less parole flexibility than determinate sentencing (Rubin, 1973). This was because many jurisdictions only employed a modified indeterminate sentence, which required inmates to serve from half to most of their maximum sentence before being eligible for parole. This was often longer than the one-third required for parole eligibility in determinate sentencing states (Rubin, 1973).

Finally, there were important drawbacks to indeterminate sentencing for inmates. Inmates were never quite sure how much time they had to serve before being eligible for parole or release (Irwin, 1980). This generated anxiety, as shown in the following statement from an ex-prisoner:

> I was sentenced to San Quentin on an indefinite term. The prisoner there has no notion during the entire year regarding the term the parole board will set for him to do. At the end of that year the parole board fixes his maximum, and may reduce it. The first year is a perfect hell for a prisoner. He keeps asking others who were convicted of a similar offense about details of their crime and of their maximum sentence. One man committed the same crime I did and he received a sentence of nine years, but he had a long previous record and was armed. Another man who was a first offender and was armed got four years. I was a first offender and was armed. Consequently I figured I would get between four and nine years. I kept thinking and worrying about it, for every year in prison makes a difference. My worry interferes with my work, and I get sent to the "hole" for inefficiency in work. That looks bad on my record and I wonder whether it will increase my maximum sentence. This worry drives a person mad. [When] . . . the sentence is fixed the prisoner can settle down to serve his time and it is a great relief to have it settled (Sutherland and Cressey, 1966, pp. 635–636).

In California offenders given release dates could have their prison terms "refixed" back to the maximum for rule violations (Irwin, 1980). This uncertainty created a great deal of unrest among inmates. If it had been removed or had been part of a clearly defined and effective treatment program, this would not have been a problem. As it was, sentencing disparities were one of the factors that were considered responsible for prison disturbances.

## Classification Was Intended to Diagnose the Causes of an Inmate's Criminal Behavior

Ideally, **classification** in a correctional institution was to parallel the process physicians used to diagnose and treat physical illnesses. It was to find out the nature of an inmate's criminality and then to prescribe a program to cure these deficiencies. First, inmates were to be "staffed" (i.e., diagnosed) by a team of correctional professionals. This required diagnostic techniques including medical, social investigation, psychiatric, psychological, educational, vocational, religious, and recreational studies. Based on this assessment, a treatment and training program was developed in a staff conference. This was then to be discussed with the inmate. This plan was tentative since classification was viewed as a dynamic process. This meant it had to be modified continually according to the inmate's changing needs (CRTM, 1959).

**THE CLASSIFICATION PROCESS HAD SEVERAL SHORTCOMINGS** In theory, this was the way classification was supposed to operate. Although attempts were made in the early rehabilitative institutions to follow this process closely, for many reasons it never operated as intended. First, social scientists were neither able to supply classification committees with valid diagnostic instruments nor to develop programs that "cured" criminality. Second, security and management concerns dominated considerations in placing offenders. Inmates might be assigned to institutions with a variety of programs, but their involvement in certain programs could be restricted because of security considerations, irrespective of whether participation might facilitate their rehabilitation. Similarly, custody considerations might result in inmates being assigned to a maximum security prison whether or not the psychological services they needed were available (Irwin, 1980; Sutherland and Cressey, 1966).

## The Correctional Treatment Program Was to Encompass All Aspects of the Institutional Milieu

In a correctional institution all aspects of the facility's milieu were to be directed toward changing the offender. The educational program was to meet the inmate's interests and needs with a heavy emphasis being placed on vocational training. The work program was to be comparable in type, variety, and pace to employment on the outside and to involve tasks with some vocational training value. Recreation was to include both indoor and outdoor activity and to be organized to promote good morale and sound mental and physical health. Institutional discipline was to be aimed at developing self-control and preparing the inmate for free life rather than merely to ensure conformity to prison rules. Therapeutic programs were also to be offered. These programs were to be directed at changing inmate behavior and attitudes to enable them to better deal with the frustrations of institutional life and those facing them on return to the community (Irwin, 1980).

These facilities were supposed to have adequate buildings, equipment, and resources to enable treatment staff to achieve their program objectives. Finally, they were also to be staffed with adequate and competent personnel, carefully selected and trained to operate under conditions promoting a degree of efficiency and morale (CRTM, 1959). Much variation existed in the extent to which correctional institutions met these criteria. As noted, some merely changed the sign on the institutional door, and others tried to create a true correctional environment. The central feature of most correctional programming involved therapeutic, academic, and vocational training components.

**THERAPEUTIC PROGRAMS WERE TO BE THE PRIMARY AGENT FOR BEHAVIORAL AND ATTITUDINAL CHANGE** Therapeutic programs were to include individual and group therapy and counseling, under the direction of psychologists and psychiatrists (or other trained counselors and therapists). Although some jurisdictions planned to employ psychiatrists and clinical psychologists, low salaries and undesirable working conditions made it almost impossible to attract them (Irwin, 1980). States like California, which required large numbers of therapy group leaders, were forced to use all categories of prison staff, including correctional officers, to fill these positions (Kassebaum, Ward, and Wilner, 1971). Thus, nonprofessional staff with no training in psychology or social work directed most group sessions.

In these institutions **group counseling** usually involved ten or twelve inmates (and a staff member) meeting at least weekly for a one- or two-hour session to discuss their problems. These groups were supposed to develop sufficient confidence and cohesiveness to enable participants to express true feelings without fear of any adverse repercussions. During this process inmates examined the ways they had solved problems in the past and explored new socially acceptable methods and solutions for dealing with them (Kassebaum *et al.*, 1971). This is how group sessions were supposed to operate, but in reality many failed to do so. Even if they had, there is no guarantee that they would have succeeded in their rehabilitative purpose.

Although participation in group sessions was voluntary, many inmates felt compelled to attend because treatment staff and parole board members led them to believe that parole was contingent on participation. The effectiveness of counseling depends on whether participants feel secure enough to discuss candidly their problems, conflicts, and feelings. However, Kassebaum *et al.* (1971) found the men involved in the counseling sessions they studied were afraid to reveal too much about themselves because they were concerned that both staff and inmates would use it against them. Many inmates also believed it was "unmanly" to talk about feelings and discomforts, and others were unable to express themselves sufficiently to do so. The Close-Up on "An Inmate's Perspective on Group Counseling" gives us a viewpoint on these sessions, which shows that group sessions tended to be very superficial and not particularly meaningful. The following comments by inmates further suggest why these sessions were not too effective:

> The counseling leader is usually an incompetent member of the staff, especially when dealing with socially maladjusted people. Lack of qualified psychiatrists to get into the deeper emotional problems. . . availability of leaders (adequate) for such widespread activity is limited. More professional personnel is necessary. Groups as they stand don't have any leadership to prod inmates toward areas requiring attention. Consequently many hours are spent just bitching about this bull [correctional officer] or that bull and nothing concrete is really established.
>
> In eighteen months of group counseling, I've only learned more ways to commit crimes—heard all about other inmates' crimes and all they had—new cars, etc.—and yet they bummed cigarettes—it's just a process of wasting time and attempted brainwashing. (Kassebaum *et al.*, pp. 137–139).

*The Effectiveness of Treatment Programs Was Questionable*  The effectiveness of these treatment sessions was affected by the fact that participants were frequently quite adept at "conning." If given a chance by an inexperienced therapist, many inmates were quite good at playing the role of a good "therapee" (Prettyman, 1981). That is, inmates learned what the therapist expected of them and then went through the process of "being cured." Usually they viewed it as a sophisticated form of conning. Some inmates under an indeterminate sentence believed in the following formula for being released:

> In California, one formula (believed to be foolproof by inmate adherents) prescribed a short period of intense "messing up" upon entering prison followed by a mixture of half group therapy and half group vocational training. This was followed with a gradual reduction of prison behavior and a few carefully written letters to close kin. (Martinson, 1972, as cited by Prettyman, 1981, p. 79).

Thus, for some inmates, involvement in treatment and other programs was not aimed at self-improvement, but was part of "playing the game" necessary to achieve release. Even in California, which was committed to providing treatment and where programs were administered by a renowned expert, supervision and training were relegated to social workers who had low status and only modest training in group therapy. In some states both staff turnover and inmate transfers—which were done for purposes of effecting population adjustments—adversely affected many programs (Conrad, 1965).

Group counseling has been the dominant form of treatment in adult correctional settings because it is inexpensive and easy to implement. By the end of the 1950s prisons began to experiment with the more intense therapy technique of milieu therapy. This involved the conversion of prisons or units within prisons into "therapeutic communities." (See our Close-Up on "Synanon at the Nevada State Prison," which provides a brief discussion on this process.) Later, other forms of therapy, including behavior modification and attack therapy, were introduced (Irwin, 1980). For a variety of reasons, these forms of therapy usually have been poorly implemented and have had limited success.

## Close Up — An Inmate's Perspective on Group Counseling

Group therapy was held for an hour each week, and the group I joined numbered ten. . . . By the time we were all gathered, sitting in a circle on wooden folding chairs, usually ten minutes of the therapeutic hour had already gone by. . . . Our circle here. . . was supposed to have no head, for the remaining fifty minutes we were all equally free to say anything we liked, but naturally we polarized toward the therapist. His equal voice might be heard by the Adult Authority. We all knew the Adult Authority took special interest in these programs.

[T]he therapist . . . was a psychologist. . . . The position he had given himself was difficult. His therapeutic stance was passive. Every session began the same. We sat silently. We smoked and stared at the bland cream walls. Sometimes the therapist would attempt to melt the impasse by asking briskly, "What were we talking about last week?" The Wit would say, "Our chances for immediate parole. . . ."

Often half the hour would pass in this willful silence. We had been told that even as we sat silent the therapy was working. If we each accepted responsibility for the waste . . . [it] . . . would help us grow. But time was the one thing we had to waste. And the one thing we were truly seeking here was not an understanding of our problem, but the appearance of the search. This was obvious from the question we asked again and again of the therapist. "Does this therapy help us with the Adult Authority? The therapist has an answer to this. "Do you think it should?" "I don't know about 'should'—does it?" "I don't really know." "What do you think?" "What do you think?" "Well, let me put it to you like this, do you make a report to the Adult Authority?" "Not directly." "Who do you report to?" "The head of the Psychiatric Department." "And does he make a report to the Adult Authority?" "That's my understanding." "Well, when you make this report to Crazy David for him to tell the Adult Authority, what're you going to say about me?" "What do you think I should say?" "You wouldn't say what I think you should say?" "How do you know?". . . .

When we finally did warm up and begin to talk, our direction was often idle. Someone might wander into a discussion of the way the Texas prisons compare to these in California, or how someone long ago had failed to give them a break. . . . Sometimes, but rarely, someone would begin to talk openly. . . . We didn't trust each other and that was one reason these sessions remained so tight. We knew anything we said was noted and would be retailed as gossip. We gossiped constantly, rumor moved through the joint like fog, and almost no one was entirely untouched by it. . . . Still some of us did talk, usually softly, staring at the floor. These men . . . told how the transformation had been worked on them. . . .

Almost everyone in the joint was taking the line that they had come to this because of their neuroses. I watched my former crime partner Mick, who was back, turn from a fierce young hard-ass into a quivering jelly of complaints and uncertainties. This was better for those he might have mugged in another future, but how was it better for him?. . .

(*Source:* Braly, M., *False Starts.* Boston: Little Brown, 1976, pp. 245–249).[a]

**CORRECTIONAL INSTITUTIONS HAD BETTER ACADEMIC AND VOCATIONAL PROGRAMS** Correctional institutions typically had much better academic and vocational training programs than therapeutic treatment programs (Irwin, 1980). By the 1950s innovative facilities had elementary and high school programs and had developed liaisons with colleges and universities enabling inmates to take advanced courses, usually on a correspondence basis. However, widespread use of accredited teachers did not occur until much later and in many facilities inmate teachers conducted the classes.

Vocational training programs of some type were available in all correctional institutions. In California inmates received training in dry cleaning, shoe repair, appliance repair, auto repair and body work, building trades, and food service (Irwin, 1980). However, these programs suffered from many problems (e.g., not having enough openings for the demand) and failed to prepare participants adequately for a trade on release. For example, the tasks of cooking and baking for several thousand inmates were not adequate preparation for most outside food service jobs because these usually do

## Close Up    Synanon at the Nevada State Prison

Synanon was an early drug treatment program that appeared to be successful. It consisted of former addicts living together in a drug-free environment. Life in this community centered on educational, therapeutic, and work activities designed to maintain abstinence. Addicts entering the program progressed through three stages. The first stage restricted them to the "house" with participation in all aspects of the program. The therapeutic program consisted of three weekly group meetings intended to help individuals discover and deal with the problems underlying their addiction. This group process provided support and created a feeling of mutual dependency. After developing sufficient confidence and maturity, residents entered the second stage. They could now work outside the "house" but were required to return after work and participate in the therapeutic process. In the third stage, individuals leave the house, returning only for occasional visits. One criticism of this program was that only a very small proportion of its participants ever reached the third stage. Nevertheless, this approach was seen as very successful in treating drug addiction (*Time* Magazine, 1963; Yablonsky, 1965).

### Synanon Moves into Prison

After hearing a presentation on Synanon the prison psychologist at the Nevada State Prison was so impressed he asked Chuck Dederich, Synanon's founder, to set up a group in the prison. A contingent of Synanon people from California (including several ex-cons) went to Reno to assist in developing a program. A tier of cells was set aside in the prison for the program and the Synanon people began to visit the prison to try to sell the program. Initially both inmates and guards were unreceptive; however, under the leadership of ex-cons from the Synanon group, the program took hold. At first it only attracted addicted inmates; later it also drew some nonaddicts also.

When some inmates who participated in the early sessions began to dramatically change their behavior, the resisting factions started to reappraise their initial negative reactions. Inmates who at first blasted Synanon people as "do gooders" and "snitches" began to reverse their field and many joined Synanon. This accelerated when they saw some "big-yard tough guys" responding with enthusiasm. The guards, who at first feared that Synanon would produce a laxness in security, later revised their opinion in the light of a sharp reduction in fighting and other inmate problems. . . .

The new dimension that Synanon added . . . was a change of behavior within the walls. . . . [Inmates still swore to] reverse their criminal and deviant pattern when they left the institution . . . but [this was not the major change]. . . . [what staff began to see] was fewer . . . "black eyes on the big yard . . ." meaning that the fighting problem had decreased. Many former hard-core candidates for solitary confinement began to work, maintained self-discipline, and became concerned with the fate of their Synanon "brothers." From the inmates' point of view, for the first time, many saw the vague possibility of a future without crime. . . .

[M]any Synanon members reported their feeling that Synanon's complex of activities and thought patterns gave them a hook for transcending the grim environment of the prison. In one seminar discussion that [Yablonsky] directed in the cell-block, the men told [him] that Synanon stimulated their otherwise vegetable-like existence. They began to read more, think more, and "moved toward life rather than away from it." [It] also provided a connection for many of the men with the outside world . . . (Yablonsky, 1965, pp. 338–339).[b]

Yablonsky in discussing the problems that the Synanon program needed to deal with in the prison setting, indicated that the "doing-time" adaptation presented serious obstacles to rehabilitation.

not require the preparation of large quantities of food. Other training programs failed due to obsolete equipment, inadequate techniques, and lack of skilled instructors with up-to-date knowledge. Chapter 18 deals more extensively with educational and vocational training programs.

**DIFFERENT OBJECTIVES FOR TREATMENT AND CUSTODY STAFF CAUSED CONFLICT**    In the Big House, where custodial concerns were paramount, the authority of custody was unchallenged. However, the correctional institution was also supposed to rehabilitate the offender and required a new

# Close Up

Inmates adopting a doing-time orientation emphasized criminal values and associations in prison. This, along with a rejection of the society that placed them in prison, also involved a strong aversion to treatment. This was reinforced by staff attitudes that saw inmates as unable to "change their stripes." To shake up the antitreatment, doing-time structure that surrounds the inmate, the Synanist is required, according to Yablonsky (1965), to:

almost automatically [inject] . . . a disturbing abrasive[ness] into the "doing-time" con culture. He is inviting the criminal to change, and he provides for him an "in-person" example of the fact that this is possible. The Synanist is "walking the [w]alk." He hobnobs with the prison administration and is apparently enjoying the rewards of his changed way of life. This is disconcerting to all segments of the inmate system, since it begins to crack up many long-established rationalizations and beliefs about being a con "forever" (p. 344).

Synanon attack therapy sessions were effective in changing behavior because they constantly required participants to face their problems. From the start individuals recognized that criminal or other unacceptable behavior would bring harsh criticism rather than praise.

*Candy:* What do you want in here, Shotgun?
*Shotgun:* Well, and, I thought I might change myself, you know—do the thing. I know there's something wrong with me. [Shotgun's comments are accompanied by the snarl and shoulder-shrugging of the "hip" tough guy.]
*Synanist:* Well, what's wrong with you, man?
*Shotgun:* I don't know—you know, I'm pretty crazy sometimes.
*Synanist:* Yeah, we know that, but what's wrong with you?

*Shotgun:* Well, I figured I could do something for myself. But if you don't want me here, well, I'll just go.
*Synanist:* No one said they didn't want you here. We want to know what you want to do.
*Shotgun:* Well, I'm always getting in trouble—and I want to do something about it.
*Candy:* Why do they call you Shotgun?
*Shotgun:* [Brightening up] Well, I pulled lots of robberies with a shotgun. . . .

The Synanon group then moves to another level of attack and appraisal. "Who do you hang with in the yard?" "Well, my best buddy is Joe." "Why do you hang with Joe?" "Well, he's a pretty good guy; he's a good thief." "What is a good thief?" Shotgun falls back on his criminal track and says, "A good thief is a guy who knows how to rob and will burn through anyone that gets in his way." The group begins to ridicule his relationship with "good-thief" Joe. They again allude to robbery of this sort as "insanity." Shotgun becomes increasingly hostile under the attack. . . . This may have been the first time in his life that he had experienced an attack of this kind from his criminal peer group. The attack was a double whammy, because it was against the very basis of his "reputation" (Yablonsky, 1965, pp. 348–349).

Judging from Yablonsky's comments, the Synanon program at the Nevada State Prison was successful. However, in 1964 it was terminated when a new governor, who did not support the program, was elected. Therapeutic community programs were established in other prisons. However, they failed for a variety of reasons (e.g., the programs were poorly conceived, lack of support from prison personnel). Recently a number of therapeutic community programs, like Stay'n Out, have been established successfully and like Synanon have been found to reduce recidivism (see Chapter 19) (Mullen, 1991).

emphasis on treatment staff. The new contingent, which formed a second major staff component, included counselors, group leaders, psychiatrists, psychologists, case workers, and other assorted therapists, chaplains, teachers, recreational workers, and medical personnel. Almost immediately

conflict with custodial personnel developed. Given that each component considered its functions most significant, it is not surprising that this friction developed. This was further aggravated by the major differences in their orientations and responsibilities. Treatment staff were charged with discovering and correcting the inmate's "defects." This required that inmates be viewed as having the potential for change; not as "bad people" but rather as individuals whose social circumstances caused them to commit crimes. In contrast, the custodial staff was responsible for maintaining internal control and preventing escapes. They had to be constantly alert to inmates who were attempting to use or manipulate them to their own advantage. This, coupled with their prejudices toward inmates, resulted in less than favorable attitudes toward them as well as toward treating them (Irwin, 1980).

Ideally all institution staff members were supposed to be part of an integrated treatment team whose primary objective was the rehabilitation of inmates (Cressey, 1965, as cited by Irwin, 1980). In reality, the treatment component had to be merged into an existing prison organization long dominated by a custody orientation (Irwin, 1980). Under these circumstances treatment personnel could either compromise some of their ideals and survive or be intransigent and be expelled.

*Custodial Concerns Took Precedence over Treatment Objectives* Custody concerns continued to dominate decision making, and treatment staff had to make concessions whenever real or imagined custody issues arose. This was evident in the deliberations of classification committees that usually included both custody and treatment staff. Custody staff views often prevailed because they pointed to the possible escape risks or resulting violence from contrary decisions. Treatment staff typically acquiesced, either because they shared the same concerns or recognized the futility of battling with custody staff. The administration sided with custody staff, because of its shared concerns about avoiding dangerous outcomes that might lead to adverse publicity. Thus, treatment was in a no-win situation.

To maintain their integrity, treatment staff often developed a therapeutic rationale for the custodial decisions they had to make. They continued their involvement in this charade because they wanted to maintain the appearance that the institution was operating a humane and individualized treatment program (Irwin, 1980). In this way, they could obtain maximum inmate participation and cooperation in available programs. If they did not show inmates they believed that the prison was operating an earnest rehabilitation program, then the

John Irwin, Professor Emeritus at San Francisco State University, was an inmate at Soledad for five years (during the 1950s) at the time it operated as an exemplary correctional institution.

program would fail from lack of interest and cooperation.

## CALIFORNIA MADE THE BEST EFFORT TO DEVELOP REHABILITATIVE INSTITUTIONS

During the era of rehabilitation California had the most progressive program (Sullivan, 1990). Even before other states embraced the rehabilitative ideal, this state had begun to establish these programs in the mid-1940s (Sullivan, 1990).

### Soledad Was an Exemplary Rehabilitative Institution

John Irwin's description of Soledad Correctional Institution provides an excellent portrait of a typical rehabilitation facility because it was planned and operated based on the rehabilitation model. His description is of greater significance because he spent five years there as an inmate during its "golden age." We summarize his work below.

**THE PHYSICAL PLANT MADE IT DIFFERENT THAN OTHER PRISONS** At Soledad, perimeter security consisted of a high fence and gun towers.

**Soledad Correctional Facility was a model rehabilitation institution.**

Inmates were housed in cells arranged around the outside walls of each wing so that each had an outside window, which was not barred. Instead, it was made of small panes of glass with heavy metal moldings. All cells, except one unit that housed reception, segregation, and isolation, had solid doors with small screened inspection windows.

At the outset, inmates were housed in single cells with each unit containing a desk, a bunk, and a chair. Later, many were modified to hold two occupants. In the five medium security wings, inmates were given the keys to their own cell doors. The prison's inside walls were painted in pastel colors (e.g., pale green, pale blue) rather than drab colors, such as "institutional green." The prison had two dining rooms with floors that were tiled, and octagonal oak tables. Other amenities included a well-equipped gym, several shops, a spacious library, and an education building. This provided a far less oppressive environment than the Big House and was presumed to be more conducive to the accomplishment of rehabilitation goals.

**THE ROUTINE AND PROGRAMS WERE DESIGNED TO BE CONDUCIVE TO REHABILITATION** The routine at Soledad was more relaxed, which meant inmates had opportunities to make choices rather than behave like preprogrammed robots. For example, they could choose to go to breakfast or

sleep an extra hour before going to work. Inmates had free access to many prison areas. For most of the day and on weekends, the cell blocks were open and inmates were free to go to the yard, library, or gym. Also, at night inmates were allowed out of their units for scheduled activities (e.g., gym, school, library).

Reflecting the emphasis on rehabilitation, programming included a broad selection of vocational training and good elementary and high school programs. Therapy for most inmates involved weekly group counseling sessions (although these were usually conducted by poorly trained guards and other staff). Participation was all but mandatory since parole was dependent on program involvement. By the late 1950s, sessions were held daily in an effort to intensify the treatment program.

**THE POPULATION INCLUDED MORE NON-WHITES** In the 1950s California experienced a major shift in the percentage of its nonwhite inmate population. By then nonwhites comprised more than 40% of the population, including approximately 25% percent Mexican-Americans and 15% blacks.

The Mexican-American population was composed of two groups—one raised in Texas (Tejanos) and the other primarily from Los Angeles (Chicanos). Although both groups came to be called

Chicanos, there was hostilty between them that sometimes resulted in fights. Many also harbored hostility toward white inmates because of the discrimination they had experienced from whites, particularly in the public schools. However, these attitudes were tempered by their involvement with whites in criminal and drug-related activities on the outside. Most white prisoners had come from lower and working class urban areas and some were **state-raised youth,** individuals literally raised by state agencies because they had spent most of their youth in one or more institutions. Black offenders were from Los Angeles or San Francisco or were migrants from the South and Southwest. Figure 7.1 roughly portrays the relationships between these groups. These various groups were separated by prejudice and sometimes hostility. Some white prisoners disliked Chicanos but generally respected and feared their propensity to react violently when insulted or threatened. Despite the enmity between these groups, friendly relations existed on an individual level. There was a greater rift between Chicanos and blacks because of extreme hostility and prejudice of Chicanos toward blacks. Prejudice and hostility also existed between blacks and whites. However, their collaboration on the outside also mitigated these attitudes and promoted friendships.

**THE SOCIAL STRUCTURE WAS COMPLEX** The social structure in Soledad was more complex than in the Big House because it was based on criminal orientations and ethnic/racial group identifications. The thief group, which had dominated the Big House, while still respected, was no longer dominant. Their numbers had diminished, their system of theft did not cross racial lines, and involvement in theft among whites was being replaced by drug addiction. The spread of heroin use during the late 1940s and 1950s from Mexican to working and lower class whites resulted in the development of a drug addict subculture. An addict group became very prominent in Soledad and other California prisons in the 1950s. In prison this group was very active, sociable, friendly, and verbal. This contrasted with their outside behavior which was passive, antisocial, individualistic, and frequently predatory.

Grasshoppers or wheatheads (marijuana users) were a smaller group of habitual drug users composed of young urban or lower class blacks, Chi-

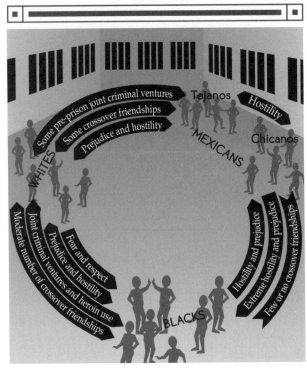

FIGURE 7.1  **Interethnic Relationships at Soledad**

*Source:* Material compiled from Irwin, J., *Prisons in Turmoil.* Boston: Little Brown, 1980, pp. 50–51.

canos, and whites who were part of a cult-like subculture involved with the "cool" jazz of the period. In prison they continued their pattern of coolness and cliquishness and were ostracized by other inmates—particularly the heroin addicts—who saw them as silly.

Black prisoners, cut off from the traditional thief subculture by segregation and prejudice, developed their own subculture that revolved around "hustling." Black thieves achieved their criminal objective through persuasion and use of their wits rather than force. Their criminal activities included such short cons as three-card monte, the pigeon drop, and rackets like the numbers and pimping. In prison they formed their own groups in which a major pastime was bragging about their hustling, pimping, and their sporting lifestyle.

State-raised youth, who comprised about 10% of the population, had their own subculture based on their experiences in youth prisons. Its features included the formation of tightly knit cliques; a propensity to threaten and use violence for protection and to increase their power, privileges, and prestige; and a preference for prison patterns and styles rather than those of the free world. In adult prisons, they formed gangs that stole from and bullied other prisoners and were actively involved in prison homosexuality.

During the 1950s most inmates at Soledad were not committed to a criminal orientation. At least 25% were "lost" young adults who drifted into crime haphazardly without fully understanding what they were doing. Frequently confused about who they were, the world in which they lived, and their position in it, they often saw themselves as losers. Although ignored in the Big House, at Soledad, while still viewed as losers, their position was improved. The diversity of the populations made it easier for them to join groups like the dope fiends or the hustlers and, for some, to rise to positions of power.

The final group consisted of mostly white inmates that had committed one felony or a few serious crimes. They did not define themselves as criminals, nor did other inmates. Known as square johns, they were typically ignored by other inmates unless they wanted to make use of their usually higher educational skills or professional backgrounds.

### SEVERAL FACTORS CONTRIBUTED TO A PRISON ATMOSPHERE THAT WAS CALM AND ORDERLY

Due to the diverse subcultural orientations, no single inmate code developed, nor did a single cohort of leaders dominate the prison. The administration, influenced by the rehabilitative ideal, also took a much greater interest in day-to-day prison operations. This affected the development of a traditional inmate power structure because it reduced such sources of inmate power as the control of information, services, and desired prison commodities. No longer could the captain's clerk secure transfers of inmates from one cell to another or could storeroom clerks steal 20% of the prison's sugar, coffee, and dried fruit to sell to other inmates. The prison was a relatively calm and orderly place. Prisoners were tolerant of each other's differences and were relatively friendly to each other. Despite racial hostility and the formation of separate groups, there were friendships and interaction between the different ethnic groups.

The peaceful and orderly mood of the prison resulted in part from the hopeful atmosphere of the correctional institution and its more relaxed routine. Most prisoners came to believe that staff members were sincere in their efforts to help offenders and would discover their basic psychological, vocational, and physical defects or problems and correct them. Thus, inmates had faith the prison was going to make a new person out of them. Many older guards changed their view of the institution and their role in it and began to see themselves as correctional agents or at least became more humane.

**Tips and cliques** were a major factor in maintaining the peace at Soledad. Tips were crowds or extended social networks of people whose association was based on preprison contacts or common subcultural involvement. These networks of people were typically interracial, overlapping, and connected. For example, Irwin was a member of a tip of Los Angeles young people involved in heroin use and theft that was connected to a tip from San Francisco through prior relationships in youthful institutions. Although not all tip members knew each other, membership involved certain obligations and provided the basis for casual associations that increased the likelihood of friendship.

Cliques were smaller primary and semiprimary groups formed by prisoners from the same tip or from several tips. Typically, cliques were composed of people who had regular contact (e.g., at work or in the yard) and shared an interest in some prison activity, subcultural orientation, and/or preprison experience. The interconnections between cliques and tips, and tips and other tips, produced extensive and overlapping networks involving bonds of friendship, communication, and obligation. This facilitated cooperative enterprises involving contraband and scarce commodities and was a major factor in reducing conflict. Open confrontations were often avoided by settling disputes through indirect negotiations between tips and cliques. Overall, the tip and clique structures replaced the old prison social structure in that they served to mitigate the differences between diverse prison groups, including those racially or ethnically based, and thereby maintained peace and promoted cooperation among inmates.

While few in number, the correctional institution had "deviants" who were not convinced of the value of rehabilitation programs. They were also not deterred from violating prison rules, despite recognizing that the indeterminate sentencing system could extend their term in prison. Persistent

## Close Up  Patuxent: A Failed Treatment Experiment

Patuxent has been refered to as "perhaps the most extreme manifestation of the medical model of correction" (Sullivan, 1990, p. 67).[c] This Maryland institution was opened in the early 1950s to house inmates convicted under the state's defective delinquent statute. Under this law extremely violent and mentally troubled offenders were to be identified and presumably treated and "cured." Patuxent was administered and operated by psychiatrists who instituted a "therapeutic milieu" to treat the inmates. It adopted a true indeterminate sentence since inmates were only released when a team of prison psychiatrists determined that they were "cured." The treatment program was organized on a graded tier system under which inmates progressed through four levels, which included increasing privileges, before attaining release.

This program had several problems. First, while the psychiatric staff evaluated each inmate, it was almost impossible to determine definitively when (or even if) an inmate was cured. Since there is no psychiatric "litmus test" by which a healthy status can be determined, it was possible for inmates to beat the system by faking

healthy behavior. In fact, many inmates serving determinate life sentences in Maryland prisons plotted continually to get into Patuxent so that they could get "cured." Sullivan does not report how many of these inmates, if indeed any did, succeeded in getting transferred there.

A second problem was that inmates who were not considered cured could unnecessarily spend the rest of their lives in the institution. Thus, they could spend many more years in Patuxent than if they had been at a prison where they might be paroled after serving a reasonable portion of their sentences. Between 1955 and 1965, of the 135 inmates paroled, almost half had served more time than comparable inmates at other institutions and only 12% were actually declared "cured." Most inmates released from this institution achieved this through recommitment hearings and not because they benefited from the treatment. The difficulties with the diagnosis and treatment, coupled with the retention of inmates for longer periods than in other institutions, led to changes in the Patuxent program in the early 1970s.

troublemakers were placed in special units called **adjustment centers.** These were segregation units where prisoners were detained for indefinite periods of time under a regimen that permitted virtually no mobility and reduced their privileges. The rehabilitation rationale for the adjustment center was that some prisoners required more intensive therapy in a more restrictive setting. However, these units were used only to detain, summarily and indefinitely, unmanageable prisoners since no intensive therapy was provided. The availability of these units, along with the rehabilitation ideal, helped to maintain peace within these prisons during the 1950s. By way of contrast, our Close-Up on "Patuxent: A Failed Treatment Experiment" looks at the problems faced by another exemplary treatment program.

## THE FAILURE OF REHABILITATIVE INSTITUTIONS

The idea that prisons could be transformed into hospitals for curing offenders was not realistic.

Since we really did not understand the causes of criminal behavior, we could not develop diagnostic instruments and programs that identified and/or changed offender behavior. Also, a highly questionable assumption was the view that all offenders could be sufficiently motivated to take full advantage of high-quality treatment programs.

Even under ideal conditions then, the correctional institution was doomed to failure. Many offenders participated in the "rehabilitation" programs, some voluntarily, while others only did so because they wanted an early release. This would not have mattered if a sufficient number of offenders had successfully been reintegrated on release, but this was not the case. It was difficult to claim rehabilitation was effective when offenders who participated in these programs were returning to prison (Irwin, 1980). However, these programs were not a total loss because many inmates did successfully complete them, like Irwin himself. As inmates became increasingly disillusioned with the rehabilitation ideal, they again blamed their involvement in crime on their life circumstances rather than on individual problems. They also recognized the "correctionalist" had gained considerable control over them by persuading them to accept the assumptions of the rehabilitative ideal. This power was used to pressure them to become involved in what they saw as "phony" treatment programs and to subscribe to so-called "chickens**t" prison routines (Irwin, 1980).

## The Paradox: Better Education Produced System Critics

The emphasis of the rehabilitative ideal on self-improvement fostered the emergence of a **prison intelligentsia.** This group served as the focal point for criticism of the rehabilitation approach. The education programs enabled many inmates with inadequate academic skills to develop their reading skills so that this became an informative and enjoyable pastime. Drawing from his own experiences and those around him, Irwin notes that most inmates began with history and then turned to other areas such as literature, philosophy, psychology, semantics, economics, and even mysticism.

After several years of this, these inmates developed a good perspective on the world scene. This increased knowledge changed their view of society,

our culture, the prison system, and even of their own criminal careers (Irwin, 1980). Some of these inmates became critical; others became bitter and cynical. Many took a new direction rather than returning to crime. Some inmates chose to become students or bohemians, whereas others, including many blacks, became activists. However, whatever direction they took, this new intelligentsia of ex-offenders and offenders continued to examine the correctional system critically and to disseminate their views. Those returning to prison were a strong force in encouraging inmate disillusionment with rehabilitation.

Inmate disenchantment with rehabilitation was not the only factor that shattered the fragile peace in the rehabilitative institution and hastened the demise of this approach. Continuing changes in the ethnic/racial composition of the prison population, along with its politicization and the administrative reaction to these changes, all hastened the death of this noble experiment (Irwin, 1980). Several other factors, among them public outrage with crime and criminals, struck the final blow in the mid-1970s. These changes are discussed in more detail in the next two chapters.

## ACKNOWLEDGMENTS

[a] ©1976 by Malcolm Braly. Reprinted by permission of Knox Burger Associates.
[b] Copyright Lewis Yablonsky. Reprinted by permission of author.
[c] *The Prison Reform Movement: Forlorn Hope* by Larry E. Sullivan. Copyright 1990 by G.K. Hall & Co. All rights reserved. Published by Twayne Publishers, a division of G.K. Hall & Co. Reproduced with permission.

## CHAPTER RECAP

**Social Changes Shaped Rehabilitative Institution**
Slum Conditions Restricted Social Mobility
　Limited Social Mobility in Urban Slums Had an Impact on the Prison System
The Manner of Dealing with Problems Began to Change
**Prison Focus Changed from Punishment to Rehabilitation**
Several Factors Gave Rise to the Shift to Rehabilitation
Some Changes Were Substantive But Others Were Only Cosmetic

**Three Components Characterized the Rehabilitative Institution**
Indeterminate Sentencing Made Release Contingent Upon Rehabilitation
　Indeterminate Sentencing Gave Rise to Several Problems
Classification Was Intended to Diagnose the Causes of an Inmate's Criminal Behavior
　The Classification Process Had Several Shortcomings
The Correctional Treatment Program Was to Encompass All Aspects of the Institutional Milieu
　Therapeutic Programs Were to be the Primary Agent for Behavioral and Attitudinal Change
　The Effectiveness of Treatment Programs Was Questionable
　Correctional Institutions Had Better Academic and Vocational Programs
　Different Objectives for Treatment and Custody Staff Caused Conflict
　Custodial Concerns Took Precedence over Treatment Objectives
**California Made the Best Effort to Develop Rehabilitative Institutions**
Soledad Was an Exemplary Rehabilitative Institution

The Physical Plant Made It Different Than Other
    Prisons
The Routine and Programs Were Designed to be
    Conducive to Rehabilitation
The Population Included More Nonwhites
The Social Structure Was Complex
Several Factors Contributed to a Prison Atmosphere
    That Was Calm and Orderly
**Failure of Rehabilitative Institutions**
The Paradox: Better Education Produced System Critics

## REVIEW QUESTIONS

**1.** Discuss the factors that led to the development of
the correctional institution.

**2.** Describe the role of indeterminate sentencing with
respect to treatment and parole. What are some of its
problems?

**3.** What is the role of classification in the correctional
institution and what are its shortcomings?

**4.** Outline the role of treatment in a correctional
setting.

**5.** What are some of the problems associated with the
use of group counseling in a correctional setting?

**6.** Discuss the basic features of prison life at Soledad
Correctional Institution.

**7.** Identify the reasons why the transformation of
prisons into "correctional facilities" was doomed to
failure.

## TEST YOUR KNOWLEDGE

**1.** Under the concept of indeterminate sentencing, an
inmate's release from prison was contingent on
    **a.** serving the entire sentence.
    **b.** the inmate's rehabilitation.
    **c.** determinations of when justice had been served.
    **d.** when overcrowding required more cell space.

**2.** Within the context of the correctional institution,
classification would ideally serve as a means of
    **a.** diagnosis.
    **b.** security.
    **c.** punishment.
    **d.** treatment.

**3.** Which of the following ethnic groups in the Soledad
prison had the most animosity toward one another?
    **a.** blacks and whites
    **b.** Chicanos and whites
    **c.** blacks and Chicanos
    **d.** whites and Asians

**4.** Which of the following groups was most predominant at Soledad prison?
    **a.** thieves
    **b.** weedheads
    **c.** murderers
    **d.** heroin addicts

**5.** The relatively peaceful coexistence between inmates
at Soledad prison was a result of
    **a.** the structure of tips and cliques.
    **b.** the brutality of the guards.
    **c.** the Big House-type inmate structure.
    **d.** the success of the rehabilitative programs.

# CHAPTER 8

# ETHNIC/ RACIAL DIVISION AND THE PRISONER MOVEMENT

## ◼ LEARNING OBJECTIVES

*After completion of this chapter, you should be able to:*

**1.** Describe the social changes that occurred in the United States from the mid-1950s to the end of the 1960s that had a major impact on prisons and outline their effects on inmates.

**2.** Identify and describe the factors that caused the demise of the traditional prison stratification system.

**3.** Explain how race relations in the prison changed during this era.

**4.** Discuss the factors that influenced the development of the "prisoner movement" during the 1970s.

**5.** Define and give examples of prisoner self-help groups. Explain why they were an important part of the prisoner movement.

**6.** Give examples of radical groups involved in the prisoner movement and briefly describe their goals and activities.

**7.** Discuss the two phases that occurred during the Attica revolt, the events surrounding the retaking of the prison, and the cover-up that followed.

**8.** Explain the difficulties that increasing inmate defiance and violence created for prison administrations.

## ◼ KEY TERMS AND CONCEPTS

Attica revolt
Authority Revolution
Black Muslims
Black Panthers
Folsom Prison strike
Half-steppers
National Lawyers Guild
Political prisoners
Prisoner movement
Prisoner rights groups
Radical groups
Self-help groups
Seven Steps
State-raised youth
Young Lords

## THE IMPACT OF THE THREE SOCIAL CHANGES ON PRISONS

From the mid-1950s to the early 1970s, the United States underwent major social and cultural changes. Three of these changes profoundly affected corrections: (1) the Authority Revolution, which eroded respect for authority; (2) the Civil Rights movement, which broke up the caste system and changed relationships between racial/ethnic groups; and (3) the Vietnam War, which engendered protests involving significant segments of the population.

### The Authority Revolution Eroded Respect for Authority

The **Authority Revolution** was manifested in decreasing respect for tradition. Not only were average citizens increasingly beginning to question the legitimacy of rules and customs once thought to be sacred, but oppressed classes relegated to a subservient position were no longer willing to accept second-class status. Additionally, those who made or administered the rules also began to question their own legitimacy (Silberman, 1978). Simply put, people became increasingly unwilling to abide blindly by a rule or practice just because this was the way it was done in the past. Neither were they willing to follow orders without question that were issued by people in positions of authority.

This situation was aggravated during the 1960s by a substantial increase in the population of fourteen- to twenty-four-year-olds, which typically includes rebellious years when youth begin to assert their independence (Silberman, 1978). Previously, most parents had exerted sufficient control over their children to make this rebellion an individual rather than a social phenomenon. Thus, when children became young adults the allure of peer activities diminished and the "grab of social institutions" took hold, and most settled down to jobs, marriage, and children. The youth cohorts were small enough to enable adults to maintain control during their more rebellious years. By the 1960s the social system was already strained by social and cultural changes. This, coupled with a more than 50% increase in the youth population, caused the control system to begin to break down. In the past, youth had looked to parents, teachers, clergymen, and other adults for advice and guid-

ance. Now, however, the youth culture itself became a major socializing force and adults became distrusted.

### The Civil Rights Movement Changed the Relationships between Racial/Ethnic Groups

In the mid-1950s blacks began to make major improvements in achieving equality in American society. In 1954 the Supreme Court, in *Brown v. Board of Education*, struck down the "separate but equal" doctrine that had supported segregation. The increasing size of the northern black vote made civil rights a key issue in national elections, resulting in the establishment of the Federal Civil Rights Commission in 1957. Martin Luther King rose to national prominence and achieved support for the Civil Rights movement through nonviolent but direct action protests against illegal segregation and discrimination. These victories made blacks feel they no longer had to accept second-class status and intensified their expectations and dissatisfaction with their current circumstances. The result was a rising tempo of nonviolent action culminating in the student sit-ins of the 1960s and the birth of the civil rights revolution [National Advisory Commission on Civil Disorders (NACCD), 1968]. By 1963 the protest movement had achieved a new sense of urgency. Blacks were no longer willing to wait for progress but began to demand immediate freedom and equality. The meteoric rise of the Black Muslims to national prominence during this period was also a major factor in awakening civil rights protests (NACCD, 1968). During this era there were massive protests in northern cities and in the South against inequities in housing, education, and employment.

**PROTESTS AGAINST INEQUITIES TURNED VIOLENT** By 1964 some movement leadership had concluded that nonviolent direct action was of limited usefulness despite major victories. Blacks remained second-class citizens, no better off economically nor in their treatment by the criminal justice system. Feeling as though the nation was moving toward two societies—one black and one white—that were separate and unequal, blacks took to the streets to express dissatisfaction with their current circumstances. During 1966 and 1967 there were 207 disorders and riots. The NACCD (1968) attributed the cause of these disturbances to pervasive segregation, discrimination, poverty, and frustration over failures to achieve concrete progress despite major judicial and legislative victories.

### The Vietnam War Engendered Protest by Significant Segments of the Population

From the mid-1960s to early 1970s the United States also experienced violent and nonviolent reactions to the Vietnam War. The growing widespread opposition involved a variety of individuals and social groups (e.g., youths and students, prestigious leaders, academic and literary figures, radical groups, and religious groups) (Brooks, 1969). Resistance to the war escalated to a point that a large part of the population opposed it, with some more radical opponents questioning the legitimacy of the political system conducting the war and using violence to oppose it.

### The Ongoing Social Movements Had a Profound Effect on the Prisons

The prison system did not escape the influence of these events. Those on the inside became aware of what was going on through the extensive coverage in newspapers and on television. Many inmates coming into prisons during the late 1960s and early 1970s in large industrial states had taken part in riots, had been exposed to nationally known civil rights leaders, had been involved in political movements, and were familiar with the language of social and political protest (Jacobs, 1977). Those who had been politically involved continued the civil rights struggle from their cells. Many were charismatic personalities, and inmates could not help but be affected by the presence of individuals who defined their situation as that of **political prisoners** (i.e., individuals who commit criminal acts to further a political cause). Inmates began to emulate outside groups and started to assert themselves and protest their conditions of confinement. Some even rejected the legitimacy of the prison system itself.

### FACTORS THAT CAUSED THE DEMISE OF THE TRADITIONAL PRISON STRATIFICATION SYSTEM

Changes in the traditional prison stratification system were the result of changes in the racial/ethnic

makeup of the prison population and of the development of a new sense of pride and self-respect on the part of these minority group inmates.

### A New Self-Image Led Blacks to Develop Racial Pride

Before the 1960s minority group prisoners suffered the normal pains of imprisonment in addition to the humiliations of racial discrimination. Blacks had previously been relegated to the lowest positions in inmate society and to the most menial jobs in prison, and they were expected to behave in a docile manner. The black prisoner movement resulted from the same conditions that produced the black Civil Rights movement but the dimensions of racial consciousness and black separatism were more significant in the prison. Also, as this movement achieved prominence, the proportion of blacks in prison was growing and they were becoming the dominant group. A major factor in the black prisoner movement was the emergence of a new self-image among blacks. This resulted from dramatic cultural changes among black Americans, including views on their identity, heritage, and relationship to American society. Some of these inmates adopted African names, wore African clothing and jewelry, changed to a natural or "afro" hairstyle, and adopted the general view that "black is beautiful" (Carroll, 1974; Silberman, 1978; Irwin, 1980).

### The Black Muslim Movement Attracted Many Black Inmates

Until the emergence of the Muslims, religious groups had not typically served as a basis for collective black inmate behavior in prison (Jacobs, 1976). Undoubtedly, the **Black Muslims** are the biggest and best organized group ever to reside in prisons. Although many black community groups doubled as protest organizations, the Black Muslims represented the best organized and most articulate militant group on the radical side of the political spectrum (Lincoln, 1973).

During the 1950s and 1960s under the leadership of Elijah Muhammad, the Black Muslims strove to become a broad-based mass movement and did considerable recruiting in the jails and prisons (Lincoln, 1973). Black inmates were attracted to this group because it provided an explanation of criminal behavior which removed the guilt from the individual and shifted it to white racism and oppression (Jacobs, 1976). This is illustrated by the following excerpt from Malcolm X, one of Muhammad's chief lieutenants, who became a Muslim in prison.

> You let this caged up black man start thinking, the same way I did when I first heard Elijah Muhammad's teachings: let him start thinking how, with better breaks when he was young and ambitious he might have been a lawyer, doctor, social scientist, anything. You let this caged up black man start realizing, as I did how from the first landing of the first slave ship, the millions of black men of America had been like sheep in a den of wolves. That's why black prisoners become Muslims so fast when Elijah Muhammad's teachings filter into their cages by way of other Muslim convicts. "The white is the devil" is a perfect echo of that black convict's lifelong experience (Malcolm X, 1965, pp. 184–185).

Black inmates became Muslims because it gave them the opportunity to be involved in something uniquely black that provided a rationale for their status and a positive self-identity. The Muslims also provided a program enabling them to break the drug/crime cycle in which many had been caught. To join the group, inmates had to take vows not to return to drugs or crime. On release, Muslim temples helped offenders keep their vows by assisting them in getting housing and jobs. Work, coupled with responsibilities to the temple, left little time for regression to their previous criminal lifestyle (Lincoln, 1973).

**INITIALLY MUSLIMS WERE VIEWED AS A THREAT TO PRISON ORDER BUT EVENTUALLY THEY BECAME A STABILIZING FORCE** During the 1960s Black Muslims became a sizable faction in many prisons, organizing themselves into distinctive groups characterized by a high degree of commitment and discipline among their members. Muslims characteristically shaved their heads, were impeccably clean, followed dietary laws prohibiting the eating of pork or any food cooked in its by-products, and gathered together, when possible, to carry on teachings, prayer, recruitment, and other organizational activities (Irwin, 1980; Jacobs, 1977). Although adopting a hostile stance, Muslims rarely initiated violence and generally reacted violently only to protect a group member.

Both prison administrators and white inmates felt threatened, frightened, and antagonized by the rhetoric of the Muslims who condemned and vilified whites and white society (Irwin, 1980). An organized group of blacks now threatened whites who were not organized and who still controlled the best positions in the prison. At some prisons, whites responded by developing activist groups (New York State Special Commission on Attica, 1972)[1]. Instead of recognizing the Black Muslims' potential for maintaining peace and for reforming offenders, prison administrators reacted only to its rhetoric and demands for basic rights. They refused Muslim demands despite the fact their requests only asked for access to Muslim ministers, for food prepared within their dietary rules, to practice their religion, and for fairer parole decisions. Agreement to these demands would have recognized that inmates had certain rights and freedoms, which conflicted with long-held ideas that inmates were a degraded caste with no constitutional rights (Jacobs, 1977).

The fact that these demands were made by the most subjugated individuals in the prison, by those who were expected to "know their place," frightened prison officials even more. Many prisons introduced rules against belonging to the Muslims. Arguing that they were denied their constitutional right to practice their religion, the Muslims took their fight to the courts. In *Cooper v. Pate* (1964), the first modern prisoner rights case, the Supreme Court recognized the rights of the Muslims to challenge prison restrictions on religious freedom under the Civil Rights Act of 1871 (see Chapter 15). Court rulings eventually forced prison administrators to recognize the Muslims as a religious organization and to allow them to practice their religion in prison since none of their activities presented a clear and present danger[2] (*Banks v. Havener*, 1964; *Knuckles v. Prasse*, 1969; Jacobs, 1980).

Over time, the Muslims modified their more extreme black supremacy and nationalistic doctrines. They began placing major emphasis on the religious character of the movement and deemphasizing its political motives. This change was also evident in the prisons (Jacobs, 1977). By the 1970s Muslims were considered one of the more stable prison groups, and it was not uncommon for guards to consider them among the best inmates. As the Muslims became less politically oriented, some black inmates became dissatisfied with their conservative position. They became involved in more violent radical groups that emerged during the late 1960s (e.g., the Black Panthers).

## Race Relations within Prisons Changed

During the 1960s a number of factors set into motion changes that transformed the nature of racial/ethnic relations in our nation's prisons.

**BLACK INMATES VIEWED BOTH WHITE INMATES AND CORRECTIONAL OFFICERS AS A THREAT** Since most correctional officers (COs) were white, racial hostility in prisons was further aggravated by their prejudices and sometimes discriminatory behavior. White COs viewed black inmates with a combination of hostility, fear, and prejudice (Carroll, 1974). They saw them as conspiring, dangerous revolutionaries whose only purpose was to challenge the authority of COs and possibly to attempt to take over prisons by open rebellion. Although COs held negative views of white inmates, they did not see them as enemies liable to provoke open warfare. Blacks saw the racial identification between white prisoners and COs as having the potential for an antagonistic alliance against them. Thus, black solidarity represented not only a desire to cultivate the unique aspects of black culture but was also a response to the perceived threat of an alliance between white staff and prisoners.

**THERE WAS SOME RACIAL INTEGRATION IN PRISON BUT LITTLE INTERACTION** At this point what was going on in the prison was out of sync with what was happening on the outside. While many free-world institutions were officially moving to promote racial equality and eliminate segregation, inmates were informally establishing rigid patterns of informal segregation. These conflicting forces resulted in some integration in prison, but interracial interaction remained limited to settings where there was a high degree of administrative control, for example, work details and cell assignments. Even here contact was superficial (Carroll, 1974). White and black inmates often worked side by side, but communication was almost exclusively job related. They now shared the same cell blocks, but social interaction was limited to their own ethnic/racial group. Thus, in many prisons there was a clear pattern of informal segregation wherever this was possible, for example, in dining rooms, day rooms, at the movies, while waiting in line, and informal gatherings (Carroll, 1974; Irwin, 1980; Attica Commission, 1972). Figures 8.1 and 8.2 provide some examples.

**INTERRACIAL TENSION INCREASED PRISON VIOLENCE** During this period of rising racial tensions, the composition of the prison population not only affected how well a given group fared but the total environment of the institution. For example, in California, there was an alliance between whites and Chicanos that placed blacks in an unfavorable position in prisons where they were outnumbered by this coalition (Irwin, 1980). In facilities where blacks comprised half the population, they were in a more equitable position. When blacks were in the majority, they claimed the best spots in areas where they gathered informally (such as the yard), and whites had to accept inferior locations. With increasing racial hostility, there was a precipitous increase in racial violence.

**STATE-RAISED YOUTH CLIQUES ACHIEVED PROMINENCE** An unfortunate consequence of the disintegration of the tip and clique network, as discussed in Chapter 7, was the rise to prominence of a group of young hoodlums, many of whom were **state-raised youth**—inmates who grew up spending substantial time in juvenile facilities. They formed cliques and hung out in the prison yard spending most of their time boasting about their exploits and exaggerating their abilities. Always presenting a demeanor of toughness, these youth were typically more violent than the average inmate and, although not respected, were feared for their violent outbursts. By wheeling, dealing, and theft they infiltrated the prison economy controlled by older inmates. Until the racial hostility of the 1960s, this group's power group was curtailed by two factors: their fear that older and more respected inmates would become violent and murderous when pushed too far, and the solidarity of other inmates against them (Irwin, 1980).

This group always displayed a high level of prejudice, even during the era of racial tolerance (Irwin, 1980). When the prison's climate was changed by racial conflict and violence, they began openly displaying racist attitudes by calling themselves Nazis and tattooing their bodies with swastikas. Similarly, black cliques manifested open racial hostility. The position of the hoodlums was further enhanced when both black and white prisoners, even respected and older inmates, joined these cliques in self-defense or became associated with them because they felt threatened by rising racial hostilities. The ranks of white groups were further swelled by the imprisonment of increasing

FIGURE 8.1 **Racial Segregation of Prisoners in the Gym**

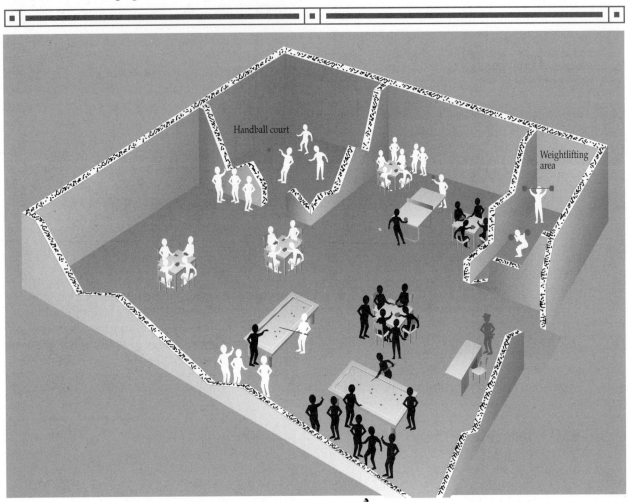

SOURCE: Carroll, L., *Hacks, Blacks, and Cons*. Lexington, MA: Lexington Books, 1974, p. 160.[a]

numbers of outlaw motorcycle gang members who held extreme racist views and sometimes assumed leadership of these groups.

**MEXICAN-AMERICANS ALSO DEVELOPED CLIQUES** The situation among the Mexican-American (Chicano) inmates was different because of their ambivalence about their racial position (Irwin, 1980). Chicanos were more hostile and prejudiced toward blacks than toward whites because they had close friendships with some white criminals. By associating with whites and adopting their racist attitudes toward blacks, they could enhance their own position.

Chicano inmates formed neighborhood-based cliques whose major concern was controlling drug trafficking rather than racial hatred and violence. These groups fought among themselves to achieve

FIGURE 8.2 **Racial Segregation of Prisoners at the Movies**

SOURCE: Carroll, L., *Hacks, Blacks, and Cons*. Lexington, MA: Lexington Books, 1974, p. 162.[a]

dominance in this area but not until the demise of the prisoner movement in the 1970s did these violent cliques and gangs become a major force in prisons (see Chapter 10). The objectives of the prisoner movement provided a basis for inmate harmony by redirecting the violence and hostility they felt toward each other against outside forces (i.e., prison administration) (Irwin, 1980). This movement temporarily halted the growing trend toward racial/ethnic division.

## THE PRISONER MOVEMENT: THE POLITICIZATION OF INMATES

The **prisoner movement** to be discussed in the remainder of this chapter spanned the period from 1970 to 1975 and involved (1) a change in inmate self-concept from subservient participants to active reformers and (2) a focus on reforming prison conditions by both free-world and inmate groups.

### The New Left's Focus on Prisons and a New Breed of Inmate Were Primary Factors in the Development of the Prisoner Movement

Inmates' views of themselves and their identification by correctional officials as "political prisoners" were alien to American corrections until the 1950s. Previously, inmates in this country were not sentenced for crimes having any political motivation. Much of this changed with the Civil Rights movement in the 1950s and continued with the protests against the Vietnam War in the 1960s (Glaser, 1971). These movements considered crimes by their members to be politically motivated, that is, committed to further their political objectives, thus justifying them. However, they were not viewed as political by the authorities, so when they were jailed or imprisoned they were treated no differently than other criminals.

Left-wing political groups formed in the 1960s in opposition to the Vietnam War, unlike traditional political parties, were not interested in developing a voter constituency. Instead they were looking to persuade individuals that the solution to existing problems was to change the system. They focused on prisons because these facilities incarcerated predominantly lower class minorities, which they felt presented a clear and glaring manifestation of the inequities, injustices, and prejudices that "charac-

terized" U.S. society (Irwin, 1980). The involvement of the New Left movement in prisons provided leaders and workers for a variety of both old and new inmate organizations: lawyers to develop the new area of prison law and people to participate actively in and to be a part of audiences at movement conferences, rallies, and other staged events (Irwin, 1980). The development of politically oriented groups in the institutions during this brief period was not surprising considering the conditions described earlier.

### Inmate Groups Critically Examined Their Circumstances

While all inmate racial/ethnic groups began to critically examine the circumstances surrounding their confinement, their reaction to the society that placed them there varied greatly.

**BLACK INMATES MOVED IN A MORE RADICAL DIRECTION**　In many prisons, like Attica, blacks were confronted with conditions more repressive than they had experienced on the streets. It is not surprising they were attracted to radical groups who "explained" their status. By 1970 black inmates had generally become disillusioned with the inability of the Civil Rights movement to accomplish any major changes and with the Muslims who, while explaining their plight, failed to provide any cogent strategies for dealing with the problems blacks faced (Berkman, 1979).

**PUERTO RICAN INMATES EMBRACED THE OBJECTIVES OF THE CIVIL RIGHTS MOVEMENT**　In the Northeast, particularly in New York, Puerto Ricans represented another minority group dissatisfied with its position. Most of these inmates were natives of Puerto Rico who were unaccustomed to the pervasive racism they encountered on the mainland (Attica Commission, 1972). These proud Puerto Rican males were discriminated against in the same way blacks were. Thus, before the Civil Rights movement, Puerto Ricans also seethed in silent bitterness. The objectives of the Civil Rights movement were not lost on Puerto Ricans, who found them easily adaptable to their own situation. They were prompted to assert themselves in government, education, and in the cultural life of American society. Puerto Rican inmates also began to demand that prison authorities deal with problems specific to their group including English language training, Spanish language broadcasts and publications, insistence that English-speaking staff be trained to understand the problems they faced, and permission to correspond with their families in Spanish—the only language many knew. By the 1970s the Puerto Rican prisoner, like the African-American inmate, was seeking to explain his current circumstances.

**CHICANO INMATES DEVELOPED A SENSE OF RACIAL PRIDE** In the Southwest, Chicanos represented a dominant group in state prisons. In the late 1960s Chicano inmates (particularly in California) began developing an ethnic consciousness and promoting their own special interests (Irwin, 1980). Inspired by other groups, they developed a sense of pride about their ethnic identity and the unique aspects of their culture. During this period self-help groups emerged to unify Chicano inmates and raise their cultural consciousness. Only a few of the more militant Chicanos adopted the extremely hostile attitude toward whites manifested by black militants. Instead, most Chicano activists adopted a moderate position becoming less hostile toward blacks and less willing to support whites in their hostile stance toward black prisoners.

**A NEW BREED OF WHITE INMATES ENTERED THE PRISONS** A new type of white inmate was entering prison who was younger, better educated, and more involved in drugs than earlier groups (Attica Commission, 1972). White inmates who previously dominated prisons believed felons generally got what they deserved (although they themselves might personally have gotten a "bum deal"). This is summed up by the phrase "if you can't do the time, don't do the crime." While recognizing that most people sent to prison were poor, they believed this was a matter of fate. This attitude changed in the 1960s when they became painfully aware that the criminal justice system apparently discriminated against certain segments of the population. Most whites in prison at this point were the most disadvantaged members of white groups. They were resentful of the higher status members of their racial group who committed crimes and used their position to avoid punishment. Thus, they too felt discriminated against because of their lower class status (Irwin, 1980).

## Inmates Redefined Their Status to That of Political Prisoners

Clearly, the early 1970s was a period when inmates critically examined their position in society and in prison. The Attica Commission (1972) noted that many prisoners viewed themselves as "political prisoners." Although not convicted of offenses having political motives or significance, many still felt they were not personally responsible for their criminal behavior. They blamed society for victimizing them by failing to provide equal educational opportunities, adequate housing, and the chance to compete effectively in society. They claimed correctional rehabilitation efforts were misdirected since it was not them but society that needed reforming. Consequently, they saw many prison programs (such as job training) as confirming their status as second-class citizens instead of helping them become equal members of society. However, even though many inmates felt victimized by society, most failed to endorse the revolutionary ideology calling for government overthrow. Instead, they subscribed to a position that called for working within the existing system to make it share some of its power and influence. Although devoid of revolutionary intent, these inmates employed strong rhetoric and violence to pressure the system to meet their demands (Berkman, 1979).

**SOME INMATES ADOPTED A MORE RADICAL POSITION** A much smaller group adopted a class-oriented Marxist position that espoused a revolutionary political ideology (Berkman, 1979). This position was more attractive to blacks and other minorities because it also explained their current social and economic circumstances. It maintained that racism was historically rooted in a capitalistic economic system because this economic strategy required a "reserve army" of labor. This prevented the rise of the working class and kept the labor force divided, which meant that no meaningful change could occur as long as our economic and political system was based on capitalism.

This ideology also provided an explanation for the conflicts between ethnic/racial minorities. It argued that the ruling elite, by controlling government and the workplace, effectively set one group of exploited people against another in the same way prison officials turned blacks against whites in order to maintain control. Thus, racial differences provided a basis for dividing these populations (Berkman, 1979). However, racism was not the primary means used by the dominant economic class to control society. The major strategy was controlling the means of production. By dominating the means of production and controlling the wealth of society, the capitalist elite could control the labor force and dictate the terms under which they worked. The result was a system under which workers either endured exploitation or were excluded from the workplace. Within this framework, prisoners were one segment of the working class who were systematically excluded from participation in the economic system. Further, blacks experienced more exploitation because of racist attitudes. Even those blacks adopting Marxism still felt racism was not completely dealt with by this position. Other minorities, including Chicanos, Puerto Ricans, Native-Americans, women, and many white workers, were also exploited under this system, thus providing the basis for a coalition of exploited groups that could jointly struggle against oppression (Berkman, 1979).

## PRISONER MOVEMENT ORGANIZATIONS

The prisoner movement thus consisted of many groups, running the gamut from revolutionary groups to those that tried to operate within the current system. The widespread publicity associated with the prisoner movement, along with its lofty goals, tended to draw together and radicalize all the organizations working on prison issues. However, most groups managed to maintain their own philosophies, identities, strategies, goals, and memberships.

### Self-Help Groups Focused on Individual Improvement

Emerging several years before the prisoner movement, **self-help groups** were primarily concerned with the improvement of the life circumstances of ex-prisoners. **Seven Steps,** founded by Bill Sands, a former inmate at San Quentin, is considered one of the earliest of these organizations to be established. Modeled after the twelve steps of the Alcoholics Anonymous program, these seven steps were developed to guide inmates in maintaining their

freedom (Sands, 1964). This group spread to prisons in other parts of the country and today is one of the largest inmate self-help organizations. It sparked the development of many other self-help groups, some of which were broad-based (e.g., the Fortune Society) and others that were racially and ethnically based (e.g., SATE for black inmates).

Ethnically based self-help groups typically emphasized ethnic themes to attract and motivate individual prisoners (Moore, 1978). For example, the Chicano cultural group EMPLEO operates on the principle that by awakening the group identity of Mexican-Americans and a sense of obligation toward their group, constructive change for ex-convicts and addicts can be achieved. It emphasizes discipline, education, self-development, training in public speaking, self-esteem, pride, and cultural awareness. It directs its efforts toward developing a cohesive group by instilling feelings of brotherhood among all Chicano inmates to reduce intra-Chicano violence and toward the improvement of prison conditions. This group also maintains contact with outside community groups to provide inmates with motivational models and with resources to help them on release.

Self-help groups were important for the prisoner movement in two ways (Irwin, 1980). First, they constituted the largest prisoner organizations. Prison administrators accepted and frequently encouraged these organizations because they represented a much safer alternative to the more radical political groups. Many inmates also preferred these organizations because they were more oriented to self-advancement than to political change. They also brought people into the prisons to help their members who, when witnessing unexpected abuses, frequently became more active in prison reform.

These groups also provided ex-cons with encouragement to "come out." Previously, most convicts tried to hide or live down their ex-convict status because most people saw them as no better than convicts. However, Bill Sands and the Seven Steps program did a great deal to reverse the negative attitudes and prejudices held regarding ex-cons. This enabled them to reveal publicly, without embarrassment, their prior criminal status. Many took advantage of the new acceptance of their status and, like Bill Sands, developed careers as professional ex-convicts (Irwin, 1980). This also gave them the opportunity to enter many conventional activities, including those of a political nature.

## Prisoner Rights Groups Focused on Improving the Offenders' Constitutional Rights and Social Position

The number of **prisoner rights groups** began to increase just before the emergence of the prisoner movement (Irwin, 1980). They inherited a legacy of reform dating back to the beginning of prisons in the United States. The groups emerging in the 1960s were quite different than their predecessors. The major focus of the earlier groups was providing prison inmates, who were viewed as psychologically inferior, with a prison environment that was not excessively cruel and offered them opportunities for reform. The later groups were influenced by the Civil Rights movement and had a new view of criminals as essentially the same as other individuals, except they were victims of reduced life chances and excessive discrimination. Their goal was to reduce the disparities between the legal and social circumstances of prisoners and members of conventional society. They also sought an increase in inmate constitutional rights and the development of meaningful prison industries programs with reasonable wages. For released offenders they wanted to restore to them the rights and privileges accorded to all citizens. They did not generally advocate rehabilitation because this implied criminals were different from other citizens, and that society was justified and had the means to reform them (Irwin, 1980).

## Radical Groups Advocated Changing Society

**Radical groups** focused on changing society rather than on helping the inmate or changing prison conditions (Irwin, 1980). They viewed the prison as an illustration of the oppression and exploitation of the poor and nonwhites by a capitalist economic system. In fact prisons were seen as representing the most negative consequences of this system. Also, based on early contacts with inmates, many felt they could recruit inmate leaders to be active in radical activities on release (Irwin, 1980). A perspective on the nature of these radical groups can be gleaned from examining two inmate groups (the Black Panthers and Young Lords) and one outside group, the National Lawyers Guild.

**THE BLACK PANTHERS ATTRACTED BLACK INMATES** The **Black Panthers** originated in Oakland, California, in 1966 in reaction to police brutality in the black community (Stratton, 1973). It represented itself as a Marxist/Leninist revolutionary party, directed toward freeing blacks from their current state of suppression by corporate capitalism. Panther leaders saw inmates as embittered and disgruntled, making them ripe for involvement in revolutionary political activity (Jacobs, 1976). Leaders like George Jackson felt inmates were an important segment of the revolutionary movement. Jackson stated:

> I feel that the building of revolutionary consciousness of the prisoner class is paramount in the overall development of a hard left revolutionary cadre (Committee on Internal Security, 1973a, p. 181).

They appealed to apolitical prisoners by offering them the more positive status of political prisoner. This enabled them to redefine their status from offender to victim and view prison and its administration as a manifestation of the repressive organizations characteristic of American society. Their objective was to unite all prisoner movement groups through an inclusive ideology emphasizing their similarities and minimizing their differences. At Attica, prior to the riot, between 200 and 300 inmates were estimated to be members, and at San Quentin, under George Jackson's leadership, a similar number were involved (Stratton, 1973; Hughes, 1973; Hankins, 1973). Former members of the Black Panthers from New York State prisons reported joining for several reasons including status, protection, and a search for identity (Stratton, 1973).

**THE YOUNG LORDS WERE SIMILAR TO THE BLACK PANTHERS** The **Young Lords** emerged from a street gang in Chicago in 1969 and spread to other states. In New York prisons, the Young Lords primarily attracted Puerto Rican inmates, but it was open to inmates of all ethnic backgrounds. This organization was revolutionary in nature and guided by Marxist/Leninist/Maoist principles. Prisoners joined for protection and because it enhanced cultural awareness (Committee on Internal

## Close Up · The Legacy of the Black Panthers: Fugitive Surfaces Thirteen Years Later

George Jackson was a black inmate who was imprisoned in Soledad prison in California in 1961. By 1970 he had embraced Marxism and became a leader of the Black Panther Party. In 1970, a Soledad tower CO had fired into a group of black inmates who were involved in a fight, killing three of them. In retaliation a CO was beaten and thrown to his death from a tier. Jackson and two other inmates were charged with this crime and became known as the "Soledad Brothers." To many radicals, this whole case symbolized the racial oppression of blacks in U.S. prisons (Morain, 1986; Lindsey, 1986; Stein 1990).

Stephen Bingham, a radical Yale educated lawyer who espoused Marxism, had become involved in efforts to help black prisoners in the late sixties which eventually led to his attempts to help Jackson. During 1971 Bingham visited Jackson six times at San Quentin. During his last visit Bingham was alleged to have smuggled a gun and some ammunition to Jackson. Shortly after this last meeting between them, guards testified that Jackson pulled a gun and took over the Adjustment Center wing of the prison. In 30 minutes six people, including Jackson, two other inmates and three COs were killed. Six inmates were charged in what was referred to as an escape attempt. One of the inmates was convicted of murder, two of assault and three were acquitted. Bingham was named as a co-conspirator in this incident but disappeared and lived as a fugitive until 1984 when he surrendered to authorities (Morain, 1986; Stein, 1990). At his trial he testified that he went underground because he believed that Jackson had been killed by the San Quentin COS to end his revolutionary activity and that his own life was in danger. He surfaced in 1984 because he thought that he could now get a fair trial. At the 2-1/2 month trial, the jury found him not guilty of murder and conspiracy. Following his acquittal, Bingham indicated that the verdict represented some encouragement to people involved in unpopular causes (Lindsey, 1986). What do you think the verdict would have been if the trial had been held immediately following the prison incident? If it had been held today?

Security, 1973a). At Attica, prior to the riot, it had from twenty-five to seventy-five members. It also helped negotiate a truce between the Black Muslims and Black Panthers.

**THE NATIONAL LAWYERS GUILD PROVIDED LEGAL ASSISTANCE AS A MEANS OF FURTHERING THE REVOLUTION** The **National Lawyers Guild** was established in 1936 and was affiliated with the International Association of Democratic Lawyers. It was reported by the Committee on Internal Security of the House of Representatives (1973b) to be a Communist front organization. In the early 1970s it claimed about 3500 members organized into 20 or more law school and independent chapters. Its political orientation is captured by a statement made at its 1971 convention: "We are a body of radicals and revolutionaries who propose to carry the struggle for social change into our lives and our professions" (Committee on Internal Security, 1973b). It initiated its involvement with prisons in 1971. It also officially added jailhouse lawyers—inmates who provide legal assistance for other prisoners—to its membership because their work in the prison further supported the revolutionary movement.

During the 1970s the activities of the Lawyers Guild in the prison movement included initiating class action suits in instances in which it felt prisoners' rights were violated; providing legal representation for prisoners involved in revolutionary activity; and negotiating with prison administrators in order to achieve inmate objectives. They first played an open role in the Folsom Prison strike in 1970 by holding press conferences and contacting the news media in support of the strike, and by being present during picketing and demonstrations. Also, during the Attica riot, they served on the observation committee and provided defense attorneys for inmates involved in the riot.

**RADICAL GROUPS ONLY HAD A FEW TRUE IN-MATE MEMBERS** Most radical groups were established outside the prisons. Only a few inmates were members of these groups and they were forced to keep their membership a secret because most prison administrators banned them. Outside members typically came from the New Left. They included two groups: some actively committed members of radical organizations, and a much larger segment of less committed part-time activists not regularly involved in movement activities. Inmate membership was limited primarily to nonwhite inmates. Most whites did not join due to their politically conservative ideas. They also tended to be racist and resented the attention these groups gave to racism and black prisoners.

In fact, only a few black inmates were true revolutionaries (Carroll, 1974; Irwin, 1980). These inmates were oriented to the future, directing their efforts to preparing for the eventual revolution. They adopted a spartan lifestyle, and their cells were typically devoid of decorations containing only necessities such as a desk, bed, typewriter, radio, and revolutionary books. They stopped participating in the prisoner economy because they felt it was a sign of weakness for inmates to deal with the deprivations of prison life (e.g., by obtaining extra food from the kitchen, using drugs, involvement in homosexuality). To better prepare themselves to be more effective in the revolution, they pursued self-improvement activities. They sought to develop a positive identity by learning about black culture through cultural programs offered by black organizations. While suspicious of prison programs, they still participated in those that could result in an outside job or an early parole.

The majority of black inmates leaned toward revolutionary ideas but were unwilling to adopt the regimented and spartan lifestyle of true revolutionaries. Thus, they were best described as **half-steppers** (Carroll, 1974). Publicly, they manifested an intense commitment to the revolution by decorating their cells with revolutionary posters that included phrases such as "The Revolution Is Now" and "Power to the People." In open conversations on the yard and in the wings, they denounced the "racist pigs" in loud voices and advocated revolution. However, a closer look at this group revealed they were oriented to the present and were more concerned with opportunities for self-expression within the institution (e.g., dress, music, and the use of nicknames) than with future revolutionary concerns. For them the function of revolutionary organizations was to make doing time easier and to "keep them whities off our backs" (Carroll, 1974, p. 109).

## PRISONER MOVEMENT ACTIVITIES

Prisoner movement activities included activities inside the prisons that ranged from inmate strikes to sporadic violence and riots. Nevertheless, outside organizations and individuals really provided the major support base for movement activities since inmates were limited in the degree to which they could influence changes in criminal justice policy.

### Inmate Strikes Were Organized to Focus Public Attention on Prison Conditions

Prison strikes occurred in many states and involved the following chain of events. Initially, a group of inmates prepared a list of grievances that were directed at making dramatic changes in existing relationships and structures. They tried to maintain a coalition of inmates from all major racial groups who were supportive of their demands and strategies and attempted to obtain outside support from prisoner support groups in the area. These coalitions sought to organize various forms of collective protest (such as strikes) to pressure the prison administration into negotiations and to attract public attention and sympathy for their grievances and circumstances (Irwin, 1980).

The longest of these strikes, the **Folsom Prison strike** in 1968, lasted nineteen days and involved nearly all 2400 inmates at Folsom. It commenced when inmates refused to go to work or to the yard after having smuggled out a list of twenty-nine demands relating to (1) constitutional rights such as changing policies to reflect federal court decisions (e.g., due process in disciplinary sentencing); (2) political freedom (e.g., ending persecution or segregation of inmates because of political beliefs); and (3) economic demands that focused on prison industries.[3]

The warden reacted by locking down the prison, which meant keeping inmates in their cells. Outside groups supported the strike by organizing picket lines at the Folsom Prison entrance, making contacts with other groups, and providing the media with a description of the strike, the issues involved, and prisons in general. Although enthusiasm was high at the beginning of the strike, it dropped off dramatically after two weeks as supplies of cigarettes and food were consumed and as batteries for their portable radios—their only means of outside information—wore out. Thus, when the warden offered to unlock the prison if inmates went back to work, most of them acquiesced (Irwin, 1980).

Other strikes and demonstrations associated with the prisoner movement occurred in many state and federal institutions, and in city and county jails (Irwin, 1980; Committee on Internal Security, 1973a). The Attica revolt was most significant because, unlike many disturbances, it involved injuries, extensive property damage, and many deaths. We conclude this section by discussing it.

### The Attica Revolt: A Riot and a Political Demonstration

The **Attica revolt** occurred in 1971 at the end of a summer marked by increasing tensions between inmates and COs yet characterized by rising inmate expectations based on improving prison conditions (Attica Commission, 1972). This unrest was caused by the changing relationships between Attica's all-white, primarily rural staff who were unprepared and untrained to deal with the new breed of young, urban black and Puerto Rican inmates who were unwilling to accept their authority without question. A small cadre of the inmates was also involved in radical political groups like the Black Panthers and the Young Lords. This disturbance was not planned but rather sparked by inmates rebelling against disciplinary actions taken by COs.

**A CHAOTIC RAMPAGE BECAME AN ORGANIZED DEMONSTRATION**  During the first phase of the riot, hundreds of prisoners went on a wild rampage destroying property, taking over parts of the prison, pillaging the commissary and officer's mess, and taking fifty officers and civilians hostage. While most prisoners were milling around, partying, and destroying property, the Muslims assumed responsibility for protecting the hostages

The Attica Correctional Facility in New York became prominent after the inmate riot of 1971. The flag is flying at half-mast to honor the ten correctional officers killed in that riot.

and arranged for the release of the seriously injured. Anarchy prevailed for more than three hours until one inmate, recognizing the disastrous consequences of this continuing situation, attempted to bring some order. Calling for the inmates to pull together, he gave instructions for various groups to gather certain items needed to continue the protest. A tenuous coalition developed between leaders of the various prison factions including the Black Panthers, Young Lords, Five Percenters, and Muslims, which constituted about 200 of the 1200 inmates involved in the disturbance. They developed a policy for treatment of hostages, rules governing inmate activities, and also formed a security force to assure compliance. This brought organization back to the prison yard. They also developed the demands put forth to Commissioner

Inmate negotiating committee talking with Commissioner Russell Oswald about their demands for ending the riot.

of Corrections Russell Oswald, which initially included requests for complete amnesty, safe and speedy transportation out of confinement to a "non-Imperialist" country, placement under federal jurisdiction, and the establishment of a negotiating committee comprised of people that inmates trusted—from the media, radical organizations (e.g., Black Panther Party), and politicians sympathetic to their cause.

The final negotiating committee consisted of thirty members and included members from some of the requested groups and some chosen by Governor Nelson Rockefeller. The members met with the inmates and attempted to sift through their demands and develop a list of proposals to submit to Commissioner Oswald. The only demands he rejected were for the removal of the superintendent, inmate transportation to a foreign country, complete amnesty, unconditional release of inmates eligible for parole, and the release of the remaining 1200 inmates so that they could join the rioting group.

On the third day of the riot the observers' committee presented the inmates with the twenty-eight points to which Commissioner Oswald had agreed. The inmates rejected his offer for a variety of reasons. First, they did not trust Oswald's promises of no physical or administrative reprisals or criminal charges for property damage. Second, the inmates wanted amnesty (immunity) from prosecution because they feared mass prosecutions for all crimes relating to the riot. The local district attorney promised no mass prosecutions and that charges would only be brought if there was substantial evidence to link specific inmates with a specific crime. Although amnesty was a major concern, a poll found that more than two-thirds of the inmates would have given up this demand to get out of the yard safely. Third, fear of dissenting prevented many inmates who approved the twenty-eight points from expressing their views. They felt obligated to support their leaders and were afraid to risk the harsh discipline that the leadership committee might impose on them for nonsupport. Finally, there was a sense of unreality. Inmates suddenly had freedom, prominence, and power, which led many to believe that by holding out they would be granted all their demands.

Many of the men in D-yard probably did not believe the 28 points really represented the best deal they could make.... They had hostages; the state had not moved against them. If they could [pry] ... those 28 points out of the state, might they not yet get more—even amnesty? (Wicker, 1975, p. 175).

With the rejection of the compromise proposal on the fourth day of the riot, some negotiating committee members requested that Governor Rockefeller come to the prison to meet with them to avert a bloodbath if the prison was taken by force. The governor refused feeling the key issue was amnesty, which was beyond his power to grant. Nevertheless, Bell (1985)[b] asserts that had he come and assured the inmates that only those involved in the death of the one guard who was fatally assaulted by inmates would be prosecuted, the inmates might have surrendered peacefully.

**THE RETAKING OF THE PRISON WAS LIKE A TURKEY SHOOT**   On the night of the fourth day, when negotiations had reached an impasse, the decision was made to take the prison by force the next morning. Although officials from the governor down insisted that this assault employ only the minimum amount of force necessary to restore order, this was not translated into effective restraints. The state police major who briefed the troops before the assault admonished them not to turn this into a "turkey shoot," that is, a game in which people are rewarded for drawing blood.[4] Moreover, four minutes into the assault a helicopter loudspeaker told inmates if they surrendered peacefully they would not be harmed. Although most men involved in retaking the prison acted with restraint, evidence from three state investigations and one trial concluded that the force used was excessive.

When the troopers retook the prison, 127 inmates and hostages were killed or wounded. The shooting was done in the midst of clouds of tear gas by troopers wearing gas masks making it difficult for them to see, much less know, at what they were aiming their weapons (Deutsch, Cunningham, and Fink, 1991). Evidence at a later trial showed the shooting was unnecessary because the gas was expected to immobilize the inmates and force them to the ground within ten to fifteen seconds. Further, the troopers knew inmates had only knives and clubs and there was no evidence of inmate attacks (Bell, 1985). Thus, the state's highest

court upheld a lower court finding that there was overpowering evidence that the state had used excessive force in retaking the D-yard (*Jones v. State*, 1983). In this regard an inmate reported watching as a helicopter discharged a cloud of tear gas and while advancing officers fired directly at inmates and hostages. Even when no one was left standing, the shooting continued and one officer shot an inmate at point-blank range (Glaberson, 1991).

Given the indiscriminate shooting, it is amazing that only thirty-nine persons (ten hostages and twenty-nine inmates) died of state-inflicted bullet wounds, and three hostages and eighty-five inmates suffered nonlethal gunshot wounds. Although warned by the inmates they would be killed *no hostages were killed by inmates during the assault*. In fact, some hostages reported inmate guards throwing their bodies on top of them to prevent their being injured.

The tragedy of Attica did not end when the shooting stopped. Despite promises of no reprisals, inmates continued to be kicked, prodded, beaten, and subjected to verbal abuse after the revolt was crushed. This abuse was still evident when the Attica Commission completed its investigation and held public hearings five months after the riot.

**THE STATE COVERED UP THE USE OF EXCESSIVE FORCE AND INFLICTION OF UNNECESSARY INJURY**   While sixty-two inmates were indicted for 1289 crimes arising out of the Attica riot, only one state trooper was indicted for the killings. This appeared to be an injustice since troopers killed ten hostages while inmates killed one. This discrepancy may be related to a public view that inmates brought this on themselves and thus deserved what was done to them.

To make matters worse, the state police were given the pivotal responsibility for investigating whether their own officers used excessive force when retaking the prison and while bringing it under control. This is akin to giving the fox responsibility for guarding the hen house. In what was called the "Hindering Case," state investigative prosecutors blamed the four ranking state police officers responsible for collecting evidence on the shooting for tampering with it. "They concluded their effort was not to enforce the law but to protect their own" (Bell, 1985, p. 202).[b]

A special state grand jury was impaneled to reexamine this question and the reckless endangerment

In the aftermath of the riot, police herded prisoners into a yard where they were made to crawl on their stomachs prior to being stripped and searched.

case against state police and corrections officers. Despite continued allegations of a cover-up, in the end a new governor decided to close the book on Attica, which had become one of New York's more embarrassing blunders. He then pardoned inmates convicted of crimes during the riot and closed the investigation. Although this appeared fair and equitable, it actually put culpable police officers and state officials beyond the reach of the law (Bell, 1985). Our Close-Up, "Attica Update and Its Legacy," by Michael Deutsch (1993), one of the attorneys for the inmate plaintiffs in the civil rights suit brought against the state, provides another chapter in the continuing Attica saga.

### Increasing Defiance and Violence Led to a Crisis in Control

Along with other social changes, the prisoner movement created an atmosphere charged with hostility and violence in many prisons. Many young inmates entering prison, particularly minorities, were notably belligerent toward all institutional authority (Irwin, 1980). As we noted, prisoners, like many other young people, rejected traditional norms regarding respect for authority. This, along with prisoner movement views that inmates had rights, could not be treated arbitrarily, and were victims rather than perpetrators, produced inmates prone to challenge staff authority and to attack

## Close Up  **Attica Update and Its Legacy**

A civil lawsuit was brought on behalf of the prisoners and their families, but the case was delayed for 20 years before it went to trial. After a four-month trial, the jury found that the prisoners' Eighth Amendment right to be free from cruel and unusual punishment was violated by the systematic beatings, denial of medical care, and shootings and killings of the defenseless prisoners. The jury, however, could only agree as to the liability of one prison official, the assistant deputy warden.

Faced with the prospect of further delays because of retrials of the claims upon which the jury was unable to reach a unanimous verdict, counsel for the plaintiffs attempted to negotiate a settlement so that the prisoner-plaintiffs could finally obtain some compensation for their injuries. The governor of New York, Mario Cuomo, however, refused to authorize any settlement, and the plaintiffs are now forced to go back to court for further litigation. This litigation will include individual damage hearings for those who were brutalized during the "rehousing" of the prisoners after the assault. This was as a result of the one verdict against the assistant deputy warden who was in charge of the "rehousing" and a retrial of the claim against the commander of the assault force.

Despite the inconclusive findings and the prospect of further delay and more litigation, the civil trial served as a forum for the prisoners to tell the real story of Attica. It allowed them to expose for the first time the true extent of the killing and brutality and placed all public officials on notice that they will be held accountable in the public record, no matter how long it takes, for their complicity in mass murder and torture.

In fact, in almost every prison rebellion since Attica, and there have been many, the lesson of avoiding the use of deadly force and keeping communication going has been followed. Attica has taught state authorities that the use of deadly force, even against convicted criminals, will have serious political fallout and must be avoided. In prison hostage situations waiting the prisoners out is clearly the course that Attica has established. Prisoner hostage taking is caused by legitimate prisoner grievances that result in desperate acts to gain the attention of the authorities and the public. While the acts are desperate, the underlying issues are real and must be addressed.

The agreements reached with the prisoners involved in the Lucasville, Ohio,[5] riot in 1993 were vague and depend on the good faith of the authorities. The willingness of the Lucasville prisoners, however, to accept more promises and end the stalemate, may also have been a lesson that they have learned from Attica. The Attica prisoners refused to accept less than all their demands. They wanted the warden fired, something the officials refused to consider. The Lucasville prisoners also wanted the warden fired, but by the eleventh day, they surrendered without obtaining that demand.

The Lucasville prisoners of the 90s, not infused with the revolutionary rhetoric and hopes of the 60s, may well have realized that certain things were possible and certain demands were not. Even at Attica, however, the prisoners' nonnegotiable demands to replace the warden or for passage out of the prison to a non-imperialist country, may well have been also forgotten after eleven days of waiting.

One lesson that clearly has not been learned from Attica is that prisoners must be treated with human dignity, respect, and with basic standards. Additionally, if you deny prisoners fairness and humane treatment you will cause rebellion, violence, and hostage taking. One can only wonder how long prison rebellions caused by inhumane and degrading treatment will go on before those in authority learn this most important lesson.

*Source:* Prepared especially for *Corrections: A Comprehensive View* by Michael E. Deutsch, Attorney At Law- Active in the defense of Attica Prisoners for over 20 years.

them. While violence against guards had been relatively rare, attacks in the 1970s became more frequent, reaching their highest level in prison history. In the past violence between inmates and guards usually occurred after some hostile confrontation; now guards were randomly attacked without any provocation. Inmates also openly and belligerently defied the authority of prison guards.

Violence, particularly in its extreme forms (e.g., the killing of COs), was an outgrowth of the revolutionary activities advocated by more radical groups who believed it was an inevitable part of the forthcoming revolution. For some, violence was a necessary evil and served as a "cleansing force" (Irwin, 1980). The difficulties in controlling the behavior of these groups is similar to dealing with guerrilla bands and terrorist groups: It is almost impossible to obtain accurate intelligence on these organizations and anticipate when and where they will strike next. Acts of violence and other incidents of defiance significantly influenced administrative reactions to the prisoner movement because they represented a serious threat to prison control.

## Activities That Occurred Outside the Prison

Most organized activities associated with the prisoner movement were controlled and supported by persons outside the prison. Without the support and involvement of outsiders, the movement would not have had a significant impact because prisoners did not possess the mobility, resources, or access to channels of communication necessary to plan and carry out successful movement activities. Not surprisingly, prison administrators were threatened and irritated by outside scrutiny of prison activities and practices because their authority had never been previously questioned. Outsiders associated with the prison movement were involved in three basic types of activities. First, sizable numbers of attorneys, enticed by the movement to focus on this area, contributed to the more rapid recognition of the constitutional rights of prisoners. This litigation changed the conception of

the prisoner from noncitizen or slave to a citizen with a temporarily reduced legal status.

Second, involvement in the publicized trials of a few well-known political prisoners rallied support for the movement by focusing attention on unethical and illegal procedures employed in investigating and prosecuting these cases. The objective was to substantiate the existence of unjust practices against the poor or members of racial minorities. These actions were viewed as manifestations of the general injustice and oppressiveness of the power structure in the United States (Irwin, 1980). Finally, from 1968 to 1975 conferences to call attention to prison problems and issues ("prisoner rights," "racism in prison," "abolishing prisons") were held. Irwin (1980), who planned and participated in many of these meetings, claimed that while some organization, education, and recruitment occurred, they fell short of what the planners had hoped to achieve.

This chapter has examined how changes in the ethnic/racial composition of the prison population, along with the prisoner movement and its accompanying politicization of inmates, changed the nature of the prison environment. These and other external factors shaped the nature of the contemporary prison to be examined in the next chapter.

## Endnotes

1. From now on this will be cited as the Attica Commission.
2. Currently, issues related to the practice of religion are regulated by the Religious Freedom Restoration Act. See Chapter 20 for a discussion.
3. This is only a partial list of demands included in the Folsom Manifesto. For a complete list, see Irwin (1980).
4. A turkey shoot is a contest in which the first shooter to draw blood from the head or neck of the turkey gets the animal. Special prosecutor Malcolm Bell, writing after years of investigating the revolt, entitled his book on the revolt *The Turkey Shoot*.
5. See Chapter 13 for further discussion of this riot.

## Acknowledgments

[a] Reprinted by permission of Waveland Press, Inc. from L. Carroll, *Hacks, Blacks and Cons.* (Prospect Heights, IL; Waveland Press, Inc., 1974 [reissued 1988]). All rights reserved.
[b] ©1985 by Malcolm Bell. Reprinted by permisson of Knox Burger Associates.

## Chapter Recap

**The Impact of Three Social Changes on Prisons**
The Authority Revolution Eroded Respect for Authority
The Civil Rights Movement Changed the Relationships
   Between Racial/Ethnic Groups
   Protests Against Inequities Turned Violent
The Vietnam War Engendered Protest by Significant
   Segments of the Population
The Ongoing Social Movements Had a Profound Effect
   on the Prisons
**Factors That Caused the Demise of the Traditional**
   **Prison Stratification System**
A New Self-Image Led Blacks to Develop Racial Pride
The Black Muslim Movement Attracted Many Black
   Inmates

Initially Muslims Were Viewed as a Threat to Prison Order But Eventually They Became a Stabilizing Force

Race Relations Within Prisons Changed

Black Inmates Viewed Both White Inmates and Correctional Officers as a Threat

There Was Some Racial Integration in Prison But Little Interaction

Interracial Tension Increased Prison Violence

State-Raised Youth Cliques Achieved Prominence

Mexican-Americans Also Developed Cliques

**The Prisoner Movement: The Politicization of Inmates**

The New Left's Focus on Prisons and a New Breed of Inmate Were Primary Factors in the Development of the Prisoner Movement

Inmate Groups Critically Examined Their Circumstances

Black Inmates Moved in a More Radical Direction

Puerto Rican Inmates Embraced the Objectives of the Civil Rights Movement

Chicano Inmates Developed a Sense of Racial Pride

A New Breed of White Inmates Entered the Prisons

Inmates Redefined Their Status to That of Political Prisoners

Some Inmates Adopted a More Radical Position

**Prisoner Movement Organizations**

Self-Help Groups Focused on Individual Improvement

Prisoner Rights Groups Focused on Improving the Offenders' Constitutional Rights and Social Position

Radical Groups Advocated Changing Society

The Black Panthers Attracted Black Inmates

The Young Lords Were Similar to the Black Panthers

The National Lawyers Guild Provided Legal Assistance as a Means of Furthering the Revolution

Radical Groups Only Had a Few True Inmate Members

**Prisoner Movement Activities**

Inmate Strikes Were Organized to Focus Public Attention on Prison Conditions

The Attica Revolt: A Riot and a Political Demonstration

A Chaotic Rampage Became an Organized Demonstration

The Retaking of the Prison Was Like a Turkey Shoot

The State Covered Up the Use of Excessive Force and Infliction of Unnecessary Injury

Increasing Defiance and Violence Led to a Crisis in Control

Activities That Occurred Outside the Prison

## REVIEW QUESTIONS

1. What are the social changes that occurred in the United States from the mid-1950s to the beginning of the 1970s that had a major impact on the prison? How did these changes affect inmates?

2. Briefly describe the factors that caused the demise of the traditional prison stratification system.

3. How did race relations in the prison change during this era?

4. What factors influenced the development of the "prisoner movement" during the 1970s?

5. Identify some prisoner self-help groups and discuss their significance for the prisoner movement.

6. Identify examples of radical groups involved in the prisoner movement and briefly describe their goals and activities.

7. Outline the sequence of events that occurred during the Attica revolt. Discuss the cover-up that followed.

8. How did increased inmate defiance and violence affect prison operations?

## TEST YOUR KNOWLEDGE

1. Which of the following statements *best characterizes* the relationship between white and black inmates during the era of increased racial integration in "free society"?

a. There was no racial integration in prisons and little interracial interaction.

b. There was some racial integration in prisons, but little interracial interaction.

c. There was no racial integration in prisons but much interracial interaction.

d. There was complete racial integration in prisons and much interracial interaction.

2. When extended tip networks declined in prisons because of increasing interracial hostilities, what became the *main purpose* of inmate cliques?

a. self-defense

b. rehabilitation

c. keeping inmates in touch with the free world

d. racial integration

3. In earlier times, this subgroup of the inmate population held the belief that, while personally they may have gotten a "bum deal," generally felons got what they deserved.

a. black inmates

b. Puerto Rican inmates

c. Chicano inmates

d. white inmates

4. Which of the following political/economic orientations provided a basis for a coalition of exploited groups that could jointly struggle against oppression?

a. capitalism

b. Nazism

c. Marxism

d. conservatism

5. The prisoner self-help group Seven Steps

a. focuses on awakening the identity of Chicano inmates.

b. is modeled after Alcoholics Anonymous.

c. is an inmate subgroup of the Black Muslims.

d. focuses on raising the political awareness of white inmates.

# CHAPTER 9

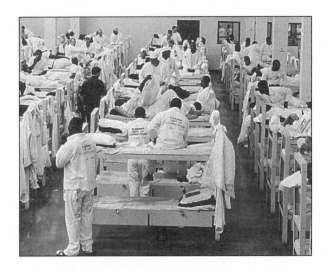

# THE ENVIRONMENT OF PRISONS IN THE LAST QUARTER OF THE TWENTIETH CENTURY

## ■ LEARNING OBJECTIVES

*After completion of this chapter, you should be able to:*
1. Identify the factors that gave rise to the contemporary prison and its present population characteristics.
2. Discuss overcrowding and the social environment within these prisons.
3. Specify the various factors that gave rise to ethnic hostility within contemporary prisons and the different reactions of the major ethnic groups to this prison situation.
4. Discuss aspects of ethnicity that have a definitive impact on the adaptation of blacks, Latins, and whites to prison.
5. Enumerate the major types of formal prisoner organizations in today's prisons and discuss the roles they play.
6. List, describe, and discuss the various roles played by inmates in the prison social structure.
7. Contrast and discuss the prisons' legal and illicit economies, their currencies, and effects on inmates and the administration.
8. List the various forms of inmate contraband and describe the major ways they are made or brought into prisons.
9. Describe and discuss the various sexual adaptations and roles of contemporary prison inmates.

## ■ KEY TERMS AND CONCEPTS

Black rage
Contraband
Convict code
Convict/hog
Deviance amplification
Ethnic/racial organizations
Homeboy orientation
Hustling
Illicit/sub-rosa economy
Independents
Inmate "credit cards"
Overcrowding
Pluralistic prison environment
Prop friendships
Punk, sissy, or kid
Religious organizations
Script
Self-Help organizations
Special interest organizations
State-raised youth/inmate
Withdrawal

The turmoil in contemporary prisons has its roots in the historical and recent events discussed in the preceding chapters. The substantial increase in crime rates during the 1960s and 1970s helped to increase the public's fear of being victimized and hardened attitudes toward punishment, both of which resulted in growing pressure to imprison more offenders. By the late 1980s prison construction could not keep up with the increasing number of offenders entering these facilities. This led to **overcrowding,** which forced the early release of serious offenders, a process that increased public frustration. This release process was complicated by the presence of large numbers of offenders serving mandatory sentences in the prisons who could *not* be considered for early release.

As indicated in Chapter 1, surveys have shown that crime was the primary public concern in the mid-1990s. This concern manifested itself as follows: strong pressure on lawmakers to get tougher on crime; statutes mandating increased rates of incarceration and longer sentences (e.g., "three strikes and you're out); changes in the manner of dealing with habitual and violent juvenile offenders; and the building of more prisons (What Are Prisons, 1982; U.S. Department of Justice, 1988a; Egan, 1994; Fisher, 1994).

The "war" on drugs and the changes in incarceration policy caused the U.S. prison population to rise from approximately 329,821 in 1980 to over one million by the year end 1994 (Gilliard, 1993; Beck and Gilliard, 1995). At the end of 1994, state prisons were estimated to be operating at 117% of their highest capacities and the federal system was 25% over its stated capacity (Beck and Gilliard, 1995).

## FACTORS THAT CHANGED THE CHARACTER OF CONTEMPORARY PRISONS

The issues we have referred to here began to affect the nature of prisons and the composition of their population. The major factors contributing to these changes included overcrowding, the increasing proportion of minority inmates, increased court oversight of prisons, and the reaction of prison staff and administration to the inmate population resulting from the radicalization of inmates.

## Overcrowding Became a Chronic Problem

Overcrowding has plagued American corrections from its Walnut Street Jail beginnings. Almost every era has had too many inmates for the available space, programs, and resources. The present costs of dealing with overcrowding have caused correctional systems to struggle with supervising and controlling offenders remanded to their custody. In 1993 the average daily cost per inmate was $52.38. New facilities ranged in average cost from $80,000 per bed for maximum security to $58,000 for medium security to $28,000 for minimum security prisons (Camp and Camp, 1994). These high operating and construction costs have made it difficult for most systems to incarcerate offenders for more than a fraction of their sentences.

**THE CAUSES OF PRISON CROWDING WERE ROOTED IN SOCIAL CHANGES** Although it is tempting to conclude that the increasing number of prison inmates at the end of the twentieth century was merely due to the hard line taken toward criminals in this era, other factors have also contributed.

Changes in several aspects of society, including the demographic makeup of the U.S. population, social attitudes, and criminal justice policy, have contributed to the overcrowding. The demographic variable making the most significant contribution was the "Baby Boom." The large number of males born between 1945 and 1960 reached their most crime-prone ages during the 1960s and 1970s. A number of this group became career criminals. As noted earlier, the Civil Rights movement, the Authority Revolution, and the protests against the Vietnam war created behavior patterns and attitudes that increased the probability that more baby boomers would become criminals. Illicit drug use by large numbers of this cohort further contributed to their involvement in crime. Additionally, many poor and minority youths became increasingly alienated and angry. This anger, combined with the greater availability of weapons (from trafficking in drugs), created a lethal mixture.

A general distrust of authority and adults also helped to increase antisocial behavior. This behavior was aggravated by an accelerated breakdown of families, which materially affected their ability to adequately socialize and supervise significant numbers of these young people. All of these factors had an impact on the increase in crime.

At the same time that more people were being sent to prison for longer periods of time, court decisions restricted the number of offenders that could be housed in existing facilities, which added to the problem. Some prisons failing to meet minimum constitutional standards were closed.

Jurisdictions across the United States began trying to provide sufficient numbers of prison beds for the rising inmate population. Although many new prisons were built, the demand for space grew faster than construction. Inmates not serving minimum mandatory sentences were released earlier and earlier, with some serving as little as 25% of their sentences.

**CROWDING HAD SEVERAL CONSEQUENCES**
Camp and Camp (1989) interviewed ninety administrators of crowded prisons to obtain a perspective on the problem. Their study focused on identifying the impact of crowding on facilities, staff, and inmates.

Two major facility problems were associated with crowding: space deficits which impacted housing and program space; and maintenance. Housing problems resulted in double bunking in one-man cells, crowding bunks into dormitory areas, and using program areas for housing. Administrators felt this reduction of living and program space caused further problems (e.g., less privacy, less program participation, more tension). Maintenance problems were particularly felt in older prisons because of the additional strain on plumbing and electrical systems that were already overburdened. Repeated breakdowns in these systems added to the tension within these prisons.

The increased number of inmates places heavier demands on existing staff because the need to maintain acceptable levels of supervision and services continues. Although recruitment and training were not adversely affected by crowding, turnover and excessive overtime were problems. The need to maintain appropriate staffing in crowded prisons required many correctional officers (COs) to work excessive numbers of hours. Overtime work leads to more mistakes by staff because they are more fatigued. Fatigue tends to increase staff use of sick leave, which in turn increases the need for overtime—a classic "Catch-22" situation.

The inability to adequately supervise the increasing number of inmates led staff to believe that many inmates were "getting away" with more rule violations. Increases in staff turnover further aggravated these circumstances. Suggested solutions have included hiring new staff to keep up with population increases and reallocating existing staff in terms of working hours and areas in which they work (Camp and Camp, 1989).

The findings regarding the effects of crowding on inmates (and consequently on staff too) have not been straightforward. Increased levels of stress, idleness, and contraband have been blamed on crowding, but violence, suicide, and escapes have gone down during the period of greatest population growth. Several authors have examined the stressful effects of living in and dealing with crowded prison conditions but their findings have not always been in agreement with each other (Megargee, 1971; Toch, 1977; Clements, 1979; Thornberry and Call, 1983; Johnson, 1987; Cox and Rhodes, 1990). A variety of problems ranging from increased blood pressure levels among inmates to increased prison violence have been blamed on stress.

Regarding violence, a 1994 national survey (Lillis, 1994), which included 41 states, the federal system, and the District of Columbia, indicated the following: the overall number of violent deaths had dropped from 235 in 1983 to 150 in 1993. Of the 1993 deaths, 47 were inmates killed by other inmates, one inmate was killed by a CO, two staff were killed by inmates, and 100 inmates committed suicide. These figures seem to indicate a significant reduction in violent deaths even though the inmate population more than doubled in that 10-year period. During the same ten-year period inmate assaults on correctional staff decreased from 6,047 in 1983 to an estimated 5,840 in 1993. Reported inmate assaults on one another, which constitute a relatively large problem, also went down from approximately 14,000 to about 10,000. The inescapable conclusion that can be derived from this data is that the frequency of killings and assaults decreased despite the apparent crowding caused by prison population increases.

Camp and Camp (1989) reported that during the early 1980s there was a large increase in the suicide rate in crowded prisons. However, Lillis (1994) indicated that between 1983 and 1993 the annual number of suicides dropped from 131 to 100. With the increased number of inmates in the prisons, this translates into a significantly lower rate of suicide. Regarding escapes, the Camps found that during the first half of the 1980s, escapes and attempted escapes also declined. They attributed this to increased perimeter security motivated by the crowding and to the greater use of electronic security systems. While providing no escape data for the 1980s, Lillis (1994) reported that escapes fell dramatically between 1991 and 1993, dropping from 5,793 to less than one thousand. He attributed this decrease to physical plant improvements, improved training, and a tightening of prison rules.

Increased inmate idleness is a major consequence of crowding. The lack of constructive use of time is a problem even in noncrowded prisons, and it is intensified by population increases for several reasons. First, even uncrowded prisons do not have enough jobs and services to keep many inmates occupied. When populations rise, programs (e.g., education, counseling) frequently are not expanded to accommodate the increased population and may even be reduced since program space may be used for inmate housing, for example, a gym may be used as a dormitory. The Camps (1989) found that, for a variety of reasons, about 20% of the inmates in their study were unassigned and that many of those who were assigned were in jobs with little to do.

Staff also found it difficult to keep track of inmates (Camp and Camp, 1989). Their reduced ability to supervise various prison areas led to increased thefts in living areas and more difficulty controlling the introduction of contraband—drugs, money, and weapons. The problem of drugs being passed from visitors was particularly hard to control in crowded visiting areas. Finally, the difficulty in coping with the rigors of crowding increased the number of inmates seeking protective custody, causing a shortage of this type of space (Camp and Camp, 1989).

Thus, through the mid-1990s prison overcrowding has not resulted in increases in certain types of behavior often thought to be associated with overcrowding (i.e. violent deaths, assaults and escapes). In the short run, improved staff, tightened prison rules and physical improvements appear to have controlled these behaviors. However, there is no way of knowing if these factors will be sufficient to deal with the stress on staff and inmates of living and working under crowded conditions for an extended period of time. An answer to this question may well depend on the extent to which: prison construction can keep up with the rising prison population; states follow the lead of Florida which has passed a bill allowing an increase in the crowding of its prisons from 135% to 150%; experienced correctional staff leave the profession due to deteriorating conditions.

## A Major Proportion of Prison Population Growth Consisted of Minorities

A substantial proportion of the prison population increase consisted of minorities, particularly African-Americans. Data for males, who have comprised about 95% of the prison population during the last ten years, show that, although in 1978 black males represented about 6% of the general population, they constituted 45.7% of the inmate population (Innes, 1988). In 1992 blacks (both males and females) represented 54% of those admitted to state prisons and 48% of the prison population (Perkins, 1994; Snell, 1995) while accounting for about 12% of the general population.

**SEVERAL FACTORS LED TO INCREASES IN THE PROPORTION OF AFRICAN-AMERICAN INMATES** The disproportionate number of blacks in prison can be attributed to various factors, including the seriousness of their crimes, extensive prior criminal records, and participation in street-level drug dealing. Their disproportionate involvement with crime and the criminal justice system can be traced in some measure to the socioeconomic conditions under which many of them live (Petersilia and Turner, 1988). An update of the 1968 National Advisory Commission Report on Civil Disorders reported that the proportion of poor blacks in the United States rose by 24% between 1970 and 1980, whereas that of poor whites fell by 20%. This disparity has continued to increase into the 1990s and the United States has become more racially divided. Life for inner-city blacks grew worse as the social and economic gap between the races increased. These conditions resulted in large numbers of dysfunctional and disorganized families whose children were poorly prepared for school, which increased the likelihood of their failure there. These conditions perpetuated the criminogenic environment (Wilkerson, 1988).

The pervasive racism most blacks have been subjected to has generated deep-seated feelings of rage (Grier and Cobbs, 1969; Silberman, 1978; Carroll, 1990). Until recently these feelings of **black rage** have been repressed by a variety of cultural devices (e.g., identification with the aggressor), but during the last several decades these devices have broken down. As a consequence many black adolescents and young men are now acting out the violence and aggression that was previously contained and sublimated. After 350 years of being afraid of whites, blacks have now learned that whites are intimidated by and actually fear them. This revelation had an extraordinary impact on black expression of anti-white feelings (Silberman, 1978).

During this same period the dismantling of legal segregation in the United States changed the nature of most predominantly black communities from multiple-class neighborhoods (including middle class and stable working class families) to largely lower class areas with few positive influences. In these communities there were many children who, largely unsupervised, vented their rage and frustration through acts of violence and criminality. Further, many of these individuals turned to a variety of drugs (e.g., heroin, crack cocaine) to deaden their pain (Silberman, 1978). Finally, the increasing availability of firearms contributed to this volatile mix (Hull, 1993). The result was that drive-by shootings, gunplay, and killings in schools (even at the elementary level), shopping malls, and restaurants became more common.

The contemporary prison has been affected by this new mix of inmates. African-American inmates now comprise about half of the prison population. They harbor feelings of rage for their current position and blame it on whites, against whom they are no longer afraid to use violence. The violence, however, is not restricted to blacks—significant numbers of Hispanic and white inmates are also predisposed to use violence.

## Staff Reactions to the Prisoner Movement Affected Contemporary Prisons

Administrative and staff reaction to the prisoner movement (Irwin, 1980), discussed in the last chapter, affected contemporary prisons by disturbing the prison's status quo in two ways. First, COs in some institutions were attacked without provocation, verbally harassed, and portrayed by radical inmates as the lowest level of humanity. A majority of these acts were committed by black inmates, aggravating racist sentiments among the predominantly rural white COs. Second, these institutions were now being watched by a group of influential outsiders including lawyers, judges, politicians, and reporters (Irwin, 1980) who had the knowledge and clout to restrict the methods employed by COs to control inmates.

## The Prisoner Movement Increased Court Oversight of Prisons

Another legacy of the prisoner movement was the assistance provided by lawyers to inmates filing writs and briefs directed toward changing institutional conditions. The resulting court intervention generated anger among prison personnel. COs felt that these court decisions curtailed their ability to maintain order in the prison by making it more difficult to find inmates guilty of infractions and to impose punitive sanctions (Irwin, 1980).

Continued court oversight has provided inmates with basic protections and has eliminated the draconian practices of just a few decades ago (see Chapters 15 and 16). Regardless of the effects of these decisions, however, they were perceived as a threat to the control of prisons. These judicial actions, inmate violence, and inmate condemnation of them pushed custodial personnel to reassert their authority and impose a stricter regime. As a result, some states, such as California, abolished any group (especially ethnic/racial ones) that made critical statements and/or was involved in political activities. Also, individuals suspected of political activities were segregated, transferred, or paroled. In other states repressive practices were not quite as extensive (Irwin, 1980).

**NOT ALL GROUPS THAT WERE ABOLISHED THREATENED PRISON SECURITY** Irwin (1980) contends most prison personnel failed to recognize that the majority of inmates and groups involved in politically related activities were not threats to prison security. Most directed their efforts toward stopping cruel, unjust, and racist practices in prisons and to developing a system of incarceration that was more humane and equitable. Their suppression caused a collapse of the informal inmate system of social control since it was no longer relevant. Irwin contends that if the benign political groups had survived, their influence might have made prisons more peaceful. These groups contained a multi-ethnic mix of inmates who would have worked toward formal accommodation between the different ethnic/racial groups. Although they might have presented problems, they would have caused far less turmoil than the violent cliques and gangs that did develop. To fully understand the current state of the contemporary prison it is necessary to examine its social environment, racial/ethnic relations, the violent cliques and gangs (discussed in Chapter 10), and the nature of adjustments to the prison environment.

## THE SOCIAL ENVIRONMENT OF THE PRISON

With the collapse of previous prison social structures, divisiveness became a major characteristic of contemporary prisons. This was primarily driven by extreme hatred and distrust among the racial and ethnic groups (Irwin and Austin, 1994). Another contributing factor is the criminal orientation of various inmates who now comprise the inmate population. These include bikers, dealers and dopers, violent predators, state-raised youths, and street gang members. These individuals and groups compete for power and respect. Given the fragmented social structure, it is surprising that prisons are not characterized by total chaos (Irwin, 1980; Irwin and Austin, 1994).

To survive in these violent, racially divided, hate-filled environments, most inmates limit their interactions to small cliques of friends or units such as gangs. These groups usually attract members of their own ethnic/racial group. Inmate associations are also determined by such factors as proximity (based on work or cell assignments), shared prison interests, similar criminal orientations, or shared preprison experiences, such as being homeboys (Irwin, 1980; Silberman, 1995).

### Ethnic/Racial Relations Changed in Modern Prisons

The changing racial proportions in contemporary prisons had several effects. These included domination of whites by blacks in many prisons, perceived racism by black inmates, and informal segregation by the inmates themselves. Additionally, racial/ethnic considerations appear to have an important influence on inmates' adaptations to prison life.

**BLACK INMATES APPEAR TO DOMINATE WHITES IN MANY PRISONS**   There is relative agreement among criminologists that in the interracial violence in prison (including rape), whites are more likely to be the victims of blacks (Adams, 1992;

Carroll, 1990; Lockwood, 1980; Van Voorhis, 1993). According to Lockwood (1980) and Carroll (1977), the clearest indication of black rage is the level of homosexual assaults on whites by blacks. Blacks view these assaults as particularly gratifying because of the humiliation that white inmates suffer as a consequence of losing their "manhood." These feelings are expressed in the following statement by a black inmate:

> It's getting even I guess. . . . You guys (whites) been cuttin' our balls off ever since we been in this country. Punkin' whites is just one way of getting even. To the general way of thinking it's 'cause we're confined and we got hard rocks. But it ain't it at all. It's a way for the black man to get back at the white man. It's one way he can assert his manhood. Anything white, even a defenseless punk, is part of what the black man hates. It's part of what he's had to fight all his life just to survive, just to have a hole to sleep in and some garbage to eat. . . . It's a new ego thing. He can show he's a man by making a white guy into a girl (Carroll, 1977, p. 422).

Several writers suggest that the views expressed by Lockwood and Carroll regarding sexual victimization of whites by blacks may not be entirely correct. For example, a study of an Ohio prison found that size and weight rather than race predicted which individuals would most fear sexual assault (Tewksbury, 1989). Further, interviews with prereleasees in Minnesota focusing on sexual victimization in prisons concluded that those inmates perceived to have "feminine" characteristics (e.g., young, weak, scared) were most likely to be victimized (Chonco, 1989). Eigenberg (1990) argues that existing data on rape in male prisons significantly underestimate the actual amount of rape in prison and thereby obscure who the victims are. Thus, because of the stigma attached to being sexually victimized, individuals who do not fit the typical victim profile will either not report a sexual assault or will not be believed by COs who may hold stereotypical views of rape victims. Silberman (1995)[a] indicates that strong inmates of both races are likely to victimize weaker inmates.

White inmates may or may not be prejudiced or racially hostile when they enter prison but they tend to develop racist attitudes after experiencing the hate, hostility, and violence directed against them by black inmates. Silberman (1995) indicates that what is emerging in the 1990s in prison for whites is an increasingly right-wing religious and social ideology. This is similar to the left-wing ideology which emerged for blacks in the 1960s in that it promotes racial hatred both inside and outside the prison.

**OTHER FACTORS CONTRIBUTED TO RACIAL TENSIONS** In the past, racial tensions in institutions have been increased by black inmates' perceptions that correctional staff were biased toward white inmates. Thus, a major factor contributing to black solidarity was their fear that an alliance existed between white prisoners and staff (Carroll, 1974). One black inmate in Rahway State Prison in New Jersey put it this way:

> Between the inmates, as far as racial discrimination, it's not like it used to be. It's always going to be there to some extent because the mentality of certain people, both black and white agree that in order to get along, in order to survive, they have to get along. . . . Now the racial problem between inmates and the correctional officers is somewhat different. Because you have some people who keep the same kind of racial mentality, like blacks should be here and whites should be there. And they feel that many of the organizations in here are run by blacks. They feel that blacks have too much power. And as long as they have that kind of mentality there is always going to be racial conflict. They've got this thing, it's an old fable, "if you're white, you're right." The inmates are not supposed to be smart. I guess because we came to jail, we're dumb and we have to remain dumb (Fox, 1982, p. 114).

Carroll (1974, 1990) indicated that blacks were disproportionately reported for disciplinary infractions, particularly those of a serious nature. The conceptions and fears of guards regarding black inmates are likely to result in mislabeling of this group's behavior as violent (e.g., horseplay may be seen as fighting). This process of mislabeling, which has been referred to as **deviance amplification,** leads to greater surveillance and control of black inmates (Silberman, 1995). As a result, black inmates tend to accumulate larger official records of misconduct and, in turn, may see many orders issued by guards as arbitrary because they do not seem to apply equally to white inmates. This tends to increase tension and hostility, leading to a higher probability of blacks being disciplined.

Silberman (1995), in his study of a maximum security prison, cited three factors that he felt had lessened discrimination against black and other minority inmates: court actions, professionalization of COs, and increasing numbers of minorities as COs and in positions of responsibility. The evidence presented earlier regarding reductions in prison violence may well have resulted from changes in these factors.

**ONE EFFECT OF RACIAL TENSION HAS BEEN INFORMAL SEGREGATION** Divisiveness pervades all aspects of group interactions. Although prisons today are integrated, there is a pattern of self-imposed segregation. Thus, although inmates of different racial groups may work together when assigned to work areas, when given a choice, in areas like the dining room or yard they will tend to group themselves along ethnic/racial lines. Thus, having a similar ethnic origin or religious affiliation or background forms the basis for social groupings in the contemporary prison (Silberman, 1995). Part of this includes a **homeboy orientation.** This involves sharing some common experience like coming from the same town or neighborhood or having the same ethnic background. Another factor is street gang affiliations. In effect, these factors can increase the level of trust between inmates because they provide a common basis of experience, which makes establishment of social relationships more comfortable and less threatening.

**EFFECTS OF INMATES' ETHNIC BACKGROUNDS ON PRISON ADAPTATION** Carroll (1990) has analyzed the influences that shape the structure and behavior of black, Hispanic, and white inmates within prisons and concluded that it is difficult to imagine any overall code of inmate solidarity spanning the social distance between inmates in these different groups.

After reviewing the work of several authors[1] Carroll feels that conditions in black ghettos are responsible for their solidarity in prison. He states:

> The concern for safety and the instability of the family gives rise to a strong peer group orientation that is also indispensable to the maintenance of self-esteem, providing an audience to validate the young ghetto male's claims of masculinity and personal worth. . . . This orientation is also the source of special relations of mutual aid and affection which are frequently given the status of kinship, as in "going for cousins" (p. 514).

He concludes by saying that:

It is plausible to infer that the subculture of the black urban ghetto is functional for survival in the walled ghetto of the prison. The ghetto inhabitants' sense of themselves as victims, reinforced daily by the facts of their existence, provides a rationale that shifts responsibility for their acts from themselves to the system. Having been raised to be cunning and tough, they feel less vulnerable, and through their extensive involvement in peer groups they are able to monopolize the available goods and services and, to some degree, can counter the power of the guards. Moreover, their "present time orientation" inclines them to do "easy time" by absorbing themselves in the prison rather than trying to "live with their heads on the streets while their bodies are in jail" (p. 515).

According to Silberman (1995), religious affiliation also appears to play a role in the process of social relationships, especially for Muslims.

The prison behavior of Latin inmates (Puerto Ricans, Chicanos, etc.) is most influenced by the family. Their reliance on family for nurturing and support creates a dependency that influences their identity and self-esteem (Carroll, 1990). Separation from the family while in prison can create problems for them. The barrio culture, particularly street gangs and their territoriality, also have important implications for their adaptation to imprisonment (Carroll, 1990; Moore 1978; Suttles, 1968). Barrio gangs, which tend to be organized for "territorial protection," remain a primary reference group into adulthood. Marrying female relatives of gang members strengthens gang "kinship" ties that carry into prison.

In prison, Chicanos spend much of their time interacting within their gang, which becomes a surrogate family that offers support and helps them deal with problems. Since Chicano gangs arise from territorial conflict gangs, they engage in much conflict and violence within the prison. This often results from their drug trafficking in the prison. Thus, both Latins and blacks import their barrio or ghetto cultures into the prison, which helps them to maintain strong solidarity (Carroll, 1990).

The prison experience is most painful for white inmates (Johnson, 1976; Jones, 1976; Carroll, 1990). White inmates, more than blacks or Latins, tend to blame themselves for their predicament in prison (Carroll, 1990). One result is an almost "psychotic attempt to reside physically in the prison while living psychologically in the free community" (Johnson, 1976, p. 122). Until recently their position in society has not allowed them to develop a class or ethnic consciousness so there was little basis for promoting solidarity. This had two consequences for this group. First, there was fear of victimization at the hands of blacks and Latins, leading to a retreat by many whites into protective custody. Second was the development of supremacist rightwing, sometimes "religiously" based, militant racist groups, like the Aryan Brotherhood, which appears to have led to greater solidarity.

### Prisons Have Many Prosocial Organizations

We have discussed the changes in the characteristics of the inmate social world as if they are found in all prisons, but there are many variations in systems across the country. For example, gangs do not exist in many prisons or may not be large or well organized enough to dominate institutional life. Even in gang-dominated prisons, legitimate groups can have a significant influence on some inmates and, as we will see in the next chapter, can provide an alternative to involvement in disruptive groups. In some prisons the number of minority groups may be very small or nonexistent. Thus, the structure of the inmate world in a given facility is influenced by its demographic and institutional characteristics and its formal and informal prisoner organizations. Some of these groups are approved by the institutions and others operate underground (Berkman, 1979; Fox, 1982).

The structure of the contemporary inmate social world is best characterized as **pluralistic.** This is evidenced by the variety of existing authorized ethnic, religious, self-help, special interest, and other groups as well as those that are unauthorized. Our discussion of the turbulent 1960s and 1970s has suggested the conditions that accounted for the development of many of these groups.

A study of four men's prisons, in California (Soledad), Minnesota (Stillwater), New Jersey (Rahway), and Oregon (Oregon State Prison), and one women's prison, in New York (Bedford Hills), all of which were maximum security prisons, suggests the types of organizations present in these institutions around the country (Fox, 1982). In three of these institutions (Stillwater, Oregon, Bedford Hills), approximately 50% of the inmates were members of at least one organization. At Rahway and Soledad only 25% and 9%, respectively, of the inmates were involved in organizations. The low percentage of members at Soledad may have reflected California's rules, which bar a wide range of organizations, especially those organized along racial/ethnic lines. Across the five prisons, minority inmates were more often members of prisoner organizations than whites. Table 9.1 shows the number of reported prison organizations at each of these five institutions and Table 9.2 shows the extent of inmate involvement in each major type of organization.[2]

PRISONER ORGANIZATIONS: AN IMPORTANT DETERMINANT OF SOCIAL STRUCTURE IN CONTEMPORARY PRISONS Ethnic/racial organizations concentrate on cultural awareness and education. These include black inmate organizations focusing on the needs/interests of blacks and cultural awareness groups for Native Americans and Hispanics. The number and proportion of inmates

TABLE 9.1  Self-Reported Memberships by Organization and Site

| Soledad (CTF–Central) | Stillwater | Rahway | OSP | Bedford Hills |
|---|---|---|---|---|
| Alcoholics Anonymous | Advisory Council | Alcoholics Anonymous | Alcoholics Anonymous | Al-Anon |
| Aryan Brotherhood[a] | Afro-American Culture Education, Inc. | Forum | Bible Club | Alcoholics Anonymous |
| Black Guerilla Family[a] | Alcoholics Anonymous | Lifers Group, Inc. | Car Club (Racing) | Committee Against Life for Drugs |
| Crypts[a] | Asklepieion | Muslims | Gavel Club | Hispanic Committee |
| Hell's Angels[a] | Atlantis | NAACP | Jaycees | Inmate Liason Council |
| Inmate Committee on Higher Education (ICHE) | Aztalan (Hispanics) | | Keen Club | Lifers |
| Men's Advisory Council | Insight | | Lakota (Native American) | New Directions |
| Mexican Mafia[a] | Jaycees | | Lifeline | Parent Awareness |
| Muslims | Muslims | | Lifers | Reality House |
| Nuestra Familia[a] | Native American Culture Education, Inc. | | Master Men (Chess Club) | South Forty Program |
| | Sounds Incarcerated, Inc. | | Motorcycle Club | Violence Alternative |
| | Worker's Council | | Muslims | |
| | | | Seventh Club | |
| | | | Slot Car Club | |
| | | | Toastmasters | |
| | | | Uhuru (Black Culture) | |

[a]Self-reported membership in unauthorized organizations.
SOURCE: Adapted from J. G. Fox (1982), *Organizational and Racial Conflict in Maximum-Security Prisons*, Lexington, Mass.: Lexington Books, p. 142, with the permission of the author and publisher.

TABLE 9.2  Distribution of Formal Organization Memberships

| | Stillwater | | Rahway | | OSP | | Bedford Hills | | Total | |
|---|---|---|---|---|---|---|---|---|---|---|
| | N | Percent | N | Percent | N | Percent | N | Percent | N | Percent |
| Ethnic | 45 | 31.5 | 2 | 4.9 | 23 | 13.3 | 20 | 15.5 | 90 | 18.5 |
| Religious | 23 | 16.1 | 9 | 22.0 | 27 | 15.6 | 8 | 6.2 | 67 | 13.8 |
| Self-help | 37 | 25.9 | 11 | 26.8 | 30 | 17.3 | 55 | 42.6 | 133 | 27.4 |
| Special interest | 38 | 26.5 | 19 | 46.3 | 93 | 53.8 | 46 | 35.7 | 196 | 40.3 |
| Total | 143 | 100.0 | 41 | 100.0 | 173 | 100.0 | 129 | 100.0 | 486 | 100.0 |

SOURCE: Adapted from J. G. Fox, 1982, *Organizational and Racial Conflict in Maximum-Security Prisons*, Lexington, Mass.: Lexington Books, p. 143, with the permission of the author and publisher.

involved in these groups tend to vary according to the proportions of these inmates in each facility. The smaller the group, the greater the likelihood these inmates will be members of an ethnic/racial organization.

The attitudes of COs toward these organizations seem to be influenced by their experiences with them in the prison and by their contacts with racial minorities in their communities. Where these groups were predictable and furthered prison stability, COs were more positive and supportive of them. At prisons where racial/ethnic conflict or violence had occurred regularly, COs were more concerned with personal safety, so they stressed the need for greater control over the formation of these organizations (Fox, 1982).

**Religious organizations** included only formal groups existing apart from regularly scheduled religious programs. Fox (1982) found these organizations attracted only 14% of all the memberships at the five facilities he studied. Participants in these groups were predominantly white (70%), long-term inmates. Although the proportion of inmates involved in religious organizations was similar in each male prison, substantially fewer women at the Bedford Hills facility were members of these groups. More recently Silberman (1995) found that one-quarter of the inmates at the maximum security prison he studied considered religious affiliation as a major basis of association and identification. Blacks holding these views were almost all Muslim.

Involvement in these groups helped African-Americans adjust to prison life (Chapters 8 and 20 discuss the history and contemporary role of Muslims in prison). White protestant inmates were found to be associated with prison groups like the Yokefellows. As with other religious groups, the courts have used the same rules to establish the rights of Native Americans to follow traditional practices as long they do not interfere with legitimate correctional goals (Silberman, 1995). For Native Americans group affiliation is important for survival in both an emotional and a practical sense. Thus, many prisoners with some Native American background become involved in traditional Native practices. Chapter 20 discusses other religious groups, the role of prison chaplains and the Religious Freedom Restoration Act.

Correctional officers were more supportive of these groups than any of the other inmate organi-

zations regardless of the race/ethnic makeup of their membership. Thus, black organizations (e.g., Muslims) were seen to be as beneficial and non-threatening as were Hispanic or white religious organizations.

**Self-help organizations** accounted for 27% of all prison organization memberships in Fox's study. Eighty-one percent of the inmates in these groups were white. As we noted, whites do not share a similar cultural background and need some basis other than ethnicity around which they can form groups. This may explain their attraction to these organizations, which include Alcoholics Anonymous and Narcotics Anonymous.

**Special interest organizations** were involved in a greater range of activities than any other type of prison group. For example, groups in various prisons were involved in such activities as cleaning and maintaining the trailers for inmate family visits; fund-raising projects within the inmate community (e.g., visitor picture programs) to provide a range of community services; lobbying for improvement in prison conditions before the Oregon legislature; maintaining a stock car on the Pacific Northwest racing circuit. Approximately 40% of the inmates in these five institutions participated in these groups (Fox, 1982). Overall, special interest groups got more official support from management than the other organizations, but not from most COs. They were nearly unanimous in rejecting any extension of their activities on the grounds that it might compromise their ability to control the inmate population. Nevertheless, as noted in the next section, legitimate nondisruptive groups provide major viable alternatives to inmate involvement in prison gangs or security threat groups.

Also included in this category were organizations involved in providing input on resolving prison problems and changing conditions there. Fox found that prison administrators were very reluctant to give these groups that kind of power because they feared inmates would abuse it and cause serious problems. Chapter 13 discusses the problems encountered with one of these in a Washington State prison. Since the institutions in Fox's study were maximum security and their administrators regularly maintained tight control of them, it is easy to see why they were reluctant to give inmate groups the opportunity to influence their operation. The following two Close-Ups, "A Jaycee Executive Director Looks at Prison Jaycees" and "The Unlimited Gavel Club," depict different inmate special interest groups.

Fox points out that with prison populations continuing to increase dramatically, prisoner organizations may well represent a valuable asset for reducing hostility and discontent in prison. We conclude this section with a discussion of this issue.

**PRISONER ORGANIZATIONS CAN BE A POSITIVE FORCE IN THE PRISON** Prison organizations place burdens on institutional managers because their presence adds to the number of entities to be regulated. If they are to become a positive force in the prison community, administrators must change their view of them. Most inmate groups are considered potential security risks for two reasons: They might develop organized opposition to official policies and goals, and they could be used as fronts in contraband traffic (see Chapter 10).

Rigid control of these organizations has had unintended consequences. Although tight control reduces forbidden practices, excessive restrictions have resulted in inmates quitting these groups and becoming more involved in informal groups such as gangs (Fox, 1982). For example, in California ethnic/racial gangs developed in response to negative policies toward formal groups (Irwin, 1980). At Rahway, in contrast, leaders of prison organizations were allowed to maintain offices, had unrestricted use of telephones, and had substantial control over their activities. Members of these organizations had a very positive view of prison management and the opportunities offered to them. Two notable achievements of this more positive approach were a vocational training program in boxing (developed by a professional boxer who shared profits from his professional bouts) and the lifers program resulting in two TV films on "Scared Straight." Our Close-Up on "Twenty Years of Scared Straight" by Mike Israel, a member of the Lifers Group Board of Directors, presents an update on that program. There was little evidence at Rahway that greater self-determination for inmate groups resulted in their using this freedom to dominate the inmate economic system. This was the case because inmates had opportunities for involvement in legitimate activities and were pro-

Prison Jaycee chapters are pro-social groups in which inmates can develop useful social skills and make outside contacts.

vided with strong administrative support for doing so (Fox, 1982).

These prisoner organizations present a unique opportunity to channel inmate energies and use their talents in meaningful and beneficial ways (Fox, 1982). There are many inmates with potential leadership skills who might dissociate themselves from violent gangs or cliques if alternatives are available (Irwin, 1980). These inmates can provide positive direction for inmate organizations and earn the respect of their fellow inmates. They would likely surface and become involved positively in these groups if prison administration supported these organizations and encouraged membership. These organizations can thus provide the basis for a more stable prison environment.

## Close Up  A Jaycee Executive Director Looks at Prison Jaycees

The Junior Chamber of Commerce, known as the Jaycees, is an organization providing leadership training through community service. In addition to many chapters in the community, the Jaycees also had about 164 institutional (prison) chapters in the United States. Most people don't realize that prisons are also communities, says Executive Director of the Louisiana Junior Chamber, Renee M. LeGrande, and the Jaycees also service those communities.

The Jaycees is an organization of young men and women whose aims are personal growth, leadership training, and providing solutions to community problems. The Jaycee process offers a threefold benefit to its members. Through individual development programs, Jaycees try to improve family communications, leadership skills, human relations, and public and spiritual development. Management development programs offer Jaycees opportunities to study and develop skills in personnel and financial management, planning, and organization. Community development programs provide leadership experience and sensitize Jaycees to the needs of those around them. These three aspects combine to form what is known as the "Total Jaycee Concept."

Often inmates join a prison chapter because they believe it impresses the Parole or Pardons Board. After joining many become involved in the true Jaycee spirit. Therefore, they benefit from the programs offered and the whole institutional population reaps the rewards because they truly service their community within the institution.

The success of an institutional chapter often depends on the support it receives from prison administration. Prison officials often fail to understand how just the delay of processing paperwork can be a detriment to the Jaycee chapter. Usually the more successful chapters are in institutions that have total staff support from the warden to the clerical workers. In working with institutional chapters for the past 12 years LeGrande indicates she has personally witnessed the evolution of many troubled people. Through working with them she has watched what society would consider to be the worst offenders become successful, well-rounded individuals and has personally testified on their behalf at Parole Board hearings. She has also written to protest or testified against some who were either not rehabilitated or had attempted to use the Jaycees as a reference but had not truly utilized the training offered.

She states "I have also witnessed first hand many 'factions,' 'gangs,' etc., . . . engage in what I would consider common 'power struggles.' I have had wives of incarcerated members call me at home because their husband had been "set up" and thrown in solitary confinement as a result of the latest struggle. These have occurred in almost all institutional chapters that I have worked with. I might add in varying degrees and not always with such drastic results."

"Most of our chapter members are what I would consider some of the better persons institutionalized or the ones that know they need the kind of help the Jaycees have to offer. Most assuredly I am biased, but then again, I have seen the results. In the years of working with the Jaycees I have seen very few repeat offenders, a record which I feel can speak for itself. Some of these people have no family, and no future. Most of the time they are pleased to have something to do and . . . they can personally excel in. Often [their achievement in the Jaycees] . . . is the first time they ever achieved any type of success. Therefore, in working with these chapters, they have often been some of the easiest to service and by far the most appreciative of that service" (LeGrande, 1994).

### The Social World of the Inmate Has Changed

Changes in the social world within the prison reduced the importance of the convict code and created new inmate roles. The life of independent inmates has been complicated by these changes and has led to a greater level of withdrawal by many of them from normal prison activities.

THE CONVICT CODE HAS BEEN TRANSFORMED As in any society, the inmate world in the contemporary prison is governed, in part, by a set of norms sometimes referred to as the **convict code.** The old convict code, described in Chapter 6, was a product of the thieves code and was seen as applying to the majority of inmates in the prison.

## Close Up  The Unlimited Gavel Club: Inmates Learn Oratorical Skills

One inmate self-help group at the Tomoka Correctional Institution near Daytona Beach, Florida, is the Unlimited Gavel Club (UGC) sponsored by Toastmasters International. Chartered by Toastmasters in August, UGC began with 25 members in 1993 and quickly grew to 39. The club seeks to provide a supportive environment in which members can develop communication and leadership skills. Weekly club meetings consist of several parts. First is a "business" meeting during which members are instructed and acquainted with the rules of parliamentary procedures and can voice suggestions regarding club activities. Members and any guests then participate in "Table Topic discussions" where one member is called on (without prior notice) to speak extemporaneously for two minutes on the topic on tap for that meeting. This is followed by prepared presentations on the same topic given by several members who have been selected and scheduled previously. Following the speeches, the audience is polled to select various

categories of "best" speakers. In the course of several meetings, all club members have an opportunity to speak before the group and thus can learn this and the other related skills. Club members also get opportunities to speak to groups from outside the prison, further enhancing their skills and confidence. Inmate participants' comments on the value of this activity are invariably enthusiastic and tend to focus on the help it provides in enhancing positive feelings about themselves and personal growth.

Beyond the ability to speak better, what values, skills, etc. do you think these activities provide for inmates? Are you generally for or against providing inmates with these types of opportunities? Why do you feel that way?

SOURCE: Derived from *The Tomoka Times*, Vol. 1, No. 1, pp. 2, 4 (institutional newsletter); Janice La Rosa (UGC sponsor), *The Unlimited Gavel Club Newsletter* (Nov., 1993), Vol. 1.

According to Silberman (1995), the basic elements of the code remain the same but have been transformed in three ways. First, toughness has become a central focus of inmate identity. Second, the focus of loyalty has changed from the inmate population as a whole to one's group (usually the ethnic or racial group). Third, there is a new emphasis on resorting to extreme violence to protect or maintain self-respect and punish snitches even to the point of killing them. This is because snitching is now viewed as one of the worst things an inmate can do. The rise in violence in the contemporary prison can be attributed to the increasing numbers of **state-raised youth** in them. These youth graduated from youthful offender or juvenile facilities that are usually permeated by violence and degradation and are controlled by the strongest and most aggressive youth. For these youth, violence is the primary means to solve problems "and is internalized and incorporated as a way of life" (Silberman, 1995, p. 35) In gang-dominated prisons, discussed in the next chapter, youth join or form gangs based on their street or institutional experiences. For these inmates their gang membership provides

them with status. However, not all inmates in gang-dominated prisons join these gangs and not all prisons have gangs. Therefore, it is important to examine some of the social roles and adaptations that have developed in response to the contemporary prison environment. This is the focus of the rest of this section.

**THE PRISON'S SOCIAL ORGANIZATION HAS A NEW TOUGH INMATE ROLE**  Known as a **hogs,** wise guys, bad dudes, outlaws, or convicts, inmates with this status are the most respected figures in contemporary prisons and dominate the inmate world in violent prisons (Irwin, 1980; Irwin and Austin, 1994; Silberman, 1995). The major distinctive feature of these inmates is their emphasis on toughness and willingness to use violence (even committing murder) to maintain one's status. This is manifested in being able to take care of oneself and having the guts to victimize and sexually exploit weaker inmates and members of other ethnic groups (Irwin, 1980; Silberman, 1995). The essence of these attributes is captured by an early description provided by Carroll (1974) of the view

# $C\!lose\ Up$   **Twenty Years of Scared Straight**

On a stage in an East Jersey State Prison meeting room the Lifers Group, an inmate group which has been in existence for 20 years, holds encounter sessions several times a week. In the middle of the stage stand twelve adolescent males. They have all had encounters with the Juvenile Courts in the northeast and have been bused into the prison by an agency and, as the press would put it, they are being "scared straight."

A muscular black inmate with a stocking cap is yelling at them about how stupid they are for being caught. A white inmate, not quite so fierce, walks up to a trembling kid standing at the end of the line and speaks to him confidentially. The kid steps out of the line to speak to the white inmate. The black in the stocking cap barks at him to get back in line. He does. The stocking cap demands of him, "Who told you to get out of line?"

The kid points to the white inmate. Stocking cap pauses a moment, then looks at the kid, and says, "Do you know what you are?" No answer. "You're dead. You're meat." All twelve of the juveniles are surprised. They don't understand. Then stocking cap tells them why. "Because you're the worst thing there is in this s**t hole of a place. You're a snitch. You know what happens to snitches? If you die you're lucky."

The tense mood changes while the black and white inmates join each other and tell the kids that what they consider a harmless gesture can be interpreted inside a prison as the worst of all iniquities, with terrible retribution, the real retribution they will fear if they end up where they are.

Twenty-six thousand juveniles have stood on that stage and been manipulated by the Lifers Group in a series of creative game-playing encounters to reach their deepest consciousness about the consequences of a criminal life. In spite of interminable obstacles, including political and interest group criticism, inmate turnover, and Department of Correction's imposed limits, the Lifers Group still goes on. These men share a kinship and loyalty that is exceptional. Although there are no studies of the program's effect on the inmates themselves, professionals who have worked with them believe this program is the salvation of many Lifers.

The men talk of how, for the first time in their lives, they experience what it feels like to give selflessly of themselves to people who need them for no immediate personal gain. These sessions drain and exhaust them in ways they have never known before. They learn how to feel good about themselves. This group is the most stable organization in the prison. In a culture without loyalties, these men share a strong solidarity. On the outside, their bond continues in a group called "Friends of the Lifers," where they speak to youth groups and school classes. Corrections authorities generally do not want former inmates to associate with each other, but the Lifers are an exception.

*Source:* Prepared especially for *Corrections: A Comprehensive View* by Mike Israel, Member Lifers Board of Directors, Rathway Prison New Jersey & Criminal Justice Director, Kean College, Union, NJ.

of manhood held by one of the most powerful groups in a prison he studied.

> Prison, in their view, is the ultimate test of manhood. A man in prison is able to secure what he wants and protect what he has: "In here, a man gets what he can." "Nobody can force a man to do something he don't want to. . . ." Any prisoner who does not meet these standards is not a man, "has no respect for himself," and is therefore not entitled to respect from others (p. 69).

By working together in varying combinations these inmates develop loose alliances with other strong inmates of the same race or ethnic group to become a major force in the prison economy (Irwin, 1980; Carroll, 1974). They also may openly manifest their opposition to the prison administration, even if it leads to harsh punishment.

Irwin and Austin (1994) also refer to the "alienated" outlaw prisoners who present themselves as "convicts." These inmates wear society's rejection of them as a badge of honor. They seem willing to callously use violence for a variety of purposes. Jack Abbott, a self-defined state-raised inmate, describes this type of inmate as follows:

> . . . the high esteem we naturally have for violence, force . . . is what makes us effective, men whose judgment impinges on others, on the world: Dangerous

killers who act alone and *without* emotion, who act with calculation and principles to avenge themselves, establish and defend their principles with acts of murder that usually evade prosecution by law; this is the state-raised convicts' conception of manhood, in the highest sense.

The model we emulate is a fanatically defiant and alienated individual who cannot imagine what forgiveness is, or mercy or tolerance, because he has no experience of such values. His emotions do not know what such values are, but he imagines them as many "weaknesses" precisely because the unprincipled offender appears to escape punishment through such "weaknesses" on the part of society (Abbott, 1982, pp. 15–16).

Rather than developing a new label, Johnson (1987) simply uses the term **state-raised inmate** to describe the dominant type of inmate replacing the "right guy"—who was hero of the Big House—as follows:

They have made today's prisons a dangerous place for staff and fellow prisoners alike. It is they who, by their violence, intimidate other prisoners and who, again through violence, find themselves embroiled with the custodial staff. They are the prison's bastard children, and this unhappy status brings out the worst in both the prisoners and the prison. They are easily provoked to violence by the stresses of prison life, and in turn they provoke the prison staff to use violence ... to maintain law and order behind bars. . . . State-raised convicts adapt to prison life and even dominate the public culture of the prison (pp. 85–86).

Thus, their alienation and anger produces a violence that is difficult to control and earns them a high position of status within the inmate hierarchy.

Regardless of the name applied to these dominant inmates, they are remorseless and callous in their use of violence and their preying on weaker inmates. Their dominance of prisons of the 1990s has changed the character of life within them (Irwin, 1980; Irwin and Austin, 1994). Thus, when these inmates fight they normally use lethal weapons because, as one inmate put it "I don't use my fist, you either kill your opponent or don't fight because if he's not dead he might come back on you later" (Silberman, 1995, p. 37). These inmates not only control prison economies, but also activities that normally involve the entire inmate population (e.g., demonstrations).

To survive in this environment inmates must find some way to adapt to the violent lifestyle of the prison or constantly live in fear of being victimized. Some survive by adopting a convict or hog persona—which means that they respond violently to all threats to their person or self-respect. A few may adapt by becoming tough on the outside while maintaining a softer, more humane side within (Silberman, 1995, p. 38). Others may avoid the dangers of prison by joining with a powerful racial gang or clique (Irwin, 1980; Irwin and Austin, 1994). Inmate involvement in gangs is more fully examined in the next chapter. Finally, in order to survive, some inmates develop **prop friendships.** These friendships involve a close relationship between two inmates, one who may be stronger than the other, who will back one another up in violent confrontations no matter what. In the violent prison atmosphere, survival may depend on having someone you trust cover your back (Silberman, 1995).

**INDEPENDENTS TRY TO AVOID ENTANGLEMENTS  Independents** represent another category of inmates who may circulate freely within the contemporary prison (Irwin, 1980). In gang-controlled prisons some of them maintain loose friendships with a major group, which protects them from other groups. A small number of tough independents, some of whom may be state-raised toughs, can move freely in these prisons because they have been victorious in many confrontations. However, in prisons dominated by gangs these inmates must be very cautious in their contacts with more powerful gang members because no inmate is likely to survive the attacks of a gang that is bent on murdering them. Black inmates are in a much better position than whites to function in gang-dominated prisons as independents because there is a greater sense of solidarity among blacks. Chicanos, at least in California, must have a token affiliation with one of the Chicano gangs (Irwin, 1980).

Finally, some independents are able to move freely in the prison world because they present no threat to convict leaders and/or provide some valuable service. Included in this group are "jailhouse lawyers," characters, dings (who may be a source of amusement), and less desirable homosexuals. More desirable younger homosexuals must be attached to powerful groups or individuals to remain free from attack (Irwin, 1980).

In larger prisons there are some politically oriented inmates who pursue goals such as prisoner rights. These inmates refrain from violent activities and involvement in the prison economic system and are therefore tolerated by violent inmates and the gangs. Sometimes they are even able to develop coalitions between the warring gangs on issues that involve the entire prisoner community. They are safe as long as they avoid conflicts with inmate leaders and abstain from involvement in other activities of the convict world (Irwin, 1980).

**WITHDRAWAL IS A WAY OF AVOIDING TENSION AND VIOLENCE**   Many inmates in more violent prisons, rather than become associated with a gang or adopt a "hog" identity, choose a more limited style of life referred to as **withdrawal.** These inmates minimize their forays into public areas. They are not active players in the sub-rosa inmate economy but may on occasion partake of some service or activity (e.g., place a bet with gamblers, buy from inmate racketeers). However, they avoid involvement in large-scale economic activity or rackets (e.g., drugs). They also avoid responding violently to any provocations by aggressive inmates. While not completely withdrawing from the prison world, they attempt to bypass potentially dangerous situations. These inmates maintain close contact with a few friends—individuals they know from the outside, or met in their units, through shared interests, or at work. In the company of these friends, they work, eat, and participate in clubs and other activities. This lifestyle is very attractive to first-term inmates who lack gang affiliations (Irwin, 1980; Irwin and Austin 1994; Sheehan, 1978).

"Convicts" usually disrespect and ignore those who withdraw from the prison world. Inmates who choose to cope with the prison world in this way may have to be deferential in subtle ways when they come in contact with "convicts". By behaving this way they place themselves in minimal danger of attack and robbery (Irwin, 1980).

Young, effeminate inmates are in a less enviable position because their characteristics make them targets for convicts who may force them into sexual liaisons or rape them. For these inmates, withdrawal does not ensure safety. The only option may be a transfer to a protective custody unit (Irwin, 1980). In the contemporary prison there has been a significant increase in the number of prisoners who request transfer to these units for their own protection.

In addition to avoiding injury, inmates choosing to withdraw may receive other tangible benefits (Irwin, 1980). By maintaining clean disciplinary records for a specified time they can request transfer to honor blocks that usually house other inmates who have also withdrawn. Access to these units is more restricted than regular housing and inmates there usually have more privileges. Contact with the inmate world can also be restricted by joining formal inmate groups that meet in closed rooms away from the prison's public settings.

## THE PRISON ECONOMY INCLUDES LEGAL AND ILLEGAL ASPECTS

As in most eras, inmates in contemporary prisons are deprived of many things that outsiders take for granted. The state takes care of inmates' basic needs, but the quality and quantity of the things furnished by the state are often insufficient as Sheehan (1978) found from her research at Greenhaven prison in New York:

> There are many things not provided by the state that most prisoners regard as even more necessary than people on the outside do—for example, talcum power, and deodorant, because of the prisoners' more limited bathing facilities. Store-bought cigarettes, instant coffee, immersion coils for heating water, and between-meal snacks—especially for the fifteen-hour period between supper and breakfast—also seem necessary, and help to fill the empty spaces of prison life (p. 90).

Inmates try to minimize their "hardships" in any way possible. The prison economic system has both legal and illegal components, and these provide opportunities for inmates to remedy this situation (Kalinich, 1986; Davidson, 1983).

### The Legal Economic System Does Not Meet All Inmate Needs

The legitimate prison economic system consists of inmate funds and goods obtained through approved channels. Inmates can acquire money by having relatives and/or friends make deposits in their prison accounts or send them goods that can be sold or traded. Rarely can they withdraw funds from a bank account that was established prior to incarceration. Work assignments can be another source of legal funds. State prison systems vary as to how much and for what types of work inmates can be paid. Typically inmates employed in prison industries are paid the highest wages; those in institutional maintenance and school programs are the lowest paid. In some states inmates receive no pay at all. Other sources of income include benefits for veterans enrolled in education programs (Gleason, 1978), managing the inmate welfare fund, or serving as staff barber (Kalinich, 1986). Inmates can also earn money through their hobbies, by making such items as belts, wallets, or paintings, which can be sold at gift shops located outside the prison or in the visitors' area. They may also enter these items in outside crafts and art contests (Davidson, 1983). One inmate, for example, received $1500 for winning first prize in an art contest (Welch, 1990).

In the late 1970s it was estimated that it cost an average of $40 to $50 per month for inmates to live comfortably at a Michigan institution (Gleason, 1978). By the mid-1990s, considering the impact of inflation, the average cost has probably risen beyond $100. At the facility studied by Gleason, gifts and government transfer payments accounted for three-quarters of an average inmate's income. The only inmates living comfortably on income from legal sources were those who worked in prison industries, got veteran's benefits, or had family and friends to provide support. Twenty percent of the inmates worked in prison industries jobs paying an average of $63 per month compared with other jobs paying $7 to $13 (Kalinich, 1986). Moreover, since many inmates have no families, come from poor families, or have had their family ties severed while in prison, they may have no outside financial support (Gleason, 1978; Kalinich, 1986; Sheehan, 1978).

Desired allowable commodities can only be legally acquired through the canteen or prison store (at free-world prices) or from friends and relatives. These items include cigarettes, appliances (e.g., stereos), musical instruments, health kits, books, clothing, toiletries, and watches. Recently, some jurisdictions have ruled money contraband and issued **credit cards** to inmates for making commissary purchases. These usually consist of ID badges with electronically sensitive tape that are used to scan inmate accounts and deduct the appropriate amount when purchases are made.

## The Illegal Economy Attempts to Fill the Void

The **sub-rosa** or **illegal economic system** thrives because it satisfies needs and contributes to the psychological well-being of inmates (Davidson, 1983; Kalinich, 1986). It provides illegal goods and services not available through normal channels. For inmates without any resources, where institutional pay is low, or when legitimate employment is limited, the sub-rosa system represents a means for improving an otherwise depressing existence. Even inmate nonparticipants take pleasure in the fact that it defeats, through inmate ingenuity and wit, a system designed to suppress them. Inmates trafficking in contraband have the chance for creative expression, personal challenge, and enhancement of their status; to improve their lifestyle and personal security; and to keep busy, reduce the normal monotony of prison life, and temporarily forget their inmate status. Finally, the illegal economy may have a stabilizing effect on the prison environment by enhancing the behavior control abilities of inmate dealers (Kalinich and Stojkovic, 1987).

The working capital of the prison economy includes cigarettes, "green" (real money), prison script, and goods and services that may be bartered (Davidson, 1983; Gleason, 1978; Irwin, 1980; Kalinich, 1986). Many prison systems designate currency as contraband and issue **script** (nonlegal tender or "money" created for a special situation) or create the credit card systems mentioned previously to try to limit economic activity to legal purchases from the prison store. These restrictions have had a negligible impact. Cigarettes have commonly been the basic prison currency. Normally they are not contraband so inmates can legally have them.[3] They have a standard value that facilitates the exchange process. Loose cigarettes and packs are used as coins and dollar bills, while cartons serve as larger bills. However, cash is used in transactions approaching twenty to twenty-five cartons because the bulk of that many cartons may attract attention. Even inmates who are nonsmokers keep cartons for trading purposes. Vaughn and del Carmen (1993) report that 90% of state correctional facilities now restrict smoking and a number of county jails ban it (LIS, 1991). Candy and other consumables from the canteen have apparently replaced cigarettes in facilities where they are banned (Knowles, 1994). Finally, although having cash is illegal in many prison systems, that has not deterred its possession or its intrusion into the prison. Inmates prefer bills of large denominations because they are easier to handle, count, and conceal.

By **hustling,** or wheeling and dealing, many inmates earn enough money to meet their "needs and wants." There is a "hustle" in any prison job that places inmates in a position to obtain salable goods (i.e., food, clothing), to provide services such as custom pressing, or to obtain information (Davidson, 1983). When violent gangs control the prison economy, it is more difficult for independents to operate without appropriate approval and/or payment of tribute. This is discussed in more detail in the next chapter.

### Contraband Fuels the Illegal Economy

**Contraband**—anything that is declared illegal by the prison authorities—can be smuggled into institutions in a variety of ways. Liberal visiting policies allowing contact visits have made it easier for visitors to transfer contraband, such as small quantities of drugs. To bring drugs into the prison, visitors must first get past the staff assigned to process them. Visitors, inmates, and even personnel who bring drugs into the prison rely on staff searches to be quick, cursory, and superficial. Figure 9.1 shows both the criteria for searches and that 93% of the federal facilities and 87% of the state institutions search visitors' belongings for drugs. Pat-down searches are conducted at 83% of the federal and 57% of the state facilities. In the case of body cavity searches, traffickers rely on the staff's natural reluctance and distaste to do them. Nevertheless, these searches are usually conducted if visitors are suspected of smuggling drugs. Facilities using these intrusive searches report lower positive tests among inmates for drugs than those employing other methods (Harlow, 1992).

Experience shows that visitors can conceal drugs anywhere on their person, in clothing like running shoes, or in food items like potato chip bags, which may be resealed to look factory sealed. Even young children are used to bring drugs into the prison because visitors think staff may overlook drugs concealed in items like children's dirty diapers and

FIGURE **9.1  Categories of Visitor Groups Selected for Different Types of Drug Control Activities**

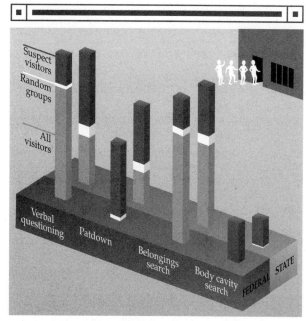

SOURCE: Adapted from C. W. Harlow (1992), *Drug Enforcement and Treatment in Prisons, 1990,* Washington, D.C.: U.S. Department of Justice.

baby bottles (Chastang, 1993). Once brought in, drugs must be passed to the inmate who must then get past searches conducted upon leaving the visiting area. Inmates can hide the drugs on their person but are safer from detection if they swallow them or insert them in a body cavity (Gunn, 1979; Kalinich, 1986).

Some correctional staff are also involved in introducing drugs and other contraband (e.g., money, escape tools, liquor, and cigarettes in facilities that have banned them) into the prison and smuggling things out—usually cash (Former prison guard, 1993; Herbeck, 1993; Three Guards, 1993; Delguzzi, 1993; York, 1992). One jail CO sold single cigarettes for $3.50 and a carton for $700 (Corrigan, 1993). COs who participate in drug smuggling do it mostly for the money or they may be coerced into it. The sale of narcotics is so lucrative, bringing prices that are two and a half to three times higher than on the street, that inmate drug dealers can pay staff well for their efforts. A typical connection involves a staff member either meeting inmate contacts on the outside to pick up or purchase the drugs from a designated dealer. The staff member brings the drugs into the prison on his person or in a personal item like a lunch pail (Davidson, 1983;

Inmate weapons represent another form of contraband. They can be made from a variety of items, some of which would not appear to pose any danger (for example, toothbrushes, pens, a bar of soap in a sock, etc.).

Kalinich, 1986). Davidson (1983) found that at San Quentin as many as 30 guards were bringing drugs in at any one time. On a yearly basis these guards could earn about $10,000 of undeclared tax-free income with some making more than $50,000. Although the irregular timing of this activity makes it fairly safe, roughly 10% of the staff who run drugs get caught (Davidson, 1983). Reluctantly recognizing that staff can be the only source of regular and large quantities of drugs and other types of contraband, some facilities have begun subjecting staff to interdiction procedures. Most of these activities only occur on suspicion of drug smuggling. Table 9.3 shows that about 50% of the federal and 40% of the state facilities question staff suspected of bringing in drugs. States were more likely to use more intrusive procedures at confinement facilities, with 23% reporting random staff frisking (Harlow, 1993).

Occasionally, staff too naive to recognize that many inmates are the masters of manipulation are duped or intimidated into bringing contraband into prison. Kalinich (1986) suggests how this can occur:

> [An inmate] becomes friendly with a guard or a professional staff member and asks the staff member to do simple favors for him; in return the resident—[inmate]—provides some kind of service for the staff member, for example, giving him contraband food. After developing this relationship, the resident continues to request favors, and each favor becomes larger, with respect to rule violation, than the last one. At some point, the resident simply advises the staff member that he is now in violation of a law. The resident threatens to inform someone higher up about the illegal activity of the staff member, unless he provides favors to a greater extent. From this time, the staff member is in the resident's "pocket" and can be continually coerced into smuggling contraband (p. 68).

## SATISFACTION OF INMATES' SEXUAL NEEDS

Earlier in this chapter we discussed the sexual nature of some violent interactions between black and white inmates; however, these represent only a part of the sexual activity occurring in prisons. Sexual interactions in prisons are, by necessity, homosexual. Their nature and quality in men's prisons are strongly influenced by attitudes and values common to the lower class cultural background of most inmates. These values include a strong masculine image, dominance and aggressiveness in sexual interactions, and a general propensity toward violence. These values are intensified in prison by racial hatred, the sexual deprivation brought about by incarceration, inaction on the part of correctional officers, and the failure of some administrators to segregate potential victims from predators.

Getting involved in sexual activities in prison can take one of several routes. As noted earlier, the contemporary prison is characterized by increased levels of violence, or the threat of it, that may also apply to the obtaining of sexual favors. This may

TABLE 9.3   Drug Interdiction for Prison Staff by Type of Facility

| Interdiction activity | Federal confinement | State Confinement | Community-based |
|---|---|---|---|
| No reported interdiction activity | 17.5% | 23.4% | 42.0% |
| Verbal questioning | 53.8 | 43.3 | 45.2 |
| Patdown | 21.3 | 49.3 | 24.4 |
| Other[a] | 35.0 | 25.0 | 11.6 |
| Number of facilities | 80 | 957 | 250 |

*Note:* Interdiction activities are overlapping categories.
[a]Includes such measures as drug testing, belongings search, and visual inspection.
*SOURCE:* Adapted from C. W. Harlow (1992), *Drug Enforcement and Treatment in Prisons, 1990,* Washington, D.C.: U.S. Department of Justice.

come from the "convict" or "hog," who tends to be extremely assertive of his masculine sexuality (Irwin, 1980). Silberman (1995) indicates that the contemporary convict code requires a violent response if one is "propositioned" and is unwilling. Since aggressive displays of manhood are used by other inmates to compensate for many of the deprivations which they suffer, sexual activity has a decidedly coercive flavor. As indicated earlier, Eigenberg (1990) feels rapes in prison are underestimated because many victims, possessing aggressive masculine self-concepts, do not meet the stereotyped model of the rape victim and are unwilling to report themselves as victims.

### Various Inmate Sexual Roles

As described in the Big House chapter, the strong emphasis of the prison value system on the maintenance and protection of one's manhood has produced two distinct sexual roles. In the contemporary prison the dominant partner maintains his self-concept of masculinity and is perceived by his peers as heterosexual. These men tend to be more athletic, less physically attractive, slightly older than their victims, black, and violent offenders. The submissive sexual role carries with it a degraded status in which the incumbent loses his manhood and becomes a "woman" (**punk, sissy,** or *kid*). Victims tend to be boyish looking, less athletic, more attractive than their victimizers, members of less powerful groups, and first-time property offenders. Both homosexual and straight individuals are squeezed into the submissive role by a variety of ploys usually involving pressure, coercion, and/or violence. Wooden and Parker (1982) indicate that:

> . . . in prison there is an institutionalized social pressure, both overt and covert, toward feminizing homosexuals and kids. This pattern serves two purposes. First, it sets the homosexual at a psychologically safe distance from the "macho" image the heterosexual convict is so desperately trying to project, and second, it makes the homosexual relationship *appear* to be heterosexual in that it is permissible for a "man" to "get down" with a "broad" but not another "dude" (p. 21).

An additional important source of pressure to "turn out" passive or less aggressive individuals and make them into "girls" comes from blacks. As noted earlier in the chapter, blacks view the making of whites into "women" as a way of denigrating them and as an important means of validating their masculinity (Carroll, 1977).

Affection and emotional involvement on the part of the dominant partner is generally viewed as being unmasculine, whereas for the "punk" or "sissy" this is seen as being in character and may be encouraged. In maximum security prisons these displays of affection, even when they are reciprocal, are usually done in private. Once hooked up with a dominant partner, the punk is essentially a slave and must do his "master's" bidding, which may include sexually servicing his friends. Almost always the sexual relationships between men in prison is exploitative. In lower security/smaller prisons, however, the structure of these relationships may not be so rigidly defined. In women's prisons sexual liaisons more likely involve emotional attachments, and displays of affection are more open and common (see Chapter 12).

There are no accurate estimates regarding the extent of homosexual behavior occurring in contemporary prisons. A survey by Nacci and Kane (1983; 1984) of 211 federal prison inmates found that 30% reported having had a homosexual experience in prison, most having played roles as the dominant partner. The small proportion of inmates who reported playing the submissive role made extensive discussion of their experiences difficult. Moreover, it is likely that the proportion of indi-

viduals engaging in homosexual behavior (willing or not) is underreported. For example, Donaldson (1993), based on extrapolations taken from surveys, estimates there are currently 290,000 prison rapes occurring annually. This estimate appears overstated. Further, there appears to be agreement that weaker, young, males who are neither gang affiliated nor part of the racial/ethnic group dominating the institution are disproportionately more likely to be targets for largely black aggressors (Nacci and Kane, 1984; Donaldson, 1993; Lockwood, 1980; Carroll, 1974). Nacci and Kane also found that state-raised youth were more likely than others to engage in prison sexual activities.

Finally Irwin (1980) suggests the long-range implications of these activities for those who are in prison for long periods:

> . . . prisoners who engage in homosexual life too long finally learn to prefer it and, in fact, become full practicing homosexuals, [playing] both ["male" and "female" roles]: "It was a jocular credo that after one year behind walls, it was permissible to kiss a kid or a queen. After five years, it was okay to jerk them off to 'get them hot.' After ten years, 'making tortillas' or 'flip flopping' was acceptable and after twenty years anything was fine" (p. 194). [Irwin asserts that the above scenario may not apply to the convict or hog in contemporary prisons].

Thus, the patterns of sexual activity and victimization occurring in the contemporary prison are likely to have a powerful effect on all concerned, but especially those who are the "victims." According to Stephen Donaldson, president of "Stop Prisoner Rape":

> The catastrophic experience of sexual violence usually extends beyond a single incident, often becoming a daily assault. Psychologists and counselors believe that the pent-up rage caused by these assaults can cause victims, especially if they don't receive psychological treatment, to erupt in violence once they return to their communities. Some will become rapists, seeking to "regain their manhood" through the same violent means by which they believe it was lost (1993, p. 11A).

We have alluded to the effect groups like gangs have on prison conditions and the inmate social world. In the next chapter we discuss in more detail, the impact of these and other disruptive groups.

## ENDNOTES

**1.** Johnson and Dorin, 1978; Dorin and Johnson, 1979; Grier and Cobbs, 1969; Anderson, 1978; Liebow, 1967; Toch, 1977a.

**2.** The populations and the proportion of inmates sampled at the five prisons studied by Fox (1982) were Soledad, 349/12.9%; Stillwater, 952/19.5%; Rahway, 1070/13.6%; Oregon, 1473/12.8%; and Bedford Hills, 412/46.4%.

**3.** California attempts to control the use of cigarettes as money by placing limits on the number of packs of cigarettes an offender can have on his person while outside of his cell. An inmate is allowed to possess no more than two packs of cigarettes, which is what is considered necessary for one day's use. If an offender is caught with more than this number he must be able to prove that he just bought them from the prison store and is on his way back to his cell. Failure to show a dated receipt can result in the confiscation of any cigarettes above the limit (Davidson, 1983).

## ACKNOWLEDGMENTS

[a] Copyright 1995 by Wadsworth, Inc. All rights reserved. Reproduced by permission of Wadsworth Publishing Co., Belmont, CA 97002.
[b] Reprinted by permission of Waveland Press, Inc. from R. Johnson and H. Toch, *The Pains of Imprisonment*. (Prospect Heights, IL; Waveland Press, Inc., [reissued 1988]. All rights reserved.

## CHAPTER RECAP

**Factors That Changed the Character of Contemporary Prisons**
Overcrowding Became a Chronic Problem
  The Causes of Prison Crowding Were Rooted in Social Changes
  Crowding Had Several Consequences
A Major Proportion of Prison Population Growth Consisted of Minorities
  Several Factors Led to Increases in the Proportion of African-American Inmates
Staff Reactions to the Prisoner Movement Affected Contemporary Prisons
The Prisoner Movement Increased Court Oversight of Prisons
  Not All Groups That Were Abolished Threatened Prison Security
**The Social Environment of the Prison**

Ethnic/Racial Relations Changed in Modern Prisons
  Black Inmates Appear to Dominate Whites in Many Prisons
  Other Factors Contributed to Racial Tensions
  One Effect of Racial Tension Has Been Informal Segregation
  Effects of Inmates' Ethnic Backgrounds on Prison Adaptation
Prisons Have Many Prosocial Organizations
  Prisoner Organizations: An Important Determinant of Social Structure in Contemporary Prisons
  Prisoner Organizations Can Be a Positive Force in the Prison
The Social World of the Inmate Has Changed
  The Convict Code Has Been Transformed
  The Prison's Social Organization Has A New Tough Inmate Role
  Independents Try to Avoid Entanglements
  Withdrawal Is a Way of Avoiding Tension and Violence
**The Prison Economy Includes Legal and Illegal Aspects**
The Legal Economic System Does Not Meet All Inmate Needs
The Illegal Economy Attempts to Fill the Void
Contraband Fuels the Illegal Economy
**Satisfaction of Inmates' Sexual Needs**
Various Inmate Sexual Roles

## REVIEW QUESTIONS

**1.** What social factors that occurred during the 1960s and 1970s contributed to the molding of the contemporary prison?

**2.** Discuss the general interactions that occur between black and white inmates in contemporary prisons. What factors seem to influence these interactions?

**3.** What factors have contributed to the crowding of prisons today?

**4.** What aspects of ethnicity appear to have a definitive impact on adaptation of blacks, Chicanos, and whites to prison?

**5.** What inmate roles and adaptations characterize contemporary prisons?

**6.** Describe the inmate sub-rosa economy, including the forms of "money" used, the types of contraband, and how it is smuggled in.

**7.** What effects does the illicit economy have on inmates and staff?

**8.** What patterns of homosexual behavior are found in prison?

## TEST YOUR KNOWLEDGE

1. By the end of 1994 the prison population in the United States had risen to _____ inmates.
    a. 565,000
    b. 880,000
    c. over one million
    d. 400,000

2. The type of formal organization within the prison to which the largest proportion of white inmates belong can be categorized as
    a. ethnic
    b. religious
    c. self-help
    d. special interest

3. The members of which of the ethnic groups listed below are most likely to best function as independents?
    a. whites
    b. blacks
    c. Hispanics
    d. all of the above do equally well

4. Which of the items below is most likely to be used as "money" in the prison sub-rosa economy?
    a. prison script
    b. real money
    c. cigarettes
    d. candy

# CHAPTER 10

# SECURITY THREAT GROUPS AND INMATE GANGS

■ **LEARNING OBJECTIVES**

*After completion of this chapter, you should be able to:*
1. Describe the development of gangs in U.S. prisons.
2. List the criteria developed by the National Institute of Corrections regarding the identification of disruptive groups.
3. Discuss the extent of contemporary gangs in U.S. prisons
4. Describe and discuss the five patterns of prison gang development.
5. Identify the various patterns of gang structure, categories of gang membership, and the gang recruitment process.
6. Discuss symbols and benefits associated with gang membership and describe gang "business" activities.
7. Discuss the types and nature of problems that gangs pose for staff and other inmates.
8. Enumerate and describe the factors involved in strategies for gang control.
9. Discuss the alternatives available for nongang inmates in a gang-dominated system.

■ **KEY TERMS AND CONCEPTS**

Aryan Brotherhood
Black Guerrilla Family
Central core members
Direct and indirect supervision
Homeboy connection
La Nuestra Familia
Marginal members
Mexican Mafia
Mexikanemi
Recognized members
Security threat groups
Strategic intelligence
Tactical intelligence
Texas Syndicate
Throw-aways
Unit management

## INMATE GANGS BECAME A PROBLEM IN THE 1960S

Prisons have always held a certain number of violence-prone individuals, typically graduates of juvenile institutions, or lower class unskilled criminals with little respect for older offenders and "regular convicts." Although they posed a constant threat to prison stability, if they went too far the older prison regulars would use force to bring them back into line. Historically, prisons have also usually held inmates who formed groups to intimidate weaker inmates and/or disrupt the prison. But these early groups were relatively ineffectual because they could usually be destroyed by transferring known leaders to other prisons. Thus, they lacked any real permanence beyond the presence of a few key core members (Buentello, 1986).

The Baby Boom substantially increased the youthful population of our urban ghettos, which, in turn, helped to fill juvenile institutions during the 1960s and 1970s. As they graduated from the juvenile justice system, adult facilities began to receive increasing numbers of these more openly aggressive, criminally unskilled urban toughs. As the number of these inmates increased, the ability of more stable elements in the prison community to control them diminished. Drawing on their street and training school experience, they formed racial or ethnically based cliques. In some cases these cliques developed into well-organized gangs (Irwin, 1980).

### Conditions That Permit Gangs to Operate in Prisons

McConville (1985) argues gangs would not have been able to flourish and dominate prisons if the following conditions had not been present:

**1.** Inmates were allowed to move relatively freely in the cell blocks and in other parts of the institution including the dining hall, yard, and workshops. This facilitated communication and intimidation.
**2.** The supervision by staff was remote rather than direct. Because COs spent most of their tour of duty in control rooms or on catwalks, rather than interacting with the inmates, there were greater opportunities for gangs to develop (e.g.,

little or poor intelligence would be gathered).
**3.** COs were unable to adequately protect general population inmates. This pushed inmates to join existing groups, which encouraged gang development.
**4.** Poor control of profitable contraband, such as drugs, encouraged gangs to monopolize its trafficking. Drugs are the commodity central to a gang's trading activity and serve as a major source of power by providing cash, control over their customers, and a pool of favors that can be dispensed to gang members and others inmates.
**5.** Relatively easy communication with the outside world enhanced ganging. This has occurred over the last twenty years as a result of less restrictive policies (e.g., regarding visiting, mail).

McConville (1985) maintains that longer prison sentences are another factor contributing to the persistence of prison gangs. There is evidence that some prison gangs have had stable leadership for ten to fifteen years (Camp and Camp, 1985). Also, for inmates serving long sentences, prisons provide few rewards for following the rules. What were once privileges are now available as a matter of institutional or court-mandated policy. In some instances the only incentive institutions offer is early release, which matters little to inmates facing twenty years or more prior to being eligible for release. Like outsiders, inmates also have ambitions and require an environment that provides challenges and want opportunities to meet some of their needs. Gang membership provides opportunities for achieving power and acquiring the many comforts that make a long stay in prison more tolerable.

### Different Terms Have Been Used to Describe Disruptive Inmate Groups

A variety of terms have been employed to describe groups that create problems for prison officials. Most recently **security threat groups** (STGs) has become the general label for inmate gangs and other disruptive prison groups. The American Correctional Association (ACA, undated) defined these groups as[1]:

> Two (2) or more inmates, acting together, who pose a threat to the security or safety of staff/inmates and/or are disruptive to programs and/or to the orderly management of the facility/system (p. 1).

Because all prisons have numerous formal and informal inmate groups it is important to distinguish disruptive from nondisruptive groups. Although both of these type groups may be organized along racial, ethnic, or cultural lines, nondisruptive groups are granted legitimate status by prison staff. However, like gangs, legitimate groups can disturb the prison by demanding special privileges. For example, if a group can have itself defined as a religion, it can demand special diets and/or special rooms to conduct religious services.[2] There is evidence some groups claiming religious status have used it as a front to cover their drug trafficking operations (McConville, 1985; ACA, undated). The ACA, in trying to develop a better understanding of the various STGs posing a threat to prison order and security, has developed the following definition:

> *Gang/Disruptive Group*—Any organization, association or groups of persons, either formal or informal, that may have a common name or identifying sign or symbol, whose members or associates engage in or have engaged in activities that include, but are not limited to, planning, organizing, threatening, financing, soliciting or committing unlawful acts or acts that violate the policies, rules, and regulations of the [corrections] department or the state code (ACA, undated, p. 74).

In our discussion we will use the terms *STG* and *gang* interchangeably. We recognize that the term *gang* may be used to describe groups commonly understood to limit their illicit activities to criminal pursuits but some groups designated as gangs also pursue political objectives.

**THE NIC HAS DEVELOPED CRITERIA TO IDENTIFY DISRUPTIVE GROUPS** The National Institute of Corrections (NIC, 1991) has identified five criteria to determine if an inmate group is a gang or constitutes a security threat group:

**1.** Does the group have an organized leadership with a clear-cut chain of command?
**2.** Does the group remain unified through good times and bad, and during conflict in the institution?
**3.** Does the group demonstrate its unity in obvious, recognizable ways?
**4.** Does the group engage in activities that are criminal or otherwise threatening to institution[al] operations?

**5.** Does the group place emphasis on member loyalty and group unity and identity; reward members for their criminal or antisocial activity? (pp. 1–2)

Although inmate groups may have some of these characteristics in common, the importance of legitimate inmate groups for prison stability requires the administration to differentiate between gangs and legitimate nondisruptive groups. Examples of recognizable nondisruptive groups include Prison Fellowship, "lifer" organizations, Black Muslims, and the Jaycee groups noted in the last chapter. Although members of these groups manifest loyalty, identity, and unity, unless they engage in criminal activities they should not be viewed nor treated as gangs. Moreover, groups such as the Cuban Marielitos may engage in criminal activity without a leadership structure. They may come together to commit one or a series of crimes but are less dangerous than gangs because their criminal group activities are short lived and, once over, they disband. This group falls within the broader category of STG.

Nevertheless, inmates are generally predisposed to manipulate the prison environment to their advantage. This means that all inmate groups, even those that lack a gang structure, bear watching since all have the potential to become disruptive and even change their focus and structure to operate as gangs.

## ORGANIZATION AND DEVELOPMENT OF STGS AND INMATE GANGS

Until about 1980 our knowledge of prison gangs was based on a few isolated studies and newspaper and magazine reports (e.g., Krajick, 1980a, 1980b; Jacobs 1977; Porter, 1982). However, there has been a flurry of recent studies (i.e., Camp and Camp, 1985, 1988; Fong and Buentello, 1991; American Correctional Association, undated[3]) some of which have gathered nationwide data. The growing interest in gathering information on prison gangs is an indicator of the problems they are posing for corrections. These studies have provided a better perspective on the nature, extent, and effects of these groups as well as strategies that have been devised to deal with them.

## The Proportion of Gang Members Is Increasing

The ACA (undated) surveyed the 50 state, the federal, and the Washington, D.C., systems in 1992. Forty jurisdictions, including the federal system, reported the presence of one or more STGs. These agencies identified 1153 individual STGs with a total membership of 46,190. The number of inmates in these groups ranged from small numbers to a high of almost one-half of a system's population. The average STG had forty members. Illinois reported the largest gang membership (14,900), followed by New Jersey (6000), California (3384), and Texas (2720). In 1992, 6% of the prison inmates were STG members, which meant the proportions since the 1985 Camp and Camp study had doubled. Table 10.1 presents a system-by-system comparison of the 1985 and 1992 surveys. In 1992 data were also obtained on forty-six jails[4] in which the number of STGs ranged from 0 to 261 and averaging 20.4 groups. Prisons averaged 22.4 per jurisdiction, while the range was 0 to 491. Thus jails and prisons averaged about the same number of STGs. Regarding inmate involvement in STGs, the range in jails was from none to one facility reporting one-third of its population as participants. Jail STGs averaged fourteen members, which was about one-third of the average in prisons. Finally, nationwide 762 different STGs were reported to be operating in our jails and prisons, of which 50 were identified as being present in two or more systems.

## Prison Gangs Have Developed According to Five General Patterns

Initially there was no connection between the development of prison gangs in different states. The first gangs appeared in the state of Washington in 1950, then in California in 1957, and in Illinois in 1969. This changed in the 1970s with the emergence of gangs in Utah, Texas, and Arizona, which were tied to gangs in California, and in Wisconsin and Iowa, which were tied to groups in Illinois. In the 1980s, gang development continued in states around Illinois and began to form in the Northeast and in the South (Figure 10.2).

**THE DEVELOPMENT OF THE MEXICAN MAFIA REFLECTS A HOMEBOY PATTERN** Gang development in prisons has taken several forms. Their emergence in California illustrates one pattern. The first gang that formed, the **Mexican Mafia,** had as its nucleus a group of Mexican-American inmates from the Marvilla section of East Los Angeles. These "homeboys" had much in common, including coming from the same barrio (neighborhood), sharing a distinctive ethnic minority status and subculture, and membership in youth gangs (Moore, 1978). Around 1956–57, a group of six to eight of these inmates at Duel Vocational Institution banded together for purposes of self-protection, operating illicit prison enterprises (e.g., narcotics, gambling, debt collecting), and to exercise control over other inmates. Initially their targets were almost exclusively black or white inmates. This organization grew by recruiting the most violent Chicano inmates.

Recognizing the threat posed by this group to prison control, the administration responded by dispersing the members to other institutions (San Quentin, Soledad, and Folsom). This had the unanticipated consequence of giving the gang new recruiting grounds and resulted in its spread throughout the California prison system. They also began to assault and rob not only blacks and whites but also other Hispanics, mainly those from rural Northern California.

**CONFLICT BETWEEN GROUPS AND THE NEED FOR SELF-PROTECTION CAN SPAWN GANGS** To defend themselves, some Northern Hispanics formed their own alliance, **La Nuestra Familia** (NF). Conflict between this group and the Mexican Mafia ensued as a result of assaults by one group on members of the other. The NF recognizing the potential profits and other advantages accruing from domination of the prison economy, particularly narcotics, began competing with the Mafia for control of these markets. This intensified the conflict. This struggle resulted in alliances developing between blacks and the NF, and whites and the Mafia. Other gangs then began to form. The white inmate gangs eventually coalesced and became known as the **Aryan Brotherhood** (AB) adopting a philosophy of white racism and neo-Nazi symbols. Black inmates, some with ties to radical groups, formed the **Black Guerrilla Family** (BGF) in order to protect and advance the position of their race. Their philosophy, drawn from the radical black political groups of the mid-1960s, advocated violence to achieve their objectives. However, despite their revolutionary goals, BGF members still par-

FIGURE 10.1 A System-by-System Comparison of STGs in 1985* and 1992

*For each state, the top row is from 1985, and the bottom row is from 1992. An empty row indicates data not available. The following states do not appear because they reported no gangs or STGs: Alaska, Louisiana, Maine, Montana, North Dakota, Vermont, and Wyoming.*

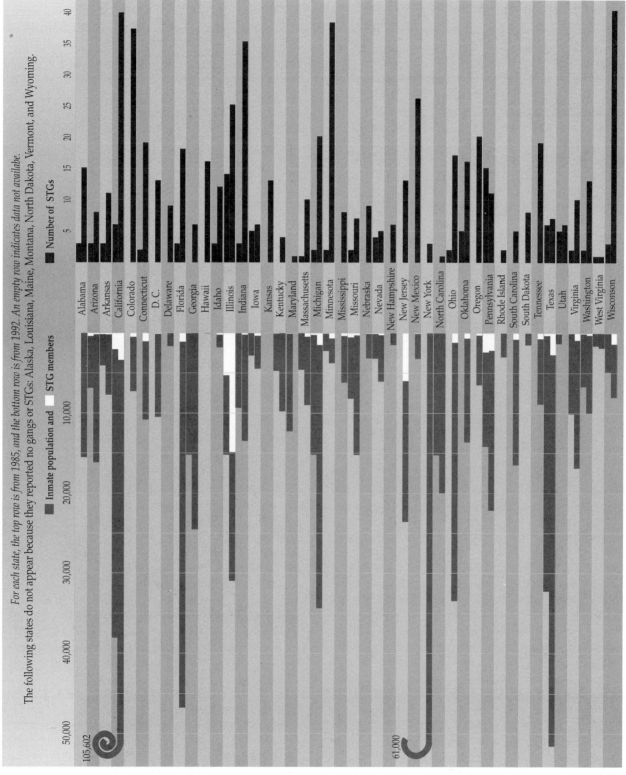

*Source:* American Correctional Association (Undated). Gangs in correctional facilities: A National Assessment (Contract No. 91-IJ-CS-0026) (Unpublished report). Washington, D.C.: National Institute of Justice, Office of Justice Programs, U.S. Department of Justice.
* The 1985 data in this figure are from Camp, G. M. and Camp. C. G., 1985. *Prison Gangs: Their Extent, Nature, and Impact on Prisons.* Washington, D.C. U.S. Department of Justice, pp. 11, 19.

FIGURE 10.2  **Development of Prison Groups between 1950 and the Early 1980s.**

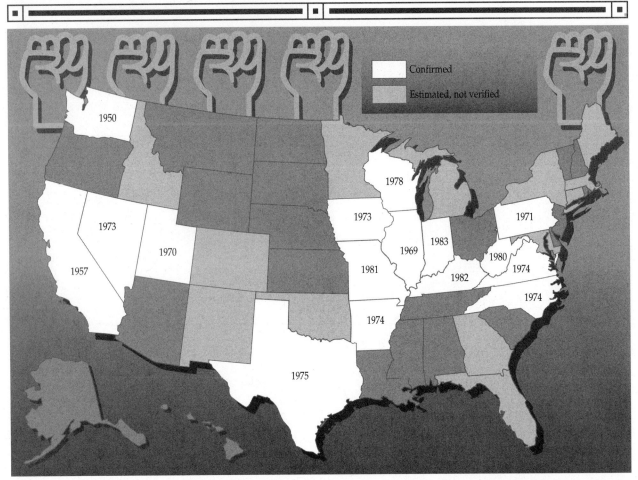

*Source:* Adapted from G. M. Camp and C. G. Camp (1985). *Prison Gangs: Their Extent, Nature and Impact on Prisons,* Washington, D.C.: U.S. Department of Justice.

ticipated in the prisoner economy (Camp and Camp, 1985; Kahn, 1978).

Gang formation in California illustrates several factors contributing to prison gang development including ethnic/racial division, self-protection, common cultural and homeboy backgrounds (coming from the same neighborhood/area) and transfer of gang members from one institution to another. The homeboy factor ties together many less organized prison groups.

**OUTSIDE GANG MEMBERS IN ILLINOIS PRISONS FORMED GANGS ON THE INSIDE**  Another pattern of gang formation is illustrated by their emergence in Illinois prisons. Gangs in this system developed, particularly at Stateville and Pontiac, as a result of the incarceration of large numbers of

inmates affiliated with four street gangs. These street affiliations provided a natural basis for these gangs to establish organizations in the prison. They quickly gathered strength and power by vigorously recruiting inmates who were not members on the outside. The recent development of the **Crips** and **Bloods** in California prisons further illustrates this pattern.

**PRISON GANG MEMBERS ENTERING NEW INSTITUTIONS FORMED GANG CHAPTERS**  Gangs developed in other Illinois prisons as a result of the transfer or rearrest of gang members. They attempted to duplicate in the new prison the groups that had provided them support and an identity.

The development of the **Texas Syndicate** (TS) in Texas also illustrates this pattern. This group was

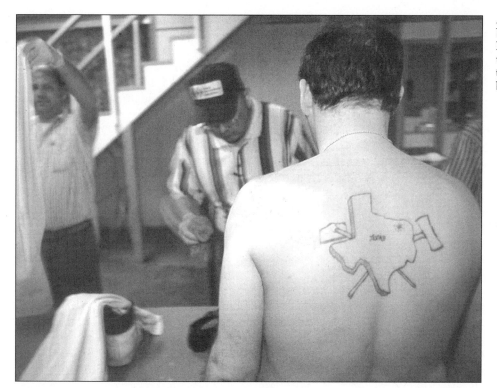

A Texas Syndicate member displays his gang logo. This is one means used by prison officials to identify gang members.

started by Texas-born Mexican-American inmates at San Quentin Prison in California in 1975. They needed protection from victimization by other California prison gangs. By 1976 it had 500 members and had spread to other California prisons. At that point it not only protected them, but was also involved in illegal activities such as drug trafficking, extortion, and contract murder. The formation of the TS in Texas is traced to several inmates who were previously associated with it in California. When reunited, they formed the Texas version of this gang, which became the second largest gang in the Texas system. Although most TS members are in Texas, the authority for making major decisions still rests with the "home office" in California. The feeling is that since the gang originated there, decisions should be made by this group (Buentello, 1986; Fong, 1990).

**COPY CAT GROUPS EMERGED IN SOME PRISONS**
Gangs with the same or similar names formed later in different systems do not necessarily constitute branches of their namesake or have any relationship between them. For example, the Mexican Mafia in California and the later formed Texas **Mexikanemi,** often also called the Mexican Mafia,

have no connection or relationship with one another. Moreover, even though the **Aryan Brotherhood** exists in various states, there is no central control of these gangs and ties exist only between a few AB gangs in different systems. Thus the Texas AB maintains some ties with its California counterpart, yet it is not controlled by it. Texas AB members entering other facilities with AB gangs are not automatically considered members and may not even be recruited by them because (1) it recruits Mexican-American inmates, which runs counter to the AB's white racist orientation or (2) members are considered lacking in basic qualities, for example, not being strong enough (Buentello, 1986).

### The Level of Organization of Prison Gangs Varies

Most prison authorities report that gangs in their institutions were not well organized, highly structured, or sophisticated groups. Nevertheless the Camps (1985) found several jurisdictions with gangs that were well organized, including the Mexican Mafia in California and the Aryan Brotherhood in Missouri. This shows the difficulty of making general statements that apply to all correctional systems.

**MEMBERSHIP IS BASED ON ONE OR MORE FACTORS**    Camp and Camp (1985) found that several factors distinguished prison gangs and formed the basis for inmate membership. Ethnic/racial origin, based on beliefs of racial superiority (e.g., Aryan Brotherhood), was the primary basis for gang membership. Next in importance was prior association or affiliation with others from the same home area, such as the gangs in Illinois. Third, was the sharing of certain strong political and/or religious beliefs (e.g., the Black Guerrilla Family). McConville (1985) notes that some religious groups have brought suit in the federal courts and have obtained permission to organize in the prison. However, some prison administrators assert that some of these groups are covers for drug trafficking operations. Another factor was a common lifestyle centering around "motorcycle machismo" as practiced by the biker gangs (e.g., Avengers). An example of a "macho" guy was an inmate McConville (1985) encountered while visiting a prison. The inmate's hands were bandaged from top to bottom as was his face. His comment to McConville was "I can take it."

Many of these gangs are organized around and attract membership based on several of these factors. For example, the AB is a white supremacist group with a motorcycle orientation, and the Mexican Mafia has both an ethnic/racial and geographical basis.

**GANG STRUCTURE CAN FOLLOW VARIOUS PATTERNS**    Leaders of these gangs are typically distinctive from their followers in several ways, including physical prowess, seniority, and the commission of violent acts. Further, members manifesting similar attributes are more likely to move up in the gang hierarchy. The leadership structure of these groups follows several patterns: (1) It is directed by a single strong leader, (2) a strong leader shares control with a council or committee, or (3) control rests with a council or committee. Gangs may also designate inmates as captains with the responsibility for a cell block (Camp and Camp, 1985).

The Texas-based Mexikanemi is structured along paramilitary lines (see Figure 10.3) All ranking positions, excluding sergeants, are elected, with the criterion being a person's leadership ability (Fong, 1990). The president, vice president, and generals control members both in and out of Texas prisons.

Each general has responsibility for a specific area of the state; Lieutenants control specific units and certain cities (Buentello, 1986).

It is important to note that, while in theory gangs demand obedience to the leadership, their ability to enforce these commands varies greatly.

**GANG MEMBERS CAN FALL INTO ONE OF SEVERAL CATEGORIES**    Commitment to the gang translates roughly into four levels of membership. First, there are **central core members** who are the most committed members. This usually includes gang leaders and their close friends who are tied together in a close-knit clique that spends a great deal of time together. A second group, **recognized members** or wanna-be's, are frequently young rookies looking for opportunities to break into the gang's inner core. This group of inmates is used by the core to show the gang's power or to assist in an attack. A third category, **throw-aways,** are inmates used by the gang to do jobs that involve high risk of injury, death, or apprehension. The fourth category, **marginal members,** can be found in prisons with large gangs. This is a relatively large group of inmates who maintain a loose association with large gangs, such as the Vice Lords or NF, who are available when a massive display of force is necessary.

**GANG CODES OF CONDUCT HELP TO CONTROL MEMBER BEHAVIOR**    All organized groups have codes of conduct that regulate member activity. Gang codes emphasize secrecy, loyalty, and sometimes require an outwardly cooperative attitude toward prison staff (Camp and Camp, 1985; Buentello, 1986; Fong, 1990). Fear, intimidation, threats, pressure, and violence, including murder, are used by members to achieve their objectives and by the gang to maintain loyalty, obedience, and order within the group. In fact, actual or threatened violence is the most potent factor in gang maintenance. True gang members have little regard for human life and are not deterred by government sanctions imposed against inmates for violent behavior. They are not controlled by the rules—the laws and sanctions that guide most other people's behavior—which allows them to disregard the law and its consequences (Camp and Camp, 1985; Fong, Vogel, and Buentello, 1992).

However, the degree to which gangs can demand obedience to their code of conduct depends

FIGURE 10.3   **The General Organizational Structure of the Mexican Mafia**

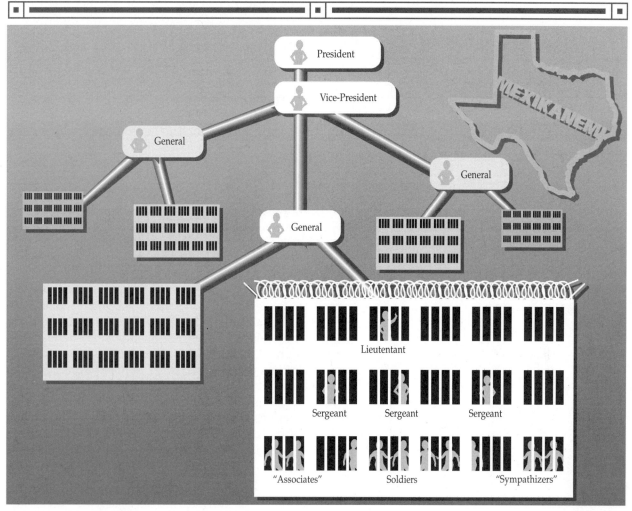

SOURCE: Based on interviews. Adapted from R. S. Fong (1990). The organizational structure of prison gangs: a Texas case study, *Federal Probation, 54*(1), p. 40.

on the organization's cohesiveness and its ability to retaliate against those breaking the code (NIC, 1991). Some gangs can enforce their code even after a member has been released from prison. For example, a Texas Syndicate member was murdered execution style in Houston, Texas, for failing to abide by the oath he took when he joined the gang (Buentello, 1986). The gang hit serves as a good example of gang expectations and the rules governing member behavior. Once someone is marked for death, a volunteer may be sought to do the job and if no one steps forward, members may be required to draw lots to decide who will do it

(Fong, 1990). The rule is if you refuse to kill someone you will be killed. A member of the Texas Syndicate told CBS reporter Ed Bradley (1986) that this applies whether it is a friend and even if "the two were raised by the same mother."

Many of the more developed groups have detailed codes of conduct and some have written constitutions. Figure 10.4 provides examples of the rules contained in the constitution of the Texas Syndicate and Mexikanemi. Fong (1990) indicates that in these gangs the "penalty for intentionally or unintentionally violating any of the established rules is death" (p. 40).

FIGURE 10.4    **The Mexikanemi Constitution**

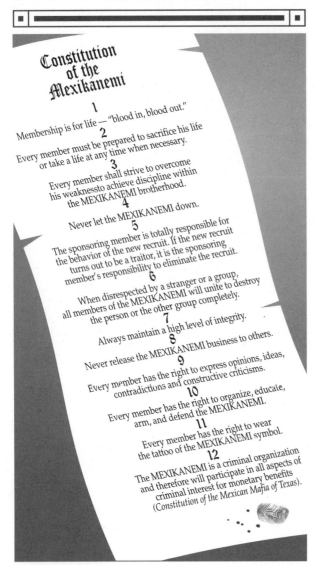

Constitution of the Mexikanemi

1
Membership is for life—"blood in, blood out."

2
Every member must be prepared to sacrifice his life or take a life at any time when necessary.

3
Every member shall strive to overcome his weakness to achieve discipline within the MEXIKANEMI brotherhood.

4
Never let the MEXIKANEMI down.

5
The sponsoring member is totally responsible for the behavior of the new recruit. If the new recruit turns out to be a traitor, it is the sponsoring member's responsibility to eliminate the recruit.

6
When disrespected by a stranger or a group, all members of the MEXIKANEMI will unite to destroy the person or the other group completely.

7
Always maintain a high level of integrity.

8
Never release the MEXIKANEMI business to others.

9
Every member has the right to express opinions, ideas, contradictions and constructive criticisms.

10
Every member has the right to organize, educate, arm, and defend the MEXIKANEMI.

11
Every member has the right to wear the tattoo of the MEXIKANEMI symbol.

12
The MEXIKANEMI is a criminal organization and therefore will participate in all aspects of criminal interest for monetary benefits (Constitution of the Mexican Mafia of Texas).

SOURCE: Adapted from R. S. Fong (1990). The organizational structure of prison gangs: a Texas case study, *Federal Probation, 54*(1), p. 40.

## The Recruitment Process Varies from Gang to Gang

Fong (1990) provides a picture of the recruitment process in the Texas system, which suggests patterns that may be operative in other gangs. In the Texas Syndicate, all prospective members must have a **homeboy connection**—an active member must have been a childhood friend of the prospect. If this requirement is met, the new member is taken in on a probationary basis. During this time a thorough background investigation is conducted

by the unit chairman. This is done by contacting other chairmen and members who may have knowledge of the prospect. If the prospect is "clean," all members are polled and if the vote is unanimous the prospect is admitted. However, if it is found that the prospect was a police informant, or has a questionable sense of loyalty, membership is denied. Moreover, he may be forced by the gang to pay protection or be used as a prostitute.

The Mexikanemi has the same requirements and procedures for membership as the TS, but it does not adhere to them as rigidly. In fact, many of their prospects are TS rejects. They do require homeboy connections, but their background investigations are often not thoroughly conducted and membership is based only on a majority vote. These less demanding criteria are considered a major factor in this gang being the largest in the Texas system (Fong, 1990).

**GANG INITIATIONS MAY REQUIRE VIOLENCE**
The Camps (1985) obtained information on the initiation practices of twenty-three gangs they studied. Nine groups used a nonviolent form of initiation, but eight others required "prospects" to commit a violent act against another inmate or staff member. The "hit," which is not necessarily fatal, requires blood be drawn. It appears to serve three purposes: It shows the candidate is "really solid," it gives gangs an opportunity to conduct their business, and it guarantees that only those who are cold-hearted, violent, and loyal will be accepted as gang members (Buentello, 1986). Finally, for six gangs, the group's needs determined whether a violent or nonviolent act was required.

## Group Operations Are Defined by Symbols, Power, Activities, and Communication

The cohesiveness of inmate gang organizations depends on the lifetime commitment required of members. They are further united by their symbols, the services they provide their members, and their ability to maintain lines of communication with group affiliates within and between different cell blocks and institutions.

**GANG MEMBERSHIP ENTAILS A LIFETIME COMMITMENT**    Gang membership often represents a lifetime commitment (Camp and Camp, 1985; Buentello, 1986; Fong, 1990). This was the case for

FIGURE 10.5   **Prison Gang Insignias**

Nuestra Familia ("Our Family")

Texas Syndicate

Arayan Brotherhood

nearly two-thirds of the gangs studied by the Camps. In these groups, leaving represented an act of betrayal that frequently had severe consequences. In fact, in more than one-half of the gangs it is reputed that the only way to leave the group is by death, natural or otherwise—blood in, blood out. For example, La Nuestra Familia members are required to take the following oath when admitted:

> If I go forward, follow me, If I hesitate, push me, If they kill me, avenge me, If I am a traitor, kill me (Camp and Camp, 1985, p. 99).

In actuality, quitting these gangs may not be so brutal. Many gang members leave the gang when they are released from prison without severe consequences. Those who remain in prison after quitting tend to seek safety in protective custody units.

**GANG IDENTIFICATION INCLUDES A VARIETY OF SYMBOLS**  Administrators of prisons with gangs report that members of these groups can usually be identified by distinctive characteristics including tattoos, clothing, jewelry, insignias, and emblems (ACA, undated). For example, while visiting one gang prison, McConville (1985) noted that there was a chessboard laid out in the front of some cells with a white king in the middle, denoting the inmate was a member of the Latin Kings. Although this form of identification may change from place to place, the gang "colors" remain constant. For example, inmates often paint their cells in these colors. They also can be recognized by their demeanor (typically hostile, rebellious, and arrogant) and distinctive tattoos, which include the gang logo, members' nicknames, and those indicating a specific criminal speciality. Graffiti, which is often called the newspaper of the street, marks gang territory and describes gang exploits. Inside prison, graffiti takes the form of inmate drawings.

**GANGS HAVE METHODS FOR PERPETUATING THEIR EXISTENCE AND POWER**  Most gangs are oriented to the prison rather than the outside world because a substantial number of gang members have long prison sentences. This partially explains their choice of tactics to maintain and perpetuate their existence and increases their influence in the prison. As members continue their gang associations and adjust to the reality of their position (i.e., the prison is going to be their home for many years), some may lose concern about having their sentences extended for ten or twenty years. They present an image of being unafraid of prison administration, other inmates, or the consequences of their violence. This stance enables them to intimidate most other inmates and some staff, and to kill with impunity (Camp and Camp, 1985).

Gangs typically base their power and prestige on their ability to control other inmates and certain prison activities. Drugs, money, and property are considered tangible evidence of their ability to accomplish these aims. Thus, they derive their image from the acquisition of power and from their emphasis on "ganghood," a concept that centers around the significance of belonging to the gang. For example, the TS's constitution states that "nothing is to be put before the [TS] and its business. Not god, religion, parole or family" (Bradley, 1986).

*Trafficking in the Inmate Economy Serves to Perpetuate the Gang* Gangs also maintain themselves by providing essential services (e.g., protection for members) and through their capacity to obtain and distribute contraband, particularly drugs (Camp and Camp, 1985). Where these groups exist, they control the majority of the drug trafficking in the institution. Many gangs bribe prison staff to bring drugs into the prison. COs receive a commission on everything they bring in and those involved can almost double their weekly salary (Crouch and Marquart, 1989) A member of the Mexikanemi describes co-opting a young inexperienced CO:

> When a young officer is assigned to a cell block, one of us would start watching him for few days. Then, I would go up to him in order to find out where he is coming from. I would borrow a cigarette or a pen from him. If he goes for it, next thing I would do is ask him to mail a letter for me. If he goes for it I would start showing him pictures of some woman which I claimed to be my friend. I would tell him to give her a call because she would show him a real good time. If he calls her and gets some sex favors from her, I know I have him. (Fong, as cited by Crouch and Marquart, 1989, p. 211.) [At that point the officer will be asked to bring in drugs. If he refuses he will be exposed to higher ranking officers as having been involved with an inmate's wife, sister, or other close relative. This usually means termination. Moreover, once involved the gang does not allow these officers to terminate their courier activities unless they resign from their prison jobs because anytime an officer refuses to cooperate he is threatened with exposure (Fong, 1990)].

Other money-making endeavors include the protection rackets, thievery, and prostitution. These activities often involve intimidating and abusing weaker inmates (Camp and Camp, 1985; Buentello, 1986). For example, a gang member in Texas showed a new recruit how gang members raise money. He took two loaves of bread and made "mayonnaise sandwiches" and went down the tier and asked those guys who had money if they wanted to "buy a sandwich." A lot of guys didn't want them but whether they wanted them or not they bought them. When asked by Ed Bradley (1986) of "60 Minutes," "What would have happened if they refused?" the gang member replied "they'd get their heads torn off. They are going to buy the sandwiches, there ain't no if."

*Open Lines of Communication Are Necessary to Maintain Continuity* Gangs have employed a number of channels to communicate with members in different units. The most common has been the U.S. mail. However, since prison officials can intercept and censor outgoing mail under certain circumstances, gangs developed codes for their letters. (see the Close-Up on "How Gangs Use the Mail to Communicate"). Prison rules can prohibit inmate-to-inmate correspondence,[5] but gangs have gotten around these rules by using wives, girlfriends, other visitors, and inmates being transferred from one unit to another to carry messages between units.

## Gang Membership Has Several Benefits

Inmates derive many benefits from joining gangs, particularly in institutions in which they dominate the inmate world (Irwin, 1980; Jacobs, 1974; Porter, 1982). Gangs provide their members with protection from physical and sexual assault and extortion and theft. Independents and members of other gangs know that if a gang member is attacked or has property stolen his comrades will retaliate. Gangs also have "private stores" and provide new inmates and those without outside resources with candy, cigarettes, pies, canned food, and other things that make prison life more tolerable. Gang members, unlike independents, are not expected to pay back these debts at 100% interest.

Gangs also serve as a source of information for their members. By getting members assigned to strategic jobs (e.g., positions as clerks in the administration building), the gang can amass valuable

## Close Up How Gangs Use the Mail to Communicate

Both the Texas Syndicate and the Mexican Mafia operate in secretive ways in the prison environment. On the unit level, instructions and decisions are relayed through verbal communications. For inter-unit communication, however, the most commonly known method is the use of the U.S. mail. Coded messages are hidden in letters. For the Texas Syndicate, the most frequently used coded method is the number code. The following coded letter is an example of this communication strategy.

Dear Bro,
Haven't heard nothing from ya for almost 4 weeks. . . . Remember Big Al, he just got back from the hospital after spendin 3 weeks there for a major heart attack. Said it was a change. Really liked it there. The room was nice and even had a 19 inch color TV. . . . Said he wouldn't mind staying there for 1/2 a year.

Guess what, he said when he woke up in his room the first time, he almost had a second heart attack cause couldn't believe what he saw, a real cute nurse with Dolly Parton's figure. Said she was taller, about 5 foot 8 inches in her early 20's. Big Al said they got to be real good friends. Said she even hugged him a dozen times or so a day. . . . Said would divorce his old lady if things get juicy with this cutie. What a two-timer. So much for Big Al.

I am getting a visit this weekend. My old man is bringing my son to see me cause next Monday is his B-day. Gonna to be 10 years old. Wish I could be out there with him. Been away for almost 5 years since I got busted for rapping that 19 year old slut down in that Motel 6. Got 3 more years to go and I'll be a free man. . .

Well, such is life! Like they say, life is a bitch and you die, sometimes if ya lucky, ya marry one. Gonna put the brakes on for now. Give my best to the best and f___ the rest.
Your bro till death

In interpreting the underlying message of this letter, one must first learn the number codes. It is assumed that the number codes are broken down as follows:

| A | B | C | D | E | F | G | H | I | J | K | L | M | N |
|---|---|---|---|---|---|---|---|---|---|---|---|---|---|
| 8 | 1 | 7 | 26 | 18 | 9 | 13 | 3 | 19 | 20 | 14 | 22 | 5 | 16 |

| O | P | Q | R | S | T | U | V | W | X | Y | Z |
|---|---|---|---|---|---|---|---|---|---|---|---|
| 12 | 17 | 23 | 2 | 10 | 6 | 36 | 15 | 21 | 11 | 27 | 34 |

The number 4 in the beginning of the letter is a code indicator. Having understood the number codes, the letter reveals the following numbers:

1st paragraph: 3, 19, 6 (1/2 year = 6)
2nd paragraph: 5, 8, 20, 12, 2
3rd paragraph: 10, 5, 19, 6, 3

Applying these numbers to the letter designations will reveal the following message:

| 3 | 19 | 6 | | 5 | 8 | 20 | 12 | 2 | | 10 | 5 | 19 | 6 | 3 |
|---|----|---|---|---|---|----|----|---|---|----|---|----|---|---|
| H | I | T | | M | A | J | O | R | | S | M | I | T | H |

Decoded message: "Hit Major Smith"

*SOURCE: B. Fong (1990), The organizational structure of prison gangs: a Texas case study, Federal Probation, 54(1), pp. 41–42.*

information on decisions affecting them. Gang affiliation allows members to operate within the prison economy. Although gangs do not always control all illicit activities in the institutions they dominate, independents are not likely to operate without approval of gang leaders. In one Texas prison, for example, an inmate who was a drug dealer on the street entered prison thinking he would continue his trafficking activity on the inside. He soon learned that the TS controlled trafficking in this prison. To deal he had to become a member of this gang or else be killed (Bradley, 1986). Thus, an affiliated inmate who wishes to operate in the prison economy can easily establish connections and can muscle in on independents who are not paying off other gangs.

Visitors and correspondents are typically arranged for inside gang members who have no outside family or other contacts. Outside gang members also send money and arrange to have drugs and other contraband smuggled into the prison. Members of gangs with outside affiliates can expect to receive assistance when released.

When asked what the gang provides its members that are released one Texas Syndicate member stated:

"They get them an old lady. They get them dope. They get them on their feet" (Bradley, 1986).

Some gangs have education programs to teach members how to read and write. For many gang members the group's primary function is providing psychological support: a feeling of belonging, a source of identification, and an air of importance. For inmates who are products of unstable families and have poor self-concepts, the gang allows them to "feel like a man" and be part of a family they never had.

### Some Gangs Have Street Affiliates, with a Few Meeting Criteria for Organized Crime Groups

Close to three-quarters of the thirty-nine jurisdictions in the Camps' study (1985) reported that some or all of the gangs in their prisons had counterpart gangs on the streets. One-half of the jurisdictions reported there was no evidence that these groups used the prison as a base for outside criminal activities, those reporting such activities had the most extensive gang involvement. Several states, including California, Texas, Arizona, and Illinois, indicated that some gangs are evolving, or have evolved, into organized crime syndicates.

The President's Commission on Organized Crime (1986) identified five prison gangs meeting criteria for organized crime groups: the Mexican Mafia, La Nuestra Familia, the Aryan Brotherhood, the Black Guerrilla Family, and the Texas Syndicate. These gangs are sophisticated and self-perpetuating groups, are involved in illegal acts for power and profit, and have operations both inside and outside of the prison. In contrast to ordinary criminal gangs, they (1) are organized to operate beyond the lifetime of individual members and to survive leadership changes and (2) have a hierarchical structure that is distinguishable and ordered by ranks based on power and authority similar to a corporation. This structure insulates gangs leaders from direct involvement in criminal activity, making it difficult to use traditional law enforcement techniques to charge and prosecute them.

Gangs with outside counterparts are involved in drug trafficking, extortion, robbery, prostitution, murder, and weapons trafficking (Camp and Camp, 1985; Buentello, 1986). At some point, if it has not already occurred, these gangs, particularly those designated as organized crime groups, will use the money generated from these highly profitable illegal enterprises to invest in high cash flow legitimate businesses, such as bars and restaurants.

The California-based Mexican Mafia successfully infiltrated and eventually controlled, several federally funded projects directed toward assisting ex-convicts, parolees, youthful offenders, and addicts. In one program designed to assist ex-convicts to readjust to society, project funds were used to purchase heroin from Mexico and airline tickets for drug couriers. Program clients were induced to establish dealerships in East Los Angeles and give a percentage of their profits back to the gang. Project-owned vehicles were used by gang members in at least six murders (Camp and Camp, 1985).

The existence of street counterparts serves a number of purposes for the gang and individual members. For member releasees it provides a support network to assist them in settling back into the community. For example, for TS members this means having a place to go, financial assistance, and opportunities to join in illegal activities with other TS members. For prison gangs this represents another source of income since outside members are often required to send a portion of the profits from their criminal activities to gang members on the inside. For example, the TS requires members to contribute 10% of their street income, while Mexikanemi requires 15% (Fong, 1990). Also some of the money from outside activities is believed to be used to pay attorneys to assist members with their cases and to post bond when a gang member is arrested (Buentello, 1986).

## PRISON GANGS CAUSE A NUMBER OF PROBLEMS

The difficulties gangs can create for prison administrators vary from state to state, with some reporting no problem and others claiming gangs account for up to 50% of the problems. The major problems created by these groups are drug trafficking, intimidation of weaker inmates, and strong-arm tactics for extortion. These latter activities present problems because of the violence and the fact that many inmate victims request placement in protective custody. Finally, the violence connected with gang activities is often intensified because of the racial character of gangs (Camp and Camp, 1985).

## Problems Occur as a Result of Gangs' "Business" Activities

The problems experienced by prison staff from gang activity are not usually the result of direct actions against staff but result from gangs pursuing their business interests. Gangs do not usually try to disrupt prison operations, yet they are determined to carry on "business" regardless of how this effects prison order (Camp and Camp, 1985). Nevertheless, some groups do actively disrupt the prison. Buentello (1986) notes that TS has continually attempted to undermine prison officials by filing frivolous litigation falsely alleging prison mismanagement, harassment, and brutality by COs. Also, the TS has tried to disrupt prison order by instigating food and work strikes and major disorders.

Older gang members generally recognize the value of cooperating with institutional staff to maintain a stable environment because that is "good for business." This may be lost on younger members who may challenge prison authority to validate their tough guy image (NIC, 1991). Stronger gangs tend to control their younger members to avoid these problems.

## Prison Administrators May Be Ambivalent about Recognizing the Existence of Gangs

The Camps (1985, 1988) indicate that it sometimes appears as if some gangs and the prison administration have unofficial pacts of mutual noninterference. Hence, some systems report gangs are not a problem in their institutions because they do not openly disrupt prison routine. It seems prison administrators in these circumstances may be unaware of the harm gangs can cause. Perhaps they feel there are no obvious problems, thus they cannot hurt the institution. It is also possible they feel these groups are part of the informal inmate structure and should only be dealt with when their actions become overt and confrontational. It is no surprise that some administrators are reluctant to acknowledge that gangs represent a problem because this suggests they are not in control of their institutions. For example, in the Texas system gangs did not become an administrative priority

until there were eight gang-related homicides within eight days (Peltz, 1986).

## Inmate-to-Inmate Problems Are Also Created By Gangs

The Camps' study (1985) found gangs were more likely to engage in confrontations with nongang inmates. Of 119 confrontations reported by ninety agencies in 1983, nearly three-quarters involved nongang members and the remainder were intergang disputes. Retaliatory action among gangs varies widely, suggesting that alliances exist in some prisons, while in others there is much competition and disagreement. Fong *et al.* (1992) suggests the kinds of problems that can arise when gangs battle for dominance. From 1982 to 1985, in Texas, of seventy-two inmate homicides, gangs accounted for fifty-one and for a high proportion of the nonfatal inmate stabbings. The ACA (undated) study likewise found a high percentage of inmate-to-inmate violence was gang related in both prisons (40%) and jails (42%).

Despite the fact that many gangs follow a policy of avoiding conflicts with prison staff, gang activity resulted in fifty-one staff injuries in four states and two staff deaths in 1983 (Camp and Camp, 1985). Moreover, other data from Fong *et al.* (1991) show that between 1983 and 1988 there was a yearly average of 2918 assaults by inmates on officers in the Texas system, most of which were gang related. Nationwide data for 1992 show that gangs accounted for about one-fifth of the violent acts against staff (ACA, undated).

## CONTROL OF PRISON GANGS IS ACHIEVED IN VARIOUS WAYS

California was the first system to experience major gang problems. In the 1960s, gangs became entrenched in its institutions before administrators realized the danger these groups posed to order and security. Since this early period and with the spread of gangs to other systems, a variety of strategies have evolved in attempts to control them. Not all tactics have been effective in all jurisdiction because of the great variation between systems including size and nature of the gang problems; ethnic/racial variation in the inmate population; number, training, and experience of staff; and funding and physical plant capabilities.

## Two Views Characterize How Gangs Are Dealt with By Prison Administration

Despite variations in the methods employed to deal with STGs, the Camps (1985, 1988) have identified two views that characterize the basic strategies systems employ in controling these groups.[6]

**ONE BASIS FOR GANG POLICY IS MEMBERSHIP** This viewpoint makes several assumptions. It maintains that inmates should be free to walk the prison yard and engage in constructive activity. Because gang members victimize other inmates, they thereby restrict that freedom of movement. Whether or not a gang has violated specific prison rules, the fact that it is "organized" is reason enough to consider it to be a threat and thereby antiadministration. These groups become more of a threat when they publicly and violently confront staff and inmates. Since gangs encourage such tactics, any inmate's membership, association, or support of the gang's actions and values constitutes a violation of institutional rules.

Prisons adopting this position are likely to take what the ACA (undated) labels a proactive "security threat group specific" (STGS) management style. States adopting this approach have management procedures to identify select groups as STGs and distinguish them from nondisruptive groups. They also have criteria for identifying STG members and policies placing sanctions on these individuals. This is dealt with in more detail later.

**ANOTHER BASIS FOR GANG POLICY IS BEHAVIOR** This second orientation considers gangs as much a fact of life in the prison as in the neighborhoods from which most of these offenders come. This is because grouping, associating, and identifying with one's peers is a natural phenomenon. Ganging is simply an outgrowth of this pattern along with the continued maintenance of friendships and associations formed prior to imprisonment. Therefore, gang members are allowed the same privileges as other inmates including freedom to move about the prison and to participate in activities.

The prison is viewed as a community in which staff and inmates have to coexist and which re-

quires appropriate police action against rule breaking. Thus, a gang member's behavior determines how he is treated rather than his group membership, even if this group is thought to be involved in illegal or rule-breaking behavior. This does not mean that collective acts by gang members that violate prison rules—such as recruiting gang members, or intimidating in the name of the gang—will not be punished. This stance comes closest to what the ACA (undated) designated as the "existing policy" philosophy, under which agencies add restrictions on STGs to their policies. This might include prohibiting activity that is characterized by:

- Involvement in group demonstrations or unauthorized organization(s)
- Intentional participation by inmate[s] in any activity with the purpose of identifying themselves with an inmate STG
- Poses or display of any materials, symbols, colors or pictures of any identified STG (ACA, undated, p. 28).

This strategy does not call for the wholesale segregation of gang members to combat gang activity. However, it does not preclude segregating inmates posing a threat to the prison's security as a result of gang-related crimes. It may involve many of the features of the more proactive STGS approach and also recognizes the need to do the following: gather intelligence on gang operations and activities; control contraband; monitor and resist gang efforts to manipulate housing and program assignments; and discipline rule violators in a prompt and certain manner.

Thus, some jurisdictions take a more proactive approach toward gangs (specifically) and STGs (generally) by controlling and/or, if possible, eliminating them because they encroach on the right of all inmates to a safe and secure prison environment. In other jurisdictions, gangs are seen as part of the prison community and control focuses on dealing with those activities that violate prison rules. The Camps suggest that these divergent views may reflect individual differences in gang behavior and in prison environments. Furthermore, although an administrator or jurisdiction may initially adopt a particular strategy, over time they may change policies based on experience. Therefore, at any point it is possible for elements of both views to be simultaneously part of an institution's strategy.

It is important to note that the behavioral approach may reflect an exceedingly naive view of the contribution gangs make to the social organization and control of prisons. Gangs provide COs with much information they would normally not receive and they promote a certain semblance of stability in prisons they dominate. But this dominance may mean that they, rather than staff, exercise control over major prison activities (e.g., control and/or influence of job and cell assignments) and over the inmate economy. In some cases prison authorities have accepted the fact that gangs "run" the prison and feel the need to negotiate with gang leaders in order to maintain order. Although this promotes stability and makes prison life more bearable for gang members, particularly the inner core, this is done at the expense of the rest of the inmate population. McConville (1985) notes several examples of the kind of "stability" promoted by gang control in some Illinois prisons: inmates being sold as slaves to other people and a brothel operation involving men dressing in lingerie to advertise their trade with all the proceeds going to a gang.

**THE REACTION TO GANGS AND STGs OFTEN FOLLOWS THREE STAGES** The views just described represent very different approaches to and perceptions of gangs and STGs by prison administrators. The ACA (undated) survey of STGs concluded that correctional personnel sometimes go through three stages in reacting to these groups, which may explain these different perceptions:

◾ *Denial:* This stage is found primarily on the East Coast and west to Ohio. Simply put, correctional administrators in these states tend to deny that gangs exist. [It is likely that these administrators will deal with gangs on a behavioral basis.]
◾ *Acknowledgment:* Midwest states acknowledge that gangs are present; however, they have few, if any, specific procedures designed to identify, track, or control them. [They are also likely to respond on a behavioral basis.]
◾ *Recognition:* "Yes we have them, now what do we do?" This tends to be the attitude of states west from Colorado. They are aware that gangs exist in their systems and are attempting to control their activities. [They are likely to deal with them on a membership basis.] (p. 2).

## Several Factors Dictate Strategies for Controlling Gangs

In a substantial number of correctional systems, gangs are a major disruptive force threatening inmate and staff security and safety. They account for a substantial amount of the violence and can undermine prison management by corrupting its staff. While control of gangs is not easy, the alternative can be a situation in which inmates control the inside and staff controls the perimeter. This results in inhumane and unconstitutional conditions. Thus, the question of gang control partially revolves around the issue of how to provide a safe and constitutional environment for the general prison population in institutions with major gang problems. The general population of a prison should not have to go into protective custody in order to feel safe and secure. This may require a number of changes in management policies and procedures as well as structural changes in a prison's physical plant. In the remainder of this chapter, we present recommendations made by the various authors and entities who have studied the prison gang problem (see, e.g., Camp and Camp, 1985, 1988; Buentello, 1986; Fong, 1990; ACA, undated).

**THE FIRST PRIORITY IS TO ESTABLISH A POLICY AND STRATEGY** Recognition followed by employing the STGs strategy takes a proactive approach to dealing with gangs. The policy statement for this approach might include the following:

Inmates who are members of [STGs] shall be identified according to established criteria. Alterative methods of management of [STGs] . . . shall be applied to prevent [them] . . . from disrupting the order and security of a facility. Facility staff shall be trained in identification and management of security threat groups.

[STGs] . . . are a threat to public safety, the security of the institutions, and the safety of other offenders and staff within both the institutions and the community. . . . [I]t is the policy of the Department of Corrections to identify and monitor those offenders who are members and/or leaders of STGs within the institutions and under field supervision. This information will be shared . . . [with] institutions, the field supervisors . . . and local law enforcement. Within [prisons] . . . per existing policy inmates are prohibited from engaging in any activity or behavior associated with . . . [STGs] . . . [including] collection of dues or fines, publishing and/or possessing threat group material, photos, or literature; communication by inventive language, code, or hand signals; and possessing or wearing clothing or jewelry designed to identify [group membership]. . . . Within the community probation and parole clients are strongly encouraged not to become affiliated or interact with . . . STGs. As appropriate, agents may develop rules of supervision that specifically prohibit any association or identification with STGs. . . (ACA, undated, pp. 69–70).

The development of an official position about gangs and the strategies needed to deal with them requires an assessment by the best qualified staff regarding the extent and nature of the problem and its effects on institutional operations, other inmates, and staff. A strategy should be broad enough to include both policies designed to deter gang activity and incentive programs to encourage nongang involvement.

**GOOD INTELLIGENCE PROVIDES NECESSARY INFORMATION** To prevent gang activity, a better identification and information system is needed. This includes techniques for detecting early signs of STG activity and determining which inmates are gang members. In states with major or growing STG problems, monitoring of these activities requires a systemwide intelligence unit and an institutional intelligence officer. However, ACA found that these units are not well accepted within many systems and are usually underfunded and staffed.

To monitor these groups, the establishment of specific criteria to designate a group as an STG is required. For example, it is necessary to identify the

[G]roups, gangs, or inmate organizations that have been observed as acting in concert to promote violence, escape, criminal, drug or terrorist activity. . . (ACA, undated, p. 73).

Next, criteria have to be established to identify inmates. These generally may include:

1. Self-admissions by inmates of STG membership
2. Possession of STG paraphernalia, e.g., membership lists, constitutions, insignia, training materials, "hit lists," etc.
3. Information from outside law enforcement, internal investigations, other prisons, and confidential informants

4. Inmate correspondence or outside contacts, e.g., visits from persons with STG affiliations
5. Individual or group STG picture (ACA, undated).

Generally, agencies require two or more criteria to designate an inmate as an STG member. To meet constitutional standards, agencies placing restrictions on these inmates must (1) inform them of their STG status and hold due process hearings, (2) give them an opportunity to appeal the results of this hearing, and (3) have methods for periodic reviews of and reclassification of those who drop out of these groups.

Identifying STGs and their members is the first step in developing an intelligence system, which is the key element in recognizing the threats posed by these groups and in forging a response.

"Intelligence" in the correctional environment is selectively processed information that is of strategic value in making informed decisions regarding security management (Trout and Meko, 1990, p. 16).

As Trout and Meko (1990) note the increasing sophistication of inmates entering our prisons requires that intelligence not be limited to STG-related activity.

[T]his "new" type of inmate [may have] . . . advanced technological skills in illicit communications, computers, security electronics, explosives fabrication, paramilitary tactics, and automatic weaponry . . . [of] greater concern, particularly with the drug cartels, is the specter of extraordinary levels of outside tactical and logistical support. . . . [Security planing must consider] defense against outside assault and the use of helicopters in . . . escape efforts (p. 16).

The complexity of the information required for a prison's intelligence system will vary based on the extent and nature of the problems within that facility. To be effective an intelligence system must be raised from the level of information "kept in the heads" of a few staff to a system that uses computers to organize and store the information. Two types of intelligence—strategic and tactical—comprise a good information system. **Strategic intelligence** focuses on developing a detailed information base about the characteristics of STGs, their members, and activities. More specifically it includes identity of [STGs] . . . membership strength, recruiting efforts, recognition features [e.g.] tattoos . . . skill levels, tactics, outside support, treaties, feuds with other groups . . . foreknowledge of emerging STGS [just entering the system or prison] (Trout and Meko, 1990, p. 18).

Operational or **tactical intelligence** involves informed knowledge of current criminal activity including drug introductions, escapes, planned violence, and work and food stoppages. The following illustrates the value of these processes:

"strategic intelligence" indicated that members of certain domestic terrorist groups were present in [a prison's population] specially one member had been active in . . . escape plots involving outside support. Existing intelligence indicated that his outside group was known to have access to heavy arms, explosives, and coordinated support from other domestic groups. . . . Operations intelligence . . . developed from a confidential informant . . . indicated that yet another violent escape was planned . . . [Based on prior strategic intelligence the agency already had information on the primary domestic terrorist group and other STGs known to be pledged to mutual aid agreements.] [A]nalysis of available information resulted in the hypothesis [that] at least two members of other [STGs] would support the . . . escape effort[s] and [might] . . . participate . . . [Direct surveillance] . . . determined that at least three members of suspected groups were involved . . . [As a result of these intelligence gathering efforts the escape was prevented and the terrorist leader and several members were successfully prosecuted] (Trout and Meko, 1990, pp. 19–20).

Intelligence information may be acquired from a variety of other sources including (1) responsible informants; (2) dropout inmates who are repudiating gang membership (they are usually quite willing to provide information on gang operations and members); and (3) observation of visitors' dress, colors, and home address. Some strategies found effective in Texas have been the designation of (1) intelligence officers for each unit to gather information for the administration and (2) a special prosecutor whose mandate was to aggressively prosecute in-prison violence. Two new statutes that have helped this effort (1) make it a felony for an inmate to possess to a weapon and (2) require that any inmate convicted of a crime serve that sentence consecutively. As Buentello (1992) notes, the intelligence officer system:

let gangs know we no longer were taking a reactive stance. [The result] was an increasing number of gang members willing to provide information. Individual gang members understood that if ordered . . . by their leaders . . . they would have to commit acts of violence and [be] subject to prosecution. As a result they would give information . . . allowing staff to stop potentially violent situations. . . . [Further], as gang members began receiving additional consecutive sentences, more inmates defected from the groups. They no longer believed that being in the gang was an advantage, and they became concerned about being prosecuted and receiving additional time (p. 60).

Finally, the establishment of a national central depository serving as a clearing house and repository for information on STGs, their members, and activities would represent a valuable intelligence resource. Consistent with constitutional requirements, state statutes, and policies, this would involve state and local jurisdictions feeding information on STGs and their members into a centralized computer system, probably under the auspices of a federal agency. This would require a system of review to remove groups as they disband and members as they drop out.[7] Part of this effort would involve centralized screening for interstate transfers of known gang leaders and members so that the inadvertent spread of STGs can be controlled. This can be done through the development of an Interstate Compact Transfer Clearing House (Camp and Camp, 1985; ACA, undated).

**JURISDICTIONS FOLLOWING AN STG SPECIFIC MANAGEMENT APPROACH RESTRICT THE ACTIVITIES OF STG MEMBERS**  To control and make life less comfortable for STGs and their members, jurisdictions adopting an STG specific management approach may place some of the following restrictions on inmates designated as members of these groups (ACA, undated; NIC, 1991):

**Searches.** Strip searches and cell and living area searches are conducted at least once every seven days to control contraband and to look for any STG-related information (e.g., notes, graffiti, lists of customers). Also, some systems use canines trained in detecting drugs and metal detectors to find hidden weapons. Canines are increasingly being used not only in housing units but also in visiting areas. Urinalysis is also used by many systems to control drug use.

**Mail and Telephone Monitoring.** Opening and reading incoming and outgoing (except legal) mail and monitoring and recording telephone calls for the purpose of detecting information on STG-related activity (e.g., incoming contraband, escape attempts, assaults and murders) is carried out.

**Custody Increases.** This can involve reclassification to maximum security or to a special administrative segregation unit to restrict or totally stop STG member contact with the general population. In Texas a policy of removing gang members from the general population and placing them in administrative segregation resulted in reduced anxiety and fear among the general inmate population, and in the number of inmates requesting protective custody and unit transfers (Buentello, 1992). Nevertheless, ACA (undated) cautions that "locking up gang leaders or security threat group members in segregation units creates a void for new leaders to emerge and can lead to continuing disruption within the facility" (p. 2).

**Monitoring of Inmate Accounts.** Like all well-organized criminal groups, STGs do not usually maintain large stashes of money because it can represent proof of their involvement in illicit activities, and in many prison systems money is contraband. These groups use a variety of methods to conduct their business. One method is to have inmates transfer money to the accounts of STG members. Thus monitoring inmate accounts can provide information on STG customers, suppliers, those subject to extortion, and outside sources of funds. Well-organized groups may also maintain outside bank accounts. Monitoring these accounts can furnish details on gang activity and can assist staff in short-circuiting some gang endeavors. For example, a large deposit or withdrawal can indicate a major drug deal is about to "go down." By instituting special security procedures COs may be able to intercept the drugs before they enter the prison (Camp and Camp, 1988).

**Work or Program Limitations.** This can involve restricting STG members from certain activities and requiring ongoing supervision in assigned program areas. STG members may be restricted from participation in any industry programs where weapons can be made or stolen, maintenance activities, and jobs outside the prison's perimeter. Also some prisons may prohibit gangs members or their affiliates from participation in programs offered to the general prison population. Addition-ally, monitoring program assignments can avoid placement of too many STG members in one program so that they gain control of it. When they gain control, they may charge inmates fees to participate or use the program as base for operating their prison rackets (NIC, 1991; Camp and Camp, 1988).

**Restricted Visits.** STG members may have "no contact visits" to restrict the flow of contraband, which, as we noted, can be smuggled into the prison by visitors in body cavities. Visits may be restricted to attorneys and their authorized staff and immediate family members—parents, siblings, and spouses (including common-law wives), and children. This may control the ability of gangs to use intermediaries to pass information between prisons and from outside affiliates.

**Restrictions on Sentence Credits.** STG members may be restricted from receiving meritorious or extra good time and from having any forfeited good time restored. The objective of this is to penalize inmates for membership in STG groups and thereby discourage membership.

**Within and Out-of-State Transfers.** To disrupt and fragment STG operations and communication, some systems separate and isolate gang leaders by transferring them to other prisons.

Out-of-state transfer of prominent gang members is a common control strategy where gangs are either attempting to organize or are not yet fully entrenched in a facility's social structure. [This strategy] ... may help to stop or interrupt gang development and activity.... Where gangs are considered to be well established, out-of-state transfers are used primarily to create a power vacuum or to remove leaders or members who present a substantial danger to the smooth operation of the institution. However, the involved jurisdictions recognize that, while such transfers may relieve them of particularly problematic cases, they have little impact on their gang situation as a whole. In addition, some correctional administrators believe that the policy of transferring gang members to other jurisdictions [or facilities] fosters the spread of gangs to receiving agencies [or prisons] and may lead to the formation of nationwide [or system-wide] gang organizations (NIC, 1991, pp. 9–10).

**PROGRAMS AND ACTIVITIES CAN REDUCE TIME DEVOTED TO GANG ACTIVITIES** Institutions must also develop more programs, particularly work programs that provide inmates with a more attractive alternative to involvement in gang activities. It is important to recognize that idle inmates have nothing else to do but plot ways to subvert the prison administration. Programs should be designed to provide inmates with more benefits than they receive from the gang reward structure. One reward that gangs can't provide is early release, which can be extremely attractive for inmates with relatively short sentences (Camp and Camp, 1988). For long termers a meaningful work program with reasonable monetary compensation and the possibility for learning and advancement could be an effective incentive to avoid gang involvement. In STG-dominated prisons, prison programs must be closely supervised to prevent these groups from gaining control of them.

**CHANGES IN HOUSING ARRANGEMENTS CAN ALSO HELP** STG members, like other inmates, spend a considerable amount of time in housing areas and transact a substantial amount of their business there. Control strategies for managing these units include changes in their design and size. Smaller institutions and housing units make control of all inmates easier. Inasmuch as gang strength is directly related to the amount of space they control, staff must control housing units. This requires units designed to facilitate maximum staff observation and supervision. Older prisons may require renovations, such as subdividing older cell blocks to reduce their size. For large multitiered cells blocks, flooring over these units to divide them vertically into two or more floors or inserting vertical barriers can reduce their size (Camp and Camp, 1988).

At new maximum security prisons in California smaller housing units have become an integral part of control strategies at this custody level. In both California and Washington this design has resulted in a reduction in the number of inmate requests for placement in protective custody. Smaller units also permit the placement of nongang inmates in units where they will not be pressured to join gangs. Housing units with single cells or rooms also serve to limit movement and facilitate better supervision and control. "Closed-cell fronts" also provide protection for inmates and staff from assaults (e.g., with spear-like devices) by cell occupants when passing along narrow walkways by open-front cells. The chances of inmates locked in their cells being fire bombed or subject to other types of

assaults are also reduced (Camp and Camp, 1988). This involves the use of strong acrylic shields over existing cells and the use of solid doors on rooms.

The availability of sufficient space to isolate inmates, particularly STG members, who are behavior problems plays a major role in managing violence. While all institutions require special detention/administrative segregation units, insufficient space to segregate violent inmates reduces the ability of staff to maintain control of the prison (Camp and Camp, 1988).

**CLOSE SUPERVISION AND STAFFING OF HOUSING UNITS IS ESSENTIAL** Prison physical design is of little value if a lack of adequate supervision permits gangs to control housing units. Although the amount of direct contact and interaction with gang members will vary, continuous supervision is generally required in order to maintain good control (Camp and Camp, 1988).

**Unit management** provides an effective means of increasing accountability and of obtaining information on gang plans and activities. This involves (1) assigning staff permanently to housing units; (2) giving them decision-making responsibility; and (3) placing staff in direct contact with inmates as opposed to supervising them from a remote location such as a control booth (Camp and Camp, 1988). Increasing staff/inmate contact by placing them in closer proximity for longer periods of time can also help. Staff need to be trained to be sensitive to "emerging security threats" so they can develop sight recognition skills to detect and deter them (Trout and Meko, 1990, p. 16). This training enables staff to perceive subtle changes in inmates, which may be indicative of impending assaults and other activities:

> hoarding of canteen [goods] and other preparations for lockdowns; unusual huddles; extreme quiet or extreme noise; rise in weapons confiscations; increases in requests for protection/or transfers; unusual disciplines; fewer inmates going to meals and programs; more sick calls and 'lay-ins'; parades and chants by gangs; more classification hearing requests; and increases in requests for personal interviews (Camp and Camp, 1988, p. 48).

Unit management also facilitates the development of trust between staff and inmates, which can result in staff receiving useful information for preventing certain gang activities. Staff can also thwart the efforts of gangs to recruit new members by orienting new inmates with no prior STG affiliation to the disadvantages of gang membership including its problems and risks, the privileges available to nongang inmates, and ways of handling pressure to join and avoiding extortion (Camp and Camp, 1988).

## ALTERNATIVES FOR NONGANG MEMBERS

Finally, there is the question of providing the general inmate population of gang/STG-dominated prisons with the level of security mandated by federal courts under the eighth amendment. The prison's general population should not have to go to protective custody to feel safe and secure (ACA, undated). The idea is to provide inmates an opportunity to make a rational choice as to whether to join an STG. This can be accomplished by a prison system that has a series of prisons with decreasing levels of control. At one end of the spectrum would be an "STG prison" housing no more than 500 inmates. It would have a high level of direct supervision by staff, house inmates in small units, greatly curtail opportunities for inmate contact, and have few privileges and strict regulations. At the opposite end might be a village-type, minimum security prison providing inmates with opportunities for involvement in a wide variety of educational, vocational, industrial, and recreational programs. This range of institutions would give offenders facing terms of 10 to 25 years a choice of how they want to spend their time (McConville, 1985).

The question facing prison administrators regarding STGs revolves around the extent to which they are willing to recognize and exert control over them. As we have seen in this chapter, a number of effective responses can be employed to make these prisons with STGs safer and more manageable. Finally, the likelihood is that the number of STGs will grow since there are indications that street gang members presently entering prison are more likely to form their own group than to join established groups.

---

### ENDNOTES

**1.** The ACA (undated) decided to use this concept in their research for three reasons. "[First their] advisory group concluded that the word 'gangs' could be misleading because it had many different meanings. [Second their] . . . advisory group further recognized that a select number of correctional administrators deny "gangs" exist in their system. [Third because] the term "security threat group" would be more universally accepted and would facilitate a higher response rate to project inquiries than the term 'gangs.' " (pp 1–2). The differences between the ACA conceptualization of STGs and the narrower definition of gangs by Camp and Camp may not make the data from these two studies entirely comparable.
**2.** The issue of the exercise of religious freedom in prison is dealt with in Chapter 20.
**3.** See the reference list for their reports.
**4.** Using the ACA directory, all forty-three mega-jails (1000+) were polled because they resembled prisons. Additionally 10 jails were randomly selected from jails designated by the size of their inmate population as small (0–249), medium (250–499), and large (500–1000). Responses were received from forty-six jails: thirty-one mega, five large, five medium, and five small (ACA, undated).

**5.** See Chapter 16 for a discussion of the restrictions on inmate correspondence and Chapter 15 (the *Turner v. Safley* decision) for a discussion on the Supreme Court ruling related to inmate-to-inmate correspondence.
**6.** These approaches are ideal types so that rarely if ever are there any systems that actually hold these views in their pure form.
**7.** Other issues involved in the establishment of this system would include determining access criteria; developing agreed on definitions and criteria for the veracity of information; and dealing with the problems of gangs with the same name but who are not affiliated, like the Aryan Brotherhood.

### CHAPTER RECAP

**Inmate Gangs Became a Problem in the 1960s**
Conditions That Permit Gangs to Operate in Prisons
Different Terms Have Been Used to Describe Inmate
   Groups
   The NIC Has Developed Criteria to Identify Disruptive Groups
**Organization and Development of STGs and Inmate Gangs**
The Proportion of Gang Members Is Increasing
Prison Gangs Have Developed According to Five General Patterns

The Development of the Mexican Mafia Reflects a
   Homeboy Pattern
Conflict Between Groups and the Need for Self-
   Protection Can Spawn Gangs
Outside Gang Members in Illinois Prisons Formed
   Gangs on the Inside
Prison Gang Members Entering New Institutions
   Formed Gang Chapters
Copy Cat Groups Emerged in Some Prisons
The Level of Organization of Prison Gangs Varies
   Membership Is Based on One or More Factors
   Gang Structure Can Follow Various Patterns
   Gang Members Can Fall Into One of Several Catego-
   ries
   Gang Codes of Conduct Help to Control Member
   Behavior
The Recruitment Process Varies from Gang to Gang
   Gang Initiations May Require Violence
Group Operations Are Defined by Symbols, Power, Ac-
   tivities, and Communication
   Gang Membership Entails a Lifetime Commitment
   Gang Identification Includes a Variety of Symbols
   Gangs Have Methods for Perpetuating Their Exist-
   ence and Power
   Trafficking in the Inmate Economy Serves to Perpetu-
   ate the Gang
   Open Lines of Communication Are Necessary to
   Maintain Continuity
Gang Membership Has Several Benefits
Some Gangs Have Street Affiliates, With a Few Meeting
   the Criteria for Organized Crime Groups
**Prison Gangs Cause a Number of Problems**
Problems Occur as a Result of Gangs' "Business" Ac-
   tivities
Prison Administrators May Be Ambivalent About Rec-
   ognizing the Existence of Gangs
Inmate-to-Inmate Problems Are Also Created by Gangs
**Control of Prison Gangs is Achieved in Various Ways**
Two Views Characterize How Gangs are Dealt with by
   Prison Administration
   One Basis for Gang Policy Is Membership
   Another Basis for Gang Policy Is Behavior
   The Reaction to Gangs and STGs Often Follows
   Three Stages
Several Factors Dictate Strategies for Controlling Gangs
   The First Priority Is to Establish a Policy and Strategy
   Good Intelligence Provides Necessary Information
   Jurisdictions Following an STG Specific Management
   Approach Restrict the Activities of the STG Mem-
   bers
   Programs and Activities Can Reduce Time Devoted
   to Gang Activities
   Changes in Housing Arrangements Can Also Help
   Close Supervision and Staffing of Housing Units Is
   Essential
**Alternatives for Nongang Members**

## REVIEW QUESTIONS

**1.** What criteria have been developed by the National Institute of Corrections to help in the identification of disruptive groups in the prison?
**2.** Discuss and compare the two patterns of prison gang development.
**3.** List and describe the various categories of gang membership.
**4.** What are the various gang business activities and what purposes do they serve in the "life" of the gang?
**5.** Enumerate and discuss the problems that gangs pose for prison administration and staff.
**6.** What are the major strategies involved in gang control?

## TEST YOUR KNOWLEDGE

**1.** Prison gangs first developed in the state of
   **a.** Illinois
   **b.** Washington
   **c.** California
   **d.** New York
**2.** Which of the statements below regarding prison groups is one of the NIC criteria for the identification of gangs?
   **a.** Has an organized leadership with a clear-cut chain of command.
   **b.** Engages in criminal or threatening activities.
   **c.** Places emphasis on member loyalty and group unity.
   **d.** All of the above are NIC criteria.
**3.** Which of these prison gangs was the first to develop?
   **a.** The Black Guerrilla Family
   **b.** La Nuestra Familia
   **c.** The Blackstone Rangers
   **d.** The Mexican Mafia
**4.** Which of the following prison gangs meet the President's Commission on Organized Crime criteria for an organized crime group?
   **a.** The Texas Syndicate
   **b.** The Outlaw Bikers
   **c.** The Black Panthers
   **d.** The Bloods and Crips
**5.** A prison that adopts gang membership as a strategy to control these groups takes which of the following positions?
   **a.** Allows gangs the same privileges as other groups.
   **b.** Gangs are organized groups and are therefore a threat to administration.
   **c.** The prison is viewed as a community and everyone must coexist.
   **d.** Does not call for the segregation of gangs.

# PART FOUR

## CORRECTIONAL CLIENTELE

# CHAPTER 11

# MALE AND SPECIAL CATEGORY OFFENDERS

■ **LEARNING OBJECTIVES**

*After completion of this chapter, you should be able to:*
**1.** Contrast the composition of the U.S. prison population to that of the U.S. population in general and explain why differences exist.
**2.** Describe six major background characteristics that are common among prison inmates.
**3.** Identify the problems that special category offenders pose for correctional institutions.
**4.** Outline the major issues involved in the treatment of mentally disordered inmates.
**5.** Define the label "mentally handicapped" and explain the problems associated with inmates who have this condition.
**6.** Explain why the sex offender presents such a difficult problem to the correctional system.
**7.** Contrast the characteristics and special needs of mature and youthful offenders.
**8.** Explain how the characteristics and problems of long-term offenders differ from those of other inmates.

■ **KEY TERMS AND CONCEPTS**

Career criminals
Civil commitment procedures
Cottage industries
Criminally insane
Functionally illiterate
Jitterbug
Long-term offenders
Mainstreaming
Mature offenders
Mentally disordered
Mentally handicapped
Organic disorders
Pedophiles
Psychotic disorders
Special management
Youthful offender

While there are many ways to categorize the prison population (e.g., based on the offenses committed), we have chosen to describe inmates by gender (i.e., adult male, adult female). The rationale for this is based on the different problems that men and women bring to corrections. This chapter deals with the male segment of the inmate population and Chapter 12 discusses females. However, before examining these groups we will briefly review some salient characteristics of the general population from which they come.

## U.S. PRISON POPULATION DIFFERS FROM THE GENERAL U.S. POPULATION

The population of the United States is an aggregate of many racial, ethnic, and national groups that lend uniqueness to the character of our society. This is manifested in many customs, languages and accents, dress, lifestyles, food preferences, and styles of personal interaction. This population is also characterized by wide variations in socioeconomic class. According to government figures, about 10% of the population lives in poverty, an income below $14,228 for a family of four (Bureau of the Census, 1993a). The lowest segment of the poverty group is sometimes referred to as the "underclass," and is characterized by extreme poverty and little hope of bettering itself. Most of the population falls within the middle socioeconomic levels or higher, has a median age of 32, and is composed of approximately 49% males and 51% females. While it is also predominantly non-Hispanic white (about 76%), this segment of the population is far from homogeneous because it consists of people of many different national origins. The nonwhite group is largely composed of blacks (about 12%). Native-born African-Americans are the predominant segment of this group, but it also includes blacks from other countries (e.g., Jamaica and Haiti). Other nonwhites, which account for approximately 3% of the national population, include Orientals (Chinese, Japanese, Vietnamese, etc.) and Native Americans. Hispanics, who comprise about 9% of the population, also include individuals from many nations (mainly Puerto Rico and Mexico), who can also be separated according to race. The nonwhite and Hispanic groups are overrepresented in the lowest socioeconomic classes (Bureau of the Census, 1993b).

## The Prison Population Is Not Representative of the General Population[1]

In contrast to the figures just given, the prison population is predominantly male (94%), poorly educated, underemployed, has lived in or on the edge of poverty, is disproportionately young, and is black and Hispanic. However, trends during the past twelve years show that the average age of the prison population is rising even while the number of juveniles entering the system is increasing (Snell, 1993). These characteristics merit close attention and study so that prisons can appropriately plan for the special needs of this changing population.

**THE PROPORTIONS OF FEMALE, OLDER, HISPANIC, AND UNMARRIED INMATES HAVE BEEN INCREASING**   Surveys of inmates in state prisons in 1979, 1986, and 1991 showed that the prison population almost tripled between 1979 and 1991. Table 11.1, which compares these three time periods, shows that while there are many similarities among the offenders in these time periods, the data shows some differences and suggest some interesting trends (Innes, 1988; Snell, 1993, Beck, Gilliard, Greenfeld, Harlow, Hester, Jankowski, Snell, Stephan & Morton, 1993). The inmate profiles show that they remained overwhelmingly male, slightly under 50% were black, and were likely to be unemployed or underemployed at the time of arrest. The trends that can be noted in Table 11.1 include:

1. An increasing proportion of female inmates. Although the number of females in prison is still relatively small their representation in the prisons increased (and has continued to do so). Between 1980 and 1995 their proportion in the prisons has increased by about 50% (Beck and Gilliard, 1995.]
2. There was a very substantial increase in the proportion of Hispanics in the prisons during this time period while the proportion of whites went down and that of blacks remained about the same. The growth in the proportion of Hispanic inmates is likely due to their larger representation in the U.S. population.

TABLE 11.1   Characteristics of State Prison Inmates

|  | 1979 | 1986 | 1991 |
|---|---|---|---|
| **Prison Population** | | | |
| Facilities | | 903 | 1,239 |
| Inmates | 274,563 | 450,416 | 711,643 |
| **Sex** | % | % | % |
| Male | 96.0 | 95.6 | 95.0 |
| Female | 4.0 | 4.4 | 5.0 |
| **Race** | | | |
| White Non-Hispanic | 49.6* | 49.7* | 35.0 |
| Black Non-Hispanic | 47.8+ | 46.9+ | 46.0 |
| Other Non-Hispanic | 2.6 | 3.4 | 2.0 |
| Hispanic | 9.9 | 12.6 | 17.0 |
| **Age** | | | |
| 17 or younger | 0.8 | 0.5 | 1.0 |
| 18–24 | 35.6 | 26.7 | 21.0 |
| 25–34 | 42.4 | 45.7 | 46.0 |
| 35–44 | 13.8 | 19.4 | 23.0 |
| 45–54 | 5.1 | 5.2 | 7.0 |
| 55–64 | 1.7 | 1.8 | 2.0 |
| 65 or older | .5 | .6 | 1.0 |
| **Marital Status** | | | |
| Married | 22.4 | 20.3 | 18.0 |
| Widowed | 2.3 | 1.9 | 2.0 |
| Divorced | 16.9 | 18.1 | 19.0 |
| Separated | 8.6 | 6.0 | 6.0 |
| Never married | 57.9 | 53.7 | 55.0 |

|  | 1979 | 1986 | 1991 |
|---|---|---|---|
| **Education** | | | |
| 8th grade or less | 61.6 | 21.0 | 19.0 |
| Some high school | | 51.0 | 46.0 |
| High school graduate | 38.4 | 18.0 | 22.0 |
| Some college or more | | 11.0 | 12.0 |
| **Work Before Arrest** | | | |
| Employed | 70.5 | 69.0 | 67.0 |
| Full time | 57.4 | 57.0 | 55.0 |
| Part time | 11.6 | 12.0 | 12.0 |
| Not employed | 29.5 | 31.0 | 33.0 |
| Looking for work | 14.0 | 18.0 | 16.0 |
| Not looking | 15.5 | 13.0 | 16.0 |
| **Income** (Annual income for inmates free at least a year) | | | |
| No Income | 1.6 | 1.6 | 3.0 |
| Less than $3,000 | 24.5 | 25.0 | 19.0 |
| $ 3,000–$4,999 | 37.9 | 12.0 | 10.0 |
| $ 5,000–$9,999 | | 22.0 | 21.0 |
| $10,000–14,999 | 36.0 | 16.0 | 17.0 |
| $15,000–$24,999 | | 13.0 | 16.0 |
| $25,000 or more | | 11.0 | 15.0 |
| **Veteran Status** | | | |
| Veterans | 23.8 | 20.0 | 16.0 |
| Vietnam era | — | 5.0 | 3.0 |
| Other | — | 15.0 | 14.0 |
| Nonveterans | 76.2 | 80.0 | 84.0 |

*This includes Hispanic whites.
+This includes Hispanic blacks.

*Source:* C.A. Innes (Jan., 1988) *Profile of State Prison Inmates, 1986,* Washington, D.C.: U.S. Department of Justice.
Beck et al. (Mar., 1993) *Survey of Prison Inmates, 1991* Washington, D.C.: U.S. Department of Justice.

**3.** There was a noticeable increase in the age of the prison population. The thirty-five and over age group grew from about one-fifth to about one-third of the inmate population and this included increases in the proportions of all the older age categories.

**4.** There was a steady decline in the proportion of inmates who were married, matching a trend that is evident in the free society.

**5.** There was a noticeable drop in the educational level of the inmates during the early 1980s, but this level rebounded somewhat by 1991.

These surveys also show interesting trends regarding the distribution of offenses for which these inmates were imprisoned. Drug-related offenses constituted a larger and larger portion of the reason for incarceration over this time period. In fact, other research shows that in 1992, the 102,000 commitments for drug offenses almost equaled those for property crimes (104,300) and exceeded those for violent crimes (95,300). Between 1980 and 1992, increased drug admissions accounted for close to half of the growth in commitments (Gilliard and Beck, 1994). The characteristics of the 1990s prison population are summarized in Figure 11.1.

## Inmates are Disproportionately Young, Male, and from Minority Groups

Young minority males constitute the largest proportion of the prison population. Inmates are likely

FIGURE 11.1 **Characteristics of the Prison Population, 1991**

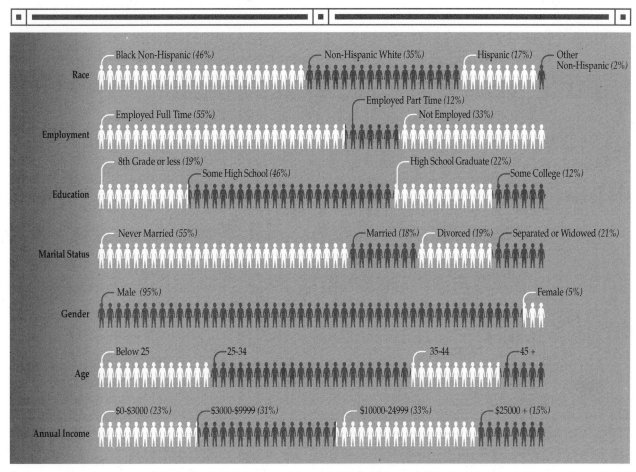

*Source:* Data taken from Beck et al. (March, 1993). *Survey of Prison Inmates, 1991.* Washington, D.C.: U.S. Department of Justice.

to come from poor, disorganized, or dysfunctional families, to be recidivists, and to have a violent crime in their criminal histories.

**MOST PERSONS ARRESTED FOR CRIMINAL BE-HAVIOR ARE MALE** In the United States, as in other countries, men are arrested far more frequently than are women. This disparity has existed historically and has been true for almost all offenses. Current statistics show that men account for about four out of five of all persons arrested and of the arrests for index crimes; almost nine out of ten of the arrests for index crimes of violence; and three-fourths of the arrests for index property crimes [Federal Bureau of Investigation (FBI), 1994]. At the end of 1993 men made up almost 19 out of every 20 of all inmates in the United States (Gilliard and Beck, 1994).

**YOUNGER PEOPLE MORE OFTEN COMMIT CRIMES** Table 11.2 shows that almost 48% of all persons arrested for serious (index) crimes in 1993 were under 21. It also shows the proportion of offenders in the various age groups. Arrest rates in general peak at an early age and then decline precipitously (FBI, 1994). However, they peak and decline earlier for property offenses than for violent offenses (see Figure 11.2). Regardless of age, the proportion of offenders sentenced to prison is greater for violent offenses than for other types of crimes. For property crimes, particularly burglary, the proportion of younger inmates is greater, whereas for violent crimes the proportion of inmates rises with age (Snell, 1993).

Older recidivists are likely to be sent to prison for less serious offenses because of their prior records. However, as offenders grow older they

TABLE 11.2  **Male Arrests Distribution by Age, 1993**

| Offense Charged | Under 18 | 18–20 | 21–24 | 25–29 | 30–34 | 35–49 | 50+ |
|---|---|---|---|---|---|---|---|
| Murder and nonnegligent manslaughter | 3,093 | 4,155 | 3,693 | 2,541 | 1,708 | 2,437 | 748 |
| Forcible rape | 5,212 | 3,848 | 4,718 | 5,282 | 4,854 | 6,679 | 1,514 |
| Robbery | 39,493 | 25,637 | 22,591 | 21,240 | 15,632 | 14,451 | 1,084 |
| Aggravated assault | 55,731 | 45,139 | 56,958 | 62,101 | 56,388 | 79,035 | 17,205 |
| Burglary | 104,871 | 49,126 | 39,131 | 38,618 | 33,404 | 36,326 | 3,226 |
| Larceny-theft | 269,690 | 107,458 | 90,579 | 97,980 | 97,557 | 147,749 | 31,645 |
| Motor vehicle theft | 66,117 | 25,884 | 18,297 | 15,334 | 11,469 | 11,588 | 1,243 |
| Arson | 6,975 | 1,325 | 1,108 | 1,056 | 1,111 | 1,704 | 459 |
| Violent crime[a] | 103,529 | 78,779 | 87,960 | 91,164 | 78,582 | 102,602 | 20,551 |
| Percent distribution[b] | 18.4 | 13.9 | 15.6 | 16.2 | 14.0 | 18.2 | 3.8 |
| Property crime[c] | 446,653 | 183,793 | 149,115 | 152,988 | 143,541 | 197,367 | 36,573 |
| Percent distribution[b] | 34.1 | 14.1 | 11.4 | 11.7 | 11.0 | 15.1 | 2.8 |
| Crime index total[d] | 550,182 | 262,572 | 237,075 | 244,152 | 222,123 | 299,969 | 57,124 |
| Percent distribution[b] | 29.4 | 14.0 | 12.6 | 13.0 | 11.9 | 16.1 | 3.0 |

[a]Violent crimes are offenses of murder, forcible rape, robbery, and aggravated assault.
[b]Because of rounding, the percentages may not add to total.
[c]Property crimes are offenses of burglary, larceny-theft, motor vehicle theft, and arson.
[d]Includes arson.

*Source:* Federal Bureau of Investigation (1994). *Crime in the United States 1993 (Uniform Crime Report).* Washington D.C.: U.S. Department of Justice.

FIGURE 11.2  **Arrest Rates for Male Inmates 1983–1985**

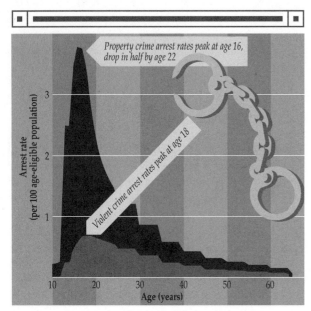

*Source:* U.S. Department of Justice (1988). *Report on to the Nation on Crime and Justice,* Washington, D.C.: U.S. Department of Justice.

commit proportionally fewer crimes and pose a lesser threat to society than younger criminals. This is noteworthy because the currently popular "three strikes and you're out" laws would most likely be applied to the older age group and not affect younger (and much more criminally active) offenders as much. The age distribution of the inmate population in the adult prison system is truncated because many offenders under eighteen are housed in juvenile institutions. However, with the increasingly violent nature of juvenile crime and a growing public intolerance of it, many violent juveniles will likely be tried as adults and sent to adult prisons.

**MINORITY GROUPS ARE DISPROPORTIONATELY INCARCERATED**  Any casual observer of American prisons would be struck by the disproportionate numbers of black and other minority individuals housed there. Blacks accounted for 43.4% of the jail inmates and 46% of the prison inmates; Hispanics accounted for 14.2 and 16.8 %, respectively, in 1991 (Maguire, Pastore, and Flanagan, 1993).

Langan (1991) estimated that there had been an eightfold increase in black admissions to prisons between 1926 and 1986, which resulted in a doubling of the proportion of blacks relative to whites. Although white admissions increased threefold during this period, their overall proportions in prison decreased. In the 1980s and early 1990s the black male incaceration rate more than doubled, rising from 1111 per 100,000 in 1980 to 2920 in 1993. In comparison the white rate went from 168 per 100,000 to 372 per 100,000 (Gilliard and Beck, 1995).

A recent study of the New York State Correctional System [Correctional Association of New York (CANY), 1990] found that almost one-fourth of the young black men in that state were under some form of correctional supervision with 11% being held in jail or prison. This represents more than twice the number of black male full-time college enrollees in the state. For Hispanic males, 12% were under some form of correctional supervision with 6% being held in jails or prisons. Thus, African-American and Hispanic young men are twenty-three and eleven times more likely than young white males to be imprisoned. The CANY study concludes that drug arrest policies that concentrate on "crime in the streets" rather than on "crime in the suites" and the deteriorating social conditions that affect poor minorities have contributed most directly to this situation. The proportion of young black males under some form of correctional supervision has continued to increase. A 1995 study showed that the figure had grown to one in three nationwide (Butterfield, 1995).

## INMATES OFTEN HAVE HISTORIES OF FAMILY DISORGANIZATION AND ARE AT THE LOWER END OF THE ECONOMIC SCALE

There is controversy regarding the impact of certain sociodemographic factors (e.g., disrupted families, abuse, family criminality, educational insufficiency) on criminal behavior. However, it is probably fair to say that individuals with many of these characteristics are at high risk for involvement in crime.

The proportion of prison inmates raised in families with only one parent or with other relatives is about two and a half times the proportion found in the general population (Beck et al., 1993). Several studies also show that many inmates report having been abused extensively as children (Mouzakitis, 1981; Straus, Gelles, and Steinmetz, 1980). Moreover, regarding overall abuse, females are more likely to report being victimized than males. A 1991 inmate survey found that three times as many female inmates (43%) reported being victims of physical or sexual abuse compared with males (Snell, 1993). The role models provided by family members also appear to play a part in an individual becoming a criminal (Glueck and Glueck,

1974). In 1991 almost four out of ten inmates had an immediate family member [parent, sibling (almost always brothers), spouse or child] who had been incarcerated, with blacks outnumbering both whites and Hispanics (Beck et al., 1993). Less than one-fifth of the prison inmates were married compared with almost half of the general population (Snell, 1993). About one-quarter of all inmates were divorced or separated; more than half had never been married. However, more than two-thirds of the females and 56% of the males had children. Males (90%) more often reported these children to be living with the other parent or a grandparent than did women (50%) (Beck et al., 1993). Just over one-third of the inmate population had completed high school compared with 85% of U.S. males between the ages of 20 and 29 (Beck et al., 1993). Additionally, one-fourth of the inmate population reported having received a general equivalency diploma, but one-fifth had not gone beyond eighth grade.

Inmates also tend to more often be employed in blue collar occupations than the general population (two-thirds versus one-third) (BJS, 1988), be concentrated in the lower socioeconomic groups, and have experienced high levels of unemployment. Beck et al. (1993) found that 45% of state prison inmates in 1991 were either unemployed or underemployed before arrest. Forty percent of the inmates in one study had either never worked or had held a variety of short-term jobs (Rolph and Chaikin, 1987). On the average this group had committed more crimes than groups with a more stable employment history. Finally, an estimated 38% of the women and 13% of the male inmate population in 1991 reported receiving some type of support from social security, welfare, or charity before being admitted to prison. More than half of these inmates had a preprison income of less than $10,000 (Beck et al., 1993).

## MANY INMATES HAVE COMMITTED VIOLENT CRIMES

The 1991 inmate survey found that about half of the inmates were in prison for violent offenses. Of this group, 17% had previously been incarcerated for a violent crime, and 13% of those presently in for a property crime had been previously sentenced for a violent offense (Beck et al., 1993). Violent offenders did not differ significantly from nonviolent offenders with respect to sex, age, marital status, or education. However, they were more likely to be black (51%) than nonviolent offenders (42%). Almost 60% of the violent offenders were robbers who had victimized strangers, and an additionl one-fourth were imprisoned for a homicide (Innes and Greenfeld, 1990).

**EXTENSIVE PRIOR ARREST HISTORIES INCREASE THE LIKELIHOOD OF FUTURE RECIDIVISM**   An often used measure of the success of prison programs, or even imprisonment itself, is recidivism. Beck and Shipley (1989) followed more than 108,000 state prisoners for three years after they were released in 1983. They found that close to two-thirds were rearrested during that period with 46% reconvicted and 41% returned to prison or jail. The majority had been repeat offenders before their release in 1983. About 15% of the rearrests were for violent offenses. Recidivism rates were highest in the first year and among males, blacks, Hispanics, high school dropouts, younger releasees, and those with extensive priors. Most were rearrested for crimes similar to those for which they had been previously imprisoned. A more recent self-report survey of inmates in 1991 found that 60% had been incarcerated in the past, and for the vast majority this had been within five years prior to their current offense (Beck *et al.*, 1993).

## SPECIAL CATEGORY OFFENDERS

Many inmates have characteristics, problems, and/or needs that set them apart from others in the prison population. As a result, there are many distinctive categories of inmates. We have decided to examine four inmate groups that represent significant problems for corrections: (1) inmates with some form of psychiatric or psychological disability that exists in combination with criminal behavior (e.g., mental disturbance or retardation); (2) younger versus mature inmates; (3) inmates with physical or medical conditions; and (4) inmates incarcerated for long terms (ten or more years). We recognize that we are not covering all special inmate categories, but with these four groups we can provide a perspective on the management approaches used to deal with special types of inmates, the problems they pose to prison personnel, and the adjustments and accommodations made by them to prison living. We also recognize that they may overlap somewhat and will also apply to women.

### Inmates with Psychological or Behavioral Disorders Can Be Management Problems

Inmates in this category include the psychologically disturbed, the retarded, and various classes of sexual offenders. They often require some form of **special management** because many may act unpredictably and/or in bizarre ways. These offenders suffer from disorders that have emotional, intellectual, cognitive, and/or behavioral ramifications. Their disorders result in behavior or mental states that tend to place them at greater than normal risk of being victimized or otherwise getting into trouble (e.g., disregarding rules). They can also engage in unpredictable or violent behavior, placing other inmates and staff at risk of injury or worse. Thus, they may need specialized help and programs to function within the prison.

**PUBLIC POLICY REGARDING THE MENTALLY DISORDERED HAS CHANGED OVER THE YEARS** We will use the term **mentally disordered** to describe those individuals who are classed as mentally or emotionally disturbed. The treatment of mentally disordered individuals has varied throughout American history, usually due to some combination of the treatment philosophy and economics of the era. In the 1700s, families tried to keep disordered individuals at home, sending them to almshouses when they became too unmanageable. In these facilities, they were likely to be locked in cellars or attics (Rothman, 1971). During the 1800s, Dorthea Dix toured prisons and other institutions holding the mentally disordered and concluded they could not receive appropriate care in prisons. Her efforts resulted in the development of institutions specifically for the mentally disordered. From 1860 until approximately 1970 there were separate institutions for the severely mentally disordered and often for those who were **criminally insane.**

In the 1950s the development of antipsychotic drugs eventually led to an emphasis on community-based treatment, and many mental hospitals were closed or reduced their services and patient caseloads. One outcome of this has been that many former mental patients become homeless street people who, when not taking their medication, may engage in behavior that makes them public nuisances (e.g., screaming, starting fires, urinating and defecating on the street, and accosting and assaulting people). As a result, this sometimes brings them into contact with the criminal justice system and they may be placed in jails or prisons.

**SOME INMATES SUFFER FROM A VARIETY OF SERIOUS MENTAL DISORDERS** In the Diagnostic and Statistical Manual (DSM-IV) published by the American Psychiatric Association (1994), mental disorders can roughly be divided into **psychotic disorders** including the various forms of schizophrenia, severe mood disorders, and various **organic disorders;** less serious disorders formerly called neuroses, which include anxiety, depression, somatoform, and dissociative disorders; and a variety of other disorders that include personality disorders, sexual disorders, and adjustment disorders. The psychotic disorders represent the most serious psychological disturbances, whereas antisocial personality disorders pose the greatest crime problems.

According to Jemelka, Rahman, and Trupin (1993), lack of agreement regarding the definition of mental disorders and variations in the manner in which inmates are classified, diagnosed, and tested have made it difficult to determine the number of offenders with mental disorders. After reviewing studies on the incidence of mental disorders among inmates, they found two that provided a better basis for estimating this population size because they directly assess the extent of mental illness through diagnostic interviews.

Extrapolating from a probability sample of 413 California inmates, it was estimated that 14.1% of them were severely mentally disturbed (i.e., could be diagnosed as having severe organic brain syndrome, schizophrenia, a major depressive disorder, or a bipolar disorder). Somewhat over half of this group was showing symptoms of their disturbances at the time of the study while the rest were not actively symptomatic (Independent Research Consortium, 1989).

A second study tested 3332 inmates and found that 8% had severe psychiatric disabilities requiring mental health treatment. An additional 16% were diagnosed as having significant psychiatric disabilities needing periodic services (Steadman, Fabisiak, and Dvoskin 1987). After reviewing studies of the incidence of mental disorders among prison inmates, Jemelka *et al.* (1993) concluded that "it is clear that the best methodological studies suggest that at any given time 10 to 15 percent of state prison populations are suffering from a major

mental disorder and are in need of the kinds of psychiatric services associated with these illnesses" (p. 11). These rates are five to six times higher than those found in the general population.

## Prisons Have Some Mentally Handicapped Inmates Who Require Special Programming

The **mentally handicapped** (retarded) constitute another group who may require special services and programs in or out of prison. As a group, they appear to commit crimes at about the same rate as nonhandicapped people. However, they may be overrepresented in correctional systems because they tend to be disproportionately poor and quite naive regarding their rights. As inmates, the mentally handicapped present special management problems including illiteracy; lower levels of understanding of concepts, rules, and correctional regulations; being more prone to victimization and more susceptible to manipulation by others; and poor impulse control.

**THERE ARE DIFFERENT LEVELS OF RETARDATION** The most widely accepted definition of mental retardation is that developed by the American Association on Mental Deficiency (AAMD). This definition states that mental retardation is based on ". . . significantly subaverage general intellectual functioning existing concurrently with deficits in adaptive behavior. . ." (1983, p. 1). For purposes of measuring the deficit in intellectual functioning for retardation, an IQ level below 70 is the criterion.[2] Approximately 2.3% of the general population of the United States is identified as retarded. Four levels of retardation are recognized, but only individuals from the highest two levels—the mildly retarded and the moderately retarded—are usually found in correctional institutions (Garcia and Steele, 1988). This is because the limited mental capacity of the lowest two categories makes it difficult to prove criminal intent (DeVolentine, 1993).

Mildly retarded individuals have IQs ranging from 55 to 69 [based upon a Wechsler Adult Intelligence Scale (WAIS) IQ] and can essentially function on an independent basis. As adults, if they have received appropriate training and education, they can often hold a job, marry, raise children, speak fluently, read easy material, and do simple arithmetic. More than 93% of all people who are labeled as retarded are in this category. Moderately retarded individuals have IQs between 40 and 54 (based on a WAIS IQ) and can learn to care for themselves but are not usually fully independent. As adults they can work in sheltered workshops, rarely marry or become parents, can learn to care for their own needs, read a few words, and carry out simple tasks. Very few of the severely or profoundly retarded (IQ 39 or below) are likely to be in prison because they usually require placement in special institutions for the retarded.

**MENTALLY RETARDED INDIVIDUALS TEND TO BE OVERREPRESENTED IN THE PRISON POPULATION**   The proportion of mentally retarded inmates in U.S. prisons has been difficult to determine because the manner in which this condition is measured varies from state to state. If IQs are derived from a group test the number of persons labeled as retarded will be higher than if an individual test (e.g., the WAIS) is used (Conley, Luckasson, and Bouthilet, 1992). Thus, states using group tests to evaluate inmate IQs will report a greater number of retarded inmates. According to Conley *et al.* (1992) about 2% of the prison population (14,500) is retarded, and 12,550 other retarded criminals are held in facilities for the retarded. Thus, proportionally there are about one and one-half times as many retarded offenders in prisons and other facilities as are found in the general population. The major reasons for the overrepresentation of the retarded in correctional populations include the fact that they are much more likely to be poor and thus to live in high crime areas; cannot think quickly so are more likely to get caught; confess more readily and less often plea bargain so are more likely to be convicted and receive longer sentences; serve a much greater proportion of their sentences compared to nonretarded inmates; are not likely to be paroled because they are poor candidates for jobs; and sometimes get more status for being a criminal than just being retarded (Santamour, 1990).

**PRISONS HAVE TYPICALLY FAILED TO CONSIDER THE NEEDS OF RETARDED INMATES**   Retarded individuals are not likely to be treated with sympathy or understanding by other inmates. Instead they are likely to be ridiculed, sexually assaulted, have their commissary items taken, or otherwise

be victimized. Often they do not understand the consequences of their actions and break rules continually or become involved in altercations. They also tend to have difficulties adjusting to regular prison programs (DeVolentine, 1993). These difficulties suggest the need for special placement and programs for many of the retarded inmates. Our Close-Up on "A Retarded Inmate's Dilemma" illustrates some problems faced by these inmates.

Experts differ as to whether to place these offenders in segregated institutions and housing or to mainstream them with the general population. Whatever the approach taken, there is a need to protect their safety (Anno, 1991a) and teach them the rudimentary social, daily living, and work skills that they may lack. Achieving these skills may allow many of them to become independent and avoid being reincarcerated. Unfortunately, most prisons do not have special programs to deal with these inmates' problems, and without them these inmates will likely regress and lose some vital life skills (Ellis and Luckasson, 1985).

## Sex Offenders Are Problems for the Community and Corrections

Imprisoned sex offenders are likely to present a mixed bag of management problems. Sex offenders are extremely diverse. They cannot be characterized by any one motivational or causal factor. While these offenders can be classified in a variety ways we choose the FBI system because it presents an easy-to-understand method of distinguishing them. This system divides major sex offenders into two categories, child molesters (**pedophiles**) and rapists. A major concern with these offenders is their propensity to repeat the offense once released. Less serious offenders include exhibitionists and voyeurs. When rapists and pedophiles are convicted they may receive long prison sentences, whereas exhibitionists and voyeurs, if convicted, will likely only be jailed.

**SOME STATES HAVE PASSED LAWS TARGETING SEX OFFENDERS AFTER THEIR RELEASE FROM PRISON**   The presence in the community of violent sexual offenders tends to stir up strong public concerns that impact lawmakers. For example, the state of Washington reacted to public concerns by passing a law requiring that communities be alerted of the imminent release of "violent sex

# *Close Up*   **A Retarded Inmate's Dilemma**

On a cold steel bench in a maximum security state prison sits Richard, a 28-year-old man with mild mental retardation. Richard has just had 6 months of good time taken away for fighting. This is the fourth infraction in the last 6 months, and the prison disciplinary review board is becoming increasingly more punitive toward Richard. The guards assigned to Richard's cell block know that something is not quite right with Richard, but they don't know how to keep him out of trouble. Richard isn't sure either, but he feels he can't stop fighting or else the other inmates will harass him even more and he will never be safe. The judge who sentenced Richard to 3 1/2 to 7 years in prison for second-degree criminal mischief did so because he didn't know what else to do with Richard. After five arrests in three years he felt he had no choice but to incarcerate Richard. Staff from the community residence where Richard was living told the judge that they had tried everything they could to help Richard but that he was resistive to services and they did not know what else to offer. The police officer who arrested Richard was willing to work out an informal disposition but nobody seemed to have any suggestions about what to do with Richard. So Richard sits, and the best minds in both criminal justice and human services are at a loss about what to do with him.

One thing is clear. For the next 3 1/2 to 7 years Richard will be the responsibility of a correctional institution. The prospects of how that time will be spent are far from encouraging. Richard has become part of an enigma. Society says "We should be kind to persons with disabilities and give them assistance to meet their needs." Society also says "Criminals should be severely punished." To unravel the enigma we must be able to discriminate between the person with mental retardation who is having trouble with the law and the criminal who may also have mental retardation (Finn, 1992, p. 8).

How would you handle Richard? Do you think there should be special facilities and programs to deal with retarded inmates?

Source: Exum, J. G., Turnbull, H. R. ,III, Martin, R., & Flinn, J. W. Point of view: Perspectives on the judicial system, mental retardation services, law enforcement, and correctional systems. In R. W. Conley, R. Luckasson, & G. N. Bouthilet, The Criminal Justice System and Mental Retardation: Defendants and Victims. (pp. pp. 1-16). Baltimore, MD: Paul H. Brookes Publishing Co. Reprinted by permission of the publisher.

offenders" from prison (Booth Gardner Inks, 1990). Laws such as this are controversial. A Washington newspaper reported that newly freed child molesters had been targets of vandalism, harassment, and assault because their identities were made known under the new law (Vigilantism Threatens, 1990). One released and identified Washington child molester had his house burned down and was driven from another community in Washington and one in New Mexico when his criminal background was made known (Driven Out, 1993). These reactions by citizens would appear to make the release of identified sex offenders very difficult. While many people have seen these responses to newly released molesters as "poetic justice," some proponents of the law feel that such behavior could lead to its being overturned. These reactions point to the need for appropriate, effective treatment of these offenders. By December 1993, 22 states had laws requiring offenders to register their names, ad-

dresses, and other information with police on release from prison. However, only two states other than Washington (Maine and Louisiana) had laws specifically targeting sex offenders and allowing the information to be released to the public. Louisiana law even requires the paroled sex offenders to personally notify all their neighbors of their addresses and criminal records. Those living in urban areas must mail letters to people within a three-block radius of their homes, while in rural areas the requirement is a one-mile radius (Protests Force, 1993).

***Sex Offenders Released from Prison Have Been Civilly Committed in Some States***   Washington State passed yet another law a year later directed at controlling repeat sex offenders (London, 1991). Under this new law, the state could detain an inmate beyond his release date while criminal justice personnel conduct a hearing to determine whether he should face a civil commitment proceeding. It also applies retroactively meaning that those who were released from prison years ago can be arrested, detained, and subjected to this proceeding. At this hearing a judge and jury hear evidence regarding the offender's potential for committing further sexual acts. To be committed, the prosecution is required to prove, beyond a reasonable doubt, that the offender is:

a person who has been convicted or charged with a crime of violence and who suffers from "mental abnormality or personal disorder which makes the person likely to engage in predatory sexual violence" (London, 1991, p. 16).

Those found to meet these criteria are committed indefinitely to a special 36-bed unit in the state prison at Monroe. Here they are separated from other inmates, do not eat their meals with them, and do not wear prison uniforms. They are not allowed to participate in work or any activities outside the prison compound. These offenders receive treatment consisting of individual and group therapy. To be released, offenders can periodically petition the court to determine if their treatment has worked. However, many sex offenders have antisocial personalities that require the more aversive and intensive forms of behavior therapy to be successful.[3] The state psychiatric association has contended that as a result many of these offenders will be confined for life.

Those favoring this law argue that it is as much a vehicle for offender treatment as it is for community protection. Its critics, however, view it as a means of circumventing traditional **civil commitment procedures**. In Washington, as in other states, these procedures require showing that an individual has a clinically recognizable disorder and represents a danger to himself or others as a result of this illness. The success of the treatment aspect of this program has yet to be determined.

Four other states have passed or are considering laws that follow Washington's sex offender civil law. These include Massachusetts (Murphy, 1992), Oregon (Gustafson, 1993), New Jersey (Brown, 1994), and Minnesota (Minnesota Statutes, 1993).[4] Florida has taken a different approach by proposing that twice-convicted sex offenders be subject to chemical castration when paroled. These offenders would be required to have weekly shots of Depo-

Provera, a drug that presumably reduces the sex drive by lowering the production of the male hormone testosterone (Reuters, 1994). A problem with this approach is that the drug is ineffective on sex offenders who have an antisocial personality disorder or those motivated by feelings of anger, power, or violence (Besharov, 1992). The proposed Florida law did not pass, but it is likely some groups will press for passage in the future.

**THERE ARE A SUBSTANTIAL NUMBER OF SEX OFFENDERS IN U.S. PRISONS**  A survey of U.S. prisons found that in 1993, 98,000 (11.5%) of 850,000 inmates in U.S. prisons were adult sex offenders. These prisons also held 720 juvenile sex offenders. Taken together this represents a 15% increase in the number of these offenders in prison since 1990 (Lillis, 1993a). However, the actual number of sex offenders may be underestimated because many of these offenders are strongly motivated to seek plea bargains that allow them to plead guilty to a non-sex offense (Vaughn and Sapp, 1990). In this way they avoid the low status given these offenders in the prison hierarchy and the potential violence directed toward them, particularly child sexual abusers. Of course, by entering prison as non-sex offenders they are unlikely to receive any treatment and will likely relapse on release. A good classification system (see Chapter 17) can identify these offenders and provide treatment for them.

**VARIOUS APPROACHES ARE AVAILABLE FOR TREATING SEX OFFENDERS**  Many jurisdictions have recently increased prison programming for sex offenders.[5] Programs available include individual counseling (42), group counseling (46), medical treatment (11), and victim-offender reconciliation (4). Eighteen also offered other treatments such as relapse prevention, Depo-Provera , aversion therapy, victim empathy, anger management, and therapeutic community (Lillis, 1993a). Twenty-six report the following types of recent changes in sex offender treatment:

making sex offender programming follow a continuum from pretreatment, through treatment, to community aftercare; starting a sex offender program for female inmates[6]; residential treatment; additional training for officers; new facilities; mandatory programming; emphasis on relapse prevention; increased focus on victim concerns (Lillis, 1993a, p. 7).

Treatment of sexual offenders is controversial because much of the public believes they should be punished, not treated. However, the maladaptive behaviors of sex offenders are likely to be further aggravated rather than deterred by imprisonment alone. Studies show that untreated, incarcerated sex offenders will more likely recidivate compared to those who are treated (Schwartz and Cellini, 1988). Libstag (1994) reports the following recidivism rates for 473 outpatient sex offenders treated at the Vermont Treatment Program for Sexual Aggressors between November 1982 and March 1991: for all offenders combined, 6%; for 195 pedophiles, 7%; for 190 incestuous offenders, 3%. These impressive figures indicate that sex offender treatment should become a priority for corrections. The pattern of success found by Libstag is supported by the findings of Marshall and his colleagues. They suggested that treatment is more likely to be successful with child molesters and exhibitionists than with rapists (Marshall, Jones, Ward, and Johnson, 1991).

*Treatments Recognize the Complexity of Sexual Deviance* A variety of approaches are employed in treating sex offenders (Lange, 1986; McGrath and Carey, 1987; Salter, 1988; Krauth and Smith, 1988; Bohn, 1993). Most programs include both individual and group psychotherapy, but individual therapy is not used extensively because sex offenders tend to engage in a great deal of denial and secrecy. Several behavioral techniques are used to reduce the deviant sexual arousal experienced by many sexual offenders (Krauth and Smith, 1988). The penile plethysmograph, a pressure-sensitive device that attaches to the penis to detect erections, is used to indentify an offender's deviant sexual interest. Behavior therapy is used to recondition an offender's arousal patterns "increasing arousal to nondeviant adult stimuli while decreasing arousal to deviant stimui such as children or of aggression toward women" (Marques, Day, Nelson and Miner, 1989, p. 28). An example of behavior therapy is:

> Covert sensitization: . . . the offender is asked to fantasize about a highly arousing deviant sexual scene [i.e., involving situations and victims most arousing to the individual] and then asked to imagine a highly negative scene [something that includes images that are frightening or nauseating, etc.]. Over time pairing the highly negative scene and the deviant fantasy reduces the strength of the deviant fantasy (Krauth and Smith, 1988, p. 12).

Our Close-Up on the Vermont sexual offender treatment program presents a look at a currently operating program for this group of difficult offenders.

**INMATES TREAT CHILD MOLESTERS DIFFERENTLY THAN RAPISTS** Vaughn and Sapp (1990)[a] surveyed adult sex offender treatment administrators to obtain a perspective on the position of sex offenders in the inmate status hierarchy. Robbers and drug offenders were found to be accorded the most respect. On the lower end of the spectrum are sex offenders. However, there is a distinction made between rapists, who ranked higher than the more passive sex offenders such as child molesters. The latter group is seen as socially degraded by their fellow inmates and they are dehumanized such that they are fair game for violence-prone inmates (see Figure 11.3) (Toch, 1978, pp. 23–24). Vaughn and Sapp relate this, in part, to their passive personalities.

Sex offenders often lack the basic social skills to enable them to function adequately. "By being a target for the ventilation of anger, sex offenders allow inmates who are themselves rejected by society-at-large to denigrate and reject them. Not belonging to the brotherhood of criminality, the sex offender is the outcast of the outcasts [because he deviates substantially] . . . from other inmates" (Vaughn and Sapp, 1990, p. 82). Thus, he is condemned by both the public and the inmate

**FIGURE 11.3   Correctional Status Hierarchy**

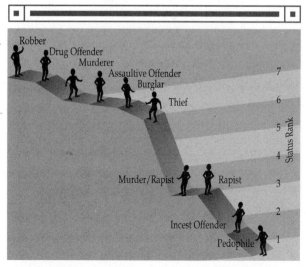

*Source:* Vaughn, M. S., and Sapp, A. D. (1990). Less than utopian: Sex offender treatment in a milieu of power struggles, status positioning, and inmate manipulation in state correctional institutions, pp. 73–89, *The Prison Journal,* July. Reproduced with permission of Sage Publications, Inc.

---

## Close Up    The Vermont Treatment Program for Sexual Aggressors

The Vermont Treatment Program for Sexual Aggressors (VTPSA) was created in 1982 and is housed on the grounds of the Northwest State Correctional Facility in Swanton, Vermont. Fifty incarcerated sex offenders, usually with sentences of at least five years, participate in treatment at this location. Program participants are selected from incarcerated sex offenders who accept responsibility for their offense and express an interest in treatment.

The program also employs a closely monitored transition process as the inmate moves from the in-patient facility to an outpatient sex offender group. All services are provided by therapists and parole officers specially trained in dealing with sex offenders.

In residential treatment the primary treatment modality employed in VTPSA is group psychotherapy. The group process allows treatment staff to provide a variety of intensive therapeutic interventions with the greatest number of residents and provides participants an opportunity to interact with their peers who can give feedback and prevent denial and rationalization. Each resident also has one hour of individual psychotherapy and participates in a peer group and unit meeting weekly. The group therapies at VTPSA focus on a number of core areas.

In core area programs, each inmate is taught to monitor closely his own deviant behavior and to deal with various problems that impact it. They learn to recognize and deal constructively with various emotions, especially anger. There is a strong cognitive emphasis in the treatment, which focuses on correcting the faulty thinking in which sexual offenders tend to engage. Misconceptions regarding human sexuality are corrected. Life skills are taught and the offender is exposed to the victim's point of view and those who were victims themselves are helped to deal with its effects. Deviant arousal patterns are addressed through behavior modification techniques. Finally, each offender is taught to recognize and understand the factors that are likely to cause a relapse and how to deal with them.

Upon completing the VTPSA program requirements (typically no less than two years), the resident transitions back to the regional facility where he was originally incarcerated. There he participates in a "transition group" while awaiting a reduction in custody level to community status. After establishing a residence and securing employment, his programming continues in an outpatient relapse prevention group until parole status ends.

*Source:* Prepared especially for *Corrections: A Comprehensive View* by Kraig Libstag, Psychologist, Vermont Treatment Program for Sexual Offenders

---

population. Most child molesters who are in prison are in great danger of being subjected to violence.

### Mature Inmates Differ from Their Younger Counterparts

Both the proportion of older Americans in the U.S. population and the average age of the general population have been increasing dramatically since the end of the Baby Boom. It's no surprise, then, that the average age of prison inmates has also increased along with the number of inmates over age 50. During the nine years between 1985 to 1994 the proportion of inmates 55 and over increased by 170% (American Correctional Association, 1986; 1995). This represents a substantial increase in their proportion despite an almost 100% increase in the total prison population. Further, the Florida Department of Corrections reported that in 1990 the proportion of inmates over fifty was increasing faster than the total inmate population. As of June 1992 there were 2230 male inmates over fifty out of a population of 44,508 (representing about 5% of the population). This reflected an almost 38% increase over a two-year period (Florida Department of Corrections, 1990, 1992). Additionally, an Illinois Department of Corrections (DOC) survey of eighteen states found that the proportion of inmates age fifty or over ranged from 2 to almost 8% (as cited by Anno 1991). In 1987 it was conservatively estimated that there were 20,000 prisoners nationwide over fifty years of age and Turley (1990) estimates that by the year 2000 there will be more than 125,000 older inmates in prison. However, other writers (e.g., Kratcoski and Pownall, 1989; Washington, 1989) have predicted considerably smaller numbers for the near future. If mid-1990 sentencing laws, like three strikes and you're out,

Elderly inmates may require different types of programs and services than are normally available for younger inmates.

continue to be expanded and enlarged for any length of time, however, the larger estimates may even be too small.

**OLDER INMATES OFTEN HAVE MORE PHYSICAL PROBLEMS THAN OUTSIDERS OF COMPARABLE AGE** The definition and labeling of older offenders have presented some problems to criminologists. This group has been designated by names such as "older," "elderly," and "mature." The cutoff age has ranged from forty-five to sixty-five with most authors deciding to use ages fifty or fifty-five. Anno (1991a) notes that "experienced correctional health practitioners have argued for a lower age definition of elderly as applied to those incarcerated on the grounds that . . . inmates' biological ages frequently are considerably higher than their chronological ages owing to substance abuse, smoking, poor nutrition and lack of prior care, among other factors" (p. 145). We are designating as older or mature those inmates who are age fifty or over simply because this is the most commonly used age and provides us with a greater range of information. We will also use the term *mature* because it avoids some semantic baggage associated with the terms older and elderly.

**OFFENSE PATTERNS OF MATURE OFFENDERS DIFFER FROM THOSE OF YOUNGER INMATES** According to the FBI (1993), only 4.4% of those arrested during 1992 were fifty and over although this age group constitutes more than 26% of the total U.S. population. These offenders represent 3.4% of the arrests for index crimes and constitute 4.8 and 4.7%, respectively, of the arrests for murder and aggravated assault. As a result of the relatively serious crimes for which they are convicted, this population tends to have proportionally longer average sentences than other inmates.

**THERE ARE THREE TYPES OF OLDER OFFENDERS** **Mature offenders** can be classified into three groups based on their incarceration histories (Morton, 1992a; Flynn, 1992; Dugger, 1988). The first group consists of offenders who have usually committed and were imprisoned for their first crime after age fifty. Their crimes often involve murder, manslaughter, rape, or other sexual offenses. Nevertheless, they are likely to see their crimes as spontaneous and perceive themselves as noncriminals (Teller and Howell, 1981). As newcomers to prison they are naive regarding prison life, which often makes them easy prey for more prison-wise inmates. Thus, they may find adjustment to prison difficult. Frequently they have community ties, making placement easier for them on release than the other two groups of older inmates. A subcategory of this group is mentally disordered, suffering from various mental illnesses and brain impairments that can produce aggressive behavior, disorientation, and frequent frustration.

The second group is part of the long-term offender (LTO) group. It consists of individuals who committed very serious crimes at an early age, were sentenced to long terms, and have grown old in prisons. Although their adjustment to prison is often relatively good, their extended sentences weaken or destroy their ties with family and friends. This, combined with a lack of appropriate work experience, makes their readjustment to the community on release difficult. The LTO group is discussed in more detail in a later section.

The third group consists of **career criminals,** or habitual offenders who serve life in prison in installments, i.e., they are in and out of prison all of their lives. They usually adjust well to prisons and present few management problems. Frequently they have substance abuse problems—usually alcohol addiction—which becomes more serious as they age. They also lack the necessary social, life, and coping skills to be successful on the outside, which results in recidivism. Their community ties are weak or nonexistent depending on the tolerance of family and friends. In addition, their poor employment record makes it difficult for them to obtain meaningful jobs and makes reintegration difficult.

**A MAJOR QUESTION IS WHETHER TO SEGREGATE MATURE INMATES OR PLACE THEM IN THE GENERAL PRISON POPULATION** Although it seems obvious that, because of their age and other factors, these inmates should be segregated from the general prison population there are many issues that must be considered when making this decision. First, while chronologically fifty or over, this group is far from uniform. Like the general population, the mental and physical condition of older inmates varies widely, with some being both mentally and physically old at age fifty while others are young in body and mind at sixty, seventy, or even older (White and Abeles, 1990). Second, placement and programming of these inmates must be consistent with the Federal Rehabilitation Act of 1973 and the Americans With Disabilities Act of 1990. Both acts prohibit discrimination against people with disabilities, which are more often found in an older population. These acts call for mainstreaming people with these disabilities whenever possible and require that they have equal access to all services and programs (Flynn, 1992; Morton, 1992a).

**Mainstreaming,** or placement in the general population, of these inmates has historically had a stabilizing effect on prisons because mature inmates have had a calming and settling effect on younger inmates (Flynn, 1992; Kratcoski and Babb, 1990). However, a decline in the respect for elders by inmates has reduced this effect. Mainstreaming also ensures that mature inmates have the same access to programming and services as younger inmates and allows placement at a prison closer to the inmate's home community, which facilitates visits from family and friends.

There are also persuasive arguments for establishing special units to house and provide programming for older inmates. First, many existing physical plants often fail to meet the needs of older inmates. Historically, prisons have been designed to accommodate healthy, young, dangerous, and violent offenders. These large institutions have multitiered cell blocks that are poorly equipped to deal with aging inmates who may be impaired in some way (Flynn, 1992). Second, older inmates are less vulnerable to victimization and likely to be less fearful for their safety in special units (Flynn, 1992; Morton, 1992a). Third, even though many elderly inmates are serving time for serious violent crimes, a large proportion do not pose high security risks and could be placed in less secure settings, allowing the expensive facilities to be used for those who really require them (Vito and Wilson, 1985; Flynn, 1992). Finally, there is a need to provide for the special health requirements of this group including identifying, monitoring, and treating chronic ailments and geriatric medical problems as they develop (Lipson, 1990; Flynn, 1992).

In the final analysis, for systems with sizable numbers of older inmates the programming should offer two options. First, mainstreaming for a majority of older inmates. Second, the placement of a small number of older inmates who need a "protected" environment in special units. As with all programming, the key to meeting the needs of both the system and the inmate is a good classification system because it offers the maximum degree of flexibility in inmate placement (Morton, 1992a). The need for programs for this population is clear if we look at current trends in sentencing. In 1994 alone there were 219,122 inmates serving long-term sentences including twenty years, natural life, and life without parole , which represented almost 23% of the prison population. With continued public intolerance of crime and such bills as "three strikes and you're out," it is likely that

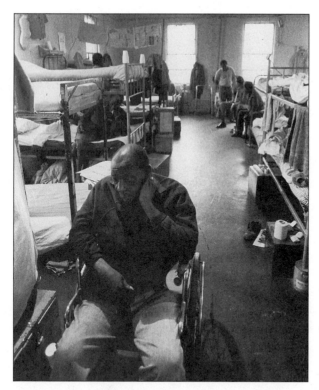

**With growing numbers of elderly inmates, prisons may need to develop facilities for the large number of these inmates who are disabled or are in poor health.**

sizable numbers of inmates will be growing old in our state and federal prison systems (Camp and Camp, 1994a; Flynn, 1992).

Finally, the pursuit of early release programs for older inmates, based on such risk factors as potential recidivism and other considerations, appears to be desirable. Age is an extremely reliable predictor of recidivism because, generally, younger males are 4.8 times more likely to be rearrested than those forty-five and over. Also, on humanitarian grounds the early release of older inmates, particularly the infirm and terminally ill, gives them the opportunity to spend their last months or years with family and friends or at least provides a more normal living setting. Cost is also a factor. Nationally it costs an average of $67,000 annually to incarcerate elderly inmates, which is three times that for younger inmates (Turley, 1990).

### The Youthful Offender Has Been Treated Differently Than Other Inmates

Young offenders have been accounting for an increasing share of violent crime in the United States. This includes substantial increases in their arrests for murder, manslaughter, aggravated assault, and robbery. These increases are beginning to have a serious impact on adult correctional systems around the country. A chain reaction has occurred similar to that for adults in the 1980s and early 1990s, which tremendously increased the prison population. The progression we are seeing is from public outrage, to demands for harsher punishment, to new legislation that increases the proportion of juveniles to be dealt with as adults. At the end of this progression, state DOCs are facing the task of managing this spate of serious youthful offenders, which, from all indications, will continue to grow (Lis, Inc., 1995).

There are no universally agreed on definitions as to what constitutes a **youthful offender.** Almost 40% of the states have no legal definition of youthful offenders. In the rest of the states, these are offenders who fall somewhere between the ages of thirteen and twenty-four with little agreement as to what the upper and lower ages should be. Of the thirty-one states designating a youthful offender status, eleven limit it to those who are under eighteen, five exclude those under eighteen, and the rest include a variety of ages both over and under eighteen (Lis, Inc., 1995).

In 1993 about 55% of all arrests for index crime involved offenders under the age of twenty-five. This age group accounted for about 47% of violent index and 58% of property index crime arrests (FBI, 1994). With respect to those convicted and sent to prison, inmates eighteen to twenty-four accounted for almost 21% of state prison inmates during 1992, 27% in 1986, and 35.6% in 1979 (Innes, 1988; Snell, 1995). The downward trend has generally been accounted for by falling property crime rates. However, if the age of new admissions to prison is considered, the figures show that the median age of violent offenders dropped one year (from twenty-seven to twenty-six) between 1986 and 1991. This decrease was fueled mainly by a 30% increase in the proportion of those under eighteen being committed to prison for violent offenses, which included an almost 70% increase in the commitment of individuals under eighteen for homicide (Perkins, 1992, 1994).

Although the youthful offender group shares many characteristics and problems with the general inmate population, it also differs in several ways, which justifies considering them as a special population. There is a tendency for older inmates

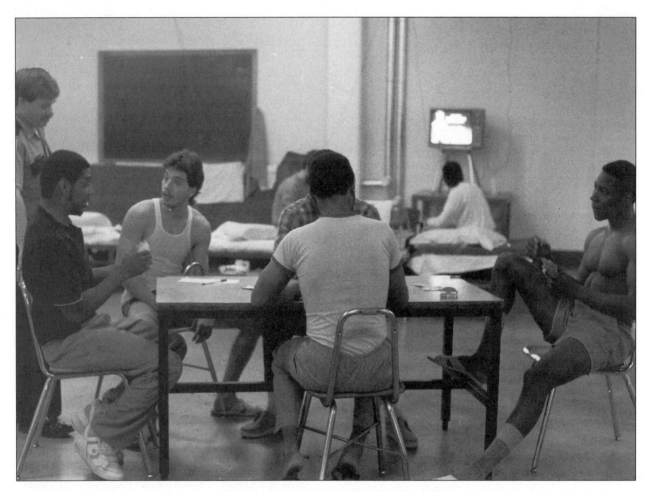

Today there is an increasing number of youthful offenders, (even younger than the ones shown) convicted of violent crimes and sent into the adult system. Less tolerant community attitudes toward violent juveniles are likely to result in even greater numbers of these offenders in adult facilities.

to shun the **jitterbugs,** as many youthful inmates are called. This is probably due to the more active, frantic, and raucous style of interpersonal interactions that is characteristic of many of these young adults. This higher level of activity manifests itself in higher levels of prison rule infractions. An NIC study indicated that of eleven states responding, ten reported higher infraction levels for the youthful offender group when compared with older groups (Lis, Inc., 1995). Other differences manifest themselves in the level and direction of their interests, their different nutritional needs, and their greater need for educational opportunities. The younger age and lack of sophistication of many members of this group make them more vulnerable and subject to be repeatedly victimized even in institutions specifically for youthful offenders. In adult institutions, unless protected (e.g., placement

in protective custody) many will be coerced to engage in homosexual activity and some will be made into "girls" by stronger, older, and more experienced inmates. Given that the majority of states do not have youthful offender institutions, the sad fact is that the scenario presented here is all too true.

The proportion of individuals under eighteen in the adult correctional system is relatively small, but growing. As of June 1994 there were approximately 75,000 inmates aged twenty-one and under incarcerated as adults, with about 5500 of those under the age of eighteen (LIS, Inc., 1995). Given the present concerns about juvenile crime and violence, their proportion in the adult system is likely to keep increasing. At present very few states (e.g., Colorado, Georgia, and Florida) are providing or developing programs specifically targeting the needs of youthful offenders. Especially for those

FIGURE 11.4 Housing of Inmates Under 18 Who Have Been Sentenced as Adults*

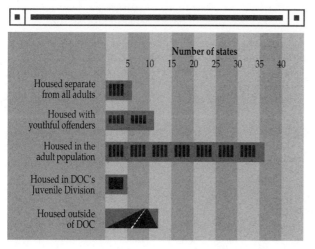

*Source:* Data for this figure derived from LIS, Inc. (1995).
* Some states house juveniles adjudicated as adults in both the adult and juvenile systems.

under eighteen, these needs involve their immaturity, poor education, and low employability, all of which require help or remediation. Most also require enhancement of their self-concept, help in anger control, drug abuse counseling, and medical care. In a number of systems those with academic deficiencies are required to go to school, and vocational training is provided to improve their ability to obtain jobs on release; intensive drug treatment programs have been established; better and greater quantities of food are given; and improved medical and dental care is offered. Some states have designated separate prisons for this group staffed by personnel specially trained to deal with them. Of course, when separated like this, these younger inmates would also not be "contaminated" by the older, more experienced criminals. Figure 11.4 shows how inmates under the age of eighteen sentenced as adults are housed in the various state systems in the United States.

## Physically or Medically Handicapped Offenders Require More Resources Than Other Inmates

Inmates with some form of physical disability or chronic or acute medical problems are a continuing challenge to the various correctional systems. Those with physical disabilities include people who are mobility impaired (e.g., those who are wheelchair-bound or walk with the help of some assistive device such as a walker) and those who

are visually, hearing, or speech impaired (Anno, 1991a). The chronically ill may have conditions that run the gamut from pulmonary disease (such as emphysema), diabetes, epilepsy, heart and hypertension disorders to AIDS. Correctional institutions may have to make special provisions to meet the needs and limitations of these inmates. Further, their physical limitations may also make them easy prey for more predatory inmates, requiring special provisions for their protection.

Many older inmates suffer from these kinds of disabilities, but younger inmates can also be affected. Thus, having special programs just for older inmates will not suffice. Also applicable is the Americans With Disabilities Act of 1990 (ADA), which, as for older inmates, prohibits correctional institutions from denying qualified disabled persons access to programs and services. This includes ensuring program accessibility and usability for all persons including inmates, staff, and visitors.

According to Anno (1991a) most states do not systematically identify the number of chronically ill or disabled in their correctional systems, which means little is known about this population. While the number of disabled inmates is unknown, a survey of twenty-eight correctional systems reported that levels of mobility impaired inmates ranged from 0.04 to 1.2% of the inmate populations (Hall, 1990). While estimates of those with visual, hearing, and speech impairments were not provided, their rates tend to be lower than for the mobility impaired (Veneziano, Veneziano, and Tribolet, 1987). Thus, to assess the extent and nature of this population, information on the prevalence and incidence of the various medical conditions in federal, state, and local correctional systems is needed. To comply with the requirements of ADA, facilities need to be modified so that those with disabilities can have access to appropriate programs and services. In states with large populations this can probably be achieved through the designation of one or more facilities as having the appropriate level of accessibility to accommodate these inmates.

## The Number of Long-Term Offenders in Prisons Is Increasing

Since the late 1970s sentencing patterns emphasizing determinate and minimum mandatory sentences have resulted in an increasing number of inmates being imprisoned for longer periods of

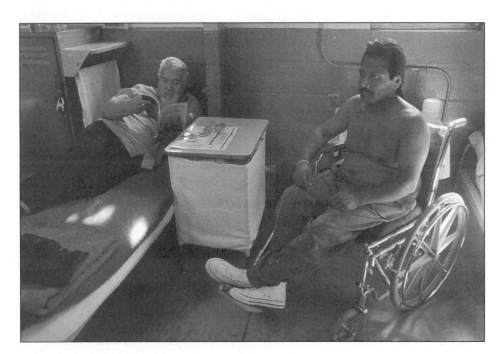

Under the American with Disabilities Act (ADA), institutions must make accomodations for disabled inmates.

time (Flanagan, 1990; Porporino, 1990; Dugger, 1990). In the federal system, with a population of 59,000 inmates in 1990, the number expected to serve a ten-year term grew from 11.4 to 15% of the population in one year. Those expecting to spend fifteen years grew by 74% from approximately 2300 inmates to 4000 (Quinlan, 1990).

Problems have arisen in defining this population because there is no agreement about what constitutes "long term." Some writers suggest five or more years, some seven or more, and some ten or more. Irrespective of the minimum amount of time required to qualify as a long-termer, inmates serving long sentences require increasing attention simply because there are greater numbers of them. They are also likely to cause unique management problems and require different programming approaches than short-term inmates.

### LTOs ARE DIFFERENT FROM OTHER INMATES

A perspective on the **long-term offender** population can be gleaned from a description of this group in Florida prisons (Dugger, 1990). Defining LTOs as inmates serving sentences of twenty-five years or longer, in 1990 these inmates constituted more than 20% (8111) of the prison population (40,078) and their number was anticipated to triple by the year 2000. They had the following characteristics: slightly more than one-half were black;

almost 98% were males; one-half were lifers or on death row; 45% were murderers; and 22% were sex offenders.

Because LTOs are initially considered escape risks, they are usually assigned to more secure institutions and classified as close custody on admission. However, their classification is reviewed every six months. If they demonstrate adjustment they can be moved to less secure institutions and after several years of good behavior have their custody status reduced. LTOs tend to have better disciplinary records than short termers, especially once they have adapted to prison life.

Dugger feels that LTOs can be divided into five program groups: younger inmates with long sentences; middle-aged inmates, frequently career criminals with long sentences; elderly inmates who have grown old in prison; elderly inmates who were old when sentenced, the vast majority sentenced for either murder or child molestation; and women with long sentences.

### LTOs FACE DIFFERENT PROBLEMS THAN OTHER INMATES 

Although LTOs are far from a homogeneous group, their long terms of confinement result in the development of certain common attitudes and coping strategies (Cowles, 1990a; Gaes, 1990a; Flanagan, 1990). They seem to shift their orientation from the outside world to the world inside the prison because of the difficulties that they face in maintaining outside relationships (Cowles, 1990b). That is, since family and friends cannot expect to resume normal relationships with them in the near future, this can reduce their motivation to continue relationships (Flanagan, 1990; Cowles, 1990b). Thus, a vital link is lost with the outside world (Flanagan, 1990). This usually means a loss of financial resources as well, which may force many LTOs to depend on illegitimate activities for their money. One way of providing outside contact for LTOs is through citizen volunteers who can help LTOs maintain a connection with the outside and reduce feelings of abandonment. This may be one way of educating the public about these forgotten inmates (McGinnis, 1990). The M-2 sponsor's program, to be discussed in Chapter 21, was established for just this purpose.

**MOST LTOs GO THROUGH PHASES OF ADJUSTMENT TO PRISON LIFE** Upon entering prison, LTOs manifest certain problem behavior and attitudes that typically change over time. Those with longer criminal records are more likely to be violent, especially during the early part of their sentences, and to maintain more procriminal attitudes. This places them at higher risk for suicide and for committing murder than shorter term inmates (Porporino, 1990). However, as LTOs get older in prison, their criminal attitudes diminish regardless of their previous criminality.

Gaes (1990a, 1990b) notes that LTOs first entering prison are typically in a state of denial. They work on and file appeals and try to figure out other ways of getting out of prison. At some point most of them accept their imprisonment and begin to look for ways to make it on a daily basis. They develop a perspective that involves focusing on the "here and now." This is reinforced by associating with other LTOs. The behavioral manifestations of this coping strategy take the form of doing one's own time, which involves avoiding trouble (e.g., minding your own business); using time profitably (involvement in work, education, etc.); and, where possible, maintaining interaction with outsiders.

LTOs face problems in trying to avoid the sense of isolation characteristic of prison life. Although establishing relationships on the inside is an obvious solution, this can run counter to the inmate's efforts to avoid trouble and do his own time (Gaes,

1990b). Inmates recognize that prison is a very dangerous place and that relationships there tend to be very shallow. Thus, there is always the danger of attack or victimization against which they will use violence. LTOs who establish close friendships face the devastation of having these relationships severed by transfers and releases (Flanagan, 1990). To avoid this pain, they may either develop guarded relationships with other inmates or adopt a solitary lifestyle labeled the "behavioral deep freeze of incarceration" (Zamble and Porporino, 1988; Gaes, 1990a).

**SPECIAL SERVICES ARE REQUIRED FOR LTOs** It is important to consider how LTOs perceive the prison and its services because of the permanency of their confinement. Most people can put up with unpleasant conditions for short periods of time, but this ability to cope can change when the conditions have to be endured for a lifetime. Many persons reading this book are students who may currently live under unfavorable conditions and eat food in a college cafeteria that is not particularly to their liking. For you, these conditions are temporary, but consider how it might feel if you were going to have to put up with them for ten, twenty, or more years without respite. This gives you some idea how LTOs may feel about prison conditions. All inmates find prison conditions such as crowding, noise, and lack of privacy distasteful; however, for LTOs these discomforts are magnified because this is their long-term home. LTOs expressed some concern regarding food quality, but Sabath and Cowles (1990) found that their greatest concern regarding services was about medical treatment. They found that treatment professionals also had concerns about the quality of medical care received by LTOs. Both felt this was a consequence of the generally slow and inefficient state of service delivery in prison. The following comments from LTOs suggest some of the pain, frustration, and hatred that results from inadequate care, while those from treatment personnel indicate some reasons for this substandard care:

**Long-Term Inmates**

I've had trouble getting help on this subject. My kidney has been giving me hell. The only thing that has ever been done for me is a urine test. I'm not a doctor, but I know pain. I've got to watch what I drink. At night it's really bad.

Long-termers have to take what they can get. They can't shop around for doctors and hospitals.

### Treatment Professionals

The staff is highly motivated and very dedicated to providing quality health care, but our resources are predicated on an inmate population of 636, and we have over 1800 inmates. We provide a very high quality care, given limitations of staff and budget, and the lack of resources. Our segregation sick call and doctor's appointment procedure is the result of a court ordered consent decree and was made without consulting medical staff. There are elements inconsistent with standards of medical practice, and others which are physically impossible given the ratio of inmates to medical staff.

I am very concerned about the medical care available. Inmate fears of what goes on at the Department of Corrections hospital is not rumor-based. Treatment for potentially critical problems is too slow. Why there are not more lawsuits than there are is beyond me (Sabath and Cowles, 1990, p. 70).[b]

In our discussion of medical services in Chapter 19, we discuss some ways by which this system can be improved. On the other hand, the comments of a correctional officer reflect skepticism regarding inmate medical problems and views inmates as abusing medical services.

### Correctional Officer

No inmate is constantly ill day after day; yet, on every sick call the same names appear. Some inmates make several hospital trips a day. For what? (Sabath and Cowles, 1990, p. 70).

These relatively negative views suggest a need to educate correctional staff regarding the handling of inmates with medical problems, particularly LTOs. This may well reflect poor inmate–staff communication and relations at the institution in which this study was conducted. Given that LTOs will be at this prison for some time and interacting with staff regularly, it is critical to try to resolve this conflict (Cowles, 1990a).

**LTOs CAN BENEFIT FROM PROGRAM PLANNING THAT CONSIDERS THEIR EXTENDED PRISON TERMS**   It is also important, in dealing with the adjustment of LTOs to structure their prison careers rather just assign them to jobs or programs. This requires LTO "career planning." One approach involves offering them the opportunity for education tied to vocational training. This training is then related to the requirements of a job in an industry program that has promotion possibilities (McGinnis, 1990; Gaes, 1990b). Another option that has been successful is to involve LTOs in high-technology kinds of programs that require long-term skill development. For example, in a Missouri facility, Cowles (1990a) experimented successfully with a program involving LTOs in video production. While there were initial reservations about bringing expensive video equipment into the prison, he reports that these inmates maintained the equipment, created viable products, and behaved maturely and responsibly. Another option for LTOs is to legitimize the prison's **cottage industries** such as tailoring, legal research, and correspondence, which are currently part of the illegitimate prison economy. If these activities are legitimized and put under the control of prison administration, they could provide LTOs with viable and meaningful jobs and facilitate a smoother functioning prison (Cowles, 1990a).

Finally, Flanagan (1990) proposes that we must reduce the secondary sanctions associated with imprisonment (idleness, noxious environmental conditions, etc.). This would limit the punishment of imprisonment to its purpose: to remove offenders from society and deprive them of their liberty. Thus, where possible, inmates should be given choices and opportunities to pursue meaningful lives within the institutions and to interact with the outside world.

## UNDERSTANDING THE DIVERSITY OF THE MALE INMATE POPULATION

Our discussion of male inmates reveals a widely divergent group of individuals with a variety of problems and needs. If the correctional systems housing this collection of inmates are to develop just and humane institutions, they must develop information to describe adequately all the important inmate segments, minister to their needs, and cope with their problems. It is with this information in hand that corrections may keep from being overwhelmed.

## ENDNOTES

**1.** Data from several surveys are included in this section, some of which are from 1991 and some from later years. Thus, there may be some small discrepancies in the data presented, but the trends are consistent.

**2.** We should note that there is some controversy regarding the use of intelligence tests as definitive measures of intellectual potential, especially with minority group individuals.

**3.** Our Close-Up later in this chapter on "The Vermont Treatment Program for Sexual Aggressors" notes some of these techniques.

**4.** However, the constitutionality of this and other similar statutes is in question. In 1995, a federal district court declared the Washington law unconstitutional on the grounds that it violated a person's due process rights, because it allows the indefinite commitment of individuals who suffer from a mental abnormality, antisocial personality, or other personality disorders but are not mentally ill (*Bigham v. Young*, 1995). However, the judge in this case decided not to release the inmate plaintiff since he was found dangerous by other courts. The state is filing an appeal with the 9th circuit court which will decide whether the district court judge's ruling on the constitutionality of this statute is valid (March, 1995).

**5.** Fifty states, the Federal Bureau of Prisons, and the District of Columbia were surveyed. Only Ohio and Montana failed to respond (Lillis, 1993).

**6.** Arizona reports beginning a program for women (Lillis, 1993a).

**7.** Chapter 17 discusses the issues associated with classifying inmates according to security and custody concerns.

## ACKNOWLEDGMENTS

[a] M. Vaughn and A. Sapp. Less than Utopian: Sex offender treatment in a milieu of power struggles. *The Prison Journal*, Fall/Winter 1990. © 1990 Reproduced by permission of Sage Publications, Inc.

[b] M.J. Sabath and E.L. Cowles. Using multiple perspectives to develop strategies for managing long term inmates. *The Prison Journal*, pp. 58–72. © 1990 Reprinted by permission of Sage Publications, Inc.

## CHAPTER RECAP

**U.S. Prison Population Differs from General U.S. Population**

The Prison Population Is Not Representative of the General Population
  The Proportions of Female, Older, Hispanic, and Unmarried Inmates Have Been Increasing
Inmates Are Disproportionately Young, Male, and from Minority Groups
  Most Persons Arrested for Criminal Behavior Are Male
  Younger People More Often Commit Crimes
  Minority Groups Are Disproportionately Incarcerated
  Inmates Often Have Histories of Family Disorganization and Are at the Lower End of the Economic Scale
  Many Inmates Have Committed Violent Crimes
  Extensive Prior Arrest Histories Increase the Likelihood of Recidivism
**Special Category Offenders**
Inmates with Psychological or Behavioral Disorders Can Be Management Problems
  Public Policy Regarding the Mentally Disordered Has Changed over the Years
  Some Inmates Suffer from a Variety of Serious Mental Disorders
Prisons Have Some Mentally Handicapped Inmates Who Require Special Programming
  There Are Different Levels of Retardation
  Mentally Retarded Individuals Tend to be Overrepresented in the Prison Population
  Prisons Have Typically Failed to Consider the Needs of Retarded Inmates
Sex Offenders Are Problems for Community and Corrections
  Some States Have Passed Laws Targeting Sex Offenders After Their Release from Prison
    Sex Offenders Released from Prison Have Been Civilly Committed in Some States
  There Are a Substantial Number of Sex Offenders in U.S. Prisons
  Various Approaches Are Available for Treating Sex Offenders
    Treatments Recognize the Complexity of Sexual Deviance
  Inmates Treat Child Molesters Differently Than Rapists
Mature Inmates Differ from Their Younger Counterparts
  Older Inmates Often Have More Physical Problems Than Outsiders of Comparable Age
  Offense Patterns of Mature Offenders Differ from Those of Younger Inmates
  There Are Three Types of Older Offenders

A Major Question Is Whether to Segregate Mature Inmates or Place Them in the General Prison Population

The Youthful Offender Has Been Treated Differently Than Other Inmates

Physically or Medically Handicapped Offenders Require More Resources Than Other Inmates

The Number of Long-Term Offenders in Prisons Is Increasing

    LTOs Are Different from Other Inmates

    LTOs Face Different Problems Than Other Inmates

    Most LTOs Go Through Phases of Adjustment to Prison Life

    Special Services Are Required for LTOs

    LTOs Can Benefit from Program Planning That Considers Their Extended Prison Terms

**Understanding the Diversity of the Male Inmate Population**

## REVIEW QUESTIONS

1. To what extent does the population of our prisons represent the composition of our society? Why do differences occur?

2. What are the main categories of offenders who require special programs and/or management in a correctional setting?

3. What kinds of mental disorders are found in prisons and what proportion of the inmate population may be suffering from them?

4. What are mentally retarded offenders? How are their needs different from more normal inmates?

5. What is a pedophile and how are they different from rapists?

6. How are older inmates different from younger ones with respect to prison program needs?

7. What are the special requirements of physically or medically handicapped inmates?

8. How are long-term offenders different from other inmates and what adjustments do they make?

## TEST YOUR KNOWLEDGE

1. The inmate population differs from the general U.S. population most markedly with respect to which of the following?
    a. age
    b. gender
    c. racial-ethnic background
    d. socioeconomic status

2. Which of the following trends is/are occurring in the U.S. inmate population?
    a. there are proportionately more female inmates
    b. the inmate population is getting older
    c. there are proportionally more Hispanic inmates
    d. all of the above

3. Which of the following occurrences was apparently *most responsible* for the present volume of mentally disordered individuals in prison?
    a. the abolishment of the insanity defense
    b. new laws passed against erratic behavior in public
    c. the development of antipsychotic drugs
    d. the rapid spread of psychiatric therapy programs inside prisons

4. The Americans with Disabilities Act (ADA) of 1990
    a. applies to staff but not inmates
    b. applies to mature and handicapped offenders but not others
    c. applies to all inmates, staff, and visitors
    d. does not apply within a correctional institution

# CHAPTER 12

# THE FEMALE OFFENDER

*read*

## ■ LEARNING OBJECTIVES

*After completing this chapter, you should be able to:*
**1.** Estimate the proportion of female offenders arrested and incarcerated for crimes.
**2.** Discuss the evidence relating to the debate over whether women are given preferential, harsh, or equal treatment by the criminal justice system.
**3.** Trace the evolution of correctional institutions for female offenders.
**4.** Describe the characteristics and criminal behavior of incarcerated women.
**5.** Describe the types of "family" relationships that develop among women in prison.
**6.** Identify the types of services and programs offered in women's prisons.
**7.** Identify the various problems of incarcerated mothers and their children.
**8.** Evaluate the advantages and disadvantages of co-corrections.
**9.** Assess the variation in community-based correctional programs for women.

## ■ KEY TERMS AND CONCEPTS

Co-corrections
Cottage plan
Eliza Farnham
Matron
Parity/disparity
Paternalistic bias
Prisonization
Pseudofamilies

*This chapter was authored by Gerasimos Gianakis, Assistant Professor, Department of Political Science, Kent State University.*

## FEMALE OFFENDERS AND THE CRIMINAL JUSTICE SYSTEM

For every woman in prison there are approximately nineteen men. As a result, women's prisons are fewer in number than male facilities, usually smaller than the average prison for men, and likely to be different in structure and programming. Consequently, this segment of the corrections system has not received much attention until recently.

Historically, the proportion of women coming into contact with the criminal justice system has been low because many fewer women than men are arrested in comparison to their proportion in the population. This led early criminologists to devote little attention to women and their crimes. When they did attempt to account for their criminality, they generally employed sexist-oriented explanations. Recently, as feminist criminologists and others have challenged these widely held unscientific notions about female crime and its relative scarcity, more objective and acceptable perspectives have been developed.

### Current Female Criminality Is Low But Increasing Faster Than for Men

Although arrests of women during the past two decades have grown steadily as a proportion of total arrests, women still comprise a small proportion of the criminal population (see Figure 12.1). Women represent a small percentage of persons arrested for violent crimes, but they represent a substantial proportion of the arrests for larceny among the index crimes, and prostitution, fraud, embezzlement, forgery, and counterfeiting among the Part II crimes. For drug-related arrests, which contributed heavily to rising incarceration rates in the early 1990s, women comprised slightly under 17% of the total (Federal Bureau of Investigation, 1994).

### Different Factors Affect the Sentencing of Women and Men

There is a debate as to whether women have been treated more leniently than men. Housewives and those who had committed multiple offenses were thought to be treated more leniently by Kruttschnitt (1981, 1982, 1984). In contrast, a study by Crew (1991) found no significant differences in treatment between male and female groups. Crew concluded:

> It appears that different factors affect the sentencing of men and women; these factors are tied to the sexual division of labor in the larger society. Therefore, for men, economic roles are an important consideration in legal processing: presentencing recommendations often are based at least partially on the offender's work history or current employment. Women, on the other hand, are likely to be judged according to the roles they play within the family. Even so, mere occupancy of selected . . . statuses . . . is not highly predictive of legal sanctions. Instead, sex roles represent different criteria by which defendants are evaluated. Leniency may be extended to female offenders who occupy the traditional female roles . . . [while] . . . women who do not enact traditional female roles or whose crimes contradict those roles are likely to be denied such . . . [treatment] (p. 78).

Crew asserted that the relationship between gender and sentencing is best viewed as involving a greater concern for maintaining families and protecting children than with merely discriminating on the basis of sex. If Crew's assertion is correct, this places the courts in the position of determining and reinforcing the social roles of females in our society. This latter view is further supported by the results of a study conducted by the Ninth Circuit Gender Bias Task Force (1993). They found that females were more likely than males to receive consideration for lower sentences in this federal circuit on the basis of being the primary caregiver, pregnant, or subjected to violence and/or duress.

Finally, Pennsylvania court data on the relationship between gender and court decisions showed that the sentencing practices of Pennsylvania judges were based on two major concerns: blameworthiness (e.g., extent of prior record, the extent and nature of the woman's participation in the crime) and practicality (e.g., extent to which personal factors may result in the sentence causing more harm than warranted; presence of children, pregnancy, emotional problems; lack of jail space) (Steffensmeier, Kramer, and Streifel, 1993). Although their data do not address the issue, these researchers contend that men and women appearing in court under similar circumstances and charged with similar offenses are likely to be treated in basically the same way.

FIGURE 12.1    **Proportion of Males and Females Arrested for Part I and Part II Crimes, 1993**

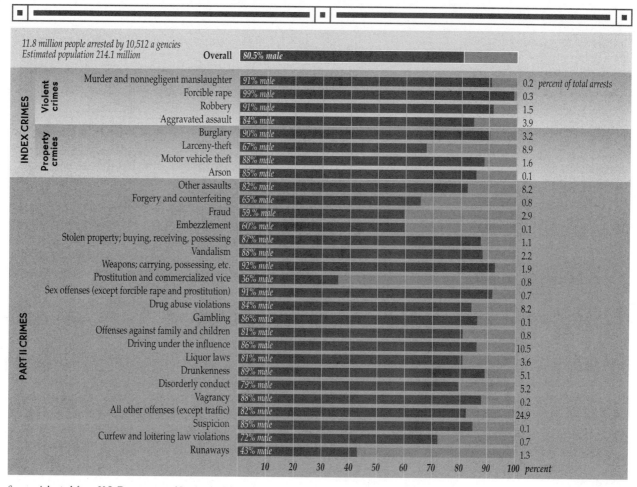

Source: Adapted from U.S. Department of Justice (1994). Uniform Crime Reports, 1993. Washington, D.C.: Author.

## WOMEN AND THE CORRECTIONAL SYSTEM

The treatment accorded women by corrections has evolved over time. However, because of their small numbers, they were likely to be neglected and placed in inferior facilities. Most recently, legal challenges by female inmates have improved their position relative to male inmates. The typical female inmate has similar demographic characteristics to her male counterparts.

### Historical Overview Shows a Familiar Pattern

The history of the incarceration of women shows a pattern of neglect and lack of concern. Houses of correction were the first confinement facilities and were intended for the idle, destitute, and criminals of both sexes. With some exceptions (e.g., the Maison de Force and the Amsterdam Spinhouse) these early facilities made no provision to separate the sexes. Typically, men and women were housed together in large rooms where survival of the strongest was the norm. This often meant that women were victimized by male inmates (Grunhut, 1972). An appalling early example of the exploitation of female convicts occurred when the London Bridewell was leased briefly to some businessmen who turned it into a brothel. Women refusing to cooperate were beaten into submission (Dobash, Dobash, and Gutteridge, 1986).

In Colonial America, as in England, provisions were not usually made for separating women incarcerated in county jails from men. This pattern continued even after the Revolution. For example, prior to the reforms initiated at the Walnut Street

**Women in a middle 19th century English prison producing knitted goods. In this system they worked under a rule of silence.**

Jail in 1790, twenty to thirty prisoners were housed in the same rooms with no segregation by age and sex. Shocked by this and other factors, reformers of the Philadelphia Society devised a new plan for the Walnut Street Jail (see Chapter 4). Women at this newly designed facility were housed in a separate section consisting of five rooms (Lewis, 1922/1967; Barnes, 1927/1968). Although this was a major improvement, the reformist zeal that characterized the birth of the penitentiary did not benefit women. Even after the development of these new institutions, where men were separated into single cells, women generally continued to be housed congregately in large cells in separate sections of men's prisons. Rafter (1985) paints the following picture: "Whereas male prisoners were closely supervised, women seldom had a **matron** [the chief supervisor of women's units]. Often idleness rather than hard labor was their curse" (p. 4).

**WOMEN TOOK THE LEAD IN REFORMING PROGRAMS FOR INCARCERATED FEMALES** Elizabeth Fry, an English Quaker, began a movement in England in 1813 to improve the conditions under which women were incarcerated. Until her death in 1845, Fry traveled widely, both in Europe and the United States, campaigning for separate female facilities, which would be supervised and staffed by women, classify women into specific treatment groups; and provide religious instruction, work, education, and preparation for employment after release (Feinman, 1986).

Reformers in the United States moved to adopt Fry's program. In 1825, when the New York House of Refuge for juveniles was opened, a separate building was set aside for female delinquents who were to be supervised by two women. This was the first institution to be operated based on the idea that females could be reformed, separated from males, and taught by women (Feinman, 1986).

**REFORMS CREATED SEPARATE PRISONS FOR WOMEN**  In 1826, a female inmate at New York's Auburn Penitentiary was raped by a guard and later killed by him after he found out she was five months pregnant. Her death prompted reforms in that state. They culminated in the construction of Mount Pleasant Female Prison in 1839, the first separate prison for women. This facility was next to the Sing Sing men's prison and administratively dependent on it. The facility had its own staff and chief matron. The women were housed in cells that were modeled after those at Auburn. It had a nursery for children (the first of its kind in the United States), which meant that women did not have to be separated from their babies or care for them in their single cells as in other prisons (Rafter, 1990). This recognized the special need of women to care for their children while in prison, which continues to be an issue in contemporary women's prisons.

The first matron at Mount Pleasant was unable to control her charges, but her replacement, **Eliza Farnham,** accomplished control with a combination of firmness and kindness. (Rafter, 1990). She was the matron from 1844 to 1848 and transformed Mount Pleasant into a model facility based on the premise that the environment should be homelike and interaction between staff and inmates should be like that of a family (Feinman, 1986). She also modified the rule of silence, introduced nonreligious reading material, and allowed visitors to teach the women to read and write. These reforms proved to be too controversial and she was forced to resign (Rafter, 1985).

**THE REFORMATORY MOVEMENT BROUGHT CHANGES FOR FEMALE CORRECTIONS**  In 1863, the House of Shelter was opened as a part of the Detroit House of Corrections. Although not an independent structure, it was under the superintendency of Zebulon R. Brockway, a leading reformer and first superintendent of the Elmira Reformatory. He employed female officers who could serve as appropriate role models and divided women into small "family" groups in which they received domestic training. He also began using a graded system by which obedient inmates were rewarded by promotion to better living conditions (Rafter, 1990).

**PAROLE WAS FIRST APPLIED TO WOMEN**  In 1867, Michigan passed an indeterminate sentencing law allowing Brockway to hold prostitutes for up to three years. However, depending on their degree of reformation, they could be released early. This law provided an opportunity for introducing a system of modified parole for women. The women who were granted early release were not released outright but were sent to the more benign House of Shelter to finish their sentences. Although not involving traditional parole, this program provided a model for reforming female and male offenders. This unit closed after five years because the space was needed to house male inmates (Rafter, 1985).

Following the Cincinnati meeting of the National Prison Association in 1870, major correctional reforms were called for, including separate institutions for women. With this as an impetus and pressure from female reformers, the penal treatment of women began to change significantly. In 1873, the first of these facilities, the Indiana Reformatory for Women and Girls, was opened. It duplicated some features of the Detroit House of Corrections including its use of female personnel.

**THE COTTAGE PLAN WAS USED IN THE CONSTRUCTION OF WOMEN'S PRISONS**  In the final quarter of the nineteenth century, three independent women's prisons were built—one in Massachusetts and two in New York. Based on the idea that females could be reformed through domestic training, an architectural modification of the **cottage plan**—borrowed from an earlier reform school for girls in Massachusetts—was slowly incorporated into the newer adult institutions. Cottage plan institutions consisted of several small units, each housing approximately thirty inmates, surrounding a central building that had regular cells.

The cells were used to hold new inmates until they were ready to be moved into the cottages. These institutions, which provided a more relaxed disciplinary atmosphere, were used for females under age thirty who had committed minor crimes. Between 1900 and 1930, twenty-five of these facilities for women were built, primarily in the Northeast and Midwest (Freedman, 1981).

In the South, because women were not wanted by private contractors, they were kept in central prisons, which also held old and sick males who were unable to work. After World War II, a few reformatories were built in this region. These facilities essentially terminated the co-correctional arrangements that had initially characterized most of women's corrections. Many facilities built during this era are still in use today. Their outdated architecture and lack of many of the amenities present in more modern construction impose program and treatment limitations. These limitations make it difficult to meet the needs of today's female inmates and also increase the probability of litigation (Chesney-Lind, 1986, 1987).

### Legal Challenges by Inmates Have Improved Female Prisons

Most recent correctional reform efforts involving women have focused on gaining **parity** (equality in programming and resources) with male prisoners. The impetus for these reforms has come from three sources. First, feminist criminologists exposed the disparities in the treatment received by women and were instrumental in initiating change (see, e.g., Adler, 1975; Simon 1975; Feinman, 1986; Smart, 1979; Chesney-Lind, 1982). Second, the American Correctional Association developed guidelines and recommendations for providing programs for female offenders including programs for pregnant women and for establishing sound family relationships; nontraditional vocational training and career counseling; child and family services; and the full range of diversional and other community correctional services. The third major source for these reforms was inmate litigation.

Beginning in the mid-1970s, legal challenges by female inmates to conditions of confinement resulted in some significant changes. One area addressed was the **disparity** (inequality) in the programs (e.g., vocational training) in women's institutions as compared to those for men. In a New Mexico decision (*Barefield v. Leach*, 1974), the court found that the state had failed to provide parity in its vocational programming and its paid work for inmates. The state was not allowed to justify the disparity just because it cost more to provide programs in the smaller female facilities

(see also *Canterino v. Wilson*, 1989). The courts also rendered several decisions supporting adequate and appropriate medical care and parity with men's institutions in programming, conditions, and opportunities in women's prisons (*Estelle v. Gamble*, 1976; *Glover v. Johnson*, 1991; *Moorhead v. Lane*, 1991; *Molar v. Gates*, 1979). Although these decisions are encouraging they have been implemented very slowly. According to Muraskin (1989) this slow implementation has resulted, in part, from the disproportionately small number of women prisoners.

### Female Inmates in Jails and Prisons Differ from Their Male Counterparts

Between 1980 and 1994, the number of women in federal and state prisons grew from 13,420 to 64,403. From 1980 to 1989 the yearly increase in the percentage of women in prisons was higher than for males: The percentage for women increased 202%; males increased 112%. The female percentage of the prison population rose from 4.1 to 5.7%. From 1990 to 1992, however, the male rate increase was higher, and the percentage of women in the prison population remained at 5.7%. In 1993, and 1994, the female rate of increase again topped males and their percent of the prison population reached 6.1 (Greenfeld and Minor-Harper, 1991; Cohen, 1991; Gilliard, 1993; Gilliard and Beck, 1994, Beck and Gilliard, 1995).

The number of women in jail also grew, from 15,628 (7% of the jail population) in 1983, to 48,879 in 1994, representing 10% of the population (Bureau of Justice Statistics, 1984; Perkins, Stephan, and Beck, 1995). In 1985 there were 272,638 women on probation constituting 17.5% of this population. Although this rose to 397,640 in 1992, the proportion of women probationers dropped to 16.7. There were 17,147 on parole in 1985 (6.5% of the parolees). This number rose to 63,461 in 1992, representing 10.7% of this population (Bureau of Justice Statistics, 1987; Snell, 1995). These figures show that the population of female inmates has been growing fairly rapidly and (except for probation) the proportion of women under correctional supervision vis-à-vis males has continued to increase. Numerically, however, males still make up the vast majority of those under correctional supervision.

Like their male counterparts, women have not escaped the tougher stance taken by the criminal justice system in reaction to public outrage with the drug problem. Immarigeon and Chesney-Lind (1990) attributed the increases in arrests and incarceration of women during the 1980s to property and drug crimes rather than to crimes of violence. However, the proportion of females incarcerated for violent crimes has increased in the 1990s (Snell and Morton, 1994).

Crawford (1988) conducted a study for the American Correctional Association on women's corrections in the mid-1980s and provided the following profile of the female inmate:

▣ *Personal history:* Fifty-seven percent were from minority groups; their median age was between 25 and 29; 37% were never married, and 62% were single parents with between one and three children. Most were planning to maintain custody of their children.

▣ *Home life:* The majority came from broken homes or single parent families; half had other family members who were incarcerated; almost two-thirds had been runaways; almost 40% admitted using drugs to feel good; and one quarter had attempted suicide at least once.

▣ *Physical and sexual abuse:* More than one-third of the women reported being sexually abused, with a majority reporting it happened at least three times. For one-half the abuser was a male relative; the majority indicated that reporting the incident resulted in no change or made matters worse.

▣ *Alcohol/drug history:* The average female offender began using alcohol or drugs between the ages of thirteen and fourteen. Three-quarters drank at least occasionally and almost one-half used cocaine, many on a daily basis; 40% used speed and almost 60% used marijuana, many on a daily basis.

▣ *Criminal history:* More than 50% were arrested between two and nine times; over one-third began their criminal careers between the ages of fifteen and nineteen. They were commonly arrested for property crimes (39%), largely larceny/theft. Violent crimes (largely murder/manslaughter of a significant other) accounted for 22%. One-half were serving sentences of between two and eight years of which they had served about one-fourth. Most of the crime committed by these women was to pay for drugs or relieve economic pressures.

▣ *Educational background:* The average female offender is a high school dropout; about one-fourth had GEDs; one-third dropped out because they were pregnant and most of the rest because they were bored with school. About one-half had attended some vocational programs pursuing training in "women's" fields (e.g., cosmetology, secretarial).

▣ *Work history:* About three-fourths of these women had previous work experience, particularly in clerical and service-related jobs; many jobs were short-lived with low pay. Sixty percent had received welfare assistance.

▣ *Treatment programs:* About two-thirds had participated in either drug or alcohol programs; many had also been in the Job Corps and educational programs while in prison. The most helpful prison programs were felt to be education programs, followed by substance abuse, AA, and chaplaincy/church programs.

In summary then, incarcerated women represent a portion of the population characterized by economic marginality, ethnic minority status, drug dependency, poor education and work skills, a history of abuse at the hands of the men in their lives, and having sole responsibility for their children. This combination of characteristics tends to push them into committing economic crimes to meet their needs or into violent crimes either from frustration or to cope with abusive significant others.

**MOST WOMEN ARE NOW BEING INCARCERATED FOR DRUG AND VIOLENT CRIMES** The proportion of women incarcerated for the various offenses fluctuated during the 1980s and into the 1990s. Between 1979 and 1986, the percentage went up for property, drug, and public order offenses and down for violent crimes (Greenfeld and Minor-Harper, 1991). Between 1986 and 1991 the downward trend continued for violent crimes and there was a reversal in the property crime category, which showed a 41% decrease. There was a significant increase in the proportion of women incarcerated for drug offenses during this period with one in three women serving time for these crimes (Snell and Morton, 1994). Also, despite the drop in the proportion of violent female inmates in the prison population, those sentenced for violent crime rose by more than 5%.

Women and men committed to prison share similar characteristics. However, regarding the crimes resulting in their incarceration, the three most frequent for men were robbery, drug trafficking, and burglary, whereas those for women were drug trafficking, murder/manslaughter, and drug possession. Thus, compared to men, most women are imprisoned for drug-related crimes and some form of homicide. Their violent crimes often tend to be very personal and frequently involve defensive reactions to continuing violence from abusive significant others. Specifically, in more than 60% of the cases their victims were males, many being husbands or significant others. In 37% of the violent incidents strangers were victims, with more than one-half of these occurring during robberies (Greenfeld and Minor-Harper, 1991; Snell and Morton, 1994).

In 1991, an estimated 72% of the women in prison had previously been incarcerated or on probation as compared with 81% of the males. Further, their prior involvement in violent crime (26 %) was much lower than that of their male counterparts (50%). Female inmates also had less extensive records than males. About two-thirds had two or fewer prior offenses compared to 39% of the males (Snell and Morton, 1994). Thus, women are less frequently recidivists, have shorter prior records, and are less likely to commit violent crimes.

## FEMALE INMATES HAVE MORE SERIOUS DRUG USE HISTORIES THAN MALES

In 1991, 54% of the female inmates sampled reported they had used drugs in the month before their current offense, with 41% reporting daily use and close to two-thirds of them saying they were regular drug users. Both the proportion of users and the levels of use were slightly higher for females than for males. Crack or cocaine (36%) topped the list of drugs used by female inmates, followed by marijuana (20%), and heroin or opiate derivatives (16%). About one in four inmates was in prison for committing a crime to get money to buy drugs and more than one-third were under the influence of drugs when they committed their crimes. Inmate drug users differed from nondrug users in that users were less likely to be in prison for violent crimes (Snell and Morton, 1994).

## Contemporary Prisons for Women Provide Better Conditions Than in the Past

The increasing number of women being arrested and sentenced to terms in prison has resulted in an expansion in the number of prisons for them. Nationally, at the end of 1993 there were 101 prisons for women, most of which were relatively small (i.e., having fewer than 500 inmates). There were also 68 co-correctional facilities (those holding both men and women) across the country, the large majority holding fewer than 100 females each (Lillis, 1994c). In 1979 there were only 29 state and 4 federal women's institutions (American Correctional Association, 1980).

## TIGHTER SECURITY IS BECOMING A CONCERN FOR MODERN WOMEN'S PRISONS

While men's prisons tend to hold a relatively narrow range of custody levels, women's facilities often have multiple levels of custody because most states have only one or two women's prisons. Consequently, security considerations that would normally apply only to the strictest custody levels are often felt by all female inmates. However, overall security has been less rigidly enforced in women's prisons. To some extent this is attributable to the cottage design of many women's prisons, which does not lend itself to tight security. However, concern with tight security has recently begun to spread to women's prisons, and now some that once had a single fence are ringed by double chain-link fences draped with rolls of razor wire. In December 1993, thirty-four U.S. jurisdictions holding 31,700 females reported that 11% of these women were held in maximum security, 39% in medium security, and 49% in minimum security (Lillis, 1994c). It is not surprising that almost half of the female inmates are housed in minimum security facilities because women are generally not considered a threat to each other or to the staff, they cause less property damage, and they typically serve their time with fewer disciplinary reports than male inmates. A 1992 survey of eighty-five institutions in forty-six jurisdictions found that in the previous twelve months only six disturbances, three demonstrations, and seventy-nine incidents involving serious staff injuries were reported. (Jones-Brown, 1992).

The growing size of the female inmate population has prompted the need for more women's prisons. Two-thirds of the states report they plan either to build new facilities or add on to existing women's facilities. This affords these jurisdictions an opportunity to build facilities that take into consideration the unique needs of women while resolving a number of inequities when compared with male facilities. These improvements include:

designing facilities comparable to male institutions and that deal with programming needs of female inmates; are more residential and have more normal furnishings due to the fewer control and security problems posed by women; have medical and mental health facilities providing the services women require; consider the special need for visiting arrangements that facilitate contact between these women and their children; consider the greater concerns women have for privacy particularly in housing units and living areas (Nesbitt, 1992).

Some of these concerns are discussed further later in the chapter.

## Females Adapt to Imprisonment in Different Ways

Inmate adaptations to prison vary from facility to facility depending on such factors as institutional and administrative programs, personal philosophy, and inmate characteristics. These adaptations can be grouped under the concept of **prisonization,** which describes the degree to which inmates participate in and adopt the prison subculture. Research related to female adaptations has been criticized for focusing principally on homosexuality and for tending to assume that the variables involved in the men's prison subcultures are applicable to women's prisons (Giallombardo, 1966; Pollock-Byrne, 1990). The lack of applicability of the variables is likely a result of the different social roles played by men and women and the manner in which these roles influence adaptive reactions to prison. These adaptive roles have been described by Giallombardo (1966), Heffernan (1972), and Ansay (1994).

**INVOLVEMENT IN PSEUDOFAMILIES REPRESENTS ONE FORM OF ADAPTATION**   Based on a study of the Women's Federal Reformatory in West Virginia, Giallombardo (1966) concluded that females in prison developed links with each other as "family" networks and in homosexual marriages. Referred to as **pseudofamilies,** these groups tended to satisfy the social, psychological, and physiological needs related to the cultural roles women were expected to play. Women participating in these "families" adopted a variety of roles (e.g., father, mother, sister, brother) and displayed behavior consistent with those roles. Within these primary "family" groups, women formed strong bonds and had little need to identify with the total inmate subculture. This bonding has been interpreted as an adaptation to the way in which women in general society sustain themselves emotionally. These family-type groupings involved close emotional relationships not usually found in men's prisons.

**THREE ADAPTIVE ROLES ARE IMPORTED FROM OUTSIDE THE PRISON**   Heffernan (1972) identified three adaptive roles at a Washington, DC, women's reformatory that were referred to in argot (slang) terms as "square," "the life," and "cool." Squares were individuals who held and followed conventional norms and values. Generally they had no criminal background but had committed a serious crime, like killing their husbands during a heated argument. These women tried to sustain a conventional life in prison, maintain respectful relations with prison staff, and be seen as good Christians.

Inmates in "the life" represented 50% of the prison's population. They were women who had habitually committed offenses such as prostitution, possession or sales of illegal drugs, or shoplifting and had been in prison before. These inmates became totally immersed in the prison world. They tended to interact with persons of similar backgrounds and be hostile or negative in their dealings with correctional officers. As on the street, they had no remorse about breaking the rules even if it meant extending their sentences. Cool inmates, were professional criminals who viewed their incarceration as a temporary experience that was a part of being involved in crime. They wanted to minimize their time in prison and essentially do easy time. To do this, they sought to manipulate the system without endangering their chances for early release. This meant remaining on the fringes of inmate activities, but at the same time following whatever inmate code existed within the prison.

Heffernan (1972) felt that these three roles were imported into the prison from the community and that these three cultural subsystems were not necessarily antagonistic toward each other. While all three groups adapted differently, each represented an attempt to create a familiar, comfortable set of relationships with which to alleviate the rigors of imprisonment. Superficially, these three adaptations resembled those found in men's prisons. However, the behavioral expression of the roles that characterize them was quite different. This included much less violence, fewer racial tensions, higher levels of informal integration, and a less formalized sub-rosa economy.

**CONTEMPORARY PSEUDOFAMILIES ARE BECOMING MORE GANG-LIKE**   In an exploratory study of a southern prison, Ansay (1994) interviewed thirty-six female inmates to determine the status of the "prison family" in the 1990s. From verbal descriptions and crude diagrams of the family groups described by the women, she determined that there were five family-like groupings. One group consisted of a well-respected Christian family of twenty "older sisters" who were noted for their caring role in helping "little sisters" and newcomers to the prison. Second, she found several biological families, consisting of individuals who were related. One of these groups included a mother and daughter who were cell mates. A third group, composed of Hispanics, had a family-like structure and was headed by a "Mommie" and "Poppie." It was noted for its unity, the members' concern for one another, and for the security they provided for themselves. A fourth group, which she labeled "surrogate," consisted of various, loosely structured, egalitarian units that bonded in mutual trust and showed care and concern for each other. These "families" were primarily matricentric and included a "mother" and one or two "daughters." The most commonly occurring groups, which Ansay labeled "game families," appeared more gang-like than family-like. Each had a core group of six to twelve long-term inmates who had become a stable, well-recognized force within the prison. The core group's influence was expressed through a complex network of interrelated "children," "in-laws," "cousins," "do-girls," and other "associates." Illegal activities included such things as "loan sharking." Ansay concludes that the "play families" described earlier by Giallombardo appear to have evolved into various types of organizations, some with elements that are similar to those of organized prison gangs.

**THE NATURE AND AMOUNT OF HOMOSEXUAL ACTIVITY IS UNCERTAIN**   Restrictions on sexual and emotional contact with the opposite sex, which generate homosexual liaisons in men's prisons, have similar effects in women's prisons but with different consequences. In women's prisons, homosexual relations are generally noncoercive and involve close emotional ties. These liaisons range from "marriage" to "dating" to "tricking" (indiscriminate sexual activity, perhaps for economic gain). The form of the relationships also varies, with some pairs involving a "male" and "female" role and others making no such distinction. In pairs having role differentiation, the woman assuming the male role often takes on the characteristics ascribed to it (e.g., she is domineering and dresses and grooms more like a man). Several studies (e.g., Halleck and Herski, 1962; Ward and Kassebaum, 1965; Giallombardo, 1966; Nelson, 1974; Propper, 1976, 1982) have examined various aspects of female inmates' homosexual activities. They report levels of participation in homosexual behavior ranging from about 20 to more than 85%. Women engaging in it were younger, more likely black, and had their first homosexual encounters outside the prison.

Most recent studies suggest a much lower incidence of homosexuality than reported by earlier studies. This difference, according to Pollock-Byrne (1990), may be related to "the almost prurient curiosity of so many [early] researchers in the females' sexual identity and activity" (p. 130).

## Services and Programs at Women's Prisons Often Lack Parity with Male Facilities

The nature, quality, and number of programs and services in women's prisons have been less adequate than those for men almost since the beginning of the imprisonment of women in the United States. A 1984 study of programming for women in Kentucky captured the essence of the problem when it asserted that "The programs offered women are limited in number, traditional in nature and clearly not equivalent to program choices available to men" (Community Research Center, 1984, p. 37, as cited by Rafter, 1990, p. 186). Thus, it is not surprising that women have instituted suits to obtain parity with programming in men's prisons. These suits brought by female inmates have changed the conditions under which women are incarcerated and have mandated expansion of the programs and services in women's prisons. One recent result of the move toward parity has been the development of a boot camp program for females in South Carolina (Brown, 1994).

**MOST WOMEN'S PRISONS OFFER EDUCATION PROGRAMS**   As with males, a majority of female inmates are deficient in academic skills. Several

Calls for equity in programs prompted some women's prisons to offer non-traditional vocational training.

studies (Glick and Neto, 1977; Chapman, 1980; Crawford, 1988) show that between one-half and three-fourths of the female inmates studied had not finished high school, and their tested educational levels were lower than the grades they reported completing. For example, data on a sample of female inmates, constituting 89% of the women incarcerated in Florida between 1985 and 1987, found that the average reported grade level was 10.1 while the tested level was 7.4. (Blount, Danner, Vega, and Silverman, 1991). A 1993 national study of women's prisons found that of the forty-nine systems responding all offered General Equivalence Diploma (GED), Adult Basic Education (ABE), and other educational programs. Forty-one of the systems offered college-level courses in some form, for example, by correspondence - (Lillis, 1994d). Five of the state systems also reported requiring inmates to attain certain minimum educational levels before being considered for sentence reductions and/or release (Lillis, 1994d).

Another part of the educational programming is life skills and related courses. In women's prisons these courses are very popular, particularly those dealing with parenting, visitation, and other family relations skills. Their popularity stems from the fact that they are seen to have a direct positive impact on an inmate's ability to maintain family relationships.

**VOCATIONAL TRAINING PROGRAMS STILL OFFER MAINLY "WOMEN'S WORK"** The vocational training programs available in women's prisons have long been a source of controversy and criticism because they fall far short of those offered to men in terms of quantity, quality, variety, and availability (Ross and Fabiano, 1986). Some reasons offered for these inequalities include the expense of establishing many programs, the small number of women's prisons, and sexist beliefs regarding the work women should perform (Ross and Fabiano, 1986).

Lillis (1994d) found that all but one of the forty-nine systems responding to her survey had at least one vocational education program. The most common programs, according to Ryan (1984) and Weisheit (1985), included sewing, food services, secretarial, domestic, and cosmetology, with all of these programs existing in from 36 to 86% of the institutions surveyed. Thus, the most frequently offered programs were those that trained women for jobs that are normally considered "women's work." Coincidentally, since these jobs tend to be low paying, they make it more difficult for the woman to be self-sufficient upon release. Cosmetology programs present a strange contradiction because, in many states offering this program, individuals with felony records cannot obtain licenses to work in this profession and thus are unable to earn a living.

Litigation aimed at achieving parity has begun to change some of these discrepancies. For example, Weisheit (1985) reported that the number of women's prisons offering nontraditional programs (e.g., auto repair, carpentry) had increased from none in 1973 to fifteen in 1985. By the late 1980s the parity movement had made some progress because corrections departments were faced with a growing number of women entering prison who had few skills yet would have to support both themselves and their children upon release (Rafter, 1990). This led systems to supplement traditional female training programs with vocational education programs that included small engine repair, masonry and drafting, and canine training. Today, as our economy is less dominated by heavy industry and more oriented toward jobs involving service and technology, vocational training programs have had to shift their emphasis to training women for jobs in this new environment. This requires development of verbal, reading, and computer skills to enable women to obtain telemarketing jobs, do office work, or be employed in other service industries (Carp and Davis, 1989).

**INMATE WORK PROGRAMS SERVE VARIOUS PURPOSES** Work involves a variety of activities with different purposes (e.g., keeping inmates busy, reducing costs, training for future employment). Work programs include institutional maintenance (e.g., cleaning, repair, mowing, landscaping, laundry, food preparation, clerical work) and working in a prison industry. Unless extenuating circumstances exist (e.g., a medical disability or special status), inmates are presently being given program and/or work assignments in all of the states except Vermont (Lillis, 1994d).

The majority of inmates work at jobs related to operating the prison. Most of the maintenance work is repetitive and menial and can be done very quickly, so to keep inmates busy these tasks are slowed and unnecessarily repeated. Food service, described in Chapter 20, requires a relatively large number of workers since meals are prepared every day of the week. The laundry also requires many inmate workers and it is one of the worst jobs in a prison because it is physically demanding work in a hot and humid environment.

Few prisons pay inmates for institutional jobs. Thus, for inmates with no other source of money to buy the few "luxuries" available in prison, a paying industry job may represent manna from heaven. Prison industries in women's prisons have tended to involve activities seen as women's work (e.g., sewing factories). However, recently developed programs have expanded the range of these jobs. An example of this is a lens grinding operation in a Florida prison for women, which gives qualified inmates a marketable skill and produces the glasses distributed to all institutionalized individuals in the state who need them.

Like vocational education programs, prison industries have had to face concerns of parity and the changes in the job sector from hard industries to more emphasis on technical and service jobs. To provide for the interests and needs of female inmates, Carp and Davis (1989) suggest that women's prisons need to develop work programs that include a garment shop, food service, and a data entry or telemarketing shop. In this regard, several jurisdictions have used female inmates to staff information lines that answer questions from callers about state tourism opportunities and as reservations agents for TWA and Best Western motels. Additionally, to increase work opportunities for women, some jurisdictions allow female inmates to work in programs with males (Davis, 1992a). Women who participate in occupational rehabilitation programs "earn more and stay out of prison longer than those who do not" (Bartolo, 1991, p. 2).

**RECREATIONAL ACTIVITIES ARE OFTEN PASSIVE AND NONPHYSICAL** Women's prisons also lag behind those for men with regard to recreational activities. While appropriate recreation and exercise are seen as healthy and important activities, most women engage in leisure activities that are sedentary (e.g., watching television and playing board games) (Mann, 1984). More physical games and sports are often shunned by the women when offered. Alternative activities found to be successful at women's facilities include aerobics classes, exercise rooms with stationary bicycles, treadmills, and weight equipment. One Minnesota prison had a bowling alley. Also popular are hobby and craft programs featuring macrame, ceramics, and jewelry making (Carp and Davis, 1989).

**MEDICAL SERVICES ARE GENERALLY INADEQUATE** The quality and quantity of health care received by all inmates have been questioned and generally found wanting (see Chapter 19). Because women commonly need and avail themselves of more medical services than men, the problem of poor medical services for the female inmate is even greater than it is for the male. The street lifestyle of many female inmates (e.g., drug and alcohol abuse, poor diet, possibly indiscriminate sexual behavior, restricted access to medical services, and the tendency to neglect medical problems) means that women entering prison are likely to require medical attention and education to help them take better care of themselves on release to the community (Carp and Davis, 1989). The literature is replete with examples of disparity in medical care for women. It is an issue that has often been related to and justified by the smaller size of many women's prisons. National standards mandate that:

> "females have access to the same basic and specialty care as males *in addition to* services designed to meet their special needs [e.g., obstetrical/gynecological care] (Anno, 1991a, p. 143).

Correctional systems failing to comply with these standards can expect litigation on these issues, especially with the growing numbers of women entering prison.

Research shows that during the last two decades medical services for women have been improving. A 1975 study by Glick and Neto (1977) of medical service delivery found that these services ranged from limited to minimal in about 60% of the prisons they surveyed. Seven years later Ryan (1984) reported that more than 90% of the facilities responding to her survey had medical care that included some of the following: intake screening, annual checkups, OB/GYN services, and round-the-clock emergency service. She concluded that this represented a doubling of these types of services during the seven-year period between the two studies. By 1993, conditions had improved substantially. At this point, forty-nine of fifty-two U.S. state and federal correctional systems responding to a Corrections Compendium study of female facilities reported that forty-seven systems had on-site medical staff; forty-two systems provided OB/GYN care; and forty-six had available prenatal and postpartum care (Lillis, 1994d).

### Pregnancy Represents a Dilemma for Both Incarcerated Women and the Corrections System

In 1991, about 6% of women in prison reported they were pregnant when they entered the institution (Snell and Morton, 1994). Most of these women had received both routine GYN and prenatal care. In 1993, forty-two systems reported there were 594 pregnant offenders (Lillis, 1994d). During

this period, in thirty-two of these systems women gave birth to 789 babies.

Pregnancy imposes strains on both the inmate mother-to-be and the relatively limited prison health care resources. Most pregnant inmates arrive at prison in that condition, but a few women become impregnated while in prison, (e.g., being raped by a male staff member; during a conjugal visit) (Holt, 1981-82). Since the health status of many women entering prison is poor, pregnant inmates may face complications during their pregnancy (Huft, Faukes, and Lawson, 1992).

Regarding the care of pregnant inmates, Jay Anno (1991a), chair of the National Commission on Correctional Medical Care, asserts that:

> Consistent with state and federal regulations, [they] should retain the right to choose abortion or continuation of pregnancy. Pregnancy counseling and abortion must be available. They must have access to regular prenatal care and receive dietary supplements (e.g., milk, extra food, prenatal vitamins) as prescribed by a physician (p. 142).

Also, guidelines on the care of pregnant inmates are provided by the American Medical Association and the American Public Health Association. These guidelines prohibit any form of discipline or punishment that might cause harm to the fetus or to a nursing baby (Holt, 1981-82). Generally, when a pregnant inmate goes into labor she is transported, sometimes in irons, to a local medical facility to deliver her baby.

**MOST INMATE MOTHERS ARE SEPARATED FROM THEIR NEWBORN BABIES**   Once she has had the baby, in all but a few U.S. prisons, the inmate mother will be sent back to the prison and separated from her child within two days to three weeks. This is typically very traumatic for the mother. It can also have harmful consequences for the child because it interferes with the bonding process that is necessary for the child's appropriate psychosocial development. Generally, each mother must select an approved family member or friend to take responsibility for the child's care. Failing this, the state selects a foster home or other placement. The New York correctional system, at its Bedford Hills and Taconic facilities, provides space for women who give birth while in prison to keep their newborns until they are one year old (New York State Department of Correctional Services,

## Close Up   Pregnant in Prison: An Inmate's Experience

My name is Dana. I am incarcerated at a federal prison camp in Bryan, Texas.

I came to prison pregnant. . . . I thought that it was the end of the world, but it wasn't. The psychologist and chaplain counseled me and gave me advice. They told me about a program where I could spend time with my child and form a mother/child bond. The name of the program is MINT, which stands for Mothers and Infants Together. . . . They explained that I would spend two months with my child after it was born. . . .

To make a long story short, I left Bryan on July 2 and went to the Community Corrections Center (CCC) in Fort Worth, Texas, where the MINT program is located. . . . I was scared at first, but the staff knew my situation and helped me in more ways than I could imagine. I was introduced to a staff member who I didn't know would have such an impact in my life—I'll use her first name only.

Thava was one of the warmest, nicest, and sincerest persons who I had met since being incarcerated. We hit it off from the start. . . . We talked and I told her how I felt at the time, which wasn't too great. She gave me some thoughtful words. It was then that I realized I had someone to talk to. As the days passed, Thava did so much for me. She set up my doctor's appointments and had films that I could watch - the subjects included mothers using drugs, the birthing process, breastfeeding, and so on. Thava was a hardworking and dependable woman. She was even in the delivery room when I gave birth to my precious son. . . . When my son was a week old, he had bad stomachaches. Thava would come at any hour, day or night, to take him to the doctor. She made sure that he had milk and Pampers. I don't know what I would have done without her.

I am grateful for having the opportunity to spend two months with my son and establish a mother/child bond. When my son turned two months old, it was time for us to say our farewells. Thava took us to the airport and waved at us until we were gone. . . .

I am back in Bryan, Texas, finishing my time. My son is now six months old. Programs like the MINT program help mothers in prison and their children (Huft, Fawkes, and Lawson, 1992, p. 53).

1993). Most of the services and supplies needed to care for the babies are provided and the mothers are thoroughly involved in caring for and nurturing their children. However, at the end of the one year these children must be placed with relatives, friends, or in a foster home to await the release of the mother. A 12-month follow-up study of twenty-eight inmate mothers in this program showed that fewer than 10% were returned as parole violators, none with new criminal charges (Grossman, 1984). The participants generally agreed that the program benefited both the inmates and children by keeping the families together.

Programs to help mothers bond with their newborns exist in various places. Our Close-Up on "Pregnant in Prison: An inmate's experience" describes one federal program.

### Visitation Enables Women to Maintain Ties with Children and Other Family Members

Chapter 21 deals with general visiting issues and thus the major focus here is on mother/child con-tacts. Because about three-fourths of the women in prison have children, two-thirds of whom are under eighteen, this is an important issue.

When mothers are imprisoned the effect on their children is likely to be greater than when the father is imprisoned because in many instances, prior to imprisonment, females are the primary caregivers. Studies conducted during the 1970s and 1980s indicated that most inmates' children (more than 80%) lived with relatives, most often those of the mother (Baunach, 1979; Bloom, 1988; Koban, 1983; Crawford, 1988). A 1991 study found that one-fourth of the children lived with the father, half resided with a grandparent, and the rest lived in a variety of other situations (e.g., other relatives, foster parents) (Snell and Morton, 1994). Inmates with children in foster homes suffered more frustration because foster parents were less likely to bring the children to visit or inform them about the children's lives.

Visitation provides a potent release from the stress and worry these women may have regarding the emotional and physical condition of their children (Davis, 1992a). However, because most states

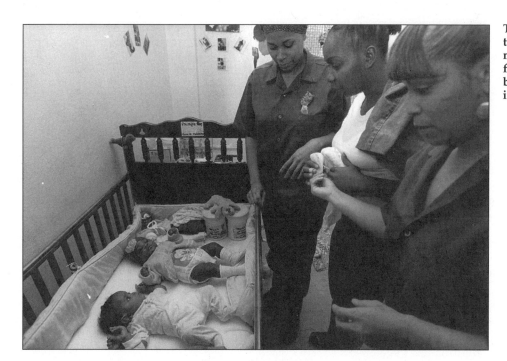

The few prison programs that allow female inmates to keep and care for their newborns help both the child and the inmate.

have only one or two women's prisons, they may be too far to allow frequent visitation (Carp and Davis, 1989). The generally poor economic conditions of inmate families and lack of public transportation to most prisons create more barriers to visitation.

Despite the many impediments that decrease the frequency of visits, they do occur and there is a need to provide programming and facilities that help maintain mother/child ties during these visits. Many jurisdictions recognize this. Thus in 1993, forty-eight of the forty-nine systems responding to a Corrections Compendium survey allowed contact visits at women's prisons, twenty-four allowed extended mother/child visits, and ten allowed some form of conjugal or family visitation (Lillis, 1994d).

**PARENT/CHILD PROGRAMS ARE DESIGNED TO FOSTER MOTHER/CHILD RELATIONS**  Both special programming and a dedicated environment are key elements in mother/child visiting arrangements. These elements should provide:

[a non-] intimidating place for children and inmates [that] should feel comfortable [for them] to bring their children to. . . Space [that] should be available so that mothers and children can spend private time together in a normalized, home-like atmosphere (Carp and Davis, 1989, p. 51).

Mother/child programs take many forms. To maintain the bonds between inmate mothers and their children "My Mother's Home" provides long-term foster care especially for children of mothers incarcerated in New York State correctional facilities. Bedford Hills Correctional Center in New York has a ten-week summer camp program for inmate children. This provides mothers the opportunity to visit with their children and take part in a regular day camp from 9:00 to 3:00 in the afternoon. The children live with volunteer host families near the prisons or are transported daily. Some hosts found this summer program so gratifying that they have volunteered to host a child one Saturday night a month. The children arrive by bus in the morning and can visit with their mothers until 3:30 P.M. returning home the next day (Roulet, 1993; Bloom and Steinhart, 1993).

"In Pennsylvania, parent/child visits are held in a trailer on the facility grounds. . . . These trailers are divided into areas for infants, young children, and adolescents. . . . [Visits are] conduct[ed] under the supervision of a social worker" (Carp and Davis, 1989, pp. 51–52). Several other states have programs that allow children to visit overnight with their mothers. The Mother-Offspring Life Development (MOLD) program, which has operated in Nebraska and Kentucky, is an example of this type of program. In addition to permitting overnight visits by their mothers, the MOLD program includes nursery programs, child care classes for the mothers, and counseling and evaluation (Stanton, 1980; Bloom and Steinhart, 1993).

Finally, a Maryland women's prison established a Girl Scout program to help foster contact between inmate mothers and their daughters. On a biweekly basis, thirty imprisoned mothers meet with their daughters to engage in Girl Scout activities. Community volunteers help to maintain the program by hosting meetings during the weeks the girls do not visit the prison. All involved consider this program a success (Moses, 1993).

**TRANSITION FROM PRISON TO SOCIETY CAN BE DIFFICULT FOR INMATE MOTHERS** The transition from the prison into society poses additional problems for many inmate mothers because the majority have insufficient finances to establish themselves upon release. California has developed the Community Prisoner Mother Program. With facilities in seven cities, these programs help inmate mothers with the transition to the community. The mothers receive employment training and counseling, and their children, up to six years of age, can live with them. Unfortunately, the criteria for admittance into these programs are so rigorous that not all operate regularly at full capacity (Bloom and Steinhart, 1993).

For mothers who lose custody of their children while in prison, the inability to provide support may make regaining custody a more difficult task. The inmate mother will face a Catch-22 situation as a single parent because if she has employment that enables her to support the child, she may be faulted for not providing adequate supervision while she is working. Finally, women who attempt to live independently may be forced, for economic reasons, to live in poverty ridden, high-crime areas that could entice them to become reinvolved in criminal behavior (Pollock-Byrne, 1990).

## Co-Correctional Institutions House Men and Women in the Same Prison

With the opening of the **co-correctional** program at the Federal Correctional Institution in Ft. Worth, Texas, in 1971, the housing of females in the same

prison with men had come full circle. As noted earlier, women had been housed in men's facilities during most of the nineteenth century. Although a few states housed some women in male facilities prior to the 1970s, there were few or no shared programs in these facilities. The increasing pressure on many systems to achieve some kind of parity, particularly in providing programs and services, prompted some systems to experiment with co-correctional programs because this offered a cost-effective solution to this problem. They also offer a more normal environment enabling both men and women to be more easily reintegrated into society. In 1993, there were sixty-eight co-correctional facilities in operation in thirty states (Lillis, 1994c).

**PROGRAMS ARE SHARED, BUT SLEEPING ARRANGEMENTS ARE SEPARATE** In contemporary co-correctional institutions men and women are housed separately but normally participate in most programs and share services. The public has many misconceptions about co-correctional institutions, among which are that there is extreme promiscuity, the two sexes share sleeping quarters, and there are many illegitimate births (Halford, 1984). The fact is that rules in these institutions prohibit male/female contact beyond holding hands and the supervision is relatively strict. Illicit sexual activity and some pregnancies do occur, but these are relatively rare.

**THESE PROGRAMS HAVE ADVANTAGES AND DISADVANTAGES FOR BOTH SEXES** Supporters of co-corrections assert that it benefits both men and women. The more relaxed atmosphere decreases tension and violence and reduces or eliminates homosexual behavior among men. Women tend to benefit from greater availability of medical, psychological, legal and social services, and educational and vocational programs. Some drawbacks for women include increased control and security (to control sexual activity), less opportunity for leadership, and avoidance of nontraditional programs because of the perception they are unfeminine (Schweber, 1984). Smykla (1980), also feels that in these facilities women may be exploited because they continue to be seen as men's sexual objects.

## Community Correctional Programs for Both Sexes Are Similar

Community correctional programs available for women are similar to those for men and are based on the same premises. That is, since incarceration disrupts family ties and creates dependency, reintegration into the community is difficult and the offender needs help to reenter the community successfully. This can be more difficult for females because the roles women perform tend to restrict employment opportunities and require them to be more responsible for their children. Also these women tend to be poorly educated, have unstable employment records, and suffer a variety of health problems including TB, sexually transmitted diseases, and AIDS. Further, many leave prison or jail either homeless or lacking safe, drug-free housing (Austin, Bloom, and Donahue, 1992). Thus, they are likely to need specialized programs that address their unique needs.

Community-based programs, which can enable women to avoid the disruptions of going to prison to begin with or ease their transition from prison to freedom, can be particularly valuable. Since women tend to commit proportionally fewer serious crimes than men, a greater number are likely to be eligible for community-based programs.

**COMMUNITY PROGRAMS SERVE PRE-PRISON AND POST-PRISON FUNCTIONS AND CAN BE RESIDENTIAL OR NONRESIDENTIAL** Austin *et al.* (1992) surveyed 100 existing community programs for female offenders. Figure 12.2 shows that these programs serve both pre- and post-prison functions, are small, and most are operated by private, nonprofit organizations. Table 12.1 provides a profile of program clients showing that they are predominantly black, divorced/separated, have children, and have problems and deficits that make adjustment to the community difficult. Most of these programs are residential and provide programs that include alcohol/drug treatment, parenting, and job-seeking skills. Also offered are:

> counseling services . . . consist[ing] of individual and group sessions and [dealing with] general life issues [and] . . . domestic violence and sexual abuse.
> . . . living skills employment services [in which they] learn and practice money management, meal planning and preparation, job and housing search skills, household management, health and hygiene, use of

community sources and other tasks of daily living. . . . employment services . . . vocational assessments, job readiness, job skill training and job placement . . . [some] programs required clients [to] work and/or have stable employment before successfully completing the program (Austin *et al.*, 1992, p. 14).

Since placement in these programs is often viewed as an intermediate sanction, courts expect strict compliance with certain specific conditions. To meet this requirement, three-fourths of these programs provide supervision and residential security. In the other 25%, offenders are supervised by probation and parole officers. Some specific monitoring strategies used by programs include:

> us[ing] urine tests and "breathalyzers" to detect alcohol/drug use . . . and workplace and home visits and telephone checks to verify participants' whereabouts (Austin et al., 1992 p. 14).

ARC Community Services Treatment Alternative Program in Madison, Wisconsin, is an example of a nonresidential diversion program that provides addiction treatment services to women arrested for drug law violations and those arrested for prostitution. Program participants are counseled for six months, must report regularly, and are required to undergo urine tests. Court sentenced programs can be divided into residential (for the offender alone or the offender and her children) or nonresidential. Residential programs are usually small with average daily populations of less than twenty and often serve both offenders directly sentenced there and those released from jail or prison. Project Greenhope in New York is an example of this type of program. Treatment is aimed at dealing with addiction, HIV education, job readiness, and parenting. Offenders are retained for three to six months and those sentenced are supervised in the community for an additional six months.

Nonresidential or day treatment programs provide or broker services for women living at home. Most programs focus on addiction treatment and life skills training and provide counseling, child care, and employment services. Genesis II, for women in Minneapolis, Minnesota, provides these services along with a children's center that has a child development program for infants and children through the age of twelve. Part of this

FIGURE 12.2 **Characteristics of 100 Community Programs for Women Offenders**

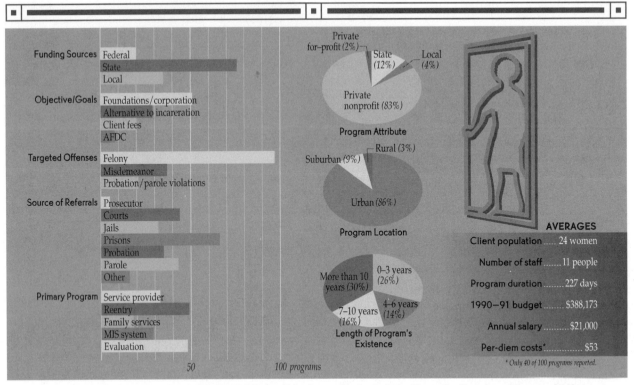

*Source:* J. Austin, B. Bloom, and T. Donahue (1992), *Female Offenders in the Community: An Analysis of Innovative Strategies and Programs*, Washington, D.C.: National Institute of Corrections, U.S. Department of Justice, p. 11.

program involves observing mother/child interactions to teach these women how to avoid or prevent abusive situations.

**POST-PRISON RELEASE PROGRAMS FOCUS ON RELAPSE PREVENTION** Aftercare programs that provide reentry into the community from jails or prisons can also be divided according to whether they are residential or nonresidential and if children can reside with their mothers. Austin *et al.* (1992) found that residential programs ranged in size from 6 to 140 beds. The Duval Community Correctional Center in Jacksonville, Florida, is a residential work release center for women released from Florida prisons. This program provides employment services and focuses on substance abuse treatment and relapse prevention. It also has 24-hour security and monitors participants' community activities.

Residential programs for offenders and their children are similar to those that accommodate only women except that they provide services for chil-

dren that may include education, mentoring, drug education, and counseling. Most nonresidential/day treatment reentry programs serve women who are either on probation or on parole. They tend to emphasize employment and life skills training and may be operated by private agencies through contractual agreements.

## Future Correctional Programming for Women Should Consider Their Special Needs

The differing needs and expectations of men and women, the expectations of society, and the patterns of female crime will continue to influence the directions taken by corrections programs for women as we move into the twenty-first century. A recognition of these differences and their implications for dealing with the crime committed by women will give courts and correctional administrators a basis for making choices about the sentencing and correctional alternatives that best serve society and these women. Among the issues re-

TABLE **12.1**   **Population Characteristics of Women in Community Corrections Programs***

| Average age | 28 years | | Clients with children under age 6 | 68% |
|---|---|---|---|---|
| | | | Clients who are pregnant | 12% |
| | | | Clients who gave birth within six months of entering the program | 18% |
| **Ethnicity** | | | | |
| African-American | 50% | | | |
| White | 37% | | **Client Service Needs** | |
| Hispanic | 16% | | Alchohol/drug treatment | 82% |
| Native American | 5% | | Employment | 80% |
| Asian | 2% | | Education | 69% |
| Other | 4% | | Housing | 69% |
| | | | Legal Aid | 48% |
| **Marital Status** | | | | |
| Married | 19% | | | |
| Divorced/separated | 45% | | | |
| Single | 75% | | | |
| Other | 5% | | | |

*Note:* The percentages represent the average percnetage reported by all programs for a specific item. Hence, they will not total 100%.

*Source:* J. Austin, B. Bloom, and T. Donahue (1992), *Female Offenders in the Community: An Analysis of Innovative Strategies and Programs,* Washington, D.C.:National Institute of Corrections, U.S. Department of Justice, p. 13.

quiring consideration so female offenders can more effectively be dealt with are the following:

**1.** To what extent do we need to imprison women convicted of crime instead of placing them in community programs?
**2.** What are the effects of incarceration on the children of inmate mothers?
**3.** What are the medical needs of the female inmate population and how can these best be met?
**4.** What is the role of drug use and abuse in the criminality of women and how can this problem be best dealt with?
**5.** What patterns of vocational training are most appropriate for female inmates?

These and a number of related questions must be addressed to deal effectively with the problems posed by female offenders.

It is likely that the arrest rates of women will continue to increase, given a continued tough stance on crime. However, because we are dealing with an initially small number of women, the proportion in the system will continue to be small, at least for the foreseeable future. The recent pattern of crimes committed by women shows they are increasingly being arrested for drug-related crimes. Thus, this is a programmatic need that will have to be addressed. There is little to suggest that the characteristics of female inmates are changing

in any drastic way. Thus, we can expect this inmate population to have the same traits, deficits, and needs in the immediate future.

**REDUCED INCARCERATION OF WOMEN IS RECOMMENDED**   It has been suggested that many of the women currently serving prison terms could safely and more economically serve their sentences in community-based programs. For those with drug problems there is a need to expand treatment programs. For many others, the economic crimes they committed resulted from their disadvantaged position and lack of marketable skills. For many of these women, as well as for society, incarceration may serve no useful purpose, especially if it fails to resolve their drug problems or enhance their economic position. This is particularly true of female offenders with children, whose offspring may be the ones to suffer most from their mothers' criminal behavior and subsequent incarceration. Many children of incarcerated mothers suffer from a variety of debilitating problems, which tend to be later expressed in school failure and delinquency. If these mothers, particularly those who are single parents, can acquire vocational skills resulting in jobs paying enough to enable them to support their children, they will no longer need to resort to criminal behavior. If they can also enhance their parenting skills their children may be more likely to escape from the cycle of criminality.

## Chapter Recap

**Female Offenders and the Criminal Justice System**
Current Female Criminality Is Low But Increasing
Faster Than for Men
Different Factors Affect the Sentencing of Women and Men
**Women and the Correctional System**
Historical Overview Shows a Familiar Pattern
Women Took the Lead in Reforming Programs for
Incarcerated Females
Reforms Created Separate Prisons for Women
The Reformatory Movement Brought Changes for
Female Corrections
Parole Was First Applied to Women
The Cottage Plan Was Used in the Construction of
Women's Prisons
Legal Challenges by Inmates Have Improved Female
Prisons
Female Inmates in Jails and Prisons Differ from Their
Male Counterparts
Most Women Are Now Being Incarcerated for Drug
and Violent Crimes
Tighter Security Is Becoming a Concern for Modern Women's Prisons
Female Inmates Have More Serious Drug Use Histories Than Males
Contemporary Prisons for Women Provide Better Conditions Than in the Past
Tighter Security Is Becoming a Concern for Modern
Women's Prisons
Females Adapt to Imprisonment in Different Ways
Involvement in Pseudofamilies Represents One Form
of Adaptation
Three Adaptive Roles Are Imported from Outside the
Prison
Contemporary Pseudofamilies Are Becoming More
Gang-Like
The Nature and Amount of Homosexual Activity Is
Uncertain
Services and Programs at Women's Prisons Often Lack
Parity with Male Facilities
Most Women's Prisons Offer Education Programs
Vocational Training Programs Still Offer Mainly
"Women's Work"
Inmate Work Programs Keep the Prison Operating
Recreational Activities Are Often Passive and Non-physical
Medical Services Are Generally Inadequate
Pregnancy Represents a Dilemma for Both Incarcerated
Women and the Corrections System
Most Inmate Mothers Are Separated from Their
Newborn Babies

Visitation Enables Women to Maintain Ties with Children and Other Family Members
Parent/Child Programs Are Designed to Foster
Mother/Child Relations
Transition from Prison to Society Can Be Difficult for
Inmate Mothers
Co-Correctional Institutions House Men and Women in
the Same Prison
Programs Are Shared, But Sleeping Arrangements
Are Separate
These Programs Have Advantages and Disadvantages for Both Sexes
Community Correctional Programs for Both Sexes Are
Similar
Community Programs Serve Pre-Prison and Post-Prison Functions and Can Be Residential or Non-residential
Post-Prison Release Programs Focus on Relapse Prevention
Future Correctional Programming for Women Should
Consider Their Special Needs
Reduced Incarceration of Women Is Recommended

## Review Questions

**1.** In what ways have female offenders received preferential treatment from the criminal justice system? In what ways have they received equally harsh or harsher treatment than men?
**2.** How have female inmates adapted to imprisonment?
**3.** Which services and programs have women's prisons been most successful in offering to female inmates? Which programs have proven inadequate and why have they been so inadequate for women?
**4.** What are the primary problems facing inmate mothers and their children? What has been the result of allowing children to stay with their mothers in prison?

## Test Your Knowledge

**1.** Differences in the sentencing of male and female offenders can best be explained by
  a. blatant gender discrimination.
  b. the chivalry factor.
  c. concern for maintaining the families of female offenders.
  d. a lack of understanding of gender roles.
**2.** Co-corrections is
  a. the housing of men and women in the same prison.
  b. the sentencing of offenders to both jail time and community-based programs.

c. the use of male correctional officers in women's prisons.

d. a radical new prison plan where male and female inmates share sleeping quarters.

3. Incarcerated women are characterized by
   a. a history of abuse.
   b. drug dependency.
   c. poor education and work skills.
   d. all of the above.

4. The main difference between the pseudofamilies in the women's prisons of the 1960s and those of the 1990s is that
   a. there is more homosexuality now than before.
   b. "families" are becoming more gang-like.

c. these "families" no longer exist.

d. there is more abusive and violent behavior now than before.

5. Vocational training programs in women's prisons
   a. generally offer a greater variety than men's prisons.
   b. attract women mostly to nontraditional types of work.
   c. generally offer access to low-paying "women's work."
   d. are at least as good if not better than in men's prisons.

# PART FIVE

---

# INSTITUTIONAL
# ADMINISTRATION
# AND
# MANAGEMENT

# CHAPTER 13

# CORRECTIONAL ADMINISTRATION

## ◼ LEARNING OBJECTIVES

*After completion of this chapter, you should be able to:*

1. Discuss the three levels of correctional systems (federal, state, and local).

2. Explain why there is ambiguity and lack of consensus about the goals of corrections.

3. Discuss the role of private corporations in modern corrections.

4. Provide an explanation of the four basic levels of correctional administration: system wide, institutional, middle level, and first level.

5. Compare and contrast the three approaches to correctional management: authoritarian, bureaucratic, and participative.

6. Discuss what is meant by "proactive corrections management."

7. Describe the essential characteristics of successful correctional administrators.

8. Compare and describe the riots at the New Mexico penitentiary, Camp Hill, and Lucasville.

9. Specify the procedures felt to be necessary by the ACA in preventing or controlling prison riots.

10. Discuss why Oak Park Heights is considered a well-run prison.

## ◼ KEYS TERMS AND CONCEPTS

Authoritarian model
Bureaucratic model
Delegation model
Executive management team
First-line supervisors
Line personnel
Management by walking around
Middle managers
Organizational culture
Participative model
Proactive management
Staff personnel
Unit management

"[W]hether prisons and jails are safe and civilized, on the one hand, or riotous and wretched, on the other, depends mainly on how they are organized and managed . . ." (DiIulio, 1991, p. 33).[a] As DiIulio indicates, the most important factors in the success of any enterprise are the manner in which it is structured and the qualities of the people who run it. In prison, it is that structure and the individuals who manage it that create the environment in which all interactions among staff and between staff and inmates take place. It is imperative that administrators and managers and those who work under them hold similar views of the mission of the prison and its achievement. It is their task to provide the leadership by which this unity of purpose is defined and attained. In the correctional setting, this leads to prisons in which staff and inmates can work or do their time in safety and with dignity.

Because corrections is a governmental rather than a private enterprise function, there are many ways in which it operates differently from a commercial enterprise. However, both public and private organizations function most effectively under professional managers who can recognize and react to environmental pressures, coordinate organizational relationships, manage and motivate people, and apply technologies germane to their fields.

## U.S. CORRECTIONAL SYSTEMS OPERATE ON THREE LEVELS

Governmental functions and responsibilities in the United States are divided among federal, state, and local entities. Each of these levels of government generally operates and maintains its own correctional programs and facilities. As a result corrections in the United States is divided into many different systems, programs, and has diverse goals. This makes it difficult to describe, in any more than general terms, the corrections systems in this country.

### The Federal Correctional System Houses Offenders Convicted of Federal Crimes

Before 1895, federal prisoners were held in state and local facilities. Between 1895 and 1930, the Department of Justice acquired or constructed four federal penitentiaries, but there was little central leadership and each was run according to the

whims of its warden. In 1930, Congress created the Federal Bureau of Prisons (BOP) and made it responsible for supervising those individuals who were convicted of violating federal laws. The BOP grew steadily and presently consists of facilities that include detention centers, halfway houses, prison camps, correctional institutions, and penitentiaries. Because the BOP currently has only a few detention facilities, it uses state and local jails to house most federal pretrial detainees. The organization of the BOP is centralized, but because of the tremendous size of the country, it is broken down into six regions. The BOP employs regionalization to make the system more responsive to the central office (DiIulio, 1991). The map in Figure 13.1 shows the six regions and the location of BOP facilities in 1992.

Since its inception, the BOP has provided strong and innovative leadership in the correctional field. The National Institute of Corrections (NIC) was created as a division of the BOP in order to provide state and local correctional systems with information and technical assistance. One of the innovations developed by the BOP in the early 1970s was **unit management.** Unit management is a form of correctional administration in which a team of correctional workers, including correctional officers, counselors, and others, works within a particular wing or cell block of a prison. The team is headed by a unit manager who, in effect, is the warden of that unit. Each team is responsible for managing the inmates living within its unit and makes the decisions and performs all of the activities associated with this function (e.g., counting, locking, monitoring inmate records, overseeing program activities, keeping track of release dates, and so on). When instituted by the BOP, many conditions in federal prisons appeared to improve for both inmates and staff. It also has had positive results in most other places where it has been tried (DiIulio, 1991).

### Each State Has Its Own Correctional System

Each of the fifty states has developed and operates its own correctional system. These systems run the gamut from the massive California system with its many facilities and over 125,000 inmates to the very small North Dakota system with its few facilities and about 38 inmates (Beck and Gilliard, 1995). With these differences, variation in the organization of these systems is not surprising. While

FIGURE 13.1   **Federal Regions and Facilities**

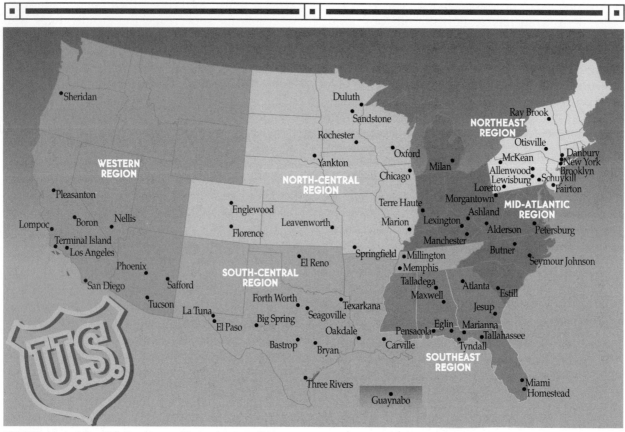

SOURCE: Adapted from U.S. Department of Justice (1992). *Facilities 1992,* Washington, DC: U.S. Department of Justice.

varying in complexity and the types of programs they have, almost all state systems consist of a department of corrections, which is headed by a politically appointed state director who develops policy and oversees the operation of state-mandated facilities and programs. The structure of the Florida system is presented in Figure 13.2 and can serve as an organizational example.

### Local Correctional Systems House PreTrial Detainees and Misdemeanants

Approximately 3300 jails and stockades in the United States make up the local correctional systems. Each jurisdiction, which maintains facilities for holding pretrial detainees and convicted misdemeanants, is thus operating a "correctional system." More than 80% of these are operated by counties in forty-four states. Almost all of these are operated by elected sheriffs. The rest are operated by municipalities, some are administered by police,

and others are run by a locally constituted corrections department. (Six states—Alaska, Connecticut, Delaware, Hawaii, Rhode Island, and Vermont—administer the jails within them at the state level.) Local systems also range from very large, for example, Los Angeles, California, or New York City, which may have daily inmate populations that surpass 20,000, to those whose daily population may not reach 10. The administrative organization of larger systems may resemble that of state corrections while that of the smallest may be quite different and perhaps even informal. Jails and local corrections are more fully discussed in Chapter 22.

## MOST CORRECTIONAL ORGANIZATIONS ARE IN THE PUBLIC DOMAIN

In the United States, as in most countries, government is responsible for establishing sanctions and

FIGURE 13.2   The Florida Department of Corrections Organizational Chart

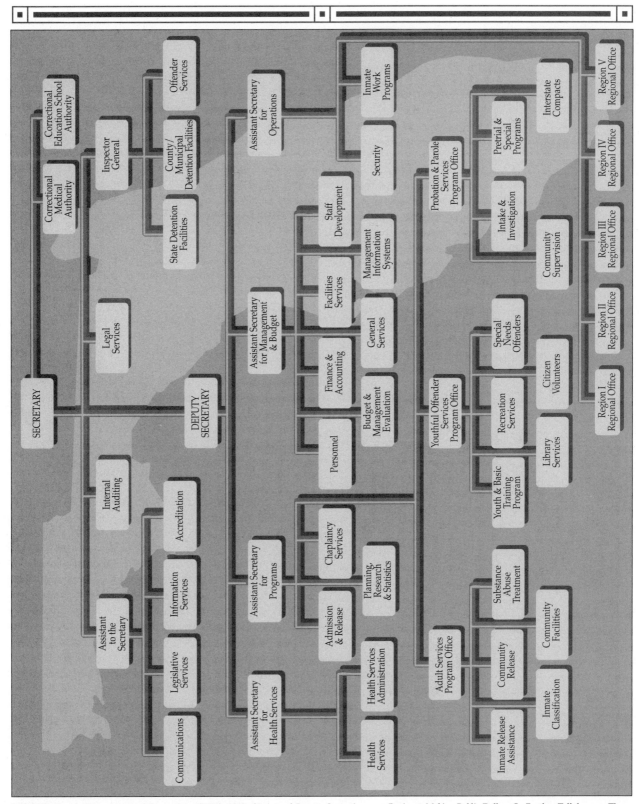

SOURCE: Florida Department of Corrections (1993). *1992–93 Annual Report: Corrections as a Business: Making Public Dollars Go Further.* Tallahassee, FL: Author, p. 6.

imposing them on those convicted of violating the laws. As a rule, governments have established and operated the agencies responsible for sanctioning law violators. Recently, however, some governmental entities have employed private companies to deal with some aspects of corrections.

## The Government Is Responsible for the Punishment of Convicted Offenders

Incarceration is the major sanction for convicted offenders, and represents a modern version of the older practice of banishing offenders because prisons are designed to separate inmates from the outside community. The U.S. Constitution mandates that this separation occur under relatively humane conditions with respect for the fundamental human rights of the banished. Since incarceration is usually for a limited time, there is an implicit concern that the government entity responsible for imprisonment not make inmates less fit for society than they were when they entered the prison. There is a tendency to forget that imprisonment itself exerts a very powerful influence on inmates and in essence defines them. Any prison in which managers cannot control the prison environment may well abandon the inmates to the criminogenic influences of the inmate culture.

The foregoing spotlights the importance of having the purpose and direction of the correctional enterprise stated in specific terms. Thus, a mission statement, which delineates the purpose, goals, and objectives of the organization, should be in place before it begins operation. The federal BOP views its mission as:

> [protecting] society by confining offenders in controlled environments of prisons and community-based facilities that are safe, humane, and appropriately secure, and that provide work and other self-improvement opportunities to assist offenders in becoming law-abiding citizens (Federal Bureau of Prisons, 1994, p. 27).

This statement suggests that the organization has responsibilities to its dual constituencies—protecting citizens and inmates through the governmental entities that are directly responsible for its functioning. It also suggests the direction in which it is heading. For example, it looks toward releasing inmates who are prepared to be law

Private corrections companies, like CCA, operate a number of jails and prisons in the U.S.

abiding. In 1993 the BOP established eight strategic goals based directly on this mission statement, that were used to guide its operations, programming, and budgeting for that year.

## Ambiguous Correctional Goals Have Caused Problems

In the broadest sense, correctional policy is set by legislators who often lack correctional expertise to write laws that contain detailed instructions regarding correctional operations. Instead, they often specify that something be done and then authorize their correctional agency to figure out exactly how and what to do (Meier, 1987). This is made more difficult by the fact that there is no public consensus on what a successful corrections system should be doing aside from banishing offenders. Thus, the environment in which much corrections policy (i.e., missions and goals) is developed contains much public ignorance, emotion, apathy, and disagreements among the experts and politicians.

## The Private Sector Has Again Become Involved in Corrections

A trend that began in the early 1980s and has been growing rapidly in the 1990s is private involvement in corrections. There was private involvement in corrections in the nineteenth century in the convict lease systems. However, it differed from the present in that it involved assignment of inmates to work in on-site factories in Auburn-type prisons, or to contractors in the South who assumed total responsibility for them. Modern privatization involves private entrepeneurs in three ways: First, some jurisdictions or facilities contract with companies to provide specific services such as food, medical attention, education, and training. For example, as we note in Chapter 19, some systems contract with private companies to provide medical services. Second, some jurisdictions use private firms to manage a facility. Thus, for example, Corrections Corporation of America (CCA) is responsible for operating several jails in the state of Florida. Finally, private companies have designed, obtained the financing for, and built correctional institutions and leased them back to the jurisdiction. In some instances, they also manage them. Proponents of this approach feel that these private entities can save the state money and be more efficient in building new facilities than the state (Schramek, 1993).

The cost savings associated with privatization are achieved in several ways. One is through building efficiently designed facilities to fulfill specific needs. An efficient design can reduce the number of personnel needed to staff the institution, thereby reducing costs. Second, private companies can circumvent state bureaucratic requirements that add to the cost of building facilities and make state purchases more expensive. Additional savings may also come from a reduction in the usually costly state benefits packages required for government employees.

Since the inception of privatization, the firms involved in this area (e.g., CCA, Wackenhut Corporation) have consistently been able to bring facilities, even major ones, on-line in a much shorter length of time than the state. This efficiency has provided the facilities when needed and has also lowered planning, building, and equipment costs by eliminating many bureaucratically mandated steps that are part of the construction and opening of state facilities. For example, when the state of Florida asked for proposals for the building of two 750-bed medium security facilities it received detailed proposals from eight firms within six weeks. All proposals indicated that these facilities could be brought on-line within twelve to fifteen months, would save the state at least 10% of the audited cost of operating them, and would meet the standards for achieving ACA accreditation (Thomas, 1994).[b]

The prison management segment of the private corrections industry was initiated in 1983. By 1993 there were seventy-three facilities with a rated capacity of about 25,000 under contract to private firms. These figures were expected to rise to eighty-six facilities with a rated capacity of 31,500 by mid-1995. Although this represents only a small proportion of the total correctional population, the numbers have been increasing at the rate of about 25% each year (Thomas, 1994). The types of facilities under contract range from jails to state and federal secure facilities. In general, these facilities are managed by correctional professionals who have been lured away from the public sector.

Twenty viable corrections management firms are competing and submitting proposals to a wide variety of jurisdictions around the country. Thus far, the industry's relative infancy has not permitted extensive cost-effectiveness studies, but Thomas (1994) indicates that studies of jurisdictions in Tennessee and Texas found cost savings of 5.37 and 14.35%, respectively. Critics of privatization have predicted that any cost savings would result from reductions in the amount and quality of service provided. However, Thomas (1993) discusses several indicators showing that the opposite is true:

1. *The renewal of existing contracts:* In terms of the contracts negotiated since the inception of privatization, only one has resulted in the closing of a facility and in another case a contract was transferred to a different firm. Neither of the firms involved in these failures is presently in business. The vast majority of contracts have been renewed.

2. *Inmate litigation:* He found no evidence of successful prisoner ligation against a private firm or of one having entered into a consent decree or being placed under a court order as a consequence of a finding of unconstitutional jail or prison conditions in a facility for which it was responsible.

3. *Accreditation:* Forty-seven percent of the private facilities operating in the United States have been accredited by the Commission on Accreditation of the ACA. An additional 13% have applied for accreditation. While accreditation does not automatically confer a mantle of quality, it does represent a willingness on the part of these facilities to open themselves to public inspection.

4. *Quality of confinement:* A study of three women's prisons (one private, one state, one federal) examining the quality of confinement found that the private institution outperformed the other two across nearly all of the dimensions measured.

The private operation of correctional facilities raises several ethical and legal questions. One question is whether government should delegate the legal responsibility to punish convicted offenders to private entrepreneurs. That is, with all of the legal and moral questions surrounding the care and treatment of offenders, should the government entrust these duties to a for-profit entity? With respect to its legality, federal law permits it, as do the laws of about three-fourths of the states (Houston, 1995).

Several major legal issues have been raised regarding private prison management and services contracts. First is the issue of whether inmates housed in correctional facilities managed by or receiving services from private companies may in some way be limited in seeking damages for constitutional violations of their rights under Section 1983 of the Federal Civil Rights Act (see Chapters 15 and 16). In effect, these workers are viewed as if they were working for a local or state government agency. Relevant state laws authorize them to provide various correctional services and other state statutes specifically authorize these contractual arrangements between private companies and state and local agencies. Further, their conduct is "attributable to state or [a local jurisdiction] since this government entity has aid[ed], encourage[ed] or require[ed] them to do what they do" (Thomas, 1990, p. 15). Second, every governmental entity is responsible for the facilities and services operated under its authority even if they are run directly by a private contractor. Thus, if an inmate dies or is injured, both the contractor and state or local jurisdiction are likely to be sued. In short, a governmental entity is responsible for both public and private facilities under its authority (Patrick, 1986). To reduce their liability jurisdictions typically require a private company to include an indemnification clause in their contact that guarantees that it will pay liability costs (e.g., attorneys fees and settlement costs) related to their contractual responsibilities (Thomas, 1990).

With respect to discipline, Houston (1995) indicates that state correctional policymakers should establish a disciplinary system that follows due process and encourages institutional tranquility. Private contractors should be specially authorized by the state to handle disciplinary matters and their employees be should be required to receive training in state policies and procedures. This

should protect them from liability. Another solution to this problem, of course, is for the state to maintain control of the disciplinary process, with the private contractor acting as the "police officer."

The use of force in maintaining the security of correctional facilities presents a different set of problems. Here, opponents assert that private contractors lack the authority to use the force necessary (especially deadly force) to prevent escapes, thereby endangering the community. In other words, under normal circumstances private correctional officers (COs) only have the same rights as ordinary citizens in dealing with prison disturbances and escapes. Houston (1995) suggests that one remedy to the above problem is for the state to statutorily authorize private COs to use legitimate force to deal with those situations.

The final issue regards the extent to which the profit motive might result in lobbying efforts by private businesses to influence the making of correctional decisions and policy. Examples of this manipulation are pressures to build or keep open unnecessary facilities and/or programs, or to promote policies that increase prison/program populations rather than decrease them. This pressure, which is commonly found in the interaction of private enterprise with government, will have to be guarded against, especially during periods when there are strong public sentiments regarding crime and its punishment.

Based on our present knowledge, it would appear that private management of correctional facilities is a viable option. Given the apparent early results showing that they are able to provide a higher quality of service at lesser costs, this option may constitute the wave of the future. Further, there are indications that private facilities may be an option for handling certain special offender populations—the mentally or physically handicapped. Also, by leasing space, jurisdictions can relieve problems of overcrowding without the long-term commitment of building new facilities (Bronick, 1989).

## ADMINISTRATIVE AND MANAGERIAL PERSONNEL

Various groups of administrators and managers exist within correctional systems. First, there are system-wide administrators and their staff who are

**Harry Singletary, Jr. has been the Chief Executive Officer of the Florida Department of Corrections since 1990. His policies have emphasized training, staff development, and community partnerships.**

charged with operating the entire system. Next, there are institutional administrators (superintendents/wardens and their major department heads) who run the individual institutions. Then there are the middle-level managers (e.g., educational administrators or security personnel of the rank of lieutenant or higher). Finally there are the first-line supervisors who oversee the day-to-day activities of personnel who work directly with inmates.

### System-Wide Administrators Create Policy and Programs

Heads of state correctional systems are usually correctional professionals, normally appointed by the governor, who have titles like director, commissioner, administrator, or secretary. Their primary duties are to provide expert advice to the governor and legislature regarding correctional policy, implement the correctional policy that emerges from this political process, secure sufficient resources to operate the system effectively, and coordinate the corrections system with other interdependent agencies such as law enforcement, courts, and human welfare services.

The structure of state correctional systems is strongly influenced by the structure of state government. Political pressures not only come from the governor and legislators but also from county sheriffs. Although the formulation of corrections policy is mainly the responsibility of elected legislators, corrections administrators should certainly lend their expertise to this process. A good correctional administrator attempts to bring rationality and knowledge of what works to the legislative policy-making process.

State correctional departments may perform a variety of functions. For example, they may only oversee adult prisons or may administer all adult services, or they may supervise all correctional functions for both adults and juveniles. In some states even the local jails are controlled at the state level.

### Institutional Administrators Implement Policies and Programs

Although the philosophy of the management of prisons has evolved from autocratic to bureaucratic to participative (greater involvement of COs and other staff in planning and policy development), the general administrative structure of prisons has remained the same for a long time. This structure normally includes a top administrator, an executive management team, middle managers, first-level supervisors, line correctional supervisors, and other workers (see Figure 13.3)

The top administrator of a prison (i.e., the superintendent or warden) is typically appointed by the head of the department of corrections. **Superintendents** are responsible for the running of the entire prison (e.g., implementation of policy and responsibility for all personnel, programs, and activities within the prison). Wardens frequently must also spend time dealing with matters external to the direct management of their facility. In some instances they may be involved in the development of the system's master plan for the year. For example, on a yearly basis federal BOP wardens are asked to review current goals and identify strategies to submit to their regional administrators. The results of these regional meetings are, in turn, passed up the chain of command to the BOP's Executive Staff Strategic Planning Group. This, in turn, is used to identify strategic issues and to develop the BOP's overall goals for the coming

FIGURE 13.3 **Example of an Institutional Organizational Chart**

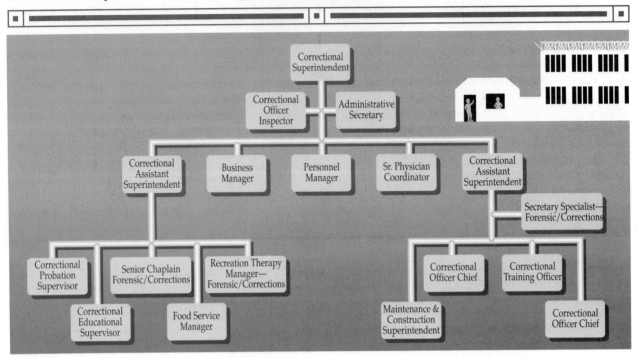

year. At these regional meetings wardens also provide input for tentative budgets for funding for the next two years. Once yearly system goals are developed, divisions like health services, industries, education, and vocational training identify specific objectives they hope to achieve during the next year. Wardens, along with their executive staffs, formulate specific local objectives that will facilitate the achievement of system-wide goals. For example, in 1993 one of the strategic goals was to proactively manage its offender population to ensure a safe and secure population. To accomplish this, some new specialized facilities were built or added to existing facilities, community programs were expanded, classification programs were adjusted, and the importance of communication skills continued to be stressed (Houston, 1995; Federal Bureau of Prisons, 1994). Superintendents also often have to serve as a spokesperson for their facility, which means speaking at meetings of local civic organizations about the general problem of crime and allaying the fears of community groups as to whether their facility is secure enough to hold its inmates or that its residents are nondangerous.

It is in the oversight of programs, activities, and personnel that wardens can have the greatest im-

pact on the ambiance of the prison. Their influence is likely to depend on the extent to which they are fair, tough-minded, able to develop a strong management team, and practice a hands-on style of management. These characteristics also determine the extend to which the goals that have been set will be achieved.

The **executive management team** selected by the warden is very important. This team includes assistant superintendents who specialize in managing certain prison functions such as security, treatment programs, business operations, or prison industries. They are responsible for supervising the operations of their specific areas. This level of management can help to develop comprehensive plans for their facility and also to evaluate and coordinate institutional programs and personnel.

### Middle-Level Managers Oversee Specific Programs

The middle-level correctional manager occupies a variety of positions at a number of levels within the prison. They carry such titles as department head, captain, lieutenant, manager, coordinator, etc. **Middle managers** oversee the delivery of specific

The food service manager oversees the food production process. Like other department heads, they are middle-level managers.

services in the prison. For instance, a prison's organization will include specialized units such as custody, treatment, food services, etc. Each of these units is then responsible to an executive administrator (e.g., assistant superintendent for custody). These subunits may be even further divided with a manager for each subdivision. For example, the assistant superintendent for treatment may have individuals who supervise drug treatment programs, psychological services, or educational programs reporting to him or her.

### First-Line Supervisors Oversee Line Personnel

**First-line supervisors** hold positions that constitute the lowest level of administration within the prison, and are usually called unit managers, supervisors, corporals, or section leaders. Their responsibilities include assigning specific jobs, overseeing the training of personnel working primarily with inmates, constructing short-range plans, and implementing policy at the employee level. They are involved in critical correctional operations since they translate organizational policy directly into action through their influence on line personnel. Finally there are line personnel, such as COs or teachers, who have the most direct daily contact with inmates. While they supervise inmates, these

personnel are not considered part of the administration hierarchy (although they may be seen by inmates in that capacity). Chapter 14 describes the functions of COs and the problems they face.

## VARIOUS APPROACHES TO CORRECTIONAL ADMINISTRATION

The lack of scientific knowledge about corrections management has hampered rational decision-making regarding alternative correctional policies. Policy debates have tended to focus on the nature of crime and the role of public institutions in crime control, but rarely has the organization of these institutions been examined. Alvin Cohn (1973, 1979, 1981, 1991) stated that corrections administrators did not learn management theory and practice, but rather applied techniques learned as they rose through the ranks. This view of administrators, which assumes that they rarely possess professional managerial skills that allow them to anticipate and plan for the future, is much less true today. This is probably due to the increased complexity of the entire correctional process and its legal implications. As a result, most prison administrators are professionals who, while they may

## Close Up    Joe Ragen—The Ultimate Authoritarian

The authoritarian style was found in its purest form in the classic Big House prison. This model was demonstrated most clearly by Joe Ragen, the warden of the Stateville (Illinois) Penitentiary from 1936 to 1961 (Jacobs, 1977). Ragen operated under a system of innumerable and very detailed rules. However it was he, and not the rules, who was the source of authority, and he refused to share that authority with anyone. As Jacobs (1977) notes, Ragen established a patriarchal organization based on his own charismatic authority. He ran an autonomous institution that was not accountable to other public agencies nor the public at large and which had no contact with outside groups concerned about prison conditions. He demanded absolute personal loyalty from his subordinates, but neither the guards nor the inmates had any real rights under Ragen's stewardship. He believed that the inmates were only due the bare necessities of life. However, both the inmates and guards were relatively secure at Stateville.

In his classic study of Stateville, James Jacobs (1977) characterized Ragen's rule as a prebureaucratic form of administration in that his power was based on his personal charisma. When Ragen retired, he took the authority that held the prison together with him and the fabric of the Stateville organization began to unravel. The organization's personnel had formed working relationships only through Ragen and his departure led to a loss of their authority. The conditions at Stateville following Ragen's departure were chaotic and the inmates "ran" the prison for more than a decade. The organization was so dependant on Ragen's idiosyncratic power that it had no structure to continue functioning in any effective way.

have risen through the ranks, have sought and achieved college degrees (including PhDs) and also taken training programs sponsored by professional organizations (e.g., the ACA).

### Structural Concepts Help to Identify the Administrative Hierarchy

Thus far, we have looked at the correctional endeavor in terms of its gross structure and its levels of management. To better comprehend how it accomplishes its goals, we will now consider various models developed to manage organizations. It is important to recognize that an organizational structure is necessary to assure that the various tasks needed to accomplish the missions and goals of the organization are performed. The structure represents the formal hierarchical network of relationships that exists among the various components, units, and positions of authority within the organization. Generally, this network is represented by an organizational table, which graphically presents these aspects of the institution as seen earlier in Figure 13.2. Several concepts are associated with hierarchically structured organizations which are helpful in defining how these organizations work.

*Unity of command* refers to the view that workers should only have to report directly to one boss (i.e., a worker only has one boss). The rationale for this type of command structure is that it reduces the confusion for workers if they are only responsible for following the orders of one superior.

The second concept, *chain of command,* is related to the first. This recognizes that in order to maintain control of a large organization a leader must delegate oversight of its many workers and activities to executive managers who, in turn, delegate authority to middle managers and they give authority to first-line supervisors. Thus, when a warden of a prison wants a particular action implemented, such as a change in the time inmates are to be locked down for the night, he or she will instruct the appropriate assistant warden who will pass the order to the appropriate middle manager, and so on down the line so that the action is taken. *Span of control* defines the limits of supervision by one person. That is, the number of programs or personnel that can be effectively supervised by one person is limited. Thus, managers at each level have a relatively small number of subordinates directly responsible to them.

**Line personnel** are the workers who are directly responsible for furthering institutional goals. In

## Close Up   George Beto and the Texas System

The Texas Prison System under the direction of Dr. George Beto from 1962 to 1972 has been considered the quintessential bureaucratic corrections organization (Barak-Glantz, 1986; Dilulio, 1987). In one sense, the inmates were part of the organization because they were treated as if they occupied a position in the bureaucratic hierarchy. The responsibility and duty of the inmate was to "do his own time," and he was rewarded for following the rules and punished for "messing up." A few carefully selected inmates had formal positions in the organization by being appointed "building tenders" (BTs). Their job was to help the guards control the other inmates in that particular unit. This system was intended to co-opt the process by which inmates select their own leaders, and to replace them with ones less likely to be violent or exploitative. In spite of these precautions, BTs used violence and intimidation to control their units. Unlike other systems that reward powerful inmates for their help in maintaining order, the building tenders were rewarded openly rather than secretly and their actions were presumed to be more subject to administrative controls.

The Texas system gained the reputation of being among the safest and best run in the nation during Beto's tenure. However, during the tenure of his successor, W. J. Estelle, the system deteriorated and became chaotic and violent. There were several reasons for this change for the worse (Dilulio, 1987). First, the population of the system nearly doubled in a very short time. Second, and more important, Estelle was not able to maintain the close working relationships and support that Beto had cultivated with powerful Texas legislators. Finally, and perhaps most importantly, Estelle managed the prisons from a distance. He was "an office-bound executive" in contrast to the close, hands-on management style that Beto had developed. In fact, as Dilulio notes:

> Inmates came to know him [Beto] as the "preacher with a baseball bat in one hand and a bible in the other." Wardens and division heads came to respect (and fear) "Dr. Beto," as they called him, and he earned the nickname Walking George for his habit of showing up (always unannounced) at the prison gates for a surprise inspection, or, as he put it, [a] "look-see" (p. 27).

Under Beto, the central goal was control. Reintegration of inmates into the community and rehabilitation were important, but Beto believed that these latter goals could only be achieved in stable and safe prisons. After Beto's departure, his carefully crafted control system began to disintegrate and neither inmates nor guards felt safe. Thus, there was a reversion to a repressive authoritarian model to keep inmates from attaining control of the prison. At its worst, the bureaucratic prison can become as punitive as an authotitarian one.

prisons, these would be the COs, teachers, counselors, and others who have direct contact with inmates. **Staff personnel** are the workers who provide the support services for line workers. These services include training, communications, accounting, and so on. These five concepts help bring to life the organizational structures referred to earlier.

### There Are Three Major Organizational Models

Organization theory concerns the manner in which power and authority within an organization are distributed and used to accomplish organizational objectives. The models to be examined also deal with management styles used to get workers to achieve organizational goals.

Organizations range from those whose structure is idiosyncratic and totally dependent on the characteristics of their leaders to those whose structure is determined by a set of very specific rules and regulations. We will examine three different organizational models: the authoritarian model, the bureaucratic model, and the participative model. It is important to remember that these models do not typically exist in their "pure form." Instead, it is likely that a given correctional organization will contain elements of at least two of these approaches. Nearly all contemporary organizations use some form of the bureaucratic model. This organizational approach can accommodate a variety of managerial styles and, therefore, provides the basic structure for contemporary corrections.

**THE AUTHORITARIAN MODEL IS CHARACTER-IZED BY A STRONG AUTOCRATIC LEADER** In authoritarian organizations, decision-making power is in the hands of one person or a small number of high-level "bosses." The authoritarian style dominated corrections management in the United States from the birth of prisons until the middle of the twentieth century (Barak-Glantz, 1986). It was associated with a correctional policy characterized by harshness and punishment. This organizational arrangement was first employed by Elam Lynds, who was often considered to be the architect of the Auburn correctional model (Lewis, 1922/1996).

The principal feature of the **authoritarian model** is strict control over both the inmates and staff (Barak-Glantz, 1986). Since all power and authority is in the hands of the boss, the influence of any group (either inside or outside of the prison) is minimal. Historically, authoritarian correctional administrations had goals that were quite simple: the temporary incarceration of offenders and the avoidance of critical incidents. This was done by creating a very repressive internal environment. When correctional goals began to become more complicated (e.g., rehabilitation and court mandates regarding prisoner rights) the authoritarian style could not deal effectively with this more complex organizational environment.

The organizational structure that emerges from the authoritarian approach is based on personal power relationships and the resulting organizational climate is ultimately corrupt. In theory, this arrangement can yield a safe and orderly institution in which both guards and inmates can "do their time" in relative security, if everyone "plays the game." However, the present level of politicalization of both staff and inmates has decreased the chances that this will happen. While the banishment goal of corrections is likely to be achieved through the authoritarian approach, other goals (e.g., protection of constitutional rights) are likely to be severely compromised. In this environment inmates are little more than "products" of the organization and often come out of the prison more bitter and crime-prone than when they entered it. Our Close-Up on Joe Ragen profiles this type of manager (see page 280).

**UNDER THE BUREAUCRATIC MODEL CONTROL IS MAINTAINED BY THE BOOK** The **bureaucratic model** establishes a formal organizational structure that permits smooth changes in leadership. This structure avoids the major disruptions that often occur when there are leadership changes in an authoritarian organization. The essential elements of a bureaucratic organization include a hierarchical structure (positions with varying levels of authority) with a formal chain of command; a vertical authority and communication structure that flows from the top of the hierarchy to the bottom, that is, there are clearly defined power relationships between subordinates and superiors (e.g., sergeants and COs) and strict channels of communication; and written job descriptions and standard operating procedures that describe the specific duties and responsibilities for each position in the organization. In its purest form, a bureaucratically structured prison is run in terms of standard operating procedures defined by "the book." The functions and authority vested in each position are based on that position's job description.

The ideal type of bureaucratic prison organization is similar to a military unit. Rules and procedures direct the flow of all operations and authority is legitimized by the power of the state. Further, "legislators and governors demand that principles, rules, and regulations be formulated to rationalize . . . correctional policy and practice" (Barak-Glantz, 1986, p. 45) See our Close-Up on George Beto, page 281.

In reality, both authoritarian and bureaucratic approaches rely on control for the maintenance of social order inside the prison. Under the authoritarian model control is maintained by fear of the warden's response to disobedience. Within a bureaucratic system, control will most likely be maintained by the rules under which the institution is organized. In theory, these standardized policies should result in consistency and fairness, but in practice, because the corrections environment is very complicated, they usually do not. Although COs enforce rules and regulations in terms of their position rather than their relationship to the warden, their ability to obtain cooperation from inmates is still based on the individual bargains they make with them. Thus, in bureaucratic organizations COs use their discretion in applying the rules to negotiate fairness. The rules may dictate that all cases be treated the same, but because the rules can never anticipate all contingencies, "going by the book" does not always guarantee fairness and the COs' discretion allows some equalization. Institutions where there is only rigid adherence to regulations are paralyzed by the inability to do anything creative or adapt to change (Burrell and Morgan, 1979).

DiIulio suggests that rules and formal organization are particularly necessary when people cannot be expected to cooperate spontaneously, as in prisons. However, with its increasingly complex and changing environment, corrections must encourage some minimal level of participation in decision making by all staff members. According to a number of writers (e.g., Lombardo, 1989; DiIulio, 1987) corrections is beginning to require the participation of as many members of the organization as possible in solving the problems within it. This forms the basis of the participative model, which we examine next.

**THE PARTICIPATIVE MODEL ALLOWS STAFF TO CONTRIBUTE TO PROBLEM SOLVING**   "The control dilemma faced by prison authorities is that they can neither expect cooperation from inmates nor govern without it" (Silberman, 1978, p. 392). This appears to be at the heart of the problems experienced in prison management and seems to pave the way for the coercive and harsh approach to control prisoners. The **participative model** is one approach that explicitly allows for input from all members of the organization in the way it is run. Inmates can also be treated as a formal component of the organization and, thus have some input. This is felt to be important because formal inmate organizations are easier to deal with than informal ones. Although the administration may not be able to get the spontaneous cooperation of all the inmates, a measure of formal cooperation may be a realistic goal. The fact that informal bargaining goes on between inmates and guards shows that some basis for cooperation exists.

An important aspect of the participative approach is that even entry-level correctional workers are given the opportunity to contribute ideas to the solution of organizational problems. This increases their commitment to helping meet organizational goals. Advocates of the participative approach believe it is more systematic and can better conditions for staff by providing for meaningful interaction between them and administration.

The participative model is based on the assumption that organizational goals are best achieved when all of the groups having a stake in their achievement contribute to the means by which they are accomplished. It recognizes that within

any organization there are conflicting values and goals. There are three ways to deal with these conflicts: attempting to resolve them, ignoring them, or neutralizing them by appealing to individuals' self-interests as an alternative to collective goal seeking. The traditional approach to correctional administration has almost always employed the latter two options.

The ideal participative organization is based on formal and open negotiations that include all organizational components (e.g., managers, treatment staff, COs). Thus, instead of depending on a set of inflexible rules for dealing with problems, those most closely involved with these problems (e.g., COs, teachers) are asked to recommend solutions for them. This can result in increased feelings of solidarity among all components and less likelihood of their being tied to groups outside the organization such as unions, prison reform groups, or legislatures. A presumed effect of this scenario is that the morale (and productivity) of correctional workers will be raised.

Ideally, a participative organization should include all groups (including inmates in a prison). However, prisons in which this has been tried have experienced problems. These have generally occurred when prison administration or COs did not buy into the notion of inmate participation. An informative example of this is the inmate self-government experiment that is profiled in our Close-Up on the Washington State Penitentiary at Walla Walla.

Of course, the participative approach can be used without inmate input. This would be accomplished by a management philosophy that encourages workers at all levels of the correctional organization to contribute ideas to the solution of problems or the achievement of institutional goals.

All three models described here have had both successes and failures. Douglas McGregor (1960), an early proponent of participative management, contends that one's managerial style ultimately rests on his or her assumptions regarding human nature, and to an extent his or her system of management encourages behavior consistent with these assumptions. McGregor's (1960) concept of management by integration and self-control rather than by direction and control is based on the idea that an organization should create the conditions that allow employees to realize that they can best achieve their own goals by pursuing the goals of

---

## *Close Up* Washington State Penitentiary—An Example of Inmate Participation That Did Not Work

In the early 1970s, the newly appointed director of the Department of Institutions in the state of Washington mandated that a Resident Government Council (RGC) be created at the Washington State Penitentiary. This was done over the opposition of the prison's administration. A constitution was drawn up and in April 1971 the first RGC, consisting of eleven members, was elected by the inmates. The RGC then chose its own officers. The RGC, led by its president, was to represent inmate interests and concerns in the resolution of prison problems and the improvement of conditions for inmates. At the beginning, inmate input was accepted by the prison administration and a series of reforms were agreed to. At this time, the officers of the RGC appeared to be trusted by both the inmates and administration. The RGC managed to propose various reforms that were accepted by the administration. These included permission to conduct religious services on Death Row, allow inmates to keep musical instruments in their cells, donate cigarettes and coffee to inmates in segregation, solicit outside therapists to conduct mental health programs, and purchase and receive commercially printed posters through the mail. The gaining of early concessions from the superintendent resulted in a great deal prestige for the RGC among inmates. This was especially true because the suggested changes benefitted the entire inmate population.

After the first year administration support for the RGC began to falter and the RGC was less and less able to extract concessions from the superintendent. The superintendent's waning support was apparently related to the stepping down of the director of the Department of Institutions who initially forced the creation of the RGC. It may also have been that all of the easy concessions were made during that first year and the administration felt that it could not continue along such a path. To protest the situation, the RGC resigned en masse and reconstituted itself but the results were to no avail because the superintendent was no longer willing to share his power, and the trust of the inmates was lost. The RGC continued to exist for about two years but was controlled by inmates who were self-serving and there was little general inmate interest in or support for it. It was formally disbanded in early 1975 (Bowker, 1982).

---

the organization. The bureaucratic and authoritarian approaches can work, but they tend to result in organizations with little flexibility or potential for improvement. The participative model allows for adaptive growth because it builds the necessary values as the participants demonstrate their capacity to act responsibly. Thus, it would appear that administrators, COs, and inmates can find enough common ground to reach a negotiated accommodation on most issues.

In the 1990s, there has been a movement toward using the team concept of management within corrections. The team concept is an offshoot of participative management and stresses the need for correctional leaders to build stable management teams that are spirited, cohesive, and actively involved in planning and decision making. K. Wright (1991) emphasizes, however, that leaders should not abdicate responsibility for what happens within the prisons but instead should facilitate the participation and involvement of others in their search for solutions to the problems they face. He feels that encouraging participation increases trust and effectiveness, helps to train future managers, and reduces turnover.

The **delegation model** is a form of participatory management stressing that input from all workers is critical, because line workers (officers) can be your best "idea" people for solving real problems. The model also empowers employees so that they feel they are part of the team and can offer solutions. Another key for the administrator is that he or she offers participation to employees, even if they only wish to complain. As one correctional manager put it, "I believe and need the participatory management model, because I recruit talented people who know more about their jobs than I do. I need their thoughts, ideas and commitment. However, we are not a democracy, I reserve 51% of the vote on issues I feel I cannot totally delegate.

George Beto, shown here talking to inmates, kept informed about prison conditions by visiting prison facilities frequently.

My staff and I are clear on which issues are participatory vs. democratic." (DeVolentine, 1993).

### Proactive Corrections Management Is Analagous to Preventive Maintenance

Managers can respond to organizational problems in one of two ways: reactively or proactively. A reactive manager waits until a problem manifests itself before taking action, whereas a proactive one tries to anticipate and correct problems before they develop. Styles (1991) asserts that the federal BOP has avoided many inmate lawsuits by continually evaluating programs. Wardens and their executive staff are responsible for regularly monitoring their own facilities and the bureau's Program Review Division conducts periodic inspections of each facility. If a reviewer finds a problem (e.g., an inoperative thermostat subjecting inmates to extreme temperatures) he or she immediately reports the problem while on site so that it can be fixed immediately. Inmates can thus see problems being

dealt with rapidly and may likely be less inclined to file suits.

Access to information is the basis for proactive organizational action. Normally, prison managers react to problems as they occur. When this is the case, problem inmates initiate managerial action and the organizational environment is reactive. Reactive organizations do not often have an open flow of information, particularly that which details problems, from the bottom of the chain of command. That is, if there are problems, managers do not want to hear about them. This reduces the effectiveness of planning and proactive problem solving. In contrast, **proactive management** requires open relationships between management and staff so that subordinates feel free to communicate problems without fear they will be evaluated negatively.

In addition to anticipating problems, proactive administrators also plan for and create opportunities for the organization to develop its capacity to pursue its mission. This includes creation of goals and objectives, ongoing evaluation of the progress being made to achieve them, and the communication of the outcomes of these evaluations to all organizational members. This approach was illustrated earlier in our discussion of the wardens at the BOP who helped to develop system plans for the next year.

## Characteristics of Successful Correctional Administrators

There is no overall agreement regarding the precise approach to good prison administration or the ideal management style. At the beginning of this chapter, we quoted John DiIulio regarding the importance of good management in the operation of safe and civilized penal institutions. We shall lean heavily on his findings and conclusions in this section (DiIulio, 1987, 1991). He cites a number of individuals who have managed or are presently managing safe, high quality-of-life prisons but whose management styles differ. In evaluating the success of their management approaches he concluded that they share one common trait: devotion to the building and maintenance of an **organizational culture,** which is defined by Wilson (1989) as "a persistent, patterned way of thinking about the central tasks of, and human relationships in, an organization" (p. 91). This culture is to the organization what personality is to the individual. Once the culture develops it is passed from one managerial "generation" to the next (Wilson, 1989). Obviously, once that happens, the culture becomes a highly unifying force within the organization.

DiIulio has further identified six key behavioral patterns that characterize the organizational culture of a well-managed prison system or institution. These are things that successful leaders do to make their institutions or systems operate more effectively.

First, successful leaders focus on outcomes by establishing an overall mission statement for the organization that specifies its primary objectives. For example, under James Bennett and Norman Carlson, the mission of the Federal Bureau of Prisons was safety, humanity, and opportunity (DiIulio, 1991). In this system, institutions were organized around meeting these objectives. Good leaders inspire their subordinates to focus on actually producing measurable results and rewarding them for accomplishing specific tasks or goals (e.g., whether inmates are safe, whether prison indus-

tries have reached production goals, etc.). Excuses for failing (e.g., too few resources, overcrowding) are not accepted.

Secondly, a core feature of this organizational culture was that, above all else, institutional security and custody were viewed as the top priorities. This means that *all* workers within the institution (e.g., teachers, doctors, secretaries) are given the necessary skills and trained to think of themselves as correctional officers first. This is referred to as the correctional worker concept (Hambrick, 1992). Because they all share a similar viewpoint, there is a strengthening of morale. Although this strong sense of mission may sometimes impede needed changes, DiIulio and Hambrick believe that the net effect of this "togetherness" is positive.

A third characteristic is what DiIulio refers to as the MBWA principle: **management by walking around.** This involves administrators going out into the institution(s) to obtain a first "foot" look at and a real feel for what is actually going on in the institution(s). This keeps them from having to rely on second-hand, possibly distorted and incomplete reports from subordinates. MBWA allows leaders to be seen by both line officers and inmates, to interact with them, and to answer directly any questions staff might have. Frank Wood, a former warden of Oak Park Heights, a high-risk, maximum security Minnesota correctional facility, reported spending about one-fourth of his time "eyeball-to-eyeball" with inmates and employees. This included his conducting the last meeting of each orientation for new inmates, so that they could understand their responsibilities while at Oak Park Heights and the facility's responsibilities to them (Ward, 1987).

Successful administrators also make strong alliances with powerful figures in the world outside of the organization. Thus, they will have to develop relationships with individuals who can affect the institution's resources, legal standing, and public image (i.e., key politicians, judges, journalists, and reformers). They also invite these movers and shakers, and other interested people, to visit their institutions so that they can see for themselves the conditions (both good and bad) that exist within these facilities. In some cases, the results of these visits are positive, but in other instances they may result in more problems.

A fifth characteristic is that successful leaders do not often innovate, but when they do, the changes they make are likely to be far-reaching. To prepare inmates and staff for these changes, they are made slowly so that both can be told about them and have plenty of time to "learn the new ways." It is important when making changes in a correctional setting to be sensitive to the fact that correctional officers always look at impending changes in terms of what they will do for them versus how they will benefit inmates. For example, providing inmates with opportunities to take college courses without improving staff opportunities for advanced education, can have negative consequences (e.g., erode staff support for administration).

A final characteristic is longevity (i.e., good leaders remain in their positions long enough to understand and to make necessary changes in the organization's internal operations and its relationships with outsiders). DiIulio indicates that most of the successful leaders have served at least six years. This length of tenure is sometimes difficult to achieve in political organizations that change leadership based on elections and political appointments.

## DISORDER IN THE PRISON: A SIGN OF POOR MANAGEMENT

■

The importance of good management in the maintenance of prison order prompts us to include a discussion of prison riots in this chapter. Correctional systems in the United States have experienced major disturbances since 1774 when a riot occurred at a facility built around an abandoned mine in Simsbury, Connecticut. Riots reflect a breakdown in control of the prison. Most prison riots have resulted from some combination of mismanagement and poor conditions. These disturbances have tended to become more frequent and destructive since the 1950s (American Correctional Association, 1981, 1990a; Martin and Zimmermann, 1990). While the riots during the 1950s tended to be in protest of specific prison conditions, most of those occurring in the 1960s and 1970s had racial overtones and began to reflect the politicalization associated with the Civil Rights movement (see chapter 8).

Martin and Zimmermann (1990) constructed a typology of six conceptual models to account for prison riots. They drew on the work of many authors and criticized the shortcomings of each explanatory approach. The models include the following:

1. *The environmental conditions model* is based on a 1981 American Correctional Association study that concluded that the causes of riots and other disturbances could be classified into four categories: institutional environment, inmate population characteristics, administrative practices, and non-institutional causes.

2. *The spontaneity model* says that riots are unplanned, spontaneous events caused when some predisposing environmental factors (such as poor food) create a "time bomb" that is set off by some precipitating event (e.g., an inmate fight).

3. *The conflict model* focuses on the impact of the repressive power structure of prisons, which creates subcultural value conflicts and limits the ways in which they can be resolved.

4. *The collective behavior and social control model* says that control within the prison is maintained through a series of informal and symbiotic social relationships among inmates, staff, and administration. Disruption of these relationships, whether for better or worse, changes the balance of control and may result in an outbreak of violence.

5. *The power vacuum model* focuses on the role of sudden changes in the balance of power among inmate groups. Martin and Zimmerman feel that the changes usually result from changed institutional goals and/or replacement of top administrators.

6. *The rising expectations model* focuses on differences between inmates' expectations regarding the quality of the prison environment and the reality of that environment. It closely resembles the concept of relative deprivation.

An evaluation of these models shows that the management or environment of the prison (i.e., the manner in which inmates are dealt with or controlled) plays a significant role in the occurrence of riots. Thus, poorly managed prisons with weak or changing leadership are most likely to have riots.

The most renown prison disturbances occurring since 1970 have been those at Attica, New York, and Santa Fe, New Mexico, where many lives were lost and extensive damage done to the facilities. The riot at Attica, discussed in Chapter 8, involved many conditions and/or issues that have since

During the 1980 New Mexico penitentiary riot, inmates controlled the inside of the prison for 36 hours. Thirty-three inmates were killed by their fellow inmates.

been addressed by the courts and resolved in favor of the inmates. In our discussion of the New Mexico, Camp Hill, and Lucasville riots we focus on the management problems that existed at the time of their occurrence.

## The New Mexico Riot Was One of the Most Savage in U.S. History

The factors that precipitated the riot at the Penitentiary of New Mexico at Santa Fe were enunciated by Raymond Procunier, a former prison administrator in California and Texas, who evaluated the institution just three weeks before the riot (Serrill and Katel, 1980). He reported the prison was overcrowded, understaffed, and many of its COs were untrained. Mr. Procunier was prophetic in saying

that New Mexico state officials were "playing Russian roulette with the lives of inmates, staff and the public" (as cited in Serrill and Katel, 1980, p. 7). This riot, which occurred in February 1980, was one of the most savage in U.S. penal history.

While Procunier may have identified the factors precipitating the New Mexico riot, Colvin (1982) argues that it was a product of changes in the control structure of the prison and the inmate social structure that had begun five years before the riot. Prior to 1975, control had been maintained by accommodating two powerful groups of inmates. The first group controlled inmate selection for participation in adult education programs, a "college prep" program, and outside contact programs. This group helped to maintain order in these programs to ensure that they continued to operate. The second group controlled drug trafficking in the prison. This group also realized if order broke down it would jeopardize their sources of supply and bring the heat down on traffickers.

This changed when a new administration took over the prison in late 1975 and began to wrest control of the prison from the inmates. They removed all inmates from positions controlling inmate placement, tightened restrictions on inmate movement, and canceled outside contact programs. Additionally, drug searches were increased, and efforts were made to eliminate possible drug supply sources. Inmate protests quickly followed these changes. In this environment, inmates' willingness to engage in violence grew, which encouraged formation of cliques for self-protection. These cliques adopted an ideology based on a willingness to use violence against other inmates, to confront and resist guards, and to "tough it out" in disciplinary confinement. The combative relations led staff to develop a system of snitches whose information was virtually unquestioned. Inmates took advantage of this to settle grudges or get favors by feeding the intelligence officer bogus information. Consequently, many inmates spent up to six months in segregation based on another inmate's unproven allegations (Hirliman, 1982). These tactics increasingly created a climate of suspicion and isolation among inmates in the period leading up to the riot.

Other factors contributing to the riot included security lapses (e.g., the renovation of a high security cell block during which dangerous inmates were transferred to a less secure dormitory); gross understaffing (it was estimated that the prison had only about 50% of the staff required to operate it safely; a modification of the control center where steel grillwork windows were replaced with windows that were bulletproof and shatterproof, but breakable. These factors merely helped spark what was already an explosive prison atmosphere (Colvin, 1982).

W. G. Stone, an inmate at the time of the riot, provided an eyewitness account of the events in the book *The Hate Factory*. He reported that several inmates, drunk on home brew, hatched a plan to overpower the guards when they came that night for count. At 1:30 A.M., when the guards arrived, they were overpowered as were others on duty at other dormitories. The inmates quickly captured seven of the staff members on duty. To get to the north wing of the prison, inmates attacked the control center, breaking the recently installed glass windows, and gaining control of the prison nerve center and the keys to the entire prison. Leaderless and uncontrolled, various groups of inmates roamed the prison, looting and destroying almost everything in sight (Hirliman, 1982; Serrill and Katel, 1980).

The rampaging inmates directed their fury and violence against both guards and inmates. Eleven of the fourteen staff inside the prison that night were taken hostage. While none of these guards was killed, they did not escape injury. Some were brutally assaulted. According to Stone, the most severely assaulted were three members of the guard "goon squad" who were beaten and repeatedly sodomized.

As in other riots, some inmates protected guards from other inmates. In the north wing of the prison three guards were given food, coffee, cigarettes, and protection. Further, with the help of sympathetic inmates, four of the hostages escaped during the riot.

Inmate violence against one another was even more brutal. Inmates killed 30 of their fellow inmates, and some 200 others were beaten and raped. The killings were reportedly carried out by about 25 to 50 inmates. Some organized into "death squads" while others acted alone. Thirteen of the slain inmates were identified as snitches but the motives for the rest of the killings could not be officially determined. Stone asserts that many were in retaliation for old injuries. Many inmates who died were not only killed but were horribly tortured and mutilated as well.

Unlike the Attica riot there were no clear-cut leaders who took control of all the inmates at any point during this insurrection. Even though they did not have the support of all those in the prison, several inmates contacted authorities and began negotiations. These negotiators made a variety of demands including requests for better food; federal oversight to ensure no retaliation; improved visiting, education, and recreation programs; an end to harassment; and the opportunity to talk to the press. Prison officials agreed to some of these demands, and in return hostages were gradually released. In the end the inmates got their news conference at which they told of conditions in the prison. The negotiators were promised that they would be transferred out of state because they

The New Mexico penitentiary riot caused tens of millions of dollars worth of damage. This picture shows some of that damage.

feared for their safety. After 36 hours the riot ended. State police SWAT teams entered and without resistance assumed control. Perhaps the words of a National Guard soldier, who searched the prison after the riot was over, summarized this most bloody riot:

> I was in 'Nam for two years, and like I've seen some hellacious sights over there, and it's my personal opinion and belief that these inmates out here made Nam look like a play pen ("Death in a Southwest Prison," ABC-TV, 1980 as cited by Hirliman, 1982).

In addition to the carnage and pain, the damages incurred by the state because of the riot were well over $100 million (Saenz and Reeves, 1989; Serrill and Katel, 1980). In the aftermath of the riot it was acknowledged that the New Mexico corrections system had been neglected and the New Mexico penitentiary had been dangerously overcrowded and understaffed. The prison had had five wardens in the previous five years, a strong indication that

leadership in dealing with existing problems was essentially lacking (Serrill and Katel, 1980).

### The Riot at Camp Hill Was Precipitated by Policy Changes

One of the last major disturbances of the 1980s occurred in October 1989, at the Camp Hill Correctional Institution (CHCI) in Pennsylvania. Two policy changes served to hasten the riot: (1) food could no longer be brought in by inmate relatives on "Family Day" and (2) inmate access to the "sick line" was restricted to every other day. These changes, although appearing to be innocuous, created a high level of inmate resentment. They were issued without explanation, in an already tense prison, and in what inmates perceived to be an arbitrary exercise of power by prison management. The riot began on October 25 when an inmate who attacked a correctional officer was helped by other inmates to keep from being taken into "custody." This disturbance was quelled that evening but erupted again the next morning. The second disturbance lasted until October 27. During the three days of the disturbance, 120 inmates and staff were injured and twelve buildings were destroyed.

After the riot, the Judiciary Committee of the Pennsylvania Senate suggested that two clusters of factors had contributed to the disturbance. First, there were systemic and institutional factors that included overcrowding, idleness, inadequate security, lack of staff, poor staff training, substandard facilities, and lack of programs. Second, there were poor administrative practices that included vague lines of authority and administrative responsibility; absence of clearly defined and easily understood rules and regulations; poor communication, particularly in dealing with inmates and staff; lack of familiarity by top staff with the institution, its staff, and inmates; and indecisive action on legitimate grievances (Adams Commission, 1989).

### The Lucasville Riot May Have Been Curtailed If Staff Had Responded Sooner

The eleven-day riot at the Southern Ohio Correctional Facility at Lucasville, Ohio, continued the trend of bloody riots sparked by management problems. The riot, in which nine inmates and one correctional officer were killed, was touched off on Easter Sunday, April 11, 1993, when two guards were attacked by inmates at the end of the afternoon recreation period. Previously, tension within the prison had escalated when Warden Arthur Tate decided to force 159 Muslim inmates to take a TB skin test, which they refused to take on religious grounds.

A report issued by the Ohio Department of Rehabilitation and Correction showed that the prison had a long history of violence and security problems. It faulted prison staff for responding too slowly to the Easter disturbance in that they took too long to establish a command post; they did not respond to calls for help from COs trapped inside the prison; and the warden did not arrive at the prison until three hours after the riot had begun.

The Department of Corrections reports indicated that many long-standing problems also contributed to the uprising:

**1.** Warden Tate did not have confidence in his administrative and middle management staff.

This resulted in a disruptive tension among prison workers.

**2.** The practice of double celling (due to overcrowding) was seen by most prison staff to be a cause of the disturbance.

**3.** Force had been frequently used to control inmates. This was particularly true for black inmates who made up 57% of the inmate population.

**4.** There was a lack of communication between staff and inmates resulting from racial and cultural differences.

**5.** The security of the institution was diminished by having inmate clerks who had access to sensitive personnel, disciplinary, and operational information. This included inmate assignment to the area in which Warden Tate had a confidential meeting to discuss a lockdown plan during which the TB tests would be completed.

These problems are examples of things that can lead to dangerous levels of tension. With this tension existing unabated, almost any spark can set off a major disturbance. This, and the other two examples of significant prison disorder presented earlier, demonstrate the importance of adequate management in maintaining control in prisons. Later in this chapter we present an example of a well-managed prison to serve as a contrast.

### The Control of Group Violence Requires a Plan

Dealing with riots and other forms of group violence requires a relatively precise set of responses from correctional personnel. The American Correctional Association (ACA), in its publication "Causes, Preventive Measures, and Methods of Controlling Riots and Disturbances in Correctional Institutions" (ACA, 1990a),[c] suggests the following responses for dealing with serious prison disturbances.

Prevention begins with good management. This means that the institutional environment must be safe, sanitary, humane, and the administration must be respectful of the rights of both staff and inmates. Further, overall comprehensive staff training along with teaching staff to recognize and deal with crises are necessary. Special training in riot control principles and the use of riot equipment (gas guns, grenades) enables them to be prepared

The three-day Attica riot resulted in an armed assault to retake the prison. There were 39 deaths (29 inmates and 10 COs) and many wounded, most at the hands of the assault force. In contrast, the riot at Lucasville lasted eleven days. It appears prison officials decided on negotiating a settlement rather than taking the prison back by force. This averted the carnage that occurred at Attica. When the riot was over, nine inmates and one CO had been killed. Several of the negotiation sessions were televised, as shown in this picture.

to handle disturbances. Some facilities have an "emergency response team" that is specially trained to respond to prison crises, such as fights and disturbances. Also, staff dealing with inmates must be tuned into signs of tension (e.g., increased purchases of foodstuffs at the inmate commissary). Staff behavior during times of increased tension should be aimed at reducing the tension or at least not exacerbating it. Another approach is to correct some design flaws in older facilities. Things such as painting, improving lighting, and soundproofing in areas with excessive noise can help to make the environment more bearable for all concerned.

Additionally all staff, including administrators, should make themselves visible and available to inmates. This allows them to deal promptly with inmate questions and concerns and can help reduce tensions. Effective communication, both among staff and between staff and inmates, is imperative. Since a riot is a final form of communication, any improvement in listening skills will likely forestall this form of violence. ACA also suggests that reliable intelligence be gathered on a routine but systematic basis, particularly from respected inmates. The intelligence information should be regularly disseminated to top staff so that decision makers can keep a constant finger on the pulse of the institution. Finally, mechanisms should be in place for the prompt and specific handling of complaints and grievances brought forth by inmates, a process that helps to improve their morale.

The security issues involved in the prevention of riots have been discussed in more detail elsewhere in this book. These include design factors that, for example, reduce the size of units to be managed, reduce indefensible space, or encourage direct supervision; a well-designed classification system; tool, key, and contraband control; effective search procedures for both persons and areas; systems of effective inspections of all physical security aspects; effective systems of communication, including personal body alarms; and effective inmate programs.

According to the ACA, each disturbance is distinctly different and, as such, requires different tactics. While uniqueness may limit the creation of a specific plan that is to be followed in all disturbances, there is the need to have a master riot plan. This plan should "be sufficiently flexible so that the response can be tailored to each individual situation" (ACA, 1990a, p. 35). The objective of any response is to ensure that the appropriate personnel and equipment are deployed to the problem area as rapidly as possible. Once a disturbance has begun, efforts are normally directed toward containing it, evacuating nonessential personnel, and protecting critical areas, such as the prison's control center, the protective custody unit, or the pharmacy. If the disturbance is not quickly resolved, specific plans for retaking the areas under inmate control are developed. Consideration is given to such factors as hostages, the conduct of negotiations, dealing with the media, the use of force, and the post-riot activities (e.g., placement of the inmates, investigating the incident, debriefing, etc.) necessary to return the facility to normal operations. Usually in major disturbances there has been severe damage to parts of the institution, which requires the movement of large portions of the prison's population to other facilities. The ACA (1990a) concludes that the resolution of prison riots is not an easy matter.

### A Well-Run Prison: Oak Park Heights

There is no question that safe, orderly prisons are a necessity for society, the prison staff, and the inmates. The basic features required to achieve this include appropriately designed institutions, decisive but humane administrators, well-trained correctional personnel, sensible rules, and well-planned programs. As described next, an important factor in the running of safe, orderly prisons lies in the leadership and type of approach used in managing them.

The Oak Park Heights facility, a maximum security prison in Minnesota designed to hold 406 inmates, has been an example of a well-run institution under the leadership of Warden Frank Wood. Put into service in 1982 it was billed as a "new generation" prison. It employs high-tech security combined with a tough code of discipline, a highly trained corps of correctional officers, and a personal and direct management style that extends to interactions with inmates. The essence of "new generation" architecture is that it keeps prisoners in small groups under close and constant surveillance in single cells. There are small distinct housing areas in which inmates have considerable freedom of movement. It resembles a podular direct

supervision type of structure and design (see Chapter 22) (Rutherford, 1985).

Oak Park Heights houses extremely dangerous inmates. Eighty-five percent had records of violence and many were transferred from other prisons where they had caused problems. The mission of the prison, according to its former warden Frank Wood (1985), was "to accept from the other adult male facilities, all inmates classified as maximum custody, or categorized as risks to the public. . . . Our program is designed to control, evaluate and facilitate the transfer of inmates to less secure facilities after they have demonstrated a satisfactory adjustment over an established time period at Oak Park Heights" (p. 3). It has been very successful in controlling these inmates.

The institution is renowned worldwide for its earth-shelter design (i.e., the facility is built into a hillside). It has a sophisticated computerized security system that makes escape virtually impossible, a strict but direct and humane approach to management, and a well-trained staff. It is the latter two features that appear to make the major difference. Warden Wood strongly disapproved of staff violence toward inmates unless their own safety was threatened. He dealt directly with cases of staff violence requiring that closely monitored incident reports be filed in all cases in which staff-inmate violence occurred. He believed that inmates will only be reinforced in their violent behavior if they are reacted to violently. Thus, staff were trained to resolve problems by nonphysical means, and those unable to deal with inmates on that basis were not retained. Wood feels that staff are the key ingredient of inmate control and insists that they be in constant and direct contact with inmates (Northam, 1985).

There was a heavy emphasis on full programming that included work, education and training, treatment, and recreation. Many inmates had jobs that paid from $0.40 to more than $2 per hour. Other inmates were assigned to an education unit. If inmates refused to work or participate in their assigned activities, they were locked in their cells. The accent of this programming was to keep inmates as busy as possible (Bottoms and Light, 1987). The incidence of violence by inmates, against one another and toward staff, was low at Oak Park Heights. Interviews with inmates indicated that this prison was perceived as a safe place (Northam, 1985; Wood, 1985).

**THE MECKLENBURG DESIGN WAS SIMILAR TO THAT AT OAK PARK HEIGHTS BUT ITS MANAGEMENT STYLE WAS NOT** The Mecklenburg Correctional Center, a state prison in southern Virginia, serves as a comparison for Oak Park Heights. Mecklenburg, built in 1977, was architecturally designed as a "new generation" institution with a podular structure. Although it was billed as an "escape-proof" prison capable of segregating inmates into small groups to enable them to live and work together, it was beset by continual control problems. There were numerous reports of staff brutality (many of which were corroborated), and six Death Row inmates had successfully escaped. Further this prison was characterized by a management style that minimized staff contact with inmates and did not discourage staff brutality (Rutherford, 1985). It is no surprise that from the early to mid-1980s, the National Prison Project of the ACLU received more inmate complaints from here than from any other U.S. prison. This culminated in nine guards being held hostage for 20 hours in 1984. A statement by inmates described the takeover "as a quest to bring to light [the] inhuman, cruel, barbaric treatment at this institution." Al Bronstein of the ACLU was able to persuade the inmates to release their hostages and surrender which avoided "a blood bath of Attica dimensions" (Rutherford, 1985, p. 410). This comparison points out very clearly that it is management and not architecture that is important in running a safe, violence-free prison.

## SOUND MANAGEMENT PRINICIPLES IMPROVE CORRECTIONAL SYSTEMS

Changes in the orientation of corrections administration are essential if prisons are to develop into truly adaptive and effective organizations. The findings and concepts of organizational theory can be employed to highlight the role of management in this regard. An active corrections management can also serve to deflect some of the instability in its environment through the development of managerial technologies and the opening of the organization to environmental groups. A science of corrections administration would also serve to better inform the political process regarding the development of correctional policy.

An examination of three different perspectives on correctional administration (Duffee, 1980; DiIulio, 1991; Kalinich, Stojkovic, and Klofas, 1988) yields similar conclusions regarding the key factors that need to be considered in developing a sound approach to correctional management:

1. The workings of the correctional institution must be approached holistically. This means that the functioning of all the components that interact within the institution must be considered, because that is the only way a complex system can be understood.
2. The study of prisons as organizations must include relevant groups outside the organization, because it is impossible to understand an organization apart from its environment (e.g., the legislature).
3. The managerial roles of correctional administrators must be reexamined, because the ultimate role of management is to ensure that the various components of the organization operate with minimum conflict in pursuit of compatible goals. If managers are to function effectively in the correctional environment, they must be armed with knowledge that includes sound methods that can be taught to both subordinates and peers.
4. We cannot know what methods will work within the correctional organization until we know how that organization works. This calls for the system to be "self-adjusting." That is, the organization must be able to use the information generated by its own successes and failures to modify itself toward increased effectiveness.

Given the importance of these aspects of the correctional enterprise, it is surprising that so little attention has been devoted to the topic of correctional organization and administration.

ACKNOWLEDGMENTS

[a] Selected excerpts from *No Escape: The Future of American Corrections* by John H. Diiulio, Jr.. Copyright © 1991 by Basic Books, Inc. Reprinted by permission of Basic Books, a division of Harper Collins Publishers, Inc.
[b] Corrections Compendium, Vol. XIX, Number 4 (April 1994).
[c] Reprinted from the American Correctional Association, 1990. *Causes, Preventive Measures, and Methods of Controlling Riots and Disturbances in Correctional Institutions* (3rd ed.), with permission of the American Correctional Association, Lanham, MD.

## CHAPTER RECAP

**U.S. Correctional Systems Operate on Three Levels**
The Federal Correctional System Houses Offenders Convicted of Federal Crimes
Each State Has Its Own Correctional System
Local Correctional Systems House Pretrial Detainees and Misdemeanants
**Most Correctional Organizations Are in the Public Domain**
The Government Is Responsible for the Punishment of Convicted Offenders
Ambiguous Correctional Goals Have Caused Problems
The Private Sector Has Again Become Involved in Corrections
**Administrative and Managerial Personnel**
System-Wide Administrators Create Policy and Programs
Institutional Administrators Implement Policies and Programs
Middle-Level Managers Oversee Specific Programs
First-Line Supervisors Oversee Line Personnel
**Various Approaches to Correctional Administration**
Structural Concepts Help to Identify the Administrative Hierarchy
There Are Three Major Organizational Models
    The Authoritarian Model Is Characterized by a Strong Autocratic Leader
    Under the Bureaucratic Model Control Is Maintained by the Book
    The Participative Model Allows All Staff to Contribute to Problem Solving
Proactive Corrections Management Is Analogous to Preventive Maintenance
Characteristics of Successful Correctional Administrators
**Disorder in the Prison: A Sign of Poor Management**
The New Mexico Riot Was One of the Most Savage in U.S. History
The Riot at Camp Hill Was Precipitated by Policy Changes

The Lucasville Riot May Have Been Curtailed If Staff Had Responded Sooner
The Control of Group Violence Requires a Plan
A Well-Run Prison: Oak Park Heights
    The Mecklenburg Design Was Similar to That at Oak Park Heights But Its Management Style Was Not
**Sound Management Principles Improve Correctional Systems**

## REVIEW QUESTIONS

**1.** Identify the three levels of correctional systems that operate in the United States.
**2.** How does the political nature of a correctional agency's environment impact its policies and operations?
**3.** Compare the authoritarian, bureaucratic, and participative approaches to management of prisons.
**4.** What does proactive corrections management entail?
**5.** Describe the key variables associated with effective leadership.
**6.** What characteristics are associated with successful correctional management?
**7.** Describe and compare the riots at the New Mexico penitentiary and at Camp Hill in Pennsylvania.

## TEST YOUR KNOWLEDGE

Match the following:
_____ 1. Bureaucratic management
_____ 2. Authoritarian management
_____ 3. Proactive management
_____ 4. Participative management
_____ 5. Unit management
    a. management by an idiosyncratic manager
    b. management by the book
    c. giving teams responsibility for managing housing units
    d. management by shared responsibility
    e. management by anticipation of problems
**6.** Public organizations such as corrections have to be successful in order to survive and continue to receive state resources.
    a. true
    b. false
**7.** Unity of command refers to the limited number of persons that one supervisor can effectively oversee.
    a. true
    b. false
**8.** Which of the following represents an important characteristic of successful correctional administration?
    a. focuses on outcomes
    b. develops an organizational culture
    c. has a direct hands-on approach
    d. creates alliances
    e. all of the above

# CHAPTER 14

# CUSTODIAL PERSONNEL

## ■ KEY TERMS AND CONCEPTS

Bona fide occupational qualifications (BFOQ)
CO subculture
Cultural diversity
In-service-training
Job bidding
Occupational stressors
On-the-job training
Sexual safety
Structured conflict
Veterans preference system
Working ideologies

## STATUS OF CORRECTIONAL OFFICERS

Correctional officers (COs) work in an environment unfamiliar to the vast majority of Americans. Even most people working in other parts of the criminal justice system have not seen this component first-hand. COs provide human services to inmates, security, and a semblance of order among unwilling captives—some of whom are dangerous and desperate. They represent the backbone of prison staffs and serve a key social control function. In the past, COs have often seen themselves—and have been viewed by others—as being on the lowest rung of the criminal justice occupational hierarchy. Until the 1970s and 1980s, little effort was made to deal objectively with COs either as people working at a difficult and demanding job or as subjects of empirical studies. Philliber (1987) feels it would be beneficial for researchers to look for the positive aspects of COs and their work.

Because prisons are isolated and are perceived to be dangerous, some people find it difficult to understand why anyone would want to work as a CO given the social, psychological, and physical factors involved in this job. These include the closed nature of the prison itself, including its physical isolation; supervision of individuals who can be dangerous, tend to reject you and your value system, and generally have to be coerced into doing many of the things required by the institution; working in a relatively punitive environment; and working alone with inmates for large portions of the day. However, in spite of the apparently negative aspects of the job, a 1994 national survey of correctional systems found that three-fourths of the systems reported having no problem recruiting qualified individuals for CO positions (Corrections Compendium, 1994b). This suggests that the individuals who take and keep jobs as COs may see the work as a challenge and feel a sense of pride in being able to deal successfully with the inmate population.

### Most Correctional Officers Are White Males in Their Mid-Thirties

As of June 30, 1993, there were 307,246 correctional officers employed in state and federal prisons. Approximately 83% of the COs were male. This high proportion is related to the fact that about 94% of the inmate population is male and the work has traditionally been seen as "man's work." This pattern has been changing since the 1970s due to court-mandated equal opportunity requirements [American Correctional Association (ACA), 1994; Corrections Compendium, 1994a]. Correctional officers are predominantly white (70.4%), with blacks (22.01%) and Hispanics (5.8%) constituting a relatively small proportion of this workforce. Although the proportion of black COs is greater than their percentage in the general population, the 22.01% is still a long way from the percentage of blacks in the inmate population (about 50%). This has fueled criticisms of prisons as institutions in which whites imprison blacks and which are, therefore, racist.

The median age of COs is mid-thirties, and the vast majority have completed high school or received a General Equivalency Diploma (GED). Although salaries for COs have traditionally been low, recent increases have brought the level of pay close to that for police officers. The average starting salary in 1994 was $19,076 and ranged from $13,668 in Kentucky to $29,700 in New Jersey. The average annual salary was $22,848, with a range of $17,004 in Wyoming to $34,062 in New York (Corrections Compendium, 1994a; ACA, 1994).

### Recruiting Qualified Correctional Officers Has Become Easier

The recruitment of COs has been difficult until recently for a number of reasons (e.g., salaries were low, which made the applicant pool small). This made it hard to be highly selective in screening and hiring. Conditions changed in the 1980s and 1990s for a number of reasons, and the current applicants are more highly qualified.

State requirements for the position of correctional officer are quite similar across the nation. Requirements include a high school diploma or GED, age 21 or older, no felony convictions, residency within the state and U.S. citizenship, and, perhaps, previous work experience or additional education. A Corrections Compendium survey (1994b) found that 60% of the states reporting said that their CO recruits typically exceeded these minimum requirements in education. Applicants typically had degrees from two- or four-year colleges and some had graduate degrees. They also exceeded the requirement for work experience, having worked in military or federal prisons and/or had prior training in law enforcement or corrections. These changes in the applicant pool have allowed more sophisticated screening and evaluation of applicants. Recent reductions in turnover rates, which are at about 13% nationwide, and improvements in the wages and status of COs (Corrections Compendium, 1994a) has made it easier to hire COs with good people-handling skills. This has enhanced their ability to control inmates without resorting to force. As the time and cost of training COs has escalated, the need to be more selective in recruiting quality COs and to retain them for longer periods has increased. A job market flooded with more qualified applicants than employment opportunities has enabled many jurisdictions to be more selective. This has resulted in "a team of correctional officers who are better educated and more experienced than in the past" (Corrections Compendium, 1994b, p. 11). In 1994 only one-fourth of the states reported they had problems recruiting COs. Most often, this problem was attributed to a lack of applicants for positions in isolated areas of a state and/or noncompetitive salaries.

In the 1980s the boom in prison construction led to a large increase (37%) in the demand for new COs. Combined with a 13% annual turnover rate, the corrections field was one of the fastest growing sectors of government employment. As a result, the need for preemployment assessments increased. Preemployment assessments ensure that new CO applicants have the appropriate skills and traits to perform their jobs. By 1992 fourteen states[1] conducted preemployment screening to obtain the best applicants, with another five indicating an intent to do so in the future. The screening done by these states varied and was either conducted by in-house staff or was done by privately contracted psychologists/psychiatrists. The instruments used in this process have included the Minnesota Multiphasic Personality Inventory (MMPI) and other personality tests and questionnaires. The fourteen states using this screening improved their ability to select candidates, lowered turnover rates, and screened out inappropriate applicants (Davis, 1992b, p. 17; Corrections Compendium, 1994b). This advantage has been recognized for some time (Morgenbesser, 1984; Shusman, Inwald, and Landa, 1984).

This occupation has generally appealed to individuals who are looking for job features that in-clude security, adequate pay, and a military type of environment (Wicks, 1980). More recently it has been attracting individuals interested in human services type of work (Gilbert, 1993, 1995). A career in corrections, because of the growth in the number of criminals being incarcerated, has been relatively easy to obtain, now pays relatively well (considerably better than minimum wage), is secure, and has decent benefits. In an era in which jobs providing a high degree of permanency are shrinking, the value of jobs in the correctional field has risen considerably.

The quasimilitary structure of jails and prisons appeals to a variety of potential workers. For retired military personnel looking for second careers, the prison—with its strict rules, its chain of command, and uniforms—offers a very comfortable and familiar work environment.

Finally, recent studies of CO job satisfaction (see, e.g., Cullen, Lutze, Link, and Wolfe, 1989; Hepburn and Knepper, 1993) indicate that many COs either derive more satisfaction from working in a human services capacity than a custodial one or are supportive of rehabilitation. This apparent shift in orientation may be a result of the changing nature of the CO applicant pool as discussed earlier.

## TRAINING OF CORRECTIONAL OFFICERS

The recognition that specialized training for correctional officers was required in order for corrections to be considered a profession dates back to 1870 when these principles were enunciated at the National Prison Congress meeting in Cincinnati. However, it took more than 100 years before any major attempts were made to realize this objective. With the help of federal funding through LEAA,[2] junior colleges and universities began to offer programs that better enabled COs to meet the newer job requirements. Between 1971 and 1975 the number of these programs grew from 43 to 115. The Attica riot in 1971 also focused national attention on the inadequacies of the prison system and its staff (Johnson, 1993). Recognizing the need for better training, the U.S. attorney general directed LEAA to establish a corrections academy, which resulted in the creation of the National Institute of Corrections (NIC) in 1977. During its first year NIC had provided training for more than 1000 correctional practitioners, and during fiscal year 1994 more than 3639 participated in conferences and workshops (Gustafson, 1994).

Organizations such as the American Correctional Association (ACA), the American Jail Association (AJA), and the International Association of Correctional Officers (IACO) have also contributed to the professionalization of COs. By the mid-1970s the ACA was deeply involved in developing standards and accreditation programs for correctional facilities. Little formal training was available during this period except for that offered at ACA conferences and meetings. These yearly events included courses ranging from corrections-based management to skill level training (e.g., use of force and defensive tactics). Today, ACA, which has more than 20,000 members (about one-fourth of whom are COs), publishes a journal, *Corrections Today*, seven times annually, that deals with correctional issues. It also publishes numerous training materials and puts on two annual conferences at which training seminars for all levels of correctional personnel are presented.

AJA, which has 5000 members, tends to focus on jail personnel and also contributes to CO training and professionalism. It publishes a journal, *American Jails*, that deals with jail issues, conducts an annual meeting, and puts on two training conferences each month for jail COs and managers. The IACO is an organization of 26,000 COs that brings together correctional experts and personnel from the United States, Canada, and other countries with the purpose of enhancing CO professionalism. It publishes a newsletter, *The Keepers' Voice*, which provides a forum for COs, has developed a "Correctional Officer's Creed," which extols the virtues of professional CO behavior, and is presently pressing for the development of a standardized curriculum to be used in the training of COs (Maghan, 1994; Hahn, 1994). Other organizations (e.g., American Society of Criminology, Academy of Criminal Justice Sciences, National Council on Crime and Delinquency), while not specifically concerned with corrections, have also contributed to professionalism by promoting and generating research to inform practitioners in the field.

Training also received an additional boost in the 1970s when federal judges began ordering correctional agencies to implement or to improve existing training programs. By the 1980s there was less emphasis on merely requiring training programs

and more on the effectiveness of the training provided (Johnson, 1993b).

Correctional officers receive two types of training, formal and informal. Formal training is provided by departments of corrections in each jurisdiction, whereas informal training is furnished on the job after the new CO has gone to work within the institution. This informal **on-the-job training** is accomplished in the daily interactions with special training officers as well as with the inmates.

## Formal Training Involves Classroom Instruction

Formal training is generally required by the state in order for the new recruit to become a qualified officer and is continued after employment in the form of in-service training. This usually begins with classroom instruction, which ranges from two weeks in North Dakota to twelve weeks in Florida (ACA, 1994). A 1992 survey of fifty-one training academies found that training included self defense, crisis management, firearms, professionalism, radio communication, race relations, inmate mental health awareness, security devices and procedures, physical fitness, report writing, first aid, substance abuse awareness, and special inmate populations (e.g., HIV/AIDS) (Vild, 1992). Training time is also devoted to teaching communication skills. The average cost of basic training per student was $2784 with a range of from $240 in Colorado to $10,000 in California (Vild, 1992; Crouch, 1980; Zane, 1987).

New officers also receive training in the general procedures used in each of the different duty areas within the institution. In addition, recruits are instructed in the ways inmates can place them in compromising situations or corrupt them so as to get them to violate institutional rules. By and large, then, formal training gives new recruits the nuts-and-bolts knowledge of the day-to-day activities in which they will engage and a hint of the "realism of prison work" (Crouch, 1980). To complete training successfully, recruits must pass a test on the material taught (Jones, 1992).

Over and above the training received by new recruits is the recognition by many in the field of the importance of continued staff development through **in-service training** within the facility, at outside workshops, seminars, and training programs; and from specially developed correspondence courses. In 1992 forty-one states and the federal Bureau of Prisons reported providing some form of annual in-service training for 125,000 COs. Some of the courses offered included:

weapons, self defense and security procedures training, racial sensitivity, social/cultural life styles of inmates and race relations, crisis management, narcotics and drug awareness, first aid, professionalism, inmate mental health and special populations, communications skills, legal issues/courtroom demeanor and supervisor/officer relationships.

While in-service training ranges from 18 hours in North Carolina to 160 in Wyoming, thirty jurisdictions provide 40 hours. This suggests that despite the importance placed on training by many in the field for the purpose of professional development, it appears to have a low priority in most agencies (Lillis, 1993c; Corrections Compendium, 1993). Johnson (1993b) notes that while "training may be high on administrators' wish lists, it is also high if not first on the list for budget reductions" (p. 16). With states worrying about finding money to house and maintain an ever growing prison population, training often takes a back seat. Also, since many facilities are already short staffed, administrators may not want to take COs away from their assigned duties for in-service training because this might compromise prison custody and security. Nevertheless, as we move toward the next century, with all the challenges and changes facing corrections, the need to place greater emphasis on career development through training and education will become more important. For agencies this will result in:

greater use of employee skills; increased loyalty, better communications and retention of valued employees. . . . [Also it will be viewed] as a "people organization," where recruiting is enhanced and organizational goals are clarified (Rosazza, 1993, p. 11).

Although it has been a long-term problem in the correctional arena, **cultural diversity** has become one of the newest concerns (Moriarity, 1991; Curry, 1993). Also known as "multiculturalism," this view involves a:

recognition that it is neither necessary nor desirable for different ethnic groups to shed their cultural identities to participate in the larger community. [This reflects a] trend away from assimilation by way of the

so called melting pot, and toward the goal of a cooperative pluralism that enables each ethnic group to preserve its cultural identity without viewing others as a threat (Cesarz and Madrid-Bustos, 1991).

Four trends are producing a more diverse population that will increasingly impact the American workforce and therefore affect corrections:

**1.** A significant aging of the workforce so that by the year 2000 its median age will be 39. It should be expected that the correctional workforce, as well as the inmate population, will likewise become older.
**2.** The proportion of women entering the workforce will continue to increase. Thus, there will also likely be more women as COs and as inmates.
**3.** By the year 2000 the proportion of minorities entering the workforce will increase, for blacks by 29%, for Hispanics by 74%, and for other minorities by 70%. This augurs for increasing numbers of these groups among correctional personnel.
**4.** More workers with disabilities will enter the workforce and will likely impact corrections in terms of the inmate population (Curry, 1993).[a]

Add to these trends the fact that the inmate population is also changing, and it makes sense for corrections to provide training that sensitizes staff to the cultural, sexual, and other differences of groups in their systems. "It is not enough to assume that familiarity leads to acceptance; education is essential to foster acceptance and overcome the tendency to regard others as threats" (Cesarz and Madrid-Bustos, 1991, p. 68). Further, from the standpoint of employment, it is predicted that by the year 2000 there will be a shortage of skilled employees. This means that corrections departments, like other employers, will be at a competitive disadvantage if their recruitment fails to include men and women from all ages and race/ethnic groups. Also, a diverse correctional staff that mirrors the inmate population will be better able to communicate with and relate to inmates, and assess, and predict inmate behavior (Curry, 1993).

A final aspect of improving the skills and capabilities of correctional officers is to encourage them to upgrade their education by taking college courses and pursuing advanced degrees. Rewards in the form of advancement and pay incentives can motivate them to do this. This can help advance professionalization and bring greater recognition and respect for the individuals engaged in this challenging task.

## Informal Training Provides a Different Orientation

The informal training received by new recruits prepares them for the job in a very different way. There is a "welcome to the real world" quality about this training, which is usually provided by training officers in the institution. This may contrast sharply with the "book learning" in the academy. While prisons vary in their structure, conditions, and general environment, when new officers enter them their senses may be overwhelmed by the sights, sounds, and smells in their new work world. They may see the racial balance within their prison is heavily tilted toward minorities. They may not even be able to hear themselves think because of the cacophony of sounds (doors clanging shut, the prison's loudspeakers blaring orders) that permeates many prisons. Added to this they may be bombarded by the mixed odors of urine, feces, disinfectant, sweat, and food. As they adapt to these sights, sounds, and odors they may find their attitudes toward inmates becoming more negative, a change which, depending on the CO subculture, may be reinforced by some of their coworkers.

Although help received from the training officers or experienced officers will vary, recruits may be told to "forget what they learned in the academy." Lombardo (1981, 1989) found that, in the eight years between his two studies of corrections officers in a New York prison, changes had occurred in the relationships established between rookies and experienced officers. Prior to the 1980s, rookies were sometimes placed with a veteran officer only for a day or two before working on their own. The advice they received was often general and sometimes consisted only of "learn for yourself, the way I did" (Lombardo, 1981, p. 29).[b] COs beginning their careers in the 1980s received a much more positive reception from experienced officers. This reduced the reliance of rookie officers on inmates to orient them to the prison world.

In his follow-up study of Auburn COs, Lombardo (1989) also found that the newer correctional officers were more likely to maintain a greater social distance from inmates and go "by the book" in dealing with them. This increased social distance may well dampen any positive influence that COs may exert on inmates. However, Lombardo (1981, 1989) noted that because many jobs performed by correctional officers place them in isolated contact with inmates, they may discover that many inmates do not fit the usual stereotype applied to them. This discovery may make it easier for the new officer to accept help from inmates in dealing with unfamiliar routines and procedures.

## THE VARIOUS ROLES OF CORRECTIONAL OFFICERS

Correctional officers play a variety of roles in carrying out their delegated responsibilities. These include security, discipline, treatment, supervision (of housing, work, etc.), transportation, and management. COs are in a paradoxical situation of being the lowest level workers in the organization but having the greatest responsibility for managing and supervising inmates. The nature of their roles and attached responsibilities often place officers in ambiguous and conflicting situations with respect to inmates, administration, and sometimes themselves.

The development of officer work styles or **working ideologies** is the result of interactions with the other groups in the institution (Poole and Regoli, 1980). An examination of these relationships will provide a better understanding of the contemporary correctional officer.

### Relationships between Correctional Officers and Inmates Have Changed

Characteristically the relationship between keeper and kept has been described as one of **structured conflict.** This stems from attempts by COs to prevent disciplinary problems (Jacobs and Kraft, 1978). As a result of the need to be alert constantly to respond to inmate violations, they experience a great deal of tension. This, coupled with policy changes that have expanded prisoner rights, has created a sense of frustration among COs. The policy changes, intended to protect inmates from abuses, are seen by the correctional officers as detrimental to their own interests and welfare.

Poole and Regoli (1980) report that COs also felt these changes had compromised their authority and safety. As a result they dealt with inmates on a more formal basis and developed a defensive posture and more negative attitudes toward them (Friel, 1984; Freeman and Johnson, 1982; Nacci and Kane, 1984; Lombardo, 1989).

Gilbert (1995),[3] on the basis of 25 years of experience working with COs, asserts that the negativism and "enforcer" (punitive) demeanor seen in COs is a public facade that they take on because it is expected of them. In reality, Gilbert feels that COs are much more likely to respect and emulate their colleagues who are able to use communication skills, human decency, and concern about inmate welfare to control their inmate charges. If the CO subculture is indeed characterized by these humanistic concerns, it is likely that COs will welcome and socialize into their group recruits who can emulate them. In doing so, according to Gilbert, they will reduce the danger and stress in their work environment.

Gilbert's view may be right because a certain degree of understanding exists between COs and inmates, and many COs still attempt to help inmates when problems arise, at least within the guidelines established by the institution. A CO at Auburn, New York, put it this way:

> Before I'd help out with a problem I'd try to see what he's tried on his own. If he's had no luck, and it depends on the inmate. If he's working for me and he did go through proper channels, I might tell him to wait a couple of days and then, if he doesn't hear, I'll check it out. If it's a money problem have him bring his printout and I'll go over it with him, and if there is a problem, I'll handle it. I take the time for a good worker because they can't pay him more than $1.55 and this is a benefit. Overall, there's a lot more formal procedures now, but I've been around, and I know where and how to get hold of people. Kind of going beyond just getting information. That's what happens when you've been here for 20 years. But I don't abuse it. It's a matter of habit, even though it's not policy. Procedures were set up because of the constant abuse, to keep people (officers) under control (Lombardo, 1989, p. 87).

Another officer at the same prison described inmate-officer relations:

> What's changed in this regard is the younger officers. Older guys still call around and point inmates in the right direction. They (the younger officers) don't realize that if an inmate works for you, you should handle the problems. Those are the problems they should take care of and now they send the inmate to the sergeant (p. 88).

Lombardo indicates that the changes in the newer COs have tended to increase the social distance between officers and inmates. Thus, more formalized relationships have replaced more personalized, informal relationships. "Helping is now 'part of the job,' but helping is now limited by suspicion and concerns for procedure rather than being limited by more general human concerns" (Lombardo, 1989, p. 87).

A different view is espoused by Gilbert (1993) in his study of CO work style preferences. He found that a majority of COs now tend to perform their jobs in a highly professional manner. This includes consistently enforcing the rules but taking some reasonable exceptions when necessary. As noted earlier, it also involves being genuinely concerned for the human condition of the inmates. If Gilbert's findings are correct, this would imply that the social distance between the keepers and the kept may not be as great as Lombardo has suggested. Gilbert attributes the differences between himself and Lombardo (and others) to the fact that COs maintain the facade noted earlier (negative and punitive attitudes toward inmates) because they do not want to be perceived as "soft" on inmates.

## Correctional Officers, Lacking a Role in Policy Making, Often Feel Unsupported by Administration

The organizational structure of correctional institutions is generally based on a quasimilitary bureaucratic hierarchy in which inmates occupy the lowest position and administration the highest, with correctional officers in between.

Lombardo (1981), using measures of job satisfaction and role strain, found that the New York COs he studied saw themselves at the bottom of the hierarchy. Hepburn (1987) also found that job satisfaction for correctional officers was tied to their perception of the level of influence they had within the institution. The greater they perceived their influence to be (and that of administration) vis-à-vis inmates, the greater their job satisfaction. In his 1981 study, Lombardo suggested that any management strategy that would allow COs to help decide policy would significantly reduce the problems referred to earlier. By 1989 he found that these changes had occurred at Auburn. Thus, improved advancement opportunities, greater recognition for their work, and more opportunities for input resulted in much greater levels of job satisfaction. Hepburn and Knepper's (1993) findings cast additional light on the changing role of COs. They found that the COs they studied who were human services oriented were more satisfied in their job role than those who were custody oriented. Human services oriented officers (HSOs)

> advise, support, console, refer or otherwise assist inmates with their problems and crisis of adjustment produced by imprisonment (Johnson and Price, 1981, p. 316).

Hepburn and Knepper (1993) felt that the satisfaction of HSO officers derived from some of the intrinsic rewards of the work, the degree of authority they had over inmates, their autonomy, and the informality of the job. Thus, the everyday duties of HSO officers involve high levels of friendliness, informality, and interpersonal skills. These COs pursue a more direct and routine contact with inmates and assist them in solving their problems. This creates a more active and self-directive job, which enables these COs to use their skills and abilities in working with inmates. Their authority is based on their relationships with inmates and on using their interpersonal skills to maintain order and help solve problems (Hepburn and Knepper, 1993). These findings support the views espoused by Gilbert (1993, 1995).

In contrast, the authority of security oriented officers derives from the uniform they wear. Their relationships with inmates are more formal and distant. They control inmates by employing the limited rewards and sanctions at their disposal and choose to suppress rather than solve inmate problems. These COs are dependent on administrative and legal systems to control inmates.

It is not surprising that HSO officers derive more satisfaction from their work since they are actively using problem-solving skills to assist and control inmates, which is more satisfying than simply policing inmates. Further, more highly educated COs are more likely to be human services oriented (Jurik, Halemba, Musheno, and Boyle, 1987). This suggests that as corrections attracts more highly educated (particularly college educated) recruits, CO orientation will likely shift even more in the

HSO direction. This also implies a greater emphasis on professionalism. This may also require a shift in orientation for administrators, because more highly educated and professionally oriented staff will want to be more involved in the organizational decision-making process. Failure to allow these COs more input in decisions may result in more disgruntled workers and affect the stability of the institution.

While allowing subordinate staff input in organization decision making may be inconsistent with the quasimilitary structure, in our Close-Up on "The Prison: A Paramilitary Versus Human Services Organization," we explore this question further.

### Correctional Officer Subcultures Tend to Vary from System to System

The work environment of COs would appear to foster a strong, tightly knit **CO subculture,** but there is some controversy as to whether this is the case (Poole and Regoli, 1980; Lombardo, 1989; Gilbert, 1993, 1995). Obviously, the nature and strength of this subculture varies from prison to prison and even from system to system. For example, the Texas and federal systems are perceived as having tightly knit CO subcultures. On the other hand, at Auburn, a New York prison studied by Lombardo, it was perceived as weak. Gilbert (1995) believes that beneath the tough independent exterior, the CO subculture is held together by mutual respect engendered by COs' ability to control inmates without coercion. Thus, they share the feeling that by their behavior they are responsible for each others' safety and the well-being of the entire facility. Remember, however, that regardless of the strength of the subculture, expectations of high solidarity exist when crisis situations arise within the prison (Lombardo, 1989).

Two reasons have been given for the absence of a strong CO subculture. First, interaction among officers tends to be minimal, usually occurring briefly between shifts, during staff meetings, or in the dining room. Because officers tend to work alone in their assigned areas (e.g., cell blocks, prison shops), they tend to remain isolated from one another. The second reason relates to the perceived expectations of administrators (and many officers), who feel that officers should be self-reliant and autonomous. Personal accountability may be stressed more than cooperation and collective responsibility. When this is the case, it

## Close Up   The Prison: A Paramilitary Versus Human Services Organization

Gilbert (1993) suggests that the paramilitary structure of correctional organizations may be more symbolic than substantive. He suggests they are human service organizations. Although the military symbolism

provides an image of control and efficiency . . . its impact is to largely erode control and generate inefficiency by focusing attention on factors which have little to do with effective correctional operations. The security, control, safety, and effective delivery of correctional services within these organizations is largely dependent on the ability of . . . correctional officers to perform specific job related, and definable skills involving human communications and security functions; they are not dependant on rank, uniform, military bearing, command voice, or other characteristically military attributes (pp. 60–61).

It is his contention that the effective operation of a complex organization is dependent on personnel at all levels interacting as colleagues rather than as superiors and subordinates.

The security and control of the institution and safety of everyone who lives or works there, depends on the ability of staff at all levels to interact in an open manner to check and cross-check each other. Individuals must be [allowed] . . . to make reasonable discretionary decisions . . . as long as [they] are reasonable, consistent with a common set of values and legal. . . . This is especially important where strict adherence to the rules. . . . would make little sense or would actually risk security, control or safety of the facility (pp. 62–63).

This suggests a new conception of prisons and a new role for COs. That of decision makers and problem solvers rather than as merely someone who watches inmates and represses inappropriate behavior by using the limited control devices available. This is consistent with unit management in prison systems and direct supervision jail models (see Chapter 22). Do you think a career as a CO would be more attractive to you if you were able to work in a facility where COs were encouraged to follow a human relations approach?

leads to reduced opportunities to develop close working relationships among officers. While the nature of the COs' work will continue to isolate them from one another, group solidarity may increase if more COs adopt a human relations orientation and prisons give officers more opportunities to contribute to organizational decision making (Hepburn and Knepper, 1993; Gilbert, 1993, 1995).

### Correctional Officers Perform Many Different Jobs

The complexity of the correctional officer's job has changed from earlier times when they were merely expected to watch the inmates, count them, lock them in, supervise them in the prison yard, or sit in a gun tower. Lombardo (1981) identified seven general categories of job assignments, which are distinctive, based on their location in the institution, the duties required, and the type of contact with inmates. Each of these is examined briefly.

Officers who supervise inmate living units are referred to as *block officers* or sometimes as dormitory officers if they oversee multiple-occupancy living units. In the cell blocks, which may contain as many as 300 to 400 inmates, these COs supervise and care for inmates, lock and unlock cells, make rounds to inspect cells and other areas, and handle inmate problems as they occur. They also supervise inmate cleanup crews, may distribute linens and clothing, and attempt to maintain some degree of order and security. Dormitory officers perform similar functions except they work in a more stressful environment because they are sometimes surrounded by as many as 80 to 100 inmates and have no means of temporarily isolating inmates who become belligerent or assaultive. Their only option is to have the inmates removed to administrative segregation (i.e., a solitary confinement unit). However, in some prisons COs who do this may be viewed as not being able to control their units.

The control room is the nerve center of the prison. Here a CO is monitoring various areas inside and outside the prison. He or she is responsible for alerting staff when problems arise.

Correctional Officers perform supervisory and other duties in cell blocks and housing areas. Effective control is best maintained when COs constantly interact with inmates.

*Work detail supervisors* oversee inmate work crews, act as inventory managers, order and distribute supplies for inmates, and keep account books. *Industrial shop* and *school officers* generally perform order maintenance and security functions. They tend to work in groups of two or three, usually in conjunction with civilian foremen, industrial supervisors, teachers, and counselors.

This shows a CO overseeing a wall post. In newer facilities, perimeter security is more often provided by mobile patrols and electronic devices.

They are in charge of groups of inmates, ranging from as few as 30 to as many as 300. Their functions include taking counts, checking the whereabouts of absentees, designing and maintaining record-keeping systems for inmate payrolls, and managing inmate interactions, problems, and complaints.

*Yard officers* spend most of their time dealing with security matters and maintaining order. They are responsible for observing inmates and controlling rule breaking in the yard or recreational areas. Although this is an easy task in small groups, it can be very difficult and potentially dangerous in a yard, in which several hundred inmates may be roaming around freely. In this situation it may be hard to determine if a rule is being broken, which inmates are involved, and how to take disciplinary action without causing a disturbance. The fact that officers assigned to yard duty usually have the least seniority and experience makes this an even more dangerous situation.

*Administrative officers* have little, if any, contact with inmates. They normally work in the administration building and deal with such tasks as handling finances, processing paperwork, working the switchboard, and controlling keys and weapons. They are indirectly involved with security, most often when emergency situations arise.

*Perimeter security officers* occupy the wall posts and guard towers, go on mobile outside patrols, or monitor electronic security devices. They usually spend their eight-hour shift watching the facility's perimeter to prevent escapes and the intrusion of contraband. This removes them from the ongoing activities inside the prison. A major problem with this job is boredom. Newer prisons have generally opted to use mobile patrols and electronic motion sensors to provide perimeter security because this is more cost effective than towers both from the standpoint of construction and manpower (NIC, 1987). Most institutions use two patrols during active program hours and only one when inmates are asleep. Towers are manned 24 hours a day.

The *relief officer* performs a variety of jobs in the institution. These officers fill in for other COs who might be on sick leave, vacation, days off, etc., and perform the duties associated with those positions. Since they move throughout the institution, they are likely to have no personal identification with any one task and may find it difficult to establish personal relationships with inmates or with other officers. The exceptions are the relief officers who work in the same areas on a weekly basis.

## Custodial Procedures and Disciplinary Actions Are the Mechanisms by Which COs Maintain Order

With respect to social control, prisons are like any other community in that they have rules and regulations and mechanisms for their enforcement. Rules and regulations vary from prison to prison but cover almost all aspects of inmates' daily routines from the time they arise until lights out at the end of the day. These rules are usually specified in inmate handbooks, which also contain the sanctions for those found guilty of violating these rules. The "law" (control and order) is maintained by COs through a variety of custodial and disciplinary processes. Custodial processes are daily activities and procedures designed to control and keep track of the inmates. Disciplinary actions are responses to the breaking of rules and regulations.

**CUSTODIAL PROCEDURES CONTROL INMATE MOVEMENT AND CONTRABAND** Custodial procedures include control of prisoner movement within the institution; movement in and out of the institution; counts; searches, shakedowns, and other forms of contraband control; and supervision of living quarters, work, and any other activities. Control of prisoner movement in institutions varies according to their custody level. Inmates' custody designations determine their freedom of movement within the prison and the conditions under which they can move around without supervision. Maximum custody inmates are allowed little, if any, unsupervised movement. They are generally always confined to their cells and handcuffed and accompanied by one or more officers during periods when they are outside their cells. For other inmates a system of passes is generally used to control movement from one location to another, except for certain things (e.g., to go to meals).

Keeping track of inmates at any given time is an important custodial function that is accomplished through counts. Counts are conducted several times during the day and night at specific hours. At maximum security prisons, counts may occur as often as every 2 hours while at minimum security facilities they may occur as few as two or three times every 24 hours. During count, inmate activities in the prison usually stop until the location of every inmate is determined. If all inmates are accounted for, the count, is cleared and normal activities resume. If any inmates are unaccounted for, there is an immediate recheck, and escape proceedings are initiated if they remain unaccounted for.

Searches of individuals and their cells, often called "shakedowns," are conducted at frequent irregular intervals in most facilities. Their purpose is to discover contraband. Many things can be defined by the institution as contraband including

Here a female CO conducts a pat search of an inmate. This is one method used to control contraband.

many innocuous items as well as those that are obviously dangerous. Since maintenance of order is a paramount objective, these searches may take precedence over inmates' Fourth Amendment rights.[4]

Control of tools and keys is very important, especially in maximum and medium security prisons. The easiest way to control tools would be to ban them from the prison. However, this is not feasible because certain tools are needed to perform required maintenance, in the various industries, and in vocational training classes. Control is achieved in various ways (e.g., careful check-out/check-in procedures, searches of inmates, use of metal detectors). Inmates who are assaultive are frequently not permitted to work in areas such as the kitchen and shops where knives and tools are available. Keys are also subject to rigid control. When one is lost, locks must be immediately changed to retain control of that particular area.

Contraband often enters through the visitation

process, so procedures are put in place to control it. These procedures include restricting visitor lists; denying contact visitation, particularly for those inmates in maximum security facilities; searching all visitors before entering the visiting park; and searching inmates returning from the visiting park. The search of incoming materials, including mail, for contraband is also a standard practice.

## DISCIPLINARY PROCEDURES ARE USED TO DEAL WITH RULE VIOLATORS

Rule violations, resulting in some formal action by correctional personnel, are quite common. A 1986 survey of state prisons found that 53% of the inmates had been charged at least once under their current sentences and the proportion of violators had remained constant over a period of time (Stephan, 1989). Violators were typically younger, had more extensive criminal careers and/or drug histories, were housed in larger or maximum security prisons, were more likely to be recidivists, and slightly more likely to be male. Whites were as likely as blacks to be charged and disciplined. Petersilia, Honig, and Hubay (1980) found that about half the rule violations they studied involved administrative infractions (e.g., being in the wrong place, insolence), one-fifth dealt with contraband, one-fifth entailed violence without injury, while the remaining 10% were incidents of escape or of violence with injury.

When an inmate commits an infraction, the CO dealing with the problem has several alternatives depending on the system in which he or she works and the nature of the violation. In Florida, for example, the officer may issue a verbal warning; a corrective consultation (CC), which is a written reprimand that becomes a part of the inmate's record; or a disciplinary report (DR), which entails a formal hearing and can result in a sanction if guilt is determined. If an inmate breaks a state law, the case may be referred for prosecution to the state attorney in the jurisdiction in which the prison is located. The American Bar Association recommends that when an inmate has committed an offense, the prosecutor be notified to help decide whether to charge the inmate (Krantz and Brantham, 1991). For example, a fistfight between two inmates in which there is no serious injury will generally be handled as an institutional disciplinary matter. A fight involving a weapon, in which the victim is cut or otherwise injured, is likely to be turned over to the state attorney. The courts have consistently ruled that inmates can be subject to prison disciplinary proceedings as well as subsequent criminal prosecution without incurring double jeopardy. The rationale is that the two punishments serve different purposes; i.e., one is to maintain prison discipline and the other is to uphold the criminal law (Mushlin, 1993; Krantz, 1988; *United States v. Smith*, 1972).

An inmate receiving a DR will be interviewed by one of the duty sergeants to determine the inmate's version of the offense and to get a list of witnesses to be interviewed. A formal disciplinary hearing follows, conducted either by a hearing officer or a hearing team, to "try" the case and make a determination of guilt or innocence.[5] If the inmate is found guilty, a sanction is imposed, and the DR becomes a part of the inmate's file. If found innocent, the DR is destroyed. Depending on the seriousness of the disciplinary breach, the inmate may be kept in administrative confinement while awaiting the hearing. Stephan (1989) reported that 94% of all inmates charged with violations of prison rules were found guilty.

The formal consequences of rule violations and criminal acts run the gamut from none to the death penalty—in jurisdictions in which capital punishment can be imposed. The more common consequences involve loss of privileges, loss of good time (in jurisdictions that award it), and confinement in disciplinary confinement. Good time is accumulated by all inmates except for those serving minimum mandatory sentences and those in disciplinary confinement. Loss of good time, or the inability to accumulate it, means inmates will serve a longer part of their current sentence.

## THE ACID TEST OF STAFF TRAINING INVOLES THE ABILITY OF COs TO CONTROL INMATES

While both the custody and disciplinary procedures discussed may help contribute to prison social control, in the final analysis it is the ability of COs to put these procedures into action that dictates the extent to which they will work. As Cohen (1991) notes:

The best video monitoring system in the world never broke up a fight in an exercise yard. The most modern construction cannot prevent a suicide. Computerized security scanning cannot prevent escapes. It is the people who watch the video monitors, walk the pods or mods or quads, and read and interpret the computer printouts who stop fights and prevent suicides and escapes. It is the officers who spend their shifts in living units talking to and watching inmates or wards who are the real fail-safe mechanisms (p. 88).

To increase these skills, training programs have been developed to help correctional personnel who deal with inmates on a daily basis.

In dealing with violent or potentially violent situations, for example, correctional workers must be prepared verbally and physically to handle the situation. Rice, Harris, Varney, and Quinsey (1989), as a function of their work in an institution for the criminally insane, developed a training program designed to help those working with violent individuals. Their program, which consists of training in violence prevention, includes following specific security guidelines; learning verbal "calming" techniques; dealing with individuals who are "blowing up" either by "defusing" their violence verbally or controlling them through physical intervention; and conducting a post-violence analysis, which pinpoints the causes of the incident and reestablishes a relationship with the perpetrator. Rice *et al.* (1989) found that institutional personnel who had been trained to use their program not only could defuse these situations but also suffered fewer injuries than those who were untrained.

## FEMALE AND MINORITY CORRECTIONAL OFFICERS

In the last two decades many correctional systems in this country have been required by the Equal Employment Opportunity Commission and other related affirmative efforts to hire minorities and female correctional officers. This has altered the traditional white male CO structure of many prisons. Many white male COs reacted strongly to and resisted the introduction of these minority and female officers into the prison. This hampered or retarded their assimilation into the officer workforce (Owen, 1985; Crouch, 1980).

Individuals from minority groups constitute approximately 30% of the correctional officer workforce. The largest percentage of minority staff were found in New Mexico (70%), Washington, D.C. (95%), Mississippi (81%), and Arkansas (45%) (ACA, 1994). As indicated earlier, the diversifica-

tion of the CO workforce will likely strengthen it and help it better deal with the demographic changes predicted for the early twenty-first century. In that respect, a consideration of the following changes in the CO workforce in adult institutions between 1982 and 1993 is enlightening:

**1.** There was about a 40% increase in the proportion of women in the CO workforce. The majority of this increase was accounted for by African-American and Hispanic women.
**2.** There was a 10% increase in the proportion of African-American COs, with the greater part of this increase accounted for by females.
**3.** The number of Hispanics in the CO workforce more than doubled so that by 1993 they represented almost 6% of the COs (ACA, 1983, 1994).

If these trends continue, the CO workforce will indeed become diversified. The hiring of minority officers will not only diversify the CO workforce but may also have a salutary effect on the corrections field. Thus, in addition to reducing the "white keeper–minority inmate" image of corrections and providing appropriate role models, research by Jackson (1992) indicates that minority COs may bring a less punitive orientation toward inmates into the correctional environment.

### Increasing Numbers of Female Correctional Officers Are Working in Male Prisons

Women have served as correctional workers from the time of the Walnut Street Jail, where Mary Weed was the principal keeper in the 1790s, to the present (Morton, 1992b). Their roles in corrections have, however, been limited until recently. Before the early 1970s, female COs worked almost exclusively in prisons for women or in the women's section of jails. The number of female officers employed in men's prisons began to increase when the Civil Rights Act was amended in 1972 to prohibit discrimination in the workplace. In 1993 women constituted around 17% of the correctional officer workforce (ACA, 1994), with Mississippi reporting the largest percentage (44%) and Rhode Island reporting the smallest (4%) (Corrections Compendium, 1994a). As of May 1994, 42% of the female COs were working in male institutions (in a survey of thirty-nine states and the Federal Bureau of Prisons) (Corrections, Compendium, 1994a). In more than one-fourth of the systems, over 50% of the female COs worked in male institutions.

Resistance to female COs has been especially strong when it involves their working in higher security men's institutions. For example, the Supreme Court supported the State of Alabama in its efforts to deny women the right to work in its maximum security prison for men (*Dothard v. Rawlinson*, 1977). The Court concluded that the jungle-like environment of this maximum security institution, where sex offenders were scattered throughout the population, was so dangerous that female COs might be raped and would be less able than men to maintain order. The Court also required Alabama to correct these unconstitutional conditions (Pollock, 1986). *Dothard*, far from being a precedent, was subsequently viewed as an isolated case by later court decisions because of the extreme circumstances in that Alabama prison. It has not been used to exclude women from jobs in other men's prisons (Collins, 1986, 1993).

Title VII of the Civil Rights Act of 1964 was used by women to overcome discriminatory hiring in the criminal justice field. Nevertheless, this act provides that if **bona fide occupational qualifications** (BFOQ) exist for a position, women could be excluded from a job if those BFOQs were based on gender. However, using a person's sex as a reason for denying them a job on a BFOQ basis has been very narrowly defined. Collins (1993)[c] suggests

> a good [justified] example . . . might be . . . a single-sex post in an institution . . . where the post (specific task) involved very close scrutiny of inmates in states of undress. In this situation use of officers of the opposite sex of the inmates would be seen as an invasion of inmates' privacy rights (p. 125).

Thus, only rarely can a person's sex be legitimately used to deny them a job on a BFOQ basis. In most cases, doing so represents discrimination.

The barriers women faced in attempting to compete with men for positions in corrections have included the Veterans Preference System, physical requirements, sexual stereotyping, concerns regarding the safety of women in male correctional environments, inmate rights to privacy, and the issue of equality of assignment between the sexes (Rafter and Stanko, 1982; Bernat and Zupan, 1989; Walters, 1990).

The underlying rationale of the **Veterans Preference System** (VPS) has been to reward veterans for

their military service and assist them in readjusting to civilian life. Civil service jobs, which include corrections officer positions, use the VPS as an inducement for veterans to apply. Since relatively few women have been in the military, they cannot receive the VPS points on hiring or promotional exams and are consequently discriminated against.

Until they were banned by the courts, physical requirements, such as minimum height, weight, and strength, were used by many corrections departments to exclude women from CO positions. Many male officers resented the intrusion of women into what they felt was a male domain. They also felt women were too weak physically to protect themselves or their fellow officers in situations involving inmate violence. A male CO in Oregon reflected this view:

> I don't believe a woman should hold down a correctional officer's job that means coming in contact with prisoners. If I'm in trouble out here, particularly in the yard, and I blow my whistle and here comes some woman running up to me, this isn't a very good help at all, and I don't care whether she's a black belt or not. As you know, if somebody slapped her on the jaw it would probably bust up her face. She doesn't have the strength, number one. Number two, some of these men—and I'm sure I would feel the same way after being here so long, and actually have the urge, they haven't been around women. I think it's just temptation to put a sexy looking broad working around them (Fox, 1982, p. 68).

The concern of some males that female COs would be unable to defend themselves or respond during a crisis is somewhat unrealistic (Fox, 1982). They fail to consider that many male officers may also not fare well in these situations by virtue of their age, weight, and lack of exercise. Furthermore, as a result of the Court's decision in *Dothard v. Rawlinson* (1977), states could no longer use height and weight as BFOQs in the hiring of COs. This meant neither males nor females could be denied employment on the basis of their size. Further, research conducted with police found that women can train themselves to achieve a level of strength and fitness well within the normal requirements of the police profession (Holeman and Kreps-Hess, 1983). If this is the case, there is no reason to believe that female correctional officers could not do the same. Moreover, Fox (1982) found that newer male correctional officers and those with more education and on-the-job knowledge were less concerned about this issue than older, less educated officers. Simon and Simon (1993) also noted that newly hired male COs were more likely to accept women COs as equals when compared with "old timers." A recent description by a young, white, middle-class female CO of her experiences in a men's prison provides an answer to many of the questions about women working in male prisons:

> In retrospect, my overall assessment of whether female corrections officers carry their weight in men's prisons and whether they are accepted by their male colleagues is positive. I never saw a male officer threatened or endangered by having to work alongside a female officer. Female officers were as likely to assume their responsibilities, stand up to prisoners, and enforce the rules as males officers; and for the most part, male and female officers recognized the absence of differences. As for the prisoners, most of them like having women around; it humanizes the institutions (Simon and Simon, 1993, pp. 240–241).

**Sexual safety** is another sexist rationalization offered by male officers for not assigning women to direct contact positions in male prisons. Fox noted that this perception by male COs, that inmates have "uncontrollable" sexual desires, that will put female COs at risk of rape, may partly reflect their own sexual appetites, which are constrained by social and organizational restraints. That is, the inmate may be a handy mirror revealing the sexual fantasies of these male COs.

While male officers may be concerned for the sexual safety of women, Fox reported that this concern has not been shared by female officers. Many female COs have reported that they viewed the possibility of sexual assault as a job-related risk and were much less concerned about it than their male counterparts. A number of female officers indicated that they had accepted the threat of sexual violence in the prison in the same way as they had in the community.

Although some inmates have welcomed the presumed humanizing effects of female COs, others resent being reminded of their sexual deprivation by the constant presence of women. According to Potter (1980), however, the crux of the matter has been the issue of privacy. Many inmates do not want to be watched by women when they are engaged in activities such as going to the toilet, showering, and sleeping. Potter (1980) quoted a Delaware inmate who summed up the female CO's

dilemma: "The issue is, should you let her (the woman CO) come down on the tier and violate my rights, or keep her off the tier and violate hers?" (p. 30).

The issues of opposite sex observations and searches of inmates have usually involved male inmates objecting to the presence of female officers on the grounds of their right to privacy. In deciding this issue, the courts have had to balance inmate privacy rights against the provision of equal employment for female COs, reasonable attempts to accommodate an institution's need to allocate responsibilities among male and female officers, and security concerns (Mushlin, 1993). The courts have tended to view female CO employment rights as more important. At the very least, they have allowed inadvertent or infrequent viewings by opposite-sex COs of inmates who are naked or using the toilet (Krantz and Branham, 1991). Some courts have gone further, approving a prison policy allowing female COs to be assigned to areas where they might see inmates partially or totally nude, showering, being strip-searched, or using toilet facilities. They ruled this did not violate male inmate rights (*Grummett v. Rushen,* 1985). Under those circumstances women could be assigned to supervise men in these areas.

Another area of concern regarding privacy involves opposite-sex searches by COs. The courts have allowed female officers to pat search male inmates, even to the extent of brief touching of the groin and anal area (e.g., *Timm v. Gunther,* 1990).

While the issue of violations of inmate privacy rights versus the rights of females to equal employment in the correctional system has received a modicum of attention, much less attention has been focused on this issue for male COs in women's prisons. The double standard of sexual propriety that is present in society (i.e., more concern surrounds the sexual protection of women) also appears to be applied in prison. Thus, decisions regarding dormitory supervision of one gender by another are more likely to favor the female CO. These decisions are motivated by the fact that restricting women COs in the supervision of males closes nearly twenty times more job and advancement opportunities for them than similar restrictions would for male COs. Not all female COs agree with the issues discussed here regarding cross-gender supervision. Modlin (1991) quotes a female CO regarding the assignment of women to cell areas in male prisons:

The double standard in corrections which allows female officers a wider range of job functions in male prisons than male officers in female prisons is an injustice to everyone. Implementation of such practices creates animosity toward female officers and are an insult to the professionalism of male officers (p. 76).

The courts have taken a somewhat different position on male COs dealing with female inmates. At least one court has found it unconstitutional for male COs to frisk female inmates (*Jordan v. Gardner,* 1992).[6] The reasoning here, as with another decision involving banning males from working in female housing units, has been that a high percentage of female inmates have been sexually abused by males. Thus, allowing them to search women or work in female housing would be traumatic and counterproductive to their rehabilitation (*Torres v. Wisconsin Dept. of Health and Social Services,* 1989).

## THE WORK ENVIRONMENT OF CORRECTIONAL OFFICERS

As in many industries and workplaces, the dissatisfaction of correctional employees with their treatment by administrators, pay, and working conditions has prompted many to join unions. Working in prisons has also been recognized as being highly stressful.

### COs Have Joined Unions to Obtain Representation in Matters Affecting Them

Unionization in the corrections field began in the 1950s but was slow to develop, particularly outside of the Northeast. This was because many states either had laws prohibiting these types of employees from organizing in this manner and/or prohibiting them from striking. It was not until the 1970s, when some of these restrictions began to be eased as a result of court decisions, that collective bargaining became a reality for many in the field (Fisher, O'Brien, and Austin, 1987). Correctional officers are represented by a variety of groups including the American Federation of State, County, and Municipal Employees (AFSCME), the International Brotherhood of Teamsters (AFL-CIO),

the Police Benevolent Association (PBA), and a variety of state and local employee organizations, for example, the California Correctional Peace Officers Association (Corrections Compendium, 1994b). In some institutions treatment and custodial staff have been represented by different unions, a condition resulting in conflicting goals and actions by the two groups. A 1993 Corrections Compendium survey (1994b) of the District of Columbia, the Federal Bureau of Prisons, and all states reported that in thirty-two of these jurisdictions correctional officers were represented by a union.

Where unions exist, the contractual agreements with the jurisdictions may give employees certain rights relating to grievance procedures, seniority and job assignments, overall working conditions, and layoffs. However, unlike labor management negotiations in private industry, the subjects open to bargaining are controlled by state law. Typically, these laws allow bargaining over working conditions and personnel-related matters. Generally both workload and safety are considered by unions to be mandatory subjects to be dealt with in the bargaining process. Issues that are viewed as managerial are not open to negotiation (e.g., applicant qualifications). However, often the line between these subjects is not very clear (Collins, 1993).

Strikes represent a strong lever used by unions to derive favorable contracts for their members and serve as a graphic way for workers to express their grievances. The extent of the grievances can be seen in some systems by the number of strikes occurring. Ohio's correctional system, for example, suffered ten strikes during a five-year period in the late 1970s. However, many states, while permitting collective bargaining, still bar their employees from striking (Fisher *et al.,* 1987). These prohibitions have been sidestepped by the use of other types of work stoppages or slowdowns such as "sickouts." For example, while their neighbors in Ohio were striking, Pennsylvania correctional officers, who were prohibited from this tactic, staged more than a dozen sickouts during which large numbers of COs would call in sick on the same day. The pressure of strikes and other work slowdowns by corrections workers has brought about both animosity as well as a greater understanding of the problems in correctional work, according to Wicks (1980).

**CONCERNS OF UNIONIZED COs FOCUS ON A WIDE RANGE OF ISSUES** The issues that concern corrections personnel differ from those concerning union members in other areas (Potter, 1979). For example, a strike in the New York system a few years ago focused on deep, long-standing issues relating to working conditions and participation in the decision-making process rather than to economic factors. In corrections the labor-management relationship involves an element (i.e., inmates) that is missing for other labor groups. The recent growth of prisoner rights and privileges has been seen by COs as a loss of their own rights and of a lowering of their status both in the eyes of the inmates and the general public. To strengthen their position vis-à-vis inmates, unions have opposed the expansion of improvement programs for inmates; established **job bidding,** which allows senior officers to bid for jobs within the institutions (they usually opt for jobs that reduce or eliminate inmate contact); and pushed for job safety. This last concern has led these unions to lobby legislators and the U.S. attorney general's office to look into the root causes of violence. The overall objectives of this effort have been to make prison work less dangerous and generate public support "on a national basis" for system-wide reforms in corrections (McEntee, 1993). Union contracts have also required mandatory training. One New York agreement, following a strike provided for stipends for preservice and in-service training and stipulated that content and delivery of training would be subject to union review (Maghan, 1981). Collins (1993) indicates that in the 1990s issues that are likely to be the subject of CO union negotiations will include employee urine testing and making the workplace smoke free. Urine testing of employees is a highly controversial issue. The Supreme Court has ruled that, at least in some instances, urine testing can be conducted without there being any specific cause or suspicion that an employee is using drugs. Based on this case, other courts have generally ruled that random drug testing for employees involved in jobs relating to public safety can be required without violating Fourth Amendment protections. However, labor agreements may require, prior to the implementation of testing, that union consent be obtained (Collins, 1993).

The unionization of correctional officers and the establishment of collective bargaining has had some major effects on the field (Crouch, 1980).

First, it has helped to create more job security, improved training, and better working conditions. Second, and perhaps more importantly, unionization has undermined the prison's authoritarian hierarchical management system and created a tripolar structure consisting of administration, officers, and inmates. As a result, officers now have more power in shaping policy, which has improved their morale.

**Prison Work Is Stressful**

It has been recognized for some time that working in prison affects correctional officers physically, psychologically, and emotionally (Cheek and Miller, 1982). Correctional officers suffer abnormally high rates of heart attacks, ulcers, hypertension, depression, alcoholism, and divorces. Woodruff (1993) points out that the average age of death for correctional personnel is fifty-nine while the average life-span of the population at large is seventy-five. These serious health and social problems and the shortened life-spans are commonly thought to result from the **occupational stressors** found in the correctional environment. This has resulted in an increasing emphasis on recognizing and controlling these stressors.

Occupational stressors can be divided into two categories, those associated with the characteristics of the job itself and those that are part of the organizational environment. Among the stressors associated with the corrections job are negative inmate behaviors such as defiance and attempted manipulation of COs, having to maintain inmate discipline, having to comply with inmate rights, overcrowding, and being confined within the jail or prison environment along with the inmates. Those relating to correctional organizations include poor communication with and/or lack of support from supervisors and/or administrators, little or no input in decision making, low pay, role ambiguity (e.g., lack of sufficient information and resources to perform their jobs), and role conflict (e.g., conflict between treatment and security). These stressors heighten the probability of burnout, a chronic condition characterized by emotional exhaustion, depersonalization, decreased competence, and detachment from the job (Maslach, 1982; Maslach and Jackson, 1981). Burnout increases the likelihood that mistakes will be made in the course of the workday, increasing the danger to all concerned.

To combat stress and burnout in the correctional setting, Woodruff (1993) opts for a multifaceted approach. The first step in this approach involves identification of specific stressors. He suggests giving all correctional workers the opportunity to express, in an anonymous way, their concerns and problems. The next steps entail getting feedback from all workers regarding the development of goals and policies that will reduce ambiguity, allow straightforward communication, and foster participation in the decision-making process. Other steps involve requiring increased training and education for the CO job, thorough training for managers, stress management training, consistent and fair evaluation practices, and a wellness program that encourages good health practices through prevention programs. Thus, the task of reducing stress becomes one of creating a consistent environment in which all workers are made aware of problems and can contribute to their solutions and which encourages wellness-oriented activities. In view of the expense involved in recruiting and training correctional officers, these attempts to deal with stress and burnout appear to be very necessary.

Corrections officer roles have changed significantly in the last few decades. They receive better training, more pay, and greater recognition for the work they do. They now have a greater voice in the running of the institutions in which they work and appear to stay in the career longer. They deal with inmate populations that have become progressively more difficult to handle in an environment that is highly legalistic. The future of the correctional officer profession thus appears to be heading in the direction of greater professionalization and more complicated criteria for the hiring of new recruits. These trends would appear to have significant implications for the types of individuals that will be recruited for these positions in the future.

## ENDNOTES

1. The fourteen states that do psychological screening include Alaska, Arizona, Arkansas, California, Iowa, New Hampshire, New Jersey, New Mexico, New York, Ohio, Pennsylvania, Rhode Island, Tennessee, and West Virginia.
2. In 1968 the U.S. Congress passed the Safe Streets and Crime Control Act, which provided funding for the Law Enforcement Assistance Administration Act.
3. Mike Gilbert, Ph.D., is currently an assistant professor at the University of Texas in the Division of Social and Policy Studies. His views are based on nearly 25 years of work with correctional officers both in the military and in several state systems as well as his extensive research (Gilbert, 1993) on the role and function of correctional officers in jails and prisons.
4. Chapter 16 delves more thoroughly into inmate rights with respect to search and seizure.
5. Chapter 16 discusses in more detail the procedural aspect of the disciplinary hearing process.
6. See Chapter 16 for a thorough discussion of these issues.

## ACKNOWLEDGMENTS

[a] Reprinted with permission of the American Correctional Association, Lanham, MD.
[b] L. X. Lombardo, (1989). *Guards imprisoned: Correctional officers at work, 2nd ed.* Cincinnati, OH: Anderson Publishing Co., © 1989. All rights reserved. Reprinted by permission of Anderson Publishing Co., Cincinnati, OH.
[c] Reprinted from W.C. Collins, 1993, *Correctional Law for the Correctional Officer,* with permission of the American Correctional Association, Lanham, MD

## CHAPTER RECAP

**Status of Correctional Officers**
Most Correctional Officers Are White Males in Their Mid-Thirties
Recruiting Qualified Correctional Officers Has Become Easier
**Training of Correctional Officers**
Formal Training Involves Classroom Instruction
Informal Training Provides a Different Orientation
**The Various Roles of Correctional Officers**
Relationships Between Correctional Officers and Inmates Have Changed
Correctional Officers, Lacking a Role in Policy Making, Often Feel Unsupported by Administration
Correctional Officer Subcultures Tend to Vary from System to System
Correctional Officers Perform Many Different Jobs
Custodial Procedures and Disciplinary Actions Are the Mechanisms by Which COs Maintain Order
Custodial Procedures Control Inmate Movement and Contraband

Disciplinary Procedures Are Used to Deal with Rule
  Violators
The Acid Test of Staff Training Involves the Ability
  of COs to Control Inmates
**Female and Minority Correctional Officers**
Increasing Numbers of Female Correctional Officers
  Are Working in Male Prisons
**The Work Environment of Correctional Officers**
COs Have Joined Unions to Obtain Representation in
  Matters Affecting Them
  Concerns of Unionized COs Focus on a Wide Range
    of Issues
Prison Work Is Stressful

## REVIEW QUESTIONS

1. What are the demographic characteristics of correctional officers in the United States?
2. What is the difference between the formal and informal training of correctional officers?
3. In what ways are new correctional officers trained by both training officers and inmates?
4. What are the essential components of an effective CO training program?
5. Why have correctional officers' relationships with inmates become more formal?
6. What are the various jobs performed by correctional officers?
7. What is the "sexual safety" argument against using female correctional officers in male prisons?
8. What are the main concerns of correctional officer unions?
9. What are the sources of stress for correctional officers?

## TEST YOUR KNOWLEDGE

1. Which of the following combinations of demographic characteristics best describes correctional officers?
   a. white males in their mid-thirties
   b. black males in their mid-twenties
   c. white males in their mid-twenties
   d. black females in their mid-thirties
2. For which of the following reasons are people most likely to become correctional officers?
   a. to stop crime
   b. job security
   c. to rehabilitate criminals
   d. to have a high status job
3. More formal relationships between correctional officers and inmates have resulted from
   a. rising crime rates.
   b. prison overcrowding.
   c. increased inmate rights.
   d. better educated correctional officers.
4. _____ are responsible for supervising inmates when they are in their housing units.
   a. Yard officers
   b. Wall post officers
   c. Administrative officers
   d. Block officers

*BFOQ — can we advertise for male or female prison.*

# CHAPTER 15

# HISTORY OF PRISONER RIGHTS, COURT ACCESS, AND REMEDIES

■ **LEARNING OBJECTIVES**

*After completion of this chapter, you should be able to:*

**1.** Discuss the hands-off, hands-on, hands-restrained doctrine, and approaches to inmates' rights.

**2.** Spell out what courts would consider an adequate plan for providing inmates with access to a law library and the restrictions that would be constitutionally acceptable.

**3.** Explain the circumstances under which inmates are entitled to court-appointed attorneys and the role played by "jailhouse lawyers" in assisting inmates in preparing court actions.

**4.** Describe the circumstances under which inmates can bring tort actions in a correctional setting and the reasons inmates prefer to bring civil rights actions rather than tort actions.

**5.** Explain the conditions that are required for an inmate to have a valid claim under the Federal Civil Rights Act.

**6.** Identify the types of relief that inmates who are successful in civil rights actions can expect.

**7.** Recount the types of legal challenges that are typically brought by inmates using a habeas corpus petition.

**8.** Describe some problems that the courts face in enforcing judicial decisions to improve prison conditions.

**9.** Discuss the use of contempt citations by the courts to achieve compliance with judicial orders to improve prison conditions.

**10.** Provide an explanation of the roles and functions of "special masters" in institutional reform cases.

■ **KEY TERMS AND CONCEPTS**

Consent decree
Contempt of court
Due process clause
Federal Civil Rights Act, Section 1983
*Habeas corpus*
Hands-off doctrine
Hands-on doctrine
Injunction
Jailhouse lawyers
Legitimate correctional objectives
Reasonableness test
Restrained hands-on doctrine
Section 1983 actions
Selective incorporation
Slaves of the state
Special masters
Tort
Totality of conditions

To many, the concept of prisoner rights may seem a contradiction in terms. Many people believe that inmates should have no rights because their crimes violated the rights of others. However, the framers of the Constitution decided prisoners do have some constitutional rights. This view is reflected in two ways: in the Eighth Amendment, which prohibits "cruel and unusual punishment" and in the objective of the Constitution to preserve human dignity. Of course, with heinous offenders (e.g., serial murderers, sadistic rapists) it is difficult to argue that there is any dignity to preserve. Nevertheless, by imposing no limits on the mistreatment of prisoners, the society in which this takes place is degraded (Krantz and Branham, 1991).

Legal concerns in corrections have two perspectives: that of correctional staff and that of the inmate. For example, inmates want to know if their mail will be censored or what actions will result in their being placed in solitary confinement. Correctional staff and administrators want to know the circumstances under which they can be held liable (e.g., for confining an inmate to administrative segregation or searching a cell). These concerns relate to the question of "Which rights must inmates be allowed in a correctional facility?" If this chapter had been written thirty years ago, the answer would have been "Only those the prison chooses to allow them."

## THE EVOLUTION OF PRISONER RIGHTS

Until the 1960s the federal courts basically refused to intervene in matters relating to prison conditions. This had the effect of making inmates "slaves of the state." However in the 1960s an era began in which the courts discarded their hands-off approach and recognized that inmates did not lose all their constitutional rights upon imprisonment. By the 1970s, after restoring some basic constitutional rights, which included forbidding states to incarcerate inmates under inhumane conditions, the courts became reluctant to further expand inmate rights. At this point they took the position that while inmates retained their basic constitutional rights, these rights had to balanced against the legitimate operational needs of prison officials to maintain order, security, and discipline.

### Under the Hands-Off Doctrine, the Courts Refused to Consider Inmate Claims of Unconstitutional Prison Conditions

The history of prisoner rights in the United States has gone through several phases (see Table 15.1). From the birth of our nation until the 1900s, the prevailing view as enunciated in *Ruffin v. Commonwealth* was that prisoners had no rights and, in effect, imprisonment made them **"slaves of the state":**

> A convicted felon. . .punished by confinement in the penitentiary instead of with death, is subject while undergoing that punishment, to all the laws which the Legislature in its wisdom may enact for the government of that institution and the control of its inmates. . .during his term of service in the penitentiary, he is in a state of penal servitude to the State. He has, as a consequence of his crime, not only forfeited his liberty, but all his personal rights except those which the law in its humanity accords to him. He is for the time being the slave of the State. . .The bill of rights is a declaration of general principles to govern a society of freemen, and not of convicted felons and men civilly dead. Such men have some rights it is true, such as the law in its benignity accords to them, but not the rights of free men (*Ruffin v. Commonwealth*, 1871, pp. 795–796).

The **hands-off doctrine,** though not a legal principle, aptly described the judicial position regarding intervention in prisoner matters. During this period, while stopping short of stating that inmates had no constitutional rights, the courts felt that they had neither the power nor the obligation to define what rights inmates had. Additionally, they were not obliged to protect them (Krantz and Branham, 1991). As we noted in Chapter 1, the courts took this position for several reasons.

One reason involved the issue of separation of powers. Some judges felt that by considering prisoner complaints they were violating this doctrine, which specifies distinct functions for each branch of government—executive, legislative, and judicial. This gives responsibility to the courts for deciding issues of law and to the executive branch for controlling agencies such as prisons. Another reason involved states' rights. Many inmate claims brought to federal courts were sent back to state courts because it was felt that consideration of these claims encroached on the states' sovereign domain. Additionally, judges felt they lacked training and

TABLE 15.1  **Evolution of Prisoner Rights**

| Period | Inmate | Court Action |
|---|---|---|
| Hands-off, 1776–1964 | Slaves of the state: entitled only to those rights prisons allowed them. | Dismissed most cases involving claims by inmates regarding prison conditions. |
| Hands-on, 1964–1979 | Recognition by the courts that inmates were persons and entitled to basic constitutional rights. | Federal and state courts considered inmate claims that they were denied basic constitutional rights. |
| Hands Restrained, 1979– | Inmate rights not as broad as those enjoyed by non prisoners; can be restricted by legitimate prison needs to maintain order, security, discipline. | Day-to-day correctional operations left to prison officials. Court action limited to instances in which basic constitutional rights were abridged, e.g., adequate food, medical care, sanitation, and safety. |

experience in the complexities of prison administration. Therefore, they might not recognize the need for certain prison rules and practices. Thus, they did not want to substitute their opinions for those of correctional experts. It was also felt that correctional staff might not take the necessary steps to maintain prison order if their actions were subject to judicial review and personal liability.

Some judges were afraid that if they began reviewing inmate claims they would be deluged by a torrent of frivolous inmate claims (Gobert and Cohen, 1981; Krantz and Branham, 1991). Finally, the hands-off doctrine greatly simplified the job of the courts since all suits involving prison conditions could automatically be dismissed (Krantz and Branham, 1991). Although these reasons appeared to justify the hands-off doctrine, each was flawed. This doctrine was sustained until the 1960s. Even at that point, in only a few cases were the courts sufficiently troubled to abandon this position (Krantz and Branham, 1991).

### The Hands-Off Doctrine Was Discarded in the 1960s

In the 1960s, the courts began to discard their hands-off approach and established what has been called a **hands-on doctrine** by beginning to focus on prison conditions. Beginning with *Cooper v. Pate* (1964), the Supreme Court reversed a circuit court decision dismissing a Muslim inmate's petition that he was denied access to the Koran and of

opportunities to worship. In reversing this decision, the Court recognized that Muslim inmates had the right to sue prison officials for religious discrimination under the Civil Rights Act of 1871.

The 1960s and early 1970s were very turbulent times in American history. As we noted in Chapter 8, the Civil Rights movement and its violent aftermath prompted most minority groups, including prisoners, to demand that they be accorded their constitutional rights. Inmates became militantly assertive in demanding their rights. Prison reform groups and social-minded lawyers inspired, supported, and tutored prisoners in filing the petitions that would bring their cases before the courts. Riots, particularly the Attica riot in 1971, brought the problems and injustices of our prisons to the attention of judges.

**THE WARREN COURT EXTENDED CONSTITUTIONAL RIGHTS TO MINORITY GROUPS**  The key ingredient that caused change was the activity of the federal judiciary, particularly the Supreme Court. In 1953, the Warren Court began a period in which constitutional rights were extended to disenfranchised minority groups. It began with the *Brown v. Board of Education* (1954) decision that rejected the "separate but equal" doctrine and mandated school desegregation. This was followed by rulings expanding the rights of accused criminals. These included landmark decisions such as *Miranda v. Arizona* (1966); *Mapp v. Ohio* (1961), and *In re Gault* (1967). The same libertarian views that prompted the court to extend constitutional rights to those accused of crimes also made them more willing to recognize that "[t]here is no iron curtain drawn between the constitution and the prisons in this country" (*Wolff v. McDonnell*, 1974, p. 2974). Thus, the court acknowledged an obligation to protect the rights of the incarcerated.

Several other legal developments contributed to the discarding of the hands-off doctrine (Krantz and Branham, 1991; Gobert and Cohen, 1981). The most important was the Supreme Court's decision in *Monroe v. Pape* (1961), which resurrected a Civil War statute providing legislative justification for individuals to seek redress in federal court when their state civil rights were violated. The section of the federal **Civil Rights Act** of 1871 that applied was 42 United States Code Section 1983 (commonly referred to as **Section 1983**). This decision allowed individuals who were deprived of their rights by a state officer, acting under color of state law, irrespective of the official's actual authority to engage in the behavior in question, to bring action in federal court. This meant that state officials who violated an inmate's constitutional rights while performing their duties could be held liable for their actions in federal court regardless of whether these actions were approved by state law or policy (University of Illinois Law Forum, 1980; Gottlieb, 1985). Also, claimants were not required to exhaust state remedies before seeking redress in federal courts.

**PROVISIONS OF THE BILL OF RIGHTS WERE SELECTIVELY INCORPORATED INTO THE DUE PROCESS CLAUSE MAKING THEM BINDING ON THE STATES**   A second important development during this period was the extension of most provisions in the Bill of Rights, through their **selective incorporation** into the **Due Process clause** of the Fourteenth Amendment, making them binding on the states. With previous decisions, this enabled state prison inmates to bring actions in federal courts for constitutional rights violations including freedom of speech, of religion, from unreasonable search and seizure, and from cruel and unusual punishment (Gobert and Cohen, 1981).[a] This meant that jails and prisons could not deprive offenders of all their constitutional rights.

During the hands-on period, from the 1960s to the late 1970s, when the courts first looked at prison conditions they found flagrant constitu-

tional violations. The courts began by limiting, on a case-by-case basis, the extent to which prison authorities could restrict rights. During this time prisoners were given such rights as:

> meaningful access to the courts; freedom of religion; the right to a reasonable standard of medical care; limited rights to privacy and freedom of personal appearance; some due process rights in disciplinary hearings; the right to correspond with the courts, lawyers, and government officials; freedom from arbitrary censorship of mail and publications; and the right not to be subject to cruel and unusual punishment (Bronstein, 1985).

The courts also recognized that many specific conditions, although offensive, might not be individually bad enough to violate constitutional rights. When taken together, however, they saw that the totality of these conditions might represent a constitutionally unacceptable state of imprisonment. First, in *Holt v. Sarver* (1970)[1] the courts found that the conditions of confinement at two Arkansas prisons, when taken as a whole, represent cruel and unusual punishment. Later, in *Pugh v. Locke* (1976), the entire Alabama prison system was found to be operating in violation of the Eighth Amendment's "cruel and unusual punishment" clause (Bronstein, 1985).

## By the Mid-1970s the Courts Were Reluctant to Further Expand Inmate Rights

By the mid-1970s the Supreme Court became reluctant to further expand the rights of inmates and even began to somewhat restrict them. This was occasioned by several factors. First, prison populations more than doubled between 1972 and 1982. While this growth was anticipated to continue through the 1980s, most jurisdictions had fewer financial resources. There was also a hardening of public attitudes and a movement toward more punitive treatment of offenders. The character of the Supreme Court was also changed as several liberal justices appointed during the 1950s and 1960s retired and were replaced by more conservative ones. This combination of factors forced improvements in prison conditions to take a backseat. *Bell v. Wolfish* (1979) and *Rhodes v. Chapman* (1981) were the cases seen as confirming the Court's new direction.

**TWO PIVOTAL DECISIONS SIGNALED THE COURT'S NEW DIRECTION** In changing to a more restrictive interpretation of inmate rights, the *Bell* and *Rhodes* cases were major turning points. This new direction attempted to balance institutional operational requirements with inmate constitutional rights.

*The Bell Case Recognized That Institutional Need Justified Restriction of Inmates Rights* In *Bell v. Wolfish* (1979), the Supreme Court reviewed a variety of conditions, some resulting from overcrowding, at a new federal detention center.[2] The Court noted that (1) problems in the daily operation of a correctional facility are not easily solved and (2) judges do not have the authority to devise plans for the operation of corrections systems. "The inquiry of federal courts in prison management must be limited to the issue of whether a particular system violates any prohibition of the constitution ... The wide range of judgment calls that meet constitutional and statutory requirements [are the responsibility] of officials outside of the Judicial Branch of Government" (p. 1886).

In examining the constitutionality of prison conditions and restrictions in *Bell,* the Court held that:

**1.** Simply because inmates retain certain constitutional rights does not mean that those rights are not subject to restrictions and limitations. [However] there must be mutual accommodation [i.e., a balance] between institutional needs and the objectives and provisions of the Constitution.... This principle applies equally to pretrial detainees and convicted prisoners (pp. 1877–1878).
**2.** Maintaining institutional security and preserving internal order and discipline are essential goals that may require limitation or retractions of the retained constitutional rights of both convicted prisoners and pretrial detainees.... Prison officials must be free to take appropriate action to ensure safety of inmates and correctional personnel and to prevent escape or unauthorized entry (p. 1878).

Finally, the Court focused on the types of restrictions and conditions that would constitute punishment for pretrial detainees. This is important because these inmates were not convicted and therefore could not be subject to punishment. The court reasoned that for something to constitute punishment the restriction/condition must be shown to have been imposed for purposes of punishment. However, if the restriction/condition relates to a "legitimate government objective," it does not, without proof of intent to punish, constitute a violation of due process. On this basis the following practices were upheld: double-bunking, body searches, restricting incoming publications, searches of cells in the absence of the prisoners, and regulations on incoming packages. The key consideration in determining if these conditions constituted punishment was whether they were reasonably related to institutional interests in maintaining security, order, and discipline.

*The Rhodes Case Recognized That Imprisonment Includes Harsh and Restrictive Conditions* In *Rhodes v. Chapman* (1981) the Supreme Court reinforced its position in the *Bell* case. This case involved an overcrowded new facility in Ohio whose population was 38% more than its designed capacity. More than one-half the population was housed two to a cell, which inmates alleged constituted cruel and unusual punishment. For inmate claims to be valid, the Court noted that they had to show that their confinement conditions either inflicted "wanton and unnecessary" pain or were grossly disproportionate to the severity of the crime.

In this case, rather than focusing on double-bunking, the Court looked at how the crowding affected prison life. While noting that it resulted in minor deprivations such as limited hours of work and access to education programs, the Court found it did not inflict pain and was not of a wanton and unnecessary nature. More important, there was no deprivation of food, medical services, or sanitation; nor was there an increase in inmate violence. The Court felt that the **totality of conditions** created by overcrowding did not constitute cruel and unusual punishment. It further noted that:

> "the constitution does not mandate comfortable prisons [nor does it require that jurisdictions] aspire to [meet] this ideal."

Justice Powell, in writing for the majority, stated that incarceration of

> "persons convicted of crimes [even in one of the better prisons] cannot be free of discomfort. [In fact] to the extent that such conditions are restrictive and even harsh, they are part of the penalty that criminals pay for their offenses against society" (p. 347).

Powell concluded the opinion by stating that lower courts should continue to examine prison conditions. However, unless contemporary standards of decency are not met, the running of prisons should be left to legislatures and prison officials rather than to judges.

These two decisions brought to an end intensive court scrutiny of prison conditions and ushered in an era of judicial restraint.

**THE COURT TOOK A MORE RESTRAINED HANDS-ON APPROACH** It seems clear that the Court has taken a more balanced approach to inmates which could be labeled "one hand on, one hand off" or a **restrained hands-on doctrine.** This approach embodies several principles that recognized (1) inmates do not forfeit all constitutional rights; (2) inmate rights are not as broad as those enjoyed by nonprisoners because inmates are imprisoned; and (3) prison officials need to maintain order, security, and discipline in their facilities. Finally, the Supreme Court suggested that lower courts use a "reasonableness test" to resolve conflicts between inmate rights and the legitimate interests of the prison officials to maintain control.

*The Reasonableness Test Determined the Acceptability of Restrictions on Inmate Rights* The **reasonableness test,** set forth in *Turner v. Safley* (1987), involved four factors. At issue in *Turner* was a ban on inmate-to-inmate correspondence. The standards the Supreme Court established for determining the "reasonableness" of a regulation were:

**1.** *Rational connection:* "There must be a valid rational connection between the prison regulation and legitimate government interests put forth to justify it" (p. 2262). The rule was justified because it advanced the goals of institutional security and safety because mail between inmates can be employed to discuss escape plans and to arrange assaults and other violent acts. Also, this could help control growing prison gang problems by restricting communication between gang members, by transferring them, and limiting correspondence. Further, this facility was used to provide protective custody. Allowing correspondence between facilities could compromise the safety of these inmates.

**2.** *Alternative means:* There must be an alternative means of exercising this right. This ban on inmate-to-inmate correspondence "does not de-

prive inmates of all means of expression. . .it only bars communication between a limited class of people with whom prison officials have particular cause to be concerned" (p. 2263). Inmates can still correspond with family members outside the prison system.

**3.** *Impact on rights:* What impact will the accommodation of this asserted right have on other inmates and staff? Prison officials asserted correspondence between prisons facilitates the formation of informal organizations, threatening staff's ability to maintain safety and internal security. Also considered was the ripple effect, i.e., the granting of correspondence to a few inmates would only be exercised at the cost of significantly less liberty and safety to staff and other inmates at this and other facilities. The Court viewed protecting the safety of many (versus abridging the rights of a few) as within the province and professional expertise of prison officials.

**4.** *Absence of alternatives:* The absence of ready alternatives to the regulation is evidence of its reasonableness. The Court noted there was no easily instituted alternative to this policy and that other systems such as the Federal Bureau of Prisons had similar restrictions. The only option, offered by inmate claimants, was for prison officials to monitor inmate correspondence. That meant reading all these letters, which prison authorities argued was impossible.

Thus, the Supreme Court said it would not intervene in prison operations as long as the restrictions placed on inmates are reasonably related to **legitimate correctional objectives,**[3] that is, the need to maintain order, security, and discipline. This does mean that the Court is giving prison officials free rein, i.e., it is not taking its hands completely off.

*The Wilson Case Reinforced the Court's Decision in Turner* This latter position is clearly reinforced by the decision in *Wilson v. Seiter* (1991). At issue in this case were two considerations (Alexander, 1991). First, the inmate contended that his Eighth Amendment rights were violated by poor conditions in the prison (e.g., overcrowding, inadequate heating and cooling, unsanitary dining facilities and food preparation, housing with mentally and physically ill prisoners). The Supreme Court, in reversing a lower court decision, reaffirmed in *Holt v. Sarver* (1970) that the totality of conditions can be constitutionally unacceptable.

The most important issue in this decision involved the liability of prison officials for constitutionally offensive conditions. The Court said that to be held liable inmates had to prove that prison officials were "deliberately indifferent" in permitting these unconstitutional conditions to exist. In fact, an opinion by Justice O'Connor[4] concluded that to demonstrate "deliberate indifference" requires showing that prison officials had knowledge of constitutional violations and then failed to act (Alexander, 1991). A case meeting this test was one in which:

> "prison officials. . .were aware that the inmate had inadequate toilet facilities, but it was two months before any significant attempt to modify toilet facilities took place and three months before the prisoner was transferred to a room with adequate facilities" (*LaFaut v. Smith*, 1987).

Finally we believe it's fair to conclude that courts will consider the following factors in making their decisions. They will defer to prison officials when they can show that a restriction is related to legitimate correctional goals, particularly facility security. Inmate suits relating to basic constitutional issues such as adequate medical care, food, sanitation, and inmate safety will continue to be considered.

**CONSTITUTIONAL CHALLENGES MAY NOW BE TAKEN TO STATE COURTS**   Most recently, some sources, including Cohen (1990) and the American Civil Liberties Union, have noted that state courts may become the new arenas where constitutional questions on prison conditions will be decided. These include claims for damages for failure to provide adequate medical or psychiatric services; claims relating to the failure to protect an inmate; and relief from conditions of overcrowding. It is important to note that Supreme Court rulings either set minimum standards relating to a particular right or deny that the Constitution requires that it be provided. While this means that rights must be provided to the extent specified by the Supreme Court, state courts can still set higher standards for their jurisdiction. For example, while the Supreme Court has not required the provision of attorneys for capital offenders in death penalty appeals, a state supreme court may decide that they should be furnished in its jurisdiction (Holmes, 1991).

The rest of this chapter examines how inmates gain access to the courts, and the next chapter focuses on substantive rights, that is, the extent of basic constitutional rights granted inmates.

## COURT ACCESS PROVIDES A BASIS FOR INMATES TO SECURE THEIR RIGHTS

The courts provide inmates with an arena in which they can bring complaints regarding the abridgement of their rights. Without court access, inmates have no mechanism to effectively force prison officials to provide them these rights. This would be like the fox guarding the henhouse in that complaints would be limited to those approved by prison authorities.

Inmates are guaranteed meaningful access to the courts by the Constitution under the Sixth and Fourteenth (due process) Amendments (Project, 1991). Prison officials are required to assist inmates in preparing and filing legal papers by either (1) establishing a law library or (2) providing individuals who are trained in the law (*Bounds v. Smith*, 1977). It is important to note that the state has the discretion to decide which of the two options is used (Marke, 1988).

### Various Issues Surround the Adequacy of and Access to Law Libraries

Questions regarding law libraries include the following: What constitutes an adequate library and sufficient time and access to use it? What restrictions can be placed on individual inmates? What types of materials are inmates entitled to in preparing their briefs?

Although the Supreme Court has not provided specific guidelines, the plan it affirmed for North Carolina prisons in *Bounds v. Smith* (1977) suggests what it would consider adequate. This plan included the establishment of law libraries (with relevant federal and state cases since 1970) in various prisons around the state. Also, inmates at other facilities were to be given transportation and housing to these prisons, if necessary, to allow for a full day's research (see also *Miller v. Evans*, 1992).

Although *Bounds* failed to specify the books necessary to meet minimum requirements, most courts have required prison law libraries to provide

The law library serves as a focal point for inmates working on appeals of their convictions or suits related to prison conditions.

the basic resources specified in *Bounds.* To be acceptable:

> [this must] include federal and state statutes . . . relevant to prisoners. . .federal and state law reporters from the past thirty years . . . essential secondary tools for the case materials in the collection and basic treatises on criminal law, habeas corpus, and prisoners rights (Mushlin, 1993, p. 21).

Despite the high cost of law books, the courts have not excused prison officials from maintaining an adequate law library exclusively on the grounds of lack of funding (*Bounds v. Smith,* 1977). They have only required that jurisdictions provide one of the above options. However, states failing to meet court requirements for the adequacy of an option chosen may be ordered to make available the other alternative. When North Carolina failed to establish adequate libraries, the Court of Appeals upheld a district court requirement that

inmates be accorded the help of attorneys (*Smith v. Bounds,* 1988).

The courts have recognized that legal research takes time. Thus, the question of adequate legal access has revolved around such issues as the length of time the library is open and its availability to different classes of inmates. A court-approved plan for Georgia prison libraries mandated that: (1) they be open a minimum of nine hours per week; (2) inmates who wished to use them be allowed the equivalent of eight hours every three weeks; and (3) the hours be varied to accommodate inmates involved in work, education, and other programs (*Mercer v. Griffin,* 1981). Access must also be provided to inmates confined in long-term segregated units (e.g., protective custody, Death Row). Also, security concerns have not been viewed as a valid basis for denying inmates from going to the library, limiting them to checking out books by citation, or from taking part in legal training programs (*DeMallory v. Cullen,* 1988). Finally, the courts have required that inmates be provided such basic resources as paper and pens to assist them in filing complaints and some have even required the limited availability of copying facilities (Mushlin, 1993).[b]

**IT IS QUESTIONABLE WHETHER INMATES CAN PREPARE THEIR OWN CASES** The high rate of inmate illiteracy makes it questionable whether the average inmate can use a law library without assistance. At least one court has had these same reservations:

> access to the fullest law library anywhere is useless and meaningless to the great mass of prisoners. To expect untrained nonprofessionals to work with entirely unfamiliar books, whose content they cannot understand, may be worthy of Lewis Carroll, but hardly satisfies the substance of the constitutional duty.
>
> Access to full law libraries makes about as much sense as furnishing medical services through books like: "Brain Surgery Self-Taught," or "How to Remove Your Own Appendix," along with scalpels, drills, hemostats, sponges and sutures (*Falzerano v. Collier*, 1982, p. 803).

Case law on this question is far from clear. Some courts have required trained paralegals to help inmates in using libraries (*Harrington v. Holshouser*, 1984). However, the Supreme Court has ruled that the presence of a law library is sufficient to provide even Death Row inmates with court access to challenge their death sentences. Thus, there is no requirement that attorneys be provided (*Murray v. Giarratano*, 1989).

Finally, while most jurisdictions have opted to provide law libraries, many of them do not meet court standards for adequacy because an acceptable library can cost tens of thousands of dollars and require substantial space to house the books required and for inmates to do research. These deficient libraries continue to operate because no one has filed suit challenging their adequacy (Collins, 1993).[c] When challenges have occurred, the courts have, in the absence of other alternatives, required prisons to provide inmates with the services of an attorney (*Canterino v. Wilson*, 1989).

### Prison Officials May Not Unreasonably Restrict Access to Attorneys

In federal and most state courts there is no requirement that inmates have counsel appointed to pur-

sue appeals of their cases. The appointment of counsel is totally within the discretion of the court (Mushlin, 1993). Inmates formally charged with offenses committed in prison, like any accused person, are entitled to counsel. This right is not extended to disciplinary actions or to placement in administrative segregation when an inmate is suspected of criminal activity (Collins, 1993).[5] When inmates have attorneys, prison officials may not unreasonably restrict them from meeting in private and communicating with their counsel (*Ching v. Lewis*, 1990). Also, courts have usually allowed unrestricted correspondence between inmates and their attorneys. Incoming mail from attorneys may be opened (but not read) in the inmate's presence to inspect for contraband. To enable prison officials to make this determination, the courts have required that correspondence be clearly marked as from an attorney. Since outgoing mail presents no threat it cannot be censored or confiscated (*Wolff v. McDonnell*, 1974; *Lemon v. Dugger*, 1991; Mushlin, 1993).

**THE COURTS UPHELD ACCESS TO INMATE ASSISTANCE IN FILING CASES** Because many inmates are functionally illiterate and cannot file claims on their own, it is not surprising that many seek assistance from other inmates. Correctional officials have not always viewed **jailhouse lawyers** (JHLs) positively. To deter JHLs from assisting inmates, some prison officials did such things as impose disciplinary actions, plant evidence on inmates so they could take disciplinary action (*Morrison v. LeFevre*, 1984), and spread rumors that a jailhouse lawyer was a snitch so that other inmates would retaliate against him (*Harmon v. Berry*, 1984).

In *Johnson v. Avery* (1969), the precedent-setting case in this area, the Supreme Court ruled that lacking reasonable alternatives, it was unconstitutional to restrict inmates' access to the courts by forbidding inmate assistance. While providing some leeway, the courts approved some limitations: restricting the time and place where assistance can take place (e.g., a requirement that all legal work be done in a writ room) and not permitting compensation (Palmer, 1991; Mushlin, 1993).

### Jailhouse Lawyers Assist Inmates in Filing Their Cases

A jailhouse lawyer is an inmate who has learned legal skills and is recognized by other inmates as a legal resource.

**THERE ARE TWO TYPES OF JHLs**   Based on his research in Illinois prisons, Thomas (1988)[d] divided JHLs into two types. The first are law clerks, who are inmates assigned by the prison to litigation tasks. These inmates are given formal recognition and are paid a nominal sum (starting at $45 per month). Of course, accomplished practitioners can creatively increase their income. Their official position gives them reasonable access to their clients and legal resources but little control over their case loads or clients. However, if they are too vigorous or successful in pursuing inmate complaints, prison officials may retaliate against them by terminating or reassigning them.

Freelancers, the second type, are inmates more closely resembling the popular stereotype of inmate writ writers. They are not formally assigned but instead use their own time to study the law and work on their own cases and those of other inmates. Freelancers are likely to be older, more experienced and capable than law clerks, since they frequently started as law clerks (Thomas, 1988). Like independent practitioners, they can be selective in their choice of clients, exert greater control over them, and can negotiate more favorable levels of compensation. They also develop a reputation based on how successfully they litigate inmate cases.

**JHLs SERVE A NUMBER OF FUNCTIONS**   The stereotypical JHL is an inmate scurrying around the prison looking for unacceptable conditions and then locating precedents with which to file a suit. While this applies to some JHLs, it is not the way most work. JHLs help inmates deal with many legal problems that are external to the prison including being the victim of unfair divorce proceedings depriving them of child visitations or having to deal with inheritance issues, taxes, compensation claims, property liens, and name changes (Thomas, 1988). They, like any successful professional, must also be therapists and diplomats to develop trust and ferret out the true problems of their clients.

The high status of JHLs enables them to be able to discover and resolve potentially violent situations. For example, Thomas (1988) found that they serve as mediators who negotiate to resolve volatile situations before they explode and take a more dangerous path (e.g., preventing a "hit"—an intentional assault—on a guard). JHLs also help inmates deal with some nonlegal prison problems (e.g.,

being unable to add a name to the visitors list, difficulties in contacting a counselor). Besides legal tasks, JHLs are involved in a variety of activities that require conflict resolution and management skills. These activities serve to reduce frustration, defuse potentially violent situations, and help the administration manage the tensions of prison life. Thus, JHLs can help foster a more secure and humane prison environment consistent with the interests of their keepers (Thomas, 1988).

**INMATES BECOME JHLs FOR A VAREITY OF REASONS**   Inmates do not become JHLs for monetary reasons alone, but opportunities for rewards may motivate them to continue. Prison regulations forbid inmates to be paid for privately rendered services. However, it is generally recognized that this service entails some economic reward and is further justified by the difficulty of securing funds in prison. Because cash is commonly considered contraband in most prisons, JHLs typically require clients to have it sent to an outside contact. A second less risky form of payment involves favors, commissary items, or other commodities, (Thomas, 1988).

Other factors motivating JHLs include gaining status, power, and prestige in the inmate culture; perhaps getting a coveted single cell; and feeling a sense of pride over preparing a first-rate case, particularly if it sets a precedent. As one JHL put it "I'm telling you that I've put together a document that an architect would put together. *I'm a legal architect*" (Thomas, 1988, p. 217). Finally, for JHLs, "practicing law" provides an opportunity for self-improvement. This happens because, to become proficient, they have to learn the law, how to do legal research and prepare briefs, and have to sharpen their reading and writing skills.

## POSTCONVICTION ACTIONS

A court will not necessarily review a claim on its merits alone. To be reviewed, a claim must be filed in a specific way with a certain court. This is made more difficult because there are several claims that inmates can file and decisions about where to file the petition—state or federal court—have to be made. Gobert and Cohen (1981) note that it is difficult, even for a lawyer, to choose the most effective legal and tactical means of postconviction litigation. Thus, for the untrained inmate with no legal assistance, this task may be impossible. Courts and legislatures have been sensitive to these problems. They have tried to streamline and simplify this process for inmates by developing model forms and placing more emphasis on the facts in the inmate complaint than on how it is drafted or the supporting legal theory (Gobert and Cohen, 1981).

### Tort Actions Are One Form of Legal Relief

A **tort** is a civil wrong arising from a claim by one party that another party has negligently, maliciously, or deliberately inflicted some sort of injury to him or her. The most typical tort action results from automobile accidents where one party negligently operates a car and injures another. In a correctional setting, tort actions against corrections personnel may arise out of claims by inmates relating to failure to protect them from harm, negligent loss of property, medical maltreatment, and other breaches of reasonable care that they are entitled to expect from correctional staff (Collins, 1993). Thus, an inmate may sue a CO for gross negligence if she were injured when the officer negligently closed her cell door, for example, when playing a game that involved seeing how close he could come to her heels as he closed the door while putting her in a cell (Fisher, O'Brien, and Austin, 1987).

Typically, since a tort action seeks only damages, it is filed in a state court. Often an inmate's claim can either be pursued as a tort action or as a civil rights claim. The nature of the proof for each action is different. For example, an inmate believing that she has received inadequate medical care could pursue a tort action by claiming that the treatment was negligent. In contrast, in a civil rights action, she would have to claim "deliberate indifference" to serious medical needs, which is harder to prove than mere negligence.

In spite of the greater difficulty, inmates often prefer to bring civil rights actions (commonly called Section 1983 actions) because (1) these suits are typically brought in federal courts, which have historically been more sympathetic than state courts to inmates; and (2) the relief available is much broader than in a tort action. Since no injunctive relief is possible in a tort action, prison officials are not required to change the conditions that led to the suit. For example, although an inmate may be paid damages for negligent medical care the prison is not required to improve health services. Also, although state restrictions may limit the damages and/or prevent punitive damages, these restrictions are not applicable in federal civil rights cases (Collins, 1993).

### Inmates Can Bring Cases to the Federal Courts under Section 1983 of the Civil Rights Act

During the hands-on era, inmates gained the right to challenge prison conditions in the federal courts through Section 1983 of the Civil Rights Act. A successful Section 1983 suit requires proof that a person, acting under the color of state law, deprived the claimant of a constitutional or federal statutory right. This means that suits can be brought against government employees—those under contract—for actions they engage in while employed by the state, even if those actions are not authorized by the state. Thus, a legitimate claim can arise out of an event in which a guard beats an inmate, even though prison rules forbid this action.

**AN INJUNCTION REQUIRES ACTS TO BE PERFORMED OR TERMINATED** In civil rights actions court orders for relief generally take the form of an **injunction,** which is a court order requiring defendants to perform or stop a specific act. Because the courts recognize that this litigation can take time to resolve, it is possible to obtain a preliminary injunction or temporary restraining order. This prevents institutional officials from continuing to engage in certain conduct or keeping an inmate in a designated status (e.g., solitary confinement). Because this is viewed by the courts as an extraordinary remedy it is usually issued only when inmate plaintiffs can show their case is likely to succeed or that there will be possible irreparable injury. However, when the victims are suffering substantial hardship, a temporary order may be obtained by showing a "substantial chance of success" (Krantz, 1988). For example, in *Smoak v. Fritz* (1970), the judge considered the following in issuing a temporary order:

> [f]or over five weeks. . .[these inmates have] been held in solitary confinement. No charges have been lodged against them, nor have they been found guilty of any wrongdoing other than for which they were originally sentenced. Yet the duration of their solitary

confinement now threatens to extend for an indefinite time, with possible physical and psychological harm.

It is the belief of this court that the five weeks plus which have passed since the Auburn Prison disturbances should have been sufficient time to investigate and prepare charges against plaintiffs if any were warranted. . . (p. 612).

After a trial in which inmate plaintiffs are successful, judges may issue an injunction ordering correction of the problem. For inmates, this remedy is very important because they typically remain in custody after the suit has been resolved and this provides them with protection from further deprivations of rights of this kind. Injunctions or court orders have required a variety of changes. First, they have mandated the abolition of certain prison regulations and state statutes relating to discipline, censorship, and court access. Most courts required the defendants (the states or institutions), either on their own or under court supervision, to develop new rules that are more consistent with constitutional requirements. Second, these orders required improvements in institutions or in the services provided. Beginning in 1970 with the prisons in Arkansas (*Holt v. Sarver*, 1970), the courts ordered major prison and jail improvements including development and achievement of acceptable stan-

dards of medical care; improvement of sanitation conditions; improvements in the quality of food; and an increase in the number of correctional officers and better training for them (Krantz, 1988). Third, jails or prisons or sections of them have been ordered closed when found to confine inmates under conditions that violated protections against cruel and unusual punishment (e.g., *Inmates of Allegheny County Jail v. Wecht*, 1989).

Fourth, the courts have also ordered institutions to reduce their populations. As of January 1995, forty-two jurisdictions were under court order or consent degree to limit population and or improve either their entire system or major facilities (National Prison Project Journal, 1994/95).[6] While overcrowding per se is not unconstitutional, when it exists it is more likely that total prison conditions and services will reach a point where they become constitutionally unacceptable. To relieve chronic overcrowding the courts have set population caps at specific facilities, ordered the transfer of prisoners to other facilities, and required the release of inmates or pretrial detainees. For example, in September 1990, when the Houston County Jail exceeded its federally mandated population cap, they had to release 250 offenders. Most were misdemeanants held because they could not post bail (Suro, 1990).

When jails or prisons exceed federally mandated caps, they may be forced to release inmates. Over the course of 15 days in September 1990, Harris County Jail in Houston County, Texas, was forced to release over 250 inmates because the jail exceeded its population cap. While many of the inmates shown here were overjoyed about their release, the public was dismayed and frightened, and viewed this as another indication of the criminal justice system's breakdown.

**INMATES CAN BE AWARDED DAMAGES IN SOME LEGAL ACTIONS** Inmate plaintiffs can receive damages in tort and civil rights suits. However, correctional workers can claim qualified immunity and will not have to pay damages if the claim was based on a law that was not clearly established or if they could not have reasonably been aware of or recognized that their actions were unconstitutional (*Wood v. Strickland*, 1975). Thus, the Court sustained a prison official's claim of qualified immunity in the case of an inmate claiming that his right to send and receive mail was violated because at the time the "controlling law was not established" (*Procunier v. Navarette*, 1978). In contrast, an injunction was granted when prison officials locked an inmate in a cell for ten days without notice since this was a clearly established constitutional violation (*Russell v. Coughlin*, 1990).

Inmates can be awarded three types of monetary damages in civil rights actions (Collins, 1993):

*Nominal damages* are awarded when inmates have sustained no actual damages, but there is clear evidence showing that their rights have been violated. This token payment is usually only $1.

*Compensatory damages* relate to actual loss and can include payments for out of pocket expenses the inmate incurred or for pain and suffering and mental anguish. For example, in *Sostre v. McGinnis* (1971), a federal appeals court sustained an award of $9300 imposed on the warden and a commissioner of corrections. This amount was calculated based on awarding $25 per day to each inmate who had spent 372 days in solitary confinement under conditions the court viewed as cruel and unusual punishment (Palmer, 1991).

*Punitive damages* are awarded when the wrongful act was done intentionally and maliciously or with reckless disregard for the rights of the inmate. For example, in *Smith v. Wade* (1983), a corrections officer placed an inmate (who was in protective custody because he was vulnerable to attack) in a cell with two other inmates—one of whom had been put in segregation for fighting. They went on to harass, beat, and sexually assault him. In this case, the jury awarded the inmate $25,000 in compensatory damages and $5000 in punitive damages. In sustaining the $5000 award, the Supreme Court affirmed the right of juries to award punitive damages in cases involving "reckless indifference to the rights of others." These

damages were justified because the guard knew, or should have known, that an assault was likely under these conditions.

**FEES ARE AWARDED TO PLAINTIFF ATTORNEYS BUT RARELY ARE THEY ASSESSED AGAINST INMATES** The prevailing party in a federal civil rights action may be awarded attorney's fees. This provision primarily benefits attorneys for inmates. Most federal or state laws limit awarding fees to defendants in cases that show the plaintiff's case was frivolous, unreasonable, or without foundation (Krantz and Branham, 1991; Collins, 1993). Recognizing that inmates are not trained in the law, the Supreme Court further suggested that lower courts should be very hesitant in assessing attorneys' fees against inmates who file *pro se*—act for themselves—as their own attorneys (*Hughes v. Rowe*, 1980; Mushlin, 1993). Note that JHLs are not entitled to attorneys' fees (Mushlin, 1993).

**CONSENT DECREES ARE AGREEMENTS THAT SETTLE DISPUTES** Instead of going to trial, an inmate plaintiff may have constitutionally unacceptable conditions rectified relatively quickly and easily by working out a **consent decree** with the defendant. This involves both parties agreeing to work out the terms of the settlement subject to court approval. This spares both parties the expense and uncertainty of a trial. It also gives them the opportunity to work out a mutually acceptable solution rather than have one imposed on them by the courts. There is no assurance that prison authorities will make the changes, but if they fail to do so, the court can impose fines or other sanctions.

## Habeas Corpus Actions Are Used to Challenge Convictions and Confinement Conditions

Literally translated as "you have the body," **habeas corpus** is an action enabling inmates to request a hearing before a judge to air claims of illegal incarceration due to a constitutional violation regarding their conviction or conditions of confinement. Habeas actions are brought by inmates who have exhausted state remedies and feel some constitutional issue exists to challenge their conviction. These challenges really represent a form of appeal beyond the normal appeal process. Death Row inmates repeatedly use this option to challenge the basis of their conviction or sentence.

Typically, inmates choose Section 1983 over habeas actions to pursue claims involving prison conditions or regulations because (1) there is no requirement that all state judicial and administrative remedies be exhausted before bringing this action and (2) in habeas actions no damages are awarded. Nevertheless, the Supreme Court broadened the relief available from habeas corpus actions to include release from custody and to rectify unconstitutional regulations. Thus, in *Preiser v. Rodriguez* (1973), the Court indicated that in cases involving restriction of good time, relief should be sought through habeas rather than a Section 1983 action. Inmates seeking release from solitary confinement have also used it (*Krist v. Ricketts,* 1974; *Tasker v. Griffith,* 1977).

## There Are Many Misconceptions Regarding Prisoner Litigation

Inmate ligation dramatically increased beginning in the mid-1970s, but many misconceptions remain regarding the nature and character of this growth. It is commonly believed that most state suits by inmates are attempts to get out of prison, which would make most of these habeas actions. It is also presumed that most inmate suits are frivolous and ought to be dismissed because they tie up the criminal justice system (Thomas, Aylward, Casey, Moton, Oldham and Wheetley, 1986). Although research on these issues is limited, Thomas (1988) sheds some important light on these questions.

**THE RELATIVE NUMBER OF HABEAS CORPUS COMPLAINTS HAS BEEN DECLINING**   First, habeas complaints have declined from 91% of all state prisoner suits in 1965 to less than one-third in 1981. Though the number of habeas filings has generally increased with the rise in prison population, their proportion has been declining from about five suits per 100 prisoners in 1970 to less than two per 100 in 1984. This refutes the popular view that inmates spend their time in prison looking for technicalities to secure their release. This decline may be a result of Supreme Court decisions narrowing the circumstances under which lower federal courts can review state convictions under the federal habeas corpus statutes (McMillian, 1985). For example, in *Keeney v. Tomayo-Reyes* (1992) the Court ruled that federal courts handling habeas petitions from state inmates no longer have to grant a hearing, even if it

is shown that their lawyers failed to properly present facts crucial to their case in a state court appeal. Since many state inmates are represented by overworked, and sometimes inadequate attorneys, this deprived inmates of an important route for having their cases reviewed. Further, since the mid-1970s, many states tightened their criminal codes, particularly those regarding capital offenses, which reduced ambiguities, eliminated obvious discrepancies, and brought their laws up to federal standards.

## A RISE IN CIVIL RIGHTS ACTIONS INDICATES GREATER CONCERN WITH PRISON CONDITIONS

Several conclusions can be drawn from looking at national filing trends regarding Civil Rights litigation (Thomas, 1988). First, compared with habeas corpus filings, the annual proportion of civil rights actions increased from less than 20% in the 1960s to more than two-thirds in 1986. This suggests that state prisoners may be more concerned with correcting perceived wrongs than they are in seeking to overturn their convictions.[7] Second, although the number of civil rights filings by state prisoners have increased dramatically during this period, the rate of increase has begun to slow. The number went from 218 in 1966 to 20,072 in 1986 (a 9100% increase); however, most increases occurred between 1966 and 1980 and then leveled off. The large increase during the first fourteen years occurred because this was the first opportunity inmates had to file complaints about unconstitutional prison conditions and because of the substantial rise in the inmate population during this period (from 199,654 to 545,133) (Bureau of Justice Statistics, 1982, 1988b).[8] There were major differences between states in the numbers, proportion, and rates of cases filed. In the states with the highest increases, particularly those in the South, this may have meant that greater improvements were necessary in these states to provide constitutionally acceptable conditions (Thomas, 1988).

Thomas (1988) found that 40% of the civil rights complaints involved inadequate health care, violence, and unjust disciplinary proceedings. There were few complaints about racism, overcrowding, rehabilitation programs, lockdowns, and segregation. This indicates that prisoners were more concerned with issues that involve fundamental conditions of confinement than with those that are political or social.

Thomas found it impossible to decide whether a suit was legally frivolous by examining the alleged nature of the violations. However, in most filings, there was a clear-cut substantive grievance to justify the complaint. A further indication of the legitimacy of inmate suits was the fact that of 2628 suits filed in Illinois' Northern District between 1977 and 1986, two-thirds survived preliminary judicial screening successfully. Also, almost two-thirds of those that passed this review process were either settled successfully out of court, or the inmate obtained relief by prevailing at trial. These positive results suggest that there are far fewer frivolous cases filed than commonly assumed.

## ENFORCEMENT OF JUDICIAL ORDERS

The potential remedies judges can impose as a result of consent agreements or Section 1983 actions can vary extensively. The problem is not with finding an appropriate remedy, however, but with enforcing it. The fact that courts have stated that inmates are entitled to basic constitutional rights means little if no effective mechanisms exist to enforce the orders to remedy these situations. This would be analogous to inmates being given radios and the right to use them but not allowing them to have the batteries that make them work.

### The Enforcement of Judicial Orders Is Not Easy

One out of every four state facilities in 1990 was under court order or consent degree to limit the number of inmates and/or improve conditions relating to confinement (Stephan, 1992). This fact increases the significance of the enforcement issue. Enforcing judicial orders is also a problem because it can involve the separation of powers between the executive, legislative, and judicial branches of government and states' rights (Krantz, 1988).

To avoid extensive involvement in carrying out large-scale institutional changes, early court decisions generally involved injunctions prohibiting or compelling the performance of specific, easily defined acts. However, this did not begin to rectify the very poor conditions plaguing some institutions and prison systems. Thus, in the early 1970s, an increasing number of judges became so out-

raged that they ordered prison officials to make basic improvements to rectify these conditions. These judges learned that merely requiring substantial improvements in prison conditions rarely resulted in major changes. This resulted, in part, because prison administrators, even those agreeing and wanting to make these ordered improvements, were usually not in a position to do. They were dependent on other officials (e.g., the governor or the legislature, who were not parties in the lawsuit) who were unwilling to provide the funds necessary to comply with these court orders. The courts could forcefully threaten jurisdictions failing to make ordered improvements, but their bark was worse than their bite, that is, they usually did no more than threaten. This issue is complicated because if federal courts insist on enforcing their orders, and these facilities claim there is no money to make the improvements, they must be ready to force counties or states to provide it. This gets into issues relating to the setting of priorities for use of public funds and even of raising taxes. This raises further questions regarding separation of powers and federal intervention in state functions.

Despite these concerns, a recent Supreme Court decision involving a school system (*Missouri v. Jenkins,* 1990) suggests that under certain circumstances courts may justify ordering a jurisdiction to levy taxes to rectify unconstitutional conditions. In this case a Missouri school district had unconstitutionally operated a segregated school system. The district court agreed to a new school program (at a cost of $380 million) proposed by the school system to remedy this situation. The court ordered property taxes be raised to secure the required funds. In upholding the district court's ruling, the Supreme Court stated:

> the [school district] may be ordered to levy taxes despite the statutory limitation on its authority in order to compel the discharge of an obligation imposed on [it]...by the Fourteenth Amendment. To hold otherwise would fail to take account of the obligation of local governments, under the Supremacy Clause, to fulfill the requirements that the Constitution imposes on them ... Even though a particular remedy may not be required in every case ... where [it is] (as here) ... the State cannot hinder the process by preventing a local government from implementing that remedy (*Missouri v. Jenkins,* 1990, p. 1666).

Thus, if similar circumstances prevailed in a county jail or state prison, the Court might be inclined similarly to require that taxes be raised to remediate unconstitutional conditions.

## Court Orders against Resistant Defendants Are Enforced by Two Methods

In a number of instances, jurisdictions fail to respond to court orders requiring that certain conditions be corrected. In these instances the courts can respond by issuing a contempt of court citation or they can supervise compliance with their orders or appoint an agent to do so.

**RESISTANT DEFENDANTS CAN BE HELD IN CONTEMPT**  The aim of **contempt of court,** in prison cases, is to pressure defendants to provide the court-ordered relief. To achieve compliance, courts can imprison defendants or impose a fine. They can also fine for purposes of compensating inmate plaintiffs for losses or damages they sustained due to noncompliance (see *Newman v. State of Alabama,* 1982; *Hutto v. Finney,* 1978). The courts generally use their contempt power when a community or institution makes no effort to correct conditions as agreed to in a consent decree or which the court has ruled to be unconstitutional. However, judges are reluctant to issue contempt orders when defendants have made diligent efforts to do what is ordered. Thus, in only a few cases have the courts done more than threaten to use their contempt power (Krantz, 1988). For example, in *Benjamin v. Sielaff* (1990), a district court found New York county officials in contempt for not complying with a ten-year-old order barring the housing of inmates in dayrooms, gymnasiums, and program rooms (Boston, 1991). While not imposing coercive fines, the judge put the county on notice that any future offenders held more than 24 hours under these conditions would be entitled to collect $150, and $100 for each subsequent 12-hour period or segment thereof.

**JUDGES CAN SUPERVISE COMPLIANCE OR APPOINT AGENTS TO DO SO**  When judges prepare and issue orders or accept consent decrees, they have four options. (Levinson, 1982). First, they can do all the work themselves. They can evaluate the situation, prepare the order, and administer its implementation. For example, in a case involving the Mississippi State Penitentiary, Judge William Keady issued the order and regularly visited the prison to make certain the standards he established were being met. When units did not conform to these standards, he used his power to close them.

Second, a judge has the option of placing a prison system into the receivership of the state's governor. In 1979, when the Alabama State Correctional Board failed to carry out previous court orders, the judge appointed the governor as receiver for the Alabama State Correctional System (*Newman v. Alabama,* 1979). This made the governor directly responsible for making changes in the system.

Third, parties to a legal action can hire a consultant to monitor changes within the institution. In 1979, the New Mexico Department of Corrections did that after signing a consent decree (Levinson, 1982). Fourth, judges can appoint a master to assist in executing the court's responsibilities. The next section discusses the roles and functions of special masters.

## Special Masters Assist the Courts in Certain Legal Actions

Masters are persons "appointed to act as representatives of the court in some particular action or transaction" (Black, Nolan, and Nolan-Haley, 1991, p. 673). The use of **special masters** is not a new idea. Initially, they were employed in England to hear the facts in civil cases involving the maritime trade. In the United States, they have frequently been used by the federal courts in many circumstances. However, more recently, they have been used in institutional reform litigation (e.g., public school segregation cases and local jail and prison reform cases).

**MASTERS HAVE PLAYED THREE ROLES IN CORRECTIONAL CASES**  In institutional reform cases, masters may function in at least three different roles (Nathan, 1978). First, judges may appoint a master to collect information to aid the court in making a decision regarding the occurrence of a constitutional violation in a complex case. In this fact-finding capacity, a master is responsible for compiling a report that provides an independent statement of the nature and extent of the alleged constitutional violations. For example, a federal court in Florida appointed a medical administrator and physician to survey the medical care in the state's prisons. They also assisted the court in determining whether prison medical services met constitutional standards [National Institute of Corrections (NIC), 1983].

Second, a court may employ a master after ruling that a jurisdiction was operating an institution(s) with constitutionally unacceptable conditions but before ordering improvements. Here the judge relies on the master's expertise to assist in developing an acceptable and effective remedial decree. Masters also function as mediators between the two parties to work out an acceptable agreement. Thus, in a Tennessee case a state court judge used a master as a court consultant to help fashion an order that rectified proven violations (NIC, 1983).

Third, a master may be employed after the court has issued a remedial decree to monitor and/or enforce it. In these instances assignments occur following a court mandate that a correctional facility or an entire system make certain improvements. Also, judges may decide to appoint a master after defendants have refused to make the ordered improvements or have shown themselves incapable of doing so. In both instances the master may do one or more of the following: fact-finding, interpreting the decree, negotiation, mediation, or assisting the defendants in planning the court-ordered changes or improvements.

**COURTS APPOINT MASTERS FOR SEVERAL REASONS** The courts appoint masters for a variety of reasons. Most often it is because the defendants stubbornly resist making mandated improvements. Other reasons include the court's lack of resources and expertise to evaluate whether defendants have fully and fairly made changes ordered. In some larger cases, the scope of ordered improvements makes it impossible for judges to supervise their implementation (NIC, 1983). By the middle of 1988 court-appointed masters or monitors were supervising as many as fourteen adult state correctional systems or institutions. Additionally there were four active in state juvenile systems or institutions and a number were functioning in jail systems in New York, Los Angeles, Houston, and Philadelphia, and in dozens of smaller facilities and systems around the country (Keating, 1990).

Keating (1990), who worked as a master in a variety of cases, says that the diversity of the functions that masters perform means there is no single model or blueprint to follow in all cases. Thus, when courts assign masters to monitor a particular case, the organization and structure of their operations can vary from a single part-time individual to a staff of eleven attorneys and investigators. Budgets can range from several thousand to millions of dollars. In choosing masters, judges have employed a variety of individuals (including former correctional administrators or lawyers) whose experience in corrections varies widely. Masterships can be brief or can go on for years. For example, when Judge Justice found the entire Texas prison system unconstitutional in 1980 (*Ruiz v. Estelle*, 1980), he appointed a master who supervised the changes he ordered the system to make for almost ten years. Although some judges are inclined to appoint masters and-or accede to inmate plaintiff requests for their involvement, others are indifferent or downright hostile toward their use (Nathan, 1978; Keating, 1990).

## Several Types of Actions Are Possible against Resisters

We conclude by discussing other powers held by the federal courts that can be employed to obtain compliance from reluctant or obstinate county or state officials. First, federal courts can threaten to stop or actually cut off the flow of federal funds to state programs. Secondly, the courts can order that state assets be seized and used to make ordered improvements. As a last resort, as in civil rights cases, the courts can order that federal troops be used to take over a facility or system to back up an order. For example, federal troops were used in Little Rock, Arkansas, in the 1960s to desegregate the schools. It is exceedingly unlikely, however, that any of these latter options will be employed in institutional reform cases, given the nation's prevailing view on crime and criminals. In fact, this view is reflected in recent presidents taking a harder line on the treatment of offenders and in the more conservative position taken by politicians around the country as well as by the Supreme Court and lower federal courts.

## ENDNOTES

**1.** See Chapter 5 for a more thorough discussion of these conditions and this case.

**2.** While *Bell v. Wolfish* (1979) and *Rhodes v. Chapman* (1981) represent pivotal cases in the Court's more restricted approach to prisoner rights, this position can be first seen in its rulings in the cases of *Meachum v. Fano* (1976) and *Jones v. North Carolina Prisoners' Union* (1977). In *Meachum,* the Court indicated that unless state law or policy guaranteed an inmate's right to due process before being deprived of a given status, the state could change an inmate's condition of incarceration without regard to how deprecating this change was. Thus prison officials could transfer inmates to any facility without regard to how this changed an inmate's living conditions. In *Jones,* the Court signaled (1) its deference to prison officials and the need to allow them discretion in managing prison operations and (2) recognition that constitutional rights may be restricted if they are consistent with an inmate's status as a prisoner or with the legitimate penological objectives of the correctional system.

**3.** Courts use the terms legitimate government, correctional, penological interests/objectives in corections cases to refer to what is construed as necessary requirements for institutional operations i.e security, custody and maintenance of discipline.

**4.** *Patzner v. Burkett,* 779 F.2d 1363, 1367 (8th Cir. 1985); *Fiacco v. City of Rensselaer,* N.Y., 783 F.2d 319 (2d Cir. 1986); *Languirand v. Hayden,* 717 F.2d 220, 226–227 n. 7 (5th Cir. 1983); *Wellington v. Daniels,* 717 F. 2d 932, 936 (5th Cir. 1983).

**5.** In certain parole revocation proceedings, fundamental fairness requires that an attorney be provided (Project, 1994).

**6.** Thirty-three jurisdictions were under court order for overcrowding or other conditions in at least one of their major prisons, and in nine jurisdictions the court orders covered the entire system.

**7.** While inmates can use this as a vehicle to challenge their conviction, this occurs only rarely. Under Section 1983 inmates can bring complaints of due process violations that relate to their original conviction. Typically these claims allege violations that occurred prior to or during the original trial and include allegations involving improper arrest or seizure of evidence or other police misconduct, perjury of witnesses, or conspiracy of judge and defense counsel or prosecuting attorneys (Turner, 1979; Thomas, 1988).

**8.** These figures include both federal and state prisoners since separate data on these populations has not been published. Some idea of the proportion of state to federal inmates can be gleaned from the following (Bureau of Justice Statistics, 1981; 1983; 1986; 1988):

| Year | Federal | State | Total |
|------|---------|---------|---------|
| 1979 | 26,371 | 287,360 | 313,731 |
| 1982 | 29,673 | 384,689 | 414,362 |
| 1984 | 34,263 | 430,304 | 464,567 |
| 1986 | 44,408 | 500,725 | 545,133 |

## ACKNOWLEDGMENTS

[a] Taken from *Rights of Prisoners*, by James J. Gobert and Neil P. Cohen © 1981 by permission of Shepard's/McGraw-Hill. Further reproduction of any kind is strictly prohibited. For subscription information, please contact Shepard's/McGraw-Hill, Inc., 555 Middle Creek Parkway, Colorado Springs, Colorado, 1-800-525-2474.
[b] Taken from *Rights of Prisoners, 2nd Edition*, by Michael Mushlin © 1993 by permission of Shepard's/McGraw-Hill. Further reproduction of any kind is strictly prohibited. For subscription information, please contact Shepard's/McGraw-Hill, Inc., 555 Middle Creek Parkway, Colorado Springs, Colorado, 1-800-525-2474.
[c] Reprinted from W. C. Collins, *Correctional Law for the Correctional Officer*, with permission of the American Correctional Association, Lanham, MD.
[d] Copyright 1988 by Rowman and Littlefield Publishers.

## CHAPTER RECAP

### The Evolution of Prisoner Rights
Under the Hands-Off Doctrine, the Courts Refused to Consider Inmate Claims of Unconstitutional Prison Conditions
The Hands-Off Doctrine Was Discarded in the 1960s
   The Warren Court Extended Constitutional Rights to Minority Groups
   Provisions of the Bill of Rights Were Selectively Incorporated into the Due Process Clause Making Them Binding on the States
By the Mid-1970s the Courts Were Reluctant to Further Expand Inmate Rights
      Two Pivotal Decisions Signaled the Courts' New Direction
     The *Bell* Case Recognized That Institutional Need Justified Restriction of Inmate Rights
    The *Rhodes* Case Recognized That Imprisonment Includes Harsh and Restrictive Conditions

The Court Took a More Restrained Hands-On
Approach
The Reasonableness Test Determined the Accept-
ability of Restrictions on Inmate Rights
The *Wilson* Case Reinforced the Court's Decision
in *Turner*
Constitutional Challenges May Now Be Taken to
State Courts
**Court Access Provides a Basis for Inmates to Secure
Their Rights**
Various Issues Surround the Adequacy of and Access to
Law Libraries
It is Questionable Whether Inmates Can Prepare
Their Own Cases
Prison Officials May Not Unreasonably Restrict Access
to Attorneys
The Courts Upheld Access to Inmate Assistance in
Filing Cases
Jailhouse Lawyers Assist Inmates in Filing Their Cases
There are Two Types of JHLs
JHLs Serve a Number of Functions
Inmates Become JHLs for a Variety of Reasons
**Postconviction Actions**
Tort Actions Are One Form of Legal Relief
Inmates Can Bring Cases to the Federal Courts Under
Section 1983 of the Civil Rights Act
An Injunction Requires Acts to Be Performed or Ter-
minated
Inmates Can Be Awarded Damages in Some Legal
Actions
Fees Are Awarded to Plaintiff Attorneys But Rarely
Are They Assessed Against Inmates
Consent Decrees Are Agreements That Settle Dis-
putes
Habeas Corpus Actions Are Used to Challenge Convic-
tions and Confinement Conditions
There Are Many Misconceptions Regarding Prisoner
Litigation
The Relative Number of Habeas Corpus Complaints
Has Been Declining
A Rise in Civil Rights Actions Indicates Greater In-
mate Concern with Prison Conditions
**Enforcement of Judicial Orders**
The Enforcement of Judicial Orders Is Not Easy
Court Orders Against Resistant Defendants Are En-
forced by Two Methods
Resistant Defendants Can Be Held in Contempt
Judges Can Supervise Compliance or Appoint Agents
To Do So
Special Masters Assist the Courts in Certain Legal Ac-
tions
Masters Have Played Three Roles in Correctional Re-
form Cases
Courts Appoint Masters for Several Reasons
Several Types of Actions Are Possible Against Resisters

**REVIEW QUESTIONS**

1. Why did courts take a "hands-off" approach to prisoner rights and what prompted them to begin taking a more restrictive approach?
2. List the elements of a court-accepted plan for providing inmates with access to a law library and the restrictions that would be constitutionally acceptable.
3. What are the circumstances under which inmates are entitled to court-appointed attorneys?
4. Discuss the roles that jailhouse lawyers play in assisting their fellow inmates.
5. Describe the circumstances under which inmates can bring tort actions in a correctional setting and the reasons inmates prefer to bring civil rights actions rather than tort actions.
6. What are the circumstances under which inmates can bring valid claims under the federal Civil Rights Act?
7. In Civil Rights actions, what types of relief will the courts grant inmates whose rights have been abridged?
8. What issues are raised by inmates when they file a habeas corpus petition?
9. What problems do the courts face in enforcing judicial decisions to improve prison conditions?
10. How have the courts used contempt citations to enforce orders to improve prison conditions?

**TEST YOUR KNOWLEDGE**

1. At the present time the general consensus is that the courts have taken which of the following positions regarding prisoner rights?
    a. a hands-off approach
    b. have returned to a position in which inmates are considered slaves of the state
    c. radical hands-on approach
    d. hands restrained approach
2. Which of the following postconviction actions is most likely to be used by inmates to pursue claims of unconstitutional prison conditions?
    a. torts
    b. Section 1983
    c. injunctions
    d. habeas corpus
    e. all of the above
3. In *Bounds v. Smith* the Court established the conditions under which special masters can be appointed.
    a. true
    b. false
4. Most recently inmates have been more likely to use civil rights petitions as opposed to habeas actions to rectify unconstitutional prison conditions.
    a. true
    b. false

# CHAPTER 16

# PRISONER SUBSTANTIVE AND PROCEDURAL RIGHTS

## ■ LEARNING OBJECTIVES

*After completion of this chapter, you should be able to:*

**1.** Recount how the courts have tried to balance inmates' First Amendment rights with the need of correctional institutions to limit inmates' use of mail and the receipt of publications.

**2.** Explain how the courts have tried to balance inmates' Eighth Amendment rights with the need for correctional institutions to use isolated confinement as a tool for maintaining discipline and control and for segregation.

**3.** Discuss the broad issues associated with the use of force by correctional officers in the prison environment.

**4.** Describe the levels of control correctional staff may employ on inmates and the circumstances under which they can be used.

**5.** Specify the circumstances under which correctional institutions and their staff can be held liable for inmate-on-inmate assaults.

**6.** Explain how prison rules can violate substantive due process requirements.

**7.** Define constitutionally protected liberty and property interests and the due process procedures required to deprive inmates of them.

**8.** Outline the Fourth Amendment safeguards that govern urine tests, and cell, pat-down, strip, and body cavity searches.

## ■ KEY TERMS AND CONCEPTS

Administrative confinement
Censorship
Clear and present danger
Control
Cruel and unusual punishment
Deadly force
Deliberate indifference test
Disciplinary detention
Due process procedures
Empty hand control
Excessive force
Less than lethal force
Liberty interests
Publisher-only rule
Reasonable force
Resistance
Restraints
Substantive due process
Substantive predicates
Vagueness
Verbal direction

This chapter focuses on the extent to which inmates and pretrial detainees are accorded basic constitutional rights. As noted in Chapter 15, although inmates are entitled to basic constitutional rights, legitimate prison operational needs, such as requirements for maintaining order, security, and safety, may justify restriction of these rights. This chapter examines how the courts have balanced these legitimate institutional operational concerns against inmate attempts to exercise their constitutional rights.

## RESTRICTIONS ON FIRST AMENDMENT RIGHTS

The First Amendment to the U.S. Constitution guarantees that no laws will be enacted that restrict or abridge our freedom of religion, speech, and the press. However, under certain circumstances, courts have restricted these rights when they unduly interfere with competing and important government interests. Since these rights are viewed as fundamental, the Court has required very compelling reasons for their restriction. The operational objectives of prisons have been among those compelling reasons.

### Inmates Have Certain Rights Relating to the Use of Mail

Although books and letters offer inmates the opportunity, even if briefly, to psychologically escape the rigors of the prison environment, until recently their use was severely restricted. Neither the Pennsylvania nor Auburn systems allowed inmates to receive or send letters. By the end of the nineteenth century, more liberal letter writing privileges were instituted (McKelvey, 1977). However, heavy **censorship** of both incoming and outgoing letters was practiced and continued into the 1950s (Fox, 1983). This process involved prison staff opening inmate mail, reading it, deleting objectionable material, and confiscating disapproved items.

Limitations were placed on persons with whom inmates could correspond, the number of letters received and sent, and the types of items inmates could receive in letters and packages. Inspection of incoming inmate mail was justified because it enabled prison officials to confiscate instruments of escape, any material that might incite inmates (e.g., pornography), and drugs. It also provided prior knowledge of upsetting news so staff could prepare the prisoner for it. Reasons given for inspecting outgoing mail included protecting the public from inmate scams or threats, insults, obscene letters,

Mail provides an important link with the outside world for inmates, and its use is protected by the First Amendment. COs can examine mail for contraband.

preventing letters casting an unfavorable or inaccurate light on the prison, and obtaining information on possible escapes, riots, and inmate dissatisfactions (*Palmigiano v. Travisono*, 1970; Palmer, 1991).

By the mid-1970s the courts had abandoned support for unregulated censorship of prison mail. In a series of cases, the Supreme Court established rules regulating the official inspection of inmate mail (*Procunier v. Martinez*, 1974; *Turner v. Safley*, 1987; *Thornburg v. Abbott*, 1989; Project, 1994). In the Procunier case the Court said institutional restrictions on correspondence abridged the rights of inmates and also of those nonprisoners who want to correspond with inmates. Although prison staff could still inspect mail, their actions with respect to enclosed materials were to be controlled by how strongly these materials threatened legitimate government interests. For example, while one court upheld the refusal to distribute a revolutionary publication during a period of prison turmoil (*Hernandez v. Estelle*, 1986), another found no valid basis for withholding periodicals containing no objectionable reading material from an inmate (*Sizemore v. Williford*, 1987).

The general rule on incoming correspondence, whether from inmates or noninmates, is that it may be rejected if found to be detrimental to the security, good order, or discipline within the institution or if it might facilitate criminal activity (*Thornburgh v. Abbott*, 1989). The Court upheld a complete ban on inmate-to-inmate correspondence on the same basis (*Turner v. Safley*, 1987).[1] As a rule, outgoing correspondence cannot be restricted because it generally poses no threat to internal prison security or other legitimate government interests. The Court held that only outgoing mail containing escape plans, information concerning criminal activity, threats of blackmail or extortion, encoded messages, or requests to nonfamily members for goods or money can be censored because this supports legitimate government interests (*Procunier v. Martinez*, 1974).

### Some Restrictions on Publications and Literature Have Been Justified

While First Amendment protections include the right to receive information and ideas, these rights are restricted under certain conditions. For example, pornographic material is not protected. Another unprotected activity is one that constitutes a **clear and present danger** of inciting or producing lawless actions (e.g., books about making weapons, explosives, alcoholic beverages, or drugs or books that describe escape methods). This view was upheld in *Thornburg v. Abbott* (1989).

Additionally, although staff members can screen publications, only wardens can reject them. Further, no "hit list" of publications that are absolutely barred from distribution in the prison is permitted. Clearly the courts will not uphold a total ban on any publications but will require prison officials to examine each issue of a magazine to determine the suitability of its content. Thus, a magazine cannot be banned because it provides information on illicit drugs, but a particular issue can be if it advocates drug usage (Collins, 1993; Gobert and Cohen, 1992). With regard to sexually explicit material, it is unlikely that a ban on all material that simply displays the naked body, like *Playboy*, will be upheld because it can hardly be justified on grounds reasonably relating to security or to rehabilitation concerns (Collins, 1993). Nevertheless, sexually oriented publications that advocate sexual relationships between adults and juveniles or homosexuality can be excluded.

The Court has recognized that publications can also be used to smuggle contraband into the prison and upheld a **publisher-only rule,** which mandates that inmates could only receive hardback books if they were mailed directly by publishers, book clubs, or bookstores (*Bell v. Wolfish*, 1979). In sustaining this rule, the Court noted the ease with which contraband could be concealed in the bindings of these books and the burden on prison officials if they had to search them.

First Amendment protections relating to religious freedom are discussed in Chapter 20, and Chapter 21 deals with visitation issues.

### EIGHTH AMENDMENT PROHIBITION AGAINST CRUEL AND UNUSUAL PUNISHMENT

The Eighth Amendment protects us from **cruel and unusual punishment.** Beyond this very general prohibition there is no specific legal definition as to what this phrase means. This clause was initially written to ban the inhumane and barbarous punishments existing when it was adopted (e.g., breaking at the wheel, burning at the stake); today it is interpreted to include physical punishment and various prison practices and conditions (Luise, 1989). Typically, Eighth Amendment cases have focused on conditions and practices such as solitary confinement, corporal punishment, use of force by guards, conditions of confinement (e.g., medical care, food service, and personal safety), overcrowding, and escapes. In defining or clarifying the meaning of cruel and unusual punishment, the courts have applied a variety of "tests" which focus on:

1. Punishment that is incompatible with the evolving standards of decency that mark the progress of a maturing society (*Trop v. Dulles*, 1958)
2. Punishment involving the infliction of unnecessary and wanton pain (*Gregg v. Georgia*, 1976)
3. Punishment that is excessive or disproportionate to the offense (*Trop v. Dulles*, 1958)
4. Punishment that is incompatible with broad and idealistic concepts of dignity, civilized standards, humanity, and decency (*Estelle v. Gamble*, 1976)
5. Deliberate indifference to the needs of the inmates (used in terms of prison services: medical, food, and personal safety) (*Estelle v. Gamble*, 1976)
6. Conditions that deny inmates the minimal civilized measure of life's necessities (*Wilson v. Seiter*, 1991).

These broad concerns are used by the courts when deciding cases involving this type of violation. However, their meaning can best be understood by examining how they apply to specific prison rules and conditions. Chapter 5 covered issues relating to the unconstitutionality of corporal punishment as enunciated in cases such as *Jackson v. Bishop* (1968), and Chapters 19 and 20 deal with issues related to medical care and food service, while the following sections examine other concerns.

### Isolated Confinement Has Been Used for a Long Time

Isolation of inmates has long been used by prison officials as a form of discipline. Today inmates can be isolated: in administrative segregation while awaiting a disciplinary hearing or because they are dangerous to other inmates or staff; and in disciplinary detention for rule violations.

The use of a dark or isolated cell for punishing those who violate prison rules dates to the use of the medieval dungeon. Known in prison jargon as the "hole," it probably represents the most universally employed form of punishment in the history of American corrections. For a long time, placement in solitary confinement meant the individual was put in a bare, unlit, and unventilated cell, and given a diet of bread and water, sometimes a blanket, and a bucket for bodily needs (Barnes and Teeters, 1951; Rothman, 1980). Confinement was supposed to be for short periods—from a few days to two weeks. Wardens easily got around these rules by keeping inmates in the hole for the allowable limit (e.g., six days), removing them, and then putting them back in again. This routine could go on for months.

**SOLITARY CONFINEMENT IS NOT USUALLY CONSIDERED UNCONSTITUTIONAL** The practice of isolating inmates for disciplinary purposes has been legally challenged. However, the federal courts have refused to consider it unconstitutional because it represents a valid means of protecting the general prison population, staff, and specific inmates and also helps prevent disobedience or escapes (Palmer, 1991; Krantz, 1988).

The courts have intervened in cases in which the duration and/or conditions of confinement were felt to constitute cruel and unusual punishment. Some combinations of the following have been found to be violations (Gobert and Cohen, 1981; Palmer, 1991; Mushlin, 1993): (1) diet—bread and water and certain restrictive diets not meeting basic daily nutritional requirements; (2) personal hygiene—lack of soap, water, towel, toilet paper, toothbrush, and clothing; (3) physical state of the cell—lack of lights, windows, mattresses, and general lack of cleanliness; (4) limited opportunity for exercise; (5) exposure to cold—lack of heat and keeping inmates nude; and (6) the presence of mice, rats, roaches, and other vermin. There are no strict rules about which combination of these factors will be considered cruel and unusual punishment. In fact, the Supreme Court has held that harsh conditions and rough disciplinary treatment are part of the price convicted criminals pay for their offenses against society (*Rhodes v. Chapman*, 1981; *Whitley v. Albers*, 1986).

Not every hardship or harsh act may be seen as unconstitutional (Project, 1992). Thus, a district court failed to find objectionable an inmate's claim that he was not given toilet paper for five days, was without soap, toothpaste, or toothbrush for ten days, and was kept in a filthy roach-infested cell (*Harris v. Fleming*, 1988). If confinement is short, the courts are more willing to allow much harsher conditions. Other decisions have allowed segregation in refuse-strewn cells for one day and a flooded cell for two days (*Evans v. Fogg*, 1979; Gobert and Cohen, 1992). The overriding standard appears to be the health of the inmate. If conditions jeopardize an inmate's physical or mental health, they have universally been condemned (*Young v. Quinlan*, 1992). However, although a nutritious diet has been mandated, some courts have allowed inmates in solitary to be fed a monotonous diet (Mushlin, 1993).

Generally, there are no agreed on time limits as to the length of detention as long the conditions of this segregation do not constitute cruel and unusual punishment. One New Hampshire district court imposed a limit of fourteen consecutive days in isolation, but other courts have upheld periods of twelve months, two years, five years, and even indefinite confinement (Gobert and Cohen, 1981; Mushlin, 1993). However, the longer an inmate is confined, the more likely it is that the court will examine the reason for confinement to see if it justifies these circumstances (Gobert and Cohen, 1990). The key is whether the punishment is disproportionate to the inmate's offense or constitutes repression of some basic right, for example, seven months for refusing to handle pork on religions grounds (Gobert and Cohen, 1981, 1992). Finally, the Courts will generally uphold long or indefinite confinement when an inmate's status is regularly reviewed and they can work their way out of these units by their own behavior[2]

**ISOLATION OF INMATES MAY HAVE ADVERSE PSYCHOLOGICAL EFFECTS** The disastrous results of the experiment at Auburn during the early 1800s indicated the potentially damaging psychological effects of extended isolation under certain conditions. However, as long as an inmate's basic needs are met, the courts have been reluctant to consider the psychological effects of isolation as constituting cruel and unusual punishment. This is despite evidence showing that solitary confinement can result in emotional damage and deterioration in mental functioning and may even cause hallucinations and depersonalization (Luise, 1989). Long periods of isolation also tend to increase resentment and rage resulting in more numerous and severe breeches of prison discipline on release.

This suggests the need to consider the psychological impact when inmates are isolated for extended periods. Thus, the court agreed, in the case of an inmate kept in managed segregation for 12 years, that prison officials bear a burden to explore feasible alternative custodial arrangements in these instances (*Sheley v. Dugger*, 1987).

### The Courts Approve Use of Force in a Correctional Setting under Certain Circumstances

The use of force in a correctional setting is affected by a variety of factors. These include an inmate population with a propensity for violence; court decisions limiting the circumstances in which force can be employed; and correctional standards and training that provide more concrete guidelines on the types of force that can be employed in response to controlling inmate violence and ensuring compliance with staff directives. In this section we briefly examine these issues. Our discussion is divided between a general examination of the issues affecting the use of force and specific levels of force used to control inmates.

Correctional officers (COs) are responsible for large numbers of inmates, many with a propensity for violence. It is no surprise that they are confronted with situations requiring the use of force. To understand both the appropriate and the excessive and punitive use of force requires that we examine both the legally relevant factors and the informal CO subculture.

**THE USE OF FORCE BY COs RANGES FROM JUSTIFIED TO UNJUSTIFIED** Like police officers, COs are permitted and expected to use force under certain circumstances and in self-defense. The issue is not the use of force per se but its use in excessive or brutal ways.

Most instances of the use of **excessive force** occur in unusual circumstances, such as riots, protests, or punitive transfers in which inmates challenge the staff's authority to control them. When unjustified force is employed in these circumstances, it may represent the staff's way of reestablishing administrative authority. It is understandable, although not acceptable, that staff will occasionally use excessive violence when involved in altercations with inmates. A more serious problem involves circumstances in which inmates are brutalized for extended periods as a means of

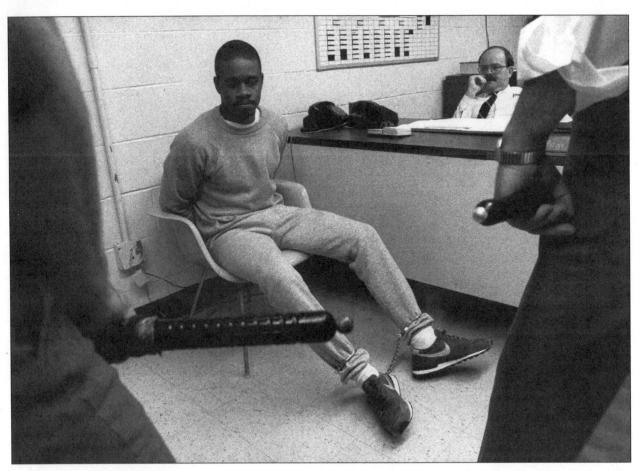

**The degree of force and restraint used by COs when dealing with inmates is covered by the Eighth Amendment, which prohibits the use of excessive force.**

punishment or control (Bowker, 1980). For example, as long as five months after the Attica riot inmates were still being punished for their participation. Reprisals of this kind have also occurred following other riots.

**THE STAFF SUBCULTURE CAN INFLUENCE THE USE OF FORCE**   The dynamics of the use of force in correctional settings have not been well explored. Available information suggests that its use is governed by a combination of subcultural and bureaucratic factors that are tolerated because of public and governmental indifference to prison conditions. Within any work environment a subculture develops with norms that broadly define expected and/or acceptable behavior. In a correctional setting, these norms are initially transmitted as part of the socialization process sometime during training. Before being given control of a unit,

new officers are usually teamed with an experienced officer who shows them the ropes. New officers learn as much by observing how their trainers handle situations as by what they are told. Toch (1977b) asserts that, as in a police setting, the excessive use of force by COs is based on norms in the officer subculture, which may justify its use for managing inmates.

As was the case in Texas prior to the *Ruiz* decision, discussed in Chapter 5, administrative concerns for expediency and control can result in unacceptable and even brutal practices. Crouch and Marquart (1989) assert the only way to ensure that prison structure and practices will keep pace with evolving standards of inmate treatment is to require continued oversight by outsiders. This assures that administrative policies are not merely given lip service but instead are enforced (Crouch and Marquart, 1989; Marquart, 1986). We will see later that, despite its conservative bent, the Supreme Court does not tolerate the physical abuse of inmates (*Hudson v. McMillian*, 1992).

## CIRCUMSTANCES AND AMOUNT EMPLOYED GOVERN THE ACCEPTABLE USE OF FORCE

Whether force used by staff in an institutional setting is considered to be **reasonable force** is governed by two factors: the circumstances under which it is used and the amount employed. Generally, when COs use excessive force beyond what is reasonably required in a given situation, inmates may (1) sue for damages in a civil suit or (2) bring a civil rights suit under Section 1983 claiming the excessive force violated either their Eighth Amendment protection against cruel and unusual punishment or a liberty interest under the Fourteenth Amendment (Collins, 1986).[3]

In determining a CO's need to use force it is important to recognize their rights as citizens to defend themselves. Further, they have police authority in a prison setting because of their control and enforcement responsibilities. Thus, COs can justifiably use force (1) in self-defense and in defense of other COs or prison personnel, inmates, or visitors; (2) to prevent a crime; (3) to detain or arrest inmates; (4) to enforce prison rules and discipline; and (5) to protect property and prevent inmates from harming themselves [American Correctional Association, (ACA), 1989; Collins, 1993].

COs have to walk a tight rope, however, since inmates have the constitutional right not to be subjected to force that is excessive, inhumane, malicious or sadistic, or employed solely for purposes of harming them. This is because no fixed line exists showing how much force is constitutionally acceptable—the amount depends on the circumstances present in each incident. Even as little force as a push or shove may be unconstitutional if done completely without any basis and causes even minimal injury. For example, it was considered an Eighth Amendment violation for a CO to beat a juvenile inmate who was giggling and protesting the treatment another inmate was receiving (*Hewett v. Jarrard*, 1986); dump an inmate on the floor, causing substantial injury, for failing to get out of bed (*Musgrave v. Broglin*, 1986); or beat an inmate for refusing to return to a housing unit in which he had been threatened with sexual assault (*Wilson v. Lambert*, 1986). In contrast, serious and even deadly force has been viewed by the courts as acceptable if

it was necessary and not employed with the intent to cause needless harm. For example, COs were not held liable when they accidentally strangled an inmate while attempting to subdue him (*Williams v. Kelley*, 1980).

*Several Key Cases Have Defined the Parameters for the Use of Force*  Several key cases have provided the parameters for what constitutes excessive force. *Johnson v. Glick* (1973) spelled out four factors applied by the courts in determining whether the force used was constitutional:

> (1) The need for the use of force; (2) The relationship between the need and the amount of force used; (3) The extent of injury inflicted; (4) Whether the force was applied in a good faith effort to maintain or restore discipline or maliciously and sadistically to cause harm . . . [It also noted] not every push or shove . . . violates a prisoner's constitutional rights (pp. 1028, 1033).

Upholding *Johnson* standards, the Court stated, in *Whitley v. Albers* (1986), that not all actions by staff against inmates constitute Eighth Amendment violations. It is only when these actions involve the infliction of pain that is unnecessary and wanton that this line is crossed. In this regard, several factors must be considered:

**1.** The force must be evaluated in light of the circumstances in which it was employed. Force applied to control a riot or disturbance has to be viewed in light of the threat this inmate action poses to "the safety of staff and inmates as reasonably perceived by responsible officials on the basis of the facts known to them" (p. 1085).
**2.** Secondly, it must be decided "whether the force was applied in a good faith effort to maintain or restore discipline or maliciously and sadistically for the purpose of causing harm" (p. 1085).

The Court recognized that under trying circumstances, prison staff must be able to make decisions without worrying whether they will be held liable later for what at the time appeared appropriate. Of course, there is a difference between the good faith use of force that later proves unreasonable and its use for retaliation and punishment.

In *Hudson v. McMillian* (1992) the Court added that for force to be unacceptable the injury does not

*Close Up* **"When Is Force Repugnant":
The *Hudson v. McMillian* Case**

Keith Hudson was an inmate at Angola, a Louisiana State prison. He got into an argument with a guard, Jack McMillian, who, with assistance from Officer Woods, placed Hudson in handcuffs and shackles. On the way to the confinement area, Hudson claimed that McMillian punched him repeatedly while Woods held him in place and kicked and punched him from behind. The beating was watched by a supervisor who told these officers "not to have too much fun." Hudson's injuries from the beating included minor bruises, swelling of his face, mouth and lip, loosened teeth, and his partial dental plate was cracked making it unusable for several months.

In deciding this case the Supreme Court indicated there is no requirement that injuries be serious to be constitutionally unacceptable. Their decision was prompted by several factors. First, there was no reason for the force to be used, meaning it must have been for punishment. Second, it was observed and condoned by a supervisor. A third reason which was not directly related to the case, but important because it shows a continuing problem, was that officers Wood and McMillian beat another inmate shortly after they had beaten Hudson. This adds weight to Crouch and Marquart's (1989) assertion that the only way to assure that prisons operate constitutionally is to maintain oversight by the courts and other agencies.

have to be serious or significant. Here again the Court recognized not every malevolent touch by a CO is a constitutional violation, but the line is crossed when the force employed is "of the sort repugnant to the conscience of mankind." Our Close-Up on this case clarifies this issue.

**THE VARIOUS LEVELS OF CONTROL ARE DETERMINED BY THE TYPE OF RESISTANCE** Although it is important for staff to be aware of the relevant court decisions and state statutes, these fail to provide concrete guidelines as to how COs should respond when confronted with cooperative and passive versus noncooperative, hostile, aggressive, and dangerous inmates. To assist in making these decisions CO training typically includes instruction that focuses on the parameters of resistance and control. These variables enter into any situation in which staff attempt to compel inmates to do something or to refrain or desist from certain actions (Ross, 1989).[a]

**Resistance** refers to the actions manifested by a prisoner who is attempting to evade an employee's efforts to control him or her. The amount and type of resistance will vary based on such factors as the inmate's: state of agitation; propensity to violence; mental stability; state of intoxication; view of the consequences and rewards of stopping a particular action or of following a staff member's request. Also important is the way in which a staff member approaches inmates. If the staff member is hostile and antagonistic, this may alter the situation from one of compliance to one requiring the use of force. Resistance may range from verbal refusal to comply to nondeadly or even deadly force.

**Control** is the action taken by a staff member to influence or neutralize the verbal and physical actions of the prisoner. The extent of the resistance displayed directly affects the level of reasonable (legally justifiable) control, which may range from verbal direction to physical force including the use of chemical agents, mechanical restraints, intermediate weapons, and deadly force.

Given that force is used as a last resort, the decision to use it and how much to use are severely restricted. This decision is based on the staff member's interpretation of the situation and the danger posed by it. For force to be used justifiably, resistance must be evident. For example, because an inmate was following orders during a shakedown it was considered cruel and unusual punishment for him to be grabbed and thrown by guards causing him to suffer permanent nerve damage (*Williams v. Luna*, 1990).

Whether inmate resistance is verbal or physical plays a major role in deciding the permissible control strategy in overcoming the resistance. Thus, inmates, by their behavior, determine the legal level of control employed by staff. Also, the use of force must decrease as inmates are brought under control and must cease when resistance stops or control is achieved. It is not constitutionally acceptable to beat or kick inmates once they cease resisting, or are unable to resist due to being physically restrained by correctional officers, or in restraints such as handcuffs. The remainder of this section focuses on the appropriate levels of control employed in response to different forms of resistance.

*Verbal Direction Should Be Employed First*   Today, the emphasis is on using communication skills as the primary tool for handling most inmate resistance. As a rule, staff can get inmates to comply with their instructions by using proper **verbal direction** to persuade them (Ross, 1989). Indeed, patience and good communication skills are considered the primary methods of preventing a potentially volatile situation from escalating into a violent confrontation. COs with good people-handling skills can often calm down confused and angry inmates so that they stop their violent behavior and/or comply with the CO's orders.

One of the keys to defusing rather than escalating resistance is to learn to be assertive rather than aggressive. Thus, guards should avoid being argumentative, threatening, or degrading and instead concentrate on lowering the emotional tone or level of the situation. Failing this, to show force by calling for backup sends a message to the inmate that lack of voluntary compliance will be met with more compelling methods (Ross, 1989).

*There Are Several Levels of Physical Force*   The lowest level of physical control has been labeled **empty hand control techniques.** These range from gently guiding inmates or temporarily immobilizing them by the use of force such as kicks or strikes, which are used against aggressive inmates. The courts have found this type of force acceptable if it is proportional to the circumstances. Thus, even an inmate's accidental death might not be viewed as constitutionally unacceptable (*Williams v. Kelley,* 1980), whereas abrasions, small lacerations, and loss of consciousness inflicted on a handcuffed inmate who refused to sit down might be (*Brown v. Triche,* 1987).

When empty hand control techniques are insufficient to overcome inmate resistance, COs move to the next level of force—the use of **less than lethal force,** which includes the use of, for instance, impact weapons (batons), chemical agents, and electrical disablers. These weapons are to be used to temporarily disable the inmate and not to inflict permanent injury. Their use is more restricted because of the greater potential for serious injury or death (Ross, 1989).

Impact weapons (batons, nightsticks, riot clubs) can be justifiably used when inmates are physically attacking staff or other inmates. The potentially fatal results of striking an inmate on the head, throat, neck, or clavicle require that blows to these areas only occur in instances when deadly force is allowed. Nevertheless, courts will evaluate their use based on circumstances and the resulting injuries. In *Brown v. Smith* (1987) placing a riot baton against a prisoner's neck and pinning him to the wall was not considered excessive force because this was necessary to get him to return to his cell.

Chemical agents employed in correctional settings typically include mace and three types of gas. Normally, they require authorization by the warden or ranking security officer and frequently require that the inmate(s) be warned and given time (e.g., five minutes) to cease their disruptive behavior before the gas is discharged. Mace, which comes in aerosol cans, is the mildest of these chemical agents. It is sprayed in the face of disruptive inmates causing intense burning in their eyes and requiring them to use their hands to rub them. This immobilizes inmates for eight to ten seconds, enough time to restrain and handcuff them. A federal appeals court (*Soto v. Dickey,* 1984) found:

> the . . . use of non-dangerous quantities of mace in "situations which are reasonably likely to result in injury to persons or to a substantial amount of property" does "not constitute an unnecessary and wanton infliction of pain" (p. 1270).

The court was also influenced by the policy and practice of an institution that provided maced inmates with prompt medical attention and a change of clothes and also cleaned the affected cells or removed inmates from them. The courts have also approved the use of mace on unruly inmates refusing to be locked in their cells and to compel an inmate to submit to a strip search when being transferred from one facility to another.[4]

Tear gas comes in two forms (CS and CN)[5] and is generally used for quelling riots and disturbances because it suppresses inmates without requiring higher levels of force (ACA, 1990a). CN gas is the least potent and is more likely to be used in enclosed areas. Its only drawback is that prison-wise inmates can avoid its effects for a while by putting a wet towel over their faces. CS, dubbed "super tear gas," is seven times more powerful than CN. It is normally used outdoors and employed indoors only if necessary because its symptoms are more severe. The courts have viewed the use of tear gas as appropriate in situations requiring several officers to subdue a violent inmate or where inmate actions have exacerbated dangerous tensions.[6]

Currently two new nonlethal alternatives are being employed by some systems. One is devices like taser and stun guns, which deliver nonlethal shocks. Although evidence regarding the long-term effects of tasers is inconclusive, at least two circuit courts have approved their use (Mushlin, 1993). Stun guns can temporarily incapacitate a person when pressed against their body. Jurisdictions using them (e.g., Florida) believe they provide a safer and less injurious method of dealing with unruly inmates. Sometimes the mere display of the device may stop a combative or uncooperative inmate's behavior. Pepper spray (or Oleoresin Capsicum, OC), a more recent nonlethal gas, is becoming more popular among law enforcement and correctional agencies. CN and CS cause painful tearing and respiratory discomfort, however, OC produces inflammation and swelling effects, making it more effective on the extremely agitated, the mentally ill, or inmates under the influence of drugs because they may not otherwise feel pain (Bryan, 1994).

While both OC and stun guns have the potential for misuse as punishments, when used properly they may prove to be effective in reducing both staff and inmate injuries. Only further research will provide data on both abuses and potentially harmful effects.

*Various Types of Restraints Are Used to Control Inmates* **Restraints** used in correctional settings include handcuffs, belly chains, leg irons, straitjackets, leather restraints, and flex cuffs. These devices temporarily restrain inmates to prevent escapes when transporting or escorting high-security inmates, injury to themselves or others, and serious damage to property. They are also used to control unruly or dangerous behavior. Courts have permitted inmates to be placed in flex cuffs to restore order after a disturbance, and for one inmate to be placed in four-point restraints with gauze padding in his mouth to stop the spread of a prison riot he incited (*Steward v. McManus*, 1991; *Williams v. Burton*, 1991). As with other forms of force, these devices can be used to discipline or punish inmates and, hence, could represent an Eighth Amendment or statutory violation (see, e.g., California Code of Regulations, 1991). However, the courts have usually dismissed cases involving prisoners alleging uncomfortable or excessively tight handcuffs wherein no serious injury has occurred (Boston and Manville, 1995). In dealing with high-security inmates, the courts have also approved handcuffing and leg shackles when outside the cells, security belts and handcuffs during visits, and leg irons and waist chains when in the law library and even while in their cells in cases of serious misconduct.[7] Finally the courts have approved the forced use of antipsychotic drugs on inmates dangerous to themselves or others (*Washington v. Harper*, 1990; see Chapter 19).

An area of greater concern involves the use of restraints such as straitjackets, leather straps, or chains to confine inmates to their beds and keep them in their cells. In examining their use, the courts consider the reasons they are employed, the availability of other control methods, the mental state of the inmate (e.g., the likelihood of suicide or self-injury; risk of injury to others), the inmate's security status, length of time restrained, the monitoring by doctors or supervisory staff, and regular observations by COs.[8] The need for continued oversight by courts and other government agencies of restraint procedures is suggested by the following barbaric practices present at the Indiana reformatory at Pendleton, prior to court intervention in the early 1980s:

> At this facility, inmates who threatened suicide or who were physically disruptive were placed in restraints (*French v. Owens*, 1985). These inmates were often stripped and chained spread-eagle to their bed for from 12 to 30 hours. Some inmates were forced to lie on bed frames without mattresses and were not allowed to use a toilet which meant that they lay in their own feces and urine.[9]

*Deadly Force Can Only Be Used in Certain Situations as a Last Resort* **Deadly force** is force that is considered likely or intended to cause death or great bodily harm. While any control methods thus far discussed can result in serious injury or death, when guns are fired at inmates the probability of causing death or serious injury is high. Although state and local regulations differ somewhat as to when deadly force is authorized, its use is generally limited to preventing an inmate from seriously injuring or killing another inmate or staff member or from committing a felony, which includes escaping. Moreover, the lethal result of the use of guns dictates that they will only be used as a last resort.

In a correctional setting, officers do not carry guns (except for those few facilities that have enclosed gun walks) because of the danger of being overpowered by inmates. As a rule, firearms are only available to COs who patrol the institution's perimeter, have guard tower duty, or are transporting inmates outside the facility. These officers are issued weapons primarily to stop escaping inmates. On the inside COs are given weapons in rare instances, such as during riots, disturbances, or hostage situations, in which control of the facility is threatened or actually lost.

In 1986, in *Whitley v. Albers*, the Supreme Court clarified the issues regarding the use of force in riots and disturbances. This case grew out of a prison disturbance in which a guard was taken hostage by several inmates. In retaking the unit, Albers, an inmate who was not involved in the riot and had attempted to help the authorities, was shot by a CO. Albers brought suit claiming excessive force was used and that no warning shot was fired so that this action constituted cruel and unusual punishment. In rejecting Albers' claim, the Court suggested its future position on the use of force in these situations. Recognizing that prison officials have to make on-the-spot determinations in emergency situations, it indicated that they must be given substantial latitude in the choices made at the time of the incident. It also noted that after-the-fact analysis may well show that the degree of force used or authorized was unnecessary, in a strict sense. However, unless it was applied in a manner that was unnecessary and wanton it was not cruel and unusual punishment. The test is "whether the force was applied in a good faith effort to maintain or restore discipline or maliciously and sadistically (i.e., with deliberate indifference) for the purpose of causing harm" (p. 1085). With the "unnecessary and wanton" standard, the Court required proof of maliciousness and sadism. Since there was no indication that the shooting was motivated by any of these factors, Albers' claims of an Eighth Amendment violation was rejected.

Although we mentioned that deadly force can be used to stop escapes, a 1985 Supreme Court decision muddled this issue as it applies within a correctional setting. In this case (*Tennessee v. Garner*) the Court ruled that a police officer could only use deadly force to prevent the escape of a fleeing felon if the officer had probable cause to believe that the suspect posed a threat of serious bodily harm to the officer or to others. With respect to corrections, the question that arises is "Do the COs responsible for perimeter security around correctional institutions have to make that same decision?" A clear answer has yet to emerge from the courts. The implication, however, is that inmates escaping from a prison or jail may have grounds for a suit against the institution if deadly force is used against them and they can show that they did not pose a threat of serious bodily harm to anyone.

Until the Court puts forth more definitive guidelines, jurisdictions will have to rely on their own statutes and local court decisions regarding the use of deadly force in escapes. The American Correctional Association (1989) indicates that most jurisdictions have adopted some variation of the following procedures.[10] An officer dealing with an escaping inmate must warn the escapee verbally (e.g., "Halt or you will be shot"). If they do not respond to the verbal warning, a warning shot must be fired. If the escapee disregards the warning shot the CO will only shoot to wound, not to kill (e.g., shoot at the legs). The Federal Bureau of Prison's (1988) policy suggests another variable, the security level of the facility, that some groups, including the American Bar Association and ACA, feel should be considered in these circumstances:

> Firearms will not ordinarily be used in minimum security level institutions except when authorized by the warden or designee. This will occur only when a judgment has been made that such use is necessary to protect the public or to prevent the loss of life or grievous bodily harm, (Federal Bureau of Prisons, 1988, p. 2).

While this and ACA policy fail to mandate that no deadly force be used in minimum security facilities, a policy forbidding its use on escapees would seem to be in order since a major criterion for placing inmates at these facilities is that they are nondangerous (Walker, 1994).

*Kinney v. Indiana Youth Center* (IYC) (1991) provides an example of a suit by an inmate subjected to deadly force during an escape.

In June, 1988 Kinney and another inmate attempted to escape from IYC, a double fenced, secure youthful offender institution with guard towers manned by armed officers. As Kinney and his companion approached the inner fence the tower officer yelled at them, asking "What are you doing?" The two inmates did not respond and continued toward the fence and climbed over it. As the inmates began climbing the second fence the officer, who had selected a 22 rifle instead of a shotgun, yelled at them "Halt, or I'll shoot!" As the 2 inmates reached the top of the second fence, ready to jump out the officer fired 2 shots attempting to only wound them. They both fell to the ground and neither made any further move. Only Kinney was hit and he suffered a severe injury to his mouth.

The court found that the officer's conduct in shooting Kinney while escaping did not amount to cruel and unusual punishment because he gave notice to Kinney he would be shot if he ventured over the fence. It also noted this facility housed violent offenders and the escape area was near the entrance to the administration building. Thus, if successful, the escapees could easily take staff or visitors as hostages. Finally, the court indicated that any prisoner who is escaping may pose a danger serious enough to justify using deadly force. Since the CO did not shoot the inmate with intention of punishing or maliciously or sadistically causing the inmate harm, its use was justified. This factor may be the basis by which these types of cases are decided (Walker, 1994).

California's recent addition of electrified fences to a maximum security prison (Caliptria) (and its planned construction of twenty more at maximum and medium security institutions in the next few years) adds another dimension to the use of deadly force in escapes. The 13-foot-high fence is located between two 12-foot-high fences topped with razor wire, and carries 4000 volts and 650 milliamperes—only 70 milliamperes are required to kill someone. Signs warning inmates that this fence is dangerous "show a man hit by a bolt of electricity falling backwards [and say] 'Danger, Peligro, Keep Out. Alto Voltaje, No Entre'" (Buzbee, 1993, p. A-18). California estimates saving $2 million by reassigning ten of the prison's twelve tower guards to other duties. The question arises as to whether the courts will find the use of deadly force without human decision making constitutional or will the fact that prisons hold dangerous people be sufficient to apply current case precedents to escape?

## Inmates Have a Right to Protection against Assault

Correctional facilities are dangerous places because they hold people either accused or convicted of crimes against other members of society. In fact, a major reason people are in prison is to protect the public from these behaviors. The question is who protects an inmate from being victimized by other prisoners since not all inmates are predisposed to violence, nor have they all threatened or injured other citizens? For COs, experience has shown this may be a no-win situation. When they attempt to protect inmates by intervening in fights their actions may be challenged as cruel and unusual punishment. However, if no action is taken, they may be accused of indifference amounting to cruel and unusual punishment. Also, some staff may feel the risk of assault is part of the cost of being convicted of a crime (Gobert and Cohen, 1981). Thus, one CO told a nineteen-year-old inmate who had been repeatedly sexually assaulted that he had three choices: submit, fight back, or escape (Lay, 1990). While inmates may be prosecuted for assaulting other inmates, for long-termers or gang members an added sentence may have little deterrent value (Gobert and Cohen, 1992).

The responsibility of prison officials to protect inmates from assaults is supported by court decisions and, in some jurisdictions, it is mandated by statute or codes of regulation:

Every employee, regardless of his or her assignment is responsible for the safe custody of the inmates confined in the institutions of the department [of corrections] (California Code of Regulations, 1991, p. 140).

**DELIBERATE INDIFFERENCE IS REQUIRED TO HOLD PRISON OFFICIALS RESPONSIBLE FOR FAILURE TO PROTECT INMATES FROM HARM** A 1994 Supreme Court decision clearly states its view that inmates are entitled to protection from assaults by other inmates:

[H]aving stripped [inmates] of virtually every means of self-protection and foreclosed their access to out side aid, government officials are not free to let the state of nature take its course.... [G]ratuitously allowing the beating or rape of one prisoner by another serves no "legitimate penological objective[s] any more than it squares with evolving standards of decency ... [nor is it] part of the penalty criminals pay for their offense against society" (*Farmer v. Brennan,* 1994, p. 4447).

This case involved a transsexual inmate, who had feminine characteristics (including having silicone breast implants and wearing "his" shirt off one shoulder). He had been placed in the general population of the federal prison at Terre Haute where he was beaten and raped.[11] Although not objecting to this placement, the inmate alleged that it was made despite knowledge on the part of prison officials that this facility had a violent environment and a history of assaults, and that he would be particularly vulnerable to attack due to projecting female characteristics. The issue before the court was whether it was safe for prison officials to place anyone with this inmate's appearance in the prison's general population [Correctional Law Reporter (CLR), 1994a] . To be held liable required a showing under the Eighth Amendment of **deliberate indifference,** the meaning of which was far from clear. Adopting a subjective standard of recklessness the court indicated that:

> [to find prison officials had] den[ied] an inmate humane conditions requires [that they] ... know ... of and disregard ... an excessive risk to inmate health and safety. Whether a prison official had the requisite knowledge of a substantial risk is a question of fact subject to demonstration in the usual ways including inference from circumstantial evidence.... [A judge or jury] may conclude that a prison official knew of a substantial risk from the fact the risk was obvious (*Farmer v. Brennan,* 1994, pp. 4448, 4449).

Thus inmates can prevail in these cases even without warning prison officials if the risk is obvious, that is, if staff should have known. This puts prison officials on notice that willful ignorance will not suffice as a defense in these cases. Some examples of conditions considered an "obvious risk" by a court include a jail's failure to lock down inmates at night, control access to wire brooms (potential weapons), or have no more than one CO on duty at night (*Berry v. City of Muskogee,* 1990). Additionally, the Court further elaborated on the meaning of circumstantial evidence:

> ... if an [inmate presents] evidence ... that circumstances suggest ... [prison] officials had been exposed to information concerning the risk and thus 'must have known about it', then such evidence could be sufficient to ... find [they] had actual knowledge of the risk (*Farmer v. Brennan,* 1994, p. 4450).

Thus, in the *Farmer* case, the inmate alleged that his feminine appearance and the violent atmosphere of the prison were "circumstances" that should have alerted prison officials to the substantial risk he faced of rape and violence by placement in the general prison population (Rifkin, 1995). The court went on to state that:

> it does not matter whether the risk comes from a single or multiple sources ... [or] whether a prisoner faces an excessive risk from attack for reasons personal to him or because all prisoners in his situation face such a risk (*Farmer v. Brennan,* 1994, p. 4450).

Boston (1994) asserts that this ruling "ratifies a broad body of case law ... [holding] ... prison officials liable for violence resulting from generalized failures of prison administration" (p. 7), which would include deficiencies such as the following (Boston and Manville, 1995):

**1.** Failure to appropriately classify and segregate particularly violent or vulnerable inmates including not screening for gang involvement; classifying inmates by any method, resulting in a young first-time offender being assaulted and raped by more violent experienced inmates; distinguishing violent and nonviolent offenders or segregating inmates likely to be sexually victimized when assigning cells.[12]
**2.** Not providing for the adequate supervision of inmates including inadequate staffing; the failure to lock inmates in at night; insufficient staffing and failure in stationing staff so they can monitor inmates in housing areas or shower areas; allowing inmates to have authority over other inmates.[13]
**3.** Failure to deal with high rates or particular patterns of assault(s) including not developing policies to protect inmates in high-risk areas; disciplining or prosecuting assailants; adequately responding to a known pattern of rape; appropriately controlling contraband.[14]
**4.** The open and less secure nature of dormitory housing has led courts to require greater and

more direct staff supervision, e.g., two COs in open dormitories to better control homosexuality.[15]

**5.** Overcrowding, which produces such conditions as unreasonable risk of assault or precludes effective classification, resulting in an inmate being the victim of an attack.[16]

**6.** Insufficient control of tools and items that can be used as weapons, i.e., failure to enforce a tool control policy or search inmates exiting a shop area.[17]

The Court's decision implied that administrative responsibility may be expanded to include both knowledge of conditions inside their facilities and "prison officials' broad knowledge of the dynamics of prison life." Thus a warden's liability may revolve around not merely whether inmates were at risk of assault but "Whether [he or she knew that] failure to classify inmates can itself create or aggravate a risk" (Boston, 1994, p. 7). For example, prison staff would be expected to know they are creating a situation with a high potential for violence (i.e., are acting with deliberate indifference) by placing a white biker with a swastika tattoo in a cell with an outspokenly anti-white black inmate (CLR, 1994). The courts may also give closer scrutiny to cases involving a high potential for sexual assault given the rising prevalence of HIV and AIDS, because this can mean a death sentence to those victimized (Rifkin, 1995). Given the trend toward confining more offenders, if states attempt to stuff more inmates in existing facilities, violence levels are likely to increase. This will undoubtedly result in more inmate suits alleging cruel and unusual punishment as a result of the deliberate indifference of prison officials to protect them from known risks of serious injury.

Finally, Boston and Manville (1995) assert that because courts recognize that prisons house dangerous people, it is unreasonable to assume that all assaults result from reckless or deliberate disregard by prison staff for inmate safety. Thus, instances in which assaults are isolated cases or have resulted from a guard's temporary inattentiveness or when prison officials have temporarily failed to act or to examine information in their possession are seen by some courts as mere negligence—the failure to exercise ordinary care that a reasonable person would use—rather than deliberate indifference.[18]

**OFFICIALS WHO ENCOURAGE OR PASSIVELY OBSERVE INMATE ASSAULTS CAN BE HELD RESPONSBILE FOR THE RESULTING HARM TO AN INMATE**  Clearly, officials or staff who obviously or actively permit or encourage an inmate assault or stand by while one occurs may be held liable (Boston and Manville, 1995). For example, a court considered as valid an inmate's claim that a correctional officer instigated other inmates to beat him when the officer directed them to do so (*Durre v. Dempsey*, 1989). Nevertheless, the courts recognize prison staff may not always be able, nor may it be wise for them, to intervene in all situations. Thus, no Eighth Amendment violation was found when several COs, surrounded by dozens of inmates, failed to break up a fight because they felt this would have increased their risk of injury and that of other inmates (*Williams v. Willits*, 1988).

### Certain Conditions Caused by Overcrowding May Be Unconstitutional

Prisons and jails in the United States are bulging at the seams. At the end of 1994 state prisons were estimated to be operating at 117% of their highest capacity and 129% of their lowest capacity (Beck and Gilliard, 1995). In 1995 the Florida legislature passed a statute allowing its state prisons to increase their capcity to 150%. The question is "Does over crowding per se constitute cruel and unusual punishment in violation of the Eighth Amendment?" In rejecting the use of standard criteria to assess prison conditions in *Rhodes v. Chapman* (1981), the Court signaled its refusal to consider any one or a combination of conditions as *automatically* unconstitutional. Its view was that overcrowded conditions may make prison life uncomfortable, but this is part of the penalty inmates pay for their criminality.

Most recently, in *Wilson v. Seiter* (1991), the Court has reiterated its view that only when overcrowding results in deprivation of one or more basic needs (e.g., food, warmth, or exercise) is it considered an Eighth Amendment violation. Thus, it is not overcrowding per se that courts find objectionable, but whether one or several conditions in combination—a "totality of conditions"—deprives inmates of the "minimal necessities of civilized life." The conditions the courts will typically focus on include the following (Collins, 1993):

## Consider This. . .
## Do Some People Who Go to Jail Deserve What They Get?

[A young white man, Stokes, was arrested with three of his friends on a charge that one of them had thrown a bottle from a moving truck. They slept in the day room area the first night while the other inmates were locked in cells. The next morning at 7:00 A.M. the cells were unlocked and all the other inmates, who were black and almost all facing felony charges, were released. While Stokes, and one of his friends, Shows, were watching television,] Otis Howard, a black male charged with burglary and armed robbery, entered the cell. As Stokes started to stand, Otis without warning struck him in the face with his fist, breaking his nose. As Otis pummeled Stokes, "Boo Boo" Dixon, a . . . [250 pounder] . . . jailed on charges that included aggravated rape, began to slug Shows. He also shoved Stokes, causing Stokes to strike his head and cut his scalp, [which bled] profusely. . . . Despite much screaming and yelling, no jailer came. Stokes made his way back to the bull pen leaving a trail of blood . . . [and then] . . . to one of the cells. Lunch was served by the trusties but no jailer came in.

Stokes [testified] that he asked the other prisoners for help [but] was refused. . . . Boo Boo had told him if he complained he would be sent out on a stretcher and . . . suggested . . . it would be difficult for him to talk with his throat cut. At Boo Boo's direction, Stokes washed his clothes in the urinal in an effort to remove the fresh blood. [Deputy] Romero . . . testified that he saw Stokes after the "fight," but that Stokes refused assistance saying it was just a little "scrimmage." At approximately 6:00 P.M., a jailer entered the bull pen area and, at the direction of Boo Boo, Stokes requested a carton of cigarettes. This was the first time according to Stokes that he had seen a jailer since breakfast. The cigarettes were delivered and were taken by Boo Boo [who] . . . then sexually assaulted Stokes, compelling him to engage in anal and oral sex. Wayne Shows suffered a similar fate.

## Consider This. . .
## Continued

The next morning, weak from loss of blood and feigning illness, Stokes attempted to attract attention when breakfast was served. When Romero, the deputy on duty, was shown his cut, Boo Boo, who was standing immediately beside Stokes, asserted that Stokes had fallen from his bunk. Romero asked if that was what happened and Stokes, fearful of saying otherwise, agreed. Romero then said, "I can't let you go to the hospital. I sent a boy to the hospital yesterday and they couldn't find anything wrong with him. Go back to your cell." [No person had been sent to the hospital the previous day.] Later, two trusties carried Stokes from the cell block where he was handcuffed and taken to the hospital. Late that afternoon, Stokes' parents arrived from Mississippi and obtained his release. (p. 1123)

In affirming the district court ruling, the Fifth Circuit Court of Appeals found Stokes, who was arrested for what was at worst a childish prank, was confined in a jail where terror reigns and that this constituted cruel and unusual-punishment (*Stokes v. Delcambre*, 1983, pp. 1120–1129). Do you think that it is OK for pretrial detainees being held in jail to be "punished" in this way? What should happen to Romero, the jail administrator, and inmates Dixon and Otis?

1. *Food:* Is it nutritionally balanced, and prepared and served under sanitary conditions?
2. *Shelter:* This category deals with the overall prison or jail environment and includes noise levels, lighting, ventilation, plumbing, overall building conditions, cell size, etc. These issues most often involve older facilities.
3. *Sanitation:* Is the facility infested with vermin; are proper food preparation and handling practices followed; does sanitation threaten inmate health?
4. *Health care:* This concerns the extent to which medical, dental, and mental health services are deficient and thus show deliberate indifference to the serious health needs of the inmates.

**5.** *Personal safety:* Are inmates reasonably safe from serious risk of assault, rape, or other serious injury from other inmates?

The courts may also examine conditions not normally considered as constitutional entitlements because in overcrowded conditions they may contribute to producing an unacceptable living environment. For example, although prisons are not required to occupy inmates productively, idleness in overcrowded prisons may heighten violence, thereby creating an unacceptable condition. Also, double-bunking may increase a prison population to the point that services are overtaxed and not providing for an inmate's basic needs. These factors contributed to a district court ruling that six housing units at the Tennessee State Prison were unconstitutionally overcrowded. It noted that:

> Inmates are double celled in tiny cages like so many animals in a zoo, with an average of about 23 square feet in which each man lives, sleeps, performs his bodily functions, and spends a great portion of each day. Beyond the deplorable lack of space, the cells are noisy, poorly lit, often in a state of disrepair and equipped with plumbing that is dangerous to the prisoner's health.... Violence at the prison is rampant, including frequent episodes of assault and sexual attack upon cellmates. With pervasive idleness, inmates have few alternatives but to sit in their tiny cells and brood ... [The court] conclude[d] that the only way in which [these] units can be constitutionally adequate is to cease double celling in [them] (*Grubbs v. Bradley*, 1982, pp. 1125–1126).[19]

In refusing to view overcrowding per se as unconstitutional, the courts have generally followed the precedent set in *Rhodes v. Chapman* (1981), in which the Supreme Court refused to view a prison's conditions as cruel and unusual just because its population exceeded its capacity by 38%. Other lower courts refused to consider facilities unconstitutional despite their operating at 30% over capacity when no averse effects were found (*Lopez v. Robinson*, 1990) Even combined with unpleasant conditions, overcrowding has not been viewed as an Eighth Amendment violation when these conditions do not deprive inmates of basic needs (*Hassine v. Jeffes*, 1988) Finally, the courts use the deliberate indifference test to determine liability in these cases. This requires evidence of knowledge of constitutional violations and then a failure to act (*Wilson v. Seiter*, 1991) (see Chapter 15).

## DUE PROCESS PROCEDURES IN INSTITUTIONS

Institutions are required to afford inmates certain due process rights. The rules that govern inmate behavior and the procedures that are employed to determine guilt or innocence when rules are violated and punishment is imposed may be subject to due process protections. This section discusses those due process safeguards.

### Rules and Regulations Must Be Clearly Stated and Be Related to Legitimate Penal Objectives

Prisons are closed communities whose populations include a disproportionate number of society's most dangerous members. By their behavior most inmates have shown a disregard for normal legal constraints. Thus, developing rules that effectively control conduct, ensure staff and inmate safety, promote orderly and efficient prison operations, and prevent escapes is not an easy task. Also, this population's tendency toward violent and predatory behavior requires rules governing behavior normally not regulated on the outside (e.g., removing pepper from dining rooms because it can be used to blind someone). Because many rules are written in ambiguous or vague language, interpreting them causes problems when attempting to enforce them and determine guilt. Examples of ambiguous regulations include rules forbidding inmates to engage in "vicious eyeballing," "insolence," "ill language" toward any officer, or engaging in conversation with another inmate (American Bar Association, 1977). The **vagueness** or ambiguity of these rules becomes clear when trying to define "insolence." While one CO views an inmate's request as insolent because of its assertive tone, another CO may see it as a display of an independent attitude.

Prison rules bearing no rational relationship to legitimate penal objectives would appear to violate requirements of **substantive due process** since to be constitutional legislation must be fair and reasonable in content and application (Mushlin, 1993; Black et al., 1991). Thus, if rules do not directly affect institutional order, they may violate an inmate's right to be free from arbitrary and unreasonable actions. For example, in one prison there was a ten-year-old rule forbidding inmates from sitting on a bench in the prison yard. This rule, intended to keep inmates from sitting on a freshly painted bench, remained in effect long after the paint dried and an inmate got five days in solitary confinement for violating it. Rules so incomprehensible that individuals of ordinary intelligence find them hard to understand violate constitutional due process restrictions against **vagueness.** Examples include prohibitions on "poor conduct" (*Laaman v. Helgemoe,* 1977) or "the possession of any article or paraphernalia which by its unusual nature gives reasonable grounds to believe escape is planned" (*Rabi v. LeFevre,* 1986). However, while there may be problems with prison regulations, courts rarely entertain cases in this area because they do not want to become involved in the daily management of prisons. To be fair, prison rules should be clear, intelligible, and only prohibit behavior that threatens important institutional interests such as order, security, and safety.

Some courts have considered failure to provide inmates with copies of rules and/or to read them to illiterate inmates as violations of due process (Gobert and Cohen, 1981; Mushlin, 1993). While most jurisdictions provide inmate handbooks indicating the disciplinary rules few include the sanctions for these violations. This raises questions of how penalties for violations are decided and undermines the deterrent effects of these rules. Consequently it "has been held that inmates have the right to know the scope of punishment possible for infractions" (Mushlin, 1993, p. 428).

## Inmates Retain the Right to Procedural Due Process

Most cases dealing with due process involve the procedures and methods by which guilt is determined for rule violations and the imposition of penalties (Collins, 1993). In other words, they involve the steps taken by the state in making decisions depriving inmates of a right, privilege, or property interest. In prison the kinds of punishments, deprivations, or restraints that can be imposed range from temporary loss of minor privileges (e.g., commissary privileges or viewing television) to more substantial ones (e.g., restriction to one's cell for a week) to the most substantial punishments (e.g., placement in disciplinary segregation and loss of statutory good time, which extends an inmate's confinement). Since privileges in prison are few, inmates are very concerned about retaining them. Like persons charged with crimes on the outside, inmates

charged with a prison rule violation may be innocent. Two concerns are relevant here: (1) defining the liberty, property, and other interests requiring **due process procedures** before the inmate can be deprived of them; and (2) whether disciplinary procedures addressing these liberty interests meet due process requirements.

**DUE PROCESS PROCEDURES ARE REQUIRED TO DEPRIVE AN INMATE OF CERTAIN TYPES OF INTERESTS** "Interests" that require due process protection, are defined by the Constitution, court orders, statutes, regulations, or standard practices, policies or customs (Project, 1994). In the case of statutes or regulations, what determines whether a liberty interest exists is the presence of mandatory language and **substantive predicates**—specific conditions or requirements (*Hewitt v. Helms,* 1983). Thus, in order to avoid creating liberty or other interests, which require due process procedures, a state or prison must exclude these factors from the wording of their statutes or rules. **Liberty interests** recognized by the courts as falling within these categories include the following:

1. *Constitutional:* These interests flow from rights granted under all amendments and can involve policies relating to visitation, mail, segregation, transfer to mental hospitals, ingestion of psychotropic drugs, and so on.
2. *Court orders:* For example, a court decision established disciplinary hearing procedures that were to be followed prior to depriving inmates of certain privileges (*Kelsey v. Minnesota,* 1980).
3. *Statutes:* For example, a statute mandating specific guidelines for placing inmates in administrative segregation created an inmate right not to be transferred without meeting these criteria (*Hewitt v. Helms,* 1983).
4. *Administrative regulations:* For example, rules containing mandatory language specifying conditions for placement in administrative segregation establish an inmate's right to remain in the general population unless these criteria have been met (*McQueen v. Tabah,* 1988).
5. *Standard practices, policies, or customs:* For example, a prison's policy required that antipsychotic drugs be administered under certain conditions. Inmates had the right to expect these conditions be met prior to being given these drugs (*Washington v. Harper,* 1990).

**DUE PROCESS IN PRISON DOES NOT REQUIRE ANY SPECIFIC PROCEDURES**    In correctional facilities due process does not necessarily involve any specific procedures. Therefore, the same protections accorded defendants in a criminal trial or parole revocation are not required in prison proceedings involving deprivation of protected interests. The degree of due process required varies from one situation to another. In making a determination in these cases the courts try to balance an inmate's interests "against the government's interest in being able to make decisions quickly and efficiently" (Collins, 1993, p. 42). Generally, the greater the consequences for inmates, the more extensive the due process requirements are likely to be. Transfer of an inmate to a mental hospital involves a greater loss of liberty than placement in administrative confinement and therefore the former action would require greater procedural safeguards.

In *Wolff v. McDonnell* (1974), the Supreme Court dealt with the procedures to be employed when inmates could be deprived of good time or placed in disciplinary confinement. This and later decisions have required that inmates:

**1.** Receive at least 24-hour advance written notice of the charges.
**2.** Have a right to be heard, i.e., the right to a hearing at which the truth of the allegations is investigated.
**3.** Have an opportunity to call witnesses, present evidence, and confront and cross examine accusers. This means inmates can call other inmates as witnesses and present evidence unless this would be "unduly hazardous" to institutional safety or correctional goals. The courts allow prison officials to decide whether to permit inmates to confront and cross examine their accusers. This recognizes the increased risk of reprisals when allowing inmates to examine informants.
**4.** Have access to assistance. Inmates are not normally entitled to have attorneys in disciplinary proceedings because they are felt to unduly complicate and delay them. However, in complex cases or those involving illiterate inmates, assistance is required and can be gotten from fellow inmates or staff.
**5.** Be treated with impartiality. The courts have required that the hearing officer or committee be impartial, which excludes those involved in the incident, e.g., victims or witnesses or those who have a strong personal animosity toward an inmate.
**6.** Be found guilty on the basis of evidence. In *Superintendent v. Hill* (1985), the Supreme Court held due process requires "some evidence" to support a disciplinary board finding of guilt (e.g., the eyewitness testimony of a guard).
**7.** Have the right to appeal an adverse disciplinary finding. Administrative review of disciplinary findings is not required but is good policy because it provides a check on the fairness of disciplinary decisions and may satisfy inmates that they received a fair hearing.
**8.** Written record. Following Wolff, it was required that a written statement be made by the hearing board detailing the evidence relied on in making the decision and if disciplinary action was taken, the reasons for it (Collins, 1993; Gobert and Cohen, 1981, 1992).

## FOURTH AMENDMENT RIGHTS TO PRIVACY

The Fourth Amendment was designed to protect people from unreasonable searches and seizures of property by government officials. Although the courts have required warrants prior to most searches, they have recognized the need for warrantless searches under limited conditions, for example, stop and frisk or during an arrest (Inbau, Thompson, Zagel, and Manak, 1984).

The courts have considered jail and prison settings, by their nature, to justify warrantless searches under some conditions, for instance, to control contraband (*Hudson v. Palmer*, 1984). Thus, anyone entering or moving about in prison (e.g., staff, inmates, and visitors) should expect some intrusion into their privacy. The courts have recognized the need to balance requirements for maintaining order and security against the intrusiveness of searches (e.g., a pat-down search is less intrusive than a strip search). Also relevant are the circumstances of the search and the manner in which it is conducted (Collins, 1993). Thus, while strip searches are sometimes done on visitors suspected of bringing in contraband, there is no justification for making rude comments during this process.

## Cell Searches Are Conducted to Search for Contraband

The Supreme Court has ruled pretrial detainees and convicted offenders have no expectation of privacy or Fourth Amendment protection in their cells (*Bell v. Wolfish*, 1979; *Hudson v. Palmer*, 1984). Thus, cell searches, or "shakedowns," can be conducted by prison officials on a random and routine basis outside the presence of the inmate. No specific justification for these searches is required. However, the Court has cautioned prison officials not to "trash"—leave in shambles—an inmate's cell while searching it nor do searches to harass inmates. If this occurs, inmates can file claims under the Eighth Amendment's cruel and unusual punishment clause and sue to have destroyed property replaced under state tort law (*Hudson v. Palmer*, 1984; Project, 1994).

## Pat-Down or Frisk Searches of Inmates and Urine Tests to Determine Illegal Drug Use Are Permitted in Prisons

As a rule, the courts have allowed COs to randomly or routinely conduct frisk searches for contraband. The question of whether COs can search inmates of the opposite sex raises legal as well as social issues. Because of this, the ACA (1989) recommended that where possible these searches be conducted by staff of the same sex as the person searched. Chapter 14 examined the issue of cross-gender pat searches.

For some time institutions have been randomly requiring inmates to "drop urine" (provide a urine specimen) to screen for drug use. The courts have upheld these practices because of their importance for maintaining order and security and the reliability of these tests. They have required samples to be obtained in ways that do not humiliate inmates; to be truly random; and to not subject inmates to harassment. They can also be justified when based on information that an inmate is using drugs (Collins, 1993; Mushlin, 1993).

## The Courts Recognize Strip Searches Are Needed to Control Contraband

Strip searches involve visual examination of the inmate's naked body and, in the case of males, require that they lift their genitals and bend over

and spread their buttocks as well. With females the vaginal and anal cavities are inspected and they may be required to lift their breasts. The courts have reluctantly allowed strip searches when there is reasonable suspicion that inmates are concealing contraband and when conducted in a reasonable manner. The Supreme Court approved these searches in circumstances in which inmates or pretrial detainees have opportunities to obtain contraband (e.g., during contact visits or trips to court or the hospital) (*Bell v. Wolfish*, 1979). Because inmates in segregation units and maximum security are more dangerous, searching them upon entering or leaving their cells has been justified. Strip searches have also been upheld when they have continued to uncover contraband. Thus, a prison policy of searching all inmates returning to their cells was considered justified when large quantities of dangerous contraband (knives and hacksaw blades) continued to be found and there was evidence these searches reduced violence (*Bruscino v. Carlson*, 1988).

The more sensitive nature of these searches by opposite-sex officers raises more compelling privacy concerns than pat searches. The courts have recognized that the rights of female officers to equal opportunity in employment may require they view inmates who are in a state of undress, such as during body cavity searches. However, a reading of several decisions suggests most courts draw the line at cross-gender strip searches and view inmate's privacy rights as generally outweighing other considerations (*Grummett v. Rushen*, 1985; *Michenfelder v. Summer*, 1988). However, a district court allowed a strip search of a male inmate by female officers suggesting this view is not universal. It argued that:

> If women guards behave in professional manner . . . they will engender respect from inmates, who will recognize that their privacy is being invaded no more than if a woman doctor examines them (*Canedy v. Boardman*, 1992).

Of course, in emergency situations, such as following a riot or disturbance, the need for quick action and for all officers to be employed in the most efficient manner justifies cross-sex searches. Further, recognizing that this type of search is humiliating enough, the courts have admonished prison officials that inmates may have cause for legal action if they are conducted in a cruel or malicious manner or with intent to harass, humiliate, or intimidate the inmate (Gobert and Cohen, 1981; Mushlin, 1993). Evidence of this might include rude and insulting comments by guards during these searches or their use to punish uncooperative inmates.

While the *Bell* decision approved strip searches of pretrial detainees already in jail populations, it did not address searching of arrestees during booking. In view of the range of offenses for which people are arrested (from traffic violations to murder) the courts have been unwilling to approve blanket strip search policies (Collins, 1993; Project, 1992). To strip search arrestees, "reasonable suspicion" that they are concealing contraband is normally required. Felony charges per se may not justify strip searches, but most courts allow them for drug-related offenses or violent offenders. However, placement of those arrested for minor offenses, including property felonies, in the general jail population may not automatically justify routine strip searches (Collins, 1993). Thus the courts appear to be saying a pat-down is sufficient for nonviolent arrestees and that strip searches are only necessary when there is reason to believe they have contraband. Of course, if COs find something suspicious during a pat-down a more intrusive search is justified.

### Body Cavity Probes Must Be Conducted by Trained Medical Staff

There is ample evidence that inmates occasionally use body cavities to hide contraband. For example, in *Bruscino v. Carlson* (1988) inmates testified to what they called "Keistering," i.e., concealing of such items as hacksaw blades, handcuff keys, and drugs in their rectums to bring them into the prison. Since this is the most intrusive type of search short of surgery, to conduct it there must reasonable cause or a clear indication that the inmate is hiding contraband in a body cavity. In high security control units—those housing a system's most difficult to control inmates—the Supreme Court approved routine searches of this kind whenever inmates return from trips outside of the prison (*Bruscino v. Carlson,* 1988).

Although not mandating that these examinations be conducted by physicians, the courts require they be done by trained medical staff, under sanitary conditions, and in a manner that respects the inmate's dignity and privacy (Gobert and Cohen, 1981, 1992). For example, in *Tribble v. Gardner* (1988) a court viewed as unconstitutional the use of these searches as a threat to influence inmate behavior (e.g., a guard's remark to an inmate that was to be searched that "Today you meet Mr. Big Finger"). Finally, while these searches should not generally be conducted with the assistance of opposite-sex officers, emergency situations can override inmate rights to privacy.

### The Courts Have Restricted the Items That Can Be Taken from Inmates

Only prohibited items can be confiscated and inmates must be provided with a list of seized items. While many things can be viewed as threatening institutional security, the courts will generally view as unreasonable the seizure of religious and legal materials, such as trial transcripts and legal papers (Palmer, 1992; Gobert and Cohen, 1992).

### ENDNOTES

1. See Chapter 15 for a complete discussion of the basis for the decision.

2. Our discussion of the Federal Prison at Marion in Chapter 17 describes how inmates work their way out of this super-max prison.

3. Convicted offenders can bring action under the Eighth Amendment or the Fourteenth Amendment. However, pretrial detainees are not protected by the Eighth Amendment so that their claims are limited to the Fourteenth Amendment. However, in *Whitley v. Albers* (1986) the Supreme Court stated that, at least with respect to prison inmates, there is no difference in the level of force that would constitute an Eighth versus a Fourteenth Amendment violation. Thus, since prison inmates are afforded no greater protection under the due process clause versus the cruel and unusual punishment clause, there is no advantage to bringing a dual action. Therefore, inmates will typically bring action under the Eighth Amendment.

4. *Norris v. District of Columbia*, 1984;, *Colon v. Schneider*, 1990.

5. CN stands for chloraceophenone and CS is short for orthorchlorobenzalmalononitrile.

6. *Greear v. Loving*, 1975; *Peterson v. Davis*, 1982; *Lock v. Jenkins*, 1981; *Blair-El v. Tinsman*, 1987.

7. *Bruscino v. Carlson*, 1989; *Hanna v. Lane*, 1985; *Tubwell v. Griffith*, 1984; *Stenzil v. Ellis*, 1990.

8. One court even found constitutionally acceptable the chaining of an inmate (considered a high escape risk) to a hospital bed for several days. No doubt this decision hinged on the fact that the chain was long enough to enable the inmate to eat, move around, sleep, and get to a toilet (*Guerrero v. Cain*, 1983). In contrast, another court considered unreasonable the shackling of an inmate to his bed for three days during which it was difficult for him to rest and use the toilet. COs justified this action because he was violent, strong, and disruptive but the court rejected this argument because a less restrictive alternative (i.e., a single cell) was available but not used (*Picariello v. Fenton*, 1980).

9. In this regard in *Ferola v. Moran* (1985), although the district court recognized the possible medical justification for shackling an inmate to his bed, they objected to the manner in which it was carried out. Specifically, they found fault with the fact that the inmate was chained spread-eagle to his bed for twenty hours without adequate medical monitoring or supervision. The unpadded chains used caused nerve damage when he attempted to move in his agitated state. He was also denied access to a toilet for fourteen hours.

10. See, for example, state regulations in Florida and California (California Code of Regulations, 1991; Florida Department of Corrections, 1991).

11. The Court remanded the case, which was dismissed by two lower courts, back for retrial, at which point the inmate would have the opportunity to show that these assaults were the result of the deliberate indifference of officials at the federal prison at Terre Haute, Indiana.

12. *Walsh v. Mellas*,. 1988; *Stokes v. Delcambre*, 1983; *Vosburg v. Solem*, 1988.

13. *Berry v. City of Muskogee*, 1990; *Vosburg v. Solem*, 1988; *Stokes v. Delcambre*, 1983; *Gillard v. Owens*, 1989.

14. *Vosburg v. Solem*, 1988; *Redmond v. Baxley*, 1979; *LaMarca v. Turner*, 1987.

15. *Williams v. Edwards*, 1977; also see *Finney v. Mabry*, 1982).

16. *Morgan v. District of Columbia*, 1987; *Ryan v. Burlington County, NY*, 1988.

17. *Berry v. City of Muskogee*, 1990; *Goka v. Bobitt*, 1988; *Shrader v. White*, 1985; *Tillery v. Owens*, 1989.

18. This does not suggest that an inmate cannot bring tort action under state law. To be successful, inmates would have to prove all the elements required by statute, which usually include a duty to exercise due care on the part of a defendant, or a failure to exercise such care; negligence or intentional misconduct; and injury. As noted earlier, many states have statutes or regulations that impose a responsibility on correctional employees for the safe custody of inmates.

19. In a later case (*Tillery v. Owens*, 1990), a court found an institution unconstitutionally overcrowded based on the following conditions: deficient lighting, ventilation, plumbing, fire safety, medical and mental health care; limited opportunities for outside recreation; double-bunking for long periods of time; inadequate screening, resulting in "fatal pairings" in which violent, delusional, or predatory inmates were often placed in cells with inmates who were unable to protect themselves. To relieve these constitutionally intolerable conditions, the court ordered the institution to stop double-bunking inmates. We should also note that the antiquated Tennessee State Prison was finally closed in 1992 (Bonnyman, 1993).

## ACKNOWLEDGMENTS

[a] D.L. Ross, (1989). A Model Policy on the Use of Non-deadly Force in Corrections: Based on a Comprehensive Analysis of Correctional Non-deadly Force Policies Nationwide. Big Rapids, MI: Criminal Justice Institute, Ferris State University. Reprinted by permission of publisher.

## CHAPTER RECAP

**Restrictions on First Amendment Rights**
Inmates Have Certain Rights Relating to the Use of Mail
Some Restrictions on Publications and Literature Have Been Justified
**Eighth Amendment Prohibition Against Cruel and Unusual Punishment**
Isolated Confinement Has Been Used for a Long Time
Solitary Confinement Is Not Usually Considered Unconstitutional
Isolation of Inmates May Have Adverse Psychological Effects
The Courts Approve Use of Force in a Correctional Setting Under Certain Circumstances
The Use of Force by COs Ranges from Justified to Unjustified
The Staff Subculture Can Influence the Use of Force
Circumstances and Amount Employed Govern the Acceptable Use of Force
Several Key Cases Have Defined the Parameters for the Use of Force
The Various Levels of Control Are Determined by the Type of Resistance
Verbal Direction Should be Employed First
There Are Several Levels of Physical Force

Various Types of Restraints Are Used to Control
Inmates
Deadly Force Can Only Be Used in Certain Situations as a Last Resort
Inmates Have a Right to Protection Against Assault
Deliberate Indifference Is Required to Hold Prison
Officials Responsible for Failure to Protect Inmates
from Harm
Officials Who Encourage or Passively Observe Inmate Assaults Can Be Held Responsible for the
Resulting Harm to an Inmate
Certain Conditions Caused by Overcrowding May Be
Unconstitutional
**Due Process Procedure in Institutions**
Rules and Regulations Must Be Clearly Stated and Be
Related to Legitimate Penal Objectives
Inmates Retain the Right to Procedural Due Process
Due Process Procedures Are Required to Deprive an
Inmate of Certain Types of Interests
Due Process in Prison Does Not Require Any Specific
Procedures
**Fourth Amendment Rights to Privacy**
Cell Searches Are Conducted to Search for Contraband
Pat-Down or Frisk Searches of Inmates and Urine Tests
to Determine Illegal Drug Use Are Permitted in
Prisons
The Courts Recognize Strip Searches Are Needed to
Control Contraband
Body Cavity Probes Must Be Conducted by Trained
Medical Staff
The Courts Have Restricted the Items Than Can Be
Taken from Inmates

## REVIEW QUESTIONS

1. How have the courts tried to balance inmates' First
Amendment rights with the needs of correctional institutions to limit inmates' use of mail and the receipt of
publications?
2. What restrictions have the courts imposed on the
use by correctional institutions of isolated confinement?
3. Discuss the broad concerns associated with the use
of force by correctional officers in the prison environment.
4. What types of control are employed in a correctional
facility and what major considerations influence which
level of control is employed by COs in given situations?
5. Under what circumstances can correctional officials
and COs be held liable for inmate-on-inmate assaults?

6. What types of prison rules would violate substantive
due process requirements?
7. Give examples of constitutionally protected liberty
and property interests and discuss the due process procedures required to deprive inmates of them.
8. Under what circumstances can prison officials conduct urine tests and cell, pat-down, strip, and body
cavity searches?

## TEST YOUR KNOWLEDGE

1. Which of the following is false? Prisons can prevent
inmates from receiving publications that
   a. are published by a revolutionary organization.
   b. are a clear and present danger to institutional
   order or security.
   c. contain information about narcotic and hallucinogenic drugs.
   d. are not sent directly from the outside publishers.
2. Choose the false statement. Correctional officers can
use force
   a. in self defense.
   b. to enforce prison rules.
   c. to prevent prisoners from harming themselves.
   d. to punish disruptive inmates.
3. The _____Amendment protects inmates from
being subjected to cruel and unusual punishment.
   a. First
   b. Fourth
   c. Fifth
   d. Eighth
4. The discussion of the use of force in corrections
indicated that
   a. deadly force can never be used inside a prison.
   b. for force to be used, resistance must be evident.
   c. tear gas is regularly used as means of controlling
   disruptive inmates.
   d. restraints are regularly used a means of punishing disruptive inmates.
5. Regarding inmate-on-inmate assaults, staff can be
held liable
   a. for mere negligence.
   b. in all instances in which inmates are seriously
   injured.
   c. when evidence is presented of deliberate indifference.
   d. in no cases because of state immunity statues.

# CHAPTER 17

# CLASSIFICATION AND CUSTODY

## ▣ LEARNING OBJECTIVES

*After completion of this chapter, you should be able to:*
1. Describe the reception and orientation process.
2. Outline the history of classification as it developed in the United States.
3. Define classification, discuss its purposes, and list the characteristics of objective classification systems.
4. Describe and discuss the three basic elements of the classification process.
5. Differentiate between custody and security and describe the five levels of security and five levels of custody.
6. Define and discuss the issues with which minimum security facilities must deal.
7. Explain the concept of needs assessment and its measurement.
8. Describe the reclassification process and discuss its functions.
9. Discuss the similarities and differences between the National Institute of Corrections classification model and the Federal Bureau of Prisons model.

## ▣ KEY TERMS AND CONCEPTS

Certified court orders
Classification
Classifications committee
Custody levels
Detainer
Inmate handbook
Objective classification systems
Orientation process
Overclassification
Predictive variables
Reception and diagnostic center
Reclassification
Security levels
Summary admission report
Super-maximum security facilities
Underclassification

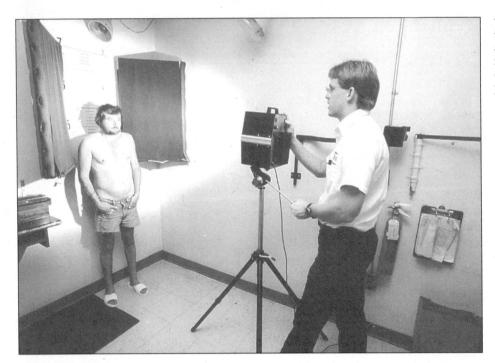

"Mug shots" are part of the admission process and become part of the inmate's file developed during the classification process.

Whenever people are placed in an institution, it is necessary to obtain certain information about them so they can be integrated into the organization. Corrections systems accomplish this task in a variety of ways. In some systems central **reception and diagnostic centers** are where inmates are assessed, classified, and then transferred to appropriate facilities. In other systems the process is carried out in a prison reception unit where inmates are kept until it is completed. Inmates are then placed in the facility's general population. Regardless of the approach used, certain procedures need to be followed before the offender's first institutional placement.

## RECEPTION AND ORIENTATION

Smooth and well-organized admission procedures make the offender's transition from the free world to institutional life less traumatic. The American Correctional Association (ACA, 1981a) recommends that admission procedures facilitate the adjustment of inmates to the system and reduce their anxiety. This can be accomplished by having staff explain to the offender each step in the admission process.

When inmates enter corrections, **certified court orders** committing them to the department of cor-

rections must be verified. A complete search is conducted of the individual and his or her clothing and other possessions to detect any contraband. Thorough strip searches are conducted, including body cavities if necessary. All personal property is sorted so it can be stored until an inmate's release, disposed of, or returned home at the inmate's expense. Inmates then shower and are issued clothing and personal items such as soap, toothbrushes, etc. This is followed by photographing, fingerprinting, and noting of identifying marks or unusual physical characteristics (e.g., scars, deformities, and tattoos). An initial medical screening is usually done at admission. Complete medical, dental, and mental examinations follow later in the reception and classification process.

The reception and **orientation process** (1) provides information required to initially place new inmates and (2) tells inmates what is expected of them and what they can anticipate from their institutional experience. They are informed about institutional rules, the disciplinary process (e.g., why reports are written, rules and appeals), and given a copy of the **inmate handbook.** They are also assisted in notifying their families of their admission, and informed of both temporary and permanent regulations regarding mail and visitation. Approved lists of visitors and correspondents are also prepared. Discussions are held to acquaint inmates with institutional services and programs (e.g., educational, religious, vocational, industrial, and recreational) and the requirements for participation. A **summary admission report** is prepared as the first step in the development of a file that includes an account of the legal aspects of the inmate's case, a summary of his or her criminal history, demographics, family and personal history data, occupational interests, recreational preferences and needs, and a summary of the assessments and recommendations made by classification staff. During the orientation period, inmates are kept separate from the general prison population but can exercise and/or work within their units.

## CLASSIFICATION PROCEDURES

Although classification has a long history, its effectiveness as a tool for correctional management can be tied to the more recent development of objective systems. This section shows that these systems not only help determine an inmate's security, custody, and program needs but also serve to protect the public from inmates, and inmates from each other, make more efficient use of prison resources, and guide future planning.

### Basic Forms of Classification Have a Long History

The history of classification dates back to the mid-1500s when workhouses and houses of correction were first opened in England and Europe. Initial forms of classification resulted from demands of reformers who were trying to eliminate prisoners' vices (e.g., gambling, drinking) and reduce the mistreatment and corruption of younger and weaker offenders (Sutherland and Cressey, 1966; Wines, 1895). These early classification systems separated juveniles from adults, first offenders from repeaters, and men from women. Classification was also used for making work assignments. However, overcrowding made separation of offenders less feasible. This simple system served these institutions because they functioned as pretrial/presentence facilities.

When prisons developed in the United States, classification was not a major factor. In the Penn-

sylvania system inmates were completely separated from each other so classification was not necessary. At Auburn-type prisons little classification was needed because offenders were housed similarly, worked at productive labor, and harsh discipline was used to maintain order [National Institute of Corrections (NIC), 1981a]. By the mid-1850s, several factors (e.g., changing views about the causes and treatment of deviant behavior, increasing humanitarian concerns) led to the removal of certain groups of offenders from jails and prisons for placement in specialized institutions. Facilities were established for juvenile delinquents, insane offenders, young adults, blacks, women, defective delinquents, and the sick or infirm.

In Chapter 6, we focused briefly on the roots of the contemporary classification process and the important role played by the development of the social sciences in this process. By 1950, as we noted in Chapter 7, with the emergence of rehabilitative institutions and their general focus on treatment, most jurisdictions had developed systems for classifying inmates, at least for purposes of unit and work assignments. Further, rehabilitation-oriented facilities developed elaborate classification systems centering around the placement of offenders into treatment programs. In the better correctional systems, systematic program planning was done by **classification committees.** Through the mid-1970s most classification in the United States was based on subjective judgments by correctional practitioners, with experience, intuition, and "clinical" skills being the basis of these decisions. The general lack of documentation and accountability of these systems led to many inappropriate inmate program and housing assignments, inconsistency regarding offenders in similar situations, high levels of **overclassification**—placement of inmates under more supervision (custody) and control (security) than required—and inefficient use of facilities (Solomon and Camp, 1993).[a] These subjective systems suffer from several additional problems: their constitutionality (the misclassification of inmates might place them at risk for potential injury); arbitrariness, inconsistency, and validity. It is impossible to test the validity of subjective systems (Austin, 1993).

Enthusiasm for rehabilitation declined in the early 1970s because prisons were not succeeding in their attempts to rehabilitate criminals. Also, rising crime rates and violence resulted in public disillusionment with the effort. Many states passed legislation that increased the number of offenders sent to prison and the length of their sentences. Growing populations strained existing facilities, many of which were outdated and designed to warehouse offenders. These overcrowded and increasingly dangerous institutions were subjected to court scrutiny that often found them violating constitutional standards of confinement. This combination of pressures required correctional systems to plan new facilities and to make more efficient use of existing ones so inmates, staff, and the public could be better protected. **Classification** was recognized by both prison administrators and the courts as a major tool for making decisions about facility planning, managing violence and overcrowding, and making institutions constitutionally acceptable (Solomon and Camp, 1993; Correctional Services Group, 1985; NIC, 1981a; Austin, 1994). The recognition by the courts of the importance of classification is best expressed in *Palmigiano v. Garrahy,* (1977):

> Classification is essential to the operation of an orderly and safe prison. It is a prerequisite for rational allocation of whatever program opportunities exist within the institution. It enables the institution to gauge the proper custody level of an inmate, to identify the inmate's educational, vocational, and psychological needs, and to separate nonviolent inmates from the more predatory. . . . Classification is also indispensable for any coherent future planning.

### Modern Classification Systems Analyze and Organize the Diverse Inmate Population

> Prison classification is the sorting out procedure that results in matching a prisoner to the appropriate level of supervision [custody], institution [security], programs, and services to meet his/her needs, and periodically reviews the inmate's placement to achieve the most appropriate assignments possible (NIC, 1981a, p. 2).

On any given day about 1.5 million people are incarcerated in our prisons and jails. These people come from all sectors of society and represent a broad spectrum of educational, social, and economic levels. They range from the scholarly to the illiterate, the unskilled worker to the professional, the psychotic to the well adjusted, the minor offender to the career criminal, nonviolent property offenders to serial murderers, and from prison-wise offenders with extensive involvement in the criminal or prison subcultures to "naive" first offenders. Classification is the primary mechanism for categorizing and ordering this diverse inmate population so that inmates can be dealt with efficiently. Jails and prisons transform citizens into inmates through the classification process. This process assesses their risks and needs and enables them to be assigned to appropriate institutions, housing units, and programs (Brennan, 1987, 1993; NIC, 1981a).

**OBJECTIVE SYSTEMS BEGAN TO BE DEVELOPED IN THE 1970s**  **Objective classification systems** began to appear in the late 1970s. These systems employ an evaluation instrument containing explicit criteria that can be uniformly applied to all offenders to make decisions. This system should:

**1.** Contain instruments that have been validated for prison populations.
**2.** Be equally applicable and usable for all offenders.
**3.** Base decisions on factors related to the placements that are made.
**4.** Make security assignments based on offender backgrounds.
**5.** Be reliable.
**6.** Involve inmates.
**7.** Be easily understood.
**8.** Have systematic and efficient monitoring (follow-up) capabilities. (Solomon and Camp, 1993)

Moreover, from a management perspective, a classification system found to be acceptable and useful by administrators and which is based on a system's resources can be a significant factor in helping that system achieve its correctional objectives (Burke and Adams, 1991).

**CLASSIFICATION PROTECTS INMATES FROM EACH OTHER**  A safe environment is a high-priority objective for both jails and prisons (Brennan, 1987, 1993; Austin, 1994). Although effective classification cannot totally eliminate prison violence, it can influence the factors that aggravate it, which include failure to separate predators from victims, placement of severely disturbed inmates in the general population, and failure to separate rival gang members. Screening for special risk offenders (e.g., those with suicidal tendencies, the aged, substance abusers) identifies inmates who require special monitoring, treatment, or program assignments (Austin, 1994).[c] In using this knowledge, prisons can become constitutionally acceptable by giving inmates reasonable protection from assault, and services for medical, substance abuse, and psychiatric problems.

**CLASSIFICATION PROTECTS THE PUBLIC** Classification also helps to protect the public from high-risk offenders (Solomon and Camp, 1993). This requires valid methods of determining levels of dangerousness. When coupled with appropriate assignments relating to security, custody, and release recommendations, it can reduce the probability of escape, erroneous community placement, and serious crimes against the public. Decisions that release high-risk offenders into the community can generate adverse media attention, public outrage, strong criticism of the prison system, and possibly adverse political consequences. This was exemplified in the case of Willie Horton, discussed earlier. Incidents like this, in which **underclassified** (placement of inmates under lower levels of supervision and control than required), high-risk offenders commit violent crimes, jeopardize community correctional programs and result in undue restrictions on many deserving inmates.

The prediction of dangerousness is not an exact science, and its use is very controversial. A review of studies on the accuracy of prediction in corrections and human behavior concludes that the value of "prediction of unusual human behavior such as serious crime is limited" (Clear, 1988 , p. 9). Nevertheless, in a prison setting, staff must make determinations of an inmate's "public risk"—the potential that he/she will commit a crime, particularly a violent one, upon escape or release. Typically, past violent behavior figures prominently in assessing an inmate's risk potential, which is used to make decisions about institutional placement, release, etc.

When a decision regarding the risk posed by an inmate is made, it can be either right or wrong. If the decision is to declare the inmate too much of a risk for release or reduction in custody, he or she will remain within the present status. Under this condition it will be impossible to know if the right or wrong decision was made because the error is

invisible and the inmate's behavior will not be "tested" under the appropriate conditions (she will not be in the community). Only if the inmate is released or given a reduction in custody and/or security level can we know if an error was made—*if* he or she victimizes someone after release or reduction in custody/security. This type of mistake is very visible and can have severe consequences for the corrections system. When correctional practitioners are concerned about this latter type of error, they generally require high cut-off scores on risk assessment scales that assure that a high proportion of offenders are placed in the high-risk category. This reduces the potential visible errors, that is, escapes and subsequent offenses by releasees, but drastically increases the invisible ones; that is, many inmates may be overclassified and kept in expensive higher security facilities. These inmates may resort to violent behavior to protect themselves or be victimized in their overplaced situation. Thus, this system suffers because expensive space is being misused and there may be control problems.

As we increase our use of sophisticated management information systems, Brennan (1993)[b] asserts there will be "a quantum leap in predictive accuracy." Yet, even these new tools should still be advisory according to Brennan because: "The human judge must always have an override capacity to introduce the intuitive, holistic, integrative role and take into account any extraneous issues" (p. 66).

**CLASSIFICATION INCREASES THE EFFICIENT USE OF PRISON RESOURCES** The growth of prison populations has strained corrections, requiring more efficient distribution of resources. Effective classification can maximize efficiency and provide inmates with the most impartial, consistent, and equitable placements.

New classification systems use criteria that determine inmates' custody needs and place them at appropriate levels. Their goal, including those currently in use in Minnesota, Tennessee, New York, and other states, is the elimination of overclassification (NIC, 1981a). A review of studies by NIC (1981a) of older classification systems revealed that many systems held 40 to 50% of their inmates in maximum custody. However, when objective criteria on the danger posed by these inmates were used, only 8 to 15% of them were found to require this placement. This type of overclassification can cause a shortage of expensive high security or custody placements for inmates who require them. Valid placements are the primary means of protecting inmates and staff from violent assaults and reducing the anxiety caused by unanticipated victimizations. This allows for the development of a more orderly, predictable, cost effective, and controlled prison environment (Brennan, 1987).

**CLASSIFICATION IS USED FOR INMATE CONTROL** Classification assists in several social control functions. Specifically, it is linked to the control of inmate behavior since it can be used to reward or punish. Inmates who frequently break prison rules can be reclassified to a custody status with fewer privileges and job opportunities. Those with a good record can be rewarded by placement in an honor unit or in a community program. Appropriate security and custody assignments can also help to reduce fear, violence, escapes, abuse, and litigation (Austin, 1994; Solomon and Camp, 1993).

**CLASSIFICATION IS A SOURCE OF PLANNING INFORMATION** Objective classification systems are invaluable for coherent planning regarding budgets, the types of institutions that need to be built, staffing, programs, and services. Growing prison populations have forced most states to make decisions about construction of new facilities. Formerly, planning was often based only on projected trends of prison population increases. However, objective classification systems can provide more accurate information on the characteristics of the prison population, which can be used to make projections regarding security, custody, staffing needs for new institutions, and the expansion of existing prisons (Austin, 1994). They also help assess medical, mental, substance abuse, and educational program and service needs. For example, the number of sex offenders, older offenders, and long-term offenders seems to be increasing. This type of information can assist correctional systems in planning for the special needs of these inmates (see Chapters 11 and 19) (Solomon and Camp, 1993). This avoids errors made by planners in the past who overestimated the need for expensive maximum security cells while underestimating the need for less expensive minimum security ones (Brennan, 1987). It can also assist systems in avoiding unnecessary litigation (Austin, 1994). Classification is not a panacea for all

institutional problems, but it can satisfy various needs of corrections systems, inmates, staff, courts, and the public.

## ELEMENTS OF THE CLASSIFICATION PROCESS

Classification can be divided into two phases: (1) initial determinations regarding the level of security and custody needed and program recommendations; and (2) periodic reclassification. Both phases require that appropriate scales be used to measure inmates' need.

### Distinctions between Security and Custody Are Not Always Clear

Many states and the federal government currently employ objective classification systems but may not use standardized designations for **security** and **custody levels** in their facilities. Some even fail to distinguish between these two concepts. For example, the federal institutions at Alderson, West Virginia, and El Reno, Oklahoma, were formerly labeled reformatories. However, Alderson was a minimum security facility for women, and El Reno was a youthful offender institution with a perimeter security including a double fence and towers with armed guards. Conversely, two facilities can have identical architectural plans and the same security levels, yet be given different names, for example, the Federal Correctional Institution at Lompoc, California, and the U.S. Penitentiary in Terre Haute, Indiana. A review of the ACA directory found that adults and juveniles in the fifty states, the federal system, and the District of Columbia are sent to twenty-nine "different" places of confinement (Levinson and Gerard, 1986). Failure to distinguish between security features and labels can be confusing within a given correctional system, can adversely affect the ability to use a sophisticated classification system, and can result in serious management problems and wasted resources (Levinson and Gerard, 1986).

To solve these problems and eliminate confusion, the ACA and the National Institute of Corrections recommend that all jurisdictions make a distinction between custody and security and develop uniform criteria distinguishing between levels. ACA has provided the following two core definitions for these concepts:[1]

*Facility Security Level:* The nature and number of physical design barriers available to prevent escape and control inmate behavior.

*Inmate Custody Category:* The degree of staff supervision necessary to ensure adequate control of the inmate (NIC, 1987).

The central concern of security is the danger posed by inmates to the community if they escape. The major focus of custody is the danger inmates pose to staff and other inmates. Although inmates who pose a substantial threat to the community may appear to represent a danger to the prison community, this is not necessarily the case (Correctional Services Group, 1985). There can be a difference between an inmate's street behavior and his or her institutional behavior. Many systems (e.g., California) recognize this distinction and make two independent classification determinations. They first assign inmates, based on the risk to the community, to a facility with the appropriate security constraints and then determine the required level of supervision in this facility. This conserves valuable supervisory resources.

So that some differences between custody and security levels can be clarified, we summarize the designations used by ACA and NIC, recognizing that not all jurisdictions use five distinct categories of security and custody. To distinguish clearly between these categories ACA uses numerical levels to designate facility security levels [i.e., I (low) to V (high)] and titles to label custody levels.

## Security Focuses on Protecting Society from Inmates

Distinctions between security levels rest on six criteria: (1) physical barriers that surround the facility perimeter; (2) presence of gun towers with armed guards; (3) mobile patrols; (4) detection devices (e.g., TV cameras, high-mask lighting, electronic sensing devices in the ground or on fences); (5) type of housing; and (6) internal architecture/ security (e.g., sally ports, secure glazing materials, electronic steel doors, physical barriers between staff and inmates). These dimensions describe the constraints separating inmates from the community and reducing the likelihood of escape.

**MAXIMUM SECURITY RESTRICTS INMATE ACTIVITY AND CLOSELY CONTROLS THEM** Level V is most secure and represents an end-of-the-line facility, meaning that its inmates need to be separated

In super-maximum and maximum-security prisons, inmates spend most of their time locked in their cells. This shows a cell block in the Super-Max Federal Prison at Marion, Illinois.

from the general prison population. Inmates here require secure housing in the most secure perimeter, and separate management for activities such as work, exercise, and food service. Thus, inmates assigned to a work area need strict supervision and should pass through metal detectors before exiting work areas. These facilities should be small, with inmate populations under 500; however, older facilities are often larger.

Inmate Housing is normally in single, inside cells (as was common in Auburn-type prisons). If inmates escape from their cells, they are still confined within the cell house. The cells generally have heavy-duty hardware (e.g., secure doors and windows, tamper-proof locks). Frequent searches for contraband and weapons are required. These

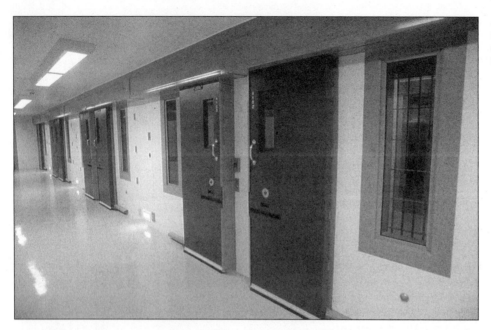

An interior view of the new super maximum federal prison at Florence, Colorado.

An aerial view of the Florence, Colorado federal super-max prison and the surrounding complex, which includes a medium security prison, a special purpose administrative facility, and a minimum security camp. A multi-prison complex like this allows the various units to share services, which makes them more cost effective. For example, one unit may prepare all of the food for the entire complex, which eliminates the need for kitchens in each of the facilities.

facilities have secure perimeters, which in newer facilities usually consist of double fences with razor wire and strategically placed towers. Older fortress-type facilities have high thick walls with gun towers. Both may have electronic detection devices. Perimeter security is maintained 24 hours a day by armed correctional officers (COs) in towers and/or external mobile patrols. Other security precautions include metal detectors for persons entering the institution, sally ports for vehicles entering and exiting the prison where they can be thoroughly searched, and high-mark lighting. Ideally, COs assigned to these prisons are specially trained to manage and meet the needs of this population (NIC, 1987). Our Close-Up on "Marion, A Super-Maximum Security Facility" (see pages 367-368) describes a

A minimum security federal prison. Note the lack of a high fence and the openness of the institution.

prison that is one security level above a standard maximum security prison. These super-maxis exist in twenty-five states (and are planned in six others) and are designed for a system's most predatory inmates (Clines, 1994).

**CLOSE SECURITY FACILITIES HOUSE INMATES WITH DIFFERENT CUSTODY DESIGNATIONS** Inmates sent to Level IV facilities require extensive security so perimeter security is the same as for Level V. Although housing may be in single cells, outside cells can be used, and the hardware may not be as secure as that used in Level V facilities.

When inmates are not in their cells, they are normally under direct supervision in the prison, but when taken outside the facility they are under full restraint (i.e., cuffs and leg irons) and accompanied by an armed escort. From a security standpoint, there are few differences between maximum and close security facilities. The primary distinctions are that close security facilities usually have inmates of different custody categories, more inmate programming, and may have larger populations (NIC, 1987).

**MEDIUM SECURITY PRISONS PROVIDE A WIDE VARIETY OF PROGRAMS** Level III facilities usually have external perimeter security that is similar to Levels IV and V. Housing may be in single cells, rooms, or dormitories. These prisons are distinctive from the preceding two levels because they provide a wider variety of programs and activities, depending on an inmate's custody status, and allow greater freedom of movement within the facility.

**LEVEL II MINIMUM SECURITY PRISONS ARE OPEN INSTITUTIONS** The hallmark of these facilities is their open design with perimeters consisting of a single fence or clearly designated unarmed "posts." They have no detection devices, although they may use intermittent external mobile patrols. Housing is in open units and varies from dormitory style to single- or multiple-occupancy rooms. These prisons typically place heavy emphasis on programs and activities.

**LEVEL I COMMUNITY SECURITY FACILITIES ARE OPEN PROGRAMS** Community-based facilities include a variety of institutions: prerelease centers (such as work release or educational release), halfway houses, private residences and special programs such as drug treatment, and other nonsecure settings appropriate to the needs of inmates at this level. They all have open housing units that may include single- and/or multiple-occupancy rooms or dormitory-style living. These facilities are discussed in more detail in Chapter 24, which deals with community correctional programs.

## Custody Deals with Levels of Supervision

The second major consideration in classification is an inmate's custody requirements. The concern here is the risk the inmate poses to staff and other inmates, which establishes the degree of supervision and restrictions placed on his or her key activities. ACA and NIC identify five levels of supervision. It is important to remember that most institutions, especially those at levels III and IV, can house inmates assigned to different custody levels (NIC, 1987).

**MAXIMUM CUSTODY INMATES ARE CLOSELY SUPERVISED AND HAVE LIMITED FREEDOM AND MOVEMENT** Inmates assigned this status pose the most serious threats to other inmates or staff and/or may be high escape risks who dictate direct supervision. Inmates may be temporarily placed in this status or receive a special custody assignment when they are awaiting a disciplinary or criminal offense hearing for a serious offense, are in immediate physical danger, are awaiting transfer to another facility, or have just arrived at a facility and require a period of observation.

These inmates are confined in single cells and only removed for authorized activities to which they are escorted by at least one staff member. When they leave the prison, they are escorted by two armed COs and placed in full physical restraints (handcuffs, leg irons, and waist chains). Supervision requirements entail the following restrictions: (1) involvement only in programs conducted in their cells, cell blocks, or in secure adjacent areas; (2) eating of meals in their cells; and (3) noncontact visits only.

**CLOSE CUSTODY INMATES CAN PARTICIPATE IN PROGRAMS UNDER SUPERVISION** This custody status is reserved for inmates with past assaultive and/or escape histories. They require constant supervision and full restraints when leaving the facility. During the day these inmates are permitted to leave their cells and go to other parts of the institution on a check-out/check-in basis under staff observation. At night, they can only move with the approval of the watch commander and under escort. They have limited access to selected day jobs, programs, and activities inside the facili-

ty's perimeter and are permitted noncontact visits. Meal arrangements vary by prison and include eating in cells (or cell blocks) or being escorted to a dining area and directly supervised.

**MEDIUM CUSTODY INMATES CAN PARTICIPATE IN INSTITUTIONAL PROGRAMS AND DO NOT REQUIRE DIRECT SUPERVISION** Inmates assigned to this status can move in the institution during the day within sight of a CO. They are eligible for all programs and activities within the main perimeter. When in program and activity areas they are under frequent supervision and direct observation. At night their movement is regulated by a check-out/check-in system. Indoor contact visits are permitted under staff supervision. When leaving the facility they are handcuffed and accompanied by a correctional officer.

**MINIMUM CUSTODY INMATES CAN MOVE ABOUT THE INSTITUTION UNSUPERVISED** This category is for inmates not posing risks associated with higher custody levels but who cannot be placed in community custody for various reasons, such as being psychologically unprepared for community release or community resistance to certain categories of violent offenders. For example, some murderers are one-time offenders whose violence was situational and pose little or no community threat. However, the label murderer frightens people, and placement of these individuals in community programs is opposed. During the day, these inmates can move about the facility without being directly within the view of staff. They are eligible for all inside jobs and supervised assignments outside the prison's perimeter. They also have access to all inside and selected community-based programs and activities. Their contact visits can be indoors or outside as long as they are supervised, and they are eligible for escorted furloughs.

**COMMUNITY CUSTODY INMATES ARE ALLOWED TO BE UNSUPERVISED IN COMMUNITY FACILITIES** Inmates given this classification pose the least danger to staff, inmates, and the community. While at the facility they may require intermittent supervision under certain circumstances. They are eligible for daily unescorted participation in outside jobs and programs and are permitted unescorted furloughs. Their contact visits can take place indoors or outdoors under periodic supervision.

# Close Up  Marion, A Federal Super-Maximum Security Facility

Marion was the first of the modern super-max facilities in the United States. The main facility has an average population of 350 male inmates,[2] all of whom exhibit extreme antisocial behavior (50% have murder and 79% assault records), are serious escape risks (36% have escaped or attempted it), or have lengthy, complex sentences. In 1978, prompted by the need to deal with the most violent and disruptive inmates, the federal system decided to "concentrate" these inmates in one place and to designate this a Level VI (most secure) facility. Marion was chosen because it was more suitable for high-security operations than other federal prisons. All federal inmates unable to adapt to other prisons were transferred there for disciplinary reasons, as were some from various state systems.

Initially, the prison operated as a standard maximum security facility. However, by 1983 increasing violence (e.g., inmate murders and assaults and the murder of 2 COs) and other incidents (e.g., work stoppages and prison take-over attempts) brought about the initiation of a regimen that rigidly controlled inmates (Holt and Phillips, 1991).

Marion is a self-contained complex of reinforced concrete buildings surrounded by a double reinforced fence, overseen by eight armed towers, electronic detection devices, and perimeter patrols (Holt and Phillips, 1991). The facility is organized into nine units: three general population units, two transfer units, a protective custody unit, a disciplinary unit, a special housing unit, and a control unit. Seven of the units contain sixty-eight cells divided into four cell houses of seventeen cells. The special unit houses seven inmates and the control unit houses fifty-eight.

Marion has a stratified housing system to give inmates an incentive to conform to the high-security program. Newly admitted inmates are placed in one of three general population units. Their daily routine includes an average of two hours per day out of their cells (Millard, 1988). They can make phone calls, receive mail, and are permitted noncontact visits. Each inmate has a TV mainly used as a closed-circuit system providing religious, educational, and self-improvement programs.

This progressive program allows inmates to work themselves out of the institution by demonstrating nondangerous, responsible behavior through compliance with prison rules. After a year in a general population unit with no infractions they can be trans-

ferred to the intermediate pretransfer unit. Six months of good behavior in this unit can lead to a transfer to the pretransfer unit. After another infraction-free six months they are eligible for transfer to a less highly controlled institution. All transfers are at the discretion of the administration of the prison. The pretransfer units are less restrictive, giving inmates opportunities to show they can behave more responsibly with fewer restrictions. On the intermediate unit inmates are trained for work in UNICOR prison industries, have increased out-of-cell time, and eat together on the unit. On the pretransfer unit inmates either work a daily seven-hour schedule at the UNICOR plant, are employed as barbers, or serve as unit orderlies. They eat in the prison's dining hall and are allowed out of their cells during the day.

Most inmates eventually conform to the behavioral requirements of this program and are transferred out. The average length of stay in the prison is 35.6 months. Of the 378 inmates released since 1983 only 55 had returned as of 1990 (Holt and Phillips, 1991).

There are four confinement units at Marion. The administrative/disciplinary confinement unit and the protective custody (PC) unit normally hold inmates for short periods either for disciplinary purposes, while on holdover status, or for protective purposes. Inmates held for disciplinary purposes are denied certain privileges available to the general population. For example, all those under administrative confinement have radios but are denied TVs, while those in disciplinary segregation have neither.

The control unit is reserved for the most dangerous, assaultive inmates at Marion. Inmates are placed here, for a given period of time, only after they have displayed an inability to control their behavior. The unit classification committee imposes this punishment after a full due process hearing and on the approval of an executive review board panel. This panel interviews these inmates monthly and approves all transfers from this unit. While these inmates have access to the same programs as those in the general population, their recreation is limited to seven hours per week and all showers and other activities are done in isolation.

The special PC unit provides high security for inmates requiring special protection. Most of these inmates have committed high-profile offenses that had extensive media coverage (e.g., spies) and are likely to be at special risk. They are always separated from the

## Close Up, *continued*

rest of the population. Placement in and removal from this unit requires the approval of the director of the Bureau of Prisons (BOP). Conditions on this unit are less restrictive than in the control unit (e.g., inmates have the same amount of recreation time as those in the general population).

Conditions at Marion have been challenged by inmate suits alleging "cruel and unusual punishment" (e.g., *Bruscino vs. Carlson,* 1988; *Hewitt v. Helms,* 1983), but the institution's policies have been upheld by the courts. The high-security system has reduced the level of violence. In the 43 months before implementing the high security operation, six inmates and two COs were killed in the prison. In the 43 months after its implementation three inmates were killed (Karacki, 1987).

Holt and Phillips (1991) note that Marion is not ideal for its high-security mission because it was not originally designed to handle highly dangerous inmates. However, they indicate a facility designed for this purpose would offer the following advantages:

**1.** Day-to-day activities would be more readily available to inmates; proper design would allow easy, safe movement from program to program without cumbersome handcuffing procedures.
**2.** The amount of direct physical access necessary to manage potentially disruptive inmates can be reduced, making life and work safer for inmates and staff.
**3.** Safe staff contact with inmates would increase the ability of employees to interact effectively with inmates and create a more normal atmosphere.
**4.** In a well-designed facility, inmates themselves feel safe and, therefore, respond to staff more normally (p. 36).

The new facility built at Florence, Colorado, to replace Marion opened in 1994 and incorporated these features. This is a 416-bed facility divided into nine units similar to those at Marion. As at Marion, inmates are sent to Florence for being uncontrollably violent or having committed a high-profile/notorious offense. It was designed to provide the highest level of security for the inmate population in the federal system. Inmates can work their way out of Florence and into less stringent facilities after a minimum of three years by modifying their violent behavior. Support services include administration, visitation, health services and education, religious, and recreational programs. The facility is relatively compact with approximately 428,250 square feet of building, which sits on a developed area of about 37 acres on the high plains desert in Colorado. It is situated on the downward face of a slope, which affords enhanced views into the facility from the perimeter road and towers (Patrick, 1994). Once Florence is fully operational, Marion will be used to house inmates who have demonstrated an inability to adjust satisfactorily to other secure BOP facilities. Security and control will be greater than at other BOP high security level facilities but less than the strict controls being employed at Florence (King, 1995).

Following the lead of the Federal Bureau of Prisons, several states have built or converted facilities (or are in the process of doing so) to handle their most dangerous inmates. These jurisdictions justify the operation of super-max facilities because staff and inmates in other facilities are safer by having these inmates removed. As with Florence, inmates can, by conforming to prison rules, work their way out of these facilities too (Clines, 1994).

## There Are Several Issues Related to Minimum Security Facilities

There are several problems associated with the operation of community-level minimum security facilities. The openness of these facilities raises questions about their use for long-term inmates and their location in the community. Another problem surrounding placement of inmates at these facilities is their limited programming.

**CAN MINIMUM SECURITY FACILITIES ACCOMODATE LONG-TERM INMATES?** The advent of objective classification systems made more inmates eligible for placement in minimum security or community-based facilities. Placement is often based on the absence of a recent history of violence and/or prior or attempted escapes. Consequently, many inmates convicted of serious offenses become eligible for minimum security placement several years before they are eligible for release. This situation raises several questions.

First, can minimum and community security facilities provide adequate programming for long-term inmates? Most minimum and community security facilities have limited programming, which largely consists of work and study release. Although these facilities seem ideal for long-term, low-risk inmates, this placement can pose serious problems. They have little supervision during the day and may even be allowed day or weekend home visits. The temptations (e.g., drugs, peer pressure) during these periods may be overwhelming for some inmates. The danger is that if inmates are caught engaging in prohibited behavior they may hurt someone or abscond.

NIC (1981a) recommends having two types of minimum security facilities as a solution. Type I facilities would serve inmates who have a short period before release. Their major focus would be on facilitating reintegration into the community. Thus, they would have little or no programming but instead use community programs and services. Type II minimum security facilities would be designated for inmates who pose no security risk and are scheduled for release or parole within 18 months or less. They would provide extensive on-site programming and could be placed next to medium security facilities to share medical, psychological, and other services. Program emphasis would be on developing a good self-concept, confidence, and skills facilitating successful adjustment in the community. To reduce temptation, inmates would be allowed outside the facility only for short periods under supervision. A good work program would also make these facilities appropriate for long-term inmates who pose a minimum risk to the community. This would make room in the more secure facilities for inmates who pose greater risks.

**MINIMUM SECURITY FACILITIES MUST DEAL WITH COMMUNITY OPPOSITION**  A second issue involves how state correctional systems respond to community opposition to having inmates "in their midst." Most often communities resist facilities that house violent, sex, and drug offenders, but there is generally resistance to all types of inmates. Even though newer classification systems provide behavioral criteria for the risk posed by these offenders, this may not allay community fears. As NIC (1981a) notes, the role that community pressures should play in assigning inmates to programs is highly controversial, with no clear guidelines. Cor-

rections must be responsive to community concerns because failure to do so can result in programs being canceled. One solution to this problem is for administrators of minimum and community-based facilities to conduct public relations activities to educate the community about the facility and its programs. People are not as likely to be afraid when they understand the type of inmates housed in these facilities and the nature of their programs.

**CAN MINIMUM SECURITY FACILITIES PROVIDE ADEQUATE PROGRAMS?**  A third question centers on the limited availability of programs and services at minimum security facilities. This is a problem when classification review determines an inmate is eligible for transfer to a minimum security facility that does not have programs or services the inmate needs. Objective classification systems cannot resolve this type of issue. This decision requires that the classification committee determine, in consultation with the inmate, the course of action that would best benefit the inmate in terms of being successful upon release.

### Segregation of Some Inmates Helps Protect Them and Others

Prisons use several forms of segregation, in which classification plays a part, to deal with certain categories of inmates. Administrative segregation (AS) is a form of separation from the general population sometimes imposed by classification committees for inmates who pose serious threats to themselves, staff, or other inmates or to institutional security; are pending investigation for serious rule violations; or are pending transfer. Disciplinary detention (DD) involves separation of inmates who have been found guilty of serious rule violations and are often punished by being segregated in special secure units for limited periods of time. They are typically housed in single cells or rooms and receive basic necessities and services such as food, clothing, showers, medical care, visitation by the prison chaplain, and are allowed limited exercise, reading materials, and mail. However, they may be deprived of visitation privileges, participation in work and education programs, other privileged activities (e.g., TV), and personal items that might be fashioned into weapons (ACA, 1990b).

Protective custody (PC) did not become a discernable correctional format until the 1960s and now contains about 6% of the population in the thirty-seven states with PC units (Henderson and Phillips, 1990). PC involves the segregation of a variety of inmates who are in serious danger of being harmed for reasons that include their offense (e.g., child molestation), gambling debts, sexual orientation, being identified as a snitch, notorious but naive criminals, and vendettas of various sorts. While conditions of confinement for PC and AS inmates are usually more restrictive than for the general population, more programs and services have become available for them during the 1980s and 1990s.

The role of classification in PC is threefold. First, a good classification system can help reduce the conditions that spawn the need for PC. This can be accomplished by "preventing an unmanageable combination of weak and strong, sophisticated and unsophisticated, old and young inmates from coming into contact with each other" (Henderson and Phillips, 1990, pp. 21–22). In fact, good classification has resulted in a lowering of the proportion of PC inmates during the 1980s and into the 1990s.

Second, the classification process can identify verified and unverified PC cases. In verified cases, the victim's attacker and/or source of threat can be identified and the need for protection established. Verified cases receive top priority for PC program resources. Protection can be for either the short or long term depending on the nature of the threat. Unverified PC cases involve inmates who refuse to disclose the source of the alleged threat. They may do this to manipulate the system (e.g., get a transfer to another institution) or to get at a PC inmate whom they may want to harm. Thus, proper screening is very important.

A third classification function involves the continuing evaluation of these inmates both in terms of their confinement status and for participation in programs. For inmates in protective custody, and even for those in administrative segregation and on death row, the courts have required reasonable levels of programs and services, in some cases comparable to those available to the general population (Johnson, 1990; NIC, 1981a). In fact, ACA (1990b) standards stipulate that inmates in PC and administrative segregation should have access to programming and activities that include library, educational, religious guidance, social, and recreational services. Our Close-Up on "Conditions of Confinement" describes a case dealing with this problem.

Litigation has also changed confinement conditions for Death Row inmates. The most far reaching suit occurred in Texas in 1986. It initiated a program whereby Death Row inmates were divided into two groups. Those deemed work-capable (about 60%) were to be furnished with "a reasonably balanced range of recreation, work, and other out-of-cell activity" (Johnson, 1990, p. 41). They were employed in a garment factory adjacent to their housing unit. Those judged to be Death-Row-segregation (about 40%), were allowed three hours daily on weekdays for out-of-cell activity and were furnished with educational and religious programming in their cells (Johnson, 1990). Responding to calls that all inmates should have to work, Alabama recently put 12 work-capable Death Row inmates to work in the Holman Prison metal fabricating plant (CIA Newsletter, 1994).

### Needs Assessment Determines an Inmate's Program and Service Requirements

Assessment for program planning was recognized as important after World War II during the rehabilitation era. The role of needs assessment is to determine inmate strengths and weaknesses so that he or she can be placed in the most advantageous programs.

**DETERMINING INMATE NEEDS LEADS TO PROPER PROGRAM PLACEMENT** Assessment of an inmate's program and service requirements is the third facet of the classification process. The needs of inmates are almost as diverse as those of the free-world population. This has led to confusion regarding the most effective programs for inmate populations. When coupled with traditionally meager correctional budgets, this has curtailed programming dealing with inmate problems or providing them marketable skills (NIC, 1981a). Currently, this problem has been further aggravated by an increasing prison population, which is straining resources and placing major emphasis on simply providing bed space.

The American Bar Association and the ACA have created standards that call for effective screening and reasonable programming covering areas ranging from education and training to health services to work assignments (NIC, 1981a; ACA, 1990b). Pressure to provide programming has also been heightened by litigation that has required systems (or put them on notice) to pro-

# Close Up   Conditions of PC Confinement

[In] *Williams v. Lane* [(1989), an appeals court] strongly affirmed correctional administrators' responsibility to provide substantially equivalent programs in many areas to inmates in protective custody . . . the court held that restrictions placed on the opportunity of protective custody inmates to attend religious services, use the law library, and participate in vocational, educational, and recreational programs were unreasonable. . . . The appeals court [also] affirmed the general principles of equal access to truly equivalent programs [for PC inmates].

**Williams provides an interesting indication of the direction in which protective custody programs may be headed, and of solutions that may be worthy of consideration by other agencies. . . . [T]he parties in that case developed a two-tiered system of PC . . . which . . . provid[es] access to equivalent programs for [legitimate] . . . long-term PC [inmates] . . . without creating a system that is unduly attractive to spurious cases.**

In the system devised as a remedy in this case, an inmate requesting PC placement is held for 30 days in what may be characterized as the "brief" PC program, pending evaluation of the actual protective needs the case presents. During that 30-day period, the inmate is held in relatively spartan circumstances and is provided only basic services and privileges, generally comparable to those offered any inmate in administrative segregation. An inmate whose claimed need for protection cannot be verified is returned to the general population. If that individual makes subsequent requests for protection, another 30-day evaluation period commences each time. By not making a full panoply of PC programs available during this evaluation period, there is less motivation for inmates to seek this status without true need.

In each case of an inmate seeking protection, staff first consider other available methods for problem resolution, such as transfer to another housing unit or to another facility. Reliance on these alternate solutions is the first and best course of action, in order to continue to provide the inmate with typical access to a general population.

The second tier, or "full" program status, is entered only when it is clear that a verified protection case cannot be re-introduced into a general population setting. In these cases, the strategy is to offer a full range of programs and services comparable to those offered in the general population. This is done through a wide range of program offerings that are comparable [in quality, although they may be customized as to form, location, or times offered. This program is used only when it is clear that long-term PC status is the only viable option for a given offender.]

As a final note on conditions of confinement, there have been a number of cases in which PC inmates have challenged double-celling in a PC unit. The general principles to keep in mind are that as long as internal screening ensures reasonable precautions against housing together inmates who pose a potential threat to each other, and as long as reasonably equivalent access is provided to necessary programs, there is no constitutional right to a single cell in PC status.

In summary, there are clearly a number of potentially serious legal problems in the area of managing PC cases. Specific state laws and agency regulations will inevitably shape the individual application of the broad legal principles discussed above. Clearly defined, consistently implemented procedures that cover day-to-day facility management, the screening of prospective PC cases, and operation protections against liability [are necessary].

Source: J. Henderson. and R.L. Phillips. (November 1990) Protective custody management in adult correctional facilities, pp. 19–20. Washington, D.C.: National Institute of Corrections. Reproduced with permission.

vide certain programs and/or services to alleviate unconstitutional prison conditions (see Chapters 15 and 16).

State correctional systems have different procedures for screening and placing inmates. Many systems make distinctions between available programs and the security levels appropriate for placement in them. In some systems an inmate's cell block assignment may impose restrictions on program placement. In others the availability of programs is extremely limited. Programming is discussed in more detail in Chapters 18 through 21, but two points need to be made here. First, inmate idleness has been a key factor in institutional disturbances. Second, it is indisputable that most inmates lack marketable skills and have other problems and deficits contributing to their involvement in crime. Denying them an opportunity to remedy these problems while in prison and expecting them to "go straight" upon release is ludicrous.

**FINDING THE RIGHT PROGRAMS TO MEET INMATE NEEDS IS IMPORTANT** Appropriate placement of inmates should involve a balance between security, inmate needs, and program availability. One reason states consider inmate needs in their classification schemes is to avoid lawsuits. To settle these suits, states with few programs have often had to spend considerable money to develop even minimal programming. Systems and institutions should strive to achieve balance between the resources used for inmate programs and the inmates' legitimate needs. Determining an inmate's programming needs requires information from various sources including presentence or admission investigations, intake interviews, intelligence and achievement tests, psychological tests, and psychological/psychiatric evaluations of the psychologically disturbed.

## CLASSIFICATION MODELS

Over time an inmate's behavior, attitudes, interests, and desires may change. While they may enter prison with hostile attitudes and no desire to change, at some point they may decide to cease their criminal pursuits. If this occurs, they may want to take advantage of institutional programs that prepare them for a job on release. Long-term inmates may also decide to become involved in prison programs because they offer challenges, opportunities to earn income and/or privileges, and/or reduce the monotony of prison life. Periodic reclassification enables inmates to take advantage of a desire to change. Several court decisions (e.g., *Pugh v. Locke*, 1976) have held that reclassification is as important as initial classification in establishing a prison system's constitutional acceptability. Typically reclassification reviews take place every sixty days for those with sentences of five years or less; and for those with longer terms every three to six months. A national survey of state correctional systems, the federal system, and the District of Columbia found that thirty-nine of these jurisdictions employed objective classification systems (Buchanan and Whitlow, 1987; Buchanan, 1986).

Table 17.1 lists factors employed by most systems in making security and custody determinations. It is beyond the scope of this text to discuss all of the different classification systems currently employed. However, a brief examination of the two most often used objective systems—those devised by the National Institute of Corrections (adopted by twelve systems) and the Federal Bureau of Prisons (FBP) (adopted by nine) (Austin, 1993)—will provide a perspective on the operation of newer classification systems.

### The National Institute of Corrections Model Is a Management Tool

In 1982, the NIC developed a classification system that is distinctive in several respects.[3] It is based on the premise that classification is an important component of corrections management systems. It is comprehensive and incorporates elements such as custody, security, needs assessment, program monitoring and assessment, reclassification, and a management information system. Under this model, inmates are classified based on their custody needs and are then placed in institutions where the security rating is appropriate for their custody requirements. Inmates are placed in the least restrictive custody category necessary to protect society, staff, and other prisoners.

**INMATES ARE RATED ON PREDICTIVE VARIABLES** The NIC system uses two scales to classify inmates. An initial scale emphasizes **predictive variables** dealing with an inmate's past criminal and institutional history to effect an initial placement within the system. The second scale reclassifies by giving greater weight to present institutional behavior. Therefore, this model takes a "just deserts" approach to classification; i.e., past behavior affects initial placement, whereas subsequent changes relate to an inmate's disciplinary record. Those posing few problems are moved to lower custody levels, while those creating more problems remain at their present level or are moved to higher levels (Correctional Services Group, 1985).

The custody status of a new inmate is decided initially by an eight-item classification scale (see Figure 17.1). In the NIC model, only inmates with histories of violence are placed in close and maximum custody. Initially, a new inmate is first rated on four items:

Table 17.1 Comparison of Initial Classification Factors Employed by Major Objective Prison Classification Models

| Factor | NIC Model | FBP Model | Correctional Classification Profile | Illinois Model | Florida Model |
|---|---|---|---|---|---|
| Severity of current offense | X | X | | X | |
| Degree of violence in current offense | | | X | | X |
| Use of weapon in current offense | | | X | | |
| Nature of sexual offense | | | X | | |
| Current offense | | | | X | X |
| Type of sentence[a] | | | | | X |
| Length of sentence | | | X | | X |
| Expected length of incarceration | | X | | X | |
| Type of detainer | X | X | X | | |
| Severity of prior commitments | | X | | | |
| Number of prior commitments | | | X | | |
| Number of prior convictions | | | | X | |
| Number of prior felony convictions | X | | | | |
| Number of convictions for violence against person | | | | X | |
| Number of convictions for burglary/theft | | | | X | |

| Factor | NIC Model | FBP Model | Correctional Classification Profile | Illinois Model | Florida Model |
|---|---|---|---|---|---|
| History of Violence | X | X | X | | X |
| History of institutional violence | X | | | | |
| History of escape | X | X | X | X | X |
| History of prior supervision | | | X | X | |
| Institutional adjustment | | | | | X |
| Behavior characteristics during incarceration[b] | | | | | X |
| Demonstrated skills in escape/assault[c] | | | | | X |
| Pre-commitment status[d] | | X | | | |
| Psychotic | | | | | X |
| Substance abuse | X | | X | | |
| Age | X | | | X | |
| Education | X | | X | | |
| History of employment | X | | X | X | |
| Program/service needs | X | X | X | X | X |
| Other | | e | | f | |

[a] That is, death, life, or consecutive.
[b] Behavior observed during confinement in jail and/or reception center; e.g., suicidal, abusive, paranoid, manipulative.
[c] For example, firearms, explosives, martial arts, electronics.
[d] That is, own recognizance, voluntary surrender, not applicable.
[e] Includes types of sentence requiring a management designation (e.g., misdemeanor, narcotic addict, split sentence, psychiatric) and considerations such as medical health, mental health, aggressive sexual behavior, and involvement in disruptive group.
[f] Includes gang affiliation, protective custody, and underrated security designation score.

Source: R. A. Buchanan and K. L. Whitlow (1987), Guidelines for Developing, Implementing, and Revising an Objective Prison Classification System. Washington D.C.: U.S. Department of Justice, National Institute of Corrections.

## FIGURE 17.1  Initial Inmate Classification: Custody

NAME _____   NUMBER _____
      Last          First          MI

CLASSIFICATION CASEWORKER _____   DATE _____ / _____ / _____

**1. HISTORY OF INSTITUTIONAL VIOLENCE**    *score*
(Jail or prison, code most serious within last five years)
None. . . . . . . . . . . . . . . . . . . . . . . . . . . . . . . . . . . . . . . . . . . . . . . . . . . . . . . . . . . . . . . . . . . 0
Assault and battery not involving use of a weapon or resulting in serious injury . . . . . . . . . . . . . . . . 3
Assault and battery involving use of a weapon and/or resulting in serious injury or death . . . . . . . . . . 7

**2. SEVERITY OF CURRENT OFFENSE**    *score*
(Refer to the Severity of Offense Scale on back of form. Score the most serious offense if there are multiple convictions.)
Low . . . . . . . . . . . . . . . . . . . . . . . . . . . . . . . . . . . . . . . . . . . . . . . . . . . . . . . . . . . . . . . . . . . . 0
Low Moderate . . . . . . . . . . . . . . . . . . . . . . . . . . . . . . . . . . . . . . . . . . . . . . . . . . . . . . . . . . . . . 1
Moderate . . . . . . . . . . . . . . . . . . . . . . . . . . . . . . . . . . . . . . . . . . . . . . . . . . . . . . . . . . . . . . . . . 2
High . . . . . . . . . . . . . . . . . . . . . . . . . . . . . . . . . . . . . . . . . . . . . . . . . . . . . . . . . . . . . . . . . . . . . 4
Highest . . . . . . . . . . . . . . . . . . . . . . . . . . . . . . . . . . . . . . . . . . . . . . . . . . . . . . . . . . . . . . . . . . . 6

**3. PRIOR ASSAULTIVE OFFENSE HISTORY**    *score*
(Score the most severe in inmate's history. Refer to the Severity of Offense Scale on back of form.)
None, Low, or Low Moderate . . . . . . . . . . . . . . . . . . . . . . . . . . . . . . . . . . . . . . . . . . . . . . . . . . . . 0
Moderate . . . . . . . . . . . . . . . . . . . . . . . . . . . . . . . . . . . . . . . . . . . . . . . . . . . . . . . . . . . . . . . . . 2
High . . . . . . . . . . . . . . . . . . . . . . . . . . . . . . . . . . . . . . . . . . . . . . . . . . . . . . . . . . . . . . . . . . . . . 4
Highest . . . . . . . . . . . . . . . . . . . . . . . . . . . . . . . . . . . . . . . . . . . . . . . . . . . . . . . . . . . . . . . . . . . 6

**4. ESCAPE HISTORY** (Rate last 3 years of incarceration.)    *score*
No escapes or attempts (or no prior incarcerations) . . . . . . . . . . . . . . . . . . . . . . . . . . . . . . . . . . . . . 0
An escape or attempt from minimum or community custody, no actual or threatened violence:
  Over 1 year ago . . . . . . . . . . . . . . . . . . . . . . . . . . . . . . . . . . . . . . . . . . . . . . . . . . . . . . . . . . . . . 1
  Within the last year . . . . . . . . . . . . . . . . . . . . . . . . . . . . . . . . . . . . . . . . . . . . . . . . . . . . . . . . . . 3
An escape or attempt from medium or above custody, or an escape from minimum or community custody with actual or threatened violence:
  Over 1 year ago . . . . . . . . . . . . . . . . . . . . . . . . . . . . . . . . . . . . . . . . . . . . . . . . . . . . . . . . . . . . . 5
  Within the last year . . . . . . . . . . . . . . . . . . . . . . . . . . . . . . . . . . . . . . . . . . . . . . . . . . . . . . . . . . 7

**CLOSE CUSTODY SCORE** (Add items 1 through 4)
(if score is 10 or above inmate should be assigned to close custody. If score is under 10, complete items 5 through 6 and use medium/minimum scale)

**5. ALCOHOL/DRUG ABUSE**    *score*
None. . . . . . . . . . . . . . . . . . . . . . . . . . . . . . . . . . . . . . . . . . . . . . . . . . . . . . . . . . . . . . . . . . . . . . 0
Abuse causing occasional legal and social adjustment problems . . . . . . . . . . . . . . . . . . . . . . . . . . . . 1
Serious abuse, serious disruption of functioning . . . . . . . . . . . . . . . . . . . . . . . . . . . . . . . . . . . . . . . 3

**6. CURRENT DETAINER**    *score*
None. . . . . . . . . . . . . . . . . . . . . . . . . . . . . . . . . . . . . . . . . . . . . . . . . . . . . . . . . . . . . . . . . . . . . . 0
Misdemeanor detainer . . . . . . . . . . . . . . . . . . . . . . . . . . . . . . . . . . . . . . . . . . . . . . . . . . . . . . . . . 1
Extradition initiated—misdemeanor. . . . . . . . . . . . . . . . . . . . . . . . . . . . . . . . . . . . . . . . . . . . . . . . 3
Felony detainer. . . . . . . . . . . . . . . . . . . . . . . . . . . . . . . . . . . . . . . . . . . . . . . . . . . . . . . . . . . . . . . 4
Extradition initiated—felony . . . . . . . . . . . . . . . . . . . . . . . . . . . . . . . . . . . . . . . . . . . . . . . . . . . . . 6

**7. PRIOR FELONY CONVICTIONS**    *score*
None. . . . . . . . . . . . . . . . . . . . . . . . . . . . . . . . . . . . . . . . . . . . . . . . . . . . . . . . . . . . . . . . . . . . . . 0
One. . . . . . . . . . . . . . . . . . . . . . . . . . . . . . . . . . . . . . . . . . . . . . . . . . . . . . . . . . . . . . . . . . . . . . . 2
Two or more. . . . . . . . . . . . . . . . . . . . . . . . . . . . . . . . . . . . . . . . . . . . . . . . . . . . . . . . . . . . . . . . . 4

**8. STABILITY FACTORS**    *score*
(Check appropriate box(es) and combine for score.)
  Age 26 or over . . . . . . . . . . . . . . . . . . . . . . . . . . . . . . . . . . . . . . . . . . . . . . . . . . . . . . . . . . . . . . -2
  High school diploma or GED received . . . . . . . . . . . . . . . . . . . . . . . . . . . . . . . . . . . . . . . . . . . . . . -1
  Employed or attending school (full or part-time) for six months or longer at time of arrest . . . . . . . . . . . -1

**MINIMUM/MEDIUM SCORE** (Add items 1 through 8.)

                                                            TOTAL SCORE

MEDIUM/MINIMUM SCALE:
Medium Custody . . . . . . . . . . . . . . . . . . . . . . . . . . . . . . . .  7-22
Minimum Custody . . . . . . . . . . . . . . . . . . . . . . . . . . . . . . . .  6 or less

*Source:* National Institute of Corrections (1981a). *Prison classification: A model systems approach.* Washington, D.C.: Department of Justice.

1. *History of institutional violence:* for the five years prior to current admission.
2. *Severity of current offense:* most severe offense for which individual was sentenced—based on a scale that gives the highest ratings to offenses involving violence—in instances of multiple convictions.
3. *History of prior assaultive offenses:* an assaultive crime is any incident in which bodily harm occurred or was attempted, despite the degree of actual injury; an offense in which a weapon was present; or any offense so defined by state statute.
4. *Escape history:* only escapes and/or attempts occurring in the last three years of incarceration are counted.

With a score of 10 or greater, assignment to close custody is recommended. Those with 9 points or less are further evaluated on the following four items with the two scores totaled to decide their assignment to medium or minimum custody:

5. *Alcohol/drug-abuse problems:* individual is rated on whether drugs and/or alcohol were a factor in convictions, cessation of employment, or commitment to jail or treatment facilities in the past three years.
6. *Current detainer[4] :* these are scored based on how many detainers there are, whether they are for a felony or misdemeanor and whether an action for extradition has been initiated.
7. *Prior felony convictions:* all prior convictions are counted.
8. *Stability factors:* age 26 or over; high school diploma or GED; employment or attending school (full or part-time) for six months or longer at time of arrest.

NIC also has an initial needs assessment screening instrument that rates inmates in the following areas: educational needs, vocational needs, health needs, mental ability, psychiatric problems, alcohol abuse, and drug abuse (see Figure 17.2). The material gathered from this instrument may be used to initiate further study so that a comprehensive picture of the offender can be obtained.

**INMATES' MEDICAL NEEDS AND INTELLECTUAL LEVELS CAN AFFECT FACILITY PLACEMENT**
The NIC classification process requires appropriate examinations to learn the inmate's medical needs and any physical disabilities and/or special medical needs because these may limit the ability to participate in certain programs. They also may dictate assignment to a prison with appropriate hospital facilities or access for handicapped offenders (e.g., wheelchair ramps). If appropriate facilities are unavailable in a correctional setting, humanitarian and legal considerations may dictate placement in a hospital or other appropriate facility. An intellectual assessment can identify inmates who are mentally retarded. Institutional and program placement of these inmates considers their level of retardation, their social maturity, and program availability.

**INMATE PROGRESS IS MONITORED THROUGH THE RECLASSIFICATION PROCESS** Under the NIC model **reclassification** provides a vehicle for monitoring inmate progress, dealing with problems as they arise, and where appropriate, reassigning inmates based on changes in behavior and attitudes. Input for these periodic reviews should be solicited from an inmate's work, program, and custody supervisors and his or her classification case worker. These assessments are usually reviewed and summarized by the classification officer who also scores inmates on the NIC custody reclassification form and evaluates them on the needs assessment form. Custody reclassification uses a rating system similar to that employed at initial classification. Inmates are rated on their official history of institutional violence, the severity of current offenses, prior assaultive offense history (noninstitutional), and any assaults occurring six months before the review date.[5] Inmates who score 15 points or above on these four items are placed in maximum custody, those scoring between 10 and 14 points go to close custody, and those with scores of 9 or below are further assessed on other behavioral factors. Based on the points received on these other factors, inmates can be assigned to custody statuses ranging from close to community.

**The Federal Prison System Classification Model Contains Objective Criteria with Staff Overrides**

The federal prison system model is based on several principles including confinement of inmates in the least restrictive, appropriately secure facility; separation of security and custody dimensions;

FIGURE 17.2   **Initial Inmate Classification: Assessment of Needs**

NAME _____   NUMBER _____
         Last              First              MI

CLASSIFICATION CHAIRMAN _____   DATE _____/_____/_____

TEST SCORES:                                                                  I.Q. _____

                                                                             Reading _____

NEEDS ASSESSMENT: Select the answer which best describes the inmate           Math _____

HEALTH
1 Sound physical health, seldom ill     2 Handicap or illness which interferes      3 Serious handicap or chronic illness,
                                          with functioning on a recurring basis       needs frequent medical care           _____
                                                                                                                              code

INTELLECTUAL ABILITY:
1 Normal intellectual ability, able to   2 Mild retardation, some need for          3 Moderate retardation, independent
  function independently                   assistance                                 functioning severely limited          _____
                                                                                                                              code

BEHAVIORAL/EMOTIONAL PROBLEMS
1 Exhibits appropriate emotional         2 Symptoms limit adequate                  3 Symptoms prohibit adequate
  responses                                functioning, requires counseling,           functioning, requires significant
                                           may require medication                      intervention, may require medication
                                                                                       or separate housing                   _____
                                                                                                                              code

ALCOHOL ABUSE:
1 No alcohol problem                     2 Occasional abuse, some disruption        3 Frequent abuse, serious disruption
                                           of functioning                              needs treatment                       _____
                                                                                                                              code

DRUG ABUSE:
1 No drug problem                        2 Occasional abuse, some disruption        3 Frequent abuse, serious disruption
                                           of functioning                              needs treatment                       _____
                                                                                                                              code

EDUCATIONAL STATUS:
1 Has high school diploma or GED         2 Some deficits, but potential for         3 Major deficits in math and/or
                                           high school diploma or GED                  reading, needs remedial programs      _____
                                                                                                                              code

VOCATIONAL STATUS:
1 Has sufficient skills to obtain and    2 Minimal skill level, needs              3 Virtually unemployable, needs
  hold satisfactory employment             enhancement                               training                                _____
                                                                                                                              code

*Source:* National Institute of Corrections (1981a). *Prison classification: A model systems approach.* Washington, D.C.: Department of Justice.

standardized objective instruments; and staff judgments that can override placements based on objective confinement criteria.[6]

**INITIAL CLASSIFICATION IS BASED ON SECURITY CONSIDERATIONS**  Under this system a new inmate's initial classification is based on security considerations. The federal system specifies six distinct levels of security and rates all institutions based on seven security attributes (see Table 17.2) (Levinson and Williams, 1979). Each new commitment is given points on six items:

**1.** *History of escapes or attempts:* the degree of seriousness of the escape or attempt and how long ago it occurred.

**2.** *Type(s) of* **detainer(s):** degree of severity of lodged detainer which is based on the seriousness of the offense for which the offender was convicted.

**3.** *Severity of the current offense:* most serious offenses resulting in the current incarceration (this is determined by a severity of offense scale).

**4.** *Expected length of incarceration:* average percent of sentence served for offenses in the severity category in which it falls.

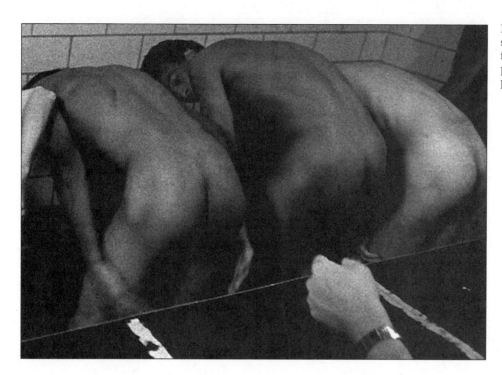

Inmates are strip searched in an attempt to find contraband. This is part of the admission process.

**5.** *History of violence:* the seriousness of any act against a person or property resulting in a fine or conviction, and when it happened.
**6.** *Type of prior commitment(s):* the seriousness of the offenses resulting in prior imprisonment.

An inmate's security level is decided by the range within which his or her total score falls. Within security levels such factors as offender's residence, level of overcrowding, age, racial balance, and need to separate certain inmates from each other are important.

Initially, a new inmate's custody status is determined by the custody levels available at the institution to which he or she is assigned which may (but not always) include Maximum, Out, In, Community. Newly committed inmates start with the highest custody level at their designated institution: inmates requiring Level V or VI[7] start their confinement in maximum custody[8]; those requiring Level IV, III, or II commence with In custody[9] and can later be changed to Out custody[10]; lastly, the inmate can be changed to Community custody.[11] The initial review (reclassification) for a possible custody level change normally does not take place for at least six months after institutional placement; subsequent reviews depend on custody status. Each time inmates are reclassified, they are

rated on the six factors reviewed above and on the following six custody factors:

**1.** *Percent of time served:* portion of projected period of incarceration that the inmate has already served.
**2.** *Involvement with drug/alcohol abuse:* history or current indications of dependency on drugs or alcohol (includes drug trafficking).
**3.** *Type and frequency of disciplinary reports:* [any] received during the past year.
**4.** *Responsibility demonstrated by inmate:* based on reports from work and program assignments of inmate's general demeanor and behavior.
**5.** *Family/community ties:* nature of inmate's established and continuing family and community involvement.
**6.** *Mental/psychological status:* based on current reports, if any, concerning an inmate's degree of mental stability (Levinson and Williams, 1979, p. 43).

Custody factors measure whether an inmate has moved in a positive or negative direction since admission or last review. Meaningful movement in one direction or the other will typically result in a reduction or increase of custody level. This may require transfer to a different institution if the new custody level is not available at the present facility.

**TABLE 17.2  Inmate classification: security/custody considerations**

| Level of Security | 1 | 2 | 3 | 4 | 5 | 6 |
|---|---|---|---|---|---|---|
| Type of Perimeter security | None | One Fence or bldg. facade | Double fence | Double fence or single + | Double fence or wall | Double fence or wall |
| Towers | None or not manned | Manned less than 24 hours | Manned less than 24 hours | Manned full & part-time | Manned 24 hours | Manned 24 hours |
| And/or external patrol | No | No | Yes | Yes | & or yes | Yes |
| Detection devices | No | No | Yes | Yes | Yes | Yes |
| Housing | Open | Open to Medium | Medium | Secure | Secure | Secure |
| Quarters/cells | Single & multiple + dorms | Single & multiple + dorms | Single & multiple + dorms | Single & multiple + dorms | Single & multiple + dorms | All single |
| Staffing per population size | Low | Low | Low to medium | Low to medium | Low to high | High |

| Type of Custody* | | Out Community | In, Out, Community | In, Out Community | In, Out | Maximum, In | Maximum, In |
|---|---|---|---|---|---|---|---|
| Facilities | NE | Allenwood Morgantown | Danbury | Petersburg | Otisville | Lewisburg | |
| Identified with each level of security | SE | Eglin Lexington Maxwell | Tallahassee | Ashland Miami | Memphis Talledega | Atlanta | |
| | NC | | Sandstone | Milan Springfield (gen. pop.) | Oxford | Leavenworth Terre Haute | Marion |
| | SC | Ft. Worth Seagoville | La Tuna | Texarkana | Bastrop El Reno | | |
| | W | Florence (Camp) And all CTCs and all satellite camps | Terminal Island | Englewood | McNeil Island | Lompoc | |

* Custody levels as of 1979. These may have changed since then (e.s. Florence has replaced Marion as a Level VI facility)

Administrative Facilities (having all levels of security and custody):

| | | |
|---|---|---|
| Alderson | El Paso | Florence (Detention) |
| New York | Pleasanton | Springfield (Medical/Psychiatric) |
| Butner | San Diego | All Pre-Trial detention units |
| Chicago | Terminal Island (Psychiatric) | |

*Source:* Levinson, R., Williams, J. (1979). Inmate classification: Security/custody considerations, *Federal Probation*, pp. 37–43.

Recommendations to change custody status are made to the inmate's unit/classification team, which can agree with or change them. When the team decides not to follow recommendations inmates must be given written notice of the reason (Austin, 1993; Buchanan and Whitlow, 1987; Levinson and Williams, 1979; Correctional Services Group, 1985).

**THE FEDERAL SYSTEM HAS RECEIVED POSITIVE EVALUATIONS**  The acid test of any classification system is whether it improves efficiency and reduces management problems. The federal model succeeded in several areas: (1) it confined more inmates in less secure facilities with no concurrent increases in assaults or escapes; (2) it better balanced each facility's racial composition; (3) it curtailed the number of transfers between institutions (this system removed a warden's transfer authority, eliminating preferential transfers); (4) it provided more current, consistent, and relevant information, enabling determination of the type of facilities that were needed, adjustment of staffing patterns, and more specific budget justifications; and (5) it found there was a need for fewer secure beds, which enabled the postponement of the building of a Level VI prison; instead, a new nonsecure facility was built at a savings of $13 million. Only in the area of protective custody did this system not have any positive impact (i.e., the number of inmates in this status was not reduced) (Levinson, 1980).

A study by Kane and Saylor (1983) found that the items used to assign inmates to different security level institutions were also related to postadmission behavior. That is, inmates who were classified by this method were distinguishable from each other in terms of their institutional behavior, justifying their assignment to different security level institutions. There are several reasons inmates create management problems when inappropriately classified. Inmates placed in less secure facilities than they require may exploit the less aggressive and unsophisticated inmates in these facilities. Conversely, the inmates assigned to higher security institutions than they require may act out in response to pressure from the more sophisticated and aggressive inmates at these custody levels. They may need to be more violent to be accepted by peers in these facilities and/or to avoid being exploited (i.e., for self-protection). Inmates who are unable to protect themselves may need to be transferred (Buchanan and Whitlow, 1987; Cor-

rectional Services Group, 1985). Currently, the need for appropriate placement is particularly critical because it is important to eliminate as many management problems as possible under the current overcrowded prison conditions.

## Objective Classification Systems Had a Positive Impact

While research is limited, a review of eighteen studies on systems employing objective classification suggest that overall the objective method had a positive impact on systems using it[12] :

**1.** Significant decreases were seen in overclassification. The proportion of inmates classified at minimum or lower custody levels was much higher than previously believed. Most systems found that 25 to 40% of their inmates could be safely housed in minimum custody.
**2.** There were increases in the consistency of classification decision-making, and staff errors and misinterpretations of classification policy were reduced.
**3.** No increases, and even some reductions were seen in rates of escapes and institutional misconduct.
**4.** There were modest but important improvements in a system's ability to house inmates according to level of risk; yet there continue to be difficulties in developing criteria that are predictive of risk.
**5.** There has been staff acceptance of objective classification instruments as useful tools in managing a rapidly increasing prison population.
**6.** While there is evidence that inmate misconduct is predicted by classification criteria, there is evidence from a California study that the institutional environment may be an equally or more important contributor to inmate misconduct.
**7.** The ability, since most systems are automated, to more effectively determine future resource needs including staffing levels, inmate programs, and types of facilities has been enhanced (Alexander and Austin, 1992).

## FUTURE OF CLASSIFICATION

Despite the gains, Austin (1993) suggests that if objective classification is to be improved and more widely used in the future, there is a need for more refined classification procedures, data, and instruments to deal with a variety of changes in corrections. First, prison systems are not only receiving more inmates but these inmates are more diverse. Systems are seeing a rapid growth in the number of African Americans, Hispanics, gang members, and women. Second, many jurisdictions are moving toward eliminating early release procedures. While this will increase the time served by inmates, some inmates will still have relatively short sentences. This, coupled with mandatory and habitual offender laws may create two distinct populations: a short-term group with relatively rapid turnover and a growing group of long-term offenders who will spend the rest of their lives in prison. Classification, programming, and work assignments for short- and long-term inmates will present major challenges to correctional systems. Finally, while current attitudes do not appear to favor a return to the rehabilitation philosophy, there is a continued recognition of the need for prison programming to deal with special offender groups such as drug addicts, sex offenders, the seriously disturbed, the chronically unemployed, and the illiterate. However, given limited resources and the view that the criminal justice system cannot break the crime cycle for all offenders, there is a need for "corrections and classification to do a better job of identifying those who can best benefit from [programming] and intervention" (Austin, 1993, p. 121).

A second set of issues involves the implementation of objective classification systems. Because objective classification is designed to alter materially the assignment of inmates to facilities and programs, it will threaten current power relationships in correctional systems. Therefore, the only way to introduce this type of change successfully is to have total support at the highest administrative levels—most importantly from the head of the system. Otherwise this effort will meet too much resistance and be rejected. There is also a need for an implementation plan that includes:

1. A system-wide Classification Advisory Committee composed of respected individuals to design and set up the new program
2. Pilot testing of the new system using a representative sample of inmates to determine the probable effect on facility functions

3. Provision for automation and inclusion in the department's management information system, which helps to reduce errors in scoring inmates and better helps to monitor them
4. A highly trained classification staff to smoothly implement the program and keep it running
5. A monitoring or evaluation plan to ensure that it works as planned, and continued monitoring to determine its impact on inmate management.

A third issue involves improving system efficiency in the placement of inmates in the community. This is important from the standpoint of reducing overcrowding in the prisons and protecting the community from victimization.

A final issue is that of internal classification. Besides system level classification, Austin (1993) suggests the need for a second layer of classification at the institution level that guides housing, work, and program assignments. These procedures are designed to be used in conjunction with an objective classification system to deal with issues such as compatibility and degree of risk presented by inmates who share a common custody designation. This helps improve the management of these groups. This second layer of classification further groups inmates at a given custody level, based on their personalities, and then devises specific housing placement and programming for these inmates within a given facility. Austin (1993) feels that, despite the fact this requires additional staff, this layer of classification will soon become a regular part of the next generation of objective prison classification systems.

## Conclusion

There is evidence that an increasing number of jurisdictions are employing objective classification systems. Not only has this occurred in prison systems but also at the local level where new-generation jails have been built and direct supervision programs have been instituted. Progress has also been noted in the reduction of overclassification. Austin (1993), in commenting on the status of classification, states:

> Despite dramatic advances much work still remains. In particular, new classification systems that govern the internal movement of inmates within a facility are required. Prison classification systems also need to

better interface with jail, probation, and parole classification systems so that critical information about offenders follows them as they move through the correctional system ... Finally, considerable experi-

mentation and research are needed to better understand the influence of the prison environment as it relates to inmate behavior (p. 123).

## ENDNOTES

**1.** The security and custody designations referred to here can be found in two NIC publications (NIC, 1981a and NIC, 1987). The 1987 publication was based on an ACA project funded by NIC.

**2.** Although Marion has a rated capacity of 440 (i.e., the number of inmates it was designed to hold) and contains over 500 cells, the nature of the inmate population has led to the BOP to restrict the number of inmates placed there to about 350.

**3.** In constructing this model, information was obtained from several sources including correctional administrators, researchers in academic and correctional settings, and attorneys from the ACLU's National Prison Project.

**4.** A warrant placed against a person incarcerated in a correctional facility, notifying the holding authority of the intention of another jurisdiction to take custody of that individual when released.

**5.** In instances in which an action pending regarding an incident and a resulting conviction would change the inmate's custody or program placement, it is suggested that inmates be maintained in their current status and that a review be scheduled following the action of the disciplinary committee.

**6.** Other factors considered are that past behavior is a predictor of future behavior; recent behavior is a better predictor of future actions than far distant behavior.

**7.** The Level VI designation referred to Marion, which was a super-max prison where all inmates were housed in single cells, the staffing per population was high, and some inmates were in their cells 23 hours per day. The designation of super-max now belongs to the federal prison at Florence, Colorado.

**8.** Maximum custody means that the inmate requires maximum control and continuous supervision. This status is for inmates who have demonstrated themselves to be assaultive, predatory, riotous, or serious escape risks.

**9.** In custody means the prisoner will be assigned to regular housing quarters (single cell, but may be doubled-bunked, multiple-cell, or cubicles in dormitories) and be eligible for all program activities under normal level supervision, but not for work or program assignments outside the institution's secure perimeter.

**10.** Out custody means the inmate may be assigned to less secure housing quarters within the institution; pris-

oner lives in open dorms, cubicles, or single rooms; is eligible for work details and program assignments outside the institution's secure perimeter with intermittent supervision.

**11.** Community custody means the inmate is eligible for the least secure housing, including that which is outside the institution's perimeter; may work on outside work details or program assignments with minimal supervision; and is eligible to participate in community-based program activities (Levinson and Williams, 1979).

**12.** While many of the studies were methodologically weak they contributed knowledge on the limitations and merits of this approach (Alexander and Austin, 1992).

## ACKNOWLEDGMENTS

[a] Reprinted from the American Correctional Association, 1993. *Classification: A Tool for Managing Today's Offenders*, with permission of the American Correctional Association, Lanham, MD.
[b] Reprinted from the American Correctional Association, 1993. *Classification: A Tool for Managing Today's Offenders*, with permission of the American Correctional Association, Lanham, MD.
[c] Reprinted from the American Correctional Association, 1993. *Classification: A Tool for Managing Today's Offenders*, with permission of the American Correctional Association, Lanham, Md.

## CHAPTER RECAP

**Reception and Orientation**
**Classification Procedures**
Basic Forms of Classification Have a Long History
Modern Classification Systems Analyze and Organize the Diverse Inmate Populations
  Objective Systems Began to Be Developed in the 1970s
  Classification Protects Inmates from Each Other
  Classification Protects the Public
  Classification Increases the Efficient Use of Prison Resources
  Classification Is Used for Inmate Control
  Classification Is a Source of Planning Information
**Elements of the Classification Process**

Distinctions Between Security and Custody Are Not Always Clear
Security Focuses on Protecting Society from Inmates
   Maximum Security Restricts Inmate Activity and Closely Controls Them
   Close Security Facilities House Inmates with Different Custody Designations
   Medium Security Prisons Provide a Wide Variety of Programs
   Level II Minimum Security Prisons Are Open Institutions
   Level I Community Security Facilities Are Open Programs
Custody Deals with Levels of Supervision
   Maximum Custody Inmates Are Closely Supervised and Have Limited Freedom and Movement
   Close Custody Inmates Can Participate in Programs Under Supervision
   Medium Custody Inmates Can Participate in Institutional Programs and Do Not Require Direct Supervision
   Minimum Custody Inmates Can Move About the Institution Unsupervised
   Community Custody Inmates Are Allowed to Be Unsupervised in Community Facilities
There Are Several Issues Related to Minimum Security Facilities
   Can Minimum Security Facilities Accommodate Long-Term Inmates?
   Minimum Security Facilities Must Deal with Community Opposition
   Can Minimum Security Facilities Provide Adequate Programs?
Segregation of Some Inmates Helps Protect Them and Others
Needs Assessment Determines an Inmate's Program and Service Requirements
   Determining Inmate Needs Leads to Proper Program Placement
   Finding the Right Programs to Meet Inmate Needs Is Important
**Classification Models**
The National Institute of Corrections Model Is a Management Tool
   Inmates Are Rated on Predictive Variables
   Inmates' Medical Needs and Intellectual Levels Can Affect Facility Placement
   Inmate Progress Is Monitored Through the Reclassification Process
The Federal Prison System Classification Model Contains Objective Criteria with Staff Overrides
   Initial Classification Is Based on Security Considerations
   The Federal System Has Received Positive Evaluations
Objective Classification Systems Had a Positive Impact
**Future of Classification**
Conclusion

## REVIEW QUESTIONS

1. Define classification and describe its various phases.
2. What are the basic elements of classification?
3. Compare and contrast the concepts of custody and security and describe the various levels of each.
4. Briefly describe the NIC and Federal Bureau of Prisons classification models.
5. Describe and discuss the reclassification process.
6. What issues must be resolved before classification can be improved?

## TEST YOUR KNOWLEDGE

1. A summary admission report on a newly arrived inmate contains all of the following types of information but one. Which is *not* included?
   a. a list of people who will be allowed to visit the inmate
   b. an account of the legal aspects of the inmate's case
   c. a summary of the inmate's legal history
   d. the recreational preferences and needs of the inmate
2. Through the mid 1970s, most classification decisions were based on:
   a. custody concerns
   b. subjective judgment
   c. convenience
   d. objective tests
3. All but one of the following are ways in which ineffective classifications can increase prison violence.
   a. failing to separate predatory offenders from victims
   b. improper placement of severely disturbed inmates in the general population
   c. failure to train prison staff adequately
   d. failure to separate rival gang members
4. The degree of staff supervision necessary to ensure adequate control of an inmate and minimize the danger that inmate may pose to the staff and other inmates is known as
   a. security level.
   b. custody category.
   c. jurisdictional label.
   d. classification status.
5. The National Institute of Corrections notes that the decision to place inmates in minimum security or community-based facilities is often based largely on
   a. the absence of a recent history of violence or escape.
   b. a psychological assessment of dangerousness.
   c. the seriousness of the inmate's offense.
   d. the community's attitude toward the offender.

# PART SIX

---

# INSTITUTIONAL PROGRAMS AND SERVICES

# CHAPTER 18

# BASIC PRISON PROGRAMS: EDUCATIONAL AND WORK

## ■ LEARNING OBJECTIVES

*After completion of this chapter, you should be able to:*

**1.** Specify and describe the various types of correctional education programs.

**2.** Discuss the role of literacy in the development of current educational programs in prisons.

**3.** Describe the benefits of GED programs for inmates who complete them.

**4.** List and describe the delivery systems that can be used to teach vocational skills.

**5.** Describe the systems of prison industry.

**6.** Outline the contemporary goals of prison industries.

**7.** Describe the constraints that the prison environment imposes on work programs.

**8.** List and describe the various models of prison industry.

## ■ KEY TERMS AND CONCEPTS

Adult basic education
Ashurst-Summers Act of 1935
Cluster courses
Controlling customer model
Corporate model
Employer model
Functionally illiterate
General Equivalence Diploma (GED)
Hawes-Cooper Act of 1929
Hilton Hotel syndrome
Life skills programs
Main customer model
No private benefit system
Peer tutoring
Principle of least eligibility
Private benefit system
Project RIO
Segmentation programs
"Time to think"

## PROVISION OF BASIC INMATE NEEDS

Major correctional institutions are like islands some distance from the mainland. They are detached from the rest of society but must provide the same basic services for their residents. Although separation is a factor, requirements for prison self-sufficiency are dictated largely by the need for security and the size of inmate populations. Because it is impractical, dangerous, and costly to transport inmates to needed services and programs in the community, prisons must provide for nearly all inmate needs on the premises. Inmates have to be fed, housed, clothed, and provided with medical care, psychiatric care and counseling, religious services and activities, education, vocational training, work, recreation, and contact with families and the world outside of the prison.

One of the most potent beliefs affecting prison programming, services, and conditions is the **principle of least eligibility,** which states that "the condition of the prisoner should be inferior, or at least not superior, to that of the lowest classes of the noncriminal population in a state of liberty" (Hawkins, 1976, p. 41). This principle has affected much common thinking about the treatment of inmates. Although many politicians, correctional administrators, and members of the public have humanitarian concerns regarding the repressive conditions of inmate confinement, most members of society feel that inmates have been treated "too well." This view is reflected in what has been called the **Hilton Hotel syndrome,** which expresses concerns that inmate living conditions are better than those enjoyed by the majority of free-world Americans. Examples of this are the complaints by many citizens that some inmates eat too well, are provided with color televisions, and are given free college educations.

### There Are Important Reasons for Providing Basic Services

Although the principle of least eligibility stimulates opposition to programs and services for inmates, there are at least three reasons for providing them: (1) the fact that they can help some inmates desist from crime, (2) the courts have mandated that they be provided, and (3) they enhance control of inmates.

**IMPROVING INMATES' SKILLS CAN REDUCE CRIME**   Why provide programs and services for inmates? Why not merely furnish them with the barest minimum needed to subsist? Some may argue this is all they deserve, but it is important to remember that most inmates will be released at some point and for some their terms of imprisonment will not be very long. If they are to be no worse on release than when they were first incarcerated, they must be provided with basic services and programs. Humane conditions can also provide inmates who are receptive to change with the opportunity to turn their lives around. The consequences of not providing these services were noted by former Chief Justice Warren Burger in his famous "Prisons Without Fences" address:

> It is predictable that a person confined in a penal institution for two, five or ten years, and then released, yet still unable to read, write, spell or do simple arithmetic and not trained in any marketable vocational skill, will be vulnerable to returning to a life of crime. And very often the return to crime begins within weeks after release. What job opportunities are there for an unskilled, functional illiterate who has a criminal record?
>
> The recidivists who return to our prisons are like automobiles that are called back to Detroit. What business enterprise, whether building automobiles in Detroit or ships in Norfolk, Virginia, or airplanes in Seattle, could continue with the same rate of "recall" of its "products" as our prisons? (Burger, 1983, p. 5).

The costs associated with these programs are outweighed by the savings to society (e.g., police services, court costs, losses from thefts, etc.) when a released offender does not return to a life of crime.

**COURTS HAVE REQUIRED BASIC SERVICES**   Recent court decisions have mandated directly that prisons provide inmates with basic services and indirectly that programs be available. These decisions were influenced by changes in our thinking about the appropriate functions of prisons. Although the most commonly supported position is that prison should punish offenders, this no longer requires that offenders be subject to harsh and inhumane conditions. Today, the prevailing view is that the prison should accomplish its retributive functions by depriving offenders of some of their constitutional rights. This position is supported by the courts, with certain limitations. Although the overriding rule is that detainees and convicted offenders retain the majority of their constitutional rights, there is a recognition that correctional officials may impose restrictions reasonably related to institutional interests in maintaining order, security, and discipline (*Bell v. Wolfish*, 1979) as discussed in Chapters 15 and 16.

**PROGRAMS INCREASE THE EFFICIENCY AND SECURITY OF THE PRISON**    Inmate programs also serve a variety of institutional functions (Embert and Kalinich, 1988; NIC, 1987). Security and custody are enhanced when inmates are involved in programs, particularly when they are offered reasonable freedom of choice and provided incentives for participation. The adage "idleness is the devil's workshop" is quite applicable here. Additionally, programs help inmates to deal with the pressures of "doing time" and contribute to order and stability, thus facilitating custody and security.

Prison services are covered in four chapters: this chapter, education and work programs; Chapter 19, health services; Chapter 20, food and religious services; and Chapter 21, visitation programs and recreational activities. These services, programs, and activities are vital components of the inmates' world and can significantly impact their future outside the prison.

## EDUCATIONAL PROGRAMS[1]

Of the prison programs available for inmates, education is probably the most important. The reasons for this lie in the fact that (1) the academic skills (reading, writing, and computation) are so important in achieving success in the world of work and (2) a very large proportion of the inmate population is deficient in these skills. This section reviews the history and development of correctional education and the range of current programs.

### Prison Education Programs Have a Long History

The recognition of education as important in reforming offenders in the United States can be traced to the Walnut Street Jail. There, religious and secular education were intertwined because if the clergy expected inmates to study the Bible, they had to first teach them to read.

The Quakers were the first to advocate secular education of offenders but they met with opposition based on the fear that education would make criminals more dangerous (Barnes and Teeters, 1951; Chenault, 1951). This argument was used in 1824 by the warden of Auburn Prison to close a school for young offenders (Lewis, 1922/1996). Before the Civil War, inmates were almost exclusively taught by prison chaplains. Education was limited because prisoners were not permitted to meet in groups and instruction was restricted to night hours. Lewis (1922/1996) provides a vivid picture of the resulting learning environment:

> The chaplain standing in the semi-dark corridor, before the cell door, with a dingy lantern hanging to the grated bars, teaching to the wretched convict in the darkness beyond the grated door the rudiments of reading or numbers (p. 341).

**AFTER THE CIVIL WAR EDUCATION CAME TO BE VIEWED AS AN IMPORTANT ELEMENT IN THE REFORMATION OF OFFENDERS**    After the Civil War, new methods for reforming offenders were sought and education came to be a key element in the development of the reformatory model. In fact, the origin of contemporary correctional education is usually traced to the establishment of academic and vocational training at the Elmira Reformatory. Although much enthusiasm was generated by the developments at Elmira, few institutions copied its programs mainly due to the heavy emphasis given work at most prisons. When restrictions were placed on prison industries during the early twentieth century, education became an acceptable substitute to keep offenders busy (Cavan, 1962). Since inmates had little or no schooling and many were illiterate, education was justified on general principles as well as for maintaining discipline. Typically, these programs were of low quality because they were not well financed or staffed. Only a few civilian teachers were hired on a part-time basis, and they usually taught evening classes after working a full day in a nearby school. Nonprofessionals (e.g., inmates, chaplains, or guards) still taught most classes, with donated books and few other basic educational materials, in chapels, mess halls, and other available space.

A nationwide study by MacCormick in 1927–1928 found no schools in thirteen out of the sixty prisons surveyed, and no adequate vocational programs in any of these facilities (Chenault, 1951). He concluded there was not one complete, adequately financed and staffed correctional education program in the whole country. This began to change as both the federal and New York systems expanded their education programs, and by 1950 most inmates in these systems who needed and wanted more education could get it. Important gains were also made in New Jersey, California, Illinois, Michigan, Wisconsin, and Minnesota (Chenault, 1951). However, programming in most states was confined to the elementary level, and instructional time was limited to between five and ten hours a week. Attempts to develop sound educational programming continued to be thwarted by inadequate facilities and staff and took a back seat to work and maintenance activities (Caldwell, 1965).

**IN THE 1960s CORRECTIONAL EDUCATION BEGAN TO RECEIVE GREATER EMPHASIS** Since the early 1960s, emphasis on both academic and vocational programs in correctional facilities has been increasing (Simms, Farley, and Littlefield, 1987). Correctional education received a major boost when Congress passed the Adult Education Act in 1964. This provided funding for programs that targeted adults who had deficiencies in communication, computation, or social relations that substantially impaired their capability of gaining or retaining employment commensurate with their real ability (Pollack, 1979). By the late 1970s, this act was credited with providing funding for the recruitment of more professional staff, development of better teaching materials, and new methods of presentation.

Three studies provide a good perspective on changes during the 1973 to 1983 period (Dell'Apa, 1973; Bell, Conard, Laffey, Lutz, Simon, Stakelon, and Wilson, 1979; Ryan and Woodard, 1987). In this time period, the pattern of enrollment was relatively constant, with the highest number of inmates participating in vocational training followed by GED, adult basic education, and postsecondary education. The average amount spent per student per year rose from $906 to $1579 between 1977 and 1983.

**IN THE 1980s SEVERAL FACTORS FURTHERED THE DEVELOPMENT OF CORRECTIONAL EDUCATION** Several factors brought correctional education to the nation's attention in the 1980s (Wolford, 1987).

First, the prison population more than doubled over a fifteen-year period. Second, the deemphasis of rehabilitation coupled with a more punitive response to crime left education as one of the few programs offering inmates a hope of change. Third, intervention by the courts in correctional facilities regularly called for improvement in education programs. Finally, the staggering levels of inmate illiteracy and related educational problems focused attention on prison education programs.

Some statistics show just how bleak this picture has been. A study of a random sample of inmates from three (two male and one female) institutions in three states (Louisiana, Pennsylvania, and Washington) found that 42% of the inmates did not appear to have the literacy skills required to function effectively in society (i.e., were at or below the fifth-grade level) (Bell, Conard, and Suppa, 1984). The vast majority of them evidenced specific learning disabilities. Their average IQ was 86, which was one standard deviation below national norms. Fifteen percent had IQs below 75, which meant many would likely be labeled as retarded. Most had little or no relevant vocational training, half lacked a consistent work history, and 80% had dropped out of school (Porter and Porter, 1984). The truly grim state of the educational attainment of offenders is reflected by the fact that in the late 1970s only 28% of the inmate population had completed high school as compared with 85% of comparably aged males in the general U.S. population (Flanagan, Hindelang, and Gottfredson, 1980; U.S. Department of Justice, 1988). Our Close-Up on "Literacy in Prison" provides a current perspective on inmate literacy.

Several other factors also helped shape correctional education programs (Wolford, 1987). First, restricted resources, staff, and expertise limited their availability. Second, relatively few inmates sought to participate in these programs with most only doing so to gain early release. The last factor prompted mandatory literacy requirements.

## There Are Several Types of Correctional Education Programs

Almost all correctional institutions offer some type of educational programming. The range of programs available is usually related to the institution's size, security level, location, and the characteristics of its inmates. A Corrections Compendium

# *Close Up*   **Literacy in Prison**

In 1991 the U.S. Congress passed the National Literacy Act, the purpose of which was to enhance the literacy and basic skills of adults to enable them to function effectively in their work and lives and to strengthen and coordinate adult literacy programs. In 1992, because national information regarding literacy levels was lacking, a study was carried out that surveyed 25,000 persons from the general population who were 16 and over and 1100 prison inmates in 80 state and federal prisons. In this study literacy was defined as:

> Using printed and written information to function in society, to achieve one's goals, and to develop one's knowledge and potential (p. 3).

Literacy was measured in terms of three scales: proficiency in prose, document, and quantitative literacy. Scores on each of the three scales were divided into five levels. Key findings included:

▣ About 70% of the inmate sample scored in the lowest two levels on all three scales, while only around 50% of the general population performed at these levels.

▣ Almost 65% of the prison population belonged to minority groups (42% black, 18% Hispanic, and 3% other) versus 24% of the general population (11% black, 10% Hispanic, and 3% other). Fifty-one percent of the inmates had a high school diploma or GED compared with 76% of the general population. However, minority adults both in and out of prisons have less education on the average than whites. Since performance is to some extent tied to educational attainment it is not surprising that this study found that (1) inmates without high school diplomas or a GED had lower levels of proficiency than those with GEDs, high school diplomas, or some postsecondary education; and (2) when the inmate and general populations were compared by educational attainment prisoners performed as well as or better than their counterparts in the general population.

▣ Although male and female inmates performed equally on the literacy scales, they both had lower proficiencies than their counterparts in the household sample.

▣ More inmates (36%), when compared with the general population (26%), had at least one disability. For prisoners this disability significantly more often involved a learning disability or mental or emotional conditions. The proficiencies of inmates with a learning disability were lower than most other inmates with disabilities and those in the general population with a learning disability.

▣ Holding race/ethnicity, sex, age, and level of education constant, prisons and household populations had similar proficiency levels on all scales. "Thus differences in overall performance between the prison and [general] populations may be attributed to differences in [race/ethnic] . . . composition and educational attainment" (p. xix).

This study concludes that even inmates with high school diplomas do not necessarily possess the literacy skills needed to function in society. Also of concern was the fact that almost four times as many inmates had a learning disability when compared to the general population. These inmates scored at the low end of the literacy scale, which meant they were only able to perform the most basic literacy tasks and suggests the need for developing programs tailored for this group. Further, this study found that one-third to one-half of the general population performing at literacy levels 1 and 2 were out of work. Because more than two-thirds of the inmates performed at these levels, unless their skill levels are improved substantially, their prospects for employment are dismal. Finally, even though this study demonstrates the need for improvement in correctional education, these researchers believe that:

> Prisons should not be expected to shoulder all the responsibility: individuals, groups, organizations, schools and colleges and businesses need to reach behind prisons walls with efforts aimed at improving the literacy skills. [To accomplish this] will take a comprehensive strategy, the purpose of which should be to prepare the whole person for succeeding in the world beyond prison walls (pp. xxiii).

Given the current emphasis on making the prison experience more punitive and on cutting programs in order to use these funds to build more prisons to house inmates, do you think legislatures will take the above recommendations seriously?

Adapted from K. Haigler, C. W. Harlow, P. E. O'Connor, and A. Campbell (1994). Literacy behind bars: Profiles of the prison population from the National Adult Literacy Survey. Washington, D.C.: U.S. Department of Education, office of Education Research and Improvement.

study found that about 210,000 inmates, constituting about 25% of the prison population, participated in education programs in 1993 (Lillis, 1994e). The systems (44 states[2] and the federal system) that provided data had a total inmate population of 803,415. Males represented 94% of the participants in this population.

Lillis (1994f) indicates that up to 90% of the total inmate population could, and perhaps should, be enrolled in these classes. In thirty-eight systems between 70 and 100% of the inmates were eligible. Steve Steurer, director of the Correctional Educational Association, indicates "if the number of eligible inmates enrolled in these programs seems small, it may be because the correctional budget has been cut dramatically in the last few years" (Lillis, 1994e, p. 5). He claims most inmates will enroll in correctional educational programs if these are available. In fact, thirty-eight systems report having waiting lists for inmates wanting to enroll but due to tight funding they now offer fewer and more crowded classes.[3] Nearly half of all inmates participate in academic education during their prison stay and about one-third are involved in vocational training (Beck, Gilliard, Greenfeld, Harlow, Hester, Janaowski, Snell, and Stephan, 1993).

**MANY JURISDICTIONS REQUIRE INMATES BELOW A CERTAIN LITERACY LEVEL TO ENROLL IN EDUCATION PROGRAMS**    At the urging of Warren Burger, former Chief Justice of the Supreme Court, the Federal Bureau of Prisons created an education task force, which established a mandatory adult basic education policy. Initially, all inmates testing below the sixth-grade level were required to enroll in the literacy program for 90 days. At that time they could leave but would not be promoted above entry-level jobs in prison industry programs or work assignments unless they had achieved a sixth-grade performance level. This requirement was later raised to the eighth-grade level because of increasing performance expectations by employers. In 1991 the minimum time inmates were required to stay in the program was raised to 120 days and a **GED** (General Equivalence Diploma) or high school diploma was required for inmates to qualify for top-level prison jobs (McCollum, 1992). All federal facilities are required to have special education instructors and to develop incentive and recognition programs to reward inmates' educational accomplishments.

By 1989 sixteen states and the District of Columbia had mandated statutory literacy programs (Hills and Karcz, 1990). The programs ranged from adult basic education and literacy training to high school completion. The critical need for these programs in prison is evidenced by the fact that, depending on how literacy is defined, from 40 to 75% of the prison population is **functionally illiterate** compared with about 25% of the free adult population (Ryan, 1990; Tracey, 1993). The functionally illiterate are not generally able to gain or maintain employment at wages sufficient to support their dependents. They also tend to lack the social skills needed to maintain normal social relationships, and to fully assume family, parenting, and citizenship responsibilities, e.g., voting (Ryan, 1990).

**BOTH ADULT BASIC EDUCATION AND LITERACY PROGRAMS FOCUS ON DEVELOPING ELEMENTARY ACADEMIC SKILLS**    Adult basic education (ABE) programs for inmates have been the mainstays of correctional education. As a result of the Adult Education Act most correctional facilities have these programs. They stress literacy and mathematical skills as a foundation for further education and training. The ABE program is generally viewed as a feeder system for GED preparatory classes. In 1993, forty-four systems offered these programs with more than 89,160 inmates participating in them (Lillis 1994f).

Literacy programs are not always distinguishable from ABE efforts because they sometimes have similar components. Basic literacy programs focus on providing basic skills to low-level readers and nonreaders. These programs vary, but they are usually personalized in their approach to learning. For example, many teachers help inmates to write letters home to serve as an impetus for future learning.

> I wanted to write my girlfriend but I didn't know how to, couldn't spell or nothing but Mrs. Smith helped me and I got to writing. I saw my success and then I wanted to keep going [in school] (as cited by Bellorado, 1986, p. 78).

One-to-one **peer tutoring** and volunteer tutoring often supplement classroom work when funds are scarce, or to reach inmates who will not attend school. In the 1980s, the number of both inmate

## Close Up   Inmates Teaching Inmates

Since 1984, education has been mandatory for those inmates who score below an eighth-grade equivalency on a reading achievement test. . . . Any inmate with a high school diploma or a GED is encouraged to apply to become a peer tutor in this program. . . . [Thus,] the peer tutoring program seeks not only to serve low-level students, but to allow tutors to experience the joy and satisfaction of helping a peer achieve in school—an opportunity lacking in the lives of most offenders. The Division of Corrections reward[s] them with an extra five days of good time for each month of sentence served. . . .

The Peer Tutoring Reading Academy trains inmates to tutor peers who function below the third-grade level in reading. The program is designed to develop basic skills and self-esteem by using real-life materials such as newspapers, sports magazines, driver's license booklets, mail-order applications, legal documents or whatever a student chooses as the basis for initial instruction. The program [uses several professionally developed programs to help learners]. . . .

Under the direct supervision of a certified reading teacher, the inmate-tutor and inmate-learner diagnose learning needs and then formulate a written education plan that includes realistic personal goals with measurable reading, writing, and, often, math objectives. Tutor-training sessions are conducted weekly and sometimes daily as the situation dictates. Tutor applicants are carefully screened and work through a probationary period. . . . The program boosts both tutor and student confidence and self-esteem, confers a sense of ownership of the educational program, and enhances tutor skills and status with other inmates. . . .

At the present time there are nine peer tutoring sites. At each site there are at least ten tutors who instruct at least two, and sometimes three, students per day. Most sites have about fifteen trained tutors. This translates into about three hundred students instructed per day in the literacy laboratory setting. The peer tutoring program is very cost-effective, as it utilizes inmate-tutors who are paid a small daily stipend (and time off their sentences) for their work. This amounts to a kind of community service behind bars. Since tutoring is a full-time job, tutors work many more hours than traditional community-based literacy volunteers. . . .

The central measure of the effectiveness of any educational program is the educational advancement of students. Data collected by the Maryland State Department of Education show that, on average, literacy laboratory students gain about three months in reading skills level for every month of instruction. . . . The quality of the program has not escaped the notice of national studies. In 1986, the National Institute of Corrections (NIC) of the United States Department of Justice cited the peer tutoring literacy laboratories in the Maryland Correctional Training Center and the Maryland Correctional Institution-Jessup as two of the nine best literacy programs in adult prisons in the United States. . . . The U.S. Secretary of Education chose the peer tutoring program as a runner-up in a 1990 competition for the most effective adult education programs. . . . (Steuer, 1991, pp. 135–139).[a]

and volunteer teachers and tutors began to increase due to the development of training programs for volunteer tutors (Wolford, 1987). Most volunteers are inmates, who are often successful because they understand the frustrations and goals of their fellow prisoners. Our Close-Up on "Inmates Teaching Inmates" profiles the Maryland Peer Tutoring Program, which has served as a model for other jurisdictions.

Community volunteers have also assisted in inmate basic literacy programs. They have the added advantage of providing inmates with free world contacts. An estimated 2000 volunteers from national organizations, including Literacy Volunteers of America, currently provide tutoring in local

and state adult and juvenile facilities. Many local organizations, such as religious groups, also furnish tutors to assist inmates (Tracey, 1993). In Pennsylvania some correctional officers (COs) are trained as tutors by the State Department of Education. They not only supplement inmate tutors, but also serve as advocates for correctional education programs (Wolford, 1987).

**GED PROGRAMS PROVIDE INMATES WITH AN OPPORTUNITY TO OBTAIN A HIGH SCHOOL DIPLOMA**   Although programs vary from state to state, most GED programs focus on the further development of reading, language arts, composition, and mathematical skills. Teachers use a variety of approaches including direct instruction, independent study, and computer-assisted instruction. Although some programs focus exclusively on preparing inmates to pass the GED test battery, others choose to emphasize lifelong learning skills and to promote problem-solving and "learning to learn" skills. Proponents of such programs claim high passing rates on the GED although the emphasis is on broad-based learning rather than just "passing the test" (Johnson, 1993c). For many uneducated inmates, receiving the GED is their first successful experience in education and represents a milestone in their lives.

A national study of GED recipients, while not specifically focused on prison, suggests the potential economic and personal value of obtaining this diploma. Based on a random sample of three Iowa cohorts earning GEDs in 1980, 1985, and 1988, this study found that, for 43% of this sample, personal income jumped more than $5000 and more than 75% of those on welfare were off public assistance by 1990. Other gains ranged from improved self-esteem, to getting jobs requiring higher skill levels, to becoming better parents (BCEL, 1992). There is every reason to believe inmates obtaining their GEDs can benefit in the same way. In 1993 more than 33,600 inmates were enrolled in GED programs (Lillis, 1994f). Some correctional facilities give inmates the option of taking regular high school diploma courses (Ryan and Woodard, 1987).

**LIFE SKILL PROGRAMS FOCUS ON PROVIDING INMATES WITH THE SKILLS TO "MAKE IT" IN SOCIETY**  A major factor in the incarceration of most offenders is their inability to function effectively in society (Shelton, 1985). For many, this may be due to deficiencies in basic academic skills; for others, however, a lack of basic "life skills" may also be a major contributing factor. Some individual prisons and state systems have developed their own **life skills programs** (e.g., California and Florida) and others have adopted "packaged" programs (e.g., Reasoning and Rehabilitation, by Ross and Associates; Adult Cross Roads, by the National Corrective Institute) (Johnson, 1994; Bellorado, 1986). These programs provide inmates with practical knowledge in areas including the following:

*Employability/job search skills* such as career/job awareness, the use of classified ads, writing business letters and resumes, filling out applica-

tions, interview techniques, and appropriate behaviors on the job.

*Consumer skills* such as money management, comparative shopping, understanding labels and bills, using credit, and shopping for food, housing, clothing, and transportation.

*The use of community resources*, such as using the telephone, obtaining help from social service agencies, interpreting postal forms, using the library, and finding child care.

*Health and safety skills* such as reading warnings, using prescription drugs, practicing first aid, and maintaining a balanced diet.

*Parenting and family skills* (sometimes included under health skills), such as child-rearing practices, understanding [the things that lead to] to child and wife abuse, and finding alternative ways to settle conflicts.

*Civic skills,* such as passing a driver's test, registering to vote, interpreting legal forms, filling out tax forms, and understanding the Bill of Rights (Bellorado, 1986, p. 96).

A 1993 Corrections Compendium study focused on two types of programs that encompass components of the life skills area. They found that thirty-six states offered job readiness training, and pre-release programs were offered by thirty-five systems (Lillis, 1994f).

*Development of "Thinking Skills" Is Sometimes Included in Life Skills Training*   According to Cheryl Johnson (1993), Director of Instructional Services for the Texas Department of Criminal Justice, offenders not only have significant academic deficits but they also have thinking deficits and attitudinal problems that are directly responsible for their being in prison. She believes that if corrections education is to be rehabilitative then it must teach offenders cognitive skills (e.g., problem solving, reasoning, and social perspective taking) in addition to academic skills.

This approach in corrections has been championed and developed by Robert Ross and Elizabeth Fabiano (Ross, 1980; Ross and Fabiano, 1982, 1986; Ross, Fabiano, and Eweles, 1988; Fabiano, 1991). They contend that many offenders fail to learn the cognitive skills necessary for developing the problem-solving and moral reasoning abilities required for effective social adaptation. To correct these deficits, offenders have to be taught how to think so that by learning to think they can come to prosocial conclusions. They tested these assumptions in a study of three groups of high-risk Canadian probationers—one group was subjected to intensive probation treatment, another to modified life skills training, and the third to the cognitive training. The group subjected to the cognitive program had a much lower rate of reincarceration compared with the other groups (30 versus 11 versus 0%, respectively).

The program they developed is one component of the Living Skills Program. As Figure 18.1 shows, cognitive skills training precedes all of the other training and is intended to facilitate the development of prosocial reasoning, evaluation, and problem solving in the other social skill areas. One program based on this model, titled **"Time To Think"** (TTT), has been implemented at the Western New Mexico Correctional Facility. It addresses thinking and social skills such as problem solving, negotiation, communication, creative thinking, management of emotions, values enhancement, and critical reasoning (DeMaret, 1991; Sanchez, 1993).

## VOCATIONAL EDUCATION PROGRAMS ARE DESIGNED TO PROVIDE INMATES WITH JOB SKILLS

The work histories of most inmates show that they have usually been employed at low-paying, low-status jobs with high and fast turnover rates or have never been employed. Correctional vocational educational programs are thought to be the best vehicles for breaking the cycle of recidivism (Simms, Farley, and Littlefield, 1987). These programs are aimed at providing inmates with up-to-date marketable skills relating to specific jobs on the outside. In contrast to academic instruction, which can use a variety of facilities for instruction, vocational programs require shops that simulate, as much as possible, real work situations. Simms, Farley, and Littlefield (1987) found that the better vocational programs are in buildings separated from cell blocks. Educators working in these programs feel that this separation helps to better simulate an authentic free-world work site, which has positive effects on inmate work attitudes and habits. However, Johnson (1993c) notes that there are advantages to having these programs in close proximity to and integrated with academic programs. Doing this enables academic and vocational instructors to work more closely together to coor-

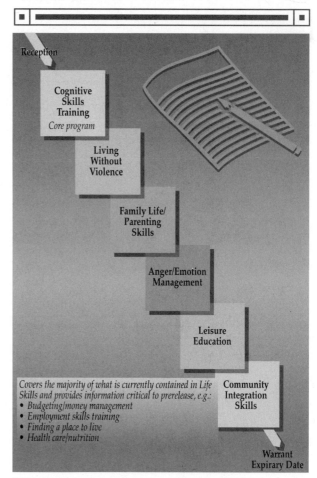

FIGURE 18.1 **Living Skills Programming within the Correctional Service of Canada**

SOURCE: Elizabeth A. Fabiano (June 1991) "How education can be correctional and how corrections can be educational, *Journal of Correctional Education*, 42(2). Adapted with permission of publisher.

dinate programming and to communicate about specific inmate problems. Good vocational training programs require materials and equipment that are similar to those currently being used in business and industry. It does the inmate little good to learn to repair typewriters when most businesses are using word processors.

The renewed concern with and expansion of prison industries has generated relationships between these programs and vocational education. In some cases, vocational training is a prerequisite to working in some of these industries. In 1993, forty-three states reported a total of 65,594 inmates involved in technical and vocational training (Lillis, 1994f). Ryan and Woodard (1987), based on data from forty-one systems, found a total of

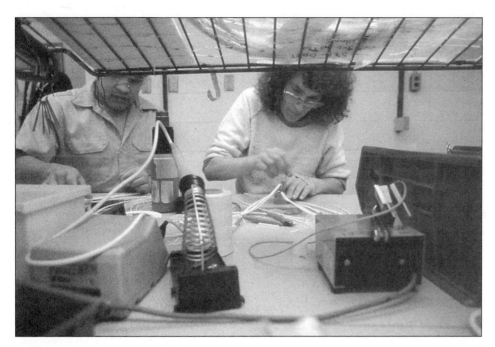

Vocational programs can teach job skills. In women's prisons, non-traditional programs can provide women with job skills for work that pays relatively high wages.

eighty different programs, with the largest enrollments being in carpentry, auto mechanics, and welding.

The acid test for these programs is whether they lead to jobs on release. Florida tracked 1572 released inmates who received a certificate of achievement in a vocational training program. Forty-eight percent were employed, of which 14% were working in occupations directly or indirectly related to their vocational training. No employment information was found on the remaining 52%. The crucial question raised by these data was why so few inmates were employed in occupations directly related to their training. Our Close-Up on "Project RIO" (Re-Integration for Offenders), is an example of a successful vocational program designed to deal with recidivism and unemployment.

The types of vocational training provided by the Texas Correctional System illustrate the possibilities for varied training that correctional systems can furnish. During the 1992–93 school year, 13,303 (of the 64,313 inmates) were enrolled in five basic program areas involving 503 different vocational training courses. The basic program areas included trades and industrial, office education, agriculture, health, and marketing. Instruction was given in traditional shop facilities and in on-the-job work areas such as industrial, construction, and farm shops (Texas Department of Criminal Justice, 1993).

Programs are offered based on their appearance on the Texas Education Agency's list of authorized priority programs and their identification as having high employment possibilities. All courses focus on the development of essential skills and knowledge.

To meet the needs of the prison population, vocational training programs are organized into four different delivery systems. **Segmentation programs** take a standard 600-hour course of study and divide it into four equal parts of approximately 150 hours, each involving a major part of the course. The curriculum of each segment is organized to teach a group of related skills and technical knowledge that is sufficient to provide employment possibilities to those completing it. For example, the automotive trade class is divided into (1) cooling systems, engine lube systems, exhaust and fuel systems; (2) brake repair; (3) engine; and (4) ignition systems. Inmates completing the brake repair segment would be qualified to work in a brake repair shop, while those completing all four segments would have opportunities to be employed as general mechanics (see Figure 18.2).

The short-term vocational program was designed to teach a specific number of skills and related knowledge in a time frame ranging from 30 to 100 hours. It was developed to give inmates who are serving short sentences, or who are about to be

## Close Up  Project Rio

Statistics from the Texas Department of Criminal Justice (TDCJ), Pardons and Parole Division, indicate that ex-offenders who secure work return to prison at a rate one-third of those who do not secure work. **Project RIO** (Re-Integration for Offenders) is a multi-agency employment initiative that matches ex-offenders with employers and was developed to increase employability. Its plan is to reduce recidivism and unemployment of ex-offenders by providing a link between education, vocational training, and services in TDCJ and job placement and training in the community. The program involves several steps:

**1.** Prospective inmates are assessed to determine eligibility. If selected, a specialist does a complete assessment that includes aptitudes, skills, interests, education and work histories.

**2.** An Employability Development Plan (EDP) is then developed based on the assessment results and availability of jobs in the community where the participant will be released.

**3.** Based on the findings of the assessment, the participants are referred to appropriate academic and/or vocational programs.

**4.** Upon inmate release, referrals are made to the Texas Employment Commission to continue training or for job placement.

RIO participants experienced a 5% reduction in recidivism. This means that about 750 releasees a year who might otherwise return to prison do not do so because of their RIO involvement. This results in a savings of over $12 million for the state (Texas Department of Criminal Justice, 1993).

---

released, an opportunity to acquire some skill training. These courses can also serve as a refresher or as skill enhancement for inmates with existing skills in the area. Eighteen different short courses are offered including word processing, short order cook, brake repair, and hospital cleaning.

**Cluster courses** offer 100-hour blocks of instruction in related but different subject areas of a given trade. For example, building maintenance is divided into seven separate clusters of instruction: electrical repair, plumbing, painting, drywall repair, installing vinyl, installing carpet, and wallpapering (Figure 18.2). Inmates successfully completing these courses either receive a certificate of participation or a certificate of achievement specifying mastery in the trade (Windham School System, 1986, 1987, 1989, 1991–1992).

Finally, the apprenticeship program offers inmates opportunities to receive training in thirty different crafts. To assure that standards are maintained, craft committees consisting of labor, management, and department representatives regularly monitor these programs. The programs require inmates to complete 2000 to 4000 hours of work and 144 to 600 hours of laboratory or classroom-related training in the theory of the craft. This training is provided after work hours.

**VARIOUS POSTSECONDARY PROGRAMS ARE OPEN TO INMATES**  Lectures given at Elmira between 1876–1900 by professors from a nearby college were the first exposure of inmates to postsecondary education (Pisciotta, 1983). In 1925 extension courses were offered at San Quentin, California. The first real college program was a joint venture between Menard Correctional Center and Southern Illinois University that began in the 1952–53 school year (Morris, 1974). During the 1960s, the number of college courses offered in prisons increased rapidly. A 1973 survey found that 218 prisons offered college programs, more than three-fourths of which involved actual in-house classes by college and university instructors (Davis, 1978).

A major contributor to expanded college offerings in prison was Project NewGate. Funded by the Office of Economic Opportunity it was first introduced in 1967 at Oregon State Prison. By 1972 programs were operating in state prisons in Minnesota, New Mexico, and Pennsylvania and at two federal youth centers. The goal of NewGate was to establish self-contained programs to prepare a sizable number of inmates for college by offering quality courses, academic and therapeutic counseling, and individual attention from staff members.

FIGURE 18.2   **The (a) Segmentation and (b) Cluster Concepts**

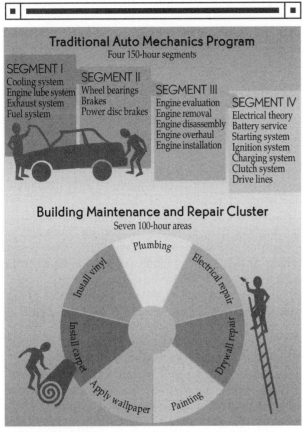

### Traditional Auto Mechanics Program
Four 150-hour segments

**SEGMENT I**
Cooling system
Engine lube system
Exhaust system
Fuel system

**SEGMENT II**
Wheel bearings
Brakes
Power disc brakes

**SEGMENT III**
Engine evaluation
Engine removal
Engine disassembly
Engine overhaul
Engine installation

**SEGMENT IV**
Electrical theory
Battery service
Starting system
Ignition system
Charging system
Clutch system
Drive lines

### Building Maintenance and Repair Cluster
Seven 100-hour areas

Plumbing
Electrical repair
Drywall repair
Painting
Apply wallpaper
Install carpet
Install vinyl

SOURCE: Windham School System (1989). *Meeting the challenge: Innovative educational programming.* Huntsville, TX: Author. Reprinted with permission of Windham School System, Texas Department of Criminal Justice.

Unique to this program was a postrelease component that assisted inmates in the transition from prison to life outside. It furnished financial and other assistance to releasees, including the initial provision of housing at release centers on or adjacent to campus, while they completed their course work (Seashore, Haberfield, Irwin, and Baker, 1976).

By the 1990s the number of inmates involved in college programs had increased substantially. In 1993, thirty-seven systems offered two-year degree programs. Of these, thirty-six reported 33,219 inmates enrolled. Four-year degree programs were offered by twenty-one systems and eighteen of these reported 3656 inmates enrolled in classes (Lillis, 1994f). Seven systems offer postgraduate courses and reported 202 inmate enrollees.

Finally, thirty-six systems offered inmates the opportunity to pursue postsecondary education on a correspondence basis. Of these, twenty reported 1274 inmate enrollees (Lillis, 1994f). The variety of offerings is as diverse as the institutions providing the courses (Wolford, 1987).

There has been little hostility toward furnishing adult basic education, GED, or related high school programs to inmates because they are available free to everyone on the outside and this is viewed as remedial. However, college programs are not seen as remedial. Since a college education may be too costly for some in the general population, there are calls to do away with this program for inmates. This is another point at which the principle of less eligibility becomes an issue. Perhaps people would be less critical if they recognized the benefits to society of allowing inmates to pursue postsecondary degrees. Thus, a follow-up study of inmate participants from New York State correctional facilities who had been in college programs in 1986–87 and had been released for at least twelve months found a significant difference between the return rates of those earning their degrees (26.4%—$n = 356$) and those who had withdrawn or were administratively terminated (44.6%—$n = 630$). Further, successful degree recipients returned at much lower rates than would be expected when compared with the overall male return rate (41.1%) (Clark, 1991). However, with the elimination by Congress of Pell grants for prison inmates in 1994, which provided a substantial amount of the funding for these types of educational programs, most systems have terminated these programs and the remaining few have substantially reduced their scope. Pell grants generally provided $1500 per year per inmate with about 26,000 inmates receiving these grants to take college courses. A study by the Office of Management and the Budget (OMB) found that despite popular views to the contrary, no college students in the free society were ever denied a Pell grant because inmates received them.

In addition to the OMB study, other studies conducted at Roosevelt University and MacMurray College, both of which offer courses in prison, found that college-educated inmates return to prison at much lower rates (5 to 10% versus 46%) than other inmates. Given that the average annual cost of keeping an inmate in prison is about $20,000, the economics of paying for inmates to attend college makes sense. Additionally, it makes the individual a productive member of society, which in the long run makes him or her into a tax contributor rather than a tax consumer. This is obviously a cost-effective way of reducing correctional and other criminal justice expenditures and all of the intangible aspects associated with crime and victimization. At this point the only opportunity that inmates appear to have for taking college courses is to attend classes that are brought into the prison via television, since most inmates do not have the money to pay tuition for colleges classes (Steurer, 1995; Copley, 1995).

## Mandatory Participation and Provisions of Incentives Are Two Issues in Correctional Education

This section focuses on issues related to the difficult problem of motivating inmates who have generally had very negative experiences and failed in school. An important question to ask is whether to make schooling mandatory for those who need it. Another consideration is the use of monetary rewards for attending school. Getting those who need the skills to attend is important because success in this endeavor may turn their lives around.

### VOLUNTARY OR COERCED ENTRY INTO BASIC EDUCATION PROGRAMS IS A DEBATED ISSUE

Typically, inmates who voluntarily participate in educational programming are more motivated than those who are required to enroll. However, there are inmates, usually dropouts, who need basic literacy skills and would not go to school if they were not required. Thus, despite test results indicating the need for basic education, inmates do not always see the urgency of participating in education programs because they may fear ridicule or may believe they are doing well enough with their limited education (Conrad, 1981). Inmate views that regard schooling either as not manly or representing conformity to the straight world may also help to reduce participation.

For many inmates, forced attendance may be a face-saving device that gives them the push they need to start. Many teachers in correctional settings report even a small taste of success can "hook" even the initially unmotivated inmate (Bellorado, 1986). Thus, there is ample justification for systems to continue requiring inmates who fall below certain basic achievement levels to attend school for at least a minimum period. The success of these

efforts can be seen in the fact that between 1981 and 1990, literacy program completions in the federal system rose 700% (McCollum, 1992).

### SHOULD INMATES RECEIVE INCENTIVES FOR PARTICIPATION IN EDUCATION PROGRAMS?

Ideally education should be pursued for the sake of learning and the help that the knowledge can provide the individual in many endeavors. For inmates who are more concretely and materially oriented, this may be too elusive as a goal. Moreover, in some systems, inmates may have to choose between earning a wage, small as it often is, or attending school. For inmates without personal resources or relatives or friends who send them money or goods, this may be too great a sacrifice. However, if wages are paid to inmates who attend school, work holds no monetary advantage to education. Other ways of resolving this problem have been to schedule education programming in the evenings or, as in Texas, to give inmates three hours per day (fifteen hours per week) off work to attend classes. Positive rewards (e.g., pay raises, etc.) for completing education programs also serve to motivate students to participate in and complete educational programs (Bellorado, 1986).

Educational programs may sometimes be subverted by some custodial staff and administration because they view the goals of the prison to be mainly security, order, and discipline. This punitive view of the prison, coupled with negative attitudes toward inmates, conflicts with educational goals aimed at helping inmates to realize their potential and may reduce the effectiveness of these programs (Bellorado, 1986). Another obstacle is that many programs operate with limited budgets, which are likely to be the first cut in times of budget shortfalls. While inmates have the right to receive certain services, Benjamin Gromes, director of Florida's Correctional Education Authority, notes that education is not seen as a protected right for inmates (Rinehart, 1990).

Despite these and other obstacles, however, many fine educational programs are currently serving inmates in many of the correctional institutions in the United States. There is evidence that educational programs tend to reduce recidivism and thereby the long-term costs of corrections. A study in Florida by the Correctional Education School Authority (1990) found that inmates completing either a GED or vocational program had a recidivism rate of 7% compared to 34% for the general inmate population, and when postrelease employment was combined with completed educational programs, there was even less recidivism. This study also estimated the net savings to the state from 377 potential recidivists who did not return to prison as a result of completing an educational program to be about $7 million over a nineteen-month period.

In the final analysis, while correctional education programs are not panaceas for all of the problems faced by inmates released from prison, they can help those who are interested in leading conventional lives. They do this by providing opportunities to develop basic academic skills and/or to learn a trade that gives them a better chance of getting and keeping a job upon release. Moreover estimates indicate that it costs about $2500 to educate an inmate versus $15,000 to keep one incarcerated (Lillis, 1994f).

## PRISON WORK PROGRAMS[4]

Prison work for inmates consists of two general types of jobs: those that maintain the institution (preparing meals, cleaning the dormitories) and those that are industrial/productive in nature. Work in prison serves several functions; it keeps the prison running, keeps inmates busy, saves the state money, produces goods and services used by other institutions and governmental agencies, and teaches a useful skill. These purposes make work a necessary and important part of any prison's program.

### The Use of Inmate Labor Has a Long History

The roots of prison labor in the United States can be traced to the English jails of the eleventh through the thirteenth centuries where inmate work actually paid for the costs of imprisonment as well as the sheriff's salary (American Correctional Association, 1986). With the establishment of the Bridewell and other workhouses in the fourteenth century, hard labor was seen to provide payment for one's keep as well as a means of reformation. Work was also an important element in programs at the Hospice of San Michele (1704) and Maison de Force (1775), which were antecedents of later juvenile and adult institutions. The types of work

selected were highly diversified and attempts were made to minimize competition with free labor even though no organized labor movement existed at that time. During the mid-1700s prison reformers such as John Howard and Cesare Beccaria viewed inmate labor as a primary method of reformation and a key factor in using imprisonment to replace capital punishment.

### Inmate Workers Help to Maintain the Institution

In the United States inmates have traditionally been occupied in work either related to the maintenance or sustenance of the institution or in workshops or item-producing industries. The rest of this section discusses prison maintenance work programs and the last part of the chapter focuses on prison industries.

**MANY MAINTENANCE/SERVICE TASKS ARE AVAILABLE**   Correctional facilities require a variety of maintenance tasks and services in order to function. While civilians could be employed to do this work, inmates have traditionally done it because they are an available and less costly source of labor. It also occupies their time, which reduces problems associated with idleness. These jobs include janitorial work, maintenance and repair of the physical plant and equipment, food preparation and service, nonconfidential clerical and stenographic work, repair, laundering, and cleaning of clothing, medical and dental assistants, landscaping, power plant operation, teaching, and serving as orderlies. Inmates may also perform domestic, maintenance, and other functions at the warden's house, assistant warden's house, and COs' quarters.

The scarcity of prison industry jobs and other work and programming tends to result in the overassignment of inmates to these activities. The result is that two, three, or even more persons may be working at a job that would normally only need one person. Conrad (1986) provides an excellent illustration:

> [In] my observations of the mess hall at the Indiana Prison at Michigan City, I had a depressing but significant dialogue with the chief steward. He told me that over-assignment to the mess hall was so serious that he had several times as many men as he could keep occupied. His solution was to assign one four-man table to each man and require him to clean it up after each meal—a task that might occupy him for

five whole minutes out of the day. Yet the Captain's assignment board would show that all these men were on full-time assignments. Was such a job meaningful, I asked? (p. 75).

The response of a correctional veteran to this description suggests how this set of circumstances has been rationalized within the correctional setting:

> If the prisoner working his table does a good job, is encouraged to do so, and praised when he does, then he is getting a job experience that he may never have had before. After all, it's the quality of the work that counts, not the mere number of hours that the prisoner puts in. A man who has learned to take pride in his work has learned something that will keep him a regular job when he gets out, right? (pp. 75–76).

Obviously this view is absurd, but it serves as a good rationale for continuing these practices. However, it does little to develop good work habits and may lead to job failure on the outside.

The problems of prison work are compounded by at least three conditions (Flanagan, 1989). First, for a variety of reasons, many inmates simply have no desire to work, and prisons are limited in their capacity to provide incentives for productive and conventional work. Second, in contrast to life on the outside where time is valued, inmates live in an environment where time is an enemy, and there are few productive/legal activities to occupy them. Third, work opportunities coming close to "real-world" employment are rare.

**EMPLOYMENT OF INMATES IN AGRICULTURAL, FORESTRY, AND ROAD WORK ACTIVITIES IS ALSO COMMON**  The employment of inmates in agricultural, forestry, and road work activities has long been a part of the prison system. As noted in Chapter 5, these were the principal activities in southern institutions. This work included picking cotton, cutting lumber, harvesting crops, building roads, fighting fires, raising livestock, and maintaining parks and state buildings.

This category of work assignments has both benefits and drawbacks for inmates and the corrections system. On the one hand, it has been argued that these activities help defray the cost of incarceration. The Texas prison system operates under a legislative mandate to be as self-sufficient as possible. As a result, its agricultural division grows most of the food that is consumed by the staff and

inmates. This division includes farms that produce millions of pounds of fresh and cannery vegetables, dairy farms, poultry farms that produced 4.9 million eggs, and cattle and swine herds. These operations are so successful that they have produced substantial surpluses (in 1993 total outside sales were $4.7 million) and kept food costs down to only $1.54 per inmate per day (Nunnellee, 1994).

This type of work has been one reason for the development of camp-type institutions that are typically minimum security. Their existence allows assignment of the inmates who are least dangerous to these less costly facilities and makes it possible to separate offenders who are young and unsophisticated from those who are seasoned and committed to a career of crime.

With the public mood currently focused on imprisoning more and more offenders, there is little doubt that these types of work assignments will continue. In fact, it would not be surprising to see correctional systems employing more inmates in these types of activities as the costs of incarcerating them continue to escalate. In this respect the Federal Bureau of Prisons is developing interagency agreements with the National Parks and Forest Services and other interested agencies in which inmates can work (Pospichal, 1991). This has even filtered down to local corrections, where the Sheriff of Manatee County, Florida, created a farm operation in which inmates work to raise vegetables and other foodstuffs for consumption in the county jail.

## Over Time Attitudes toward Prison Industries Have Changed

In the United States work was an integral part of both the Pennsylvania and Auburn systems. Individual labor characterized the Pennsylvania system, and congregate work was a key factor in the Auburn regimen. This latter feature enabled the establishment of factories in prisons with the potential for making them self-supporting and was a major reason this model became dominant in this country.

**HISTORICALLY THERE WERE TWO MAIN TYPES OF PRISON INDUSTRY SYSTEMS**  The period after the Civil War lasting until the end of the 1800s represents the heyday of prison industries in this country. Auburn-type (industrial) prisons were

Industry jobs for inmates provide wages, which helps raise morale while reducing tension. These jobs can benefit society by providing services and goods and reducing correctional costs.

most numerous in the Midwest and Northeast. Two basic types of prison industry systems operated during this era, each of which had three subtypes and were primarily distinguished by the degree of private involvement.

One of the two basic types was the **private benefit system.** Its three variations included:

**1.** *The lease system:* Under this system the state gave up the care and custody of inmates and was paid a price by the leasee. It was primarily used in the South (see Chapter 5).

**2.** *The contract system (Auburn model):* Under this system the state retained control of prisoners. Work was done within the prison under contract to private companies who paid the state a per diem charge per worker and furnished the necessary instructors, machinery, and raw material. The state usually furnished buildings, power, light, and guards for the supervision of the inmates. However, it had no responsibility for the sale of the finished product.

**3.** *The piece-price system:* Although similar to the contract system, it differed in two important ways. First, state officials had full control of the production process. The contractor furnished the raw materials but prison authorities were respon-

sible for manufacturing the product, the speed of the work process, and product quality. Second, the contractor paid the state an agreed amount for each finished article it accepted. Under this and the contract system it was customary to set a fixed amount of work as the daily task. Inmates exceeding this minimum level were paid "overtime" based on the amount of their overproduction. They were not paid directly but, depending on prison rules, could use this money to improve their comfort or pleasure, have it forwarded to their family, or held until their release (Byers, 1910; Gillin, 1935).

The second basic type of prison industry also included three subtypes and was designated **no private benefit system.** It employed inmates solely for the benefit of the state or its political subdivisions.

**1.** In the state or public account system, the state or municipality becomes a manufacturer and the prison becomes an industrial establishment operating in the same manner as any outside free industry. The institution purchases raw materials, supervises production, sets prices, and sells the product on the open market. This puts prisons in direct competition with private enterprise.

**2.** The state-use system differs from the public account system in that sales are limited to public institutions, municipalities, and political divisions of the state. The state does not compete directly with outside industries that are only indirectly affected by curtailment of sales to government agencies.

**3.** The public works and ways system is quite similar to the state-use system in that prison labor is used to benefit the governmental entity. However, instead of being employed in manufacturing products, inmates are used for construction, repair, and maintenance of prisons or other public structures, roads, and parks. This system has been used extensively in the south.

**RESTRICTIVE LEGISLATION SUPPRESSED PRISON INDUSTRIES**    Prison industries began to decline at the beginning of the twentieth century. During the next forty years, pressure from unions and business culminated in three key pieces of restrictive federal legislation:

**1.** The **Hawes-Cooper Act of 1929** allowed states to block the importation of prison-made goods.
**2.** The **Ashurst-Summers Act of 1935** prohibited the interstate transportation of convict-made goods to states where such products were prohibited and required labels on all prison products sold in interstate commerce.
**3.** The Act of October 14, 1940, prohibited the interstate transport of all prison-made products except agricultural commodities and goods produced for states and their political subdivisions (Flynn, 1951).

By 1940, restrictive legislation limiting the open-market sale of prison-made goods also existed in most states.

All of this legislation sounded the death knell for prison industries. At the beginning of the twentieth century, 85% of all inmates worked in prison industries; by 1940 this dropped to 44%. Only during World War II was there a brief resurgence of prison industries due to an executive order lifting restrictions on inmate-produced goods needed for the war effort. This order was revoked at the end of the war and prisons returned to their prewar state of idleness (Flynn, 1951). However, during the wars in Korea, Vietnam, and the recent Persian Gulf War, federal prisons produced materials for those war efforts.

Prison industries further stagnated until the 1970s due to the emergence of correctional rehabilitation, which viewed education and treatment as the primary methods for reforming offenders. Work was considered of minimal rehabilitative value and was relegated to a position of insignificance (Hawkins, 1983).

**REINTEGRATION, OVERCROWDING, AND EMPHASIS ON THE PRIVATE SECTOR HAVE REVITALIZED PRISON INDUSTRIES**    The recent resurgence of prison industries was influenced by several developments. In 1967 the President's Commission Task Force on Corrections issued a report at a time when the medical model of rehabilitation was coming under attack and losing credibility (American Correctional Association, 1986). This report stressed reintegration as the key to reforming offenders. This philosophy required an emphasis on the development of skills that would enable offenders to maintain themselves successfully in the community on release from prison. This suggested the need for programs paralleling those in the private sector that would provide inmates with the knowledge, skills, practice, and experience to "make it" in the community after release. The cycle of prison reform had come full circle, and work replaced treatment programs as the means to reform offenders. Cullen and Travis (1984) found that this coincided with public views that work had the greatest potential for rehabilitating offenders. A study of inmates during this period showed that they shared a similar view (Dinitz and Huff, 1988).

Also, during the 1970s, public attitudes shifted and supported more punitive treatment of inmates, resulting in greater use of incarceration as a sanction and the imposition of longer sentences. This increased the prison population substantially at a time when resources for adding more beds were not available. The resulting overcrowding caused prisons to focus attention on inmate work as a means of partially offsetting the increasing need for greater state funding for corrections and to reduce idleness.

Finally, an increasing emphasis on the use of the private sector to solve public problems led to private enterprise again becoming involved in prison industries and in other aspects of corrections. Two factors helped in hastening this development. First, a broadened national economy dominated by large manufacturers was not threatened by competition from relatively small prison production operations. Second, American industry had shifted its labor-intensive production operations, for which prisons are best suited, to foreign countries. This offered U.S. companies an opportunity to recapture enterprises that had gone overseas by using prison labor, which could produce many of these products at competitive prices (Dwyer and McNally, 1993). Taken together these factors enabled the rejuvenation of prison industries that had stagnated since the 1930s (Miller and Grieser, 1986; Auerbach, Sexton, Farrow, and Lawson, 1988).

## Contemporary Prison Industries Have Three Goals

Inmate labor is currently receiving support from widely divergent groups of people who view it as serving a variety of goals (Flanagan, 1989). Guynes and Greiser(1986) have classified these goals into three categories: inmate related, institutional, and societal.

**THE OFFENDER BENEFITS BY DEVELOPING WORKING SKILLS AND SAVING MONEY** Most offenders have been unsuccessful in the work world, in part because they lack exposure to the norms and practices (e.g., punctuality, individual effort) of the world of work. Prison jobs can enable inmates to learn these responsibilities and job skills.

Prison jobs based on real-world work truly provide inmates with the experiences needed to be successful on release. On these jobs inmates are supervised by free-world managers who emphasize promptness, attendance, and quality and quantity of output. A broader objective is life management experience, which gives offenders the opportunity to legitimately provide for themselves. It does this by paying them wages and requiring them to manage their income to pay for room, board, and other life needs.

Additionally, jobs that pay inmates a reasonable wage enable them to save funds for their release (gate money). Since inmates coming out of prison often have trouble getting jobs, this money can help them secure a residence, eat, and pay for transportation, clothes, etc. Ex-offenders who leave prison with sufficient gate money have a lower recidivism rate compared with those who do not. Thus, providing them with opportunities to earn release money makes good correctional sense (Guynes and Grieser, 1986).

**THE INSTITUTION CAN BENEFIT FROM PRISON INDUSTRIES** Reducing idleness has become an even greater concern today because of overcrowding. Involving inmates in prison industries gets them out of their cells and dormitories and provides a meaningful daily activity that can reduce tensions. It also structures their time, which adds an element of order to institutional life and facilitates supervision and management. When large numbers of inmates are idle, they have time for illicit pursuits, which can result in institutional violence or other rule violations. Finally, prison industries can serve to reduce net operating costs by providing the correctional system with a variety of products, reduced costs for alternative programming when inmates are employed rather than idle, and profits from the sale of industrial products and services.

**SOCIETY CAN BENEFIT FROM PRISON INDUSTRIES** Societal objectives center on the idea that criminals are responsible to the community for at least some of their incarceration costs. A different facet of this is the savings achieved when prison industry programs provide goods and/or services to governmental agencies or meet other societal needs. Road gangs work on highways, parks, and other public/government areas, and can also be viewed as attempts to realize these objectives. However, only a few states use them. Assessing convicted offenders for court costs is a more recent effort to make criminals pay some of the costs associated with their offense. For indigent inmates, wages for prison work can be used to make these payments. Another goal in states that pay inmate workers wages is for them to use part of their income to help support their outside dependents and thereby reduce the burden on the welfare system. They may also pay income taxes and social security. Finally, in line with the greater emphasis on victim rights, inmates often have restitution payments deducted from their wages.

**ATTAINING OFFENDER, INSTITUTIONAL, AND SOCIETAL GOALS FOR WORK PROGRAMS CAN CREATE PROBLEMS** The fact that prison work programs have multiple goals that can conflict with one another raises questions as to the extent to which these goals can be achieved simultaneously (Guynes and Greiser, 1986). For example, the need to reduce idleness may result in the overassignment of inmates to prison jobs, compromising goals such as providing real-world job experiences or teaching job skills. Likewise, requiring that inmate compensation include provisions for both victim restitution and dependent assistance increases expenses, adding to the cost of services and products. This reduces their competitiveness with the private sector (Guynes and Grieser, 1986; Flanagan, 1989).

### The Prison Environment Imposes Constraints on Work Programs

Operating industries in the prison environment involves factors not at issue in outside businesses (Guynes and Grieser, 1986).

#### INMATE WORKERS CAN POSE SOME PROBLEMS

Prison industries are limited to selecting workers from the institutional population. Although every system has some qualified inmates, the vast majority are underqualified. Some states have developed vocational programs that provide inmates with the training or skill development required to work in their prison industrial programs. For example, the federal prison system has linked these components by establishing an Industrial Education and Vocational Training Division (IEVT), which manages and coordinates these programs (Pospichal, 1991). IEVT conducts preindustrial programs that give inmates hands-on skill training at actual production sites before assuming their positions in a prison industrial setting. It also provides refresher, continuing, and advanced training as needed during production in addition to requiring educational achievement for promotion or other advancements.

Another problem is that many inmates have little or no motivation to work. To counteract this problem, more supervision is needed. Part of the reason for low motivation is that there is often no direct relationship between productivity and rewards for the inmate.

#### SECURITY NEEDS CAN DISRUPT PRODUCTION

Security concerns, ranging from dealing with one disruptive inmate to controlling the entire population through a lockdown, often impede production goals. Budgetary constraints may add to this problem by curtailing the number of available COs to supervise inmates. One solution to this problem, used in North Carolina, was to hire industry personnel as assistant shop foremen and train them in

the demands of prison industry shops while they supervised inmate workers. They were then eligible for promotion to shop foremen and higher level central office positions (Miller and Grieser, 1986).

Another problem is tool regulation, which is critical in a correctional facility. Some control methods can obstruct production. There are two approaches to this issue: (1) Adopt a strict tool control policy that reduces production time by an hour a day; and (2) focus on maximizing production and live with the risks of less strict control (Agresti, 1991).

Lockdowns, which are used to control serious disruptive prison situations, can be managed to minimize the disruption of industry schedules by giving prison industry inmates priority to return to their jobs when conditions permit. Callouts, counts, and meal times also make it difficult for prison industries to maintain an eight-hour work schedule. Counts can be scheduled before and after work hours and, if necessary, during the lunch hour. Several states have developed successful approaches to deal with inmate-caused callouts including pay reductions if inmates leave work for other than a parole or classification hearing or drug counseling; and evening counseling schedules. Solutions to problems caused by meals have included earlier meal schedules, having inmates "brown bag it" (Miller and Grieser, 1986; Grieser, Miller, and Funke, 1984), and creating an on-site dining area and using carts to deliver the food (Agresti, 1991).

A final problem faced by prison industries is the need for inmates to work in institutional support services (e.g., kitchen and maintenance). The Washington State correctional system attacked this issue by establishing a three-step system under which all inmates initially worked in institutional maintenance. They could then graduate to state-run tax reduction workshops, and then to private sector plants (Miller and Grieser, 1986).

#### THE INMATE WORK EXPERIENCE MUST INCLUDE REASONABLE PAY AND INCENTIVES

A requisite for industry success is reasonable compensation for inmates. The primary obstacle to appropriate inmate compensation has been the court-supported view that the state owns the inmates' labor and is not obligated to pay them for work done (Grieser, Miller, and Funke, 1984; Mushlin, 1993). In many states this has resulted in inmates receiving little

(10 to 65 cents daily) or no pay and/or good time credits (Burns, 1975). The recent emerging view of prison industries as business operations has placed greater emphasis on giving inmate workers sufficient incentives to produce quality products. Average daily inmate salary rates for 1993 ranged from $2.12 to $9.85 for industry jobs and $1.01 to $4.91 for nonindustry jobs (in systems which paid inmates for this work) (Camp and Camp, 1994a). This compared with a daily average of $28.08 to $35.93 for private industry jobs.

More states appear to be providing some form of bonus or incentive pay for performance. For example, Michigan and Montana have wage plans that include increased pay for longevity and seniority, which reportedly has reduced inmate turnover. They also pay quarterly bonuses based on profitability. A few states, such as Washington and Minnesota, pay inmates up to the prevailing market rates for work in selected industry shops. Deductions are made for room, board, restitution, and dependent support. This is designed to reinforce the real-world aspects of work that these programs are attempting to create. The federal system's industry program, UNICOR, deals with motivation through promotion/demotion, incentive pay, premium pay, and other benefits, including a scholarship and incentive awards program (Pospichal, 1991). Other state-provided incentives have included additional good-time credits and privileges such as special housing, added recreation time, extra telephone and visits, and special meals.

**THE QUALITY OF PRISON GOODS AND SERVICES HAS BEEN A PROBLEM** In the past, prison industries have been plagued with complaints regarding the poor quality of their products. This has been used as justification by state agencies for not purchasing prison-made products. The recent emphasis on operating these industries like private business has resulted in better quality control through inspections and inmate incentive programs. For example, in Oklahoma inmate incentives are tied directly to product quality. Here a certain amount of money is placed in a fund based on the production of satisfactory merchandise. However, double the amount is taken from it when faulty products are returned (Miller and Grieser, 1986). These procedures have increased the salability of inmate-produced items.

## Attempts Are Being Made to Revitalize Prison Industries

Between 1885 and 1979 the proportion of inmates employed in correctional industries dropped from 90 to 10% (Funke, Wayson, and Miller, 1982). Camp and Camp (1994a) found that almost 7% of the inmate population was employed in prisons with close to an additional 2% working in farm-related activities—some of these are considered industry programs in some jurisdictions. These figures characterize what has undoubtedly been the longest economic depression of any U.S. industry and are another consequence of overcrowding.

**PRIVATE SECTOR INVOLVEMENT IN PRISON INDUSTRY INCLUDES SEVERAL MODELS** Four basic models represent possible roles that the private sector might play in prison work.

In the **controlling customer model** the private sector is the primary or exclusive customer of a business that it owns or has helped capitalize and which it may or may not manage. The Vinyl Products Manufacturing Company, which operates a plant producing mattresses at the Northern Nevada Correctional Center (NNCC), illustrates this approach. In 1985 Vinyl Products began to experience increasing product demands. The company was using prerelease inmates to work the graveyard shift at its plant, but there were not enough eligible inmates in this prison to keep up with the increased demands. To solve the problem, it decided to establish a plant inside NNCC. Within two years the prison workforce had grown to nearly 120 inmates on three shifts. Inmates originally were restricted to production of the company's simplest product line, but satisfaction with both production and quality led the company to add to the NNCC plant both its full and custom product lines. Inmate workers earn the same pay and benefits as outside workers. Room and board is deducted from their pay. Inmates also have taxes deducted from their salaries, pay victim restitution, and support their families with this money (Auerbach et al., 1988). While economic conditions have reduced the workforce to 70 inmates in 1994 the continued operation of this program for almost ten years is indicative of its success (Skolnik, 1994).

Under the **main customer model** the private sector buys a substantial portion of the output of a prison-owned and operated business, but has no other connection with it. The Graphics and Printing Shop at the Utah State Prison at Draper fits this model. This shop employs thirty workers and is operated by Utah Correctional Industries. It sells to both the state and the public, with more than 40% of its output sold to private companies, which influenced it to operate like an outside business (Sexton *et al.*, 1985).

In the **employer model** the private sector owns and manages the business and employs inmates to produce its goods or services. Control over firing, hiring, and supervision of inmates rests with the company (Sexton *et al.*, 1985). The arrangement between TWA and the California Youth Authority illustrates how both industry and corrections can benefit. TWA required readily available trained workers to process the overflow of phone reservations during peak call periods and on holidays and weekends. Because inmates have few time commitments, are usually available on short notice, and are close to the workplace, they are more flexible than free-world workers in responding to overflows. In 1986 the Youth Authority constructed a building that it leased to the airline and TWA brought in telephones and computers. Inmate reservation agents are required to have a GED, at least a tenth-grade reading level, and must complete an eighteen-week junior college accredited training course taught by the Youth Authority prior to employment. In 1994 seventy inmates were working in the program. They are paid $5.09 per hour from which 15% is automatically deducted for victim restitution. Federal income tax is also deducted. Twenty percent of the net wages goes toward room and board and 40% goes into a savings account, the proceeds of which the youth receives on release. This program has been operating for more than eight years (Randall, 1994). Agresti (1991) notes that there are problems with programs that allow inmates access to personal and financial information because some inmates have used this credit information to purchase items by phone. This has resulted in the restriction of the information available to inmates or in the monitoring of their calls, thereby increasing costs. One other solution is to screen applicants for these jobs so that inmates with histories of fraud-related offenses are not hired. Although the incidence of these problems may not be greater than on the outside, their occurrence in a prison setting can endanger a program's continuation.

The **corporate model** represents a logical extension of current efforts to operate prison industries using free-world business practices (Grieser, 1988). It involves establishing a quasi-independent corporation that operates and manages prison industries yet is connected to the corrections department for security purposes. It is structured like a private corporation, with a chief executive that reports to a policy board. While markets are still government entities, the corporate structure provides more flexible purchasing and borrowing arrangements. UNICOR, the federal program established in 1934, is the grand-father of this approach. Other variants of this model have also been employed by Florida, California, and Georgia. Our Close-Up on "PRIDE" discusses Florida's program.

### The Future of Prison Work and Industry Programs Involves the Private Sector

Private sector involvement in prison work programs cannot solve all the problems that plague corrections. Although the goal is to achieve productive, cost-effective, and meaningful work programs, the corrections environment and inmate population place limitations on the achievement of these objectives. However, at a time when correctional budgets are stretched to the limit, private sector work programs offer opportunities to experiment with programs that might otherwise be impossible. They also represent a commitment by the business community to use its expertise "to open a pathway for those at the very bottom of the social order who might otherwise continue to fail at their own and society's expense" (Auerbach *et al.*, 1988, p. 65).

Expansion of work programs is limited by the deficiencies of the inmate labor force that require costly and nonprofitable academic and vocational training prior to employment in these programs. Added to this is the overriding concern with security in correctional facilities. When security is threatened, production will be sacrificed. Thus far, the renewed involvement of business in prison industries has not raised any major objections from labor and business groups. This may be partly due to the small scale of prison programs. However, the cries of unfair competition by labor and business may again be heard.

For all of the preceding reasons, the goal of full and meaningful employment in the prison setting is not likely to be realized (Flanagan, 1989). Still, it

# *Close Up*   PRIDE: An Example of the Corporate Model[5]

PRIDE (Prison Rehabilitative Industries and Diversified Enterprises) is a state-sponsored, not-for-profit corporation running forty-two industries and thirteen operations in twenty of Florida's prisons. It produces over 3000 products and services. In 1993, it employed 2663 of Florida's 48,000+ inmates. PRIDE has a number of problems recruiting qualified workers: some qualified inmates are not at facilities where PRIDE has programs, and some qualified inmates are employed in higher priority prison work programs. Another difficulty is most workers are short-term, medium and minimum security inmates many of whom, because of overcrowding, serve less than six months. Besides restricting the pool of workers, this severely curtails the benefits that inmates receive from those programs since twelve months is the optimum period required for inmate training (Florida Auditor General, 1991). In answer to this, PRIDE has established training that can at least be partially completed within six months. Considering such factors as the need for institutional maintenance and services, security considerations, inmate skill levels, and motivation, it is unrealistic to believe that more than 15% of the prison population would be available and could be accommodated by prison industries programs (Agresti, 1991).

### PRIDE Attempts to Reduce Inmate Idleness

One of PRIDE's primary goals is to reduce inmate idleness. Despite steady increases in the prison population, PRIDE has continued to employ the same percentage of inmates over the period 1986 to 1993. Its ability to employ more inmates has been impeded by adverse business conditions and the closing of unprofitable industries. To reduce the problem of idleness and inmate turnover and make use of long-term inmates, the establishment of new prison industries inside secure prisons has been recommended (Florida Auditor General, 1991; Florida TaxWatch, 1989).

### PRIDE Can Reduce the Costs of Incarceration

PRIDE employs male and female inmates from six to eight hours a day at wages from $0.15 to $0.50 per hour depending on seniority and job classification. An added 15% of inmate wages is contributed to victim restitution and court costs. PRIDE returns 1.5% of its annual net sales to the state general fund, which helps offset inmate incarceration costs. Inmates working for PRIDE are primarily supervised by their staff, reducing the need for correctional officers. Over a six-year period this is estimated to have saved Florida $8 million (Florida TaxWatch, 1989).

A 1985 state auditor general's report criticized PRIDE for not meeting quality standards. PRIDE responded by establishing a quality control program. A recent survey found that the major problems with quality had been resolved to the customer's satisfaction (Florida Auditor General, 1991). All PRIDE industries now guarantee that they will unconditionally take back any product with which a customer is dissatisfied. As TaxWatch notes these improvements show PRIDE's growing maturity as a corporation.

The issue of whether state agencies should be required to purchase PRIDE products must consider more than just the price of the item. Given comparable quality and prices not substantially different from those of private vendors, there are good reasons to require these purchases. These include PRIDE provides inmates with job skills that can reduce recidivism and result in substantial savings to the state; PRIDE staff supervises inmates while at work reducing the number of COs that need to be employed; employing inmates reduces tensions that can escalate to disturbances resulting in injury and property damage.

### Postrelease Employment Has Been a Difficult Goal

Another major goal of PRIDE is to prepare inmates for gainful employment upon release. Since the proportion of inmates working in PRIDE industries is small, the impact on the total prison population is likely to be small. However, for those inmates who have worked for PRIDE, the results are good. For 7893 inmates trained by PRIDE and tracked since 1991, over 3100 received one or more certificates. Of those trained, 1500 were released to the community from a PRIDE industry. Almost half these (48%) received help with job placement. After two years only 9% of these inmates returned to prison and only 3% of those with jobs were returned. This compares to a 50% return rate for Florida inmates as a whole.

To enhance inmate marketability PRIDE is pursuing a goal of having 70% of its workers receive a job completion certificate. In 1990 it established a new program called TIES (Training, Industry, Education, Support) designed to better prepare inmates for reentry into society. This program provides inmates with prerelease training and follows up released inmates placed through the PRIDE employment service (Florida Auditor General, 1991).

PRIDE of Florida employs inmates in various industry programs, providing them with work experience, and, in some cases marketable skills. This work experience can help reduce recidivism.

should be pursued because this approach holds promise of eliminating some of the debilitating effects of idleness by providing meaningful ways of "doing time" and other potential benefits for inmates. For society the cost benefits and potential reduction of recidivism are an added benefit. The results of a federal study support this view. This research focused on:

> inmates who participated in UNICOR work and other vocational training [while] in prison. This study found

that these inmates [as compared with those not participating in these activities] showed better institutional adjustment, were less likely to be revoked at the end of their first year back in the community, were more likely to be employed in the halfway house and community, and earned slightly more money in the community (Saylor and Gaes, 1992, p. 25).

Finally, one should judge prison work programs both in terms of these objectives and in the improvements made over the abysmal conditions of the recent past.

## ENDNOTES

**1.** The authors would like to thank Dr. Cheryl Johnson, director of instructional services, and Dr. Chris Tracy, acting superintendent, and Dr. Lane Murray, retired superintendent, Windham School District, Texas Department of Criminal Justice, and Martin Salisbury, director of education, Patuxent Institution, Maryland Department of Public Safety and Corrections, for providing information, reviewing this manuscript, and offering useful suggestions to improve its authenticity.

**2.** The states that either did not provide information on the number of inmate participants or failed to provide any data for this survey were Arizona, District of Columbia, West Virginia, Indiana, Maine, Nevada, Utah, Texas, and Washington and data for females from New Mexico was not available (Lillis, 1994e). Data from the 1993 annual report of the Texas Department of Criminal Justice showed the following figures for enrollment in other than college programs for 64,313 inmates: basic academic training, 34,477; vocational training, 13,905; English as second language, 922; special education for the handicapped, 1978; Chapter 1 (remedial program), 922.

**3.** For this second phase of this survey Arizona, District of Columbia, West Virginia, Indiana, Maine, Nevada, and Utah failed to provide information on ABE programs.

**4.** The authors would like to thank Tom Pospichal, division manager, UNICOR Plans and Policy, and Dr. David Agresti, formerly director of Institutional Programs PRIDE, Inc., for providing information, reviewing this manuscript, and offering useful suggestions to improve its authenticity.

**5.** The authors would like to thank Christine Reynolds, Director of Business Planning, and Patricia Foote, Director, Corporate Communications of PRIDE of Florida, for providing the information on PRIDE operations contained in this Close-Up.

## ACKNOWLEDGMENTS

[a] Quoted with permission of the Correctional Education Association.

## CHAPTER RECAP

### Provision of Basic Inmate Needs

There Are Important Reasons for Providing Basic Services
  Improving Inmates' Skills Can Reduce Crime
  Courts Have Required Basic Services

  Programs Increase the Efficiency and Security of the Prison

### Educational Programs

Prison Education Programs Have a Long History
  After the Civil War Education Came to be Viewed as an Important Element in the Reformation of Offenders
  In the 1960s Correctional Education Began to Receive Greater Emphasis
  In the 1980s Several Factors Furthered the Development of Correctional Education
There Are Several Types of Correctional Education Programs
  Many Jurisdictions Require Inmates Below a Certain Literacy Level to Enroll in Education Programs
  Both Adult Basic Education and Literacy Program Focus on Developing Elementary Academic Skills
  GED Programs Provide Inmates with an Opportunity to Obtain a High School Diploma
  Life Skill Programs Focus on Providing Inmates with the Skills to "Make It" in Society
    Development of "Thinking Skills" Is Sometimes Included in Life Skills Training
  Vocational Education Programs Are Designed to Provide Inmates with Job Skills
  Various Postsecondary Programs Are Open to Inmates
Mandatory Participation and Provision of Incentives Are Two Issues in Correctional Education
  Voluntary or Coerced Entry into Basic Education Programs Is a Debated Issue
  Should Inmates Receive Incentives for Participation in Education Programs?

### Prison Work Programs

The Use of Inmate Labor Has a Long History
Inmate Workers Help to Maintain the Institution
  Many Maintenance and Service Tasks Are Available
  Employment of Inmates in Agricultural, Forestry, and Road Work Activities Is Also Common
Over Time Attitudes Toward Prison Industries Have Changed
  Historically There Were Two Main Types of Prison Industry Systems
  Restrictive Legislation Suppressed Prison Industries
  Reintegration, Overcrowding, and Emphasis on the Private Sector Have Revitalized Prison Industries
Contemporary Prison Industries Have Three Goals
  The Offender Benefits by Developing Working Skills and Saving Money
  The Institution Can Benefit from Prison Industries
  Society Can Benefit from Prison Industries
  Attaining Offender, Institutional, and Societal Goals for Work Programs Can Create Problems

The Prison Environment Imposes Constraints on Work
  Programs
    Inmate Workers Can Pose Some Problems
    Security Needs Can Disrupt Production
    The Inmate Work Experience Must Include Reasonable Pay and Incentives
    The Quality of Prison Goods and Services Has Been a Problem
Attempts Are Being Made to Revitalize Prison
  Industries
    Private Sector Involvement in Prison Industry
      Includes Several Models
The Future of Prison Work and Industry Programs
  Involves the Private Sector

## REVIEW QUESTIONS

1. Discuss the concept of "least eligibility" and the impact it has on prison programming.
2. Describe the various educational programs that can be found in prisons.
3. What role does literacy play in education programs for inmates?
4. What is a GED and what benefits does it bring to inmate recipients?
5. Discuss the delivery systems that can be used to teach vocational skills.
6. Why is the prison environment generally not conducive to work?
7. What are the two main systems of prison industry?
8. What kind of constraints does the prison environment impose on work programs?
9. What is the corporate model of prison industry?

## TEST YOUR KNOWLEDGE

1. The Peer Tutoring Academy teaches
    a. correctional officers to assist in education programs
    b. citizen volunteers to tutor inmates
    c. qualified inmates to tutor other inmates
    d. inmates to assist instructors in vocational programs
2. Enrollment in which one of the following programs is required of inmates whose achievement falls below a certain level?
    a. Basic literacy programs
    b. Vocational training programs
    c. GED programs
    d. High school diploma programs
3. All of the following but one are reasons why the prison environment is not conducive to a meaningful work experience. Which one is *not* one of those reasons?
    a. There are not enough inmates available for labor.
    b. Many inmates have no desire or incentive to work.
    c. The value of time is less in prison.
    d. There are few opportunities for "real-world" employment experiences.
4. The system of prison industry in which a company agrees to pay a specific price for each specific article manufactured by prison labor is known as the
    a. lease system.
    b. piece-price system.
    c. the public works system.
    d. the state-use system.

# CHAPTER 19

# BASIC PRISON SERVICES: PHYSICAL AND MENTAL HEALTH AND TREATMENT

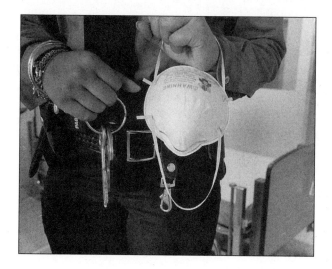

■ **LEARNING OBJECTIVES**

*After completion of this chapter, you should be able to:*
1. Describe the basis for inmate rights to adequate health care.
2. Discuss correctional treatment programs including behavior modification and cognitive approaches.
3. List and describe the issues in the provision of inmate health care.
4. Discuss the use of private care providers for inmate health care.
5. Describe drug abuse problems among inmates and the use of therapeutic communities in their treatment.
6. Discuss the incidence of infectious disease and the severe problems they pose for corrections.
7. Describe the AIDS problem in corrections and delineate the problems in dealing with HIV-infected inmates.

■ **KEY TERMS AND CONCEPTS**

Behavior modification
Cognitive therapy
Daily sick call
Deliberate indifference to serious medical need
HIV/AIDS
Multiple drug-resistant TB strains
National Commission on Correctional Health Care
Private health care providers
Ride the medical pony
Therapeutic communities

## Provision of Health Services

Outside of prison people are responsible for their own health care and, if they can afford it, may go to several practitioners until they receive the care that satisfies them. However, inmates are dependent on an institution's health services, which sometimes provides less than adequate care. This may lead to inmate court challenges. The importance of medical service can be seen in the frequency with which complaints about it head the list of riot demands and/or are the target of inmate court petitions (Anno, 1991a).

### Prison Health Care Did Not Improve Until the 1970s[1]

Like most prison activities, health care received little public scrutiny prior to the 1970s, which meant that "almost anything could go" (Prout and Ross, 1988, p. 228). This generally was justified by invoking the principle of least eligibility, as discussed in the last chapter. The Attica rebellion, often cited as a key event in prison medical reform because of the prominence given by inmates to medical grievances, prompted investigations and surveys of the health care delivery system in prisons and jails (Anno, 1989). Numerous deficiencies were found including unsanitary conditions; inadequate supplies and equipment; correctional staff impeding access to medical services; institutional physicians and other health care staff who could practice only in state institutions because they were trained abroad and were either unqualified to take or pass state licensing exams; and use of inmates as caregivers (Anno, 1989). These conditions were aggravated by the fact that 95% of the prison inmates required some type of medical attention, and two-thirds had not had medical examinations prior to imprisonment (Prout and Ross, 1988).

By the 1970s inmate medical care had improved as result of a growing recognition that everyone was entitled to adequate medical care. Also, the courts began intervening in prison matters and established an inmate's right to health care (*Newman v. Alabama*, 1972; *Estelle v. Gamble*, 1976). Since then hundreds of class action suits alleging unconstitutional medical conditions have been filed (Anno, 1989). Key professional organizations, including the American Public Health Association, the American Medical Association, the American Correctional Association, and the American Bar Association, also affirmed an inmate's right to adequate medical care and established commissions to develop standards and regulations for jails and prisons on the essentials of health care.

### Inmates Have a Constitutional Right to Adequate Medical and Mental Health Care

In *Estelle v. Gamble* (1976), the Supreme Court firmly supported the constitutional obligation of government to provide inmates with adequate medical and health care. This decision established a test to determine if the manner in which treatment was given constitutes "cruel and unusual punishment." This test required evidence of **deliberate indifference to serious medical need**. Examples of deliberate indifference include:

> 1) denial of an inmate's request for treatment; 2) failure to provide prescribed treatment; 3) delay in providing treatment; 4) inadequate treatment (e.g., giving penicillin to an inmate despite his known allergic reaction to it); 5) failure to examine new admissions appropriately and treat or isolate those with problems; 6) failure to provide and maintain adequate infirmary facilities (e.g., shortages of medication and use of antiquated equipment); 7) failure to provide appropriate and sufficient number of adequately trained, qualified, and experienced medical staff (the acid test for staffing is whether prisoners will suffer because of delay or denial of necessary medical care due to insufficient personnel); and 8) failure to provide adequate follow up care (e.g., intentional delay in removing sutures while the inmate was confined in isolation for 15 days resulting in an infected ear) (Isele, 1977; Knight, 1986; *Grubbs v. Bradley*, 1982; *Hughes v. Joliet Correctional Center*, 1991; *Warren v. Fanning*, 1991).

In general, constitutional prohibitions against cruel and unusual punishment do not require that an inmate be free from or cured of all real or imagined medical conditions while in custody. What is essential is that an inmate be provided with medical care (i.e., diagnosis and treatment) that is comparable in quality and availability to that obtainable by the general public (Anno, 1993). Recognizing that minor symptoms can escape the most skilled diagnostician, the courts hold prisons responsible only when they fail to recognize and treat "serious medical needs," i.e., a condition that would have been diagnosed by a physician as requiring treatment or one so obvious even a layperson would easily recognize the necessity for a doctor's attention (Prout and Ross, 1988; *Laaman v. Helgemoe*, 1977).

A jurisdiction cannot refuse to provide inmates with needed or essential care because funds are unavailable. However, there is no requirement that an inmate who, for example, has a heart condition has to receive the services of a foremost heart surgeon (Isele, 1979;). As Isele (1979) notes, a "rule of reason" regarding the adequacy of care is determined on a case-by-case basis. For example, if an inmate was afforded intensive medical care, the courts would not require that he receive treatment deemed to be experimental (*Hampe v. Hogan*, 1974). These decisions are helpful, but with rising health costs and new developments in medical care there is a need for a formula to assist prison health care administrators in making decisions in gray areas between "urgent and clearly elective procedures" and those that are experimental. This will help defuse public antagonism toward providing expensive services to those seen as "less deserving" (Anno, 1989).

While the *Estelle* decision related only to medical care, lower court decisions quickly extended the deliberate indifference standard to psychiatric care for serious mental or emotional illness (Lopez and Cheney, 1992; *Inmates of Allegheny County Jail v. Pierce*, 1979).

During the last two decades, the courts have made no distinction between the right to health care and to mental care for psychiatric or psychological impairments (Mayer, 1989). Thus, courts see deliberate indifference to psychological needs of inmates as unconstitutional. While there is no authoritative definition of this standard, court rulings have provided some guidance. They have not viewed an inmate's statement that he was depressed as requiring treatment since mere depression is not construed as a serious medical need (Mayer, 1989). However, conditions such as acute depressions, nervous collapse, and paranoia are considered sufficiently dramatic to represent serious medical needs. Nevertheless the "courts continue to rely heavily on [the] ... judgement [of mental health professionals] to determine whether care is adequate and defer to those judgements except in the most gross circumstances," that is,

when failure to respond to special needs produces unnecessary suffering (Mayer, 1989, p. 275).

The basic components of a correctional mental health treatment system grew out of *Ruiz v. Estelle*. These include (1) a systematic program for screening and evaluating inmates to identify those needing treatment; (2) treatment programs that entail more than segregation and close supervision of inmate clients; (3) sufficient numbers of appropriately trained mental health professionals; (4) maintenance of accurate, complete, and confidential records of the treatment process; (5) avoidance of medication in dangerous amounts or by dangerous methods, or without appropriate supervision and evaluation; and (6) a separate program for identifying, treating, and supervising inmates with suicidal tendencies (Cohen, 1988). In 1980, in *Vitek v. Jones*, the Supreme Court ruled that arbitrary transfers to a mental hospital violate the protections of the Fourteenth Amendment due process clause. The Court held that such transfers first require a hearing with adequate notice and due process safeguards (Cohen, 1993). Taken together, these court decisions have pushed corrections into a "right to treatment" posture. However, funding shortfalls resulting from the economic downturn of the late 1980s and early 1990s hampered the implementation of these programs in some areas (Jemelka, Rahman, and Trupin, 1993).

The issue of enforced psychiatric and mental health treatment in a correctional setting has also been addressed by the Supreme Court. Psychiatric drugs can be administered for treatment against an inmate's will "if the inmate is dangerous to himself or others, and the treatment is in the inmate's medical interest" (*Washington v. Harper*, 1990, p. 1033, n. 3). Treatment must be for a medical reason, however, not merely for control of inmate behavior.

Further, the Court rejected an inmate's right to a judicial hearing in this matter. Recognizing that the real question in this case involved the benefits versus the risks of antipsychotic medication, it felt that this issue could be best resolved by an administrative hearing conducted by an independent mental health professional not involved in the diagnosis or treatment of the inmate in question. The Court upheld Washington State procedures requiring that inmates be given notice of this adversary hearing and a tentative diagnosis, be present and be allowed to cross-examine witnesses,

 **Close Up** **Florida's Correctional Mental Health Facilities Use Different Approaches**

The Florida model incorporates a comprehensive approach to mentally disturbed inmates.

The Florida Department of Corrections developed comprehensive mental health facilities as part of the settlement of a class action suit brought by inmates in 1972, which claimed inadequate medical services. Today they serve the 5% of the Florida inmate population (over 53,000 in 1993) that has been diagnosed as severely disturbed.

Incoming inmates are evaluated at the reception center, which is unique in its level of medical and/or mental health care. Outpatient services are provided at thirty-five institutions where inmates without a mental health diagnosis can receive counseling. The next level of care involves outpatient treatment at seventeen facilities for inmates with a history of mental health problems, but who can function in a general population with this type of care.

Six in-patient short-term crisis stabilization units (CSUs) serve inmates who temporarily require more intense in-patient treatment to deal with acute problems. If they can be stabilized, they can be placed back in the general population under outpatient care. CSU's provide psychiatric, psychological, and psychotropic (drug) services. Five transitional care units (TCUs) serve a similar population who have been stabilized but cannot function in a general prison population. Between the CSUs and the TCUs is the Correctional Mental Health Institution (CMHI), which is a 110-bed coed facility for acute in-patient psychiatric care. Located on the grounds of Florida State Hospital (FSH) in Chattahoochee, it is a close custody prison with clinical services provided by FSH staff. CMHI is a four-story facility with six wards; one women's, one suicidal, one admissions, and three general treatment. Psychiatric, psychologic, social work, nursing, medical, rehabilitation therapy, and other staff provide a multidisciplinary approach to inmate care. A unique aspect of CMHI is that DOC security staff participate as part of the inmate patient's treatment team. Thus, CMHI is a psychiatric hospital whose patients are inmates of the DOC.

The average stay at CMHI is six to nine months, but length of stay is driven by individual need. CMHI has a mix of single- and multiple-occupancy cells, and retrofitted suicide prevention cells. In 1992–93, there were 164 admissions and 154 releases. CMHI inmates are convicted of a variety of crimes. Over one-third have committed murder, many with multiple victims. CMHI works with a very dangerous, mentally ill, often suicidal population.

*Source:* Prepared especially for *Corrections: A Comprehensive View* by Joel DeVolentine, Program Administrator. Florida Correctional Mental Health Institution.

---

and be allowed the assistance of a lay advisor (Burlington, 1991; Cohen, 1993).

The Close-Up on Florida's correctional mental health facilities highlights an example of one correctional system's responses to mental health treatment.

## CORRECTIONAL MENTAL HEALTH TREATMENT PROGRAMS

Mental health treatment in prison usually consists of some forms of psychotherapy, counseling, or behavior therapy. The goals of treatment are to relieve psychological problems that may help inmates to better adjust to the institution and/or reduce their future criminality. The efficacy of treatment in reducing criminal behavior and the role of psychological disturbance as a broad cause of criminal behavior has been questioned by criminologists and psychiatrists (see, e.g., Conklin, 1992; Szasz, 1970). This type of criticism had a hand in the demise of rehabilitation as a way to deal with criminals.

### A Variety of Treatment Modalities Have Been Used in Prisons

Some of the commonly used treatments in corrections (see, e.g., Bartollas, 1985) include behavior modification and cognitive approaches.

**THE MAIN GOAL OF BEHAVIOR MODIFICATION IS BEHAVIOR CHANGE** **Behavior modification** is based on a variety of learning principles that can

Mentally disturbed inmates may require restraint and close observation. Shown here is a schizophrenic inmate in a Rhode Island prison.

change inmate behavior. The most frequently used approaches in corrections include token economies and behavioral contracts.

Token economies involve tangible payoffs (points, tokens, etc.) to inmates who manifest certain behaviors. These tokens are accumulated over a period of time and can be spent on a variety of goods and privileges (e.g., goodies from the commissary, living in a special unit with more privacy). In this way the desirable behavior can become part of the inmate's behavior repertoire in prison and may even be generalized to behavior on the outside. Behavioral contracting is the negotiation of a written agreement between inmates and corrections personnel. This contract may specify that if inmates in correctional programs behave in certain ways they will be rewarded. If negotiated and

executed in good faith, this contract can induce the motivation needed by the inmate to achieve desired behavioral changes.

**COGNITIVE APPROACHES ARE OFTEN LEARNING BASED Cognitive therapy** has recently received increasing attention within corrections. Underlying it is the notion that much of our behavior is driven by faulty thoughts and beliefs. To change a person's behavior successfully, changes in the thoughts and beliefs supporting it are required (Ellis, 1980). Our Close-Up on "The Lifestyle Approach to Correctional Treatment" profiles a program developed by Glen Walters (1994) to teach inmates to recognize and modify various thinking patterns associated with criminals.

## ISSUES SURROUNDING THE PROVISION OF INMATE HEALTH CARE

Although the vast majority of inmates are young, they tend to have more medical problems than comparably aged persons in the general population. This is due to their lifestyles, which involve risk taking, poor diets, and drugs. Adequate medical care in prison requires appropriate assessment and follow-up care. These services can be provided by in-house medical staff, on-call private practitioners, or health care companies.

### Inmates Have More Health Problems Than the General Population

Health services delivery within prisons has been increasingly strained over the last decade primarily as a result of (1) more inmates coming into the prisons and (2) new inmates being less healthy than their counterparts of just a decade ago (Anno, 1991a). Additionally, longer sentences combined with minimum mandatory conditions, and increasing incarceration of drug offenders, many of whom are over 40, contributed to the aging of the prison population (Austin and McVey, 1989). Since older persons in general have more and chronic health problems, they require additional medical resources. Also, many of the problems of aging are likely to affect inmates earlier when compared with those leading more normal lives, i.e., "inmates grow old before their time" (Anno, 1991a). These factors have placed increased demands on prison

## Close Up    The Lifestyle Approach to Correctional Treatment

The Lifestyle approach to correctional treatment involves three steps. The first step is to interfere with criminal lifestyle activities. This is done because persons actively involved in crime have no motivation to leave that lifestyle. Therefore, lifestyle activities must be temporarily interrupted if change is to occur. This can happen when individuals become disgusted with the adverse consequences of their lifestyle (e.g., when they are temporarily prevented from committing crimes by incarceration). Then the offender is focused on beliefs regarding change. Individuals must realize that change is necessary and assume responsibility for the negative consequences of their criminal lifestyle. They must recognize that change is possible and that they can turn their lives around.

The next step is instructing the individual in basic social, coping, and life management skills. This begins by teaching the offender what can be refered to as condition-based skills (e.g., stress management, cue control, assertiveness) which can control conditions that trigger criminal behavior. Choice-based skills are taught next. These can enhance decision making by improving creative thinking, the capacity to solve problems, and goal setting.

The last skills taught are cognition-based skills. Using a cognitive restructuring approach, offenders are taught to recognize, challenge, and change eight thinking patterns that support the criminal lifestyle. An example of one of these thinking patterns is *mollification*. Through mollification, offenders justify their criminal actions by pointing out unjust or inequitable conditions in the wider social environment. By picturing themselves as victims of these conditions, offenders feel free to victimize others.

The third and final step in the treatment process is providing effective follow-up and community reintegra- tion for the offender. In this stage, through a reorienta- tion of values, a change in identity (from criminal to noncriminal), family support, and community pro- grams, the offender learns to maintain a noncriminal lifestyle.

There are three levels of groups in the Lifestyle change program. First-level groups engage in activities designed to teach offenders the beliefs, skills, and thinking patterns necessary for change. The group meetings at this level run for ten weeks. At the second level, which runs for twenty weeks, participants begin to apply what they have learned about the lifestyle approach to their own behavior both past and present. Criminally relevant movies and news segments are used to demonstrate points and maintain interest. The final level also runs for twenty or more weeks. At this stage offenders incorporate and attempt to extend what they have learned about themselves and their criminal lifestyles. There is also a relapse prevention group, which attempts to teach the clients how to cope with those things that will push them toward restarting their criminal lifestyles.

Although this program has not been in effect long enough to evaluate its impact, the author feels confident that it will prove successful because it addresses the real problems that face inmates upon release. What do you think? Can criminals be taught to change their thinking patterns and turn away from a criminal lifestyle?

*Source:* Prepared especially for *Corrections: A Comprehen- sive View* by Glen Walters, Psychology Services, Federal Correctional Institution-Schuylkill

A more extensive discussion of this approach can be found in: Walters, G. *The Criminal Lifestyle: Patterns of Serious Criminal Conduct.* Newbury Park, CA: Sage, 1994.

---

health service for both general care and expensive specialty services (Anno, 1991a).

As a result of their lower socioeconomic status and involvement in crime, the lifestyle of most inmates has likely included poor nutrition, lack of exercise, abuse of drugs and alcohol, smoking, and a lack of adequate medical care prior to incarcera- tion (Anno, 1991a). These factors place inmates at high risk for health conditions that include heart disease and strokes, tuberculosis, epilepsy, and hy- pertension[2] (a condition which when not treated, can result in heart attack, stroke, and kidney fail- ure) (Anno, 1991a).

Prisons also must care for AIDS patients who are likely to be in and out of infirmaries and hospitals and require expensive medications (AIDS will be dealt later in the chapter). This, added to an aging prison population, increases the number of inmates with progressive illnesses such as cancer.

Finally, prison health services must also provide for the special needs of handicapped inmates, women with obstetrical and gynecological prob-

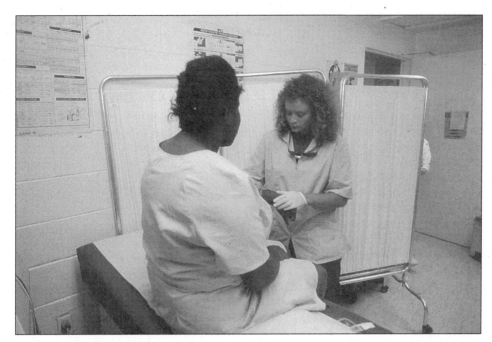

Prison clinics and infirmaries deal with an inmate's medical problems. Prompt attention to an inmate's health needs can often prevent some minor conditions from developing into major medical problems.

lems, and those with mental health problems (e.g., suicidal inmates, self-mutilators, substance abusers, the mentally ill, the retarded, and sex offenders).

Providing care for inmates with special health needs will increase the cost of furnishing these services due to the need for more staff, housing, space, and equipment (Anno, 1991a). In fact, Anno asserts that "the cost of caring for special needs patients is likely to overwhelm many [Department of Corrections] budgets in the future" (p. 154). A national survey in February 1993 confirms this prediction. It found health care costs-per-year-per-inmate were about $4296, with corrections departments allocating about 10% of their budgets to providing this care. Thirty-five jurisdictions reported budget increases in 1992 (Davis, 1993).

### Prison Medical Facilities Vary According to Institution Size

Medical facilities can be viewed on a continuum from clinics, to infirmaries, to well-equipped and staffed general hospitals—which only a few systems have (Prout and Ross, 1988; Anno, 1991a).[3] Institutions with under 100 inmates often have "clinics," staffed by nurses or paramedics who are on site or on short call during the day and on call at night. They are typically used for physical examinations, triage (to determine inmate medical needs), dressing wounds, short-term observation,

and simple minor surgical procedures. Infirmaries, the most common type of medical facility, are generally found in jails and prisons with populations of 500 or more. They provide bed care and, therefore, have around-the-clock nursing care.

The major secondary or tertiary care provider is usually a nearby general hospital. Infirmaries, and to a lesser extent clinics, can deal with minor conditions but send inmates to outside hospitals for more complicated treatment. For both security and financial reasons, prison administrators are reluctant to send inmates to outside facilities that do not have a secure ward (Anno, 1991a). As a result, prisons of all sizes have expanded their medical facilities to reduce, where possible, the use of outside facilities.

### There Are Many Facets to the Treatment of Inmate Medical Problems

Since prison health care is "free," inmates quickly develop expectations for good care (Prout and Ross, 1988). **Daily sick call** is the process by which inmates who perceive themselves to have a health problem (e.g., a headache) get permission to go to morning clinic sessions. This daily ritual may draw up to 10% of a prison's population (Anno, 1991a). This relatively high proportion of use is believed by most correctional staff to be an excessive use of health services by inmates. It may also be seen as

**Sick call is a daily activity that provides inmates the opportunity to get medical services. A good medical services program can deal with inmate abuses of this process.**

malingering. However, Anno (1991a) points to a number of valid reasons why this proportion is so high. The average inmate tends to be in poorer health than the average citizen, which means that some of this increased usage is justified. Second, the discontent associated with confinement may cause or intensify physical problems. Thus, inmates may have such general complaints as stomach or headaches, diarrhea or constipation for which no physical basis can be found. These inmates, according to Anno (1991a), are generally not faking, but "they simply do not feel well and they don't know why" (p. 119). Often, they only need someone to talk to, and referral to a counselor may resolve the problem. However, sometimes nonspecific complaints are indicative of serious illness, and when they occur, it is important that the inmate be referred to appropriate medical staff.

Some inmates **ride the medical pony** in the same way as others ride the religious pony (see Chapter 20). That is, they abuse the medical system by deliberately faking symptoms for secondary gains including opportunities to complain and receive sympathetic attention; obtain medications, particularly narcotic and sedative drugs; take time off from work details; meet inmates from other housing units; or, during a lockdown, to get out of their cells (Anno, 1991b; Prout and Ross, 1988). Those who are known abusers can be handled by being seen outside of regular sick call hours (e.g., after work). In this way, they are not denied access, avoiding the occasional legitimate medical complaint, yet still allowing sick call to be used to service those with legitimate complaints.

Overuse of health care services has also been attributed to extremely conservative prison requirements that inmates come to the health unit to receive services and products available over the counter in the free society (Anno, 1991a). By making basic over-the-counter medications for problems such as colds, heartburn, and constipation available in housing units, some states (e.g., Florida, Texas, and Illinois) have reduced the number of inmates at sick call. Having lotions, soaps, and shampoo in commissaries further reduces the need to get these items at sick call. Additionally, as Anno (1991a) notes, providing inmates the opportunity to deal with some aspects of their own health care may foster responsibility, thus reducing liability and decreasing the use of health services. Overuse of prison health care has resulted in a new correctional practice—that of billing prisoners for their medical care (see Close-Up).

A stay in the prison health unit may provide some inmates with access to items for their own drug use and opportunities to acquire items for trafficking (e.g., drugs, chemicals for preparing drugs, and needles and syringes for intravenous use). Opportunities for illicit communication with the outside world also are more possible because some of the personnel who work in these health units—nurses, physicians, consultants, lab technicians—may be less aware of the games inmates play and easier to con than correctional officers.

Finally, this unit is often a geographically separate part of the prison, and this too offers benefits. It may provide inmates with a respite from a violence-charged prison or an atmosphere that is more pleasant because they are likely to be treated more decently. Health care professionals are less

## Close Up  Billing for Medical Care

A recent trend in correctional health care is charging prisoners for basic medical care. Prisoners are usually charged $3 or $4 for attending sick call or are required to purchase over-the-counter medications and products at market prices. These fees are charged to the inmate's account. However, those who are indigent or have negative balances in their account are not denied care. Advocates of this system claim it cuts down on the abuse of sick call, reduces costs, and inmates are not charged for emergency care. Critics claim such policies ignore the need for unimpeded access to sick call and downplays the importance of prevention. Further, they claim it discourages inmates with legitimate medical concerns from seeking medical care.

SOURCE: Lopez, Mark, and Chayriques, Kara. "Billing prisoners for medical care blocks access," *National Prison Project Journal*, 9(2):1–2, 17.

likely to have punitive attitudes and more likely to be understanding of the inmates' circumstances and accepting of them as individuals than are custodial staff (Anno, 1991b).

**ADEQUATE MEDICAL ASSESSMENT IS THE KEY TO A GOOD HEALTH CARE SYSTEM**  A primary means of furnishing inmates with quality health care and dealing with the relatively large number of inmates appearing at sick call is to establish medical assessment procedures for inmates on arrival at prisons or intake facilities. The **National Commission on Correctional Health Care** (NCCHC) recommends that an inmate be screened soon after admission by a qualified health professional to determine basic health and mental health needs, including needs for immediate care and scheduling for receiving medications and/or follow-up care (NCCHC, 1992; Anno, 1991a). Such evaluations provide a record to assist physicians in diagnosing any health problems, and permit the scheduling of appointments for inmates not requiring regular treatment at times other than sick call. Finally, this preliminary process can demonstrate to inmates that health care personnel are concerned and competent, and can set a positive tone that will be carried throughout an inmate's subsequent relationships with this team (NCCHC, 1992; Prout and Ross, 1988).

### Several Factors Have Made It More Attractive for Physicians to Work in Prisons

In the past, low pay and poor working conditions in our nation's prisons tended to attract medicine's

rejects. Today, most systems have improved their working conditions, often in anticipation of, or in response to, court orders. They also pay competitive salaries to recruit and retain qualified staff. But the remote location of many prisons still impedes the recruitment of good health care personnel, particularly those with specialty and consultive care skills (Anno, 1989; Prout and Ross, 1988).

Two factors that have recently attracted young physicians to positions with health maintenance organizations in the public health area have also benefitted prison medical care. First, a larger number of medical school graduates, as a result of increased competition in more attractive communities, have begun to consider public health-type practices. Second, the stabilization of income in medicine and increasing risks in private practice (e.g., more patient lawsuits and high malpractice insurance rates) have made private practice less financially rewarding for physicians (Prout and Ross, 1988).

### Private Companies Are Now Providing More Prison Health Care

Contracts for medical care with **private health care providers** are considered another option for cost-effective and quality medical care. This requires a competitive bidding process under which health care providers submit proposals detailing the services they will provide. Under this system the company selected provides medical care at a fixed cost per year. Private providers claim there are economic advantages to contracting for these services, but, at this point, there is no independent research that confirms this assertion (Anno, 1991a).

Nevertheless, contractors have a vested interest in hiring quality doctors and nurses who can provide good care because this will minimize liability and ultimately reduce inmate health care costs. Also, large health care organizations may be better able to provide specialty care by temporarily transferring staff to a correctional facility.

There are also some potential problems associated with private health care providers. For-profit organizations may have strong motives to cut costs so that they can increase profits. This may result in measures that discourage inmate complaints and appearances at sick call; cause delay in or failure to take inmates from one health care unit to another; and transfer inmates who are expensive or difficult to treat to state facilities. Thus, care must be taken to ensure that profit motives do not jeopardize the adequacy of medical care. Strict supervision by the contracting agency and prior contractual arrangements are the keys to dealing with these problems (Prout and Ross, 1988; Anno, 1991a).

### National Accreditation Can Improve Medical Services

During the 1970s and 1980s we recognized and began to correct the often abysmal state of prison medical care. In the 1990s the problem will be how to "fine tune [these] . . . systems so the quality of inmate care will mirror that of the community" (Anno, 1989, p. 11). One way for states to upgrade care and move toward accomplishing this objective is to go through voluntary accreditation. This is offered by the NCCHC, which is composed of representatives from thirty-six organizations that have an interest in correctional health care. Accreditation involves site visits by an independent team from NCCHC to determine whether the facility is meeting standards established by this commission. To become accredited, prisons must meet all of the thirty-four "essential standards" and 85% of applicable "important standards." Facilities that initially fail to be accredited are provided with technical assistance to aid them in becoming accredited (Anno, 1993). Accredited institutions acquire the status and benefits that go with this certification, and also reduce their liability. Anno (1993) notes that no system that is currently accredited by NCCHC has been successfully sued by inmates in class action suits that have challenged

the adequacy or availability of their health care delivery system.

### Many Inmates Are Drug Offenders

Another aspect of prison medical care concerns treatment for substance abusers, especially drug offenders. There was a dramatic increase in the number of drug-abusing offenders entering the correctional system at all levels between the early 1980s and the early 1990s. While the number of state court commitments to prison almost tripled from 1981 to 1993, the number of commitments for new drug offenses grew almost tenfold (Maguire, Pastore, and Flanagan, 1993; Snell and Morton, 1992; Beck and Gilliard, 1995). Inmates sentenced for a drug offense accounted for 31% of the growth in total admissions to state prisons from 1986 to 1993 (Beck and Gilliard, 1995). A 1991 face-to-face survey of 13,986 inmates found that 79% reported having used illegal substances, 50% had used drugs within one month prior to their incarceration, 36% were daily users, and 31% reported being under the influence of drugs at the time of their crime (Snell, 1993). About 30% of the robbery, burglary, and larceny offenders reported committing their offense for drug money.

In general, there have been limited opportunities for drug-abusing inmates in jails and prisons to obtain any degree of help for their drug problems (Peters, 1993; Lipton, 1993; General Accounting Office, 1991) even though research has clearly shown that treatment works (Wexler and Lipton, 1993; Institute of Medicine, 1990; DeLeon, 1984; Hubbard, Marden, Rachel, Harwood, Cavanaugh, and Ginzberg, 1989; Office of National Drug Control Policy, 1990; Simpson and Sells, 1988). Since it has been estimated that upwards of 70% of all inmates have substance abuse problems, the need for treatment seems apparent (General Accounting Office, 1991), as discussed in detail in the next section.

## DRUG TREATMENT PROGRAMS

Responding to the problem of drug-involved offenders, all states and the federal system have developed some form of substance abuse program for convicted offenders and have planned increased programs and more comprehensive substance abuse treatment. In 1979, it was estimated that 4.4% (10,100) of all state inmates were involved in drug treatment (Chaiken, 1989). By 1991, 32.7% (228,500) of all prison inmates were enrolled in some form of drug intervention with nearly 70,000 inmates enrolled in formal drug treatment or education programs (Snell, 1993). However, due primarily to a lack of treatment beds, only about 7% of those needing it were enrolled in community residential programs (Beck *et al.*, 1993; Wexler, 1994).

### Offenders Enter Treatment Programs in Different Ways

Offenders enter correctional treatment programs in several ways. First, judges can mandate that an incarcerated offender participate in a prison treatment program. Second, inmates may be identified as having a drug problem during the classification process and be assigned to a treatment program. Third, inmates can enter a treatment program at their own request.

In-prison treatment encompasses a wide range of services and modalities. The most frequent treatment offered is group counseling conducted by professionals or by peers in a self-help program. Other treatment elements include drug education, individual counseling, and residential programs (Beck *et al.*, 1993). Almost every institution in the nation has peer support groups, usually in the form of Alcoholics Anonymous (AA), Narcotics Anonymous (NA), or Cocaine Anonymous (CA) programs (Marlette, 1990a).

### Drug Treatment Aims to Reduce Drug Use and Criminal Behavior

Treatment for addiction consists of a broad range of formal organized services that have a variety of different goals, including reducing or ending drug and alcohol use, substantially reducing violent behavior, reducing educational or vocational deficiencies, obtaining legal employment, and changing the individual's values to be more conventional regarding work, family, and the law (Institute of Medicine, 1990). All treatment programs encompass at least some of these goals. Most focus on restoring individuals to a drug-free lifestyle and helping them to improve their capacity to function effectively in society, including reducing or eliminating criminal behavior.

Technically, virtually every formal treatment program in the nation is voluntary. In other words inmates do not have to participate in treatment if they do not want to. However, there are strong pressures on an inmate to "voluntarily" participate in treatment, especially if one has been court ordered or assigned through the classification process. The available literature provides evidence that court and other legal treatment mandates have a positive effect on increasing retention in treatment (Chaiken, 1989; DeLeon, 1988; Hubbard *et al.*, 1989; Pompi and Resnick, 1987). Length of time in treatment is the single most important factor related to successful treatment outcome.

**THE THERAPEUTIC COMMUNITY MODEL IS EFFECTIVE IN TREATING SERIOUS DRUG PROBLEMS**   Available research has shown that the long-term **therapeutic community** (TC) treatment model has the best chance of success in working with hard-core drug abusers with criminal justice involvement (Lipton, 1994; Wexler and Lipton, 1993; Institute of Medicine, 1990). Best results appear to be achieved with residency of at least nine to twelve months followed by some form of aftercare (Lipton, 1994). Our Close-Up on Stay'n Out and 977 Serendipity highlights two successful programs: a prison-based TC program, and an aftercare program for graduates of this program. Multiple-year studies of a variety of in-prison TC treatment programs show that program graduates have a significantly reduced rate of parole violations in comparison to nongraduates and those not in treatment, and they have fewer rearrests, convictions and reincarcerations (Wexler and Lipton, 1993). TC prison programs have resulted in 22 to 35% reductions in rearrest rates for men and 25 to 40% reductions for women (Institute of Medicine, 1990) when compared to similar inmates who were not in treatment. These results are consistent with the more than 20 years of results showing the immediate and long-term effectiveness of community based TC treatment.

### INFECTIOUS DISEASES ARE INCREASING AMONG INMATES

A rising tide of infectious diseases in the nation has impacted jails and prisons as infected inmates enter

# Close Up The Stay'n Out and 977 Serendipity Programs

The Stay'n Out program in New York is one widely known example of a prison-based therapeutic community (Wexler and Williams, 1986). Replicated in other correctional systems, the New York program for 148 men is located at the Arthur Kill Correctional Facility on Staten Island and at the Bayview Correctional Facility in Manhattan for forty women. Originally modeled after Phoenix House, a well-known TC, inmates are recruited from various state correctional facilities. Treatment lasts six to nine months. Most program staff are graduates of TCs and ex-offenders and ex-substance abusers—a common characteristic of most TCs. These staff serve to provide successful role models, showing that successful rehabilitation is possible (Reform, 1988).

Treatment is viewed as a developmental growth process with clients taking on increasing responsibility as they advance through the program. First, clients are in an orientation or adjustment phase designed to familiarize them with program rules and expectations, and build mutual trust. This is accomplished through individual and group counseling, encounter sessions, and seminars. New clients are assigned low-level jobs with little status. As inmate-clients progress through treatment, they take on increasing responsibility for program activities and in turn receive increased status and privileges.

Clients attend daily morning and evening meetings, which function to increase communication and cohesion as well as focus on the day's activities. Daily afternoon seminars help unite the group, encourage the development of individual viewpoints, and help reduce the fear of speaking before others. These seminars include such life skill issues as how to set goals, seeking employment, and how to manage a household.

Counseling groups include about ten clients and focus on attitude, behavior, and work performance. Meeting twice a week for an hour each, these groups are less intense than the encounter groups, which are held two or more times each week. Encounter groups are confrontational and are designed to reduce individual defenses and influence meaningful behavior change. These groups focus on in-depth issues such as impulse management, self-discipline, respect for authority and others, and interpersonal relationships.

In the final period of treatment, transitional issues related to "making it" on the outside are addressed. Clients are involved with other self-help networks such as Alcoholics Anonymous and Narcotics Anonymous, and serve as role models to "newer" program participants. Once released from prison, usually on parole, there are a variety of support systems available including residential halfway houses, support groups, and outpatient counseling. Clients usually maintain close contact with program staff and become members of a "community" of recovered addicts organized by the program (Wexler and Williams, 1986; Reform, 1988).

977 Serendipity, named in part for its street address in Brooklyn, New York, is an 18- to 24-month aftercare program for graduates of the Stay'n Out program. The primary focus of the program is to successfully reintegrate the offender back into society. For the first 6 to 12 months, up to forty residents live at the 977 Serendipity center. Central to the program is a continuity of care utilizing an extensive network of community resources. Residents are restricted to the center for an initial orientation period, and are escorted to community agencies for assessments not accomplished at the center. In addition to individual, group, and family counseling, residents receive extensive vocational and employment counseling and use the community resource network to help secure job placement or vocational training. Stipends are provided for lunch and travel to and from work. Residents also receive remedial education as needed, continued drug and alcohol counseling, life skills classes in areas such as money management and installment buying, and medical care. Residents are also encouraged to do volunteer work in the community.

Each resident contracts for one year of aftercare following completion of the residential phase. For the first three months after leaving the center, the former resident is expected to attend a once-a-week evening group to discuss their adjustment and assist them in problem solving. During the second three-month period, residents attend group every other week, while for the last six months, attendance is on a monthly basis (Callender, 1993).

977 Serendipity is an example of an aftercare program that gradually reintegrates an offender back into the community prepared to successfully face the challenges of living a life free from drugs and crime.

correctional systems. Administrators are concerned about the potential spread of infectious diseases in their facilities due to close living in often over-crowded conditions, the cost of medical care, and the potential spread of such diseases to the com-munity to which inmates will return. The following sections examine the two most pressing infectious diseases problems facing corrections today: tuber-culosis and AIDS.

## Tuberculosis Is Reemerging in Jails and Prisons

Tuberculosis (TB) is an infectious disease that is spread by bacteria in the air resulting from the coughs or sneezes of infected individuals. It is the leading infectious disease killer worldwide. With the creation of anti-TB drugs in the early 1950s, it became a treatable disease. In the United States, it steadily declined in incidence for more than thirty years until the mid-1980s at which point the trend started to reverse. By 1992, over 26,000 new cases were reported nationwide representing an increase of more than 20% compared to 1984.

Although TB has always been a problem in prisons and jails, correctional systems such as New York and California have seen a five to tenfold increase in cases during the past decade. This is on top of rates that are five to ten times higher than those for the general population (Hammett and Harrold, 1994; Nadel, 1993).

The increase in TB infection among inmates is due to a number of factors, most significant being the increase in AIDS. Since AIDS-infected individu-als have weakened immune systems, this makes them more susceptible to TB. Other factors contrib-uting to the TB increase include drug abuse, prison overcrowding, homelessness, and an increase in immigrants from parts of the world with higher lev-els of TB infection (Hammett and Harrold, 1994). Failure to comply with medical treatment increases the possibility of transmission of the disease.

The emergence of **multiple drug-resistant TB strains** (MDR-TB, TB strains that are resistant to normal drug treatments) has further resulted in the reactivation of the disease. Outbreaks of MDR-TB have been documented in the medical literature and many infected individuals have died. Some correctional and health care workers have also become infected with the MDR-TB strain (Ham-mett and Harrold, 1994). Effective therapy for this new strain remains elusive. A 1993 survey of state correctional systems found more than 48,000 TB-infected inmates, with more than one-third of the systems not able to report test results. Based on such data, it appears that as many as 10% of all prison inmates may be TB-infected (Hammett and Harrold, 1994). More than 600 correctional staff have become TB-infected with forty-five active cases as of 1993.

Jails face a particularly difficult problem in re-sponding to TB because of the rapid turnover and short stays of its inmates. Due to their longer stay, virtually every state prison system screens inmates for TB. Thus, prison inmates are more likely to receive treatment for active TB. Inmates with tuber-culosis who also have HIV/AIDS are more difficult to diagnose.

**INMATES WITH ACTIVE TUBERCULOSIS MUST BE ISOLATED** Guidelines from the Centers for Dis-ease Control and Prevention (CDC) call for the immediate isolation of inmates suspected or con-firmed to have contagious TB (Hammett and Har-rold, 1994). Masks must be worn and adjacent areas must be protected to prevent contamination when doors are opened. Such arrangements have forced correctional systems to retrofit, or design and build, special facilities to care for inmates with active TB. About one-third of all prison systems have specially equipped isolation rooms, which keep infected air within them, with about another 25% of the sys-tems housing inmates in special isolation rooms.

## AIDS Is an Immune System Disease without a Known Cure

The AIDS epidemic is one of the most pressing social and public health issues facing our nation. Drug-involved offenders represent one group at high risk of contracting AIDS. **AIDS,** or Acquired Immune Deficiency Syndrome, is a condition in which the body's immune system is unable to fight illness and disease, making individuals susceptible to a host of infections that otherwise do not affect healthy people. In essence, the virus that causes AIDS, the **Human Immunodeficiency Virus** (HIV), infects and destroys the body's ability to fight disease. As a result, people die from cancers, pneu-monia, and other diseases. There is presently no cure for AIDS.

A blood test is the only way to determine if a person has the AIDS virus. Individuals testing

HIV-positive may not show any signs of being ill because it can take up to ten years for a person to manifest symptoms of the disease. However, some become sick and die after just a few years, or sooner. Once a person has the disease, they will remain infected for life. Infected individuals not showing any signs or symptoms of AIDS are considered to be asymptomatic. Asymptomatic individuals are not reported for statistical purposes. Treatment for asymptomatic individuals consists of reducing exposure to diseases and other people who are sick, and providing good medical support. When symptoms appear and persist after the initial infection, the individual is considered to be symptomatic (or to have AIDS). Early in the disease, these symptoms are usually not life threatening, however, they can affect the HIV person's lifestyle and overall health. A variety of medications are available that can reduce some AIDS-related symptoms and/or delay their onset.

As the infected individual's immune system weakens, stronger drugs are used to treat the symptoms, although many have extreme side effects. As the disease progresses, the individual is likely to develop opportunistic infections, which are very rare in the general population but are common among people with AIDS, such as certain cancers and pneumonia.

**INMATES HAVE AIDS AT TEN TIMES THE RATE OF THE GENERAL POPULATION**    As of 1993, a total of 11,565 cumulative AIDS cases were reported among state and federal correctional inmates (Hammett, Harrold, Gross, and Epstein, 1994). The AIDS incidence rate among correctional inmates was 195 cases per 100,000, about ten times the incidence rate for the U.S. population as a whole (Hammett *et al.*, 1994). HIV-infected inmates constitute about 2% or less of the inmates in most corrections systems, ranging from less than 1% in some systems to a high of about 20% (Hammett *et al.*, 1994). As of 1991, the latest published data, AIDS-related deaths among prison inmates had accounted for 28% of all reported inmate deaths in the previous twelve months; 24% of all jail deaths in 1992 were AIDS-related (Harlow, 1993).

**AIDS HAS GENERATED PROBLEMS AND CONTROVERSIES FOR CORRECTIONAL ADMINSTRATORS**    The increasing number of inmates testing positive for HIV or who have AIDS has presented correctional authorities at all levels with a range of problems and challenges. These problems affect system-wide or institutional policies, medical care, housing, inmate and staff rights, inmate and staff safety, employee training, and release considerations. Several of the more important issues are discussed next.

*Precautionary Measures Can Protect Staff and Inmates from Infection*    Correctional systems must continue to address the fears and concerns of staff and inmates regarding the possibility of being exposed to the HIV virus from an infected inmate. Reasonable precautions must be taken to protect inmates and especially staff. As people learn more about how AIDS is spread, there has been a decline in the concerns voiced by both prison staff and inmates. The CDC has issued a series of guidelines for health care and public safety workers, including correctional officers, concerning steps that should be taken as precautions when working with individuals who may potentially be HIV-positive or who may have other communicable diseases such as hepatitis B. Known as **universal precautions**, these are basic medical standards of safety and care to reduce the spread of infectious diseases. The CDC recommends that all personnel treat all prisoners as though they were HIV infected in order to protect staff and inmates from the possibility of becoming exposed to the HIV virus from an infected inmate. Universal infection control precautions are detailed in Table 19.1. Institutions must have policies for their employees regarding how to respond to occurrences such as exposure to needles and other sharp instruments, hand washing, cleaning up blood spills or other body fluids, and the use of protective equipment such as gloves for body and cell searches (Hammett, 1988a).

*Screening and Testing Inmates for HIV Is Controversial*    Perhaps the most highly charged and controversial issue is the debate over forced or mandatory HIV testing for inmates. Proponents argue that identifying infected inmates will facilitate administration of antiviral medications such as Zidovudine (AZT) and Didanosine (ddI), which are used for preemptive or early intervention treatment, and may help sustain better health for a period of time (Hammett *et al.*, 1994). It is also argued that testing is the best way to identify HIV infected inmates, offering an opportunity to provide them with education

TABLE 19.1    **Universal Infection Control Precautions**

- Avoid needlesticks and other sharp instrument injuries.
- Wear gloves when contact with blood or body fluids is likely.
- Keep all cuts and open wounds covered with clean bandages.
- Avoid smoking, eating, drinking, nail-biting, and all hand-to-mouth, hand-to-nose, and hand-to-eye actions while working in areas contaminated with blood or body fluids.
- Wash hands thoroughly with soap and water after removing gloves and after any contact with blood or body fluids.
- Clean up any spills of blood or body fluids thoroughly and promptly, using a 1:10 household bleach dilution.
- Clean all possibly contaminated surfaces and areas with a 1:10 household bleach dilution.

about how not to spread the disease. Further, it has been posited that mass screening will give correctional officials a better understanding of the scope of the problem and can thus plan for more effective institutional responses (Blumberg, 1990).

Opponents argue that because any testing method may produce inaccurate results—positive cases testing negative, and negative cases testing positive—it is not possible to identify all potentially infectious inmates. This can lead to a false sense of security over who may or may not have AIDS. It can also unnecessarily stigmatize inmates and place them in the leper-like status that comes with being identified as HIV-positive.

The issue of mass testing raises many questions with few or no clear answers for correctional administrators (Hammett, 1988b). Should correctional systems have mandatory testing when such testing is not required anywhere else in the community? What are the legal implications of screening? How costly is testing? Will mass testing allay or inflame fears? Some middle ground responses have been proposed. These include testing of inmates who engage in high-risk behavior (e.g., intravenous drug use); encouraging voluntary testing; and testing inmates who are found to engage in behaviors such as forcible rapes (Hammett, 1988b). Despite the many issues raised by mass testing, more correctional systems are conducting mass testing (by 1992, sixteen states and the federal system required inmate testing and nine other states and the federal system tested high-risk inmate groups) (Hammett et al., 1994).

**Most States House HIV-Infected Inmates with the General Inmate Population**    Until 1988 virtually every correctional institution segregated HIV-positive inmates. By 1993, however, there was an almost uni-

versal move away from such blanket policies. At that point, only two state systems automatically segregated HIV-positive inmates, Alabama and Mississippi (Hammett et al., 1994).

As of 1993, thirty correctional systems housed nonsymptomatic HIV-positive inmates with the general population; four added some restrictions to the HIV-positive inmate, such as single-cell assignment; fifteen handled HIV-positive inmates on a case-by-case basis; and, as mentioned, only two permanently segregated them (Hammett et al., 1994). Symptomatic inmates were permitted to be in the general population without restriction in 43% of the systems, while half the systems handled such inmates on a case-by-case basis. The general rule is that as inmates manifest more AIDS symptoms, they are increasingly likely to be permanently segregated from the general population. Nevertheless, nearly one-third of the systems permit AIDS-ill inmates who are not incapacitated to be housed with the general population.

**Inmates Have Legally Challenged Housing Segregation Policies for HIV and AIDS-Infected Inmates**    Housing and segregation policies for HIV-positive or AIDS symptomatic inmates, where inmates are forcibly housed apart from the general population, raise a number of issues. Segregation has been supported on the grounds that HIV-infected inmates who have weakened immune systems are at greater risk for becoming ill, and therefore need to be protected from exposure to illnesses from the general inmate population. Additionally, this can provide protection for other inmates and staff from HIV-positive inmates who may become violently, sexually or otherwise assaultive, engage in consensual sex, or may, in an encounter, expose others to their infected blood. These concerns have been the basis for lawsuits brought by both staff and inmates (see, for example, *Harris v. Thigpen*, 1990; *Ramos v. Lamm*, 1990). Most court rulings have upheld these correctional housing policies.

Many HIV-positive inmates who are not ill will complete their sentences in a relatively short period of time. This fact has significant implications for how they should be handled while in prison. It makes little sense to segregate low-risk inmates and make the prison experience more difficult than it ordinarily would be.

*Correctional Systems Are Experiencing Financial Pressures Concerning the Care of AIDS-Ill Inmates* Because inmates are not eligible for Medicaid, which is the prime public health care method of financing AIDS-related treatment, the costs of health care for AIDS inmates must be born entirely by the systems in which they are incarcerated. Thus, the increasing number of AIDS symptomatic inmates has resulted in a major escalation in medical costs as a budget item for institutions. Even though many state systems have provisions for the early release of inmates with AIDS, in a 1992–93 national survey of sixteen correctional systems that reported early release of AIDS inmates, only sixty-seven inmates were released (Hammett *et al.*, 1994).

Many observers consider the medical care of AIDS-infected inmates to be inadequate (Hammett *et al.*, 1994). While there is considerable variation in quality of care, budget and staffing also are significant factors for correctional administrators. The use of therapeutic drugs for AIDS inmates has increased sharply, with all but one state correctional system in 1993 making the most frequently prescribed AIDS prophylactic drug, AZT, available to inmates. Other AIDS drugs are available in most state prison systems. The use of such drugs, however, has put a strain on correctional medical budgets. For example, in 1992–93, New York State spent about $4 million for AZT for about 1900 inmates (Hammett *et al.*, 1994).

*Disclosure of an Inmate's HIV Status Generally Is Limited to Those with a Need to Know* Issues as to who should receive information regarding inmates' HIV test results are difficult and legally complex. Although inmates and staff have asserted their right to know the status of who is HIV positive, AIDS infected individuals have asserted their right to privacy (Hammett *et al.*, 1994; Anderson, 1990;

AIDS-infected individuals are segregated from the general population in some prisons, particularly in the last stages of the illness.

Hammett, 1988b). Decisions concerning whether to release such test results are governed by legal and policy standards and mandates.

While decisions to disclose the HIV status of inmates will be decided by state legislatures and the courts, current correctional practices permit AIDS-related medical information to be provided to those with a need to know. These include correctional administrators, physicians, other medical staff, probation officers as well as the inmate (Hammett *et al.*, 1994; Takas and Hammett, 1989). A variety of related issues can be raised, such as, how will HIV information be used? Who has access to it? Who else within the criminal justice system should know? Should public health authorities or relatives be notified? Should contact tracing of partners be instituted? These and other complex confidentiality issues will continue to confront correctional administrators.

*Half of All Prison Systems Mandate Aids Education* AIDS education is a cornerstone in the prevention effort to halt the spread of the disease. Virtually every prison system provides some AIDS education for staff. As of 1993, about half of all prison systems mandated AIDS education for inmates even though at that time 86% already offered such education (Hammett *et al.*, 1994). In a survey of thirty-one jail systems, 58% offered HIV education, while only 13% mandated inmate participation (Hammett *et al.*, 1994). High inmate

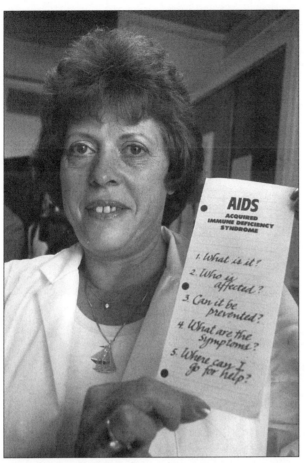

**AIDS education provides helpful information to inmates. Because inmates are at a much greater risk for contracting the AIDS virus, this education may help reduce its incidence in this population.**

turnover in jails complicates the mandating of AIDS education.

The content of AIDS education also has been a concern of correction officials. Ninety-six percent of state and federal correctional systems provide information on safer sex practices and 71% offer instruction on cleaning drug needles and drug injection equipment. Despite educational programs that have raised the levels of inmate HIV knowledge, research has consistently shown that information alone is insufficient to produce appropriate behavior change (Hammett *et al.*, 1994; Kelly and Murphy, 1992). Emphasis also must be placed on changing cultural beliefs and role expectations, particularly within a sexual context.

There is no doubt that the provision of health-related services to inmates will provide increasing burdens for the nation's correctional systems. Their response to this challenge will be influenced by fiscal realities, court mandates, humanitarian concerns, and the public beliefs as to the treatment deserved by inmates.

## ENDNOTES

1. The authors would like to thank B. Jaye Anno, Ph.D., chair, National Commission on Correctional Health Care, for providing, information, reviewing the manuscript, and offering useful suggestions to improve the accuracy of the material on medical services.
2. Anno (1991a) states that while no national prevalence rates are available it can be inferred that a "significant number of inmates" are hypertensive due to the fact that blacks make up at least half of the prison populations and their overall rates of hypertension are twice those of whites.
3. While many prisons call their medical units "hospitals," in most cases, these facilities are really only clinics or infirmaries because they are only equipped to provide ambulatory care, e.g., intake, medication distribution, chronic condition clinics, and in-patient and emergency care. They are not equipped to do full-scale surgical procedures, many diagnostic procedures, or to provide most specialized types of treatments (Anno, 1991a).

## CHAPTER RECAP

**Provision of Health Services**
Prison Health Care Did Not Improve Until the 1970s
Inmates Have a Constitutional Right to Adequate
  Medical and Mental Health Care
**Correctional Mental Health Treatment Programs**

A Variety of Treatment Modalities Have Been Used in Prisons
   The Main Goal of Behavior Modification Is Behavior Change
   Cognitive Approaches Are Often Learning Based
**Issues Surrounding the Provision of Inmate Health Care**
Inmates Have More Health Problems Than the General Population
Prison Medical Facilities Vary According to Institution Size
There Are Many Facets to the Treatment of Inmate Medical Problems
   Adequate Medical Assessment Is the Key to a Good Health Care System
Several Factors Have Made It More Attractive for Physicians to Work in Prisons
Private Companies Are Now Providing More Prison Health Care
National Accreditation Can Improve Medical Services
Many Inmate Are Drug Offenders
**Drug Treatment Programs**
Offenders Enter Treatment Programs in Different Ways
Drug Treatment Aims to Reduce Drug Use and Criminal Behavior
   The Therapeutic Community Model Is Effective in Treating Serious Drug Problems
**Infectious Diseases Are Increasing Among Inmates**
Tuberculosis Is Reemerging in Jails and Prisons
   Inmates with Active Tuberculosis Must Be Isolated
AIDS Is an Immune System Disease Without a Known Cure
   Inmates Have AIDS at Ten Times the Rate of the General Population
   AIDS Has Generated Problems and Controversies for Correctional Administrators
      Precautionary Measures Can Protect Staff and Inmates from Infection
      Screening and Testing Inmates for HIV Is Controversial
      Most States House HIV-Infected Inmates with the General Inmate Population
      Inmates Have Legally Challenged Housing Segregation Policies for HIV- and AIDS-Infected Inmates
      Correctional Systems Are Experiencing Financial Pressures Concerning the Care of AIDS-Ill Inmates
      Disclosure of an Inmate's HIV Status Generally Is Limited to Those with a Need to Know
      Half of All Prison Systems Mandate AIDS Education

## REVIEW QUESTIONS

1. What are the bases for inmate rights to adequate health care in prison?
2. Compare behavior modification and cognitive approaches to treatment.

3. What issues impact the provision of health care to inmates?
4. What are the advantages and disadvantages of having private organizations provide health services for inmates?
5. Describe the drug abuse problem among inmates and the TC approach to treating them.
6. Discuss the problem of infectious disease, including TB and AIDS, within prisons.

## TEST YOUR KNOWLEDGE

1. An inmate's right to adequate medical care is derived from
   a. state laws.
   b. constitutional guarantees.
   c. institutional rules.
   d. public opinion polls.
2. Deliberate indifference to a serious medical need has been ruled by the courts to be in violation of Constitutional guarantees.
   a. for equal protection
   b. to due process
   c. against cruel and unusual punishment
   d. for separation of powers
3. Research concerning the effectiveness of therapeutic community type programs has shown that
   a. prison-based therapeutic communities are more effective than those which are community-based.
   b. effective results can be achieved with six months of residential treatment.
   c. TC prison program graduates have reduced rearrest and recidivism rates when compared with nonprogram participants.
   d. male offenders typically have better outcomes than female offenders.
4. Which one of the following statements concerning tuberculosis is correct?
   a. Individuals who are infected but show no signs of the disease cannot transmit it to others unless they show symptoms.
   b. An individual with inactive TB has a 90% chance of developing active TB in their lifetime.
   c. Inmates with active TB are given medication and returned to the general population.
   d. Few prison systems screen every inmate for TB.
5. Which of the following statements concerning AIDS is correct?
   a. Condoms are widely available in prisons in order to reduce the spread of AIDS.
   b. Virtually every prison system screens all incoming inmates for the AIDS virus.
   c. Most prison systems isolate HIV-positive inmates from the general population.
   d. Only half of all prison systems mandate AIDS education for inmates.

# CHAPTER 20

# BASIC PRISON SERVICES: FOOD AND RELIGION

## ■ LEARNING OBJECTIVES

*After completion of this chapter, you should be able to:*
1. Explain the significance that food has for inmates.
2. Discuss the factors associated with food preparation in an institutional setting.
3. Describe the characteristics and functions of the contemporary prison chaplain.
4. Explain the complexities of ministering to a wide variety of religious beliefs in the correctional setting.
5. Discuss the legal issues associated with religious restrictions in a correctional setting.
6. Contrast the religious goals of prison chaplains with the expectations of prison administrations regarding the role of chaplains in the institution.
7. Specify the personality characteristics that are necessary for a prison chaplain to be effective.

## ■ KEY TERMS AND CONCEPTS

American Muslim Mission
Bona fide religious belief
Clinical Pastoral Education Movement
Compelling interest
Cook/chill food production system
Cycle menu
Decentralized dining
Imams
Kairos Prison Ministry
Least restrictive means
Nation of Islam
Order of Misericordia
Prison Fellowship
Reasonableness test
Religious Freedom Restoration Act
Shadow board
Special diets
Substantial burden

The basic services discussed in the previous chapter are important for maintaining inmates in a healthy physical and mental state. However, it is equally important for inmate nutritional needs and spiritual needs to be addressed because of their role in maintaining their health and general well-being. We discuss food service programs first because they have a great impact on the day-to-day aspects of the prison ambiance. This is followed by a discourse on religious programs with particular emphasis given to the role of the prison chaplain. Religious programs are additionally important because they add a moral context to the otherwise secular range of inmate activities and concerns.

## PRISON FOOD SERVICE[1]

Although all programs impact inmate life, food service may have the greatest immediate significance. Inmates may or may not go to chapel, attend GED classes, see their case workers or the prison doctor, but three times (breakfast, lunch, and dinner) every day they are affected by the food that is served (Ayres, 1988; Boss, Schechter, and King, 1986). Bad food is the primary target of inmate complaints and lawsuits; in fact, it has been a factor in most inmate riots and disturbances (Barnes and Teeters, 1951; McKelvey, 1977). For example, a riot involving 600 inmates at the Turney Center Prison in Tennessee, in which the commissary and kitchen were burned down, was ostensibly started to protest a rule requiring striped uniforms. However, the grievance included a charge that the prison was serving "rat-infested" food (Boss *et al.*, 1986).[a]

> I believe no other job in the field of corrections experiences the never-ending pressure to meet deadlines as the food service manager does. In most cases, we are given some of the most difficult inmate workers, and we are expected to produce a product that must be nutritionally adequate, properly prepared, and attractively served at a specific time three, four, five or six times a day for 500 or more inmates. This task would not be difficult . . . but then someone says, 'Make 25 of the meals Kosher, 30 a medical bland diet, 15 low sodium, 30 1800 calorie controlled, 50 no pork with protein substitute, and 10 vegetarian—and you must maintain a budget of $2.25 per person, per day (Ayres, 1988, p. 1).

**Prison kitchens are required to produce large quantities of food every day.**

The following discussion represents some issues that need to be examined regarding this vital, yet often neglected prison service.

### Food Has a Critical Role in Prisons

Food is a basic necessity of life, and in prison it becomes more important because meals are one of the few things inmates look forward to. Food has a higher priority in prisons than on a college campus, in a hospital environment, or even in the military. Unlike the free world, however, where individuals can choose what and where they eat, inmate choices are limited to what is served and to eating in the same place every day (Stokes, 1993).

Prison food services are faced with several major challenges: (1) attempting to satisfy the diverse tastes and special dietary needs of inmates, (2) providing a sufficient amount of food within budgetary constraints, (3) minimizing disruptive behavior in food service areas, (4) avoiding the sabotage of equipment, and (5) minimizing inmate lawsuits (Stokes and Associates, 1985). To meet these growing challenges, prisons and jails have modified their food service operations. Early on, a correctional officer who enjoyed cooking generally ran the kitchen. Today, most institutions employ qualified food service administrators to manage these operations. As with other services, the laissez-faire attitude toward food preparation has been replaced by a set of minimum standards. These have been either voluntarily imposed by state corrections departments or mandated by court decisions, often guided by American Correctional Association (ACA) Standards for Adult Correctional Institutions (ACA, 1981b, 1990). The expertise required to deal with the complexities of prison food preparation has resulted in the development of specialists in this area (Ayres, 1988; Boss *et al.*, 1986; Stokes *et al.*, 1985).

### Menu Planning Can Be Complex

Today, planning prison menus includes the need to meet basic nutritional requirements, to provide varied and appealing meals, and to do all of this within strict cost constraints. Most correctional systems use some type of **cycle menu** covering a certain time period, at the end of which the menu is repeated (Stokes, 1991).[2] These menus not only provide a nutritionally adequate diet but can also include popular menu items and avoid undue repetition and a monotonous diet while maintaining average daily food costs at allotted amounts. Daily costs average $3.45 per day nationally and range from a low of $1.24 in Alabama to a high of $6.51 in Hawaii (Camp and Camp, 1994a). To add variety, some systems include ethnic meals such as Mexican, Italian, Irish, Oriental, and African-American foods and plan special meals for holidays, for example, Cinco de Mayo and St. Patrick's Day (Ayres, 1988; Stokes *et al.*, 1985). Also, like outsiders, inmates are bombarded by advertising for new products that they would like to try (e.g., chicken nuggets) (Boss *et al.*, 1986).

Health trends on the outside have influenced prison menus by prompting many facilities to begin serving less red meat and fewer starches, more fish, sandwiches, and broiled foods, and adding salad bars. Food service administrators have also recognized that the stressful nature of the prison environment requires more consistent nutrients

and a more-than-adequate diet. Even though an inmate is offered a fully nutritional meal—an appetizer, an entree, two vegetables, potatoes, and dessert—he might eat only the chocolate pudding and three pieces of bread. This underscores the need to educate inmates regarding the benefits of good eating habits (Boss *et al.*, 1986).

**SOME INMATES REQUIRE SPECIAL DIETS**  Court rulings have required jails and prisons to provide inmates with **special diets** to fulfill therapeutic/medical requirements and to accommodate, where possible, the special dietary restrictions of legitimate religious groups. To protect themselves from lawsuits alleging an inmate has become ill because of not receiving a prescribed diet, many institutions require that inmates sign when receiving these meals. Thus when an inmate claims "I'm a diabetic, and the lousy diet they are feeding me is making me unhealthy," the institution can respond by producing the prescription for the diet, the menu, and perhaps show that the inmate only picked up his special diet about every fourth meal. A commissary sheet showing the purchase of loads of candy bars by a diabetic inmate can further show the fault lies with the inmate, not with the prison (Boss *et al.*, 1986). To educate inmates who have health problems (e.g., diabetics) that require a special diet, some facilities conduct therapeutic clinics or provide individual instruction regarding the proper foods to eat and the need to restrict their diet. (Stokes, 1991).

The issue of whether correctional facilities are required to provide religious diets and special meals for religious celebrations relates to the right to free exercise of religion. In the past, the federal courts have allowed religious exercises to be regulated based on legitimate institutional needs (e.g., security, expense). They have also been divided over the extent to which prison authorities can impose restrictions and the degree to which they need to substantiate their justifications (Boston, 1990). Thus, one federal court upheld a New York prison official's refusal to provide a Rastafarian diet on the grounds that its requirements were too complex (*Benjamin v. Coughlin*, 1989) despite the fact this prison system had been ordered to provide observant Jews with a nutritionally adequate kosher diet (*Kahane v. Carlson*, 1975; *Bass v. Coughlin*, 1992). Therefore, it is not surprising that the manner in which prisons have met inmate requests for religious diets has varied considerably. However, this may all change as a result of the passage of the Religious Freedom Reformation Act of 1993, which is discussed later in this chapter. Chaplains will continue to play an important part in determining the validity of inmate requests for special diets in order to meet religious prescriptions and for observance of holidays. However, prison officials will be unable to use the issue of cost and will generally not be able to deny legitimate inmate requests for diets that are an important part of practicing a religion.

The two types of diets most frequently requested are vegetarian and nonpork. By providing extra portions of protein-rich foods, vegetables, and salads, the nutritional needs of vegetarians can be met. The low cost of pork made it a staple of the prison menu until recently, but its consumption is banned by Jewish, Muslim, and some other religions (Ayres, 1988). To accommodate the requirements of these inmates, many correctional facilities label or mark with an asterisk foods containing pork, and serve these foods in such a way that they do not spill over onto other foods. They also make available alternative meat dishes, cottage cheese, or extra portions of vegetables (Stokes *et al.*, 1985). Additionally, some jurisdictions provide an alternative menu offering a substitute nonmeat entree at every meal, which accommodates both dietary concerns.

### The Feeding of Inmates Requires Close Scrutiny

> Jennings asserts "There's an old saying in . . . corrections [that] . . . any time there's a disturbance it's going to be in a cafeteria . . . [B]ecause of the large number of inmates that are there the stress level has gotten to such a point that if the soup is cold, that's going to set inmates off . . . (as cited by Boss *et al.*, 1986, p. 114).

This quote highlights the highly volatile nature of the dining area environment. Controlling this area requires an understanding of the factors that can ignite inmate populations, including both the manner in which food is prepared and serving issues.

Food should be prepared under sanitary conditions for health reasons and because the workers are also customers and will be quick to pass the word if unsanitary conditions exist (Boss *et al.*,

1986), which could spark a disturbance. Also, the emphasis placed on food by inmates makes variation, flavor, texture, appearance, palatability, and temperature vital. No one likes to eat food that is under- or overcooked, dry, or unappetizing. Stokes (1993) asserts that one major problem facilities have is maintaining appropriate food temperatures. By complying with new U.S. Department of Agriculture temperature standards this may become less of an issue.[3]

**INMATES ARE FED IN DINING ROOMS OR IN THEIR UNITS** Except for those restricted to their cells, most prisoners are fed in large dining areas. In newer prisons, these areas generally accommodate about half the prison population (i.e., about 250 to 500 inmates). They provide an informal setting where inmates eat at four- to six-person tables in two sittings. To minimize the potential for a riot or disturbance, it is felt that no more than 125 inmates should be fed at one time (Stokes, 1993). To prevent disturbances, rules regarding appropriate behavior are clearly established, often posted, and enforced through adequate and firm supervision. For example, many institutions prohibit passing food from table to table to keep some inmates from pressuring others to give them their food (Ayres, 1988).

Another trend in newer facilities is **decentralized dining** under which inmates are fed in dayrooms, cell blocks, small satellite areas, or in the pods in the new generation jails (Stokes, 1993). This reduces the number of inmates congregated in one location at a given time and enhances security by reducing inmate movement within the prison or jail (Stokes, 1991). Under this arrangement, food can be delivered to areas in any one of the following ways: insulated trays, heated carts, hot/cold carts in bulk, or by retherm systems.[4]

There are opposing views regarding centralized versus decentralized dining areas. Some favor centralized dining because it gets inmates out of their housing units, which adds variety to their day (Stokes, 1991). Others argue for the decentralized approach because of the potential for problems when numerous inmates are moved and congregate in one location. For example, if inmates in a large group are unhappy about what they are served, their disapproval might spark a serious disturbance. Stokes believes there are better ways to provide variety, including exercise opportunities in the prison yard.

Prison dining rooms with small tables provide a more normal eating atmosphere for inmates than the long tables of the past. However, with so many inmates coming together in one place, the dining room can be a dangerous place.

**SERVING LINES MUST BE CONTROLLED**  The serving line is an area where inmate behavior problems often occur (e.g., inmates skipping ahead of others). Inmate workers also normally do the serving, which can result in inequitable food distribution either due to friendship or intimidation. Both instances can spark fights and demands for extra servings by other inmates (Ayres, 1988). Stationing a correctional officer behind the serving line to pay strict attention and immediately intervene when problems arise can help (Stokes *et al.*, 1985).

**FOOD SERVICE AREAS REQUIRE SECURITY**  A prison food service department can be a potential source of contraband items including knives, tools, caustic substances, and particular food items that can be used in making alcoholic beverages. Civilian personnel supervising inmates in food preparation need to be trained in security techniques and practices. To control tools and implements such as knives, inmates are required to check these items out. When they are returned many facilities require they be placed back on a **shadow board,** which has an outline of each item so staff can tell if an item and what type of item is missing (Ayres, 1988).

Also, a secure storage area is needed for food items that can be used in making alcohol (e.g., yeast, sugar) or that are highly salable in the black market. To deter inmates from hiding items in the kitchen area, open shelves and racks are used in place of drawers and cabinets (Stokes *et. al.*, 1985). Shakedowns and searches of inmates, trash, and other items leaving the kitchen area can prevent the removal of items. Close scrutiny of inmates as they unload incoming supply trucks is important because contraband can be hidden in numerous places on these vehicles. Inexperienced staff may not see the hazards of inmates taking certain foods from the kitchen. For example, a handful of salt and pepper can be used to cause temporary blindness and animal bones can be made into weapons. Prevention requires close monitoring of all inmates in the dining area and perhaps searches to prevent removal of food or utensils.

## More Efficient Food Preparation Methods Can Deal with Overcrowding and Prison Emergencies

Overcrowding can place much pressure on food services because it must expand to meet the population increase usually without expanded kitchen facilities. At some overcrowded prisons, cooking may start early in the morning, and food may be served all day long, which means there is no break from one meal to the next. This places phenomenal stress on food service operations. Furthermore,

Inmate workers provide most of the labor in prison kitchens, which requires the use of knives and other implements that can be used as weapons. Security procedures must be established to make sure these items remain in the kitchen area.

some institutions have had to establish satellite serving areas in other parts of the facility because dining rooms cannot accommodate a larger population within allotted meal hours (Boss *et al.*, 1986). A more efficient solution is to adopt the **cook/chill method[5] of food production,** which allows large quantities of food to be precooked and stored in advance. This takes the pressure off the need to prepare food for each meal. For example, the staff can prepare enough chili to meet menu needs for an entire month at one time. Thus, as long as institutions have sufficient freezer space, existing kitchen facilities can meet food service needs (Stokes, 1993).

Finally, institutions must have contingency plans to feed inmates if the food service department is temporarily incapacitated due to a prison disturbance or other emergency. One option is a cooperative arrangement with a nearby correctional institution where each agrees to provide the other with meals in the event of emergencies (Ayres, 1988). Institutions using the cook/chill food preparation system have enough previously cooked and fast frozen food at any given time to feed their population for a week or even longer. During disturbances, these facilities can use staff instead of inmate workers to handle the feeding process (Stokes, 1993).

There is no doubt that the food service in correctional institutions is an important function. Because of this it requires constant attention from prison administrators.

## Religious Programs[6]

The remainder of this chapter focuses on how institutions accommodate the many and varied religious needs and practices of inmates and discusses the important role played by prison chaplains in providing basic religious and other services.

### Religious Groups Have Historically Been Concerned with Offenders

Although churches have historically provided asylum for accused individuals and religion has often tempered the treatment of criminals, the most direct influence of religion has been through the work of chaplains. As far back as 539, Church members considered it an obligation to visit those in prison despite their offenses (Wines, 1895). The **Order of Misericordia** was founded in 1488 to provide assistance and consolation to offenders condemned to death, accompany them to the gallows, furnish religious services, and provide a Christian burial (Kuether, 1951). In the United States, as prisons developed, chaplains visited offenders and/or became regular members of the prison staff. They were the earliest paid noncustodial staff and provided education and counseling in addition to religious programs (Tappan, 1960; Johnson, 1968).

The early prison chaplains worked under poor circumstances and were often thwarted in their efforts by prison administrators who considered them a hindrance to prison operations. Thus, early prisons usually failed to attract a high caliber of chaplain.

**THE INTRODUCTION OF THE TREATMENT APPROACH TO CORRECTIONS PROVIDED A NEW INCENTIVE FOR YOUNG, BETTER QUALIFIED MEN TO BECOME CHAPLAINS**   The beginning of the twentieth century ushered in a progressive era that brought changes in attitudes and practices regarding the treatment of offenders (Rothman, 1980). As other professionals (e.g., teachers) began to work in corrections, the chaplain's role became limited to ministering to spiritual needs of inmates (Kuether, 1951). Many chaplains responded by becoming part of the new treatment team/program component that developed in prisons to rehabilitate offenders. During the 1920s and 1930s, the **Clinical Pastoral Educational Movement** emerged, resulting in clinical training for clergy and the viewing of prison chaplaincy as a specialty subgroup of the clergy (Kuether, 1951). Young men began to see chaplaincy as a lifelong calling and subsequently a professional identity developed around this specialty. This made it possible for prison systems to employ young, well-trained clergy rather than the discouraged and spent clergy previously available. More than any other development in the twentieth century, this changed the standing of chaplains in penal facilities (Solomon, 1991).

### The Courts Have Dealt with Several Religious Issues

Outside of prisons, individuals do not have to ask permission to practice their religion, which might involve special diets, the wearing of medals, and attendance at religious services. In prison, uninhibited religious expression may not only conflict with concerns relating to security and safety, but may also strain limited budgets (Mushlin, 1993).

The courts have been uncomfortable in deciding whether a particular faith constitutes a religion and have hesitated to withhold recognition of any religion because this would be inconsistent with freedom of religious expression. The groundbreaking case for prisons involved the Black Muslims. Although prison officials and the courts were undoubtedly uncomfortable with Black Muslim doctrines on black supremacy and hatred of whites, there was no denying that it had the trappings of a traditional religion. For example, it had a belief in a supreme being and a bible. Thus, it was not surprising that the courts recognized it as a valid religion (Gobert and Cohen, 1981).

Not all groups claiming to be religions have been recognized by the courts. While the courts are not in agreement as to how to determine when an inmate's religious beliefs deserve First Amendment protection, two requirements seem to emanate from the salient cases: (1) that the beliefs be sincerely held; and (2) that the beliefs be religous in nature (Mushlin, 1993). Thus, an inmate's claim that a group calling itself "MOVE" was a religion was rejected by one court on the grounds that it was a quasi back-to-nature social movement of limited proportion and with an admittedly revolutionary design (*Africa v. Pennsylvania*, 1982). Further, the court found that MOVE lacked certain traditional religious characteristics, e.g., failure to address fundamental and ultimate religious questions (*Africa v. State*, 1982).

With respect to the question of providing facilities and clergy to inmates of all recognized faiths, the Supreme Court indicated that it was not necessary for prisons to do so. They were only required to afford all inmates a reasonable opportunity to be able to practice their religion (*Cruz v. Beto*, 1972). In coming to this conclusion the Court was influenced by the fact that in many prisons there might be 120 or more distinct sects, which would require an extraordinary number of clergy and facilities if prison officials had to provide them equally to each religion (*Gittlemacker v. Prasse*, 1970). Allowing groups to share facilities is one option used by prisons and approved by the courts to accommodate different faiths (*Blair-Bey v. Nix*, 1992). The new federal legislation to be discussed next is not likely to change these decisions but it will likely place a greater emphasis on the use of outside volunteer clergy and laypersons to conduct religious services.

**THE RELIGIOUS FREEDOM RESTORATION ACT WILL HAVE A MAJOR IMPACT ON THE REGULATION OF RELIGIOUS PRACTICES IN PRISON** In November 1993 the **Religious Freedom Restoration Act** (RFRA) became law. This federal legislation requires that the government show a compelling interest in restricting religious expression and employ the least restrictive measures available when curtailing religious freedoms. Twenty-five attorneys general and 49 state correctional agencies argued unsuccessfully for an amendment that would exempt prisons on the grounds that without this exception this act would:

[allow] prison gangs [to] claim religious status [and] to shield their illegal activities from prison rules and regulations. Correctional administrators will need to prove they have a compelling state interest in order to limit each request to organize, meet, distribute material, display hand signals, wear identifiable clothing or engage in other activities that promote gangs (Peters, 1993, p. 18).

[Florida's attorney general claimed that] it would make it tougher for states to win cases brought by inmates saying their religion requires everything from sex with virgins to steak and wine (Chachere and Lavelle, 1993).

While the act gives inmates a new opportunity to raise these and other issues previously litigated, its provisions enable the courts to uphold restrictions on practices that represent a serious threat to institutional order and security.

RFRA works as follows. An inmate claims that she wants to practice her religion in a way that involves certain types of rituals or practices. If the institution says no to the inmate, she must initially show that institutional restrictions have had an impact on a **bona fide religious belief** or practice to prove a RFRA violation (Straley and Morris, 1994).[b] To sustain this claim, inmates may have to "provide evidence [in the form of published theology or expert testimony] of the religious nature of their beliefs, especially when the religious practice is not one generally known" (Straley and Morris, 1994, p. 3). If the court sustains the inmate's claim, it will then examine the policy or restriction to see if it poses a **substantial (impermissible) burden** on

the inmate's ability to practice her religion. A governmental entity is considered to place an impermissible burden on an individual's religious freedom

by pressuring him or her to commit an act forbidden by the religion or preventing him or her from engaging in conduct or having religious experience which the faith mandates. This interference must be more than inconvenience: the burden must be substantial and an interference with a tenet or belief that is central to religious doctrine (Straley and Morris, 1994, p. 3).

A RFRA related court decision suggests some restrictions that may be considered as imposing a substantial burden in the exercise of religious freedom. These include denying inmates the opportunity to pray and to meet with other inmates for group worship. While placing inmates in disciplinary confinement was not viewed as imposing a substantial burden, not allowing inmates to pray and read religious texts while confined would be (*Boone v. Commissioner of Prisons*, 1994; Straley and Morris, 1994). If the court concludes that the restriction represents a substantial burden, then prison officials must show that this restriction represents a **compelling interest,** i.e., a serious threat to a prison's security, order, or discipline (*Procunier v. Martinez*, 1974). However, issues involving cost and administrative convenience are not likely to be viewed as compelling interests since the Supreme Court rejected these as considerations years ago in nonprison cases [*Memorial Hospital v. Maricopa County*, 1974; Correctional Law Reporter (CLR), 1994b]. This will enable more inmates to prevail when challenging an institution's refusal to provide a special diet to meet religious dietary requirements since cost and convenience often have been the major basis in denying these requests. As a result, Boston (1993/94) asserts that prison officials may now attempt to "manufacture security rationales for practices that are in reality based on financial or administrative factors" (p. 14). However, both the House committee and Senate committee reports suggest that this was not the intent of this legislation. The Senate report, for example, indicates that "inadequately formulated prison regulations and policies grounded on mere speculation, exaggerated fears or post-hoc rationalizations will not suffice to meet this act's requirement" (as cited by Boston, 1993/94, p. 15). This will

**A group of Native Americans are seen engaging in a religious ritual. As a result of the Religious Freedom Restoration Act, prisons will be required to make provisions for more nontraditional groups like this to practice their religion.**

require administrators to provide more convincing justifications regarding their belief that a restriction is based on security concerns (CLR, 1994b).

RFRA also requires that even if a policy is deemed to further a compelling interest that it only be sustained if prison officials demonstrate that it represents the **least restrictive means** of accomplishing this objective. In essence, since money concerns are no longer an issue, a least restrictive means can be proposed in every instance. Thus, rather than completely banning a practice this new law requires flexibility and accommodation. This opens the door for inmates to suggest alternatives that are less restrictive than those imposed by prison officials, but yet do not compromise compelling correctional objectives. For example, an alternative to banning a piece of religious literature deemed too inflammatory, because of its racist statements, might be to require an inmate to keep it in his cell or only allow him to read it in a secure area. In order to ban the material under RFRA a warden would be required to convince a court that these alternatives still jeopardize a compelling prison interest (CLR, 1994b; Straley and Morris, 1994). This approach can be seen in a recent court decision that granted a preliminary injunction on a prison rule banning the wearing of all beads including those of a religious nature. Prison officials claimed this restriction was imposed because beads serve as a means of gang membership identifica-

tion and this created friction, rivalries, and violence among inmates. However, prison officials were unable to show that a total ban was the least restrictive means of combating the spread of prison gangs. Nor could they provide persuasive evidence that the wearing of beads under clothing posed a security threat (*Campos v. Coughlin*, 1994).

Inmates who now seek damages related to violations of religious freedom may prefer to seek primary relief through RFRA rather than using Section 1983 of the Civil Rights Act.[7] Unlike Section 1983, RFRA allows inmates to recover damages not only from individuals, but also from state governments and from city or county governments without having to show the violation occurred pursuant to a municipal policy (Boston, 1995a). Thus under RFRA

> for example . . . if a state or city correctional officer bars a prisoner from religious services for a reason that is short of compelling, the prisoner can recover an award of damages from the state or city that employs [them and] attorney fees regardless of whether the officer acted pursuant to policy (Boston, 1993/94, p. 15).

Finally, there is the question regarding the future impact of RFRA on inmates' exercise of their religious freedom, previous litigation in this area, and the way in which prison officials handle inmate requests related to religious issues. This law appears to bring into question many, if not all, of the court decisions on religious issues that have been based on the **reasonableness test** first set forth in *Turner v. Safley*[8] (1987) and applied specifically to restrictions on religious practices in *O'Lone v. Estate of Shabazz* (1987). In the *O'Lone* case, prison officials prohibited inmates on work details outside the prison from returning to the institution to attend a Muslim religious service held every Friday afternoon. The prison administration demonstrated that this practice would create security problems and impede rehabilitation. These rationales were viewed as legitimate penological concerns or objectives by the district court and by the Supreme Court. Additionally, prison administrators showed that there were alternative means of exercising this constitutional right (e.g., inmates could congregate for prayer or discussion at other times). Although this alternative satisfied the standard under *Turner*, it may not do so under RFRA rules. A court of appeals decision, even though later reversed by the Supreme Court, suggests how cases of this kind might be decided under RFRA. Since the new requirements of this law place the burden of proof on prison officials to demonstrate that a restriction (1) meets a compelling interest (not including monetary issues or administrative convenience), and (2) is the least restrictive alternative, this means that some method of accommodating the practice rather than banning it must be sought. The appeals court decision referred to above reversed a district court decision saying that "the lower court should consider whether there was any reasonable method of accommodating the objective without 'creating bona fide security problems'" (*Shabazz v. O'Lone*, 1986, p. 420; CLR, 1994b).

CLR (1994b) asserts that given that RFRA "creates an entirely new set of rules for judging religious restrictions ... it may cause a new judicial 'hands on' era in matters in the area of religion" (p. 73). While one can expect that inmates who enjoy harassing their captors with frivolous lawsuits will have a "field day through ligation with RFRA cases" (p. 73) it is far from clear that correctional administrators should see this as a catastrophe. As CLR (1994b) notes, in more than one instance correctional administrators have considered certain practices in which they engaged to be essential to prison operations yet when alternatives to them were tried not only did prison operations

not break down but in some cases they were improved. The use of female officers in male institutions represents a good example of this phenomenon (see Chapter 14).

Finally, while a new round of lawsuits is inevitable, a reactive approach of waiting to be sued may result in large increases in attorney fees, losing lawsuits, wasted time in court, and even damage payments to inmates. A proactive approach involving a review of existing restrictions with an eye toward finding the least restrictive alternatives would be in keeping with good administrative principles and be the most cost-effective action. Correctional administrators should consult religious leaders, including institutional clergy and other community leaders, as to whether existing practices constitute a substantial burden and as to what might be the "least restrictive alternative" to an existing regulation (CLR, 1994b). Many systems and facilities have begun an early review and update of their restrictions. For example, following the passage of RFRA, Oklahoma rescinded its ban on long hair and beards because of the cost of litigating this issue and it did not constitute a breach of security (Straley and Morris, 1994). If institutions feel the need to have photographs of inmates clean shaven for identification purposes in case of escape "state of the art computers" can now produce these images (James, 1994). When all the dust settles RFRA is likely to improve inmates' ability to practice their religion without compromising important correctional objectives since the courts are unlikely to rescind existing restrictions or impose alternatives that represent serious threats to institutional order.

## The Contemporary Chaplain Has a Variety of Functions

Two studies of chaplains—one conducted in New York[9] (Shaw, 1990) and the other in the Federal Bureau of Prisons (BOP)[10] (Stout and Clear, 1992)—provide a contemporary look at prison chaplains. The majority of chaplains in both studies were white, male, and between the ages of thirty to fifty-nine. While half of the chaplains in the federal prison survey were married, only one-third of those in the New York System were. Seventy-nine percent of those in the federal system had attended seminary and nearly all reported some form of graduate education. In both studies, Catholic chap-

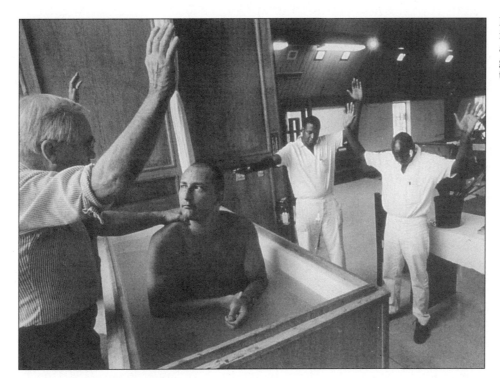

**Prison religious programs include baptisms as well as the range of most religious services and activities.**

lains comprised a substantial group (New York, 60%, versus the BOP, 37%).

**THE CHAPLAIN'S MAIN "MISSION" IS TO IMPROVE THE LOT OF INMATES** Shaw's research indicates that chaplains consider themselves advocates for inmates. Because chaplains have historically been concerned with the injustices of the criminal justice system and the living conditions of inmates, it has sometimes placed them at odds with prison administrators. Chaplains regularly walk the tiers and interact with inmates where they live. This can lead them to empathize with inmates, and for inmates to expect them to be sympathetic. Thus, chaplains may serve as a "wailing wall" or become a "court of constant complaint" for perceived injustices. These injustices are noted and responded to by chaplains. Shaw also found that chaplains express distress about simplistic public views of all offenders being "bad" and the fact that these views are not likely to change. They also see themselves as inmate advocates or ombudsmen:

> The Church is in the prison not just for the "service and maintenance" of inmates, but also to watch the government lest it sin worse than the inmates (p. VIII-10).

> [There is a] near total dependance on the chaplain to stand up for these men—and when you win them a right denied, there is a personal satisfaction of David defeating Goliath again" (p. VI-4).

> Chaplains are the only honest "snitch group in the organization" (p. VI-2). [Although made tongue in cheek, this comment does capture the essence of this point.]

In their unofficial capacity as inmate ombudsmen, chaplains encounter situations (e.g., guard abuse) that can strain relations with staff. Shaw recounts an incident in which he witnessed and reported a guard beating an inmate. Intense pressure was used to try to get him to retract his statement. He was threatened by one officer, kept locked on various tiers for hours, and locked off others.

**CHAPLAINS COORDINATE, SUPERVISE, AND RUN ALL RELGIOUS ACTIVITIES** From an administrative standpoint, the prison chaplain is responsible for coordinating and supervising all religious activities and services. During inmate orientation, they identify the inmates' religious needs and make them aware of available services.

Part of determining an inmates' religious needs involves ascertaining whether their faith group is an officially recognized religious group. This is a problem because religion may be used by some inmates for ulterior purposes (e.g., to voice objections to prison life and prison officials). To attempt to deter the formation of sham religious groups, corrections systems establish guidelines as to what is recognized as a legitimate faith group. The Texas Department of Corrections, while not excluding other considerations, uses the following factors in determining the legitimacy of a faith group:

**1.** A belief in a divine or supreme being, or transcendent power;
**2.** Societally shared common practices, with identifiable leaders or clergy in the "free world"; such practices must bear a relationship to the supreme being or transcendent power, such as worship or veneration;
**3.** An ongoing history, reference to scriptures, and trappings and practices traditionally considered religious (Texas Department of Corrections, 1985, p. 2).

*Chaplains Are Responsible for Providing Worship Services* All chaplains lead worship services for those of their own faith and may also be present at or even lead those of other faiths. Some resemble a "large unruly high school study hall" (Shaw, 1990, p. IV-22). Some of the distractions that occur include:

> [having] to stop mid sermon or mid prayer to silence conversations or disruptive activities. Officers interrupt to call inmates out for visits. Sometimes officers, there to keep inmates from being disruptive, converse with one another in a way that is more disruptive than inmates (p. IV-22).

This situation is aggravated by the fact that, in many prisons, chapel services are among the few times when inmates from different units (who normally have no contact with each other) get together. Thus, if inmates want to start a disturbance, attack another inmate, or plan an escape, religious services would present an opportunity to do so.

Some chaplains may measure the success of their services not by their impact on inmates but on whether they can "get from start to finish without any incidents" (Shaw, 1990, p. IV-22). It is not surprising that some inmates who are genuinely religious do not attend chapel because they

find the rowdy atmosphere offensive. While the disruption of services may bother some chaplains, Shaw found that most do not consider this extremely distressing because it only involves one hour of their work week.

*Outside Clergy and Volunteers Assist Chaplains* Most prisons have one full-time chaplain. To minister to inmates of faiths other than their own, chaplains attempt to recruit outside clergy or volunteers to serve these inmates (Riggs, 1989). Stout and Clear (1992) found that almost all BOP chaplains felt both comfortable and effective in ministering to inmates of other faiths. Historically, it was not easy to get mainline church groups to provide clergy to lead religious services and volunteers to assist in other religious activities. Mainline churches also tended to be disdainful of prison chaplains. This sometimes isolated these clergy from their faith groups and caused them to expect little support (Stout and Clear, 1992; Shaw, 1990).

Religious volunteers make up 95% of all volunteers in prison. Chaplain Solomon (1991) notes, however, that religious volunteers today are more sophisticated than in the past largely because of the recruitment and training done by groups such as **Prison Fellowship** (PF). Many chaplains rely on these organizations to recruit and train volunteers and to provide teaching, mentoring, and aftercare programs for released inmates. Their participation in religious activities helps inmates involved in these programs to make contact with prominent members of the community and has served to elevate the standing of chaplains among both staff and inmates (Solomon, 1991). For the volunteers, it has served to help educate them about prisons and provide a new perspective on inmates. Hands-on volunteer ministry helps citizens to understand that most inmates are not the animal-like monsters portrayed in the media but are indeed real people with hopes and dreams very often like their own.

Prison Fellowship represents an outstanding example of a national religious group with a prison focus. PF is composed of churches and volunteers involved in prison evangelism and a variety of inmate support activities both in and out of prison. It is active in more than two-thirds of our nation's prisons. Its programs include:

> three day seminars which stress spiritual renewal as well as dealing with prison problems; Bible studies;

Life Plan Seminars which stress positive goal setting; many inmate family support services (e.g., finding jobs, providing food, clothes, etc.); the "Angel Tree," which provides Christmas gifts for children of inmates; programs which involve the inmate in community programs while on furlough; and an advocacy program (The Justice Fellowship) which pushes for reform in the criminal justice system.

These and other PF programs contribute significantly to the success of many inmates upon release (Clark, 1989).

Another program, the **Kairos Prison Ministry** (KPM), emanates from mainline churches. KPM includes many professional people and puts on seminars to teach inmates religious principles. Active in 20 states, this growing volunteer program also provides significant transitional services to inmates in its programs (Solomon, 1991).

Fundamentalist religious groups have been very active in the volunteer movement. The nature of their literature, emotionally charged services, and the experience of declaring oneself "born again" makes them extremely popular with inmates (Shaw, 1990). This is further enhanced by their willingness to provide secular and religious assistance. For example, Living Witnesses For Christ volunteers minister to inmates' religious needs and assist them in legal efforts to win their freedom and, on release, help them get jobs and housing. They also visit inmate families prior to release to explain their role in the inmate's reintegration into society (Angolite, 1981).

*Inmate-Led Religious Groups Have Posed Problems*
One area causing problems and controversy involves inmate-led religious groups. The extent to which prison systems allow inmates to lead religious activities varies. In the federal system, inmates are not permitted to do this unless the prison's chaplain is of a different faith and/or no assistance is available from local community religious groups. In fact, no professional (e.g., a dentist) is allowed to practice his or her profession while incarcerated in a federal prison (Schulze, 1991). Some states allow inmates to lead religious services with a chaplain or a staff member present, but there is a tendency to require the presence of an outside clergyperson or religious representative of that faith (Mushlin, 1993). In considering the constitutionality of the sponsor requirement, the

courts have been heavily influenced by the security problems posed by inmate-led services. In *Benjamin v. Coughlin* (1990) the court noted that:

> The sponsor requirement is . . . intended to ensure that the meeting is convened for religious purposes and not to hold kangaroo courts, foster extortion, or provide a venue for the dissemination of conspiratorial information . . . the use of sponsors is thought to minimize conflicts among inmates as to the nature and content of the service (p. 577).

**BLACK MUSLIM CLERGY HAVE INCREASINGLY BECOME INVOLVED IN PRISON RELIGIOUS ACTIVITIES**   As we noted in Chapter 8, Black Muslims began seeking religious converts among inmates in the prisons in the 1960s and 1970s. According to Imam Hafiz (1993), the Black Muslims represent a hybrid religion and should be regarded as an organization begun in America in the 1930s by blacks that combined the tenets of Islam and Christianity. It was called the **Nation of Islam** by one of its early leaders, Elijah Mohammed. The name was changed to **American Muslim Mission** by his son, Imam W. D. Mohammed, who removed all racial restrictions on membership. This group is considered to represent the largest group of Muslims in America identifying with one Islamic leader. In 1979 minister Louis Farrakhan left this group and started his own Muslim sect using the resurrected name, Nation of Islam. This group is viewed as outside traditional Islamic practice since it does not follow the Qur'an (the holy book of the Muslims) but instead has its own books (Hafiz, 1993). Farrakhan's policies have been described as being reactionary and based on beliefs that include black superiority, scapegoating of Jews, and economic self-sufficiency (Terry, 1994; Holmes, 1994; Marriott, 1994). According to Hafiz (1993), Nation of Islam ministers have not been employed in state or federal prisons. Nevertheless, there are Nation of Islam groups functioning within our prisons and also those associated with the Moorish Science Temple of America, another hybrid offshoot. Hafiz cautions that chaplains need to attend meetings of these groups to ensure that the activities are of a religious nature.

The increasing presence in prison of Muslim **Imams** (qualified clergy) who are black has added a new dimension to the prison religious scene (Shaw, 1990). Initially Imams were not given a

A group of Muslim inmates engaging in one of many prayer services. They must do this several times a day.

warm welcome because they had to deal with correctional personnel (including chaplains) who had had negative experiences with some Islamic inmates (e.g., being called "white devils" or taunted and threatened by them). However, Muslim chaplains of the 1990s have not only been accepted but considered real assets in those facilities that employ them full time. They have been able to educate staff on Muslim religious matters so that requests concerning religious practices can be evaluated. This has reduced litigation by inmates based on denial of opportunities to engage in legitimate religious practices (Hafiz, 1993).

Without Imams, the Muslim religion in prison has tended to develop extremist ideas and practices that are not accepted by the faith. In some cases its members have been seen by staff as a gang using religion as a pretext to meet and run gang business.

Other inmates have seen it as an exclusive black religion. The role of the Imam chaplain has been to eliminate incorrect stereotypes and to ensure that these religious groups are operating in accordance with the tenets of the religion and prison rules. He can also encourage members of Muslim communities to do volunteer work in the prisons so inmates can have contact with blacks who are successful and will provide them with assistance when they are released (Hafiz, 1993). The Close-Up on Imams describes their role as chaplains in prisons.

**CHAPLAINS HELP REGULATE AND DISTRIBUTE RELIGIOUS ITEMS** Chaplains also function to assist inmates in obtaining literature and other materials necessary for the practice of their faith. There appears to be wide latitude on the items inmates are allowed to possess across the various systems (Texas Department of Corrections, 1985; Federal Bureau of Prisons, undated). For example, federal inmates can possess items including but not limited to beads, feathers, medicine pouches, religious headbands, prayer oils, prayer rugs, kufis, medals/chains, medallions, rosaries, phylacteries, prayer shawls, yarmulkes, and turbans. Additionally chaplains keep some items (e.g., wine) that inmates are not allowed to possess but can use in conducting religious services. Wine is required by ecclesiastical law for use in certain religious rites and the sacraments of several faith groups. BOP guidelines allow wine to be used in these ceremonies but require it to be kept in secure storage by the prison chaplain.

Despite their recognition of an inmate's First Amendment right to religious expression, the courts have recognized that restricting personal possession of items and of their use in religious services may be necessary.

### Chaplains Must Be Responsive to a Number of Inmate Needs

In serving the religious needs of prisoners, chaplains must truly be "jacks of all trades."

**COUNSELING INMATES CAN PUT CHAPLAINS INTO DIFFICULT SITUATIONS** Chaplains counsel inmates either individually or in a group setting and these sessions may focus on religious as well as secular concerns. Inmates who seek help in dealing with their problems from prison counse-

## *Close Up*  An Imam Provides Religious Leadership for Muslim Inmates

The growing number of inmate adherents to the Islamic religion, created a need for qualified clergy (Imams) to conduct worship and other activities for these inmates. According to Abu Ishaq Abdul-Hafiz—one of eight full-time Muslim Imam chaplains now in the federal prison system—the lack of Imams in prisons had led to the development of practices by inmate Muslim groups that were not accepted in the faith. Abdul-Hafiz, who serves as a chaplain at the Terminal Island Federal Correctional Institution, provides spiritual guidance to inmates of all faiths at the prison. However, he considers his main mission to be exposing the Muslim religion for what it really is—peace and harmony for all people. He feels that all religions actually are from one source, are the same, and that we're all talking about the same God.

He has touched the lives of a number of inmates both Muslim and otherwise. A 44-year-old heroin addict indicated that Hafiz had inspired him to find another life path and in effect had saved his life. Buddhist inmates credited him with reviving their interest in practicing their faith while Jewish inmates appreciated his help in securing literature for them. Hafiz has also created a strong bond between the prison and the external Islamic community, which has helped to expose inmates to a wider view of the faith.

An estimated 20% of male black inmates (between 80,000 and 100,000) claim Islam as their religious preference. Like the Christian faith, the Islamic religion has several "sects." This complicates the job of non-Muslim chaplains and reinforces the need for Imams as chaplains in prison systems with substantial black inmate populations (Rae-Dupree, 1991; *Volunteer Today*, 1993; Hafiz and Hamidullah, undated).

lors, particularly mental health professionals, are more likely to be seen as "crazy" because of the common view that anyone seeking this kind of help must be severely disturbed. In contrast, going to a counseling session with a chaplain is not seen as visiting the "shrink" because of the religious context in which these sessions are held. Further, Johnson (1968) notes that some inmates might "within the framework of religious terminology . . . accept the role of treatment client and will not resist the principles of therapy, whereas they would be repelled by the specialized language of professionalized therapy" (pp. 588–589). Also, chaplains may refer inmates to receive other types of treatment. The important role played by chaplains in inmate treatment has led some states to recognize them as integral members of prison treatment teams.

In the course of counseling and moving about the institution, chaplains invariably acquire information on an inmate's criminal history and violations of prison rules. Most state statutes view communication between minister and penitent as privileged. Thus, the minister receiving the information cannot be compelled to divulge it unless the individual giving it waives the legal right to secrecy (Kaplan and Waltz, 1987). However, while chaplains are employees of the institution and the policies and procedures governing their role consider communication with inmates as confidential, this policy is not absolute. That is, they are generally required to divulge information that threatens the safety or security of the institution, its staff, or other inmates (Federal Bureau of Prisons, undated; Florida Department of Corrections, 1982; Texas Department of Corrections, 1986). This places chaplains in a Catch-22 situation in that their effectiveness with inmates is reduced if they are seen as "snitches," but they will be seen as "traitors" by staff if they fail to divulge critical information. As the following incident suggests, this requires chaplains to tread a very fine line:

An undergraduate female student was murdered on the campus where Chaplain Shaw (1990) was completing his doctoral work. Later, in talking with an inmate in a confidential setting, he was told that another inmate, incarcerated for a minor crime, had admitted killing the girl and indicated the location of the body. The inmate informant was very afraid and commanded Shaw to remain silent. Burdened by the revelation, he tried to persuade the inmate to tell someone by appealing to his sense of responsibility to the murdered girl's mother. After about a week, the inmate acquiesced and told an investigator. While the alleged murderer denied his boast, and the information on the body location was not valid, according to Shaw (1990), this provides a "classic example of the sort of pressure such confidentiality can place on a chaplain" (p. IV-31).

## CHAPLAINS ASSIST INMATES IN DEALING WITH MANY SITUATIONS
Chaplains play an important role in helping inmates to deal with family-related issues. They counsel inmate families and meet with them during visits, and assist inmates in reestablishing family ties. Chaplains also help inmates with things such as requests for visits, clothes and commissary money, guidance for inmate families in obtaining financial or social service assistance (Texas Department of Corrections, 1986), and by recruiting qualified volunteers who are willing to work with inmates who are soon to be released (Shaw, 1990; Florida Department of Corrections, 1982). Chaplains may also receive calls reporting family problems and are usually responsible for notifying the inmate or the family of emergencies including death and serious illness. This latter aspect is one of the more stressful aspects of the chaplain's job.

Marriage of inmates also falls within the chaplain's province. While the Supreme Court in *Turner v. Safely* (1987) has upheld an inmate's fundamental right to marry, it acknowledged the right of prison officials to regulate the time and circumstances under which the marriage may take place. Since *Turner,* the courts have been unwilling to deny an inmate the right to marry unless the prison can offer powerful reasons for forbidding the inmate to do so (Mushlin, 1993). Although weddings are typically joyous events that occur in pleasant surroundings, prison does not lend itself to this.

> These weddings, when performed, are [because of the] setting, sad, ugly experiences not only for the couple, but for any minister . . . who likes to make marriage ceremonies memorable for brides and grooms. They are generally performed in an office or consultation booth, over within a few minutes; the couple newly tied in marriage are almost immediately separated and he, she, or both are returned to the tier area (Shaw, 1990, p. IV-29).

As Shaw (1990) notes, chaplains have no way of knowing which of these marriages are "made in heaven and which are done for monetary convenience or whim" (p. IV-29).

Chaplains are responsible for visiting inmates in special housing units including protective or disciplinary segregation and in the prison hospital. Recently, this has included ministering to the needs of AIDS patients. The incidence of AIDS and the aging of the prison population will result in a larger number of inmates dying in prison (U.S. Department of Justice, 1989). BOP has developed hospices at two of its prisons to ease the tension involved in the dying process.

Finally, some chaplains have to minister to the needs of inmates on Death Row. This includes working with inmate families and assisting inmates in making final decisions before their execution (e.g., disposal of personal property and trust fund money). They may also help them deal with the pain and myriad emotions they may experience during their last day (Marble, 1988).

## PRISON RELIGIOUS PROGRAMS ARE VULNERABLE TO MANIPULATION BY INMATES

> [T]he total involvement of religionists and organizations with the inmate and all of his problems has one drawback—one that everyone recognizes. It invites con and deception by insincere inmates hunting ways to secure their needs or obtain their freedom. Outside religionists and organizations promising to become totally involved with the inmate and assisting him with all his problems creates a situation ripe for exploitation by criminal and insincere inmates. The only requirement is that they ride the religious pony and, given their basic criminality, deception comes easy (Angolite, 1981, p. 49).

The literature is replete with accounts of inmates becoming involved with religion to improve their chances of parole (Shaw, 1990; Kassebaum, Ward, and Wilner, 1971). The advent of parole in Illinois saw attendance at religious services go from 35 to 80%, and a few years later it reached more than 99% (Weir and Kalm, 1936). Rabbi Leibert reports that a regular inmate member of his prison choir asked for a parole recommendation based on his religious observance. The Rabbi pointed out to the inmate that he was not Jewish to which the inmate responded:

"Look Rabbi, I know I am not a Hebrew, but a heathen. But the board doesn't give a hoot about my conscience or my beliefs. All they're interested in is whether or not I attend services. And I do, as you well know—or how come your choir sings so sweetly?" (Leibert, 1965, as cited by Shaw, 1990, p. III-24)

Because of such motivation, most prison systems have dropped the direct payoff for attendance at chapel functions by providing favorable parole recommendation (Solomon, 1991). Other factors that enhance religious attendance include an opportunity to interact with female volunteers who are sometimes brought in to assist in the service and to obtain help with getting a job and/or housing when released.

The reality of inmate manipulation causes chaplains to be on guard and constantly question inmate motives. There can be danger involved in putting trust in some inmates. Chaplain Shaw (1990) reports a case of an inmate who was imprisoned for brutally killing a store owner and his female clerk, whom he mutilated. Not long after being sent to prison, this inmate secured a job as a trusted clerk in the prison chapel. He later brutally murdered a female corrections officer. Shaw, who had contact with the offender, said he was stunned at how an inmate with his record and demeanor was able to gain the confidence of the chaplain in such a short period of time.

### Integration into the Prison Staff Can Be Difficult for Chaplains

As paid members of the prison staff, chaplains come under the direct control of the prison warden or jail commander and in the state and federal systems are also supervised by the department supervisor of chaplains. Unlike other staff who are paid by a jurisdiction, chaplains owe their primary allegiance to their religious group and must be responsive to its theology or belief system. This may create conflict with prison administrators when religious values and institutional/custodial goals are at odds (Stoltz, 1978, as cited by Shaw, 1990). In some respects, chaplains are like the proverbial person without a country in that they must be responsive to two chains of command, neither of which may be particularly supportive. As one chaplain put it, "the government does not really respect religious personnel and their pro-

grams. The church (clergy, curia) leaves us totally isolated" (Shaw, 1990, p. VI-13). The lack of understanding on the part of prison administrators results in attempts to fit religious programming into a standard program model, which involves chaplains completing reams of forms to show they are being productive.

Correctional officers (COs) do not typically view chaplains any more favorably than do prison administrators. Shaw (1990) found that chaplains tended to feel that COs viewed them as do-gooders who interfered with their routines. Nevertheless, while this attitude is frustrating, experienced chaplains can overcome it by "selling themselves to correctional staff" (Shaw, 1990, p. VIII-9). One chaplain put his finger on the real reason that chaplains and others working in the prison have so many problems:

> Often it seems that staff does not work in unity with each other toward the overall goal. There is little gathering of colleagues-chaplain/program people/ security to discuss problems. There has been no time when we gathered to set positive goals, develop an overall strategy, as a theme by which to improve the [atmosphere] of the institution. The goal [unspoken] seems to be: "leave it alone" (as cited in Shaw, 1990, p. VI-14).

Thus, the lack of communication between chaplains, administrators, and staff is the cause of much of the conflict between them (Shaw, 1990).

### Chaplains Also Minster to Staff and Their Families

While chaplains and staff may have difficulties working with each other, part of the institutional responsibilities of chaplains involves ministering to staff and their families (Federal Bureau of Prisons, undated; Texas Department of Corrections, 1986; Florida Department of Corrections, 1982). In delineating chaplain responsibilities, the BOP indicates that new staff or those who work rotating shifts, and who often may not have ties with congregations in the community, be ministered to by the prison chaplain. Being able to feel welcome in the prison chapel, and comfortable in looking to the chaplain for spiritual direction and support on occasions such as marriages, funerals, and baptisms can be of major assistance to staff. It is interesting that, despite the resentment that chaplains experience from staff, many of them feel a genuine concern for their well-being (Shaw, 1990). Further, 88% of BOP chaplains felt that their ministry was successful with staff (Stout and Clear, 1992).

Chaplains also play an important role in helping staff gain an understanding of inmate religious practices. In the federal system, they may act as sponsors and advisors to new employees during their probationary year and counsel other employees who perform poorly due to alcohol or drug abuse or other types of problems.

### Effective Chaplains Must Have Certain Characteristics

Prison chaplains have a difficult and demanding job. The essence of this is captured by Emmett Solomon (1990), administrator of the chaplaincy programs for the Texas Department of Criminal Justice, who notes:

> Since the prison is a "cold war" the chaplain has to continually be alert to his/her being used as a pawn in that conflict. This factor requires him/her always to evaluate every situation and the motivation of every request. It requires the development of "tough love" in order to function effectively in the adversarial setting [of the prison]. In this age of specialization the chaplain is still a generalist, interested in the client's overall welfare (p. 1).

Solomon's view parallels the perceptions that Shaw's chaplain respondents have of themselves.

They reported themselves to be tough and resilient individuals with strong shoulders to bear the burdens of others. Their self-defined toughness is not a traditional macho approach to their work but instead recognizes "their own vulnerability and [the] dangers associated with giving in to situations [that] could cause undue stress" (Shaw, 1990, p. IX-9). Also, like other professionals, experienced chaplains realize the need to separate themselves emotionally from inmate problems when they leave the facility and to maintain a degree of emotional distance from inmates and their problems.

One quality that appeared to be essential in dealing with the stresses of working in a prison/jail environment was a "sense of humor" (Shaw, 1990). Given these positive feelings, it is not surprising that Stout and Clear (1992) found that almost all BOP chaplains felt the job they did was important. This relates to the almost unanimous feeling among them that their ministry with inmates was successful. In fact, eight of ten indicated that they would rather work as chaplains than any other job.

Finally, with respect to chaplain effectiveness, at least one study found that "of the successful releasees who credited a specific staff member with being a major influence in their reformation, one-sixth cited the prison chaplains and religious workers." This is true despite the fact that these employees represent less than 1% of the prison staff (Glaser, 1969, pp. 93–94).

### ENDNOTES

1. The authors would like to thank Judy Ford Stokes, president of Judy Ford Stokes & Associates, Inc., Atlanta, Georgia, food management and design consultants, for providing information, reviewing the section on food services, and offering useful suggestions to improve its authenticity. Bill Bowers, food service coordinator, Florida Department of Corrections, and Jeff Vickers, director of food services, Contra Costa County Detention Division, Martinez, California, also provided some assistance.

2. It is preferable for a system or facility to have a computerized nutrient analysis of its cycle menu done by a university or some other creditable organization because this can be used to refute inmate court challenges to the nutritional value of the food served (Stokes, 1991). Also, in this respect Stokes (1991) notes that it is advisable to use a nutrient analysis database of recipes like those of the military service.

3. As of January 1994, a new standard (Hazard Analysis Critical Control Point, HACCP) requires constant temperatures to be maintained for food, from the point of receiving through storage, and through the entire food production process and in serving. Cold food must be maintained at temperatures no higher than 41°F and hot food must be served at temperatures of at least 160°F. To meet these new standards and document compliance, refrigerated work counters must be installed and used in some production areas, e.g., salad bars. In addition, rethermalization systems will need to be used in many facilities to ensure proper temperatures.

**4.** Rethermealization units are mobile and can be used to retherm bulk food or individual food serving trays. Hot food items are placed in the retherm units and cold food in separate carts and rolled to cell areas or decentralized dining rooms. The retherm units are plugged in, and 15 to 30 minutes later hot food is ready to be assembled with cold food and beverages for delivery to the inmate. This system can also be used in kitchens with adjacent dinning areas (Stokes & Associates, undated; Stokes, 1993).

**5.** The cook/chill production method, a type of cook-to-inventory system, prepares food according to inventory levels using standardized recipes. It is based on maintaining predetermined amounts (par levels) of menu items on hand at all times. For example, if the par level for chili is 400 gallons and only 150 gallons exist in storage, then 250 additional gallons would need to be prepared. Food prepared today may be served next week (Stokes, 1993). For a more complete discussion of this method consult "Your Kitchen Can Pay for Itself" prepared by Judy Ford Stokes & Associates, Atlanta, Georgia (undated).

**6.** The authors would like to thank Richard Shaw, chaplain at the New York State Summit Shock Incarceration Facility and Albany County Jail; Emmett Solomon, administrator of chaplaincy programs, Texas Department of Criminal Justice; Robert Schulze, assistant chaplaincy administrator, Federal Bureau of Prisons; Charles Riggs, chaplaincy administrator, Federal Bureau of Prisons; and Imam Abdul Hafiz, Chaplain, Federal Correctional Institution-Terminal Island, for providing information, reviewing this manuscript, and offering useful suggestions to improve its authenticity.

**7.** Under Section 1983 damages cannot be recovered against state governments—only against individual state employees—because of Eleventh Amendment restrictions on federal suits against these entities. Also, under Section 1983 damages can only be recovered against a city or county government if the plaintiff shows that the violation occurred pursuant to municipal policy. RFRA appears to be an exception to the Eleventh Amendment because it explicitly authorizes suits against state governments, and it does not require that a violation be related to a local policy (Boston, 1995b).

**8.** Note that the rules established in the *Turner* decision will continue to be the standard for evaluating inmates versus institutional concerns in cases other than those involving religious issues.

**9.** Shaw surveyed all Catholic, Jewish, and Islamic chaplains listed as official chaplains in the federal and state prisons in New York State and in county and city jails. In comparing the characteristics of his sample with data on chaplains provided by the New York Department of Corrections, Shaw (1990) found that in terms of age and sex his sample closely paralleled

chaplains in the state, however in terms of years of service, his respondents were more seasoned (9.4 average years of service versus 4.04). Out of 270 questionnaires sent out, 70 responses were received.

**10.** The Stout and Clear (1992) survey was based on 113 responses from chaplains attending a BOP chaplains meeting in June 1990—not all chaplains completed the survey.

## ACKNOWLEDGMENTS

[a] D. Boss, M. Schecter, and P. King. (1986, March) Food service behind bars. Food Management pp. 83–87. Penton Publishing with permission of the publisher.
[b] Reprinted with permission from the National Prison Project Journal.

## CHAPTER RECAP

**Prison Food Service**
Food Has a Critical Role in Prisons
Menu Planning Can Be Complex
  Some Inmates Require Special Diets
The Feeding of Inmates Requires Close Scrutiny
  Inmates Are Fed in Dining Rooms or in Their Units
  Serving Lines Must Be Controlled
  Food Service Areas Require Security
More Efficient Food Preparation Methods Can Deal with Overcrowding and Prison Emergencies
**Religious Programs**
Religious Groups Have Historically Been Concerned with Offenders
  The Introduction of the Treatment Approach to Corrections Provided a New Incentive for Young, Better Qualified Men to Become Chaplains
The Courts Have Dealt with Several Religious Issues
  The Religious Freedom Restoration Act Will Have a Major Impact on the Regulation of Religious Practices in Prisons
The Contemporary Chaplain Has a Variety of Functions
  The Chaplain's Main "Mission" Is to Improve the Lot of Inmates
  Chaplains Coordinate, Supervise, and Run All Religious Activities
    Chaplains Are Responsible for Providing Worship Services
    Outside Clergy and Volunteers Assist Chaplains
    Inmate-Led Religious Groups Have Posed Problems
  Black Muslim Clergy Have Increasingly Become Involved in Prison Religious Activities
  Chaplains Help Regulate and Distribute Religious Items
Chaplains Must Be Responsive to a Number of Inmate Needs

Counseling Inmates Can Put Chaplains into Difficult Situations

Chaplains Assist Inmates in Dealing with Many Situations

Prison Religious Programs Are Vulnerable to Manipulation by Inmates

Integration into the Prison Staff Can Be Difficult for Chaplains

Chaplains Also Minister to Staff and Their Families

Effective Chaplains Must Have Certain Characteristics

## REVIEW QUESTIONS

1. How have court rulings affected basic inmate services?

2. What are the special challenges that prison food services face?

3. Why can prison menu planning be so complex?

4. Why is security in the food service area so important?

5. How has religion influenced corrections in the past?

6. What difficulties can arise when a chaplain tries to be an advocate for inmates with problems?

7. How have the courts affected the treatment of inmate religious groups?

8. What role do volunteers play in prison ministries?

9. What social characteristics are required to be an effective prison chaplain?

## TEST YOUR KNOWLEDGE

1. Which of the following is true regarding prison food services?

a. The courts have refused to regulate prison food services.

b. Prisons can refuse to provide religious diets based on their expense.

c. One-way prisons provide varied menus is through the use of cycle menus.

d. As long as inmates are provided with sufficient amounts of food, there is no requirement that diets be nutritionally balanced.

2. Religion has historically affected corrections in all but one of the following ways. Which is *not* one of those ways?

a. Churches have been administering parole supervision.

b. Churches have tried to temper the impact of penal sanctions.

c. Churches have established prisons.

d. Chaplains have been providing religious services for prison inmates.

3. Which of the following *best describes* the chaplain's function in terms of the prison administration's expectations?

a. an advocate for inmates' rights

b. coordinator of all religious activities

c. monitor of staff treatment of inmates

d. coordinator of all rehabilitation programs

# CHAPTER 21

# FAMILY TIES, VISITING, AND RECREATION

## LEARNING OBJECTIVES

*After completion of this chapter, you should be able to:*

1. Describe the effect that visits and family ties have on recidivism.
2. Specify some of the crises that incarceration creates for inmates' wives.
3. Discuss differences in visiting conditions in various prisons and specify the types of visitors.
4. Describe how security and custody concerns affect visiting.
5. Define private family/conjugal visits and discuss the arguments for and against this program.
6. Discuss how telephones serve to augment visiting.
7. Explain the benefits of prison furlough programs.
8. Describe how prison recreation programs can be beneficial to both inmates and the institution.

## KEY TERMS AND CONCEPTS

Conjugal visits
Contact visits
Dismemberment
Furloughs
M-2 Sponsors program
Parenting programs
Social isolates
Strip searches
The yard

The gulf between the "island," which is the prison, and the "mainland," which is the free world, is bridged by contacts inmates may have with people important to them on the outside. If maintained throughout the inmate's stay in prison, these relationships can help keep inmates bonded to conventional, prosocial activities inside and outside of the prison. This chapter focuses on the conditions under which inmates may have contact with loved ones and friends. Also examined are the activities inmates engage in to keep physically fit and to deal constructively with their leisure time.

## Visitation and Inmate Family Ties

The origin of occasionally allowing friends or relatives to visit inmates is obscure. In the Walnut Street Jail and its predecessors, dating back to 1718, visitors were permitted to call on inmates (Barnes and Teeters, 1951). However, the principle of separation, central to both the Pennsylvania and Auburn prison systems, dictated that inmates be isolated from the outside world and their families and friends, hence visits and mail were not allowed. This policy was gradually modified to allow well-behaved inmates visits from friends and relatives in most prisons (Pettigrove, 1910). Thus, wide variation existed in visitation policies, with progressive wardens recognizing its importance, others merely tolerating it, and some sabotaging it.

### Family Contacts Positively Impact Inmate Prison and Postrelease Behavior

Wives, children, parents, and other relatives of inmates are sometimes viewed as "the second victims of their crimes." Although this notion may generate some sympathy, it is unlikely to engender support for family-oriented prison programs given current budgetary constraints and attitudes toward the offender population. However, with severe prison overcrowding and current antitax sentiments, programs reducing recidivism should be very attractive. Several studies have found positive relationships between the maintenance of strong family ties during imprisonment and postrelease success (Ohlin, 1951; Glaser, 1954, 1969; Adams and Fischer, 1976; Holt and Miller, 1972).

Holt and Miller (1972), conducted the most extensive of these studies on California parolees. They found that those who received visits while in prison experienced significantly fewer and less serious difficulties on release. Also, for parolees with two or more visits, the amount of money they received on release and their place of residence were also important predictors of parole success.

**FAMILY TIES PROVIDE INMATES WITH A SUPPORT SYSTEM AND THE MOTIVATION TO CHANGE** Most research justifies support for visitation programs, but it fails to explain why family contacts during imprisonment reduce antisocial behavior after release. Hairston (1988) provides a perspective on this process. Drawing from the social support literature, she notes that the social network that families provide protects a person from a variety of stressful stimuli. Abandonment by family can make the prison experience more demoralizing so on release the offender has fewer positive feelings of self-worth and resources to resist recidivating. Outside social networks can provide inmates with tangible resources (e.g., money to buy items not furnished by the state that make prison life more bearable). Additionally, families may motivate inmates to take advantage of prison programs and services that can lead to better jobs on release, improvement in interpersonal relations with family members, and/or elimination of substance abuse.

The interactionist perspective provides another explanation of the impact that family ties have on inmates by examining primary versus secondary group involvement. Primary groups, such as families, are small. Members have intimate personal ties by which they can meet basic needs for companionship, love, security, and an overall sense of well-being. These close ties tend to lead members to be more concerned with each others' welfare and to terminate certain patterns of behavior at their request. Also, individuals are apt to be accepted based on "the kind of person they are" rather than on their accomplishments. Secondary groups involve more formal relationships, fewer emotional ties, limited interaction, and place greater emphasis on economic and social accomplishment. Thus, without strong primary group contacts, a person is more likely to feel forsaken and drift into an anomic state in which they are not controlled by conventional rules and customs. By maintaining family contact, inmates can retain socially acceptable roles as brothers, sisters, parents, or children. This reinforces their sense of individual worth and can offset the stigma of the inmate role and the often negative evaluations inmates get from prison staff and society. If family ties are broken, releasees may have only the ex-convict role with all of its negative connotations.

These perspectives suggest the importance of family ties for inmates. Although these contacts cannot guarantee success, their absence can help explain the likelihood of failure.

## Incarceration Creates Crises for Prisoners' Wives

Wives comprise a primary group left behind when husbands are imprisoned. Wives must first cope with the crises of arrest and sentencing. Fishman's (1990)[a] a in-depth study of thirty prisoner wives provides a rare look at this group.

**IMPRISONMENT FOR INMATES' WIVES IS LIKE THE DEATH OF A LOVED ONE**    Initially, imprisonment produces a double crisis (dismemberment and demoralization) for wives and other family members. **Dismemberment** refers to the adjustment made to the loss of a husband or other family member, such as when a loved one dies. The obvious difference is that imprisoned husbands are alive and may one day return. Families must also deal with the demoralization caused by the shame and stigma of a family member in prison and establish new relationships with a person who is now "living while dead" (Schwartz and Weintraub, 1974).

Inmate wives also have to deal with several economic issues related to their husbands' imprisonment. They have to decide whether to get a job, remain at home, and/or apply for welfare. Most wives experience severe financial problems following their spouses' imprisonment including being on the edge of subsistence, being inundated with household and child-related expenses, and having to obtain money for their incarcerated husbands and for the costs of travel to the prison. Some also have to decide whether to move to the area where their husbands' prison is located. Those wives who do so experience added hostility and stigmatization (Fishman, 1990).

On a personal level, most inmate wives have feelings of physical deprivation, which include not having their husband's companionship and the hardships of not having them available to pay bills, provide income, or make repairs around the house. This is often compounded by sexual frustration. Wives with children experience child management problems similar to those of single mothers. They also have to decide how to explain the father's absence to the children, which tends to upset children and make them fearful and insecure. In Fishman's study (1990), those with school age children did not try to conceal the arrest or incarceration since these youngsters saw it or heard about it from other adults. As one wife put it:

> Everyone knows where he is and I don't keep it back from anyone. I tell the kids that he's in jail too. Mary would say as we rode by the jail, "Daddy's in jail! There's his house!" I say to her Daddy got into a little trouble and he's in jail (p. 132).

The family life of inmates is frequently marked by crises (e.g., substance abuse, violence, and separations). For their children, imprisonment precipitates some of the problems since, for many, this is merely their most recent crisis. Many react adversely to this separation, experiencing problems such as insomnia, nightmares, and bed-wetting. Half had school problems that included falling grades, truancy, or becoming dropouts (Fishman, 1990).

Despite the hardships experienced by these wives, they also realized some benefits. In their husbands' absence, they gained a measure of independence in managing their lives, those of their children, the household, and their resources. This gave them a new sense of competence. However, the burdens, particularly those of a financial nature, far outweighed any of these benefits (Fishman, 1990).

## VISITATION PROGRAMS AND INMATE FAMILY TIES

The opening of prisons to visitors creates security problems and therefore requires some regulation. Most often, visitors are family members and may include an inmate's children. The remote location of many prisons impedes visitation as do institutional conditions that may sometimes be inhospitable.

Visitation conditions range from noncontact situations in some maximum security prisons to totally private conjugal visits, which are allowed in several states.

## Visiting Rules Are Based on Security Concerns

Until the 1950s visits were viewed as rewards for good behavior. Since then, prison officials have begun to see visits as contributing to the rehabilitative process, to postrelease success, and to the orderly nature of prison life (Schafer, 1989; Knight, 1986). Nevertheless, prison regulations and practices continue to control visitation by restricting the who, what, when, how long, and where of it.

The courts have usually held that prison authorities can regulate this activity for security and other purposes (Project, 1994). They have upheld limitations such as types (e.g., noncontact or contact), number, and duration of visits; who may visit; the suspension of visiting to punish prison rule violators; and transfers of inmates to other prisons despite less convenient locations. Nevertheless, the courts will not permit restrictions that are arbitrary, vague, or discriminatory such as restricting visitors who are "objectionable" (Mushlin, 1993; Palmer, 1991; Knight, 1986).

## Most Often Inmates Are Visited by Family Members

Most prisons define family members as eligible to visit. However, each person, including any friend, who wants to visit must complete an application form in order to be placed on the inmate's approved visitor list. Hairston and Hess (1989) found that thirty states place some restrictions on visitation by unaccompanied children. A study of visits (Neto, 1989) in three California prisons found that the typical visitor was female (the wife, 42%; mother, 14%; or girlfriend, 11%), had an average age of thirty-five, lived in the general area (some having relocated to be near spouses), and visited the prison a couple times a week to see her husband. These women revealed "a strong sense of mission and purpose . . . that of being with their loved ones, no matter what their hardships" (Neto, 1989, p. 34).

**WIVES COMMONLY BRING THE CHILDREN WHEN THEY VISIT**   Neto further found that more than 50% of her subjects "usually" or "sometimes" brought their children, one-half of whom were six or younger. Those who did not cited added ex-

A children's special play area. Some prisons provide play areas like this for children's use while parents visit. This encourages inmate spouses and other visitors to bring children.

penses, avoiding exposure of children to the prison environment, and/or difficulty in handling the children on the bus or in the visiting area as reasons for not doing so.

Research has demonstrated the importance of frequent visits between inmates and their children for the well-being of all concerned. However, prison regulations and facilities often neglect the special needs of children, and instead focus on parental responsibility for controlling their children's behavior (Hairston and Hess, 1989; Schafer, 1991). What is required are special play areas for children. Newer prisons often include these areas, but only three states (New York, Missouri, and South Carolina) require them. At Arthur Kill Correctional Center in New York, the children's area was transformed into "Kiddie Land" through the cooperative efforts of staff and inmates. Inmate funds from vending machine profits were used to purchase toys and furniture, while prison art classes painted murals, and a floor covering class

TABLE 21.1 Distances Traveled to Prisons by Visitors

| Prison | Location | Distance Traveled | % of Visitors Traveling This Distance |
|---|---|---|---|
| San Quentin | San Francisco area | 50 miles or less | 60 |
| | | More than 50 miles | 40 |
| Norco | Prison Valley of Southern California | 150 miles or less | 80 |
| | | More than 150 miles | 20 |
| Susanville | Northern California | Less than 150 miles | 34 |
| | | 151 to 600 miles | 50 |
| | | Over 600 miles | 16 |

*Source:* V. V. Neto (1989). *Prison Visitors: A Profile*. In J. Mustin and B. Bloom (Conference Directors), The First National Conference on the Family and Corrections, Richmond, KY. Training Resource Center, Eastern Kentucky University. Reproduced with permission.

installed the carpeting. The children are supervised by volunteer "grandparents" recruited through New York City's Foster Grandparent program. President James Thorpe of the inmate Jaycees attributes the success of the center to these volunteers. During its first year the center serviced 1200 children (New York State Department of Correctional Services, 1988).

### Prison Visiting Schedules and Visiting Area Capacities Vary Widely

In a 45-state survey, Schafer (1991) found that between 1976 and 1987 visiting policies changed in a positive direction. There was an increase in the number of total available visiting hours during that period. Visiting hours vary: Only two states (Florida and Texas) restrict hours to Saturday and Sunday; in others the range is from 3 to 89 hours and up to seven days per week with twenty-three states allowing visits on five or more days per week. In prisons built before 1950 visiting areas had space for less than 20% of their prison population while those built later could accommodate up to 30%. If a visiting area has space for only 20% of its population this means that only 10% can receive visitors assuming one visitor per inmate. The American Correctional Association (ACA) (1983) recommends that a typical visiting area for an institution of 500 inmates should accommodate at least 150 people. Schafer (1991) found that most prisons allow visitors to remain in the visiting area until it closes unless there are more visitors than the area can accommodate; 60% allowed at least six hours per day. Some prisons restrict the number of visits an inmate can receive and/or the number of times a person can visit per month. However, more than one-third permit daily visits (Schafer, 1991).

### Conditions External to the Prison Affect Visitors

The economically disadvantaged status of many inmates' families makes it difficult for them to visit frequently. Transportation assistance and visitor centers sometimes help these families to overcome this problem.

**GETTING TO THE PRISON CAN BE DIFFICULT** Prisons are not normally built close to major population centers, from which most offenders come. This makes visiting difficult for relatives who are likely to be poor. Neto (1989) found that most visitors (70%) traveled by car. Their economic status means that these cars were often undependable, making trips potentially hazardous. The rest typically traveled by bus, which tended to drop them off a few miles or more from the prison. As Table 21.1 shows, prisons closest to urban areas require the shortest trips for the largest proportion of visitors. Neto found that both distance and the lack of a car reduced the frequency of visitation. Thus, more than one-half of the visitors to Norco and San Quentin came one to five times a week, compared to only one-third at Susanville. One 80-year-old mother spent 10 hours on a bus to visit her son for only a few hours. The distant location of some prisons also involves increased costs for transportation, food, and maybe even overnight lodging.

**TRANSPORTATION ASSISTANCE TO SOME PRISONS IS PROVIDED** Frequent visitation is often discouraged by lack of regular transportation or unsatisfactory transportation (i.e., a bus may leave visitors miles from the prison, with their only other options being walking or an expensive taxi ride). Public and private agencies in some states offer assistance to inmate families by providing transportation from major population centers or from public transportation drop-off points. A survey of fifty-six U.S. state and federal systems found that: in close to one-half, government or outside organizations made arrangements for free or low-cost transportation for inmate families. In more than one-half, no help was available. As an example, New York State provides cost-free transportation to thirty-seven institutions on buses with escorts trained to answer questions on visiting procedures and provide referral assistance for visitors with problems (New York State Department of Correctional Services, 1988). Centerforce, in California, operates twenty-six centers that provide transportation from local drop-off points to institutions.

A few organizations, like Centerforce, also provide financial assistance to inmate families to help defray the costs of overnight stays when they visit. Others, like Harvest House, Inc., in Boonville, Missouri, operate hospitality centers located close to prisons which provide lodging and sometimes meals (Mustin and Bee, 1992; Coombs, 1991). Finally, the rural and remote location of many prisons often means there are no adequate social service agencies to provide emergency services that may be needed by visiting families. This may also be a problem if inmate families relocate to towns close to their loved ones because some inmate wives fail to plan adequately for the move. Without adequate assistance from social services agencies, some end up homeless (Centerforce, 1993).

### Visitor Centers and Hospitality Houses Assist Visitation

A woman walks slowly up the hill toward the Washington State Reformatory in Monroe. Her husband, a new inmate, had asked her to come visit. On the phone it seemed such a small request, but the closer she gets to the prison's towering brick wall, the more forbidding it looks. As she pauses to gather her courage, her eye catches a slate blue house with a red door across the street. "The Matthew 25:36 House," a sign reads. . . . The woman knocks on the door and is greeted by the Hospitality House's director, Mary Parker Cosby. "I was on my way to visit my husband at the Reformatory," the woman stammers, "but now I'm too scared to go there. It's really not so bad," Cosby says, as she invites her inside. "Let me tell you what to expect. . . ." In a few minutes, Cosby sees the woman off with a smile and a hug and tells her, "Please stop by afterward and tell me how it went."

When the woman returns to report a successful visit she learns [about all the services Matthew 25:36 provides] (Coombs, 1991).

Located adjacent to or near prisons in only a few jurisdictions, facilities like this serve as waystations providing a variety of services for relatives and friends visiting inmates. The largest program is operated by Centerforce in California. It operates twenty-nine hospitality centers, which serviced 176,403 adults and 60,487 children in 1992. Services included the following:

*Transportation:* State vans are used to provide visitors with transportation from public transit terminals.

*Child care:* Care is provided for visitors' children while they are visiting the institution. In many cases, after a short visit involving the entire family, staff go into the prison and pick up the children thus allowing higher quality visiting for the adults, while providing the children with educational and recreational activities.

*Emergency clothing:* Clothing is provided for visitors who arrive inappropriately attired. This reduces the hostility that arises between prison officials and visitors when they are refused entry due to improper attire and enables prison officials to refer visitors who do not meet dress codes to the visitor center.

*Information on visiting regulations and processes:* Providing this information saves prison staff and visitors considerable time and reduces potential problems.

*Referral to other agencies and services:* Staff are trained to assess visitor needs and refer them to existing community agencies, which reduces their stress.

*Emergency food:* Out of hospitality and for genuine need, these centers provide this service.

*Crisis intervention:* A large number of visitors arrive unprepared financially and otherwise to stay overnight due to an unanticipated lockdown or the fact that they missed the last bus or are told to visit the next day. Also, they may fail to anticipate a child's illness requiring medical care and an overnight stay. Money and other assistance is provided to deal with these problems.

*Sheltered area:* As a way to encourage visiting, these centers provide a homelike atmosphere for

## Close Up — An Inmate's View of the Importance of Hospitality Centers

During the past two years that I have spent here incarcerated at the California Rehabilitation Center, the "Hospitality Place" has been a beneficial factor in the continuous communication and/or visitation between myself and my family.

Besides providing transportation when it's needed, this program has also assisted families with child care, clothing, and many other institutional guideline requirements that must be met in order for the inmates here at this institution to keep a prominent, and well respectful attitude while physical and mental contact is being made between them and their loved ones.

The Hospitality Place has many physical attributes which they have made available to the inmate population, but what is even more remarkable is that even though they constantly ascertain a daily sense of weariness they never seem to show a symbol of fatigue, and this is why we have always been able to count on them in every way. I personally feel that the staff of this organization should be commended for the continuous commitment towards building a sense of stability between the inmates and their families, but also for their daily participation with the few activities that are being provided here at this institution.

I would also like to acknowledge that without the Hospitality Place a vast majority of the inmate population would suffer in a most undesirable manner, whether it be family ties, transportation, regular or family visiting, or whatever information that may be required to assist during your stay at this institution.

So, on behalf of the Unit 3 inmates, myself, and last but not least, my family, I would like to thank the entire staff of the organization of Hospitality Place for being of great assistance to all of us in every way that they possibly could.

Respectfully submitted,
L*** G***
Dorm 307 Bed 46
Black Representative

*Source:* Letter provided by Centerforce. Used with permission of Peter Breen, Director.

---

visitors before and after their visits to the institution (Centerforce, 1993).

The importance of many of these services will become even clearer as we examine the internal visiting context of the prison. Our Close-Up suggests how inmates value these services.

### Visiting Rules and Conditions Relate to Institutional Security and Inmate Custody Levels

Each facility has rules relating to visiting and the processing of visitors. These rules vary according to the prison's security level and, sometimes, the inmate's custody level. Generally, the higher the security level the more restrictive the visiting conditions. These procedures are designed to maintain security and control.

**RULES SPECIFY MODE OF DRESS AND THE ITEMS VISITORS ARE PERMITTED TO BRING** All institutions require that visitors present an acceptable ID. Almost all require appropriate attire for visitors (Schafer, 1989). Most dress requirements are directed toward prohibiting attire that is sexually stimulating (e.g., see-through blouses) or can facilitate forbidden behavior (e.g., wrap-around skirts, which allow for fondling).

Many institutions limit the items that can be taken into the prison. Some provide lockers while others require that handbags and other items be locked in cars. This underscores the value of visitor centers that inform visitors about what items are forbidden and provide lockers for storing them. Schafer found all prisons to have rules dealing with contraband, eighty percent define it specifically and detail the legal penalties for those caught violating these rules. Contraband can include drugs, weapons, money, tape recorders, cameras, etc.

**VISITORS ARE FREQUENTLY SEARCHED** To prevent visitors from bringing contraband into the prison, all closed facilities typically require them and their belongings to be searched. Most facilities employ metal detectors to search for weapons (Neto, 1989). COs typically search belongings and may do external pat-down searches of visitors. Although rarely done, **strip searches** have been

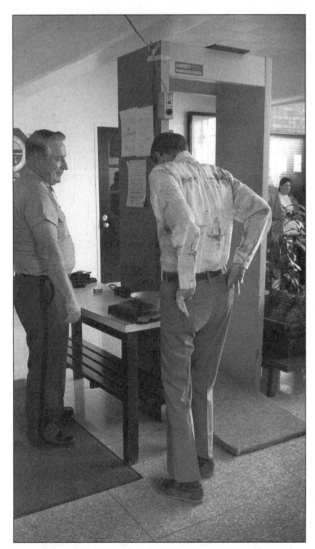

Many prisons allowing contact visitation require visitors to be searched before entering the visiting area. This may require them to empty their pockets and pass through a metal detector. They may also be subject to pat down searches.

would place them in the vicinity of their genitals or up their rectums. These wives risked detection and the humiliation of a search because they felt drugs helped their husbands do "good time." Smoking marijuana was believed to reduce the monotony and suffering of prison life. That is, drugs enabled their husbands to "mellow out" or "chill out" and thereby better adjust to prison life (Fishman, 1990).

**THERE IS A SPECTRUM OF POSSIBLE VISITING CONDITIONS** In the past, particularly through the Big House era, visitation was typically of a noncontact nature with visitors and inmates either separated by glass partitions and communicating through telephones or separated by mesh screens. Today most systems allow **contact visits** for most inmates. Schafer (1991) found 90% of the prisons she surveyed permitted contact visits for all inmates, and most others had facilities for both. As noted in Chapter 12, inmates designated as close and maximum custody are likely to be denied contact visits (National Institute of Corrections, 1987). Although the courts recognizes contact visits as desirable, no decision to date supports entitlement of convicted inmates to them (Mushlin, 1993). In fact, the Supreme Court ruled a blanket ban on jail contact visits to be constitutional as long as it was reasonably related to the security of the facility (*Block v. Rutherford*, 1984). The security issues raised in this case included preventing the introduction of contraband (e.g., drugs, weapons) and keeping detainees and their visitors from exposure to violent offenders awaiting trial.

**THE VISITING ROOM ATMOSPHERE CAN AFFECT THE OUTCOME OF THE VISIT** The Task Force on Corrections (1973) of the National Advisory Commission on Criminal Justice Standards and Goals recommended that visiting facilities provide a natural environment that encourages ease and informality of communication. Required supervision should be done in an unobtrusive manner so as not to eavesdrop on conversations or otherwise interfere with participants' privacy.

Visiting area rules usually center around the following:

**1.** *General behavior:* typically involves the control or management of children; movement around the visiting room (e.g., changing seats, moving chairs); chatting with other prisoners or visitors;

upheld by the courts when there is "reasonable cause" based on "specific objective facts" indicating a visitor will attempt to smuggle contraband into the prison on his or her person (Palmer, 1991).

Fishman (1990) found that women who smuggled drugs hid them inside their bras, in socks, on their hips, secured between their breasts, and, less frequently, hid them in their vaginas or placed on their children (e.g., taped inside a child's Pampers). The typical scenario involved these women going to the restroom early in the visit, removing the drugs and passing them to their husbands who

At some minimum security prisons inmates are permitted to picnic, and even barbecue, with their families. This normalizes the visiting process.

and control of loud voices, abusive behavior, and profanity.

**2.** *Physical contact:* usually forbid behavior such as petting, sitting on laps, prolonged kissing, sexually stimulating activity, necking, hands under clothing, or touching or stroking breasts, genitalia, or thighs (Schafer, 1989).

Fishman's description of visiting programs at five Vermont institutions suggests the effect the ambience and rules have on the visiting atmosphere. At one facility, the ambience was pleasant, but the rules prohibited movement around the room. At three other institutions the rules were restrictive, and the ambience was uninviting and dismal. Wives reported they could not help overhearing other conversations and arguments. This, along with surveillance by the guards, undermined privacy and inhibited spontaneous and authentic emotional communication. A wife's comments capture this:

> During visiting, I got the feeling that people were aware of each other constantly. They were always watching each other.... And I saw how they were watching me to see what I was doing. I felt really uncomfortable. I felt that people were tuning into what we said so I didn't want to talk to Buddy there. I began to hide things. Thinking of visiting still gives me goose bumps (Fishman, 1990, p. 159).

At only one of the five facilities did the ambience and rules encourage normal interaction between inmates and their families. Like other community facilities it provided inmates with more freedom. Thus it enforced system visiting rules less stringently but still emphasized security, and conducted visiting under the "watchful eyes of at least one guard." Visiting took place in a less structured environment. During the warmer months inmates could take their families outdoors to play with the children and have picnics. Also there were places where they could go that allowed them to be somewhat alone, facilitating greater physical and verbal intimacy.

**SEXUAL INTIMACY, ALTHOUGH PROHIBITED, CAN OCCUR DURING VISITATION** Although the rules forbid couples from engaging in anything more than casual contact, discussions with inmates and guards yield ample information that sexual relations occur during visiting at some facilities. Fishman (1990) found sixteen of the thirty wives she interviewed did more than just holding hands, hugging, or cuddling their husbands. In fact, eight managed to cuddle and fondle their mates and five had intercourse. The type of contact depended on the leniency of the guards, which varied by facility. Even when surveillance was tight at the closed facility, some women had sex with their husbands:

When I got to visit him, we would sit in the corner and a lot goes on in that corner and they can't see us. Sam blocks their view of me because he is so big. . . . We constantly look to see who's watching. . . . We don't do much talking. We had sex in the visiting rooms. We had some nice visits. I know that people who are visiting saw us have sex. Some of them get embarrassed (Fishman, 1990, p. 152).

While many women were willing to go further than the rules permitted, most felt sex was something "nice girls" did not do in public. The minority engaging in sexual relations reported doing so in response to pressure from their husbands, and a few did it to "put one over on the enemy." Regardless of the level of sexual intimacy, these women derived little satisfaction because they needed to be alert to the attention they received from guards and other visitors.

### Some Institutions Allow Private Family/Conjugal Visiting

**Conjugal visits** have been typically limited to private visits between inmates and their spouses, but programs have now been expanded to include other family members, usually children, parents, and, in a few cases, grandparents and siblings. Only two programs permit conjugal visits by "common law" wives (Lillis, 1993b). While the comments of wives in Fishman's study suggest the need for more natural and intimate visiting arrangements, there has been resistance to establishing these programs based on several issues. These include morality, misconceptions of its impact on the correctional environment, and punitive views regarding the purpose of incarceration (National Task Force on Corrections, 1973; Johns, 1971).

Few studies in the past have focused on attitudes toward this program. Bennett (1987; 1989) surveyed most institutions in eight states (California, Connecticut, Minnesota, Mississippi, New Mexico, New York, Washington, and Wyoming)[1] with conjugal programs and compared them with a random sample of prisons without this program. Almost one-half of the sample (including 34% without programs) endorsed the idea of private family visiting programs with suitable security safeguards and proper administration. Most felt these programs would not only continue but would increase in the next ten years.

Although critics consider the major purpose of these visits to be sexual satisfaction, program par-

ticipants consider as equally important, factors that include emotional closeness, a better understanding of each other, the woman's touch (Burstein, 1977). The major benefits have been viewed as the stabilization and enhancement of marital and family relationships and the provision of a support group when inmates are released (Hopper, 1989; Burstein, 1977; Bennett, 1989, 1987; Lillis, 1993b).[2]

**FAMILY VISITS CAN BENEFIT INMATES** The fact that all but one of Burstein's sample asked their wives to bring the children means that inmates do not just see those visits as opportunities for sexual intimacy. Evidence also shows these visits have an impact on marital stability after release. Burstein found that combined divorce and separation rates for nonprogram participants were four times (47%) higher than program participants. Research in New York found that 87% of the Family Reunion Program participants were scheduled to live with family members, generally their wives, on release (MacDonald, 1980). Finally, almost one-half of superintendents in Bennett's study felt these visits would reduce disciplinary problems and improve parole planning. Both inmate participants (90%) and nonparticipants (85%) agree it is an important method of behavior control:

- You don't get up in the man's face when you got conjugal visits.
- It [the visits] keeps the lid on.
- It cuts down on violence because the most important thing to a man is a woman.
- It curbs frustration and violence.
- They keep the heat off the staff (Burstein, 1977, p. 81).

This is further confirmed by New York studies, which found inmates not approved for family visiting had a larger number of and more serious disciplinary infractions than those in the program. More than a third of the inmates with poor disciplinary records who were not initially approved improved their behavior sufficiently to be approved later (Howser, Grossman, and MacDonald, 1984).

There is evidence showing a positive relationship between program participation and community adjustment. In New York the actual return rate of program participants was lower than projected, based on the rate of return of all releasees from custody (MacDonald and Bala, 1986). (See Table 20.2).

TABLE 20.2 **Recidivism Rates of Family Reunion Participants**

| | 1980 Study (%) | 1986 Study (%) |
|---|---|---|
| Projected return rate | 11.7 | 26.5 |
| Actual return rate | 3.9 | 19.6 |
| Difference | 7.8 | 6.9 |

In the past, it has been argued that a conjugal visit program would reduce homosexuality, violence, and sexual assaults. Although administrators did not agree (Bennett, 1989), inmates—particularly those participating in the program—felt that it did reduce homosexuality (Hopper, 1989; Burstein, 1977). If involvement in consensual homosexual relationships in prison is motivated by the need for sexual release, loneliness, and other emotional needs, when satisfied by private visiting, the homosexual relationships are likely to be reduced. However, when prison rape and violence are motivated by factors such as the need to dominate and to dissipate anger and aggression, these programs may not substantially reduce these behaviors except for program participants, who may refrain in order keep their visiting privileges.

**THERE ARE OBJECTIONS TO CONJUGAL VISITING** Conjugal visiting is opposed on several grounds. First, critics claim that it will generate negative attitudes on the part of inmates who are unable to participate. In Mississippi in 1963 and 1984, Hopper (1989) found fewer than 15% of the unmarried inmates were concerned about married inmates having conjugal visits. Second, concerns are raised about the increased problems of controlling the introduction of drugs and other contraband. Bennett found that administrators saw drug smuggling as a danger but not a problem requiring anything more than constant vigilance and the use of standard precautionary measures. A third set of concerns involves negative public and political reaction arising from anxiety about escapes, questions about program morality, feelings that inmates are not entitled to this privilege, and the added cost resulting from pregnancies. However, three-quarters of the facilities using public education to portray these program goals as reuniting the family and improving postrelease success encountered no such public resistance (Bennett, undated).

Finally, while the majority of these programs are state funded, several started with donations and were organized by staff and inmate volunteers (Bennett, undated). Funds also came from the inmate welfare fund and payments made by inmates when their families used these facilities. Bennett estimated yearly costs at $100,000 to operate a program with three visiting units including supervision and security, repair, upkeep, replacement of damaged furnishings, utilities, etc. While this may seem high, inmate welfare funds and maintenance by volunteers can help to reduce the cost. This seems like a small price for a program that has a positive impact on prison discipline and increases postrelease success.

Despite the benefits of conjugal visiting, the courts in all jurisdictions have held inmates have no constitutional right to conjugal visiting. They have generally rejected inmate claims that denying conjugal visiting violates the marital right to privacy, undermines the marital couple's right to practice their religion, constitutes cruel and unusual punishment, violates the equal protection clause[3] (by being available at some facilities, but not others), and unfairly places restrictions on the class of visitors permitted (Palmer, 1991; Mushlin, 1993).

**FAMILY/CONJUGAL VISITING PROGRAMS HAVE SOME COMMON CHARACTERISTICS** While these programs vary considerably, it is possible to develop a basic picture of them (Bennett, undated). Most are located in the prison but separated from the general population. They are composed of one- or two-bedroom units with bathrooms and linens, fully equipped kitchens, outside activity areas, and some even have barbecue grills. Most impose no custody restrictions. Instead inmate eligibility is tied to their disciplinary record and participation in prison programs. The following groups may be excluded and/or require special screening to participate: condemned prisoners, chronic disciplinary problems, those convicted of heinous crimes, and those with a history of family violence, sex offenses, and/or serious psychiatric problems. Depending on the space available and institutional policy, visits can occur from every two weeks to every six months (Bennett, undated). Finally, each system uses various methods to prevent HIV/AIDS, which include education, counseling, distribution of condoms, and limits on inmate and spouse participation (Lillis, 1993b).

## Some Institutions Provide Family Counseling and Parenting Programs to Strengthen Family Ties and Promote Visiting

What happens during the visiting is of equal importance to the frequency and length of visits. The way inmates interact with family members will strongly impact the continuation of these visits and maintenance or enhancement of family ties. Inmates are frequently not skilled in sustaining and enriching family relations, may lack good communication skills, and may bring anger and frustration from the prison environment to the visiting situation. Family members may harbor feelings of guilt, alienation, frustration, and anger resulting from their loved ones' imprisonment. Research shows that female inmates feel strongly about the importance of loving their children and guiding their appropriate social, behavioral, and attitudinal development (Leflore and Holston, 1990). Even male inmates serving very long sentences, most of whom were unmarried fathers with little or no contact or knowledge of their children's whereabouts, still perceived themselves as fathers and wanted to improve their parenting skills (Hairston, 1990). These factors point to the need for programs to enhance both interpersonal and parenting skills.

Several jurisdictions have established programs addressing these concerns. These include coping with having to live in a home where addiction problems exist, alternatives to violence, spouse abuse and being the victim of abuse, and written and verbal communication with wives and children (e.g., explaining to a child about incarceration). These **parenting programs** are important because few inmates had positive relationships with their parents and carry with them a disastrous legacy likely to be passed on to their children if they fail to get help (New York State Department of Correctional Services, 1988). However, despite the potential benefits of these programs only a few are currently in operation (Jorgensen, Hernandez, and Warren, 1986; Hairston and Lockett, 1987). The focus of New York's program, which is "the road back from crime is a family affair," captures the essence that family breakdown is at the root of crime.

Finally, our Close-Up on the **M-2 Sponsors program** deals with inmates who do not normally receive visitors.

## Telephones Are a Vital Link to Family and Friends

In the late 1960s and early 1970s we began to see inmates being allowed to use telephones to contact family and friends. By 1979, all states but Ohio permitted inmates to make nonemergency telephone calls and today all correctional systems in the United States and Canada permit inmates access to telephones. Telephone contacts with family and friends, whether frequent or not, according to Fishman (1990), reinforced marital ties and mitigated the pain of separation for both wives and their incarcerated husbands. Likewise, corrections systems overwhelmingly view inmate use of phones as beneficial (Davis, 1990). The topics covered during telephone use included child care, matters of discipline, and prison. However, most of the time was spent talking about intimate matters. Given the generally low literacy levels among inmates (and possibly their wives), it was easier for them to talk on the phone than to put their thoughts and feelings on paper.

Irrespective of the type of prison their husbands were in, wives felt there was never enough time during visiting to interact with their spouses in a realistic way (Fishman, 1990). Thus, telephone calls added an opportunity for more frequent communication and came to be seen as visits by most of these wives. This is illustrated by the recollections one wife had of her conversations:

> Oh, stupid things: how much we missed each other, how lonely we were. We pulled each other's hearts out! We'd listen to each other breathe. It was sort of a continuation of the talk during the visit: what the kids were doing; what did he do that day; and how we both were trying to change. . . (Fishman, 1990, p. 212).

Finally, the telephone allows husbands to more frequently interject themselves into the day-to-day functioning of the household and to maintain their positions as husbands, fathers, and heads of the households. Wives had the opportunity to place their husbands in the role of an understanding but distant observer in their lives. This made it easier to believe their relationship was worthwhile and worth waiting for until their spouses were released. Not all communication was positive and reinforcing of marital ties. Some couples who communicated regularly, argued over a variety of

## Close Up M-2 Sponsors Program Provides Visitors for Isolated Inmates

The positive impact of visiting on institutional adjustment and postrelease success has provoked the question "Can anything be done for those inmates who do not ordinarily receive visitors?" The M-2 Sponsors program, started in California for adults in 1971 and for youth in 1973, was a response to this need. Its major focus has been on improving the probability of success for inmates on release.

M-2 provides one-on-one visitation by community volunteers for inmates who, although involved in prison programs, have received few or no visitors in the previous year. Designated as **social isolates** because of their lack of outside contact, these inmates are viewed as high risk for recidivism. Volunteers serve as the inmate's link to the outside, countering feelings of isolation and loneliness by offering friendship through visiting and writing (EMT Associates, 1985, 1987).

The effectiveness of this program (EMT Associates, 1985, 1989) has been examined over a fourteen-year period. Prior to participation these inmates were more likely to be serious repeat offenders with higher rates of recidivism than other offenders. However, parolees with M-2 sponsors had higher rates of parole success (using new criminal behavior as the criterion) than comparison groups. Evidence from a 1987 study shows that, for males, parole success was directly related to the degree of contact (i.e., number of visits) the inmate had with his M-2 sponsor.

### Parole Success for Males and M-2 Sponsor Visits

| No. of Visits | Six Months After Release (%) | Twelve Months After Release (%) | Twenty-four Months After Release (%) |
|---|---|---|---|
| None | 49.3 | 38.7 | 33.3 |
| 1 or 2 | 59.1 | 34.1 | 29.0 |
| 3 to 11 | 63.3 | 44.6 | 43.3 |
| 12 or more | 63.0 | 65.5 | 57.1 |

For women (who tend to have high parole success rates to begin with), no positive relationship was found between program participation and parole success (EMT Associates, 1987).

These studies also found that inmate involvement with M-2 sponsors contributes to positive adjustment and behavior in prison for males, but not for females. This was explained by the fact that the cultural environment of female prisons facilitates friendships between women, while in male prisons this is less common. Women are thus less in need of friends from the outside and this may explain why involvement with sponsors failed to affect their parole success. In contrast, males indicate a greater need for and appreciation of the ties provided by volunteers. They mentioned that sponsors provided "news from outside," and some viewed their sponsors as their only true friends and expressed great faith in this friendship. One inmate felt that even if the program no longer existed his sponsor would continue to visit because "he is my friend" (EMT Associates, 1987).

Inmates reported that sponsors had been helpful in their preparation for release, but most only had very general plans (e.g., getting a job, starting a new life). While not obligated to provide concrete assistance for the releasee, three of the eighteen inmates interviewed indicated sponsors provided contacts with the parole authorities and arranged for job tryouts. All had made commitments to the inmate to be at the gate when he was released.

Finally, this program was also cost effective. Projected savings from not having to reincarcerate successful M-2 participants were estimated to be $1,238,858, which exceeded program costs by $288,000 and state program contributions by $460,499 (EMT Associates, 1987).

Allowing inmates the use of telephones provides them a direct contact with their loved ones (and others) on a frequent basis. This is considered by some as an extension of the visiting process, which further enables inmates to maintain family and other outside contacts.

things. Disagreements erupted over the wives resisting their husbands' attempts to dominate their lives. Overall, however, the telephone had more positive than negative effects on these relationships (Fishman, 1990). We should note that some inmates may be reluctant to make calls or be fully candid during their conversations, since the courts have allowed prison officials to record and monitor all phone contacts except those with attorneys (Mushlin, 1993).

**ALL SYSTEMS PLACE RESTRICTIONS ON PHONE CALLS** A Corrections Compendium survey (Davis, 1990) found that more than half of the systems[4] allowed either unlimited or daily telephone usage. In most remaining jurisdictions, the number of calls was limited either by institutional policies, inmate custody/security classification, and/or privilege level. *Most systems restrict calls to from 5 to 20 minutes.* Half the jurisdictions required inmates to pay for local calls and, in most of the others, calls had to be made on a collect basis. This latter rule applied to long-distance calls in all jurisdictions.

Most states report few or no problems with inmate phone usage. The few problems that did occur included threats to relatives, girlfriends, or others; drug deals; using the phone to buy merchandise with stolen credit card numbers; and obscene phone calls. Other problems have involved fights over phone use and the burden on families of long-distance bills calls they cannot afford. Also, out of loneliness, some inmates called random numbers simply to talk to someone. These problems were frequently eliminated with a collect-call-only policy. However, despite some misuse, corrections systems overwhelmingly consider inmate phone use to be beneficial (Davis, 1990).

A 1995 update of the earlier 1990 phone use survey found that the 1990 figures regarding access, use, and monitoring remain essentially the same. However, the major change was that litigation was now centered not on phone access but on the "rates charged to inmates and the people who accept collect calls from prisoners" (Wunder, 1995a, p. 6). This is because inmate phone use has become profitable for both phone companies and for most state departments of corrections. "The average DOC commission rate from the phone companies is 28.08% [and] . . . 31 responding departments of corrections received approximately $96.4 million . . . in revenues from phone companies in 1994" (p. 6). Critics contend that these exorbitant profits make rates higher and discourage inmates from maintaining ties to the outside world to which they will eventually return. However, supporters argue that the profits received by correctional facilities for phone calls are channeled into inmate welfare funds to be used for inmate programming and rehabilitation (Wunder, 1995a). Only time will tell if and how the courts will settle this controversy.

## Furloughs Let Some Inmates Temporarily Leave Prison

Prison **furloughs** are short-term escorted or unescorted trips away from the prison, granted so that inmates can find jobs and/or housing prior to release; participate in treatment and/or religious programs, recreation, or shopping; or strengthen family ties. They are different than releases for emergency purposes, which are only granted to inmates for serious family illnesses or death. Although commonly used in Europe, in this country they are a recent development (Burns, 1975). In the mid-1960s only two states had programs, but by 1987 all states, the Federal Bureau of Prisons, and the District of Columbia had some form of furlough or temporary release (Smith, undated; Contact, 1988).

These programs have several major functions. First, they foster self-esteem in inmates because of the trust they imply. This can reduce feelings of dependency and allow inmates (particularly those imprisoned for a long time) to recognize they can still make decisions about their actions. Second, they reinforce existing family ties and enable inmates with children opportunities to reassert their presence and reinforce their roles as parents. Families can also begin reaccepting the inmate as part of the household. Third, they facilitate release planning by gradually reintegrating offenders back into the community and by exposing them to the community programs and experiences that are unavailable in prison. Finally, they are also felt to promote rehabilitation and enhance crime prevention (Markley, 1973; Smith, undated). The 1988 Bush–Dukakis presidential campaign turned furlough into a dirty word.[5] Studies conducted between 1987 and 1989 show the bad press generated by the Horton incident (Contact, 1988; Marlette, 1990b; Smith, undated) negatively affected furlough policies. The number of states granting furloughs dropped from thirty-nine to thirty-four and the number of furloughs granted went from 200,000 to 170,000, while the number of inmates participating went up from 53,000 to 55,000.[6]

Furlough eligibility requirements vary by state. Approval is usually dependent on an inmate's security classification (typically offenders have a minimum, community trusty status), the amount of time served, proximity of parole, type of crime committed,[7] behavior in prison, and reviews by a facility committee and the head of the corrections department (Smith, undated; Contact, 1988; Marlette, 1990b). Some states also consider input from victims and local law enforcement. Most systems require a sponsor (e.g., a relative or some other approved person) for the inmate. Furloughs range from the 4 to 12 daylight hours allowed by Florida to 210 days allowed in Oregon, which uses them to alleviate overcrowding.

More than 80% of the systems report a 98% or higher success rate and only two had rates below 90%. Twenty-seven jurisdictions provided information on rule infractions: There were 971 revocations of furloughs reported, which equaled about 2% of all the furloughs granted. Most infractions were for late returns, alcohol or drug use, or failure to arrive at an agreed-on location. Less than 1% of the revocations were for "new crimes," most involving escapes, some property crimes, and a few assaults (Marlette, 1990b). In the thousands of furloughs studied there were two reported homicides: one involved a wife and another a girlfriend (Marlette, 1990b).

In 1988, thirty-eight jurisdictions allowed furloughs for inmates serving life terms. No data were available on revocations for lifers for 1988, but in 1987 thirty-eight jurisdictions allowed lifers furloughs and none were revoked (Contact, 1988). Virtually all systems found furloughs to be helpful in preparing inmates for release and promoting institutional morale.

## RECREATIONAL PROGRAMS[8]

Recreational activities form an important part of prison programming and have a number of benefits.

### Prison Recreation Has a Long History

For as long as offenders have been imprisoned, they have probably engaged in recreational activity, either organized on their own or by the prison staff. For example, in the early 1600s, Miguel de

Cervantes, who wrote *Don Quijote de la Mancha,* reportedly organized his fellow captives into a theater company while awaiting trial during the Spanish Inquisition. In early Colonial jails, and later in both Pennsylvania and Auburn-type prisons, provision was made for exercise.

The Elmira Reformatory, which opened in 1876, was the first institution to offer a diversified recreation and leisure program that included organized sports, an indoor gymnasium, social clubs (e.g., debating), an inmate newspaper, and drama and arts programs (Burns, 1975; Nicolai, 1981). These programs were atypical and only a few prisons had them until well into the twentieth century. More typically, recreation in prisons was limited to three areas: (1) the **yard,** described in the Big House chapter, where inmates could walk around, sit down, or congregate in small groups, and where, on weekends and holidays, outdoor sports were allowed; (2) the library, offering a limited selection of reading matter that was usually of little interest to most inmates; and (3) the auditorium, where movies were shown on Saturday evening and church services were offered on Sunday.

**PRISONS BEGAN TO DEVELOP DIVERSIFIED RECREATION PROGRAMS IN THE 1970s** Following World War II, there was a belated recognition of the significance of recreational programs in prisons by both the American Correctional and National Correctional Recreation Associations. A joint conference on recreation in correctional institutions in 1953 crystallized many ideas that later served as a basis for prison recreational programs (Committee for the Revision of the 1954 Manual, 1959; Hormachea, 1981). However, it was not until 20 years later that a sustained effort to develop diversified prison recreation and leisure programs began. The Attica riot (which focused attention on many prison problems) and court mandates regarding prison conditions forced institutions to establish new programs. During the 1970s, the membership of the National Correctional Recreation Association began to change from COs interested in recreation to full-time professional personnel with degrees in recreation or physical education (McCall, 1981).

### Recreation Benefits Both Inmates and Institutions

Recreation programs in the Federal Bureau of Prisons are intended to help reduce idleness and to keep inmates constructively occupied; to reduce personal stress and institutional tension; to increase physical fitness and positive life styles both in prison and after release; and to contribute to personal and institutional stability through maximum participation in formal and informal programs (U.S. Department of Justice, 1986).

This Federal Bureau of Prison's (BOP) policy statement suggests that recreation programs serve a variety of needs for inmates, staff, and the public. Recognizing the varied benefits of recreation programs, the BOP has the most complete facilities for recreation and the best educated and trained staffs (McCall, 1993). These programs have several important functions. First, they play a major part in alleviating the dull monotony of prison life. As an ex-inmate put it:

It is difficult for those who have not personally experienced the emotion and strains of daily life in a correctional institution to appreciate the finality of the electric gate closing behind you for a court determined period of time. In this situation, recreation is the only thing that makes today different from yesterday or tomorrow.... Without recreation each day would have the same duties and the same routine. The sameness of each day compresses long periods of confinement into a single milestoneless happening. Recreation provides a welcome reprieve from the monotony (Speckman, 1981, pp. 46–47).

Recreation provides a constructive means for inmates to use a great quantity of unstructured prison time. If not available, many inmates are likely to pursue activities threatening prison safety and security.

Second, good recreation programs function as safety valves for dissipating the tensions created by the prison's unnatural environment (McCall, 1981; Crutchfield, Garrette, and Worral, 1981). That is, they enable inmates to release pent-up energy, anger, and frustration in healthy and productive ways. Hopefully, these lessons in self-control will carry over to the outside once inmates are released (McCall, 1993).

Activities especially directed toward dealing with stress and anxiety in prison include weightlifting, softball, basketball, football, and other physical activities. A number of activities also provide opportunities to escape the prison ambiance. Movies and reading can reduce tension by allowing inmates to become involved with something other than their current circumstances so that, at

An inmate practices his "one-two" punch. This kind of physical activity by inmates is frowned upon by some because they feel it helps to make for "better" criminals. However, recreational experts argue this enables some inmates to dissipate aggression in a socially acceptable manner, which helps make the prison a safer place.

least temporarily, they can forget the oppressiveness of the prison (McCall, 1981). Concerts given by outside or inmate groups serve similar functions.

> After a concert given by the Baltimore Symphony at the Maryland Penitentiary, Glenn Grainger, a trumpet playing inmate, remarked, "Music is a very good thing here, a chance to get away from the frustrations and let off tensions. . ." (Nicolai, 1981, p. 33).

Both inmates and staff are in agreement that recreation makes prisons safer places. Ron Speckman (1981), a former prison inmate, writes that physical exertion in recreation programs reduces prison violence and disciplinary problems and results in fewer "write-ups."

McCall (1981) found that in all the riots spanning the period from Attica to New Mexico (1971–1980) better recreation was an inmate demand and in half it was among the top three demands (Gould, 1981) . In a forty-state survey of sixty-six facilities, including some for females, more than three-quarters of the administrators felt having inmates active in recreation resulted in fewer security problems (Jewell, 1981). A study of arts-related recreation programs found decreases of 54 to 100% in the monthly incident reports of program participants. Theater programs showed the greatest decreases (Nicolai, 1981). This type of program may even provide a means of reaching extremely alienated inmates.

A mentally troubled inmate at Joseph Harp Correctional Center in Lexington, OK had not talked to anyone for years and was physically filthy. [Soon after] arts and crafts programs were introduced the inmate made a rug—then started cleaning himself up, started talking, and soon the staff could not shut him up (Welch, 1990, p. 1, 5).

Staff who participated in this programming learned to appreciate the benefits of constructive leisure for inmates and the institution.

A third benefit of good recreation programs is they can have effects beyond the individual's prison stay. Constructive use of leisure time as a factor in crime participation has received little attention. We can divide a 24-hour period into three basic time blocks: a period in which the individual must work to secure funds for basic needs; a period dedicated to personal maintenance including time for eating, sleeping, and taking care of basic physical needs; and a third representing discretionary time or a period in which individuals can do as they please and which is usually designated as leisure time (Garibaldi and Moore, 1981). McCall, in an Indiana study, found that little crime is committed during either work or personal maintenance time and most is committed during leisure time. Since leisure time exceeds the other two time periods on the outside and even more so in prison, learning to use it appropriately is important (Gould, 1981). This, coupled with our previous discussion of inmate idleness, suggests that failure to provide for constructive leisure activities both in prison and on the street creates a high-risk situation for criminal and other deviant behavior.

An experiment with probationers conducted by McCall and summarized by Gould (1981) provides additional justification for this thesis:

> . . . leisure counselors [were used] to determine what people did in their leisure, what their abilities and needs were, their income, work hours, and many other factors. The probationers were given a "leisure prescription"—bowling, pleasure driving, fishing, hiking, city league softball, arts and crafts, or community service projects. . . . At the end of a two-year period, the rate of repeated offenses among one-year probationers had plummeted from 92 percent to 14 percent. . . . [McCall] found that individuals who satisfied a personal value or gained self-esteem through some sort of leisure activity had less of a tendency to commit crimes. . . .[She notes that] if you don't just go to a bar after work, but have something productive to look forward to that meets your needs, it can have an effect (pp. 22–23).

Weight lifting is one of the most popular physical activities in prison. Critics argue it should be eliminated because it builds an inmate's strength, which makes them a greater threat in prison and upon release. Recreational experts assert that it helps reduce tension and provides inmates with an activity at which they can work at their own pace and achieve some success.

In another experiment using institutionalized offenders, McCall compared 125 offenders choosing to participate in an enhanced recreation program with 125 offenders who did not. She found that, on release, there was a significant difference in the types of activities chosen by the two groups (Gould, 1981).

Recreational/arts programs can also help build an inmate's self-image and teach social skills, self-expression, how to think creatively, aggression control, self-discipline, and respect for authority (Welch, 1990). Because recreation is a voluntary activity and inmates can set their own "standard for success," there is a high probability inmates who participate will experience feelings of success.

For example, in sports like weightlifting and jogging, the individual is competing against himself and improvement is assured as long as the individual continues to participate. Team sports provide an excellent way to teach getting along with others, anger control, and how to deal with authority. Other activities, such as involvement in theater productions, can teach delayed gratification and cooperation. McCall (1993) asserts that recreation programs encourage decision making, which is critical to an inmate's "making it" on the outside.

Finally, involvement in arts and crafts programs teaches inmates hobbies and can also provide income. Inmates can sell their work through shows and gift shops and can compete in outside shows for monetary prizes. One Delaware inmate sent his pictures to a colonial ship building contest and won a $1500 first prize in competition with professional artists. This long-term inmate quit his prison gang and was expected to be released in the early 1990s (Welch, 1990). While recreation is neither a panacea for the ills of imprisonment nor a solution to the crime problem, it certainly can make prison life safer, more bearable, and provide releasees with constructive leisure options to be used in the outside world. Thus, the benefits of a good recreation program far outweigh its costs.

## Good Recreational Programming Has Many Facets

An effective recreational program requires well-trained professional staff, adequate funds for equipment and supplies, and areas and facilities for a year-round program of diversified outdoor and indoor activities.

One problem regarding the provision of recreational facilities for inmates is public and legislative views of them as luxuries—the first step toward turning the prison into a "resort hotel." Once again, we see the principle of least eligibility rearing its ugly head. For example, one warden justified the lack of a gymnasium in his institution by commenting that "some high schools in this state . . . do not have gymnasiums" (Nagel, 1973, p. 98). While it's regrettable that some schools lack gymnasiums or other recreational facilities, this is hardly a basis for not providing them in correctional institutions. Inmates are confined there for months and even years on end. Their options for recreation are limited to those available in the institution, whereas those outside have available to

Prison artists "exercising" their creativity. This activity can release tension in the inmate and create a somewhat safer environment. By selling their paintings at prison shops and outside shows, inmates can earn additional income.

them not only schools, but such things as parks, boys clubs, playgrounds, pools, lakes, theaters, mountains, seashores, and sporting events. Although many prisons lack adequate recreational facilities, it is encouraging that planners of newer correctional institutions have recognized the importance of ample recreational space and have, within budgetary limitations, attempted to provide adequate facilities.

**RECREATIONAL PROGRAMS REQUIRE ADEQUATE STAFF AND DIVERSE ACTIVITIES** The National Correctional Recreation Association (NCRA, undated) recommends that prisons of under 200 inmates be staffed by at least two recreation

persons and larger ones with commensurate numbers. The programs in these facilities should vary according to the size and security status of the prison, the number of inmates served, and the climate. NCRA has recommended both outdoor facilities (e.g., softball field, weightlifting area, basketball courts) and indoor facilities (e.g., a multipurpose building) which can provide space for a gym and theater or auditorium.

To serve inmates' interests and needs, a recreation program needs to be balanced, sufficiently diverse, and flexible enough to meet changing inmate desires and interests. Programs should include sports and athletics, music, arts and crafts, drama, literary activities, special events (such as art festivals, music festivals, special holiday programs), social games, club activities, motion pictures, radio, and television. Consideration also has to be given to the fact that some inmates prefer group activities, while others only like to engage in two-person activities (e.g., handball or checkers); still others prefer individual activities (e.g., crafts or weightlifting—the most popular activity in male institutions). While detailing the advantages of each of the many recreational activities mentioned is beyond our scope, they can all help reduce the boredom, monotony, and tension of imprisonment and introduce offenders to activities they can engage in on release.

**COMMUNITY GROUPS PARTICIPATE IN AND SUPPORT RECREATION PROGRAMS**   Prison chapters of Jaycees and Toastmasters[9] receive assistance and funds and active participation from local outside chapters. This gives inmates additional contact with the outside world, which, as we saw earlier, can reduce feelings of isolation and alienation and provide helpful community contacts (Speckman, 1981). Volunteers are a vital part of any prison recreation program since they augment program staff and may have talents not possessed by staff (McCall, 1993). With shrinking program dollars their contribution is even of greater significance.

Competition is the essence of athletics, but security considerations limit the extent to which inmate teams and athletes can compete with their community counterparts. Nevertheless, in some state and federal prisons, community teams regularly play football and softball and lift weights against inmate teams (Telander, 1987). For example, Murphy and Von Minden (1981) described an invitational softball tournament at the Correctional Center in Lincoln, Nebraska, nicknamed "cop and robbers" because it included teams from various law enforcement agencies. Some prisons also allow inmate teams to participate in outside recreational activities. While there is the risk of an inmate deciding to go deep for a football pass or a high fly in baseball and not coming back, good screening can go a long way toward avoiding this problem. In selecting inmates to compete outside the prison, ability is not the major concern but rather whether they will behave appropriately and benefit from the experience (Murphy and Von Minden, 1981). Further, inmate teams and athletes are often able to win against opponents because they have ample

Team sports such as football provide an activity that requires cooperation among team members. This can provide inmates with an opportunity to learn a valuable social skill that can be used in other life activities.

time to practice and may have been together longer than most outside teams. Sports writer Rick Telander (1987) notes that a team of guys doing time can develop closer ties than the Lakers.

Many correctional institutions are able to bring outside individuals and groups to the prison to entertain offenders. This has included such show business personalities as Johnny Cash and B. B. King and community and regional traveling groups including rock bands, theater groups, and bands and choral groups from local schools and colleges.

**INMATES NEED TO BE INFORMED ABOUT RECREATIONAL ACTIVITIES**   Given the important functions served by recreation programs, it is vital that inmates be made aware of their availability. This can be done during the orientation process by having recreation staff provide information on available programs and their value (McCall, 1993). Recreation supervisors also have to encourage inmates to be involved in recreation programs, since nonactivity may lead to physical problems and to other ways of working off their energy and tension.

## Overcrowding and Budget Constraints May Adversely Affect Recreation Programs

Finally, since prison population projections indicate a continuing rise well into the next century, the need for recreation that constructively occupies inmates and provides creative outlets for their energies is more important than ever (Hambrick, 1988). However, despite a well-substantiated need for these programs in the 1990s their survival is threatened by overcrowding, funding concerns, and the "get tough" attitude that views recreation programs as a frill. Spaces once available for recreation have been used to build temporary or permanent structures to house inmates. The paradox that exists is that the more inmates there are, the larger is the number of programs needed to teach them new skills and to relieve the tension of overcrowd-

ing. In addition, as economic hard times have resulted in shrinking revenues, the demand for prison beds and inmate programs has increased. A sad commentary to this scenario is that as resources become scarcer, we find that almost all monies are going into inmate maintenance, e.g., food, health care, bed space, etc. With funding such a critical issue in corrections today, money for recreation programs must be generated from the institution. Currently, canteen profits, telephone revenues, inmate art sales, and many other creative activities augment these meager recreation budgets (McCall, 1993).

As the "get tough" movement has gathered steam there are increased calls for the removal of recreation programs (specifically TVs, weight rooms, etc.). If this sentiment is allowed to remove these programs, their positive influences will be lost and inmates will likely become more difficult to manage (Nossiter, 1994). The consequences for prison and jail staff is that corrections work will become more difficult and dangerous.

## ENDNOTES

1. As of 1993, these eight states continue to permit conjugal visiting (Lillis, 1993b). Goetting (1982) found that the following countries reported having conjugal visiting: Mexico, all Central American countries except Panama and Belize, Cuba, Brazil, Bolivia, Columbia, Educator, Paraguay, Peru, and Venezuela; India (only in open prisons), Norway, Sweden, Finland, Denmark, Iceland, The Netherlands, Switzerland, West Germany, and Spain.
2. Wyoming found that having a conjugal visiting program reduced the sexual contact in the public visiting area.
3. The one exception involved a New York inmate claiming he had been deprived of his right to privacy by being denied access to conjugal visits because the program was not available at his prison. In deciding this case a district court noted that while the Supreme Court had granted inmates the right to marry, it had not ruled on the issue of the right to marital privacy. The district court held prison officials could not deprive inmates of this right without some rational justification. Further the inmate had noted that a local religious group was willing to donate the trailers to establish the program. The district court refused to dismiss the suit, in light of this available alternative, since

the defendants failed to indicate why they were unwilling to accept this donation. This suggests that the courts may reexamine the issue of an inmate's right to participate in this program in jurisdictions that have voluntarily initiated them (*Cromwell v Coughlin, 1991*).
4. This Corrections Compendium (1990) survey obtained responses from forty-nine states, the District of Columbia, the Federal Bureau of Prisons (only Connecticut did not respond), and nine Canadian provinces or territories (no responses from British Columbia, Manitoba, and Ontario). Unless otherwise noted the data reported will on be on the U.S. systems.
5. Bush focused on the case of Willie Horton, a Massachusetts inmate, who while serving a sentence of life without parole was given a furlough from which be absconded. Horton terrorized a Maryland couple, raping the wife and stabbing the husband. Bush accused Dukakis, the governor of Massachusetts at that time, of mismanaging the furlough program and being soft on crime.
6. This increase in the number of participants is possibly related to the fact that the prison population went up during this period.
7. Depending on the jurisdiction, offenders may be excluded from being eligible for furloughs if sentenced for crimes that include drug trafficking, child molesting

and other current sex offenses (or if they have sex offense histories), heinous or notorious crimes, capital murder, or are sentenced to death, life, and life without parole (Smith, undated).

**8.** The authors would like to thank Gail McCall, Ph.D., associate professor, Department of Recreation, University of Florida, for providing information and reviewing this manuscript.

**9.** See Chapter 9 for discussions of these programs.

### ACKNOWLEDGMENTS

[a] Reprinted from *Women at the wall,* by L.T. Fishman. Published by State University of New York, Albany © 1990. State University of New York. All rights reserved.

### CHAPTER RECAP

**Visitation and Inmate Family Ties**
Family Contacts Positively Impact Inmate Prison and Postrelease Behavior
  Family Ties Provide Inmates with a Support System and the Motivation to Change
Incarceration Creates Crises for Prisoners' Wives
  Imprisonment for Inmates' Wives Is Like the Death of a Loved One
**Visitation Programs and Inmate Family Ties**
Visiting Rules Are Based on Security Concerns
Most Often Inmates Are Visited by Family Members
  Wives Commonly Bring the Children When They Visit
Prison Visiting Schedules and Visiting Area Capacities Vary Widely
Conditions External to the Prison Affect Visitors
  Getting to the Prison Can be Difficult
    Transportation Assistance to Some Prisons Is Provided
Visitor Centers and Hospitality Houses Assist Visitation
Visiting Rules and Conditions Relate to Institutional Security and Inmate Custody Levels
  Rules Specify Mode of Dress and the Items Visitors Are Permitted to Bring
  Visitors Are Frequently Searched
  There Is a Spectrum of Possible Visiting Conditions
  The Visiting Room Atmosphere Can Affect the Outcome of the Visit
  Sexual Intimacy, Although Prohibited, Can Occur During Visitation
Some Institutions Allow Private Family/Conjugal Visiting
  Family Visits Can Benefit Inmates
  There Are Objections to Conjugal Visiting

Family/Conjugal Visiting Programs Have Some Common Characteristics
Some Institutions Provide Family Counseling and Parenting Programs to Strengthen Family Ties and Promote Visiting
Telephones Are a Vital Link to Family and Friends
  All Systems Place Restrictions on Phone Calls
Furloughs Let Some Inmates Temporarily Leave Prison
**Recreational Programs**
Prison Recreation Has a Long History
  Prisons Began to Develop Diversified Recreation Programs in the 1970s
Recreation Benefits Both Inmates and Institutions
Good Recreational Programming Has Many Facets
  Recreational Programs Require Adequate Staff and Diverse Activities
  Community Groups Participate In and Support Recreation Programs
  Inmates Need to be Informed about Recreational Activities
Overcrowding and Budget Constraints May Adversely Affect Recreation Programs

### REVIEW QUESTIONS

**1.** What are the effects of visits and family ties on recidivism?

**2.** How are wives affected by the incarceration of their husbands?

**3.** Discuss some of the differences between visiting conditions from prison to prison. Who generally comes to visit inmates?

**4.** How do security and custody concerns affect visiting?

**5.** Define private family/conjugal visits. What are the arguments for and against this program?

**6.** How do telephones serve to augment visiting?

**7.** What are the benefits of prison furlough programs?

**8.** How do prison recreation programs benefit both inmates and the institution?

### TEST YOUR KNOWLEDGE

**1.** Which of the following statements best characterizes the effects of family ties on recidivism?
  **a.** Lack of family ties can increase recidivism.
  **b.** Inmates with strong family ties never come back to prison.
  **c.** Family ties have no apparent effect on recidivism.
  **d.** Lack of family ties can reduce recidivism.

**2.** Court rulings regarding restrictions on visitation *do not* allow prisons to
  **a.** limit the number of visits.
  **b.** exclude "objectionable" visitors.

c. suspend visits as punishment.
d. limit the duration of visits.

3. Which of the following services are not provided to prison visitors?
a. transportation
b. child care
c. legal counsel
d. information on regulations

4. Which of the following best describes the official objective of conjugal visiting?
a. reduce prison rape

b. reduce prison homosexuality
c. improve inmate responsibility
d. maintain inmate family ties

5. The benefit(s) of prison recreation programs include which of the following?
a. raising the inmate's self concept
b. alleviating monotony
c. reducing inmate stress
d. teaching postrelease activities
e. all of the above

# PART SEVEN

# COMMUNITY CORRECTIONAL PROGRAMS AND FACILITIES

# CHAPTER 22

# JAILS AND DETENTION: THE AMERICAN JAIL

## ■ LEARNING OBJECTIVES

*After completion of this chapter, you should be able to:*
**1.** Specify the functions of jails and describe the types of people who tend to populate them.
**2.** Trace the history of the modern jail.
**3.** Contrast the three types of jail design and explain how each affects the supervision of inmates.
**4.** Describe the processes and problems that occur when offenders are first brought to jail.
**5.** Specify the essential issues involved in creating an effective jail staff.
**6.** Outline major jail trends and management issues.

## ■ KEY TERMS AND CONCEPTS

Booking process
Campus-style facilities
Deinstitutionalization
Design capacity
Detoxification center
Direct supervision design
Gaol
Jail diversion programs
Juvenile Justice and Delinquency Prevention Act
Linear design
Orientation process
Podular remote surveillance design
Pretrial confinement
Regional jails
Video mug shots

*The chapter was authored by Larry R. Ard, Chief Deputy (Ret.), Detention Division, (Contra-Costa County) California, Sheriff's Office, and Ken Kerle, Managing Editor, American Jail Association.*

Once police arrest lawbreakers, they are taken to either a holding facility or jail. Holding facilities generally keep people up to 48 hours and are often located in police stations for the convenience of arresting officers. Individuals held for extended investigations or charged with a criminal offense are transported to one of the 3300 plus jails in the country (Perkins, Stephen, and Beck, 1995). Most inmates are housed in jails holding over 500 inmates yet the majority of jails are small, housing fewer than 50 inmates. Thus, jails are complex institutions that hold dangerous pretrial detainees, short-term-sentenced inmates, work releasees, and those awaiting transportation to state or federal prison. They also hold the drunk, disorderly, and mentally ill. Their population includes adults and juveniles, males and females, and the elderly and sick. These facilities are administered by local officials and are designed to hold persons from a few hours to one year in most states. In contrast, prisons are state or federal facilities that hold persons serving felony sentences of generally longer than a year. Because most states and the federal government operate more than one facility, the population of prisons is typically more homogeneous than a jail with respect to the level of dangerousness of the inmates (security/custody level) and age and sex. Thus, the diversity of jail populations may, in some cases, make inmate management more difficult than in prisons.

At midyear 1994, there were an estimated 490, 442 persons—about 251 per 100,000 adults in the population—in the nation's jails. This is more than a 100% increase from 1983, when the population was 223,551. Admissions and releases on a given day average over 50,000 (Perkins, *et al.*, 1995). Since holding facilities do not exist in many places, most counties transport prisoners directly to jail.

After being booked, people are afforded an opportunity to post bail or, in many jurisdictions, obtain release on their own recognizance (ROR) upon a promise to appear in court. Those not released remain in a pretrial status until court action. Jails are maximum security facilities because offenders held there can range from shoplifters and drunk drivers to rapists and serial killers.

## THE DIVERSE POPULATION OF JAILS

Two surveys, one of jail inmates and the other of jails, provide data on jail inmates and jail popula-

tions (Beck, 1991; Perkins *et al.*, 1995). Between 1983 and 1994 the jail population rose 106% and there were significant changes in it. First, the population of females increased from 7.1 to 10%. Second, the proportion of white inmates dropped from 46.4 to 39.1%, while the proportion of blacks rose from 37.5 to 43.9% and that of Hispanic rose from 14.3 to 15.4%.

Of the 76% increase in the jail population between 1983 and 1989, more than 40% resulted from the increase in the number of persons being held for drug-related offenses. Thus, the number of drug offenders during this period rose from one in ten to one in four. Overall, more than 75% of all jail inmates reported using a controlled substance at some point in their lives. In the month prior to their offense, more than four out of ten convicted inmates had used drugs and one in four were current users. Further, at the time they committed their offense over 50% had been under the influence of drugs or alcohol. As Table 22.1 shows, as a result of the increased incarceration of drug offenders, the overall proportion of inmates incarcerated for either property or violent offenses decreased.

In 1989 women were more likely than men to be in jail for drug offenses (30 versus 20%) and larceny and fraud (24.5 versus 10.6%). Compared with women, men were more likely to be in jail for violent offenses (24 versus 13%), burglary (11.4 versus 4%), and driving under the influence (9.3 versus 3.6%). Drug offenses were more prevalent among Hispanics (one-third) and blacks than among whites (under one-sixth). Jail inmates in 1989 also tended to be older than those in 1983 (see Table 22.2). Other characteristics of this population included:

an estimated 45% of jail inmates were on probation, parole, out on bail or under some other criminal justice status at the time of their arrest. More than [3/4] ... of the jail inmates had a prior sentence to probation or incarceration. At least [1/3] ... were in jail for a violent offense or had a prior sentence for a violent offense. Among those sentenced to jail, half had received a sentence of 6 months or less. The median time that inmates sentenced to jail would serve before release was 4.8 months ... more than half (53.8%) of the inmates ... failed to complete high school ... [16%] ... reported they had been physically or sexually abused some time in their lives before their current offense [8.2% reported] ... they had been sent by a court to a mental health hospital or program. At least 1 in 8 ... had taken medication

TABLE 22.1  **Most Serious Offense of Jail Inmates by Conviction Status, 1989 and 1983**

| Most Serious Offense | Percent of Jail Inmates in 1989 | | | 1983 |
| | Convicted | Unconvicted | Total | Total |
|---|---|---|---|---|
| Violent Offenses | 16.6% | 30.4% | 22.5% | 30.7% |
| Murder[a] | 1.2 | 5.1 | 2.8 | 4.1 |
| Negligent manslaughter | .7 | .3 | .5 | .6 |
| Kidnapping | .3 | 1.5 | .8 | 1.3 |
| Rape | .7 | 1.0 | .8 | 1.5 |
| Other sexual assault | 2.7 | 2.4 | 2.6 | 2.0 |
| Robbery | 5.0 | 9.1 | 6.7 | 11.2 |
| Assault | 5.1 | 10.0 | 7.2 | 8.6 |
| Other violent[b] | 1.0 | 1.2 | 1.1 | 1.3 |
| Property offenses | 29.2% | 31.2% | 30.0% | 36.6% |
| Burglary | 9.8 | 12.0 | 10.7 | 14.3 |
| Larceny/theft | 8.5 | 7.1 | 7.9 | 11.7 |
| Motor vehicle theft | 2.8 | 2.9 | 2.8 | 2.3 |
| Arson | .5 | .9 | .7 | .8 |
| Fraud | 4.2 | 3.6 | 4.0 | 5.0 |
| Stolen property | 2.2 | 2.6 | 2.4 | 2.5 |
| Other property[c] | 1.2 | 2.1 | 1.6 | 1.9 |
| Drug offenses | 22.5% | 23.8% | 23.0% | 9.3% |
| Possession | 10.7 | 8.4 | 9.7 | 4.7 |
| Trafficking | 10.7 | 13.7 | 12.0 | 4.0 |
| Other/unspecified | 1.0 | 1.6 | 1.3 | .6 |
| Public-order offenses | 30.2% | 12.9% | 22.8% | 20.6% |
| Weapons | 2.2 | 1.5 | 1.9 | 2.3 |
| Obstruction of justice | 2.4 | 3.4 | 2.8 | 2.0 |
| Traffic | 4.1 | .9 | 2.7 | 2.2 |
| Driving while intoxicated[d] | 13.8 | 2.0 | 8.8 | 7.0 |
| Drunkenness/morals[e] | 2.0 | 1.3 | 1.7 | 3.4 |
| Violation of parole/probation[f] | 3.7 | 2.1 | 3.0 | 2.3 |
| Other public order[g] | 2.0 | 1.6 | 1.8 | 1.6 |
| Other[h] | 1.4% | 1.8% | 1.6% | .8% |
| Number of jail inmates | 218,303 | 161,858 | 380,160 | 219,573 |

Note: Excludes an estimated 15,393 jail inmates whose conviction status or offense was unknown.
[a] Includes nonnegligent manslaughter.
[b] Includes blackmail, extortion, hit-and-run driving with bodily injury, child abuse, and criminal endangerment.
[c] Includes destruction of property, vandalism, hit-and-run driving without bodily injury, trespassing, and possession of burglary tools.
[d] Includes driving while intoxicated and driving under the influeence of drugs or alcohol.
[e] Includes drunkenness, vagrancy, disorderly conduct, unlawful assembly, morals, and commercialized vice.
[f] Includes parole or probation violations, escape, AWOL, and flight to avoid prosecution.
g Includes rioting, abandonment, nonsupport, immigration violations, invasion of privacy, liquor law violations, tax evasion, and bribery.
[h] Includes juvenile offenses and unspecified offenses.
Source: Allen J. Beck (1991), *Profile of Jail Inmates, 1989,* U.S. Department of Justice, Bureau of Justice Statistics, Washington, D.C.

TABLE 22.2  **Selected Characteristics of Jail Inmates, by Conviction Status, 1983, 1989, and 1994**

| | Percent of Jail Inmates in 1989 | | | 1983 | 1994 |
|---|---|---|---|---|---|
| *Characteristics* | *Convicted* | *Unconvicted* | *Total* | *Total* | *Total* |
| **Sex** | | | | | |
| Male | 90.0% | 91.5% | 90.5% | 92.9% | 90% |
| Female | 10.0 | 8.5 | 9.5 | 7.1 | 10 |
| **Race/Hispanic origin** | | | | | |
| White non-Hispanic | 42.5% | 33.5% | 38.6% | 46.4% | 39.1 |
| Black non-Hispanic | 37.1 | 48.2 | 41.7 | 37.5 | 43.9 |
| Hispanic | 17.5 | 16.7 | 17.4 | 14.3 | 15.4 |
| Other** | 2.9 | 1.6 | 2.3 | 1.8 | 1.6 |
| **Age** | | | | | |
| 17 or younger | 1.1% | 2.0% | 1.5% | 1.3% | NA* |
| 18–24 | 30.9 | 35.1 | 32.6 | 40.4 | NA |
| 25–34 | 44.0 | 41.2 | 42.9 | 38.6 | NA |
| 35–44 | 17.0 | 16.5 | 16.7 | 12.4 | NA |
| 45–54 | 5.0 | 4.0 | 4.6 | 4.9 | NA |
| 55 or older | 2.0 | 1.2 | 1.7 | 2.4 | NA |
| **Number of jail inmates** | 218,797 | 162,441 | 395,554 | 223,552 | |

*Note:* Total includes jail inmates with an unknown conviction status or no offense. Data were missing for mental status on 0.2% of the inmates; for education, 1.7% of the inmates; and for military service, 1.2%.

*Data not available

**Includes Asians, Pacific Islanders, American Indians, Aleuts, Eskimos, and other racial groups.

*Source;* Allen J. Beck (1991), *Profile of jail inmates, 1989.* U.S. Department of Justice, Bureau of Justice Statistics, Washington, D.C.; Craig A. Perkins, James J. Stephan, and Allen J. Beck (1995), Jail and jail inmates 1993–94. U.S. Department of Justice, Washington, D.C.

prescribed by a psychiatrist or other doctor for an emotional or mental problem (Beck, 1991, pp. 2–10).

These data indicate that in addition to their criminality many jail inmates are affected by such problems as illiteracy, substance abuse, and varying degrees of mental instability. These problems tend to go untreated in the outside world. Consequently, the jail—a community agency—becomes a repository for people with these problems. Irwin (1985) indicates that since the typical jail inmate can be characterized as detached and disreputable, they are viewed as deserving of their status as jail inmates.

Finally, another reason the jail population rose considerably between 1983 and 1993 is due to crowding in state and federal prisons. While in 1983 only 2.9% of the jail population (6470) was being held due to crowding in state or federal systems, in 1993 this percentage rose to 7.4 (34,200) (Perkins *et al.*, 1995). Unless prison construction

keeps up with changes in sentencing policy, e.g., three strikes laws and requirements that inmates serve a greater percentage of their sentence, this situation is not likely to improve.

## THE LONG HISTORY OF JAILS

The English jail was the model on which American jails developed. The colonial version of these facilities was very informal and was used only to detain those awaiting trial. Later these facilities began to be used to house convicted minor offenders.

### Jails in England Originated in the Medieval Period

The **gaol,** as the jail was referred to in England, was an institution developed in medieval England. One of the first confinement facilities in the City of London (although not a gaol in the strict sense) was the Tower of London. Construction began after William I arrived following the Battle of Hastings in 1066. Various small gaols were constructed and used as the city developed under the different Norman kings (Moynahan, 1992). In 1166, Henry II ordered jails to be constructed in every shire (local government entities similar to our counties) (Pugh, 1968). As towns and cities grew, and the number of displaced persons and crime increased, more laws were passed to deal with this problem. The vagrancy laws passed between 1349 and 1743 were intended to further control the problem of displaced persons (Chambliss, 1964).

As noted in Chapter 3, during the seventeenth century, the House of Corrections was developed in England. These institutions, which were closely related to jails, served as facilities for both punishment and reform. During the eighteenth century they merged with gaols and were housed under one roof, where they served as places for both the detention of suspects and penal facilities for convicted petty offenders (Barnes and Teeters, 1951). By the nineteenth century, these houses of corrections had been completely amalgamated with jails (Goldfarb, 1973).

### Jails in America Date Back to the Colonial Period

The first jail built in America was constructed in Virginia, during the establishment of the Jamestown settlement, and began housing inmates in 1608. Colonial jails were rarely used as places of imprisonment or punishment but were instead employed for **pretrial confinement** (Rothman, 1971). Early jails had no distinctive architecture or special procedures and were located close to the stocks and pillory or whipping post. They had no cells, instead inmates were housed in small rooms holding up to thirty people.

**EARLY JAILS RESEMBLED HOMES** Consistent with the household model, the keeper and his family lived in one of the rooms, while prisoners lived in the others. Inmates were required to supply their own amenities, either by purchasing them from the jailer or getting them from their families. This practice of collecting money from inmates for services was known as the "fee system." While this

system was modified, it was used well into the twentieth century in some places.

Houses of correction and workhouses were often established near the public jail. Their functions included the punishment of rogues, vagabonds, and strangers and putting the idle poor to work (Rothman, 1971). As in England, jails and workhouses gradually merged and jails have since served both pretrial detention and correctional functions.

**ABOUT HALF THE JAILS IN THE U.S. WERE BUILT AFTER WORLD WAR II** After World War II, the United States spent billions on interstate highways and roads, undertook a large expansion of schools and universities, and initiated a monetary assault on the increasingly polluted environment. Also during this period, the jail-building industry experienced a multibillion dollar construction bonanza. From the 1950s through 1993, more than 1500 jails were built (Kerle, 1993).

## BASIC JAIL DESIGNS

Specific architectural features of jails greatly influence how inmates are supervised, protected, and managed. Like other community agencies (e.g., schools), jails must effectively manage groups of individuals. The architecture of jails and the manner of their construction can either strictly limit management options or expand opportunities for efficient and effective services. Jail architecture began to evolve dramatically in the 1970s. This evolution coincided with the intervention of the federal courts, which brought to light the fact that past design, construction, and management techniques were flawed. Today, three principal jail designs are used in the United States: linear, podular remote, and podular direct.

### A Linear Design Results in Intermittent Surveillance

The **linear design** is the older, more traditional design for jails. In linear facilities, cells are constructed in long straight rows aligned with corridors where correctional staff walk from cell to cell to supervise inmate activities (Figure 22.1). This inhibits the ability of staff to supervise inmates because they can only observe a fraction of those

**FIGURE 22.1 Linear Design/Intermittent Surveillance**

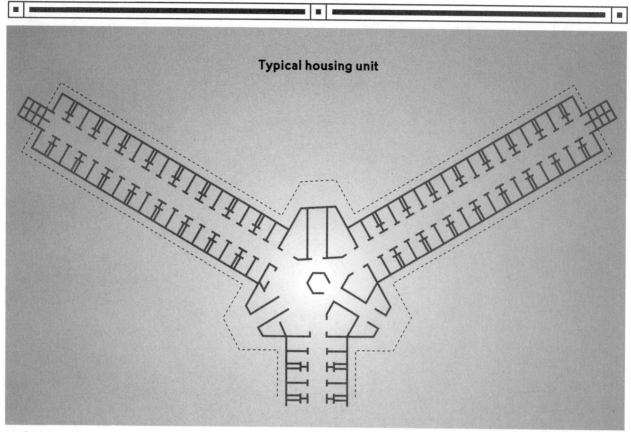

Typical housing unit

SOURCE: U.S. Department of Justice, National Institute of Corrections (1993), *Podular, Direct Supervision Jails Information Packet*, U.S. Department of Justice, Washington, D.C.

within an assigned area at any given moment. Specifically, they can only observe and supervise inmates in those cells directly in their view. It is impossible, in a linear design, to observe all cells from a single location. Therefore, inmate misbehavior, vandalism, and violence can occur when the staff are not directly in front of a given location or cell.

The traditional linear design usually lacks sufficient space for recreation, leisure, and program activities, which are vital for maintaining a calm and safe environment. Due to the lack of continuous supervision these facilities require maximum security construction, equipment, and furnishings. However, in spite of this, graffiti and vandalism remain significant problems.

**One Podular Design Uses Remote Supervision**

To enhance the ability of staff to observe the activities of all inmates within their living units,

the architectural designs of the 1970s introduced the **podular remote surveillance** style of inmate management (Figure 22.2). These facilities resolved many problems of linear intermittent design by changing the basic configuration of the inmate living areas. This was done by situating inmate cells on the exterior perimeter and providing open interior space for inmate activities. Secure control rooms allow staff to observe inmate areas and activities from a central and protected location, rather than patrolling corridors.

While this improved surveillance of inmate activities, secure control rooms effectively isolated staff from the inmate environment. Even though there was greater observation capability, this design did not improve, and perhaps even reduced, the ability of staff to supervise inmates actively and effectively. Podular remote facilities also use "secure" construction, equipment, and furnishings. However, they still experience graffiti and vandalism

FIGURE 22.2 **Podular Design/Remote Surveillance**

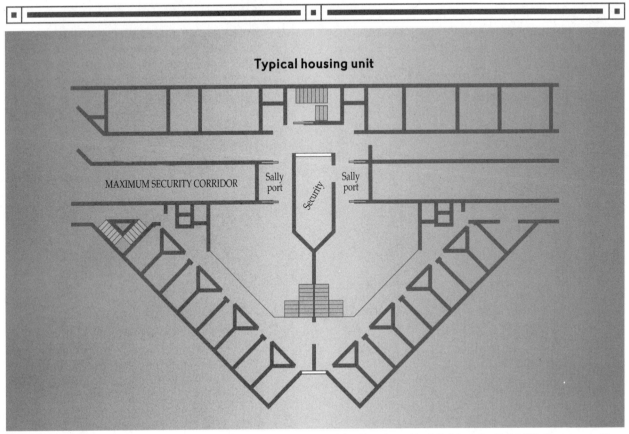

**Typical housing unit**

MAXIMUM SECURITY CORRIDOR | Sally port | Security | Sally port

SOURCE: U.S. Department of Justice, National Institute of Corrections (1993), *Podular, Direct Supervision Jails Information Packet*, U.S. Department of Justice, Washington, D.C.

as well as other problems. For example, one administrator reported that inmates considered the officers weak because they stayed out of the pod when problems arose. Also, when they called for assistance, staff responding did not know what they were walking into due to their limited contact with inmates (Heuer, 1993).

### The Newest Podular Design Uses Direct Supervision

In the 1970s, the federal government designed and constructed three pretrial federal detention centers (jails) in New York City, San Diego, and Chicago. They incorporated **direct supervision designs** that permanently situated staff among the inmates within each housing unit and used "soft" furnishings, such as wood doors, regular beds and tables, along with other furnishings that tended to normalize the living environment (Figure 22.3). In these facilities, inmates were confined fewer hours

in their rooms so they had more recreation, leisure, and program activities, and received intensive personal supervision. This design changes the traditional character of a jail and requires that inmates take more responsibility for their behavior (Nelson, 1988; Zupan, 1991). The movement of staff about the pod and their constant interaction with inmates enabled them to control these units. A survey found that administrators of these facilities report they are safer and have fewer incidents of violence than their counterparts in indirect facilities. This research also suggests that it costs an average of 45% less to build, and 33% less to staff and maintain than indirect supervision jails (Farbstein and Weiner, 1989).

Several factors slowed local adoption of the direct supervision jail concept. These included beliefs that county inmates were more violent than federal inmates, these facilities were prohibitively expensive to build and operate, and due to their normalized furnishings the public would not con-

FIGURE 22.3    **Podular Design/Direct Supervision**

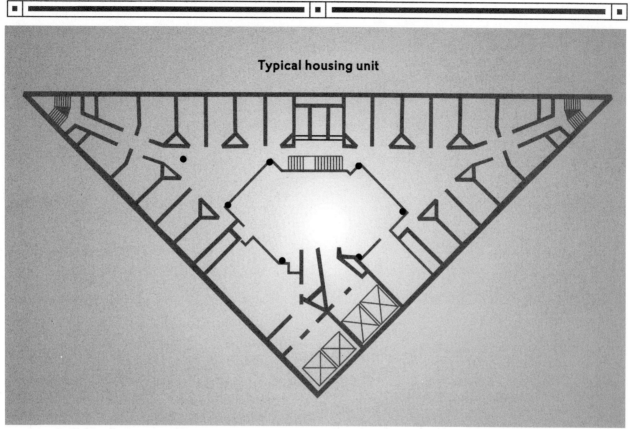

**Typical housing unit**

SOURCE: U.S. Department of Justice, National Institute of Corrections (1993), *Podular, Direct Supervision Jails Information Packet,* U.S. Department of Justice, Washington, D.C.

sider them to be punitive enough to punish offenders sufficiently. Many believed inmates would wreck the furnishings and violence would escalate. These questions were answered in 1981, when Contra Costa County, California, opened the first county-managed direct supervision facility. Since then, this style has rapidly been accepted throughout the country. Nevertheless, there is still some resistance to the adoption of these models, primarily based on the fact that these facilities provide a more normalized environment and also require COs to communicate, manage, and interact with inmates (Farbstein and Weiner, 1989).

## SECURITY AND CONTROL

The primary goal and responsibility of correctional facilities is to provide and maintain a controlled environment that ensures the safety and security

of the public, staff, and inmates. Control of inmates can be achieved in a variety of ways (e.g., the style and quality of the facility, and the presence of solid walls, bars, and locks). However, as is the case in a variety of institutions, architecture alone is a short-sighted approach to control because it fails to consider the human factor.

### Sound Perimeter Security Is a Primary Line of Control

The outer perimeter of the institution forms the first line of control. This consists of secure walls, protected windows, and controlled access to the points of entrance and exit. If it is poorly designed, not routinely inspected, or otherwise ignored, the facility will soon be unable to perform its primary function—to maintain inmates in a controlled environment. A sound and well-maintained perimeter allows maximum flexibility in the interior design and normal operations of the facility. This is

In a direct supervision jail, such as the Contra Costa County Jail, COs are in direct contact with inmates around the clock. This makes for a safer environment for both staff and inmates.

particularly important for jails because many of them are located in the downtown area of a city or in close proximity to populated areas.

In the 1990s, **campus-style facilities** have been replacing older, more traditional stone-walled jails. These jails, which house medium or maximum security inmates, are usually double fenced, with alarms, surrounded with barbed or "razor" wire, and have external mobile patrols. Inside the perimeter the buildings are arranged in a circular fashion with the inside green space often used for outside recreation. Many new jails, especially in urban downtown justice centers, are designed to blend with the surrounding court and civic architecture. These rely only on the building exterior to provide adequate security against escape.

### Control is Easier When the Population is Divided into Manageable Groups

Smaller groups of inmates are easier to control, but the cost of doing so is high. Classification of inmates into groupings based on their anticipated need for supervision allows the best allocation of resources. For the less violent and compliant, larger groupings are appropriate. For those posing a definable risk, small groupings with additional security controls and staff supervision may be necessary.

### Well-Designed Jails Facilitate the Surveillance of Inmates

Facility design that enables staff to watch and be in contact with inmates enhances control. Indefensible space (e.g., concealed alcoves and dark corridors) on the other hand has the opposite effect. Inmate spaces require continual inspection so that predatory inmates cannot use them to carry out their own agendas. The modern podular jail enables staff, at a quick glance or a short walk, to see and hear the activities within the entire living unit.

The staffing and operational costs of a facility are directly proportional to the number of inmates a single staff member can supervise. As modern jails have adopted professional standards, classification, and greater staff training, the number of inmates that can be supervised has increased. In the 1970s, most jail professionals thought that fifty inmates was the maximum number that could be safely supervised in jail living units by one CO. In the 1990s, staff in direct supervision facilities are routinely supervising sixty to eighty inmates each, depending on inmate classification. Sometimes, however, a second officer is assigned to units with more than fifty inmates.

It is difficult to establish hard and fast rules regarding the number of inmates that can be supervised by one CO (Senese, Wilson, Evans, Aquire, and Kalinich, 1992). Unfortunately, in small jails this is a very difficult problem because they lack the space and staff needed to classify inmates properly. Under these circumstances, cost-effective staff-to-inmate ratios may not be possible.

## JAIL ADMISSION PROCESS

Booking, intake, receiving, classification, and orientation are terms referring to the procedures used to introduce newly arrested individuals into local corrections.

During the intake process certain types of information must be acquired from those being admitted to ensure the health and safety of other inmates while protecting and maintaining the institution's security. This information includes who they are and whether they are who they claim to be; whether they have consumed a dangerous drug and/or alcohol; if they are injured or in some form of distress; and if they are violent or potential suicides. Knowledge of these factors and others will help determine an appropriate housing assignment.

### The Design of the Intake Area Affects the Control of Arrestees

In older and more traditional linear jails, the intake space was purposely designed with stark cells and "drunk tanks" to temporarily house new intakes. In these facilities, the violent are admitted with the nonviolent, the sophisticated with the unsophisticated, the predators with the prey, and many are intoxicated. Thus, the intake unit can be the most violent and disruptive one in the entire jail.

In direct supervision facilities, the intake unit encourages and promotes normalized behavior. This includes an open environment , reduced levels of sound, normalized furnishings, and immediate and thorough screening and supervision by professional staff. These factors have helped to reduce levels of suicide, violence, vandalism, and disruptive behavior in these facilities (Wallenstein, 1989).

### Many Offenders Spend Only a Few Hours in Jail

Drunk drivers, misdemeanants, traffic offenders, shoplifters, and others arrested on minor felony charges will often post bail or be released to a variety of programs serving as alternatives to incarceration. Even those arrested on more serious felony charges may soon be free either on bail or through a reduction or dismissal of charges. For many, then, jail is a short-term confinement experience that never goes further than the initial booking and release process. At some time during the intake process, each inmate will have the opportunity to do several things. Depending on state law and agency policy, this includes making two or more telephone calls to family, friends, or attorneys, and/or arranging either a cash, property, or bail bond within the first two hours of confinement. These calls are important because they notify family and friends of an arrestee's custody status and, for many, begin the process of obtaining the means of release. For those remaining, it can be the start of an extended incarceration experience.

### Medical and Mental Health Screening of Arrestees Is Routine in Many Jails

Jails have a legal obligation to identify and treat arrested individuals who are sick, injured, overdosed, or subject to emotional distress (Dale, 1989). Each year in the United States, many individuals who appear merely intoxicated die of a variety of causes including diabetic comas, drug overdoses, or alcohol poisoning. Many minor first offenders attempt or commit suicide when they find themselves alone, embarrassed, and depressed because of their incarceration.

In large jail systems medical examinations and mental health interviews are part of the intake process. Many small jails cannot afford to have specially trained personnel continually available to identify and treat the variety of problems experienced by many of those arrested. Chapter 19 fully discusses prison health services but it is important to mention jail medical services here because many newly arrived inmates require immediate medical attention.

Are you a diabetic? Have you taken cocaine or other illicit drugs within the last 90 minutes? Are you presently taking any prescription medication? Are you now thinking or have you ever thought about injuring or harming yourself or others? These are some examples of questions that must be answered to protect the jail against potential liability, while assisting those in distress. Once a problem

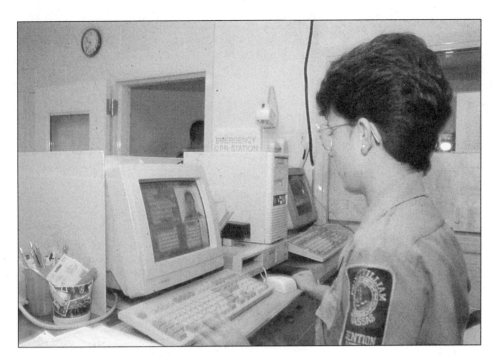

The booking process is aided by modern technology. This computer system facilitates the booking process by creating video mug shots and taking fingerprints.

is identified, prompt action by jail personnel is required to ensure against any future or further injury. Whether the problem is medical, one of drug ingestion, or psychological, a trained professional should examine and evaluate the situation (Jones, 1989).

### Accurate Identification of the Inmate Involves Several Steps

Once cleared medically, the inmate must be accurately identified through a **booking process** that obtains personal information such as age, height, weight, date and location of birth, address, next of kin, social security number, and driver's license number. For positive identification, fingerprints are taken, classified, and compared with those in local, state, and national automated fingerprint files. If a fingerprint match is confirmed, identification is complete. For first-time arrestees, a new file will be started for future reference.

A photograph or "mug shot" is taken of each person booked. In the 1990s, the integration of computer graphics and video allow **video mug shots** to be stored in an automated system and transferred for viewing to any desired location. Once identification and assessment are completed, inmates are either released on bail, on recogni-

zance, or on a promise-to-appear citation. Those not released will be thoroughly searched, all their clothing and property will be removed and stored, and they will be issued jail clothing and personal hygiene items. They are then transferred to an intake housing unit to await classification, orientation, and further housing assignment.

### Good Classification and Orientation Facilitate Control

As we discussed in Chapter 17, classification is a management process that separates inmates according to preestablished security and custody levels. It allows assignment to compatible groups, which reduces violence and conflict while enhancing facility programming. Jails that do not adequately classify inmates can expect continual violence and disruptive conduct. In smaller jails, the classification process is usually subjective, and is dependent on the experience and judgment of the intake staff. Subjective systems take many of the same factors into consideration, but are based on the limited resources available (Brennan and Wells, 1992).

During the **orientation process** inmates are acquainted with the rules and regulations applying to conduct while in custody and the requirements for and availability of work, education, religious, and substance abuse programs. This information is usually presented in small groups using videotapes, pamphlets, and/or classroom instruction. Institutions without formal orientation programs may just pass out booklets or other printed materials to inform inmates about facility rules and procedures. Once inmates have been completely processed, they can be assigned to appropriate living quarters.

## SPECIAL PROBLEMS OF CERTAIN TYPES OF INMATES

Certain categories of inmates require special attention because of the potential risks they pose to themselves and other inmates and staff. These include drug and alcohol abusers, the mentally ill, those who are potentially suicidal, and juvenile inmates. Women are also a special category because their relatively small numbers have made it difficult for jails to meet their program and service needs.

### Substance Abusers May Require Special Care

A majority of jail inmates are physically and/or psychologically dependent on one or more legal or illegal substances. Recent studies of arrestees coming into jails from various U.S. cities have shown that from 47 to 78% have used illicit drugs in the 72 hours before their arrests. Cocaine, "crack," methamphetamines, heroin, marijuana, and LSD are the major drugs of choice of those arrestees. Thus, an important task of jail personnel is to identify those under the influence and provide appropriate medical care (Peters, Kearns, Murin, and Dolante, 1992).

Addicted inmates and those selling drugs are most likely to introduce illegal drugs into a jail. While it is nearly impossible to totally eliminate drugs in jails, great care must be given to reduce the scope of the problem. The use of drugs in a jail can result in serious overdoses requiring immediate attention or even in death. Drug trafficking in a facility can also cause problems including intimidation, coercion, and possible injury to inmates who find themselves in debt to those supplying the drugs. Thus, dealing with the problem and treatment are essential (Hecht, 1992).

Typically, alcohol abusers arrested for driving a vehicle under the influence (DUI) comprise one of the largest categories of the jail inmate population—about 8.8% in 1989 (Maguire and Pastore, 1994). During 1993, some 1.5 million DUI arrests were made in the United States and many of these people were alcoholics (Samuels, 1991; Federal Bureau of Investigation, 1994).

Processing alcoholics into jails can pose difficult and potentially dangerous problems for both staff and inmates. If the addiction is severe, sudden withdrawal often results in episodes that require prompt medical treatment. In addition, some inmates who look to be heavily under the influence may not have been drinking at all, but instead are suffering from a chemical imbalance resulting from diabetes.

The loss of self-control due to alcohol intoxication makes many drunks very uncooperative during the intake and detoxification process and may even lead to violent behavior. Typically, jail personnel handling drunks during booking can expect to be assaulted at some time during their career. This is not surprising considering the National Institute on Alcohol Abuse and Alcoholism indicates that 25% of alcoholics have antisocial personality characteristics (Samuels, 1991). Thus, the training of jail staff in the nonviolent management and control of inebriates is important.

Given the high incidence of alcohol abusers entering our jails, there is a need to develop mandatory drug and alcohol screening standards (Mays, Fields, and Thompson, 1991). These regulations must make allowances for jail size, different populations, and availability of resources. For this to become a reality, states must share in funding for treatment programs because local governments lack sufficient resources to effectively screen, house, and treat drug- and alcohol-dependent inmates (Mays *et al.,* 1991).

In fact, a good detoxification treatment program should exist in every jail since so many treatment clinics refuse to deal with the violent drinker. While most megajail systems (over 1000 inmates) have detox treatment programs of some kind, small jails (under 50 inmates) lack sufficient resources for adequate detox programs. As a result, detoxification is often done without appropriate counseling or treatment.

In larger cities and counties, "common drunk" arrestees have begun to be diverted from jails into residential **detoxification centers.** This is best done if the jail works in tandem with an outside community agency. For example, the Elmwood Deuce Alcohol Treatment Program in Santa Clara County, California, combined the efforts of the Santa Clara County Bureau of Alcohol Services with the Santa Clara County Department of Correction and the Santa Clara Adult Probation Program to provide services for alcoholic arrestees (Samuels, 1991).

## Changes in Mental Health Policies Have Increased the Number of Mentally Ill in Jails

A substantial number of inmates entering jail suffer from mental illness. **Deinstitutionalization** in the mental health system during the last 30 years has resulted in relatively large numbers of mentally ill persons reentering the community without support, with many becoming homeless. In most counties, the jail is the largest repository for this population (Zupan, 1991). The impairments these inmates have can lead to behavior causing conflicts with other inmates, an inability to understand or follow instructions, and self-destructive behavior. Obviously this category of inmate can be best served in mental health facilities and institutions geared to meet their needs.

A 1992 survey of 1391 city and county jails found that more than one in fourteen people in these jails were seriously mentally ill (Torrey, Steiber, Ezekiel, Wolfe, Sharfstein, Noble, and Lauric, 1992).[a] This represented 7.2% of the inmate population—a ten-fold increase in their proportion since 1980. Thus, on any given day jails hold more than 30,700 people with serious mental conditions. Further, 29% of the jails confine seriously mentally ill persons with no criminal charges against them, often because communities lack facilities for psychiatric emergencies. Though most are arrested on criminal charges the vast majority of their offenses are trivial misdemeanors (e.g., disorderly conduct), which are manifestations of their disorders. About one-third of these individuals are homeless and jail represents part of a continuous cycle that includes the street as well as stays in jails and mental hospitals. Moreover, despite the best efforts of jail staff, many of these inmates are cruelly abused, suffering torment, rape, and beatings by other inmates. The net result is that jails are being used as dumping grounds for this group. Torrey *et al.* (1992) made the following recommendations to alleviate the problem:

1. States which fail to amend their laws to eliminate the jailing of mentally ill people not charged with a crime should lose eligibility for mental health block grants.
2. More jail diversion programs for the mentally ill.
3. Evaluation of the seriously mentally ill should occur within 24 hours after booking.
4. There should be a transfer of state mental health funds to jails in states where mental health authorities have failed to set up **jail diversion programs** [programs to remove the mentally ill from jails].
5. Follow up of the mentally ill when released from jails should be required.
6. Training should be provided for jail officers who deal with the mentally ill.
7. Mental health trainees should be required to spend a minimum of six hours in on-site training in jails.
8. Mental health professionals should be required to provide mental health services to the jail two hours each week.
9. There needs to be greatly improved federal and state statistical reporting to reflect the existence of the seriously mentally ill in jails.
10. Each jurisdiction with a jail should have a standing mental illness committee including representatives from the jail, local mental health department, local public psychiatric inpatient unit, and the local chapter of the National Alliance for the Mentally Ill.

**SOME INMATES ARE SUICIDAL**   Suicide has been the leading nonnatural cause of death within jails. In 1991 there were 131 suicides, while 124 occurred in 1992, and 234 in 1993. Suicides represented a large majority of all nonnatural deaths in jails during these years (Beck *et al.*, 1993; Perkins *et al.*, 1995). Depression, anxiety, embarrassment over their arrest, and the fear that incarceration may devastate their lives lead some to decide that suicide is a preferable alternative. An in-depth survey of jails in which 339 suicides occurred, found that 30% occurred in holding facilities with the remainder occurring in detention facilities (Hayes and Rowan, 1988). An analysis of those who committed suicide showed that:

- 72% of victims were white.
- 94% of victims were male.
- Mean age of the victim was 30.

◙ 52% of victims were single.

◙ 75% of victims were detained on nonviolent charges, with 27% detained on alcohol/drug related charges.

◙ 89% of victims were confined as detainees.

◙ 78% of victims had prior charges, yet only 10% were previously held on personal/violent offenses.

◙ 60% of victims were intoxicated at the time of incarceration.

◙ 30% of suicides occurred between midnight and 6:00 A.M.

◙ 94% of suicides were by hanging; 48% used their bedding.

◙ Two out of three victims were in isolation.

◙ 51% of suicides occurred within the first 24 hours of incarceration; 29% occurred within the first 3 hours (pp. X–XI).

Jail staff can be taught to recognize and successfully intervene in situations involving potentially suicidal inmates. They may exhibit warning signs and symptoms that include:

◙ Depression (physical signs)
  a.–sadness and crying
  b.–withdrawal or silence
  c.–sudden loss or gain in appetite
  d.–insomnia
  e.–mood variations
  f.–lethargy
◙ Intoxication/withdrawal
◙ Talking about or threatening suicide
◙ Previous suicide attempts
◙ History of mental illness
◙ Projecting hopelessness or helplessness
◙ Speaking unrealistically about future and getting out of jail
◙ Increasing difficulty relating to others
◙ Not effectively dealing with present; preoccupied with past
◙ Giving away possessions; packing belongings
◙ Severe aggressiveness
◙ Paranoid delusions or hallucinations (Hayes and Rowan, 1988, p. 41).

Professional standards and practices require that staff interview and complete a comprehensive physical and mental health survey on each inmate immediately upon entering the jail. If this indicates a suicide potential, further processing must be stopped and a mental health evaluation must be conducted. If mental health resources are not readily available, a suicide watch must be instituted so that the detainee is continually observed by staff to prevent self-injury.

It must be recognized that individuals will not always answer the initial questions truthfully (Kennedy, 1994). Therefore, it is important that all inmates be closely observed and supervised during the first 72 hours of incarceration. Failure to supervise this vulnerable population will allow them the time and certainly the opportunity to kill or seriously injure themselves (Rowan, 1991).

### Juveniles Are at Risk in Adult Jails

The placement of juveniles, usually between the ages of 14 and 17, within adult jails has been a continuing problem. In 1993, our jails housed about 3400 juveniles on any given day (Perkins *et al.*, 1995). Juveniles are admitted into jails for a variety of reasons. While they constitute less than one-half of 1% of the jail population, there are critics who say that no juveniles should be housed in adult jails (Zupan, 1991). Schwartz (1991) has proposed legislation prohibiting the placement of juveniles in jails under any circumstances. However, in many counties with small populations, juvenile institutions do not exist and the only alternative is the county jail. In larger jurisdictions, juveniles may be transferred to the jail by the order of a court due to the seriousness of their crimes.

Throughout our history, many instances of abuse of juveniles within adult institutions have occurred. Juveniles have been victims of sexual assaults, physical and emotional violence, and intimidation. There are special conditions, standards, and laws that protect juveniles when they are placed jails:

**1.** *Separation:* Strict separation by sight and sound of juveniles from the adult population. This requires jails to have separate living units, recreation, and education facilities for juveniles that totally isolates them from adults.

**2.** *Judicial review and authorization:* Juveniles cannot be incarcerated in a jail unless this confinement is reviewed and ordered by a court. Arbitrary placement in jails without judicial review and approval is almost universally prohibited.

**3.** *Nutrition:* Juveniles require different nutritional standards and, therefore, two different menus and food service policies are required to ensure proper nutrition for both populations.

Recognizing the dangers of keeping juveniles in jails, in 1974 Congress passed the **Juvenile Justice and Delinquency Prevention Act** (JJDP.) It mandated that juveniles detained in adult jails be out of the sight and sound of adult inmates. To obtain federal funds, states were required to comply with the JJDP act. That threat did not work because in 1980, most states were still out of compliance and Congress amended the JJDP act to end the practice of juvenile jailings. By 1988, thirteen states and territories were still not in compliance with these laws (Sweet, 1991). Some states, Kentucky for example, still hold juveniles in jails. Kentucky requires that jail officers who supervise juveniles undergo 40 hours of special training prior to this assignment and complete an additional 40 hours during their first year on the job (Black, 1991).

### Females Have Been the "Forgotten Inmates" of the Jail System

In 1994, females constituted 10% of the total jail population (Perkins *et al.*, 1995). Although women represent a small proportion of the inmate population, state laws require that programs and services be equally available to them (Dale, 1991). The small size of this population creates special and unique problems not usually found in managing the male population. Similar to males, women fall into many different categories requiring different levels of security. There are female inmates who are mentally and physically ill, suicidal, assaultive, require protective custody, or are otherwise in need of separation from other inmates. They must be segregated according to standards established by law. Except for a few large jurisdictions, most jails do not have the physical plant or financial resources to provide adequate separate living accommodations. In most small- and medium-sized facilities, all female inmates are either housed together or their living unit is subdivided into smaller clusters to handle the many different classifications of inmates (Schafer and Dellinger, 1993a, 1993b).

To protect women from verbal and physical harassment and potential assault, state laws and professional standards mandate that male and female inmates be housed in units separated by sight and sound. In some states this strict standard is relaxed to allow mixing of male and female inmates during periods of educational, substance abuse treatment, and other programs.

## JAIL STAFF AND MANAGEMENT

This section focuses on recent improvements in jail staffing, and issues related to management. A safe and secure jail requires qualified and well-trained correctional officers (COs) and command staff that maintains contact with COs and inmates.

### Correctional Officers Constitute the Bulk of the Staff

In 1993 jails employed a total of 165,500 people, of whom 117,000 were COs. An estimated 69% of the COs were white non-Hispanic, 23.2% were black non-Hispanic, 6.7% were Hispanic, and other groups constituted less than 1%. Male officers outnumbered females by about three to one (Perkins *et al.*, 1995).

In many communities, the public considers the jail as an agency that is "out of sight and out of mind" and, therefore, does not consider the human dynamics involved in jail operations. Many believe that COs are undereducated, poorly trained, and unsophisticated. While this may have been the case in the past, there has been considerable improvement, largely due to court action. Most states today require at least a high school diploma to work in a jail, but the people who have the potential to be the best officers cannot be attracted by paying substandard wages. One very important step in attracting them is to begin paying jail officers the same as police officers.

In 1994 salaries in 154 reporting jurisdictions for starting deputies/jail officers averaged $21,443—ranging from $11,250 in Iberia Parish, Louisiana, to $38,383 in San Bernadino County, California. Maximum salaries average $31,109—ranging from a low of $13,187 in Kenton County, Kentucky, to a high of $46,643 in Los Angeles County, California (Camp and Camp, 1994b).

**IN MANY JAILS ROAD DEPUTIES MUST FIRST SERVE AS COs** Most jails are under the control of county sheriffs and in many, jail duty is required of road deputies as the first step in their law enforcement career ladder. An advantage to this approach is that officers quickly learn the behaviors and characteristics of those with whom they will be dealing when they transfer to patrol duty. Its disadvantage is that the deputy sheriff does not see corrections as a desirable career path. The jail is only an entry assignment to be followed by a full career in law enforcement. High turnover, loss of valuable experience, and the absence of commitment to corrections are all major disadvantages of combining corrections and law enforcement into a deputy sheriff's career path (Reed, 1993).

**PROFESSIONALIZATION OF COs REQUIRES SUBSTANTIAL TRAINING**  As our jails become increasingly professionalized, the requirement for trained, quality staff becomes more important. Some states now mandate that jail correctional personnel be certified through academy training. In 1994, 143 systems reported an average of 282 preservice training hours—ranging from 1024 hours in Orange County, California, to no hours in several jurisdictions (e.g., Floyd County, Georgia) (Camp and Camp, 1994b). Even in states that require training, it still generally falls below the number of hours required for entrance into law enforcement. The reluctance of government to meet its training obligations has served as a stimulus to the American Jail Association (AJA) to fill this void by issuing monthly training bulletins. AJA also conducts two training sessions a month in different sections of the country. Refresher training is vital and offered in many areas (e.g., CPR, fire safety, riot techniques, interpersonal relations skills). In 1994, 143 systems required an average of 33 hours of in-service training—the range was from 0 to 200 (Camp and Camp, 1994b).

**THE PRIMARY ROLE OF JAIL STAFF IS SUPERVISION**  The safety and security of the jail demands that staff control the inmate population. If staff are hesitant or actually do not enter certain sections of the jail, then control of those areas is, in effect, relinquished to the inmates. A jail with adequate control rarely has escapes, maintains effective supervision, has few serious injuries, and staff are in charge of all functional inmate space.

Effective supervision of inmates requires that trained staff be in frequent, interpersonal contact and communication with inmates because, left to their own devices, predatory inmates will assume

control of their units to further their own agendas. Merely observing inmate behavior from a remote location or walking by a cell block every half hour does not constitute effective supervision (Heuer, 1993). Staff–inmate communication is nurtured by close personal and professional contact. Supervising behavior, answering questions, scheduling events, inspecting cells, assembling work details, and general conversation are methods staff can use to open lines of communication. Uncommunicative staff tend to become isolated and this makes it more difficult to obtain full cooperation from inmates.

**CONTROL IS BEST ACHIEVED BY HAVING INMATE BEHAVIOR DETERMINE CONFINEMENT CONDITIONS**  Inmates know the difference between "easy time" (having certain privileges) and "hard time" (being locked up in disciplinary confinement). Ideally inmates should be given the opportunity to decide which type of "time" they wish to do. Compliance with facility rules and regulations ensures reasonably comfortable living conditions with increased access to such things as additional freedom of movement, recreation, library, programs, television, telephones, and visiting. However, noncompliance results in increasing restrictions on personal freedom and reduction of privileges.

## Jail Management Involves a Variety of Issues

Jail management not only encompasses issues related to staff supervision but also includes such concerns as which agency should administer these facilities.

**JAIL REGIONALIZATION AND SEPARATION FROM LAW ENFORCEMENT ARE NEW TRENDS**  State jail standards, crowding, and a landslide of inmate lawsuits have given continued impetus to questions about which agency should administer county jails. Although most jails (more than 80%) now come under an elected sheriff's command, there has been a considerable movement to separate law enforcement from correctional functions (*Who's Who in Jail Management*, 1994). Three of California's 58 counties, 10 of New Hampshire's counties, 6 of Florida's 67 counties, 4 of Maryland's 23 counties, 55 of Pennsylvania's 67 counties, and 15 of New Jersey's 21 counties now operate separate departments of corrections. Six states (Vermont, Connecticut, Rhode Island, Delaware, Hawaii, Alaska) run state-operated jail systems. By the year 2000, West Virginia's 55 counties will be totally amalgamated into a series of state-operated **regional jails.** Today, Kentucky has only 76 jails in 120 counties and though the elected jailer remains a fixture in Kentucky politics, many of these jails have been downgraded to a holding facility status (*Who's Who in Jail Management,* 1994).

Much of the discussion about regional jails stems from the large number of small jails that still dot this country's landscape. According to the second edition of the American Jail Association's *Who's Who in Jail Management* (1994), more than 1000 jails still have rated capacities of twenty-five and under. In states like North and South Dakota, regional jails have been established for a number of years. North Dakota, with 53 counties, has only 30 jail facilities, South Dakota, with 66 counties, has only 32 jail facilities, while Nebraska has only 68 jails in 93 counties.

The economic arguments in favor of regionalizing many of the small jails are strong. In Iowa, 95 of the 99 counties operate jails. The rated capacities of these jails include 71 holding under 20 with 21 of these holding fewer than 10, and 1 that holds 30. Thirty-one of these jails have an average daily population of less than five. Regardless of size, each jail is required to meet state jail standards including full 24-hour staffing, initial and continuing education, and medical services (Gardner, 1992). Larger prisons and jails can reduce the per-inmate cost of providing these services compared with smaller facilities. Contrast this with Virginia, which has 12 regional jails representing a total of 24 counties and 11 cities. Virginia law permits any two or more counties or cities to establish and operate a regional jail. However, to receive maximum state reimbursement for construction of new facilities or renovation of old ones, three or more jurisdictions must participate (Leibowitz, 1991).

In some localities, regional jail arrangements are informal rather than formal. That is, a handshake between county officials cements an agreement by one county to hold another's prisoners for a fee. In fact, in some states like Nebraska, South Dakota, Kansas, and Iowa, the *de facto* regional jail constitutes a way of life. Some jails find it impossible to separate women by sight and sound from males

and so they instead arrange to ship them to other jurisdictions; in others, crowding forces jail staff to search for additional space (Crabtree, 1993).

**GOOD MANAGEMENT REQUIES FREQUENT CONTACT BETWEEN COMMAND STAFF AND INMATES** Irrespective of jail size, effective management requires that jail administrators establish and enforce policies requiring all command and supervisory jail staff to make frequent visits, each day and each shift, to inmate living areas. This approach, which has been labeled as "management by walking around," was discussed in Chapter 13. This proactive posture can prevent lazy or weak staff from retreating from inmate contact. Lack of contact by management with line staff, insufficient interaction with inmates, and failure to conduct routine inspections are management deficiencies that allow small incidents and problems to fester into major problems, for example, disturbances or riots. Proper jail management requires jail administrators to be highly visible and accessible to the public, staff, and inmates.

**CONSTITUTIONAL JAILS PROVIDE A SAFE ENVIRONMENT FOR STAFF AND INMATES**   Jails that properly classify and supervise inmates reduce tension and stress while increasing the feeling of safety among staff and inmates. A jail that fails to provide a safe environment for staff and inmates is not functioning according to constitutional standards (Catanese and Hennessey, 1989; Peed, 1989). A constitutionally acceptable environment requires adherence to standard safety codes, provides levels of supervision that adequately control violence, and corrects situations that violate basic inmate rights (Marchese, 1990). Failure to comply can often result in court-imposed judgments requiring jurisdictions to make changes far exceeding the cost of correcting and monitoring the initial problem. Tax dollars are much more effectively used when they provide safety in comparison to being paid out as damages and attorneys' fees. For example, in 1982, the federal court in San Francisco, California, fined the county $2.6 million and $300 per day for every inmate over the court-imposed population capacity. While inmates only win a few of the thousands of lawsuits filed each year against jail overcrowding and other correctional problems, the time and expense to the governments involved in these suits can be substantial (Dale, 1987; Hager, 1992).

Each jail has a rated or **design capacity,** a figure that specifies the number of inmates that the jail was built (or remodeled) to accommodate. Thus, jails contain finite amounts of space (cells/rooms/ dormitories) and support facilities to manage specified inmate populations. All too often, they are constructed without considering the impact of future community population growth or changing attitudes about crime and punishment. As a result, jails can become overcrowded and the staff's ability to supervise and manage inmates diminishes proportionally.

A crowded jail creates significant management problems. As the number of inmates in living units rises beyond design capacity, the many required support systems (e.g., such as visiting, recreation, food service, medical care) begin to deteriorate. To relieve jail overcrowding, federal and state courts have forced local governments to release more pretrial detainees or require a new building program among other things (Wilkinson and Brehm, 1992). Klofas (1991) suggests that systematic policy formulation efforts are also needed to resolve these problems.

## JAILS PROVIDE SOME PROGRAMS FOR INMATES

An increased emphasis on jail programming has resulted from a growing recognition that occupying inmates through recreation and established programs will reduce their involvement in violence and other illegal activities, may affect their return to criminal pursuits, and can even result in revenue for the jail. Today jail programs include recreation, some education, alcohol and drug abuse counseling, and in a few instances work and industry programs.

### Jails Usually Have Little Recreational Space

Access to recreation and physical exercise, within security constraints, is a constitutional right of inmates. Sufficient indoor and outdoor space and adequate time must be provided to all inmates in custody. Many jails, particularly those in downtown areas of a city, have very limited space for recreational and exercise programs and may use the jail roof for this purpose. Newer direct supervision jails often have both indoor recreational areas and outside areas with basketball hoops attached to the living units.

### Some Jails Offer Education and Substance Abuse Programs

A substantial number of inmates who come to jail have significant educational deficiencies. Some jails have education programs that include literacy, GED, health (including AIDS), parenting, and life skills classes. In fact, some of the most innovative correctional education programs today are found in jails. For example, the Hillsborough County, Florida, Detention Department uses computer-assisted instruction in addition to traditional Adult Basic Education (ABE) programs. With sixty computers in seven labs located throughout two facilities, they engage a significant number of inmates in this integrated learning approach. As with all of their programs, the computer labs provide an open entry/open exit format (inmates are allowed to enter and exit any time during their confinement instead of the traditional semester program concept). The program serves both male and female inmates, including juveniles awaiting trial in adult court. Preliminary research shows the program is well received by both staff and inmates. Inmates have been increasing their average grade levels between 1.5 and 2.0 years in sixty hours of instruction (Smith, 1994).

Given the large proportion of jail inmates with a substance abuse history, drug education classes and even short-term treatment programs can help addicts to deal with their problems. For example, the D.E.U.C.E. Program operated in Contra Costa County, California, is an intense three-phase, 90-day effort at reducing substance-abuse-related recidivism through the use of a therapeutic community in a jail setting. D.E.U.C.E. was developed for multiple-offending drunk drivers and dual/poly addicted individuals. The program focuses on substance abuse education, intervention, prevention, and employability. Traditional educational instruction is paired with individual and small group treatment and twelve-step sessions similar to those used by Alcoholics Anonymous. Each hour of the day and evening is oriented to the program. Individuals must apply for admission and are pre-screened by program staff (Blount, 1994).

### Some Jails Have Begun Industry Programs

Since the mid-1980s, an increasing number of the nation's jails have been creating productive industry programs. According to the National Institute of Justice, the concept is simple: Use inmate labor

Some jails have industry programs that help reduce inmate idleness, teach job skills, and keep jail costs down.

to produce a product or service of value that benefits inmates, jails, and communities. A 1993 national jail survey indicated that, in the jails reporting (11% of all jails), 18% of their inmates worked at least a 6-hour day (American Jails, 1994).

Hennepin County, Minnesota, houses the earliest private sector jail industries program in the nation and serves as the National Institute of Corrections Resource Center. It conducts training seminars and provides technical assistance to jails interested in developing these programs. Several exemplary programs are now in existence. In the Philadelphia Jail, the Prison Industries Program turns out furniture, mattresses, clothing, etc. Another program, is in Winona County, Minnesota (the smallest jail in the nation with an industry program—average under thirty inmates) where inmates perform light assembly and packaging services for a variety of private sector companies (American Jail Association, 1992).

### It Is Difficult to Institute Jail Programs

A number of factors impede the development of effective jail programs for all categories of inmates. Those awaiting trial are not required to participate in any ongoing programs except sanitation. Many inmates only spend a few days in jail and will not

benefit from education and substance abuse programs. Any programs for short-term inmates must be designed to provide motivation, orientation, and referral to community resources to facilitate further progress on release. Another consideration is the size of the jail. Small jails, which constitute the majority of jail facilities, often lack the resources necessary to conduct such programs (Mays *et al.*, 1991).

While jail programming can benefit many inmates, as Table 22.3 shows, even in 503 of the largest jails only a small proportion of the inmates in each system is involved in jail programs (Beck *et al.*, 1993). While 420 of these systems offered at least one of four programs only 127 offered all of them. There is no indication whether the low participation rate is due to limitations on program space or lack of inmate interest.

### THE FUTURE OF THE AMERICAN JAIL

The American public and its leadership have sent mixed signals regarding the proper role of jails. Are jails established to administer punishment, to simply warehouse offenders, or to attempt to correct past behaviors? The answers to these important

TABLE 22.3   **Jurisdictions with Large Jail Populations: Selected Jail Programs and Number of Participants, June 30, 1992**

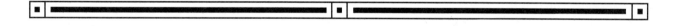

| | | Large Jail Jurisdictions | |
| | | *Number of* | |
| Programs for inmates | Number | Program Participants | Inmates in Jurisdiction |
| --- | --- | --- | --- |
| Total | 503 | b | 362,217 |
| Drug treatment[a] | 275 | 18,052 | 234,591 |
| Alcohol treatment[a] | 295 | 20,100 | 213,147 |
| Psychological counseling | 212 | 14,237 | 189,845 |
| Education program | 350 | 25,591 | 282,328 |

[a] Combined substance abuse programs and enrollment in them were classified by the substance most emphasized in the program.
[b] Not determined.

*Source:* A. Beck, T. P. Bonczar, and D. K. Gilliard (1993), *Jail Inmates 1992,* Bureau of Justice Statistics, U.S. Department of Justice, Washington, D.C., p. 8.

questions have changed from time to time and, as indicated in our discussion of the history of corrections, will likely continue to change. There is no solid evidence that punishment and/or incarceration help to reduce future jail populations or crime in the community. Thus, the current policy of building more jails and prisons as a way dealing with the crime problem is not likely to reduce significantly the level of crime. Nor will it deal with overcrowding on a long-term basis because it does not reduce the reasons people commit crimes nor will it assist them in adopting a noncriminal lifestyle. The jail of the future must strive to use the limited available community resources in its capacity as a community agency and work in tandem with other government agencies at all levels to direct the incarcerated person into a noncriminal lifestyle (Powell, 1993; Sluder and Sapp, 1994).

### ACKNOWLEDGMENTS

[a] Reprinted (or cited) by permission of the National Alliance for the Mentally Ill.

### CHAPTER RECAP

**The Diverse Population of Jails**
**The Long History of Jails**
Jails in England Originated in the Medieval Period
Jails in America Date Back to the Colonial Period
    Early Jails Resembled Homes
    About Half the Jails in the U.S. Were Built After World War II
**Basic Jail Designs**
A Linear Design Results in Intermittent Surveillance
One Podular Design Uses Remote Supervision
The Newest Podular Design Uses Direct Supervision
**Security and Control**

Sound Perimeter Security Is a Primary Line of Control
Control Is Easier When when the Population Is Divided into Manageable Groups
Well-Designed Jails Facilitate the Surveillance of Inmates
**Jail Admission Process**
The Design of the Intake Area Affects the Control of Arrestees
Many Offenders Spend Only a Few Hours in Jail
Medical and Mental Health Screening of Arrestees Is Routine in Many Jails
Accurate Identification of the Inmate Involves Several Steps
Good Classification and Orientation Facilitate Control
**Special Problems of Certain Types of Inmates**
Substance Abusers May Require Special Care
Changes in Mental Health Policies Have Increased the Number of Mentally Ill in Jails
    Some Inmates Are Suicidal
Juveniles Are at Risk in Adult Jails

Females Have Been the "Forgotten Inmates" of the Jail System

**Jail Staff and Management**

Correctional Officers Constitute the Bulk of the Staff
    In Many Jails Road Deputies Must First Serve as COs
    Professionalization of COs Requires Substantial Training
    The Primary Role of Jail Staff Is Supervision
    Control Is Best Achieved by Having Inmate Behavior Determine Confinement Conditions

Jail Management Involves a Variety of Issues
    Jail Regionalization and Separation from Law Enforcement Are New Trends
    Good Management Requires Frequent Contact Between Command Staff and Inmates
    Constitutional Jails Provide a Safe Environment for Staff and Inmates

**Jails Provide Some Programs for Inmates**

Jails Usually Have Little Recreational Space

Some Jails Offer Education and Substance Abuse Programs

Some Jails Have Begun Industry Programs

It Is Difficult to Institute Jail Programs

**The Future of the American Jail**

## Review Questions

1. What are the functions of jails and the characteristics of the people who make up the jail populations?

2. Which of the three types of jail design best enhances the supervision of inmates?

3. Which jail characteristics tend to have the greatest impact on security and control?

4. Why do jails screen incoming offenders for medical and mental problems?

5. What steps are taken to identify accurately an offender who is being booked into jail? How are jail inmates classified and why is it so important to do so?

6. What kinds of special needs and problems do inmates have?

7. Why are juveniles at risk in adult jails?

8. What are the characteristics of an effective jail staff and what role does training play in their development?

9. What are the advantages of jail regionalization?

## Test Your Knowledge

1. Early Colonial jails were used primarily for
    a. pretrial detention.
    b. rehabilitation.
    c. punishment.
    d. deterrence.

2. Which of the following jail designs appear to provide the most effective form of inmate supervision?
    a. linear intermittent
    b. podular direct
    c. podular remote
    d. all three are about the same

3. The most common crime for which alcohol abusers are jailed is
    a. homicide.
    b. assault.
    c. disorderly conduct.
    d. driving under the influence.

4. Which of the following programs can be found in contemporary jails:
    a. education
    b. substance abuse
    c. industry programs
    d. all of the above
    e. only a and b.

# CHAPTER 23

# PROBATION AND PAROLE

## ▪ LEARNING OBJECTIVES

*After completion of this chapter, you should be able to:*

**1.** Describe the history of probation including the role played by John Augustus in its development in the United States.

**2.** Discuss the use of risk prediction scales in deciding which offenders should be placed on probation.

**3.** Differentiate between control and treatment conditions.

**4.** Outline the basic organizational arrangements under which probation services are administered in different states and identify the methods that are employed in assigning cases to probation officers.

**5.** Describe the five basic uses of the PSI and the nature of the information that should be included in these reports.

**6.** Contrast the independent and the consolidated models of parole services.

**7.** Describe the types of approaches taken to predicting the success of inmates placed on parole.

**8.** Outline the variety of work roles, supervisory styles, and service delivery strategies engaged in by POs.

**9.** Summarize the general results of studies on the effectiveness of probation and parole and specific types of treatments applied to clients.

**10.** Describe the way in which probation and parole officers are hired, and some of the factors that cause them to "burn out."

## ▪ KEY TERMS AND CONCEPTS

Appointment system of selection
Benefit of clergy
Case worker model
Conditions of probation or parole
Discretionary parole
John Augustus
Judicial reprieve
Law enforcement model
Mandatory release
Merit system of selection
PO stress
Presentence investigation report (PSI)
Recognizance
Resource broker/advocate model
Revocation
Risk prediction scale
Supervision fee

One of the most critical problems affecting corrections, as indicated earlier, is the escalating number of convicted offenders combined with demands to incarcerate more of them. Although prison overcrowding has been a chronic problem, the "drug wars" of the 1980s and 1990s and hardening public attitudes toward criminals have resulted in unprecedented crowding. In spite of massive prison construction during the 1980s and 1990s, there has been a growing space shortage in our prisons due to the crush of inmates resulting from current incarceration policies.

Another contributing factor to overcrowding has been the number of offenders receiving minimum mandatory sentences. These sentences require offenders to serve a specific number of years before being eligible for release. However, lack of space in the early 1990s led to a continuing parade of inmates (those not encumbered with minimum mandatory sentences) being released well before their sentences expire to make room for the more recently convicted ones. This game of "musical cells" has led to public dissatisfaction with corrections, renewed calls for "truth in sentencing," and created pressure to resolve the problem by building more and more prisons. This has escalated the cost of corrections to a point where it may soon become unaffordable.

It would appear that probation and parole (or some type of postprison supervision) have the potential to control the soaring costs of corrections. In this chapter we will explore both probation and parole. Probation is a sentence having the function of keeping the offender from the stigmatizing effects of prison and parole is a shift in the place and type of supervision for an incarcerated offender. Although they serve very different functions, we will treat them in the same chapter because the supervisory processes involved in both are similar and often handled by the same agency. We will refer to both as POs.

## PROBATION AS AN ALTERNATIVE TO IMPRISONMENT

Of the sanctions available to sentencing judges probation is the one most frequently imposed. In the recent past approximately 60% of offenders under correctional supervision have been on probation (U.S. Department of Justice, 1994). Probation is a sentence in which the offender remains in the community under the supervision of a corrections agent and subject to conditions imposed by the court. According to Champion (1990), the correctional philosophy underlying probation gives "offenders . . . the opportunity [to] prov[e] themselves capable of refraining from further criminal activity." (p. 16). This philosophy is in keeping with the meaning of the Latin word *probare*—meaning to prove—from which the term *probation* is derived.

While serving their sentences in the community probationers are under intermittent supervision and have access to the resources and services available in the community. Probation may also provide an economical alternative to imprisonment. One of the major criticisms of probation is that keeping offenders in the community could result in additional criminality. Another criticism is that it is too lenient and may not be a deterrent or even serve a retributive purpose.

Before proceeding, it is important to note that our discussion of probation in this chapter is limited to standard probation. The next chapter addresses the intermediate sanctions that have been developed to fill the gap between regular probation and imprisonment.

## Probation and Its Antecedents Mitigated Harsh Sentences

The practices preceding probation, which emerged in England during the course of several centuries, helped mitigate the harsh punishments in effect then. These practices, which were imported to America by the English settlers, included benefit of clergy, judicial reprieve, and recognizance.

**Benefit of clergy** allowed individuals accused of serious crimes to appeal for leniency by reading the 51st Psalm in court. Benefit of clergy came into widespread use but abuses eventually led to reduction in its use and to its abolition in 1827. It was briefly practiced in America, but quickly fell into disrepute because of its arbitrary nature (Hussey and Duffee, 1980).

**Judicial reprieve** was another way judges exercised discretion. Under this practice, which grew during the nineteenth century, convicted offenders could apply for a temporary suspension of their sentence. Its purpose was to allow a defendant to apply to the Crown for a pardon while at liberty

(United Nations, 1970). In the United States, judicial reprieve was transformed so that in many cases the sentence was suspended indefinitely and the court controlled the defendant over long periods of time. In 1916 the Supreme Court declared this process unconstitutional because it interfered with legislative and executive powers to enact and enforce laws (Ex parte United States, 1916). This ruling had the effect of bringing probation practices under the provisions of state penal codes.

**Recognizance** allowed an offender to be released from custody during court proceedings. This type of release, which is still in use today, releases accused individuals who are awaiting trial from jail.

Probation, as an alternative to incarceration, was impelled by the effort to give judges flexibility and the ability to personalize the punishment process. The state of Massachusetts led the way in this regard through the work of a well-to-do Boston shoemaker and philanthropist who had a strong interest in the court process.

**JOHN AUGUSTUS WAS THE FATHER OF MODERN PROBATION**   John Augustus (1785–1859) was influenced by the temperance movement, a group dedicated to reforming drunks. He often attended sessions in the Boston Municipal Court trying to influence public drunks appearing before the court to change. In 1841 he became the first probation officer (PO) when he intervened in the case of a common drunk who had been convicted and was about to be sentenced to a six-month term in the Boston House of Corrections. Augustus asked the judge to let him supervise the man for three weeks, guaranteeing his later appearance in court and pledging to pay all court costs. The judge agreed and three weeks later Augustus and his charge returned to the courtroom. The judge, impressed with the changes the "probationer" had made, suspended the jail sentence and substituted a small fine. (United Nations, 1951).

From this modest beginning Augustus began to regularly stand bail for and assist a variety of minor offenders in the Boston Municipal Court. He continued this work until 1858, a year before his death. During this time he supervised about 2000 men and women (Lindner and Savarese, 1984; Champion, 1990). His work was not formally evaluated, but Augustus himself indicated that most of his "probationers" eventually led law-abiding lives. His work led to the statutory creation of probation services in Massachusetts. He devised the initial investigative and screening procedures, supervisory practices, and delivery of services to offenders that form the basis of probation today. After his death and until the state of Massachusetts passed probation legislation, the practice of having only volunteers work with the offenders continued (United Nations, 1951; Lindner and Savarese, 1984).

**PROBATION GREW RAPIDLY IN THE EARLY TWENTIETH CENTURY**   It was during the early part of the twentieth century that the probation movement gained momentum. By 1920 every state had passed legislation that permitted juvenile probation, and thirty-three states allowed adult probation. However, it took until 1954 before probation was available to adult offenders in all states (Rothman, 1980; Task Force on Corrections, 1967).

Following World War II, psychological concepts began to be used by POs and rehabilitation was emphasized for the next 25 years. As noted earlier, this approach had limited success, and in the late 1960s was supplanted by the reintegration model and in the 1970s treatment in prison began to be deemphasized. This model stressed placement for offenders within the community because the resources to help them were available there. The reintegration model fit well with probation since it had long been dealing with offenders in the community. However, by the late 1970s reintegration was overtaken by a new emphasis on law and order, which stressed punishment for criminals.

**PROBATION IN THE ERA OF JUST DESERTS**   As the purpose of criminal sanctions in the 1980s and 1990s shifted to retribution and just deserts, so did the focus of probation. This was reflected in the development of the intermediate sanctions described in Chapter 24. It involved a shift from the brokering of treatment services to an emphasis primarily on the strategy of risk management, which was to be accomplished through more intensive supervision and stricter conditions. Due to prison crowding during this time, a greater proportion of felony offenders began to be placed on probation. This has raised questions regarding community safety (Petersilia, 1990) and the extent to which these sanctions subject convicted offenders to retribution when they remain at relative liberty in the community. Thus, the idea of leaving convicted offenders in the community is not viewed favorably by those taking a just deserts approach to corrections.

In spite of this dislike for probation, however, it has prospered during this era for several reasons. These reasons include its popularity among corrections people, its low cost compared with incarceration, and the need for alternatives to incarceration. One problem that has resulted from its growing use is that funding has not kept up with the large number of cases sentenced to probation. McCarthy and McCarthy (1991) comment that the failure of states to provide appropriate resources for probation services to keep up with increased caseloads has resulted in a level of "probation crowding" comparable to that found in prisons.

## Probation Today Is at Record Levels

At the beginning of the 1990s a record number of adults were on probation. According to the U.S. Department of Justice (1994), more than 2.84 million adult offenders were on probation in 1993, representing an estimated 1.8% of all adults and 3.2% of all adult males. There were more than 1.47 million admissions to probation during 1993.

Table 23.1 shows a probation population increase of 1.1% during 1993. Of fifty-two jurisdictions (fifty states, Washington, DC, and the federal system), thirty-six showed increases while the rest decreased. The 1993 national rate was 1490 per 100,000 adults, with the South having the highest rate at 1745. Ten states had rates that were over 2000 per 100,000 adult residents. Although not shown in the table, the number of probationers increased 164% from 1980 to the end of 1990, an increase that is between fifteen and twenty times greater than the population increase in the United States during that period. According to *The Corrections Yearbook* (Camp and Camp, 1994c), as of January 1994 approximately 42% of the probationers were nonwhite and 19% were females.

**A SENTENCE TO PROBATION DEPENDS ON SEVERAL FACTORS**  When defendants are sentenced to probation a decision has to be made regarding ← the structure of the sentence. This decision will involve several variables: the length of the sentence, the level of supervision required by the offender, and the number and nature of the condi-

tions to be imposed. Sentence lengths, for both probation and prison, tend to vary directly with the seriousness of the crime (Cunniff, 1987).

**Risk prediction scales** may be employed to determine the level of supervision required by an offender. As indicated in Chapter 17, these scales attempt to predict the future behavior of offenders and/or the outcome of probation (Gottfredson and Tonry, 1987). Although these scales can select some individuals who will act in the manner predicted, they are never perfect. Thus, some individuals predicted to be successes will not be (false positives) and some who are predicted to be failures will succeed (false negatives). Since not all individuals who are convicted can possibly be sent to prison, any improvement in the predictive process that can reduce the number of both false positives and negatives will result in the most effective placement of offenders.

Risk assessment scales are used almost universally in the United States. Wisconsin pioneered the use of risk/needs assessment scales to assign probationers to various levels of supervision. The Wisconsin model included five components: a risk assessment scale, a needs assessment scale, a workload budgeting and deployment system, a management information system, and a standard reclassification process. When implemented in Wisconsin, this model had an impact on:

1. *How often cases were seen:* Based on both risk and need assessment scale scores, three levels of contact were developed (i.e., every 14 days, every 30 days, every 90 days).
2. *Planning and evaluation capabilities:* Information generated during the entire process of assessment and supervision was used for future planning.
3. *The Bureau of Community Corrections budgeting process:* Provided data on statewide PO workloads.
4. *Accountability measures:* This was accomplished by identifying client needs and providing information as to how well these needs were met (National Institute of Corrections, 1981b).

The risk assessment part of the scale was generally found to separate low-, medium-, and high-risk offenders moderately well in terms of predicting recidivism. It also did significantly better when compared with POs' intuitive judgments (Brown, 1984; Baird, Heinz, and Bemus, 1982). However, the

TABLE 23.1   Adults on Probation, 1993

| Region and Jurisdiction | Probation Population 1/1/93 | 1993 Entries | 1993 Exits | Probation Population, 12/31/93 | Percent Change in Probation Population, During 1993 | Number on Probation on 12/31/93 per 100,000 Adult Residents |
|---|---|---|---|---|---|---|
| **U.S. total** | 2,811,611 | 1,478,002 | 1,431,915 | 2,843,445 | 1.1% | 1,490 |
| Federal | 46,485 | 25,544 | 29,030 | 43,095 | −7.3 | 23 |
| State | 2,765,126 | 1,425,458 | 1,402,885 | 2,800,350 | 1.3 | 1,468 |
| **Northeast** | 481,594 | 209,321 | 200,606 | 487,861 | 1.3% | 1,252 |
| Connecticut | 48,567 | 28,520 | 26,183 | 50,904 | 4.8 | 2,035 |
| Maine | 8,942 | N/A | N/A | 8,650 | −3.3 | 928 |
| Massachusetts | 48,312 | 35,892 | 37,054 | 47,150 | −2.4 | 1,021 |
| New Hampshire | 4,104 | 2,061 | 2,043 | 4,122 | .4 | 490 |
| New Jersey | 108,093 | 43,151 | 41,668 | 109,576 | 1.4 | 1,831 |
| New York | 152,013 | 46,508 | 41,904 | 156,617 | 3.0 | 1,141 |
| Pennsylvania | 89,944 | 40,502 | 42,266 | 88,180 | −2.0 | 961 |
| Rhode Island[a,c] | 15,585 | 9,318 | 6,743 | 16,604 | 6.5 | 2,170 |
| Vermont[a] | 6,034 | 3,369 | 2,745 | 6,058 | .4 | 1,402 |
| **Midwest** | 589,858 | 395,481 | 381,230 | 603,391 | 2.3% | 1,341 |
| Illinois | 76,125 | 62,400 | 64,975 | 73,550 | −3.4 | 852 |
| Indiana | 79,850 | 71,326 | 68,372 | 82,804 | 3.7 | 1,951 |
| Iowa[a] | 14,084 | 10,088 | 9,620 | 14,505 | 3.0 | 697 |
| Kansas | 23,994 | 13,181 | 13,092 | 24,083 | .4 | 1,304 |
| Michigan[a] | 135,012 | 69,431 | 64,412 | 139,682 | 3.5 | 2,003 |
| Minnesota | 72,938 | 53,422 | 52,174 | 74,186 | 1.7 | 2,256 |
| Missouri[a] | 32,629 | 14,536 | 14,239 | 32,916 | .9 | 850 |
| Nebraska | 15,386 | 15,032 | 15,824 | 14,594 | −5.1 | 1,249 |
| North Dakota | 1,920 | 1,091 | 1,057 | 1,954 | 1.8 | 422 |
| Ohio[a] | 94,129 | 61,646 | 57,252 | 98,211 | 4.3 | 1,193 |
| South Dakota[b] | 3,367 | 4,307 | 3,893 | 3,781 | 12.3 | 746 |
| Wisconsin | 40,424 | 19,021 | 16,320 | 43,125 | 6.7 | 1,167 |
| **South** | 1,135,326 | 573,094 | 538,382 | 1,155,168 | 1.7% | 1,745 |
| Alabama[a] | 31,188 | 9,369 | 3,958 | 33,721 | 8.1 | 1,084 |
| Arkansas | 16,448 | 5,909 | 4,830 | 17,527 | 6.6 | 980 |
| Delaware | 14,887 | 7,992 | 7,308 | 15,571 | 4.6 | 2,966 |
| District of Columbia | 10,607 | 5,961 | 6,134 | 10,434 | −1.6 | 2,254 |
| Florida[a] | 200,471 | 123,648 | 112,363 | 199,275 | −.6 | 1,896 |
| Georgia | 153,154 | 67,597 | 75,521 | 145,230 | −5.2 | 2,861 |
| Kentucky | 10,750 | 6,230 | 5,522 | 11,458 | 6.6 | 407 |
| Louisiana | 30,468 | 12,324 | 10,358 | 32,434 | 6.5 | 1,063 |
| Maryland | 82,948 | 36,670 | 39,410 | 80,208 | −3.3 | 2,154 |
| Mississippi[a] | 8,031 | 4,644 | 3,266 | 9,943 | 23.8 | 527 |
| North Carolina | 86,371 | 43,977 | 44,136 | 86,212 | −.2 | 1,645 |
| Oklahoma[a] | 25,902 | 11,750 | 11,918 | 25,689 | −.8 | 1,088 |
| South Carolina | 35,587 | 16,481 | 13,213 | 38,855 | 9.2 | 1,444 |
| Tennessee | 38,614 | 25,608 | 23,759 | 40,463 | 4.8 | 1,056 |
| Texas | 360,702 | 173,485 | 155,664 | 378,523 | 4.9 | 2,946 |
| Virginia | 23,510 | 18,547 | 18,438 | 23,619 | .5 | 482 |
| West Virginia | 5,688 | 2,902 | 2,584 | 6,006 | 5.6 | 433 |

TABLE 23.1, CONTINUED **Adults on Probation, 1993**

| Region and Jurisdiction | Probation Population 1/1/93 | 1993 Entries | 1993 Exits | Probation Population, 12/31/93 | Percent Change in Probation Population, During 1993 | Number on Probation on 12/31/93 per 100,000 Adult Residents |
|---|---|---|---|---|---|---|
| **West** | 558,348 | 274,562 | 282,667 | 553,930 | −.8% | 1,365 |
| Alaska | 3,014 | 720 | 520 | 3,214 | 6.6 | 784 |
| Arizona | 34,647 | 13,144 | 10,976 | 36,815 | 6.3 | 1,285 |
| California | 300,635 | 165,791 | 185,677 | 280,749 | −6.6 | 1,241 |
| Colorado[a] | 33,700 | 23,132 | 22,274 | 35,494 | 5.3 | 1,351 |
| Hawaii | 10,038 | 6,066 | 6,004 | 10,100 | .6 | 1,157 |
| Idaho | 4,075 | 2,338 | 1,664 | 4,749 | 16.5 | 620 |
| Montana | 3,948 | N/A | 1,463 | 4,107 | 4.0 | 677 |
| Nevada | 8,533 | 3,772 | 3,479 | 8,826 | 3.4 | 851 |
| New Mexico[a] | 6,921 | 5,855 | 7,503 | 7,673 | 10.9 | 676 |
| Oregon | 39,019 | 11,328 | 12,445 | 37,902 | −2.9 | 1,685 |
| Utah | 6,671 | 3,866 | 3,212 | 7,325 | 9.8 | 613 |
| Washington[a] | 103,837 | 37,313 | 25,861 | 114,018 | 9.8 | 2,952 |
| Wyoming | 3,310 | 1,237 | 1,589 | 2,958 | −10.6 | 891 |

[a] Because of nonresponse, or lack of data, the population on 1/1/93 plus entries, minus exits, does not equal the population on 12/31/93.
[b] Numbers are for fiscal year 7/1/92 to 6/30/93.
[c] Numbers are for fiscal year 7/1/93 to 6/30/94.
SOURCE: Adapted from U.S. Deptartment of Justice (1994, September 11), *Probation and Parole Populations Reach New Highs*, U.S. Department of Justice, Washington, DC.

needs assessment part of the scale was found to have little predictive value (Program Services Office, 1983).

**CONDITIONS ARE THE LIMITS PLACED ON PROBATIONERS** Conditions of probation are imposed on all probationers as part of their sentences. Normally, there are two types of conditions imposed: control and treatment. Control conditions are imposed on all probationers and include:

obeying laws, not associating with known criminals, reporting regularly to the probation officer, submitting to searches, not possessing firearms, not using alcohol excessively, not leaving the jurisdiction without permission and otherwise reporting any significant changes in status (e.g., residence, employment) to the probation officer.

Treatment conditions are made to fit the problems and needs of the offender. These may include:

psychiatric treatment, payment of restitution, participation in a community work program, maintenance of employment, involvement in Alcoholics Anony-

mous, observing a curfew, participation in a training or educational program and any other specific prohibitions or requirements which the court may see fit.

The conditions imposed on offenders are supposed to help them successfully complete the probation sentence.

Financial penalties are another distinctive category of probation conditions. These include court costs, probation supervision fees, restitution, and other fees.[1] With correctional costs soaring, making convicted offenders contribute to the costs of their own supervision has gained widespread political support (Parent, 1990a). In 1991, probation agencies in twenty-eight states had statutory authority to collect fees from probationers with another seven states considering implementing them (Davis, 1991). Parent (1990a) found that these fees averaged between $20 to $25 per month and ranged from $10 to $50. In looking at the impact of fee collection on agency budgets, Parent (1990a) found that in ten jurisdictions probation agencies retained the money collected. The amounts collected made up from 3% to about half of their budgets.

With respect to conditions, a very important function of the PO is to make sure that probationers understand and adhere to the conditions placed on them. Thus, they must explain each of the conditions to their clients and inform them of the consequences (revocation of their probation) for failing to follow them.

### The Organization and Administration of Probation Services

Originally, probation services were administered by county courts. This arrangement was carried forward into the early part of the twentieth century during the development of juvenile courts. As the adult probation system expanded, however, different organizational arrangements were tried. Today there are five organizational variations of probation services across the United States. These are (1) within the state executive branch,(2) within local (county or municipal governments) executive departments, (3) under the state judiciary, (4) under local courts, and (5) under various combinations of the first four.. Thus, within each state, arrangements for probation services are either centralized (i.e., under the administration of a state agency) or decentralized (i.e., under the administration of county or municipal agency); in the judicial area or in the executive area; under the umbrella of the correctional system or separate from it; or combined with the parole function or separate from it.

The most popular form is a centralized arrangement within the executive branch under the supervision of the state department of corrections (Abadinsky, 1994). The major argument for centralization is that a uniform standard of services is available in a state compared with local programs. When probation services are combined with other state correctional services, consistency and continuity in the policies affecting all correctional services can be achieved.

Arguments for judicial and local placement of probation point out that it is a judicial disposition that should be overseen by the court. They also assert that community support for programs will be stronger when they are responsive to its input, which is obviously more likely if decisions are made locally. Flexibility will be enhanced because

there is no large, rigid bureaucratic structure with which to deal (Nelson, Ohmart, and Harlow, 1978).

**CASELOAD SIZE DETERMINES THE LEVEL OF SUPERVISION** As early as 1917 the issue of caseload size surfaced and an optimum figure of fifty cases per officer first appeared in the literature. This figure was not based on research but on the opinion of probation directors at this time. While better service and lower recidivism rates would seem to result from lower caseloads, this was too simple an answer for a fairly complex problem.

More than two decades ago, the San Francisco Project dispelled the myth that smaller caseload size improved probation effectiveness. (Robinson, Wilkins, Carter, and Wahl, 1969). This study found almost identical violation rates in caseload sizes ranging from 50 to 250. The conclusion was that the concept of caseload was meaningless without some type of classification and matching of offender type, service to be offered, and staff (Task Force on Corrections, 1973). In 1993 the average regular caseload in forty-six jurisdictions responding to a survey was 118, ranging from a high of 400 in California to a low of 13 in South Dakota (Camp and Camp, 1994c).[2]

**CASELOAD ASSIGNMENTS ARE MADE IN SEVERAL WAYS** Probation departments employ various methods of assigning cases to their officers. In some offices cases may be assigned on a random basis. That is, as cases come into the office they are assigned to probation staff. This is the most inefficient and least effective method of assignment. In some offices cases are assigned by geographic area. A PO supervises all probationers who live within a defined area. This type of arrangement may yield a more efficiently served caseload for probation officers in that they will travel less and get to know the area in which their clients live better. A third method of assigning clients is to attempt to match clients who have particular kinds of problems (e.g., drug abuse), with officers who may have special skills in dealing with them. A final way of assigning cases is based on classification. Here, each case is assigned on the basis of the level of supervision predicted, and PO caseloads are balanced on this basis. While this approach is rational, it is difficult to maintain (Abadinsky, 1994; McCarthy and McCarthy, 1991).

## The Presentence Investigation Is an Important Probation Officer Activity

At the beginning of the chapter, we alluded to the major services provided by probation officers—investigative and supervisory. We will discuss the investigative function in this section. Depending on state statutes or on the discretion of the sentencing judge, an investigation of the defendant may be conducted after conviction but before sentencing. The fruits of this investigation are embodied in the **presentence investigation report (PSI).**

**THE PSI HELPS IN SENTENCING AND TREATMENT**   The PSI has five basic purposes each of which may serve a different set of constituents.

**1.** To help the sentencing judge make the most appropriate sentence.
**2.** To establish a probation or parole supervision and treatment plan for the offender regardless of the type of sentencing disposition.
**3.** To help jail and prison personnel classify the offender.
**4.** To provide parole authorities with information that can be used in release planning including special conditions needed to insure greater success for the parolee.
**5.** To serve as a rich source of information to criminal justice and correctional researchers. (Abadinsky, 1994; Champion, 1990; McCarthy and McCarthy, 1991).

**THE PSI REQUIRES A LOT OF INFORMATION**
The information for the PSI comes from interviews with the offender, his/her family, teachers, police, etc., and from an examination of various offender records and reports. The records to be reviewed include the individual's arrest record, the police offense report, previous PSI reports, records of previous institutionalization, educational records, reports of psychological/psychiatric evaluations, and any records of treatment. From these sources the PO should develop a report that contains:

**1.** A complete account of the offense and the attendant circumstances
**2.** A description of the victim's status (impact of the crime, losses suffered, restitution due) and a statement from the victim
**3.** The offender's criminal history including juvenile training school reports

**4.** The offender's educational history and employment, including present levels of functioning
**5.** Family background, social history, marital status, dependents, religious affiliations, interests and activities, medical and psychiatric history
**6.** Special resources that might be available to assist the offender (e.g., treatment centers, special educational or vocational programs, etc.)
**7.** A summary of the significant information and the specific recommendations regarding sentencing and service needs.

The value of the PO's work lies in the significant weight his or her recommendations are likely to carry with the judge. This is as it should be because the PO has had the opportunity to see the offender in the community and develop a perspective on his or her "general lifestyle" (Carter, 1966). From this the PO has to evaluate the risks posed by the offender to the community and make decisions about several issues:

**1.** The nature of the recommended sentence: probation? prison?
**2.** The level of security required with a prison sentence
**3.** The defendant's rehabilitative potential
**4.** Any negative public reaction to a sentence of probation.

**ISSUES RELATED TO THE PSI**   The question has arisen as to whether the contents of PSIs should be disclosed to defendants and their attorneys to contest damaging information. The present trend is to make the PSI available to the defendant omitting the following: the PO's recommendations, diagnostic information that might seriously disrupt a rehabilitation program, information collected under the promise of confidentiality, and other information that could be deemed "harmful" to the defendant or others (Adair and Slawsk, 1991).

A number of criticisms have been leveled at PSI reports. Among these are that many POs are so overloaded with cases and investigations that they may not have time to produce adequate reports; judges may misuse PSIs because they may feel the information may be based on hearsay and rumor and thus distrust it; and misinformation and incomplete information may make a number of PSIs misleading (Blumberg, 1970; Dickey, 1979).

Another criticism leveled at the PSI concerns the accuracy of the diagnostic information in the report. These reports may contain clinical "impressions" regarding the subject that could be taken as fact. These "impressions" tend to be relatively unreliable in that another clinician interviewing the same subject may come to very different conclusions (Robitscher, 1980). Finally, there are for-profit agencies in some areas that prepare PSI studies on commission. This can produce a problem with respect to equal justice in that only the well-to-do can afford the required fee to commission private PSIs. (Abadinsky, 1994; McShane and Krause, 1993).

## PAROLE IS SERVED IN THE COMMUNITY

Parole involves the conditional release of inmates from prison to serve the remainder of their sentences under community correctional supervision. Normally, parole is associated with indeterminate sentences and is granted to inmates by a legally constituted parole board when they have served a prescribed minimum portion of their sentences and met certain behavioral criteria within the prison. While parole is not a sentence, it is a legal status.

Parole can fit well in either the rehabilitation or reintegration models of corrections. Because successful program participation and good behavior within the prison are prerequisites for parole consideration, there is a natural relation to rehabilitation. The fact that inmates serve part of their sentence in the community adheres to the tenets of the reintegration model. Whatever the model under which it is subsumed, parole has played an important part in the American correctional process for more than 100 years. In this section we discuss parole in terms of its development in the United States, its status today, and organization and administration.

The term *parole* comes from the French phrase *parole d'honneur*, which means "word of honor." The French used the term to denote the release of an inmate for good behavior and, based on his word of honor, that he would obey the law upon release. The roots of parole can be traced to the practices of clemency, indenture, and transportation. Each of these practices, at least in some instances, included a conditional form of release

from a penal sanction. Parole as we know it today in the United States evolved largely from practices initiated during the middle of the nineteenth century by Alexander Maconochie and Walter Crofton, whose work was described in detail in Chapter 4.

The mark system developed by Maconochie was similar to the indeterminate sentences that were developed to accompany parole in the United States. That is, it assumed that an inmate would be released from incarceration on the basis of his behavior rather than as a mere function of serving time. However, Maconochie felt that release should be unconditional (i.e., not supervised) so his system was not a direct forerunner of parole. That distinction fell upon Walter Crofton's adaptation of Maconochie's mark system for the Irish prisons. It was in this context that conditional postrelease supervision was developed.

### Developments in the United States Resulted from Changes in Philosophy

In the United States, prior to the use of parole, early release usually involved a governor's power to commute sentences and pardon inmates. Commutation was first used in 1817, when New York enacted a law permitting a 25% sentence reduction for first-time offenders serving five years or less (Burns, 1975).

In the 1870s, as noted in Chapter 4, based on the work of Maconochie and Crofton and the reforms suggested at the Cincinnati meeting, the state of New York began planning the Elmira Reformatory and introduced indeterminate sentences. The Elmira Reformatory opened in 1876 as a separate institution for youthful offenders. To be eligible for release, inmates there had to have jobs waiting for them. Releasees were supervised by volunteers, since there were no paid parole officers at that time (Pisciotta, 1983).

By 1900 approximately twenty states had enacted parole statutes. However, it was not until 1944 that every state had a parole system. The development of parole was helped by several factors. First, the parole concept was strongly supported by the correctional community. Secondly, discretionary release of inmates allowed prison authorities to better control disciplinary problems, stimulate inmate reform, and relieve overcrowding. Finally, the wide use of pardons in many states made it easy to shift to granting releases based on inmates' progress in prison.

**THE RETURN TO RETRIBUTION REDUCED DISCRETIONARY PAROLE**   As rehabilitation declined and was replaced by retribution, determinate sentencing statutes in many states led to a significant decline in the use of **discretionary parole,** release of an inmate at the discretion of a parole board. Many states that abolished discretionary parole adopted a procedure called (supervised) **mandatory release.** In this form of release inmates are placed under the supervision of a parole officer after they have served their original sentences minus earned or administratively awarded good time. The difference between parole and supervised mandatory release is that in the former a parole board makes the release decision, whereas in the latter it is made by a corrections official. Both types of releasees are treated similarly in that they must adhere to specified conditions and are supervised by a parole officer in the community after release (McCarthy and McCarthy, 1991; McShane and Krause, 1993).

### Today the Number of Parolees Is at an All-Time High

At the end of 1993 there were 671,470 adult offenders on some form of parole supervision in the United States (U.S. Department of Justice, 1994). This figure, a record high number, represents a 2% increase over 1992 and a 205% increase over the 1980 figure. According to Camp and Camp (1994c), at the beginning of 1994 53% of the parolees were nonwhite and 9.3% were female.

**THERE ARE SEVERAL TYPES OF RELEASE FROM PRISON**   Release from prison can be either conditional or unconditional. Conditional releases typically include parole, supervised mandatory release, and supervised work furloughs. The vast majority of unconditional releases occur at the expiration of inmates' sentences and most of the rest are a result of commutation. Since the late 1970s the proportion of inmates given conditional releases from prison has remained relatively stable (between 80 and 85% of all releases). However, the proportion of those released on discretionary parole has declined steadily since 1977 (from 71.9 to 40.1% in 1992), whereas supervised mandatory

releases have increased commensurately (Jankowski, 1991; Snell 1995).

### The Organization and Administration of Parole Services

Three basic services can be offered to inmates by a parole agency: release, supervision, and executive clemency. Compared with probation services, parole services are more uniformly organized in that they are centrally administered at the state level and lie within the executive branch of government.

**PAROLE IS AN EXECUTIVE FUNCTION**   Parole services are administered based on one of two models: the independent model or the consolidated model. Those that operate under the independent model may have different names in the various states (e.g., Parole Board, Parole Commission, Board of Pardons, etc.). These autonomous units have the power to make parole release decisions and to supervise all conditionally released inmates (Task Force on Corrections, 1967).

Under the consolidated model, parole services are in the state Department of Corrections and authority is split between these two administrative units. Thus, the parole authority makes release decisions and the Department of Corrections supervises all conditionally released inmates. Parole and probation supervisory services are combined under this model in states that have centralized probation services.

**THE PAROLE BOARD MAKES THE PAROLE DECISION**   In states with parole boards, members are usually appointed by the governor. Board size varies from three to fifteen members. Only a few states require any special qualifications for its parole board members (e.g., a bachelor's degree) (Parker, 1975).

In deciding whether to release an inmate, parole authorities often consider the protection of society from predatory criminals as their first responsibility. This raises the question of the predictive power of risk assessment scales, a topic discussed in Chapter 17. Release is granted or denied based on an evaluation of information that is obtained either through hearings and interviews, usually within the institutions served by the board, and/or through reviews of institutional reports. In most states the potential parolee is briefly interviewed

POs visit their clients at home to determine their compliance with the conditions of their probation or parole.

by board members or by hearing examiners who report their recommendations back to the board.

**OBJECTIVE PAROLE CRITERIA AND GUIDELINES HELP IN MAKING THE DECISION** The development of guidelines has been of great assistance to parole boards in making release decisions. Parole boards have used the following criteria in the past: the nature of the crime committed by the inmate, time served with respect to the sentence received, the inmate's age, history of substance abuse, criminal history including previous sanctions received, and adjustment and program participation.

In creating guidelines to be used in making parole decisions, a process similar to that used for constructing sentencing guidelines has been employed. These guidelines attempt to more accurately gauge the risk the parolee poses for the community (Clear, 1988).

## SUPERVISION AND SERVICE DELIVERY TO PROBATIONERS AND PAROLEES

The second major function of probation officers, and the singular function of parole officers, is the supervision of offenders placed on probation or granted parole. There are two major duties required in client supervision: surveillance, or controlling the offender, and providing social services. The first duty is similar to that of a police officer, while the second is akin to that of a social worker. These two duties appear to put POs in conflicting positions with respect to their clients and may create a dilemma. If law enforcement is emphasized, clients may develop a distrust of the PO and reject their efforts to provide help. On the other hand, by emphasizing helping, POs may overlook the risks clients are presenting to themselves or the community. Most POs probably develop an approach to supervision that lies between these two extremes.

### PO Strategies Balance Surveillance and Service

There are three major models under which POs deliver supervisory services to their clients: the law enforcement model, the case worker model, and the resource broker/advocate model (McCarthy and McCarthy, 1991; Abadinsky, 1994).

**THE PROBATION/PAROLE OFFICER AS A LAW ENFORCEMENT AGENT** Under the **law enforcement model,** law enforcement-oriented POs operate

---

*Close Up*  **Should POs Be Armed?**

As a private citizen with a working knowledge of probation and parole, I have certain concerns about personal safety—that of my family, friends, and neighbors. It is from this (I believe typical) layperson's perspective that I evaluate a p/p agency. Let me provide some typical examples. It is not unusual during the course of an office or home visit for a p/p officer to discover that a client is using heroin or cocaine. If the offender is unemployed, the drug habit is probably financed by criminal activities—the client is a clear and present danger to him- or herself and to the community. A p/p agency whose officers cannot immediately (and safely) arrest such an individual is not providing an adequate level of client service or community protection. P/p agencies also supervise offenders who have been involved in (1) sex offenses against children, (2) vehicular homicide as a result of intoxication, (3) burglary, and (4) armed robbery. A p/p agency whose officers have no responsibility to enforce prohibitions, through investigation and arrest, against (1) frequenting play areas, (2) drinking and driving, (3) carrying tools for forced entry, or who cannot (4) investigate money or a lifestyle that cannot be supported by the offender's employment status, is not providing the minimum acceptable level of community safety. Furthermore, the adult p/p client is a serious law violator who has proved to be a potential danger to the community. Many have been involved in crimes of violence, and the public and elected officials expect that probationers and parolees, if they are to remain in the community, will be under the scrutiny of p/p authorities. This is why the law of most jurisdictions empowers p/p agencies with law enforcement responsibilities (Abadinsky, 1994, pp. 341–342).[a]

Given Abadinsky's concerns do you think POs should be armed? What are the positive and negative aspects of arming POs?

Source: H. Abadinsky (1994). *Probation and Parole-Theory and Practice*, 5th ed. Englewood Cliffs, NJ: Prentice Hall.

---

under the control model of supervision (Abadinsky, 1994). This approach to supervision has become more popular and heavily used since the advent of retribution and the implementation of risk control strategies. There is considerable controversy related to this approach in that its emphasis is tilted toward surveillance and arrest activities. This tends to place POs in dangerous situations. The controversy arises because many jurisdictions in which POs are expected to be law enforcers or peace officers discourage the use of firearms in carrying out their duties. According to Parsonage (1990), however, the practice of allowing POs to carry a weapon is becoming more common.

Abadinsky is a strong advocate of both the law enforcement approach and the need for POs to carry firearms. His notions, described in the Close-Up on "Should POs be Armed?" are not only based on years of studying this area but are also drawn from his experiences as a parole officer in New York City.

**THE PROBATION/PAROLE OFFICER AS A CASE-WORKER**  The **case worker model** is centered on the provision of treatment/counseling and focuses on the development of a one-to-one relationship between the PO and the client. In developing this relationship the PO encourages rapport and trust. When clients develop trust in their POs, they may be positively influenced by them. This harkens back to John Augustus, whose work with offenders was based on the positive helping role. Allen, Eskridge, Latessa, and Vito (1985) describe this approach in the following way:

Casework is a way of working with individuals. It is consciously chosen to help the offender become better adjusted to the demands of social living. Casework in probation and parole follows the traditional medical model and remains intact in most probation and parole agencies. In reality, however, the supervising officer does not have the time or energy to devote to individual cases. Perhaps the most basic criticisms of the casework approach are that the probation or parole officer tries to be all things to all people, and does not adequately mobilize the community and its support systems. In addition, large caseloads, staff shortages, and endless report writing leave the supervising officer unable to perform all the tasks called for by casework. Coupled with the trend away from the medical model, probation and parole administrators have initiated—the brokerage approach (Allen *et al.*, 1985, p. 175).

**THE PROBATION/PAROLE OFFICER AS A RE-SOURCE BROKER/ADVOCATE** Under the **resource broker/advocate model**, POs are not required to have the time or skills to treat their clients. In place of that, they act as referral agents. Thus, they must identify client needs and problems and find the community agencies that can help meet them. A motivational tool that is often used in this approach is to have clients participate in the development of the plan to deal with their needs and problems. Beyond referring clients to community resources POs also act as advocates, supervise them, and monitor their progress. In this approach a PO's relationship with community service agencies is more important than the relationship with clients (Culbertson and Ellsworth, 1985; McShane and Krause, 1993).

The brokerage approach is based on the reintegration model. It assumes that the community is the most logical place for clients to receive the services necessary to complete probation or parole successfully. It emphasizes rehabilitation, but removes the PO from having to provide the services directly. It also has the potential to reduce the conflict inherent in the PO role. However, it also has drawbacks. The PO–client relationship is not very strong and this reduces the POs' ability to influence clients. Additionally, needed services may not be available within the community or agencies may refuse to take criminal clients. Where these conditions exist, the effectiveness of this approach will be reduced.

## Probation or Parole Can Be Revoked for Violations

When probationers or parolees fail to live up to the conditions in their contracts they can be subjected to revocation proceedings. For both probationers and parolees POs have the authority to recommend and begin the process, but the actual power

to revoke an offender's probation is in the hands of the sentencing judge. For parolees it is done by either the parole board or hearing officers. Normally, revocation can result from two types of violations, those that deal with lawbreaking and those that are technical (i.e., a violation of one or more of the conditions of the probation/parole contract). The parties involved in revocation (the PO, the hearing body, the judge) have considerable discretion. Clients are not automatically revoked when they fail to abide by some of the conditions of their contracts. If an offender violates conditions the PO can ignore it, take informal action (e.g., reprimand the offender), or report it to the sentencing judge or parole authority. If a decision is made to revoke, a formal process controlled by guidelines set by the Supreme Court must be followed.

**SEVERAL COURT DECISIONS HAVE AFFECTED THE REVOCATION PROCESS** In *Mempa v. Rhay* (1967) the Supreme Court ruled probationers are entitled to counsel at revocation hearings. This decision was important because it was the first time the Court recognized the rights of probationers. Two Court decisions in the early 1970s provided the present guidelines used in revocation hearings. The first of these decisions was *Morrissey v. Brewer* (1972), which applied to parole revocation proceedings. The due process protections that were established for parolees were extended to probationers a year later in *Gagnon v. Scarpelli*, (1973). These two cases mandated that probationers and parolees be provided with the right to a two-stage hearing, including due process protections, during revocation proceedings. In the first hearing a determination is made as to whether probable cause exists that the probationer or parolee violated any specific conditions of their contract. The second hearing consists of the general revocation proceeding. During both hearings the offender is guaranteed basic due process rights.

In parole hearings, counsel is not guaranteed but rather is decided on a case-by-case basis by the hearing body, taking into consideration the fact that uneducated clients might have difficulty presenting their version of disputed facts, particularly if the issues involved were complex, and cases in which the violation is not disputed but there are substantial reasons to justify or mitigate it. Also when required, counsel will be appointed for indigent violators (Palmer, 1991). Table 23.2 provides

TABLE 23.2  **Procedural Due Process Routinely Provided at Parole Revocation Hearings**

| Due Process Protection | Preliminary Hearing | | Final Hearing | |
|---|---|---|---|---|
| | # | % | # | % |
| Written notice of alleged violation | 45 | 88.2 | 51 | 100.0 |
| Disclosure of evidence of violations | 42 | 82.4 | 51 | 100.0 |
| Opportunity to confront and cross-examine adverse witnesses | 44 | 86.3 | 47 | 92.2 |
| Representation by counsel | 31 | 60.8 | 40 | 78.4 |
| Opportunity to be heard in person and to present evidence and witnesses | 43 | 84.3 | 51 | 100.0 |
| Written statement of reasons for the decision | 45 | 88.2 | 48 | 94.1 |

Adapted with permission from E. E. Rhine, W. R. Smith, and R. W. Jackson (1991), *Paroling Authorities: Recent History and Current Practice,* American Correctional Association, Laurel, MD[b]

TABLE 23.3  **Probation and Parole Revocations, 1993**

| | New Crimes | Technical Violations | Other Reasons | Total |
|---|---|---|---|---|
| Probation | 44,061 | 59,483 | 37,387 | 141,944 |
| Parole | 72,788 | 43,009 | 30,196 | 147,476 |

*Note:* The total presented is larger than the sum of the figures associated with the causes because some of the jurisdictions included in the survey only reported total figures.

Data taken from G. M. Camp and C. G. Camp (1994); *The Corrections Yearbook* Parole and Probation, Criminal Justice Institute, South Salem, NY, were used to construct this table.

the data on the procedural protections accorded parolees drawn from a national survey conducted by ACA of Parole Boards in 1988.

**REVOCATION RESEARCH SHOWS A STRONG SUBSTANCE ABUSE INFLUENCE**  Parolees and probationers are revoked for a variety of reasons. Research reviewed by Champion (1990) suggests that the most frequent reasons include arrest for a new crime, alcohol or drug abuse, escape, possession of weapons, traffic violations, and difficulties with probation/parole officers or halfway house staff.

Table 23.3 presents data reported in *The Corrections Yearbook* on probation and parole revocations in a variety of jurisdictions during 1993. From the figures presented it can be deduced that about 31% of probationers were revoked for new crimes, and close to 50% of the parolees were revoked for that reason. Although these data are not complete, they indicate parolees pose a greater threat proportionately since more are revoked for committing new crimes.

Revocations of offenders on probation or parole rose sharply between 1980 and 1990. According to

a survey conducted by Parent, Wentworth, Burke, and Ney (1994), in many states more persons are admitted to prison after revocation than are sentenced directly for a crime. Parent *et al.* feel that two factors account for this: the very large number of offenders on probation and parole, and increased emphasis on surveillance with better ways to detect violators. The large rise in revocations has contributed significantly to the problem of prison crowding, which, in turn, has led to early releases for many of those revoked. An additional problem has been to tend to disregard those supervisees who abscond. The discretionary manner in which these problems were handled within and across jurisdictions led to discrepancies in the way in which these cases were disposed of.

Several reforms have begun to be implemented to restructure the process:

**1.** Development of written policies regarding revocations. In states where this has been done (e.g., South Carolina), the policies: generally covered the goals of the agency, had clear definitions of the different categories of violations, and guidelines that matched categories of violations with sanctions (e.g., which violations deserve revocation, which deserve imprisonment, which deserve to remain in the community under increased supervision, etc.).

**2.** Refining procedures by which agency goals are to be accomplished. This included such things as spelling out in greater detail the types of enforcement actions POs may take on their own and those that require approval.

**3.** Expanding the choices of sanctions available to the agency. Thus, instead of just having the option of continuing supervision or imprisonment, which might be too lenient or too harsh, the whole range of community sanctions might be used.

**4.** For absconders, a more active approach has been developed in order to apprehend them. This new approach includes an expansion of POs' responsibility in trying to contact them, a greater use of existing sources of information (e.g., driver's license bureau), the development of enhanced fugitive units which target specific absconders for apprehension, and finally, the development of sanctions to match absconder risk, rather than just placing all apprehended absconders in prison (Parent *et al*, 1994).

Finally, a means of reducing the number of revocations is for POs to develop reasonable and understandable rules for clients to follow. Success can be further enhanced by specifying client objectives, defining their importance, and identifying appropriate resources to assist in their achievement. Revocation can be greatly reduced if court or parole board objectives are translated into concrete behavioral expectations that clients can understand and meet. For example, if the court orders a client to pay restitution to the victim, this can be translated into the following requirement: The client will pay the victim at least $15 per week until the amount of $575 is paid (Cohn, 1987).

### The Effectiveness of Probation/Parole Supervision

The effectiveness of correctional strategies, including probation and parole, should be measured in terms of their goals. Generally, probation and parole agencies measure effectiveness in terms of revocation and/or recidivism. Both measures have been criticized because they have shortcomings.

**MEASUREMENT PROBLEMS MAKE EVALUATION DIFFICULT** To begin with, both revocation and recidivism tend to be defined differently in different agencies (Albanese, Fiore, Powell and Storti, 1981; Maltz, 1984). Generally, **revocation** of probation or parole involves a termination of that status for cause and is likely to result either in the imposition of more stringent conditions and supervision or imprisonment. Recidivism is variously defined in terms of either a rearrest, a reconviction, or a reincarceration. The disparities in these definitions make cross-agency comparisons difficult at best and meaningless at worst. Waldo and Griswold (1979) consider that arrest and conviction for any crime is not a sufficient condition for the strict definition of recidivism. This is because rearrest of the client may result from a variety of situations that are more or less serious (e.g., a technical violation of probation or parole conditions). Additionally, the arrested client may not even be guilty. To consider an example, if revocation occurs because the client is unable or refuses to maintain employment, this will have a significantly different meaning than if it is due to an arrest for armed robbery. Yet in the gross measure of agency success both may be counted as recidivists.

As an additional consideration, McCarthy and McCarthy (1991) note that PO discretion in their responses to the violation of conditions will affect revocation. Thus, service-oriented POs may overlook relatively minor violations because they feel that the beneficial effects of remaining in the community outweigh those of imprisonment. Law enforcement-oriented officers may take the opposite tack and revoke offenders for the same violation. These considerations can also apply at the agency level, depending on its policy.

**EFFECTIVENESS STUDIES SHOW RELATIVELY HIGH LEVELS OF RECIDIVISM** Reviews of probation effectiveness studies (e.g., Geerken and Hayes, 1993; Allen, Carlson, and Parks, 1979) have indicated that findings are inconsistent. This inconsistency is the case whether probation was compared with other sanctions, whether the recidivism rates were only for probation, or whether factors that might enhance probation success were being evaluated. A number of writers (see for example Maltz, 1984; McCarthy and McCarthy, 1991) have concluded that, because of the methodological problems (noncomparable subject groups, varying definitions of recidivism), little can be generalized from findings such as these. They infer, however, that, except for individuals with several prior felony convictions, probation seemed as effective as other sanctions in terms of recidivism. With respect to specific recidivism rates, the reviewers cited earlier indicated that agency rates of 30% or below were seen as representing effective programs. Nevertheless, McCarthy and McCarthy note that in over half the studies reviewed, significant correlations were found between higher recidivism levels and the following offender characteristics: previous criminal history, youthful age, status other than married, unemployment, education below fourth grade, drug or alcohol abuse, and commission of property offenses. Of these the most significant was having a history of several felony convictions.

In reviewing the effects of specific types of treatments applied to probationers, Allen and his colleagues (1979) grouped the treatments into three categories. These included those that emphasized vocational counseling or employment, counseling, and drug treatment.

While common sense would indicate that programs enhancing employment would contribute greatly to probation success, study findings only weakly supported the effectiveness of programs (e.g., vocational evaluation, job coaching, and job referral) that concentrated on this factor alone. The same appears to be true for psychological counseling programs. Some sex offender and other types of counseling programs reported successful results but many programs found no differences between groups who received counseling and those who did not. The findings in the counseling studies were complicated by the poor definition and description of the treatment methodologies used in the studies. With respect to outpatient drug treatment there was also a mixed bag of findings. While success has been reported in some studies using an intensive level of supervision along with education and treatment, or methadone maintenance, or behavior modification, other studies did not report such findings.

*The Rand Study and Subsequent Research* A study conducted by the Rand Corporation (Petersilia, Turner, Kahan, and Peterson, 1985) examined the effectiveness of probation for more than 16,000 California offenders. Some of the major results of this study, which followed the sample for 3.5 years, were as follows:

1. During the follow-up period two-thirds of the probationers were rearrested, over half were reconvicted, and over one-third were incarcerated. Those probationers with criminal histories similar to those of prison inmates were 50% more likely to get rearrested as compared with other probationers.

2. Knowing the type of conviction, prior criminal record and use of alcohol and drugs resulted in accurate prediction of reconviction in two out of three cases for the probation sample.

3. Once information on the offenders background and criminal history was considered, the PO's sentencing recommendation contributed little to enhancing the prediction of recidivism. About two-thirds of those in each group recommended for either probation or imprisonment were rearrested.

4. When using factors associated with actual probation success, this study concluded that only 3% of the sample could have been placed on probation with at least a 75% chance of succeeding.

Based on their findings the Rand researchers concluded the following:

1. More use needed to be made of risk assessment scales along with improved case management procedures.

2. There was a need for the development of different strategies to control offenders in the community.

Compared with the California study, studies in other areas achieved dramatically different results. A study of Missouri and Kentucky felony probationers found rearrest and reconviction rates that were about one-third as high as those found in California (McGaha, Fichter, and Hirschburg, 1987). A similar study in New Jersey (Whitehead, 1989) indicated that rearrest and reconviction rates there were two-thirds as high as in California. Whitehead (1991) also found that when incarceration was used as a measure of recidivism, rates were only 17% after a four-year follow-up.

We conclude our discussion of probation effectiveness with a review of research reported by Langan and Cunniff (1992) because this is the largest follow-up study to date. Their results were based on a sample of 79,000 felons from seventeen states, sentenced to probation in 1986 and followed

FIGURE 23.1  **100 Felons Tracked through Their First Three Years of Probation**

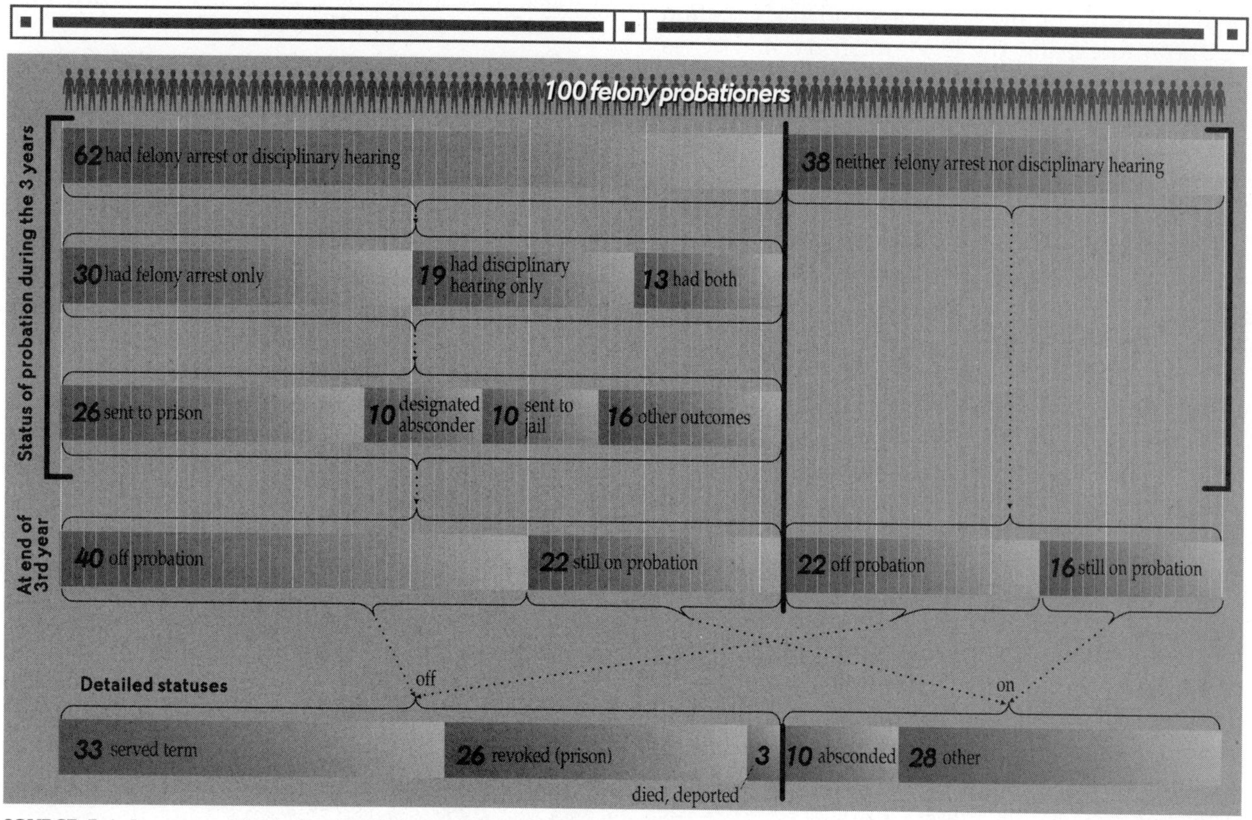

SOURCE: P. A. Lanagan and M. A. Cunniff (1992), *Recidivism of Felons on Probation, 1986–89*, U.S. Department of Justice, Bureau of Justice Statistics, Washington, DC.

through 1989. Figure 23.1 provides a graphic picture of what happened to these offenders over a three-year period. Nearly two-thirds of these felony probationers were arrested for a new felony or were charged with technical violations.

As a rule, violators who were sent to prison did more than just fail to meet some technical condition of their probation. In fact, two-thirds of those sent to jail or prison had at least one felony arrest. The types and number of offenses for which these offenders were arrested raises some serious concerns about placing them on probation. Close to half (34,000) of these probationers accounted for 64,000 felony arrests during the three-year follow-up period. About 20% of the group was arrested three or more times. The offenders most likely to commit subsequent crimes were those on probation for robbery, drug possession, and burglary.

What happened to those committing subsequent offenses is quite telling. Three-quarters of those arrested after the first felony were convicted (64%

for a felony and 11% for a misdemeanor)[3] and 88% of this group was sentenced either to prison (42%) or jail (46%). Judges sentenced 49% of them to prison after their second convictions and by their third conviction judges sent 70% to prison.

At the end of the three-year follow-up period, only 33% had completed their probation sentences. Looking at those who completed their terms of probation is far from comforting. As indicated in the following list, this group was not trouble free:

**1.** 41% had at least one felony arrest while on probation and one-third of these also had a hearing.
**2.** 24% had at least one disciplinary hearing.
**3.** 16% had at least one sentence to jail.
**4.** 31% of those with a special condition had not satisfied the condition in full.
**5.** 53% of those with a financial penalty had not paid the penalty in full (Langan and Cunniff, 1992, p. 8).

It appears, however, that regardless of the level of recidivism, the most recent trend in probation has been to expand the level, intensity, and types of supervision available in the community. These newer forms of supervision, which are often referred to as intermediate sanctions, are discussed in the following chapter.

**SOME RESEARCH COMPARES PROBATION AND PAROLE OUTCOMES** Another Rand Corporation study (Petersilia, Turner, and Peterson, 1986) compared the recidivism of probationers and parolees. Because of the differences between offenders placed on probation and those incarcerated, the samples were matched with regard to several offense criteria. This study determined that parolees recidivated more quickly and had higher rates of recidivism than probationers. However, the crimes for which they were revoked were no more serious than those committed by the probationers.

**PAROLE STUDIES ALSO SHOW HIGH RECIDIVISM** A study by Beck and Shipley (1987) shed some important light on parole effectiveness. This research, conducted in twenty-two states, was based on a sample of 3995 parolees, aged 17 to 22, who were followed for six years. Figure 23.2 shows the cumulative percentage of offenders rearrested, reconvicted, and reincarcerated by six-month intervals. The major results of this study include the following:

**1.** *Rearrests:* Over two-thirds of the parolees were arrested within six years. One-third of the group was rearrested in each of the first two years.
**2.** *Reconviction and reincarceration:* Slightly over half were reconvicted within six years and 49% of these were reincarcerated within this period.
**3.** *Volume and type of new offenses:* These parolees averaged two new arrests; over half were for property offenses, about one-third for drug offenses, and almost one-sixth for violent offenses.
**4.** *Recidivism and prior violent crime:* Offenders with prior arrests for violent crime had a greater likelihood of arrests for another violent crime. Offenders on parole for property offenses with a record of one violent crime had the highest rates of rearrest.

Several later studies have resulted in somewhat similar findings. A parole study in Hawaii (Attor-

FIGURE 23.2 **Cumulative Percent of Young Adults Paroled in 1978 Who Were Rearrested, Reconvicted, and Reincarcerated, by Twelve-month Intervals**

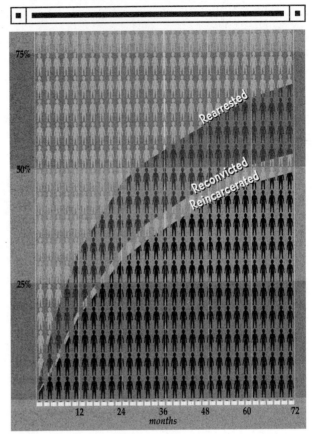

SOURCE: A. Beck and B. E. Shipley (1987), *Recidivism of Young Parolees,* U.S. Department of Justice, Bureau of Justice Statistics, Washington, DC.

ney General's Office, 1989) found that of the 366 parolees studied, 46% were arrested before their terms expired. Gould, MacKenzie, and Bankston (1991) followed 102 nonviolent offenders for 12 months after release from Louisiana prisons. They found that 25% of this sample had their parole status revoked during that period. Another Louisiana study (Geerken, Miranne, and Kennedy, 1993) followed 327 offenders convicted for burglary and armed robbery who were paroled between 1974 and 1981 for the term of their supervision. They found that 46% of them were arrested for an index offense during that period.

In summary, studies of probation and parole effectiveness tend to show an inconsistent but relatively poor outcome. That is, the proportion of felony probationers and parolees who are arrested for violations (technical and criminal) ranges up to

70% and more. As a general rule there appears to be a relationship between probation and parole failure and seriousness of criminal histories. Given that probationers are less serious criminals than parolees, they tend to recidivate less. This latter aspect is negated when probationer characteristics closely resemble those of incarcerated offenders.

The dangers posed by probationers and parolees are used by critics to attempt to curtail these programs. However, there are several reasons why they are likely to remain strong components of the system. The first is prison overcrowding and the very high cost of building prisons. The public wants to get tough on crime but may not be likely to support the tax increases necessary to incarcerate all offenders. Second, equity demands a range of punishments that matches the range of crimes committed. Thus, less serious criminals can receive a nonincarcerative sanction. Humanitarian concerns are a third reason for these types of sanctions. On this basis some offenders are spared the debilitating effects of imprisonment.

## SELECTION OF PROBATION AND PAROLE OFFICERS

At the beginning of 1994 there were about 57,200 probation workers and almost 35,000 parole workers in fifty-two jurisdictions (Camp and Camp, 1994c). Available information on the characteristics of these officers revealed that approximately half were women and 22 and 31% respectively, were nonwhite in probation and parole agencies. The average caseload of probationers on standard probation per PO was 118 versus 81 for parole officers. The average annual entry salary reported was approximately $24,000 (ranging from $16,000 to $44,000) with the average maximum salary being $40,000 (ranging from $29,000 to $109,000).

Probation and parole officers are selected either through a merit system, an appointment system, or some combination of the two (Abadinsky, 1994). The **merit system** requires applicants to qualify by meeting certain minimum requirements and scoring above a certain level on a written exam. Some systems also evaluate and rate applicants on the basis of education and experience. This method is also used by some agencies in determining promotions.

Under the **appointment system** a pool of applicants meeting certain minimum requirements is

developed (e.g., have a BA degree) but no examination is mandated. Agency administrators interview "qualified" candidates and select whomever they please from this group.

In the combined system the written exam screens candidates. Those who have qualifying scores are placed on a list from which candidates are interviewed and selected. Today the vast majority of agencies in the United States require POs to hold a bachelor's degree, usually in a specified area (e.g., criminology or one of the social sciences; Champion, 1990). In addition to educational requirements, most of the agencies around the country require both preservice and in-service training.

The requirement that newly hired POs participate in preservice training programs has grown recently. A substantial majority of the states have instituted training programs, which range from a minimum of 24 hours in South Dakota to 540 hours in Oklahoma (Camp and Camp, 1994c). In some states successful completion of training leads to certification, which is required before the individual can begin to work as a PO. Most states also require a minimum number of in-service training hours (usually 40) each year. The in-service training is intended to keep officers current with new developments.

### Stress and Burnout Are Problems

The effects of stress on police and correctional officers are well documented. POs, because they face many of the same work-related conditions as both police and correctional officers, are also felt to be exposed to high levels of stress. According to Champion (1990), stress among probation officers results from several sources including job dissatisfaction, role conflict, role ambiguity, client–officer interactions, excessive paperwork and performance pressures, low self-esteem and public image, job risks, and liabilities.

Some of the specific reasons that cause the most job dissatisfactions among POs include low pay, excessive caseloads, poor supervision, lack of control over one's job, and lack of input into agency policy. Role conflict results from being faced with job and performance expectations on the part of supervisors that conflict with those of the PO. Role ambiguity, which is related to role conflict, results from poorly defined program goals, which make it difficult for POs to remain focused.

The recent shift toward a control/law enforcement orientation in dealing with probation and parole clients is likely to make the interaction between PO and client more antagonistic. Brown (1993) indicates that mental preparation for the crises involved in this more antagonistic ambiance is likely to reduce stress. Although this antagonistic ambiance may have the effect of reducing the role conflict and ambiguity for the PO, it may also reduce greatly the positive influence that the PO can have on his or her clients.

## CONCLUSION

The supervision of offenders in the community has grown tremendously in the 150 years since John Augustus began his work in Boston. There is no question about its importance to both corrections and the community given that about three-fourths of the offenders under correctional supervision are in the community. This fact has at least one important ramification: It provides an alternative sanction that avoids the potentially debilitating effects of imprisonment while saving the taxpayer a significant amount of money. In spite of the importance of community supervision, there are nagging concerns among much of the public regarding its effectiveness, whether it is punitive enough, and whether society can be protected from victimization at the hands of those convicted offenders who remain in the community. To deal with these concerns and keep some of the advantages of community programs, there has been a proliferation of programs attempting to provide more supervision and impose tougher conditions. Thus, these more rigorous programs could be construed by the public as more punitive. It is these programs, referred to as intermediate sanctions, that we describe in Chapter 24.

## ENDNOTES

1. States authorized to collect probation fees are:
   1. Alabama*
   2. Arizona*
   3. Arkansas*
   4. California*
   5. Colorado
   6. Florida*
   7. Idaho*
   8. Illinois
   9. Indiana
   10. Louisiana*
   11. Massachusetts
   12. Minnesota
   13. Mississippi*
   14. Missouri
   15. Nebraska
   16. Nevada*
   17. New Hampshire
   18. North Carolina*
   19. Oklahoma*
   20. Oregon
   21. South Carolina*
   22. South Dakota
   23. Texas
   24. Utah
   25. Vermont*
   26. Washington*
   27. Wisconsin

   *Also authorized to levy fees on parolees. Kentucky and Montana only authorize fees for parolees.

2. More specifically these data show that:

| Number of Jurisdictions | Number of cases |
|---|---|
| 5 | 200+ |
| 19 | 91 to 199 |
| 16 | 67 to 90 |
| 6 | Below 67 |

3. Some felony charges were reduced to misdemeanors.

## ACKNOWLEDGMENTS

[a] H. Abadinsky, *Probation and Parole: Theory and Practice,* 5/e, © 1994, pp. 341-342. Reprinted by permission of Prentice-Hall, Upper Saddle River, New Jersey.
[b] Reprinted from E.E. Rhine, W.R. Smith, and R.W. Jackson, 1991, *Paroling Authorities: Recent History and Current Practice,* with permission of the American Correctional Association, Lanham, MD.

## CHAPTER RECAP

### Probation as an Alternative to Imprisonment
Probation and Its Antecedents Mitigated Harsh
Sentences
  John Augustus Was the Father of Modern Probation
  Probation Grew Rapidly in the Early Twentieth Century
  Probation in the Era of Just Deserts
Probation Today Is at Record Levels
  A Sentence to Probation Depends on Several Factors
  Conditions Are the Limits Placed on Probationers
The Organization and Administration of Probation
Services
  Caseload Size Determines the Level of Supervision
  Caseload Assignments Are Made in Several Ways
The Presentence Investigation Is an Important
Probation Officer Activity
  The PSI Helps in Sentencing and Treatment
  The PSI Requires a Lot of Information
  Issues Related to the PSI
### Parole Is Served in the Community
Developments in the United States Resulted from
  Changes in Philosophy
  The Return to Retribution Reduced Discretionary
  Parole
Today the Number of Parolees Is at an All-time High
  There are Several Types of Release from Prison
The Organization and Administration of Parole Services
  Parole is an Executive Function
  The Parole Board Makes the Parole Decision
  Objective Parole Criteria and Guidelines Help in
  Making the Decisions
### Supervision and Service Delivery to Probationers and
Parolees
PO Strategies Balance Surveillance and Service
  The Probation/Parole Officer as a Law Enforcement
  Agent
  The Probation/Parole Officer as a Caseworker
  The Probation/Parole Officer as a Resource Broker/
  Advocate
Probation or Parole Can Be Revoked for Violations
  Several Court Decisions Have Affected the
  Revocation Process
  Revocation Research Shows a Strong Substance
  Abuse Influence
The Effectiveness of Probation/Parole Supervision
  Measurement Problems Make Evaluation Difficult
  Effectiveness Studies Show Relatively High Levels of
  Recidivism
    The Rand Study and Subsequent Research
  Some Research Compares Probation and Parole Out-
  comes
  Parole Studies Also Show High Recidivism
### Selection of Probation and Parole Officers
Stress and Burnout are Problems
### Conclusion

## REVIEW QUESTIONS

**1.** Briefly summarize the history of probation. What role did John Augustus play in its development?
**2.** How are risk prediction scales used in deciding which offenders should be placed on probation?
**3.** Identify the basic organizational arrangements under which probation services are administered in this country and the methods employed in assigning cases to probation officers.
**4.** List the five basic uses of the presentence investigation and the basic types of information that should be included in each report.
**5.** Differentiate between the independent and consolidated models of parole services.
**6.** Discuss the supervisory styles and service delivery strategies characteristic of different probation and parole officers.
**7.** Summarize the general results of studies regarding the effectiveness of probation and parole.
**8.** What due process rights are probationers and parolees entitled to during the revocation process?
**9.** What different types of procedures are employed in the hiring of probation and parole officers? Discuss some of the factors that cause them stress.

## TEST YOUR KNOWLEDGE

**1.** _____ is an early antecedent of probation that allowed individuals accused of serious crimes to appeal for leniency by reading the 51st Psalm in court.
  **a.** Benefit of clergy
  **b.** Judicial reprieve
  **c.** Recognizance
  **d.** Executive clemency
**2.** Today probation and parole officers are more likely to operate under the _____ orientation.
  **a.** counseling
  **b.** law enforcement
  **c.** case worker
  **d.** broker/advocate
**3.** The most common form of organizing probation services in the United State is
  **a.** within local county executive departments.
  **b.** within the state executive branch.
  **c.** under the state judiciary.
  **d.** under the local courts.
**4.** Probationers and parolees are entitled to certain procedural due process rights at revocation hearings. Which of the following is *not* one of them?
  **a.** right to a jury trial
  **b.** right to present evidence
  **c.** right to cross-examine witnesses
  **d.** right to have a fair hearing

# CHAPTER 24

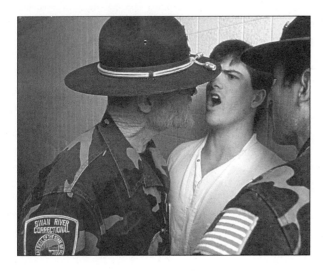

# INTERMEDIATE SANCTIONS: GETTING TOUGH IN THE COMMUNITY

## ▣ LEARNING OBJECTIVES

*After completion of this chapter, you should be able to:*

1. Discuss the reasons for the increase in intermediate sanction programs.

2. Define the term *intermediate sanction*, its historical antecedents, and the programs that comprise it.

3. Describe and discuss the goals of these programs and their philosophical underpinnings.

4. Delineate the factors that must be considered in the successful establishment of a halfway house.

5. Explain the goals and positive effects of work/study release programs and their development in the United States.

6. Explain how intensive supervision programs work and the purposes for which they were established.

7. Describe home confinement, the role that surveillance plays in it, and its advantages and disadvantages.

8. Describe the various forms of electronic monitoring, explain how they work, and discuss the ethical issues involved.

9. Describe shock incarceration and boot camps and differentiate between them.

10. Explain the functions and goals of day reporting centers.

## ▣ KEY TERMS AND CONCEPTS

Boot camps
Continuous signaling devices
Day reporting centers
Electronic monitoring
Halfway house
House arrest/home confinement
Huber Act
Intensive probation supervision
Intermediate sanctions
Net widening
Programmed contact devices
Shock incarceration
Tracking devices
Work/study release

*This chapter was authored by Linda Smith, Assistant Professor, Department of Criminal Justice, Georgia State University.*

One of the most important correctional developments in recent years has been the use and expansion of intermediate sanctions. These programs carry names such as intensive probation supervision, house arrest/home confinement, electronic monitoring, shock incarceration/boot camp, and day reporting centers. This development is attributed to three primary concerns: the prison overcrowding crisis facing many correctional systems; the growing dissatisfaction with regular probation that is viewed as too lenient on felony offenders; and fiscal conservatism and budget constraints that have forced correctional administrators and policy makers to search for less costly alternatives to incarceration without appearing to be too "soft" on crime.

Intermediate sanctions appear to have been an ideal answer to the concerns just listed because they are less costly than prison yet more punitive than standard probation. Many would agree that economics has fueled the rapid growth of these programs (Petersilia, 1987). They have received highly visible and favorable media attention at local, state, and federal levels as innovative sentencing options designed to fill the gap between regular probation and incarceration on the continuum of sanctions.

Despite the rapid growth of intermediate sanction programs, we are only beginning to evaluate systematically their efficacy. The following questions have been raised about these programs: (1) Are they cost effective? (2) Do they help reduce prison overcrowding or do they just widen the net? (3) Do they maintain enough control over offenders so that the safety of the community is not compromised? (Tonry, 1990; Clear and Hardyman, 1990; Tonry and Will 1988; General Accounting Office, 1990b; Wagner and Baird, 1993). These are some issues to be addressed in this chapter along with a description of several types of intermediate sanction programs.

## HISTORICAL DEVELOPMENT OF INTERMEDIATE SANCTIONS

Historically, intermediate sanctions are not a new idea. Some older programs, with similarities to intermediate sanctions, can be traced to sixth-century France when St. Leonard obtained the release of prisoners from the king (James, 1975). These individuals were given temporary food and shelter in St. Leonard's monastery at Limoges until they could return to their communities. During this period and throughout the Middle Ages, it was not uncommon for religious orders to assist prisoners in such a humanitarian fashion.

As early as the 1820s a need was recognized for halfway houses to assist those released from prison. However, because public opposition to this concept was too strong, they were not implemented until about 20 years later (McCarthy and McCarthy, 1991). In 1914 the first formal work release program was implemented in Wisconsin. In the 1960s, a growing emphasis on community-based corrections led to the establishment of a variety of residential treatment programs (Public Health Service, 1976). From the 1950s through the early 1970s, the first modern intensive supervision programs emerged (Clear and Hardyman, 1990). Other intensive supervision programs were developed in the mid-1980s and included house arrest/home confinement programs, boot camps, electronic monitoring, and day reporting centers (General Accounting Office, 1990b; U.S. Department of Justice, 1990).

Initially, the programs begun in the 1980s were described as intermediate *punishments*, not intermediate *sanctions*, because this terminology seemed "tougher." Legislators, pushed by public opinion, wanted these programs to appear more punitive than standard probation because the emphasis was being placed on the correctional goal of "just deserts." A complicating factor was that as these programs were being developed, rehabilitation was being rejected as a primary objective for corrections. Rehabilitation did not fit in with the "just deserts" philosophy underlying these programs. This emphasis on punishment was in direct contrast to the philosophical ideals that had characterized the community-based programs implemented earlier. A review of the philosophical underpinnings of intermediate sanctions may provide the reader with a better understanding of how earlier programs differed from later ones in concept and impact.

### The Correctional Philosophy Underlying Intermediate Sanctions Has Changed

The earliest community programs established between incarceration and release in the United

States were based on humanitarian concerns. Halfway houses were created to provide temporary shelter and food for offenders who were often too destitute to resume normal (noncriminal) residence in the community. Work release programs focused on helping offenders find employment, reestablishing familial ties, and easing the transition into the community. Later, these two programs served offenders not only as postincarceration alternatives but also as pre-incarceration dispositions. This provided them with the opportunity to change their criminal lifestyle *before* it led to incarceration.

In the 1960s, dissatisfaction with correctional practices led to a new movement among practitioners and academics to decrease the use of incarceration as punishment. These professionals agreed that incarceration was debilitating and ineffective. Some states even called for the abolition of imprisonment for some classes of offenders (Task Force on Corrections, 1973). Rather than incarcerate, emphasis was placed on the humanitarian, reintegrative, and managerial aspects of community-based corrections.

In the late 1970s, the philosophy of community-based programs began to shift from a humanitarian/rehabilitative perspective to one guided by economics and a need to be more punitive (Byrne, 1986). Thus, it is now more appropriate to call these programs "corrections in the community" because their emphasis now includes more traditional correctional objectives such as control and "just deserts." While attempts continue to be made to move intermediate sanctions back to a philosophy based on humanitarianism and rehabilitation, given current public attitudes toward correctional programming it is unlikely that this will occur.

**WHAT ARE INTERMEDIATE SANCTIONS SUPPOSED TO DO?** It has been difficult to determine exactly what intermediate sanctions and the programs representing them are supposed to accomplish. Remember that recent programs developed and grew primarily in response to the overcrowding crisis. Thus, the policies behind these programs were rarely based on logical and valid theoretical principles. Instead, most developed without any explicit theoretical rationale regarding what program outcomes should be.

Because interest in intermediate sanctions grew out of practical and expedient concerns, it is no surprise that their theoretical underpinnings are weak. This has caused confusion in defining them. What has resulted is perplexing and redundant terminology in describing these sentencing options, including terms such as "intermediate punishments," "intermediate sanctions," "alternatives to incarceration," and "sentencing alternatives" (U.S. Department of Justice, 1990; Morris and Tonry, 1990). To provide some consistency and clarity, the U.S. Department of Justice (1990) labeled these programs **intermediate sanctions** and provided the following definition: " . . . a punishment option that is considered on a continuum to fall between traditional probation and traditional incarceration" (p. 3). Defined in this way, these programs provide multipurpose sentencing options for dealing with high-risk offenders who require more surveillance and control and whose crimes require more punishment than can provided by traditional probation, but less than is provided by imprisonment. They also include elements from all the traditional goals of corrections. The punitive aspect of intermediate sanctions reflects the goals of retribution and "just deserts." Other traditional goals such as deterrence (both general and specific), incapacitation, and rehabilitation also are found in the various program rationales. Therefore, as we examine programs in this category, we must keep in mind their multipurpose functions.

## VARIOUS INTERMEDIATE SANCTION PROGRAMS EXIST

Intermediate sanction programs today meet the need for a graduated sentencing system. While some programs are new, such as the day reporting centers, others have been part of the correctional process from its earliest beginnings and had a much different focus. The older programs, residential community correctional facilities such as halfway houses and work release centers, filled the gap between probation and jail/prison sentences long before *intermediate sanctions* became the buzzword in corrections. These latter programs are discussed first so that some historical continuity is provided.

### Halfway Houses Are Treatment Oriented

**Halfway houses** were the earliest form of what are now called intermediate sanctions. Initially, halfway houses served as an intermediate step between prison and release into the community, thus the name halfway-out programs. Today, they also are used as an alternative to prison commitment, and when used in this manner, they are called halfway-in programs. Whether halfway houses function as post- or pre-incarceration programs, they are clearly transitional residential facilities that operate in community settings. The following provides a good definition of halfway houses:

> The very name halfway house suggests its position in the corrections world: halfway-in, a more structured environment than probation and parole; halfway-out, a less structured environment than institutions. As halfway-in houses they represent a last step before incarceration for probationers and parolees facing . . . revocation; as halfway-out houses, they provide services to prereleasees and parolees leaving institutions. Halfway houses also provide a residential alternative to jail or outright release for accused offenders awaiting trial or convicted offenders awaiting sentencing (Thalheimer, 1975, p. 1).

Although most halfway houses function according to this basic definition, there is great diversity in their actual operation and the services provided to offenders.

The appeal of halfway houses can be traced to three goals or ideals that are encompassed by these programs. The humanitarian ideal of halfway houses was based on the perception that removing offenders from the harsh prison environment was more beneficial than continued exposure to the criminogenic effects of incarceration. The reintegrative ideal held that temporary assistance for offenders made the transition back to the community much easier. This included assisting offenders to (1) find employment, (2) reestablish family and community ties, and (3) make rehabilitative services in the community accessible. It was felt that all these factors would facilitate the third ideal, which was the successful rehabilitation of the offender. Maintaining offenders in halfway houses also resulted in a reduction in costs compared to imprisonment (Latessa and Allen, 1982). This created positive managerial practices that were embraced by practitioners and policy makers.

**THIS TYPE OF FACILITY HAS EXISTED FOR A LONG TIME**   Public indifference, opposition by progressive organizations like the American Prison

**Individuals having a meal at a halfway house. Halfway houses emphasize a more normal, more homelike environment, as well as treatment.**

Association, and concerns about allowing exoffenders to associate with one another had a contaminating effect on the idea of halfway houses that resulted in the development of only a few halfway houses during the latter part of the nineteenth and first half of the twentieth centuries.

The first halfway house in the United States (Isaac T. Hopper House) opened in New York in 1845, followed by one in Boston in 1864 and another Philadelphia in 1889. In 1896 the first of the Hope Houses was opened in New York followed by others in seven states (Keller and Alper, 1970; McCartt and Mangogna, 1973; McCarthy and McCarthy, 1991). However, it was not until the 1950s with the opening of the Dismas House, St. Leonard's House, and 308 West Residence that we saw what has been called the real beginning of a national halfway house movement (Keller and Alper, 1970). Major boosts to this movement resulted from the endorsement of the halfway house concept in 1961 by Attorney General Robert F. Kennedy and the formation of the International Halfway House Association in 1964 (McCartt and Mangogna, 1976). Additional impetus for these programs was provided by the President's Crime Commission (Task Force on Corrections, 1967) and the National Advisory Commission Criminal Justice Standards and Goals (Task Force on Corrections, 1973). These groups supported the humanitarian, rehabilitative, and reintegrative ideals that community-based corrections provided. In addition, halfway houses were thought to be a positive managerial approach because they seemed more cost effective than incarceration. This level of support and positive view of these programs led to the presence of halfway houses in almost all states by the mid-1970s as well as an expansion of the programs offered in them and the types of clients served (Latessa and Allen, 1982). Also during this period private agencies began operating many of these programs. As a result, many standard procedures required in government programs no longer applied. General guidelines for the implementation and operation of halfway houses were developed during this time to provide consistency in program characteristics.

An important question regarding halfway houses is whether or not they realize their rehabilitative and other objectives. The most comprehensive review aimed at answering this question was initially done by Seiter, Carlson, Bowman, Granfield, and Beran (1977) and later updated by Latessa and Allen (1982). Based on an examination of 44 studies Latessa and Allen concluded that halfway houses may be as effective as any other parole strategy and for that period of time (the late 1970s) were probably more cost effective when compared with incarceration in a state prison. Donnelly and Forcshner (1992) assert that "given that halfway house clients are probably a higher risk group than parolees and that recidivism rates are similar for the two groups, halfway houses may be doing a better job than the evaluations can measure" (p. 349).

**GUIDELINES FOR OPENING AND OPERATING A HALFWAY HOUSE**    Rachin (1972) established guidelines for opening and operating halfway

houses that focused on size, site selection, community relations, and space requirements. Programs housing twenty to twenty-five clients are considered the optimum size for halfway houses. This number is based on costs, retaining small group interactions, and keeping the number of offenders down for community acceptance. Site selection is very important in successfully implementing halfway houses. Zoning, availability of public transportation, community resistance, the type of physical facility, the neighborhood environment, and availability of commercial services are important factors to be considered.

Halfway houses should make maximum use of community resources including educational, religious, vocational, recreational, and medical services. Thus, they need to become fully integrated into the community. Community relations are also enhanced by establishing boards consisting of representatives from key areas including political entities, criminal justice, religious organizations, and representatives from businesses and citizens in the community. Space requirements should meet the needs for the maximum number of offenders to be housed in the facility. Standards set by the American Correctional Association (ACA) for matters such as bathroom facilities, sleeping areas, dayrooms, etc., must be met to gain ACA accreditation. Space requirements must also conform to the standards set by local boards as well as to legislatively enacted statutes.

**THE VAST MAJORITY OF HALFWAY HOUSES TODAY ARE PRIVATELY OPERATED**    The number of halfway houses has generally declined in the 1980s and 1990s. Issues regarding costs (which are higher for halfway houses than for other intermediate sanction programs), recidivism, and public resistance have plagued these programs. Most of these programs today are privately run: A recent survey revealed that over 85% of halfway house programs presently operating are privately administered (Camp and Camp, 1994a). As a result, we can expect to see an even greater diversity in the goals, planning, implementation, programming, and operation of these programs in the future (McCarthy and McCarthy, 1991). The Close-Up on the Delancey Street program describes a private halfway house program in California. It is different from most halfway houses in that it houses several hundred residents.

## Close Up    Delancey Street Is a Very Unique Halfway House

The new Delancey Street Complex is not the usual halfway house operation. The beautiful buildings, located in the Embarcadero area of San Francisco, provide a magnificent view of San Francisco Bay. The complex was built almost entirely by Delancey Street residents.

The complex can house 600 residents. Besides the residences, there are offices to house several businesses. These businesses produce income for program operation. Delancey Street is totally self-sufficient and does not receive any tax money nor does it solicit donations.

Delancey Street was started in 1970 by John Maher, a former addict and member of Synanon (a similar program from which Maher developed the Delancey Street concept), with money borrowed from a "loan shark." Although Delancey Street is primarily for addicts, the program accepts all types of individuals—many of whom have been serious criminal offenders. While some residents enter the program by self-referral, others are interviewed in jail or prison by current residents as prospective residents.

Delancey Street operates as a therapeutic community with hard, unpaid work and "the Games" as the two primary treatment techniques. There are also a variety of educational and vocational training programs, many of the latter actually being profit-making businesses. All monies made by these businesses go into a fund for program operation. The residents generally start by working within the house in menial jobs, such as building maintenance, which are intended to cause humiliation and break down any facades that many of them have developed over the years. The program is entirely operated by the residents. Some residents learn business practices in order to run what is the equivalent of a major corporation. Many residents are rewarded with social outings and enriching experiences to facilitate their socialization process.

The Games part of the program is an adaptation of the "attack therapy" used at Synanon, which encourages residents to ventilate their hostilities and anger and to accept responsibility for their behavior.

There are three simple and universal rules that every resident must understand and follow: no violence, no threats of violence, and no drugs and/or alcohol. In addition, everyone must work and make a commitment to stay in the program for two years. Discipline is handled by twelve "barbers" who are generally veteran residents. The "barbers" divide the responsibility over the residents and give "verbal haircuts" when needed for disobedient members.

The program has received enthusiastic support from the public and the media because of the positive impact program supporters claim it has had on the lives of the residents (some of whom were viewed as hopeless, drug-addicted criminal offenders). However, empirical evidence to support these claims is not available. The criticisms of the program have centered on claims that the program cultivates a dependence on the program that is not healthy. Indeed, some refer to it as a cult experience.

What this program is trying to do in a relatively short period is what parents do when raising a child; teach residents self-respect, respect for others, self-reliance, and a work ethic that will allow them to become independent. Most parents have eighteen years to do this. Delancey Street takes an average of four years with their residents.

What do you think of the Delancey Street methods? Does the dependency issue bother you? This Close-Up is based on knowledge gained by the author during a visit to the facility.

## Work/Study Release Programs Provide Prerelease Employment or Education

**Work release,** also known as work furlough or day parole, is a program that allows specially selected inmates to work in the community while still incarcerated. Inmates participating in a work release program must meet the same job eligibility criteria as other employees. They must work under the same conditions required of their civilian counterparts and, ideally, receive the same wages. **Study release** allows inmates to go into the community to pursue educational opportunities not available inside the prison (e.g., certain vocational and college courses). Study release functions the same as work release, and the program is often conducted out of the same facility as work release. Further discussion will refer to work release only, but keep in mind that the same principles guiding work release also apply to study release programs.

During nonworking hours, inmates are confined to either a correctional institution for institutionally based programs, or to a specially designated residential facility. During confinement hours, inmates must follow all of the same rules normally required of an incarcerated population as well as adhere to the rules and regulations established for work release participants.

**EARLY WORK RELEASE PROGRAMS BEGAN IN WISCONSIN** While work release programs did not really develop in the United States until the 1960s, a form of work release operated in a few states in the early 1900s. As indicated earlier, the first work release program was established in Wisconsin in 1914 under the **Huber Act.** This law authorized counties to set up a program for misdemeanants, serving one year or less, to be released during certain hours to work in the community (McCarthy and McCarthy, 1991). These inmates were supposed to be paid wages comparable to those for civilian employees.

Although the Wisconsin program was generally considered successful, during the next forty years only Nebraska, West Virginia, and Hawaii (then the territory of Hawaii) established work release programs. Until North Carolina began an extensive work release program in 1957 for misdemeanants (later extended to felony offenders), interest in work release was largely dormant (Doeran and Hageman, 1982). By the 1960s, work release programs were used fairly extensively. With the passage of the Prisoner Rehabilitation Act of 1965, work release was established for inmates in federal institutions. By 1975, all fifty states and the federal system had some form of work release operating. In the early 1990s, approximately 21,000 inmates were participating in work release and 750 in educational release throughout the United States annually (Davis, 1993a).

**WORK RELEASE HAS VARIOUS GOALS AND OBJECTIVES** Work release was initially instituted as a postincarceration community correctional program. Although many work release programs have been established with humanitarian, rehabilitative, and reintegrative goals, earlier work release programs were meant to be punitive or retributive (Doeran and Hageman, 1982). Advocates of these early programs questioned why criminal offenders were allowed to remain idle while law-abiding citizens labored. At the time, there was a labor shortage and inmate workers were needed in the workforce. Today the reverse argument is used by those who oppose inmate work programs, that is, why should inmates work at paying jobs when law-abiding citizens are unable to find employment? Whatever the answer, work release still serves multiple goals whether the program is institutionally based or community centered. Thus, providing inmates with work can be viewed as both punitive and rehabilitative.

**HOW WORK RELEASE PROGRAMS OPERATE** Work release programs are operated by local, state, and federal authorities. Misdemeanant programs are usually operated by local authorities and generally administered by the county sheriff's office as part of the jail program. State-run programs are usually operated either out of prisons or out of specially designated residential facilities (e.g., community correctional centers, prerelease centers). These programs target felony offenders who are nearing the end of their sentences. Federal programs, administered by the Federal Bureau of Prisons, may contain misdemeanant and felony offenders. Both state and federal agencies sometimes contract with local agencies to house their inmates if they meet eligibility criteria for these programs. This is done because most state and federal prisons are located in rural areas where there may be a shortage of employment opportunities. The current trend, however, whether local, state, or federal, is to contract with private agencies to administer community correctional programs such as work release. These agencies may be nonprofit—e.g., the Salvation Army or Goodwill—or they may be for-profit companies.

The most important factor in the success of work release programs is the selection and screening of inmates who can safely and securely work in the community. Having specific guidelines and procedures for the selection of program participants in place is critical for program operation. Although potentially dangerous and violent offenders must be eliminated from program eligibility, no foolproof system is available for selecting "safe" inmates.

The selection of program participants is based on a variety of factors which must meet statutory and administrative requirements. These factors

greater control and supervision than was provided in regular probation (Empey, 1967; Public Health Service, 1976). While this idea is basically the same for the programs most recently implemented (i.e., alternative sentencing for prison-bound offenders), there are major philosophical differences between today's programs and those of the 1950s.

During the late 1950s and throughout the 1960s, popular and professional support for incarceration declined. There was greater acceptance of community-based programs and alternative measures for prison-bound offenders. These earlier programs also were intended to be rehabilitative. They were considered improvements over imprisonment and were instituted " ... to avoid the negative effects of isolation from the community, the severing of family ties and noncriminal associations, and the institutional culture" (Public Health Service, 1976, p. 520).

The belief was that increased officer contact with the offender enhances the officer's helping role and assists in promoting positive behavioral changes. In general, these experiments attempted to figure out the optimal caseload size (i.e., the one which would maximize the officer's ability to assist those offenders who needed it) (Clear and Hardyman, 1990).

The various studies in California, including the study of the Special Intensive Parole Unit (SIPU) from 1953 until 1964, the Alameda County parole experiment in Oakland in 1959, and the study of federal probation and parole conducted at Berkeley in the 1960s, showed that reducing caseload size did not increase offenders' chances for success. It also did not substantially increase the amount of officer contact with offenders in a number of cases (Carter and Wilkins, 1976; Banks, Porter, Tardin, Siler, and Unger, 1977; Clear and Hardyman, 1990).

**PROGRAMS DEVELOPED IN THE 1980s WERE DESIGNED TO INCREASE CONTROL**   While these programs appeared to fail (as evidenced by their abandonment in the 1970s), when they were revived in the 1980s, their objective was to increase control over offenders. This was done by restricting their freedom in the community. The important issue was enhancing public safety by increasing the surveillance and supervision of offenders.

While the public is skeptical about corrections' ability to effectively supervise offenders in the community, it is also aware of the limited resources and funding available to imprison all of them. The

public, legislators, and policy makers were ready to support any sanction that increased the severity of punishment for the offender while being cost effective and providing greater community safety.

To summarize, the philosophy of the programs implemented in the 1980s embodies "two overriding and ambitious goals" (Byrne, 1990). The first goal is the alleviation of prison overcrowding and its negative effects and costs. The second is the protection of the public by using surveillance and techniques that reduce opportunities for recidivism. Although Byrne says that IPS can achieve a rehabilitative end, that is not a priority with most of these programs. The questions that should be addressed in IPS programs are similar to the ones addressed in the early California programs: Do smaller caseloads increase contact with offenders? Does this increased contact work to reduce recidivism? We may find that too much is expected from current programs, and they will experience the same failures that occurred earlier.

**NEW IPS PROGRAMS ARE MORE SUCCESSFUL IN ACHIEVING SOME GOALS THAN OTHERS**   Research on the new programs shows most have not significantly reduced recidivism of participants when they were compared with true prison-bound offenders (offenders who would actually go to prison without IPS programs). This is in contrast to initial evaluations of these programs, which reported success in this area (Erwin, 1987; Pearson, 1987). Researchers conducting the recent studies on IPS have questioned both the methodologies used and the target population selected to participate in these programs (Tonry, 1990; Petersilia, 1987; Byrne, 1990; Clear, Flynn, and Shapiro, 1987; Petersilia and Turner, 1993).

One concern is that these programs may be net widening. **Net widening** occurs when a sanction extends the "net" of control over offenders who could be effectively supervised with less intrusive methods (i.e., under regular probation, which involves less surveillance and control) than those employed in IPS. This view is supported by data showing that many of these offenders have criminal characteristics more like offenders who should have been placed on "regular" probation than like those of the prison-bound population. The fact that these less serious offenders are included in IPS effectively counters claims that these programs reduce prison overcrowding. Net widening also questions the cost savings associated with placing offenders in IPS if they could have been supervised in less costly regular probation. Our Close-Up on "Does IPS Work?" focuses on a Rand study that was designed to answer these and other questions.

## House Arrest/Home Confinement Programs Make Offenders' Homes Their Jails

**House arrest/home confinement** programs have been very popular with both the public and legislatures. In these programs, offenders are confined to their home or designated residences at all times unless officially permitted to leave for employment, community service, medical needs, or other reasons. Presently, the largest intermediate sanction program of this type in the nation is Florida's Community Control Program known more popularly as "house arrest." Similar programs are being implemented across the United States, and although house arrest has many of the same characteristics as IPS programs, there are significant differences.

**MANY ARE STAND-ALONE PROGRAMS BECAUSE THEY ARE NOT ASSOCIATED WITH PROBATION PROGRAMS** In many instances, house arrest/home confinement programs are stand-alone programs. They generally operate under statutes separate from those that guide and define probation programs. The differences between intensive supervision programs and house arrest programs include the following:

1. House arrest is nearly always designed to ease prison crowding and serve a prison- bound population.
2. House arrest is usually a sentence imposed by the court; it is virtually never an administrative tool used by program administrators to manage existing caseloads.
3. Most house arrest programs are designed to be much more punitive than IPS programs.
4. House arrest represents a greater departure than IPS from the traditional model of probation.
5. House arrest is the "last chance" before imprisonment; and revocation automatically leads to prison (Petersilia, 1987).

The surveillance and supervision functions in home confinement programs are extremely important for their successful operation. While other features (e.g., offender counseling, substance abuse treatment) may be provided to offenders in these

programs, the services are secondary to enforcing restriction of offenders to their homes or designated residences. The Close-Up dealing with Florida's Community Control Program provides a better understanding of how house arrest/home confinement programs function.

## Electronic Monitoring Increases Surveillance

**Electronic monitoring** has also gained widespread acceptance both as a cost-effective alternative to incarceration (Lilly, Ball, and Wright, 1987) and as an enhancement to supervising offenders in the community (Morris and Tonry, 1990). Sometimes it is used to increase control over offenders who have violated the conditions of their intensive probation/parole, house arrest, or another form of community supervision. Although it is primarily employed to monitor offenders who have already been sentenced, in some jurisdictions it is also used for offenders awaiting trial (Schmidt, 1989a). There are several key decision points at which electronic monitoring can be chosen as a sanction ranging from pretrial to postincarceration.

A 1988 survey revealed that almost 90% of the offenders supervised by electronic monitoring were male, which is consistent with their proportion in our nation's prisons and jails (Schmidt, 1989). It also found that offenders in these programs had been convicted of a wide range of criminal offenses, with major traffic violations (i.e., DUI) comprising the largest category. The proportion of traffic offenders in electronic monitoring programs may be accounted for by the fact that these programs started at local rather than state levels.

**HISTORICAL DEVELOPMENT OF ELECTRONIC MONITORING PROGRAMS** The notion of using electronic monitors for surveillance of offenders can be traced back to the 1960s when Schwitzgebel, Pahnke, and Hurd (1964) suggested using them to track the mentally ill, probationers, and parolees. They were later tested on 100 volunteers to assess their social and psychological effects (Schmidt and Curtis, 1987). Despite Schwitzgebel's interesting results, it took almost 20 years for his idea to take hold in corrections. The first formal electronic monitoring program was implemented in 1983 when Albuquerque, New Mexico, District Court Judge Jack Love, reputedly inspired by a "Spiderman" comic strip, placed a probation violator on

# Close Up   Does IPS Work?

A study was conducted by the Rand Corporation of fourteen programs in nine states to answer the question of whether participation in this type of program affected an offender's subsequent criminal behavior versus involvement in more traditional sanctions, i.e., prison and routine probation (Petersilia and Turner, 1993). The study involved 2000 nonviolent offenders who were assigned randomly to an experimental group (i.e., an IPS program) or a control group who were either given routine probation, parole, or prison.

**IPS was found to be effective in providing surveillance.** It was designed to be much more stringent than routine supervision and in every site it delivered more contact and monitoring than routine supervision. There was no clear indication whether these increased surveillance levels reduced an offender's subsequent involvement in crime. Thus, while in Seattle face-to-face contacts averaged 3.4 per month and in Macon they numbered 16.1, at both sites almost the same percentage of IPS offenders were arrested—46 versus 42%.

**The programs were effective as intermediate sanctions.** Most IPS had significantly higher levels of features curtailing freedom, which can be construed as punishment. This examines the same factors at which we previously looked: frequent contacts and drug testing. The question is: Did these more stringent control and surveillance methods subject IPSs to more punitive action by finding and punishing those who violated their conditions? In fact, IPS did have higher rates of technical violation than controls, which meant that it did achieve its objective of being more coercive and punitive. However, these results should be interpreted with caution since their closer surveillance may increase the probability that they were caught for a larger percentage of their violations. This was substantiated by interviews with IPS participants, which found that they believed there was a higher likelihood they would be caught and treated more harshly for violation than their counterparts on routine probation.

**The effect on recidivism was not as successful.** IPS participants were subsequently arrested more often, did not have a longer time until they committed a crime, and their offenses were not less serious than control group members. Thus, 37% of IPSs were arrested as compared with 33% of the controls. However, remember that IPS offenders are more closely monitored and thus may be more likely to be caught in the enforcement net, while those on routine probation and parole may escape it. Thus, IPS offenders may well be committing the same or fewer offenses than those under routine supervision.

**Whether IPS is more cost effective depends on what it is being compared to.** When compared to routine probation, it is more expensive because caseloads are much smaller—generally about twenty-five offenders per PO or team. Comparing all the costs, including those associated with handling the higher rates of technical violations and rates of imprisonment (court costs), IPS costs per year averaged $7200 per offender versus $4700 for the controls on routine supervision. However, the costs per day for imprisonment are much more per offender than for IPS, especially when the cost of building new prisons is considered.

**IPSs were more involved in treatment and this was found to be related to a reduction in recidivism at some sites.** Comparing IPS offender involvement in programming with that of controls found IPSs had higher rates of involvement in some counseling (45 versus 22%); paid employment (56 versus 43%); and restitution 12 versus 3%). Only in the area of community service was there no difference.

**This research suggests that IPS is better at achieving some goals than others.** For jurisdictions primarily interested in reducing recidivism, prison crowding, and system costs, IPS may not meet all these objectives. On the other hand, if the objective is to develop a more comprehensive and graduated sentencing structure, IPS can assist in achieving this goal. It can take its place as one of the intermediate sanctions between prisons and probation. Like other intermediate sanctions, it may impose more stringent controls on offenders than routine probation. It may also achieve greater flexibility in sentencing decisions by providing punishments that more closely fit the crimes. However, Petersilia and Turner (1993) caution that the public must be made aware that if jurisdictions plan to use IPS programs as a means of reducing recidivism they may not accomplish that goal.

## Close Up, continued

Finally, IPS programs are still in the testing stage and need to be further refined. One way it might be more effective is to select offenders for IPS earlier in their careers. These offenders may better benefit from both the deterrent and rehabilitative aspects of IPS since they are not as committed to the criminal lifestyle.

What do you think? Also, do you think these programs should be eliminated if they do not reduce recidivism or is the fact that they provide more diversified sentencing options and more punishment than routine probation sufficient to justify their continued funding?

SOURCE: Adapted from J. Petersilia and S. Turner (1993), *Evaluating Intensive Probation/Parole: Results of Nationwide Experiment*, National Institute of Justice, Washington D.C.

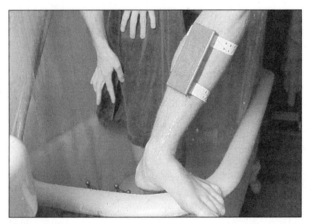

An electronic monitoring device. A probationer wearing an anklet which detects his presence or absence at home.

An individual on electronic monitoring reporting to his community control officer by using an instrument attached to his telephone.

electronic monitoring for one month. This was followed by a pilot project implemented in 1984 in Palm Beach County, Florida, initially targeting drunk drivers (Palm Beach County Sheriff's Office, 1987). Since its implementation in 1983, electronic monitoring has expanded rapidly across the United States. By 1990, it had been adopted in all fifty states by local, state, and federal correctional agencies (Renzema and Skelton, 1990).

**THERE ARE SEVERAL TYPES OF ELECTRONIC MONITORS** Electronic monitors are best described as new telemetry devices designed to verify that an offender is at a given location during specified times. Generally, a host computer is pro-grammed to electronically verify the offender's presence at home during nonworking hours, but does not operate while the offender is away from home (e.g., work). The public generally believes (and officials have done little to dispel this belief) that the whereabouts of offenders on electronic monitoring are always known by correctional officials. With present technology, this is not possible, although electronic monitoring technology is moving in that direction. A review of the current technology will help clarify just what electronic monitoring devices can and cannot do. These devices fall into one of three categories: continuously signaling with and without telephones, programmed contact, and tracking devices.

---

# Close Up  Florida's Community Control Program

In 1982, the Florida Department of Corrections was forced by federal court orders to set a maximum capacity figure not only for each individual facility but also for the prison system as a whole. Florida lawmakers, realizing that prison construction would not keep up with prison population growth, passed the Correctional Reform Act of 1983. Included within the act was a mandate for the establishment of a Community Control program.

The Correctional Reform Act defined Community Control as:

[A] form of intensive supervised custody in the community, including surveillance on weekends and holidays, administered by officers with restricted caseloads. Community Control is an individualized program in which the freedom of the offender is restricted within the community, home, or noninstitutional residential placement, and specific sanctions are imposed and enforced. (Joint Legislative Management Committee, 1983, p. 446).

The act emphasizes punishment and confinement for its target population of felony offenders, not rehabilitation. The goals of the program are (1) to help reduce prison overcrowding, (2) to reduce commitments to

prison, and (3) to provide a safe diversionary alternative to incarceration (Florida Department of Corrections, 1988, p. 3).

A major study conducted by the National Council on Crime and Delinquency focused on the issue of net widening. This study found that 54% of the program participants were true diversions from incarceration (high-risk offenders), while 46% resembled regular probationers (Wagner and Baird, 1993). Finally, a five-year recidivism study conducted by Smith and Akers (1993) reported high levels of recidivism (78%). When these rates were compared to the recidivism rates of a matched group of prisoners, the researchers found that there was no significant difference between the two groups. The recidivism rates of Community Control participants exceeded the rates reported by comparable intermediate sanction programs in other states.

During the first eight years of Florida's Community Control Program operation, more than 60,000 participants were admitted to the program. The size, longevity, and continued political endorsement of the program suggest that it is the largest and most important program of its type in the country (Morris and Tonry, 1990; Tonry and Will, 1988).

---

**Continuously signaling devices** with telephone service consist of three components: (1) A cigarette pack-sized transmitter, which may or may not be tamper-proof, is strapped to the offender's ankle or wrist. It sends an encoded signal at regular intervals; (2) A receiver-dialer, which receives the signal, is located in the offender's home. It reports the information automatically by telephone. (3) The central computer, which can be in any of various locations, accepts reports from the receiver-dialer. When any interruption in the signal occurs, it compares the report with the offender's curfews or work schedule. If the information indicates that the offender is on an unauthorized absence, the computer either records the information for review later, or alerts correctional staff immediately, depending on program policies and procedures (Schmidt and Curtis, 1987). Some continuously signaling monitors have extended options including visual telephones and alcohol detection de-

vices. The alcohol detection devices are designed to verify both the alcohol level *and* the identity of the person at the same time (Mitsubishi Electronics Inc., 1990).

A continuously signaling device without a telephone has only two components: a transmitter strapped to the offender, which sends out a continuous signal, and a portable-receiver located in the monitoring officer's car, which picks up the signal. The portable-receiver can pick up the signal within a one-block range of the offender's location allowing the officer to check on the offender both at home or other places (e.g., at his/her place of employment) (Schmidt, 1989). While this device allows flexibility in checking the offender's whereabouts, it is more expensive because it requires direct monitoring by a community control officer.

The second category of electronic monitoring equipment is the **programmed contact device,** which consists of either a wristlet or a voice verification unit and a central computer. The computer, located in a designated office, is programmed to call the offender during the hours the offender is scheduled to be monitored. The calls may be random to keep the offender offguard, or programmed for a specific time. If a wristlet is used, a telephone with a verifier box is utilized so that when the computer calls, the wristlet can be inserted into the verifier box to confirm that the offender being monitored answered the call. The voice verification unit is in a tamper- proof box attached to a handset, which can connect to any telephone in the offender's home. When the computer calls for a voice check, the offender must repeat the words the unit requests. The unit analyzes the voice pattern and compares it with words previously recorded by the offender to see if they match. If they do not match, usually a second test is made and if there is a second failure, the correctional agency is notified.

The third type of electronic monitoring device, the **tracking device,** is in the earliest stages of development (Arnold, 1991). The design of these devices is similar to those used to track endangered, wild animals. Using a geographic grid system, they can pinpoint the offender's exact location at any given time. The range of these devices will most likely encompass a city or county, greatly expanding their range of usefulness. The tracking device will no doubt increase the ability of correctional officials to exercise greater control and to satisfy the "get tough" punitive demands of the public and legislators raises ethical questions.

There are also financial costs that must be considered. In Florida, for example, offenders are required to have telephones and are expected to pay an additional $30 per month in supervision fees. Does this exempt those who cannot financially meet these obligations from participating in the program and subject them to a term of imprisonment in the place of electronic monitoring? Again, these issues have not been satisfactorily investigated.

The popularity of electronic monitoring in recent years can be attributed to both its claimed punitive and economic benefits. However, while electronic monitoring of offenders does seem to add an additional punitive measure to the continuum of sanctions, recent research calls into question the cost/benefit claims of these programs (Morris and Tonry, 1990; Tonry and Wills, 1988).

## Shock Incarceration and Boot Camp Involve Short-Term Incarceration

The terms shock incarceration and boot camp are often used interchangeably, although there are differences in the two programs. **Shock incarceration,** sometimes called shock probation/parole, consists of a short period of incarceration in a state prison followed by a return to community supervision (e.g., intensive probation supervision). **Boot camps** provide a very structured and regimented environment similar to that found in military boot camps. Inmates sentenced to boot camps are usually separated from the general prison population either by assignment to special dormitories or to special facilities.

**SHOCK INCARCERATION WAS THE PREDECESSOR OF BOOT CAMPS**　Shock incarceration grew out of the European tradition of *sursis,* the legal suspension of an offender's sentence. With sursis, the sentence is fulfilled if, after release, no further offenses are committed during a designated period. The advantage of shock incarceration over sursis is that it provides for supervision of offenders once they are released from incarceration. With sursis, authorities have little or no control or supervision over the offender once the sentence is suspended.

The first shock incarceration law was passed in Ohio in 1965. In 1974, Ohio enacted a shock parole program. Supporters of shock probation and parole programs stated that these programs:

1. impress offenders with the seriousness of their crimes without imposing a long prison term;
2. give courts a way to release offenders deemed amenable to community-based treatment, based on more extensive assessments than were available at the original sentencing;
3. let courts appropriately achieve a just compromise between punishment and leniency;
4. let courts combine treatment and deterrence purposes when sentencing offenders;
5. allow young offenders serving their first prison terms to be released before they have been socialized into the prison culture (Parent, 1989, p. 51).

**BOOT CAMPS ARE MODELED AFTER MILITARY BOOT CAMP TRAINING**　Boot camps, which emphasize military style discipline, have caught the attention of the public, legislators, and policy makers. The first boot camp programs began operating in Oklahoma in November 1983 and in Georgia one month later (Parent, 1989). By 1992, twenty-five states and the federal government were running these programs (MacKenzie and Souryal, 1994). Boot camps, like other intermediate sanctions, are designed to alleviate overcrowding, reduce recidivism, and cost less than incarceration. Additionally, in an era when the public increasingly wanted criminals to be punished, the strict military regimentation and discipline of these programs resulted in their being perceived as "tough on crime." Their growth can be attributed to the fact that politicians and the public were impressed with both their punitiveness and their cost effectiveness.

Most boot camp programs are designed for young (sixteen to twenty-five) male offenders convicted of nonviolent crimes. About one-half of the states allow female participation yet the numbers of beds available for women is limited. In 1992, in close to two-thirds of the programs, participation was voluntary while in seven out of ten dropping out was voluntary., Initially these programs emphasized a strict military regimen centering around drill, strictly controlled unquestioning behavior, physical conditioning, and hard work. This is generally accomplished by the drill sergeants who constantly supervise and discipline the inmates and keep them busy during their waking hours. Later programs have placed more emphasis on rehabilitation—e.g., education, substance abuse counseling, life skills training (MacKenzie and Souryal, 1994).

At a typical boot camp prison for adults,

> ... male inmates have their heads shaved (females may be permitted short haircuts). At all times they are required to address staff as "Sir" or "Ma'am," must request permission to speak, and must refer to themselves as "this inmate." Punishments for even minor rule violations are summary and certain, frequently involving physical exercise such as push-ups or running in place. A major rule violation can result in dismissal from the program.
>
> [The] day begins with pre-dawn reveille followed by one to two hours of physical training and drill.... [From there] they march ... to breakfast where they must stand at attention while waiting in line, [moving] in a military manner as the line advances, ... stand at attention behind their chairs until commanded to sit, and eat in silence. After breakfast they march to work sites where they participate in hard

physical labor.... When the 6 to 8 hour work day is over the inmates return to their compound where they participate in more exercise and drill. Dinner is followed by evening programs that include counseling, life skills training, academic education or drug education and treatment. There is little or no free time.

> As their performance and time in the program warrants, [boot camp] ... inmates gradually earn more privileges and responsibility. A special hat or uniform may be the outward display of their new status. Those who successfully finish the program usually attend an elaborate graduation ceremony with visitors and family invited to attend. Awards are often presented to acknowledge progress made during the program, and the inmates may perform the drill routines they have practiced throughout their time in the boot camp (MacKenzie, 1993, pp. 22–23).

The nagging question was whether or not these programs, which were touted as being tough, could realize their objectives. A multisite evaluation of eight state-level boot camp programs by MacKenzie and Souryal (1994) addressed these questions. Their study found that "the recidivism rate of boot camp graduates did not differ from ... similarly situated inmates who had served longer terms of incarceration" (p. 41). The critical factor in whether these programs successfully reduced overcrowding was related to program design. Where the Department of Corrections was allowed to select boot camp participants overcrowding was most likely to be alleviated. This was because they generally maximized the selection of offenders who otherwise would have been sent to prison. The military aspects of these program had little deterrent effect. Moreover, this overly authoritarian atmosphere was felt to be less conducive to allowing other treatment programming to achieve its desired results. Program length—six months versus three months—was felt to be related to the effectiveness of the rehabilitative programming since offenders had more time to benefit from programs such as substance abuse treatment and education. This, coupled with intensive supervision on release and continued work, education, and treatment programming, was felt to be more effective in reducing recidivism. Voluntary participation was also considered to be related to the effectiveness of rehabilitative programming. Offenders who volunteered were felt to possess a greater sense of self-control, which was believed to result in higher levels of commitment to the program.

Boot camp inmates go through a short-term, intense program that attempts to develop new behavior patterns, deal with deficiencies in education, and other problems such as substance abuse. While military activities are not always emphasized, these programs are highly regimented.

In examining inmate attitudes toward incarceration, boot camp inmates developed more positive attitudes toward their prison experience over time, which was not the case for conventional prison inmates. Interviews with boot camp inmates revealed that:

> they believed that the experience had been positive and that they had changed for the better. Although ... initially [they] entered because they would spend less time incarcerated near the end of their time in boot camp they said that the experience had changed them for the better ... and that they were proud of themselves for being able be to complete such a program (p. 41).

*Future Boot Camps Will Place Greater Emphasis on Treatment Programming and Aftercare* First-generation boot camps tended to follow a strict military regimen in response to public and political demands for programs that were punitive and tough on offenders. However, evaluators found that these programs centering around "scaring youth straight" through a tough military style boot camp program have not been effective. It is unrealistic to believe that you can take a group of 16- to 25-year-old, out-of-control youth, most of whom had been part of antisocial groups or gangs for years, and in the space of three to six months alter

their criminal lifestyle by subjecting them to an authoritarian regimen. While years ago many juvenile delinquents were coerced to join the military and did straighten up, current boot camps leave out an important element of this process: Following their boot camp experience, military recruits went on to spend at least several years in a highly structured military environment, which provided jobs, housing and the like.

Second-generation boot camp programs have capitalized on the idea of special programs, but their emphasis has changed. The time spent in military-oriented activities has been reduced to about one-quarter of a typical sixteen-hour day with the remainder of the time occupied with programming that includes education, the teaching of problem-solving skills, anticriminal role modeling, anger control, and programs dealing with substance abuse (Sharp, 1995). If they are to avoid being just another correctional fad they to have to do more than just appear to be tough. Future boot camps will have to deemphasize the idea that they are a quick fix and strengthen their treatment and aftercare programs so that they better meet the needs of boot camp inmates (Cowles, Castellano, and Gransky, 1995). Additionally, if they are used for females, they will have to be modified to meet the special needs of this population (e.g., women abused by men being placed in a situation in which

# Close Up    New York's Shock Incarceration Program: A Model for the Future

To qualify for admission offenders must be under thirty-five, eligible for parole within three years, have not committed violent or sex offenses nor have been sentenced to an indeterminate prison term. At screening inmates are informed about the program and must decide whether they want to serve their full prison term or volunteer for the program. Volunteers go through a program divided into two six-month phases.

Phase 1 involves an intensive incarceration program. All staff in these programs receive special training in military and treatment curriculum. Group teamwork and unity are emphasized to facilitate staff from different disciplines in working together as a team because this program follows a therapeutic community model.

While inmate programing includes physical training, drills, and ceremonial formations this component only comprises 26% of a sixteen-hour day. For six hours each day, inmates perform hard labor on facility and community projects. In 1994, inmates performed 1.2 million hours of work on projects that would have cost municipalities $6.3 million to complete.

The network program, which forms the basis for the therapeutic community structure of these programs, focuses on fostering responsibility for self, to others, and for the quality of one's life. Inmates are formed into platoons, and they live together as a unit. They hold daily network community meetings to resolve problems and reflect on their progress. Networks help inmates adjust to community living and develop socialization, employment, communication, and decision-making and critical thinking skills. Part of this involves teaching inmates that responsible behavior results from recognizing the difference between wants and needs and appropriate versus dysfunctional ways— e.g., crime and substance abuse—of getting needs met.

As distinguished from other boot camps, substance abuse treatment takes place in a therapeutic community context. All inmates participate in Alcohol and Substance Abuse Treatment (ASAT), which includes drug education and group counseling for a minimum of two three-hour sessions per week. ASAT is modeled after the 12-step recovery program of Alcoholics and Narcotics Anonymous and is staffed by trained substance abuse counselors.

Education achievement is a central objective of these programs. A minimum of twelve hours per week is spent on academic work, which amounts to at least 260 hours at the end of six months. The success of this component is exemplified by a 68% passing rate on the GED tests as compared with 52% and 59% rates for minimum and medium custody inmates, respectively. This occurred despite the fact that boot camp inmates were in prison for shorter periods of time than the other two groups. Finally, inmates who have been removed for disciplinary reasons or are in danger of removal for unsatisfactory program adjustment can opt to be placed in the "reevaluation program." These inmates receive refresher training, which focuses on reviewing program concepts and expectations. Satisfactory completion of this refresher course results in readmission to the program.

Phase 2 of this program is called "AfterShock" and is operated by the division of parole. Prior to an inmate's release POs work closely with inmates, their families, and community service agencies to develop sound residence and employment programs to ensure a smooth transition from the facility to the community. Further, suitable housing is provided by the division's Community-Based Residential Program for shock incarceration (SI) inmates without a suitable home environment to which they can return. POs supervising SI graduates have reduced caseloads, with two officers responsible for thirty-eight SI graduates for a six-month period. This allows increased contacts between officers and parolees for employment, curfew checks, and drug testing. Within one week of SI release, program objectives call for SI parolees to have a job, and within two weeks they are to be enrolled in an educational or vocational training program. SI graduates are also required to participate in network meetings, which are designed to reinforce the principles of positive decision-making learned at institutional meetings. They must also attend relapse counseling meetings, which focus on factors that may lead to relapse, reinforce principles of sobriety learned in shock facilities, and discuss common problems and solutions to adjustment to community life.

A major goal is cost containment. New York estimates that it saves $2.11 million per 100 inmates completing this program. With 10,927 program graduates as of September 1994, the state estimates savings of $225 million. As to the rates of return to prison, SI graduates when compared to control groups— program dropouts, inmates eligible but not entering

## Close Up

the program, and those paroled before shock incarceration was established—had higher success rates after three years and had rates that were equal to or better than comparison groups after four and five years.

Given that this program saved the state money, provided municipalities with free labor to complete needed projects, and had recidivism equal to or better than sending inmates to prison, it would seem that programs of this kind have a place in the spectrum of correctional

programming. What do you think of this program? Do you believe these programs are a fad or will they become a regular part of correctional programming?

SOURCE: Adapted from C. L. Clark, D. W. Ariz, D. L. MacKenzie (1994). *Shock Incarceration in New York: Focus on Treatment.* Washington D.C.: National Institute of Justice; New York State Department of Correctional Services and The New York Division of Parole. *Seventh Annual Shock Legislative Report.* Albany, New York N.Y.: Author.

## Close Up  The Metropolitan Day Reporting Center, Boston

At age 22, Bill is serving his second prison term, this time, two years in the Billerica House of Correction for an assault conviction. The Billerica House of Correction is run by the Middlesex County Sheriff, and serves a large urban county west of Boston. The facility houses felons with prison terms of up to 30 months. Due to crowding, officials must keep Billerica's population below a court ordered limit.

Ninety days before his minimum parole eligibility date, Bill was offered the chance to serve the rest of his prison term under the supervision of the Metropolitan Day Reporting Center (DRC), a program operated by the Crime and Justice Foundation. It is one of four similar programs funded by the Commonwealth of Massachusetts to reduce crowding in county houses of correction.

Bill lives with his mother in Framingham, about 30 miles southwest of Billerica. Today it takes him 45 minutes to drive to Billerica, where he reports to the Metropolitan Day Reporting Center office located in the work release unit, a residential facility outside the prison's security perimeter. After checking in with center staff, he fills out an itinerary, showing where he will be each moment of the next day, and giving phone numbers where he can be reached at each location.

After Bill gives a urine specimen for drug testing, he and his counselor spend 15 minutes planning Bill's budget for the coming month. He then goes to work at a metal fabrication plant, a job he got through Comprehensive Offender Employment Resources, a community program. He calls center staff at noon, and gets two additional phone calls at random times during the day from center staff. After work, Bill returns to Metro DRC offices to attend a group drug use counseling session. He then goes home. During the evening and early morning hours, he gets two random phone calls to assure he is complying with curfew requirements. Last week Bill had forty-two in-person and telephone contacts with DRC staff.

If he continues to obey all DRC rules, Bill will be paroled in six weeks when he reaches his minimum eligibility date. But, if he violates even one major rule—for example, if he has a single positive drug test or is out of contact with center staff for more than two hours—he will be returned to the House of Correction. He will also lose his minimum parole date and probably serve until the expiration of his sentence (Parent, 1990b, p. 6).

a male instructor is verbally "abusing" them) (Sharp, 1995). The Close-Up on New York's shock incarceration program suggests the direction programs this kind of program will take.

### Day Reporting Centers Are an Innovation

**Day reporting centers** (DRCs) are the newest innovation in the wide array of intermediate sanctions. They have, however, been slow to catch the attention of correctional administrators and policymakers. In 1990, a national study by Parent, (1990b) found that only fourteen day reporting centers were operating in the United States.

**THE PROGRAMS HAVE A BRITISH ORIGIN** While DRCs did not emerge in the United States until 1986, they have been widely used in other countries since the early 1970s, most notably in Great Britain. These programs were created by correctional reformers who sought alternatives for chronic minor offenders. Generally, these offenders were not dangerous and many became incarcerated primarily because judges had exhausted their sentencing options. Reformers argued that incarcerating these offenders would serve to intensify their propensity to commit criminal acts.

In 1972 Parliament created four day treatment centers (DTCs) and several similar programs were established by probation officers around England and Wales (Parent, 1990b). While most of these centers developed without central planning and standards and were diverse, collectively, their program content focused on four primary areas: social/life skills, health/welfare activities, arts and crafts, and sports (Mair, 1988). In the 1980s the British DTCs caught the attention of correctional leaders in Massachusetts and Connecticut who were searching for alternatives to ease jail and prison overcrowding. Legislators in those two states, impressed with these DTCs, appropriated funds to develop, implement, and operate DRCs (Parent, 1990b). These programs were adaptations of the British DTCs. However, while program goals and objectives were clearly defined and systematically applied, programs developed in the United States were still diverse.

**THE GOALS AND PURPOSES OF DRCs VARY** In British DTCs, the overriding goal was to provide an alternative to imprisonment for a targeted group of offenders. DTCs also reported goals that in-

cluded reduction of recidivism and development of offenders' skills (Mair, 1988). These goals are similar to those outlined in the study of DRCs in the United States (Parent, 1990b). The major functions of DRCs in the United States have been (1) to reduce jail and prison crowding, (2) to enhance probation and parole supervision, and (3) to treat offenders' problems.

DRCs are similar to work release programs, but are more cost effective because they are nonresidential. DRCs also are likely to be more program intensive than work release and generally offer a variety of programs. However, not enough research has been conducted to determine their effectiveness compared to other types of intermediate sanctions.

## FUTURE OF INTERMEDIATE SANCTIONS

As we move into the twenty-first century, we can expect intermediate sanctions to continue being an integral part of corrections. Although studies show recidivism rates in halfway house and work release programs were not significantly lower than for offenders given harsher or more lenient sentences, these programs continue to be widely used. We can expect the same pattern regarding IPS programs, house arrest/home confinement, electronic monitoring, inmate boot camps, day reporting centers, and residential community programs though they too have not led to significant reductions in recidivism. Recidivism does not appear to be the critical issue for these programs. The driving force behind the new programs centers more on economic issues. These programs seem more cost effective than incarceration. Indeed, advocates suggest that placing offenders in these programs has saved millions of dollars by eliminating the need to build new prisons. Morris and Tonry (1990), however, point out that " . . . cost comparisons are complicated [and that] glib claims about cost savings associated with intermediate punishments often do not stand up to careful scrutiny" (p. 234).

As noted earlier, we may be approaching these sanctions unrealistically. Their real focus is neither recidivism reduction nor cost savings. What intermediate sanctions are, and will continue to be, as we move into the twenty-first century, is a component of a complex sentencing system allowing for a wider range of sentencing alternatives. This reflects a more advanced, comprehensive approach to sanctioning offenders that is commensurate with the severity of their crimes. Since our laws distinguish gradations in the severity of criminal behavior, our punishments also need to reflect those gradations (Thornberg, 1990). Thus, by adding intermediate sanctions to our arsenal of sentencing alternatives, we are better able to impose the least restrictive sentencing alternative commensurate with an offender's crime.

We can expect to see intermediate sanctions expand across the country through the continued implementation of a wide variety of the programs discussed here. The enthusiastic support these pro-

grams have received from academics, correctional reformers, policy makers, legislators, the judiciary, prosecutors, and correctional administrators is a good indication that there is a wide array of people who have a vested interest in seeing intermediate sanctions "work." With this kind of support, we can expect to see impediments removed and reforms made when necessary to see that these programs continue to function properly. No longer are we prone to "throw the baby out with the bath water" as we did in the past when programs failed to reach our expectations. After all, the business of "correcting" should apply to programs as well as people.

## CHAPTER RECAP

**Historical Development of Intermediate Sanctions**
The Correctional Philosophy Underlying Intermediate Sanctions Has Changed
   What Are Intermediate Sanctions Supposed to Do?
**Various Intermediate Sanction Programs Exist**
Halfway Houses Are Treatment Oriented
   This Type of Facility Has Existed for a Long Time
   Guidelines for Opening and Operating a Halfway House
   The Vast Majority of Halfway Houses Today Are Privately Operated
Work/Study Release Programs Provide Prerelease Employment or Education
   Early Work Release Programs Began in Wisconsin
   Work Release Has Various Goals and Objectives
How Work Release Programs Operate
Intensive Probation Supervision Programs Are Designed for Prison-Bound Offenders
   These Programs Had Antecedents in California
   Programs Developed in the 1980s Were Designed to Increase Control
   New IPS Programs Are More Successful in Achieving Some Goals than Others
House Arrest/Home Confinement Programs Make Offenders' Homes Their Jails
   Many Are Stand-Alone Programs Because They Are Not Associated with Probation Programs
Electronic Monitoring Increases Surveillance
   Historical Development of Electronic Monitoring Programs
   There Are Several Types of Electronic Monitors
Shock Incarceration and Boot Camp Involve Short-Term Incarceration
   Shock Incarceration was the Predesessor of Boot Camps

   Boot Camps Are Modeled After Military Boot Camp Training
   Future Boot Camps Will Place Greater Emphasis on Treatment Programming and Aftercare
Day Reporting Centers Are an Innovation
   The Programs Have a British Origin
   The Goals and Purposes of DRCs Vary
**Future of Intermediate Sanctions**

## ACKNOWLEDGMENT

[a] J. Byrne, A. J. Lurgio, and J. Petersilia (Eds.) *Smart Sentencing: The Emergence of Intermediate Sentences*, p. 289, copyright © 1992 by Sage Publications, Inc. Reprinted by permission of Sage Publications, Inc.

## REVIEW QUESTIONS

**1.** How is the term *intermediate sanctions* defined? What types of programs are included in this set of sanctions?
**2.** What factors have contributed to the development of intermediate sanctions in the 1980s and 1990s?
**3.** Describe and discuss halfway houses, their development, organization, and present status. Compare halfway houses with work release programs.
**4.** Compare intensive probation supervision with house arrest in terms of procedure and goals.
**5.** Discuss the various types of electronic monitoring devices and the legal and ethical issues associated with their use.
**6.** Describe first- and second-generation boot camps.
**7.** What are day reporting centers and what are their objectives?

## TEST YOUR KNOWLEDGE

1. Intermediate sanctions
   a. are not intended to be punitive.
   b. fall between traditional probation and imprisonment.
   c. are designed exclusively for rehabilitative purposes.
   d. are only for convicted misdemeanants.

2. Halfway houses
   a. are rarely operated by private agencies.
   b. were only developed in the 1980s.
   c. should be designed to house between twenty to thirty-five residents.
   d. are not used as an alternative to sending offenders to prison.

3. Work release programs
   a. are generally unsuccessful because they admit too many problem inmates.
   b. have been discontinued because they are not cost effective.
   c. are sometimes operated by private agencies.
   d. are only used as an alternative to imprisoning felons.

4. Research shows that offenders in IPS programs
   a. have lower arrest rates than those on routine probation.
   b. are subject to more surveillance and control than those on routine probation.
   c. do not participate in treatment programs as frequently as those on routine probation.
   d. have fewer technical violations than those on routine probation.

5. The discussion of electronic monitoring indicated that
   a. with the technology available today, correctional officials can track offenders' specific whereabouts.
   b. legal concerns have caused some jurisdictions to discontinue these programs.
   c. these programs have been used to increase control over offenders who violated IPS conditions.
   d. these programs have replaced ordinary IPS programs in some states.

# EPILOGUE

# WHAT CAN WE EXPECT AS THE 20TH CENTURY COMES TO A CLOSE?

## TRENDS AFFECTING THE FUTURE OF CORRECTIONS

An epilogue allows us to discuss our vision of the future of corrections in the United States. However, as with any set of predictions, nothing is as unpredictable, and perhaps as subject to error, as anticipating what the future holds. Nevertheless, several of the social, political, and economic trends of the mid-1990s are likely to have a direct impact on correctional policies and issues as we move toward the end of the century. These trends include:

**1.** The public mood, as evidenced by the 1994 elections, is heavily tilted toward retribution and a reduction of "frills," which include most non-work programming.
**2.** A move is afoot to reduce those crime prevention programs that can be interpreted as being social, particularly when they deal with children. These tend to be seen as wasteful of tax dollars.
**3.** The demographic structure of the U.S. population is such that there will be a significant increase in the number of fifteen-through nineteen-year-olds by the year 2000.
**4.** Lower income neighborhoods are perpetuating criminogenic conditions that include, for example, dysfunctional families living in disorganized communities; relatively high levels of drug use; and large numbers of youths joining gangs, which become their primary groups and foster the development of antisocial values and patterns.
**5.** More and more prisons are being built, which is taking a larger proportion of tax dollars. The question is: Will the public tire of supporting this approach to crime control if this means more taxes or fewer services?
**6.** The courts are currently requiring jurisdictions to operate constitutionally acceptable jails and prisons that provide inmates with basic necessities and a reasonably safe environment. Will public pressure change their support for inmate rights and allow prison administrators more latitude in dealing with inmates?

Each of these broad issues will have a significant impact on corrections during the next ten years and beyond. We will discuss their implications and then deal with the future of corrections into the beginning of the twenty-first century.

## The Public Mood toward Criminals Is Becoming More Punitive

There is ample evidence that a substantial proportion of the public perceives crime as a major—if not the leading—problem facing our society today. A 1994 poll, for example, put crime as the number one concern, with 81% of those sampled favoring laws that would imprison repeat offenders for life. More than half of this sample said it was willing to pay more taxes to build more prisons to house these offenders (Byrne, 1994). Crime rates began rising in the mid-1970s, dropped off somewhat in the early 1980s, and began to rise again by the mid-1990s. In fact, by the early 1990s violent crime had reached an all-time high while property offenses were lower than their 1980 highs.

Regardless of the amount of crime, people are more afraid of being victimized today, as the survey quoted earlier shows. This is related to the fact that victimization is more random now, meaning that the suburbs are no longer the safe havens they once were. This has led to a growing discontent with the criminal justice system, particularly with corrections. As the pressure to get tougher with criminals has increased, legislatures around the nation have responded by creating longer and mandatory sentences. The most recent type of these laws is the "three strikes and you're out" type, which mandates life imprisonment for violent three-time felony offenders. During the 1980s and into the 1990s these types of sentences led to unprecedented growth in the prison population, which caused severe overcrowding in many of the systems. Court intervention brought about in part by conditions related to overcrowding, resulted in the placement of population caps and other restrictions on many systems. This led to early releases and major reductions in the proportion of the sentence served by many inmates. As the media highlighted the new crimes committed by these releasees, there was greater public pressure for jurisdictions to keep offenders in prison longer. This resulted in crash programs of prison building as politicians pushed for inmates to serve a longer proportion of their sentences. It appears that this cycle will continue into the near future unless the public or lawmakers become less willing to spend the dollars necessary to continue incarcerating increasing numbers of offenders for longer periods of time.

A corollary of the pressure to get tough has been the move to reduce or eliminate inmate programs, activities, and privileges because they are seen as making prison life too comfortable for inmates and/or subverting the punitive aspects of imprisonment. Thus, the emphasis is likely to be placed on reducing programs and leisure activities and mandating hard daily work for all inmates. Additionally, such activities as weight lifting, watching TV, smoking, and even drinking coffee have begun to be barred in different facilities. Although this transformation of prisons into "hard time" facilities is in its early stages, this is also a strategy that is likely to continue into the near future. Even though this will reduce program costs, any savings are likely to be absorbed by the increasing costs of maintaining security. When inmates are idle they develop their own means of entertainment, which frequently includes activities that violate prison rules, encourage gang development, and threaten control and security. Also, organized activities provide acceptable opportunities for inmates to reduce the stresses and frustrations of prison life. Thus, one likely result of the hard-line strategy may well be an increase in violence as inmate tensions mount and no acceptable methods of reducing them are available. This may also aggravate feelings of alienation and anger that many inmates harbor toward the society that imprisoned them, thereby raising the probability of recidivism. This strategy, if actualized, is likely to make the job of correctional personnel more difficult and dangerous and increase turnover rates.

## The Public Is Advocating a Reduction in Prevention Programs

The agenda of the new conservative majority in the U.S. Congress and in many states appears to include a reduction of "liberal social" programs and a shifting of responsibility for maintaining them from federal to state and local governments. The targeted programs include some that impact children who can be described as being at risk of becoming delinquent (e.g., Headstart, recreation programs for inner city youth, etc.). While programs ought to be funded on their merits (i.e., how well they accomplish their goals and objectives), care must be taken at all levels to support those that increase the chances of school success for children from disadvantaged groups. The cost ef-

fectiveness of successful programs of this type can be seen in the reduced number of the children who may become delinquent. Thus, if prevention programs that work are reduced, the long-term effects are likely to include increases in delinquency and later adult criminality. This outcome obviously will result in greater expenses for the criminal justice system, including corrections.

## The Demographic Structure of the Population Is Changing

One of the most accurate bases for making predictions about future trends can be found in the census figures that describe our population. These data provide us with facts, such as the age, gender, and race composition of the population, which can be used to plan for the future. Projections for the decade from 1995 to 2005 tell us that the number of Americans under the age of eighteen will increase from approximately sixty million to more than seventy million by the year 2000 (Krauss, 1994). Individuals below the age of twenty account for more than 26% of all arrests and those below thirty account for almost 62% (Federal Bureau of Investigation, 1994).

Thus, barring any other changes, this bulge in the youthful population alone will result in a considerable rise in crime rates for the first ten or twenty years of the next century. A survey of forty-eight U.S. correctional systems (Wunder, 1995b) indicates that present correctional populations are expected to increase by 51% by the year 2000. Further, 75% of the thirty-two systems responding to the question said they would not have sufficient space to hold that increase. Based on these figures, there is no question that corrections will continue to grapple with problems of overcrowding in the immediate future. How they are dealt with will depend on the sentencing and correctional policies in effect during this time. We must also keep in mind that the criminogenic conditions existing in the communities around the United States, have probably already affected the children and youth living in these areas.

## Criminogenic Social Conditions Will Continue to Affect Involvement in Crime

Regardless of the preparation for them or the conditions surrounding them, when children are born they are on a developmental track that will lead to their becoming adolescents and adults, unless, of course, they die first. Many developmental psychologists and other social scientists consider the first five or six years of life as the most important in that a cognitive foundation is developed that will serve the individual for the rest of his or her life. Thus, whether the child is loved and nurtured or rejected, abused, and neglected, whether it is taught a value system that results in law-abiding behavior or given an antisocial one to copy, whether drugs fog their environment, the child inevitably develops and enters the society. Once this cognitive foundation is laid down, it becomes more and more difficult as time passes for this individual to change. Thus, any criminogenic influences present during this period (and later) are likely to have a deleterious influence. The litany of criminogenic influences includes dysfunctional families; teenage pregnancies; dysfunctional neighborhoods and communities that encourage drug use, delinquency, and gang formation; impoverished status; poor schools; and inadequate opportunity structures.

The family, which has a crucial role in the criminogenic process, can be defined as that unit which has the initial and primary responsibility for socializing the child. It exists in a variety of forms: extended families that include many kinfolk; nuclear families with two parents or one parent; blended families with two parents, each with their own children; surrogate families in which children are being raised by nonbiological, perhaps unrelated, parents. Regardless of the type of family, if the child is subjected to abuse and/or neglect, is not supervised, is not given preparation to succeed in school, or is not taught appropriate coping skills, the probability of his or her developing delinquent or other deviant behavior will be increased. Thus, a family with few resources, with young, immature, or absent parents, or one that abuses drugs and/or models violent behavior will tend to be criminogenic.

Communities that cannot assist people, whether through government programs or informal networks (e.g., charitable religious programs), cannot control disruptive or violent behavior, do not have schools that can absorb and motivate students who are poorly prepared, and do not have meaningful opportunities for them after they become prepared can also be criminogenic. These are some of the conditions that, in various combinations, help to create delinquency and crime and, thus, provide greater numbers of offenders to be supervised in correctional settings.

## Will the Public Continue to Support the Most Expensive Solutions?

The public's insistence on long-term imprisonment as the solution for the crime problem will be tested in the very near future. As the cost of this approach to the problem escalates and the public balks at paying higher taxes, decisions will have to be made as to how public funds are apportioned for different programs. Are prisons more important than education? More important than infrastructure needs such as roads, water treatment, etc.? Than libraries and other cultural concerns? Than health care or programs that care for the elderly?

In 1991 the cost of incarcerating an inmate for one year (including indirect costs such as correctional officer pensions) was $30,000 (Branham, 1992). Given the 1994 level of incarceration (including jails and prisons), and assuming no increase in the per year/inmate cost, and not including community correctional costs, the yearly correctional bill for imprisonment was about $45 billion. An additional factor that is likely to increase future costs is the aging of the prison population due to inmates serving longer sentences. This will require significant increases in prison health care budgets to meet the greater health needs of older offenders.

Some idea of the effects of get-tough measures on a state's budget can be gleaned from looking at the projected effects of the California "three strikes" law. The California Department of Corrections estimates that if this law remains in effect, it will raise the state's prison population by an additional 275,000 inmates by the year 2028. The estimated costs of this are $21 billion for prison construction and $5.7 billion per year for operating costs. In 1990, when the California prison population experienced a sharp rise, taxes were not raised but the education budget was reduced by $2 billion. There is no way of knowing what will be the extent and effects of taking money from positive programs such as education to fund corrections. However, it is not hard to predict that there will be some long-term negative results. Remember that by the year 2000 the youthful population will bulge. If the educational system is not adequately funded so it can deal this population increase, crime and delinquency rates will rise as youths drop out of school and cannot find jobs because they do not have the appropriate skills.

The public may respond favorably to one of the innovations regarding cost containment: the greater use of contracting with private entities to build and/or run prisons and jails. We discussed this option in Chapter 13 and make some additional comments later.

### Will the Courts Continue to Insist on Constitutional Prisons?

The operation of contemporary correctional institutions has become very complex. The legal issues facing prison administrators, which demand that they run "constitutional prisons," contribute to this complexity and cannot be ignored. As indicated earlier in the text, the courts have gone through several changes in their manner of handling complaints regarding prison conditions. The courts have become increasingly hesitant to micromanage correctional institutions and have ruled that harsh and even overcrowded conditions are a part of the price inmates may have to pay for violating the law. However, they will intervene when inmates are denied appropriate access to basic necessities such as adequate food and medical care. They will also intervene when prison officials fail to deal with obvious risks that result in inmates being assaulted by other inmates (e.g., *Farmer v. Brennan*, 1994) and will not allow staff to unnecessarily injure inmates (*Hudson v. McMillian*, 1990). Based on the present composition of the Supreme Court, there is no reason to assume that there will be a significant change of direction in its treatment of prison issues.

However, Congress, apparently responding to public pressure to get tough on criminals, has targeted both "frivolous" prisoner litigation as well as that which is justified or meritorious. In 1995 the House passed the "Stop Turning Out Prisoners Act," and the Senate passed the "Prison Litigation Reform Act." Frivolous law suits, such as those by inmates claiming that they want crunchy rather than smooth peanut butter, should be restricted. The main thrust of this legislation, however, is to restrict the ability of federal courts to protect inmates' constitutional rights and prevent the courts from correcting the heinous wrongs that are sometimes inflicted against them (Westcott, 1995).

Specific provisions of these bills would place substantial limitations on the power of the courts to resolve class action cases involving prison conditions. Consent degrees would be limited and this would make negotiated settlements to eliminate the necessity of a trial impracticable. Even when inmate plaintiffs succeed in a court action, any court orders prohibiting practices found unconstitutional would terminate after two years even if the abusive practices have not been corrected. The only way to renew court oversight would be to go through a long and expensive new trial. Further, any current court monitoring of prison conditions would be terminated as soon as this legislation is passed. Finally, both bills severely limit the fees paid to attorneys representing inmate plaintiffs. They would not receive fees for cases settled out of court nor for the monitoring of remedial orders to correct abuses that were proven unconstitutional at trial.

In addition, the fees paid to plaintiff attorneys would be capped at the rates paid to court appointed defense attorneys in criminal cases. Unlike criminal defense attorneys, however, those representing inmates in cases involving unconstitutional prison conditions only receive fees if they win in these long, difficult and complicated cases. For these fees they are required to bear the enormous expenses associated with this ligation (e.g. expert witness fees). These financial burdens will make it difficult for organizations like the ACLU's National Prisoner Project (NPP), which takes cases involving serious breaches of prisoners' constitutional rights, to continue to effectively challenge these abuses. The operating budgets of organizations such as NPP are dependant on these fees since this area attracts little private funding. If these bills become law they will severely limit the ability of inmates to continue enjoying the constitutional guarantees accorded them by courts over the last 25 years. Even if some form of this legislation is not passed, the fact that the Senate and House each passed bills supporting these types of restrictions suggests that there is a move to limit prisoner rights by restricting their access to the courts. These restrictions, combined with the trend toward more punitive prison conditions, heighten the likelihood that inmates will be living in a more inhumane and dangerous environment. It also increases the probability that when they are released, as most will, they will be more anti-social and may commit more serious and violent crimes (Westcott, 1995).

## HOW CAN CORRECTIONS RESPOND?

According to Branham (1992), the crowding crisis and its attendant problems will continue to affect corrections as long as the following conditions remain:

1. Sentencing policies which imprison offenders for offenses that did not previously carry the penalty of incarceration
2. The imposition of lengthy sentences for a large variety of crimes
3. Minimum mandatory sentences
4. Restrictive probation and parole policies
5. High levels of probation and parole revocations
6. Demographic factors which show that the number of individuals in the population who are in their most crime-prone ages is, or will be, high.

To Branham's list we would add a seventh condition—extensive areas in the society in which criminogenic conditions continue to flourish.

To make our correctional systems more effective, Branham recommends a set of reforms that focuses on both sentencing and corrections. With respect to sentencing, these include:

1. Adoption of sentencing guidelines which ensure that prison space is generally reserved for violent offenders and which include a range of community-based sanctions
2. Expansion of the use of means-based fines [day fines] as sanctions
3. Sentencing that allows a graduated response to violations of community-based sanctions or parole—i.e., not making an automatic sanction of incarceration for violations of conditions or even for additional offenses. Branham feels that the range of options for violations (depending on the offense committed) should include increased restrictions and supervision, special conditions, and financial penalties
4. A repeal of minimum mandatory sentences
5. Require that sentencing guidelines deal with and adjust to correctional system capacities. Additionally, legislatures should prepare correctional impact statements before enacting any legislation that raises the number of people under correctional supervision.

Branham's suggestions for correctional policy reform include:

1. Adoption of a comprehensive corrections act that provides a wide range of sanctions for nonviolent offenders and probation and parole violators
2. Provision of fully funded, high-quality programs—educational, mental health, substance abuse treatment, etc.—intended to reduce recidivism
3. Any inmate not involved in education on a full-time basis should work, presumably on a full-time basis
4. Development of prerelease programs to help releasees successfully transition from prison to the "outside"
5. Requiring that from 3% to 5% of the correctional budget be earmarked for research. The intention of the research is to determine the system's effectiveness and cost efficiency and change it as the data may dictate.

To these we add a reform that we feel must also be addressed and vigorously implemented if our is society going to reduce the number and proportion of individuals subjected to some form of correctional supervision. That is, regardless of how they are funded, programs must be implemented that focus on children who are at risk for involvement in serious delinquency and crime. These programs would seek to stabilize and enrich the developmental environment of these children so they can develop the skills necessary to survive in our society without having to resort to crime.

## DILEMMAS FACING CORRECTIONS

We have alluded to several factors that will have a significant impact on the future of corrections: the public's fear of crime and its hard line toward criminals, the resulting overcrowding, and the costs of maintaining the present punitive attitude as a solution to the crime problem. There is no doubt that these three factors are interactive in that changes in any one will result in changes in the others. Thus, anything that leads to increasing crime leads to a hardening of public attitudes, which in turn leads to tougher sanctions, which tends to increase prison populations. The increased prison populations create a need for additional prison space. The costs of building prisons and maintaining more inmates increase the need for new taxes or for reductions in other programs (e.g., education) for which tax dollars are spent. This, in turn, may affect public attitudes and possibly lead to a softening of attitudes and policies.

We have mentioned that there is growing political and social pressure for corrections systems to become tougher on inmates. While it is difficult to say exactly how this pressure will manifest itself, some of the consequences have already included changes in programming such as reductions in activities that are seen as recreational or pleasurable or perhaps those associated with rehabilitation. Additionally, there have been proposals to require inmates to engage in some type of hard work. The removal of the recreational "frills" (e.g., no cable TV, ping-pong tables, smoking, etc.) will increase inmate idleness and/or take away what may be considered to be tension reducers. There may also be reductions in education programs (except for basic literacy programs) and nonspecific counseling and treatment (e.g., any treatment not specifically designed to deal with drug or sexual abusers). One unintended effect of the reduction or elimination of programming may well be to increase recidivism. Due to the fact that inmates will not be prepared to survive the return to freedom, larger numbers may well return to crime.

The issue of hard work poses several problems for corrections: what the work will consist of; which inmates will do the work; where the work will be done; what motivators can be used to encourage inmates to work; will the work be productive or simply designed to tire inmates out (e.g., "busting rocks").

We have seen the difficulty associated with providing inmates work that merely keeps them occupied and may be construed as being designed solely to tire them out. It would make more sense to create productive jobs that help to pay the costs of incarceration. There have been suggestions that labor-intensive industries with jobs that are currently being lost to countries with abundant numbers of low-paid workers be established in the prisons. The Texas model, described in Chapter 5, in which agricultural production was accomplished by large numbers of individuals on "hoe lines," might also offer a means of having significant numbers of inmates employed at hard labor. This model would employ inmates in productive work but would not serve the purpose of teaching mar-

ketable skills. However, the abuses evident in the supervision of these individuals during the pre-*Ruiz* era would have to be eliminated in order for this solution to pass constitutional muster. Also, this solution would not be feasible in many states. In our estimation it will be difficult to engage all, or even most, of the prison population in full-time work in the near future without having other types of programs (e.g., education, vocational training) to occupy their time.

Assigning all inmates in the system to work would also pose significant problems when it comes to those classified as maximum security. Further, because of the violent nature of many inmates and the gang problems in many prisons, placement of these individuals together in work groups could pose severe management problems. One solution to this problem could be to develop "cottage industry" programs in which these individuals perform the work in their cells (similar to the way it was done in the Pennsylvania system). This problem coincides with the issue of where the work is to be done. If a significant number of inmates in the system are classified as medium security or above (and they are), most of the work may have to be performed within the prison walls or fences.

Motivating inmates to work may also present significant problems. While some coercive methods can be used (e.g., suspension of privileges), none that are seen as violating Eighth Amendment prohibitions against cruel and unusual punishment are likely to be allowed. Indeed, if the hard-liners succeed in taking away the "frills," there may be very few privileges to be suspended, which will add to the motivation problem. Earlier we discussed the advantages of paying prisoners for the work they do and charging them for the goods and services they receive. We strongly endorse this approach as a means of providing inmates a work experience that is positive and more closely mirrors that which exists in the community.

Although work that simply tires inmates out carries an onerous, punitive message, it is likely to have no value beyond the immediate punishment situation. Thus, our philosophy regarding work is that it should prepare inmates to survive on the outside by teaching marketable skills. We realize that there is a proportion of the prison population who, because of their intractability and violent behavior, will not be able to participate in much general programming. Some of this group will have to be dealt with in super-max institutions (e.g., Marion, Florence, Pelican Bay, etc.), where, under strict, highly controlled conditions, they may learn to conform their behavior to more normal prison regimens. The presence of gangs and other security threat groups will continue to complicate this situation.

The notion that we can continue the present approach (i.e., imprisonment) to solve the crime crisis is untenable. There are three major factors which appear to us to support this contention. First, the vast majority of offenders under some form of correctional supervision are not in prison, but instead are in the community. Incarcerating just one-third of this group would require a doubling of the present prison capacity, the costs of which would be immense. A second factor revolves around the low crime clearance rate (currently about 20%) and the low proportion of those who are arrested who go to prison. This has two implications: The number of criminals in society is likely to remain high, which means that crime rates are likely to remain at a relatively high level, and any increase in crime clearance efficiency and in the rate of incarceration will create added pressures on corrections. A third factor revolves around the folly of concentrating on backdoor solutions. By this statement we do not mean to imply that we do not need prisons, for indeed there are a substantial number of individuals whose predatory behavior mandates that they be segregated from society, some on a permanent basis. We do mean, however, that emphasizing imprisonment and neglecting primary prevention (e.g., working to eliminate or reduce as many criminogenic conditions as possible) ignores the fact that a proportion of the children born each year will become serious delinquents and criminals. The cohort studies of Wolfgang and others have shown that approximately 6% to 7% of the individuals comprising a birth cohort become serious habitual offenders. As they become older, there will be a crop of offenders maturing each year and ready to occupy space in an ever expanding prison system. The expense of this approach can soon become unbearable.

## WHAT ARE SOME APPROACHES CORRECTIONS MIGHT TAKE?

Two diametrically opposed tasks appear to exist for corrections: Protect society from offenders who

have been convicted and sentenced and make sure the sanctions they receive are punitive; and do this in a constitutional way that will not bankrupt the various jurisdictions responsible for doing it. Accomplishment of these tasks will probably involve a variety of areas and approaches. Four directions corrections might take that we think are worth considering are: strengthening of community-based correctional services; creating tough prisons; engaging the private sector in the correctional process; and developing prisons with a humane environment. These are discussed next.

### Strengthening Community Corrections for the Twenty-First Century

Community correctional programs presently supervise about 75% of the convicted offenders and do it with about 20% of the correctional budget (Sluder, Sapp, and Langston, 1994). While these programs have been criticized in the past for not effectively supervising offenders, recent evidence indicates that probation and parole programs emphasizing or including treatment result in significantly lower levels of recidivism when compared with those emphasizing control (Petersilia and Turner, 1993). This finding, combined with increasing concerns about the currently high and growing costs of imprisonment and the increasing support for reform programs among criminologists (Sluder *et al.*, 1994), indicates that community programs with effective treatment components may enjoy strong support as we enter the twenty-first century. With these programs averaging about 20% of the cost of incarceration and appearing to effectively deal with some offenders, their use is likely to remain at a high level and perhaps even increase if certain modifications are made.

For this approach to be effective, Sluder *et al.* (1994), assert that the range of sentence options must be expanded and ranked according their severity. This graduated sanction system might include the following progression: restitution, day fine with restitution, community service, active probation, intensive probation, house arrest, residential community corrections, split sentences, jail, and prison. If used for offenders based on the severity of their crimes and danger they pose to the community and not in terms of net widening, community-based sentences are likely to have a positive impact.

## Creating Tough Prisons

Making prisons tough has been increasingly trumpeted as one of the solutions to the problem of crime. Support for this is based on at least two different notions. First, if the prisons are very uncomfortable, inmates experiencing these conditions will not want to return there. Thus, the tough prison is thought to have a deterrent function. However, there is evidence that this is not the case. A second aspect of the tough prison is that it will simply be more punitive and better serve the goal of retribution. Earlier we discussed the problems associated with making prisons tougher by reducing or eliminating inmate privileges and programs and by engaging them in hard work. In this context, hard time may have to vary from prison to prison and from inmate to inmate. Inmates in the prisons should be presented with choices which, depending on their classification, will have certain consequences. For example, increasing or decreasing specific privileges depending on the quality of the inmate's behavior. Maconochie and Crofton's model, which called for each inmate to progress through various stages, starting with a punitive one and progressing through ones requiring increasing responsibilities, might be a good starting point.

J. Michael Quinlan (1993), retired director of the Federal Bureau of Prisons, has suggested the creation of "tough time institutions" (TTIs). These facilities would resemble military boot camps but without the drill and marching. They would have a greatly enhanced program component and be characterized by a long day in which activities would include physical conditioning, half a day of work, and half a day of program participation (e.g, education, drug treatment). Inmates would live in a spartan environment where recreational opportunities would be extremely limited. Participation would be voluntary, with eligibility being limited to nonviolent offenders and those not imprisoned for high-level trafficking. The incentive for choosing this option would be that those successfully completing the program would serve only half of their sentence. Completion of this sentence would be followed by parole-like supervision in the community. Quinlan feels that the advantages of TTIs are that they confront inmates with a more rigid disciplinary structure, would be less costly because they cut time served in half, help inmates to reduce some of their problems (e.g., drug abuse), and meet public expectations regarding no-frills prisons. Offenders not volunteering or not eligible for the TTIs would be required to serve their full sentences (no good time or parole) in prisons presumably less spartan than the TTIs.

Our Close-Up on the revival of the chain gangs looks at the potential effects of another approach to toughening the prisons experience.

## Private Sector Involvement in the Correctional Process May Grow

The increasing need for prison beds has led to a variety of proposals and approaches. As indicated in Chapter 13, one of the more interesting approaches has been the development of private sector companies to provide correctional services. These services can be as narrow as contracting with a private provider for medical care or as broad as contracting with a corporation to build, staff, and operate an entire facility. As indicated, proponents of this approach feel that these private entities can save the jurisdictions that are contracting with private providers significant amounts of money in the building and operation of correctional facilities.

To the extent that these correctional enterpeneurs can deliver on their promises, it is likely that they will play an increasingly important role in the future. This expanded role will, of course, be tempered by the manner in which the private providers handle the legal/ethical issues regarding inmate care and discipline as discussed earlier. A major consideration will also be the extent to which these firms are able to turn a profit. The limited amount of information presently available appears to suggest that the private presence in corrections will continue to expand.

## Developing Prisons with a Humane Environment

Conrad and Dinitz (1978) and Dinitz (1980) have argued that the objective of the corrections system should be defined as punishment since this is a goal the system can achieve. This would involve a model of sentencing in which offenders are punished in a manner proportionate to the extent and seriousness of their crimes. Punishment would involve imposing humane restraints on an offender's liberty. Conrad and Dinitz have proposed that, given this definition, in order for prisons to be successful in the future they must be lawful, safe,

# Close Up   **The Return of Chain Gangs**

Public concern and anger with crime and criminals has led legislators to pass laws designed to toughen our response to this behavior. One of these measures has been the revival of the chain gang in Alabama, Arizona, and Florida, and its consideration in several other states. Used primarily in southern states from the late nineteenth century until the mid-1960s (see Chapter 5), inmates on these chain gangs wore leg irons, sometimes had heavy metal balls attached to waist chains and/or were chained together. They worked at jobs such as cleaning and maintaining highway rights-of-way under armed guard. This practice was abolished because of the inhumane and slave-like work and housing conditions to which inmates were subjected. These conditions were inconsistent with the evolving standards of decency that marked the progress of America's maturing as a society (*Austin v. James*, 1995).

Even though chain gangs were abolished, inmates have continued to work on roads or other projects in or outside jails and prisons, but not in chains. Thus, the present revival of chain gangs is not simply for purposes of subjecting inmates to hard work. Instead the unpleasant conditions and humiliating nature of working out in public chained together are viewed as being more punitive and designed to deter both the offenders subject to it, and those seeing the chain gangs, from further criminality.

There are major differences in the chain gangs operating in Florida, Arizona, and Alabama. In Florida, inmates work on what are termed "restricted labor squads." They are not chained together but only individually shackled at the ankles. Prison officials contend this enables inmates to be more productive and does not require that the whole group join an inmate needing to relieve himself. Currently inmates work inside the prison compound since present legislation does not require they work outside. For now, they are placed on these squads for assaulting someone, disobeying orders, or for possession of contraband. Conditions on these squads may become more punitive if some legislators have their way (Schailler, 1995; Standard Chain Gangs, 1995). Arizona does not chain its inmates to one another, either, and assigns inmates from disciplinary detention to stints of a week at a time on these squads. However, they do work outside the prison in crews of 20 under the supervision of four armed guards, making this a very costly form of

punishment. Inmates are paid 10 cents an hour. They work from 5:30 AM to 1:30 PM four days per week with a half hour for lunch. Arizona inmates have complained about the humiliation of working out in public and the difficulty of walking with chains (Davidson, 1995). Those refusing to work have their privileges revoked and are shackled and forced to stand next to those working. Nevertheless, the practices in Florida and Arizona do not appear to violate constitutional standards.

Alabama presents a different picture. They are all newly admitted inmates, except those designated maximum security, and are assigned to serve 90 days on the chain gangs. During this period they live in dormitories called "Alterative-thinking Units," because this experience is viewed as somehow altering the inmates' way of thinking. They only receive visits every two weeks and are not allowed to smoke, watch TV, have access to the law library, or to hobby material. Inmates work 10 hours a day, 5 days a week in white uniforms with the words "Chain Gang" lettered on the back. They are shackled at the ankles individually and chained together in groups of five. They pick-up papers, clean ditches, and clean highways using blades, axes and shovels (Dorman, 1995; *Austin v. James*, 1995; Alabama To Make Prisoners, 1995).

The Southern Poverty Law Center has filed a section 1983 action claiming that the chain gangs and the punishment for those refusing to work (chaining inmates to a post for 12 hours) violates inmates' rights under the Eighth and Fourteenth Amendments (*Austin v James*, 1995). The state is accused of being deliberately indifferent to the fact that these practices create a substantial risk of serious harm, even death, to inmates and deprives them of basic human needs. First, inmates are at greater risk of being injured if a motor vehicle accident occurs near them because the entire group can be dragged into the accident by the chains that bind them together. Second, these groups often include inmates with a history of violence and who sometimes have to work in the extreme heat using shovels, axes and blades. This can create a potentially volatile situation resulting in violence, which can lead to serious injuries and even death. With one guard to 40 inmates there is insufficient staff to intervene and adequately protect inmates when fights erupt. When fights do occur the guard aims his gun at the group and orders them to stop. There have been instances of warning shots being fired over the inmates'

---

## Close Up, Continued

heads. (Police no longer fire warning shots because of the possibility of injuring innocent bystanders). Third, the chains and leg irons inhibit inmates from protecting themselves from snakes, wasps, hornets or being hit by trees cut down by other inmates. The leg irons also cause physical pain by constantly rubbing and chafing their legs while they work. Fourth, the only toilet available to these inmates while working is a chamber pot, which is on the road behind a make-shift screen. Inmates remain chained together while relieving themselves. No toilet paper is provided and there are no facilities for inmates to wash their hands after use and prior to lunch. Also, if the "toilet" is inaccessible, inmates have to squat on the ground and defacate in public. Finally, inmates refusing to work on the chain gang are forced to stand in the hot sun all day shackled to a metal hitching post. Since no disciplinary hearing is held until after the inmate serves his time on the post, there is pain and loss of liberty without a due process proceeding to determine the legitimacy of the disciplinary action.

In examining the revival of chain gangs, we must consider their potential harmful effects. First, instead of correcting and deterring, the experience may have the unintended consequences of creating more anger, hatred, and alienation among people who are already angry and alienated. This may produce more management problems in prison and may increase the likelihood that these offenders will engage in more serious and violent crimes on release. Of particular concern are the practices in effect in Alabama. The question is whether they are consistent with the standards of a country that considers itself a world leader in protecting human rights. Based on previous ligation, there is evidence that these practices violate constitutional guarantees. With prison costs rising at staggering rates, the question of the cost effectiveness of these staff-intensive chain gangs must also be considered. Further, because many of these inmates lack any positive work experience, working chained together under these conditions may serve to reinforce their already negative job experiences. Finally, in assessing the motivation behind the revival of chain gangs, we must also ask you to consider whether the politicians advocating them really believe in their effectiveness, or do they simply want to appear to be hard on crime.

What do think? Do you agree with the agruments advocating the revival of the chain gang? If so, how should they operate and what limitations, if any, should be placed on them?

---

industrious, and provide inmates with reasonable care and personal dignity. They do not have to be "country clubs" but must provide inmates with decent and clean housing, sufficient clothing, adequate diets, and medical care designed to maintain an appropriate level of health. A very important aspect of the environment of these prisons is that they enhance inmates' personal dignity. This is important because most of these inmates have come from communities where their personal dignity has been shredded in their day-to-day interactions with the agents of society (e.g., unemployment officers or other government clerks). The personal dignity of inmates has also been shredded within prisons by the degradations of institutional life. Any expectations that the vast majority of inmates can become conventional members of society without enhancing their sense of self-worth and dignity are not likely to be achieved.

For prisons to be safe and lawful requires the establishment of a reasonable set of prison rules and their enforcement by staff through adequate patrols, inspections, and contact with inmates. Staff must receive training in contraband control, STG prevention, and humane control techniques. This requires training in communication and human relations skills so staff can learn how to manage inmates through verbal persuasion and avoid using humiliating and degrading methods. Further, by developing good relations with inmates, staff are more likely to be informed by inmates about potentially dangerous situations before they become major problems. They must also insist that inmates recognize and share responsibility for maintaining appropriate self-respect in their interactions within the prison. Finally, prisons must be hopeful and industrious. This means, as noted earlier, providing inmates with opportunities for educational and vocational training and meaning-ful work experiences. While this idea is not too popular because it is viewed as making prison life less punitive, we must recognize that most inmates will not spend a substantial portion of their lives in prison. Putting aside humanitarian concerns, this approach makes sense from a practical economic standpoint. As we have noted, research indicates that inmates who complete educational and voca-tional training programs have much lower recidi-vism rates than nonparticipants. This provides a method for ultimately lowering the cost of impris-onment. It is sheer folly to believe that inmates who lack educational and marketable work skills will desist from crime on their release, since their job opportunities are limited and may be close to nonexistent.

As a society we must come to recognize that inhumane prisons and rejection of inmates on re-lease are "sure fire" formulas for failure. We must punish criminals—i.e., deprive them of their liberty—but if we do this in prisons that are lawful and assure that inmates are not degraded, we stand a better chance of successfully releasing them back into the community. To this end, the legislative agenda set forth by the American Correctional Association for 1995-1996 appears to us to identify the most relevant issues in addressing crime prob-lems. We must:

**1.** Support the need for adequate funding to fa-cilitate sound correctional practice.
**2.** Support sentencing reform that streamlines the sentencing and classification processes such that nonviolent offenders are placed in the least resstrictive environment.
**3.** Support juvenile justice reforms.

**4.** Support rehabilitation and prevention pro-grams.
**5.** Oppose the harsh and mean spirited treatment of inmates (Survey Identifies, 1995).

Throughout this book, we have tried to show the effects of the various approaches used by society to sanction criminal offenders. It is evident to us that harsh, brutal sanctions have not produced a satis-factory result. The voices of reason call for proce-dures that enhance inmates' abilities to return suc-cessfully to the community. We hope these procedures will be dominant in the future of cor-rections.

## EPILOGUE RECAP

**Trends Affecting the Future of Corrections**
The Public Mood Toward Criminals Is Becoming More Punitive
The Public Is Advocating a Reduction in Prevention Programs
The Demographic Structure of the Population Is Changing
Criminogenic Social Conditions Will Continue to Affect Involvement in Crime
Will the Public Continue to Support the Most Expen-sive Solutions?
Will the Courts Continue to Insist on Constitutional Prisons?
**How Can Corrections Respond?**
**Dilemmas Facing Corrections**
**What Are Some Approaches Corrections Might Take?**
Strengthening Community Corrections for the Twenty-First Century
Creating Tough Prisons
Private Sector Involvement in the Correctional Process May Grow
Developing Prisons with a Humane Environment

# TABLE OF CASES

# GLOSSARY *

**ABOLITIONISTS:** Term applied to individuals who are against capital punishment.

**ABSCOND:** In corrections, to depart without authorization from a geographical area or jurisdiction, in violation of the conditions of probation or parole.

**ABSOLUTE PARDON:** A pardon for British subjects banished to Australia that restored all rights including the return to England.

**ACADEMY OF CRIMINAL JUSTICE SCIENCES:** A professional organization for criminal justice professionals and academics.

**ACCOMPLISHED CHARACTERS:** Big house inmates good at providing diversions and entertainment.

**ACCOMPLISHED GAMBLERS:** Inmates whose gaming skills or luck enabled them to acquire substantial winnings, putting them in a position of power relative to the inmate economy.

**ACCREDITATION:** A process by which facilities or agencies are certified by the American Correctional Association as meeting a set of standards for their physical plant, operations, performance, staffing, programs and services. *Also see* NATIONAL COMMISSION ON CORRECTIONAL HEALTH CARE.

**ACQUIRED IMMUNE DEFICIENCY SYNDROME (AIDS):** A condition in which the body's immune system is unable to fight illness and disease, making individuals susceptible to a host of infections that otherwise do not affect healthy people.

**ACQUITTAL:** The verdict in a court that the defendant is not guilty of the offenses for which he or she has been tried.

**ACT OF OCTOBER 14, 1940:** Prohibited the interstate transport of all prison-made products except agricultural commodities and goods produced for states and their political subdivisions.

**ADJUDICATION:** The process by which a court arrives at a decision regarding a case, also the resulting decision.

**ADJUSTMENT CENTERS:** The euphemism applied to segregation units in California during the rehabilitation era.

**ADMINISTRATIVE CONFINEMENT/ SEGREGATION:** A form of separation from the general population sometimes imposed by classification committees for inmates who pose serious threats to themselves, staff, or other inmates or to institutional security; are pending investigation of and disciplinary hearing for serious rule violations; are pending transfer.

**ADULT BASIC EDUCATION (ABE):** Educational programs that stress literacy and mathematical skills as a foundation for further education and training. Generally viewed as a feeder system for GED preparatory classes.

**ADULT EDUCATION ACT (1964):** A federal act that provided funding for programs targeting adults with deficiencies in communication, computation, or social relations substantially impairing their employment chances.

**AFTERCARE:** In the criminal justice system this term usually refers to postrelease supervision for juveniles but is sometimes used to denote other programs that provide reentry into the community from jails or prisons.

**AGGRAVATED ASSAULT:** Unlawful intentional inflicting of serious bodily injury or unlawful threat or attempt to inflict bodily injury or death by means of a deadly or dangerous weapon with or without actual infliction of any injury.

**AGGRAVATING CIRCUMSTANCES:** Circumstances regarding a crime which cause it to be considered more serious than that of the average instance of that offense.

**ALCOHOLICS ANONYMOUS (AA):** An independent organization established in the 1930s that uses a twelve-step program to help members overcome addiction to alcohol.

**AMERICAN CORRECTIONAL ASSOCIATION (ACA):** A professional organization, founded in 1870, for correctional personnel and others interested in corrections. Heavily involved in research, accreditation, and training.

**AMERICAN JAIL ASSOCIATION (AJA):** An organization that focuses on jail personnel and also contributes to correctional officer training and professionalism.

*AMERICAN JAILS:* Journal published by the American Jail Association (AJA) that deals with jail issues.

**AMERICAN MUSLIM MISSION:** *See* NATION OF ISLAM.

**AMERICAN PRISON ASSOCIATION:** Created in 1870 and was the forerunner of the American Correctional Association.

**AMERICAN SOCIETY OF CRIMINOLOGY:** Professional organization for academic criminologists and others. Not specifically concerned with corrections but contributes by promoting and generating research to inform practitioners in the field.

**AMERICANS WITH DISABILITIES ACT OF 1990:** A federal act that prohibited government agencies like correctional institutions from denying qualified disabled persons access to programs and services.

**AMNESTY INTERNATIONAL:** An organization that is concerned with human rights abuses (including opposition to capital punishment) and carries on campaigns to reduce or abolish them.

**AMSTERDAM WORKHOUSE:** An early Dutch workhouse.

**ANTEBELLUM PLANTATION MODEL:** A farm organized in the manner of pre-Civil War plantations.

**ANTIPSYCHOTIC DRUGS:** Any drug such as thorazine, used to relieve or control the symptoms of (e.g., delusions, hallucinations), but not "cure," psychotic disorders.

**ANTISOCIAL PERSONALITY DISORDER:** A disorder characterized by callousness, impulsiveness, lack of loyalty, and a chronic indifference to and violation of the rights of others. These individuals are often in trouble with the law.

**APPEAL:** The request (and the resulting process) that a court with appellate jurisdiction review the judgment, decision, or order of a lower court and set it aside.

**APPELLANT:** The person making an appeal.

**APPOINTMENT SYSTEM:** As used in employee hiring, a pool of applicants meeting certain minimum requirements is developed (e.g., have a B.A. degree) but no examination is mandated. Agency administrators interview qualified candidates and select whomever they please from this group.

**ARRAIGNMENT:** The court hearing at which a defendant is formally charged with an offense.

**ARREST:** The taking of a person into physical custody by authority of law for the purpose of charging him or her with a criminal offense.

**ARSON:** The intentional damaging or destruction, or attempt to do so, by means of fire or explosion of the property of another without the consent of the owner, or of one's own property or that of another with intent to defraud.

**ARYAN BROTHERHOOD (AB):** White inmate gangs that formed in reaction to the development of minority-based gangs. Their credo espouses white superiority.

**ASHURST-SUMMERS ACT OF 1935:** Prohibited the interstate transportation of convict-made goods to states where such products were prohibited and required labels on all prison products sold in interstate commerce.

**ASSAULT:** Unlawful, intentional inflicting, or attempted or threatened inflicting, of injury upon the person of another.

**ASSET FORFEITURE:** Government seizure of property derived from or used in criminal activity. Typically used to strip drug traffickers, racketeers, and white collar offenders of their economic power.

**ASSISTANT SUPERINTENDENTS:** Persons within the executive management team who specialize in managing certain prison functions such as security, treatment programs, business operations, or prison industries. Also responsible for supervising the operations of their specific area.

**ASYLUMS:** The term used to denote early facilities used to house the mentally disturbed.

**ASYMPTOMATIC:** HIV-infected individuals not showing any signs or symptoms of AIDS.

**ATTICA REVOLT, THE:** A name given the riot that occurred at the Attica correctional facility in New York in 1971.

**AUBURN SYSTEM, THE:** The approach to imprisonment, also called the congregate system, developed in New York at the Auburn penitentiary. It was designed to reform inmates through congregate labor, a strict rule of silence, harsh discipline, and isolation at night.

**AUGUSTUS, JOHN:** Considered the first probation officer. Between 1841–1858 he took responsibility for supervising and assisting offenders who were released into his custody by Boston judges.

**AUTHORITARIAN ORGANIZATIONAL MODEL:** In these organizations, decision-making power is in the hands of one person or a small number of high-level "bosses."

**AUTHORITY REVOLUTION, THE:** The erosion in respect for authority, tradition, and adults by young people that began during the 1960s.

**BABY BOOM:** Refers to the demographic changes caused by the large number of males born between 1945 and 1960 who reached their most crime-prone ages during the 1960s and 1970s.

**BACK-DOOR PROGRAM:** A community program that functions as an early release mechanism for high-risk offenders who may not meet the criteria for regular parole.

**BAGNES:** Secure stockades established at French seaports to house slaves and others. They were also used to hold crippled galley convicts while they were in port. They were eventually transformed into "workhouses" and served as a transition from the galleys to prisons.

**BAIL:** To effect the release of an arrested person in return for a promise that they will appear at required court proceedings granted by a pledge to pay the court a specified amount of money for failure to appear. Also refers to the money pledged to the court.

**BAIL BONDSMAN:** A person, usually licensed, in business to effect releases on bail for those charged with offenses and held in custody, by pledging to pay a sum of money if the defendant fails to appear in court as required.

**BANISHMENT:** A form of punishment by which the offender is expelled from his or her home area or country either temporarily or permanently. Can include enslavement or exile of offenders to a penal colony.

**BARRIO GANGS:** Neighborhood gangs organized in Mexican-American areas in California for "territorial protection."

**BATTERY:** A completed assault.

**BECCARIA, CESARE:** Italian economist/criminologist who, with Jeremy Bentham, was the founder of the classical school of criminology.

**BEHAVIOR MODIFICATION:** A technology based on the principles of learning used in the treatment of behavior problems as well as in teaching any adaptive form of behavior. The assumption is that all behavior is learned and that socially acceptable behavior can be learned as substitute for deviant behavior.

**BEHAVIORAL CONTRACTING:** The negotiation of a written agreement between inmates and corrections personnel that specifies that if the inmates behave in certain ways they will be rewarded.

**BEHAVIORAL DEEP FREEZE OF INCARCERATION:** A lifestyle adopted by long-term inmates in which they either develop guarded or no relationships with other inmates. This is to avoid facing the devastation of having relationships terminated by transfer or releases.

**BENCH WARRANT:** A court document directing that a law enforcement officer bring the person named therein before the court.

**BENEFIT OF CLERGY:** This was first practiced in England. While originally available only to religious officials, this privilege was later extended to laypersons by defining clerical status in terms of literacy. In practice, this meant, that if a prisoner could read a verse from the bible he could avoid the death penalty. In the late 1600s women could use this privilege on the same basis as males.

**BIG HOUSE:**  A pre-1950s type prison resembling a military fortress with large cell blocks. These also had a unique subculture and hierarchial inmate status systems.

**BILL OF RIGHTS:**  The first ten amendments to the U.S. Constitution.

**BILLING FOR MEDICAL CARE:**  A recent practice by which some systems charge inmates with resources for medical care.

**BLACK CODES:**  These were penal codes specifically aimed at controlling black slaves in the pre-Civil War South that inflicted more severe punishments on slaves than on whites for many offenses.

**BLACK GUERRILLA FAMILY (BGF):**  A black prison gang that formed in order to protect and advance the position of their race. Their philosophy advocated violence to achieve their objectives.

**BLACK MUSLIMS:**  An organization begun in America in the 1930s by Blacks that combined the tenets of Islam and Christianity.

**BLACK PANTHERS, THE:**  A group of dissident blacks who organized in Oakland, California, in 1966 in reaction to police brutality in the black community and to provide protection for blacks from the police. Their objective, with respect to inmates, was to unite all prisoner movement groups through an inclusive ideology emphasizing their similarities and minimizing their differences.

**BLACK RAGE:**  The deep anger and hatred that blacks have felt over being subjected to more than three and a half centuries of humiliation, prejudice, and discrimination.

**BLOOD FEUD:**  An ongoing conflict between two kinship groups. Acts against one individual were viewed as acts against that person's entire kinship group and required the victim's family, tribe, or community to take action against the other group, which in turn was required to retaliate.

**BODY CAVITY SEARCHES:**  Searches conducted of body orifices (e.g., the anus) for contraband.

**BONA FIDE OCCUPATIONAL QUALIFICATIONS (BFOQ):**  Job qualifications that are in and of themselves necessary for adequate performance of that job and can be used to exclude individuals not having them.

**BONA FIDE RELIGIOUS BELIEF OR PRACTICE:**  A belief or practice that is found in a religion's published theology or expert testimony and indicates it is associated with a particular religion.

**BOOKING PROCESS:**  A law enforcement or correctional administrative process after arrest that officially identifies the person, time, reason for arrest, and arresting authority after which he/she may be released on bail/released on recognizance, or placed in detention.

**BOOT CAMPS:**  A form of split sentence used with juveniles and youthful offenders. These programs consist of a three- to six-month residential phase in a very structured and regimented environment similar to that found in military boot camps and, in some instances, is followed by some form of community aftercare and supervision. Newer programs deemphasize the military regimen and put more stress on treatment programs such as education, work, substance abuse treatment, and developing a prosocial lifestyle.

**BRANDING:**  The practice of placing of a mark on a individual in order to identify him or her as a criminal. The marking could be done on the skin by using a hot metal brand, by sewing letters onto a garment, etc.

**BRIDEWELL:**  An old palace donated to the city of London by King Edward VI. It was renovated and opened about 1516 as the first workhouse.

**BRIDLE:**  This was an iron cage that fit over the head and had a front plate that was sharpened or covered with spikes designed to fit into the mouth of the offender. This was intended to punish the individual as well as to keep him from speaking.

**BROCKWAY, ZEBULON T.:**  A noted prison reformer who opened the first reformatory at Elmira, New York in 1877 which he headed for the next 20 years.

**BUILDING TENDERS:**  Inmates who were given the authority to maintain order within the tanks at Texas prisons. Performed functions similar to trusty-guards but did not carry firearms.

**BULLS:** *See* HACKS.

**BUREAUCRATIC ORGANIZATIONAL MODEL:** Establishes a formal organizational structure, which includes a hierarchical structure with varying levels of authority, a formal chain of command, a vertical authority and communication structure that flows from the top of the hierarchy to the bottom.

**BURGLARY:** The unlawful entry of any fixed structure, vehicle, or vessel used for regular residence, industry, or business, with or without force, with intent to commit a felony or larceny.

**BURNOUT:** A state of emotional exhaustion and cynicism that frequently occurs among individuals who are involved in "people work." This is particularly true for those who work closely with others under conditions of chronic tension and stress. It is frequently characterized by emotional exhaustion, depersonalization, decreased competence, and detachment from the job caused by stress.

**CALLOUTS:** The taking of inmates from regularly scheduled activities (e.g., work) for a special purpose (e.g., a dental appointment).

**CAMPUS-STYLE FACILITIES:** Prison facilities in which the buildings are arranged in a circular fashion with an inside green space used for recreational activities. Security levels can vary, but for the most part they are often minimum security facilities.

**CAPITAL OFFENSE:** A criminal offense punishable by death.

**CAPITAL PUNISHMENT:** The death penalty.

**CAREER CRIMINALS:** A person having a past record of multiple arrests or convictions for serious crimes, or an unusually large number of arrests for crimes of varying degrees of seriousness.

**CASE WORK:** A way of working with individuals generally used by social workers. It follows the traditional medical model. Theoretically many probation and parole agencies expect their officers to use this approach; however, large caseloads made following this approach difficult.

**CASELOAD:** In corrections, the total number of clients registered with a correctional agency or agent at a given point in time.

**CATCH-22:** A situational dilemma in which any decision made will have negative consequences. Akin to "damned if you do and damned if you don't."

**CELL BLOCKS:** A building or part of a building within a prison containing an array of cells that serves as housing for a group of inmates. Usually found in Auburn-type prisons.

**CENTRAL CORE MEMBERS:** Gang members with a very strong commitment to a gang; usually includes gang leaders and close friends.

**CERTIFIED COURT ORDERS:** Certified orders committing convicted offenders to the custody of the department of corrections.

**CHAIN GANG:** A group of inmates, usually chained together, used by Southern county and state correctional agencies for working at clearing highway rights-of-way, etc.

**CHAIN OF COMMAND:** This recognizes that in order to maintain control of a large organization a leader must delegate oversight of its many workers and activities to executive managers who in turn delegate authority to middle managers and they give authority to first-line supervisors.

**CHARGE:** An official allegation that a specified person has committed a specific offense.

**CHEMICAL AGENTS:** These include gasses that temporarily immobilize individuals subjected to them.

**CHICANOS:** The name given Mexican-Americans in general. During the rehabilitation era this applied specifically to inmates from Los Angeles.

**CHILD MOLESTER/PEDOPHILE:** An individual who sexually abuses children. This person has a preference for children as sexual objects.

**CHOICE THEORY OR RATIONAL CHOICE THEORY:** The modern version of classical theory. It emphasizes the rational weighing of the specific costs and gains in the decision-making process governing criminal events.

**CHRONIC OFFENDERS:** Originally defined by Wolfgang in his cohort studies to denote offenders arrested five or more times. Although small in number, they account for a disproportionate amount of serious crime.

**CITATION:**   A written order issued by a police officer directing an alleged offender to appear in a specific court at a specified time to answer a criminal charge.

**CITIZEN DISPUTE SETTLEMENT CENTERS:** *See* NEIGHBORHOOD JUSTICE CENTERS.

**CIVIL COMMITMENT:**   A formal nonpenal commitment to a treatment facility resulting from findings made during criminal proceedings, or civil proceedings involving the mentally ill or disturbed, the incompetent, or substance abusers.

**CIVIL RIGHTS (SECTION 1983) ACTIONS:** *See* SECTION 1983 THE CIVIL RIGHTS ACT.

**CIVIL RIGHTS ACT OF 1871:**   An act passed by the federal legislature that attempted to protect the rights of blacks following the Civil War.

**CIVIL RIGHTS ACT OF 1964:**   Prohibits discrimination in the workplace.

**CIVIL RIGHTS REVOLUTION, THE:**   The fight to gain the rights of full citizenship and reduce racism by African-Americans which began to strongly manifest itself in the late 1950s and early 1960s.

**CLASS ACTION SUITS:**   Suits that provide a means by which a large group of persons interested in a matter, where one or more of them may sue or be sued as representatives of the class without needing to join every member of the class.

**CLASSICAL THEORY:**   An eighteenth-century theory of criminal behavior that assumes that human beings have free will, are rational, and make behavioral decisions based on the consequences of their actions before engaging in them. If the consequences are positive they will engage in the behavior and if not they will avoid it.

**CLASSIFICATION:**   *See* PRISON CLASSIFICATION.

**CLASSIFICATION COMMITTEE:**   A committee composed of several correctional staff members that has the responsibility of classifying and periodically reclassifying inmates.

**CLEAR AND PRESENT DANGER:**   Doctrine in constitutional law providing that governmental restrictions on freedoms of speech and press will be upheld if necessary to prevent grave and immediate danger to interests which the government may lawfully protect.

**CLEARANCE:**   For UCR purposes the closing of a case by effecting the arrest of a suspected perpetrator. Also cases can be exceptionally cleared when some element beyond law enforcement control precludes formal charges, e.g., victim refuses to testify or the offender is being prosecuted for another crime.

**CLEMENCY:**   An executive or legislative action whereby the punishment of a person or persons is reduced or stopped.

**CLINICAL PASTORAL EDUCATIONAL MOVEMENT:**   A movement among the clergy that led to clinical training for them and which viewed prison chaplaincy as a specialty subgroup of the clergy.

**CLIQUES, PRISON:**   Primary and semiprimary groups formed by prisoners, from the same tip or from several tips, who have regular contact (e.g., at work, in the yard) and share an interest in some prison activity, subcultural orientation, and/or preprison experience.

**CLOSE CUSTODY INMATES:**   Reserved for inmates with past assaultive and/or escape histories. Constant supervision and full restraints are required when leaving the facility. During the day permitted to leave their cells and go to other parts of the institution on a check-out/check-in basis under staff observation.

**CLOSE SECURITY FACILITIES/LEVEL V:**   Perimeter security is the same as for maximum security prisons, but with single, outside cells. When not in their cells inmates are normally under direct supervision, usually have inmates of different custody categories, more programming.

**CLUSTER-TYPE VOCATIONAL TRAINING COURSES:**   Offer 100-hour blocks of instruction in related but different subject areas of a given trade.

**CN:**   A standard type of tear gas.

**CO SUBCULTURE:**   The norms, behaviors, and adaptations developed by the correctional officers to cope with their work environment. This is influenced by such factors as administrative concerns and the dangerous nature of the prison environment. These norms are initially transmitted as part of the socialization process sometime during training.

**COCAINE ANONYMOUS (CA):** Similar to narcotics anonymous.

**CO-CORRECTIONAL FACILITIES:** These are facilities that house both men and women and normally both sexes participate in most programs and share services.

**COGNITIVE APPROACHES:** Treatment approaches based on the assumption that incorrect thinking underlies and drives most behavior and that if the thinking is corrected problem behaviors will be changed.

**COGNITIVE THERAPY:** *See* COGNITIVE APPROACHES.

**COHORT STUDIES:** Studies that use a sample of individuals who have a characteristic such as year of birth in common.

**COLLECTIVE INCAPACITATION:** A form of incapacitation that would impose the same sentence on all individuals convicted of the same offense (e.g., armed robbery).

**COLONIAL PERIOD, THE:** The period of English rule over its American colonies that ended with the American revolution.

**COMBINED PREEMPLOYMENT SCREENING SYSTEM:** Written exam screens candidates. Those who have qualifying scores are placed on a list from which candidates are interviewed and selected.

**COMMISSARY:** The prison "store" where inmates can buy items such as cigarettes, shampoo, candy, etc.

**COMMITMENT:** A judicial action placing an individual in a particular type of confinement as authorized by law.

**COMMON LAW MARRIAGE:** In this context it refers to the acceptance of the existence of a marital relationship between a man and woman who have never legally married. This relationship is usually based on the fact that they lived together for some period of time.

**COMMUNITY CONTROL:** A term used to denote various forms of community supervision and known more popularly as "house arrest." *See* HOUSE ARREST for a more detailed definition.

**COMMUNITY CUSTODY INMATES:** Pose the least danger to staff, inmates, and the community. May require intermittent supervision, eligible for daily unescorted participation in outside jobs and programs, unescorted furloughs, contact visits.

**COMMUNITY SECURITY FACILITIES/LEVEL I:** These are nonsecure facilities that include prerelease centers (such as work release or educational release), halfway houses, and other nonsecure settings.

**COMMUTATION (OF SENTENCE):** An executive act changing a punishment from a greater to a lesser penalty. In corrections this usually results in the immediate release or reduction of the time to be served or changes a sentence of death to a term of imprisonment.

**COMPELLING GOVERNMENT INTEREST:** For correctional facilities this means anything representing a serious threat to a prison's security, order, or discipline.

**COMPENSATION:** An early process that attempted to circumvent blood feuds by having both the perpetrator and victim agree to some form of payment by the perpetrator to the victim or his family to compensate for the damage done.

**COMPENSATORY DAMAGES:** Used to compensate the injured party for the injury sustained and nothing more.

**CONCURRENT SENTENCE:** A sentence that is one of two or more sentences imposed at the same time. After conviction all or part of each term is served simultaneously.

**CONDITIONAL RELEASES:** Releases in which the correctional system maintains some supervision over the releasee for a specified period of time. Typically includes parole, supervised mandatory release, and supervised work furloughs.

**CONDITIONS OF RELEASE ON PROBATION/PAROLE:** These are restrictions or mandates imposed on all probationers as part of their sentences or on parolees as an aspect of their release.

**CONFIDENTIAL COMMUNICATION:** Similar to a privileged communication but the protection is not absolute. In a corrections context the recipient of the information is generally required to divulge information that threatens the safety or security of the institution, its staff, or other inmates.

**CONFINEMENT:** In corrections, the physical restriction (by barriers or guards) of a person to a clearly defined area from which he or she is lawfully forbidden to depart.

**CONJUGAL VISITS:** A visit under which inmates and their visitors (usually wives, but in some earlier circumstances prostitutes) were allowed privacy. Emotional and sexual intimacy is presumed to occur.

**CONNING:** In treatment, this involves inmate attempts to fool the counselor or therapist into believing that the treatment being received was causing positive changes in the person doing the conning. Its purpose is to achieve an early release.

**CONSECUTIVE SENTENCE:** A sentence that is one of two or more sentences imposed at the same time; after conviction the sentences are served in sequence.

**CONSENT DECREE:** A court judgment in which both parties agree to work out the terms of the settlement subject to court approval.

**CONSOLIDATED PAROLE BOARD MODEL:** Under this model the parole board makes the release decision but field parole services are in the state department of corrections and authority is split between these two administrative units.

**CONTACT VISITS:** Prison visitation that permits visitors and inmates to have a limited degree of nonsexual physical contact.

**CONTEMPT OF COURT:** Intentionally obstructing a court in the administration of justice, or acting in a way calculated to lessen its authority or dignity, or failing to obey its lawful orders. To achieve compliance with its orders, courts can imprison or fine defendants.

**CONTRABAND:** Items that are declared illegal or off-limits to inmates by prison authorities.

**CONTRACT SYSTEM:** Under this system the state retained control of prisoners. Work was done within the prison under contract to private com-

panies who paid the state a per diem charge per worker and furnished the necessary instructors, machinery, and raw material for the production of the products, which it then sold.

**CONTROL CONDITIONS:** These conditions, which are imposed on all probationers and parolees, include obeying laws, not associating with known criminals, and reporting regularly to their probation officer.

**CONTROLLING CUSTOMER PRISON INDUSTRIES MODEL:** Under this model the private sector is the primary or exclusive customer of a business, operating as part of a prison industries program, that it owns or has helped capitalize and which it may or may not manage.

**CONVICT:** A name given to inmates, also known as hogs, wise guys, bad dudes, or outlaws. Inmates with this status are the most respected figures in contemporary prisons and dominate the inmate world in violent prisons; emphasis is on toughness and willingness to use violence to maintain one's status.

**CONVICT CODE:** The dominant value system in the Big House heavily influenced by the thieves code, which included the following values: do your own time, don't rat on another prisoner; maintain your dignity and respect; help other thieves; leave most other inmates alone; and manifest no weakness.

**CONVICTION:** A court finding, based on the results of a trial or on the plea of guilty by the accused, that the defendant is guilty of the crime with which he or she has been charged.

**COOK/CHILL METHOD OF FOOD PRODUCTION:** Allows large quantities of food to be cooked in advance and then stored for later use.

**COOL INMATES:** The term applied to the prison adaptation of female inmates who were professional criminals and viewed their incarceration as a temporary experience that was a part of being involved in crime. Their goal was to minimize their time in prison and to do easy time.

**CORPORAL PUNISHMENT:** Any form of punishment applied to the body.

**CORPORATE MODEL PRISON INDUSTRIES:** A logical extension of current efforts to operate prison industries using free-world business practices. This model establishes a quasiindependent corporation that operates and manages prison industries yet is connected to the corrections department for security purposes.

**CORRECTIONAL AGENCY:**   A federal, state, or local agency of which the principal functions include intake screening, custody, confinement, treatment, or presentence investigation of alleged or adjudicated offenders.

**CORRECTIONAL FACILITY:**   A building or part thereof, set of buildings, or an area enclosing them operated by a government agency for the physical custody, or custody and treatment, or persons sentenced or subject to criminal proceedings.

**CORRECTIONAL INSTITUTIONS:**   This name came into widespread use during the rehabilitation era to connote changes in the focus of prisons from punishment to treatment. Today it continues to be a method of referring to prisons, a state system, the federal system, and even local systems that deal with detainees and offenders.

**CORRECTIONAL OFFICERS (COs):**   Custodial personnel who directly supervise inmates.

**CORRECTIONAL SIEVE:**   A method of describing the process by which apprehended offenders may be screened out of the system at different points along the way. When viewed in this way, this screening process takes the shape of a funnel, which functions like a sieve through which most cases "leak" out before they are retained in some correctional program (such as probation or prison).

**CORRECTIONALISTS:**   Penal specialists, many with college degrees, who began to work in or study prisons during the rehabilitation era.

**CORRECTIONS:**   Has at least two definitions: (1) the official responses taken by criminal justice agencies to the punishment of convicted offenders in the United States; (2) the agencies, programs, and organizations on the local, state, and federal levels that detain those accused of crimes and those convicted of them.

*CORRECTIONS TODAY:*   Journal published by the American Correctional Organization (ACA); deals with correctional and other related criminal justice issues.

**CORRUPT FAVORITISM:**   Informal control mechanism whereby guards granted special privi-leges to certain key inmates in exchange for their assistance in the maintenance of order.

**COTTAGE INDUSTRY:**   Any type of productive work that can be done by an individual alone and/or in the confines of his or her cell.

**COTTAGE PLAN:**   A correctional compound that consists of several small units, each housing approximately 30 inmates, surrounding a central building that has regular cells. It may also have buildings used for program activities. This type of facility has usually been used with women and juveniles.

**COUNTS:**   Process for determining the whereabouts of every inmate by physically counting them. These are conducted several times each day and all prison activities usually stop until all inmates are accounted for.

**COURT ORDER:**   A mandate, command, or direction issued by a court in the exercise of its judicial authority.

**COVERT SENSITIZATION:**   A behavior modification technique to change the affect associated with a deviant behavior by pairing an imagined stimulus with imagined dire consequences.

**CREATIVE SENTENCES:**   Offbeat sentences imposed by some judges (usually in misdemeanor cases).

**CREDIT CARDS:**   Some prison systems issue electronically sensitive cards that are used to scan inmate accounts and deduct the appropriate amount when purchases are made.

**CRIME IN THE SUITES:**   A term used to describe white collar or business crime.

**CRIME, ORGANIZED:**   *See* ORGANIZED CRIME SYNDICATES.

**CRIMINAL CAREER INCAPACITATION:**   A form of selective incapacitation that targets classes of criminals who, on the average, have active high rates of crime (e.g., burglars).

**CRIMINAL HOMICIDE:**   The causing of the death of another person without legal justification or excuse.

**CRIMINAL OFFENSE:**   An act committed or omitted in violation of a law forbidding or commanding it which carries possible penalties (e.g., incarceration) upon conviction.

**CRIMINALLY INSANE:** This term lumped together a number of categories of individuals that had in common the fact that they were involved in some way with the criminal justice system and had some type of mental problems. These included: those found incompetent to stand trial, persons acquitted by reason of insanity and inmates who became mentally ill while serving their sentence. These individuals were confined in either state mental hospital, special wards of these facilities or in separate institutions. Today these individuals are generally referred to as mentally ill offenders or according to their status in the criminal justice system which includes: incompetent to stand trial, insane/mentally ill and or mentally disordered.

**CRIMINOGENIC SOCIAL CONDITIONS:** Conditions within the society that are likely to produce criminal behavior in the people influenced by them, e.g., dysfunctional families, neighborhoods, and communities.

**CROFTON, SIR WALTER:** *See* IRISH OR INTERMEDIATE SYSTEM.

**CRUEL AND UNUSUAL PUNISHMENT:** Conditions and practices in prisons such as solitary confinement, corporal punishment, use of force by guards, and other conditions of confinement that go beyond the limits allowed by the U.S. Constitution.

**CS:** A super tear gas that is approximately ten times stronger than CN gas.

**CULTURAL DIVERSITY/MULTICULTURALISM:** This involves a recognition that it is neither necessary nor desirable for different ethnic groups to shed their cultural identities to participate in the larger community. It reflects a trend toward the goal of a cooperative pluralism that enables each ethnic group to preserve its cultural identity without viewing others as a threat.

**CUSTODIAL PROCESSES:** Daily activities and procedures designed to control and keep track of the inmates.

**CUSTODY:** Legal or physical control of or responsibility for a person or thing.

**CYCLE MENU:** A menu detailing daily meals and covering a relatively long time period (e.g., six weeks), at the end of which the menu is repeated. These menus provide a nutritionally adequate diet, include popular menu items, and avoid undue repetition and monotony while maintaining average daily food costs at allotted amounts.

**DADDIES:** *See* JOCKERS.

**DAILY SICK CALL:** The process by which inmates who perceive themselves to have a health problem (e.g., a headache) get permission to go to morning clinic sessions.

**DAY FINES:** A European innovation that allows judges to impose monetary sanctions that are commensurate with the seriousness of the crime while tying their amount to the offender's income and assets.

**DAY REPORTING CENTERS:** *See* NONRESIDENTIAL/DAY TREATMENT PROGRAMS.

**DEADLY FORCE:** Force that is considered likely to or intended to cause death or great bodily harm.

**DECENTRALIZED DINING:** A system for feeding inmates under which they are fed in dayrooms, cell blocks, small satellite areas, or in the pods in the new generation jails.

**DEINSTITUTIONALIZATION:** A philosophy or process of reducing or closing the number of remote state facilities that house the mentally disturbed, retarded, or delinquents and dealing with them at the community level instead.

**DELEGATION (MANAGERIAL) MODEL:** A form of participatory management stressing that input from all workers is critical, because line workers (officers) can be your best "idea" people for solving real problems.

**DELIBERATE INDIFFERENCE:** The meaning of this concept from a legal standpoint is far from clear. However, court cases suggest deliberate indifference occurs if prison officials know or should have known, because the condition is obvious, of a risk to inmate health and safety and take no action.

**DELINQUENCY:** Juvenile actions in violation of laws, status offenses, or other juvenile misbehavior.

**DEMORALIZATION FELT BY INMATE'S FAMILY:** The shame and stigma suffered by a family when one of its members is convicted of a crime and imprisoned.

**DEPARTMENT OF CORRECTIONS:** A government agency that is headed by a politically appointed director who develops policy and oversees the operation of mandated correctional facilities and programs.

**DEPO-PROVERA:** A hormone-based drug used most effectively to treat sex offenders who are attracted to young males (pedophiles) and exhibitionists. Clinical experiments have shown it reduces the intensity of deviant sexual urges and erotic fantasies. To be effective it must be used in conjunction with a program of group counseling.

**DEPRIVATION MODEL:** Argues that inmate culture is a collective response to the deprivations imposed by prison life, e.g., lack of heterosexual relations.

**DETAINEE:** Usually a person held in local, very short term confinement while awaiting consideration for pretrial release, first appearance for arraignment, trial, or sentencing.

**DETAINER:** A warrant placed against a person incarcerated in a correctional facility, notifying the holding authority of the intention of another jurisdiction to take custody of that individual when released.

**DETENTION:** The legally authorized confinement of a person subject to criminal or juvenile court proceedings, either until commitment to a correctional facility or release.

**DETERMINATE DISCRETIONARY SENTENCES:** Sentences provided by a legislative body for the courts in its jurisdiction that include a range of time to be served for each crime. Judges can then use their discretion to impose the exact term to be served by the convicted offender.

**DETERMINATE PRESUMPTIVE SENTENCE:** Specifies the exact length of time to be served by persons convicted of that offense. Judges must impose these sentences unless there are aggravating or mitigating circumstances in which case they may lengthen or shorten them within narrow boundaries and with written justification.

**DETERMINATE SENTENCE:** Imposes a specified period of time for incarceration.

**DETERRENCE:** A philosophy underlying punishment. It is based on the belief that the pain generated by the punishment will serve to discourage future criminality.

**DETOXIFICATION CENTER:** Any community facility or program, public or private, for the short-term medical treatment of acutely intoxicated persons, or drug or alcohol abusers, often substituting for jails for persons taken into custody.

**DEVIANCE AMPLIFICATION:** This process involves mislabeling of a group's behavior as a consequence of certain biases or preconceptions about group members. Thus, in some cases the conceptions and fears of guards regarding black inmates will result in mislabeling of this group's behavior as violent (e.g., horseplay may be seen as fighting).

**DEVIL'S ISLAND:** A French penal colony off the coast of French Guiana in South America.

**DIAGNOSTIC AND STATISTICAL MANUAL (DSM-IV):** A manual published by the American Psychiatric Association that contains a classification of mental disorders. It is used in the process of diagnosing mentally disordered individuals. The manual is revised about every 10 years.

**DINGBATS:** Crazy but harmless inmates.

**DISCHARGE:** To release an individual from confinement, supervision, or any legal status imposing an obligation upon the subject person.

**DISCIPLINARY CONFINEMENT/DETENTION:** The punishment given to some inmates found guilty of a serious rule violation. Inmates are usually placed in more secure units and their privileges are restricted.

**DISCIPLINARY REPORT (DR):** A written report citing an inmate involved in a relatively serious rule violation. An investigation and/or hearing is held to determine the validity of the complaint and to impose punishment where appropriate.

**DISCRETIONARY PAROLE:** The release of an inmate at the discretion of a parole board.

**DISMEMBERMENT:** (1) As a punishment it is the practice of severing a part of the body (e.g., a hand). (2) As a social condition it refers to the adjustment made to the loss of a husband or other family member, such as when a loved one dies or is incarcerated for a lengthy period.

**DISPARITY:** In corrections this term refers to the failure to provide equal programming for both male and female inmates.

**DIVERSION:** The official suspension of a criminal or juvenile procedure at any point after official intake but before an official judgment has been rendered; and the referral of that person to a nonjustice agency or no referral at all.

**DOING TIME:** A way of adapting to imprisonment involving the avoidance of trouble, i.e., situations that might result in one's sentence being extended in order to get out fast.

**DRIVING UNDER THE INFLUENCE (DUI):** The name of the uniform crime report category used to record and report arrests for offenses of driving or operating any vehicle or common carrier while drunk or under the influence of liquor or drugs.

**DRUNK TANK:** A section or cell within a jail in which inebriated arrestees are placed to sober up before being further processed.

**DUCKING STOOL, THE:** A chair suspended over a body of water into which offenders were strapped and then repeatedly plunged into the water.

**DUE PROCESS CLAUSE, FOURTEENTH AMENDMENT:** This clause protects persons from state actions. There are two aspects: procedural, in which a person is guaranteed fair procedures, and substantive, which protects a person's property from unfair governmental interference or taking.

**DUE PROCESS PROTECTION:** The protections accorded individuals being processed by the criminal justice system under the fifth, sixth and fourteenth amendments of the U.S. Constitution

**EARLY RELEASE PROGRAMS:** These are inmate release processes that include early parole or sentence reduction for certain offenders (e.g., early release of usually nonviolent offenders within a few months of sentence completion) to cope with overcrowding in accordance with court-imposed population caps.

**ECONOMIC MARGINALITY:** Refers to individuals living at or below the poverty level.

**ECONOMIC SANCTIONS:** Any sanction imposed on convicted offenders that is economically based. These include fines, restitution, court costs, surcharges on fines, and asset forfeiture.

**EIGHTH AMENDMENT, THE:** Prohibits excessive bail, excessive fines, and cruel and unusual punishment.

**ELECTRIFIED FENCES:** Fences used in prison perimeter security that are topped with razor wire and carry several thousand volts and well over the 70 milliamperes required to kill someone.

**ELECTRONIC MONITORING:** Electronic telemetry devices designed to verify that an offender is at a given location during specified times.

**EMPLOYER PRISON INDUSTRIES MODEL:** In this model the private sector owns and manages the business employing inmates to produce its goods or services. It has control over firing, hiring, and the supervision of inmates.

**EMPTY HAND CONTROL TECHNIQUES:** Control techniques that do not involve any weapons and range from: gently guiding inmates, to those that temporarily immobilize them, to force such as kicks or strikes used against aggressive inmates.

**ENFORCER DEMEANOR:** The negative and/or punitive attitude used by COs as a public facade. This facade is taken on because COs feel it is expected of them.

**EQUAL EMPLOYMENT OPPORTUNITY COMMISSION:** Federal body that oversees the hiring of minority and female correctional officers to reduce discrimination.

**EQUITY:** The belief that like treatment should be accorded similar criminals who have committed similar crimes.

**ESCAPE:** The unlawful departure of a lawfully confined person from official custody.

**EXCESS FORCE:** Force used beyond the need and circumstances of the particular event, which means it was unnecessary or was used to inflict punishment.

**EXECUTIVE CLEMENCY:** A pardon granted for meritorious conduct such as participation in medical experiments; also general clemency on major holidays.

**EXECUTIVE MANAGEMENT TEAM:** This team includes assistant superintendents who specialize in managing certain prison functions such as security, treatment programs, business operations, or prison industries.

**EXHIBITIONISTS:** Individuals (almost always male) who achieve sexual arousal by exposing their genitals to persons of the opposite sex. Usually occurs in a public place.

**EXILE:** The expulsion of an individual from a particular area or country used as a punishment for wrong done by that individual. Exile can be temporary or permanent.

**FACILITY SECURITY LEVEL:** The nature and number of physical design barriers available to prevent escape and control inmate behavior.

**FAMILY VISITS:** A program that allows private overnight visits between inmates and close family members including wives/husbands, children, parents, grandparents, and siblings.

**FARNHAM, ELIZA:** The matron at Mount Pleasant prison in 1844, which was the first separate prison for women in the United States. She transformed this into a model facility with a homelike environment.

**FEDERAL BUREAU OF PRISONS (BOP):** Organization created by Congress in 1930 that is responsible for incarcerating those individuals convicted of violating federal laws.

**FEDERAL PRISON SYSTEM CLASSIFICATION MODEL:** An objective classification system that is based on several principles including confinement of inmates in the least restrictive, appropriately secure facility; separation of security and custody dimensions; standardized objective instruments; staff judgments can override placement based on objective confinement criteria.

**FEE SYSTEM:** The practice of collecting money from inmates for services (food, bedding, etc.) rendered to them while in custody.

**FELONY:** A criminal offense punishable by death, or by incarceration for a year or more in a state prison.

**FIELD FORCE/HOE LINE:** The inmate labor force in Texas prison farms.

**FINES:** Monetary sanctions that can be imposed on convicted offenders. They can be the only sanction imposed or can be given in conjunction with others (e.g., incarceration).

**FIRST AMENDMENT, THE:** Guarantees that no laws will be enacted that restrict or abridge our freedom of religion, speech, and the press.

**FIRST-LINE SUPERVISORS:** Lowest level of administration within the prison (e.g., corporals, unit managers) who supervise line personnel.

**FISH:** A newcomer to prison.

**FLEX CUFFS:** *See* HANDCUFFS.

**FLOGGING:** Whipping, also known as scourging. Widely employed as a means of corporal punishment.

**FOLSOM PRISON STRIKE:** This was the longest of the prison demonstrations that was part of the prisoner movement. It occurred in 1968, lasted nineteen days, and involved nearly all 2400 inmates. It commenced when inmates refused to leave their cells after having smuggled out a list of twenty-nine demands. The warden locked the prison down. Despite outside assistance, the strike ended after two weeks when supplies ran low and the warden offered to lift the lockdown if inmates went back to work.

**FOURTH AMENDMENT:** Protects people from unreasonable searches and seizures of property by government officials.

**FRAUD:** Offenses of conversion or obtaining of money or some other item of value by false pretenses. As an offense this category does not include forgery, counterfeiting, or embezzlement.

**FREELANCERS:** JHLs who seek their own inmate clients.

**FRONT-DOOR PROGRAM:** A community program in which the offender is placed under increased control, generally through some type of intensive probation, instead of being sent to prison.

**FUNCTIONALLY ILLITERATE:** An individual who may have completed middle or high school but functions at a much lower level than his or her education would indicate and does not have the skills to generally gain or maintain employment at wages sufficient to support dependents.

**GAGS:**   Any device used to muzzle an individual to keep him or her from speaking.

**GALLEYS:**   Oar-driven ships used in commerce and warfare for hundreds of years until the seventeenth century by Mediterranean nations. During the Middle Ages convicts and other undesirable were sentenced to galley servitude.

**GAME FAMILIES:**   These are pseudofamilies that may be found in female prisons which appear more gang-like than family-like. Each had a core group of six to twelve long termers and was a stable, well-recognized force within the prison.

**GANG CODES OF CONDUCT:**   Gang norms that involve expected behavior and regulate member activity. These codes emphasize secrecy and intense loyalty.

**GANG COLORS:**   A color or pattern of colors that identifies a particular gang. The color is worn by gang members as part of their clothing.

**GANG/DISRUPTIVE GROUP:**   Any organization, association, or groups of persons, either formal or informal, that may have a common name or identifying sign or symbol, whose members or associates engage in or have engaged in activities that include, but are not limited to, planning, organizing, threatening, financing, soliciting, or committing unlawful acts or acts that violate the policies, rules, and regulations of the corrections system or the state code.

**GANG HIT:**   A gang "contract" to kill someone. The general rule associated with this contract is that if the person selected to do the job refuses to do the killing he will be killed.

**GANGHOOD:**   A concept that emphasizes the significance of belonging to the gang. An example of this is found in the credo of the Texas Mafia: "Nothing is to be put before the Texas Mafia and its business. Not God, religion, parole or family."

**GAOL:**   The British term for the jail, developed in medieval England.

**GAOL FEVER:**   A set of illnesses in jails of the seventeenth and eighteenth centuries caused by the unhygienic conditions found in them. These conditions produced serious epidemics of typhus as well as malignant forms of dysentery.

**GATE MONEY:**   The money an inmate has when he or she is discharged from prison.

**GATEKEEPER FUNCTION:**   Police discretionary actions (decision to arrest or not arrest) that allow them to determine how far some individuals are processed into the criminal justice system.

**GENDER BIAS:**   Bias toward or discrimination against an individual on the basis of his or her gender.

**GENERAL DETERRENCE:**   The belief that the punishment imposed on an offender shows others what will happen to them if they engage in similar acts, which will then discourage them from doing them.

**GENERAL EQUIVALENCY DIPLOMA (GED):**   Diploma given in lieu of a high school diploma. Persons who do not finish high school may instead take the general equivalency test to demonstrate they have enough knowledge to graduate.

**GLEANING:**   An adaptation to imprisonment adopted by a small number of inmates who used available prison resources to improve their minds and postprison employment potential.

**GOOD TIME:**   A statutory provision for the reduction of time served on a sentence through the accumulation of credits that are either automatic (e.g., one day for every two days served) and/or earned (e.g., given for participation in programs, exceptional conduct).

**GROUP COUNSELING:**   A therapeutic program usually involving ten or twelve inmates (and a staff member) meeting at least weekly for a one- or two-hour session to discuss their problems.

**GUILLOTINE, THE:**   An instrument developed in France used for beheading people. It was presumed to make the beheading more humane.

**GULAGS:**   A chain of prisons, labor camps, insane asylums, and villages operated in the Siberian region of Russia to confine and exile those opposing the government.

*HABEAS CORPUS:*   An action enabling inmates to request a hearing before a judge to air claims of illegal incarceration.

**HABITUAL OFFENDERS:**   In legal terms, a person sentenced under the provisions of a statute that punishes more severely anyone convicted of a given offense who has been previously convicted of other specified offenses. Sometimes also referred to as career or repeat offenders.

**HACKS:** Also called screws or bulls; this was another name for prison guards.

**HALF-STEPPERS:** This term was used describe certain black inmates during the prisoner movement era who leaned toward revolutionary ideas but were unwilling to adopt the regimented and spartan lifestyle of true revolutionaries. While they made a show of being revolutionary they were more concerned with being part of a radical group that would make doing time easier.

**HALF-TRUSTIES OR DO-POPS:** In the Arkansas prison farms, these were the inmates who had a status between the trusties and the rank men. They had duties that allowed them to avoid working in the fields.

**HALFWAY HOUSES:** Transitional residential facilities that operate in community settings and provide more intense supervision than probation or other nonresidential programs but less than incarceration. Typically they are oriented toward providing or brokering treatment services for their residents.

**HALFWAY-IN:** Halfway houses that are used as an alternative to prison commitment.

**HALFWAY-OUT:** Halfway houses that serve as an intermediate step between prison and total release into the community.

**HANDCUFFS:** Temporary restraints that help control inmates in situations where they might escape, injure themselves or others, or become unruly or dangerous.

**HANDS-OFF DOCTRINE:** The position of the courts, prior to the mid-1960s, that they had neither the power or the obligation to define or protect what constitutional rights inmates had.

**HANDS-ON APPROACH:** The term applied to the approach by the courts, after it discarded its hands-off approach in the 1960s, of dealing with prison conditions, recognizing that prisoners had certain constitutional rights, and intervening to be sure they were accorded these rights.

**HARD TIME:** Serving a sentence under conditions that cause relatively severe discomfort.

**HAWES-COOPER ACT OF 1929:** Allowed states to block the importation of prison-made goods.

**HEAD BUILDING TENDER:** The building tender in charge of a specific cell block or tank in a Texas prison.

**HIGH MASK LIGHTING:** This system is used as part of an institution's perimeter security system. Usually five to eight lights, each illuminating a large area, are placed on poles 100 to 120 feet so as to completely light the prison compound and its perimeter.

**HILTON HOTEL SYNDROME:** Expresses the concern that inmate living conditions are better than those enjoyed by the majority of free-world Americans.

**HOG:** *See* CONVICT.

**HOLDING FACILITIES:** Keep arrestees up to 48 hours and are often located in police stations for the convenience of arresting officers. Also known as lockups.

**HOLE, THE:** An inmate term for solitary confinement.

**HOMEBOY:** The term applied to individuals who share some common experience such as coming from the same town or neighborhood, having the same ethnic-minority status, or being a member of the same youth gang.

**HOMEBOY CONNECTION:** See HOMEBOY, HOMEBOY PATTERN.

**HOMEBOY PATTERN:** A pattern of prison gang membership based on relationships formed outside of the prison. Usually based on coming from or growing up in the same neighborhood or having been boyhood friends. Also see HOMEBOY.

**HOMICIDE:** A generic term meaning the killing of one person by another.

**HONOR BLOCKS:** A dormitory or area within a prison reserved for inmates who have maintained good behavior over relatively long periods of time. Inmates there usually have more privileges.

**HOOCH:** An alcoholic beverage made in prison.

**HOOSIERS:** Dull, backward, and provincial individuals with little knowledge of crime who came from rural areas.

**HOSPICE OF SAN MICHELE:** A multipurpose facility developed in the early eighteenth century in Rome, Italy. The unit that housed juveniles anticipated many features that became an integral part of early adult and juvenile systems in the United States. The cellular design of the facility is considered to represent its most lasting contribution.

**HOUSE ARREST/HOME CONFINEMENT:** An intermediate sanction that involves confinement to one's residence or some other designated location. The offender may only leave that location to go to work, attend school, see a doctor, or engage in some other mandated activity, e.g., community service. Supervision is typically done by POs with smaller caseloads who make more frequent personal and telephone contacts with offenders at work, at night, and on weekends and holidays. Control may be further enhanced through some form of electronic monitoring.

**HUBER ACT, THE:** A 1914 Wisconsin law that authorized counties to set up work release programs for misdemeanants serving one year or less.

**HULKS:** Abandoned military vessels that were used as floating prisons by the English during the eighteenth and nineteenth centuries.

**HUMAN IMMUNODEFICIENCY VIRUS (HIV):** The virus that causes AIDS. It infects and destroys the body's ability to fight disease.

**HUMAN SERVICES ORIENTED OFFICERS (HSOs):** COs who advise, support, console, refer, or otherwise assist inmates with their problems and crises of adjustment produced by imprisonment.

**HUSTLING:** (1) In a prison context this describes ways in which inmates exploit their prison jobs so as to obtain salable goods or provide special services, which are in turn sold to other inmates. (2) On the outside, an activity through which individuals achieve their criminal objectives through persuasion and use of their wits rather than force.

**ILLITERACY:** A lack of the reading, writing, and computational skills required to function adequately in society.

**IMAM:** A Muslim clergyman.

**IMPORTATION MODEL:** Asserts the inmate subculture is shaped by a socialization process involving the adoption of a criminal value system to which the inmate is exposed prior to confinement.

**INCAPACITATION:** A philosophy that advocates the use of punishments that prevent offenders from committing additional crimes.

**INCARCERATION:** Placement in a jail or prison. As a sanction it is usually imposed when it is felt the community must be protected from further victimization by the offender.

**INCOMPETENCY TO STAND TRIAL:** A person who lacks the capacity to understand the nature of the proceedings against them and to consult with and assist counsel in the preparation of their defense.

**INDENTURE SYSTEM:** The system under which an individual was forced (or volunteered for compensation) into a period of servitude, which carried with it a slave-like status. Those forced into this system were typically convicted offenders but sometimes included individuals who were kidnapped. The practice was associated with English transportation of criminals to its American colonies.

**INDEPENDENT PAROLE BOARD MODEL:** These are autonomous units that have the power to make parole release decisions and to supervise all conditionally released inmates.

**INDEPENDENTS:** Inmates who do not affiliate with a gang or other such groups.

**INDETERMINATE SENTENCE:** Under strict indeterminate sentencing, judges assign custody of the offender to the department of corrections, and their release is dependent on their readiness to function prosocially in society. In most cases it is used in a modified form which consists of a range of time, e.g., three to five years, that is defined in terms of a minimum period to be served before release can be considered, and a maximum period after which the inmate must be released. Usually associated with rehabilitation and parole.

**INDEX CRIMES:** These are the Part I crimes dealt with in the FBI's Uniform Crime Reports. These crimes include murder and nonnegligent manslaughter, rape, robbery, aggravated assault, burglary, larceny-theft, motor vehicle theft, and arson.

**INFIRMARIES:**   The most common type of medical facility in correctional settings; generally found in jails and prisons with populations of 500 or more inmates. They provide bed care for inmates and thus have round-the-clock nursing care.

**INJUNCTION:**   A court order requiring defendants to perform or stop a specific act.

**INMATE ACCOUNTS:**   These are analogous to inmate bank accounts that are managed by prison personnel. They contain any money that has been sent to the inmate by his or her family or that the inmate has legitimately earned by working.

**INMATE CUSTODY CATEGORY:**   The degree of staff supervision necessary to ensure adequate control of the inmate.

**INMATE HANDBOOK:**   A booklet containing information regarding the rules, regulations, programs, and procedures within the prison with which the inmate should become familiar.

**INMATE SOCIAL WORLD:**   The set of norms, behaviors, etc., characterizing inmate society.

**INMATE SUBCULTURE:**   Provides ways of thinking, feeling, and acting about all aspects of prison life to help inmates cope with the special circumstances of prison life.

**INMATES IN THE LIFE:**   This label was used to describe the prison adaptation of female inmates who had habitually committed offenses such as prostitution, possession or sales of illegal drugs, or shoplifting and had been in prison before. These inmates became totally immersed in the prison world. They tended to interact with persons of similar backgrounds and be hostile or negative in their dealings with correctional officers.

**INSANITY:**   A legal term connoting a mental disease or disorder of sufficient seriousness to absolve an individual of responsibility for the commission of a crime.

**IN-SERVICE TRAINING:**   Any form of specialized training to enhance the job skills of an individual occurring after the individual has assumed the day-to-day responsibilities of that job. This includes outside workshops, seminars and training programs, and participation in specially developed correspondence courses.

**INSIDE CELL DESIGN:**   A design in which cells are built back to back, sometimes five tiers high, in a hollow building. These cells have doors that open onto galleries or walkways eight to ten feet from the outer wall of the building.

**INTELLIGENCE:**   Selectively processed information that is of strategic value in making informed decisions regarding security management.

**INTELLIGENCE OFFICER:**   The individual responsible for the collection of intelligence information or who is in charge of the intelligence unit.

**INTELLIGENCE UNIT:**   A correctional organization's unit that is responsible for the collection of strategic information that can be used to deal with potential prison security problems.

**INTENSIVE PAROLE SUPERVISION:**   *See* INTENSIVE PROBATION SUPERVISION. The only difference is that this is used as an early release mechanism for high-risk offenders who do not meet the criteria for regular parole.

**INTENSIVE PROBATION SUPERVISION (IPS):**   An intermediate sanction designed to serve prison-bound offenders. It is meant to be more punitive and controlling than regular probation by reducing the size of officer caseloads thus allowing for more intensive surveillance and the imposition of stricter conditions.

**INTERMEDIATE SANCTIONS:**   A punishment option that is considered on a continuum to fall between traditional probation and traditional incarceration. This provides sentencing options for those requiring more surveillance and control than can be provided by probation, but less control than imprisonment.

**INTERMITTENT SENTENCE:**   A sentence to periods of confinement interrupted by periods of freedom.

**INTERNATIONAL ASSOCIATION OF CORRECTIONAL OFFICERS (IACO):**   An organization that brings together correctional experts and personnel from many areas around the world.

**INTERSTATE COMPACT:**   An agreement between two or more states to transfer prisoners, parolees, or probationers from the physical or supervisory custody of one state to the physical or supervisory custody of another where the state with original jurisdiction retains legal authority to confine or release the prisoner.

**IRISH OR INTERMEDIATE SYSTEM, THE:** Sir Walter Crofton's system, which punished convicts for their past crimes and also prepared them for release. This was accomplished by giving them the opportunity to earn increased responsibility and privileges while progressing through four stages.

**JAILHOUSE LAWYERS (JHL):** Inmates who, without formal training, become proficient in writing writs and briefs and who help other inmates in dealing with appeals, violations of inmate rights, and other legal matters.

**JAILING:** The adaptation to imprisonment generally adopted by a "state raised youth." These prisoners almost completely oriented themselves to the prison, which became the world around which their lives revolved.

**JAILS:** Local institutions usually run by law enforcement agencies. These institutions hold pretrial detainees, short-term (up to one year) sentenced misdemeanants, and those awaiting transportation to state or federal prison. They also hold the drunk, disorderly, and mentally ill.

**JITTERBUGS:** The term used to describe many youthful inmates by adult or older inmates.

**JOB BIDDING:** Allows senior correctional officers to bid for specific jobs within the institutions.

**JOCKERS:** Sexual aggressors who took the traditional masculine role in oral or anal intercourse during a homosexual encounter.

**JUDICIAL ORDER:** A court order that involves the exercise of judicial discretion and affects the final result of litigation.

**JUDICIAL REPRIEVE:** Under this practice, convicted offenders could apply for a temporary suspension of their sentence while they appealed to the crown for a pardon while at liberty.

**JURISDICTION:** The territory, subject matter, or persons over which lawful authority may be exercised by a court or other justice agency, as determined by statute or constitution.

**JUST DESERTS:** A term used in conjunction with retribution to indicate that offenders should be punished to repay society for the harm done by their crime.

**JUSTICE MODEL:** Takes a just deserts or retributive approach, while emphasizing a justice-as-fairness perspective. This model appears to fit the present public mood for more punishment and the use of determinate sentencing, and the shift away from rehabilitation.

**JUSTIFIABLE USE OF FORCE:** COs can use force in self-defense and in defense of others; to prevent a crime; to detain or arrest inmates; to enforce prison rules and discipline; and to protect property and prevent inmates from harming themselves.

**JUVENILES:** Individuals can be subject to juvenile court proceedings because of statutorily defined events or conditions in which these individuals were involved. The status of juvenile is statutorily defined by an age range, usually from 7 to 17.

**KAIROS PRISON MINISTRY (KPM):** Emanates from mainline churches. Puts on seminars to teach inmates religious principles. Also provides significant transitional services to inmates.

*KEEPERS' VOICE, THE:* Newsletter published by the International Association of Correctional Officers (IACO), which provides a forum for correctional officers.

**KEISTERING:** A prison term referring to the concealment of such items as hacksaw blades, handcuff keys, and drugs by inmates in their rectums to bring these items into the prison.

**KID:** An individual, usually young and weak, who has been coerced or forced into being another inmate's sex slave.

**KING'S PEACE:** A law by which the king extended his protection to those in his presence and in the local area in which he was staying.

**KITE or SNITCH:** An anonymous note to a guard's superior detailing his past derelictions of duty.

**KNOUT, THE:** A Russian wooden-handled whip typically consisting of several rawhide thongs twisted together and terminating in a single strand. Sometimes the hide was plaited with wire, dipped in liquid, and then frozen before use or the thongs had hooks or rings attached to the ends.

**LA NUESTRA FAMILIA (NF):** A group of Northern California Chicanos who formed their own gang to protect themselves from attacks by members of the Mexican Mafia. Today this group is considered an organized crime group and has units both inside and outside California prisons.

**LARCENY:** Unlawful taking or attempted taking of property other than a motor vehicle from the possession of another, by stealth, without force and without deceit, with the intent to permanently deprive the owner of the property.

**LARCENY-THEFT:** Uniform Crime Reports designation for larceny.

**LAW CLERKS:** In corrections, these are inmates assigned by the prison, as jailhouse lawyers, to litigation tasks.

**LEASE SYSTEM:** A method of contracting with a private company or individual to control and operate prison shops, or be entirely responsible for groups of convicts or for an entire prison. Contractors paid states a fee or a portion of the profits from inmate-produced goods for this privilege.

**LEAST RESTRICTIVE MEANS TEST FOR RFRA CASES:** Prison officials can only ban legitimate practices that are an important of part pursuing a religion if they show the restriction is based on a compelling government test and there is no alternative means of allowing inmates to engage in this practice that does not comprise a compelling government interest.

**LEATHER RESTRAINTS:** Used to humanely restrain agitated inmates.

**LEFT-WING POLITICAL GROUPS:** Political groups espousing a socialist or communist political philosophy.

**LEG IRONS:** Cuffs placed on inmates' legs.

**LEGITIMATE GOVERNMENT OBJECTIVES:** In corrections this refers to institutional objectives that are considered as a constitutionally acceptable basis for prison restrictions on inmate rights because they are necessary for maintaining a safe and secure facility environment. These include maintaining institutional security and preserving internal order and discipline.

**LEGITIMATE PRISON ECONOMIC SYSTEMS, THE:** Consist of inmate funds and goods obtained through approved channels. Inmates can acquire money from relatives and/or friends, work assignments, veterans's benefits, or through their hobbies (e.g., by making items that can be sold at gift shops located outside the prison). Friends and relatives can also send them goods that can be sold or traded.

**LESS THAN LETHAL WEAPONS:** These are weapons that are not likely to be lethal if properly used. They include impact weapons (batons), chemical agents, and electrical disablers used to temporarily disable the inmate and not to inflict permanent injury.

*LEX TALIONIS:* The principle of an eye for eye. This was used as a means to regulate the extent to which victims could retaliate against those who injured them.

**LIBERTY INTERESTS:** Interests that require due process protection and are defined by the Constitution, court orders, statutes, regulations, or standard practice policies or customs. In this case of statutes or regulations, liberty interests exist only if these rules have in them mandatory language and substantive predicates, i.e., that stipulate specific conditions or requirements.

**LIFE SKILLS PROGRAMS:** Educational programs that provide inmates with practical knowledge in employability/job search skills, consumer skills, the use of community resources, health and safety skills, parenting and family child skills, civic skills.

**LIFE WITHOUT PAROLE (LWOP):** A sentence intended to assure that an individual who receives it will spend the rest of his or her life in prison. It is seen by some as a feasible alternative to capital punishment.

**LINE PERSONNEL:** These are the workers who directly perform the activities that accomplish the goals and objectives of the organization (e.g., correctional officers).

**LINEAR DESIGN FACILITIES:** Jail and prison facilities in which the cells are constructed in long straight rows aligned with corridors where correctional staff walk from cell to cell to intermittently supervise inmate activities.

**LITERACY:**   The possession of the skills required to function effectively in society.

**LITERACY PROGRAMS:**   Educational programs that focus on providing basic skills to low-level readers and nonreaders.

**LOCAL CORRECTIONS:**   The system of facilities and programs dealing with convicted misdemeanant offenders and pretrial detainees.

**LOCKDOWN:**   An action taken by prison administrators consisting of keeping inmates locked in their cells when a breakdown of order appears imminent.

**LOCK-STEP:**   Convicts were marched from place to place in "close-order single file," each looking over the next man's shoulder with their faces pointed to the right to prevent conversation, and their feet moving in unison. This formation began in the Auburn era and was used in American prisons well into the 1930s.

**LONG-TERM OFFENDER (LTO):**   An offender sentenced to a long term (e.g., 25 years or life in prison). This group includes younger inmates, middle-aged inmates, and frequently career criminals with long sentences and elderly inmates who have grown old in prison.

**M-2 SPONSORS PROGRAM:**   A program in which community volunteers were trained to function as visitors for inmates who had no family or friends to visit them.

**MACE:**   A type of tear gas that is the least incapacitating of the gasses currently in use.

**MACONOCHIE, ALEXANDER:**   *See* MARK SYSTEM.

**MAIN CUSTOMER PRISON INDUSTRIES MODEL:**   Here the private sector buys a substantial portion of the output of a prison-owned and -operated business, but has no other connection with it.

**MAINSTREAMING:**   The practice of placing individuals with special needs in the general population of a facility.

**MAISON DE FORCE:**   Established in 1773 in Ghent, Belgium. It had a rudimentary classification system in which felons were separated from misdemeanants and had a separate section for women and one for children. Work was the primary method of reform.

**MANAGEMENT BY WALKING AROUND:**   This involves administrators going out into the institution(s) to obtain a first "foot" look at and a real feel for what is actually going on in the institution(s) or an entire corrections system.

**MANDATORY RELEASE:**   Under this form of release inmates are placed under the supervision of a parole officer after they have served their original sentences minus earned or administratively awarded good time.

**MANDATORY SENTENCES:**   These sentences mandate incarceration, often for specified lengths of time, for certain categories of offenders (e.g., drug traffickers). They generally do not permit judges any discretion in the sentence to be imposed.

**MANSLAUGHTER, INVOLUNTARY:**   Causing the death of another person unintentionally but with recklessness or gross negligence. Also referred to as negligent manslaughter.

**MANSLAUGHTER, VEHICULAR:**   A from of involuntary manslaughter caused by grossly negligent operation of a motor vehicle.

**MANSLAUGHTER, VOLUNTARY:**   Intentionally causing the death of another without legal justification but under conditions of extreme provocation. Also referred to as nonnegligent manslaughter.

**MARGINAL MEMBERS:**   Peripheral members of the gang who are called on when the gang needs to present a strong show of force or power.

**MARK SYSTEM, THE:**   A system developed by Alexander Maconochie under which sentences were to consist of a specified number of marks or points based on the seriousness of the offense. Marks represented a debt, and the offender had to earn enough marks to pay off the debt before he could be released.

**MARXIST POSITION:**   Pertaining to the teaching of Karl Marx. It argued that current inequities in society were rooted in the system of corporate capitalism. Under this system the ruling elite controlled government and the workplace by effectively setting one group of exploited people against another.

**MATRON:** In early women's prisons, the woman who was the chief supervisor of the women's prison or unit.

**MATURE INMATES:** Older inmates. The minimum age for this group varies according to who is defining the group and ranges from 45 to 65.

**MAXIMUM CUSTODY INMATES:** Pose the most serious threats to other inmates or staff or may be high escape risks. They are: confined in single cells; only removed for authorized activities when escorted by at least one staff member; involved only in programs conducted in their cells; eat in their cells; and allowed only noncontact visits.

**MAXIMUM SECURITY/LEVEL V:** A prison with the highest level of security, which is generally considered to be an end-of-the-line facility. Inmates here require secure housing in the most secure perimeter, and separate management for activities such as work, exercise, and food service. Inmate housing is normally in single inside cells. In correctional systems with super-max facilities they represent the highest security level.

**MAXIMUM SENTENCE:** The maximum penalty provided by law for a given criminal offense.

**MEDICAL MODEL:** An approach to dealing with crime as an illness that viewed criminals as "sick." To cure them requires a diagnostic process that identifies their problems and the program of treatment that remediates these problems.

**MEDIUM CUSTODY INMATES:** These types of inmates move about the institution during the day within sight of a CO. Eligible for all programs and activities within the main perimeter. Indoor contact visits are permitted.

**MEDIUM SECURITY PRISONS/LEVEL III:** Usually have external perimeter security that is similar to level IV and V. Housing in single cells, rooms, or dormitories. Provide a wider variety of programs and activities and allow greater freedom of movement within the facility.

**MEGA-JAILS:** A term used to denote jails with populations in excess of 1000 inmates.

**MENTAL RETARDATION:** A condition characterized by significantly subaverage general intellectual functioning existing concurrently with deficits in adaptive behavior.

**MENTALLY DISORDERED:** Individuals who are classed as mentally or emotionally disturbed. Sometimes restricted to those having a disabling mental disorder like schizophrenia or an affective disorder.

**MERCHANTS:** Inmates who obtain or manufacture scarce luxury items, both legal and illegal (e.g., cigarettes, "hooch," weapons) to be sold or traded in the inmate economy.

**MERIT SYSTEM:** As used in employee hiring, the merit system requires applicants to qualify for a specific job by meeting certain minimum requirements for that job and scoring above a certain level on a written exam.

**MEXICAN MAFIA:** A California prison gang formed by a group of Mexican-American inmates from the Marvilla section of East Los Angeles. Today it has groups throughout California prisons and is viewed as an organized crime syndicate.

**MEXIKANEMI:** A Texas gang that was an offshoot of the Mexican Mafia.

**MIDDLE MANAGERS:** Supervisors responsible for overseeing the delivery of specific services, such as education, in the prison.

**MILDLY RETARDED:** Individuals who have IQs ranging from 55 to 69 (based on a Wechsler Adult Intelligence Scale IQ) but who can essentially function on an independent basis.

**MILIEU THERAPY:** A form of therapeutic community.

**MINIMAL NECESSITIES OF CIVILIZED LIFE, THE:** The factors considered by the courts in making decisions regarding the constitutionality of the totality of prison living conditions. These include food, shelter, sanitation, health care, and personal safety.

**MINIMUM CUSTODY INMATES:** Not posing risks associated with higher custody levels. Can move about the facility without being directly within the view of staff. Eligible for all inside jobs and supervised assignments outside the prison's perimeter. Access to all programs and activities.

**MINIMUM MANDATORY SENTENCES:** Sentences that require a specific term to be served before good time credits can be accumulated or release can be considered.

**MINIMUM SECURITY PRISON/LEVEL II:** Open design with perimeters consisting of a single fence or clearly designated unarmed "posts." No detection devices, intermittent external mobile patrols. Housing is in open units varying from dormitory style to single or multiple occupancy rooms. Heavy emphasis on programs and activities.

**MINNESOTA MULTIPHASIC PERSONALITY INVENTORY (MMPI):** An objective personality test sometimes used in preemployment screening to select job candidates.

**MISDEMEANOR:** An offense less serious than a felony and which may be punished by a fine and/or incarceration, usually in a local jail, for up to one year.

**MISSION STATEMENT:** A policy statement that delineates the purpose, goals, and objectives of the organization.

**MOBILE PATROLS:** These are vehicles manned by armed correctional officers that are used to patrol the perimeter of the prison compound.

**MOBILITY IMPAIRED:** A condition under which an individual needs assistance (e.g., a wheelchair) in order to get around.

**MODERATELY RETARDED:** Individuals who have IQs between 40 and 54 (based on a Wechsler Adult Intelligence Scale IQ) and can learn to care for themselves but are not likely to function independently.

**MONASTERIES:** Religious facilities used to house members of religious orders.

**MOOD DISORDERS:** Another name used for affective disorders (e.g., depression).

**MOORISH SCIENCE TEMPLE OF AMERICA:** A hybrid offshoot of the Black Muslim movement.

**MORTIFICATION PROCESS:** The process by which prison routines deprive individuals of key aspects important for maintaining their self-concept.

**MOTHER-CHILD PROGRAMS:** These programs help to maintain the bond between a female inmate and her child.

**MUG SHOTS:** The photographs taken during the booking process.

**MULTIPLE DRUG-RESISTANT TB STRAINS (MDR-TB):** TB strains resistant to normal drug treatment.

**MURDER:** Intentionally causing the death of another person without extreme provocation or legal justification or causing that death while committing or attempting to commit another crime.

**MURTON, TOM:** A reform warden who exposed the barbaric conditions under which Arkansas prisons operated. He attempted in the late 1960s to bring these prisons up to mid-twentieth century standards.

**MUTILATION:** Any form of punishment in which the individual is mutilated, such as dismemberment.

**MUTUAL AGREEMENT PROGRAM:** A program involving a contractual agreement between a prisoner and/or state prison and parole officials by which the prisoner attempts to complete a specific self-improvement program in order to receive a definite parole date.

**NARCOTICS ANONYMOUS (NA):** A self-help organization that supports recovering addicts, which follows the twelve-step program originated by AA. This is a world-wide organization with groups operating almost everywhere. Groups hold open meetings, at which anyone is welcome, and closed meetings exclusively for members at which personal problems or interpretations of the twelve steps are discussed.

**NATION OF ISLAM:** The name given to the original Black Muslim movement in the United States by its founder, Elijah Muhammad. This was later changed to the American Muslim mission by Muhammad's son. The name was resurrected by a splinter group led by Louis Farrakhan.

**NATIONAL CENTRAL STG DEPOSITORY:** A proposed clearing house and repository for information on STGs, their members, and activities that would represent a valuable intelligence resource.

**NATIONAL COMMISSION ON CORRECTIONAL HEALTH CARE (NCCHC):** Composed of representatives from thirty-six organizations that have an interest in correctional health care, and who set standards for prison medial services. It also conducts site visits to evaluates jails and prisons for accreditation purposes, which requires that they meet certain minimum standards.

**NATIONAL CORRECTIONAL RECREATION ASSOCIATION:** A professional association of full-time professional correctional personnel who are committed to promoting professional programs and services that assist the inmate in eliminating barriers to leisure, in developing leisure skills and attitudes, and optimizing leisure participation.

**NATIONAL COUNCIL ON CRIME AND DELINQUENCY:** A professional organization consisting mainly of criminal justice personnel, many of whom are involved in community corrections and correctional research.

**NATIONAL INSTITUTE OF CORRECTIONS MODEL:** An objective classification system that incorporates elements such as custody, security, needs assessment, program monitoring and assessment, reclassification, and a management information system.

**NATIONAL LAWYERS GUILD:** A communist front organization composed of left-wing lawyers that was active in the prisoner movement.

**NATIONAL PRISON CONGRESS:** At this conference held in 1870, the leading reform ideas of the era were discussed and incorporated into a declaration of principles that advocated a philosophy of reformation as opposed to the adoption of punishment. This was the first meeting of what today is called the American Corrections Association.

**NEEDS ASSESSMENT:** Assessment of an inmate's program and service requirements.

**NEIGHBORHOOD JUSTICE CENTERS:** Centers in which volunteer mediators act as hearing officers and attempt to resolve relatively minor disputes between citizens that might otherwise wind up in the courts. The solutions that are worked out are agreed to by both parties.

**NET-WIDENING:** Net-widening occurs when a sanction extends the "net" of control over offenders who could be effectively supervised with less intrusive methods.

**NEW COURT COMMITMENT:** The imprisonment of a person being admitted on a new sentence and not being readmitted on any previous sentence still in effect.

**NEW PENOLOGY MODEL:** Model under which persistent pressures for more humane practices and programs to reform offenders were applied. This movement traced its roots to the principles enunciated in 1870 at the National Prison Congress.

**NEW YORK HOUSE OF REFUGE:** The first correctional unit in the United States developed to house juveniles apart from adults. It was opened in 1825 and had a separate building for housing women.

**NIMBY:** Acronym for "not in my back yard." The position usually taken by citizens when an attempt is made to locate some type of correctional program in a specific area of the community.

**NOLLE PROSEQUI:** A formal decision by the prosecutor not to further prosecute.

**NOLO CONTENDERE:** A plea in court in answer to a charge stating that the defendant will not contest the charges, but neither admits guilt or claims innocence. Tantamount to a guilty plea.

**NOMINAL DAMAGES:** A trifling sum awarded to a plaintiff where there is no substantial loss or injury.

**NONCONTACT VISITATION:** A condition of prison visitation in which visitors and inmates are denied physical contact either by being separated by glass partitions and communicating through telephones or separated by mesh screens.

**NONDISRUPTIVE GROUPS:** These are formal or informal groups of inmates that are not felt by prison personnel to pose a threat to the security of the prison.

**NONRESIDENTIAL/DAY TREATMENT PROGRAMS:** These are community-based programs that allow the clients participating in them to attend program functions during the day but to live at home.

**NOT GUILTY BY REASON OF INSANITY:** A plea or verdict in a criminal proceeding that the defendant is not guilty of the offense(s) charged because when the crime(s) was/were committed the defendant did not have the mental capacity to be held criminally responsible for his or her actions.

**OBJECTIVE CLASSIFICATION SYSTEMS:** Approaches to classification that provide more accurate information on the characteristics of the prison population than subjective systems, and use evaluation instruments containing explicit criteria. These systems can also be used to make projections, regarding security, custody, and staffing needs for new institutions, and the expansion of existing prisons.

**OCCUPATIONAL/JOB STRESS:** Factors associated with the job itself, e.g., negative inmate behavior, overcrowding, and those which are part of the organizational environment (e.g., lack of administrative support) that makes people feel uncomfortable, overwhelmed, unhappy, fearful, or anxious. These emotional responses to stimuli may have dysfunctional psychological (e.g., depression) or physiological consequences (e.g., heart attacks and hypertension).

**OFFENDER:** An adult (or juvenile tried as an adult) convicted of a criminal offense.

**OFFICER SUBCULTURE:** *See* CO SUBCULTURE.

**OMBUDSMAN:** An individual who acts as an advocate for a specific group.

**ON-THE-JOB-TRAINING:** Informal training of correctional officers, accomplished while working, via daily interactions with older, more experienced officers as well as with the inmates.

**OPERATIONAL OR TACTICAL INTELLIGENCE:** This involves obtaining information about the current activity of an individual or group. For example, regarding STGs this would involve acquiring knowledge of current criminal activity including drug introductions, escapes, planned violence, and work and food stoppages.

**ORDEAL BY WATER:** A torture process in which prisoners were strapped down on their backs and had a funnel forced into their mouths, into which a steady stream of water was poured.

**ORDER OF MISERICORDIA:** This group was founded in 1488 to provide assistance and consolation to offenders condemned to death, accompany them to the gallows, furnish religious services, and provide a Christian burial.

**ORGANIC DISORDERS:** A mental disorder caused by damage to the central nervous system.

**ORGANIZATIONAL CULTURE:** This is a persistent, patterned way of thinking about the central tasks of, and human relationships in, an organization.

**ORGANIZED CRIME SYNDICATES:** Sophisticated self-perpetuating organized groups, involved in illegal acts for power and profit. This includes group like La Cosa Nostra and some prison gangs with inside and outside groups. These groups provide illegal goods and services and also operate legitimate businesses. Their organizational features include the availability of large capital resources, disciplined management, division of labor, and a focus on maximum profit.

**ORIENTATION/RECEPTION PROCESS:** A period during which inmates are provided with information regarding what is expected of them and what they can anticipate from their institutional experience. This includes being informed about institutional rules, the disciplinary process and being given a copy of the inmate handbook.

**ORWELLIAN:** A term derived from the name of George Orwell, the author of a book entitled *1984* that detailed the oppressive conditions in a society in which the government was able to monitor the activities of all its citizens.

**OUTLAWS:** In medieval times men and women who either fled from justice (failed to appear in court to face the charges against them) or had been banished to the wilderness.

**OUTSIDE CELL BLOCKS:** Cells line the outside wall of each unit with doors that open onto a central corridor and may be several tiers high. Older units may have barred windows, while newer units may have windows of special unbreakable materials that allow light in but do not open.

**OVERCLASSIFICATION:**  Placement of inmates under more supervision (custody) and control (security) than required.

**PAINS OF IMPRISONMENT:**  Describes the deprivations and limits on freedom to which prisons subject inmates.

**PARCHMAN PENAL FARM:**  A Mississippi prison farm.

**PARENTING PROGRAMS:**  In prison, these are programs that improve parenting skills through a series of educational activities and may include special events involving inmates and their children. These programs include efforts to increase participants' knowledge of child development; instill effective parenting styles and techniques and family communication; strengthen inmate family relationships; and create an understanding of the impact of incarceration on children and other family members.

**PARITY:**  In corrections this term refers to equality in programming and distribution of resources between female and male inmates.

**PAROLE:**  The conditional release, by an agency that has statutory authority to grant such releases, of inmates from prison to serve the remainder of their sentences under community correctional supervision.

**PAROLE BOARD, THE:**  A panel of individuals usually appointed by the governor that makes decisions regarding the release of inmates. The decision is usually based on an evaluation of the progress made by the inmate while incarcerated, the risk posed to the community by the release, and the inmate's plan for the postprison period.

**PAROLE GUIDELINES:**  Guidelines used by parole authorities in making parole decisions, similar to those used for sentencing. They attempt to gauge accurately the risk the parolee poses to the community.

**PAROLE OFFICER:**  An employee of a parole agency whose primary duties include the supervision of parolees.

**PAROLEE:**  A person on parole status.

**PARTICIPATIVE ORGANIZATIONAL MODEL:** This approach allows for input from all members of the organization in the way it is run.

**PATUXENT:**  A correctional facility in Maryland that was originally designed to be a psychiatrically run prison.

**PEER TUTORS:**  Inmates, usually with a GED or high school diploma, who tutor other inmates with low-level academic skills. They may be specially trained and under the supervision of a certified teacher.

**PENAL SERVITUDE:**  A system of imprisonment of both black and white convicts that made them the temporary or life-long "slaves" of states, or of the employers or corporations to whom they were assigned.

**PENILE PLETHYSMOGRAPH:**  A device sometimes used in the behavior modification of sex offenders. It measures penile erection.

**PENITENTIARIES:**  Another name for prisons.

**PENNSYLVANIA SYSTEM, THE:**  The approach to imprisonment, also called the separate system, developed at the Eastern penitentiary. It was designed to reform inmates through a program of isolation, work, and penitence.

**PENOLOGY:**  The generic term for the organized body of concepts, theories, and approaches centered on the prison and the institutional experience; signifies the study of punishment. This term was used previously to denote what today is described as the study of corrections.

**PEPPER SPRAY (OC):**  A recently developed nonlethal gas that is becoming more popular among law enforcement and correctional agencies. OC is more effective on the extremely agitated, the mentally ill, or inmates under the influence of drugs.

**PERCEPTUAL RESEARCH:**  Relating to deterrence, the line of research that asks subjects to determine how certain they are that they might get caught and punished if they broke a specific law. They are then asked whether they would actually commit that crime.

**PERIMETER SECURITY:**  The structures and processes, consisting of secure walls, protected windows, and controlled access to the points of entrance and exit, that protect against escape from a prison or jail.

**PERPETRATOR:** The chief actor in the commission of a crime, that is, the person who commits the crime.

**PERSONALITY DISORDERS:** An inflexible and maladaptive pattern of behavior developed early in life causing significant impairment in overall functioning. The most important of these for the criminal justice system is the antisocial personality disorder.

**PHILADELPHIA SOCIETY FOR ALLEVIATING THE MISERIES OF PUBLIC PRISONS:** A reform group existing in the eighteenth and nineteenth centuries in Philadelphia. Today this organization is known as the Pennsylvania Prison Society.

**PIECE-PRICE PRISON INDUSTRIES SYSTEM:** Similar to the contract system except that state officials had full control of the production process. The contractor furnished the raw materials but prison authorities were responsible for manufacturing the product, which the contractor then sold.

**PILLORIES:** A device similar to the stocks by which an individual could be punished by being secured by his or her wrists and neck. These devices were usually placed in a town's square so that the offender would suffer humiliation at the hands of his or her fellow citizens.

**PLANTATION/FARM PRISONS:** Prisons organized in the manner of pre–Civil War plantations.

**PLAYING THE GAME:** *See* CONNING.

**PLEA:** A defendant's formal answer in a criminal proceeding to the charge contained in a complaint, information, or indictment, that he or she is guilty or not guilty of the offense charged.

**PLURALISTIC PRISON ENVIRONMENT:** This is used to describe the inmate world of the contemporary prison since it is characterized by ethnic, religious, self-help, special interest, and unauthorized groups.

**PODULAR DIRECT FACILITIES:** Jail or prison facilities with a direct supervision design. It permanently situates staff among the inmates within each housing unit, thus allowing the most continuous supervision.

**PODULAR REMOTE FACILITIES:** Jails and prison facilities with pods housing various numbers of inmates that are arranged in such a way as to permit observation of activities from a central, protected control room.

**POLITICAL PRISONERS:** Individuals imprisoned for engaging in political activities deemed as criminal within the society in which they occur. These acts can range from simple political dissent to murder.

**POLITICIANS, INMATE:** Prisoners who generally occupied positions in the administrative offices or worked for key officials that gave them the ability to influence decisions affecting other inmates, e.g., cell and work assignments and access to files and other sources of information.

**POPULATION CAPS:** Limits placed by the courts or by statute regarding the number of inmates that can be legally housed in a jail, prison, or prison system.

**POPULATION MOVEMENT:** In corrections, the entries and exits of adjudicated persons, or persons subject to judicial proceedings, into or from correctional facilities or programs.

**POSTCONVICTION REMEDY:** The procedures by which a person who has been convicted of a crime can challenge in court the lawfulness of that conviction or the penalty received or of a correctional agency action and thus obtain relief in situations where this cannot be done by direct appeal.

**PRELIMINARY INJUNCTION/TEMPORARY RESTRAINING ORDER:** In corrections, an injunction granted at the beginning of a suit to prevent institutional officials from continuing to engage in certain conduct or keeping an inmate in a designated status that is in dispute. It may be terminated or continued depending on the results of the court decision.

**PRESENTENCE INVESTIGATION:** An investigation of the defendant by a probation officer designed to help the sentencing judge decide on the most appropriate sentence. It may also be used for other purposes by criminal justice personnel.

**PRESERVICE TRAINING:** Any form of training occurring before the individual assumes the day-to-day responsibilities of a job.

**PRETRIAL DETAINEES:** Individuals being held in a jail or similar facility while awaiting court processing.

**PRETRIAL DETENTION:** A period of confinement occurring between arrest and any further prosecution.

**PRETRIAL INTERVENTION:** *See* DIVERSION.

**PRETRIAL STATUS:** Any status (e.g., ROR, detention) in which an accused individual finds himself or herself while awaiting court processing.

**PRIDE:** Prison Rehabilitative Industries and Diversified Enterprise is a not-for-profit corporation that runs Florida's prisons industries. It is an example of the "corporate model" by which some jurisdictions run their prison industry programs.

**PRIMARY PREVENTION:** Measures that are taken to eliminate or reduce as many of the criminogenic conditions existing within the community as possible.

**PRINCIPLE OF LEAST ELIGIBILITY:** The notion that prisoners should not be given programs and services nor live under conditions that are better than those of the lowest classes of the non-criminal population in the society.

**PRISON ADMINISTRATION:** The group of individuals that runs the prison composed of the superintendent and his or her assistants.

**PRISON CHAPLAINS:** He/she is a minister of a particular faith who is typically employed and paid by a jurisdiction to administer, supervise, and plan all religious activities and services at a particular facility and is responsible for ministering to inmates, staff, and families regardless of their religious beliefs or affiliation.

**PRISON CLASSIFICATION:** The sorting out procedure that results in matching a prisoner to the appropriate level of supervision (custody), institution (security), programs, and services to meet his/her needs, and that periodically reviews the inmate's placement to achieve the most appropriate assignments possible.

**PRISON CROWDING:** When institutions are filled beyond their rated or court-mandated capacities.

**PRISON FELLOWSHIP (PF):** A prison ministry that recruits and trains volunteers and provides teaching, mentoring, and aftercare programs for released inmates.

**PRISON FURLOUGHS:** Short-term, escorted or unescorted trips away from the prison, granted for various purposes.

**PRISON INTELLIGENTSIA:** A group of inmates who during the rehabilitation era took advantage of education programs to develop their academic skills and eventually came to enjoy reading. They expanded their knowledge by reading in all areas, which provided them with a perspective on the world scene and changed their views of themselves and society. This led them to critically examine the prison system and expose its flaws. This group was very vocal during the prisoner movement era.

**PRISON QUEENS:** Inmates who are openly homosexual and manifest their "feminine" characteristics in dress and manner.

**PRISON RULES:** To be considered constitutionally acceptable institutional rules should be clear, intelligible, and only prohibit behavior that threatens important institutional interests such as order, security, and safety.

**PRISON STUPOR:** Referred to as prison psychosis this is a mental escape from the deprivations of prison life.

**PRISON TOUGHS:** Inmates who manifested a constant hostility toward prison officials, conventional society, and most other prisoners and occasionally hurt or killed inmates, usually those without prestige or power.

**PRISONER:** A person in physical custody in a confinement facility or in the physical custody of a criminal justice official while being transported to or between confinement facilities.

**PRISONER MOVEMENT, THE:** A movement inspired by the changes that occurred in the United States during the 1960s that focused on reforming prison conditions. It included both free-world and inmate groups.

**PRISONER RIGHTS GROUPS:** These groups were influenced by the Civil Rights movement.

They directed their efforts toward reducing the disparities between prisoners and members of conventional society and sought to increase inmate constitutional rights.

**PRISONIZATION:** The socialization process by which inmates take on (to a greater or lesser degree) the folkways, mores, customs, and general culture of the penitentiary or prison.

**PRIVATE BENEFIT PRISON INDUSTRY SYSTEM:** A system of prison industry in which a private entity derives profits from its involvement in the industry.

**PRIVATE SECTOR INVOLVEMENT IN CORRECTIONS:** Some jurisdictions contract with companies to provide specific services such as food or to manage or build a facility.

**PRIVATE WRONGS:** In current usage, private wrongs are referred to as torts or civil wrongs. In preliterate times these included many things that today we consider to be criminal offenses.

**PRIVILEGED COMMUNICATION:** Statements made by certain persons in a protected relationship (e.g., priest–penitent, lawyer–client) which the law protects from forced disclosure on the witness stand unless the individual making them waives his or her legal right to secrecy.

**PROACTIVE:** A term that means to act in anticipation of an event. In corrections this refers to dealing with and correcting conditions that are known to cause problems before the problems can manifest themselves.

**PROACTIVE MANAGEMENT:** This approach to management involves trying to anticipate and correct problems before they develop by continually evaluating programs and planing for and creating opportunities for the organization to develop the capacity to pursue its mission.

**PROBATION:** A sentence that keeps the convicted offender in the community under supervision by a probation agency and usually requires compliance with legally imposed restrictions and conditions.

**PROBATION OFFICER:** An employee of a probation agency whose primary duties include the supervision of probationers and any other of the probation agency functions.

**PROBATION SUPERVISION FEES:** Statutory requirements that probationers and/or parolees contribute to their own supervision. These fees average between $20 to $25 per month.

**PROBATION WITHOUT ADJUDICATION:** Allows judges to withhold adjudication in the interests of reducing the penetration of offenders into the criminal justice system. This is similar to the use of deferred prosecution in the federal courts.

**PROBATIONER:** A person who is placed on probation status.

**PROCEDURAL DUE PROCESS:** In correctional facilities due process does not necessarily involve any specific procedures. Generally, the greater the consequences for inmates, the more extensive the due process requirements are likely to be.

**PROJECT RIO:** This is a multiagency program operated by the Texas Department of Criminal Justice. While in prison, project inmates are assessed and referred to appropriate academic and/or vocational programs. Upon release they are referred to the Texas Employment Commission to continue training or for job placement.

**PROP FRIENDSHIPS:** Involve a close relationship between two inmates, one who may be stronger than the other, but who will back one another up in violent confrontations no matter what.

**PROPORTIONALITY:** Requires that the severity of the punishment given the convicted offender match the seriousness of his or her crime.

**PROTECTIVE CUSTODY:** Involves the segregation of a variety of inmates who are in serious danger of being harmed for reasons that include their instant offense (e.g., child molestation); gambling debts; homosexual triangles; being identified as a snitch.

**PROTESTANT ETHIC:** A moral precept that required that "everyone should work."

**PRUNO:** Also called "Raisin Jack," this is an intoxicating brew made by accumulating sugar, grains, fruit, or potatoes and yeast, and allowing them to ferment for several days to a few weeks.

**PSEUDOFAMILIES:** These are adaptive groupings of female inmates that involve family-like interrelationships. Each individual within the group adopts a role as one of the family members (e.g., father, mother, daughter, etc.).

**PSYCHIATRIC OR PSYCHOLOGIC DISABILITY:** Any type of mental disturbance or disorder.

**PSYCHOPATH:** See ANTISOCIAL PERSONALITY DISORDER.

**PSYCHOTIC DISORDERS:** Severe emotional disruptions characterized by personality disorganization and significant impairment in normal functioning, e.g., schizophrenia.

**PUBLIC WORKS AND WAYS SYSTEM:** Under this system prison labor is used to benefit the governmental entity overseeing the work of the inmates. Inmates are used for construction, repair, and maintenance of prisons or other public structures, roads, and parks.

**PUBLIC WRONGS:** These would be considered crimes. In preliterate societies there were six basic categories: sacrilege and other offenses against religion, treason, witchcraft, incest and other sex offenses, poisoning, and violations of the hunting rules.

**PUBLISHER ONLY RULE:** A court ruling mandating that inmates can only receive hardback books if they are mailed directly by publishers, book clubs, or bookstores.

**PUNITIVE DAMAGES:** In a correctional setting those damages awarded over and above what would barely compensate inmates for their losses when the wrongful act was done intentionally and maliciously or with reckless disregard for the rights of the inmate. The intent is to punish the wrongdoer.

**PUNKS:** Young inmates, seduced by gifts or favors, or coerced by threats or force to provide sexual favors to other inmates. *Also see* KID.

**QUALIFIED IMMUNITY:** A situation in which correctional workers can be exempted from having to pay damages for their actions when a law is not clearly established or it is not reasonably recognized that the actions were unconstitutional.

**QUASIMILITARY MODEL:** Auburn-type prisons were organized in military fashion, which included a rigid daily schedule, inmates wearing striped uniforms, being marched to and from all activities, and harsh discipline.

**QUR'AN:** Holy book of the Muslim religion. Also referred to as the Koran.

**RADICAL GROUPS:** Left-wing groups that focused on changing society rather than helping the inmate or changing prison conditions.

**RANK-AND-FILE BUILDING TENDERS:** The head building tender's assistants in Texas prisons.

**RANK MEN:** The lowest level of inmate in the Arkansas prison farms. They were the farm laborers.

**RAPE:** Unlawful sexual intercourse with a person, by force or without legal or factual consent.

**RAPIST:** An individual who uses force or threat to have sexual intercourse with a nonconsenting victim.

**RAPOS:** Also called abnormal sex offenders, these are sex offenders sentenced for incest and child molesting. They are considered repulsive by most inmates.

**RASPHOUSES:** Workhouses in which the major form of work involved the rasping of bark off logs to produce materials that could be used in the making of dyes.

**RATED OR DESIGN CAPACITY:** A figure that specifies the number of inmates that the jail or prison was built (or remodeled) to accommodate.

**RATS:** Inmates known to inform on others to the staff.

**REACTIVE MANAGEMENT:** This involves waiting until a problem manifests itself before taking action.

**REASONABLE FORCE:** Refers to the legally justifiable amount of force that may be used in a given situation, which is determined by the amount and type of resistance displayed.

**REASONABLENESS TEST:** A judicial criterion that mandates that there be a valid rational connection between a prison rule restricting inmate rights and the legitimate government interests put forth to justify it or that there be alternative means of exercising this right.

**RECEPTION AND DIAGNOSTIC CENTERS:** Correctional facilities in which inmates are assessed, classified, oriented, and then transferred to the appropriate facilities within the system.

**RECIDIVISM:** The repetition of criminal behavior variously defined in terms of either a rearrest, a reconviction, or a reincarceration.

**RECIDIVIST:** A person convicted of one or more crimes, and who is alleged to have subsequently committed another crime.

**RECKLESS ENDANGERMENT:** An offense characterized by the willful disregard for the safety of others.

**RECLASSIFICATION:** An ongoing process of monitoring inmate progress, dealing with problems as they arise, and where appropriate, reassigning inmates based on changes in behavior and attitudes. Typically this occurs every six months and includes both a reevaluation of an inmate's security/custody status and program and service needs.

**RECOGNIZANCE:** A way in which an offender can be released from custody during court proceedings. *Also see* RELEASE ON RECOGNIZANCE.

**REFORMATION:** The idea that imprisonment or other type of punishment or treatment will change inmates by instilling a new sense of morality and purpose in them.

**REFORMATORY:** A type of prison developed in the late 1800s that was supposed to incorporate the principles advocated at the National Prison Congress meeting. It was for young, first offenders and emphasized training.

**REGIONAL JAILS:** Centralized jail facilities that serve two or more jurisdictions.

**REHABILITATION:** The process of providing inmates with a variety of services and programs (e.g., education, job training, psychological counseling) while under the supervision of the corrections system; designed to reduce the probability of future criminality and make productive members of society.

**REHABILITATIVE INSTITUTION:** In corrections, a prison that functions as a treatment facility where the major focus is to treat and "cure" the offender.

**REHABILITATIVE MODEL:** Advocates treatment to change offenders' attitudes and behavior and improve their academic and vocational skills to reduce the likelihood of their reinvolvement in crime.

**REINTEGRATION:** A correctional approach that emphasizes graduated release programs and the greater use of community facilities and programs to assist offenders released from prison to adjust to life back in the community.

**RELAPSE PREVENTION:** A treatment strategy that prepares the individual to deal with the various circumstances that can lead to resumption of the condition being treated.

**RELEASE ON RECOGNIZANCE (ROR):** A pretrial release in which the defendant signs a promise to appear in court when asked to but does not pledge anything of value to be forfeited upon nonappearance. Jurisdictions use certain criteria to screen defendants for eligibility. These include severity of the offense, previous conviction for a serious offense, family ties, residence, employment, financial condition, and mental condition. It excludes those charged with certain crimes, previously convicted serious offenders, and those with a previous violation of prerelease conditions.

**RELIGIOUS FREEDOM RESTORATION ACT (RFRA):** Federal legislation requiring that the government show a compelling interest in the restriction of religious expression and employ the least restrictive measurements available when curtailing it.

**REMOTE SUPERVISION:** *See* PODULAR REMOTE DESIGN.

**RESIDENTIAL COMMITMENT:** A sentence of commitment to a correctional facility that requires the person committed to reside there at night but permits them to leave unaccompanied during the day.

**RESIDENTIAL PROGRAMS:** These are community-based programs that require the clients to live there while participating in the program.

**RESOURCE BROKERS:** POs acting as referral agents for their clients and also acting as advocates.

**RESTITUTION:** As a sentence (or part of a sentence), the requirement that the offender repay the victim (or the community), either through money or services, so that the damages or losses caused by the criminal act can be restored.

**RESTRAINED HANDS-ON DOCTRINE:** A modification of the hands-on doctrine adopted in the mid-1970s, which recognized that while inmates do not forfeit all constitutional rights, there rights are not as broad as those enjoyed by non-prisoners. This is because inmates are imprisoned and prison officials need to maintain order, security, and discipline in their facilities, which justifies the imposition of certain restrictions on inmate rights.

**RETENTIONISTS:** A term applied to those who favor capital punishment.

**RETHERMALIZATION UNITS:** A mobile unit that is used to bring food to appropriate serving temperatures.

**RETRIBUTION:** A philosophy underlying punishment that specifies that the punishment is deserved because of the evil done by the perpetrator.

**REVOCATION:** A process that involves a termination or modification of an individual's probation or parole status for cause (violation of conditions or arrest for the commission of a crime) and is likely to result either in the imposition of more stringent conditions and supervision or imprisonment.

**RIDE THE MEDICAL PONY:** A term connoting the abuse of the prison medical system by inmates who deliberately fake symptoms for secondary gains including opportunities to complain and receive sympathetic attention; obtain medications, particularly narcotic and sedative drugs; take time off from work details; meet inmates from other housing units; or gain relief during a lockdown.

**RIGHT GUYS:** Big House inmates at the top of the prison hierarchy because they could be depended on to do right according to the inmate code. Their high prestige as thieves, tendency to cooperate with each other, and demeanor of toughness and coolness further enhanced their position.

**RIGHT TO TREATMENT:** The right of an individual who is institutionalized for the purpose of receiving some form of treatment to receive that treatment.

**RISK-PREDICTION SCALES:** Any scale employed to determine the level of supervision required by an offender by determining the risk that individual poses to those around him or her.

**ROAD DEPUTIES:** Sheriff's deputies generally responsible for conducting patrol activities within their jurisdictions.

**ROAD GANGS:** Prison or jail inmates who work on highways, parks, and other public/government areas.

**ROBBERY:** The unlawful taking or attempted taking of property that is in the immediate possession of another, by use or threatened use of force.

**ROLE CONFLICT:** In corrections, role conflict has typically been associated with the different and conflicting role expectations related to custody and treatment.

**ROLE DISPOSSESSION:** The separation of inmates from many of the roles they normally occupy in the outside world.

**RUIZ V. ESTELLE:** A district court decision that resulted in the most sweeping and detailed order in the history of prison ligation. It found almost all major aspects of the Texas prison system unconstitutional and resulted in a master being appointed to oversee the remediation of these conditions.

**SALLY PORTS:** Vehicle entrances into prison compounds that consist of double gates, only one of which is open at any time. At high-security facilities a pit or inspection well is used to allows COs to look at the undercarriage of the vehicle on mirrors or creepers used for this purpose. After the search is completed the second gate is opened allowing the vehicle to enter the prison proper.

**SANCTUARY:** A medieval practice that allowed protection to those accused of crimes by entering a city or a special building, such as a temple or church, which could not be lawfully entered.

**SCARED STRAIGHT:** A program begun at the Rahway Prison in New Jersey by the Lifer's group that brought juvenile delinquents into the institution to be confronted with the realities of being in prison.

**SCHIZOPHRENIA:** A psychotic disorder.

**SCHOOL RESOURCE OFFICER:** A law enforcement officer who is assigned to junior and senior high schools for purposes of preventing delinquency and diverting youth from contact with the juvenile justice system.

**SCREWS:** *See* HACKS.

**SCRIPT:** Nonlegal tender or "money" created for special situations. Some prison systems issue their own "script," which inmates are required to use to buy goods at the prison commissary.

**SECTION 1983, THE CIVIL RIGHTS ACT:** A part of the Civil Rights Act of 1871 that allowed individuals who were deprived of their rights by a state officer, acting under color of state law, irrespective of the official's actual authority to engage in the behavior in question, to sue them in federal court.

**SECURITY THREAT GROUPS (STG):** Two or more inmates, acting together, who pose a threat to the security or safety of staff/inmates and/or are disruptive to programs and/or to the orderly management of the facility/system.

**SEGMENTATION VOCATIONAL TRAINING PROGRAMS:** Vocational training programs that take a standard course of study and divide it into four equal segments. Each segment teaches a group of related skills and knowledge sufficient to provide employment possibilities.

**SELECTIVE INCAPACITATION:** A form of incapacitation based on predictions that certain offenders will commit serious offenses at higher rates than others convicted of the same types of crimes and thus should receive longer sentences.

**SELECTIVE INCORPORATION:** The process by which the due process aspects of the fourteenth amendment to the U.S. Constitution were incorporated into other amendments.

**SELF-HELP GROUPS:** Formal prison organizations concerned with the improvement of the life circumstances of exprisoners.

**SELF-MUTILATION:** Self-inflicted injuries by inmates designed to remove them from the harsh conditions that existed on the Texas prison farms.

**SENTENCE:** A sentence represents the punishment specified for a given crime by the legislature of a given political jurisdiction, imposed by one of its courts, and carried out by its correctional system.

**SENTENCE CREDITS:** Time deducted from an inmate's sentence that he or she has already served or on the basis of good time credits that have been earned by the inmate.

**SENTENCING DISPARITY:** A situation in which a significant difference exists in the sentences received by similar individuals convicted of similar crimes.

**SENTENCING GUIDELINES:** Statutory guides that set forth explicit policies and procedures for making decisions regarding the sentences to be imposed for each crime.

**SENTENCING REVIEW PROCEDURES:** Any set of arrangements employed to reduce sentencing inconsistencies.

**SEPARATE BUT EQUAL:** A doctrine underlying the southern system of segregation of blacks and whites until the middle of the twentieth century that justified segregation on the basis of having comparable services, facilities, etc, for both groups. It was eventually declared unconstitutional.

**SEPARATION OF POWERS:** A constitutional mandate that specifies distinct functions for each branch of government.

**SERIOUS MEDICAL NEED:** A condition that would have been diagnosed by a physician as requiring treatment or one so obvious even a layperson would easily recognize the necessity for a doctor's attention.

**SEVEN STEPS:** One of the earliest of the self-help organizations. Modeled after the twelve steps of the Alcohol Anonymous program, the seven steps were developed to guide inmates in maintaining their freedom.

**SEXUAL SAFETY:** A sexist rationalization offered by male officers for not assigning women to direct contact positions in male prisons.

**SHADOW BOARD:** A pegboard on which tools can be hung that has an outline of each item in order to know when an item is missing.

**SHAKEDOWNS:** Searches of individuals and their cells conducted at frequent, irregular intervals for the purpose of discovering contraband.

**SHAM RELIGIOUS GROUPS:**  Groups of inmates claiming to belong to a religious body that does not meet the requirements for constituting a religion. These groups have ulterior motives for wanting to be recognized as legitimate religious group.

**SHIVS:**  Knives made from materials available in the prison, including kitchen utensils, metal from the shops, and even from seemingly harmless items such as toothbrushes.

**SHOCK INCARCERATION:**  *See* SHOCK PROBATION/PAROLE.

**SHOCK PROBATION/PAROLE:**  A form of split sentence that begins with an unspecified short period of incarceration in a local jail or a state or federal prison followed by a period of community supervision.

**SIBERIA:**  An area in the extreme northeast part of Russia that was used as a penal colony.

**SICKOUTS:**  A form of strike used where strikes are prohibited in which large numbers of officers call in sick on the same day.

**SISSY:**  *See* KID.

**SLAVES OF THE STATE:**  The prevailing court view of prison inmates, as enunciated in *Ruffin v. Commonwealth*, from the birth of our nation until the 1900s, that prisoners had no rights guaranteed to them.

**SNITCH:**  An inmate informer.

**SOCIOPATH:**  *See* ANTISOCIAL PERSONALITY DISORDER.

**SOLEDAD:**  A California state prison that represented a prototype correctional facility during the rehabilitation era.

**SOLITARY CONFINEMENT:**  Often called the hole. In the past, prior to court oversight of prison conditions, these were frequently bare, unlighted, and unventilated cells used for punishment. Inmates placed there were sometimes stripped and not given blankets, which meant they slept naked on a stone floor, and were fed only bread and water. Today this term is used also to refer to units used for isolating inmates for disciplinary purposes. *See* DISCIPLINARY CONFINEMENT/DETENTION.

**SPAN OF CONTROL:**  Recognizes the limits of supervision by one person and defines the number of persons that person can effectively supervise directly.

**SPECIAL DIETS:**  Fulfill therapeutic/medical requirements and generally accommodate the special dietary restrictions of legitimate religious groups.

**SPECIAL MANAGEMENT:**  In corrections this refers to specially designed programs to deal with or care for inmates who have conditions that impair their normal functioning.

**SPECIAL MASTERS:**  Masters are persons appointed to act as representatives of the court in some particular action or transaction including to collect information; to aid the court in deciding whether a constitutional violation occurred; and to assist in developing or monitoring a remedial decree that involves constitutional violations.

**SPECIFIC DETERRENCE:**  This involves the belief that if the offenders suffer punishment that outweighs the gains resulting from the crime they will presumably not engage in subsequent crimes.

**SPECIFIC LEARNING DISABILITIES:**  A disability believed to be related to a minimal brain disorder resulting in perceptual distortions that inhibit proper learning of reading, writing, etc.

**SPIN HOUSE:**  An early Dutch workhouse for women.

**SQUARE JOHNS:**  Accidental offenders, or those who committed only a few crimes, who were often better educated than most inmates. They were not considered criminals by the inmate population and were oriented to conventional society.

**SQUARES:**  The adaptive role taken by female inmates who held and followed conventional norms and values.

**STAFF PERSONNEL:**  These are the workers who provide the support services for line workers, e.g., training, communications, accounting.

**STAFF SUBCULTURE:**  *See* CO SUBCULTURE.

**STATE OR PUBLIC ACCOUNT PRISON INDUSTRIES SYSTEM:**  The state or municipality becomes a manufacturer and the prison becomes an industrial establishment operating in the same manner as any outside free industry. The state markets and profits from the items manufactured.

**STATE-RAISED YOUTH:** Individuals literally raised by state agencies because they had spent most of their youth in one or more institutions. They are at home in prison and tend to form tightly knit cliques that threaten and use violence for protection and to increase their power, privileges, and prestige.

**STATE USE PRISON INDUSTRIES SYSTEM:** Whether managed by the state or a private entity, under this system the sales of the products made by inmates are limited to public institutions, municipalities, and political divisions of the state.

**STATES' RIGHTS:** This refers to the fact that states retain any powers not specifically delegated to the federal government by the U.S. Constitution.

**STATES' SOVEREIGN DOMAIN:** Those areas of government over which a state has exclusive control.

**STOCKS:** A device similar to a pillory by which an individual could be punished by being secured by his or her wrists and ankles. These devices were usually placed in the town's public square so that the offender would suffer humiliation at the hands of his or her fellow citizens.

**STRAP:** A leather strap attached to a handle and used for inflicting whippings.

**STRATEGIC INTELLIGENCE:** This focuses on developing a detailed information base about the characteristics of a particular group or individual. For example, regarding STGs, information is obtained about their members and activities.

**STRESS:** A state of the body caused by undue demands being placed on it by internal and environmental stressors, which can lead to physical and mental disorders.

**STRIP SEARCHES:** Require inmates or visitors to remove all clothing and submit to a visual inspection of the body, including the outer portions of orifices and cavities.

**STUDY RELEASE:** A community release program that allows inmates to go into the community to pursue educational opportunities not available inside the prison or at community residential facilities.

*SUB-ROSA INMATE ECONOMY:* The inmate black market that provides illegal (i.e., contraband) goods and services.

**SUBSTANTIAL (IMPERMISSIBLE) BURDEN ON RELIGIOUS FREEDOM:** Pressuring an individual to commit an act forbidden by the religion or preventing him or her from engaging in conduct or having a religious experience which the faith mandates. The tenet or belief must be central to the religion's doctrine.

**SUBSTANTIVE PREDICATES:** Language that delineates specific conditions or requirements.

**SUMMARY ADMISSION REPORT:** An account of the legal aspects of the inmate's case, a summary of his/her criminal history, demographics, family and personal history data, occupational interests, recreational preferences and needs, and a summary of the assessments and recommendations made by classification staff.

**SUPERINTENDENT/WARDEN:** In corrections, the person responsible for running the entire prison (e.g., implementation of policy, responsibility for all personnel, programs, and activities within the prison).

**SUPER-MAX INSTITUTIONS:** Provide the highest level of custody and security. Inmates assigned to these facilities have demonstrated an inability to adjust satisfactorily to general population units at other secure facilities. Inmates are all housed in single secure units. They typically spend twenty-three house per day in their cells with one hour for recreation. All programming involving staff is through the cell doors, e.g., religious and case work services, and other programs are provided by correspondence courses or by closed-circuit TV. When inmates are removed from their cells they are often strip searched, always placed in full restraints, and accompanied by more than one CO.

**SUPERVISION, CORRECTIONAL:** Authorized and required guidance, treatment, and/or regulation of the behavior of a person who is subject to adjudication or who has been adjudicated to be an offender, performed by a correctional agency.

**SUPREMACY CLAUSE:** The clause of Article VI of the U.S. Constitution which declares that all laws made in pursuance of the Constitution and all treaties made under the authority of the United States shall be "the supreme law of the land" and shall enjoy legal superiority over any conflicting provision of a state constitution or law.

**SURVEILLANCE BY PROBATION/PAROLE:** The process of controlling the offender through supervision.

**SUSPENDED SENTENCE:** A procedure by which a judge can either defer the pronouncement of a sentence or suspend its implementation.

**SWEAT BOX:** A torture device consisting of a coffin-like cell with just enough space to accommodate a man standing erect. Generally made of wood or tin, it was completely closed except for a hole two inches in diameter at nose level. In the heat of the Southern sun, temperature levels in these devices reached 120° F or more.

**SYNANIST:** A person involved in doing treatment within a Synanon program.

**SYNANON:** A long-term residential drug treatment program using the therapeutic community approach that is still in operation today.

**TANKS:** The housing units in Texas prison farms or the cell blocks in its prisons.

**TASER/STUN GUNS:** Electronic weapons that deliver nonlethal shocks. Stun guns can temporarily incapacitate a person when pressed against their body and discharged.

**TECHNICAL VIOLATION:** The violation of one or more of the conditions of the probation/parole contract, which may result in further sanctions.

**TEJANOS:** The name given Mexican-American inmates raised in Texas.

**TEXAS SYNDICATE:** This group was started by Texas-born Mexican American inmates, at San Quentin Prison in California in 1975, in order to protect themselves from victimization by other California prison gangs. It spread to other California prisons and to Texas prisons in which it became the second largest gang.

**THEFT:** Generally, any taking of the property of another with the intent to permanently deprive the rightful owner of its possession.

**THERAPEE:** The person receiving the therapy.

**THERAPEUTIC COMMUNITY DRUG TREATMENT PROGRAMS:** Highly structured, long-term residential programs that help residents face the fact that they are addicted to drugs and its associated lifestyle. They foster change in their personalities and behavior so they can live drug-free, socially productive lives.

**THERAPEUTIC PROGRAM:** Any program including individual and group therapy and counseling, under the direction of psychologists and psychiatrists (or other trained counselors and therapists).

**THREE STRIKES AND YOU'RE OUT LAWS:** Anticrime statutes that sentence offenders convicted of three felonies, usually involving violence, to life in prison without the possibility of parole.

**THROW-AWAYS:** Inmates that are considered expendable and are used by a gang to do jobs that involve high risk of injury, death, or apprehension.

**TICKET OF LEAVE:** A conditional pardon. For example in Australia during the transportation era convicts given "tickets" were freed from their obligation to work for the government or a master. They could work as free agents or for wages as long as they committed no new crimes and remained in the colony until their sentences ended.

**TIME SERVED:** The time spent in confinement in relation to conviction and sentencing for a given offense.

**TIME TO THINK (TTT):** An example of a cognitive skills training program that is one component of the Living Skills Program. This program addresses thinking and social skills such as problem solving, negotiation, communication, creative thinking, management of emotions, values enhancement, and critical reasoning.

**TIPS:** These were crowds or extended social networks of inmates whose association was based on preprison contacts or common subcultural involvement.

**TOKEN ECONOMIES:**  A type of behavior modification based on tangible payoffs (points, tokens, etc.) to inmates who manifest certain behavior. Tokens are accumulated over a period of time and can be spent on a variety of goods and privileges. The goal is to eliminate undesirable behavior and create desirable behavior.

**TORT:**  A civil wrong arising from a claim by one party that another party has negligently, maliciously, or deliberately inflicted some sort of injury to him/her.

**TOTAL INCAPACITATION:**  Any form of punishment that prevents an offender from ever doing the crime again (e.g., capital punishment or life imprisonment without parole).

**TOTAL INSTITUTIONS:**  A way of describing the environment that characterizes custodial hospitals, boarding schools, and military training bases and prisons. These are places in which large groups of people live and work together around the clock within a circumscribed space and under a tightly scheduled sequence of activities.

**TOTALITY OF CONDITIONS:**  A court interpretation indicating that, taken individually, conditions cited may not represent constitutional violations, but when taken together (in "their totality") they may constitute cruel and unusual punishment.

**TOUGH TIME INSTITUTIONS (TTI):**  Proposed as alternatives to prison for nonviolent offenders who would only serve one-half of their sentence if they successfully completed the program. These would be spartan facilities like boot camps without the military aspects. The program would be characterized by a long day in which activities would include physical conditioning, half a day of work, half a day of program participation (e.g., education, drug treatment), and limited recreational opportunities.

**TRANSFER:**  In corrections, the movement of a person from one correctional facility or caseload to another.

**TRANSPORTATION:**  The term used to denote banishment of prisoners to overseas or remote locations.

**TREATMENT CONDITIONS:**  These conditions are tailored to fit the problems and needs of each offender. They may include psychiatric treatment or participation in a training or educational program.

**TREATMENT PROGRAMS:**  These are programs such as education, psychological counseling, etc. that are intended to remediate inmate deficiencies that are felt to impair successful functioning in the free society.

**TRICKING:**  A term usually associated with prostitution. In women's prison usage it refers to indiscriminate sexual activity, perhaps for economic gain.

**TRUSTY:**  A jail or prison inmate who has been entrusted with some custodial responsibilities, or who performs other services assisting in the operation of the facility.

**TRUSTY GUARDS:**  These were inmates in many of the Southern prison systems who were given the responsibility of guarding other prisoners. In many instances they were armed with rifles and were rewarded for shooting escapees.

**TRUSTY-SERVANTS:**  Trusty inmates who performed household duties in the homes of prison officials.

**TRUSTY-SHOOTER:**  An armed trusty guard.

**TRUSTY SYSTEM:**  A system under which inmates were given various responsibilities for running a prison.

**TUBERCULOSIS:**  An infectious disease spread by bacteria in the air resulting from coughs or sneezes from infected individuals.

**TUCKER TELEPHONE:**  A torture device, previously used in the Arkansas prison system, that consisted of an electric generator taken from a crank-type telephone and wired in sequence with two dry cell batteries. An undressed inmate had electrodes attached to his big toe and his penis. The crank was then turned, sending an electrical charge into his body.

**TURNKEYS:**  Inmates responsible for opening and closing riot gates.

**TYPE I MINIMUM SECURITY FACILITIES:**  Designated for inmates who have a short period before release, facilitating reintegration into the community. Little or no programming.

**TYPE II MINIMUM SECURITY FACILITIES:** Designed for inmates, posing no security risk, with release or parole dates of eighteen months or less. They provide extensive on-site programming.

**UCR:** *See* Uniform Crime Reports.

**UNCONDITIONAL RELEASES:** In this type of release the releasee is free from further correctional supervision. They occur at the expiration of an inmate's sentence.

**UNDERCLASS:** The lowest segment of the poverty group, which is characterized by extreme poverty and little hope of bettering itself.

**UNDERCLASSIFICATION:** Placement of inmates under lower levels of supervision and control than required.

**UNICOR:** The federal prison system's industry program.

**UNIFORM CRIME REPORTS:** An annual statistical summary of certain types of crimes reported to the police and of persons arrested for these offenses. Published by the Federal Bureau of Investigation.

**UNIT MANAGEMENT:** A form of correctional administration in which a team of correctional workers, including correctional officers, counselors, and others, takes responsibility for managing a particular wing or cell block of a prison.

**UNITY OF COMMAND:** Refers to the view that workers should only have to report directly to one boss.

**UNIVERSAL PRECAUTIONS:** Basic medical standards of safety and care to reduce the spread of infectious diseases.

**UTILITARIAN MODEL:** Advocates the use of punishment as a way to affect, control, or change future criminal behavior.

**VERBAL DIRECTION:** Using communication skills to control inmate resistance.

**VETERANS' PREFERENCE SYSTEM:** A system that rewards veterans for their military service by giving them an advantage when applying for government jobs.

**VISITING RULES:** Institutions typically have rules that specify who can visit, their mode of dress, the items that can be brought, the frequency and length of visitation, and the extent of contact.

**VISITOR CENTERS:** Provide a variety of services to the family members of inmates that visit them in prison. These services include transportation, child care, emergency clothing, information on visiting regulations and processes, referral to other agencies and services, emergency food, crisis intervention, and a sheltered area to use before and after visitation.

**VOLUNTARY COMMITMENT:** Admission to a correctional, residential, or medical facility or program for care or treatment without a court commitment and by personal choice.

**VOYEURS:** Individuals who achieve sexual arousal and release through secretly looking at nude persons, persons who are disrobing, or persons engaging in sexual activity.

**WAIS:** The Wechsler Adult Intelligence Scale. An individually administered intelligence test.

**WALNUT STREET JAIL:** A jail in Philadelphia, Pennsylvania, that was converted to function as the first true prison in the United States.

**WANNA-BEES:** Young rookie gangs members looking for opportunities to break into the gang's core.

**WANTON AND UNNECESSARY:** In the correctional context, this means actions of correctional personnel to control or deal with inmates that are characterized by reckless or unreasonable disregard of the rights and safety of others or evil intent and not required by the circumstances of the situation.

**WARDEN:** *See* SUPERINTENDENT/WARDEN.

**WARRANT:** Any of a number of writs issued by a judicial officer that directs a law enforcement officer to perform a specified act and affords the officer protection from damage if he or she performs it.

**WARRANTLESS SEARCHES:** A search conducted without a warrant under one of a number of constitutionally permissible circumstances.

**WARREN COURT:**   The Supreme Court in the 1950s and 1960s when Earl Warren was the chief justice. During this period constitutional rights were extended to disenfranchised minority groups including accused criminals and prison inmates.

**WATTS:**   A black section of Los Angeles, California, that was the scene of widespread rioting during the summer of 1965.

**WEEKEND SENTENCE:**   A form of intermittent sentence in which the time is served on weekends.

**WERGILD:**   *See* COMPENSATION.

**WINDHAM SCHOOL DISTRICT:**   The nongeographical school district established in Texas specifically for conducting educational programs at Texas Department of Criminal Justice correctional facilities.

**WOLVES:**   *See* JOCKERS.

**WOMEN'S WORK:**   The term applied to work or jobs that have traditionally been done by women (e.g., secretary, cosmetician) which are generally low paid and have little prestige. These have been the most frequently offered training programs at women's prisons.

**WORK RELEASE:**   A community correctional program that allows specially selected inmates to work in the community without direct supervision while still incarcerated either at a prison or, most often, at a community residential facility.

**WORKHOUSES:**   These were penal facilities established in England and other European countries to reform those who were considered to be immoral, living in sin, or who had committed minor crimes.

**WORKING IDEOLOGIES:**   The development of officer work styles as a result of the beliefs developed from interactions with other groups in the institution.

**WRIT:**   A court document ordering or forbidding the performance of a specified act.

**WRIT OF DETAINER:**   An official notice from a government agency to a correctional agency requesting that the person identified was wanted by the first agency, and was not to be released or discharged without notification to the first agency and an opportunity to respond.

**YARD MAN:**   The chief trusty.

**YARD, THE:**   A feature of the Big House prison, it was typically enclosed by cell blocks and the prison's exterior wall. It was used by the inmates for recreation.

**YOUNG LORDS, THE:**   A prison gang/group that emerged from a street gang in Chicago in 1969. It was revolutionary in nature and guided by Marxist/Leninist/Maoist principles.

**YOUTHFUL OFFENDER:**   These are offenders who fall somewhere between the ages of thirteen and twenty-four with little agreement among the various jurisdictions as to what the upper and lower ages should be.

**ZIDOVUDINE (AZT)/DIDANOSINE:**   Antiviral medications used for preemptive or early intervention treatment of AIDS.

*\* Some of the definitions of these terms and concpets are adapted from Search Groups, Inc. (1981). Dictionary of Criminal Justice Data Terminology. Washington, DC: U.S. Department of Justice.*

# BIBLIOGRAPHY

A judge's view of society's 'losers.' (1988, January 7). *The New York Times.*

Abadinsky, H. (1994). *Probation and parole: Theory and practice* (5th ed.). Englewood Cliffs, NJ: Prentice Hall.

Abbott, J. H. (1982). *In the belly of the beast.* New York: Vintage Books.

Abell, P. (1991). *Rational choice theory.* Aldershot, England: Edward Elgar Publishing Limited.

Adair, D. N., & Slawsk, T. D. (1991). Looking at the law: Fact-finding in sentencing. *Federal Probation, 55,* 58–72.

Adams Commission. (1989). *The final report of the governor's commission to investigate disturbances at Camp Hill Correctional Institution.* Harrisburg, PA: Author.

Adams, D., & Fischer, J. (1976). The effects of prison residents' community contacts on recidivism rates. *Corrective and Social Psychiatry and Journal of Behavioral Technology Methods, 22,* 21–27.

Adams, K. (1992). Adjusting to prison life. In M. Tonry (Ed.), *Crime and justice: A review of research.* (pp. 275–358). Chicago: University of Chicago Press.

Adams, W. E., Barlow, R. B., Kleinfeld, G. R., Smith, R. D., & Wootten, W. W. (1968). *The western world, volume I: To 1700.* New York: Dodd, Mead & Company.

Adler, F. (1975). *Sisters in crime: The rise of the new female criminal.* New York: McGraw-Hill.

Agresti, D. (Former Director of Institutional Programs, PRIDE, Inc.) (1991). Personal communication.

Agresti, D. (undated). Liberty and justice for all? A question and answer pamphlet about the Death penalty—(compilation of seminar reports). Unpublished manuscript: University of South Florida.

Akre, B. S. (1994, September 4). Indian teens banished to islands. *Tampa Tribune/Times,* p. 1, 7.

Alabama to make prisoners break rocks. (1995, July 28). *New York Times,* p. A5.

Albanese, J. S., Fiore, B. A., Powell, J. H., & Storti, J. R. (1981). *Is probation working?* Washington, DC: University Press of America.

Alexander, E. (1991). Proving "deliberate indifference" in the wake of Wilson v. Seiter. National Prison Project, 6(1), 3–5, 12.

Alexander, J. A., & Austin, J. (1992). *Handbook for evaluating objective prison classification systems.* Washington, DC: U.S. Department of Justice, National Institute of Corrections.

Allen, H. E., Carlson, E. W., & Parks, E. C. (1979, September). *Critical issues in adult probation: Summary.* Washington, DC: U.S. Department of Justice, National Institute of Law Enforcement and Criminal Justice.

Allen, H. E., Eskridge, C. W., Latessa, E. J., & Vito, G. F. (1985). *Probation and parole in America.* New York: The Free Press.

Allen, H. E., & Latessa, E. (1982). Half-way houses and parole: A national assessment. *Journal of Criminal Justice, 10*(2), 153–163.

American Association on Mental Deficiency. (1983). *Manual on terminology and classification in mental retardation* (H. J. Grossman, Ed.). Washington, DC: Author.

American Bar Association. (1977). *Joint committee on the legal status of prisoners.* Washington, DC: Author.

American Correctional Association. (undated). *Gangs in correctional facilities: A national assessment.* (Contract 91-IJ-CS-0026, [Unpublished report]. Washington, DC: National Institute of Justice, Office of Justice Programs, U.S. Department of Justice.

American Correctional Association. (1980). *Directory of juvenile and adult correctional departments, institutions, agencies & paroling authorities.* Laurel, MD: Author.

American Correctional Association. (1981a May). *Guidelines for the development of policies and procedures for adult correctional institutions.* Laurel, MD: Author.

American Correctional Association. (1981b). *Standards for adult correctional institutions.* College Park, MD: Author.

American Correctional Association. (1983). *Design guide for secure adult correctional facilities.* Laurel, MD: Author.

American Correctional Association. (1983). *The American prison: From the beginning . . . A pictorial history.* College Park, MD: Author.

American Correctional Association. (1986a). 1985 Directory of juvenile & adult correctional departments, institutions, agencies & paroling authorities. Laurel, MD: Author.

American Correctional Association. (1986b). *A study of prison industry: History, components, and goals.* College Park, MD: National Institute of Corrections.

American Corectional Association. (1989). *Legal issues for correctional officers.* Laurel, MD: Author.

American Correctional Association. (1990a). *Causes, preventive measures, and methods of controlling riots and disturbances in correctional institutions* (3rd ed.). Washington, DC: Author.

American Correctional Association. (1990b). *Standards for adult correctional institutions.* College Park, MD: Author.

American Correctional Association. (1992). *Directory of juvenile and adult correctional departments, institutions, agencies and paroling authorities.* Laurel, MD: Author.

American Correctional Association. (1993). *Directory of juvenile & adult correctional departments, institutions, agencies & paroling authorities.* Laurel, MD: Author.

American Correctional Association (1994). Vital statistics in corrections. Laurel, MD: Author.

American Correctional Association (1995). Directory of juvenile & adult correctional departments, institutions, agencies & paroling authorities. Laurel, MD: Author.

American Jail Association. (1992a). Resolutions. *American Jails, 6*(1), 123–130.

American Jail Association. (1992). Jail industries column. *American Jails, 6*(5), 96.

American Jails (1994). Work in American jails NIJ provides first national profile. *American Jails, 8,* (2), 37.

American Psychiatric Association. (1994). *Diagnostic and statistical manual of mental disorders (DSM IV* (4th ed.). Washington, DC: Author.

Amnesty International. (1989a). *When the state kills . . . The death penalty: A human rights issue.* New York: Author.

Amnesty International. (1989b). *Amnesty International: 1988 report.* New York: Author.

Amnesty International. (1990). *Amnesty International: 1990 report.* New York: Author.

Amnesty International. (1991). *Amnesty International: 1991 report.* New York: Author.

Amnesty International. (1992). *Amnesty International: 1992 report.* New York: Author.

Anderson, A. F. (1990). AIDS and prisoners' rights laws: Deciphering the administrative guideposts. In M. Blumberg (Ed.), *AIDS: The impact of the criminal justice system* (pp. 211–225). Columbus, OH: Merrill Publishing Co.

Anderson, E. (1978). *A place on the corner.* Chicago: University of Chicago Press.

Andrews, W. (1899). *Bygone . . . punishments.* London: William Andrews & Co.

Angolite: The Prison News Magazine. (1981, January/ February). Inside Angola: "Religion in prison"—A look at the pulpit behind bars. *Angolite,* pp. 31–56.

Anno, B. J. (1989, December). Prison health care: The state of the states. A paper presented at the Federal Bureau of Prisons conference on Prison Health Care Issues, Washington, DC.

Anno, B. J. (1991a). *Prison Health Care: Guidelines for the management of an adequate delivery system.* Washington, DC: National Institute of Corrections.

Anno, B. J. (1991b, July). Secretary, National Commission on Correctional Health Care. Personal communication.

Anno, B. J. (1993, December). Chairman, National Commission on Correctional Health Care. Personal communication.

Ansay, S. (1994, January). Personal communication. Gainesville, FL: University of Florida.

Archembeault, W. G., & Archembeault, B. N. (1982). *Correctional supervision management.* Englewood Cliffs, NJ: Prentice-Hall.

Archer, D., Gartner, R., & Beittel, M. (1983). Homicide and the death penalty: A cross-national test of a deterrence hypothesis: *Journal of Criminal Law and Criminology, 74,* 991–1013.

Aric Press. (1986, October 6). Reported by D. Pederson, D. Shapiro, and A. McDaniel. Inside America's toughest prison. *Newsweek,* pp. 46–61.

Arnold, L. (1991). Florida Department of Corrections. Personal Communication.

Attorney General's Office, S. O. Hawaii. (1989). *Parole and Recidivism.* Honolulu, HI: Hawaii Criminal Justice Data Center.

Auerbach, B. J., Sexton, G. E., Farrow, F. C., & Lawson, R. H. (1988). *Work in American prisons: The private sector gets involved.* Washington, DC: National Institute of Justice.

Austin, J. (1993). Objective prison classification systems: A review. In American Correctional Association, *Classification: A tool for managing today's offenders* (pp. 108–123). Laurel, MD: American Correctional Association.

Austin, J. (1994, July). Managing offender classification: Is key to proper housing decisions. *Corrections Today, 56*(4), 94–96.

Austin, J., Bloom, B., & Donahue, T. (1992, April). *Female offenders in the community: An analysis of innovative strategies and programs.* Washington, D.C.: National Institute of Corrections, U.S. Department of Justice.

Austin, J., & McVey, A. D. (1989, December). *The impact of the war on drugs.* San Francisco, CA: National Council on Crime and Delinquency.

Ayers, E. L. (1984). *Vengeance and justice: Crime and punishment in the 19th-century American south.* New York: Oxford University Press.

Ayres, M. B. (1988). *Food Service in jails.* Alexandria, VA: The National Sheriffs' Association.

Bailey, W. C. (1990). Murder, capital punishment, and television: Execution publicity and homicide rates. *American Sociological Review, 55,* 628–633.

Baird, S. C., Heinz, R. C., & Bemus, J. (1982). *The Wisconsin case classification/staff deployment project: A two year followup report in classification.* College Park, MD: American Correctional Association.

Baldus, D. C., Woodworth, G., & Pulaski, C. A. (1990). *Equal justice and the death penalty: A legal and empirical analysis.* Boston: Northeastern University Press.

Bamford, P. W. (1973). *Fighting ships and prisons: The Mediterranean galleys of France in the age of Louis XIV.* Minneapolis: University of Minnesota Press.

Banished tribal teens sent to prison. (1995, October 2). Tampa Tribune, p.5 Nation/World.

Banks, A., Porter, J., Tardin, R., Siler, T., & Unger, V. (1977). *Summary, phase I evaluation of intensive probation projects.* Washington, DC: U.S. Government Printing Office.

Barak-Glantz, I. (1986). Toward a conceptual scheme of prison management styles. *The Prison Journal, 61,* 42–60.

Barnes, H. E. (1968). *The evolution of Penology in Pennsylvania:* A study in American social history. Montclair. New Jersey: Patterson Smith. (Original work published in 1927).

Barnes, H. E. (1969). *The repression of crime: Studies in historical penology.* Montclair, NJ: Patterson Smith. (Original work published 1926).

Barnes, H. E. (1972). *The story of punishment: A record of man's inhumanity to man.* (2nd Edition revised) Montclair, NJ: Patterson Smith. (Orginal work published 1930).

Barnes, H. E., & Teeters, N. K. (1943). *New horizons in criminology: The American crime problem.* New York: Prentice Hall.

Barnes, H. E., & Teeters, N. K. (1951). *New horizons in criminology* (2nd ed.). Englewood Cliffs, NJ: Prentice Hall.

Barnes, H. E., & Teeters, N. K. (1959). *New horizons in criminology* (3rd ed.). Englewood Cliffs, NJ: Prentice Hall.

Barry, J. V. (1958). *Alexander Maconochie of Norfolk Island: A study of prison reform.* London, England: Oxford University Press.

Barry, J. V. (1972). Alexander Maconochie (1787–1860). In H. Mannheim (Ed.), *Pioneers in criminology,* (2nd edition enlarged). Montclair, NJ: Patterson Smith.

Bartollas, C. (1985). *Correctional treatment: Theory and practice.* Englewood Cliffs, NJ: Prentice Hall.

Bartolo, A. (1991). The female offender in the bureau of prisons. In U.S. Department of Justice, *The June 7, 1991 forum on issues in corrections: Female offenders* (p. 2). Washington, DC: U.S. Department of Justice.

Bates, S. (1936). *Prison and beyond.* New York: Macmillan.

Baunach, P. J. (1979). *Mothering behind prison walls.* Paper presented at American Society of Criminology meeting, Philadelphia.

BCEL. (1992, April). GED pays off. *Newsletter for the Business and Literacy Communities,* p. 8.

Beattie, J. M. (1986). *Crime and courts in England 1660–1800.* Princeton, NJ: Princeton University Press.

Beccaria, C. (1963). *On crimes and punnishments.* (H. Paolucci, Trans.) Indianapolis, IN: Bobbs-Merrill. (Original work published 1764)

Beck, A. J. (1991, April). *Profile of jail inmates, 1989.* Washington, DC: Bureau of Justice Statistics.

Beck, A. J., Bonczar, T. P., & Gilliard, D. K. (1993). *Jail inmates 1992.* Wahington, DC: Bureau of Justice Statistics.

Beck, A. J., & Gilliard, D. K. (1995, August). *Prisoners in 1994.* Washington, DC: U.S. Department of Justice.

Beck, A., Gilliard, D., Greenfeld, L., Harlow, C., Hester, T., Jankowski, L., Snell, T., & Stephan, J. (1993, March). *Survey of state prison inmates, 1991.* Washington, DC: U.S. Department of Justice.

Beck, A. J., & Shipley, B. E. (1987). *Recidivism of young parolees.* Washington, DC: U.S. Department of Justice.

Beck, A., & Shipley, B. (1989). *Recidivism of prisoners released in 1983,* Washington, DC: Bureau of Justice Statistics.

Bedau, H. A. (Ed.) (1982). The death penalty in America (3rd ed.). New York: Oxford University Press.

Bedau, H. A., & Radalet, M. L. (1987). Miscarriages of justice in potentially capital cases. *Stanford Law Review, 40,* 21–179.

Bell, M. (1985). *The turkey shoot: Tracking the Attica cover-up,* New York: Grove Press.

Bell, R., Conard, E., Laffey, T., Lutz, J. G., Simon, C., Stakelon, A. E., & Wilson, N. J. (1979). *Correctional educational programs for inmates.* Washington, DC: U.S. Department of Justice.

Bell, R., Conard, E. H., & Suppa, R. J. (1984). The findings and recommendations of the national study on learning deficiencies in adult inmates. *Journal of Correctional Education, 35*(4), 129–137.

Bellamy, J. (1973). *Crime and public order in England in the later middle ages.* London: Routledge & Kegan Paul.

Bellorado, D. (1986). *Making literacy programs work, Vol. 1, A practical guide for correctional educators.* Washington, DC: National Institute of Corrections.

Bennett, L. A. (undated). *Problems in implementing and operating private prison visiting programs.* Sacramento, CA: Unpublished manuscript.

Bennett, L. A. (1987, November). What has happened to prison visiting? Current use of a rehabilitative tool. Paper presented at the annual meeting of the American Society of Criminology, Montreal, Canada.

Bennett, L. A. (1989). Correctional administrators' attitudes toward private family visiting. *The Prison Journal, 66,* 110–114.

Berkman, R. (1979). *Opening the prison gates: The rise of the prisoners' movement.* Lexington, MA: Lexington Books.

Berlin, F., & Meinecke, C. F. (1981). Treatment of sex offenders with antiandrogenic medication: Conceptualization, review of treatment modalities, and preliminary findings. *American Journal of Psychiatry, 138,* 601–607.

Bernat, F. P., & Zupan, L. L. (1989). An assessment of personal processes pertaining to women in a traditionally male dominated occupation: Affirmative action policies in prisons and jails. *The Prison Journal,* pp. 64–73.

Besharov, D. J. (1992, July). Sex offenders: Is castration an acceptable punishment? *American Bar Association,* p. 42.

Black, B. (1991, January/February). Juvenile confinement in Kentucky—A step in the right direction. *American Jails, 4*(5), 32–36.

Black, H. C., Nolan, J. R., & Nolan-Haley, J. M. (1991). *Black's Law Dictionary.* St. Paul, MN: West Publishing Co.

Bloom, B. (1988). *Women behind bars: A forgotten population.* Paper presented at the Academy of Criminal Justice Sciences, San Francisco.

Bloom, I., & Steinhart, D. (1993). *Why punish the children?: A reappraisal of the children of incarcerated mothers in America.* San Francisico, CA: National Council Crime and Delinquency.

Blount, W. R. (1994, July). Department of Criminology, University of South Florida. Personal communication.

Blount, W. R., Danner, T. A., Vega, M., & Silverman, I. J. (1991, Spring). The influence of substance abuse use among adult female inmates. *Journal of Drug Issues, 21*(2), 449–467.

Blumberg, A. (1970). *Criminal justice.* Chicago, IL: Quadrangle Books.

Blumberg, M. (1990). Issues and controversies with respect to the management of AIDS in corrections. In M. Blumberg (Ed.), *AIDS: The impact of the criminal justice system* (pp. 195–210). Columbus, OH: Merrill Publishing Co.

Blumenthal, W. H. (1962). *Brides from Bridewell: Female felons sent to colonial America.* Rutland, VT: Charles E. Tuttle Co.

Bohm, R. M. (1991). American death penalty opinion, 1936–1986: A critical examination of the Gallup polls. In R. M. Bohm (Ed.), *The death penalty in America: Current research* (pp. 113–145). Cincinnati, OH: Anderson Publishing Co.

Bohm, R.M. (1992). Retribution and capital punishment: Toward a better understanding of death penalty opinion. *Journal of Criminal Justice, 20,* 227–236.

Bohn, S. E. (1993, December). Corrections mental health: New techniques and technologies bring basic theories up to date. *Corrections Today, 55*(7), 8, 12.

Bonnyman, G. (1993). Reform advances in Tennessee after decades of brutality. *The National Prison Project Journal, 8*(4), 1–5.

Booth, D. E. (1989). Health status of the incarcerated elderly: Issues and concerns. *Journal of Offender Counseling, Services and Rehabilitation, 13*(2), 193–213.

Booth Gardner inks sex predator bill, & then pleads for more prisons. (1990, March 1). *Walla Walla Union Bulletin.* p. 1.

Boss, D., Schecter, J., & King, P. (1986, March). Food service behind bars. *Food Management,* pp. 83–87, 114, 120–136.

Boston, J. (1990, Fall). Case law report: Highlights of most important cases. *The National Prison Project Journal, 5*(4), 9–16.

Boston, J. (1991 Spring). Case law report: Highlights of most important cases—Crowding/damages/ contempt/pre-trial detainees. *The National Prison Project Journal, 6*(2), 6.

Boston, J. (1993/1994 Winter). Case law report. *The National Prison Project Journal, 9*(1), 13–15.

Boston, J. (1994). Highlights of most important cases. *The National Prison Project, 9*(3), 6–17.

Boston, J. (1995a, June 20). Director of the Prisoners' Rights Project, Legal Aid Society of New York. Personal communication. New York, NY.

Boston, J. (1995b, Sept. 25). Director of the Prisoners' Rights Project, Legal Aid Society of New York. Personal communicaton. New York, NY.

Boston, J., & Manville, D. E. (1995). *Prisoners self-help litigation manual.* New York: Oceania.

Bottoms, A. E., & Light, R. (1987). Introduction: Problems of long term imprisonment. In A. E. Bottoms & R. Light (Eds.), *Problems of long term imprisonment.* Aldershot, England: Gower Publishing Co.

Bowers, W. (1993). Research on the death penalty. *Law and Society Review, 27,* 157–175.

Bowers, W. J., & Pierce, G. L. (1980). Arbitrariness and discrimination under post-Furman capital statutes. *Crime and Delinquency, 26,* 563–635.

Bowker, L. H. (1980). *Prison victimization.* New York: Elsevier.

Bowker, L. (1982). *Corrections: The science and the art.* New York: Macmillan.

Boyce, R. N., & Perkins, R. M. (1989). *Cases and materials on criminal law and procedure.* Westbury, NY: The Foundation Press, Inc.

Bradley, E. (Reporter). (1986, January 27). 60 Minutes report on prison gangs. New York: CBS News.

Braly, M. (1967). *On the yard.* Boston: Little Brown and Co.

Braly, M. (1976). *False starts: A memoir of San Quentin and other prisons.* Boston: Little Brown and Co.

Branch-Johnson, W. (1957). *The English prison hulks.* London: Christopher Johnson Publishers, Ltd.

Branham, L. S. (1992). *The use of incarceration in the United States: A look at the present and the future.* Chicago: American Bar Association.

Brennan, T. (1987). Classification: An overview of selected methodological issues. In D. M. Gottfredson & M. Tonry (Eds.), *Prediction and classification: Criminal justice decision making.* Chicago: University of Chicago Press.

Brennan, T. (1993). Risk assessment: An evaluation of statistical classification methods. In American Correctional Association, *Classification: A tool for managing today's offenders* (pp. 46–70). Laurel, MD: American Correctional Association.

Brennan, T., & Wells, D. (1992). The importance of inmate classification in small jails. *American Jails, 6*(2), 49–52.

Bronik, M. J. (1989, Fall). Relieving subpopulation pressures: The Bureau of Prisons' use of private correctional facilities. *Federal Prisons Journal,* 17–21.

Bronstein, A. J. (1985). Prisoners and their endangered rights. *Prison Journal, 45*(1), 3–17.

Brooks, R. (1969). Domestic violence and America's wars: A historical interpretation. In H. D. Graham (Ed.), *The history of violence in America* (pp. 529–550). New York: Bantam Books.

Brown, C. (1965). *Manchild in the promised land.* New York: Signet Books.

Brown, M. (1984). *Executive summary of research findings from the Massachusetts risk/need classification system. Report 5.* Boston, MA: Office of the Commissioner of Probation.

Brown, P. W. (1993). Probation officer safety and mental conditioning. Federal Probation, 57(4), 17–21.

Brown, V. L. (1994, January 17). Session End Report. *New Jersey Lawyer*, p. 4.

Bryan, D. (1994). Dealing with violent inmates: Use of nonlethal force. *Corrections Compendium, 19*(6), 1–2, 23.

Buchanan, R. A. (1986, Spring). An evaluation of objective prison classification systems. (Contract 84-IJ-CX-K029) [Unpublished report under Grant from National Institute of Justice, U.S. Department of Justice]. Kansas City: Correctional Services Group.

Buchanan, R. A., Whitlow, K. L., & Austin, J. (1986). National evaluation of objective prison classification systems: The current state of the art. *Crime and Delinquency, 32*(3), 272–290.

Buchanan, R. A., & Whitlow, K. L. (1987). *Guidelines for developing, implementing, and revising an objective prison classification system.* Washington, DC: National Institute of Justice.

Buck, G. (1989). The effectiveness of the "new" intensive supervision programs. *Research in Corrections, 5,* 64–75.

Buckley, W. F. (1978, September). Humiliating criminals is worth a try. *Tampa Tribune*, p. 11-A.

Buentello, S. (1986). *Texas syndicate: A review of its inception, growth in violence and continued threat to the Texas Department of Corrections* (Confidential and unpublished report). Huntsville, TX: Texas Department of Corrections.

Buentello, S. (1992, July). Combatting gangs in Texas. *Corrections Today,* 58, 59.

Bureau of the Census. (1993a). *Money income of households, families, and persons in the United States: 1992.* Washington, DC: U.S. Department of Commerce.

Bureau of the Census. (1993b). *Statistical abstract of the United States, 1993.* Washington, DC: U.S. Government Printing Office.

Bureau of Justice Statistics. (1981, May). Prisoners in 1980. Washington, DC: U.S. Department of Justice.

Bureau of Justice Statistics. (1982). *Prisoners 1925–81.* Washington, DC: U.S. Department of Justice.

Bureau of Justice Statistics. (1983, April). Prisoners in 1982. Washington D.C.: U.S. Department of Justice.

Bureau of Justice Statistics. (1984, April). Prisoners in 1983. Washington DC: U.S. Department of Justice.

Bureau of Justice Statistics. (1984, November). The 1983 jail census. Washington, DC: U.S. Department of Justice.

Bureau of Justice Statistics. (1986, June). Prisoners in 1985. Washington, DC: U.S. Department of Justice.

Bureau of Justice Statistics. (1987, December). Correctional Populations in the United States, 1985. Washington, DC: U.S. Department of Justice.

Bureau of Justice Statistics. (1988a). Report to the nation on crime and justice (2nd ed.). Washington, DC: U.S. Department of Justice.

Bureau of Justice Statistics. (1988b, April). Prisoners in 1987. Washington, DC: U.S. Department of Justice.

Bureau of Justice Statistics. (1992, May). Prisoners in 1991. Washington DC: U.S. Department of Justice.

Burger, W. F. (1983). Factories with fences. *Pace Law Review, 4*(1), 1–9.

Burke, J. (1992, Feb. 7). Former prisoners say Russian abuses persist. *The Christian Science Monitor, The World,* p. 6.

Burke, P., & Adams, L. (1991). *Classification of women offenders in state correctional facilities: A hand book for practitioners.* Washington, DC: National Institute of Corrections.

Burlington, B. (1991, Winter). Involuntary treatment: When can mentally ill inmates be medicated against their will? *Federal Prison Journal, 2*(4), 25–29.

Burns, H. (1975). *Corrections organization and administration.* St. Paul, MN: West Publishing Co.

Burrell, G., & Morgan, G. (1979). *Sociological paradigms and organizational analysis.* London: Heineman.

Bursik, R., Grasmick, H., & Chamlin, M. (1990). The effect of longitudinal arrest patterns on the development of robbery trends at the neighbohood level. *Criminology, 25,* 431–450.

Burstein, J. Q. (1977). *Conjugal visits in prison.* Lexington, MA: Heath.

Butterfield, F. (1995, March 23) California's courts clogging under its 'three strikes' law.' *The New York Times,* pp. 1A, 9A.

Butterfield, F. (1995, October 5). More blacks in their teens and 20's have trouble with the law. *New York Times,* p. A8.

Buzbee, S. S. (1993, November 20). Prison escapees are in for a shock. *Tampa Tribune,* Sec. A, p. 1.

Byers, J. (1910). Prison labor. In C. R. Henderson (Ed.), *Penal and reformatory institutions: Correction and prevention.* New York: Charities Publication Committee.

Byrne, C. (1994, March 14). "Childish nonsense" or good politics? A punishing debate. *Washington Star Tribune,* p. 1A.

Byrne, J. (1986, March). The control controversy: A preliminary examination of intensive probation and supervision programs in the United States. *Federal Probation,* 50(1), 4–16.

Byrne, J. (1990). The future of intensive probation supervision and the new intermediate sanctions. *Crime and Delinquency,* 36, 6–41.

Byrne, J., Kelly, L., & Guarino-Ghezzi, S. (1988). Understanding the limits of technology: An examination of the use of electronic monitoring in the criminal justice system. *Perspectives, 12*(2), 30–37.

Byrne, J., Lurgio, A., & Baird, C. (1989). The effectiveness of the "new" intensive supervision programs. *Research in Corrections, 5,* 1–48.

Byrne, J., Lurgio, A., & Petersilia, J. (1992). *Smart sentencing: The emergence of intermediate sanctions.* Newbury Park, CA: Sage Publications.

Byrne, J. M., and Pattavina, A. (1992). The Effectiveness Issue: Assessing What Works in the Adult Community Corrections System. In (Eds.) J. M. Byrne, A. J. Lurgio, and J. Petersilia, *Smart Sentencing: The Emergence of Intermediate Sanctions.* Beverly Hills, CA: Sage Publications.

Caldwell, R. G. (1947). *Red hannah.* Philadelphia: University of Pennsylvania Press.

Caldwell, R. G. (1965). *Criminology* (2nd ed.). New York: The Ronald Press Co.

California Code of Regulations (1991). *Division 3. Department of Corrections.* San Francisco, CA: Barclay's Law Publishers.

California judge refuses to apply a tough new sentencing law (1994, July 20). *New York Times,* p. WA9.

Callender, D. (1993). Regional Director, New York Therapeutic Communities, Inc. Personal communication.

Camp, G. W., & Camp, C. G. (1985, July). *Prison gangs: Their extent, nature and impact on prisons.* Washington, DC: U.S. Government Printing Office.

Camp, G. W., & Camp, C. G. (1988). *Management strategies for combating prison gang violence.* South Salem, NY: Criminal Justice Institute.

Camp, G. M., & Camp, C. G. (1989, January). *Management of crowded prisons.* Washington, DC: National Institute of Corrections.

Camp, G. M., & Camp, C. G. (1992). *The corrections yearbook 1992: Adult corrections.* South Salem, NY: Criminal Justice Institute.

Camp, G. M., & Camp, C. G. (1994a). *The corrections yearbook: Adult corrections.* South Salem, NY: Criminal Justice Institute.

Camp, G. M., & Camp, C. G. (1994b). *The corrections yearbook 1994: Jail systems.* South Salem, NY: Criminal Justice Institute.

Camp, G. M., & Camp, C. G. (1994c). *The corrections yearbook 1994: Probation and parole.* South Salem, NY: Criminal Justice Institute.

Carleton, M. T. (1971). *Politics and punishment: The history of the Louisiana state penal system.* Baton Rouge, LA: Louisiana State University Press.

Carp, S. V., & Davis, J. A. (1989). *Design considerations in the building of women's prisons.* Washington, DC: Department of Justice.

Carrol, L. (1974). *Hacks, blacks and cons: Race relations in a maximum security prison.* Lexington, MA: Lexington Books.

Carrol, L. (1977). Humanitarian reform and biracial sexual assault in a maxium security prison. *Urban Life, 5*(4), 417–437.

Carroll, L., (1988). Race, ethnicity, and the social order of the prison. In R. Johnson & H. Toch (Eds.), *The pains of imprisonment* (pp. 181–203). Prospect Heights, IL: Waveland Press, Inc.

Carroll, L. (1990). Race, ethnicity, and the social order of the prison. In D. H. Kelly (Ed.), *Criminal behavior: Text and readings in criminology* (2nd ed., pp. 510–527). New York: St. Martin's Press.

Carter, R. M. (1966). It is respectfully recommended. . . . *Federal Probation, 30,* (2), 38–42.

Carter, R., & Wilkins, L. (1976). Caseloads: Some conceptual models. In R. Carter and L. Wilkins (Eds.), *Probation, parole and community corrections.* New York: John Wiley and Sons.

Castro, J. A (1992, March 9) Judge whose ideas nearly got him killed. *Time,* pp. 12, 16.

Catanese, R., & Hennessey, J. (1989). Fire safety. *Jail Operations Bulletin, 1*(3), pp. 3, 6.

Cavadino, M., & Dignan, J. (1992). *The penal system: An introduction.* London: Sage Publications.

Cavan, R. S. (1962). *Criminology* (3rd ed.). New York: Thomas Y. Crowell Co.

Centerforce (1993). *Annual report to the legislature; fiscal year 1992/93.* San Quentin, CA: Author.

Cesarz, G., & Madrid-Bustos, J. (1991). Cultural awareness—New Mexico focuses on ethnic and minority issues. *Corrections Today, 53*(7), 68–71.

Chachere, V., & Lavelle, L. (1993, October 28). Prisons lose bid on new bill: Officials failed to get an exemption on a bill that would expand religious privileges. *Tampa Tribune,* Florida/Metro, p. 1.

Chaiken, M. (1989). *Prison programs for drug involved offenders.* Washington, DC: National Institute of Justice.

Chaiken, J. M., & Chaiken, M. R. (1982). *Varieties of criminal behavior: Summary and policy implications.* Santa Monica, CA: The Rand Corporation.

Chaiken, M., & Johnson, B. (1988). *Characteristics of different types of drug-involved offenders.* Washington, DC: National Institute of Justice.

Chambliss, W. J. (1964). A sociological analysis of the law of vagrancy. *Social Problems, 12,* 67–77.

Champion, D. J. (1990). *Probation and parole in the United States.* Columbus, OH: Merrill Publishing Co.

Chapman, J. (1980). *Economic realities and female crime.* Lexington, MA: Lexington Books.

Chastang, C. (1993, February 1). Smugglers' blues. *Los Angeles Times,* Metro, p. 3.

Cheatwood, D. (1988). The life-without-parole sanction: Its current status and a research agenda. *Crime and Delinquency, 34,* 43–59.

Cheek, F. E., & Miller, M. D. (1982). *Prisoners of life: A study of occupational stress among state corrections officers.* Washington, DC: American Federation of State, County, and Municipal Employees.

Chenault, P. (1951). Education. In P. W. Tappan (Ed.), *Contemporary corrections* New York: McGraw-Hill.

Chesney-Lind, M. (1982). Guilty by reason of sex: Young women and the juvenile justice system. In B. Price & N. Sokoloff (Eds.). *The criminal justice system and women* (pp. 77–105). New York: Clark Boardman.

Chesney-Lind, M. (1986). Women and crime: The female offender. *Signs: Journal of Women in Culture and Society, 12,* 78–96.

Chesney-Lind, M. (1987). Female offenders: Paternalism reexamined. In L. L. Crites & W. L. Hepperle (Eds.), *Women, the courts, and equality* (pp. 114–139). Newbury Park, CA: Sage Publications.

Chiricos, T., & Waldo, G. (1970). Punishment and crime: An examination of some empirical evidence. *Social Problems, 18,* 200–217.

Chonco, N. R. (1989). Sexual assaults among male inmates: A descriptive study. *The Prison Journal,* 72–82.

CIA Newsletter. (1994, Spring). Death row inmates join Alabama's correctional industries program. *CIA Newsletter, 11*(2), 3.

Civil Rights Act of 1871 (42 U.S.C. Sec. 1983).

Clark, C. L., Aziz, D. W., & MacKenzie, D. L. (1994, August). *Shock incarceration in New York: Focus on treatment.* Washington, DC: National Institute of Justice.

Clark, D. (1989, July). Chuck Colson: Born again prison reformer. *Corrections Today,* 80, 81, 84.

Clark, D. D. (1991). *Analysis of return rates of the inmate college program participants.* Albany, NY: State of New York Department of Correctional Services.

Clark, M. (1986). Missouri's sexual offender program. *Corrections Today, 48*(3), 84, 85, 89.

Clear, T. R. (1988). Statistical prediction in corrections. In J. Petersilia (Ed.), *Research in corrections* (Vol. 1, 1–35).

Clear, T., Flynn, S., & Shapiro, C. (1987). Intensive supervision probation: A comparison of three projects. In B. McCarthy (Ed.), *Intermediate punishments: Intensive supervision, home confinement and electronic surveillance.* Monsey, NY: Criminal Justice Press.

Clear, T., & Hardyman, P. (1990). The new intensive supervision movement. *Crime and Delinquency, 36*(1), 42–60.

Clements, C. B. (1979). Crowded prisons: A review of psychological and environmental effects. *Law and Human Behavior, 3,* 217–225.

Clemmer, D. (1958). *The prison community.* New York: Holt, Rinehart & Winston, (Originally published in 1940.)

Clines, F. X. (1994, October 17). A futuristic prison awaits the hard core. *The New York Times,* Sec. A. p. 1, 12.

Cloward, R. A. (1969). Social control in prison. In. L. E. Hazelrigg (Ed.), *Prison within society: A reader in penology.* Garden City, NY: Anchor Books.

Cohen, F. (1988, November). *Legal issues and the mentally disordered prisoner.* Washington, DC: National Institute of Corrections.

Cohen, F. (1990). Correctional law in the 90's: My murky crystal ball says bodies will be the issue. *Correctional Law Reporter,* 1, 10–12.

Cohen, F. (1993). The legal context for mental health services. In H. J. Steadman & J. J. Cocozza (Eds.), *Mental illness in America's prisons.* Seattle, WA: National Coalition for the Mentally Ill in the Criminal Justice System.

Cohen, J. (1983). Incapacitating criminals: Recent research findings. Washington, DC: U.S. Department of Justice, National Institute of Justice.

Cohen, R. L. (1991, May). Bureau of Justice Statistics Bulletin: Prisoners in 1990. Washington, DC: U.S. Department of Justice.

Cohen, S. B. (1991). Behind every good security system stand the people who make it work. *Corrections Today, 53*(4), 86, 88–90.

Cohn, A. W. (1973). The future of correctional management. Crime and Delinquency, 19, 323–331.

Cohn, A. W. (1979). The future of correctional management revisited. Federal Probation, 33, 10–15.

Cohn, A. W. (1981). The future of correctional management reconsidered. Criminal Justice Review, 6, 55–61.

Cohn, A. W. (1987). Behavioral objectives in probation and parole: A new approach to staff accountability. *Federal Probation, 51,* 40–49.

Cohn, A. W. (1991). The future of correctional management. Federal Probation, 45, 12–16.

Collins, W. C. (1986). *Correctional law 1986: An analysis and discussion of the key issues and developments in correctional law over the past year.* Olympia, WA: Author.

Collins, W. C. (1993). *Correctional law for the correctional officer.* Laurel, MD: American Correctional Association.

Colvin, M. (1982). The 1980 New Mexico prison riot. *Social Problems, 29*(5), 449–461.

Committee for the Revision of the 1954 Manual (1959). *Manual of correctional standards.* New York: The American Correctional Association.

Committee on Internal Security House of Representatives (1973a). *Staff study on revolutionary activity directed toward the administration of penal or corrections systems.* Washington, DC: U.S. Government Printing office.

Committee on Internal Security House of Representatives (1973b). *Staff study: The National Lawyers' Guild.* Washington, DC: U.S. Government Printing office.

Conklin, J. E. (1992). *Criminology.* New York: Macmillan Publishing Co.

Conley, R. W., Luckasson, R., & Bouthilet, G. N. (1992). *The criminal justice system and mental retardation.* Baltimore, MD: Paul H. Brookes Publishing Co.

Conrad, J. P. (1965). *Crime and its correction: An international survey of attitudes and practices.* Berkley, CA.: University of California Press.

Conrad, J. P. (1981). *Adult offender education programs.* Washington, DC: U.S. Department of Justice.

Conrad, J. P. (1986). Research and development in corrections. *Federal Probation, 1*(3), 74–77.

Conrad, J. P., & Dinitz, S. (1978, September). The state's strongest medicine. Paper presented at the Colloquium on the Criminal Justice System, Columbus, OH.

Contact. (1988a, August). Furlough programs success rate high: Majority furlough lifers. *Corrections Compendium, 13*(3), p. 11.

Contact. (1988b, September–October). Furlough programs success rate high: Majority furlough lifers. *Corrections Compendium, 13*(3), 12–18.

Contact. (1992a, October). Correctional officers, Part I—Numbers, salaries. *Corrections Compendium, 17,* 9–11.

Contact. (1992b, October). Correctional officers, Part II—Requirements, training. *Corrections Compendium, 17,* 12–14.

Cook, P. J., and Slawson, D. B. (1993). Study finds each death penalty cost North Carolina more than $250,000. Durham, NC: Duke University News.

Coombs, E. (1991). The Simon of Cyrene Society: Stretching a helping hand to reformatory visitors. *Corrections Today, 53*(5), 114, 116, 118.

Cooper, W. M. (1870). *A history of the rod in all countries.* London: John Camden Hotten.

Copeland, R. C. (1980, August). *The evolution of the Texas Department of Corrections.* Unpublished master's thesis, Sam Houston State University.

Copley, E. W. (1995, July 3). State prisons inmates have to pay for part of college costs: Federal budget cuts force drops in courses. *State Journal-Register (Springfield, IL),* Local, p. 7.

Cornish, D. B., & Clarke, R. V. (Eds.) (1986). The reasoning criminal: Rational choice perspectives on offending. New York: Springer-Verlag.

Correctional Association of New York. (1990, September). *Imprisoned generation: Young men under criminal justice custody in New York State.* New York: Author.

Correctional Educational School Authority. (1988–1989). *Annual report.* Tallahassee, FL: Author.

Correctional Educational School Authority. (1990). *Academic and vocational program completers released from prison during fiscal year 1986–88: Employment, recidivism and cost avoidance.* Tallahassee, FL: Author.

Correctional Law Reporter. (February 1994a). Supreme Court accepts "I didn't know" as defense to failure to protect claim. *Correctional Law Reporter, 5*(2), 17–18, 26–29.

Correctional Law Reporter. (February 1994b). New rules, new law suits: RFRA means litigation and change for corrections. *Correctional Law Reporter, 5*(5), 65–66, 72–73.

Correctional Law Reporter. (February 1994c). What's a warden to do about RFRA? Well, don't just wait to be sued. *Correctional Law Reporter, 5*(5), p. 69.

Correctional Services Group, I. (1985). *Overview of objective prisoner classification.* Unpublished report. Kansas City, MO: Author.

Corrections Compendium. (1993, July). Survey: Correctional officer training—Pre-service/curricula hours. Author, pp. 5–15.

Corrections Compendium. (1994a, September). Hiring of correctional officers increasingly more selective—Part I: Numbers and salaries of C.O.s. *Corrections Compendium,* pp. 8–11.

Corrections Compendium. (1994b, September). Hiring of correctional officers increasingly more selective—Part II: Requirements, recruitment and training of C.O.s. *Corrections Compendium,* pp. 11–16.

Corrigan, P. (1993, February 9). Police accuse county jail guard of supplying drugs to inmates. *St. Louis Post-Dispatch,* p. 1A.

Coste, C. (1976). Prison health care—Part of the punishment? *The New Physician, 25,* 29–35.

Cowles, E. L. (1990a, December). Program needs for long-term inmates. In Federal Bureau of Prisons, *Long term confinement and the aging inmate population* (pp. 17–25). Washington, DC: Federal Bureau of Prisons.

Cowles, E. L., (1990b, December). Programming for long-term inmates: Executive summary. In Federal Bureau of Prisons, *Long term confinement and the aging inmate population* (pp. 114–119). Washington, DC: Federal Bureau of Prisons.

Cowles, E. L., Castellano, T. C., & Gramsky, L. A. (1995). "Boot Camp" drug treatment and aftercare intervention: An evaluation review. Washington, D.C.: U.S. Department of Justice.

Cox, G. H., Jr., & Rhodes, S. J. (1990). Managing overcrowding: Corrections administrators and the prison crisis. *Criminal Justice, 4*(2), 115–143.

Crabtree, J. (1993). A small county jail: Wasecha, Minnesota. *American Jails, 7*(5), 62–66.

Crawford, J. (1988). *Tabulation of a nationwide survey of state correctional facilities for adult and juvenile female offenders.* College Park, MD: American Correctional Association.

Crawford, W. (1969). *Report on the penitentiaries of the United States.* Montclair, NJ: Patterson Smith. (Original work published 1835)

Crew, B. K. (1991). Sex differences in criminal sentencing: Chivalry or patriarchy? *Justice Quarterly, 8*(1), 59–83.

Cromwell, P., Marks, A., Olson, J., & Avary, D. W. (1991). Group effects on decision making by burglars. *Psychological Reports, 69,* 579–588.

Cromwell, P., Olson, J., & Avary, D.W. (1991). *Breaking and entering, an ethnographic analysis of burglary.* Newbury Park, CA: Sage Publications.

Crouch, B. M. (1980). *The keepers: Prison guards and contemporary corrections.* Springfield, IL: Thomas.

Crouch, B. M., & Marquart, J. W. (1989). *An appeal to justice: Litigated reform of Texas prisons.* Austin, TX: University of Texas Press.

Crutchfield, E., Garrette, L., & Worral, J. (1981, February). Recreation's place in prisons: A survey report. *Parks and Recreation,* 35–39, 73.

Culbertson, R., & Ellsworth, T. (1985). Treatment innovations in probation and parole. In L. Travis (Ed.), *Probation, Parole and Community Corrections*. Prospect Heights, IL: Waveland Press.

Cullen, F. T., & Gilbert, K. E. (1982). *Reaffirming rehabilitation*. Cincinnati, OH: Anderson Publishing Co.

Cullen, F. T., Lutze, F. E., Link, B. G., & Wolfe, N. T. (1989). The correctional orientation of prison guards: Do officers support rehabilitation? *Federal Probation, 53*, 33–41.

Cullen, F. T., & Travis, L. F. (1984). Work as an avenue of prison reform. *New England Journal On Criminal and Civil Confinement, 9*(1), 1–20.

Cunniff, M. A. (1987). *Sentencing outcomes in 28 felony courts*. Washington, DC: National Association of Criminal Justice Planners.

Curry, T. H., II. (1993). Dealing with diversity. *Corrections Today, 55*(5), 168–172.

Cusson, M., & Pinsonneault, P. (1986). The decision to give up crime. In D. B. Cornish & R. V. Clarke (Eds.), *The reasoning criminal: Rational choice perspectives on offending* (pp. 72–82). New York: Springer-Verlag.

Dale, M. J. (1987). Who are these people and why are they suing us? *American Jails, 1*(3), 23–24.

Dale, M. J. (1989). Inmate medical care: Defining the constitutionally permissible level of care. *American Jails, 3*(2), 61–64.

Dale, M. J. (1991). The female inmate: An introduction to legal rights and issues. *American Jails, 4*(4), 56–58.

Darnton, J. (1993, February 6). After nearly 4 years, Rushdie has hope. *The New York Times*, p. 4.

Davidson, M. (1995, June 18). Chain-gang debate clangs; Inmates: Work is 'humiliating.' *Arizona Republic*, p. B1.

Davidson, T. R. (1983). *Chicano prisoners: The key to San Quentin*. Prospect Heights, IL: Waveland Press. (Originally published in 1974)

Davis, E. K. (1978). Offender education in the American correctional system: An historical perspective. *Quarterly Journal of Corrections, 2*(2), 7–13.

Davis, S. P. (1990, April). Inmates use of phones in prison "a positive that outweighs negatives." *Corrections Compendium, 15*(3), 9–16.

Davis, S. P. (1991, July). Survey: Number of sex offenders in prison increases 48%. *Corrections Compendium*, pp. 9–19.

Davis, S. P. (1992). Survey: Programs and services for female offenders. *Corrections Compendium*, September (9), pp. 7–20.

Davis, S. P. (1993a). Health care costs—10% Of the pie. *Corrections Compendium, 18*(5).

Davis, S. P. (1993b, April). Survey: Work and educational release, 1993. *Corrections Compendium, 18*(4), 5, 22.

Death Penalty Information Center. (1993). *Sentencing for life: Americans embrace alternatives to the death penalty*. Washington, DC: Author.

Death Penalty Information Center. (1995, March). *Facts about the death penalty*. Washington, DC: Author.

Del Carmen, R., & Vaughn, J. (1986). Legal issues in the use of electronic surveillance in probation. *Federal Probation, 50*(2), 60–66.

deLangy, G. (1854). *The knout and the Russians*. New York: Harper & Brothers, Publishers.

DeLeon, G. (1984). *The therapeutic community: Study of effectiveness*. Rockville, MD: National Institute of Drug Abuse.

DeLeon, G. (1985). The therapeutic community: Status and evolution. *International Journal of Addictions, 20*, 823–844.

Delguzzi, K. (1993, May 21). Prison guard accused of smuggling ammo inside. *The Cincinnati Enquirer*.

Dell'Apa, F. (1973). *Educational programs in adult correctional institutions: A survey*. Boulder, CO: The Western Interstate Commission for Higher Education.

DeMaret, W. F. (1991). Time to think: Social/cognitive skills programming in transition in New Mexico. *Journal of Correctional Education, 42*(2), 107–110.

Deming, B. (1966). *Prison notes*. Boston: Beacon Press.

Deutsch, M. E. (1993). Attorney for the inmate plaintiffs in Attica civil rights suits. Personal communication.

Deutsch, M. E., Cunningham D., & Fink, E. M. (1991). Twenty years later—Attica civil rights case finally cleared for trial. *Social Justice, 18*(3), 13–25.

DeVolentine, J. (1993). Program Director, Florida Correctional Mental Health Institution. Personal communication.

Dickey, W. (1979). The lawyer and the accuracy of presentence reports. *Federal Probation, 43*, 28–38.

Dieter, R. C. (1995, October). With justice for few: The growing crisis in death penalty representation. Washington, DC: Death Penalty Information Center.

DiIulio, J. J., Jr. (1987). *Governing Prisons*. New York, NY: McMillan.

DiIulio, J. J., Jr. (1991). *No escape*. New York: Basic Books.

Dinitz, S. (1980). Are safe and humane prisons possible? The John Vincent Barry Memorial Lecture, University of Melbourne, Australia.

Dinitz, S., & Huff, C. R. (1988). The Figgie report part VI: The business of crime: The criminal perspective. Richmond, VA: Figgie International, Inc.

Dison, J. E. (1991, November). *A brief history of the Arkansas prison system through the mid 1960s*. Paper presented at the annual meeting of the American Society of Criminology, San Francisco.

Dobash, R. P., Dobash, R. E., & Gutteridge, S. (1986). *The imprisonment of women*. Oxford, England: Basil Blackwell, Ltd.

Doeran, S., & Hageman, M. (1982). *Community corrections*. Cincinnati, OH: Anderson Publishing Co.

Donaldson, S. (1993, December 29). The rape crisis behind bars. *The New York Times*, p. 11A.

Donnelly, P. G., & Forschner, B. R. Predictors of success in a co-correctional halfway house: A discriminant analysis. In T. Ellsworth (Ed.), *Contemporary community corrections*. Prospect Heights, IL: Waveland Press.

Dooley, E. E. (1981, Winter). Sir Walter Crofton and the Irish or intermediate system of prison discipline. *New England Journal on Prison Law*, 72.

Dorin, D., & Johnson, R. (1979). The premature dragon: George Jackson as model for the new militant inmate. Contemporary Crises, 3, pp. 295–315.

Dorman, M. (1995, June 18). On the chain gang. *Newsday*, p. 7.

Driven out sex offender returns to town. (1993, August 14). New York Times-Final, 1, p. 23.

Duffee, D. (1980). *Correctional management*. Englewood Cliffs, NJ: Prentice Hall.

Dugger, R. L. (1988, June). The graying of America's prisons: Special care considerations. *Corrections Today*, pp. 26–28.

Dugger, R. L. (1990). Life and death in prison. *The Prison Journal*, 70(1), 112–114.

Dwyer, D. C., & McNally, R. B. (1993, June). Public policy, prison industries, and business: An equitable balance for the 1990s. *Federal Probation*, 30–36.

Earle, A. M. (1969). *Curious punishments of bygone days*. Montclair, NJ: Patterson Smith. Originally published 1896.

Earley, P. (1992). *The hot house: Life inside Leavenworth Prison*. New York: Bantam Books.

Egan, T. (1994, February 15). It's not as simple as it seems. *The New York Times*, p. 1.

Eigenberg, H. (1990, July). Male rape: An empirical examination of correctional officers' attitudes toward rape in prison. *The Prison Journal*, 39–56.

Ekirch, A.R. (1987). *Bound for America: The transportation of British convicts to the colonies 1718–1775*. Oxford: Clarendon Press.

Ellis, A. (1980). An overview of the clinical theory of rational-emotive therapy. In R. Greiger, & J. Boyd (Eds.), *Rational-emotive therapy: A skills based approach*. New York: Van Nostrand Reinhold.

Ellis, J. W., & Luckasson, R. A. (1985). Mentally retarded defendents. *George Washington Law Review*, 53(3–4), 483.

Embert, P. S., & Kalinich, D. B. (1988). *Behind the walls*. Salem, WI: Sheffield Publishing Co.

Empey, L. (1967). *Alternatives to incarceration*. Washington, DC: U.S. Department of Health, Education and Welfare, Office of Juvenile Delinquency and Youth Development.

EMT Associates, Inc. (1985). *Evaluation of the M-2 sponsors program*. Sacramento, CA: Author.

EMT Associates, Inc. (1987). *Evaluation of the M-2 sponsors program: Final report*. Sacramento, CA: Author.

Erwin, B. (1987). *Evaluation of intensive probation supervision in Georgia*. Atlanta, GA: Department of Offender Rehabilitation.

Erwin, B. (1990). Old and new tools for the modern probation officer. *Crime and Delinquency, 36*(1), 61–74.

Exum, J.G., Jr., Turnbull, H.R., III, Martin, R. and Finn, J.W. (1992). Point of view: Perspectives on the judicial, mental retardation services, law enforcement, and correctional systems. In R.W. Conley, R. Luckasson, & G.N. Bouthilet (Eds.), *The criminal justice system and mental retardation: Defendants and Victims* (pp. 8–16). Baltimore, MD: Paul H. Brookes Publishing Co.

Fabiano, E. A. (1991). How education can be correctional and how corrections can be educational. *Journal of Correctional Education, 42*(2), 100–106.

Farbstein J., & Wiener, R. (1989, June 1). *A comparison of corrections "direct" and "indirect" supervision correctional facilities. Final report Grant GG-1*. Washington, DC: U.S. Department of Justice, National Institute of Corrections.

Faucheaux, R. (1994, March). Analysis: The politics of crime. *Campaigns and Elections, Inc.* 15(4), 5.

Federal Bureau of Investigation. (1994). *Crime in the United States 1993 (Uniform Crime Report)*. Washington, DC: U.S. Department of Justice.

Federal Bureau of Prisons. (undated). *A working manual of day-to-day procedures for field chaplains*. Washington, DC: Author.

Federal Bureau of Prisons. (1988). *Program statement: Firearms and badges*. Washington, DC: Author.

Federal Bureau of Prisons. (1994). *State of the Bureau—1993*. Washington, DC: U.S. Department of Justice.

Feinman, C. (1986). *Women in the criminal justice system*. New York: Praeger.

Fickenauer, J. O. (1988). Public support for the death penalty: Retribution as just deserts or retribution as revenge? *Justice Quarterly, 5*, 81–100.

Finger, M. (1993, February 26). A judge's sentence may be, write one. *The New York Times*, p. B10.

Finn, P. (1989). Decriminalization of public drunkenness: Response of the healthcare system. *Journal of Studies on Alcohol, 46*, 7.

Finn, P., & Sullivan, M. (1988). *Police response to special populations*. Washington, DC: National Institute of Justice.

Fisher, I. (1994, January). Why '3-strike' sentencing is a solid hit this year. The *New York Times*, p. A16.

Fisher, M., O'Brien, E., & Austin D. T. (1987). *Practical law for jail and prison personnel*. St. Paul, MN: West Publishing Co.

Fishman, J. F. (1934). *Sex in prison: Revealing sex conditions in American prisons*. New York: National Library Association.

Fishman, L. T. (1990). *Women at the wall*. Albany, NY: State University of New York Press.

Flanagan, T. J. (1989). Prison labor and industry. In L. Goodstein & D. L. MacKenzie (Eds.), *The American prison*. New York: Plenum Press.

Flanagan, T. J. (1991, Spring). Long-term prisoners: Their adaptation and adjustment. *Federal Prison Journal*, 45–51.

Flanagan, T. J., Hindelang, M. J., & Gottfredson, M. R. (1980). *Sourcebook of criminal justice statistics—1979*. Washington, DC: U.S. Department of Justice.

Florida Auditor General Department of Corrections. (1994, March 4). *Performance audit of the prison industries program administered by Prison Rehabilitative Industries and Diversified Enterprises, Inc.* Tallahassee, FL: Author.

Florida Department of Corrections. (1982, March). *Policy and procedure directive: Chaplaincy services.* Tallahassee, FL: Author.

Florida Department of Corrections. (1988). *Annual report 1987/88.* Tallahassee, FL: Author.

Florida Department of Corrections. (1991, November 22). *Rules of the Department of Corrections: Use of force—rule No. 33-3.0066.* Tallahassee, FL: State of Florida.

Florida Department of Corrections. (1991). *Annual report 1989/90.* Tallahassee, FL: Author.

Florida Department of Corrections. (1993). *Annual report 1991/92.* Tallahassee, FL: Author.

Florida Department of Law Enforcement. (1990). *School resource officer student guide.* Tallahassee, FL: Author.

Florida TaxWatch Inc. (1989). *PRIDE—Is Florida's prison industries experiment succeeding.* Tallahassee, FL: Author.

Florida TaxWatch Inc. (1991). *Making our correctional education investment pay off.* Tallahassee, FL: Author.

Flynn, E. E. (1992). The graying of America's prison population. *The Prison Journal, 72*(1&2), 77–98.

Flynn, F. T. (1951). Employment and labor. In P. W. Tappan (Ed.), *Contemporary correction.* New York: McGraw-Hill.

Fogel, D. (1979). *We are the living proof: The justice model for corrections.* Cincinnati, OH: Anderson Publishing Co.

Fong, R. (1990). The organizational structure of prison gangs: A Texas case study. *Federal Probation, 54*(1), 36–43.

Fong, R. S., & Buentello, S. (1991, March). The detection of prison gang development: An empirical assessment. *Federal Probation*, pp. 66–69.

Fong, R. S., Vogel, R. E., & Buentello, S. (1992). Prison gang dynamics: A look inside the Texas Department of Corrections. In P. J. Benekos & A. V. Merlo (Eds.), *Corrections: Dilemmas and directions.* Cincinnati, OH: Anderson Publishing Co.

Fong, R. S., Vogel, R. E., Little, R. E. & Buentello, S. (1991). Prison violence and disruption: An analysis of hispanic, black and white prison gangs. Paper presented at the annual meeting of the Academy of Criminal Justice Sciences, Nashville, TN.

Former prison guard admits accepting bribes from inmates. (1993, July 9). United Press International,

Foster, C. D., Siegel, M. A., & Jacobs, N. R. (Eds.) (1992). *Capital punishment: Cruel and unusual?* Wylie, TX: Information Plus.

Fox, J., Radalet, M., & Bonsteel, J. (1990). Death penalty opinion in the post-Furman years. *New York University Review of Law and Social Change, 18,* 499–528.

Fox, J. G. (1982). *Organizational and racial conflict in maximum security prisons.* Lexington, MA: Lexington Books.

Fox, V. (1956). *Violence behind bars.* Westport, CT: Greenwood Press.

Fox, V. (1983). *Correctional institutions.* Englewood Cliffs, NJ: Prentice Hall.

Frase, R. S. (1993, February). Prison population growing under Minnesota guidelines. *Overcrowded Times, 4*(1), p. 1.

Freedman, E. (1981). *Their sisters' keepers: Women's prison reform in America, 1830–1930.* Ann Arbor, MI: University of Michigan.

Freeman, R. W., & Johnson L. (1982). Health related knowledge, attitudes and practices of correctional officers. *Journal of Prison and Jail Health, 2*(2), 125–138.

Friedrichs, D. (1989). Comment—Humanism and the death penalty. *Justice Quarterly, 6,* 197–211.

Friel, J. (1984). Staff perceptions of prisoner life tasks in a Canadian penitentiary. *Canadian Journal of Criminology, 26*(3), 355–357.

Funke, G., Wayson, B., & Miller, N. (1982). *Assets and liabilities of correctional industries.* Lexington, MA: Lexington Books.

Gaes, G. (1990a, December). Fact finding information. In Federal Bureau of Prisons, *Long term confinement and the aging inmate population* (pp. 5–12). Washington, DC: Federal Bureau of Prisons.

Gaes, G. (1990b, December). Long term inmates—A preliminary look at their programming needs and adjustment patterns. In Federal Bureau of Prisons, *Long term confinement and the aging inmate population* (pp. 82–93). Washington, DC: Federal Bureau of Prisons.

Garcia, S. A., & Steele, H. V. (1988). Mentally retarded offenders in the criminal justice system and mental retardation services systems in Florida: Philisophical, treatment and placement issues. *Arkansas Law Review, 41*(4), 809–859.

Gardner, E. (1992). Regional jails. *American Jails, 6*(2), 45–47.

Gardner, R. (1981). Guard stress. *Corrections Magazine, 7,* 6–14.

Garibaldi, M., & Moore, M. (1981, April). The treatment team approach. *Journal of Physical Education and Recreation, 52*(4), 28–32.

Garrett, D. G. (1993, November 15). Pretrial Programs Director State Attorney's Office, Duval County, Florida. Personal communication.

Geerken, M. R., & Hayes, H. D. (1993). Probation and parole: Public risk and the future of incarceration alternatives. *Criminology, 31*(4), 549–564.

Geerken, M., Miranne, A., & Kennedy, M. B. (1993). *The New Orleans offender Study: Development of official databases.* Washington, DC: National Institute of Justice.

General Accounting Office. (1990a). *Death penalty sentencing: Research indicates pattern of racial disparities.* Washington, DC: Author.

General Accounting Office. (1990b). *Intermediate sanctions: Their impacts on prison crowding, costs and recidivism are still unclear.* Washington, DC: Author.

General Accounting Office. (1991). *Mentally ill inmates: Better data would help determine protection and advocacy needs.* Washington, DC: Author.

General Accounting Office. (1993). *Prison inmates: Better plans needed before felons are released.* Washington, DC: Author.

Gettinger, S. (1978, March). The Windham school district. *Corrections Magazine,* pp. 14–15.

Giallombardo, R. (1966). *Society of women: A study of a women's prison.* New York: Wiley.

Gibbs, J. (1968). Crime, punishment and deterrence. *Social Science Quarterly, 48,* 515–530.

Gilbert, M. J. (1993, March). *Discretionary workstyle preferences among correctional officers: Implications for correctional training and management.* Paper presented at the annual meeting of the Academy of Criminal Justice Sciences, Kansas City, MO.

Gilbert, M. J. (1995, March 27). Assistant Professor, The University of Texas at San Antonio. Personal communication.

Gilliard, D. K. (1993). *Prisoners in 1992.* Washington, DC: U.S. Department of Justice.

Gilliard, D. K., & Beck, A. J. (1994, June). *Prisoners in 1993.* Washington, DC: U.S. Department of Justice.

Gillin, J. L. (1935). *Criminology and penology.* New York: D. Appleton-Century Company.

Glaberson, W. (1991, December 9). Violence at Attica Prison echoes in the courtroom. The *New York Times,* pp. A1, A17.

Glaser, D. (1954). *A reformulation and testing of parole prediction factors.* Unpublished doctoral dissertation, University of Chicago.

Glaser, D. (1969). *The effectiveness of a prison and parole system.* Indianapolis, IN: The Bobbs-Merrill Co.

Glaser, D. (1971, November–December). Politicalization of prisoners: A new challenge to American penology. *American Journal of Correction, 33,* 6–9.

Glasser, W. (1965). *Reality therapy.* New York: Harper and Row.

Gleason, S. E. (1978, June). Hustling: The "inside" economy of a prison. *Federal Probation, 42*(2), 32–40.

Glick, R., & Neto, V. (1977). *National study of women's correctional programs.* Washington, DC: U.S. Government Printing Office.

Gluckstern, N. B., Neuse, M. A., Harness, J. K., Packard, R. W., Patmon, C., & Coleman, M. (1979). *Health care in correctional institutions.* Washington, DC: U. S. Department of Justice.

Glueck, S., & Glueck, E. (1974). *Of delinquency and crime.* Springfield, IL: Thomas.

Gobert, J. J., & Cohen, N. P. (1981). Rights of Prisoners. Colorado Springs, CO: Shepard's/McGraw-Hill, Inc.

Gobert, J. J., & Cohen, N. P. (1992). *Rights of prisoners: 1992 cumulative supplement.* Colorado Springs, CO: Shepard's/McGraw-Hill.

Goetting, A. (1982, September). Conjugal association in prison: A world view. *Criminal Justice Abstracts,* pp. 406–416.

Goffman, E. (1961). *Asylums: Essays on the social situation of mental and other inmates.* New York: Anchor Books.

Goldfarb, R. (1973). *Jails: The ultimate ghetto.* Garden City, NY: Anchor Press/Doubleday.

Gottfredson, D. M., & Tonry, M. (1987). *Prediction and classification: Criminal justice decision making.* Chicago, IL: University of Chicago Press.

Gottlieb, D.J. (1985). The legacy of Wolfish and Chapman: Some thoughts about "big prison case" litigation in the 1980s. In I. D. Robbins (Ed.), *Prisoners and the law.* New York: Clark Boardman Co. Ltd.

Gottlieb, D.J. (1991). A review and analysis of the Kansas sentencing guidelines. *Kansas Law Review, 39,* 65–89.

Gottlieb, D. J. (1993, June). Kansas adopts sentencing guidelines. *Overcrowded Times, 4,* p. 1, 10–12.

Gould, J. (1981, June). How to keep prisoners from returning to lockup. *Today—University of Florida, 6*(3), 21–23.

Gould, L. A., MacKenzie, D. L., & Bankston, W. (1991). *A comparison of models of parole outcome.* Paper presented at the annual meeting of the American Society of Criminology, San Francisco.

Grasmick, H., & Bursik, R. (1990). Conscience, significant others and choice: Extending the deterrence model. *Law and Society Review, 24,* 837–861.

Greek, C. (1992). Drug control and asset seizures: A review of the history of forfeiture in England and colonial America. In T. Mieczkowski (Ed.), *Drugs, crime and social policy.* Boston: Allyn and Bacon.

Greene, J. (1992). The Staten Island day-fine experiment. In D. C. McDonald (Ed.), *Day fines in American courts: The Staten Island and Milwaukee experiments.* Washington, DC: U.S. Department of Justice, Office of Justice Programs.

Greenfeld, L. (1985). *Examining recidivism.* Washington, DC: U.S. Government Printing Office.

Greenfeld, L. A., & Minor-Harper, S. (1991, March). *Women in prison.* Washington, DC: Bureau of Justice Statistics.

Greenfeld, L. A., & Stephan, J. J. (1993). *Capital punishment 1992.* Washington, DC: U.S. Department of Justice.

Grier, W. H., & Cobbs, P. M. (1969). *Black rage.* New York: Bantam Books.

Grieser, R. C. (1988, August). Model approaches: Examining prison industry that works. *Corrections Today,* pp. 174–178.

Grieser, R. C., Miller, N., & Funke, G. S. (1984, January). *Guidelines for prison industries.* Washington, DC: U.S. Department of Justice, National Institute of Corrections.

Grossman, J. (1984, March). *An examination of the trends of female new commitments: 1960–1982.* Report prepared for the New York State Department of Correctional Services.

Grossman, J. (1984). *Bedford Hills mothers follow-up.* Albany: New York State Department of Correctional Services.

Groth, N. A. (1979). *Men who rape: The psychology of the offender.* New York: Plenum Press.

Grunhut, M. (1972). *Penal reform: A comparative study.* Montclair, NJ: Patterson Smith. (Orginal work published 1948)

Gunn, B. (1979). *Identification & control of drugs in correctional institutions.* Sacremento, CA: California Department of Corrections.

Gustafson, A. (1993, January 5). Law would allow indefinite imprisonment of sex predators. *The Salem Statesman Journal,*

Gustafson, J. I. (1994, August). Specialist, National Institute of Corrections. Personal communication.

Guynes, R. G., & Grieser, R.C. (1986, January). Contemporary prison industry goals. In American Correctional Association (Eds), *A study of prison industry: History, components, and goals.* Washington, DC: National Institute of Corrections.

Hackett, J., Hatry, H. P., Levinson, R. B., Allen, J., Chi, K., and Feigenbaum, E. D. (1987). *Issues in contracting for the private operation of prisons and jails.* Washington, DC: U.S. Department of Justice.

Hafiz, A. (1993). Chaplain, Federal Correctional Institution Terminal Island. Personal Communication.

Hafiz, A., & Hamidullah, M. (undated). Practicing Islam in prison. In Federal Bureau of Prisons, *African American work group report.* Washington, DC: U.S. Department of Justice.

Hager, J. (1992). Proactive jail management. *Jail Managers Bulletin, 2*(9).

Hahn, P. H. (1994, August). A standardized curriculum for correctional officers: History and rationale. Paper presented at the American Congress on Corrections, St. Louis, MO.

Haigler, K., Harlow C.W., O'Connor P.E., & Campbell, A. (1994, October). *Literacy behind bars: Profiles of the prison population from the National Adult Literacy Survey.* Washington, DC: U.S. Department of Education, Office of Education Research and Improvement.

Hairston, C. F. (1988, March). Family ties during imprisonment: Do they influence future criminal activity? *Federal Probation, 52*(1), 48–52.

Hairston, C. F. (1990). Men in prison: Family characteristics and parenting views. *Journal of Offender Counseling, Services and Rehabilitation, 14*(1), 23–29.

Hairston, C. F., & Hess, P. M. (1989). Regulating parent-child communication in correctional settings. In J. Mustin & B. Bloom (Conference Directors), *The First National Conference on the Family and Corrections* (pp. 29–32). Richmond, KY: Training Resource Center, Department of Correctional Services, Eastern Kentucky University.

Hairston, C. F., & Lockett, P. W. (1987). Parents in prison: New directions for social services. *Social Work, 32*(2), 162–164.

Halford, S. C. (1984). Kansas co-corrections concept. *Corrections Today, 46,* 44–46.

Hall, M. (1990, December). *Special needs inmates: A survey of state correctional systems.* Boulder, CO: National Institute of Corrections.

Halleck, S., & Herski, M. (1962). Homosexual behavior in an institution for adolescent girls. *American Journal of Orthopsychiatry, 32,* 911–917.

Haly, K. (1980). Mothers behind bars: A look at the parental rights in incarcerated women. In S. K. Datesmen & F. Scarpitti (Eds.), *Women, crime and justice.* New York: Oxford University Press.

Hambrick, M. C. (1988, December). Correctional recreation: Get your program off and running. *Corrections Today, 134,* 136.

Hambrick, M. (1992, Winter). The correctional worker concept: Being connected in the 90's. *Federal Prison Journal,* 11–14.

Hammett, T. M. (1988a). *Precautionary measures and protective equipment: Developing a reasonable response.* Washington, DC: National Institute of Justice.

Hammett, T. M. (1988b). *AIDS in correctional facilities: Issues and opinions* (3rd ed.). Washington, DC: National Institute of Justice.

Hammett, T. M., & Harrold, L. (1994, January). *Tuberculosis in correctional facilities.* Washington, DC: U.S. Department of Justice, National Institute of Justice.

Hammett, T. M., Harrold, L., Gross, M., & Epstein, J. (1994). *1992 update: AIDS in correctional facilities: Issues and opinions.* Cambridge, MA: Abt Associates.

Hammett, T. M., & Lynne, H. (1994). *1992—Tuberculosis in correctional facilities.* Cambridge, MA: Abt Associates.

Hammett, T. M., & Moini, S. (1990). *Update on AIDS in prisons and jails.* Cambridge, MA: U.S. Department of Justice.

Hankins, W. E. (1973, July 24 & 25). *Testimony before the Committee on Internal Security of the House of Representatives. Hearings on revolutionary activities directed toward the administration of penal or correctional systems.* Washington, DC: U.S. Government Printing office.

Harland, A. (1992, Summer). Toward the rational assessment of economic sanctions. In National Institute of Corrections (Eds), *Topics in community corrections.* Washington, DC: National Institute of Corrections.

Harlow, C. W. (1992, July). *Drug enforcement and treatment in prisons, 1990.* Washington, DC: U.S. Department of Justice.

Harlow, C. W. (1993). *HIV in U.S. prisons and jails.* Washington, DC: U.S. Department of Justice.

Harlow, C. W. (1994). *Comparing federal and state prison inmates, 1991.* Washington, DC: U.S. Department of Justice.

Hawkins, G. (1976). *The Prison.* Chicago: University of Chicago Press.

Hawkins, G. (1983). Prison labor and prison industries. In M. Tonry & M. Norval (Eds.), *Crime and justice, an annual review of research* (Vol. 5). Chicago, IL: University of Chicago Press.

Hayes, L. M., & Rowan, J. R. (1988). *National study of jail suicides: Seven years later.* Alexandria, VA: National Center on Institutions and Alternatives.

Hecht, F. (1992). Substance abuse program development—A direct supervision approach. *American Jails, 6*(4), 53–55.

Heffernan, E. (1972). *Making it in prison: The square, the cool, and the life.* New York: Wiley.

Henderson, J. D., & Phillips, R. L. (1990, November). *Protective custody management in adult correctional facilities: A discussion of causes, conditions, attitudes and alternatives.* Washington, DC: American Correctional Association.

Hepburn, J. R. (1987). The prison control structure and its effects on work attitudes. *Journal of Criminal Justice, 15,* 49–64.

Hepburn, J. R., & Knepper, P. E. (1993). Correctional officers as human service workers: The effect on job satisfaction. *Justice Quarterly, 10*(2), 315–335.

Herbeck, D. (1993, October 17). Jail aide held in connection with drug scam: Cocaine seized in sting. *The Buffalo News, Section—Local.*

Heuer, G. (1993). Direct supervision. *American Jails, 7*(4), 57–60.

Hills, A., & Karcz, S. (1990, May). Literacy survey. *ASFDCE National Agenda,* pp. 6–7.

Hillsman, S. T., & Greene, J. A. (1988). European "day fines" as method for improving the administration of monetary penalties in American criminal courts. *American Probation and Parole Association Perspectives,* pp. 35–38.

Hillsman, S. T., Mahoney, B., Cole, G. F., & Auchter, B. (1987). Fines as criminal sanctions. Washington, DC: U.S. Department of Justice, National Institute of Justice.

Hippchen, L. J. (1978). Trends in classification philosophy and practice. In L. J. Hippichen (Ed.), *Handbook on correctional classification: Treatment and reintegration.* Washington, DC: American Correctional Association.

Hirliman, I. (1982). *The hate factory.* Agoura, CA: Paisano Publications, Inc.

Hirst, J. B. (1983). *Convict society and its enemies.* Sydney, Australia: George Allen & Unwin.

Holeman, H., & Krepps-Hess, B. J. (1983, January). *Women correctional officers in the California Department of Corrections.* Sacramento, CA: California Department of Corrections.

Holmes, S.A. (1991, September 30, p. A14). Frustrated by federal courts, A.C.L.U. looks to states on individual rights. *The New York Times.* See page 14.

Holmes, S. A. (1994 March 4). As Farrakkan groups land jobs from government, debate grows. *The New York Times,* pp. 1A, 10A.

Holt, K. E. (1981–82). Nine months to life—The law and the pregnant inmate. *Journal of Family Law, 20*(3), 523–543.

Holt, N., & Miller, D. (1972). *Explorations in inmates family relationships.* Sacramento, CA: California Department of Corrections.

Holt, R., & Phillips, R. (1991). Marion: Separating fact from fiction. *Federal Prison Journal, 2*(1), 29–35.

Hopper, C. B. (1969). *Sex in prison: The Mississippi experiment in conjugal visiting.* Baton Rouge, LA: Louisiana State University Press.

Hopper, C. B. (1989). The evolution of conjugal visiting in Mississippi. *The Prison Journal, 66,* 103–109.

Hormachea, C. R. (1981, April). Recreation programming for local jails. *Journal of Physical Education and Recreation, 52*(4), 45–46.

Houston, J. (1995). *Correctional management: Functions, skills and systems.* Chicago: Nelson-Hall Publishers.

Houston, R., & Koch, J. (1993, March). *Work release adjustment: Predicting a headache.* Paper presented at the annual meeting of the Academy of Criminal Justice Sciences, Kansas City, MO.

Howard, J. (1792). *The state of prisons in England and Wales with preliminary observations and an acount of some foreign prisons and hospitals* (4th ed.) London, England: J. Johnson, C. Dilly, and T. Cadell. (Reprinted by Patterson Smith, Monclair, NJ: 1973).

Howser, J., Grossman, J., & MacDonald, D. (1984). Impact of family reunion program on institutional discipline. *Journal of Offender Counseling, Services and Rehabilitation, 8*(1/2), 27–36.

Hubbard, R. L., Marsden, M. E., Rachal, J. V., Harwood, H. J., Cavanaugh, E. R., & Ginzberg, H. M. (1989). *Drug abuse treatment: A national study of effectiveness.* Chapel Hill, NC: University of North Carolina Press.

Huft, A. G., Fawkes, L. S., & Lawson, W. T. (1992). Care of the pregnant offender. *Federal Prisons Journal, 3*(1), 49–53.

Hughes, H. H. (1973, March 29 & May 1). *Testimony before the Committee on Internal Security of the House of Representatives. Hearings on revolutionary activities directed toward the administration of penal or correctional systems.* Washington, DC: U.S. Government Printing Office.

Hughes, R. (1987). *The fatal shore.* New York: Alfred A. Knopf.

Hull, J. D. (1993, August 2). A boy and his gun. *Time,* pp. 20–27.

Hussey, F. A., & Duffee, D. E. (1980). *Probation, parole and community field service: Policy, structure and process.* New York: Harper and Row.

Ibrahim, Y. M. (1989, February 16). Khomeini's judgment: Iranian leader's instruction to kill writer may reflect a calculation rooted in politics. *The New York Times*, pp. 1, 7.

Immarigeon, R., & Chesney-Lind, M. (1990). *Women's prisons: Overcrowded and overused*. A paper presented at the American Society of Criminology, Baltimore, MD.

Inbau, F. E., Thompson, J. R., Zagel, J. B., & Manak, J. P. (1984). *Criminal law and its administration* (4th ed.). Mineola, NY: The Foundation Press.

Independent Research Consortium. (1989). *Current description, evaluation and recommendations for treatment of mentally disordered criminal offenders*. San Francisco, CA: Standard Consulting Corp.

Innes, C. A. (1988, January). *BJS special report: Profile of state prison inmates, 1986*. Washington, DC: U.S. Government Printing Office.

Innes, C. A., & Greenfeld, L. A. (1990, July). *Violent state prisoners and their victims*. Washington, DC: U.S. Department of Justice.

Institute of Medicine, Committee for the Substance Abuse Coverage Study. (1990). *Treating drug problems*. Washington, DC: National Academy Press.

Irwin, J. (1970). *The felon*. Englewood Cliffs, NJ: Prentice Hall.

Irwin, J. (1980). *Prisons in turmoil*. Boston: Little Brown.

Irwin, J. (1985). *The jail: Managing the underclass in American society*. Berkeley, CA: University of California Press.

Irwin, J., & Austin, J. (1994). *It's about time: America's imprisonment binge*. Belmont, CA: Wadsworth Publishing Co.

Irwin, J., & Cressey, D. (1962). Thieves, convicts, and the inmate culture. *Social Problems, 10*, 145–147.

Isele, W. P. (1977). *Legal obligations to the pre-trial detainee*. Chicago, IL: American Medical Association.

Isele, W. P. (1979). Constitutional issues of the prisoner's right to health care. In N. B. Gluckstern, M. A. Neuse, J.K. Harness, R.W. Packard, C. Patmon, & M. Coleman (Eds.), Health care in correctional institutions. (pp. 3–23). Washington, DC: U.S. Department of Justice.

Ives, G. (1970). *A history of penal methods: Criminals, witches, lunatics*. Montclair, NJ: Patterson Smith. (Orginal work published 1914)

Jackson, J. E. (1992, November). *Female and minority officers' attitudes toward treatment programs in the Texas correctional system*. Paper presented at the annual meeting of the American Society of Criminology, San Francisco.

Jacobs, J. B. (1974). Street gangs behind bars. *Social Problems, 21*(3), 395–409.

Jacobs, J. B. (1976). Stratification and conflict among prison inmates. *Journal of law and Criminology, 6*, 476–482.

Jacobs, J. B. (1977). *Stateville: The pentitentiary in mass society*. Chicago: University of Chicago Press.

Jacobs, J. B. (1978). What prison guards think: A profile of the Illinois force. *Crime and Delinquency, 24*, 185–196.

Jacobs, J. B. (1980). The prisoner rights movement and its impact, 1960–1980. In N. Morris & M. Tonry (Eds.), *Crime and justice: An annual review of research* (Vol. 2), Chicago: University of Chicago Press.

Jacobs, J. B., & Kraft, L. S. (1978). Integrating the keepers: A comparison of black and white prison guards in Illinois. *Urban Life, 7*, 304–318.

Jacobs, J. B., & Retsky, H. G. (1975). Prison guards. *Urban Life, 4*, 5–29.

James, G. (1994, December 29). Computer replaces Rabbi's picture. *The New York Times*, p. A15.

James, J. T. L. (1975). The halfway house movement. In G. R. Perlstein & T. R. Phelps (Eds.), *Alternatives to prison: Community based corrections*. Pacific Palisades, CA: Goodyear Publishing Co.

Jankowski, L. (1991). *Probation and parole 1990*. Washington, DC: U.S. Department of Justice, Bureau of Justice Statistics.

Jankowski, L. (1992). *Correctional populations in the United States, 1990*. Washington, DC: U.S. Department of Justice, Bureau of Justice Statistics.

Jemelka, R. P., Rahman, S., & Trupin, E. W. (1993). Prison mental health: An overview. In H. J. Steadman & J. J. Cocozza (Eds.), *Mental illness in America's prisons*. Seattle, WA: National Coalition for the Mentally Ill in the Criminal Justice System.

Jewell, D. L. (1981, February). Behind the leisure eight ball in maximum security. *Parks and Recreation*, pp. 41–45, 77.

Johns, D. R. (1971). Alternatives to conjugal visiting. *Federal Probation, 36*(1), 48–52.

Johnson, C. (1993). Director of Instruction, Windham School District, Texas Department of Criminal Justice. Personal communication.

Johnson, C. (1994). Director of Instruction, Windham School District, Texas Department of Criminal Justice. Personal communication.

Johnson, D. (February 6, 1989). Iowa inmates granted right to read porn. *The Tampa Tribune*, Sec. A, pp. 1, 4.

Johnson, E. L. (1968). *Crime, correction, and society*. Homewood, IL: Dorsey Press.

Johnson, H. A. (1988). *History of criminal justice*. Cincinnati, OH: Anderson Publishing Co.

Johnson, P. M. (1993a). Corrections should take the lead in changing sentencing practices. *Corrections Today, 52*, 54–55, 130–131.

Johnson, R. (1976). *Culture and crisis in confinement*. Lexington, MA: Lexington Books.

Johnson, R. (1987). *Hard time: Understanding and reforming the prison*. Monterey, CA: Brooks/Cole.

Johnson, R. (1990). *Death work: A study of the execution process*. Pacific Grove, CA: Brooks/Cole.

Johnson, R. (1993b, Spring). A history of correctional training: A national perspective. *Journal of Correctional Training,* Spring, pp. 12–17.

Johnson, R., & Dorin, D. (1978). Dysfunctional ideology: The black revolutionary in prison. In D. Szabo & S. Katzenelson (Eds.), *Offenders and corrections.* Lexington, MA: DC Heath.

Johnson, R., & Price, S. (1981). The complete correctional officer: Human service and the human environment of prison. *Criminal Justice and Behavior, 8*(3), 343–373.

Johnson, R., & Toch, H. (1982). *The pains of imprisonment.* Beverly Hills, CA: Sage Publications.

Johnston, N. (1969). Introduction to Crawford, W. Report on the Penitentiaries of the United States. Montclair, NJ: Patterson Smith.

Joint Legislative Committee. (1983). *Laws of Florida, Chapter 83–131.* Tallahassee, FL: State of Florida.

Jones, D. A. (1976). *The health risks of imprisonment.* Lexington, MA: DC Heath.

Jones, S. T. (1992, October). Evaluating correctional officer training: Is it working? *Corrections Compendium,* pp. 1, 4–8.

Jones, W. R. (1989). Mentally ill offenders. *American Jails, 3*(3), 47–56.

Jones-Brown, P. (1992). Most female offenders incarcerated for non-violent drug and alcohol related offenses. *Corrections Compendium, 27*(8), p. 11.

Jorgenson, J. D., Hernandez, S. H., & Warren, R. C. (1986). Addressing the social needs of families of prisoners: A tool for inmate rehabilitation. *Federal Probation, 50,* 47–52.

Jurik, N. C., Halemba, G. J., Musheno, M. C., & Boyce, B. V. (1987). Educational attainment, job satisfaction, and the professionalization of correctional officers. *Work and Occupations, 14*(1), 106–125.

Kahn, B. (1978, June 14). *Prison gangs: A briefing document for the Board of Corrections.* Sacramento, CA: State Board of Corrections.

Kalinich, D. B. (1986). *Power, stability, & contraband: The inmate economy.* Prospect Heights, IL: Waveland Press.

Kalinich, D. B., & Stojkovic, S. (1987). Prison contraband systems: Implications for prison management. *Journal of Crime and Justice, 10*(1), 1–21.

Kalinich, D. B., Stojkovic, S., & and Klofas, J. (1988). Toward a political-community theory of prison organization. *Journal of Criminal Justice, 16,* 217–230.

Kane, T., & Saylor, W. (1983). *Security designation: A validation study.* Washington, DC: U.S. Bureau of Prisons.

Kaplan, J., & Waltz, J. R. (1987). *Evidence: Cases and materials* (6th ed.). Mineola, NY: The Foundation Press.

Karacki, L. (1987, May). *An assessment of the high security operation at USP–Marion, Illinois.* Washington, DC: Federal Bureau of Prisons.

Kassebaum, G. W., Ward, D.A., & Wilner, D.M (1971). *Prison treatment and parole survival: An empirical assessment.* New York: John Wiley & Sons.

Keating, J. M. (1990, Fall). How to work with special masters. *National Prison Project Journal, 5*(4), 1–3.

Keil, T. J., & Vito, G. F. (1991). Kentucky prosecutor's decision to seek the death penalty: A LISREL model. In R. M. Bohm (Ed.), *The death penalty in America: Current research.* Cincinnati, OH: Anderson Publishing Co.

Keller, O. J., & Alper, B. S. (1970). *Halfway houses: Community-centered correction and treatment.* Lexington, MA: Heath Lexington Books.

Kelly, J. A., & Murphy, D. A. (1992). Psychological interventions with AIDS and HIV: Prevention and treatment. *Journal of Consulting and Clinical Psychology, 60,* 576–585.

Kennedy, D. B. (1994). Rethinking the problem of custodial suicide. *American Jails, 7*(6), 41–45.

Kerle, K. (1993). Jails and minorities—An editorial. *American Jails, 7*(2), 5.

King K. (1995). Administrative Assistant to the Assistant Director for Administration, Federal Bureau of Prisons. Personal communication.

Kittrie, N. M., & Zenoff, E. H. (1981). *Sentencing, sanctions and corrections: Law, policy and practice.* Mineola, NY: The Foundation Press.

Klepper, S., & Nagin, D. (1989). Tax compliance and perceptions of the risks of detection and criminal prosecution. *Law and Society, 23,* 209–240.

Klofas, J. M. (1991). Disaggregating jail use: Variety and change in local corrections over a ten year period. In J. A. Thompson & G. L. Mays (Eds.), *American jails: Public policy issues* (pp. 40–58). Chicago: Nelson-Hall Publishers.

Knight, B. B. (1986). *Prisoners' rights in America.* Chicago, IL: Nelson-Hall Publishers.

Knowles, F. (1994, May 17). Sergeant, Hillsborough County Sheriff's Office, Tampa, FL, Detention Division. Personal communication.

Koban, L. A. (1983). Parents in prison: A comparative analysis of the effects of incarceration on the families of men and women. *Research in Law, Deviance and Social Control, 5,* 171–183.

Koeninger, R. C. (1951, April). What about self-mutilation? *Prison World.*

Korn, R. K., & McCorkle, L. W. (1959). *Criminology and penology.* New York: Holt, Rinehart and Winston.

Krajick, K. (1978, March). Profile Texas. *Corrections Magazine,* pp. 5–8, 10–25.

Krajick, K. (1980a, June). At Stateville, the calm is tense. *Corrections Magazine, VI,*(3), 6–9.

Krajick, K. (1980b, June). The menace of the supergangs. *Corrections Magazine, VI*(3), 11–12.

Krantz, S. (1988). *The law of corrections and prisoners' rights in a nutshell* (3rd ed.). St. Paul, MN: West Publishing Co.

Krantz, S., & Branham, L. S. (1991). *The law of sentencing, corrections and prisoners' rights.* (4th ed.). St. Paul, MN: West Publishing Co.

Kratcoski, P. C. (1989, November). *Adjustment of older inmates in long term correctional institutions.* Paper presented at the meeting of the American Society of Criminology, Reno, NV.

Kratcoski, P. C., & Babb, S. (1990). Adjustment of older inmates: An analysis by institutional structures and gender. *Journal of Contemporary Criminal Justice, 6*(3), 139–156.

Kratcoski, P. C., & Pownall, G. A. (1989). Federal Bureau of Prisons programming for older inmates. *Federal Probation, 53*(2), 28–35.

Krauss, C. (1994, November 13). No crystal ball needed on crime. *The New York Times*, Sec. E, p. 4.

Krauth, B., & Smith, R. (1988, October). *An administrator's overview: Questions and answers on issues related to the incarcerated male sex offender.* Washington, DC: U.S. Department of Corrections.

Kruttschnitt, C. (1981). Social status and sentences of female offenders. *Law and Society Review, 15* (2), 247–265.

Kruttschnitt, C. (1982). Respectable women and the law. *Sociological Quarterly, 23*, 221–234.

Kruttschnitt, C. (1984). Sex and criminal court dispositions: The unresolved controversy. *Journal of Research in Crime and Delinquency, 21*(3), 213–232.

Kuether, F. B. (1951). Religion and the chaplain. In P. W. Tappan (Ed.), *Contemporary correction* (pp. 254–265). New York: McGraw-Hill.

Labaton, S. (1993, June 29). Justices restrict ability to seize suspects' goods. *The New York Times*, pp. A1, A8.

Lacayo, R. (1992, March 23). Sentences inscribed on flesh. *Time*, p. 54.

Langan, P. A. (1991, May). *Race of prisoners admitted to state and federal institutions 1926–1986.* Washington, DC: U.S. Department of Justice.

Langan, P. A., & Cunniff, M. A. (1992). *Recidivism of felons on probation, 1986–1989.* Washington, DC: U.S. Department of Justice.

Langan, P. A., & Dawson, J. M. (1993). *Felony sentences in state courts, 1990.* Washington, DC: U.S. Department of Justice, Bureau of Justice Statistics.

Langan, P. A., & Solari, R. (1993). *National Judicial Reporting Program, 1990.* Washington, DC: Bureau of Justice Statistics.

Lange, A. (1986). *Rational-emotive therapy—A treatment manual.* Rockville, MD: National Institute of Mental Health.

Latessa, E., & Allen, H. (1982). Halfway houses and parole: A national assessment. *Journal of Criminal Justice, 10*(2), 153–163.

Laurence, J. (1960). *A history of capital punishment.* New York: The Citadel Press.

Laws, D. R. (1985). *Prevention of relapse in sex offenders.* Washington, DC: National Institute of Mental Health.

Lay, D. P. (1990, October 22). Our justice system, so called. *The New York Times*, p. A19.

Layson, S. K. (1986). United States time-series regressions with adaptive expectations. *Bulletin of the New York Academy of Medicine, 62*, 589–600.

Leflore, L., & Holston, M. A. (1990). Perceived importance of parenting behaviors as reported by inmate mothers: An exploratory study. *Journal of Offender Counseling, Services and Rehabilitation, 14*(1), 5–21.

LeGrande, J. L. (1973). *The basic process of criminal justice.* Beverly Hills, CA: Glencoe.

Leibert, J. A. (1965). *Behind bars: What a chaplain saw in Alcatraz, Folsom and San Quentin.* Garden City, NY: Doubleday and Co.

Leibowitz, M. J. (1991). Regionalization in Virginia.*American Jails, 5*(5), 42–43.

Libstag, K. (1993). Licensed Psychologist, The Vermont treatment program for sexual aggressors. Personal communication.

Libstag, K. (1994). Licensed Psychologist, The Vermont treatment program for sexual aggressors. Personal communication.

Liebow, E. (1967) Tally's corner: A study of Negro streetcorner men. Boston: Little, Brown.

Levinson, M. R. (1982). Special masters: Engineers of court ordered reform. *Corrections Magazine, 7*(4), 7–18.

Levinson, R. (1980, September). Security designation system: Preliminary results. *Federal Probation*, 26–30.

Levinson, R. B., & Gerard, R. E. (1986, July). Classifying institutions. *Crime and Delinquency, 32*(3), 272–290.

Levinson, R., & Williams, J. (1979, March). Inmate classification: Security/custody considerations. *Federal Probation*, 37–43.

Lewis, O. L. (1996). *The development of American prisons and prison customs, 1776–1845.* Montclair, NJ: Patterson Smith. (Original work published 1922)

Likert, R. (1961). *New patterns of management.* New York: McGraw-Hill.

Lillis, J. (1993a, November). Incarcerated sex offenders total nearly 100,000. *Corrections Compendium, 28*(11), pp. 7–16.

Lillis, J. (1993b, November). Family visitation evolves. *Corrections Compendium, 28*(11), pp. 1–4.

Lillis, J. (1993c, July). Survey: Corrections training budget approaches $57 million. Corrections Compendium, 28(7), pp. 4, 15.

Lillis, J. (1994a, July). Sentencing guidelines determine penalties in 19 systems: Survey summary. *Corrections Compendium, 29*(7), pp. 7–14.

Lillis, J. (1994b, June). Prison escapes and violence remain down. *Corrections Compendium, 29*(6), pp. 6–21.

Lillis, J. (1994c, January). Female inmates: A current overview. *Corrections Compendium, 29*(1), pp. 6–13.

Lillis, J. (1994d, February). Programs and services for female inmates. *Corrections Compendium, 29*(2), pp. 6–13.

Lillis, J. (1994e, March). Education in U.S. prisons: Part one. *Corrections Compendium, 29*(3), pp. 5–6.

Lillis, J. (1994f, March). Education in U.S. prisons: Part two. *Corrections Compendium, 29*(3), pp. 10–16.

Lilly, J. R., Ball, R., & Wright, J. (1987). Home incarceration with electronic monitoring in Kenton County,

Kentucky: An evaluation. In B. McCarthy (Ed.), *Intermediate punishments: Intensive supervision, home confinement and electronic surveillance*. Monsey, NY: Criminal Justice Press.

Lincoln, C. E. (1973). *The Black Muslims in America*. Chicago, IL: University of Chicago Press.

Linder, C. L., & Savarese, M. (1984, June). The evolution of probation. *Federal Probation, 48*(2), 3–10.

Lindsey, R. (1986, June 28). Bingham cleared in 1971 shootout. *The New York Times*, pp. 1, 8.

Lipson, S. (1990, December). Aging inmates: The challenge for corrections. In Federal Bureau of Prisons, *Long term confinement and the aging inmate population* (pp. 47–49). Washington, DC: Federal Bureau of Prisons.

Lipton, D. S. (1994). The correctional opportunity: Pathways to drug treatment for offenders. *Journal of Drug Issues, 24* (1–2), 331–348.

LIS, Inc. (1991, September). Smoke-free jails: Collected resources. Boulder, Colorado: U.S. Department of Justice, National Institute of Corrections.

LIS, Inc. (1995). *Offenders under age 18 in state correctional systems: A national picture*. Longmont, CO: U.S. Department of Justice, National Institute of Corrections Information Center.

Lockwood, D. (1980). *Prison sexual violence*. New York: Elsevier.

Lombardo, L. X. (1981). *Guards imprisoned: Correctional officers at work*. New York: Elsevier.

Lombardo, L. X. (1989). *Guards imprisoned: Correctional officers at work* (2nd ed.). Cincinnati, OH: Anderson Publishing Co.

London, R. (1991, February 8). Strategy on sex crimes is prison, then prison. *The New York Times*, Law, p. 16.

Lopez, M., & Chayriques, K. (1994). Billing prisoners for medical care blocks access. National Prison Project Journal, 9(2), 1–2.

Lopez, M., & Cheney, C. (1992, Summer). Crowded prisons and jails unable to meet needs of mentally ill. *National Prison Project Journal, 8*(3), 15–16.

Low, P. W., Jeffries, J. C., Jr., & Bonnie, R. J. (1986). *Criminal law: Cases and materials* (2nd ed.). Mineola, NY: The Foundation Press.

Luise, M. A. (1989). Solitary confinement: Legal and psychological considerations. *New England Journal on Criminal and Civil Confinement, 15*(2), 301–324.

Lurgio, A. (1990). Intensive probation supervision: An alternative to prison in the 1980s. *Crime and Delinquency, 36*(1), 3–6.

MacDonald, D. (1980, May). *Follow-up survey of post-release criminal behavior of participants in family reunion program*. Albany, NY: New York Department of Correctional Services.

MacDonald, D., & Bala, G. (1986, March). *Follow-up study sample of family reunion participants*. Albany, NY: New York Department of Correctional Services.

MacDonald, J., & Gifford, R. (1989). Territorial cues and defensible space theory: The burglar's point of view. *Journal of Environmental Psychology, 9*, 193–205.

Mackay, D. (1985). *A place of exile: The European settlement of New South Wales*. Melbourne: Oxford University Press.

MacKenzie, D. L. (1993, November). Boot camp prisons in 1993. *National Institute of Justice Journal*, 21–28.

MacKenzie, D. L, Shaw, J., & Gowdy, V. (1993). *An evaluation of shock incarceration in Louisiana*. Washington, DC: National Institute of Justice.

MacKenzie, D. L., & Souryal, C. (1994, November). *Multisite evaluation of shock incarceration*. Washington, DC: National Institute of Justice.

Maghan, J. (1981). Guarding in prison. In D. Fogel, & J. Hudson (Eds,.) Justice as Fairness. Cincinnati, OH: Anderson Publishing Co.

Maghan, J. (1994, July). Measuring training. *Corrections Compendium*, pp. 1–3.

Maghan, J. (1994, September 30). Vice President, International Association of Correctional Officers. Personal communication.

Maguire, M., Pastore, A. L., & Flanagan, T. L. (1993). *Sourcebook of criminal justice statistics, 1992*. Washington, DC: U.S. Department of Justice.

Maguire, M., & Pastore, A. L. (1994). *Sourcebook of criminal justice statistics, 1993*. Washington, DC: U.S. Department of Justice.

Mair, G. (1988). *Probation day centres*. London, England: HMSO Books.

Malcolm, A. H. (1989, May 3). Tainted trials stir fears of wrongful executions. *The New York Times*, p. 9.

Malcolm X (1965). *The autobiography of Malcolm X*. New York: Grove Press.

Maltz, M. D. (1984). *Recidivism*. Orlando, FL: Academic Press.

Mann, C. (1984). *Female crime and delinquency*. Birmingham, AL: University of Alabama Press.

Marble, G. (1988, June). Chaplain ministers to Texas death row. *Corrections Today*, pp. 96–97.

March, J. (1995, Sept. 11). Public Affairs Officer, Washington Attorney General's Office. Personal communication.

Marchese, J. D. (1990). Emergency preparedness planning for jail officers. *Jail Operations Bulletin, 2*(9).

Marke, J.J. (1988). Prisoner's right of access to law libraries. *New York Law Journal, 200*(118), 4–5.

Markley, C. W. (1973). Furlough programs and conjugal visiting in adult correctional institutions. *Federal Probation, 37*(1), 19–26.

Markman, S., & Cassell, P. (1988). Protecting the innocent: A response to the Bedaau-Radalet study. *Stanford Law Review, 41*, 121–170.

Marlette, M. (1990a). An essential part of corrections: Drug treatment programs for inmates. *Corrections Compendium, 15*(6), pp. 1, 5–20.

Marlette, M. (1990b). Furloughs tightened—Success rates high. *Corrections Compendium, 15*(1), pp. 1, 6–8.

Marquart, J. W. (1986). Prison guards and the use of physical coercion as a mechanism of prisoner control. *Criminology, 24*(4), 347–366.

Marquart, J. W. (1990). Prison guards and the use of physical coercion as a mechanism of prisoner control. In D. H. Kelly (Ed.), *Criminal behavior: Text and readings in criminology* (2nd ed., pp. 528–544). New York: St. Martin's Press.

Marquart, J. W., & Crouch, B. M. (1984). Coopting the kept: Using inmates for social control in a southern prison. *Justice Quarterly, 1*(4), 491–509.

Marques, J. K., Day, D. M., Nelson, C., & Miner, M. H. (1989). *The sex offender treatment and evaluation project.* Sacramento, CA: Department of Mental Health.

Marriott, M. (1994, March 5). 'Manhood' classes at Mosque: Hope, discipline and defiance. *The New York Times*, pp. 1A, 8A.

Marshall, I. H., & Horney, J. (1991). *Motives for crime and self-image among a sample of convicted felons.* Paper presented at the annual meeting of the American Society of Criminology, San Francisco.

Marshall, W. L., Jones, R., Ward, T., & Johnson, P. (1991). Treatment outcome with sex offenders. *Clinical Psychology Review, 11*, 465–485.

Martin, R., & Zimmerman, S. (1990, December). A typology of the causes of prison riots and an analytical extension to the 1986 West Virginia riot. *Justice Quarterly, 7*(4), 711–738.

Martin, S. J., & Eckland-Olson, S. (1987). *Texas prisons: The walls came tumbling down.* Austin, TX: Texas Monthly Press.

Martinez, R., & Wetli, C. V. (1982). Santeria: A magico-religious system of Afro-Cuban origin. *The American Journal of Social Psychiatry II, 3*(Summer), 32–38.

Martinson, R. (1975). What works?—Questions and answers about prison reform. *Public Interest, 35*, 22–54.

Maslach, C. (1982). *Burnout: The cost of caring.* Englewood Cliffs, NJ: Prentice Hall.

Maslach, C., & Jackson, S. E. (1981). The measurement of experienced burnout. *Journal of Occupational Behavior, 2*, 99–113.

Mason, G. L. (1990). Indeterminate sentencing: Cruel and unusual punishment, or just plain cruel. *New England Journal on Criminal and Civil Confinement, 16*(1), 89–120.

Mauer, M. (1994, July) "3 Strikes and You're Out." *Corrections Compendium*, pp. 15–16.

Mayer, C. (1986). Legal issues surrounding private operation of prisons. *Criminal Law Bulletin*, pp. 309–325.

Mayer, C. (1989). Survey of case law establishing constitutional minima for the provision of mental health services to psychiatrically involved inmates. New

England Journal of Criminal and Civil Confinement, 15(2), pp. 243–275.

Mays, G. L., Fields, C. B., & Thompson, J. A. (1991). Preincarceration patterns of drug and alcohol use by jail inmates. *Criminal Justice Policy Review, 5*(1), 30–52.

McCall, G. (1981, April). Leisure restructuring. *Journal of physical education and recreation, 52*(4), 38–39.

McCall, G. (1988, December). The history of the NCRA 1966 through 1988 22 years of growth. *Correctional Recreation Today, 3*(4), 9–10.

McCall, G. (1993, December). Associate Professor, Department of Recreation, University of Florida. Personal communication.

McCarthy, B. (1985, March). Mentally ill and mentally retarded offenders in corrections. In New York State Department of Corrections (Ed.), *Source book on the mentally disordered prisoner* (pp 13–30). Washington DC: National Institute of Corrections.

McCarthy, B. R., & McCarthy, B. J. (1991). *Community based corrections* (2nd ed.). Pacific Grove, CA: Brooks/Cole.

McCartt, J., & Mangogna, T. (1973). *Guidelines and standards for halfway houses and community treatment centers.* Washington, DC: U.S. Government Printing Office.

McCollum, S. G. (1992). Mandatory literacy: Evaluating the Bureau of Prisons' long standing commitment. *Federal Prisons Journal, 3*(2), 33–36.

McConville, S. (1985, October). *Prison gangs.* Symposium conducted at the annual meeting of the Midwestern Criminal Justice Association, Chicago.

McDonald, D. C. (1992). Introduction: The day fine as a means of expanding judges' sentencing options. In D. C. McDonald (Ed.), *Day fines in American courts: The Staten Island and Milwaukee experiments.* Washington, DC: U.S. Department of Justice, Office of Justice Programs.

McEntee, G. W. (1993, July). President's column. *AFSCME Public Employee, 58*(5), 3.

McFarland, S. G. (1983). Is capital punishment a short term deterrent to homicide? A study of the effects of four recent American executions. *Journal of Criminal Law and Criminology, 74*, 1014–1032.

McGaha, J., Fichter, M., & Hirschburg, P. (1987). Felony probation: A reexamination of public risk. *American Journal of Criminal Justice, 11*, 1–9.

McGinnis, K. L. (1990) Programming for long-term inmates. *Prison Journal, 70*(1), 119–120.

McGrath, R. J., & Carey, C. H. (1987). Treatment of men who molest children—A program description. *Journal of Offender Counseling, 7*(2), 23–33.

McGregor, D. (1960). *The human side of enterprise.* New York: McGraw-Hill.

McKelvey, B. (1977). *American prisons: A history of good intentions.* Montclair, NJ: Patterson Smith.

McMillian, T. (1985). Habeas Corpus and the Burger court. In I.P. Robbins (Ed.), *Prisoners and the law.* New York: Clark Boardman Co.

McShane, M. D., & Krause, W. (1993). Community Corrections. New York: MacMillan Publishing Co.

McShane, M. D., Williams, F. P., & Wagoner, C. P. (1992, January). Prison impact studies: Comments on methodological rigor. *Journal of Crime and Delinquency, 38*(1), 105–120.

Megargee, E. I. (1971). Population density and disruptive behavior in a prison setting. In A. Cohen, G. Cole, & R. Bailey (Eds.), *Prison violence.* Lexington, MA: DC Heath.

Meier, K. J. (1987). *Politics and the bureaucracy.* Monterey, CA: Brooks/Cole.

Millard, P. (1988, July). Inside Marion: Warden Gary Hennan talks about BOP's most secure prison. *Corrections Today,* pp. 92–94, 96–98.

Miller, F. W., Dawson, R. O., Dix, G. E., & Parnas, R. I. (1976). *Criminal justice administration.* Mineola, NY: The Foundation Press.

Miller, N., & Grieser, R. C. (1986). The evolution of prison industries. In American Correctional Association (Eds.), *A study of prison industry: History, components, and goals.* Washington, DC: National Institute of Corrections.

Miller, S., Dinitz, S., & Conrad, J. P. (1982). *Careers of the violent few: The dangerous offender and criminal justice.* Lexington, MA: Lexington Books.

Minnesota Statutes. (1993). Criminal sentences, conditions, duration, appeals: Supervised release term. *Minnesota Statutes 244.05,* St. Paul, MN.

Mitsubishi Electronics Inc. (1990). The comprehensive tools for breath alcohol monitoring in home detention programs. Sunnyvale, CA Author.

Modlin, B. (1991, Fall). Naked men and uniformed women: The erotic element in cross gender supervision. *Odyssey,* pp. 67–78.

Moore, J. W. (1978). *Homeboys: Gangs, drugs, and prison in the barrios of Los Angeles.* Philadelphia: Temple University Press.

Moos, M. C. (1942). *State penal administration in Alabama.* Tuscaloosa, AL: Bureau of Public Administration, University of Alabama.

Morain, D. (1986, September 26). Inmate convicted in prison killings gets retrial. Los Angeles Times, Part 1, p. 3.

Morgenbesser, L. (1984). Psychological screening mandated for New York correctional officer applicants. *Corrections Today, 46,* 28–29.

Moriarty, D. (1991). Jail training—Preparing officers for today's inmates. *Corrections Today, 53*(7), 72–75.

Morris, D. W. (1974). The univerity's role in prison education. In A. Roberts (Ed.), *Readings in prison education.* Springfield IL: Charles C. Thomas.

Morris, N., & Tonry, M. (1990). *Between prison and probation: Intermediate punishments in a rational sentencing system.* Oxford, England: Oxford University Press.

Morse, W. (Ed.) (1940). *The attorney general's survey of release procedures.* Washington, DC: U.S. Government Printing Office.

Morton, J. B. (1992a, August). *An administrative view of the older inmate.* Washington, DC: National Institute of Corrections.

Morton, J. B. (1992b, August). Women in corrections: Looking back on 200 years of valuable contributions. *Corrections Today,* pp. 76–87.

Moses, M. C. (1993, August). Girl scouts behind bars: New program at women's prison benefits mothers and children. *Corrections Today,* pp. 132–135.

Mouzakitis, C. M. (1981). Inquiring into the problem of child abuse and juvenile delinquency. In R. J. Hummer & Y. E. Walker (Eds.), *Exploring the relationship between child abuse and delinquency.* Montclair, NJ: Allanheld.

Moynahan, J. (1992). An American gaoler in London: A self guided tour American gaolers may take of gaol-related pubs in and around the central London district. *American Jails, 6*(4), 79–86.

Mullen, R. (1991, September). Therapeutic communities in prison: Dealing with toxic waste. *Proceedings for the 14th World Conference on Therapeutic Communities.*

Muraskin, R. (1989). *Disparity of correctional treatment: Development of a measurement instrument.* Unpublished doctoral dissertation, City University of New York.

Murphy, S. P. (1992, June 30). Weld proposal on sex criminals will be challenged, lawyers say. *The Boston Globe,* pp. 17–18.

Murphy, W. D., & Von Minden, S. (1981, April). Hard time and free time. *Journal of Physical Education and Recreation, 52*(4), 50–52.

Murray, C., & Cox, L. (1979). *Beyond probation: Corrections and the chronic delinquent.* Beverly Hills, CA: Sage Publications.

Murton, T., & Hyams J. (1969). *Accomplices to the crime: The Arkansas prison scandal.* New York: Grove Press.

Mushlin, M. (1993). *Rights of prisoners* (2nd ed.). Colorado Springs, CO: Shepard's/McGraw-Hill.

Mustin, J. W., & Bee, C. W. (1992). *Directory of programs serving families of adult offenders.* Washington, DC: U.S. Department of Justice.

Nacci, P. L., & Kane, T. R. (1983, December). The incidence of sex and sexual aggression in federal prisons. *Federal Probation, 47*(4), 31–36.

Nacci, P. L., & Kane, T. R. (1984, March). Sex and sexual aggression in federal prisons: Inmate involvment and employee impact. *Federal Probation, 48*(1), 46–53.

Nadel, B. (1993, July). Architectural group addresses state's TB problem. *CorrectCare, 7*(3), 4.

Nagel, W. G. (1973). *The new red barn: A critical look at the modern American prison.* New York: Walker and Co.

Nathan V.M. (1978). The use of masters in institutional litigation. *The University of Toledo Law Review, 10,* 419–464.

National Advisory Commission on Civil Disorders. (1968). *Report.* New York: Bantam Books.

National Commission on Correctional Health Care. (1992). *Standards for health services in prisons.* Chicago: Author.

National Correctional Recreation Association. (undated). *National mission statement, policy statement, personnel standards, facility standards for correctional recreation.* Author.

National Institute of Corrections. (1981). *Prison classification: A model systems approach.* Washington, DC: Department of Justice.

National Institute of Corrections. (1983, May). *Handbook for special masters: Judicial version.* Washington, DC: U.S. Department of Justice.

National Institute of Corrections. (1987, July). *Guidelines for the development of a security program.* Washington, DC: U.S. Department of Justice.

National Institute of Corrections. (1991). *Management strategies in disturbances and with gangs/disruptive groups.* Washington, DC: U.S. Department of Justice.

National Prison Project Journal. (1994/95, Winter). Status Report: State prisons and the courts January 1. 1995. Author, 10(1), p. 5.

Nelson, C. (1974). *A study of homosexuality among women inmates at two state prisons.* Ph.D. dissertation, Temple University, Philadelphia.

Nelson, E. K., Ohmart, H., & Harlow, N. (1978). Promising Strategies in Probation and Parole. Washington, D. C.: U. S. Government Printing Office.

Nelson, R. W. (1988). The origins of the podular direct supervision concept: An eyewitness account. *American Jails, 2*(1), 8–16.

Nelson, V. F. (1933). *Prison days and nights.* Garden City, NY: Garden City Publishing Co.

Nesbit, C. A. (1992). The female offender: Overview of facility planning and design issues and considerations. *Corrections Compendium, 27*(8), 1, 5–7.

Neto, V. V. (1989). Prison visitors: A profile. In J. Mustin & B. Bloom (Conference Directors), *The First National Conference on the Family and Corrections* (pp. 33–39). Richmond, KY: Training Resource Center, Department of Correctional Services, Eastern Kentucky University.

Neto, V., & Banier, L. M. (1983). Mother and wife locked up: A day with the family. *The Prison Journal, 63*(2), 124–141.

New York State Department of Correctional Services. (1988, April). Grandmas' key helpers at Arthur Kill. In *Inmate family service programs* (pp. 14, 22). Albany, NY: Author.

New York State Department of Correctional Services. (1993, October). *Bedford Hills Correctional Facility Children's Center fact sheet.* Bedford Hills, NY: Author.

New York State Department of Correctional Services & New York Division of Parole. (1995). *Seventh annual shock legislative report.* Albany, NY: Author.

New York State Special Commission on Attica (1972). *Official Report.* New York: Bantam Books.

Newman, D. J. (1975). *Introduction to criminal justice.* Philadelphia: J. B. Lippincott Co.

Newman, G. (1978). *The punishment response.* New York: J. B. Lippincott Co.

Nicolai, S. (1981, April). Rehabilitation and leisure in prisons. *Journal of Physical Education and Recreation, 52*(4), 33–35.

Ninth Circuit Gender Bias Task Force. (1993, July). *The final report of the 9th Circuit Gender Bias Task Force.*

Northham, G. (1985, April). America's new generation prisons: Can we learn any lessons from death row? *The Listener,* pp. 5–7.

Nossiter, A. (1994, September 17). Making hard time harder, states cut jail TV and sports. *The New York Times,* pp. 1a, 10a.

Nunnellee, D. (1994, November 12). Public Information Officer, Texas Department of Criminal Justice. Personal communication.

Office of National Drug Control Policy. (1990). *Understanding drug treatment.* Washington, DC: The White House.

Ohlin, L. E. (1951). *Selection for parole.* New York: Russell Sage Foundation.

Oppenheimer, H. (1975). *The rationale of punishment.* Montclair, NJ: Patterson Smith. (Original work published 1913).

Owen, B. (1985). Race and gender relations among prison workers. *Crime and Delinquency, 31,* 147–159.

Palm Beach County Sheriff's Office. (1987). Palm Beach County's in-house arrest work release program. In B. McCarthy (Ed.), *Intermediate punishments: Intensive supervision, home confinement and electronic surveillance.* Monsey, NY: Criminal Justice Press.

Palmer, J. W. (1977). *Constitutional rights of prisoners.* Cincinnati, OH: Anderson Publishing Co.

Palmer, J. W. (1991). *Constitutional rights of prisoners.* Cincinnati, OH: Anderson Publishing Co.

Palmer, T. (1978). *Correctional intervention and research.* Lexington, MA: Lexington Books.

Palmer, T. (1992). *The re-emergence of correctional intervention.* Newbury Park, CA: Sage Publications.

Parent, D. G. (1989). *Shock incarceration: An overview of existing programs.* Washington, DC: U.S. Department of Justice.

Parent, D. G. (1990a, May). *Residential community corrections: Developing an integrated policy*. Washington, DC: U.S. Department of Justice.

Parent, D. G. (1990b, September). *Day reporting centers for criminal offenders: A descriptive analysis of existing programs*. Washington, DC: U.S. Department of Justice.

Parent, D. G. (1990c). *Recovering correctional costs through offender fees*. Wahington, DC: U.S. Department of Justice.

Parent, D. G., Wentworth, D., Burke, P., & Ney, B. (1994). *Responding to probation and parole violators*. Washington, DC: U.S. Department of Justice.

Parker, W. (1975). *Parole*. College Park, MD: American Correctional Association.

Parry, L. A. (1975). *The history of torture in England*. Montclair, NJ: Patterson Smith. (original work published 1934.)

Parsonage, W. H. (1990). *Worker safety in probation and parole*. Longmont, CO: National Institute of Corrections.

Paternoster, R. (1991). Prosecutorial discretion and capital sentencing in North and South Carolina. In R. M. Bohm (Ed.), *The death penalty in America: Current research*. Cincinnati, OH: Anderson Publishing Co.

Patrick, A. L. (1986). Private sector—Profit motive vs. quality. *Corrections Today, 48*(2), 68–71.

Patrick, W. J. (1994, January 21). Senior Deputy Director for Administration, Federal Bureau of Prisons. Personal communication.

Pearson, F. (1987). Taking quality into account: Assessing the benefits and costs of New Jersey's intensive supervision program. In B. McCarthy (Ed.), *Intermediate punishments: Intensive supervision, home confinement and electronic surveillance*. Monsey, NY: Criminal Justice Press.

Pearson, F., & Harper, A. (1990). Contingent intermediate sanctions: New Jersey's intensive supervision program. *Crime and Delinquency, 36*(1), 75–85.

Peed, C. (1989). Inmate classification procedures. *Jail Operations Bulletin, 1*(6),

Peltz, M. E. (1986, March). *When brotherhood leads to violence: Managing inmate gangs in the Texas prison system*. Paper presented at the annual meeting of the Southwestern Sociology Association, San Antonio, TX.

Perkins, C. (1992). *National corrections reporting program, 1986*. Washington, DC: U.S. Department of Justice.

Perkins, C. (1993). *National corrections reporting program, 1990*. Washington, DC: U.S. Department of Justice.

Perkins, C. (1994, Feb.). *National corrections reporting program, 1991*. Washington, DC: U.S. Department of Justice.

Perkins, C. (1994, October). *National corrections reporting program, 1992*. Washington, D.C.: U. S. Department of Justice.

Perkins, C. A., Stephan, J. J., & Beck, A. J. (1995, April). *Jails and jail inmates 1993–94*. Washington, DC: Bureau of Justice Statistics.

Peters, H. A. (1993, November 1). Caution on prison religious freedom. *Chicago Tribune*, p. 18.

Peters, R. H. (1993). Drug treatment in jails and detention settings. In J. Inciardi (Ed.), *Drug treatment and criminal justice* (pp. 44–80). Newbury Park, CA: Sage Publications.

Peters, R., Kearns, W. D., Murin, M., & Dolante, D. (1992). Effectiveness of in-jail substance abuse treatment: Evaluation results from a national demonstration program. *American Jails, 6*(1), 98–104.

Petersilia, J. (1983). *Racial disparities in the criminal justice system*. Santa Monica, CA: The Rand Corp.

Petersilia, J. (1987). *Expanding options for criminal sentencing*. Santa Monica, CA: Rand Corp.

Petersilia, J. (1988). *House arrest: Crime file study guide*. Washington, DC: U.S. Department of Justice, National Institute of Justice.

Petersilia, J. (1990). Conditions that permit intensive supervision to survive. *Crime and Delinquency, 36*(1), 126–145.

Petersilia, J., Greenwood, P., & Lavin, M. (1978). *Criminal careers of habitual felons*. Washington, DC: U.S. Department of Justice, National Institute of Law Enforcement and Criminal Justice.

Petersilia, J., Honig, P., & Hubay, C. (1980). *Prison experience of career criminals*. Washington, DC: National Institute of Justice.

Petersilia, J., & Turner, S. (1988, June). Research perspectives—Minorities in prison. *Corrections Today, 50*(3), 92–95.

Petersilia, J., & Turner, S. (1990). Comparing intensive and regular supervision for high-risk probationers: Early results from an experiment in California. *Crime and Delinquency, 36*(1), 87–111.

Petersilia, J., & Turner, S. (1993). *Evaluating intensive supervision Probation/parole: Results of a nationwide experiment*. Washington, DC: U.S. Department of Justice.

Petersilia, J., Turner, S., Kahan, J., & Peterson, J. (1985). *Granting felons probation: Public risks and alternatives*. Santa Monica, CA: Rand Corporation.

Petersilia, J., Turner, S., & Peterson, J. (1986). *Prison versus probation in California: Implications for crime and offender recidivism*. Santa Monica, CA: Rand Corporation.

Peterson, R. D., & Bailey, W. C. (1991). Felony murder and capital punishment. *Criminology, 29*, 367–395.

Pettigrove, F. G. (1910). State prisons of the United States under separate and congregate systems. In C. R. Henderson (Ed.), *Penal and reformatory institutions*. New York: Russell Sage Foundation.

Philliber, S. (1987. Thy brother's keeper: A review of the literature on correctional officers. *Justice Quarterly, 4*, pp. 9–37.

Pike, L. O. (1968). *A history of crime in England, illustrating the changes of the laws in the progress of civilization*. (Vols. 1–2). Montclair, NJ: Patterson Smith. (Original work published 1873–76)

Pisciotta, A. W. (1983, October). Scientific reform: The 'new penology' at Elimira, 1876–1900. *Crime & Delinquency, 29*(4), 613–630.

Pollack, R. (1979). The ABCs of prison education. *Corrections Magazine, 5*(3), 60–66.

Pollock, J. (1986). *Sex and supervision: Guarding male and female inmates.* New York: Greenwood Press.

Pollock-Byrne, J. (1990). *Women, prison and crime.* Pacific Grove, CA: Brooks/Cole.

Pompi, K., & Resnick, J. (1987). Retention in a therapeutic community for court referred adolescents and young adults. *American Journal of Drug and Alcohol Abuse, 13*(3), 309–326.

Poole, E., & Regoli, R. M. (1980). Work relations and cynicism among prison guards. *Criminal Justice and Behavior, 7*, 303–314.

Porporino, F. J. (1990). Difference in response to long-term imprisonment: Implications for the management of long-term offenders. *The Prison Journal, 70*(1), 35–44.

Porter, B. (1982, December). California Prison gangs: The price of control. *Corrections Magazine, VIII*(6), 6–19.

Porter, R. F., & Porter, J. G. (1984). Survey of attitudes of incarcerated felons on dropping out of public schools. *Journal of Correctional Education, 35*, 80–82.

Pospichal, T. (1991). Division Manager, UNICOR, Plans and Policies, Federal Bureau of Prisons, Personal communication.

Potter, J. (1979, Sept.). Guards' unions: The search for solidarity. *Corrections Magazine, 5*, pp. 25–35.

Potter, J. (1980, Sept.). Should women guards work in prisons for men? *Corrections Magazine, 6*, pp. 30–38.

Powell, J. C. (1970). *The American Siberia or fourteen years experience in a southern convict camp.* Montclair, NJ: Patterson Smith. (Original work published 1891)

Powell, R. L. (1993). City shock—Corrections XXI. *American Jails, 7*(5), 9–13.

Powers, E. (1959, July–August). Halfway houses: A historical perspective. *American Journal of Correction, 21*(4), 20–22, 35.

President's Commission on Organized Crime. (1986, April). *The impact: organized crime today.* Washington, DC: U.S. Government Printing Office.

Prettyman, E. B. (1981). The indeterminate sentence and the right to treatment. In D. Fogel & J. Hudson (Eds.), *Justice as fairness: Perspectives on the justice model.* Cincinnati, OH: Anderson Publishing Co.

Prison guard gets 55 months in contraband caper. (1992, October 30). United Press International.

Program Services Office. (1983). *Probation classification and service delivery approach.* Los Angeles, CA: Los Angeles County Probation Department.

Project. (1991). Twentieth annual review of criminal procedure: United States Supreme Court and Courts of Appeals 1989–1990, Part VI: Prisoners' rights. *Georgetown Law Journal, 79*(4), 1253–1305.

Project. (1992). Twenty-first annual review of criminal procedure: United States Supreme Court and Courts of Appeals 1990–1991, Part VI: Prisoners' rights. *Georgetown Law Journal, 80*(4), 1677–1734.

Project. (1994). Twenty-third annual review of criminal procedure: United States Supreme Court and Courts of Appeal 1992–1993, Part VI: Prisoners' rights. *Georgetown Law Review, 82*(3), 1365–1419.

Propper, A. (1976). *Importation and deprivation perspectives on homosexuality in correctional institutions: An empirical test of their relative efficacy.* Ph.D. dissertation, University of Michigan, Ann Arbor.

Propper, A. (1982). Make believe families and homosexuality among imprisoned girls. *Criminology, 20*(1), 127–139.

Protests force sex offender to move. (1993, July 20). *The New York Times*, p. 8.

Prout, C., & Ross, R. N. (1988). *Care and punishment: The dilemmas of prison medicine.* Pittsburgh, PA: University of Pittsburgh Press.

Public Health Service. (1976). Community-based correctional programs. In R. Carter and L. Wilkins (Ed.), *Probation, parole and community corrections.* New York: John Wiley and Sons.

Public whipping proposed. (1989, January 29). *Tampa Tribune*, p. 2A.

Pugh, R. B. (1968). *Imprisonment in medieval England.* London: Cambridge University Press.

Quinlan, J. M. (1990, December). Welcome. In Federal Bureau of Prisons, *Long term confinement and the aging inmate population* (pp. 7–8). Washington, DC: Federal Bureau of Prisons.

Quinlan, J. M. (1993, December). News of the future: Carving out new territory for American corrections. *Federal Probation, 57*(4), 59–63.

Rachin, R. (1972). So you want to open a halfway house. *Federal Probation, 36*(1), 30–37.

Radelet, M. L., Bedau, H. A., & Putnam, C. E. (1992). *In spite of innocence: Erroneous convictions in capital cases.* Boston: Northeastern University Press.

Rae-Dupree, J. (1991, Dec. 13). He's putting his faith behind bars. *Los Angeles Times*, Sec. B, p. 3.

Rafter, N. H. (1985). *Partial justice: State prisons and their inmates, 1800–1935.* Boston, MA: Northeastern University Press.

Rafter, N. H. (1990). *Partial justice: Women, prisons and social control* (2nd ed.). New Brunswick, NJ: Transaction Publishers.

Rafter, N. H., & Stanko, E. A. (1982). *Judge, lawyer, victim, thief: Women, gender roles and criminal justice.* Boston: Northeastern University Press.

Randall, C. (1994). Director, Prison Industries, California Youth Authority. Personal communication.

Reed, S. O. (1993). The plight of jail deputies in a sheriff's office. *Sheriff, 48*(1), 10–13.

Reform. (1988). Major outcome study of "Stay'n Out. *Reform - National Program to Develop Comprehensive Prison Drug Treatment*, 1(3), p. 1, 11.

Renzema, M., & Skelton, D. (1990). *Final report: The use of electronic monitoring by criminal justice agencies, 1989.* Washington, DC: U.S. Department of Justice.

Reuters Limited. (1994, March 1). *Florida politicians mull castration for rapists.* Tallahassee, FL: Author.

Reynolds, M. O. (1992, December). *Why does crime pay?* Dallas, TX: National Center for Policy Analysis.

Rice, M., Harris, G., Varney, G., & Quinsey, B. (1989). *Violence in institutions: Understanding, prevention and control.* Toronto, Canada: Aogrefe and Huber.

Rickards, C. (1968). *The man from devil's island.* New York: Stein and Day.

Rifkin, M. (1995). Farmer v. Brennan: Spotlight on an obvious risk of rape in a hidden world. *Columbia Human Rights Law Review* 26(2), 273–307.

Riggs, C. (1989, Fall). Chaplaincy in the 1990s: A changing calling. *Federal Prisons Journal*, pp. 4–6.

Rinehart, E. (1990, May 16). Budget cuts may threaten programs to educate inmates. *The Tampa Tribune*, Sec. A, pp. 1, 13.

Robinson, J., Wilkins, L. T., Carter, R. M., & Wahl, A. (1969). *The San Francisco project: A study of federal probation and parole.* Berkley, CA: University of California, School of Criminology.

Robitscher, J. (1980). *The power of psychiatry.* Boston, MA: Houghton Mifflin.

Roehl, J., & Ray, L. (1986, July). *Toward the multi-door courthouse—Dispute resolution intake and referral.* Washington, DC: U.S. Department of Justice, National Institute of Justice.

Rolph, J.E., & Chaiken, J. M. (1987). *Identifying high-rate serious criminals from official records.* Washington, DC: U.S. Department of Justice.

Rosazza, T. (1993, Summer/Fall). Career development: The new frontier. *The Journal of Correctional Training*, pp. 10–11.

Rosenthal, A. M. (1989, May). Into the heart of the Gulag. *Reader's Digest*, pp. 71–75.

Ross, D. L. (1989). *A model policy on the use of non-deadly force in corrections: Based on a comprehensive analysis of correctional non-deadly force policies nationwide.* Big Rapids, MI: Criminal Justice Institute, Ferris State University.

Ross, H., & McKay, B. (1981). The correctional officer: Selection through training. In R. Ross (Ed.), *Prison guard/correctional officer: The use and abuse of the human resources of prisons* (pp. 259–272). Toronto, Canada: Butterworth.

Ross, H. L., McCleary, R., & LaFree, G. (1990). Can mandatory jail laws deter drunk driving? The Arizona case. *Journal of Criminal Law and Criminology, 81,* 156–167.

Ross, R. R. (1980). *Socio-cognitive developments in the offender: An external review of the UVIC program at Matsqui Penitentiary.* Ottawa, Canada: The Solicitor General.

Ross, R. R., & Fabiano, E. (1982). *Effective correctional treatment: Cognitive components.* Ottawa, Canada: Department of Criminology.

Ross, R. R., & Fabiano, E. (1986). *Female offenders: Correctional afterthoughts.* Jefferson, NC: McFarland and Co.

Ross, R. R., Fabiano, E., & Eweles, C. (1988). Reasoning and rehabilitation. *The International Journal of Offender Therapy and Comparative Criminology, 32,* 29–35.

Rothman, D. J. (1971). *The discovery of the asylum; Social order and disorder in the New Republic.* Boston: Little Brown.

Rothman, D. J. (1980). *Conscience and convenience: The asylum and its alternatives in progressive America.* Boston: Little Brown.

Roulet, E. (1993, October). *Bedford Hills Correctional Facility fact sheet.* Unpublished manuscript, New York State Department of Corrections, Bedford Hills, NY.

Rowan, J. R. (1991). Beware the halo effect of mental health personnel when they say "not suicidal." Recommended: A national policy change. *American Jails,* 4(5), 24–27.

Royko, M. (1995, March 10). Life sentence fits the crime: Being a jerk. *The Tampa Tribune*, Nation/World, p. 13.

Rubin, S. (1973). *Law of criminal correction.* St. Paul, MN: West Publishing Co.

Rusche, G., & Kirchheimer, O. (1967). *Punishment and social structure.* New York: Russell and Russell. (Original work published 1939)

Rutherford, A. (1985, September). The new generation of prisons. *New Society, 20,* pp. 408–410.

Ryan, T. A. (1984). *Adult female offenders and institutional programs: A state of the art analysis.* Washington, DC: National Institute of Corrections.

Ryan, T. A. (1990, November). Literacy training and reintegration of offenders. *Forum on Corrections Research.*

Ryan, T. A., & Woodard, J. C. (1987). *Correctional education: A state-of-the-art analysis.* Washington, DC: National Institute of Corrections.

Sabath, M. J., & Cowles, E. L. (1990). Using multiple perspectives to develop strategies for managing long-term inmates. *The Prison Journal,* 70(1), 58–72.

Saenz, A. B., & Reeves, T. Z. (1989, July). Riot aftermath: New Mexico's experience teaches valuable lessons. *Corrections Today,* pp. 66, 67, 70, 88.

Salter, A. C. (1988). *Treating child sex offenders and victims: A practical guide.* Newbury Park, CA: Sage Publications.

Samuels, H. (1991). Criminal histories and addiction addressed in a rehabilitative setting. *American Jails,* 5(4), 33–38.

Sanchez, C. S. (1993, August). Teaching inmates thinking skills. *Corrections today,* pp. 162–165.

Sands, B. (1964). *My shadow ran fast.* New York: Signet Books.

Santamour, M. B. (1990). Mentally retarded offenders: Texas program targets basic needs. *Corrections Today, 52*(1), 52, 92, 106.

Saylor, W. G., & Gaes, G. G. (1992). Prison work has measurable results on post-release success. *Federal Prisons Journal, 2*(4), 32–36.

Schafer, N. E. (1989). Prison visiting: Is it time to review the rules? *Federal Probation, 53,* 25–30.

Schafer, N. E. (1991). Prison visiting policies and practices. *International Journal of Offender Therapy and Comparative Criminology, 35*(3), 263–275.

Schafer, N. E., & Dellinger, A. B. (1993a). Jail classification: Is it time to include women? (Part I). *American Jails, 7*(4), 31–35.

Schafer, N. E., & Dellinger, A. B. (1993b). Jail classification: Is it time to include women? (Part II). *American Jails, 7*(5), 33–38.

Schafer, S. (1969). *Theories in criminology: Past and present philosophies of the crime problem.* New York: Random House.

Schafer, S. (1976). *Introduction to criminology.* Reston, VA: Reston Publishing Co.

Schafer, S. (1977). *Victimology: The victim and his criminal.* Reston, VA: Reston Publishing Co.

Schailer, R. (1995, November 22). Florida's latest chain gangs toil on prison grounds. *Tampa Tribune.* Florida/Metro, p. 3.

Schmidt, A. (1989). Electronic monitoring. *Journal of Contemporary Criminal Justice, 5*(3), 133–140.

Schmidt, A., & Curtis, R. (1987). Electronic monitors. In B. McCarthy (Ed.), *Intermediate punishments: Intensive supervision, home confinement and electronic surveillance* (pp. 137–152). Monsey, NY: Criminal Justice Press.

Schneider, V., & Smykla, J. O. (1991). A summary analysis of executions in the United States, 1608–1987: The Espy file. In R. M. Bohm (Ed.), *The death penalty in America: Current research.* Cincinnati, OH: Anderson Publishing Co.

Schramek, L. (1993, March). If not government, then who? Private sector corrections. *Corrections Compendium, 28*(3), p. 1.

Schulze, R. R. (1991). Assistant Chaplaincy Administrator, Federal Bureau of Prisons. Personal communication.

Schwartz, B. K., & Cellini, H. R. (Eds.). (1988, February). *A practitioner's guide to treating the incarcerated male sex offender: Breaking the cycle of sexual abuse.* Washington DC: U.S. Department of Justice.

Schwartz, I. M. (1991). Removing juveniles from adult jails: The unfinished agenda. In J. A. Thompson & G. L. Mays (Eds.), *American jails: Public policy issues* (pp. 216–226). Chicago: Nelson-Hall Publishers.

Schwartz, M. C., & Weintraub, J. F. (1974, Dec.). The prisoner's wife: A study in crisis. *Federal Probation, 26,* 20–26.

Schweber, C. (1984). Beauty marks and blemishes: The coed prison as a microcosm of integrated society. *The Prison Journal, 64*(1), 3–15.

Schwitezgebel R. K., Pahnke, W. N., & Hurd, W. S. (1964). A program of research in behavioral electronics. *Behavioral Science, 9,* 233–238.

Scott, G. R. (1938). *The history of corporal punishment.* London: T. Werner Laurie Ltd.

Seashore, M. J., Haberfeld, S. I., Irwin, J., & Baker, J. (1976). *Prisoner education: Project Newgate and other college programs.* New York: Praeger Publishers.

Seiter, R. P., Carlson, E. W., Bowman, H. H., Granfield, J. J., & Beran, N. J. (1977, January). *National evaluation program, Phase 1 report: Halfway houses.* Washington, DC: U.S. Department of Justice, National Institute of Law Enforcement and Criminal Justice.

Sellin, T. (1930). The house of correction for boys in the Hospice of Saint Michael in Rome. *Journal of the American Institute of Crininal Law and Criminology, 20,* 533–553.

Sellin, J. T. (1976). *Slavery and the penal system.* New York: Elsevier.

Senese, J. W., Wilson, J., Evans, A. O., Aguirre, R., & Kalinich, D. B. (1992). Evaluating jail reform: Inmate infractions and disciplinary response in a traditional jail and a podular direct supervision jail. *American Jails, 6,* 14–23.

Serrill, M., & Katel, P. (1980). New Mexico: The anatomy of a riot. *Corrections Magazine, 6*(2), 6–24.

Sexton, G. E., Farrow, F. C., & Auerbach, B. J. (1985, August). The private sector and prison industries. *National Institute of Justice Research in Brief.*

Shane-Dubow, S., Brown, A. P., & Olsen, E. (1985). *Sentencing reform in the United States: History, content and effect.* Washington, DC: U.S. Government Printing Office.

Shapiro, P., & Votey, H. (1984). Deterrence and subjective probabilities of arrest: Modeling individual decisions to drink and drive in Sweden. *Law and Society Review, 18,* 111–149.

Sharp, D. (1995). Boot camps-punishment and treatment. *Corrections Today, 57*(3), special pullout between pp. 80–81.

Shaw, A. G. L. (1966). *Convicts and the colonies.* London: Faber and Faber.

Shaw, R. D. (1990). *The jail/prison ministry and stress.* Unpublished doctoral dissertation, State University of New York at Albany.

Sheehan, S. (1978). *A prison and a prisoner.* Boston: Houghton Mifflin.

Shelton, E. (1985). The implementation of a life coping skills program within a correctional setting. *Journal of Correctional Education, 36,* 41–45.

Shenon, P. (1994, April 1). Flogging upheld for U.S. youth in Singapore. *The New York Times,* p. A5.

Sherman, L., & Berk, R. (1984). The specific deterrent effects of arrest for domestic assault. *American Sociological Review, 49, 261–272.*

Shusman, E. J., Inwald, R., & Landa, B. (1984). Correction officer job performance as predicted by the IPI and the MMPI. *Criminal Justice and Behavior, 11*(3), 309–329.

Silberman, C. E. (1978). *Criminal justice, criminal violence.* New York: Vintage Books.

Silberman, M. (1995). *A world of violence.* Belmont, CA: Wadsworth Publishing Co.

Simms, B. E., Farley, J., & Littlefield, J. R. (1987). *Colleges with fences: A handbook for improving corrections education programs.* Columbus, OH: National Center for Research in Vocational Education.

Simon, R. J. (1975). *Women and crime.* Lexington, MA: D. C. Heath/Lexington Books.

Simon, R. J., & Simon, J. D. (1993). Female guards in men's prisons. In R. Muraskin & T. Alleman (Eds.), *It's a crime: Women and justice* (pp. 226–259). Englewood Cliffs, NJ: Regents/Prentice-Hall.

Simpson, D. D., & Sells, S. B. (1988). Legal status and long term outcomes for addicts in the DARP follow-up project. In C. G. Leukefeld, & F. M. Tims (Eds.), *Compulsory treatment of drug abuse: Research and clinical practice.* Rockville, MD: National Institute of Drug Abuse.

Singer, R. G., & Statsky, W. P. (1974). *Rights of the imprisoned: Cases, materials and directions.* Indianapolis, IN: Bobbs-Merrill.

Skolnick, H. (1994). Assistant Director, Prison Industries, Nevada Department of Corrections. Personal communication.

Slaying suspects on early release. (1993, September 23). *Bradenton Herald,* Sec. B, p. 6.

Sluder, R. D., & Sapp, A. D. (1994). Peering into the crystal ball to examine the future of America's jails. *American Jails, 7*(6), 81–87.

Sluder, R. D., Sapp, A. D., & Langston, D. C. (1994, June). Guiding philosophies for probation in the 21st century. *Federal Probation, 58*(2), 3–10.

Smart, C. (1979). The new female criminal: Reality or myth? *British Journal of Criminology, 19*(1), 50–57.

Smith, A. E. (1963). *Colonists in bondage: White servitude and convict labor in America, 1607–1776.* Chapel Hill, NC: The University of North Carolina Press. (original work published 1947).

Smith, D., & Gartin, P. (1989). Specifying specific deterrence: The influence of arrest in future criminal activity. *American Sociological Review, 54,* 94–105.

Smith, L. (1994, July). Department of Criminology, University of South Florida. Personal communication.

Smith, L., & Akers, R. (1993). A comparison of Florida's community control and prison: A five year survival analysis. *Journal of Research in Crime and Delinquency, 30*(3), 267–292.

Smith, R. R. (undated). *American prisoner home furloughs.* Unpublished manuscript, West Virginia College of Graduate Studies: West Virginia Institute of Justice Studies.

Smith, W. E. (1989, February 27). Hunted by an angry faith: Salman Rushdie's novel cracks open a fault line between east and west. *Time,* pp. 28–32.

Smykla, J. O. (1980). *Coed prisons.* New York: Human Sciences Press.

Snell, T. L. (1993, August). *Correctional populations in the United States, 1991.* Washington, DC: U.S. Department of Justice.

Snell, T. L. (1995, January). Correctional populations in the United States, 1992. Washington, D.C.: U.S. Department of Justice.

Snell, T. L., & Morton, D. C. (1992, March). *Prisoners in 1991.* Washington, DC: Bureau of Justice Statistics.

Snell, T. L., & Morton, D. C. (1994, March). *Survey of state inmates, 1991: Women in prison.* Washington, DC: Bureau of Justice Statistics.

Solari, R. (1992). *National judicial reporting program, 1988.* Washington, DC: U.S. Department of Justice, Bureau of Justice Statistics.

Solomon, E. (1990). Administrator of Chaplaincy Programs, Texas Department of Criminal Justice. Personal communication.

Solomon, E. (1991). Administrator of Chaplaincy Programs, Texas Department of Criminal Justice. Personal communication.

Solomon, L., & Camp, A. T. (1993). The revolution in correctional classification. In American Correctional Association, *Classification: A tool for managing today's offenders* (pp. 1–16). Laurel, MD: American Correctional Association.

Souryal, C., & MacKenzie, D. (1993, March). *Shock incarceration and recidivism: An examination of boot camp programs in four states.* Paper presented at the annual meeting of the Academy of Criminal Justice Sciences, Kansas City, MO.

Southwick, K. (Aug. 2, 1992). Use Norplant, don't go to jail: Judges, social workers and medical professionals debate the ethic. *The San Francisco Chronicle,* pg. 13/Z1.

Speckman, R. (1981, April). Recreation in prison—A panacea? *Journal of Physical Education and Recreation, 52*(4), 46–47.

Spierenburg, P. (1991). *The prison experience: Disciplinary institutions and their inmates in early modern Europe.* New Brunswick, NJ: Rutgers University Press.

Stanton, A. (1980). *When mothers go to jail.* Lexington, MA: Lexington Books.

Steadman, H. J., Fabisiak, S., & Dvoskin, J. (1987). A survey of mental disability among state prison inmates. *Hospital and Community Psychiatry, 38,* 1086–1090.

Steffensmeier, D. (1992, December). More PA prisoners did not reduce violent crime. *Overcrowded Times, 3*(6), 1, 7–9.

Steffensmeier, D., Kramer, J., & Streifel, C. (1993). Gender and imprisonment decisions. *Criminology, 31*(3), 411–446.

Stein, M. A. (1990, April 24). High court won't restore conviction of former Panther. *Los Angeles Times*, Part A, p. 3.

Stephan, J. (1989, December). *Prison rule violators.* Washington, DC: Bureau of Justice Statistics.

Stephen, S. (1992, May). Census of state and federal correctional facilities, 1990. U. S. Department of Justice, Bureau of Justice Statistics, Washington, DC: U. S. Government Printing Office.

Stephan, S., Brien, P., & Greenfeld, L. A. (1994, December). *Capital punishment 1993.* Washington, DC: U.S. Department of Justice, Bureau of Justice Statistics.

Steurer, S. J. (1991). Inmates helping inmates: Maryland's peer tutoring reading academies. *Yearbook of Correctional Education*, pp. 133–139.

Steurer, S. J. (1995, August). Executive Director, Corrections Education Association. Personal communication.

Stokes, J. F., & Associates. (undated). *Your kitchen can pay for itself!* Atlanta, GA: Author.

Stokes, J. F., & Associates. (1985). *Control food services: Costs and courts.* Atlanta, GA: Author.

Stokes, J. F. (1991, July). President, Judy Ford Stokes & Associates Inc., Atlanta, GA, Food Management and Design Consultants. Personal communication.

Stokes, J. F. (1993, December). President, Judy Ford Stokes & Associates Inc., Atlanta, GA, Food Management and Design Consultants. Personal communication.

Stoltz, B. A. (1978). *Prisons as political institutions—What are the implications for prison ministry?* College Park, MD: American Correctional Association.

Stone, A. (1994, March 10). Whipping penalty judged too harsh—by some. *USA Today*, Sec. A, p. 3.

Stout, B. D., & Clear, T. R. (1992, Winter). Federal prison chaplains: Satisfied in ministry but often undervalued. *Federal Prisons Journal*, pp. 8–10.

Straley, N., & Morris, S. (1994). New legal standard set on religious rights of prisoners. *The National Prison Project Journal, 9*(4), 2–5.

Stratton, J. (1973, March 29 and May 1). *Testimony before the Committee on Internal Security of the House of Representatives. Hearings on revolutionary activities directed toward the administration of penal or correctional systems.* Washington, DC: U.S. Government Printing office.

Straus, M., Gelles, R., & Steinmetz, S. (1980). *Behind closed doors: Violence in the American family.* New York: Anchor.

Streib, V. L. (1992, January 17). *Capital punishment for female offenders: Present female death row inmates and death sentences and executions of female offenders, January 1, 1973 to December 31, 1991.* Unpublished paper, Cleveland State University, Marshall College of Law, Cleveland, OH.

Styles, S. (1991, Summer). Conditions of confinement suits: What has the Bureau of Prisons learned? *Federal Prisons Journal*, pp. 41–47.

Sullivan, L. E. (1990). *The prison reform movement: Forlorn hope.* Boston: Twayne Publishers.

*Sun-Sentinel* (1995, June 9). Standard chain gangs not in Florida's plans: Alabama study instructive for prison chief, p. 16A.

Suro, R. (1990, October 1). As inmates are freed, Houston feels insecure. *The New York Times*, p. A16.

Survey identifies relevant issues in support of '95–'96 priorities. (1995, Nov.). *On the Line*, 18(5), p. 1.

Sutherland, E. H. (1924). *Criminology.* Philadelphia: J. B. Lippincott Co.

Sutherland, E. H., & Cressey, D. R. (1966). *Principles of criminology* (7th ed.). New York: J.B. Lippincott Co.

Suttles, G. D. (1968). *The social order of the slum: Ethnicity and territory in the inner city.* Chicago: University of Chicago Press.

Sweet, R. W., Jr. (1991). Juvenile jailing: Federal compliance. *American Jails*, 5(1), 92–96.

Sykes, G. M. (1956). *Crime and society.* New York: Random House.

Sykes, G. M. (1958). *The society of captives: A study of a maximum security prison.* Princeton, NJ: Princeton University Press.

Sykes G. M., & Messinger, S. L. (1960). The inmate social system. In D. R. Cressey, G. H. Grosser, R. McCleery, L. E. Ohlin, G. M. Sykes, S. L. Messinger, & R. A. Cloward (Eds.), *Theoretical Studies in Social Organization in the Prison.* New York: Social Science Research Council.

Szasz, T. (1970). The Manufacture of Madness. New York, NY: Harper and Row.

Takas, M., & Hammett, T. M. (1989). *Legal issues affecting offenders and staff.* Washington, DC: National Institute of Justice.

Tannenbaum, F. (1924). *Darker phases of the south.* New York: Putnam.

Tappan, P. W. (1960). *Crime, justice and correction.* New York: McGraw-Hill.

Task Force On Corrections (1967). Task force report: Corrections. Washington, D. C.: President's Commission on Law Enforcement and the Administration of Justice, U.S. Goverment Printing Office.

Task Force on Corrections (1973). *Corrections.* Washington, DC: National Advisory Commission on Criminal Justice Standards and Goals.

Task Force on the Courts (1973). Task force report: Courts. Washington, DC: National Advisory Commission on Criminal Justice Standards and Goals.

Taylor, S. (1993, August 23). "Taking issue" in the drug wars: Small minds go after small fry; can Reno muster the courage to end mandatory-minimum madness? *The Connecticut Law Tribune*, p. 14.

Taylor, S. J. (April 23, 1987). Court, 5–4, rejects racial challenge to death penalty. *The New York Times*, pp. 1, 13.

Taylor, W. B. (1978, Spring). Alexander Maconochie and the revolt against the penitentiary. *Southern Journal of Criminal Justice*, 3(1),

Taylor, W. B. (1984, March). *In pursuit of profit: Observation on convict labor in Mississippi 1907–1934*. Paper presented at the annual meeting of the Academy of Criminal Justice Sciences, Chicago.

Taylor, W. B. (1993). Brokered Justice: Race, Politics, and the Mississippi Prisons, 1798–1992. Columbus, OH: Ohio State University Press.

Teeters, N. K. (1970). The passing of Cherry Hill: Most famous prison in the world. *The Prison Journal*, 50(1), 3–12.

Telander, R. (1987, October). Sports behind the walls. *Sports Illustrated*, pp. 82–88.

Teller, F. E., & Howell, R. J. (1981). Older prisoners: Criminal and psychological characteristics. *Criminology*, 18, pp. 549–555.

Terry D. (1994 March 3). Farrakhan: Fiery separatist in a somber suit. *The New York Times*, pp. 1A, 8b.

Tewksbury, R. (1989). Fear of sexual assault in prison inmates. *The Prison journal*, pp. 62–71.

Texas Department of Corrections. (1977). *Texas Department of Corrections: 30 years of progress*. Huntsville, TX: Author.

Texas Department of Corrections. (1985, July). *Administrative directive: Religious policy statement*. Huntsville, TX: Author.

Texas Department of Corrections. (1986, January). *Basic job analysis for the position of Chaplain II*. Huntsville, TX: Author.

Texas Department of Criminal Justice. (1993). *Annual report 1993*. Austin, TX: Author.

Thalheimer, J. (1975). *Cost anaysis of corrections standards: Halfway houses* (Vol. 1). Washington, DC: National Institute of Law Enforcement and Criminal Justice.

Thibaut, J. (1982). To pave the way to penitence: Prisoners and discipline at the Eastern State Penitentiary 1829–1835. *Pennsylvania Magazine of History and Biography*, 106, 187–221.

Thomas, C. W. (1990). Prisoners' rights and correctional privatization: A legal and ethical analysis. *Business & Professional Ethics Journal*, 10(1), 3–45.

Thomas, C. W. (1993, Winter). Are "doing well" and "doing good" contradictory goals of privatization? *Large Jail Network Bulletin*, pp. 3–7.

Thomas, C. W. (1994, April). Growth in privatization continues to accelerate. *Corrections Compendium*, pp. 5–6.

Thomas, C. W., and Logan, C.H. (1991). *The development, present status, and future potential of correctional privatization in America*. A paper presented at the Conference of the American Legislative Exchange Council held in Miami, FL, March 23, 1991.

Thomas, C. W., & Petersen, D. W. (1977). *Prison organization and inmate subcultures*. Indianapolis, IN: Bobbs-Merrill Co.

Thomas, J. (1988). *Prisoner litigation: The paradox of the jailhouse lawyer*. Totowa, NJ: Rowman and Littlefield.

Thomas, J., Aylward, A., Casey, M.L., Moton, D., Oldham, M., and Wheetley, G.W. (1985). Rethinking prisoner litigation: Some preliminary distinctions between habeas corpus and civil rights. *The Prison Journal*, 65, 83–106.

Thornberg, D. (1990). Opening remarks by the Attorney General of the United States. Presented at the National Drug Conference.

Thornberry, T. P., & Call, J. E. (1983). Constitutional challenges to prison overcrowding: The scientific evidence of harmful effects. *Hastings Law Journal*, 35, 313–351.

Three guards arrested in contraband bust. (1993, June 12). *The Times-Picayune*, Metro, p. B2.

Tittle, C., & Rowe, A. (1974). Certainty of arrest and crime rates: A further test of the deterrence hypothesis. *Social Forces*, 52, 455–462.

Toch, H. (1977a). *Living in prison: The ecology of survival*. New York: The Free Press.

Toch, H. (1977b). *Police, prisons, and the problem of violence*. Washington, DC: Government Printing Office.

Toch, H. (1978). Social climate and prison violence. *Federal Probation*, 42(4), 21–25.

Tonry, M. (1990). Stated and latent features of ISP. *Crime and Delinquency*, 36(1), 174–191.

Tonry, M. (1992). Mandatory penalties. In M. Tonry (Ed.), *Crime and justice: A review of research* (Vol. 16, pp. 243–273). Chicago: The University of Chicago Press.

Tonry, M., & Will, R. (1988). *Intermediate sanctions: Preliminary report*. Washington, DC: National Institute of Justice.

Torrey, E. F., Steiber, J., Ezekiel, J., Wolfe, S., Sharfstein, J., Noble, J. E. & Lauric, M. (1992). *Criminalizing the seriously mentally ill—The abuse of jails as mental hospitals*. Washington, DC: National Alliance of the Mentally Ill.

Tracey, A. (1993, August). Literacy volunteers share a belief in rehabilitative effect of education. *Corrections Today*, pp. 102–109.

Tracy, P. E., Wolfgang, M. E., & Figlio, R. M. (1985). *Delinquency in two birth cohorts: Executive summary*. Washington, DC: U.S. Department of Justice.

Trout, C., & Meko, J. A. (1990, Spring). The uses of intelligence: Every staff member is a vital part of the network. *Federal Prison Journal*, pp. 16–21.

Turley, J. (1990). Alternative solutions. In U.S. Department of Justice, Federal Bureau of Prisons, (Ed.). *The December 7, 1990 forum on issues in corrections-Long term confinement in the aging inmate population*. Washington, DC: U.S. Department of Justice.

Turner, W. B. (1979, June). When prisoners sue: Prisoner section 1983 suits in Federal Courts. *Harvard Law Review, 92,* 610–63.

United Nations. (1951). *Probation and related matters.* New York: Author.

United Nations. (1970). Probation and related measures. *United Nations, IV,* 15–26.

U.S. Department of Justice. (undated). *Federal prison industries: Meeting the military's needs when quality really counted.* Washington, DC: Federal Bureau of Prisons.

U.S. Department of Justice. (1986, September). *Program statement: Inmate recreation programs.* Washington, DC: Author.

U.S. Department of Justice. (1988, March). *Report to the nation on crime and justice.* Washington, DC: Author.

U.S. Department of Justice. (1989). *The December 12, 1989 conference on issues in corrections.* Washington, DC: Author.

U.S. Department of Justice. (1990, September). *A survey of intermediate sanctions.* Washington, DC: Author.

U.S. Department of Justice, National Institute of Corrections (1993). *Podular Direct Supervision Jails Information Packet.* Washington, D. C.: Author.

U.S. Department of Justice. (1994, September 11). *Probation and parole populations reach new highs.* Washington, DC: Author.

U.S. Department of Justice, Bureau of Justice Statistics. (1980). *Capital punishment 1979: National prisoner statistics.* Washington DC: Author.

University of Illinois Law Forum. (1980). *Prieser v. Rodriguez in retrospect.* In D. P. Robbins (Ed.), *Prisoners' rights source book,* New York: Clark Boardman Co.

Van Den Haag. E. (1975). *Punishing criminals: Concerning a very old and painful question.* New York: Bssic Books.

Van der Slice, A. (1936, June). Elizabethan house of correction. *Journal of Criminal Law and Criminology, 27,* 45–67.

Van der Zee, J. (1985). *Bound over: Indentured servitude and American conscience.* New York: Simon and Schuster.

Van Voorhis, P. (1993). Psychological determinants of the prison experience. *The Prison Journal, 73*(1), 72–101.

Van Yelyr, R. G. (1942). *The whip and the rod.* London: Gerald G. Swan.

Vaughn, M. S., & del Carmen, R. V. (1993, April). Research note: A national survey of correctional administrators in the United States. *Crime and Delinquency, 39*(2), 225–239.

Vaughn, M. S., & Sapp, A. D. (1989, Fall/Winter). Less than utopian: Sex offender treatment in a milieu of power struggles, status positioning, and inmate manipulation in state correctional institutions. *The Prison Journal,* pp. 73–89.

Velimesis, M. I. (1981). Sex roles and mental health of women in prison. *Professional Psychology, 12*(1), 128–135.

Veneziano, L., Veneziano, C., & Tribolet, C. (1987). Special needs of inmates with handicaps: An assessment. *Journal of Offender Counseling Services and Rehabilitation, 12*(1), 61–72.

Vera Institute of Justice. (1977). *Felony arrests: Their prosecution and disposition in New York City's courts.* New York: Author.

"Vigilantism" threatens sex offender law. (1990, October 30). *Walla Walla Union Bulletin,* p. 1.

Vild, D. R. (1992, July). *A comparative study of state academies for basic correctional officer training.* Unpublished report to the Arizona Department of Corrections.

Vito, G., & Allen, H. (1981). Shock probation in Ohio: A comparison of outcomes. *International Journal of Offender Therapy and Comparative Criminology, 25,* 70–76.

Vito, G. F., & Wilson, D. G. (1985). Elderly inmates. *Federal Probation, 49*(1), 18–24.

Volunteer Today. (1993, Summer). Islamic volunteers work to meet diverse needs. *Volunteer Today,* p. 4.

Wagner, D., & Baird, C. (1993, January). *Evaluation of the Florida Community Program.* Washington, DC: National Institute of Justice Journal.

Waldo, G., & Chiricos, T. (1974). *Work as a rehabilitation tool: An evaluation of two state programs, final report.* Washington, DC: U.S. Department of Justice.

Waldo, G., & Griswold, D. (1979). Issues in the measurement of recidivism. In L. Sechrest, S. O. White, & E. D. Brown (Eds.), *The rehabilitation of criminal offenders: Problems and prospects.* Washington, DC: National Academy of Sciences.

Walker, J. T. (1994). *Police and correctional use of force: Parity or parody.* Paper presented at the annual meeting of the Academy of Criminal Justice Sciences, Chicago.

Walker, P. N. (1973). *Punishment: An illustrated history.* New York: Arco Publishers.

Wallerstein, A. M. (1989, Spring). New generation/ direct supervision correctional operations in Bucks County. *American Jails, 1*(1), 34–36.

Walters, G. (1994). *The criminal lifestyle: Patterns of serious criminal conduct.* Newbury Park, CA: Sage Publications.

Walters, S. (1990). *Factors affecting the acceptance of female prison guards by their male counterparts.* Unpublished manuscript, University of Wisconsin-Platteville.

Ward, D., & Kassebaum, G. (1965). *Women's prison: Sex and social structure.* Chicago: Aldine-Atherton.

Ward, D. A. (1987). Control strategies for problem prisoners in American penal systems. In A. E. Bottoms & R. Light (Eds.), *Problems of long-term imprisonment.* Aldershot, England: Gower Publishing Co.

Washington, P. A. (1989). Mature mentally ill offenders in California jails. *Journal of Offender Counseling, Services and Rehabilitation, 13*(2), 161–173.

Weinstein, M. (1989, June). Executive Director, State Attorney's Office, Duval County, FL: Personal communication.

Weir, E., & Kalm, L. (1936). *Crime and religion: A study of criminological facts and problems.* Chicago: Franciscan Herald Press.

Weis, B. (1985, March). *The Cleveland prosecutor mediation program.* Washington, DC: National Institute of Justice.

Weisheit, R. (1985). Trends in programs for female offenders: The use of private agencies as service providers. *International Journal of Offender Therapy and Comparative Criminology, 29*(1), 35–42.

Welch, R. (1990, December). The arts in prison. *Corrections Compendium, 15*(10), 1, 5–6.

Wells, C. (1993). *Manatee inmate boot camp.* Bradenton, FL: Manatee County Sheriff's Office.

Wenk, E. A., Robison, J. D., & Smith, G. W. (1972). Can violence be predicted? *Crime and Delinquency, 9,* 171–196.

Westcott, K. (1995, November 10). Legislative Liason, Coalition Against STOP, National Prison Project. Personal communication.

Wetli, C. V., & Martinez, R. (1981). Forensic sciences aspects of santeria, a religious cult of African origin. *Journal of Forensic Sciences, 26*(3), 506–514.

Wetli, C. V., & Martinez, R. (1983). Brujeria: Manifestations of Palo Mayombe in South Florida. *Journal of Florida Medical Association, 70*(8), 629–634.

Wexler, H. K. (1994) Progress in prison substance abuse treatment: A five year report. *Journal of Drug Issues.* 24 (1&2), 349–360.

Wexler, H. K., Falkin, G. P., & Lipton, D. S. (1990). Outcome evaluation of a prison therapuetic community for substance abuse treatment. *Criminal Justice and Behavior, 17*(1), 71–92.

Wexler, H. K., & Lipton, D. S. (1993). From reform to recovery: Advances in prison drug treatment. In J. Inciardi (Ed.), *Drug treatment and criminal justice* (pp. 209–227). Newbury Park, CA: Sage Publications.

Wexler, H. K., & Williams R. (1986). The Stay'N Out therapuetic community: Prison treatment for substance abusers. *Journal of Psychoactive Drugs, 19*(3), 221–230.

What are prisons for? (1982, Sept. 13). *Time Magazine,* pp. 38–41.

White, R. M., & Abeles, R. P. (1990, November 26). *The behavioral and social research program at the National Institute on Aging: History of a decade.* Bethesda, MD: National Institute on Aging, Behavioral and Social Research Program.

Whitehead, J. T. (1989). *The effectiveness of felony probation.* A paper presented at the annual meeting of the American Society of Criminology, Reno, NV.

Whitehead, J. T. (1991). The effectiveness of felony probation. *Justice Quarterly, 4,* 525–543.

Who's Who in Jail Management. (1994). Hagerstown, MD: American Jail Association.

Wicker, T. (1975). *A time to die.* NY: Quadrangle/The New York Times Press.

Wickersham Commission Reports. (1931). *Report on Penal institutions, probation, and parole.* Washington, DC: U.S. Government Printing Office.

Wicks, R. J. (1980). *Guard! Society's professional prisoner.* Houston, TX: Gulf Publications.

Wilkerson, I. (1987, April 29). Detroit crime feeds on itself and youth. *The New York Times,* Sec. Y, pp. 1, 14.

Wilkerson, I. (1988, March 1). Two decades of decline chronicled by Kerner follow-up report. *The New York Times,* p. 5.

Wilkinson, K., & Brehm, D. (1992). Overcrowding—A cooperative approach. *American Jails, 6*(1), 89–91.

Williams, J. E. H. (1970). *The English penal system in transition.* London: Butterworth & Co.

Wilson, D. W. (1948). *My six convicts.* New York: Rinehart and Co.

Wilson, J. Q. (1975). *Thinking about crime.* New York: Basic Books.

Wilson, J. Q. (1989). *Bureaucracy: What government agencies do and why they do it.* New York: Basic Books.

Wilson, M. (1931). *The crime of punishment.* New York: Jonathan Cape Harrison & Smith.

Wilson, R. (1980). Who will care for the mad and bad? *Corrections Magazine, 6* (1), 5–9, 12–17.

Windham School System. (1986). *Windham school system: The national leader in correctional education.* Huntsville, TX: Texas Department of Criminal Justice.

Windham School System. (1987). *Annual performance report.* Huntsville, TX: Texas Department of Criminal Justice.

Windham School System. (1989). *Meeting the challenge: Innovative educational programming.* Huntsville, TX: Author.

Windham School System. (1991–1992). *Annual performance report.* Huntsville, TX: Texas Department of Criminal Justice.

Wines, E. C., & Dwight, T. (1867). *Report on the prisons in the United States and Canada.* Albany, NY: Van Benthuysen.

Wines, F. H. (1895). *Punishment and reformation: A historical sketch of the rise of the penitentiary system.* New York: Thomas Crowell.

Winterfield, L. A., & Hillsman, S. T. (1991). *The effects of instituting means-based fines in a criminal court: The Staten Island day-fine experiment.* New York: Vera Institute of Justice.

Wolfgang, M. E., Figlio, R. M., & Sellin, T. (1972). *Delinquency in a birth cohort.* Chicago: University of Chicago Press.

Wolford, B. I. (1987). Correctional education: training and education opportunities for delinquent and criminal offenders. In C. M. Nelson, R. B. Rutherford, and B.I. Wolford, Columbus, OH: Merrill Publishing Co.

Wood, A. W., & Waite, J. B. (1941). *Crime and its treatment: Social and legal aspects of criminology.* New York: American Book Company.

Wood, F. (1985, Summer). Oak Park Heights sets high super-max standards. *The National Prison Project Journal,* pp. 3–6.

Wooden, W. S., & Parker, J. (1982). *Men behind bars: Sexual exploitation in prison.* New York: Plenum.

Woodruff, L. (1993, September/October). Occupational stress for correctional personnel, Part I. *American Jails,* pp. 15–20.

Worzella, C. (1992). The Milwaukee Municipal Court day fine project. In D. C. McDonald (Ed.), *Day fines in American courts: The Staten Island and Milwaukee experiments.* Washington, DC: U.S. Department of Justice, Office of Justice Programs.

Wright, C. D. (1899). Prison labor. *The Catholic University Bulletin, V*(4), 403–423.

Wright, J. H., Jr. (1991). Life without parole: The view from death row. *Criminal Law Bulletin, 27,* 334–367.

Wright, K. (1991). Successful prison leadership. *Federal Probation, 55*(3), 5–7.

Wright, K. N., & Saylor, W. G. (1991). Male and female employees' perceptions of prison work: Is there a difference? *Justice Quarterly, 8* (4), 505–524.

Wunder, A. (1995a, May). Inmate phone use: Calling collect from America's prisons and jails. *Corrections Compendium, 20*(5), 6–7.

Wunder, A. (1995b). Corrections systems must bear the burden of new legislation. *Corrections Compendium, 20*(3), 4–20.

Yablonsky, L. (1965). *The tunnel back : Synanon.* New York: The Macmillan Co.

York, M. (1992, April 28). D.C. Jail officers admit smuggling: Drug sting caught seven guards. *The Washington Post,* p. B1.

Zamble, E., & Porporino, F. (1988). *Coping, behavior, and adaptation in prison inmates.* New York: Springer-Verlag.

Zane, T. (1987, September). Personal communication.

Zedlewski, E. W. (1987). *Making confinement decisions.* Washington, DC: National Institute of Justice.

Zimmer, L. (1986). *Women guarding men.* Chicago: The University of Chicago Press.

Zimring, F. E., & Hawkins, G. J. (1973). *Deterrence.* Chicago: University of Chicago Press.

Zupan, L. L. (1991). *Jails: Reform and the new generation philosophy.* Cincinnati, OH: Anderson Publishing Co.

# NAME INDEX

# Subject Index

Abnormal sex offenders in prison, 127

Absolute pardon, 63

Academic programs in correctional institutions, 147–48

Academy of Criminal Justice Sciences, 299

Accused
definition of, 3
as a responsibility of corrections, 3–4

American Civil Liberties Union, National Prison Project of, 294

Adjustment centers, 153–54

Administrative officers, 306

Administrative segregation (AS), 132, 369

Admission process
in jails, 481–83
in prisons, 125, 126, 358–59

Adult basic education (ABE) programs
in jails, 489
in prisons, 389–90

Adult Education Act (1964), 387

African American inmates
development of racial pride, 159
dominance over white inmates, 181
in rehabilitative institutions, 152
increases in the proportion of in corrections, 179–80
in prison population, 226
in jail population, 473
in prisoner movement, 163, 166

*Africa v. Pennsylvania*, 433

*Africa v. State*, 433

Agriculture, employment of inmates in, 398

Augustus, John, 495

AIDS
education of inmates about, 424
effects on prison health care costs, 424
nature of, 421–22
precautions to protect staff and inmates from, 422

proportion of inmate population with, 423
role of chaplains in caring for inmates with, 442
screening and testing of inmates for, 422–23
segregation of inmates infected with, 423

Alcohol in prison, 129

Alcoholics Anonymous (AA), 419

Alderson, West Virginia, federal institution at, 362

Alger, Horatio, myth, 141

Alternative means and restrictions of religious practices, 321

American Bar Association on prison health care, 410

American Correctional Association (ACA)
American Prison Association, as forerunner of. 143
on controlling prison riots, 291–93
*Manual of Correctional Standards*, 143
on prison health care, 410
and professionalization of correctional personnel, 299
on recreational programs, 462
on standards for halfway houses, 518

American Federation of State, County, and Municipal Employees (AFSCME), correctional officers in, 312

American Jail Association (AJA), 299

*American Jails*, 299

*American Journal of Corrections*, 143

American Medical Association on prison health care, 410

American Muslim Mission, 439

American Prison Association, 143

American Public Health Association on prison health care, 410

American Revolution
effect on English corrections, 61
search for new methods of social control after, 73–74

American Society of Criminology, 299

Americans With Disabilities Act (1990), 241

Amnesty International
on capital punishment, 34
and legality of whipping, 53
on use of mutilation, 57

Amsterdam Workhouse, 67

Appointment system in selection of probation and parole officers, 511

ARC Community Services Treatment Alternative Program in Madison, Wisconsin, 263

Arkansas, prison system history, 103–7
conditions in system when Murton assumed control, 103–4
Murton's efforts to reform the system, 105–6
the system is declared unconstitutional, 106–7
the system today, 107

Aryan Brotherhood (AB), 202, 205, 212

Ashurst-Summers Act (1935), 400

Assault, inmate right to protection from, 346–48

Asylums, tracing roots of imprisonment to, 66

Attica prison riot, 169–72, 287–88, 289
legacy of, 173
and prison health care, 410
and recreation programs, 462

Attorneys for indigents, 33

Auburn System, 58, 69, 76–80
alternative programs experimented with, 78
and censorship of mail, 336
classification in, 359
debate over superiority of, 79–81
education program in, 386
females in, 251
becomes model for prisons in U.S., 80–81